COLLINS WORLD ATLAS CONCISE EDITION

Collins

An imprint of HarperCollinsPublishers
77-85 Fulham Palace Road
London
W6 8JB

First Published 2002

Copyright © HarperCollinsPublishers 2002
Maps © Bartholomew Ltd 2002

Collins ® is a registered trademark of HarperCollinsPublishers Ltd

The contents of this edition of the Collins World Atlas Concise Edition
are believed correct at the time of printing. Nevertheless the publisher
can accept no responsibility for errors or omissions, changes in the detail
given, or for any expense or loss thereby caused.

Printed in Italy

British Library Cataloguing in Publication Data.
A catalogue record for this book is available from the British Library.

ISBN 0 00 714498 9

PH11309 Imp 001

The maps in this product are also available for purchase in
digital format from Bartholomew Mapping Solutions.
For details and information visit
http://www.bartholomewmaps.com
or contact
Bartholomew Mapping Solutions
Tel: +44 (0) 141 306 3162
Fax: +44 (0) 141 306 3130
e-mail: bartholomew@harpercollins.co.uk

Everything **clicks** at
www.collins.co.uk

Collins

WORLDATLAS
CONCISE EDITION

contents

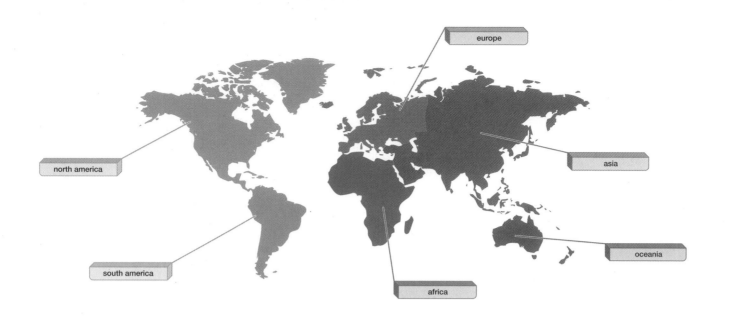

north america

south america

europe

asia

africa

oceania

title	scale	page#
map **symbols**		4

world

world physical features		6–7
world countries		8–9
world earthquakes and volcanoes		10–11
world climate and weather		12–13
world environment		14–15
world population and cities		16–17
world communications		18–19
world indicators		20

europe

europe landscapes		22–23
europe locations		24–25
europe reference maps		
map_1 **russian federation**	1:18 000 000	26–27
map_2 **russian federation** west	1:7 500 000	28–29
map_3 **europe** northwest	1:7 500 000	30–31
map_4 **iceland, norway, sweden, finland** and **denmark**	1:4 500 000	32–33
inset: **iceland**	1:6 000 000	
map_5 **united kingdom** and **republic of ireland**	1:3 000 000	34–35
inset: **faroe islands**	1:3 000 000	
map_6 **europe** north central	1:3 000 000	36–37
map_7 **france** and **switzerland**	1:3 000 000	38–39
map_8 **europe** south and the **mediterranean**	1:9 000 000	40–41
map_9 **spain** and **portugal**	1:3 000 000	42–43
map_10 **italy, slovenia, croatia** and **bosnia-herzegovina**	1:3 000 000	44–45
map_11 **europe** southeast	1:3 000 000	46–47
europe states and territories		48

asia

asia landscapes		50–51
asia locations		52–53
asia reference maps		
map_1 **asia** east and southeast	1:20 000 000	54–55
map_2 **asia** southeast	1:13 000 000	56–57
map_3 **indonesia** west, **malaysia** and **singapore**	1:6 000 000	58–59
inset: **singapore**	1:400 000	
map_4 **myanmar, thailand, laos** and **vietnam**	1:6 000 000	60–61
map_5 **asia** east	1:13 000 000	62–63
map_6 **asia** northeast	1:6 000 000	64–65
map_7 **china** south	1:6 000 000	66–67
inset: **hong kong**	1:700 000	
map_8 **asia** central and south	1:20 000 000	68–69
map_9 **asia** south	1:12 500 000	70–71
map_10 **india** south and **sri lanka**	1:6 000 000	72–73
map_11 **india** north, **bangladesh** and **nepal**	1:6 000 000	74–75
map_12 **asia** southwest	1:13 000 000	76
map_13 **middle east**	1:3 000 000	77
map_14 **turkey, iraq** and **trans-caucasian republics**	1:6 000 000	78–79
map_15 **iran, afghanistan** and **pakistan**	1:6 000 000	80–81
asia states and territories		82

title	scale	page#

africa

africa landscapes		84–85
africa locations		86–87
africa reference maps		
map_1 **africa** northeast	1:8 000 000	88–89
map_2 **africa** northwest	1:8 000 000	90–91
map_3 **africa** west	1:8 000 000	92–93
inset: **cape verde**	1:8 000 000	
map_4 **africa** west central	1:8 000 000	94–95
map_5 **africa** east central	1:8 000 000	96–97
map_6 **africa** south	1:8 000 000	98–99
inset: **madagascar**	1:8 000 000	
africa states and territories		100

oceania

oceania landscapes		102–103
oceania locations		104–105
oceania reference maps		
map_1 **australia** and **pacific** southwest	1:18 000 000	106–107
map_2 **australia** west	1:7 500 000	108–109
map_3 **australia** east	1:7 500 000	110–111
map_4 **australia** southeast	1:7 500 000	112
map_5 **new zealand**	1:5 000 000	113
oceania states and territories		114

north america

north**america** landscapes		116–117
north**america** locations		118–119
north**america** reference maps		
map_1 **canada**	1:16 000 000	120–121
map_2 **canada** west	1:7 000 000	122–123
map_3 **canada** central and east	1:7 000 000	124–125
map_4 **united states of america**	1:12 000 000	126–127
map_5 **united states of america** east	1:6 500 000	128–129
map_6 **united states of america** northeast	1:3 000 000	130–131
map_7 **united states of america** central	1:6 500 000	132–133
map_8 **united states of america** west	1:6 500 000	134–135
inset: **hawaii**	1:6 500 000	
map_9 **united states of america** southwest	1:3 000 000	136–137
map_10 **central america** and the **caribbean**	1:12 500 000	138–139
north**america** states and territories		140

south america

south**america** landscapes		142–143
south**america** locations		144–145
south**america** reference maps		
map_1 **south america** north	1:8 250 000	146–147
map_2 **south america** central	1:8 250 000	148–149
map_3 **south america** east	1:8 250 000	150–151
map_4 **south america** south	1:8 250 000	152–153
inset: **south georgia**	1:8 250 000	
south**america** states and territories		154

oceans and poles

oceans features		156–157
poles features		158–159
oceansand**poles** reference maps		
map_1 **atlantic** ocean	1:40 000 000	160–161
map_2 **indian** ocean	1:40 000 000	162–163
map_3 **pacific** ocean	1:45 000 000	164–165
arctic ocean	1:26 000 000	166
antarctica	1:26 000 000	167
oceansand**poles** statistics		168

index

index		169–248

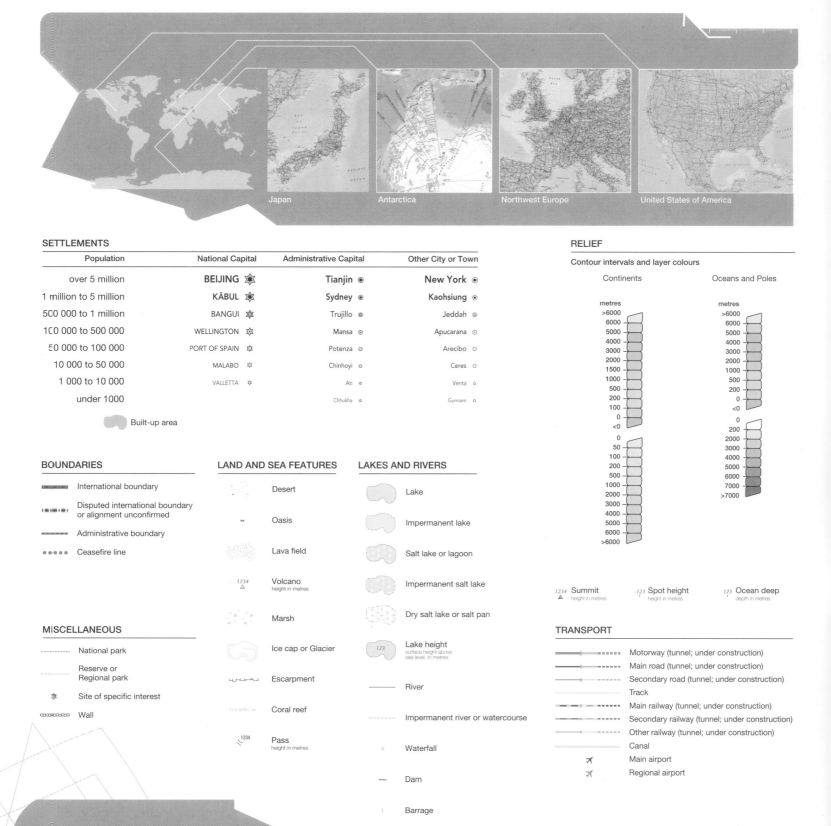

Japan | Antarctica | Northwest Europe | United States of America

SETTLEMENTS

Population	National Capital	Administrative Capital	Other City or Town
over 5 million	**BEIJING** ✶	**Tianjin** ◉	**New York** ◉
1 million to 5 million	**KĀBUL** ✶	**Sydney** ◉	**Kaohsiung** ◉
500 000 to 1 million	BANGUI ✶	Trujillo ◉	Jeddah ◎
100 000 to 500 000	WELLINGTON ✫	Mansa ◉	Apucarana ⊙
50 000 to 100 000	PORT OF SPAIN ✩	Potenza ◉	Arecibo ○
10 000 to 50 000	MALABO ✿	Chinhoyi ○	Ceres ○
1 000 to 10 000	VALLETTA ✾	Ati ○	Venta ○
under 1000		Chhukha ○	Gunnam ○

◗ Built-up area

BOUNDARIES

▭▭▭ International boundary

▬▭▬ Disputed international boundary
or alignment unconfirmed

▬▬▬ Administrative boundary

••••• Ceasefire line

MISCELLANEOUS

- - - - - National park

.... Reserve or
Regional park

✿ Site of specific interest

▭▭▭ Wall

LAND AND SEA FEATURES

Desert

⌄ Oasis

Lava field

△ 1234 Volcano
height in metres

Marsh

Ice cap or Glacier

⌐┐└┘ Escarpment

Coral reef

╷╵ 1234 Pass
height in metres

LAKES AND RIVERS

Lake

Impermanent lake

Salt lake or lagoon

Impermanent salt lake

Dry salt lake or salt pan

123 Lake height
surface height above
sea level, in metres

——— River

- - - - - Impermanent river or watercourse

‖ Waterfall

— Dam

╎ Barrage

RELIEF

Contour intervals and layer colours

Continents | Oceans and Poles

metres | metres
>6000 | >6000
6000 | 6000
5000 | 5000
4000 | 4000
3000 | 3000
2000 | 2000
1500 | 1000
1000 | 500
500 | 200
200 | <0
100 |
0 | 0
<0 | 200
 | 2000
0 | 3000
50 | 4000
100 | 5000
200 | 6000
500 | 7000
1000 | >7000
2000 |
3000 |
4000 |
5000 |
6000 |
>6000 |

△ 1234 Summit
height in metres

· -123 Spot height
height in metres

· 123 Ocean deep
depth in metres

TRANSPORT

▬▬▶ ⋯⋯ Motorway (tunnel; under construction)

▬▬▶ ⋯⋯ Main road (tunnel; under construction)

▬▬▶ ⋯⋯ Secondary road (tunnel; under construction)

⋯⋯⋯⋯ Track

▬▬ ⋯⋯ Main railway (tunnel; under construction)

▬▬ ⋯⋯ Secondary railway (tunnel; under construction)

▬▬ ⋯⋯ Other railway (tunnel; under construction)

▬▬▬ Canal

✈ Main airport

✈ Regional airport

satellite imagery

The thematic pages in the atlas contain a wide variety of photographs and images. These are a mixture of 3-D perspective views, terrestrial and aerial photographs and satellite imagery. All are used to illustrate specific themes and to give an indication of the variety of imagery, and different means of visualizing the Earth, available today. The main types of imagery used in the atlas are described in the table below. The sensor for each satellite image is detailed on the acknowledgements page.

satellite/sensor name	launch dates	owner	aims and applications	web address	additional web address
Landsat 4, 5, 7	July 1972-April 1999	National Aeronautics and Space Administration (NASA), USA	The first satellite to be designed specifically for observing the Earth's surface. Originally set up to produce images of use for agriculture and geology. Today is of use for numerous environmental and scientific applications.	geo.arc.nasa.gov ls7pm3.gsfc.nasa.gov	asterweb.jpl.nasa.gov earth.jsc.nasa.gov earthnet.esrin.esa.it
SPOT 1, 2, 3, 4 (Satellite Pour l'Observation de la Terre)	February 1986-March 1998	Centre National d'Etudes Spatiales (CNES) and Spot Image, France	Particularly useful for monitoring land use, water resources research, coastal studies and cartography.	www.cnes.fr www.spotimage.fr	earthobservatory.nasa.gov eol.jsc.nasa.gov modis.gsfc.nasa.gov
Space Shuttle	Regular launches from 1981	NASA, USA	Each shuttle mission has separate aims. Astronauts take photographs with high specification hand held cameras. The Shuttle Radar Topography Mission (SRTM) in 2000 obtained the most complete near-global high-resolution database of the earth's topography.	science.ksc.nasa.gov/shuttle/countdown www.jpl.nasa.gov/srtm	seawifs.gsfc.nasa.gov topex-www.jpl.nasa.gov visibleearth.nasa.gov
IKONOS	September 1999	Space Imaging	First commercial high-resolution satellite. Useful for a variety of applications mainly Cartography, Defence, Urban Planning, Agriculture, Forestry and Insurance.	www.spaceimaging.com	rsi.ca www.usgs.gov

SPOT

Landsat

Space Shuttle
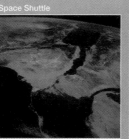

IKONOS

world

contents

6–7   **world** physical features

8–9   **world** countries

10–11   **world** earthquakes and volcanoes

12–13   **world** climate and weather

14–15   **world** environment

16–17   **world** population and cities

18–19   **world** communications

20   **world** indicators

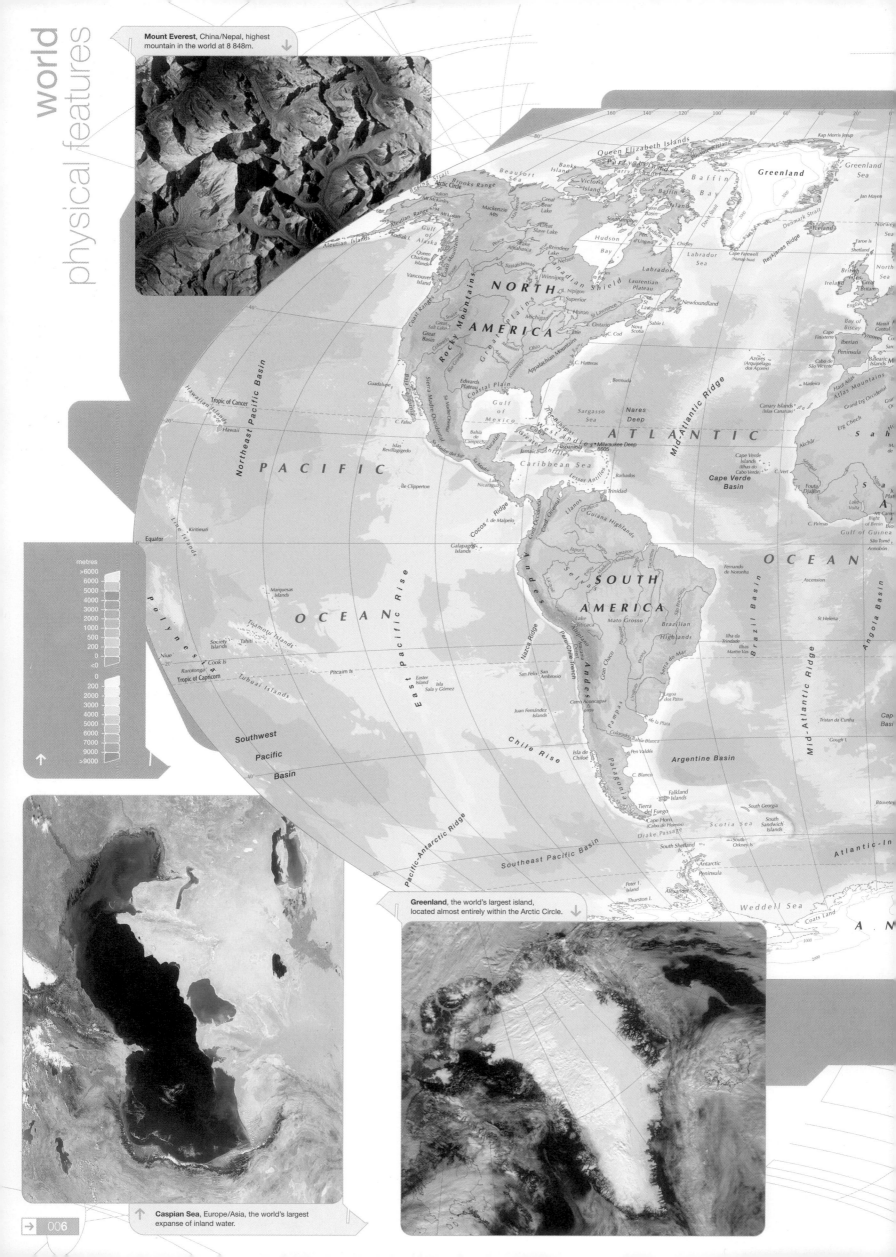

Mount Everest, China/Nepal, highest mountain in the world at 8 848m.

Caspian Sea, Europe/Asia, the world's largest expanse of inland water.

Greenland, the world's largest island, located almost entirely within the Arctic Circle.

metres
>6000
6000
5000
4000
3000
2000
1000
500
200
0
<0
0
200
2000
3000
4000
5000
6000
7000
8000
9000
>9000

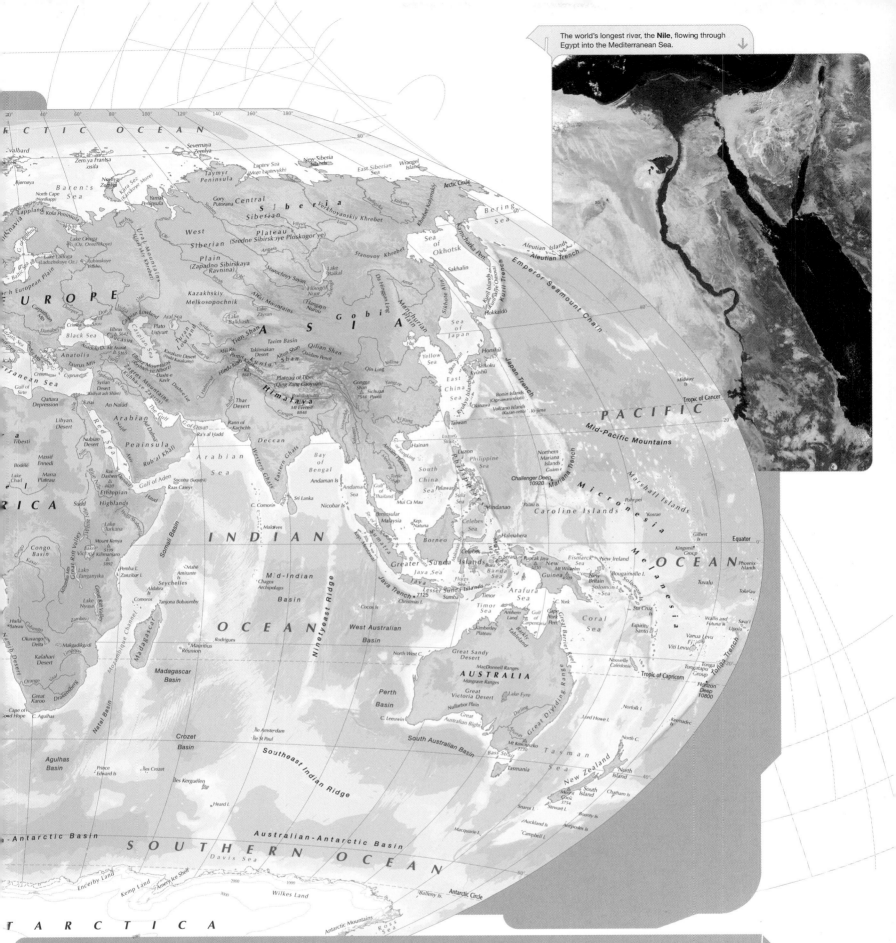

The world's longest river, the **Nile**, flowing through Egypt into the Mediterranean Sea.

world

HIGHEST MOUNTAINS

	metres	feet	map
Mt Everest, China/Nepal	8 848	29 028	75 E4
K2, China/Jammu and Kashmir	8 611	28 251	74 C2
Kangchenjunga, India/Nepal	8 586	28 169	75 F4
Lhotse, China/Nepal	8 516	27 939	75 E4
Makalu, China/Nepal	8 463	27 765	75 E4
Cho Oyu, China/Nepal	8 201	26 906	75 E3
Dhaulagiri, Nepal	8 167	26 794	75 D3
Manaslu, Nepal	8 163	26 781	75 E3
Nanga Parbat, Jammu and Kashmir	8 126	26 660	74 B2
Annapurna I, Nepal	8 091	26 545	75 D3

LONGEST RIVERS

	continent	km	miles	map
Nile	Africa	6 695	4 160	89 F2
Amazon	South America	6 516	4 049	150 B1
Yangtze	Asia	6 380	3 964	67 G2
Mississippi-Missouri	North America	5 969	3 709	133 D6
Ob'-Irtysh	Asia	5 568	3 459	26 G3-27 I5
Yenisey-Angara-Selenga	Asia	5 550	3 448	27 I2-K4
Yellow	Asia	5 464	3 395	63 J4
Congo	Africa	4 667	2 900	95 B6
Rio de la Plata - Paraná	South America	4 500	2 796	152-F3
Irtysh	Asia	4 440	2 759	26 G3

LARGEST ISLANDS

	location	sq km	sq miles	map
Greenland	North America	2 175 600	840 004	121 O2
New Guinea	Oceania	808 510	312 167	57 J7
Borneo	Asia	745 561	287 863	59 F2
Madagascar	Africa	587 040	266 657	99 J3
Baffin Island	North America	507 451	195 927	121 L3
Sumatra	Asia	473 606	182 860	58 C3
Honshū	Asia	227 414	87 805	55 D6
Great Britain	Europe	218 476	84 354	35 E5
Victoria Island	North America	217 291	3 897	121 H2
Ellesmere Island	North America	196 236	75 767	121 K2

LARGEST LAKES

	continent	sq km	sq miles	map
Caspian Sea	Asia/Europe	371 000	143 243	68 C2
Lake Superior	North America	82 100	31 698	132 D2
Lake Victoria	Africa	68 800	26 563	96 B5
Lake Huron	North America	59 600	23 011	128 C2
Lake Michigan	North America	57 800	22 316	128 B3
Aral Sea	Asia	33 640	12 988	70 A2
Lake Tanganyika	Africa	32 900	12 702	95 F6
Great Bear Lake	North America	31 328	12 095	122 F1
Lake Baikal	Asia	30 500	11 776	27 K4
Lake Nyasa	Africa	30 044	11 600	97 B7

EARTH'S DIMENSIONS

Mass	5.974 x 10²¹ tonnes
Total area	509 450 000 sq km / 196 672 000 sq miles
Land area	149 450 000 sq km / 57 688 000 sq miles
Water area	360 000 000 sq km / 138 984 000 sq miles
Volume	1 083 207 x 10⁶ cubic km / 259 875 x 10⁶ cubic miles
Equatorial diameter	12 756 km / 7 926 miles
Polar diameter	12 714 km / 7 900 miles
Equatorial circumference	40 075 km / 24 903 miles
Meridional circumference	40 008 km / 24 861 miles

CONNECTIONS

Europe landscapes	22—23
Asia landscapes	50—51
Africa landscapes	84—85
Oceania landscapes	102—103
North America landscapes	116—117
South America landscapes	142—143

CONNECTIONS

World population and cities	16—17
Europe locations	24—25
Asia locations	52—53
Africa locations	86—87
Oceania locations	104—105
North america locations	118—119
South america locations	144—145

ABBREVIATION KEY

A.	ANDORRA	HUN.	HUNGARY	ROM.	ROMANIA
AL.	ALBANIA	ISR.	ISRAEL	SL.	SLOVENIA
ARM.	ARMENIA	JOR.	JORDAN	SLA.	SLOVAKIA
AUST.	AUSTRIA	L.	LUXEMBOURG	SUR.	SURINAME
AZER.	AZERBAIJAN	LAT.	LATVIA	SW.	SWITZERLAND
B.	BURUNDI	LEB.	LEBANON	TAJIK.	TAJIKISTAN
BEL.	BELGIUM	LITH.	LITHUANIA	TURKM.	TURKMENISTAN
B.H.	BOSNIA-HERZEGOVINA	M.	MACEDONIA	U.A.E.	UNITED ARAB EMIRATES
BULG.	BULGARIA	MOL.	MOLDOVA	U.K.	UNITED KINGDOM
CR.	CROATIA	NETH.	NETHERLANDS	U.S.A.	UNITED STATES OF AMERICA
CZ.F.	CZECH REPUBLIC	N.Z.	NEW ZEALAND	UZBEK.	UZBEKISTAN
EST.	ESTONIA	R.	RWANDA	YU.	YUGOSLAVIA
GEOR.	GEORGIA	R.F.	RUSSIAN FEDERATION		

Washington D.C., leading international political centre and capital city of the United States of America.

La Paz, the world's highest capital city, and joint capital of Bolivia with Sucre.

Cape Town, legislative capital of the Republic of South Africa.

world

LARGEST COUNTRIES BY AREA	sq km	sq miles	map	SMALLEST COUNTRIES BY AREA	sq km	sq miles	map	JOINT CAPITALS	country	map
Russian Federation	17 075 400	6 592 849	26–27	Vatican City	0.5	0.2	44	Amsterdam/The Hague	Netherlands	36 B2
Canada	9 970 610	3 849 674	120–121	Monaco	2	1	39	Kuala Lumpur/Putrajaya	Malaysia	58 C2
United States of America	9 809 378	3 787 422	126–127	Nauru	21	8	107	La Paz/Sucre	Bolivia	148 C4 / 148 D4
China	9 584 492	3 700 593	62–63	Tuvalu	25	10	107	Pretoria/Cape Town	South Africa	99 F5 / 98 C7
Brazil	8 547 379	3 300 161	150–151	San Marino	61	24	44			
Australia	7 682 395	2 966 189	106–107	Liechtenstein	160	62	39			
India	3 065 027	1 183 414	70–71	St Kitts and Nevis	261	101	139			
Argentina	2 766 889	1 068 302	152–153	Maldives	298	115	71			
Kazakhstan	2 717 300	1 049 155	26–27	Grenada	378	146	147			
Sudan	2 505 813	967 500	88–89	St Vincent and the Grenadines	389	150	147			

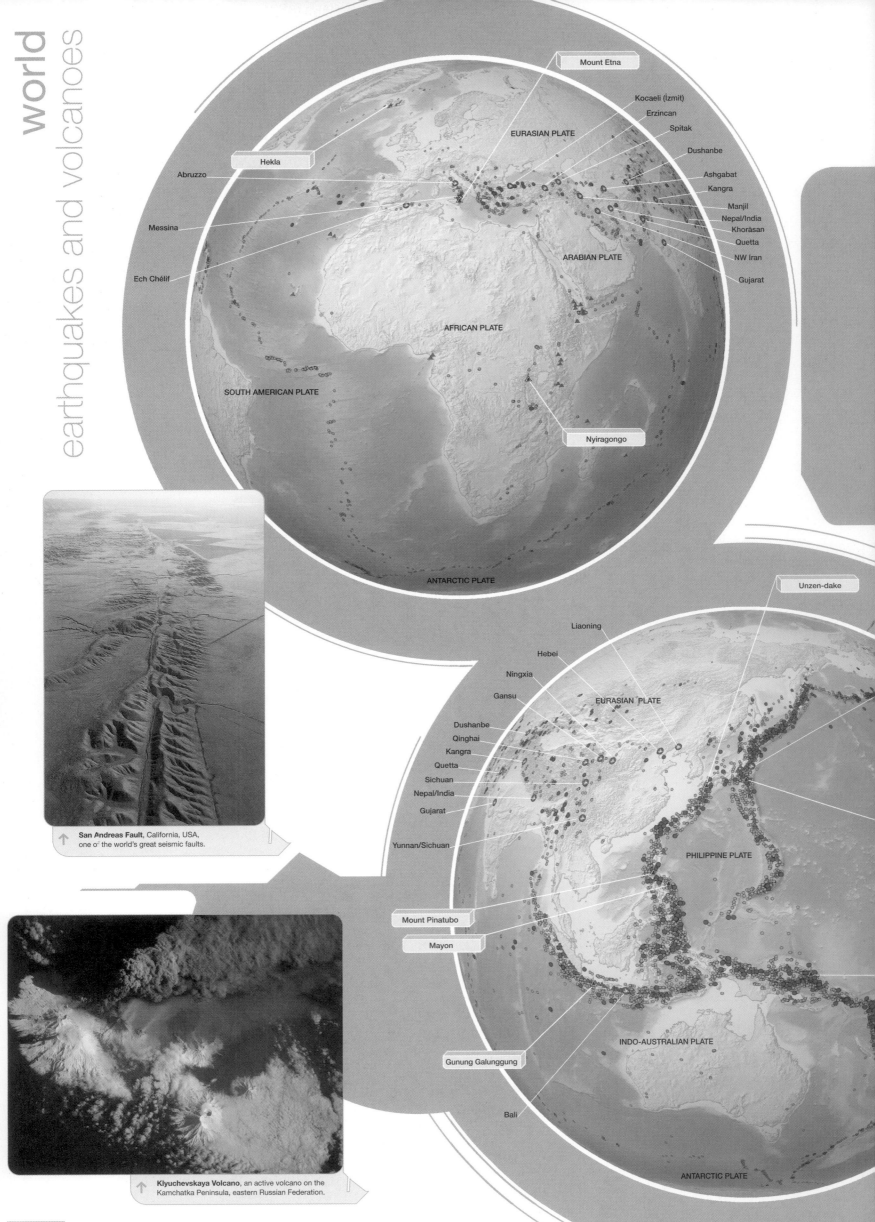

Mount Etna

Kocaeli (İzmit)

Erzincan

Spitak

Dushanbe

Ashgabat

Kangra

EURASIAN PLATE

Hekla

Abruzzo

Messina

Manjil

Nepal/India

Khorāsan

Quetta

NW Iran

Gujarat

ARABIAN PLATE

Ech Chélif

AFRICAN PLATE

SOUTH AMERICAN PLATE

Nyiragongo

ANTARCTIC PLATE

San Andreas Fault, California, USA,
one of the world's great seismic faults.

Unzen-dake

Liaoning

Hebei

Ningxia

Gansu

EURASIAN PLATE

Dushanbe

Qinghai

Kangra

Quetta

Sichuan

Nepal/India

Gujarat

PHILIPPINE PLATE

Yunnan/Sichuan

Mount Pinatubo

Mayon

Gunung Galunggung

INDO-AUSTRALIAN PLATE

Bali

ANTARCTIC PLATE

Klyuchevskaya Volcano, an active volcano on the
Kamchatka Peninsula, eastern Russian Federation.

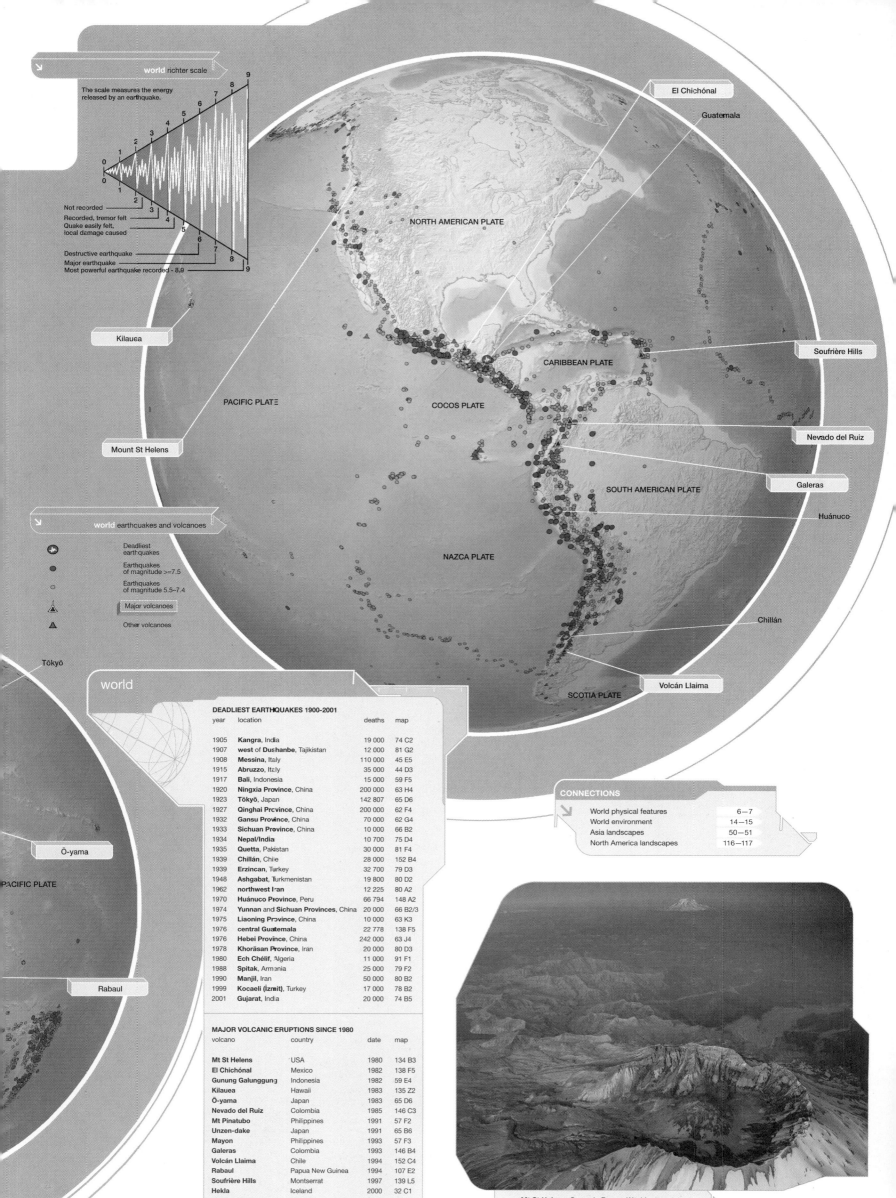

world richter scale

The scale measures the energy released by an earthquake.

9
8
7
6
5
4
3
2
1
0

Not recorded
Recorded, tremor felt
Quake easily felt, local damage caused
Destructive earthquake
Major earthquake
Most powerful earthquake recorded - 8.9

Kilauea

Mount St Helens

PACIFIC PLATE

NORTH AMERICAN PLATE

El Chichónal

Guatemala

Soufrière Hills

CARIBBEAN PLATE

COCOS PLATE

Nevado del Ruiz

Galeras

SOUTH AMERICAN PLATE

Huánuco

NAZCA PLATE

Chillán

Volcán Llaima

SCOTIA PLATE

world earthquakes and volcanoes

- Deadliest earthquakes
- Earthquakes of magnitude >=7.5
- Earthquakes of magnitude 5.5–7.4
- △ Major volcanoes
- ▲ Other volcanoes

Tōkyō

Ō-yama

PACIFIC PLATE

Rabaul

world

DEADLIEST EARTHQUAKES 1900-2001

year	location	deaths	map
1905	**Kangra**, India	19 000	74 C2
1907	west of **Dushanbe**, Tajikistan	12 000	81 G2
1908	**Messina**, Italy	110 000	45 E5
1915	**Abruzzo**, Italy	35 000	44 D3
1917	**Bali**, Indonesia	15 000	59 F5
1920	**Ningxia Province**, China	200 000	63 H4
1923	**Tōkyō**, Japan	142 807	65 D6
1927	**Qinghai Province**, China	200 000	62 F4
1932	**Gansu Province**, China	70 000	62 G4
1933	**Sichuan Province**, China	10 000	66 B2
1934	**Nepal/India**	10 700	75 D4
1935	**Quetta**, Pakistan	30 000	81 F4
1939	**Chillán**, Chile	28 000	152 B4
1939	**Erzincan**, Turkey	32 700	79 D3
1948	**Ashgabat**, Turkmenistan	19 800	80 D2
1962	**northwest Iran**	12 225	80 A2
1970	**Huánuco Province**, Peru	66 794	148 A2
1974	**Yunnan** and **Sichuan Provinces**, China	20 000	66 B2/3
1975	**Liaoning Province**, China	10 000	63 K3
1976	**central Guatemala**	22 778	138 F5
1976	**Hebei Province**, China	242 000	63 J4
1978	**Khorāsān Province**, Iran	20 000	80 D3
1980	**Ech Chélif**, Algeria	11 000	91 F1
1988	**Spitak**, Armenia	25 000	79 F2
1990	**Manjil**, Iran	50 000	80 B2
1999	**Kocaeli (İzmit)**, Turkey	17 000	78 B2
2001	**Gujarat**, India	20 000	74 B5

MAJOR VOLCANIC ERUPTIONS SINCE 1980

volcano	country	date	map
Mt St Helens	USA	1980	134 B3
El Chichónal	Mexico	1982	138 F5
Gunung Galunggung	Indonesia	1982	59 E4
Kilauea	Hawaii	1983	135 Z2
Ō-yama	Japan	1983	65 D6
Nevado del Ruiz	Colombia	1985	146 C3
Mt Pinatubo	Philippines	1991	57 F2
Unzen-dake	Japan	1991	65 B6
Mayon	Philippines	1993	57 F3
Galeras	Colombia	1993	146 B4
Volcán Llaima	Chile	1994	152 C4
Rabaul	Papua New Guinea	1994	107 E2
Soufrière Hills	Montserrat	1997	139 L5
Hekla	Iceland	2000	32 C1
Mt Etna	Italy	2001	45 E6
Nyiragongo	Democratic Republic of Congo	2002	94 F5

CONNECTIONS

World physical features	6—7
World environment	14—15
Asia landscapes	50—51
North America landscapes	116—117

↑ **Mt St Helens**, Cascade Range, Washington state, USA which erupted violently in May 1980.

Computer generated image of **Hurricane Floyd** near the Florida coast, 1999, the deadliest US hurricane since 1972.

CONNECTIONS

World physical features   6—7
World environment   14—15
Oceans features   156—157
Poles features   158—159

world major climatic regions and sub-types

Polar		Cooler humid		Warmer humid		Köppen classification system

Polar	Cooler humid	Warmer humid
EF Ice cap	DcDd Subarctic	CbCc Temperate
ET Tundra	Db Continental cool summer	Ca Humid subtropical
	Da Continental warm summer	Cs Mediterranean

Dry	Tropical humid
BS Steppe	Aw As Savanna
BW Desert	Af Am Rain forest

Köppen classification system

A Rainy climate with no winter: coolest month above 18°C (64.4°F).

B Dry climates; limits are defined by formulae based on rainfall effectiveness: BS Steppe or semi-arid climate. BW Desert or arid climate.

*C Rainy climates with mild winters: coolest month above 0°C (32°F), but below 18°C (64.4°F); warmest month above 10°C (50°F).

*D Rainy climates with severe winters: coldest month below 0°C (32°F); warmest month above 10°C (50°F).

E Polar climates with no warm season: warmest month below 10°C (50°F). ET Tundra climate: warmest month below 10°C (50°F) but above 0°C (32°F). EF Perpetual frost: all months below 0°C (32°F).

a Warmest month above 22°C (71.6°F).
b Warmest month below 22°C (71.6°F).
c Less than four months over 10°C (50°F).
d As 'c', but with severe cold: coldest month below -38°C (-36.4°F).
f Constantly moist rainfall throughout the year.
*h Warmer dry; all months above 0°C (32°F).
*k Cooler dry: at least one month below 0°C (32°F).
m Monsoon rain: short dry season, but is compensated by heavy rains during rest of the year.
n Frequent fog.
s Dry season in summer.
w Dry season in winter.

* Modification of Köppen definition

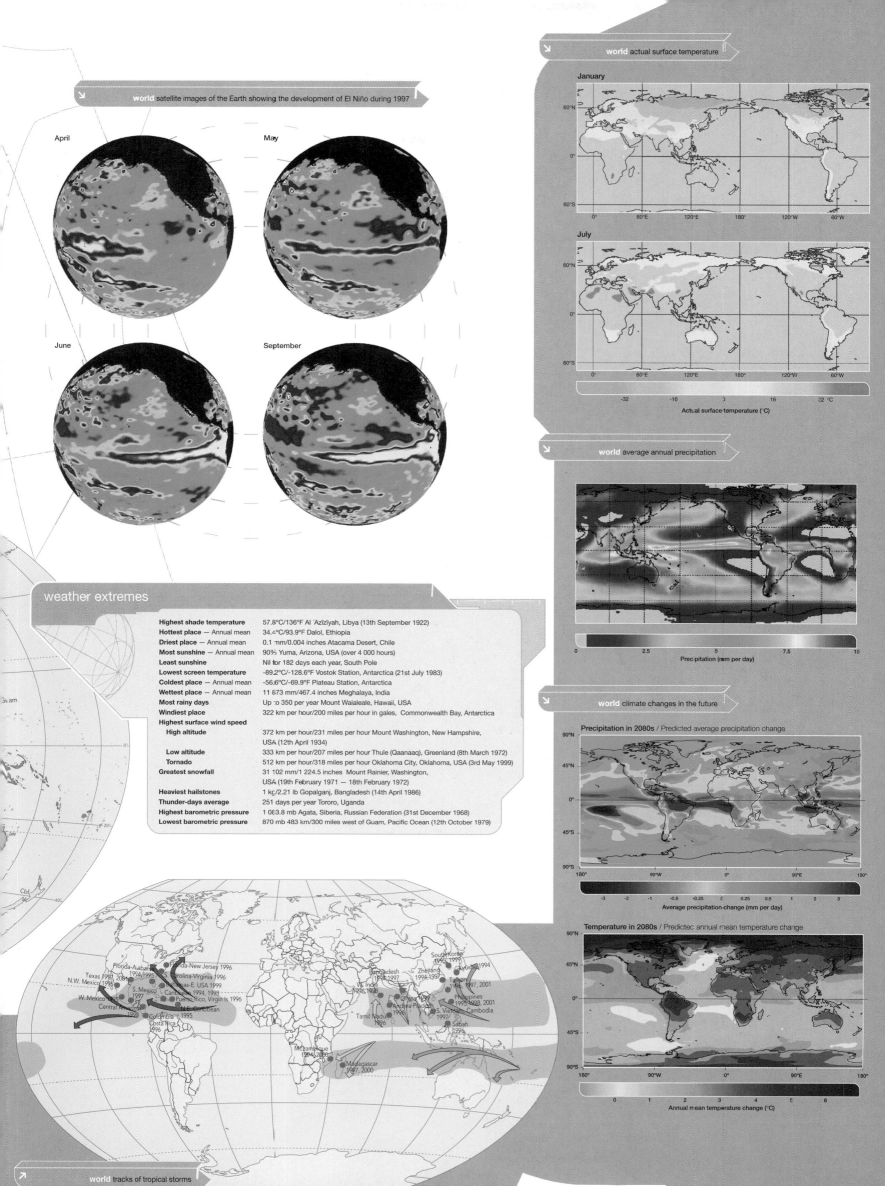

April

May

June

September

January

July

-32   -16   0   16   32 °C

Actual surface temperature (°C)

0   2.5   5   7.5   10

Precipitation (mm per day)

Precipitation in 2080s / Predicted average precipitation change

-3   -2   -1   -0.5   -0.25   0   0.25   0.5   1   2   3

Average precipitation change (mm per day)

Temperature in 2080s / Predicted annual mean temperature change

0   1   2   3   4   5   6

Annual mean temperature change (°C)

weather extremes

Highest shade temperature	57.8°C/136°F Al 'Aziziyah, Libya (13th September 1922)
Hottest place — Annual mean	34.4°C/93.9°F Dalol, Ethiopia
Driest place — Annual mean	0.1 mm/0.004 inches Atacama Desert, Chile
Most sunshine — Annual mean	90% Yuma, Arizona, USA (over 4 000 hours)
Least sunshine	Nil for 182 days each year, South Pole
Lowest screen temperature	-89.2°C/-128.6°F Vostok Station, Antarctica (21st July 1983)
Coldest place — Annual mean	-56.6°C/-69.9°F Plateau Station, Antarctica
Wettest place — Annual mean	11 873 mm/467.4 inches Meghalaya, India
Most rainy days	Up to 350 per year Mount Waialeale, Hawaii, USA
Windiest place	322 km per hour/200 miles per hour in gales, Commonwealth Bay, Antarctica
Highest surface wind speed	
High altitude	372 km per hour/231 miles per hour Mount Washington, New Hampshire, USA (12th April 1934)
Low altitude	333 km per hour/207 miles per hour Thule (Qaanaaq), Greenland (8th March 1972)
Tornado	512 km per hour/318 miles per hour Oklahoma City, Oklahoma, USA (3rd May 1999)
Greatest snowfall	31 102 mm/1 224.5 inches Mount Rainier, Washington, USA (19th February 1971 — 18th February 1972)
Heaviest hailstones	1 kg/2.21 lb Gopalganj, Bangladesh (14th April 1986)
Thunder-days average	251 days per year Tororo, Uganda
Highest barometric pressure	1 083.8 mb Agata, Siberia, Russian Federation (31st December 1968)
Lowest barometric pressure	870 mb 483 km/300 miles west of Guam, Pacific Ocean (12th October 1979)

Wind speeds often over 160 km per hour

⇨ Cyclone track   ⇨ Willy-willies   ☐ Source area of tropical storms

⇨ Typhoon track   ⇨ Hurricane track   ● Major tropical storm (1994–2001)

↑ **Urban**, La Paz, Bolivia.

↑ **Barren/Shrubland**, Death Valley, California, USA.

Forest/Woodland, Amazonian rainforest, Peru, South America. ↓

One of Africa's largest bodies of water, **Lake Chad**, West Africa in 1973. ↓

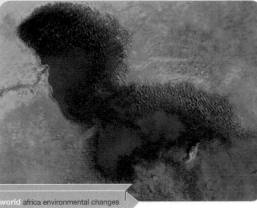

→ world africa environmental changes

↑ **Lake Chad**, 1997, reduced in size as a result of massive irrigation projects and an increasingly dry climate.

CONNECTIONS

World physical features	6 — 7
World climate and weather	12 — 13
World population and cities	16 — 17
Oceans features	156 — 157
Poles features	158 — 159

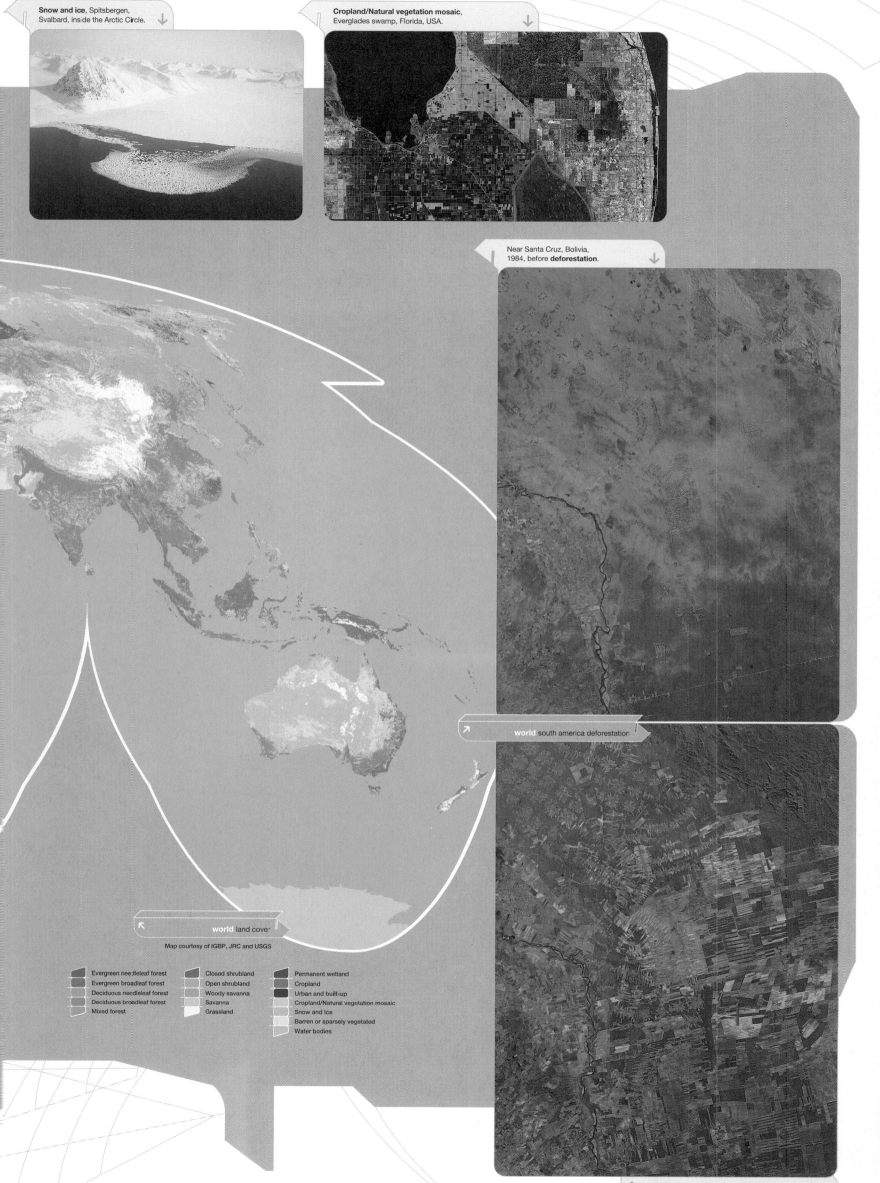

Snow and ice, Spitsbergen, Svalbard, inside the Arctic Circle.

Cropland/Natural vegetation mosaic, Everglades swamp, Florida, USA.

Near Santa Cruz, Bolivia, 1984, before **deforestation**.

world south america deforestation

world land cover

Map courtesy of IGBP, JRC and USGS

- Evergreen needleleaf forest
- Evergreen broadleaf forest
- Deciduous needleleaf forest
- Deciduous broadleaf forest
- Mixed forest
- Closed shrubland
- Open shrubland
- Woody savanna
- Savanna
- Grassland
- Permanent wetland
- Cropland
- Urban and built-up
- Cropland/Natural vegetation mosaic
- Snow and Ice
- Barren or sparsely vegetated
- Water bodies

Near Santa Cruz, Bolivia, 1998, after extensive **deforestation**.

world

TOP TEN COUNTRIES

country	rank	population
China	1	1 270 082 000
India	2	1 025 096 000
United States of America	3	285 926 000
Indonesia	4	214 840 000
Brazil	5	172 559 000
Pakistan	6	144 971 000
Russian Federation	7	144 664 000
Bangladesh	8	140 369 000
Japan	9	127 335 000
Nigeria	10	116 924 000

KEY POPULATION STATISTICS FOR MAJOR REGIONS

	population (millions) 2001	growth (per cent) 2000-2005	*infant mortality rate 1995-2000	**total fertility rate 1995-2000	life expectancy (years) 1995-2000
World	6 134	1.23	57	2.82	65.0
More developed regions	1 194	0.16	9	1.57	74.9
Less developed regions	4 940	1.48	63	3.10	63.0
Africa	813	2.33	87	5.27	51.4
Asia	3 721	1.26	57	2.70	65.8
Europe	726	-0.18	12	1.41	73.2
Latin America and the Caribbean	527	1.42	36	2.69	69.3
North America	317	0.88	7	2.00	76.7
Oceania	31	1.24	24	2.41	73.5

*Deaths of infants less than one year old per 1000 live births
**Estimate of number of children a woman will bear through her child-bearing years

CONNECTIONS

World countries	8—9
World indicators	20
Europe states and territories	48
Asia states and territories	82
Africa states and territories	100
Oceania states and territories	114
North America states and territories	140
South America states and territories	154

Village settlement in sparsely populated area of Côte d'Ivoire, West Africa.

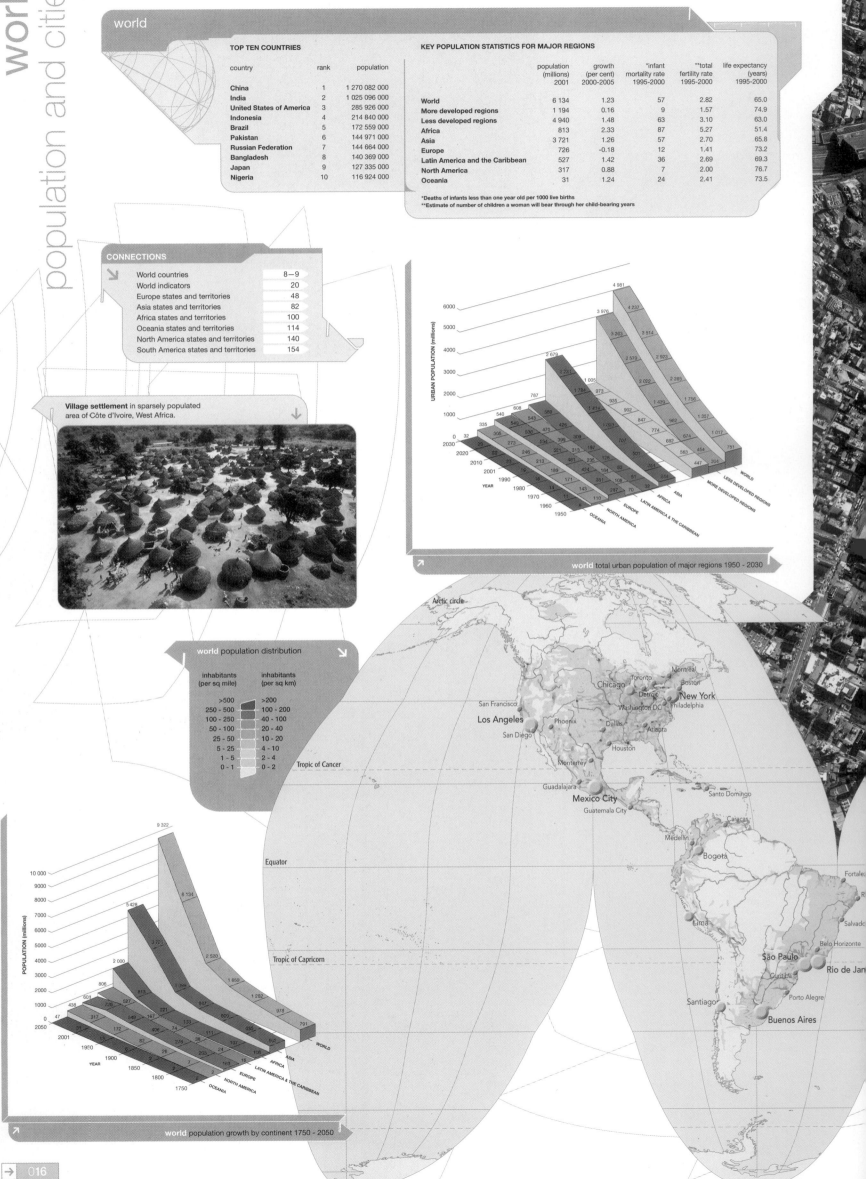

world total urban population of major regions 1950 - 2030

world population distribution

inhabitants (per sq mile) | inhabitants (per sq km)
- >500 | >200
- 250 - 500 | 100 - 200
- 100 - 250 | 40 - 100
- 50 - 100 | 20 - 40
- 25 - 50 | 10 - 20
- 5 - 25 | 4 - 10
- 1 - 5 | 2 - 4
- 0 - 1 | 0 - 2

world population growth by continent 1750 - 2050

Densely populated urban agglomeration of Tōkyō, Japan, the **world's largest city.**

1930

1975

2050

Each dot on the map represents a city with over 5 million inhabitants

world growth of cities

world

St Petersburg

Düsseldorf Hamburg
London Berlin
Paris Essen Katowice Moscow
Cologne Frankfurt
Stuttgart Milan
Barcelona Rome İstanbul
Lisbon Naples Ankara
Madrid Athens
Casablanca Algiers Kābul
Alexandria Baghdād Tehrān
Cairo Lahore Delhi
Riyadh
Jeddah Ahmadabad Karachi
Khartoum Kanpur Dhaka
Mumbai Surat Kolkata
(Bombay) Pune (Calcutta)
Hyderabad Chittagong
Addis Bangalore Chennai
Abidjan Ababa
Lagos Ha Nôi
Bangkok
Rangōon
Kinshasa
Luanda Ho Chi
Minh City
Singapore
Jakarta
Bandung
Johannesburg
Cape Town

Harbin
Changchun
Shenyang
Beijing P'yŏngyang Nagoya
Tianjin Dalian Seoul Tōkyō
Xian Taiyuan Zhengzhou Taegu Ōsaka
Chengdu Nanjing Pusan Kita-Kyūshū
Chongqing Wuhan
Guiyang Shanghai
Guangzhou T'aipei
Hong Kong
Manila

LARGEST CITIES

city	country	population
Tōkyō	Japan	26 444 000
Mexico City	Mexico	18 066 000
São Paulo	Brazil	17 962 000
New York	USA	16 732 000
Mumbai (Bombay)	India	16 086 000
Los Angeles	USA	13 213 000
Kolkata (Calcutta)	India	13 058 000
Shanghai	China	12 887 000
Dhaka	Bangladesh	12 519 000
Delhi	India	12 441 000
Buenos Aires	Argentina	12 024 000
Jakarta	Indonesia	11 018 000
Ōsaka	Japan	11 013 000
Beijing	China	10 839 000
Rio de Janeiro	Brazil	10 652 000
Karachi	Pakistan	10 032 000
Manila	Philippines	9 950 000
Seoul	South Korea	9 888 000
Paris	France	9 630 000
Cairo	Egypt	9 462 000

Sydney
Melbourne

inhabitants

over 20 million

10 - 20 million

5 - 10 million

2.5 - 5 million

world urban agglomerations

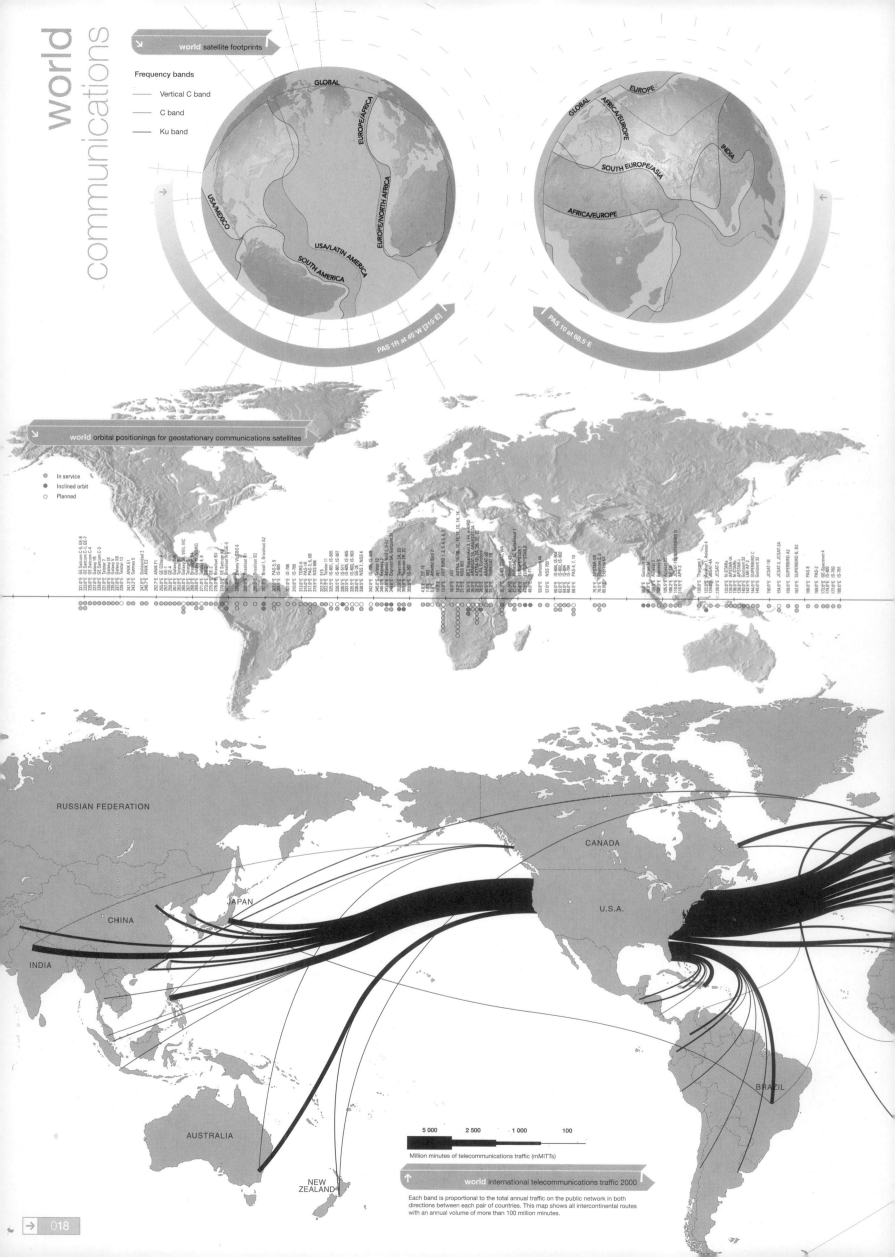

world satellite footprints

Frequency bands

— Vertical C band
— C band
— Ku band

GLOBAL

EUROPE/AFRICA

EUROPE/NORTH AFRICA

USA/MEXICO

USA/LATIN AMERICA

SOUTH AMERICA

PAS 1R at 45° W (315° E)

EUROPE

AFRICA/EUROPE

GLOBAL

INDIA

SOUTH EUROPE/ASIA

AFRICA/EUROPE

PAS 10 at 68.5° E

world orbital positionings for geostationary communications satellites

○ In service
● Inclined orbit
○ Planned

RUSSIAN FEDERATION

CANADA

JAPAN

CHINA

U.S.A.

INDIA

BRAZIL

AUSTRALIA

NEW
ZEALAND

5 000   2 500   1 000   100

Million minutes of telecommunications traffic (mMiTTs)

world international telecommunications traffic 2000

Each band is proportional to the total annual traffic on the public network in both
directions between each pair of countries. This map shows all intercontinental routes
with an annual volume of more than 100 million minutes.

NORTH
AMERICA

EUROPE

ASIA

OCEANIA

SOUTH
AMERICA

AFRICA

world

San Francisco airport, California, USA,
ninth busiest airport in the world.

THE WORLD'S BUSIEST AIRPORTS	country	number of passengers
Atlanta Hartsfield	USA	80 162 407
Chicago O'Hare	USA	72 144 244
Los Angeles	USA	66 424 767
London Heathrow	UK	64 606 826
Dallas/Fort Worth	USA	60 687 122
Tokyo Haneda	Japan	56 402 206
Frankfurt	Germany	49 360 630
Paris Charles de Gaulle	France	48 246 137
San Francisco	USA	41 040 995
Amsterdam	Netherlands	39 606 925
Denver	USA	38 751 687
Las Vegas Mccarran	USA	36 865 866
Minneapolis/St Paul	USA	36 751 632
Seoul Kimpo	South Korea	36 727 124
Phoenix Sky Harbor	USA	36 040 469
Detroit Wayne County	USA	35 535 080
Houston	USA	35 251 372
New York Newark	USA	34 188 468
Miami	USA	33 621 273
Madrid	Spain	32 893 190
New York JFK	USA	32 856 220
Hong Kong	China	32 752 359
London Gatwick	UK	32 065 685
Orlando	USA	30 823 509
St Louis Lambert	USA	30 561 387
Bangkok	Thailand	29 616 432
Toronto Lester B. Pearson	Canada	28 930 036
Singapore Changi	Singapore	28 618 200
Seattle-Tacoma	USA	28 408 553
Boston	USA	27 412 926

RUSSIAN FEDERATION

CHINA

SAUDI
ARABIA

INDIA

REPUBLIC OF
SOUTH
AFRICA

millions
10 000

1 000

100

10

1

6134

1044
941
495

141

Population
Main lines
Cellular subscribers
PCs
Internet host computers

1970 1973 1976 1979 1982 1985 1988 1991 1994 1997 2001

world telecommunications equipment

Regional distribution of population (%)

| 14.9 | 30.6 | 7.8 | 8.5 | 4.9 | 22.4 | 10 |

World population: 6 057 000 000

Regional distribution of land area (%)

| 24.2 | 12.2 | 18.1 | 15.3 | 8.2 | 3.9 | 18.1 |

World land surface area: 133 806 000 sq km

Regional distribution of Gross National Income (%)

| 79.8 | 6.3 | 3.0 | 6.0 | 2.0 | 1.0 |
1.9

World Gross National Income: 31 315 000 million $

world regional distributions

High-income economies
East Asia and Pacific
Europe and Central Asia
Latin America and the Caribbean
Middle East and North Africa
South Asia
Sub-Saharan Africa
No data

world regions / as defined by the World Bank

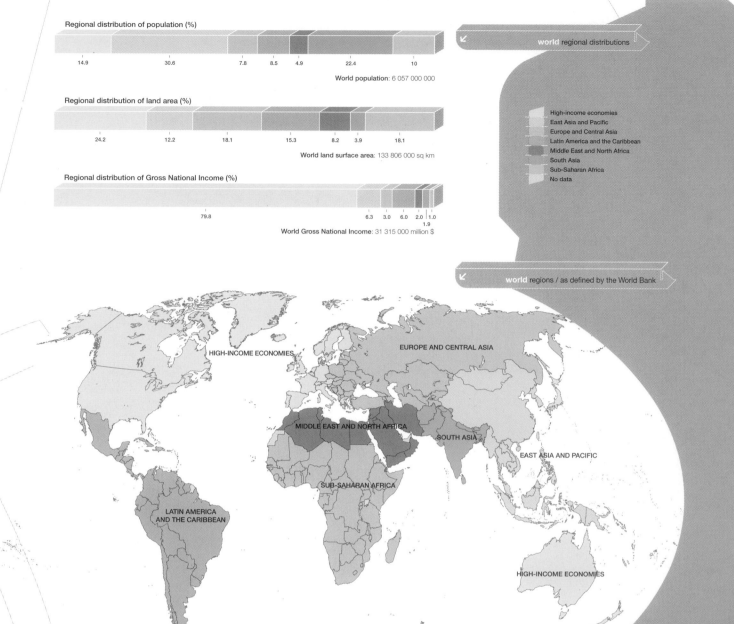

HIGH-INCOME ECONOMIES
EUROPE AND CENTRAL ASIA
MIDDLE EAST AND NORTH AFRICA
SOUTH ASIA
EAST ASIA AND PACIFIC
SUB-SAHARAN AFRICA
LATIN AMERICA AND THE CARIBBEAN
HIGH-INCOME ECONOMIES

world indicators / by region

	World	High-income economies	East Asia and Pacific	Europe and Central Asia	Latin America and the Caribbean	Middle East and North Africa	South Asia	Sub-Saharan Africa
Population 2000 (millions)	6 057	903	1 855	474	516	295	1 355	659
Annual population growth (%)	1.31	0.68	0.95	0.07	1.53	1.90	1.92	2.43
Surface area (thousand sq km)	133 806	32 315	16 385	24 217	20 459	11 023	5 140	24 267
Gross National Income (million $)	31 315 000	24 994 000	1 962 000	953 000	1 895 000	618 000	595 000	310 000
Gross National Income per capita ($)	5 170	27 680	1 060	2 010	3 670	2 090	440	470
Life expectancy (years)	66	78	69	69	70	68	62	47
Infant mortality rate (per 1 000 live births)	54	6	35	20	29	43	73	91
Access to safe water (% of total population)	80	-	75	90	85	89	87	55
Adult illiteracy rate (% of population over 15 years)	-	-	14	3	12	35	45	39
Aid per capita (US $)	-	-	4.56	22.91	9.67	15.61	3.13	20.42

World Bank Headquarters, Washington DC

European Central Bank, Frankfurt

UN Headquarters, Washington DC

European Parliament, Strasbourg

europe

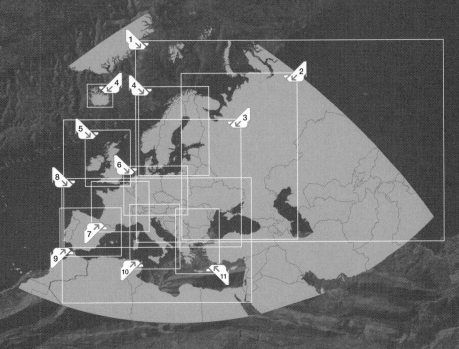

contents

		map coverage	scale
22–23	landscapes		
24–25	locations		
26–27	map_1	**russian federation**	1:18 000 000
28–29	map_2	**russian federation** west	1:7 500 000
30–31	map_3	**europe** northwest	1:7 500 000
32–33	map_4	**iceland, norway, sweden, finland** and **denmark**	1:4 500 000
34–35	map_5	**united kingdom** and **republic of ireland**	1:3 000 000
36–37	map_6	**europe** north central	1:3 000 000
38–39	map_7	**france** and **switzerland**	1:3 000 000
40–41	map_8	**europe** south and the **mediterranean**	1:9 000 000
42–43	map_9	**spain** and **portugal**	1:3 000 000
44–45	map_10	**italy, slovenia, croatia** and **bosnia-herzegovina**	1:3 000 000
46–47	map_11	**europe** southeast	1:3 000 000
48	states and territories		

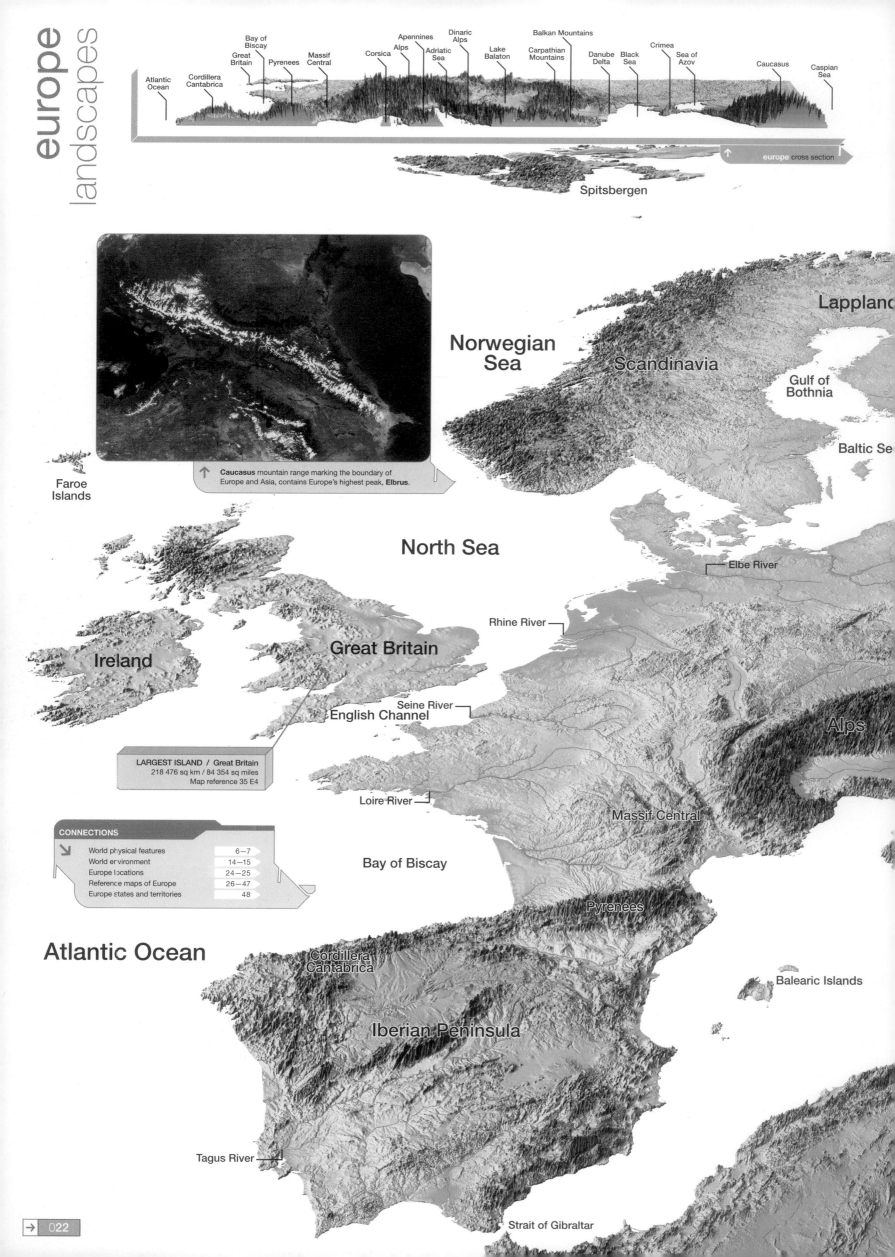

Atlantic Ocean

Cordillera Cantabrica

Great Britain

Bay of Biscay

Pyrenees

Massif Central

Corsica

Alps

Apennines

Adriatic Sea

Dinaric Alps

Lake Balaton

Balkan Mountains

Carpathian Mountains

Danube Delta

Black Sea

Crimea

Sea of Azov

Caucasus

Caspian Sea

europe cross section

Spitsbergen

Lappland

Norwegian Sea

Scandinavia

Gulf of Bothnia

Baltic Sea

Caucasus mountain range marking the boundary of Europe and Asia, contains Europe's highest peak, **Elbrus**.

Faroe Islands

North Sea

Elbe River

Rhine River

Ireland

Great Britain

Seine River

English Channel

Alps

LARGEST ISLAND / Great Britain
218 476 sq km / 84 354 sq miles
Map reference 35 E4

Loire River

CONNECTIONS

World physical features   6—7
World environment   14—15
Europe locations   24—25
Reference maps of Europe   26—47
Europe states and territories   48

Massif Central

Bay of Biscay

Pyrenees

Atlantic Ocean

Cordillera Cantabrica

Balearic Islands

Iberian Peninsula

Tagus River

Strait of Gibraltar

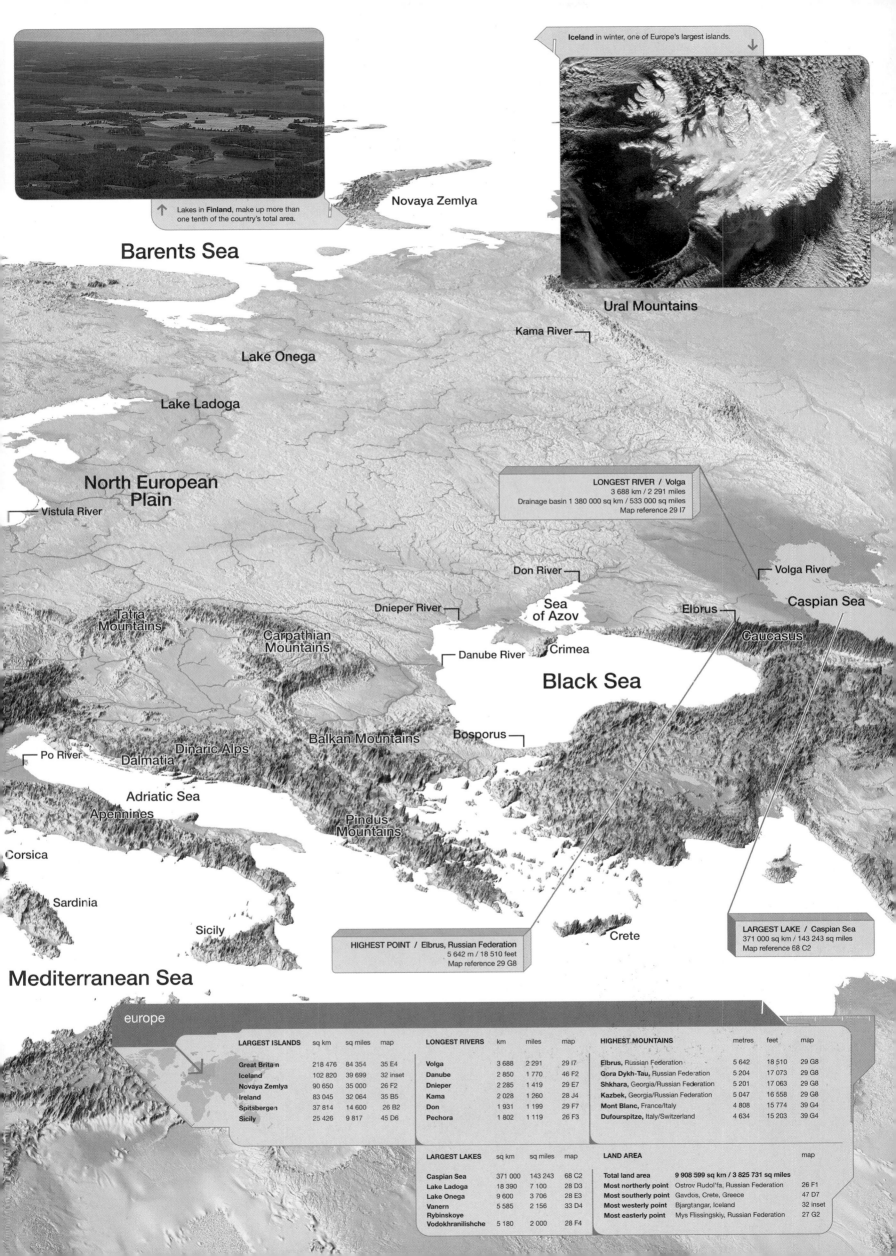

Lakes in **Finland**, make up more than one tenth of the country's total area.

Iceland in winter, one of Europe's largest islands.

Novaya Zemlya

Barents Sea

Ural Mountains

Kama River

Lake Onega

Lake Ladoga

North European Plain

Vistula River

LONGEST RIVER / Volga
3 688 km / 2 291 miles
Drainage basin 1 380 000 sq km / 533 000 sq miles
Map reference 29 I7

Don River

Volga River

Dnieper River

Sea of Azov

Elbrus

Caspian Sea

Tatra Mountains

Carpathian Mountains

Danube River

Crimea

Caucasus

Black Sea

Balkan Mountains

Bosporus

Dinaric Alps

Po River

Dalmatia

Adriatic Sea

Apennines

Pindus Mountains

Corsica

Sardinia

Sicily

Crete

LARGEST LAKE / Caspian Sea
371 000 sq km / 143 243 sq miles
Map reference 68 C2

HIGHEST POINT / Elbrus, Russian Federation
5 642 m / 18 510 feet
Map reference 29 G8

Mediterranean Sea

europe

LARGEST ISLANDS	sq km	sq miles	map		LONGEST RIVERS	km	miles	map		HIGHEST MOUNTAINS	metres	feet	map
Great Britain	218 476	84 354	35 E4		Volga	3 688	2 291	29 I7		Elbrus, Russian Federation	5 642	18 510	29 G8
Iceland	102 820	39 699	32 inset		Danube	2 850	1 770	46 F2		Gora Dykh-Tau, Russian Federation	5 204	17 073	29 G8
Novaya Zemlya	90 650	35 000	26 F2		Dnieper	2 285	1 419	29 E7		Shkhara, Georgia/Russian Federation	5 201	17 063	29 G8
Ireland	83 045	32 064	35 B5		Kama	2 028	1 260	28 J4		Kazbek, Georgia/Russian Federation	5 047	16 558	29 G8
Spitsbergen	37 814	14 600	26 B2		Don	1 931	1 199	29 F7		Mont Blanc, France/Italy	4 808	15 774	39 G4
Sicily	25 426	9 817	45 D6		Pechora	1 802	1 119	26 F3		Dufourspitze, Italy/Switzerland	4 634	15 203	39 G4

LARGEST LAKES	sq km	sq miles	map		LAND AREA		map
Caspian Sea	371 000	143 243	68 C2		**Total land area**	9 908 599 sq km / 3 825 731 sq miles	
Lake Ladoga	18 390	7 100	28 D3		**Most northerly point**	Ostrov Rudol'fa, Russian Federation	26 F1
Lake Onega	9 600	3 706	28 E3		**Most southerly point**	Gavdos, Crete, Greece	47 D7
Vänern	5 585	2 156	33 D4		**Most westerly point**	Bjargtangar, Iceland	32 inset
Rybinskoye Vodokhranilishche	5 180	2 000	28 F4		**Most easterly point**	Mys Flissingskiy, Russian Federation	27 G2

↑ Snow-capped mountains in the Swiss **Alps**.

↑ **Venice**, northeastern Italy, city of lagoons and islands connected by numerous canals and bridges.

Space Imaging

CONNECTIONS

World countries	8—9
Europe landscapes	22—23
Reference maps of Europe	26—47
Europe states and territories	48
Atlantic Ocean	160—161
Arctic Ocean	166

↑ Rugged, mountainous landscape of southern Greece and the **Peloponnese Peninsula**.

ARCTIC OCEAN

Spitsbergen
LONGYEARBYEN
Svalbard
(Norway)

Bjørnøya
(Norway)

Jan Mayen
(Norway)

Ba

Denmark Strait

North Cape

REYKJAVIK
ICELAND

*Norwegian
Sea*

ATLANTIC

OCEAN

N
O
R
W
A
Y

S
W
E
D
E
N

FINLAN

Gulf of Bothnia

Faroe Islands
(Denmark) ·TÓRSHAVN

Shetland

Orkney

Outer
Hebrides

Skagerrak

Kattegat

OSLO

STOCKHOLM

HELSINKI

TALLINN

ESTONIA

Lake
Peipus

RIGA

LATVIA

Glasgow
Edinburgh

North
Sea

Ålborg

DENMARK

COPENHAGEN

Bornholm

Baltic Sea

RUSSIAN
FEDERATION

Kaliningrad

LITHUANIA

VILNIUS

MIN

Belfast

REPUBLIC
OF IRELAND
DUBLIN

UNITED

Liverpool
Leeds

Odense

Hamburg

Gdańsk

Grodno

Białystok

BE

Birmingham
Manchester

NETHERLANDS
AMSTERDAM
THE HAGUE

Bremen

Hannover

Poznań

Łódź

WARSAW

Brest

Cardiff

KINGDOM

LONDON

Rotterdam

Essen

BERLIN

Bydgoszcz

POLAND

Channel Islands
(U.K.)

English Channel

BRUSSELS
Lille

Cologne

GERMANY

Leipzig

Wrocław

Rivne

Brest

BELGIUM
Bonn

Katowice

Kraków

Lviv

Rennes

LUXEMBOURG·LUXEMBOURG

PARIS

Strasbourg

Stuttgart

PRAGUE

CZECH
REPUBLIC

Dniester

A Coruña

Bordeaux

Bay
of Biscay

FRANCE

Orléans

Dijon

Munich

VIENNA

Brno

SLOVAKIA

BRATISLAVA

Košice

Debrecen

Nantes

BERN

Zürich

Innsbruck

Salzburg

AUSTRIA

BUDAPEST

HUNGARY

Oradea

ROMAN

Bilbao

ANDORRA

Geneva

SWITZERLAND

LIECHTENSTEIN

Lyon

SLOVENIA

LJUBLJANA

ZAGREB

Szeged

Timișoara

Oporto

Salamanca

Toulouse

Milan

Turin

Venice

Trieste

CROATIA

BELGRADE

Brașov

Craiova

Pleven

BUCHARES

PORTUGAL

SPAIN

MADRID

Zaragoza

ANDORRA
LA VELLA

Nice

MONACO

Bologna

Florence

BOSNIA-
HERZEGOVINA
SARAJEVO

Split

YUGOSLAVIA

BULG

LISBON

Lugus

Tagus

Marseille

VATICAN CITY
ROME

SAN
MARINO

I
T
A
L
Y

Adriatic Sea

Podgorica

SKOPJE

SOFIA

Seville

Córdoba

Valencia

Barcelona

Corsica

TIRANA

MACEDONIA

Thessaloniki

Ibiza

Majorca

Sardinia

Naples

Bari

ALBANIA

GREECE

Aege

Cádiz

GIBRALTAR
(U.K.)

Málaga

Minorca

Balearic
Islands

Tyrrhenian
Sea

Ionian
Sea

Cre

Ceuta
(Spain)

Melilla
(Spain)

Cartagena

Cosenza

Palermo

Messina

icily

Syracuse

M e d i t e r r a n e a n S

VALLETTA
MALTA

ATHENS

Larisa

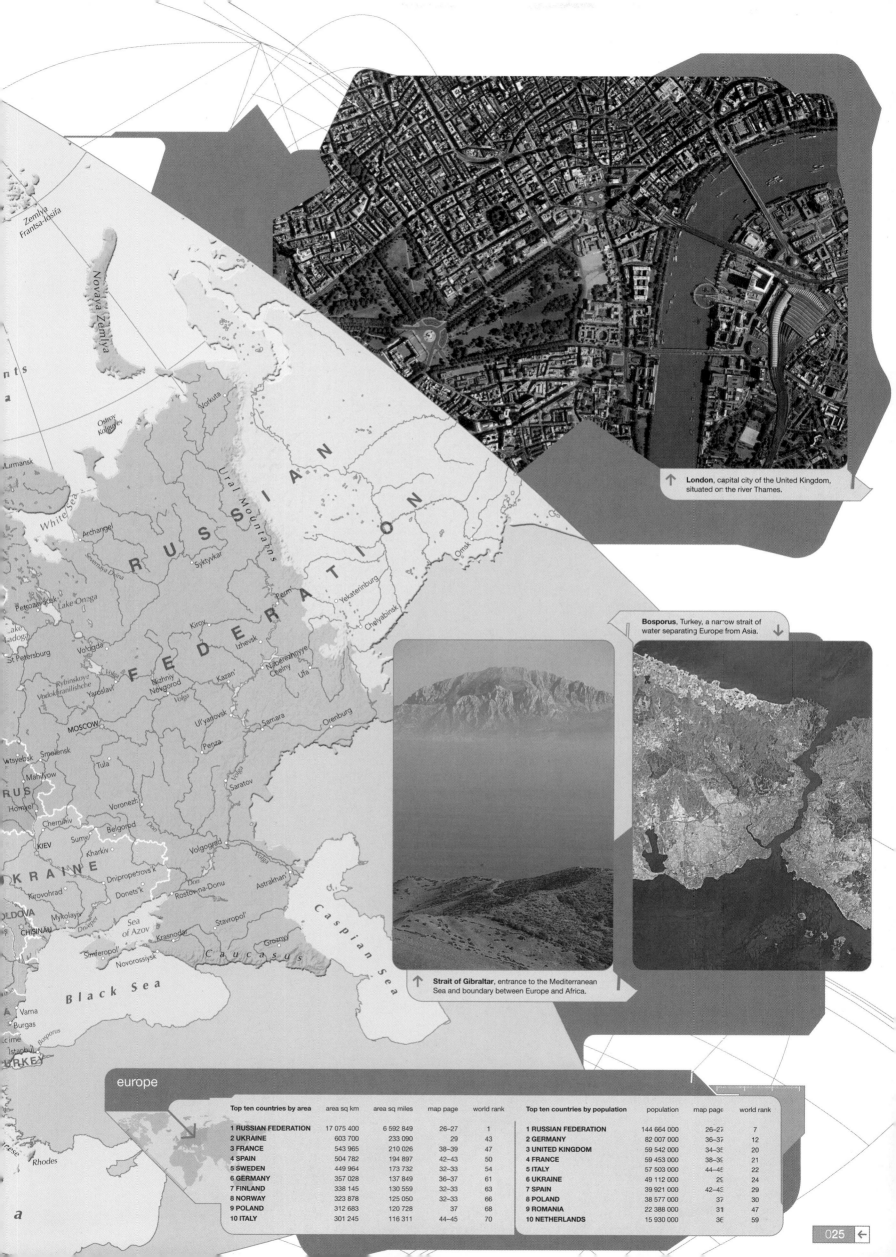

↑ **London**, capital city of the United Kingdom, situated on the river Thames.

Bosporus, Turkey, a narrow strait of water separating Europe from Asia. ↓

↑ **Strait of Gibraltar**, entrance to the Mediterranean Sea and boundary between Europe and Africa.

europe

Top ten countries by area	area sq km	area sq miles	map page	world rank	Top ten countries by population	population	map page	world rank
1 RUSSIAN FEDERATION	17 075 400	6 592 849	26–27	1	1 RUSSIAN FEDERATION	144 664 000	26–27	7
2 UKRAINE	603 700	233 090	29	43	2 GERMANY	82 007 000	36–37	12
3 FRANCE	543 965	210 026	38–39	47	3 UNITED KINGDOM	59 542 000	34–35	20
4 SPAIN	504 782	194 897	42–43	50	4 FRANCE	59 453 000	38–39	21
5 SWEDEN	449 964	173 732	32–33	54	5 ITALY	57 503 000	44–45	22
6 GERMANY	357 028	137 849	36–37	61	6 UKRAINE	49 112 000	29	24
7 FINLAND	338 145	130 559	32–33	63	7 SPAIN	39 921 000	42–43	29
8 NORWAY	323 878	125 050	32–33	66	8 POLAND	38 577 000	37	30
9 POLAND	312 683	120 728	37	68	9 ROMANIA	22 388 000	31	47
10 ITALY	301 245	116 311	44–45	70	10 NETHERLANDS	15 930 000	36	59

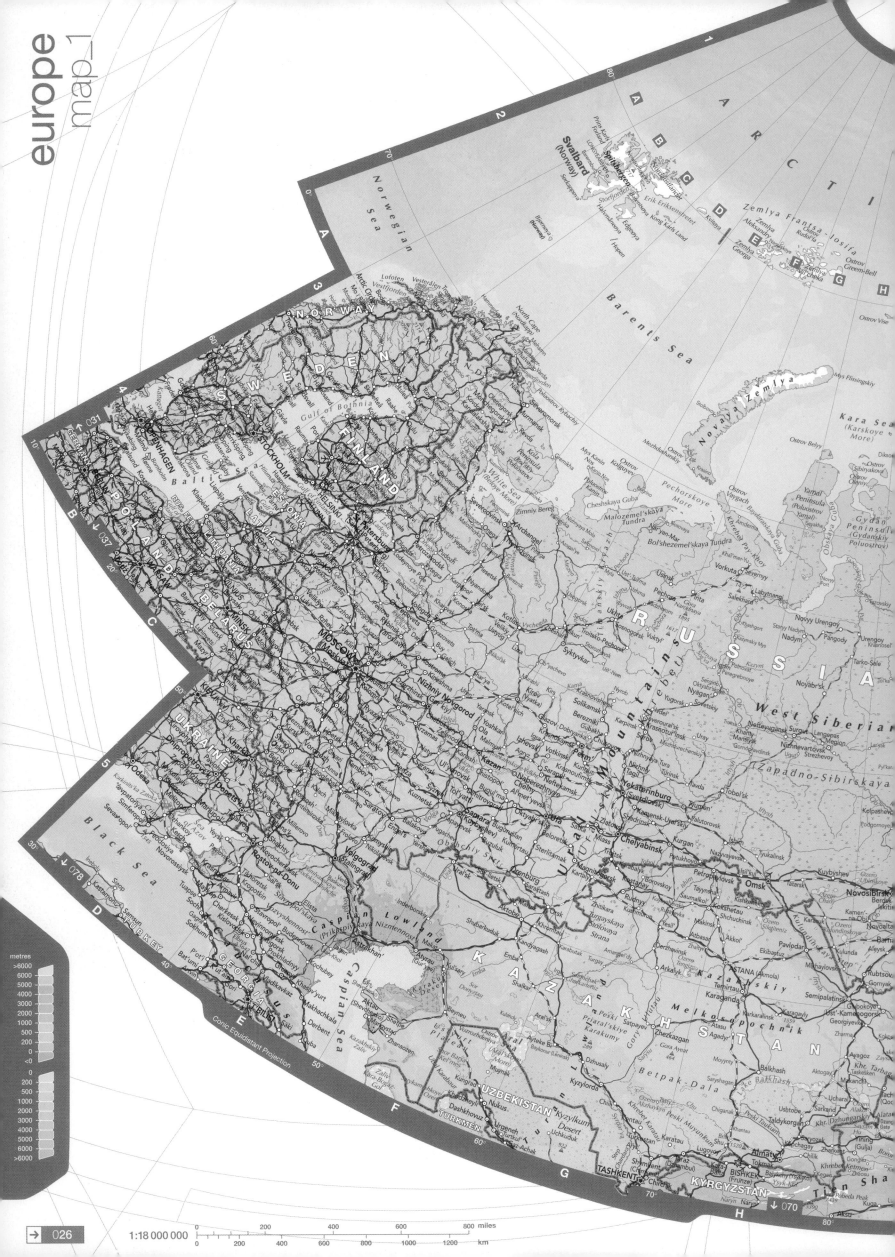

1:18 000 000

metres
>6000
6000
5000
4000
3000
2000
1000
500
200
<0
0
200
500
1000
2000
3000
4000
5000
6000
>6000

Conic Equidistant Projection

| 0 | 200 | 400 | 600 | 800 miles |

| 0 | 200 | 400 | 600 | 800 | 1000 | 1200 | km |

OCEAN

Bering Sea

Chukchi Sea

Bering Strait

East Siberian Sea
(Vostochno-Sibirskoye More)

New Siberia Islands
(Novosibirskiye Ostrova)

Laptev Sea
(More Laptevykh)

Severnaya Zemlya

Taymyr Peninsula
(Poluostrov Taymyr)

North Siberian Lowland
(Severo-Sibirskaya Nizmennost')

Momskiy Khrebet

Khrebet Cherskogo

Kamchatka Peninsula
(Poluostrov Kamchatka)

Sea of Okhotsk
(Okhotskoye More)

Central Siberian Plateau
(Sredne-Sibirskoye Ploskogor'ye)

Verkhoyanskiy Khrebet

Stanovoy Khrebet

Patomskoye Nagor'ye

RUSSIAN FEDERATION

SIBERIA (SIBIR')

Yakutsk

Noril'sk

Sakhalin

JAPAN

Hokkaido

Severo-Baykalskoye Nagor'ye

Stanovoye Nagor'ye

Vitimskoye Ploskogor'ye

Lake Baikal
(Ozero Baykal)

Da Hinggan Ling

Sikhote-Alin'

Khabarovsk

Sapporo

Tomsk
Kemerovo
Leninsk-Kuznetskiy
Kiselevsk
Novokuznetsk
Biysk
Gorno-Altaysk

Krasnoyarsk
Achinsk
Kansk
Bratsk
Ust'-Ilimsk
Ust'-Kut

Abakan
Minusinsk
Chernogorsk

Irkutsk
Angarsk
Usol'ye-Sibirskoye

Ulan-Ude

Chita

Nerchinsk

Blagoveshchensk

Belogorsk

Svobodnyy

Birobidzhan

Komsomol'sk-na-Amure

Qiqihar

Daqing
Anda

Harbin

Jilin

Changchun

Vladivostok

Ussuriysk

Nakhodka

Sea of Japan
(East Sea)

NORTH KOREA

Zapadnyy Sayan

Vostochnyy Sayan

Altai Mountains

Tannu-Ola

ULAN BATOR
(Ulaanbaatar)

MONGOLIA

Gobi

CHINA

Chifeng
(Ulanhad)

Fuxin

Shenyang

Anshan
Benxi

Ürümqi

Turpan

Gobi

Govĭ Altayn Nuruu

Bayan Obo

90°   100°   110°   120°   130°

↓ 032

→ 031

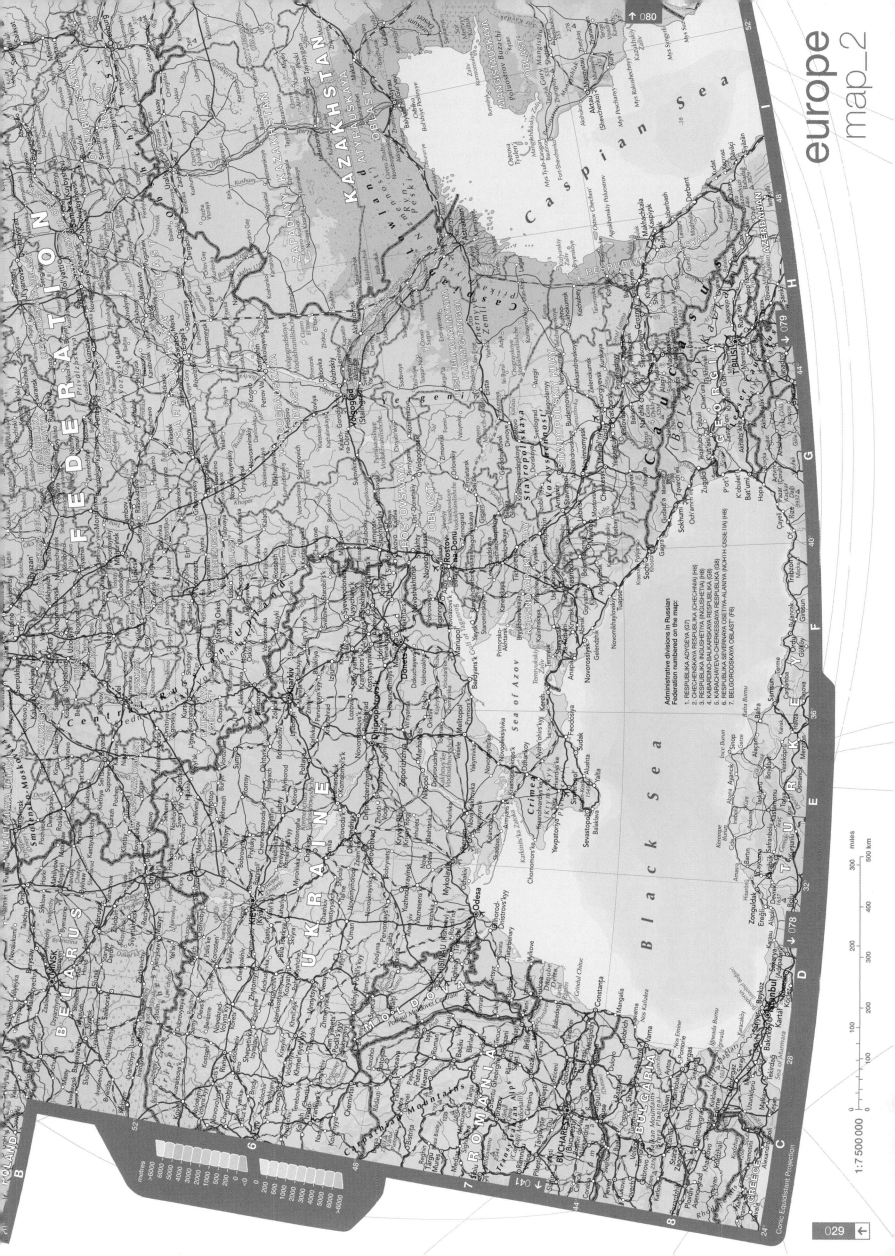

Administrative divisions in Russian
Federation numbered on the map:

1. RESPUBLIKA ADYGEYA (G7)
2. CHECHENSKAYA RESPUBLIKA (CHECHNYA) (H8)
3. RESPUBLIKA INGUSHETIYA (INGUSHETIA) (H8)
4. KABARDINO-BALKARSKAYA RESPUBLIKA (G8)
5. KARACHAYEVO-CHERKESSKAYA RESPUBLIKA (G8)
6. RESPUBLIKA SEVERNAYA OSETIYA-ALANIYA (NORTH OSSETIA) (H8)
7. BELGORODSKAYA OBLAST (F6)

1:7 500 000

North Sea

Atlantic Ocean

Bay of Biscay

Gulf of Gascony

English Channel (La Manche)

Irish Sea

UNITED KINGDOM

SCOTLAND

NORTHERN IRELAND

REPUBLIC OF IRELAND

WALES

ENGLAND

FRANCE

SPAIN

PORTUGAL

ANDORRA

BELGIUM

NETHERLANDS

LUXEMBOURG

Mar Cantábrico

Mediterranean Sea

Golfe du Lion

metres
>6000
6000
5000
4000
3000
2000
1000
500
200
0
0
200
500
1000
2000
3000
4000
5000
6000
>6000

Conic Equidistant Projection

↓ 042

1:7 500 000

0   100   200   300 miles
0 100 200 300 400 500 km

1:4 500 000

Conic Equidistant Projection

200 miles

km

↓ 037

↓ 036

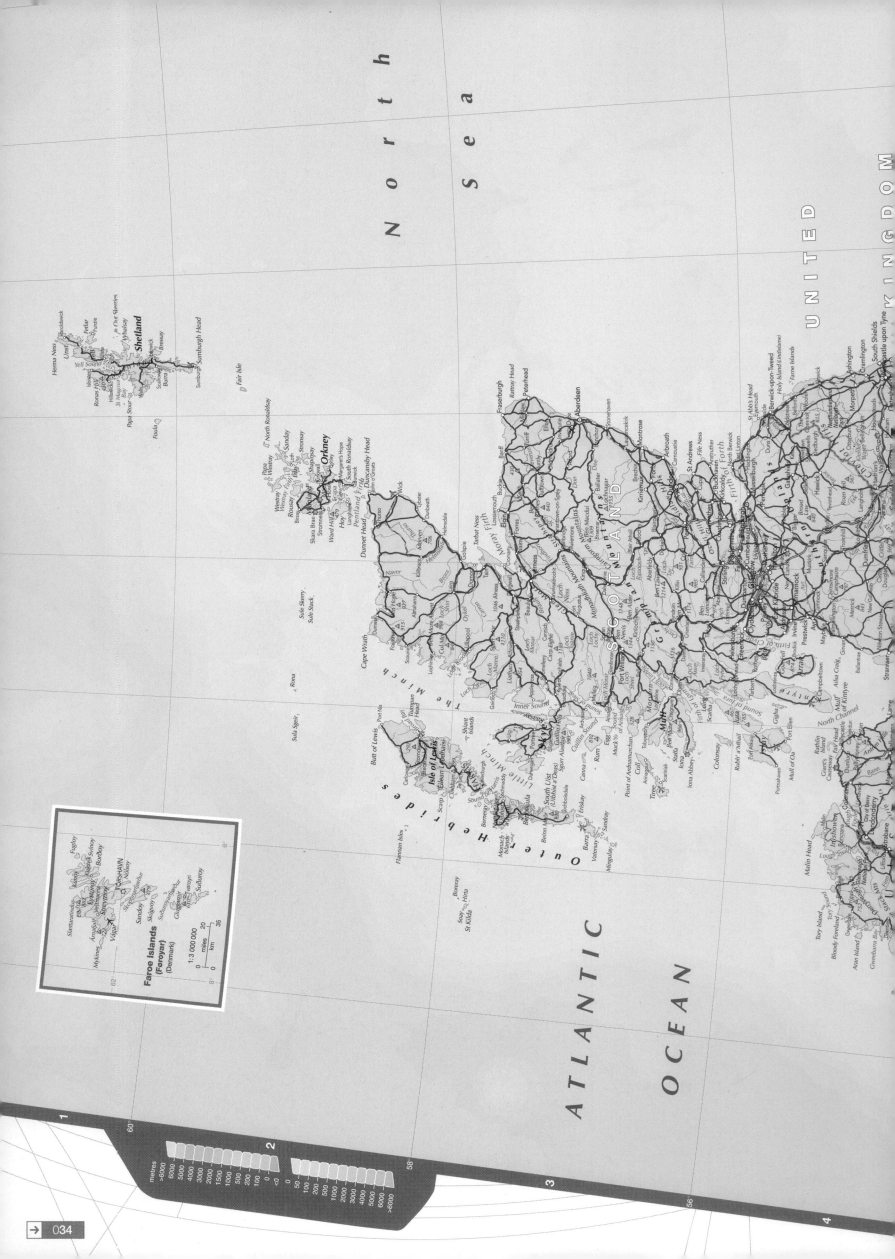

North Sea

ATLANTIC

OCEAN

UNITED KINGDOM

S C O T L A N D

Shetland

Herma Ness
Unst
Fetlar
Out Skerries
Yell Sound
Whalsay
Lerwick
Bressay
Burra
Foula
Sumburgh Head

Fair Isle

Orkney
North Ronaldsay
Papa Westray
Westray
Sanday
Stronsay
Rousay
Shapinsay
Eday
Kirkwall
Stromness
Scapa Flow
Hoy
South Ronaldsay
Duncansby Head
Pentland Firth
John o'Groats

Cape Wrath
Dunnet Head
Thurso
Wick

The Minch

Butt of Lewis
Port Nis
Sula Sgeir
Rona
Sule Skerry
Sule Stack

Isle of Lewis
Eilean Leodhais
Stornoway
Tarbat Ness

Little Minch

Shant Islands
North Uist
Benbecula
South Uist
(Uibhist a Deas)
Barra
Vatersay
Mingulay

Outer Hebrides

Flannan Isles
Monach Islands

Skye

Mull
Iona
Colonsay
Jura
Islay
Sound of Jura

St Kilda
Soay
Hirta
Boreray

Moray Firth
Elgin
Lossiemouth
Nairn
Inverness

Grampian Mountains
Aberdeen
Fraserburgh
Peterhead
Rattray Head
Banff

Ben Nevis
1344
Fort William

Firth of Forth
Edinburgh
Dundee
Perth
Stirling
Glasgow
St Andrews
Montrose
Arbroath

Mull of Kintyre
Kintyre
North Channel
Campbeltown
Ailsa Craig
Giant's Causeway

Malin Head
Tory Island
Bloody Foreland

Faroe Islands
(Føroyar)
(Denmark)

TÓRSHAVN
Vágar
Streymoy
Sandoy
Suðuroy
Mykines
Fugloy

1:3 000 000
miles 20
km 35

metres
>6000
6000
5000
4000
3000
2000
1500
1000
500
200
0
<0
0
50
100
200
500
1000
2000
3000
4000
5000
6000
>6000

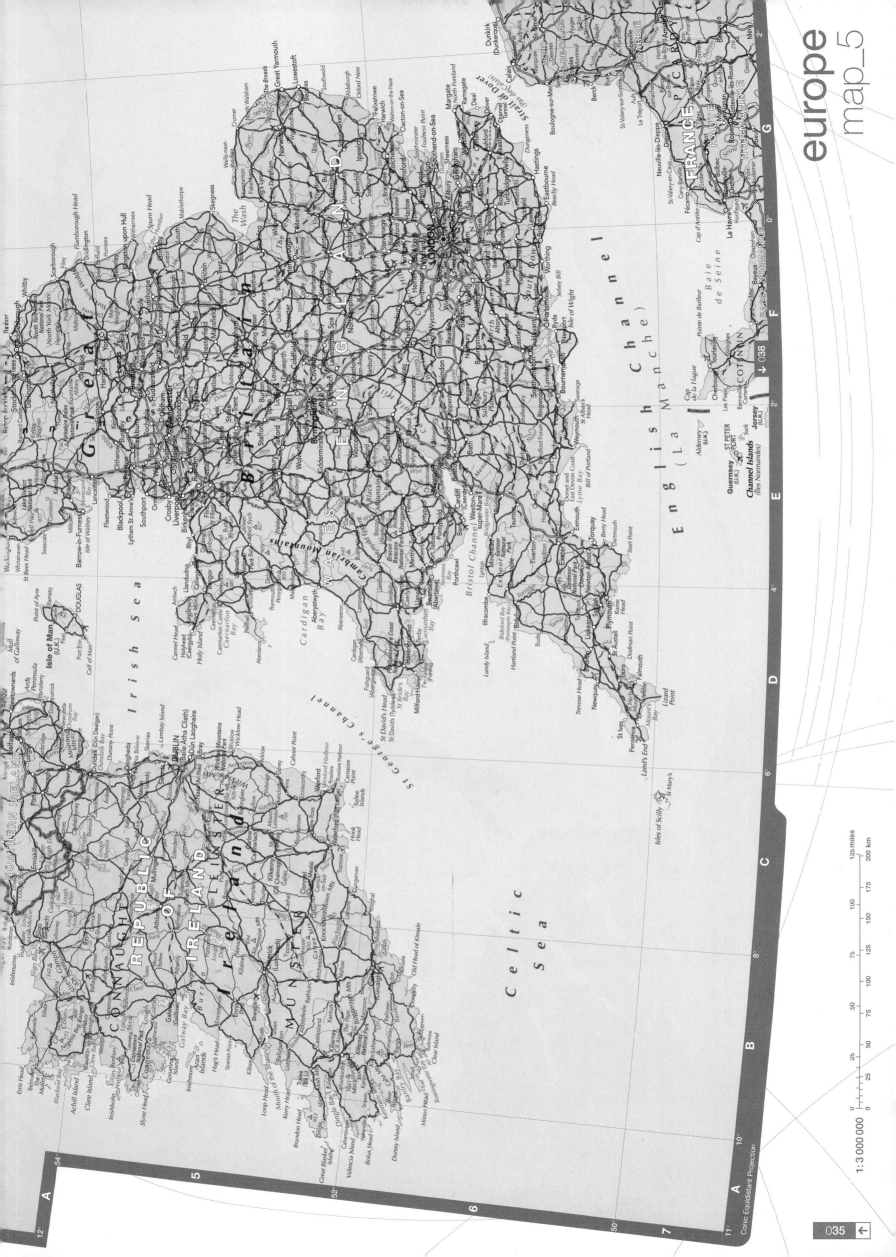

1:3 000 000

Conic Equidistant Projection

125 miles
200 km

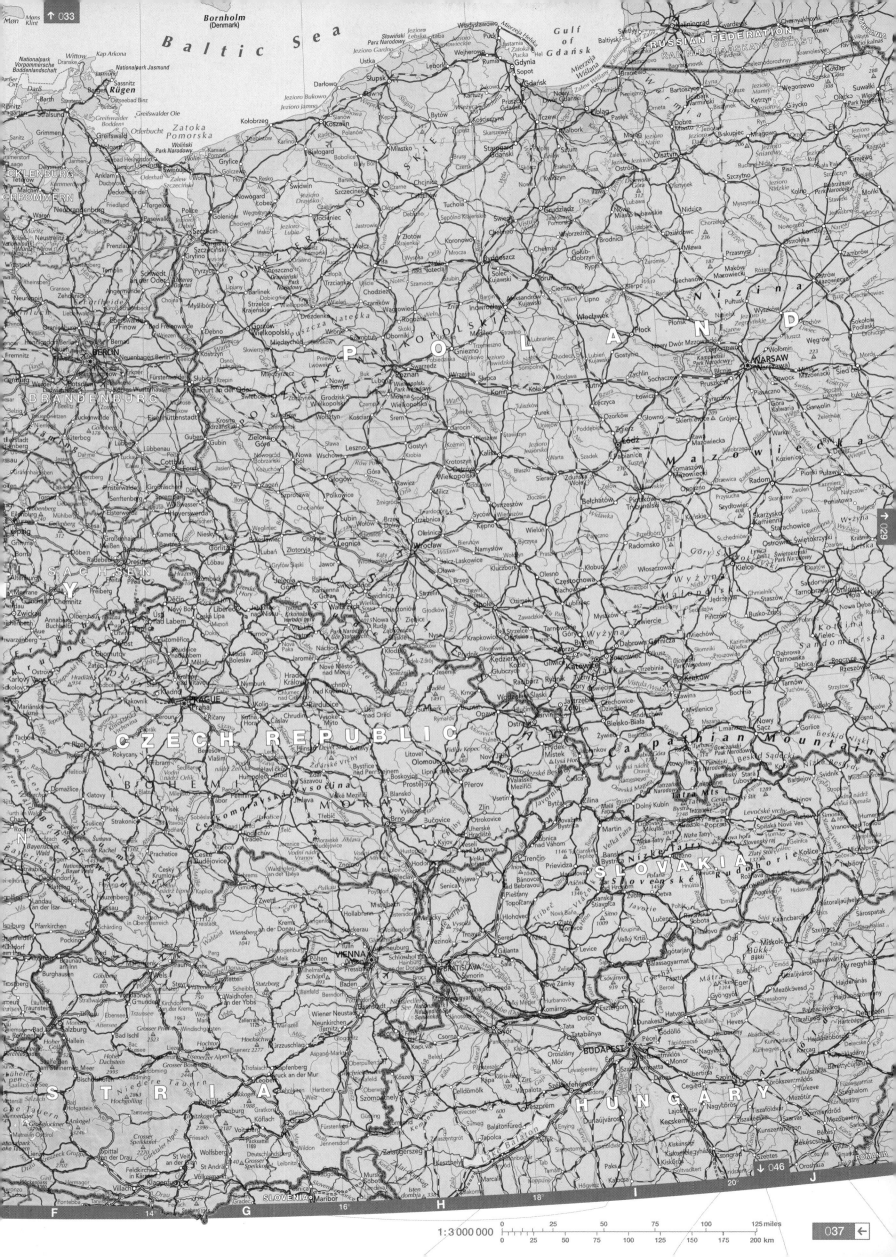

1:9 000 000

Conic Equidistant Projection

↑ 079

↑ 047

G

F

E

D

C

B

18°

16°

14°

12°

10°

8°

I o n i a n   S e a

T y r r h e n i a n   S e a

M e d i t e r r a n e a n   S e a

Sicilian Channel

SICILY
(SICILIA)

SARDINIA
(SARDEGNA)
(Italy)

Golfo di Taranto

CALABRIA

BASILICATA

Catanzaro

Palermo

Catania

Syracuse (Siracusa)

MALTA

TUNIS

TUNISIA

ALGERIA

Cagliari

Sassari

Isole Lipari

Isole Egadi

Isole Pelagie
(Italy)

Golfe de Tunis

Golfe de Hammamet

Mount Etna

Bizerte

Sousse

↓ 091

↓ 091

36

5

6

7

40°

38°

metres
>6000
5000
4000
3000
2000
1500
1000
500
200
100
0
0
100
200
500
1000
2000
3000
4000
5000
6000
>6000

1:3 000 000

Conic Equidistant Projection

0   25   50   75   100   125 miles
0   25   50   75 100 125 150 175 200 km

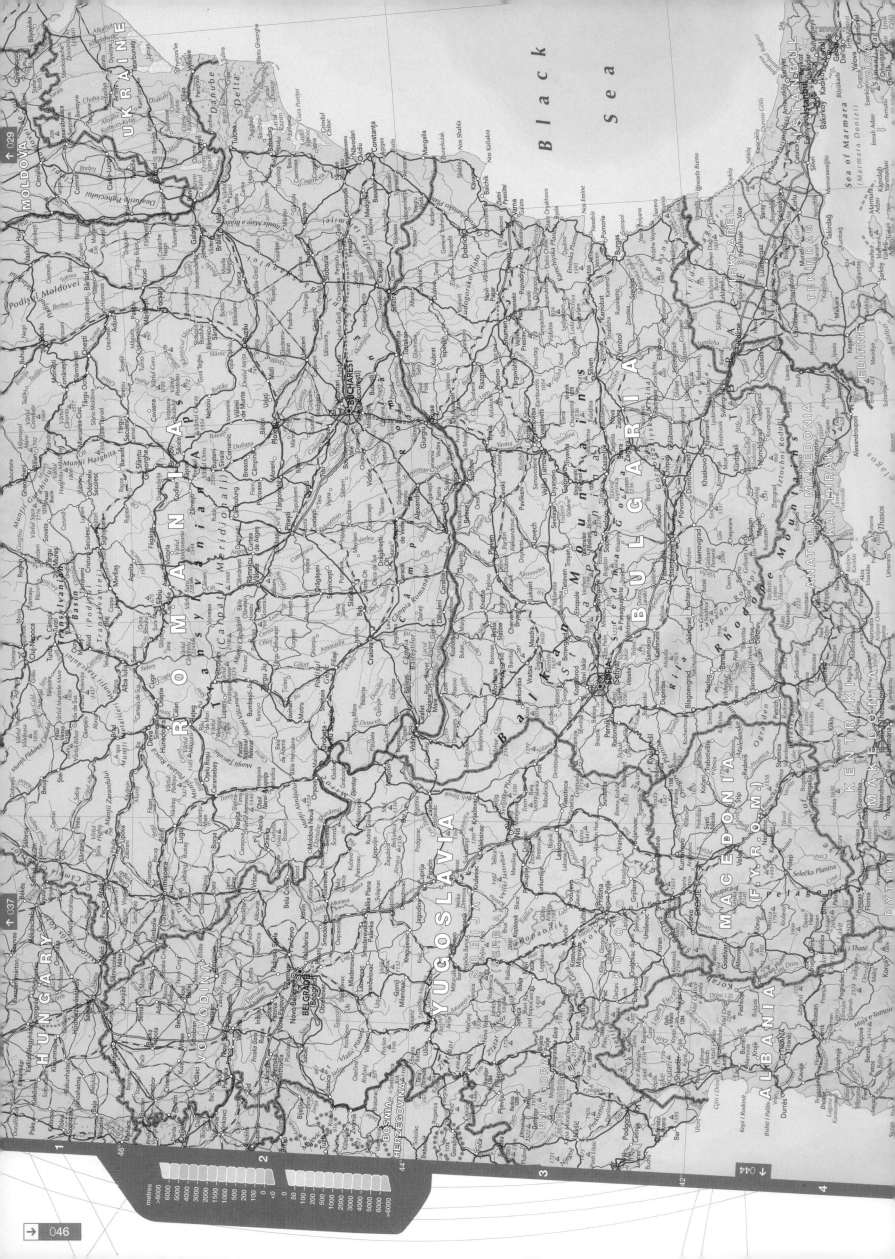

Conic Equidistant Projection

1:3 000 000

0   25   50   75   100 125 miles

0   25 50 75 100 125 150 175 200 km

↓ 088

Italy

Paris, France

Amsterdam, Netherlands

Brussels, Belgium

COUNTRIES		area sq km	area sq miles	population	capital	languages	religions	currency	map
ALBANIA		28 748	11 100	3 145 000	Tirana	Albanian, Greek	Sunni Muslim, Albanian Orthodox, Roman Catholic	Lek	46–47
ANDORRA		465	180	90 000	Andorra la Vella	Spanish, Catalan, French	Roman Catholic	Euro	43
AUSTRIA		83 855	32 377	8 075 000	Vienna	German, Croatian, Turkish	Roman Catholic, Protestant	Euro	36–37
BELARUS		207 600	80 155	10 147 000	Minsk	Belorussian, Russian	Belorussian Orthodox, Roman Catholic	Belarus rouble	31
BELGIUM		30 520	11 784	10 264 000	Brussels	Dutch (Flemish), French (Walloon), German	Roman Catholic, Protestant	Euro	36
BOSNIA-HERZEGOVINA		51 130	19 741	4 067 000	Sarajevo	Bosnian, Serbian, Croatian	Sunni Muslim, Serbian Orthodox, Roman Catholic, Protestant	Marka	44
BULGARIA		110 994	42 855	7 867 000	Sofia	Bulgarian, Turkish, Romany, Macedonian	Bulgarian Orthodox, Sunni Muslim	Lev	46
CROATIA		56 538	21 829	4 655 000	Zagreb	Croatian, Serbian	Roman Catholic, Serbian Orthodox, Sunni Muslim	Kuna	44
CZECH REPUBLIC		78 864	30 450	10 260 000	Prague	Czech, Moravian, Slovak	Roman Catholic, Protestant	Czech koruna	37
DENMARK		43 075	16 631	5 333 000	Copenhagen	Danish	Protestant	Danish krone	33
ESTONIA		45 200	17 452	1 377 000	Tallinn	Estonian, Russian	Protestant, Estonian and Russian Orthodox	Kroon	33
FINLAND		338 145	130 559	5 178 000	Helsinki	Finnish, Swedish	Protestant, Greek Orthodox	Euro	32–33
FRANCE		543 965	210 026	59 453 000	Paris	French, Arabic	Roman Catholic, Protestant, Sunni Muslim	Euro	38–39
GERMANY		357 028	137 849	82 007 000	Berlin	German, Turkish	Protestant, Roman Catholic	Euro	36–37
GREECE		131 957	50 949	10 623 000	Athens	Greek	Greek Orthodox, Sunni Muslim	Euro	46–47
HUNGARY		93 030	35 919	9 917 000	Budapest	Hungarian	Roman Catholic, Protestant	Forint	31
ICELAND		102 820	39 699	281 000	Reykjavik	Icelandic	Protestant	Icelandic króna	32
IRELAND, REPUBLIC OF		70 282	27 136	3 841 000	Dublin	English, Irish	Roman Catholic, Protestant	Euro	34–35
ITALY		301 245	116 311	57 503 000	Rome	Italian	Roman Catholic	Euro	44–45
LATVIA		63 700	24 595	2 406 000	Riga	Latvian, Russian	Protestant, Roman Catholic, Russian Orthodox	Lats	33
LIECHTENSTEIN		160	62	33 000	Vaduz	German	Roman Catholic, Protestant	Swiss franc	39
LITHUANIA		65 200	25 174	3 689 000	Vilnius	Lithuanian, Russian, Polish	Roman Catholic, Protestant, Russian Orthodox	Litas	33
LUXEMBOURG		2 586	998	442 000	Luxembourg	Letzeburgish, German, French	Roman Catholic	Euro	36
MACEDONIA (F.Y.R.O.M.)		25 713	9 928	2 044 000	Skopje	Macedonian, Albanian, Turkish	Macedonian Orthodox, Sunni Muslim	Macedonian denar	46
MALTA		316	122	392 000	Valletta	Maltese, English	Roman Catholic	Maltese lira	45
MOLDOVA		33 700	13 012	4 285 000	Chişinău	Romanian, Ukrainian, Gagauz, Russian	Romanian Orthodox, Russian Orthodox	Moldovan leu	29
MONACO		2	1	34 000	Monaco-Ville	French, Monegasque, Italian	Roman Catholic	Euro	39
NETHERLANDS		41 526	16 033	15 930 000	Amsterdam/The Hague	Dutch, Frisian	Roman Catholic, Protestant, Sunni Muslim	Euro	36
NORWAY		323 878	125 050	4 488 000	Oslo	Norwegian	Protestant, Roman Catholic	Norwegian krone	32–33
POLAND		312 683	120 728	38 577 000	Warsaw	Polish, German	Roman Catholic, Polish Orthodox	Zloty	37
PORTUGAL		88 940	34 340	10 033 000	Lisbon	Portuguese	Roman Catholic, Protestant	Euro	42
ROMANIA		237 500	91 699	22 388 000	Bucharest	Romanian, Hungarian	Romanian Orthodox, Protestant, Roman Catholic	Romanian leu	31
RUSSIAN FEDERATION		17 075 400	6 592 849	144 664 000	Moscow	Russian, Tatar, Ukrainian, local languages	Russian Orthodox, Sunni Muslim, Protestant	Russian rouble	26–27
SAN MARINO		61	24	27 000	San Marino	Italian	Roman Catholic	Euro	44
SLOVAKIA		49 035	18 933	5 403 000	Bratislava	Slovak, Hungarian, Czech	Roman Catholic, Protestant, Orthodox	Slovakian koruna	37
SLOVENIA		20 251	7 819	1 985 000	Ljubljana	Slovene, Croatian, Serbian	Roman Catholic, Protestant	Tólar	44
SPAIN		504 782	194 897	39 921 000	Madrid	Castilian, Catalan, Galician, Basque	Roman Catholic	Euro	42–43
SWEDEN		449 964	173 732	8 833 000	Stockholm	Swedish	Protestant, Roman Catholic	Swedish krona	32–33
SWITZERLAND		41 293	15 943	7 170 000	Bern	German, French, Italian, Romansch	Roman Catholic, Protestant	Swiss franc	39
UKRAINE		603 700	233 090	49 112 000	Kiev	Ukrainian, Russian	Ukrainian Orthodox, Ukrainian Catholic, Roman Catholic	Hryvnia	29
UNITED KINGDOM		244 082	94 241	59 542 000	London	English, Welsh, Gaelic	Protestant, Roman Catholic, Muslim	Pound sterling	34–35
VATICAN CITY		0.5	0.2	480	Vatican City	Italian	Roman Catholic	Euro	44
YUGOSLAVIA		102 173	39 449	10 538 000	Belgrade	Serbian, Albanian, Hungarian	Serbian Orthodox, Montenegrin Orthodox, Sunni Muslim	Yugoslav dinar	46

DEPENDENT TERRITORIES		territorial status	area sq km	area sq miles	population	capital	languages	religions	currency	map
Azores		Autonomous Region of Portugal	2 300	888	243 600	Ponta Delgada	Portuguese	Roman Catholic, Protestant	Euro	160
Faroe Islands		Self-governing Danish Territory	1 399	540	47 000	Tórshavn	Faroese, Danish	Protestant	Danish krone	34
Gibraltar		United Kingdom Overseas Territory	7	3	27 000	Gibraltar	English, Spanish	Roman Catholic, Protestant, Sunni Muslim	Gibraltar pound	42
Guernsey		United Kingdom Crown Dependency	78	30	64 555	St Peter Port	English, French	Protestant, Roman Catholic	Pound sterling	35
Isle of Man		United Kingdom Crown Dependency	572	221	76 000	Douglas	English	Protestant, Roman Catholic	Pound sterling	35
Jersey		United Kingdom Crown Dependency	116	45	89 136	St Helier	English, French	Protestant, Roman Catholic	Pound sterling	38

asia

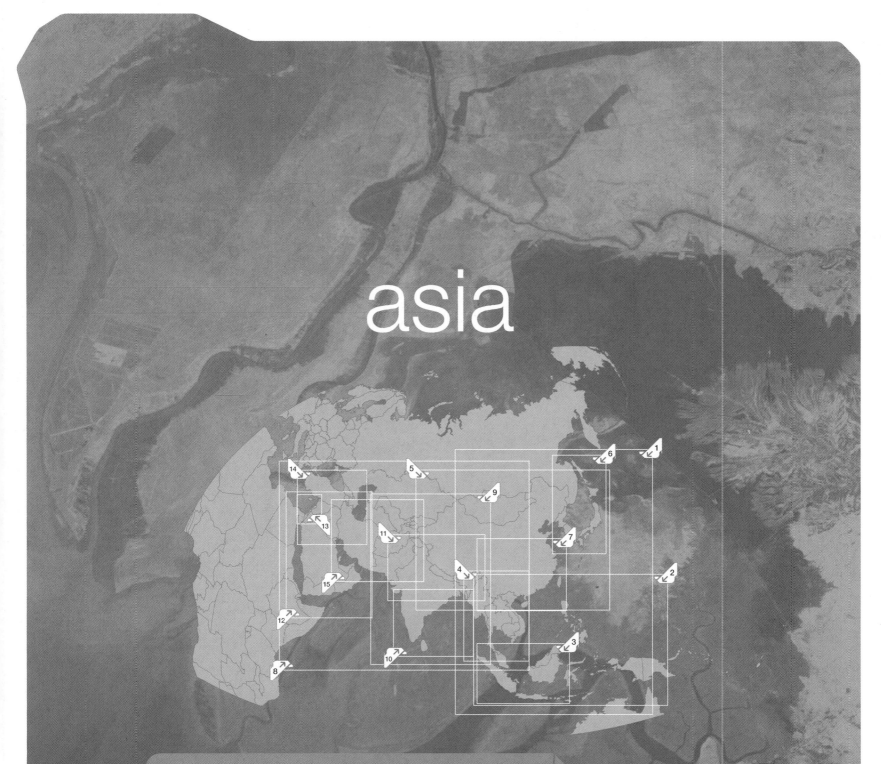

contents

		map coverage	scale
50–51	landscapes		
52–53	locations		
54–55	map_1	**asia** east and southeast	1:20 000 000
56–57	map_2	**asia** southeast	1:13 000 000
58–59	map_3	**indonesia** west, **malaysia** and **singapore**	1:6 000 000
60–61	map_4	**myanmar, thailand, laos** and **vietnam**	1:6 000 000
62–63	map_5	**asia** east	1:13 000 000
64–65	map_6	**asia** northeast	1:6 000 000
66–67	map_7	**china** south	1:6 000 000
68–69	map_8	**asia** central and south	1:20 000 000
70–71	map_9	**asia** south	1:12 500 000
72–73	map_10	**india** south and **sri lanka**	1:6 000 000
74–75	map_11	**india** north, **bangladesh** and **nepal**	1:6 000 000
76	map_12	**asia** southwest	1:13 000 000
77	map_13	**middle east**	1:3 000 000
78–79	map_14	**turkey, iraq** and **trans-caucasian republics**	1:6 000 000
80–81	map_15	**iran, afghanistan** and **pakistan**	1:6 000 000
82	states and territories		

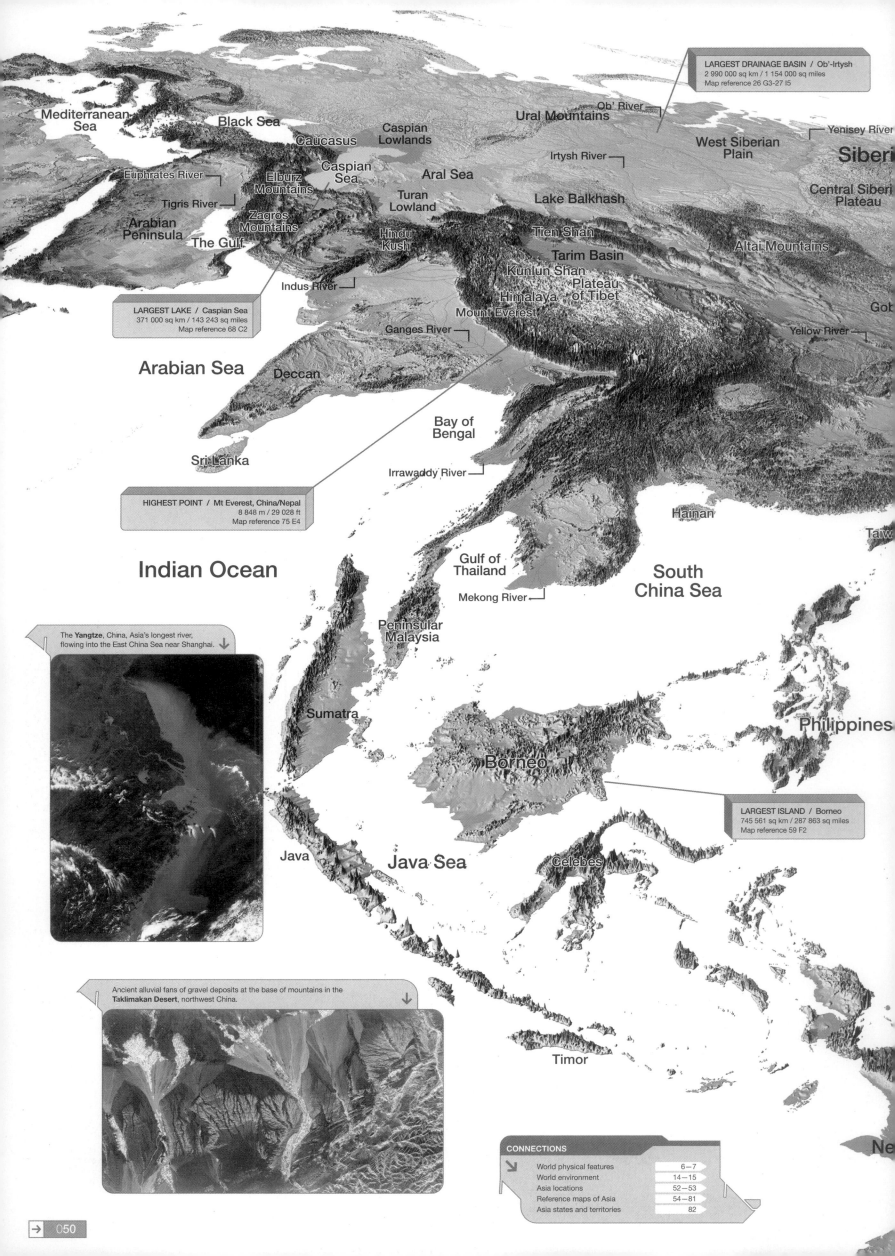

Mediterranean Sea

Black Sea

Caucasus

Caspian Lowlands

LARGEST DRAINAGE BASIN / Ob'-Irtysh
2 990 000 sq km / 1 154 000 sq miles
Map reference 26 G3-27 I5

Ob' River

Ural Mountains

Yenisey River

Irtysh River

West Siberian Plain

Siberi

Euphrates River

Elburz Mountains

Caspian Sea

Aral Sea

Central Siberi Plateau

Tigris River

Turan Lowland

Lake Balkhash

Arabian Peninsula

Zagros Mountains

The Gulf

Hindu Kush

Tien Shan

Altai Mountains

Tarim Basin

Gob

Indus River

Kunlun Shan

Plateau of Tibet

LARGEST LAKE / Caspian Sea
371 000 sq km / 143 243 sq miles
Map reference 68 C2

Himalaya

Mount Everest

Yellow River

Ganges River

Arabian Sea

Deccan

Bay of Bengal

Sri Lanka

Irrawaddy River

HIGHEST POINT / Mt Everest, China/Nepal
8 848 m / 29 028 ft
Map reference 75 E4

Hainan

Taiw

Indian Ocean

Gulf of Thailand

Mekong River

South China Sea

Peninsular Malaysia

The **Yangtze**, China, Asia's longest river, flowing into the East China Sea near Shanghai. ↓

Sumatra

Philippines

Borneo

LARGEST ISLAND / Borneo
745 561 sq km / 287 863 sq miles
Map reference 59 F2

Java

Java Sea

Celebes

Ancient alluvial fans of gravel deposits at the base of mountains in the **Taklimakan Desert**, northwest China. ↓

Timor

Ne

CONNECTIONS

World physical features	6—7
World environment	14—15
Asia locations	52—53
Reference maps of Asia	54—81
Asia states and territories	82

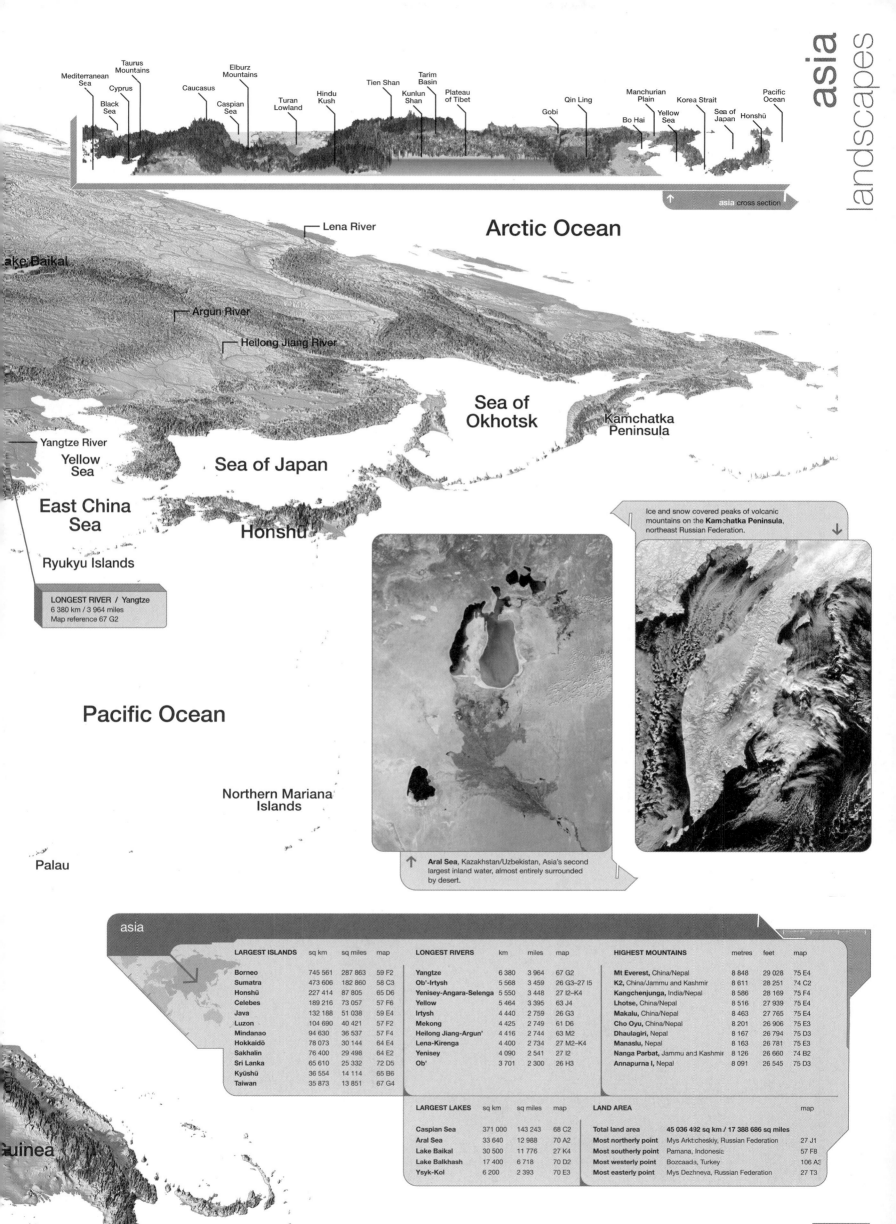

asia cross section

Mediterranean Sea
Taurus Mountains
Cyprus
Black Sea
Caucasus
Elburz Mountains
Caspian Sea
Turan Lowland
Hindu Kush
Tien Shan
Tarim Basin
Kunlun Shan
Plateau of Tibet
Gobi
Qin Ling
Manchurian Plain
Bo Hai
Yellow Sea
Korea Strait
Sea of Japan
Honshū
Pacific Ocean

Lena River

Arctic Ocean

ake Baikal

Argun River

Heilong Jiang River

Sea of Okhotsk

Kamchatka Peninsula

Yangtze River

Yellow Sea

Sea of Japan

East China Sea

Honshu

Ryukyu Islands

LONGEST RIVER / Yangtze
6 380 km / 3 964 miles
Map reference 67 G2

Ice and snow covered peaks of volcanic mountains on the **Kamchatka Peninsula**, northeast Russian Federation.

Pacific Ocean

Northern Mariana Islands

Palau

↑ **Aral Sea**, Kazakhstan/Uzbekistan, Asia's second largest inland water, almost entirely surrounded by desert.

Guinea

asia

LARGEST ISLANDS	sq km	sq miles	map
Borneo	745 561	287 863	59 F2
Sumatra	473 606	182 860	58 C3
Honshū	227 414	87 805	65 D6
Celebes	189 216	73 057	57 F6
Java	132 188	51 038	59 E4
Luzon	104 690	40 421	57 F2
Mindanao	94 630	36 537	57 F4
Hokkaidō	78 073	30 144	64 E4
Sakhalin	76 400	29 498	64 E2
Sri Lanka	65 610	25 332	72 D5
Kyūshū	36 554	14 114	65 B6
Taiwan	35 873	13 851	67 G4

LONGEST RIVERS	km	miles	map
Yangtze	6 380	3 964	67 G2
Ob'-Irtysh	5 568	3 459	26 G3–27 I5
Yenisey-Angara-Selenga	5 550	3 448	27 I2–K4
Yellow	5 464	3 395	63 J4
Irtysh	4 440	2 759	26 G3
Mekong	4 425	2 749	61 D6
Heilong Jiang-Argun'	4 416	2 744	63 M2
Lena-Kirenga	4 400	2 734	27 M2–K4
Yenisey	4 090	2 541	27 I2
Ob'	3 701	2 300	26 H3

HIGHEST MOUNTAINS	metres	feet	map
Mt Everest, China/Nepal	8 848	29 028	75 E4
K2, China/Jammu and Kashmir	8 611	28 251	74 C2
Kangchenjunga, India/Nepal	8 586	28 169	75 F4
Lhotse, China/Nepal	8 516	27 939	75 E4
Makalu, China/Nepal	8 463	27 765	75 E4
Cho Oyu, China/Nepal	8 201	26 906	75 E3
Dhaulagiri, Nepal	8 167	26 794	75 D3
Manaslu, Nepal	8 163	26 781	75 E3
Nanga Parbat, Jammu and Kashmir	8 126	26 660	74 B2
Annapurna I, Nepal	8 091	26 545	75 D3

LARGEST LAKES	sq km	sq miles	map
Caspian Sea	371 000	143 243	68 C2
Aral Sea	33 640	12 988	70 A2
Lake Baikal	30 500	11 776	27 K4
Lake Balkhash	17 400	6 718	70 D2
Ysyk-Köl	6 200	2 393	70 E3

LAND AREA		map
Total land area	45 036 492 sq km / 17 388 686 sq miles	
Most northerly point	Mys Arkticheskiy, Russian Federation	27 J1
Most southerly point	Pamana, Indonesia	57 F8
Most westerly point	Bozcaada, Turkey	106 A3
Most easterly point	Mys Dezhneva, Russian Federation	27 T3

Top ten countries by area	area sq km	area sq miles	map page	world rank	Top ten countries by population	population	map page	world rank
1 RUSSIAN FEDERATION	17 075 400	6 592 849	26–27	1	1 CHINA	1 270 082 000	62–63	1
2 CHINA	9 584 492	3 700 593	62–63	4	2 INDIA	1 025 096 000	70–71	2
3 INDIA	3 065 027	1 183 414	70–71	7	3 INDONESIA	214 840 000	56–57	4
4 KAZAKHSTAN	2 717 300	1 049 155	68–69	9	4 PAKISTAN	144 971 000	70–71	6
5 SAUDI ARABIA	2 200 000	849 425	76	13	5 RUSSIAN FEDERATION	144 664 000	26–27	7
6 INDONESIA	1 919 445	741 102	56–57	15	6 BANGLADESH	140 369 000	75	8
7 IRAN	1 648 000	636 296	80–81	17	7 JAPAN	127 335 000	64–65	9
8 MONGOLIA	1 565 000	604 250	62–63	18	8 VIETNAM	79 175 000	60–61	13
9 PAKISTAN	803 940	310 403	70–71	34	9 PHILIPPINES	77 131 000	56–57	14
10 TURKEY	779 452	300 948	78–79	36	10 IRAN	71 369 000	80–81	15

Terraced agricultural land, **Bali**, Indonesia.

Tōkyō, administrative financial and cultural centre, capital city of Japan.

British Indian Ocean Territory

ARM.   ARMENIA
AZ.   AZERBAIJAN
U.A.E.   UNITED ARAB EMIRATES

The **Great Wall**, 2 400 km, northern China.

Space Imaging

↑ Kowloon Peninsula and harbour area of **Hong Kong**, China.

Space Imaging Middle East

↑ The grand mosque, **Mecca**, holiest city of Islam, Saudi Arabia.

CONNECTIONS

World countries	8–9
Asia landscapes	50–51
Reference maps of Asia	54–81
Asia states and territories	82
Indian Ocean	162–163
Pacific Ocean	164–165
Arctic Ocean	166

↑ The world's highest mountain range, **Himalaya**, South Asia.

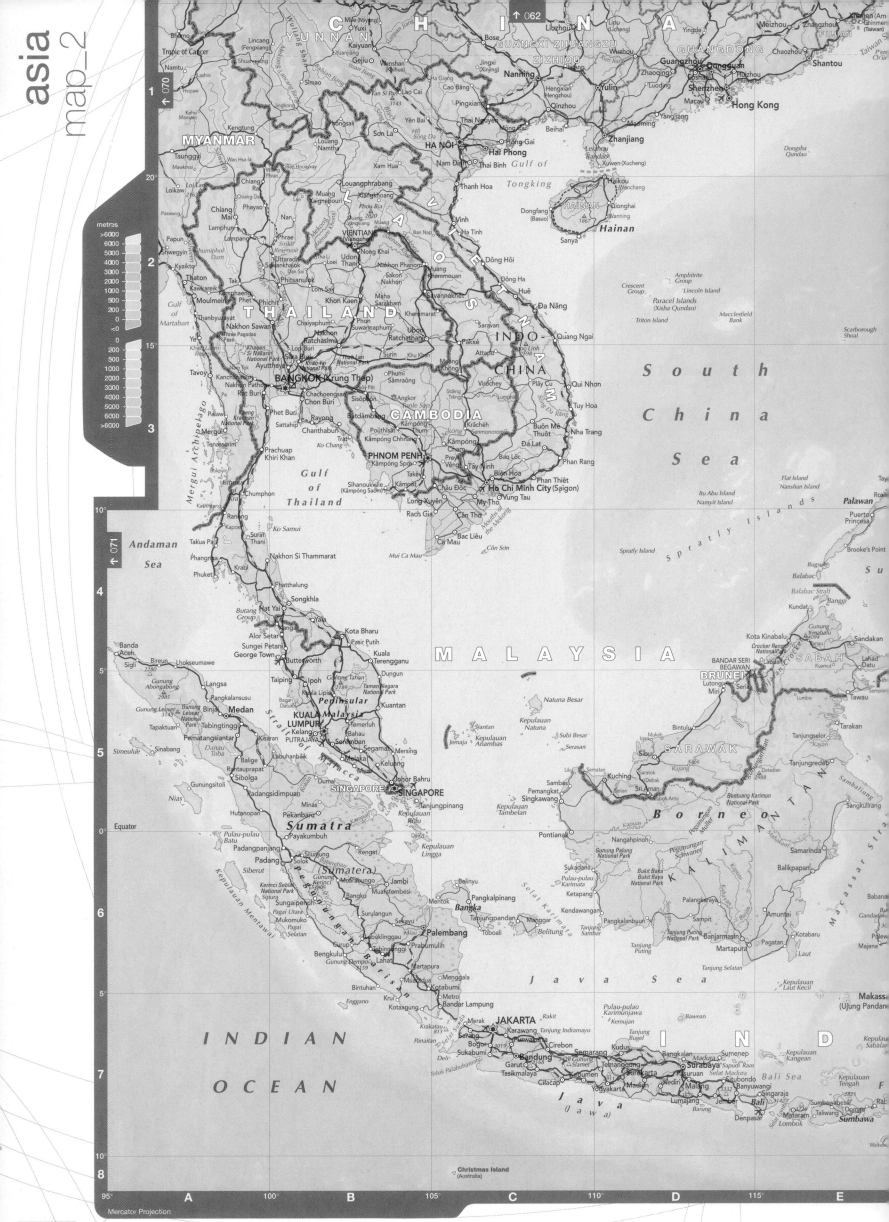

↑ 062

↑ 070

↑ 071

metres
>6000
6000
5000
4000
3000
2000
1000
500
200
0
<0

200
500
1000
2000
3000
4000
5000
6000
>6000

C H I N A

YUNNAN

GUANGXI ZHUANGZU ZIZHIXOU

GUANGDONG

FUJIAN

Taiwan

Nanning

Guangzhou Dongguan

Shantou

Shenzhen

Macau

Hong Kong

MYANMAR

Zhanjiang

Gulf of Tongking

HAINAN

Hainan

Dongsha Qundao

THAILAND

LAOS

VIÊTNAM

VIENTIAN (Viangchan)

BANGKOK (Krung Thep)

INDO-CHINA

Amphitrite Group

Crescent Group

Lincoln Island

Paracel Islands (Xisha Qundao)

Triton Island

Macclesfield Bank

Scarborough Shoal

South China Sea

CAMBODIA

PHNOM PENH

Ho Chi Minh City (Saigon)

Gulf of Martaban

Gulf of Thailand

Mergui Archipelago

Andaman Sea

Flat Island
Nanshan Island

Itu Abu Island
Namyit Island

Palawan

Puerto Princesa

Spratly Island

Spratly Islands

Brooke's Point

Balabac Strait

MALAYSIA

Kota Kinabalu

SABAH

Sandakan

Lahad Datu

Tawau

BANDAR SERI BEGAWAN

BRUNEI

Banda Aceh

George Town

KUALA LUMPUR

SINGAPORE

Natuna Besar

Kepulauan Natuna

SARAWAK

Kuching

Sri Aman

B O R N E O

K A L I M A N T A N

Sumatra

Sumatera

Equator

Pontianak

Palembang

Bangka

J a v a   S e a

INDIAN OCEAN

JAKARTA

Bandung

J a v a (Jawa)

Surabaya

Bali Sea

Bali

Denpasar

Lombok

Sumbawa

Christmas Island (Australia)

Mercator Projection

PACIFIC

OCEAN

**Northern
Mariana
Islands
(U.S.A.)**

Okino-Daitō-jima

Volcano Islands
(Kazan-rettō)
(Japan)   Minami-ō-jima

Okino-Tori-shima
(Japan)

Farallon de Pajaros

Maug Islands

Asuncioa

Agrihan

Pagan

Alamagan

Guguan

Sarigan

Anatahan

Farallon
ce Medinilla

Saipan
Tinian   CAPITOL HILL

Rota

HAGÅTÑA
Guam
(U.S.A.)

Aguijan

TAIWAN
T'aichung
T'ai'nan
Hualien
T'aitung
Oluan Pi

Sakishima-
shotō
Yaeyama-retto

Ryukyu Islands
(Nansei-shotō) (Japan)

Bashi Channel

Luzon
Strait

Balintang Channel

Itbayat
Batan
Islands
Batan

Calayan
Babuyan

Babuyan Islands

Camiguin

Babuyan Channel

Laoag

Vigan
Bontoc
Mount
Pulog
2929

Tuguegarao
Ilagan

Philippine

Sea

San
nando
Tarlac
Bayombong
Cabanatuan

Daet
Quezon City
MANILA
San Pablo
Lucena   Naga
Boac   Lopez
Calapan   Legaspi
Mount   Mayon
Halcon   Calauag
2585

Catanduanes

Sorsogon
Irosin
Catarman
Calbayog

Colonia
Yap

FEDERATED STATES

OF MICRONESIA

Ulithi

Fais

Gaferut

Faraulep

West Fayu
Olimarao

Ifalik   Lamotrek
Eleto   Satawal

Bongabo
Batangas
Lucena
Mindoro
Roxas

Polillo Islands

Siliyan
Sea

Masbate
Masbate

Tacloban
Ormoc

Guiuan

Ngulu

Sorol

Woleai

Eauripik

C a r o l i n e

Islands

PHILIPPINES

Fredoro Strait
Cuyo
Islands
San Jose
de Buenavista

Iloilo
Bacolod

Roxas
Panay
Cebu

Negros
Bais ay
Tanjay

Sibuyan
Sea

Visayan
Sea

Leyte

Cebu
Bohol

Dinagat

Siargao

Surigao

Ngeruangel

Kayangel Atoll
Kossol Reef

Palau Islands   Babeldaob
KOROR

PALAU

Angaur   Peleliu
Peleliu

Lamacan

Durraguete

Cauayan

Tagbilaran
Dipolog

Bohol Sea

Cagayan
de Oro
Iligan
Mindanao

Butuan

Sea

Ozamiz
Pagadian
Cotabato
Zamboanga   Datu Piang
Isabela
Basilan

Mount
Apo
Davao
Davao
Gulf

Mati

Moro
Gulf

General Santos

Sarangani
Islands

Sonsorol
Islands

Pulo Anna

Merir

Jolo
Jolo

Sulu Archipelago

C e l e b e s

Sea

Tawitawi

Kepulauan
Nanusa

Karakelong   Kepulauan
Talaud

Sangir

Kaburuang

Tobi

Helen

Helen Reef

Siau
Sangir
1784
Siaur

Kepulauan
Sangir

Tahulandang

Manado
Tondano

Morotai

Tolitoli
Kwandang

Ternate
Sao-Siu   Daruba
Halmahera
Makian
Kayoa

INDONESIA

Gorontalo

Dumago Bore
National Park

Semenarjung Minahase

Molucca Sea

Tobelo
Akelamo

Teluk
Tomini

Kepulauan Togian

Tanjung
Pangkalsiang

Gebe

Waigeo

Selat Dampir
Sorong

Kwoka
3000

Manokwari

Supiori
Numfoor   Biak

M o l u c c a s

Obi
Salawati

Jazirah Doberai
Teminabuan

Num
Biak

Selat Yapen

Tanjung d'Urville

Ninigo
Group   Pelleluhi Is

Admiralty
Islands

Hermit Is   Manus
Island

Wuvulu Island

Mangole
Kepulauan
Banggai

Taliabu
Sulabesi

Kepulauan
Sula

Mispöl   Babo

Jayapura
Vanimo

Gunung Dom
1340

Pegunungan Van Rees

Sarmi

Wewak

Schouten Islands

Bismarck
Archipelago

Manam I.

Bismarck

Sea

Karkar Island

Namlea
Buru

Wahi
Seram   Gunung
Binaija
3019

Bula

Semenanjung
Bomberai
Fakfak

Teluk
Berau

Nabire
Enarotali

Teluk
Cenderawasih

Pegunungan Maok

Puncak Jaya
Tembagapura   5100

Puncak Trikora
4730

Puncak
Yamin
Puncak
Mandala
4595   4700

Tariku

Taritatu

Maprik

Pagwi
Sepik

Begia

Madang

Ambon
Ambon

Kepulauan
Gorong

Adi

Teluk
Kamrau

Uta
Lorentz
National Park
Amamapare

New
Central Range

Mount Hag
Goro

PAPUA

Long Is

Mount Wilhelm
4509

Mount
Giluwe
4359

Celebes

Palu
Poso
Uekuli
Koloredale
Teluk
Towori

Malili
Palopo

Peleng

Manui
Wowoni

Kendari
Kolaka

Namosi

Kepulauan
Banda

Kepulauan
Watubela

Seram Sea

Kepulauan
Kai

B a n d a   S e a

Kai
Besar

Wokam

I R I A N

Kumbe

Klunga
Lake
Murray

Digul

New GUINEA

Guinea

Balimo

Mount Hac

Kaiapit   Kaiapo

Peninsula
Wau

Mualli
Watampone

Raha
Buton

Manui

Sinjai
Bulukumba

Muna

Kabaena
Baubau

Kepulauan
Tukangbesi

Kai
Kecil

Dobo

Benjina
Kobroor

Kepulauan
Aru

Trangan
Workai

Sia

Tanjung
Deyong

Komoran

Guinea

Kiwai
Island

Kerema

Bulolo

Kepulauan
Salayar

Bentong

Tanahjampea

Kalao
Kepulauan
Bonerate

Kepulauan
Barat Daya

Damar
Roma

Wuliaru

Larat

Molu

Kepulauan
Tanimbar

Saumlaki

Tanjung Vals

Merauke
Morehead

Kiunga

Kiwai
Island

PORT
MORESBY

Tepa
Kawati

Babar

Tanjung d

Mari

Daru

Torres Strait

*Gulf
of
Papua*

Kalaotoa

Komba
1659

Lomblen

Kalao

Kepulauan
Alor
Alor

Lirangan
Atapupu
Huaki

Wetar

Kepulauan Leti
Kisar

Kepulauan
Babar

Arafura Sea

Melville
Island
(Aus.)

Saibai I.
Badu I.

Boigu I.
Daumori

Torres Strait
Cape York

AUSTRALIA

Flores

Ende

Endeh
2149

Kepulauan Solor
DILI   Manatuto

EAST TIMOR

Gunung Tata Mailau
2960

Maliana

EAST TIMOR

Timor

Kupang

Sawu Sea

Rote

Savu

Melville
Island
(Aus.)

Thursday Island
Prince of Wales Island

Moa I.

Sawu

Panarua

Sumba

120°   **F**   125°   **G**   130°   **H**   135°   **I**   140°   **J**   145°   **K**

1:13 000 000

0   100   200   300   400   500 miles

0   100   200   300   400   500   600   700   800 km

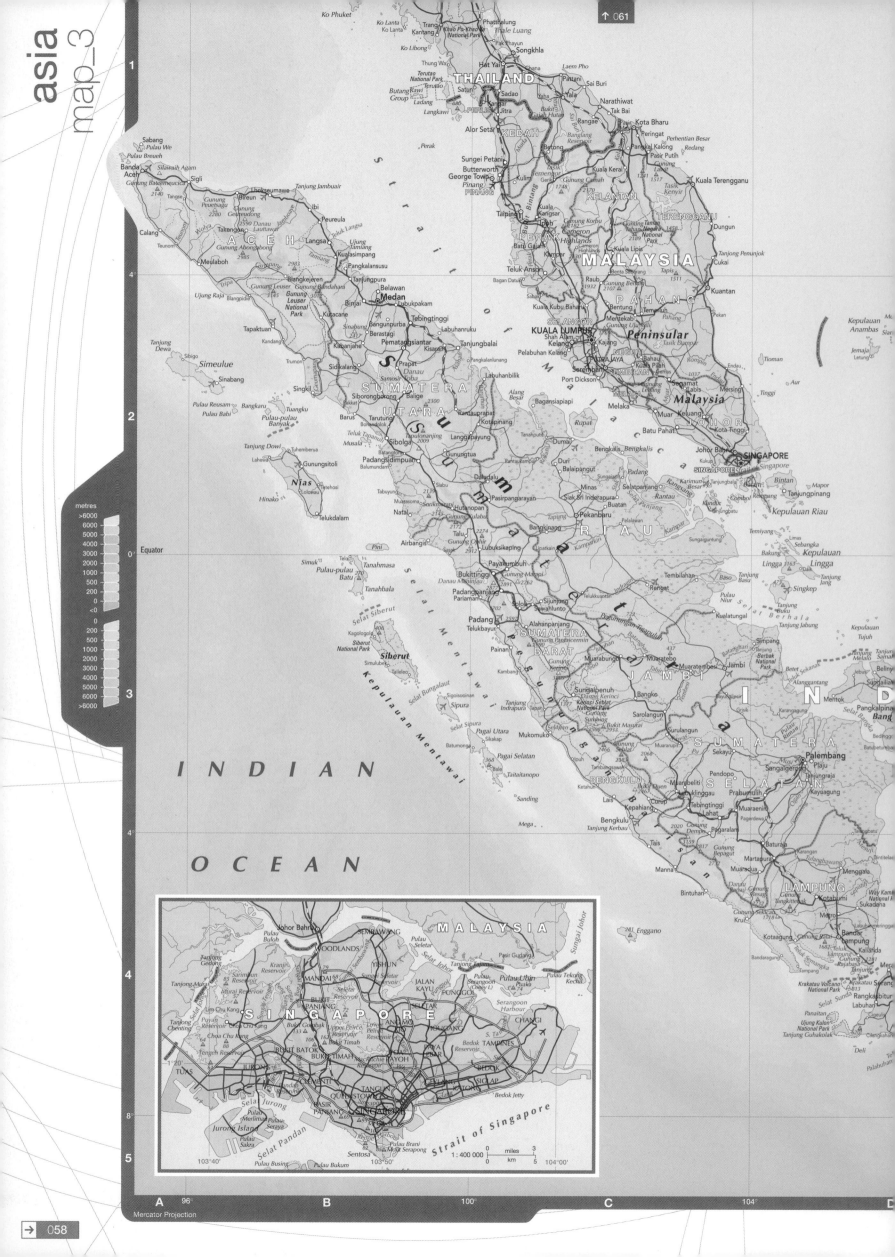

South China

Sea

Sulu Sea
PHILIPPINES

Celebes

Sea

MALAYSIA
SABAH
SARAWAK

Celebes
(Sulawesi)

KALIMANTAN
TIMUR

BRUNEI
BANDAR SERI
BEGAWAN

Borneo

KALIMANTAN BARAT

KALIMANTAN
TENGAH

KALIMANTAN
SELATAN

RANTAU

ONESIA

Java Sea

JAKARTA

JAWA BARAT

JAWA TENGAH

JAWA TIMUR

YOGYAKARTA

Java

(Jawa)

Bali Sea

Flores
Sea

BALI

Lombok

Sumbawa

108°   E   112°   F   116°   G

1 : 6 000 000

0   50   100   150   200   250 miles
0   50   100 150 200 250 300 350 400 km

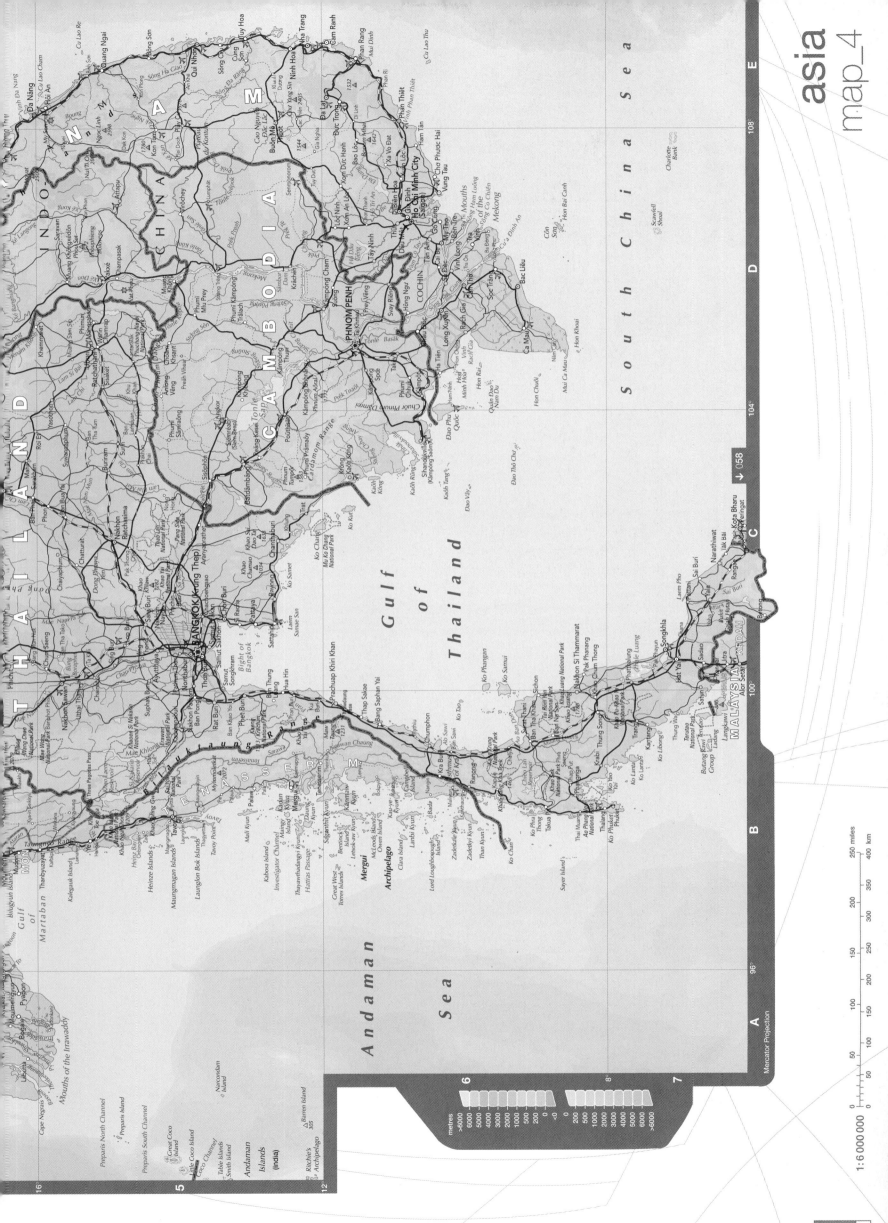

↓ 058

1 : 6 000 000
Mercator Projection

0 50 100 150 200 250 miles
0 100 200 300 350 400 km

metres
>6000
5000
4000
3000
2000
1000
500
<0
0
200
500
1000
2000
4000
5000
>6000

South China Sea

Gulf of Thailand

Andaman Sea

Gulf of Martaban

THAILAND

CAMBODIA

VIETNAM

INDO-CHINA

MALAYSIA

BANGKOK (Krung Thep)

PHNOM PENH

Ho Chi Minh City (Saigon)

Mergui Archipelago

TENASSERIM

Andaman Islands (India)

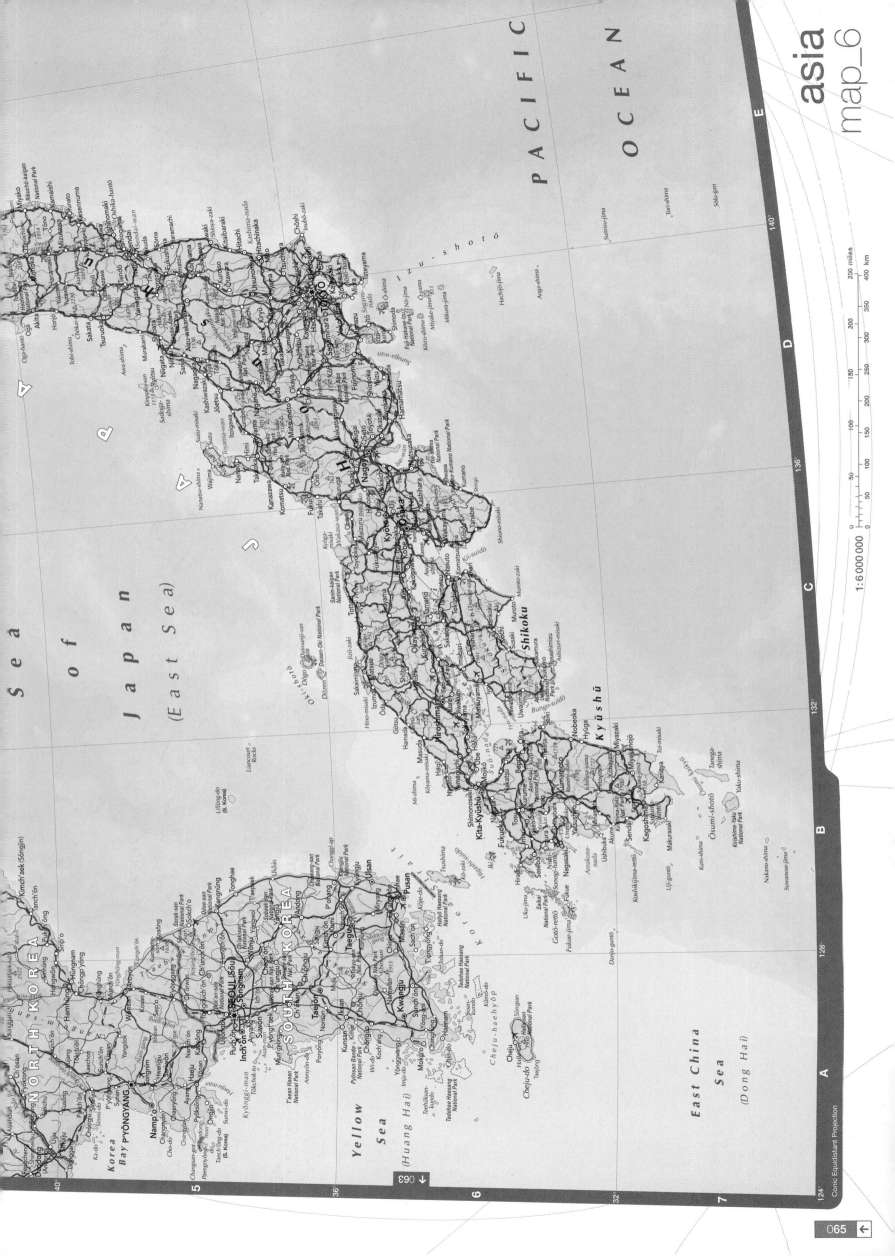

PACIFIC

OCEAN

Sea of Japan (East Sea)

NORTH KOREA

SOUTH KOREA

SEOUL (Sŏul)

Inch'ŏn

Taejŏn

Taegu

Pusan

Kwangju

Yellow Sea
(Huang Hai)

East China Sea
(Dong Hai)

Korea Bay
PYŎNGYANG

Honshū

Sendai

TŌKYŌ

Nagoya

Ōsaka

Kyōto

Kōbe

Hiroshima

Shikoku

Kyūshū

Fukuoka

Kita-Kyūshū

Kumamoto

Kagoshima

Izu-shotō

Hachijō-jima

Sumisu-jima

Tori-shima

Sōfu-gan

1 : 6 000 000

250 miles
400 km

Conic Equidistant Projection

A   B   C   D   E

124°   128°   132°   136°   140°

40

36

32

5

6

7

↓ 063

↓ 061
↑ 060

Conic Equidistant Projection

metres
>6000
6000
5000
4000
3000
2000
1000
500
200
0
<0
0
200
500
1000
2000
3000
4000
5000
6000
>6000

QINGHAI

GANSU

XIZANG ZIZHIQU
(TIBET)

SICHUAN

CHINA

SICHUAN PENDI

Chengdu

Chongqing

CHONGQING

GUIZHOU

Guiyang

INDIA

KACHIN

The Triangle

MYANMAR

SAGAING

SHAN

Mandalay

Shan Plateau

KAYAH

THAILAND

Chiang Mai

PEGU

YUNNAN

Kunming

VIETNAM

TONKIN

HÀ NỘI

Hai Phong

Gulf of

LAOS

Annam Highlands

THAILAND

Tropic of Cancer

Mekong

Salween

Yangtze

Gulf o

Hengduan Shan

Nu Shan

Qingshuiliang Shan

↑ 056

INDONESIA

Sumatra
(Sumatera)

Banda Aceh · Sigli
Sigli
Simeulue

Andaman
Sea

ANDAMAN AND NICOBAR ISLANDS (India)

North Andaman
Middle Andaman
South Andaman · Port Blair
Little Andaman

Nicobar
Islands

Tillanchong Island
Teressa Island · Nancowry
Camorta
Little Nicobar
Great Nicobar

Car Nicobar

Ten Degree Channel

Great Coco Island
Little Coco Island
Preparis Island
Preparis North Channel
Preparis South Channel

Narcondam Island
Barren Island
Ritchie's Archipelago

Cape Negrais
Bassein (Pathein)

MYANMAR

RANGOON (Yangon)

Mouths of the Irrawaddy

Chittagong
Cox's Bazar

WEST BENGAL

Kolkata (Calcutta)
Khulna

Mouths of the Ganges

B a y   o f   B e n g a l

I N D I A

ORISSA

Bhubaneshwar
Cuttack
Puri
Ganjam
Brahmapur

Vishakhapatnam

Srikakulam
Vizianagaram
Bobbili

ANDHRA PRADESH

Kakinada
Rajahmundry
Eluru
Machilipatnam

Coromandel Coast

Chennai (Madras)

Pondicherry (Puducherri)
Cuddalore
Karaikal
Kumbakonam
Nagapattinam
Thanjavur

TAMIL NADU

Madurai

SRI JAYEWARDENEPURA KOTTE

SRI LANKA

Jaffna
Trincomalee
Batticaloa
Kalmunai

Anuradhapura
Colombo
Moratuwa
Galle
Matara
Hambantota

Palk Strait
Gulf of Mannar

I N D I A N   O C E A N

A r a b i a n   S e a

Administrative divisions in India
numbered on the map:

1. DADRA AND NAGAR HAVELI (D7)
2. DAMAN AND DIU (D7)

Mumbai (Bombay)

MAHARASHTRA

Hyderabad

Bangalore

KARNATAKA

KERALA

Cochin (Kochi)
Trivandrum (Thiruvananthapuram)
Cape Comorin

Malabar Coast

LAKSHADWEEP (India)

Laccadive Islands
Amindivi Islands

Minicoy
Nine Degree Channel
Eight Degree Channel

MALDIVES

Male Atoll
MALE

One and a Half Degree Channel

Addu Atoll

Equator

0°

1:12 500 000

Albers Conic Equal Area Projection

500 miles
800 km

metres
>6000
6000
5000
4000
3000
2000
1000
500
0
<0
<0
500
1000
2000
4000
6000
>6000

Conic Equidistant Projection

metres
>6000
6000
5000
4000
3000
2000
1000
500
200
< 0
0
200
500
1000
2000
3000
4000
5000
6000
>6000

Arabian

Sea

MAHARASHTRA

Mumbai
(Bombay)

Pune
(Poona)

Ratnagiri

GOA

Marmagao

Madgaon

Karwar

KARNATAKA

Mangalore

Bangalore

Mysore

Sesostris Bank

Bassas de Pedro
Padua Bank

Cherbaniani
Reef

Byramgore Reef

Laccadive

Islands

Tree
Island
Bitra
Par

Kilttan

Chetlat

Amindivi Islands

Kadmat

Amini

Peremul
Par
Sand
Cay

Bingaram
Agatti

Timakara

Pitti

Kavaratti

LAKSHADWEEP
(India)

Andrott

Kavaratti

Kalpeni

Suheli Par
North
South Island Island   Cannanore Islands

Cheriyam
Kalpeni

Nine Degree Channel

Minicoy

Eight Degree Channel

Ihavandhippolhu
Atoll

Kelai

Thiladhunmathee Atoll

MALDIVES

Makunudhoo

Miladhunmadulu Atoll

North
Maalhosmadulu
Atoll

Faadhippolhu Atoll

Maalhosmadulu Atoll

INDI

Nagpur

Surat

Nashik

Aurangabad

Deccan

Solapur

Gulbarga

Hyderabad

Secunderabad

ANDHRA PRADESH

Kurnool

Nellore

Coromandel Coast

Chennai
(Madras)

Pondicherry
(Puducherry)

Cuddalore

TAMIL
NADU

Coimbatore

Salem

KERALA

Calicut (Kozhikode)

Cochin
(Kochi)

Madurai

Palk Strait

Jaffna

Tuticorin

Gulf of
Mannar

Trivandrum
(Thiruvananthapuram)

Cape
Comorin

Kanniyakumari

Nagercoil

SRI LANKA

SRI JAYEWARDENEPURA KOTTE

Colombo

Moratuwa

Galle

Dondra Head

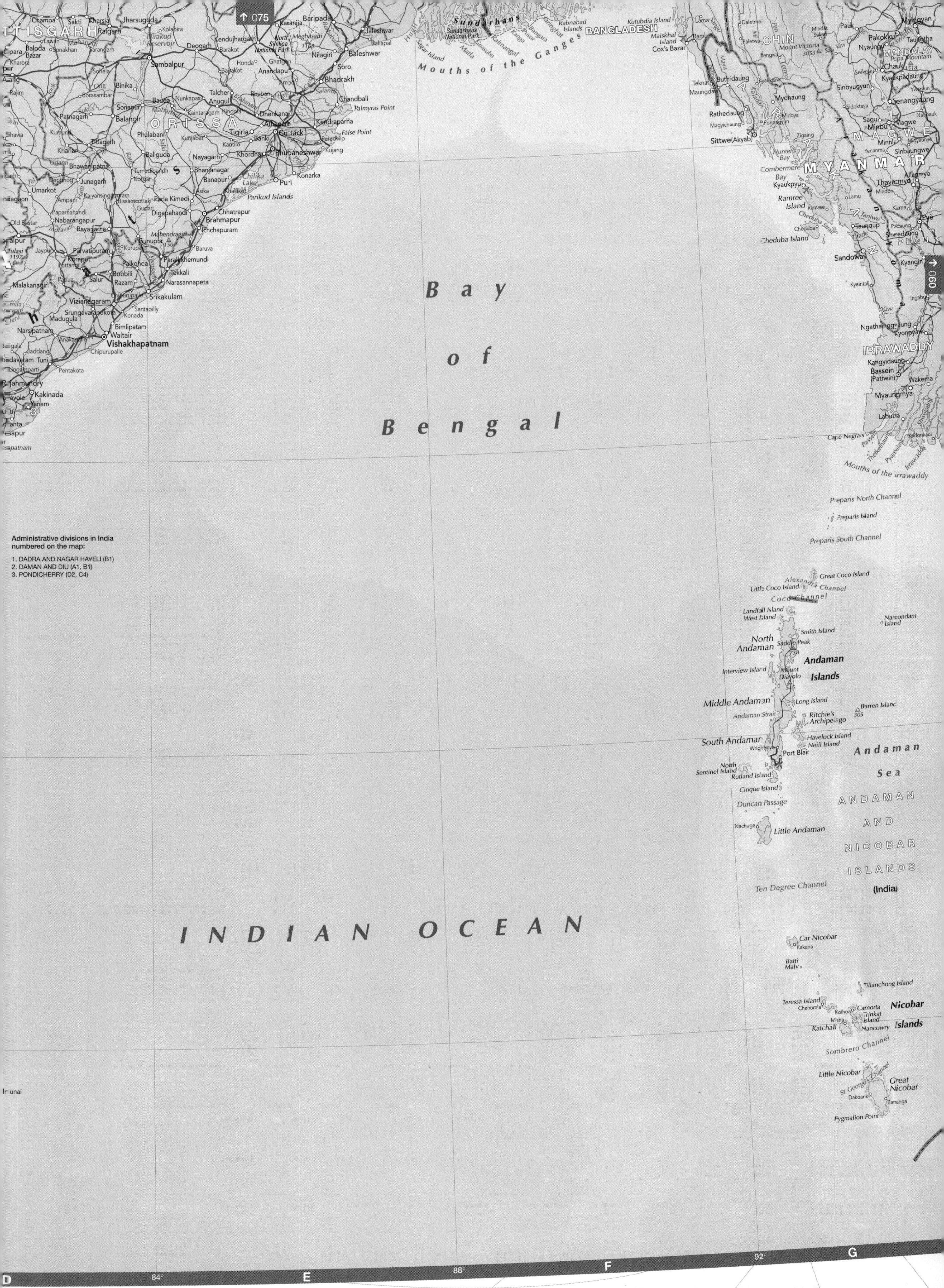

Bay

of

Bengal

INDIAN OCEAN

Administrative divisions in India
numbered on the map:

1. DADRA AND NAGAR HAVELI (B1)
2. DAMAN AND DIU (A1, B1)
3. PONDICHERRY (D2, C4)

CHATTISGARH

ORISSA

Champa · Sakti · Kharsia · Jharsuguda
Raigarh · Kolabira · Baripada
Lawan · Barakot · Kendujhargarh
Khariar · Sonakhan · Deogarh · Honda · Ghatgon · Nilagiri · Baleshwar
Kharora · Bazar · Sambalpur · Barakot · Kaintaragarh · Hindola · BHADRAKH
Rajim · Binika · Sonapur · Balangir · Talcher · Anugul · Dhenkanal · Chandbali
Kumuti · Balangir · Nunkapasi · Dhenkana · Salang
Khariar · Bauda · Nayagarh · Khordha · Tigiria · Banki · CUTTACK · Paradwip
Umarkot · Bhawanipatna · Baliguda · Nayagarh · Khordha · Kujang
Nilagaon · Kayansingram · Phulbani · Bhubaneshwar
Parla Kimedi · Asika · Chilika · Lake · Puri · Konarka
Ampani · Paparbahandi · Digapahandi · Balikhai · Parikud Islands
Nabarangapur · Rayagama · Chhatrapur · False Point
Jaypur · Parvatipuram · Ichchapuram · Baruva
Tulasi · Korput · Palkonda · Kurupam · Paralakhemundi
Bobbili · Razam · Narasannapeta · Srikakulam
Malakanagiri · Salur · Tekkali
Vizianagaram · Bimlipatam · Santapilly · Konada
Madugula · Narsipatnam · Srungavarapukota
Chipurupalle · Waltair · Vishakhapatnam
Madula · Anakapalli
Rajahmundry · Kakinada · Yanam
Pentakota

Sundarbans
Sundarbans
National Park

Mouths of the Ganges

BANGLADESH

Sagar Island
Matla
Kutubdia Island
Rabnab Islands
Kutubdia Island
Cox's Bazar

Maiskhal
Island

CHIN
Lama · Ramu · Daletme
Mindat · Pakokku · Myanaung
Mount Victoria · Nyaung-U
3053 · MANDALAY
Pepa mountain
Teknaf · Buthidaung · Chauk
Maungdaw · Myohaung
Rathedaung · Magyichaung
Magyichaung · Ponnagyun
Sittwe (Akyab) · Zigaing
Hunters' Bay
Combermere Bay
Kyaukpyu
Ramree Island · Ramree
Cheduba Strait
Cheduba Island
Sandoway
Cape Negrais
Kyeintali

MYANMAR

IRRAWADDY

Kangyidaung
Bassein (Pathein)
Wakema
Myaungmya
Labutta

Mouths of the Irrawaddy

MAGWE
Pakokku · Taungtha
Minhla · Minbu · Magwe
Shwedaung · PEGU
Thayetmyo · Allanmyo
Kyangin

Preparis North Channel
Preparis Island
Preparis South Channel

Alexandra Channel
Great Coco Island
Little Coco Island
Coco Channel
Landfall Island
West Island
North Andaman
Saddle Peak
Smith Island
Interview Island
Mount Diavolo
Andaman Islands
Middle Andaman
Long Island
Andaman Strait
Ritchie's Archipelago
South Andaman
Havelock Island
Neill Island
Wrightmyo
Port Blair
North Sentinel Island
Rutland Island
Cinque Island
Duncan Passage
Nachuge · Little Andaman

Narcondam Island

Barren Island
305

Andaman Sea

ANDAMAN AND NICOBAR ISLANDS
(India)

Ten Degree Channel

Car Nicobar
Kakana

Batti Malv

Tillanchong Island
Teressa Island
Chanumla
Koliong · Camorta
Trinkat Island
Misha · Nancowry
Katchall

Nicobar Islands

Sombrero Channel

Little Nicobar
St George's Channel
Dakoark
Great Nicobar
Bananga
Pygmalion Point

1:6 000 000

| 0 | 50 | 100 | 150 | 200 | 250 miles |
| 0 | 50 | 100 | 150 | 200 | 250 | 300 | 350 | 400 km |

D   E   88°   F   92°   G

84°

↑ 081

AFGHANISTAN

PAKISTAN

INDIA

Arabian Sea

Tropic of Cancer

Gulf of Kachchh

Gulf of Khambhat

Rann of Kachchh

Little Rann

BALOCHISTAN

SINDH

PUNJAB

GUJARAT

RAJASTHAN

HARYANA

PUNJAB

HIMACHAL PRADESH

UTTARANCHAL

UTTAR PRADESH

MADHYA PRADESH

JAMMU AND KASHMIR

ZANSKAR

LADAKH

NORTHERN AREAS

BALTISTAN

HUNZA

NORTH WEST FRONTIER

TRIBAL AREAS

PAKTIA

PAKTIKA

GHAZNI

VARDAK

LOWGAR

NANGARHAR

KONAR

LAGHMAN

PARVAN

KAPISA

BADAKHSHAN

TAKHAR

BAGHLAN

AKSAI CHIN
Claimed by India
under Chinese
administration

LINE OF CONTROL

KABUL (Kabul)

ISLAMABAD

Rawalpindi

Peshawar

Lahore

Faisalabad

Multan

Jammu

Srinagar

NEW DELHI

Delhi

Jaipur

Agra

Kanpur

Lucknow

Jodhpur

Ahmadabad

Vadodara (Baroda)

Surat

Bhopal

Indore

Nagpur

Jabalpur

Hyderabad

Chandigarh

Ludhiana

Amritsar

Meerut

Gwalior

Udaipur

Hindu Kush

Karakoram Range

Thar Desert

Administrative divisions in India
numbered on the map:

1. DADRA AND NAGAR HAVELI (B5)
2. DAMAN AND DIU (A5, B5)

↓ 072

Albers Conic Equal Area Projection

1:13 000 000

| 0 | 100 | 200 | 300 | 400 | 500 miles |

| 0 | 100 | 200 | 300 | 400 | 500 | 600 | 700 | 800 km |

↑ 029

↑ 047

↑ 088

↓ 089

metres
>6000
6000
5000
4000
3000
2000
1000
500
200
0
0
200
500
1000
2000
3000
4000
5000
6000
>6000

Administrative divisions numbered on the map:

EGYPT
10. AD DAQAHLĪYAH (B5)
11. AL BUḤAYRAH (B5)
12. AL GHARBĪYAH (B5)
13. AL ISKANDARĪYAH (B5)
14. AL QĀHIRAH (B5)
15. AS SUWAYS (C5)
16. BŪR SAʿĪD (C5)

17. DUMYĀṬ (B5)
18. ISMĀʿĪLIYAH (C5)
19. KAFR ASH SHAYKH (B5)
20. MINŪFĪYA (B5)
21. QALYŪBĪYA (B5)
22. SHARQĪYAH (B5)

IRAN
23. CHAHĀR MAḤALL VA BAKHTĪĀRĪ (G4)
24. KOHKĪLŪYEH VA BŪYER AḤMADĪ (G5)

Conic Equidistant Projection

1 : 6 000 000

0   50   100   150   200   250 miles
0 50 100 150 200 250 300 350 400 km

↑ 079

AZERBAIJAN

BAKU

Caspian
Sea

Administrative divisions
numbered on the map

AFGHANISTAN
1. KÂBUL (G3)
2. KÂPISA (G3)
3. LAGHMÂN (G3)
4. LOWGAR (G3)
5. PARVÂN (G3)

IRAN
6. CHAHÂR MAHÂLL VÂ BAKHIÂRÎ (B3)
7. KOHKÎLÛYEH VA BÛYER AHMADÎ (B4)

UZBEKISTAN
8. FERGANSKAYA OBLAST' (G1)
9. SYRDAR'INSKAYA OBLAST' (G1)
10. TASHKENTSKAYA OBLAST' (G1)

ARMENIA

AZERBAIJAN

TURK

BALKANSKAYA
OBLAST

Tabriz

AZARBAYJAN-E
SHARQI

ARDABIL

GILAN

MAZANDARAN

GOLESTAN

ELBURZ MOUNTAINS

KORDESTAN

ZANJAN

QAZVIN

TEHRAN

SEMNAN

Dasht-e Kavir

KERMANSHAH

HAMADAN

MARKAZI

QOM

KHO

LORESTAN

ARAK

ESFAHAN

YAZD

ILAM

IRAQ

KHUZESTAN

I R A N

Esfahan

Shiraz

KERMAN

KUWAIT

KUWAIT (Al Kuwayt)

FARS

BUSHEHR

T h e   G u l f

Bandar-e
'Abbas

HORMOZGAN

Strait of Hormuz

SAUDI

ASH
SHARQIYAH

ARABIA

BAHRAIN

MANAMA (Al-Manâmah)

Gulf
of
Bahrain

QATAR

DOHA
(Ad Dawhah)

Gulf of Oman

RIYADH
(Ar Riyâd)

AR RIYAD

OMAN

UNITED
ARAB
EMIRATES

ABU DHABI
(Abū Zabī)

OMAN
AL BATINAH

Dubai (Dubayy)

↓ 076

Conic Equidistant Projection

1: 6 000 000

| 0 | 50 | 100 | 150 | 200 | 250 miles |

| 0 | 50 | 100 | 150 | 200 | 250 | 300 | 350 | 400 km |

Indian subcontinent

Ganges Delta, India

Forbidden City, Beijing, China

Cyprus, eastern Mediterranean

Space Imaging

COUNTRIES		area sq km	area sq miles	population	capital	languages	religions	currency	map
AFGHANISTAN		652 225	251 825	22 475 000	Kābul	Dari, Pushtu, Uzbek, Turkmen	Sunni Muslim, Shi'a Muslim	Afghani	81
ARMENIA		29 800	11 506	3 788 000	Yerevan	Armenian, Azeri	Armenian Orthodox	Dram	79
AZERBAIJAN		86 600	33 436	8 096 000	Baku	Azeri, Armenian, Russian, Lezgian	Shi'a Muslim, Sunni Muslim, Russian and Armenian Orthodox	Azerbaijani manat	79
BAHRAIN		691	267	652 000	Manama	Arabic, English	Shi'a Muslim, Sunni Muslim, Christian	Bahrain dinar	80
BANGLADESH		143 998	55 598	140 369 000	Dhaka	Bengali, English	Sunni Muslim, Hindu	Taka	75
BHUTAN		46 620	18 000	2 141 000	Thimphu	Dzongkha, Nepali, Assamese	Buddhist, Hindu	Ngultrum, Indian rupee	75
BRUNEI		5 765	2 226	335 000	Bandar Seri Begawan	Malay, English, Chinese	Sunni Muslim, Buddhist, Christian	Brunei dollar	59
CAMBODIA		181 000	69 884	13 441 000	Phnom Penh	Khmer, Vietnamese	Buddhist, Roman Catholic, Sunni Muslim	Riel	61
CHINA		9 584 492	3 700 593	1 270 082 000	Beijing	Mandarin, Wu, Cantonese, Hsiang, regional languages	Confucian, Taoist, Buddhist, Christian, Sunni Muslim	Yuan, HK dollar*, Macau pataca	62–63
CYPRUS		9 251	3 572	790 000	Nicosia	Greek, Turkish, English	Greek Orthodox, Sunni Muslim	Cyprus pound	77
EAST TIMOR		14 874	5 743	750 000	Dili	Portuguese, Tetun, English	Roman Catholic	United States dollar	108
GEORGIA		69 700	26 911	5 239 000	T'bilisi	Georgian, Russian, Armenian, Azeri, Ossetian, Abkhaz	Georgian Orthodox, Russian Orthodox, Sunni Muslim	Lari	79
INDIA		3 065 027	1 183 414	1 025 096 000	New Delhi	Hindi, English, many regional languages	Hindu, Sunni Muslim, Shi'a Muslim, Sikh, Christian	Indian rupee	70–71
INDONESIA		1 919 445	741 102	214 840 000	Jakarta	Indonesian, local languages	Sunni Muslim, Protestant, Roman Catholic, Hindu, Buddhist	Rupiah	56–57
IRAN		1 648 000	636 296	71 369 000	Tehrān	Farsi, Azeri, Kurdish, regional languages	Shi'a Muslim, Sunni Muslim	Iranian rial	80–81
IRAQ		438 317	169 235	23 584 000	Baghdād	Arabic, Kurdish, Turkmen	Shi'a Muslim, Sunni Muslim, Christian	Iraqi dinar	79
ISRAEL		20 770	8 019	6 172 000	Jerusalem	Hebrew, Arabic	Jewish, Sunni Muslim, Christian, Druze	Shekel	77
JAPAN		377 727	145 841	127 335 000	Tōkyō	Japanese	Shintoist, Buddhist, Christian	Yen	64–65
JORDAN		89 206	34 443	5 051 000	'Ammān	Arabic	Sunni Muslim, Christian	Jordanian dinar	77
KAZAKHSTAN		2 717 300	1 049 155	16 095 000	Astana	Kazakh, Russian, Ukrainian, German, Uzbek, Tatar	Sunni Muslim, Russian Orthodox, Protestant	Tenge	26
KUWAIT		17 818	6 880	1 971 000	Kuwait	Arabic	Sunni Muslim, Shi'a Muslim, Christian, Hindu	Kuwaiti dinar	79
KYRGYZSTAN		198 500	76 641	4 986 000	Bishkek	Kyrgyz, Russian, Uzbek	Sunni Muslim, Russian Orthodox	Kyrgyz som	70
LAOS		236 800	91 429	5 403 000	Vientiane	Lao, local languages	Buddhist, traditional beliefs	Kip	60–61
LEBANON		10 452	4 036	3 556 000	Beirut	Arabic, Armenian, French	Shi'a Muslim, Sunni Muslim, Christian	Lebanese pound	77
MALAYSIA		332 965	128 559	22 633 000	Kuala Lumpur, Putrajaya	Malay, English, Chinese, Tamil, local languages	Sunni Muslim, Buddhist, Hindu, Christian, traditional beliefs	Ringgit	58–59
MALDIVES		298	115	300 000	Male	Divehi (Maldivian)	Sunni Muslim	Rufiyaa	71
MONGOLIA		1 565 000	604 250	2 559 000	Ulan Bator	Khalka (Mongolian), Kazakh, local languages	Buddhist, Sunni Muslim	Tugrik (tögrög)	62–63
MYANMAR		676 577	261 228	48 364 000	Rangoon	Burmese, Shan, Karen, local languages	Buddhist, Christian, Sunni Muslim	Kyat	60–61
NEPAL		147 181	56 827	23 593 000	Kathmandu	Nepali, Maithili, Bhojpuri, English, local languages	Hindu, Buddhist, Sunni Muslim	Nepalese rupee	74–75
NORTH KOREA		120 538	46 540	22 428 000	P'yŏngyang	Korean	Traditional beliefs, Chondoist, Buddhist	North Korean won	64–65
OMAN		309 500	119 499	2 622 000	Muscat	Arabic, Baluchi, Indian languages	Ibadhi Muslim, Sunni Muslim	Omani riyal	76
PAKISTAN		803 940	310 403	144 971 000	Islamabad	Urdu, Punjabi, Sindhi, Pushtu, English	Sunni Muslim, Shi'a Muslim, Christian, Hindu	Pakistani rupee	70–71
PALAU		497	192	20 000	Koror	Palauan, English	Roman Catholic, Protestant, traditional beliefs	United States dollar	57
PHILIPPINES		300 000	115 831	77 131 000	Manila	English, Pilipino, Cebuano, local languages	Roman Catholic, Protestant, Sunni Muslim, Aglipayan	Philippine peso	56–57
QATAR		11 437	4 416	575 000	Doha	Arabic	Sunni Muslim	Qatari riyal	80
RUSSIAN FEDERATION		17 075 400	6 592 849	144 664 000	Moscow	Russian, Tatar, Ukrainian, local languages	Russian Orthodox, Sunni Muslim, Protestant	Russian rouble	26–27
SAUDI ARABIA		2 200 000	849 425	21 028 000	Riyadh	Arabic	Sunni Muslim, Shi'a Muslim	Saudi Arabian riyal	76
SINGAPORE		639	247	4 108 000	Singapore	Chinese, English, Malay, Tamil	Buddhist, Taoist, Sunni Muslim, Christian, Hindu	Singapore dollar	58
SOUTH KOREA		99 274	38 330	47 069 000	Seoul	Korean	Buddhist, Protestant, Roman Catholic	South Korean won	65
SRI LANKA		65 610	25 332	19 104 000	Sri Jayewardenepura Kotte	Sinhalese, Tamil, English	Buddhist, Hindu, Sunni Muslim, Roman Catholic	Sri Lankan rupee	72
SYRIA		185 180	71 498	16 610 000	Damascus	Arabic, Kurdish, Armenian	Sunni Muslim, Shi'a Muslim, Christian	Syrian pound	78–79
TAIWAN		36 179	13 969	22 300 000	T'aipei	Mandarin, Min, Hakka, local languages	Buddhist, Taoist, Confucian, Christian	Taiwan dollar	67
TAJIKISTAN		143 100	55 251	6 135 000	Dushanbe	Tajik, Uzbek, Russian	Sunni Muslim	Somoni	81
THAILAND		513 115	198 115	63 584 000	Bangkok	Thai, Lao, Chinese, Malay, Mon–Khmer languages	Buddhist, Sunni Muslim	Baht	60–61
TURKEY		779 452	300 948	67 632 000	Ankara	Turkish, Kurdish	Sunni Muslim, Shi'a Muslim	Turkish lira	78–79
TURKMENISTAN		488 100	188 456	4 835 000	Ashgabat	Turkmen, Uzbek, Russian	Sunni Muslim, Russian Orthodox	Turkmen manat	68
UNITED ARAB EMIRATES		83 600	32 278	2 654 000	Abu Dhabi	Arabic, English	Sunni Muslim, Shi'a Muslim	United Arab Emirates dirham	76
UZBEKISTAN		447 400	172 742	25 257 000	Tashkent	Uzbek, Russian, Tajik, Kazakh	Sunni Muslim, Russian Orthodox	Uzbek som	70
VIETNAM		329 565	127 246	79 175 000	Ha Nôi	Vietnamese, Thai, Khmer, Chinese, local languages	Buddhist, Taoist, Roman Catholic, Cao Dai, Hoa Hao	Dong	60–61
YEMEN		527 968	203 850	19 114 000	Şan'ā'	Arabic	Sunni Muslim, Shi'a Muslim	Yemeni rial	76

*Hong Kong dollar

DEPENDENT AND DISPUTED TERRITORIES		territorial status	area sq km	area sq miles	population	capital	languages	religions	currency	map
British Indian Ocean Territory		United Kingdom Overseas Territory	60	23	uninhabited					162
Christmas Island		Australian External Territory	135	52	2 135	The Settlement	English	Buddhist, Sunni Muslim, Protestant, Roman Catholic	Australian dollar	55
Cocos Islands (Keeling Islands)		Australian External Territory	14	5	637	West Island	English	Sunni Muslim, Christian	Australian dollar	55
French Southern and Antarctic Lands		French Overseas Territory	439 580	169 723	uninhabited					163
Gaza		Semi-autonomous region	363	140	3 311 000*	Gaza	Arabic	Sunni Muslim, Shi'a Muslim	Israeli shekel	77
Heard and McDonald Islands		Australian External Territory	412	159	uninhabited					163
Jammu and Kashmir		Disputed territory (India/Pakistan)	222 236	85 806	13 000 000					74
West Bank		Disputed territory	5 860	2 263			Arabic, Hebrew	Sunni Muslim, Jewish, Shi'a Muslim, Christian	Jordanian dinar, Israeli shekel	77

africa

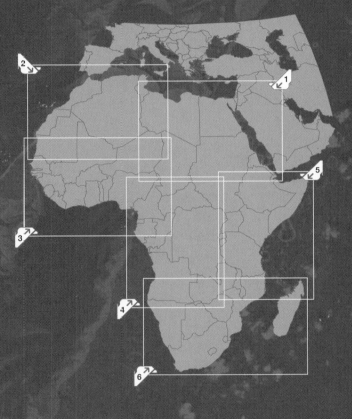

contents

		map coverage	scale
84–85	landscapes		
86–87	locations		
88–89	map_1	**africa** northeast	1:8 000 000
90–91	map_2	**africa** northwest	1:8 000 000
92–93	map_3	**africa** west	1:8 000 000
94–95	map_4	**africa** west central	1:8 000 000
96–97	map_5	**africa** east central	1:8 000 000
98–99	map_6	**africa** south	1:8 000 000
100	states and territories		

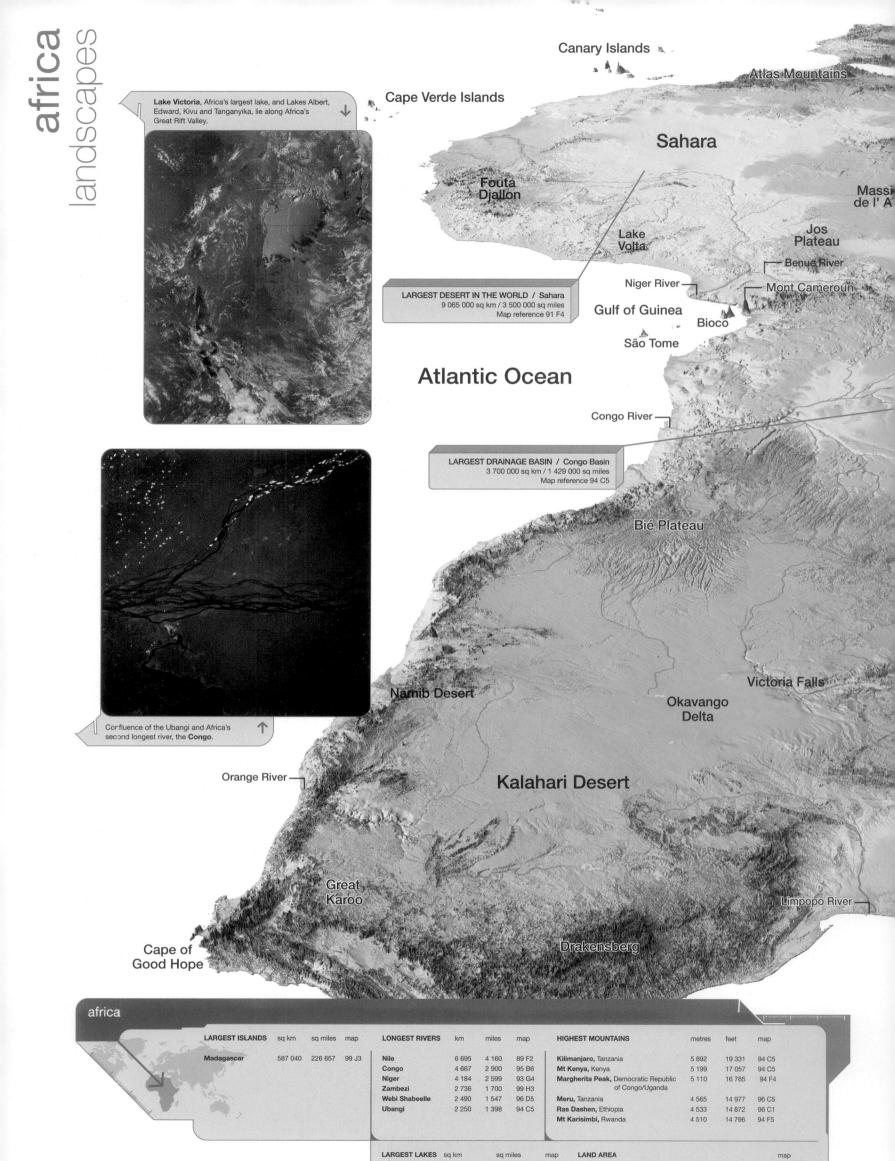

Lake Victoria, Africa's largest lake, and Lakes Albert, Edward, Kivu and Tanganyika, lie along Africa's Great Rift Valley.

Canary Islands

Atlas Mountains

Cape Verde Islands

Sahara

Fouta Djallon

Lake Volta

Jos Plateau

Massif de l' A

Benue River

LARGEST DESERT IN THE WORLD / Sahara
9 065 000 sq km / 3 500 000 sq miles
Map reference 91 F4

Niger River

Mont Cameroun

Gulf of Guinea

Bioco

São Tome

Atlantic Ocean

Congo River

LARGEST DRAINAGE BASIN / Congo Basin
3 700 000 sq km / 1 429 000 sq miles
Map reference 94 C5

Bié Plateau

Confluence of the Ubangi and Africa's second longest river, the **Congo**.

Victoria Falls

Namib Desert

Okavango Delta

Orange River

Kalahari Desert

Great Karoo

Limpopo River

Cape of Good Hope

Drakensberg

africa

LARGEST ISLANDS	sq km	sq miles	map
Madagascar	587 040	226 657	99 J3

LONGEST RIVERS	km	miles	map
Nile	6 695	4 160	89 F2
Congo	4 667	2 900	95 B6
Niger	4 184	2 599	93 G4
Zambezi	2 736	1 700	99 H3
Webi Shabeelle	2 490	1 547	96 D5
Ubangi	2 250	1 398	94 C5

HIGHEST MOUNTAINS	metres	feet	map
Kilimanjaro, Tanzania	5 892	19 331	94 C5
Mt Kenya, Kenya	5 199	17 057	94 C5
Margherita Peak, Democratic Republic of Congo/Uganda	5 110	16 765	94 F4
Meru, Tanzania	4 565	14 977	96 C5
Ras Dashen, Ethiopia	4 533	14 872	96 C1
Mt Karisimbi, Rwanda	4 510	14 796	94 F5

LARGEST LAKES	sq km	sq miles	map
Lake Victoria	68 800	26 563	96 B5
Lake Tanganyika	32 900	12 702	95 F6
Lake Nyasa	30 044	11 600	97 B7
Lake Chad	10 000—26 000	3 861—10 039	93 I2
Lake Volta	8 485	3 276	92 F4
Lake Turkana	6 475	2 500	96 C4

LAND AREA		map
Total land area	30 343 578 sq km / 11 715 721 sq miles	
Most northerly point	La Galite, Tunisia	91 H1
Most southerly point	Cape Agulhas, South Africa	98 D7
Most westerly point	Santo Antao, Cape Verde	92 inset
Most easterly point	Raas Xaafuun, Somalia	96 F2

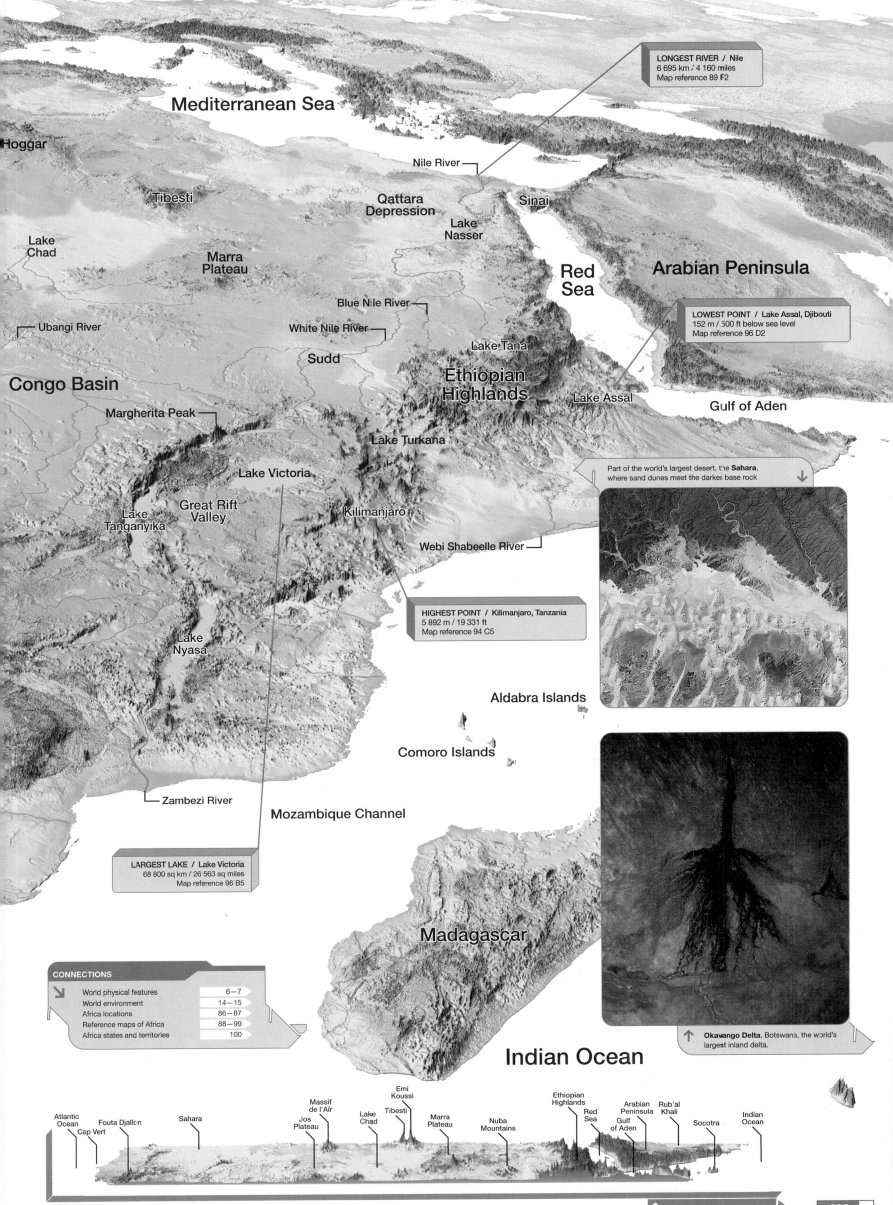

Mediterranean Sea

Hoggar

Tibesti

Qattara
Depression

Sinai

Lake
Nasser

Lake
Chad

Marra
Plateau

Red
Sea

Arabian Peninsula

LONGEST RIVER / Nile
6 695 km / 4 160 miles
Map reference 89 F2

Nile River

Blue Nile River

LOWEST POINT / Lake Assal, Djibouti
152 m / 500 ft below sea level
Map reference 96 D2

Ubangi River

White Nile River

Lake Tana

Sudd

Ethiopian
Highlands

Lake Assal

Congo Basin

Gulf of Aden

Margherita Peak

Lake Turkana

Part of the world's largest desert, the **Sahara**,
where sand dunes meet the darker base rock

Lake Victoria

Great Rift
Valley

Lake
Tanganyika

Kilimanjaro

Webi Shabeelle River

Lake
Nyasa

HIGHEST POINT / Kilimanjaro, Tanzania
5 892 m / 19 331 ft
Map reference 94 C5

Aldabra Islands

Comoro Islands

Zambezi River

Mozambique Channel

LARGEST LAKE / Lake Victoria
68 800 sq km / 26 563 sq miles
Map reference 96 B5

Madagascar

CONNECTIONS

World physical features	6—7
World environment	14—15
Africa locations	86—87
Reference maps of Africa	88—99
Africa states and territories	100

Okavango Delta, Botswana, the world's
largest inland delta.

Indian Ocean

Atlantic
Ocean
Cap Vert

Fouta Djallon

Sahara

Massif
de l'Aïr

Emi
Koussi

Jos
Plateau

Tibesti

Lake
Chad

Marra
Plateau

Nuba
Mountains

Ethiopian
Highlands

Red
Sea

Arabian
Peninsula

Gulf
of Aden

Rub' al
Khali

Socotra

Indian
Ocean

Namib Desert, arid region along the entire coast of Namibia, southwest Africa.

CONNECTIONS

World countries	8–9
Africa landscapes	84–85
Reference maps of Africa	88–99
Africa states and territories	100
Atlantic Ocean	160–161
Indian Ocean	162–163

Uninhabited island group, Aldabra Islands, part of the Seychelles, Indian Ocean.

The Great Pyramids, on the west bank of the river Nile near Giza, Egypt.

Space Imaging

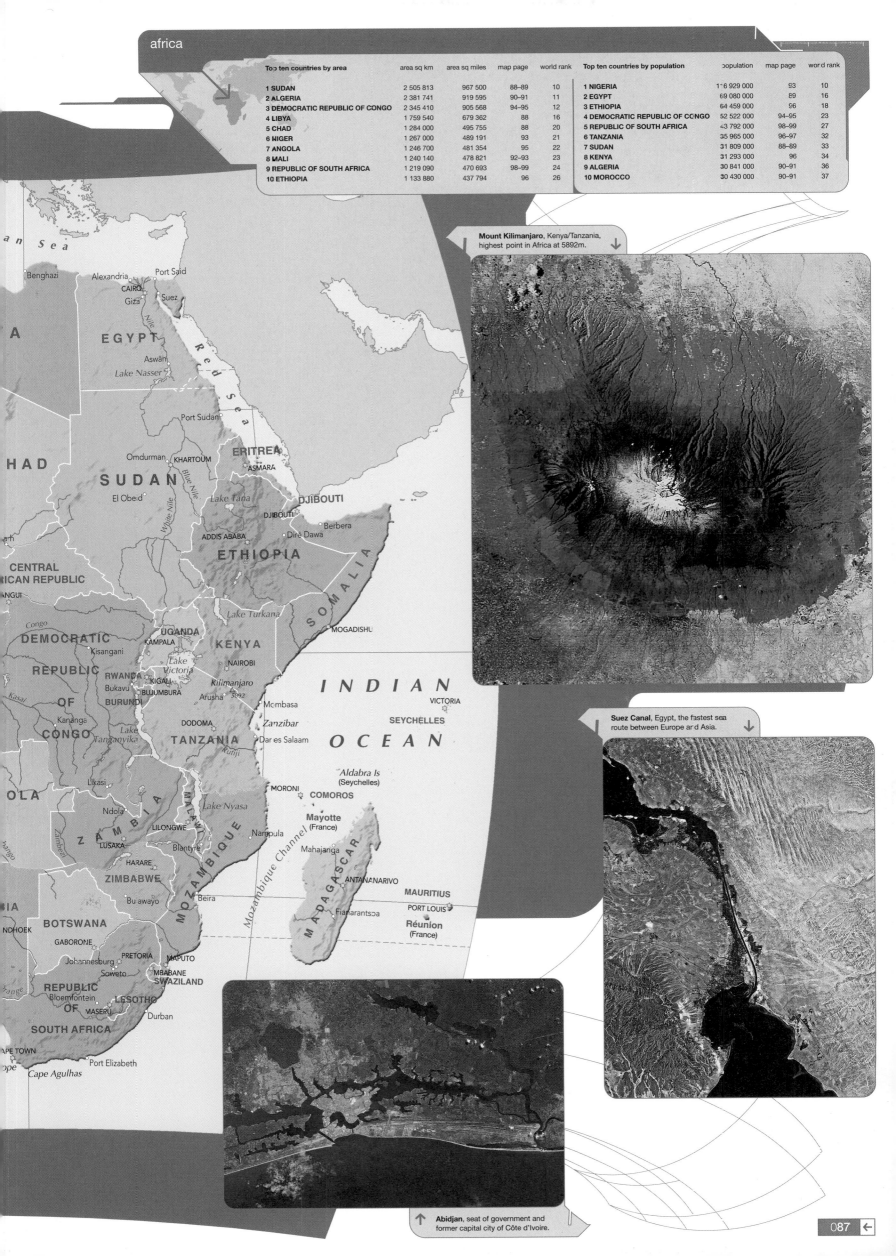

Top ten countries by area	area sq km	area sq miles	map page	world rank
1 SUDAN	2 505 813	967 500	88–89	10
2 ALGERIA	2 381 741	919 595	90–91	11
3 DEMOCRATIC REPUBLIC OF CONGO	2 345 410	905 568	94–95	12
4 LIBYA	1 759 540	679 362	88	16
5 CHAD	1 284 000	495 755	88	20
6 NIGER	1 267 000	489 191	93	21
7 ANGOLA	1 246 700	481 354	95	22
8 MALI	1 240 140	478 821	92–93	23
9 REPUBLIC OF SOUTH AFRICA	1 219 090	470 693	98–99	24
10 ETHIOPIA	1 133 880	437 794	96	26

Top ten countries by population	population	map page	world rank
1 NIGERIA	116 929 000	93	10
2 EGYPT	69 080 000	89	16
3 ETHIOPIA	64 459 000	96	18
4 DEMOCRATIC REPUBLIC OF CONGO	52 522 000	94–95	23
5 REPUBLIC OF SOUTH AFRICA	43 792 000	98–99	27
6 TANZANIA	35 965 000	96–97	32
7 SUDAN	31 809 000	88–89	33
8 KENYA	31 293 000	96	34
9 ALGERIA	30 841 000	90–91	36
10 MOROCCO	30 430 000	90–91	37

Mount Kilimanjaro, Kenya/Tanzania, highest point in Africa at 5892m.

Suez Canal, Egypt, the fastest sea route between Europe and Asia.

Abidjan, seat of government and former capital city of Côte d'Ivoire.

Lambert Azimuthal Equal Area Projection

1:8 000 000

| 0 | 100 | 200 | 300 | miles |

| 0 | 100 | 200 | 300 | 400 | 500 km |

← 091

↓ 094

ean Sea

EGYPT

SUDAN

SAUDI ARABIA

JORDAN

ISRAEL

SYRIA

LEBANON

IRAQ

ERITREA

ETHIOPIA

YEMEN

DJIBOUTI

Western Desert
(Aş Şahrā' al Gharbīyah)

Eastern Desert
(Aş Şahrā' ash Sharqīyah)

Nubian Desert

Baiyuda Desert

HIJAZ

RED SEA

Gulf of Suez

Gulf of Aqaba

SINAI
Jabal at Tīh

NORTHERN

NILE

KASSALA

GEDAREF

SENNAR

WHITE NILE

NORTHERN KORDOFAN

WESTERN KORDOFAN

TIGRAY

AMHARA

AFAR

Alexandria (Al Iskandarīyah)

CAIRO (Al Qāhirah)

Giza (Al Jīzah)

DAMASCUS (Dimashq)

AMMAN

JERUSALEM (El Quds)

Tel Aviv-Yafo

GAZA

Port Said (Būr Saʿīd)

Suez (As Suways)

Luxor (Al Uqşur)

Aswān

Medina (Al Madīnah)

Mecca (Makkah)

Jeddah (Jiddah)

Ţāʾif

Port Sudan (Būr Sudan)

KHARTOUM

Omdurman

Khartoum North

ASMARA

Hodeidah (Al Hudaydah)

A T L A N T I C

O C E A N

metres
>6000
6000
5000
4000
3000
2000
1000
500
200
0
<0
0
200
500
1000
2000
3000
4000
5000
6000
>6000

PORTUGAL
Alcácer do Sal
Zafra
Azuaga
Sierra Morena
Estrella
Linares
Córdoba
Andújar
Jaén
S P A I N
Cabo de Sines
Serpa
Fuente del Río
Écija
Alcaudete
Seville (Sevilla)
Huelva
Granada
Sierra Nevada
Lagos
Faro
Ayamonte
Utrera
Antequera
Vélez-Málaga
Cabo de São Vicente
Olhão
Golfo
de Cádiz
Cádiz
Jerez de la Frontera
Málaga
Marbella
San Fernando
Algeciras
Tarifa
Gibraltar (U.K.)
Isla de Alborán (Spain)
Tangier (Tanger)
Ceuta (Spain)
Tétouan
Al Hoceima
Melilla (Spain)
Cap des Trois Fourch
Nador
Larache
Chaouen
Ksar el Kebir
Taourirt
Souk el Arbaâ du Rharb
Ouezzane
Taza
Taounate
Guercif
RABAT
Sidi Kacem
Volubilis
Kénitra
Meknès
Casablanca
Khemisset
Azrou
Ben Slimane
Ifrane
El Jadida
Berrechid
Azemmour
Boulemane
Dutat Oued el Hj
Settat
Moyen Atlas
Missour
Beni Guil
Sidi Bennour
Khouribga
Oued Zem
Safi
Youssoufia
Beni Mellal
Azilal
Khenifra
M O R O C C O
Chemaïa
Benguerir
El Kelaâ
des Srarhna
Plaine de
Essaouira
Ounara
Chichaoua
Marrakech
Er-Rachidia
Tamanar
Parc National
Toubkal
Aït Benhaddou
Ouarzazate
Errachidia
Cap Rhir
Tarqudannt
Taliouine
Tazenakht
Zagora
Abadla
Agadir
Oulad Teima
Irherm
H a u t
Atlas
Taïta
Tata
Béchar
Tiznit
A n t i - A t l a s
Akka
Sidi Ifni
Bou Izakarn
Guelmine
Tan-Tan
Assa
Zag
H a m m a d a d u D r â a
Tabelbala

LAÂYOUNE
El Haggoûnia
G'ydat al Jhoucha
Al Mahbas
Tindouf
Hamada ed Douakel
Es Semara
Haouza
W E S T E R N
S A H A R A
Boujdour
Al Matmaïna
Hassi Arida
Amasine
Aoufist
Bir Lahmar
Tiarity
Atonyia
Ayoûn
'Abd el Mâlek
Zug
Galtat Zemmour
Bir Aïdiat
Bir Mogreïn
Bir Bel Guerdâne
Ain
Ben Tili
Zamlat Amagraj
Skaymat
T I R I S
Z E M M O U R
Sebkhet Iguetti
El Beyyed
El Ghallâoûïya

Tropic of Cancer
Ad Dakhla
Adrar Soutlou
La Râygat
Sebkhet Oumm
ed Drous Guebli
Sebkhet
ej Jill
Fderik
Zouérât
Tiguesmat
Maqteïr
Bir 'Amrâne
Mejaouda
A
o
u
k
â
r
Oumm el Asel
Agârakmet
Bir Chali
El Gçaib

Nouâdhibou
Râs Nouâdhibou
Cansado
DAKHLET
NOUÂDHIBOU
Parc
National
du Banc
d'Arguin
INCHIRI
Bû Gandous
Tichla
Chami
Ben Amira
Choûm
Ouadâne
Chreïrik
Guelb
Chemchâm
A D R A R
Atâr
Chinguetti
Dhar
Ioûrène
Jbel Fçâl
El Khnâchich
Bir Ounâne
El Guettara
TOMBOUCTOU
M A

MAURITANIA
Akjoujt
Oujeft
Tat'raoun
M A U R I T A N I A
T A G A N T
Tidjikja
Aghouavil
HODH
ECH CHARGUI
Oued el Hajâr

Nouâmghar
Râs Timirist
TRARZA
Sebkhet
Te-n-Dghamcha
NOUAKCHOTT
Damâne
Tourirma
Lekhcheb
Tichit
Dhar Tichît
Aratâne
Aghrijit
BRAKNA
Keur Massène
Rosso
Richard Toll
St-Louis
Lac de Guier
SENEGAL
GORGOL
ASSABA
EL GHARBI
HODH
EL-GHARBI
Kiffa
Néma

Lambert Azimuthal Equal Area Projection

1:8 000 000

0   100   200   300 miles
0   100   200   300   400   500 km

metres
>6000
6000
5000
4000
3000
2000
1000
500
200
0
◁ 0
200
500
1000
2000
3000
4000
5000
6000
>6000

MAURITANIA

INCHIRI

A D R A R

TAGANT

HODH
ECH CHARGUI

HODH
EL GHARBI

ASSABA

TRARZA

BRAKNA

NOUAKCHOTT

St-Louis

DAKAR

SENEGAL

THE GAMBIA
BANJUL

GUINEA-BISSAU
BISSAU

GORGOL

GUIDIMAKA

KAYES

KOULIKORO

SEGOU

GUINEA

MOYENNE-GUINEE

HAUTE-
GUINEE

GUINÉE-
MARITIME

CONAKRY

GUINÉE-FORESTIÈRE

SIKASSO

BAMAKO

NORTHERN

SIERRA
LEONE

WESTERN AREA
FREETOWN

EASTERN

SOUTHERN

**CÔTE
D'IVOIRE**

YAMOUSSOUKRO

LIBERIA

MONROVIA

Abidjan

A T L A N T I C   O C E A N

Equator

Ponta do Sol
Santo Antão
Mindelo
São Vicente
Santa Luzia
São Nicolau
Sal
Santa Maria

**CAPE
VERDE**

Boa Vista
Vila da Sal Rei

Ilhas do Cabo Verde

Vila do Tarrafal
Assomada
Maio
Porto Inglês
Fogo
São Filipe
Vila Nova Sintra
Brava
São
Tiago
PRAIA

0   miles   60
1 : 8 000 000
0   100
km

1 : 8 000 000

0   100   200   300 miles
0   100   200   300   400   500 km

Lambert Azimuthal Equal Area Projection

ATLANTIC

OCEAN

africa
map_4

1:8 000 000

Lambert Azimuthal Equal Area Projection

094 ↓

1 : 8 000 000

Lambert Azimuthal Equal Area Projection

metres
>6000
6000
5000
4000
3000
2000
1000
500
200
<0
0
200
1000
2000
3000
4000
5000
6000
>6000

Administrative divisions in Tanzania
numbered on the map:
1. PEMBA NORTH (C6)
2. PEMBA SOUTH (C6)
3. ZANZIBAR NORTH (C6)
4. ZANZIBAR SOUTH (C6)
5. ZANZIBAR WEST (C6)

INDIAN OCEAN

Mozambique Channel

SEYCHELLES

Providence Atoll
St Pierre
Farquhar Islands (Seychelles)
Farquhar Atoll
Cosmolédo Atoll
Aldabra Islands (Seychelles)
Aldabra Atoll
Îles Glorieuses (Seychelles)

COMOROS
Nzizidja (Grande Comore)
MORONI
Mbéni
Mutsamudu (Anjouan)
Fomboni
Mwali (Mohéli)
Mayotte (France)
Grande Terre
DZAOUDZI

MADAGASCAR
ANTSIRANANA
MAHAJANGA
Mahajanga
TOAMASINA

TANZANIA
Mombasa
Dar es Salaam
Zanzibar Island
Pemba Island
DODOMA
IRINGA
MBEYA
Great Rift Valley
Lake Malawi

MALAWI
LILONGWE

ZAMBIA

MOZAMBIQUE
NIASSA
CABO DELGADO
NAMPULA
Pemba
Nacala
Nampula
Quelimane
TETE
SOFALA
MANICA

ZIMBABWE
HARARE

DEM. REP. OF CONGO

Lake Tanganyika

→ 099

50 miles
500 km

ATLANTIC

OCEAN

Lambert Azimuthal Equal Area Projection

1:8 000 000

0   100   200   300   miles
0   100   200   300   400   500 km

metres
>6000
6000
5000
4000
3000
2000
1000
500
200
0
<0
0
200
500
1000
2000
3000
4000
5000
6000
>6000

Sinai Peninsula, Egypt   Madagascar   Niger Delta, Nigeria   Victoria Falls, Zambia/Zimbabwe

COUNTRIES		area sq km	area sq miles	population	capital	languages	religions	currency	map
ALGERIA		2 381 741	919 595	30 841 000	Algiers	Arabic, French, Berber	Sunni Muslim	Algerian dinar	90–91
ANGOLA		1 246 700	481 354	13 527 000	Luanda	Portuguese, Bantu, local languages	Roman Catholic, Protestant, traditional beliefs	Kwanza	95
BENIN		112 620	43 483	6 446 000	Porto-Novo	French, Fon, Yoruba, Adja, local languages	Traditional beliefs, Roman Catholic, Sunni Muslim	CFA franc*	93
BOTSWANA		581 370	224 468	1 554 000	Gaborone	English, Setswana, Shona, local languages	Traditional beliefs, Protestant, Roman Catholic	Pula	98–99
BURKINA		274 200	105 869	11 856 000	Ouagadougou	French, Moore (Mossi), Fulani, local languages	Sunni Muslim, traditional beliefs, Roman Catholic	CFA franc*	92–93
BURUNDI		27 835	10 747	6 502 000	Bujumbura	Kirundi (Hutu, Tutsi), French	Roman Catholic, traditional beliefs, Protestant	Burundian franc	94–95
CAMEROON		475 442	183 569	15 203 000	Yaoundé	French, English, Fang, Bamileke, local languages	Roman Catholic, traditional beliefs, Sunni Muslim, Protestant	CFA franc*	94
CAPE VERDE		4 033	1 557	437 000	Praia	Portuguese, creole	Roman Catholic, Protestant	Cape Verde escudo	92
CENTRAL AFRICAN REPUBLIC		622 436	240 324	3 782 000	Bangui	French, Sango, Banda, Baya, local languages	Protestant, Roman Catholic, traditional beliefs, Sunni Muslim	CFA franc*	94
CHAD		1 284 000	495 755	8 135 000	Ndjamena	Arabic, French, Sara, local languages	Sunni Muslim, Roman Catholic, Protestant, traditional beliefs	CFA franc*	88
COMOROS		1 862	719	727 000	Moroni	Comorian, French, Arabic	Sunni Muslim, Roman Catholic	Comoros franc	97
CONGO		342 000	132 047	3 110 000	Brazzaville	French, Kongo, Monokutuba, local languages	Roman Catholic, Protestant, traditional beliefs, Sunni Muslim	CFA franc*	94–95
CONGO, DEMOCRATIC REP. OF		2 345 410	905 568	52 522 000	Kinshasa	French, Lingala, Swahili, Kongo, local languages	Christian, Sunni Muslim	Congolese franc	94–95
CÔTE D'IVOIRE		322 463	124 504	16 349 000	Yamoussoukro	French, creole, Akan, local languages	Sunni Muslim, Roman Catholic, traditional beliefs, Protestant	CFA franc*	92
DJIBOUTI		23 200	8 958	644 000	Djibouti	Somali, Afar, French, Arabic	Sunni Muslim, Christian	Djibouti franc	96
EGYPT		1 000 250	386 199	69 080 000	Cairo	Arabic	Sunni Muslim, Coptic Christian	Egyptian pound	89
EQUATORIAL GUINEA		28 051	10 831	470 000	Malabo	Spanish, French, Fang	Roman Catholic, traditional beliefs	CFA franc*	93
ERITREA		117 400	45 328	3 816 000	Asmara	Tigrinya, Tigre	Sunni Muslim, Coptic Christian	Nakfa	89
ETHIOPIA		1 133 880	437 794	64 459 000	Addis Ababa	Oromo, Amharic, Tigrinya, local languages	Ethiopian Orthodox, Sunni Muslim, traditional beliefs	Birr	96
GABON		267 667	103 347	1 262 000	Libreville	French, Fang, local languages	Roman Catholic, Protestant, traditional beliefs	CFA franc*	94
THE GAMBIA		11 295	4 361	1 337 000	Banjul	English, Malinke, Fulani, Wolof	Sunni Muslim, Protestant	Dalasi	92
GHANA		238 537	92 100	19 734 000	Accra	English, Hausa, Akan, local languages	Christian, Sunni Muslim, traditional beliefs	Cedi	92–93
GUINEA		245 857	94 926	8 274 000	Conakry	French, Fulani, Malinke, local languages	Sunni Muslim, traditional beliefs, Christian	Guinea franc	92
GUINEA-BISSAU		36 125	13 948	1 227 000	Bissau	Portuguese, crioulo, local languages	Traditional beliefs, Sunni Muslim, Christian	CFA franc*	92
KENYA		582 646	224 961	31 293 000	Nairobi	Swahili, English, local languages	Christian, traditional beliefs	Kenyan shilling	96
LESOTHO		30 355	11 720	2 057 000	Maseru	Sesotho, English, Zulu	Christian, traditional beliefs	Loti, S. African rand	99
LIBERIA		111 369	43 000	3 108 000	Monrovia	English, creole, local languages	Traditional beliefs, Christian, Sunni Muslim	Liberian dollar	92
LIBYA		1 759 540	679 362	5 408 000	Tripoli	Arabic, Berber	Sunni Muslim	Libyan dinar	88
MADAGASCAR		587 041	226 658	16 437 000	Antananarivo	Malagasy, French	Traditional beliefs, Christian, Sunni Muslim	Malagasy franc	99
MALAWI		118 484	45 747	11 572 000	Lilongwe	Chichewa, English, local languages	Christian, traditional beliefs, Sunni Muslim	Malawian kwacha	97
MALI		1 240 140	478 821	11 677 000	Bamako	French, Bambara, local languages	Sunni Muslim, traditional beliefs, Christian	CFA franc*	92–93
MAURITANIA		1 030 700	397 955	2 747 000	Nouakchott	Arabic, French, local languages	Sunni Muslim	Ouguiya	90
MAURITIUS		2 040	788	1 171 000	Port Louis	English, creole, Hindi, Bhojpurī, French	Hindu, Roman Catholic, Sunni Muslim	Mauritius rupee	162
MOROCCO		446 550	172 414	30 430 000	Rabat	Arabic, Berber, French	Sunni Muslim	Moroccan dirham	90–91
MOZAMBIQUE		799 380	308 642	18 644 000	Maputo	Portuguese, Makua, Tsonga, local languages	Traditional beliefs, Roman Catholic, Sunni Muslim	Metical	99
NAMIBIA		824 292	318 261	1 788 000	Windhoek	English, Afrikaans, German, Ovambo, local languages	Protestant, Roman Catholic	Namibian dollar	98
NIGER		1 267 000	489 191	11 227 000	Niamey	French, Hausa, Fulani, local languages	Sunni Muslim, traditional beliefs	CFA franc*	93
NIGERIA		923 768	356 669	116 929 000	Abuja	English, Hausa, Yoruba, Ibo, Fulani, local languages	Sunni Muslim, Christian, traditional beliefs	Naira	93
RWANDA		26 338	10 169	7 949 000	Kigali	Kinyarwanda, French, English	Roman Catholic, traditional beliefs, Protestant	Rwandan franc	94
SÃO TOMÉ AND PRÍNCIPE		964	372	140 000	São Tomé	Portuguese, creole	Roman Catholic, Protestant	Dobra	93
SENEGAL		196 720	75 954	9 662 000	Dakar	French, Wolof, Fulani, local languages	Sunni Muslim, Roman Catholic, traditional beliefs	CFA franc*	92
SEYCHELLES		455	176	81 000	Victoria	English, French, creole	Roman Catholic, Protestant	Seychelles rupee	162
SIERRA LEONE		71 740	27 699	4 587 000	Freetown	English, creole, Mende, Temne, local languages	Sunni Muslim, traditional beliefs	Leone	92
SOMALIA		637 657	246 201	9 157 000	Mogadishu	Somali, Arabic	Sunni Muslim	Somali shilling	96
SOUTH AFRICA, REPUBLIC OF		1 219 090	470 693	43 792 000	Pretoria/Cape Town	Afrikaans, English, nine official local languages	Protestant, Roman Catholic, Sunni Muslim, Hindu	Rand	98–99
SUDAN		2 505 813	967 500	31 809 000	Khartoum	Arabic, Dinka, Nubian, Beja, Nuer, local languages	Sunni Muslim, traditional beliefs, Christian	Sudanese dinar	88–89
SWAZILAND		17 364	6 704	938 000	Mbabane	Swazi, English	Christian, traditional beliefs	Emalangeni, S. African rand	99
TANZANIA		945 087	364 900	35 965 000	Dodoma	Swahili, English, Nyamwezi, local languages	Shi'a Muslim, Sunni Muslim, traditional beliefs, Christian	Tanzanian shilling	96–97
TOGO		56 785	21 925	4 657 000	Lomé	French, Ewe, Kabre, local languages	Traditional beliefs, Christian, Sunni Muslim	CFA franc*	93
TUNISIA		164 150	63 379	9 562 000	Tunis	Arabic, French	Sunni Muslim	Tunisian dinar	91
UGANDA		241 038	93 065	24 023 000	Kampala	English, Swahili, Luganda, local languages	Roman Catholic, Protestant, Sunni Muslim, traditional beliefs	Ugandan shilling	96
ZAMBIA		752 614	290 586	10 649 000	Lusaka	English, Bemba, Nyanja, Tonga, local languages	Christian, traditional beliefs	Zambian kwacha	95
ZIMBABWE		390 759	150 873	12 852 000	Harare	English, Shona, Ndebele	Christian, traditional beliefs	Zimbabwean dollar	98–99

DEPENDENT AND DISPUTED TERRITORIES		territorial status	area sq km	area sq miles	population	capital	languages	religions	currency	map
Canary Islands		Autonomous Community of Spain	7 447	2 875	1 606 522	Santa Cruz de Tenerife, Las Palmas	Spanish	Roman Catholic	Euro	90
Ceuta		Spanish Territory	19	7	68 796	Ceuta	Spanish, Arabic	Roman Catholic, Muslim	Euro	90
Madeira		Autonomous Region of Portugal	779	301	259 000	Funchal	Portuguese	Roman Catholic, Protestant	Euro	90
Mayotte		French Territorial Collectivity	373	144	144 944	Dzaoudzi	French, Mahorian	Sunni Muslim, Christian	Euro	97
Melilla		Spanish Territory	13	5	59 576	Melilla	Spanish, Arabic	Roman Catholic, Muslim	Euro	90
Réunion		French Overseas Department	2 551	985	732 000	St-Denis	French, creole	Roman Catholic	Euro	162
St Helena and Dependencies		United Kingdom Overseas Territory	121	47	6 000	Jamestown	English	Protestant, Roman Catholic	St Helena pound	160
Western Sahara		Disputed territory (Morocco)	266 000	102 703	260 000	Laâyoune	Arabic	Sunni Muslim	Moroccan dirham	90

oceania

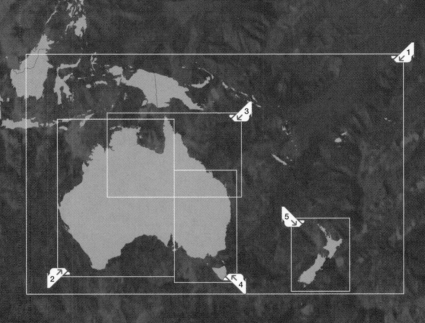

contents

		map coverage	scale
102–103	landscapes		
104–105	locations		
106–107	map_1	**australia** and **pacific** southwest	1:18 000 000
108–109	map_2	**australia** west	1:7 500 000
110–111	map_3	**australia** east	1:7 500 000
112	map_4	**australia** southeast	1:7 500 000
113	map_5	**new zealand**	1:5 000 000
114	states and territories		

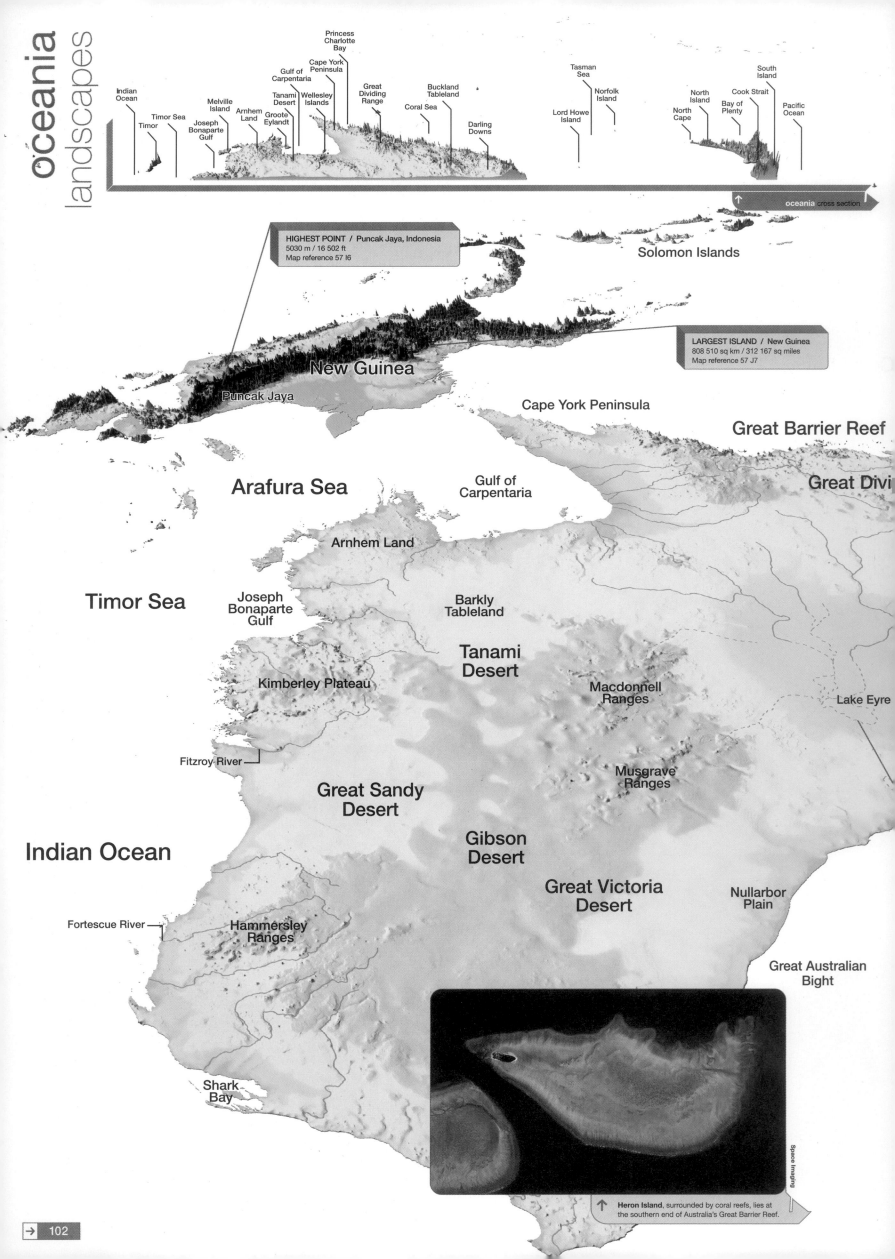

Indian Ocean

Timor

Timor Sea

Joseph Bonaparte Gulf

Melville Island

Arnhem Land

Groote Eylandt

Tanami Desert

Gulf of Carpentaria

Cape York Peninsula

Princess Charlotte Bay

Wellesley Islands

Great Dividing Range

Coral Sea

Buckland Tableland

Darling Downs

Tasman Sea

Lord Howe Island

Norfolk Island

North Cape

North Island

Bay of Plenty

Cook Strait

South Island

Pacific Ocean

oceania cross section

HIGHEST POINT / Puncak Jaya, Indonesia
5030 m / 16 502 ft
Map reference 57 I6

LARGEST ISLAND / New Guinea
808 510 sq km / 312 167 sq miles
Map reference 57 J7

Solomon Islands

New Guinea

Puncak Jaya

Cape York Peninsula

Great Barrier Reef

Great Divi

Arafura Sea

Gulf of Carpentaria

Arnhem Land

Timor Sea

Joseph Bonaparte Gulf

Barkly Tableland

Tanami Desert

Kimberley Plateau

Macdonnell Ranges

Lake Eyre

Fitzroy River

Great Sandy Desert

Musgrave Ranges

Indian Ocean

Gibson Desert

Great Victoria Desert

Nullarbor Plain

Fortescue River

Hammersley Ranges

Great Australian Bight

Shark Bay

Space Imaging

↑ **Heron Island**, surrounded by coral reefs, lies at the southern end of Australia's Great Barrier Reef.

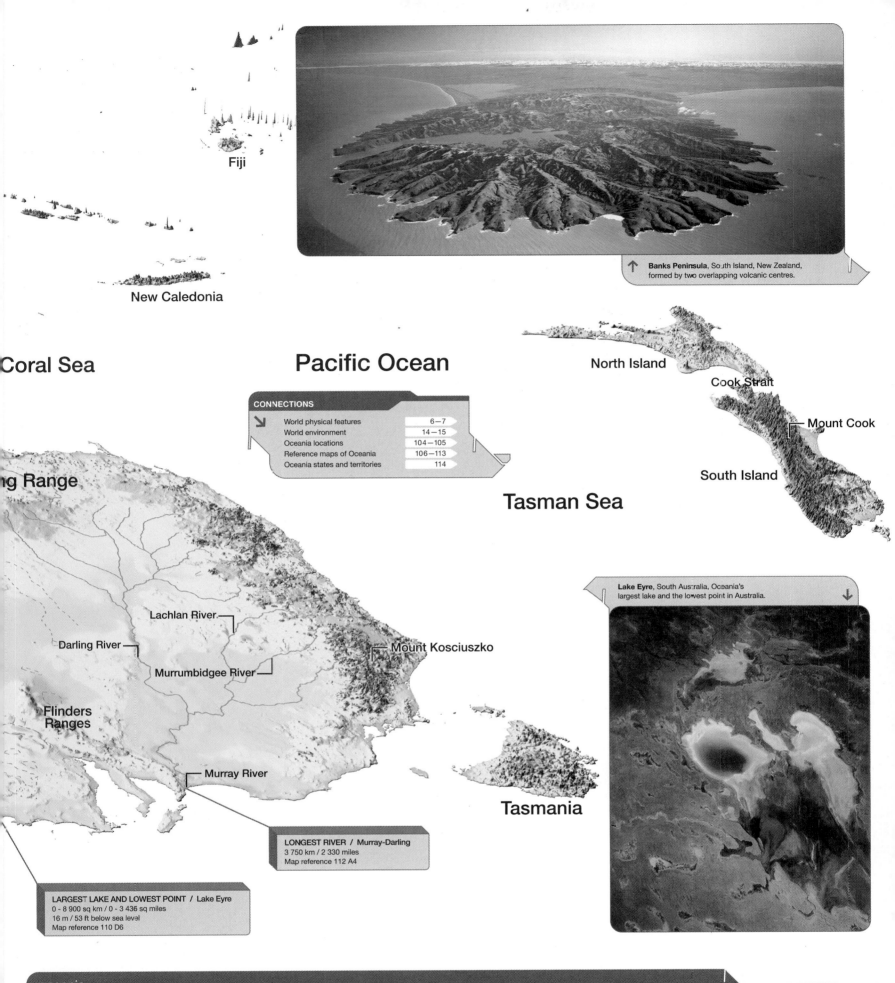

Fiji

New Caledonia

Coral Sea

Pacific Ocean

North Island

Cook Strait

Mount Cook

South Island

ng Range

Tasman Sea

CONNECTIONS

World physical features	6—7
World environment	14—15
Oceania locations	104—105
Reference maps of Oceania	106—113
Oceania states and territories	114

Lachlan River

Darling River

Murrumbidgee River

Mount Kosciuszko

Flinders
Ranges

Murray River

Tasmania

Banks Peninsula, South Island, New Zealand, formed by two overlapping volcanic centres.

Lake Eyre, South Australia, Oceania's largest lake and the lowest point in Australia.

LONGEST RIVER / Murray-Darling
3 750 km / 2 330 miles
Map reference 112 A4

LARGEST LAKE AND LOWEST POINT / Lake Eyre
0 - 8 900 sq km / 0 - 3 436 sq miles
16 m / 53 ft below sea level
Map reference 110 D6

oceania

LARGEST ISLANDS	sq km	sq miles	map	LONGEST RIVERS	km	miles	map	HIGHEST MOUNTAINS	metres	feet	map
New Guinea	808 510	312 167	57 J7	Murray-Darling	3 750	2 330	112 A4	Puncak Jaya, Indonesia	5 030	16 502	57 I6
South Island, New Zealand	151 215	58 384	113 B4	Darling	2 739	1 702	112 B4	Puncak Trikora, Indonesia	4 730	15 518	57 I6
North Island, New Zealand	115 777	44 702	113 C2	Murray	2 589	1 608	112 A4	Puncak Mandala, Indonesia	4 700	15 420	57 J6
Tasmania	67 800	26 178	112 C6	Murrumbidgee	1 690	1 050	112 C4	Puncak Yamin, Indonesia	4 595	15 075	57 I6
				Lachlan	1 480	919	112 B4	Mt Wilhem, Papua New Guinea	4 509	14 793	57 J7
				Macquarie	950	590	112 C6	Mt Kubor, Papua New Guinea	4 359	14 301	57 J7

LARGEST LAKES	sq km	sq miles	map	LAND AREA		map
Lake Eyre	0-8 900	0-3 436	110 D6	Total land area	8 844 516 sq km / 3 414 887 sq miles (includes New Guinea and Pacific Island nations)	
Lake Torrens	0-5 780	0-2 232	112 A3	Most northerly point	Eastern Island, North Pacific Ocean	164 G4
				Most southerly point	Macquarie Island, South Pacific Ocean	164 E9
				Most westerly point	Cape Inscription, Australia	109 A6
				Most easterly point	Île Clipperton, North Pacific Ocean	165 K5

Space Imaging

Nikumaroro, Kiribati, uninhabited coral atoll, part of the Phoenix Islands group. ↓

↑ **Great Barrier Reef**, northeast coast of Queensland, Australia.

INTERNATIONAL DATE LINE

CONNECTIONS
↘
World countries	8–9
Oceania landscapes	102–103
Reference maps of Oceania	106–113
Oceania states and territories	114
Pacific Ocean	164–165
Antarctica	167

Wake I. (U.S.A.)

Pagan

Northern Mariana Islands
Tinian · Saipan
Rota
Guam (U.S.A.)

MARSHALL ISLANDS

Bikini

Ralik Chain
Rarak Chain

Gaferut
Pikelot
Hall Is
Chuuk
Yap
Pohnpei ✿ PALIKIR
Kosrae

Caroline Islands

DELAP-ULIGA-DJARRIT

Nomoi Is

FEDERATED STATES OF MICRONESIA

Tarawa ✿ BAIRIKI

YAREN NAURU

Gilbert Islands

Admiralty Is
New Ireland
Wewak
Bismarck Sea
Rabaul
New Guinea
Mt Wilhelm Madang
4509m
New Britain
Bougainville I.
Lae
PAPUA NEW GUINEA
Solomon Sea
SOLOMON ISLANDS
Daru
Gulf of Papua
HONIARA
Malaita
Guadalcanal
Torres Strait
PORT MORESBY
Santa Cruz Is

Nanumea
Niutao
TUVALU
Nukufetau
VAIAKU
Nukulaelae
Funa
Niulakita
Vaitupu

Rotuma
Wallis and Futuna I. (France)

Coral Sea Islands Territory (Australia)

Banks Is
Espíritu Santo
Malakula
VANUATU
PORT VILA
Éfaté
Tanna

Vanua Levu
Viti Levu
FIJI
SUVA

Melville I.
Bathurst I.
Darwin
Gulf of Carpentaria

Timor Sea

Cape Londonderry

New Caledonia (France)
NOUMÉA
Îs Loyauté

Cairns
Townsville
Mackay
Rockhampton
Brisbane

NORTHERN TERRITORY
QUEENSLAND

Broome

AUSTRALIA

Alice Springs

Port Hedland

Barrow I.
North West Cape
Newman

WESTERN AUSTRALIA

SOUTH AUSTRALIA

Lake Eyre
Lake Torrens
Port Augusta
Port Pirie

NEW SOUTH WALES

Darling
Murray
Albury
CANBERRA
A.C.T.
Newcastle
Sydney

Norfolk I. (Aust.)

PACIFI

Kermadec Is (N.Z.)

Lord Howe I. (Australia)

Geraldton
Kalgoorlie

Great Australian Bight

Adelaide

VICTORIA
Geelong
Melbourne
Murray
Bass Strait

Raoi

Great Barrier I.
Auckland
Rotorua
North Island
WELLINGTON

Perth
Fremantle
Cape Leeuwin
Albany

Kangaroo I.

Tasman Sea

Blenheim
South Island
Christchurch
NEW ZEALAND
Dunedin

Launceston
TASMANIA
Hobart

Stewart I.

Antipodes Is

Auckland Is

Campbell I. (N.Z.)

Bou
Is

↑ **Canterbury Plains** and **Southern Alps**, South Island, New Zealand.

Top ten countries by area	area sq km	area sq miles	map page	world rank
1 AUSTRALIA	7 682 395	2 966 189	106–107	6
2 PAPUA NEW GUINEA	462 840	178 704	106–107	53
3 NEW ZEALAND	270 534	104 454	113	74
4 SOLOMON ISLANDS	28 370	10 954	107	140
5 FIJI	18 330	7 077	107	151
6 VANUATU	12 190	4 707	107	156
7 SAMOA	2 831	1 093	107	165
8 TONGA	748	289	107	171
9 KIRIBATI	717	277	107	172
10 FEDERATED STATES OF MICRONESIA	701	271	164	173

Top ten countries by population	population	map page	world rank
1 AUSTRALIA	19 338 000	106–107	51
2 PAPUA NEW GUINEA	4 920 000	106–107	110
3 NEW ZEALAND	3 808 000	113	122
4 FIJI	823 000	107	152
5 SOLOMON ISLANDS	463 000	107	161
6 VANUATU	202 000	107	172
7 SAMOA	159 000	107	173
8 FEDERATED STATES OF MICRONESIA	126 000	164	176
9 TONGA	99 000	107	178
10 KIRIBATI	84 000	107	181

Space Imaging

↑ **Sydney,** largest city in Australia, main port, cultural and industrial centre.

Melbourne, capital city of Victoria state, Australia ↓

↑ **Alofi,** Capital of Niue, self-governing Overseas Territory of New Zealand.

INDONESIA

Borneo

Celebes (Sulawesi)

Moluccas (Maluku)

New Guinea

PAPUA NEW GUINEA

PORT MORESBY

INDIAN OCEAN

Timor Sea

East Timor
DILI
EAST TIMOR
Timor

Arafura Sea

Gulf of Carpentaria

Cape York Peninsula

NORTHERN TERRITORY

Darwin

Arnhem Land

QUEENSLAND

Cairns

Townsville

Great Sandy Desert

Tanami Desert

Alice Springs

Simpson Desert

WESTERN AUSTRALIA

Gibson Desert

SOUTH AUSTRALIA

Great Victoria Desert

Nullarbor Plain

Perth
Fremantle

NEW SOUTH WALES

Broken Hill

CANBERRA

Great Australian Bight

Adelaide

VICTORIA

Melbourne

Bass Strait

TASMANIA
Hobart

metres
>6000
6000
5000
4000
3000
2000
1000
500
200
0
<0
200
1000
2000
3000
4000
5000
6000
>6000

oceania
map_1

1:18 000 000

0   200   400   600   800 miles

0   200   400   600   800   1000   1200 km

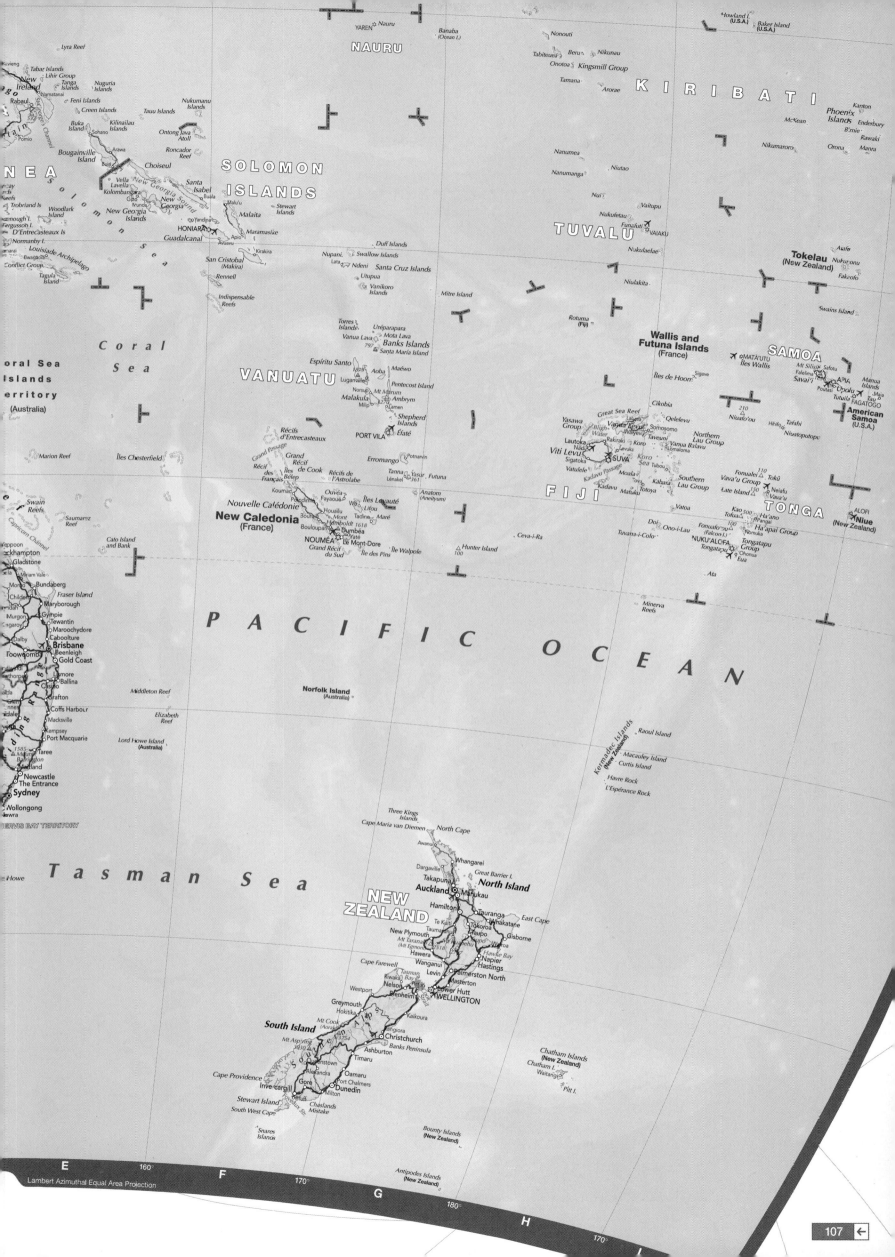

NAURU

YAREN • Nauru
Banaba
(Ocean I.)

Nonouti
Beru
Nikunau
Tabiteuea
Onotoa • Kingsmill Group
Tamana •
Arorae •

K I R I B A T I

Howell I.
(U.S.A.)
Baker Island
(U.S.A.)

Kanton
Phoenix
Islands
Enderbury
B'nie

Rawaki

Nikumaroro
Orona • Manra

New
Ireland
Rabaul

Tabar Islands
Lihir Group
Tanga
Islands
Feni Islands
Green Islands

Nuguria
Islands

Nukumanu
Islands
Tauu Islands

Ontong Java
Atoll

S O L O M O N
I S L A N D S

Roncador
Reef

NEA

NEW
GUINEA

Bougainville
Island
Buka Island
Sohano

Arawa
Buin

Choiseul

Santa Isabel
Buala

Vella
Lavella
Kolombangara
Gizo
New Georgia
Islands

Munda
Yandina

HONIARA
Guadalcanal
Aruvuu

Malaita

Maramasike

Kirakira

San Cristobal
(Makira)

Rennell

Indispensable
Reefs

Woodlark
Island

Trobriand Is
Fergusson I.
D'Entrecasteaux Is
Normanby I.

Bwagaoia

Louisiade Archipelago
Conflict Group
Tagula
Island

Duff Islands

Nupani •
Lata
Ndeni

Swallow Islands

Utupua

Santa Cruz Islands
Vanikoro
Islands

Nanumea

Nanumanga •

Niutao •

Nui •

Vaitupu •

Nukufetau •
Funafuti • VAIAKU

Nukulaelae •

T U V A L U

Niulakita •

NMāta'utu
ÎLES WALLIS
Sigave
Wallis and
Futuna Islands
(France)

Tokelau
(New Zealand)

Atafu
Nukuonu

Fakaofo

Swains Island

S A M O A

Mt Silisili
Savai'i
Falelima
Poutasi

Safotu
Upolu
APIA
Tutuila FAGATOGO

Manu'a
Islands
Ofu Tau

American
Samoa
(U.S.A.)

Mitre Island

Rotuma
(Fiji)

Îles de Hoorn

Niuafo'ou •

Tafahi •
Niuatoputapu •

Hihifo

Torres
Islands
Vanua Lava
Ureparapara
Mota Lava
797
Banks Islands
Santa María Island

C o r a l   S e a

Coral Sea
Islands
Territory
(Australia)

Marion Reef

Îles Chesterfield

Récifs
d'Entrecasteaux

Espíritu Santo
Luganville
Norsup
Malakula
Milip
Lamen

1829
Aoba
Maéwo
Mt Marum
Pentecost Island
Ambrym

Shepherd
Islands

V A N U A T U

PORT VILA
Éfaté

Erromango

Tanna
Lénakel
Yasur
361

Futuna
Anatom
(Aneityum)

Great Sea Reef
Labasa
Vanua Levu
Somosomo
Taveuni

Yasawa
Group
Lautoka
Nadi
Sigatoka
Vatulele

Blight
Water
Rakiraki
Waiyevo
Levuka
Koro

Qelelevu

Northern
Lau Group
Vanua Balavu
Lomaloma

V i t i   L e v u
SUVA

Koro
Sea

Kadavu Passage
Kadavu

Moala
Matuku

Tubou
Totoya

Southern
Lau Group

F I J I

Vatoa

Doi • Ono-i-Lau

Tuvana-i-Colo

210

Fonualei 110
Vava'u Group
Late Island 150
Neiafu

Vava'u • Tokū

Kao 500
Tofua
Ha'ano
Ha'apai Group

Fonuafo'ou
(Falcon I.) 100

NUKU'ALOFA
Tongatapu
Group
'Eua
Ohonua

T O N G A

ALOFI
• Niue
(New Zealand)

Nouvelle Calédonie

Grand
Récif
de Cook

Récif
des
Français

Grand
Passage

Koumac

Île Belep

Poindimié

Ouvéa
Houaïlou
Mont
Humboldt 1618
Boulouparis
Tadine

We
Lifou
Maré

Îles Loyauté

New Caledonia
(France)

NOUMÉA
Dumbéa
Yaté
Le Mont-Dore
Grand Récif
du Sud
Île des Pins

Île Walpole

Hunter Island
100

Ata

Minerva
Reefs

Swain
Reefs

Saumarez
Reef

Cato Island
and Bank

Ceva-i-Ra

Capricorn Channel
Rockhampton
Gladstone

Mt Larcom
Miriam Vale
Monto
Bundaberg
Childers
Fraser Island
Maryborough
Murgon
Gympie
Kingaroy
Tewantin
Maroochydore
Dalby
Caboolture
Toowoomba
Brisbane
Beenleigh
Gold Coast
Warwick
Beaudesert
Lismore
Ballina
Casino
Grafton

Coffs Harbour

Armidale

Middleton Reef

Elizabeth
Reef

Lord Howe Island
(Australia)

1585
Mt Barrington

Macksville
Kempsey
Port Macquarie
Taree

Maitland
Newcastle
The Entrance

Gosford

SYDNEY
Wollongong
Nowra

JERVIS BAY TERRITORY

P A C I F I C   O C E A N

Norfolk Island
(Australia)

Kermadec Islands
(New Zealand)
Raoul Island
Macauley Island
Curtis Island

Havre Rock
L'Espérance Rock

T a s m a n   S e a

Howe

Three Kings
Islands
Cape Maria van Diemen
North Cape

Awanui
Dargaville
Takapuna

Whangarei

Great Barrier I.

North Island

Auckland
Manukau

Hamilton
Te Kuiti

Taumarunui

New Plymouth
Mt Taranaki
(Mt Egmont) 2518
Hawera

Ruapehu
Taupo
Tokoroa

Tauranga
Whakatane

East Cape

Gisborne

Rotorua

Wanganui
Levin

Palmerston North
Masterton

Hawke Bay
Napier
Hastings

NEW
ZEALAND

Cape Farewell

Tasman
Bay

Nelson

Kaikoura

Lower Hutt
WELLINGTON

Westport
Blenheim

Greymouth
Hokitika

South Island

Mt Cook
(Aoraki) 3754

Mt Aspiring
3010

Kaiapoi
Rangiora
Christchurch
Banks Peninsula
Ashburton
Timaru

Chatham Islands
(New Zealand)
Chatham I.

Waitangi

Pitt I.

Cape Providence
Invercargill
Gore
Bluff
Milton
Alexandra
Queenstown

Oamaru
Port Chalmers
Dunedin

Stewart Island
South West Cape

Chaslands
Mistake

Snares
Islands
(New Zealand)

Bounty Islands
(New Zealand)

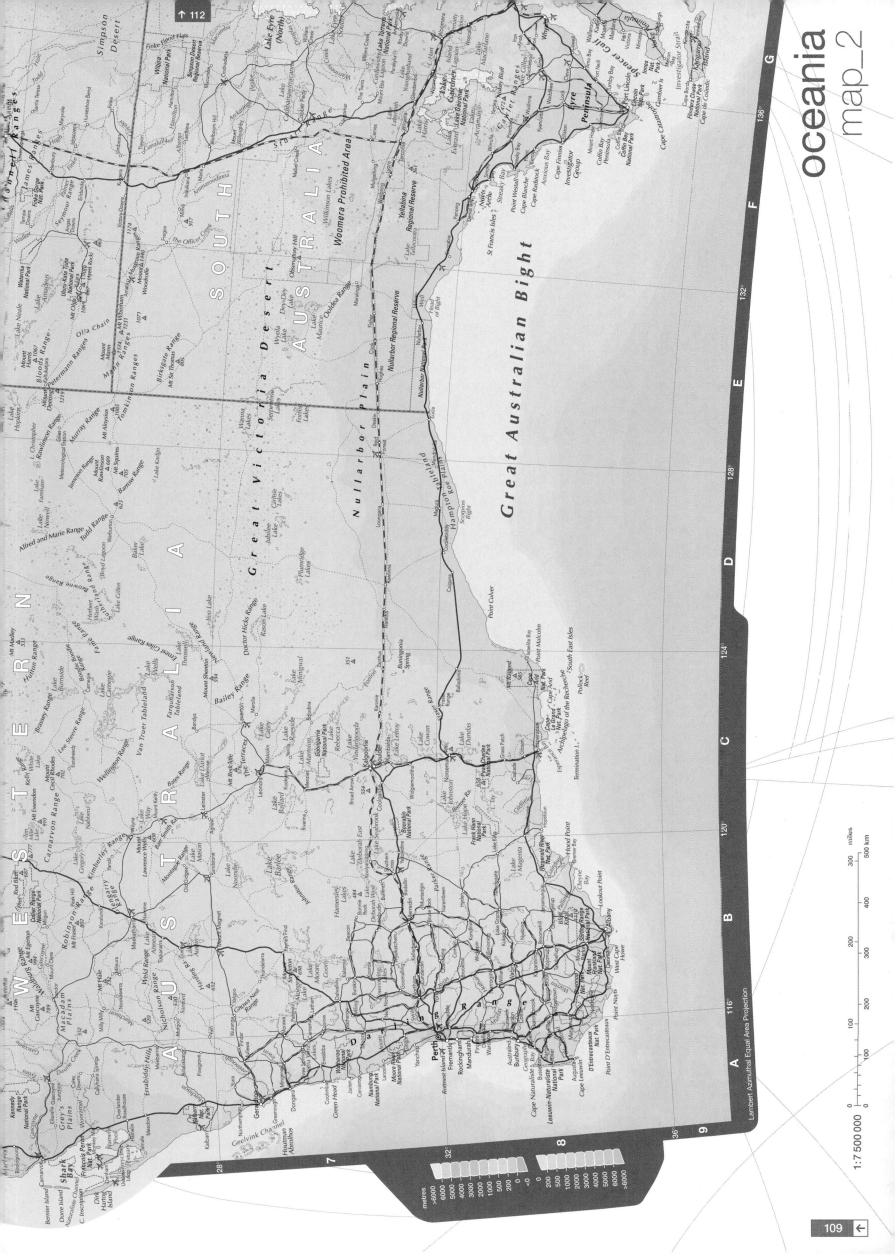

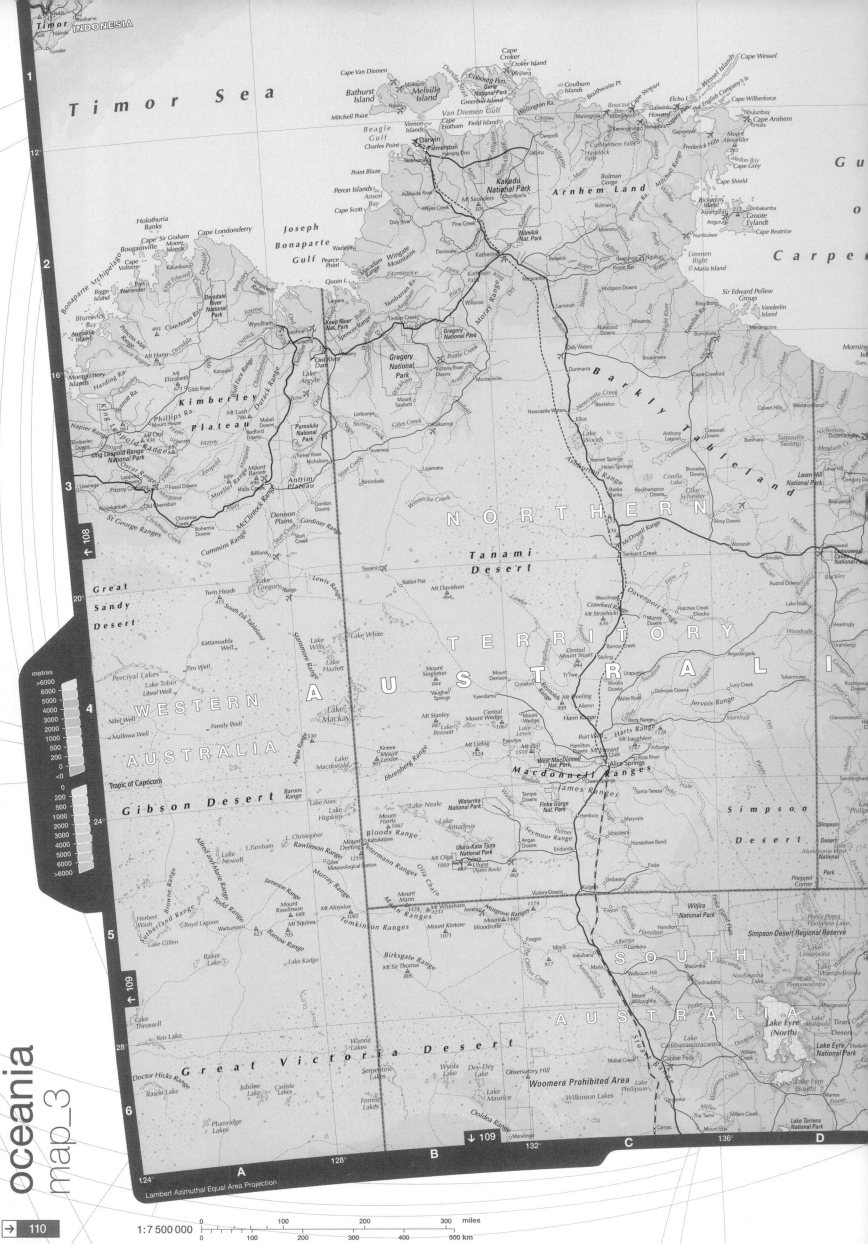

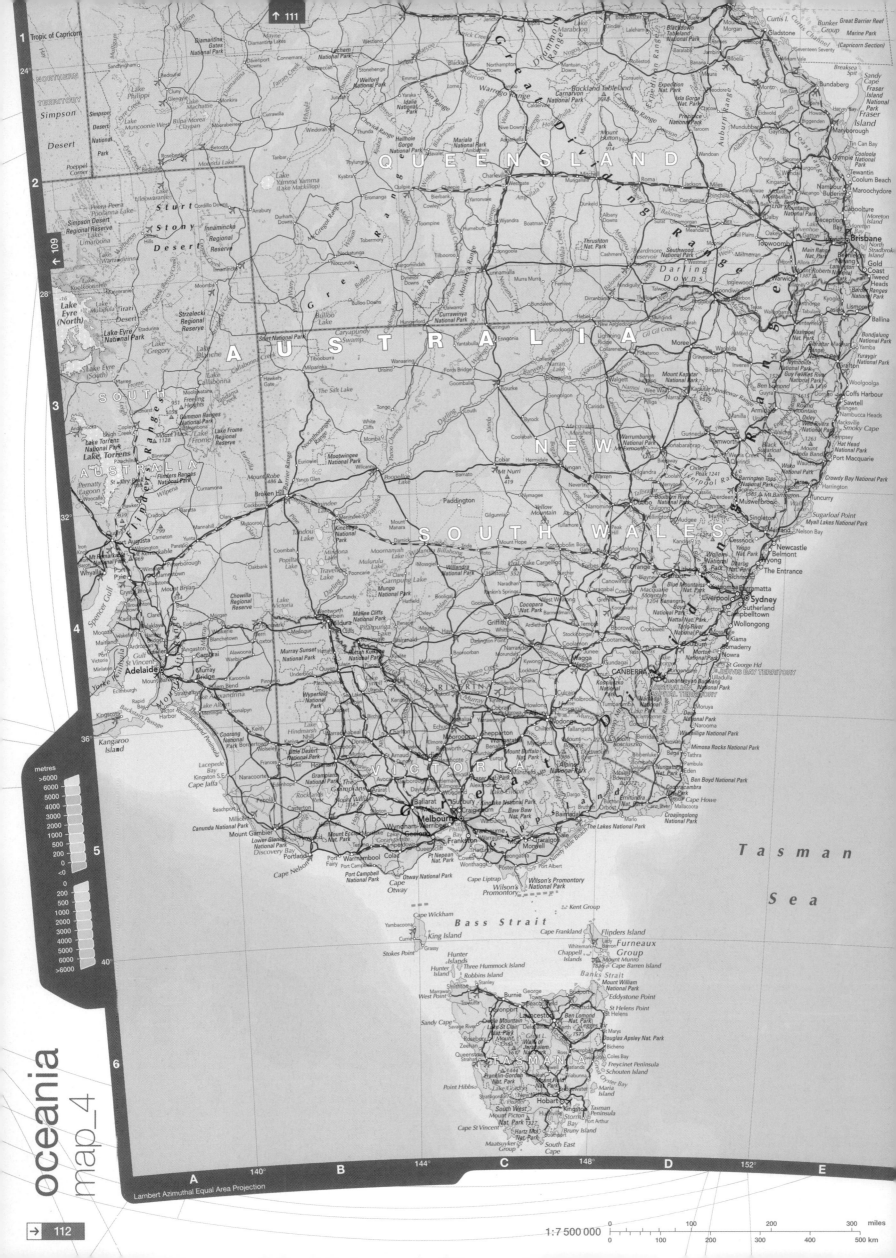

oceania
map_4

Lambert Azimuthal Equal Area Projection

1:7 500 000

Three Kings Islands

Cape Maria van Diemen
North Cape

Te Paki
Rangaunu Bay
Cape Karikari
Doubtless Bay
Ahipara Bay
Tauroa Point
Kaitaia
Broadwood
Russell
Kawakawa
Cape Brett

T a s m a n

Donnellys Crossing
Whangarei
Poor Knights Islands

Dargaville
Bream Bay
Mokohinau Islands

S e a

Tangaehe
Mangaturoto
Wellsford
North Head
Orewa Harbour
Warkworth
Leigh
Little Barrier Island
Port Fitzroy
Great Barrier Island
Colville Channel

North

East Coast Bays
Takapuna
Auckland
Manukau
Papatoetoe
Papakura
Waiuku
Port Waikato
Hauraki Gulf
Waiheke Island
Whitianga
Colville
Coromandel
Peninsula
Mercury Islands
The Aldermen Islands

Island

Tuakau
Te Kauwhata
Huntly
Ngaruawahia
Whatawhata
Hamilton
Raglan
Kawhia Harbour
Awakino
Mokau
Waingaro
Te Awamutu
Otorohanga
Te Kuiti
Pio Pio
Cambridge
Waiharoa
Mangakino
Thames
Paeroa
Waihi
Whangamata
Matakana Island
Motiti Island
Mayor Island
Tauranga
Te Puke
Rotorua
Mount Tarawera
Whakaari
1075
Bay of Plenty
Whakatane
Opotiki
Cape Runaway
Hicks Bay
Te Araroa
East Cape
Ruatoria
Tokomaru Bay

N E W

North Taranaki Bight
Waitara
New Plymouth
Mount Egmont (Mt Taranaki)
2518
Cape Egmont
Opunake
Stratford
Eltham
Inglewood
Taumarunui
Okahukura
Waitahanui
Taupo
Lake Taupo
Turangi
Tongariro National Park
Whanganui National Park
Mount Ruapehu 2797
Tarawera
Murupara
Urewera National Park
Wairoa
Gisborne
Poverty Bay
Table Cape
Mahia Peninsula

Z E A L A N D

Hawera
South Taranaki Bight
Patea
Waverley
Pipiriki
Waiouru
Taihape
Hawke Bay
Bay View
Napier
Hastings
Cape Kidnappers
Havelock North
Waimarama

Wanganui
Turakina
Marton
Apiti
Waipukurau
Waipawa
Takapau
Feilding
Dannevirke
Waimarama

Cape Farewell
Farewell Spit
Cape Stephens
Palmerston North
Foxton
Levin
Porangahau
Cape Turnagain

Kahurangi Point
Golden Bay
Collingwood
Takaka
Abel Tasman National Park
D'Urville Island
French Pass
Tasman Bay
Kapiti Island
Otaki
Paraparaumu
Upper Hutt
Masterton
Castlepoint

Karamea
Tasman Mountains
Kahurangi National Park
Riwaka
Motueka
Nelson
Richmond
Wakefield
Picton
Havelock
Mount Tapuae-o-Uenuku
1571
Tararua Range
WELLINGTON
Lower Hutt
Wairarapa
Mount Ross 983
Te Wharau

Karamea Bight
Seddonville
Hope Saddle
Murchison
Owen River
Buller
Wairau
Blenheim
Cloudy Bay
Palliser Bay
Cape Palliser

Westport
Charleston
Wangapeka
Nelson Lakes National Park
Mount Travers 2338
Renwick
Seddon
Cape Campbell

P A C I F I C

Paparoa National Park
Reefton
Springs Junction
Lewis Pass
Hanmer Springs
Arthur's Range
2231
Inland Kaikoura Range
2885
Manakau
2610
Clarence
Kaikoura

Greymouth
Ahaura
Grey
Moana
Rotomanu
Otira
Arthur's Pass National Park
Springfield
Rangiora
Rotherham
Waiau
Culverden
Cheviot
Waipara
Waikari
Amberley

Hokitika
Lake Brunner
Ross
Pukekura
Pegasus Bay
Oxford
Rangiora
Belfast
Christchurch
Sumner
Banks Peninsula
Akaroa

Abut Head
Harihari
Mount Arrowsmith 2795
Sheffield
Darfield
Canterbury Plains
Lincoln
Rolleston
Lake Ellesmere

Franz Josef Glacier
Westland National Park
Fox Glacier
Mount Cook/Aoraki 3754
Mount Cook National Park
Rangitata
Methven
Mayfield
Ashburton
Canterbury Bight

Jackson Head
Mount Ward 2644
Mount Tasman 3498
Lake Pukaki
Lake Tekapo
Geraldine
Temuka
Pleasant Point
Timaru

Awarua Point
Mount Aspiring/Tititea 3027
Mount Aspiring National Park
2347
Lake Hawea
Lake Wanaka
The Hunters Hills
Pareora
Makikihi
Waimate

Milford Sound
Mount Christina 2502
Lake Wanaka
Cardrona
Tarras
Cromwell
Omarama
Otematata
Kurow
Studholme Junction
Glenavy

South

George Sound
Mount Tutoko 2723
The Key Summit
Queenstown
Arrowtown
James Peak 1695
Dunstan Mts
Alexandra
Roxburgh
Ranfurly
Naseby
Hyde
Middlemarch
Palmerston
Moeraki Point
Oamaru
Cape Wanbrow

Secretary Island
Doubtful Sound
Fiordland
Lake Te Anau
National
Park
Manapouri
Te Anau
The Eyre Mountains
Kingston
Garston
Lumsden
Mandeville
Beaumont
Lawrence
Milton

Island

Breaksea Sound
Resolution Island
Lake Manapouri
Mossburn
Winton
Gore
Clinton
Balclutha
Kaitangata
Nugget Point

Cape Providence
Puysegur Point
Caroline Peak 1722
Te Waewae Bay
Tuatapere
Orepuki
Riverton
Otautau
Invercargill
Edendale
Mataura
Wyndham
Mount Pye
Fortrose
Chaslands Mistake

Solander Island
Foveaux Strait
Bluff

O C E A N

Codfish Island
Mason Bay
Ruapuke Island
Halfmoon Bay

Muttonbird Islands
Stewart Island
Shelter Point

South West Cape
North Trap

1:5 000 000

0   50   100   150   200   250 miles
0   50 100 150 200 250 300 350 400 km

Conic Equidistant Projection

A   168°   B   172°   C   176°   D

metres
>6000
6000
5000
4000
3000
2000
1000
500
200
0
<0
0
200
500
1000
2000
3000
4000
5000
6000
>6000

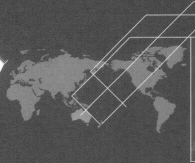

New Zealand

Tahiti and Moorea, French Polynesia

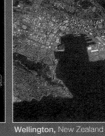

Wellington, New Zealand

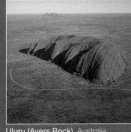

Uluru (Ayers Rock), Australia

COUNTRIES		area sq km	area sq miles	population	capital	languages	religions	currency	map
AUSTRALIA		7 682 395	2 966 189	19 338 000	Canberra	English, Italian, Greek	Protestant, Roman Catholic, Orthodox	Australian dollar	106–107
FIJI		18 330	7 077	823 000	Suva	English, Fijian, Hindi	Christian, Hindu, Sunni Muslim	Fiji dollar	107
KIRIBATI		717	277	84 000	Bairiki	Gilbertese, English	Roman Catholic, Protestant	Australian dollar	107
MARSHALL ISLANDS		181	70	52 000	Delap-Uliga-Djarrit	English, Marshallese	Protestant, Roman Catholic	United States dollar	164
MICRONESIA, FEDERATED STATES OF		701	271	126 000	Palikir	English, Chuukese, Pohnpeian, local languages	Roman Catholic, Protestant	United States dollar	164
NAURU		21	8	13 000	Yaren	Nauruan, English	Protestant, Roman Catholic	Australian dollar	107
NEW ZEALAND		270 534	104 454	3 808 000	Wellington	English, Maori	Protestant, Roman Catholic	New Zealand dollar	113
PAPUA NEW GUINEA		462 840	178 704	4 920 000	Port Moresby	English, Tok Pisin (creole), local languages	Protestant, Roman Catholic, traditional beliefs	Kina	106–107
SAMOA		2 831	1 093	159 000	Apia	Samoan, English	Protestant, Roman Catholic	Tala	107
SOLOMON ISLANDS		28 370	10 954	463 000	Honiara	English, creole, local languages	Protestant, Roman Catholic	Solomon Islands dollar	107
TONGA		748	289	99 000	Nuku'alofa	Tongan, English	Protestant, Roman Catholic	Pa'anga	107
TUVALU		25	10	10 000	Vaiaku	Tuvaluan, English	Protestant	Australian dollar	107
VANUATU		12 190	4 707	202 000	Port Vila	English, Bislama (creole), French	Protestant, Roman Catholic, traditional beliefs	Vatu	107

DEPENDENT TERRITORIES		territorial status	area sq km	area sq miles	population	capital	languages	religions	currency	map
American Samoa		United States Unincorporated Territory	197	76	70 000	Fagatoga	Samoan, English	Protestant, Roman Catholic	United States dollar	107
Ashmore and Cartier Islands		Australian External Territory	5	2	uninhabited					108
Baker Island		United States Unincorporated Territory	1	0.4	uninhabited					107
Clipperton, Île		French Overseas Territory	7	3	uninhabited					165
Cook Islands		Self-governing New Zealand Territory	293	113	20 000	Avarua	English, Maori	Protestant, Roman Catholic	New Zealand dollar	165
Coral Sea Islands Territory		Australian External Territory	22	8	uninhabited					107
French Polynesia		French Overseas Territory	3 265	1 261	237 000	Papeete	French, Tahitian, Polynesian languages	Protestant, Roman Catholic	CFP franc*	165
Guam		United States Unincorporated Territory	541	209	158 000	Hagåtña	Chamorro, English, Tapalog	Roman Catholic	United States dollar	57
Howland Island		United States Unincorporated Territory	2	1	uninhabited					107
Jarvis Island		United States Unincorporated Territory	5	2	uninhabited					165
Johnston Atoll		United States Unincorporated Territory	3	1	uninhabited					164
Kingman Reef		United States Unincorporated Territory	1	0.4	uninhabited					165
Midway Islands		United States Unincorporated Territory	6	2	uninhabited					164
New Caledonia		French Overseas Territory	19 058	7 358	220 000	Nouméa	French, local languages	Roman Catholic, Protestant, Sunni Muslim	CFP franc*	107
Niue		Self-governing New Zealand Territory	258	100	2 000	Alofi	English, Polynesian	Christian	New Zealand dollar	107
Norfolk Island		Australian External Territory	35	14	2 000	Kingston	English	Protestant, Roman Catholic	Australian Dollar	107
Northern Mariana Islands		United States Commonwealth	477	184	76 000	Capitol Hill	English, Chamorro, local languages	Roman Catholic	United States dollar	57
Palmyra Atoll		United States Unincorporated Territory	12	5	uninhabited					165
Pitcairn Islands		United Kingdom Overseas Territory	45	17	68	Adamstown	English	Protestant	New Zealand dollar	165
Tokelau		New Zealand Overseas Territory	10	4	1 000		English, Tokelauan	Christian	New Zealand dollar	107
Wake Island		United States Unincorporated Territory	7	3	uninhabited					164
Wallis and Futuna Islands		French Overseas Territory	274	106	15 000	Matā'utu	French, Wallisian, Futunian	Roman Catholic	CFP franc*	107

Tasmania, Australia

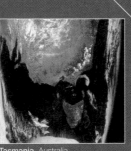

Kiritimati island, Kiribati

Mount Cook, New Zealand

Canberra, Australia

northamerica

contents

		map coverage	scale
116–117	landscapes		
118-119	locations		
120–121	map_1	**canada**	1:16 000 000
122–123	map_2	**canada** west	1:7 000 000
124–125	map_3	**canada** central and east	1:7 000 000
126–127	map_4	**united states of america**	1:12 000 000
128–129	map_5	**united states of america** east	1:6 500 000
130–131	map_6	**united states of america** northeast	1:3 000 000
132–133	map_7	**united states of america** central	1:6 500 000
134–135	map_8	**united states of america** west	1:6 500 000
136–137	map_9	**united states of america** southwest	1:3 000 000
138–139	map_10	**central america** and the **caribbean**	1:12 500 000
140	states and territories		

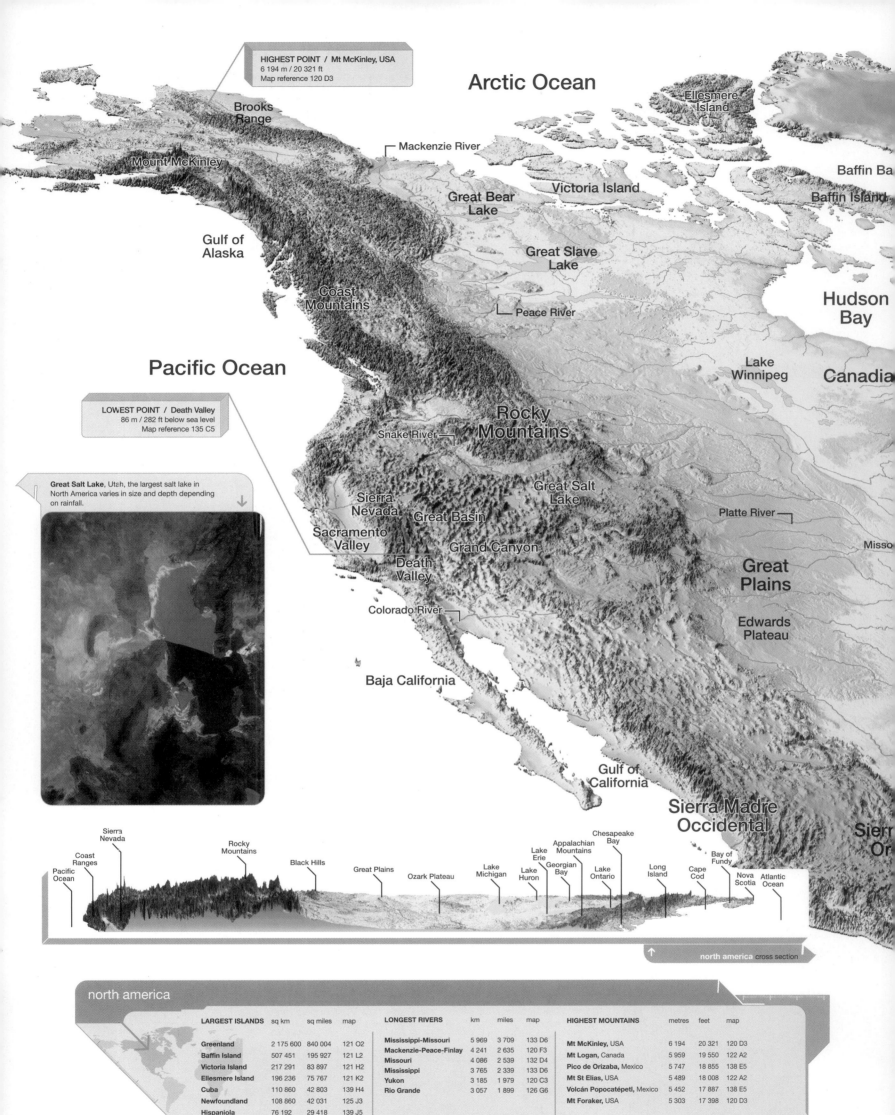

Arctic Ocean

HIGHEST POINT / Mt McKinley, USA
6 194 m / 20 321 ft
Map reference 120 D3

Brooks Range

Ellesmere Island

Mackenzie River

Baffin Ba

Baffin Island

Mount McKinley

Victoria Island

Great Bear Lake

Gulf of Alaska

Great Slave Lake

Hudson Bay

Coast Mountains

Peace River

Pacific Ocean

Lake Winnipeg

Canadia

LOWEST POINT / Death Valley
86 m / 282 ft below sea level
Map reference 135 C5

Snake River

Rocky Mountains

Great Salt Lake

Platte River

Great Salt Lake, Utah, the largest salt lake in North America varies in size and depth depending on rainfall.

Sierra Nevada

Great Basin

Sacramento Valley

Grand Canyon

Death Valley

Misso

Great Plains

Colorado River

Edwards Plateau

Baja California

Gulf of California

Sierra Madre Occidental

Sier Or

Sierra Nevada

Rocky Mountains

Chesapeake Bay

Coast Ranges

Black Hills

Appalachian Mountains

Bay of Fundy

Pacific Ocean

Great Plains

Ozark Plateau

Lake Michigan

Lake Erie

Lake Huron

Georgian Bay

Lake Ontario

Long Island

Cape Cod

Nova Scotia

Atlantic Ocean

↑ north america cross section

north america

LARGEST ISLANDS	sq km	sq miles	map
Greenland	2 175 600	840 004	121 O2
Baffin Island	507 451	195 927	121 L2
Victoria Island	217 291	83 897	121 H2
Ellesmere Island	196 236	75 767	121 K2
Cuba	110 860	42 803	139 H4
Newfoundland	108 860	42 031	125 J3
Hispaniola	76 192	29 418	139 J5

LONGEST RIVERS	km	miles	map
Mississippi-Missouri	5 969	3 709	133 D6
Mackenzie-Peace-Finlay	4 241	2 635	120 F3
Missouri	4 086	2 539	132 D4
Mississippi	3 765	2 339	133 D6
Yukon	3 185	1 979	120 C3
Rio Grande	3 057	1 899	126 G6

HIGHEST MOUNTAINS	metres	feet	map
Mt McKinley, USA	6 194	20 321	120 D3
Mt Logan, Canada	5 959	19 550	122 A2
Pico de Orizaba, Mexico	5 747	18 855	138 E5
Mt St Elias, USA	5 489	18 008	122 A2
Volcán Popocatépetl, Mexico	5 452	17 887	138 E5
Mt Foraker, USA	5 303	17 398	120 D3

LARGEST LAKES	sq km	sq miles	map
Lake Superior	82 100	31 698	132 D2
Lake Huron	59 600	23 011	128 C2
Lake Michigan	57 800	22 316	128 B3
Great Bear Lake	31 328	12 095	122 F1
Great Slave Lake	28 568	11 030	123 H2
Lake Erie	25 700	9 922	130 C2

LAND AREA		map
Total land area	24 680 331 sq km / 9 529 129 sq miles (including Hawaiian Islands)	
Most northerly point	Kap Morris Jessup, Greenland	121 P1
Most southerly point	Punta Mariato, Panama	139 H7
Most westerly point	Attu Island, Aleutian Islands	164 F2
Most easterly point	Nordøstrundingen, Greenland	166 I1

Greenland

Iceland

Davis Strait

LARGEST ISLAND / Greenland
2 175 600 sq km / 840 004 sq miles
Map reference 121 D2

Labrador

hield

LARGEST LAKE / Lake Superior
82 100 sq km / 31 698 sq miles
Map reference 132 D2

Newfoundland

Great Lakes

St Lawrence River

Appalachian
Mountains

Atlantic Ocean

er

Ozark
Plateau

Red River

Mississippi River

Brazos River

LONGEST RIVER / Mississippi-Missouri
5 969 km / 3 709 miles
Map reference 133 D6

Rio Grande River

Florida

The Bahamas

Gulf of
Mexico

Cuba

Hispaniola

Madre
al

Yucatan

Bahía de Campeche

Caribbean Sea

Sierra Madre
del Sur

Isthmus
of Panama

North America's longest river system, the
Mississippi-Missouri, flows into the Gulf
of Mexico through the **Mississippi Delta**.

Baffin Island, the world's fifth largest island,
separated from mainland Canada by the Davis Strait.

Volcán Popocatépetl, North America's fifth highest mountain,
located seventy kilometres southeast of Mexico City.

CONNECTIONS

World physical features | 6—7
World environment | 14—15
North America locations | 118—119
Reference maps of North America | 120—139
North America states and territories | 140

Alaska, the largest state in the USA, in the far northwest of North America.

CONNECTIONS

World countries	8–9
North America landscapes	116–117
Reference maps of North America	120–139
North America states and territories	140
Atlantic Ocean	160–161
Pacific Ocean	164–165
Arctic Ocean	166

Bering Sea

St Lawrence Island

Bering Strait

Point Hope

Barrow

Nome

Nunivak Island

A L A S K A

Yukon

Mount McKinley

Anchorage

Aleutian Islands

Bristol Bay

Kodiak Island

Gulf of Alaska

Alexander Archipelago

Juneau

Prince Rupert

YUKON TERRITORY

Whitehorse

Fort Nelson

BRITISH COLUMBIA

Prince George

Kamloops

Vancouver

Victoria

Seattle

Olympia

WASHINGTON

Portland

Salem

Columbia

OREGON

IDAHO

Twin Falls

Great

Salt Lake

Reno

Carson

NEVADA

Sacramento

San Francisco

CALIFORNIA

Las Vegas

Los Angeles

San Diego

Tijuana

ARIZONA

Phoe

Tucson

Guadalupe (Mex.)

Gulf of California

Baja California

Hermos

La Paz

PACIFIC OCEAN

HAWAII (U.S.A.)

Honolulu

Hawaiian Islands

Islas Revillagigedo (Mex.)

The **Panama Canal**, Panama, linking the Pacific Ocean to the Atlantic Ocean.

Los Angeles, USA, the world's eighth largest city, lying just south of the San Andreas Fault.

Manhattan and the East River in **New York**, USA, the sixth largest city in the world.

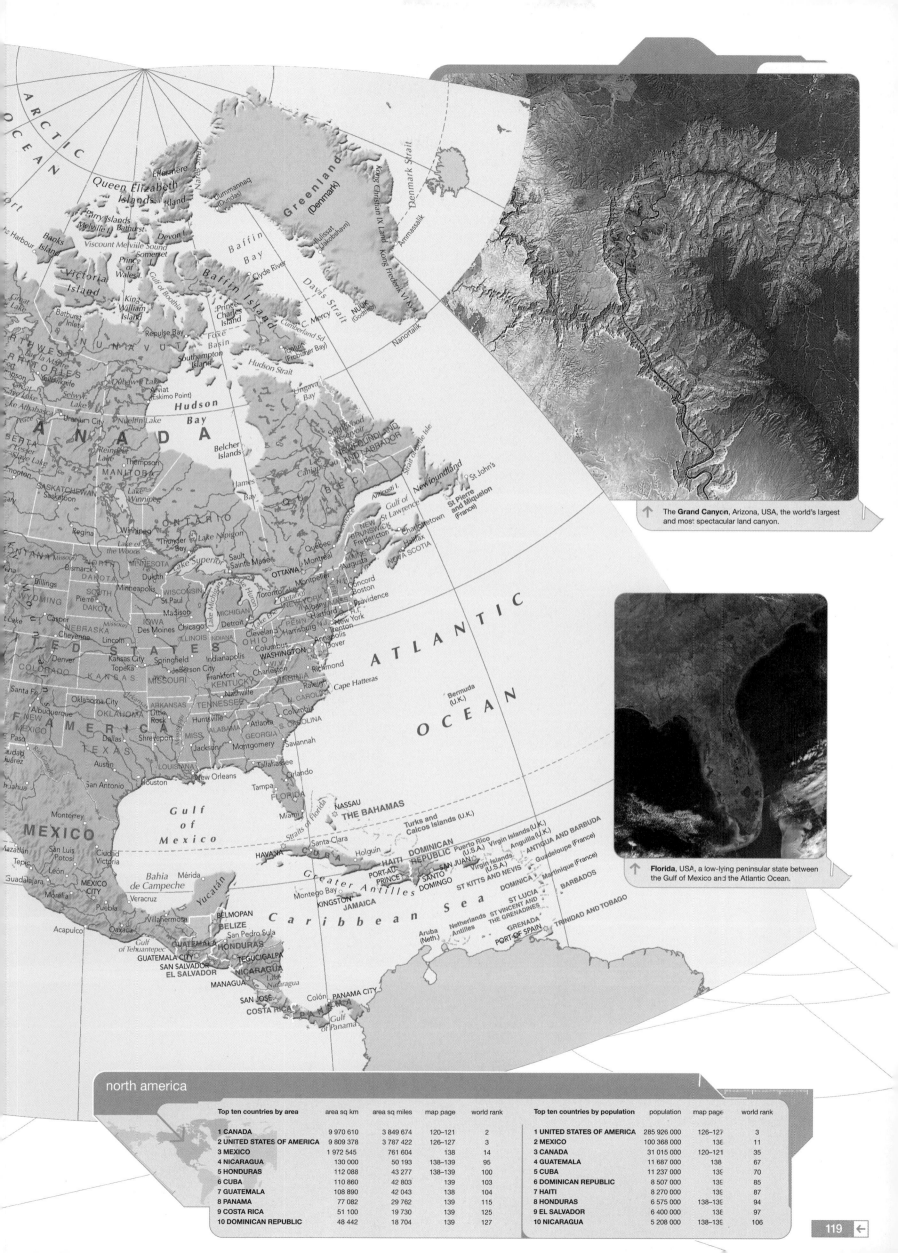

↑ The **Grand Canyon**, Arizona, USA, the world's largest and most spectacular land canyon.

↑ **Florida**, USA, a low-lying peninsular state between the Gulf of Mexico and the Atlantic Ocean.

north america

Top ten countries by area	area sq km	area sq miles	map page	world rank	Top ten countries by population	population	map page	world rank
1 CANADA	9 970 610	3 849 674	120–121	2	1 UNITED STATES OF AMERICA	285 926 000	126–127	3
2 UNITED STATES OF AMERICA	9 809 378	3 787 422	126–127	3	2 MEXICO	100 368 000	138	11
3 MEXICO	1 972 545	761 604	138	14	3 CANADA	31 015 000	120–121	35
4 NICARAGUA	130 000	50 193	138–139	95	4 GUATEMALA	11 687 000	138	67
5 HONDURAS	112 088	43 277	138–139	100	5 CUBA	11 237 000	139	70
6 CUBA	110 860	42 803	139	103	6 DOMINICAN REPUBLIC	8 507 000	139	85
7 GUATEMALA	108 890	42 043	138	104	7 HAITI	8 270 000	139	87
8 PANAMA	77 082	29 762	139	115	8 HONDURAS	6 575 000	138–139	94
9 COSTA RICA	51 100	19 730	139	125	9 EL SALVADOR	6 400 000	138	97
10 DOMINICAN REPUBLIC	48 442	18 704	139	127	10 NICARAGUA	5 208 000	138–139	106

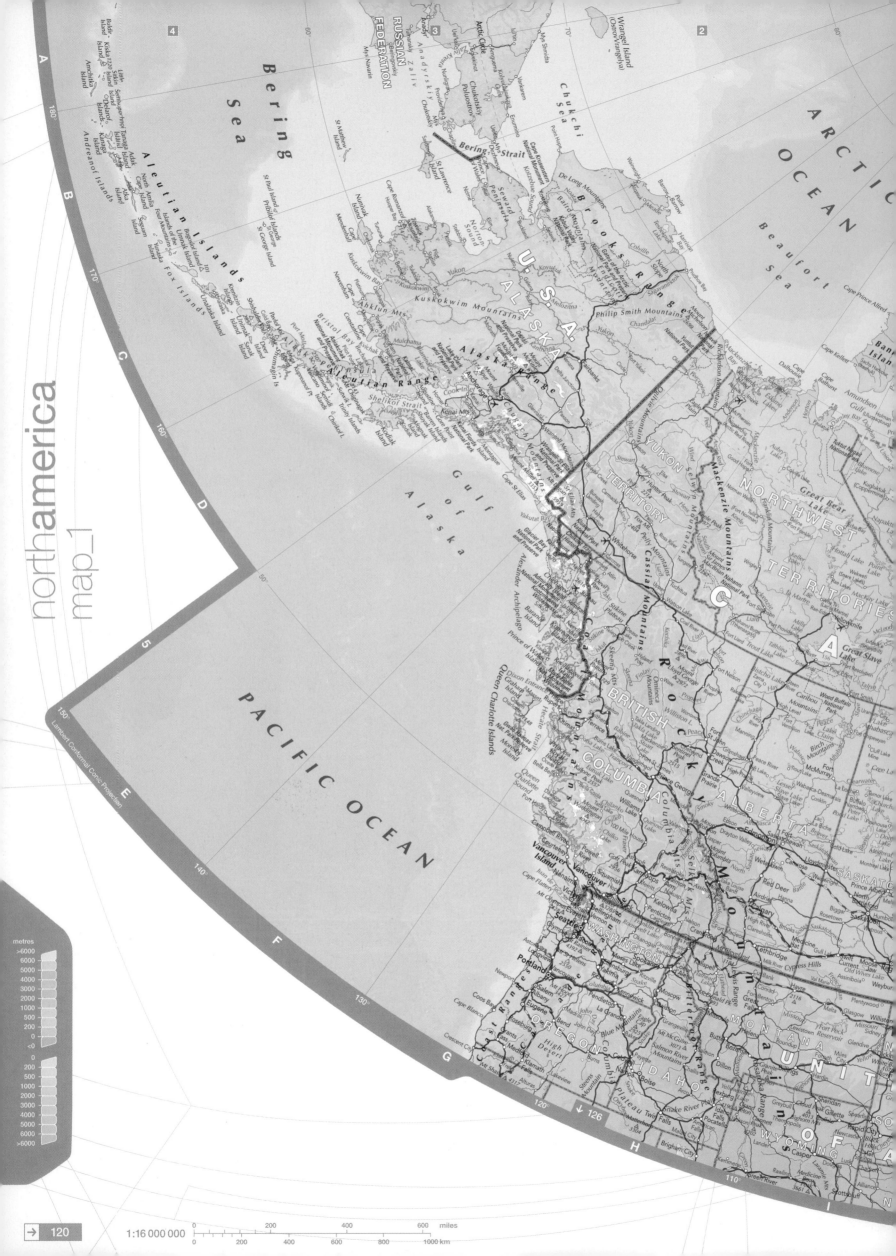

1:16 000 000

Greenland
(Kalaallit Nunaat)
(Denmark)

ICELAND

NUNAVUT

N A D A

C A N A D A

Queen Elizabeth Islands

Parry Islands

Victoria Island

Baffin Bay

Davis Strait

Greenland Sea

Denmark Strait

Labrador Sea

ATLANTIC OCEAN

MANITOBA

ONTARIO

QUÉBEC

NEWFOUNDLAND AND LABRADOR

Newfoundland

Labrador

Hudson Bay

James Bay

Péninsule d'Ungava

Ungava Bay

Foxe Basin

Foxe Channel

Hudson Strait

Lake Winnipeg

Lake Superior

Lake Michigan

Lake Huron

Lake Erie

Gulf of St Lawrence

Cabot Strait

Winnipeg

Thunder Bay

Ottawa

Montréal

Toronto

Detroit

Chicago

Milwaukee

Minneapolis

St Paul

Duluth

Boston

Québec

Halifax

UNITED STATES OF AMERICA

MINNESOTA

WISCONSIN

IOWA

MICHIGAN

NEW YORK

MAINE

NOVA SCOTIA

NEW BRUNSWICK

NORTH DAKOTA

SOUTH DAKOTA

NEBRASKA

Administrative divisions in the
U.S.A. numbered on the map:

1. RHODE ISLAND (L5)
2. MASSACHUSETTS (L5)
3. NEW HAMPSHIRE (L5)

↑ 120

Arctic Circle

PACIFIC

OCEAN

YUKON

TERRITORY

ALASKA

U.S.A.

C A N A D A

BRITISH

COLUMBIA

Alexander

Archipelago

Queen Charlotte Islands

Hecate Strait

Dixon Entrance

Vancouver
Island

WASHINGTON

Liard
Plateau

metres
>6000
6000
5000
4000
3000
2000
1000
500
200
0
<0
0
200
500
1000
2000
3000
4000
5000
6000
>6000

Conic Equidistant Projection

1:7 000 000

0   100   200   300   miles
0   100   200   300   400   500 km

↓ 134

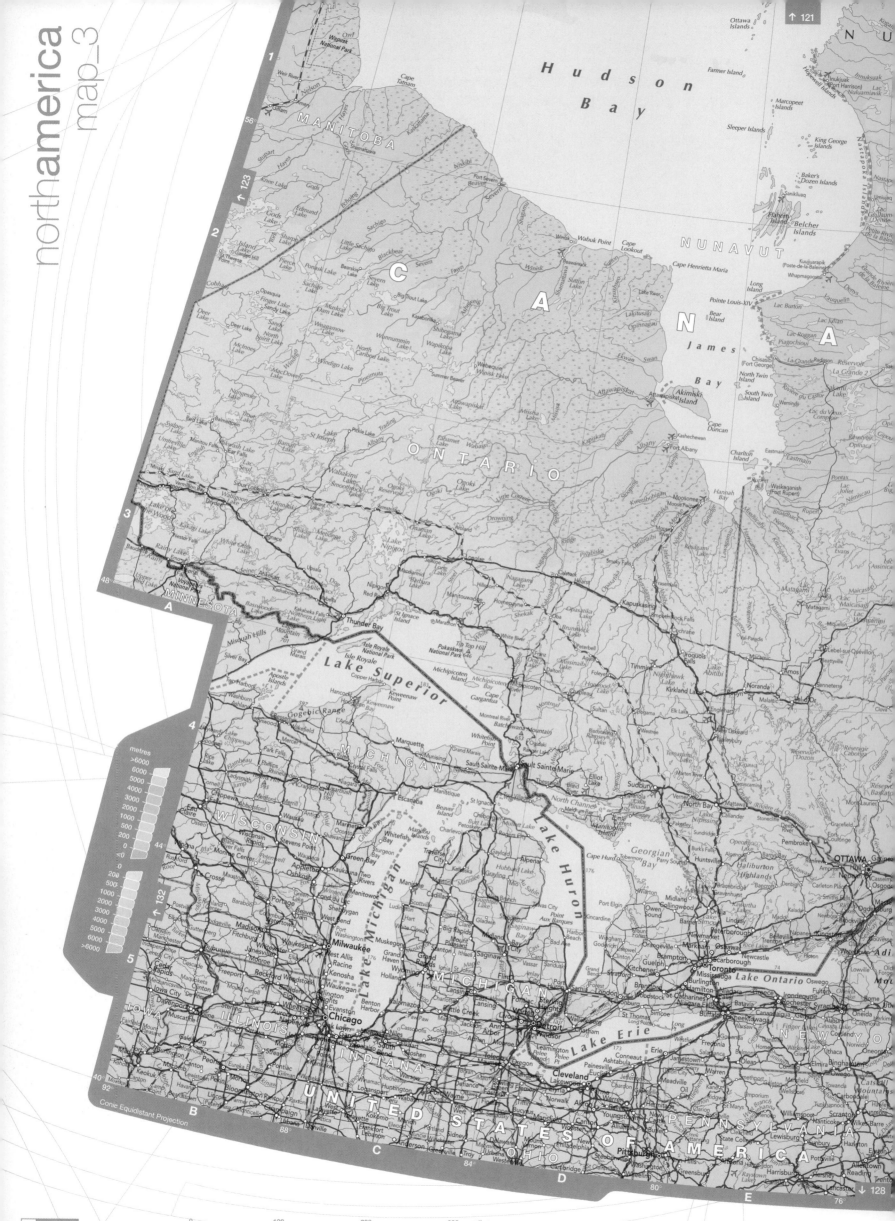

↑ 121

N

U

H u d s o n
B a y

MANITOBA

C

A

N

A

NUNAVUT

James
Bay

ONTARIO

Belcher
Islands

King George
Islands

Lake
Nipigon

Lake Superior

MINNESOTA

WISCONSIN

MICHIGAN

Lake Michigan

Lake Huron

Georgian
Bay

Thunder Bay

Isle Royale
National Park

Sault Sainte Marie

Sudbury

North Bay

Lake
Nipissing

OTTAWA

Lake Ontario

Milwaukee

Green Bay

Toronto

Hamilton

Madison

Chicago

Detroit

Lake Erie

Cleveland

NEW YO

IOWA

ILLINOIS

INDIANA

MICHIGAN

OHIO

PENNSYLVANIA

UNITED STATES OF AMERICA

metres
>6000
6000
5000
4000
3000
2000
1000
500
200
0
<0
0
200
500
1000
2000
3000
4000
5000
6000
>6000

↑ 123

↑ 132

→ 128

Conic Equidistant Projection

1:7 000 000

0   100   200   300   miles
0   100 200 300 400 500 km

A   B   C   D   E
1
2
3
4
5

Administrative divisions in the
U.S.A. numbered on the map:
1. CONNECTICUT (F5)
2. MASSACHUSETTS (F5)
3. NEW JERSEY (F5)
4. RHODE ISLAND (G5)

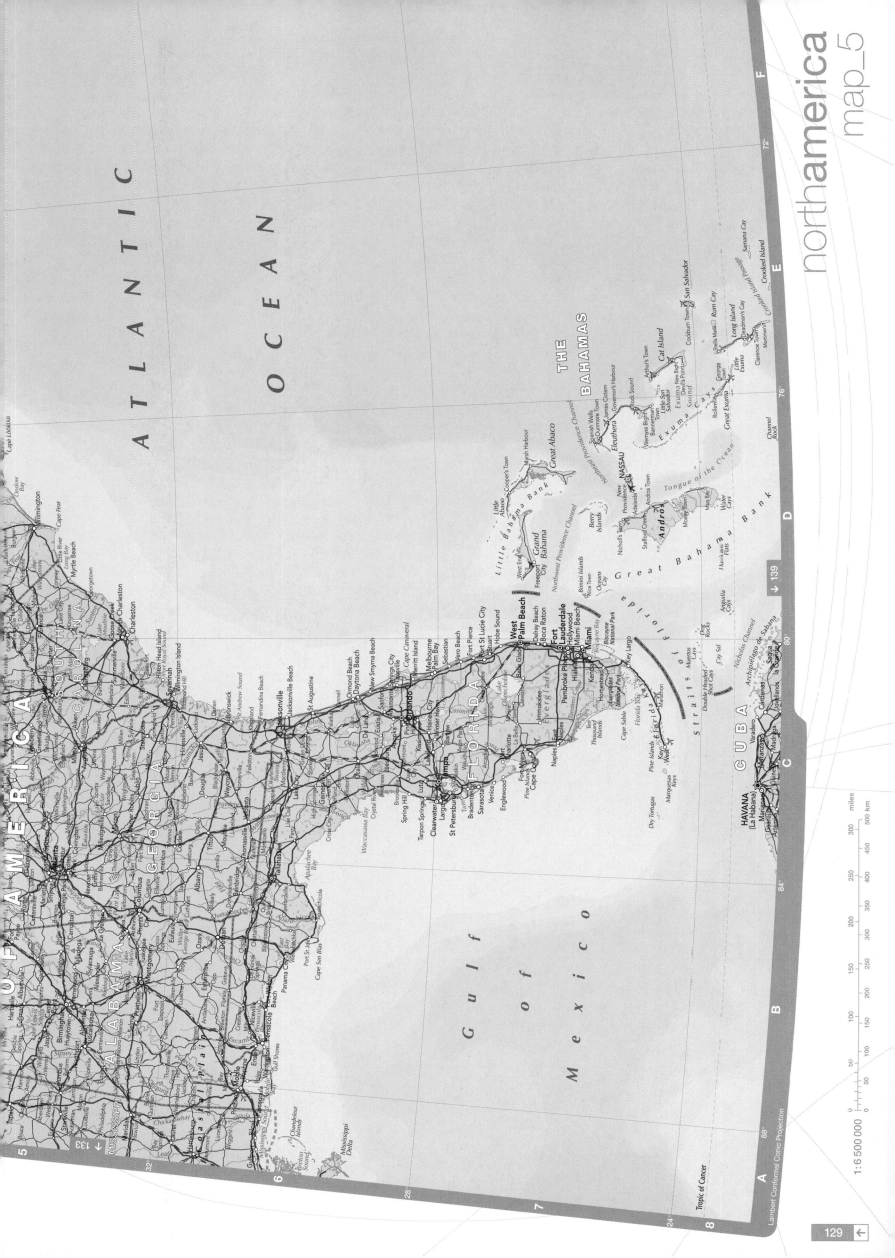

ATLANTIC

OCEAN

Gulf

of

Mexico

THE
BAHAMAS

NORTH AMERICA

ALABAMA

GEORGIA

SOUTH
CAROLINA

FLORIDA

CUBA

Cape Lookout

Wilmington
Cape Fear

Onslow
Bay

Myrtle Beach
Georgetown

Charleston

Hilton Head Island

Savannah

Brunswick

Jacksonville Beach
Jacksonville

St Augustine

Ormond Beach
Daytona Beach
New Smyrna Beach

Cape Canaveral
Merritt Island

Melbourne
Palm Bay

Sebastian
Vero Beach

Fort Pierce

Port St Lucie City
Stuart
Hobe Sound

West
Palm Beach
Delray Beach
Boca Raton
Fort
Lauderdale
Hollywood
Miami Beach
Miami
Homestead

Key Largo

Tallahassee

Tampa
St Petersburg
Clearwater
Largo
Bradenton
Sarasota

Venice

Englewood

Fort Myers
Cape Coral

Naples

Orlando
Kissimmee

Gainesville

Ocala

Panama City

Pensacola
Mobile

Montgomery

Columbus

Albany

Atlanta

Birmingham

Grand
Bahama
Freeport

West End

Little
Abaco
Cooper's Town

Marsh Harbour
Great Abaco

NASSAU
New
Providence

Andros

Berry
Islands

Bimini Islands
Alice Town

Eleuthera

Cat Island

San Salvador

Exuma Cays
Great Exuma
Little
Exuma

Long Island

Crooked Island

HAVANA
(La Habana)

Matanzas

Cárdenas

Great Bahama Bank

Straits of Florida

Tropic of Cancer

Lambert Conformal Conic Projection

1:6 500 000

0   50   100   150   200   250   300   miles

0   100   200   300   400   500 km

129

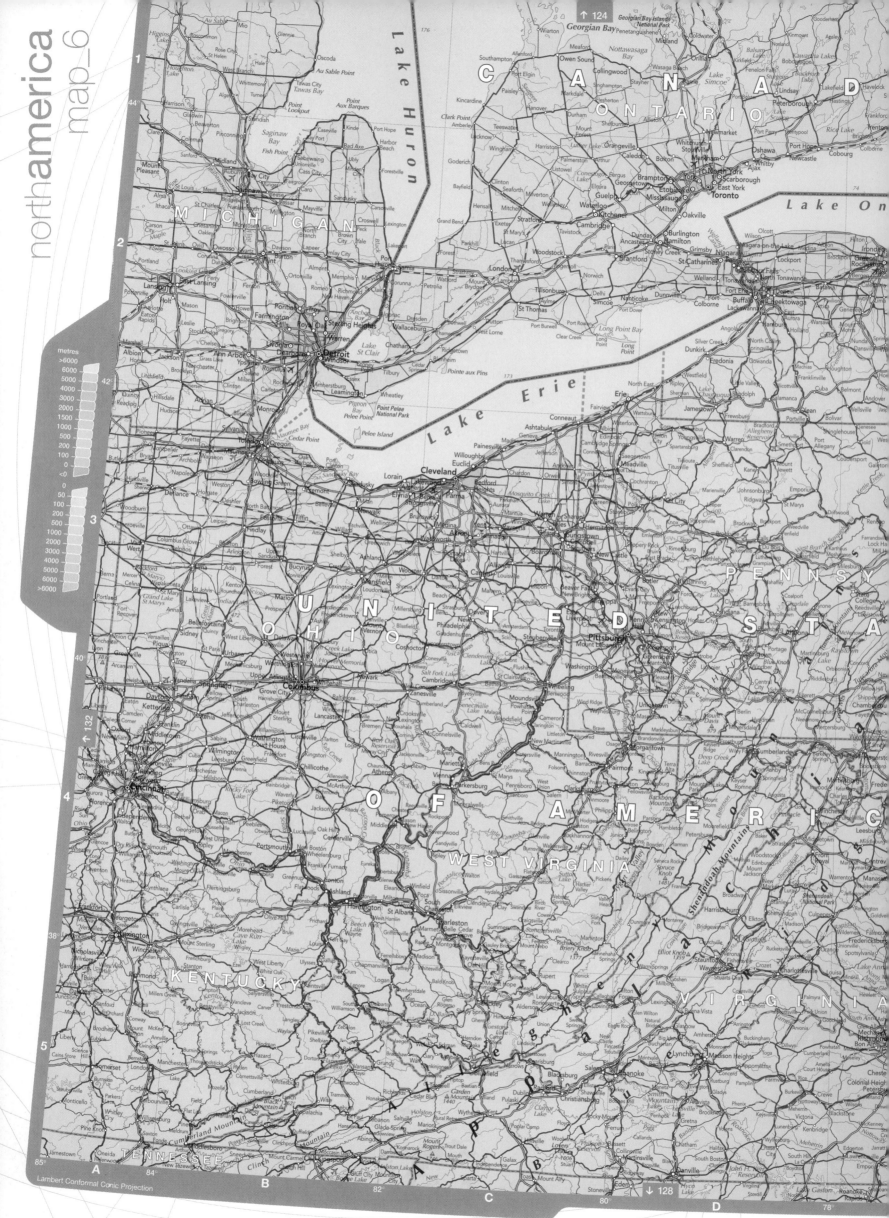

↑ 124

↑ 132

↓ 128

Lambert Conformal Conic Projection

1:3 000 000

| 0 | 25 | 50 | 75 | 100 | 125 miles |

| 0 | 25 | 50 | 75 | 100 | 125 | 150 | 175 | 200 km |

metres
>6000
6000
5000
4000
3000
2000
1500
1000
500
200
100
0
<0

0
50
100
200
500
1000
2000
3000
4000
5000
6000
>6000

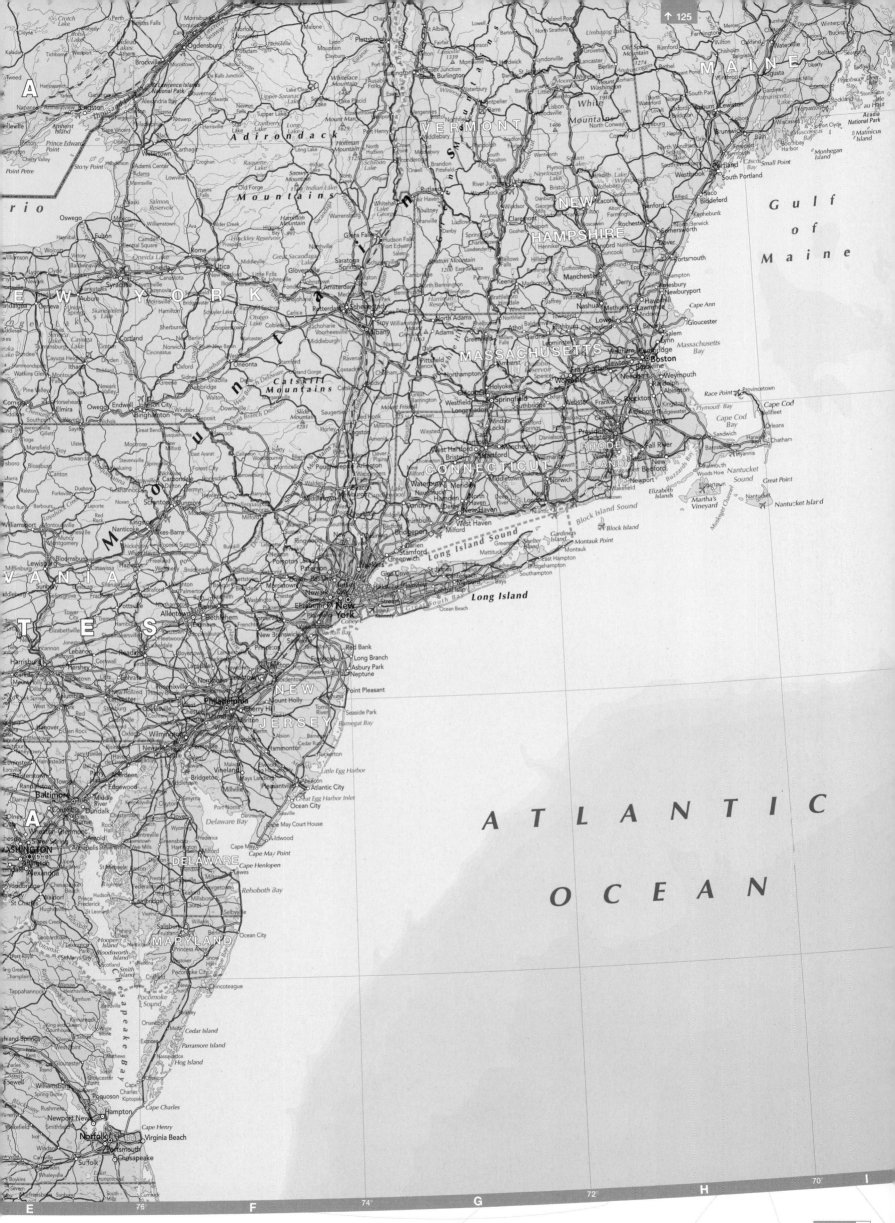

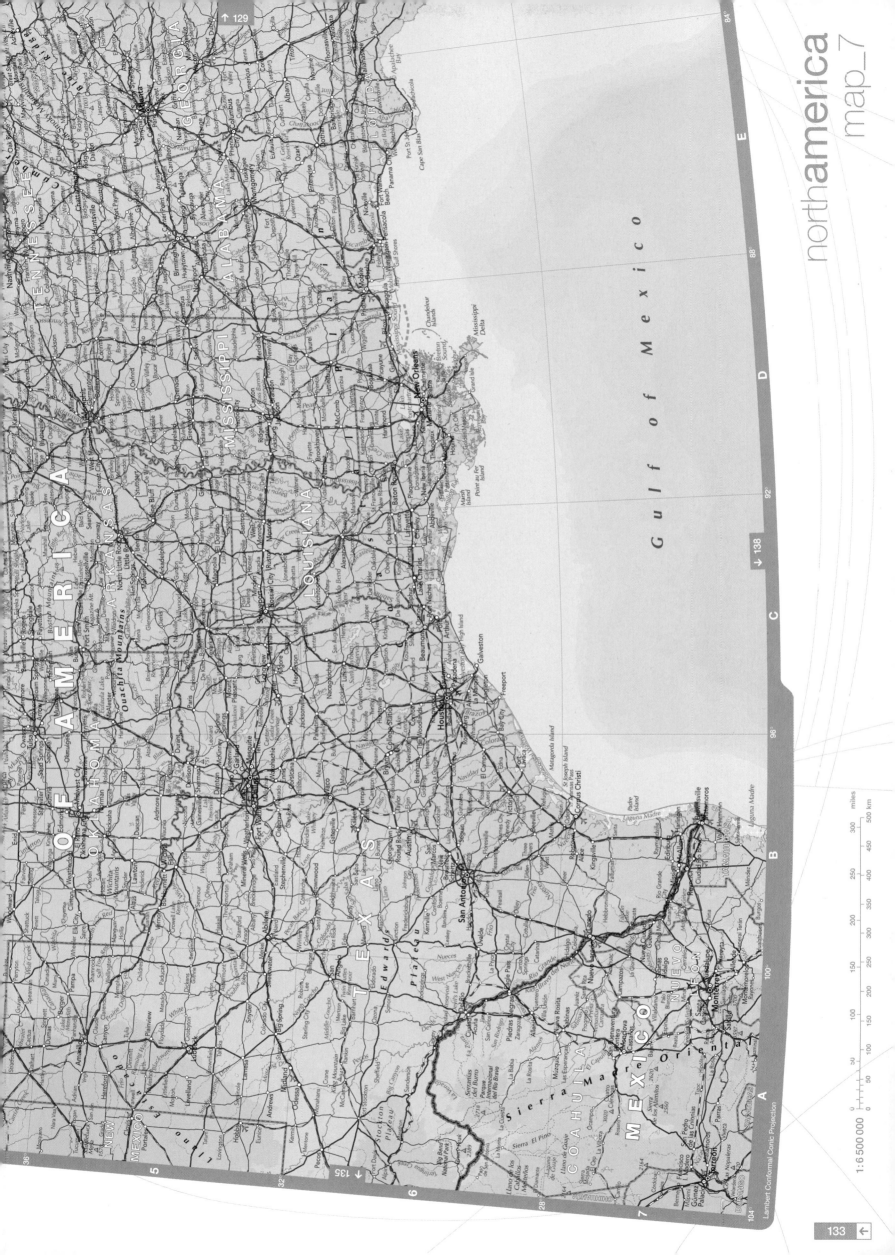

Lambert Conformal Conic Projection

1:6 500 000

miles

500 km

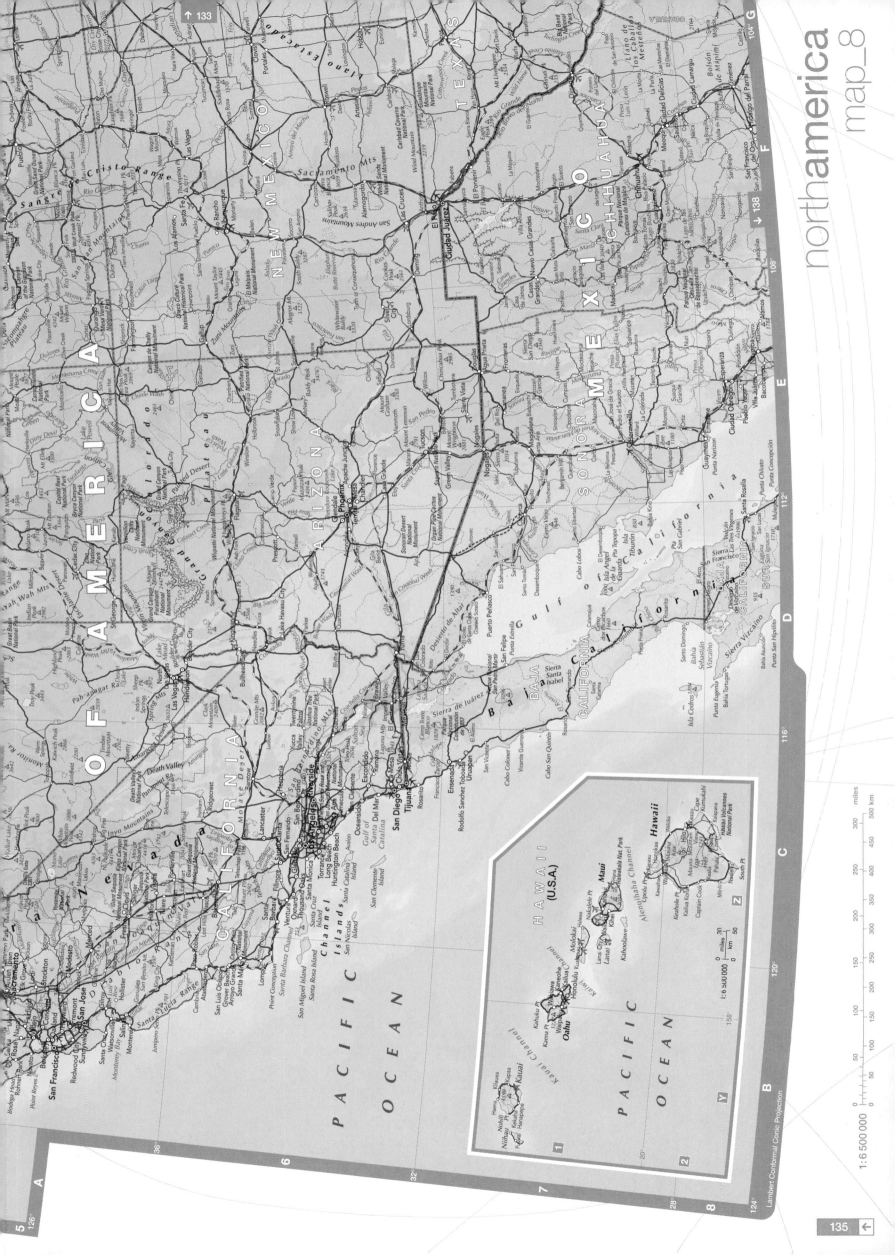

1:6 500 000

Lambert Conformal Conic Projection

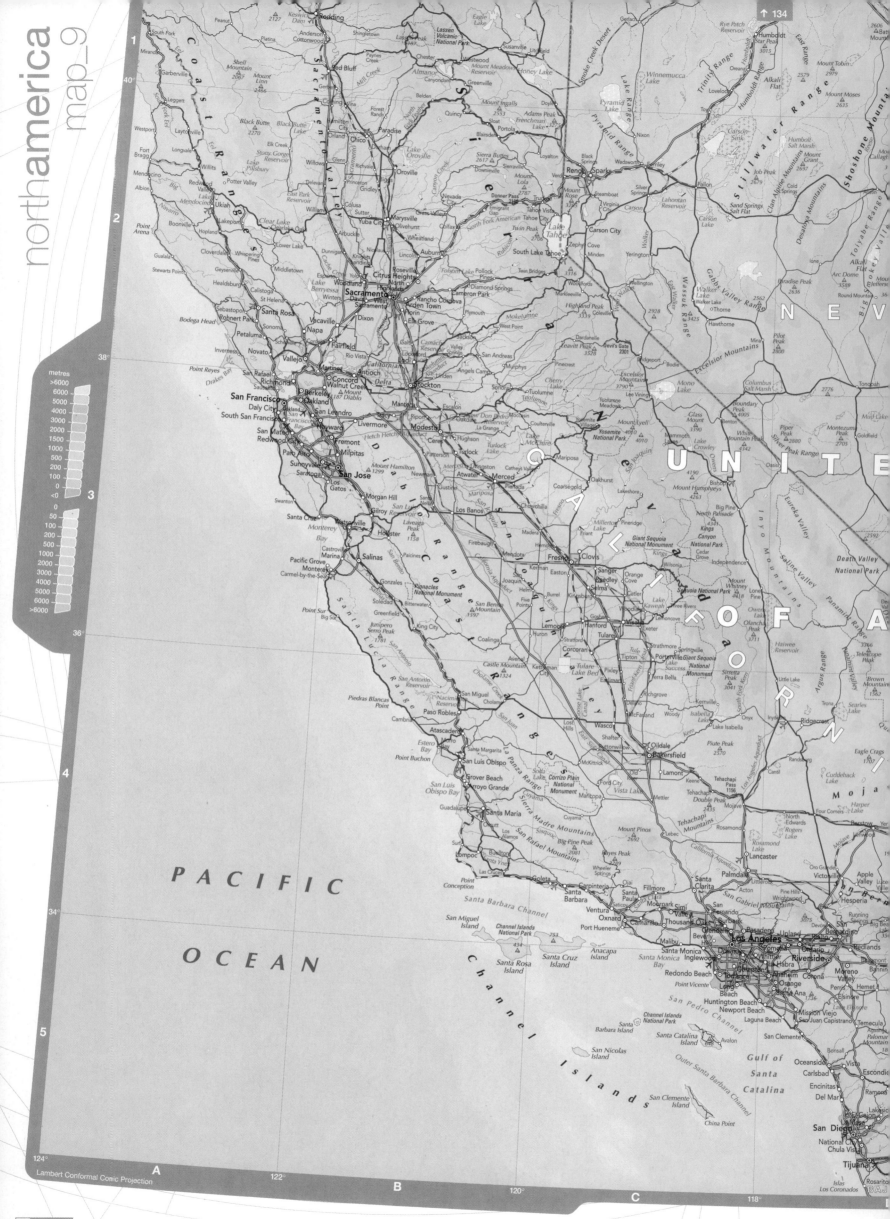

metres
>6000
6000
5000
4000
3000
2000
1500
1000
500
200
100
0
<0

0
50
100
200
500
1000
2000
3000
4000
5000
6000
>6000

PACIFIC

OCEAN

UNITE

OF A

C A L I F O R N

N E V

1   2   3   4   5

A   122°   B   120°   C   118°

Lambert Conformal Conic Projection

1:12 500 000

A T L A N T I C

O C E A N

Bermuda
(U.K.)
HAMILTON

THE
BAHAMAS

W   e   s   t   I   n   d   i   e   s

Turks and
Caicos Islands
(U.K.)

Leeward Islands

Virgin Is
(U.K.)   Anguilla
(U.K.)
SAN
JUAN   THE VALLEY
St Martin (Fr.)
ST JOHN'S   ANTIGUA
AND BARBUDA
Puerto Rico   Virgin Is   Antigua
(U.S.A.)   (U.S.A.)
Montserrat
(U.K.)

Hispaniola

HAITI

PORT-AU-
PRINCE   DOMINICAN
REPUBLIC
SANTO
DOMINGO

Guadeloupe
(France)
BASSE-TERRE
DOMINICA
ROSEAU
Martinique (Fr.)
FORT-DE-FRANCE
ST LUCIA   CASTRIES
Soufrière   BARBADOS
ST VINCENT   BRIDGETOWN
AND   KINGSTOWN
THE GRENADINES
GRENADA
ST GEORGE'S

CUBA

HAVANA
(La Habana)

Cayman Islands
(U.K.)
GEORGE TOWN

G   r   e   a   t   e   r

JAMAICA
KINGSTON

C   a   r   i   b   b   e   a   n   S   e   a

A   n   t   i   l   l   e   s

L   e   s   s   e   r   A   n   t   i   l   l   e   s

Lesser   Antilles
Netherlands
Aruba   ORANJESTAD Antilles
(Neth.)   Bonaire
WILLEMSTAD
Curaçao

Windward Islands

TRINIDAD
AND
PORT OF   TOBAGO
SPAIN
Trinidad

CARACAS

VENEZUELA

COSTA RICA

PANAMA
CITY
PANAMA

COLOMBIA

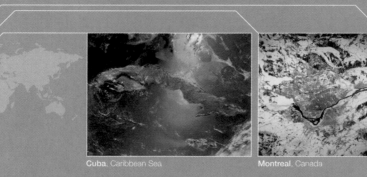

Cuba, Caribbean Sea Montreal, Canada The Pentagon, Washington DC, USA Mexicali, Mexico/USA border

COUNTRIES		area sq km	area sq miles	population	capital	languages	religions	currency	map
ANTIGUA AND BARBUDA		442	171	65 000	St John's	English, creole	Protestant, Roman Catholic	East Caribbean dollar	139
THE BAHAMAS		13 939	5 382	308 000	Nassau	English, creole	Protestant, Roman Catholic	Bahamian dollar	139
BARBADOS		430	166	268 000	Bridgetown	English, creole	Protestant, Roman Catholic	Barbados dollar	139
BELIZE		22 965	8 867	231 000	Belmopan	English, Spanish, Mayan, creole	Roman Catholic, Protestant	Belize dollar	138
CANADA		9 970 610	3 849 674	31 015 000	Ottawa	English, French	Roman Catholic, Protestant, Eastern Orthodox, Jewish	Canadian dollar	120–121
COSTA RICA		51 100	19 730	4 112 000	San José	Spanish	Roman Catholic, Protestant	Costa Rican colón	139
CUBA		110 860	42 803	11 237 000	Havana	Spanish	Roman Catholic, Protestant	Cuban peso	139
DOMINICA		750	290	71 000	Roseau	English, creole	Roman Catholic, Protestant	East Caribbean dollar	139
DOMINICAN REPUBLIC		48 442	18 704	8 507 000	Santo Domingo	Spanish, creole	Roman Catholic, Protestant	Dominican peso	139
EL SALVADOR		21 041	8 124	6 400 000	San Salvador	Spanish	Roman Catholic, Protestant	El Salvador colón, United States dollar	138
GRENADA		378	146	94 000	St George's	English, creole	Roman Catholic, Protestant	East Caribbean dollar	139
GUATEMALA		108 890	42 043	11 687 000	Guatemala City	Spanish, Mayan languages	Roman Catholic, Protestant	Quetzal, United States dollar	138
HAITI		27 750	10 714	8 270 000	Port-au-Prince	French, creole	Roman Catholic, Protestant, Voodoo	Gourde	139
HONDURAS		112 088	43 277	6 575 000	Tegucigalpa	Spanish, Amerindian languages	Roman Catholic, Protestant	Lempira	138–139
JAMAICA		10 991	4 244	2 598 000	Kingston	English, creole	Protestant, Roman Catholic	Jamaican dollar	139
MEXICO		1 972 545	761 604	100 368 000	Mexico City	Spanish, Amerindian languages	Roman Catholic, Protestant	Mexican peso	138
NICARAGUA		130 000	50 193	5 208 000	Managua	Spanish, Amerindian languages	Roman Catholic, Protestant	Córdoba	138–139
PANAMA		77 082	29 762	2 899 000	Panama City	Spanish, English, Amerindian languages	Roman Catholic, Protestant, Sunni Muslim	Balboa	139
ST KITTS AND NEVIS		261	101	38 000	Basseterre	English, creole	Protestant, Roman Catholic	East Caribbean dollar	139
ST LUCIA		616	238	149 000	Castries	English, creole	Roman Catholic, Protestant	East Caribbean dollar	139
ST VINCENT AND THE GRENADINES		389	150	114 000	Kingstown	English, creole	Protestant, Roman Catholic	East Caribbean dollar	139
TRINIDAD AND TOBAGO		5 130	1 981	1 300 000	Port of Spain	English, creole, Hindi	Roman Catholic, Hindu, Protestant, Sunni Muslim	Trinidad and Tobago dollar	147
UNITED STATES OF AMERICA		9 809 378	3 787 422	285 926 000	Washington DC	English, Spanish	Protestant, Roman Catholic, Sunni Muslim, Jewish	United States dollar	126–127

DEPENDENT TERRITORIES		territorial status	area sq km	area sq miles	population	capital	languages	religions	currency	map
Anguilla		United Kingdom Overseas Territory	155	60	12 000	The Valley	English	Protestant, Roman Catholic	East Caribbean dollar	139
Aruba		Self-governing Netherlands Territory	193	75	104 000	Oranjestad	Papiamento, Dutch, English	Roman Catholic, Protestant	Arubian florin	146
Bermuda		United Kingdom Overseas Territory	54	21	63 000	Hamilton	English	Protestant, Roman Catholic	Bermuda dollar	139
Cayman Islands		United Kingdom Overseas Territory	259	100	40 000	George Town	English	Protestant, Roman Catholic	Cayman Islands dollar	139
Greenland		Self-governing Danish Territory	2 175 600	840 004	56 000	Nuuk (Godthåb)	Greenlandic, Danish	Protestant	Danish krone	121
Guadeloupe		French Overseas Department	1 780	687	431 000	Basse-Terre	French, creole	Roman Catholic	Euro	139
Martinique		French Overseas Department	1 079	417	386 000	Fort-de-France	French, creole	Roman Catholic, traditional beliefs	Euro	139
Montserrat		United Kingdom Overseas Territory	100	39	3 000	Plymouth	English	Protestant, Roman Catholic	East Caribbean dollar	139
Navassa Island		United States Unincorporated Territory	5	2	uninhabited					139
Netherlands Antilles		Self-governing Netherlands Territory	800	309	217 000	Willemstad	Dutch, Papiamento, English	Roman Catholic, Protestant	Netherlands guilder	146
Puerto Rico		United States Commonwealth	9 104	3 515	3 952 000	San Juan	Spanish, English	Roman Catholic, Protestant	United States dollar	139
St Pierre and Miquelon		French Territorial Collectivity	242	93	7 000	St-Pierre	French	Roman Catholic	Euro	125
Turks and Caicos Islands		United Kingdom Overseas Territory	430	166	17 000	Grand Turk	English	Protestant	United States dollar	139
Virgin Islands (U.K.)		United Kingdom Overseas Territory	153	59	24 000	Road Town	English	Protestant, Roman Catholic	United States dollar	139
Virgin Islands (U.S.A.)		United States Unincorporated Territory	352	136	122 000	Charlotte Amalie	English, Spanish	Protestant, Roman Catholic	United States dollar	139

southamerica

contents

		map coverage	scale
142–143	landscapes		
144–145	locations		
146–147	map_1	**south america** north	1:8 250 000
148–149	map_2	**south america** central	1:8 250 000
150–151	map_3	**south america** east	1:8 250 000
152–153	map_4	**south america** south	1:8 250 000
154	states and territories		

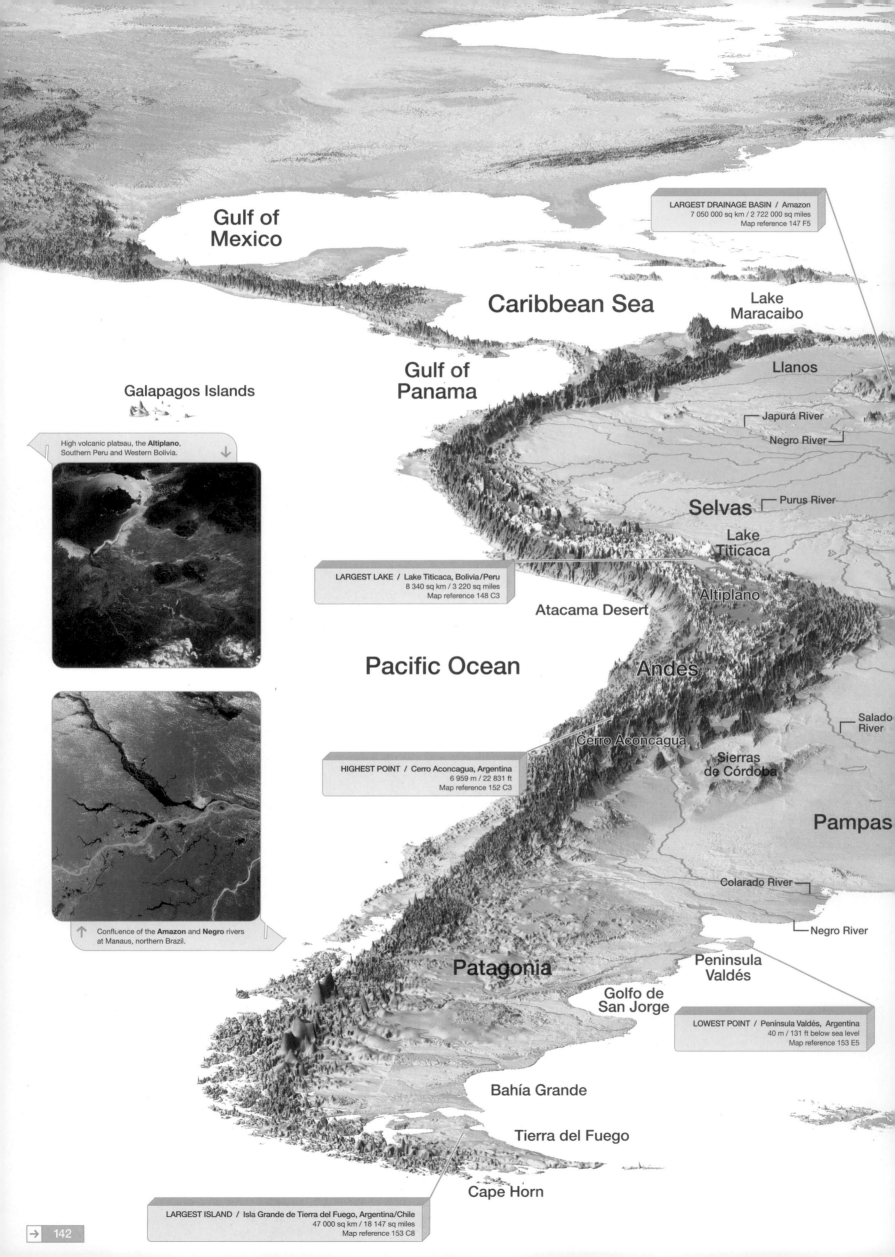

Gulf of
Mexico

Caribbean Sea

Lake
Maracaibo

LARGEST DRAINAGE BASIN / Amazon
7 050 000 sq km / 2 722 000 sq miles
Map reference 147 F5

Gulf of
Panama

Llanos

Galapagos Islands

Japurá River

Negro River

High volcanic plateau, the **Altiplano**,
Southern Peru and Western Bolivia.

Purus River

Selvas

Lake
Titicaca

LARGEST LAKE / Lake Titicaca, Bolivia/Peru
8 340 sq km / 3 220 sq miles
Map reference 148 C3

Altiplano

Atacama Desert

Pacific Ocean

Andes

Salado
River

Cerro Aconcagua

Sierras
de Córdoba

HIGHEST POINT / Cerro Aconcagua, Argentina
6 959 m / 22 831 ft
Map reference 152 C3

Pampas

Colarado River

Confluence of the **Amazon** and **Negro** rivers
at Manaus, northern Brazil.

Negro River

Peninsula
Valdés

Patagonia

Golfo de
San Jorge

LOWEST POINT / Península Valdés, Argentina
40 m / 131 ft below sea level
Map reference 153 E5

Bahía Grande

Tierra del Fuego

Cape Horn

LARGEST ISLAND / Isla Grande de Tierra del Fuego, Argentina/Chile
47 000 sq km / 18 147 sq miles
Map reference 153 C8

Isla Grande de Terra del Fuego, South America's largest island, situated at the southern most tip of the continent.

Lake Viedma, Argentina, located on the Patagonian Plateau at over 300m above sea level.

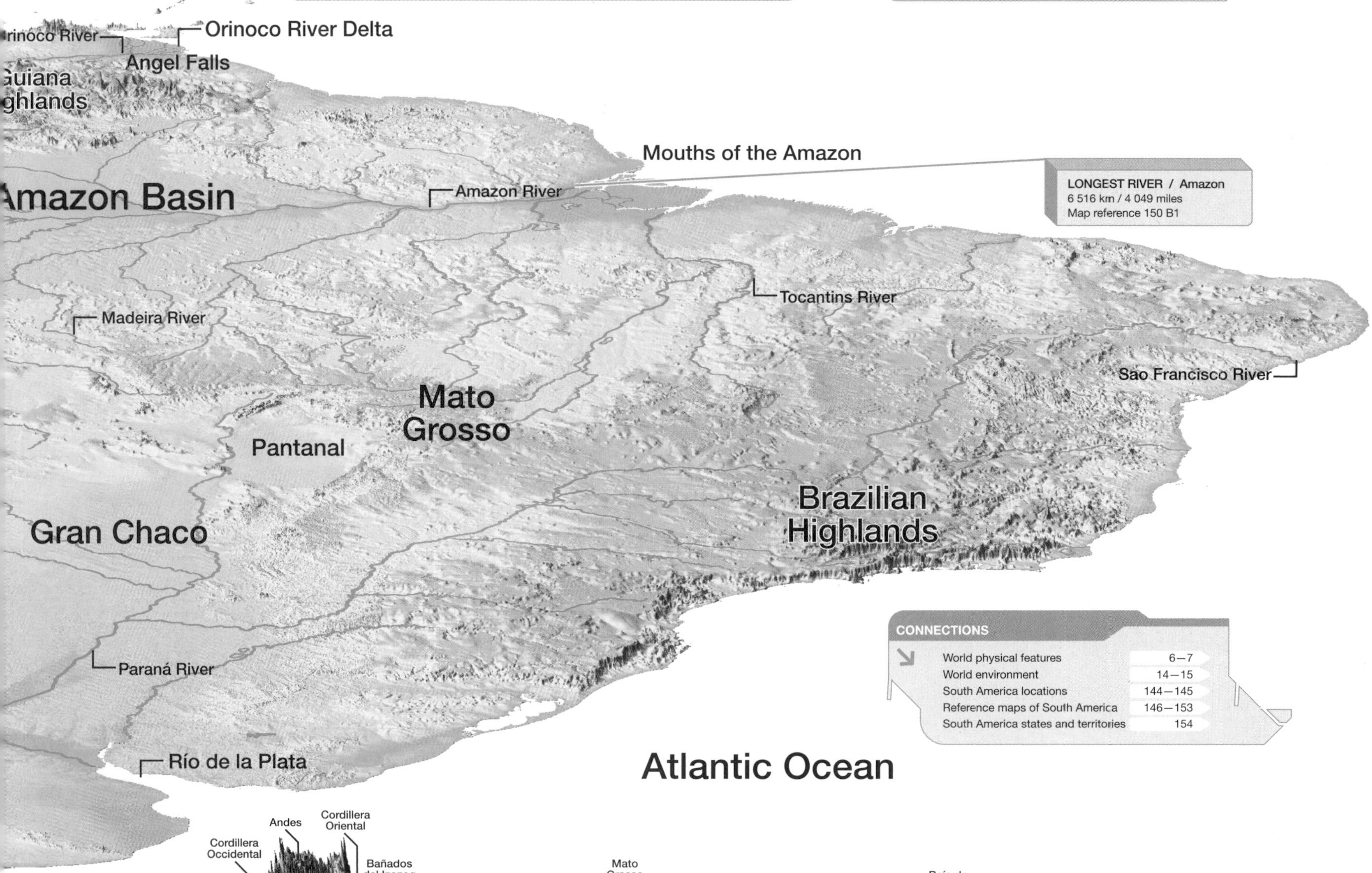

Orinoco River

Orinoco River Delta

Angel Falls

Guiana Highlands

Mouths of the Amazon

Amazon Basin

Amazon River

LONGEST RIVER / Amazon
6 516 km / 4 049 miles
Map reference 150 B1

Tocantins River

Madeira River

São Francisco River

Mato Grosso

Pantanal

Gran Chaco

Brazilian Highlands

Paraná River

CONNECTIONS

World physical features	6—7
World environment	14—15
South America locations	144—145
Reference maps of South America	146—153
South America states and territories	154

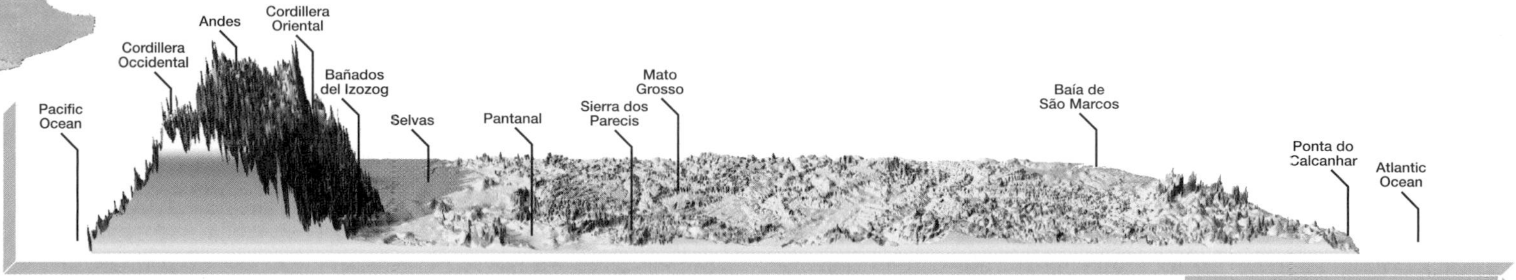

Río de la Plata

Atlantic Ocean

Cross section labels:
Pacific Ocean · Cordillera Occidental · Andes · Cordillera Oriental · Bañados del Izozog · Selvas · Pantanal · Sierra dos Parecis · Mato Grosso · Baía de São Marcos · Ponta do Calcanhar · Atlantic Ocean

south america cross section

south america

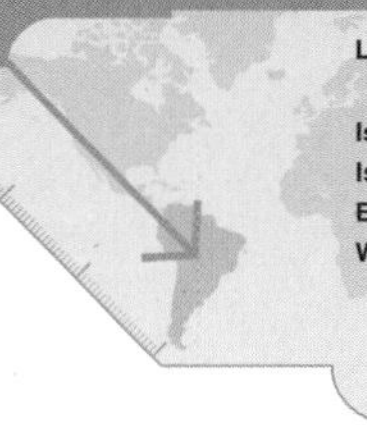

LARGEST ISLANDS	sq km	sq miles	map
Isla Grande de Tierra del Fuego	47 000	18 147	153 C8
Isla de Chiloe	8 394	3 240	153 B5
East Falkland	6 760	2 610	153 F7
West Falkland	5 413	2 090	153 E7

LONGEST RIVERS	km	miles	map
Amazon	6 516	4 049	150 B1
Río de la Plata-Paraná	4 500	2 796	152 F3
Purus	3 218	1 999	147 F5
Madeira	3 200	1 988	147 G5
Sao Francisco	2 900	1 802	150 E4
Tocantins	2 750	1 708	150 B2

HIGHEST MOUNTAINS	metres	feet	map
Cerro Aconcagua, Argentina	6 959	22 831	152 C3
Nevado Ojos del Salado, Argentina/Chile	6 908	22 664	152 C1
Cerro Bonete, Argentina	6 872	22 546	152 C1
Cerro Pissis, Argentina	6 858	22 500	152 C1
Cerro Tupungato, Argentina/Chile	6 800	22 211	152 C3
Cerro Meredario, Argentina	6 770	22 211	152 B3

LARGEST LAKES	sq km	sq miles	map
Lake Titicaca	8 340	3 220	148 C3

LAND AREA		map
Total land area	17 815 420 sq km / 6 878 572 sq miles	
Most northerly point	Punta Gallinas, Colombia	146 D1
Most southerly point	Cape Horn, Chile	153 D8
Most westerly point	Galapagos Islands, Ecuador	160 H6
Most easterly point	Ilhas Martin Vas, Atlantic Ocean	161 M7

Parallel ranges of South America's longest mountain system, the **Andes**.

Galapagos Islands, Ecuador, a group of volcanic islands lying on the equator in the eastern Pacific Ocean.

Isla de Coco

Galapagos Islands
(Ecuador)

PAC

OC

Rio de Janeiro, southeast Brazil, third largest city in South America.

south america

Top ten countries by area	area sq km	area sq miles	map page	world rank	Top ten countries by population	population	map page	world rank
1 BRAZIL	8 547 379	3 300 161	150–151	5	1 BRAZIL	172 559 000	150–151	5
2 ARGENTINA	2 766 889	1 068 302	152–153	8	2 COLOMBIA	42 803 000	146	28
3 PERU	1 285 216	496 225	148	19	3 ARGENTINA	37 488 000	152–153	31
4 COLOMBIA	1 141 748	440 831	146	25	4 PERU	26 093 000	148	38
5 BOLIVIA	1 098 581	424 164	148–149	27	5 VENEZUELA	24 632 000	146–147	40
6 VENEZUELA	912 050	352 144	146–147	32	6 CHILE	15 402 000	152–153	60
7 CHILE	756 945	292 258	152–153	37	7 ECUADOR	12 880 000	146	64
8 PARAGUAY	406 752	157 048	149	58	8 BOLIVIA	8 516 000	148–149	84
9 ECUADOR	272 045	105 037	146	73	9 PARAGUAY	5 636 000	149	100
10 GUYANA	214 969	83 000	147	82	10 URUGUAY	3 361 000	152	127

Massive deforestation in the **Amazonian rainforest**, Rondônia, Brazil.

Caribbean Sea

Golfo
del
Darién
Isla
de Malpelo
(Colombia)

Gulf
of
Panama

Barranquilla
Cartagena
Maracaibo
Montería
Medellín
San Cristóbal
Tunja
Ibagué
BOGOTÁ
Cali
Neiva
Pasto

CARACAS
Cumaná
Maracay
Ciudad Bolívar

VENEZUELA

Orinoco

GEORGETOWN
PARAMARIBO
CAYENNE

GUYANA
SURINAME
French
Guiana

QUITO
Manta
Guayaquil
de Guayaquil
ECUADOR
Cuenca
Iquitos

COLOMBIA
Puerto Ayacucho
Boa Vista

Orinoco

Branco

Putumayo
Japurá
Tonantins
Amazon

Negro

Amazon
Santarém
Manaus

Belém
São Luís
Parnaíba

Yavari
Marañón
Carauari
Juruá
Purus

Tapajós

Tocantins

Xingu

Chiclayo
Trujillo
PERÚ
Cruzeiro do Sul
Pucallpa
Rio Branco
Porto Velho
Madeira

BRAZIL

Maraba
Teresina
Fortaleza
Natal
João Pessoa
Floresta
Recife
Maceió
Aracaju
Salvador

Huancayo
LIMA
Ica
Cusco
Juliaca
Trinidad
Guaporé
Cuiabá
BRASÍLIA
Goiânia

Araguaia
Tocantins
São Francisco

Juàzeiro
Teófilo Otôni

Arequipa
LA PAZ
Cochabamba
SUCRE
Potosí
Santa Cruz
BOLIVIA
Mamoré

Patos
de Minas
Uberaba
Campo
Grande
Belo Horizonte

Arica
Iquique
Tarija
Campinas
Vitória

San Salvador
de Jujuy
Antofagasta
PARAGUAY
Pedro Juan
Caballero
Araçatuba
Maringá
São Paulo
Rio de Janeiro

Ilha
da Trindade
(Brazil)
Ilhas
Martin Vas
(Brazil)

Islas de los
Desventurados
(Chile)

Teuco
ASUNCIÓN
Paraguay
Iguaçu
Curitiba
Florianópolis

San Miguel
de Tucumán
Catamarca
La Rioja
Corrientes
Posadas
Santa Maria
Porto Alegre

Archipiélago
Juan Fernández
(Chile)

Cerro
Aconcagua
6959
San Juan
Mendoza
Córdoba
Paraná
Concordia
Rio Grande

Valparaíso
SANTIAGO
Rosario
URUGUAY
BUENOS AIRES
MONTEVIDEO

Salado
Paraná
Santa
Fé
Salado

Concepción
Santa Rosa

ATLANTIC

OCEAN

Bahía Blanca
Mar del Plata

ARGENTINA
Neuquén
Colorado
Negro
Viedma

Golfo San Matías

Isla de Chiloé
Trelew

Chubut
Golfo
de San Jorge

Archipiélago
de los Chonos
Comodoro
Rivadavia

PACIFIC OCEAN

Bahía
Grande
STANLEY
Falkland Islands
(U.K.)

Puerto Natales
Punta Arenas
Isla Grande
de Tierra del Fuego
Ushuaia
Cape Horn

South Georgia
and
South Sandwich
Islands
(U.K.)

Santiago, capital city and main industrial
centre of Chile.

Atacama Desert, north central Chile,
the driest place on earth.

CONNECTIONS

World countries — 8–9
South America landscapes — 142–143
Reference maps of South America — 146–153
South America states and territories — 154
Atlantic Ocean — 160–161
Pacific Ocean — 164–165

Administrative divisions
numbered on the map:

COLOMBIA
1. BOGOTÁ (C3)
2. QUINDO (C3)
3. RISARALDA (C3)

ECUADOR
4. BOLÍVAR (B5)
5. CHIMBORAZO (B5)
6. TUNGURAHUA (B5)
7. ZAMORA-CHINCHIPE (B5)

metres
>6000
6000
5000
4000
3000
2000
1000
500
200
0
<0
0
200
500
1000
2000
3000
4000
5000
6000
>6000

PACIFIC

OCEAN

Caribbean Sea
Lesser Antilles

PANAMA
PANAMA CITY
Gulf of Panama

COLOMBIA

ECUADOR

PERU

↓ 148

Lambert Azimuthal Equal Area Projection

1 : 8 250 000

0   50   100   150   200   250   300   miles
0   100   200   300   400   500 km

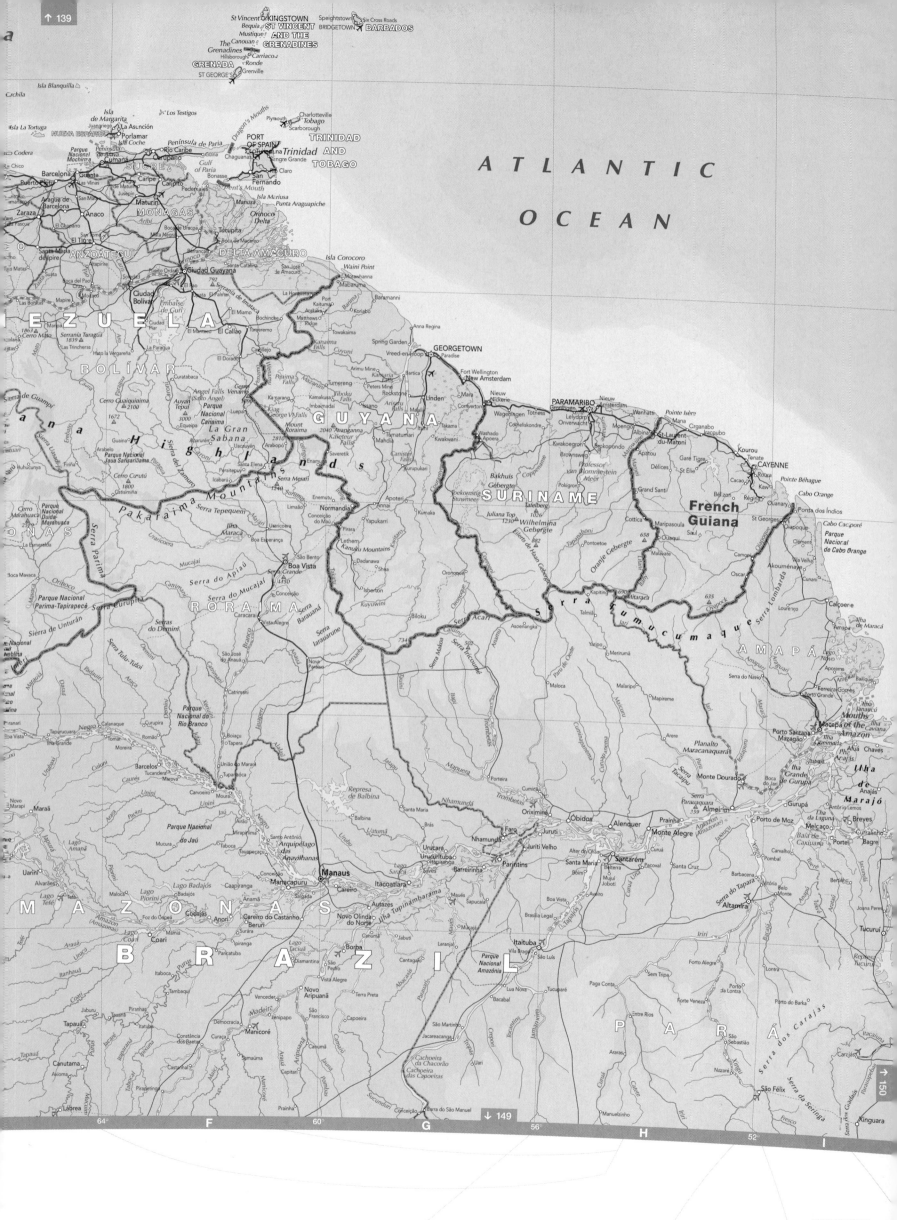

ATLANTIC

OCEAN

PACIFIC

OCEAN

Tropic of Capricorn

metres
>6000
6000
5000
4000
3000
2000
1000
500
200
0
<0
0
200
500
1000
2000
3000
4000
5000
6000
>6000

Lambert Azimuthal Equal Area Projection

1:8 250 000

| 0 | 50 | 100 | 150 | 200 | 250 | 300 | miles |
| 0 | 100 | 200 | 300 | 400 | 500 | km | |

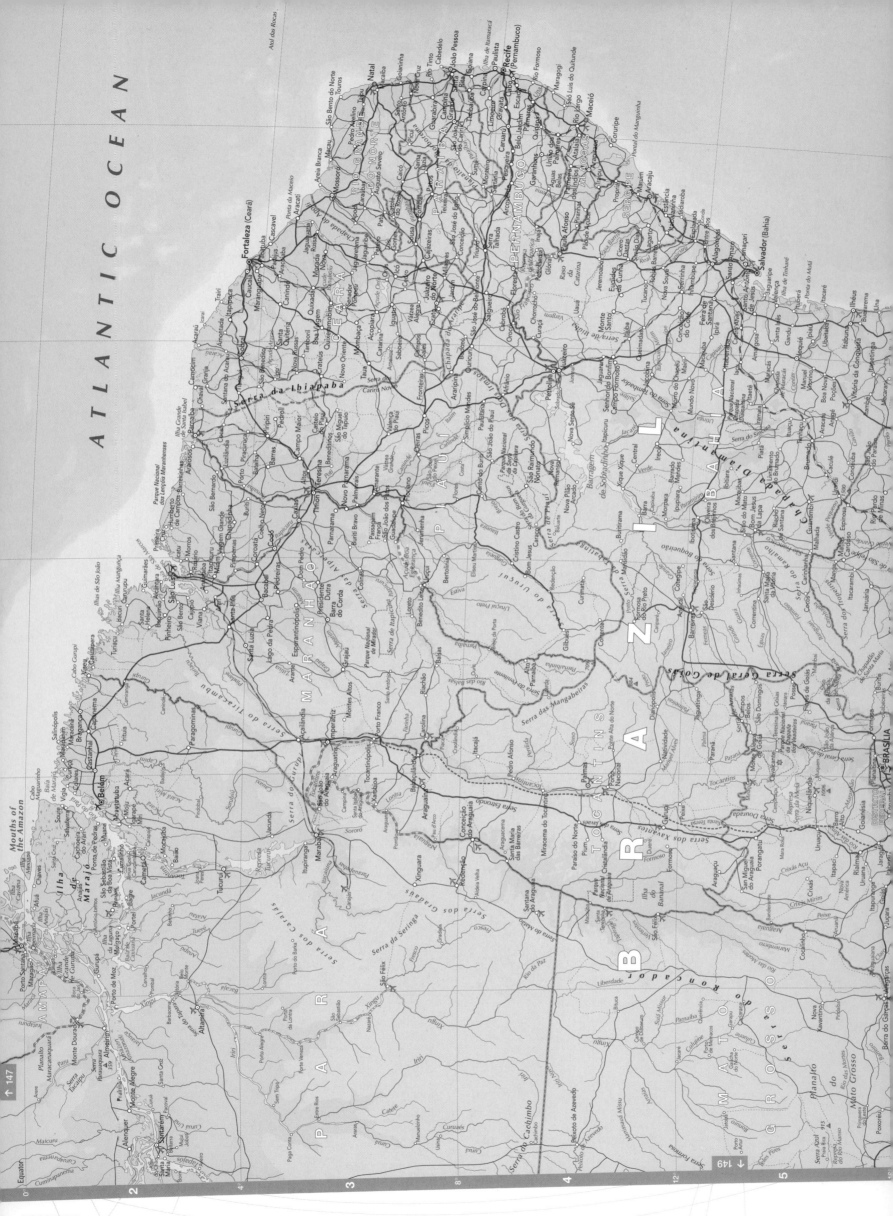

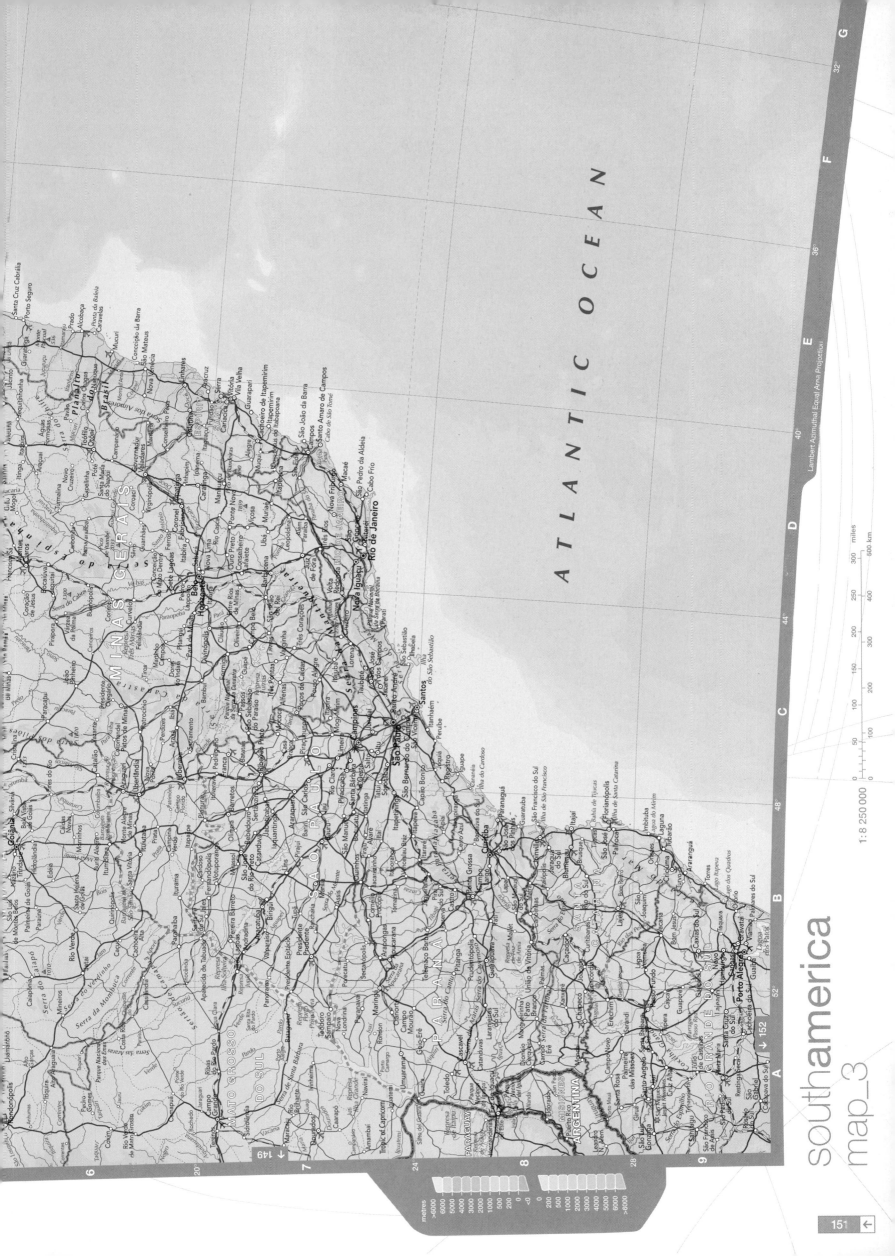

southamerica
map_3

ATLANTIC OCEAN

Lambert Azimuthal Equal Area Projection

1:8 250 000

metres
>6000
6000
5000
3000
2000
1000
500
200
<0
0
200
500
1000
2000
3000
4000
5000
6000
>6000

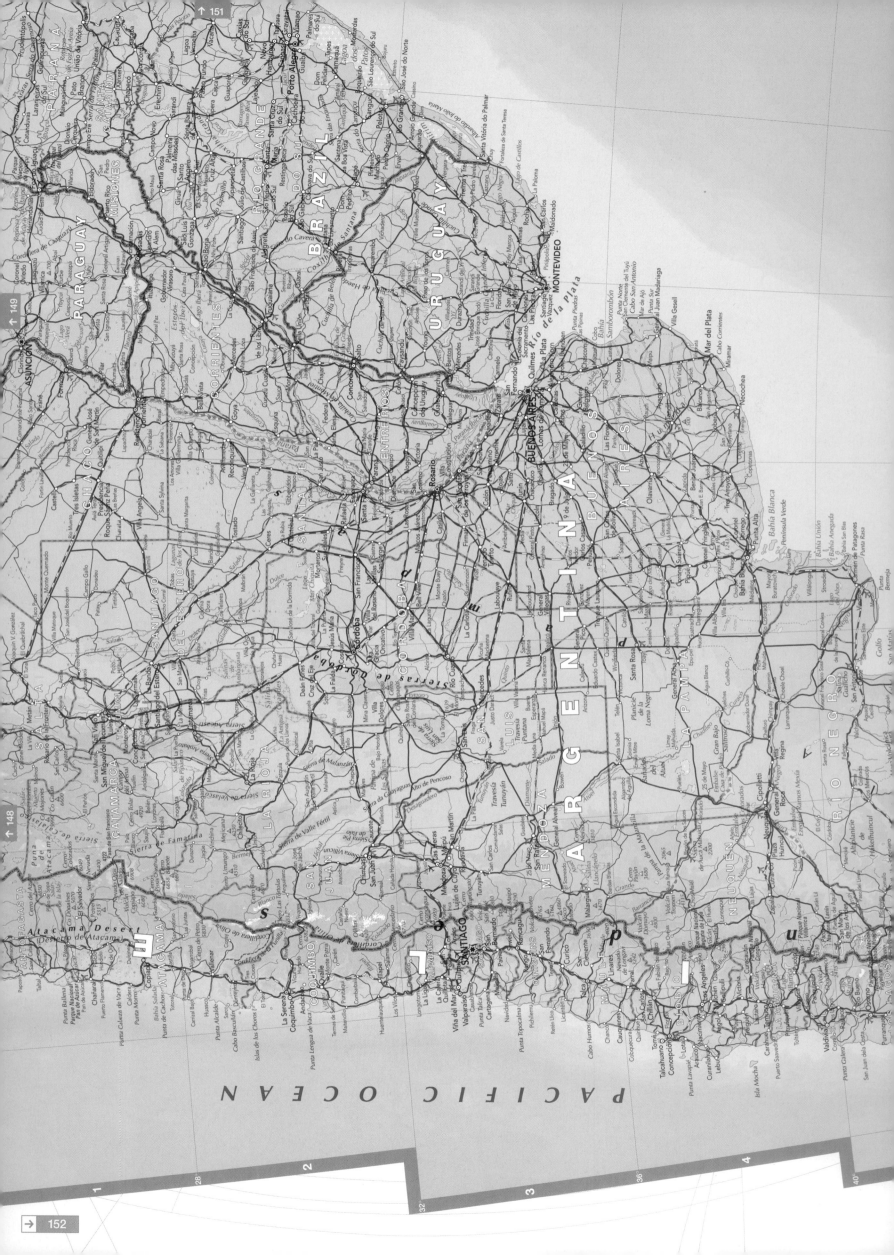

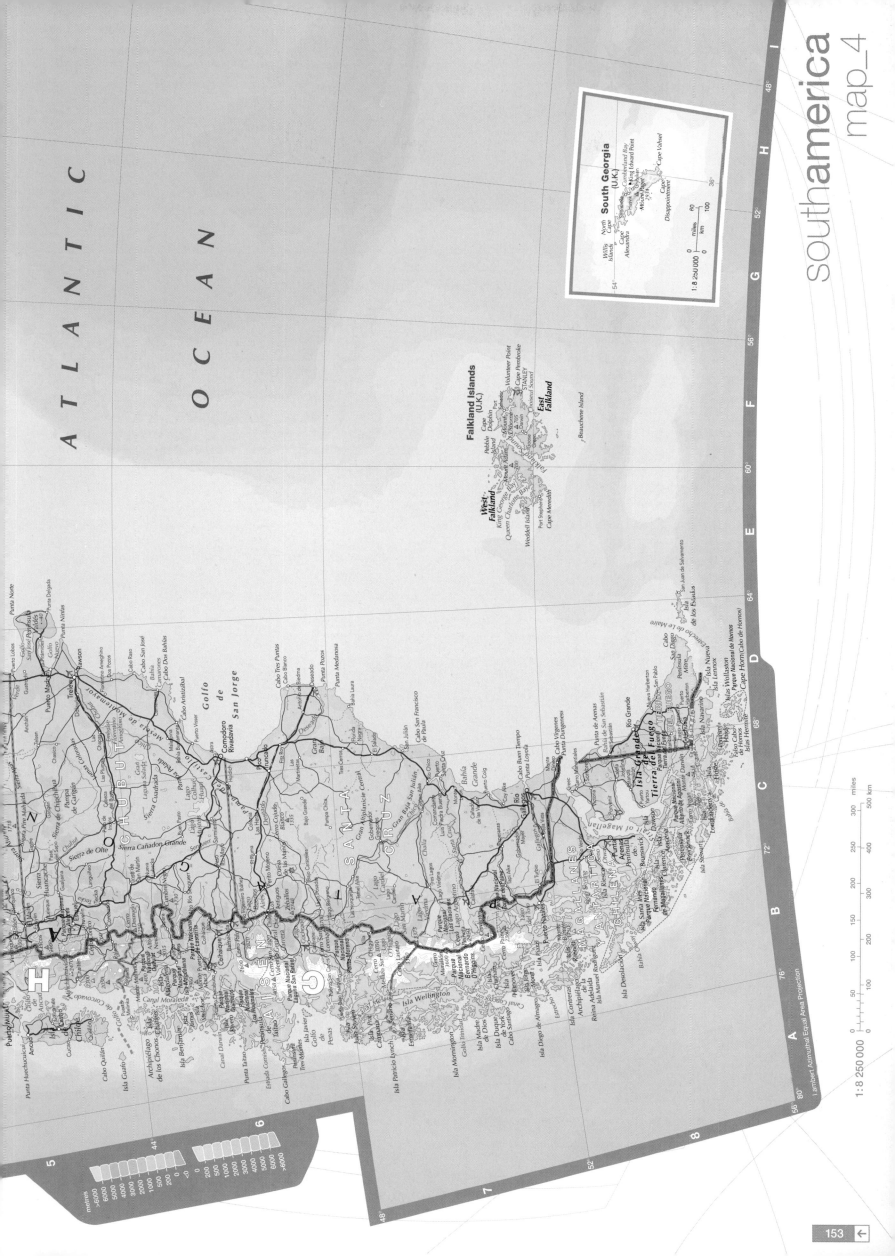

ATLANTIC

OCEAN

South Georgia (U.K.)

North Willis Cape Cumberland Bay
Islands Cape Alexandra King Edward Point
Husvik Grytviken
Mount Paget
2935 Cape Vahsel
Cape Disappointment

miles 0 60 100
km 0 60 100
1:8 250 000

36°

Falkland Islands (U.K.)

West Falkland
King George Bay
Queen Charlotte Bay
Weddell Island
Port Stephens
Cape Meredith

Cape Dolphin
Port Louise
Mount Adam 700
Mount Usborne 705
Darwin
Choiseul Sound

Volunteer Point
Cape Pembroke
STANLEY
East Falkland

Beauchene Island

ATLANTIC OCEAN

Punta Norte
Puerto Lobos
Golfo San José
Península Valdés
Punta Delgada
Punta Ninfas

Puerto Madryn
Rawson
Trelew
Golfo Nuevo
Cabo Raso
Bahía Camarones
Cabo Dos Bahías

Cabo San José

Golfo de San Jorge

CHUBUT

Comodoro Rivadavia

Cabo Blanco
Cabo Tres Puntas
Deseado
Punta Medanosa

SANTA CRUZ

Puerto San Julián
San Julián

Bahía Grande

Río Gallegos
Cabo Vírgenes
Punta Dungeness

Punta de Arenas
Bahía de San Sebastián
Río Grande

Isla de los Estados
Estrecho de Le Maire
Cabo San Diego

AISÉN

MAGALLANES Y ANTÁRTICA CHILENA

Punta Arenas
Strait of Magellan
Isla Grande de Tierra del Fuego
TIERRA DEL FUEGO

Isla Wollaston
Islas Hermite
Cape Horn (Cabo de Hornos)

ATLÁNTICO

Puerto Montt
Chiloé
Isla de Chiloé
Archipiélago de los Chonos

Golfo de Penas
Isla Wellington

Parque Nacional Bernardo O'Higgins

Puerto Natales

Parque Nacional Los Glaciares

metres
>6000
6000
5000
4000
3000
2000
1000
500
200
0
<0
0
200
500
1000
2000
3000
4000
5000
6000
>6000

1:8 250 000
Lambert Azimuthal Equal Area Projection

miles 0 50 100 150 200 250 300
km 0 100 200 300 400 500 km

Falkland Islands,
South Atlantic Ocean

Lake Titcaca, Bolivia/Peru

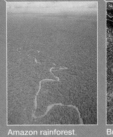

Amazon rainforest,
Ecuador

Buenos Aires, Argentina

COUNTRIES		area sq km	area sq miles	population	capital	languages	religions	currency	map
ARGENTINA		2 766 889	1 068 302	37 488 000	Buenos Aires	Spanish, Italian, Amerindian languages	Roman Catholic, Protestant	Argentinian peso	152–153
BOLIVIA		1 098 581	424 164	8 516 000	La Paz/Sucre	Spanish, Quechua, Aymara	Roman Catholic, Protestant, Baha'i	Boliviano	148–149
BRAZIL		8 547 379	3 300 161	172 559 000	Brasília	Portuguese	Roman Catholic, Protestant	Real	150–151
CHILE		756 945	292 258	15 402 000	Santiago	Spanish, Amerindian languages	Roman Catholic, Protestant	Chilean peso	152–153
COLOMBIA		1 141 748	440 831	42 803 000	Bogotá	Spanish, Amerindian languages	Roman Catholic, Protestant	Colombian peso	146
ECUADOR		272 045	105 037	12 880 000	Quito	Spanish, Quechua, other Amerindian languages	Roman Catholic	US dollar	146
GUYANA		214 969	83 000	763 000	Georgetown	English, creole, Amerindian languages	Protestant, Hindu, Roman Catholic, Sunni Muslim	Guyana dollar	147
PARAGUAY		406 752	157 048	5 636 000	Asunción	Spanish, Guaraní	Roman Catholic, Protestant	Guaraní	149
PERU		1 285 216	496 225	26 093 000	Lima	Spanish, Quechua, Aymara	Roman Catholic, Protestant	Sol	148
SURINAME		163 820	63 251	419 000	Paramaribo	Dutch, Surinamese, English, Hindi	Hindu, Roman Catholic, Protestant, Sunni Muslim	Suriname guilder	147
URUGUAY		176 215	68 037	3 361 000	Montevideo	Spanish	Roman Catholic, Protestant, Jewish	Uruguayan peso	152
VENEZUELA		912 050	352 144	24 632 000	Caracas	Spanish, Amerindian languages	Roman Catholic, Protestant	Bolívar	146–147

DEPENDENT TERRITORIES		territorial status	area sq km	area sq miles	population	capital	languages	religions	currency	map
Falkland Islands		United Kingdom Overseas Territory	12 170	4 699	2 000	Stanley	English	Protestant, Roman Catholic	Falkland Islands pound	153
French Guiana		French Overseas Department	90 000	34 749	170 000	Cayenne	French, creole	Roman Catholic	Euro	147
South Georgia and South Sandwich Islands		United Kingdom Overseas Territory	4 066	1 570	uninhabited					161

Orinoco River,
Colombia/Venezuela

Angel Falls, Venezuela

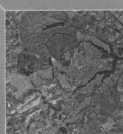

Machupicchu, Peru

Brasília, Brazil

oceansandpoles

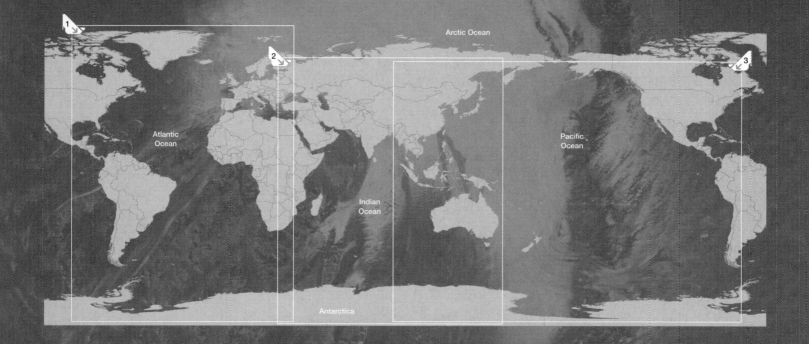

Arctic Ocean

Atlantic
Ocean

Pacific
Ocean

Indian
Ocean

Antarctica

contents

		map coverage	scale
156–157	**oceans** features		
158–159	**poles** features		
160–161	map_1	**atlantic ocean**	1:40 000 000
162–163	map_2	**indian ocean**	1:40 000 000
164–165	map_3	**pacific ocean**	1:45 000 000
166	the **arctic**	**arctic ocean**	1:26 000 000
167	antarctica	**antarctica**	1:26 000 000
168	**oceans** and **poles** statistics		

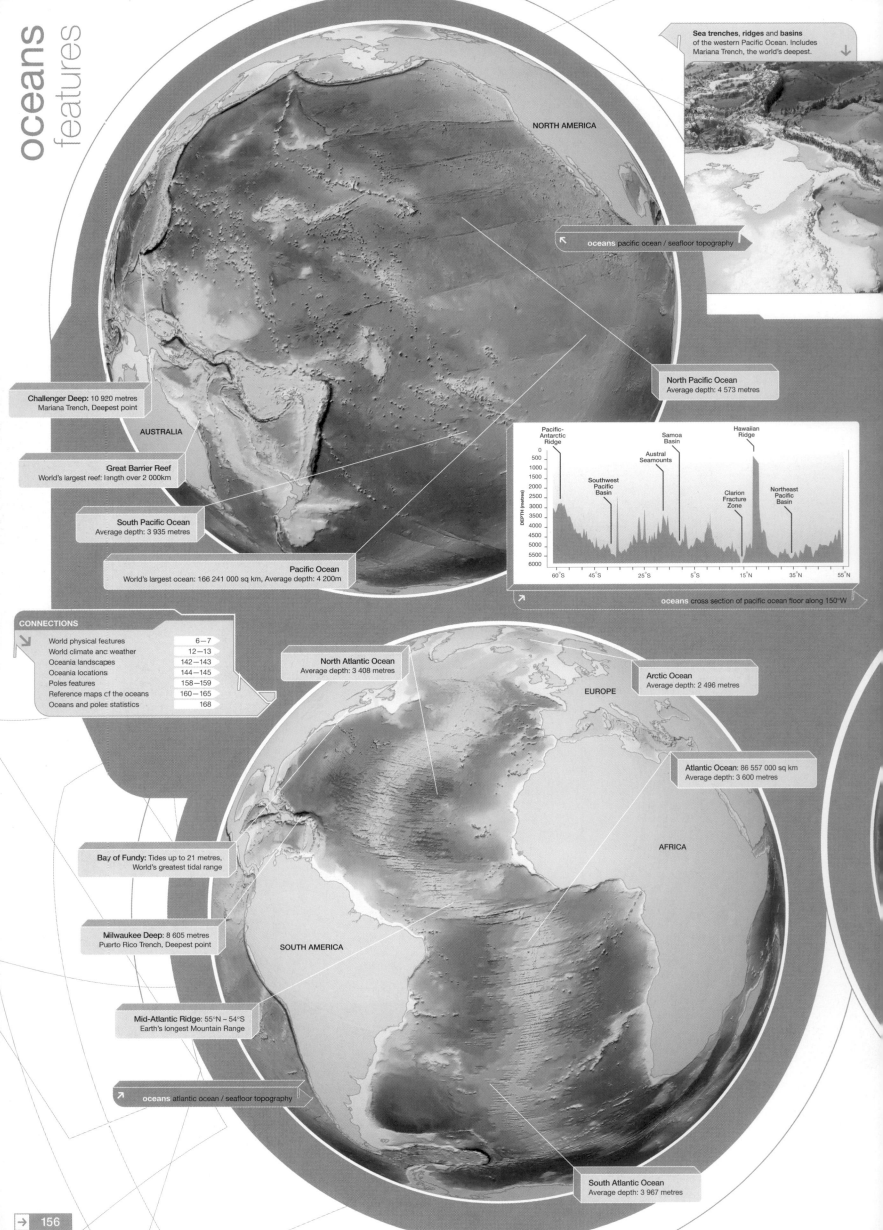

NORTH AMERICA

Sea trenches, ridges and basins of the western Pacific Ocean. Includes Mariana Trench, the world's deepest.

oceans pacific ocean / seafloor topography

North Pacific Ocean
Average depth: 4 573 metres

Challenger Deep: 10 920 metres
Mariana Trench, Deepest point

AUSTRALIA

Great Barrier Reef
World's largest reef: length over 2 000km

South Pacific Ocean
Average depth: 3 935 metres

Pacific Ocean
World's largest ocean: 166 241 000 sq km, Average depth: 4 200m

Pacific-Antarctic Ridge

Southwest Pacific Basin

Austral Seamounts

Samoa Basin

Hawaiian Ridge

Clarion Fracture Zone

Northeast Pacific Basin

DEPTH (metres)

0
500
1000
1500
2000
2500
3000
3500
4000
4500
5000
5500
6000

60°S   45°S   25°S   5°S   15°N   35°N   55°N

oceans cross section of pacific ocean floor along 150°W

CONNECTIONS

World physical features	6–7
World climate and weather	12–13
Oceania landscapes	142–143
Oceania locations	144–145
Poles features	158–159
Reference maps of the oceans	160–165
Oceans and poles statistics	168

North Atlantic Ocean
Average depth: 3 408 metres

Arctic Ocean
Average depth: 2 496 metres

EUROPE

Atlantic Ocean: 86 557 000 sq km
Average depth: 3 600 metres

AFRICA

Bay of Fundy: Tides up to 21 metres,
World's greatest tidal range

Milwaukee Deep: 8 605 metres
Puerto Rico Trench, Deepest point

SOUTH AMERICA

Mid-Atlantic Ridge: 55°N – 54°S
Earth's longest Mountain Range

oceans atlantic ocean / seafloor topography

South Atlantic Ocean
Average depth: 3 967 metres

Wind speed (m per second)

0   6   12   >15

Pacific Ocean / August 1999   Atlantic Ocean / August 1999   Indian Ocean / August 1999

Arctic Circle

Labrador

North Atlantic Drift

Gulf Stream

California

Tropic of Cancer

North Equatorial

Equator

South Equatorial

Tropic of Capricorn

Peru

Brazil

Benguela

Agulhas

Somali

Equatorial Counter

0°

East Australia

Kuroshio

Oyashio

Antarctic Circumpolar   Antarctic Circumpolar

Antarctic Circle

→ Warm current
→ Cold current
→ Seasonal drift
during northern winter

The **Intertropical Convergence Zone**, near the equator, where winds from the northern and southern hemispheres merge.

ASIA

AFRICA

AUSTRALIA

ANTARCTICA

Java Trench: 7 125 metres
Deepest point

Indian Ocean: 73 437 000 sq km
Average depth: 4 000 metres

Southern Ocean
Average depth: 3 239 metres

Red Sea
Hottest underwater temperature: 22°C (at 1.5 km below sea level)

Tropical cyclone Dina, January 2002, northeast of Mauritius and Réunion, Indian Ocean.

poles features

CONNECTIONS

World climate and weather	12—13
World environment	14—15
Arctic reference map	166
Antarctica reference map	167
Oceans and poles statistics	168

poles **cross section of Arctic Ocean from northwest Canada to northwest Russia**

Elevation (m)

Canada · Beaufort Sea · Canadian Basin · Alpha Range · Amunsden Basin · North Pole · Nansen Basin · Barents Sea · Russian Federation

Arctic Circle · Arctic Circle

poles **cross section of West Antarctica from Ronne Ice Shelf to Ross Ice Shelf**

Elevation (m)

Weddell Sea · Ronne Ice Shelf · Ellsworth Mountains · Bentley Subglacial Trench · Roosevelt Island · Ross Ice Shelf · Ross Sea

Antarctica, frozen continent lying around the South Pole.

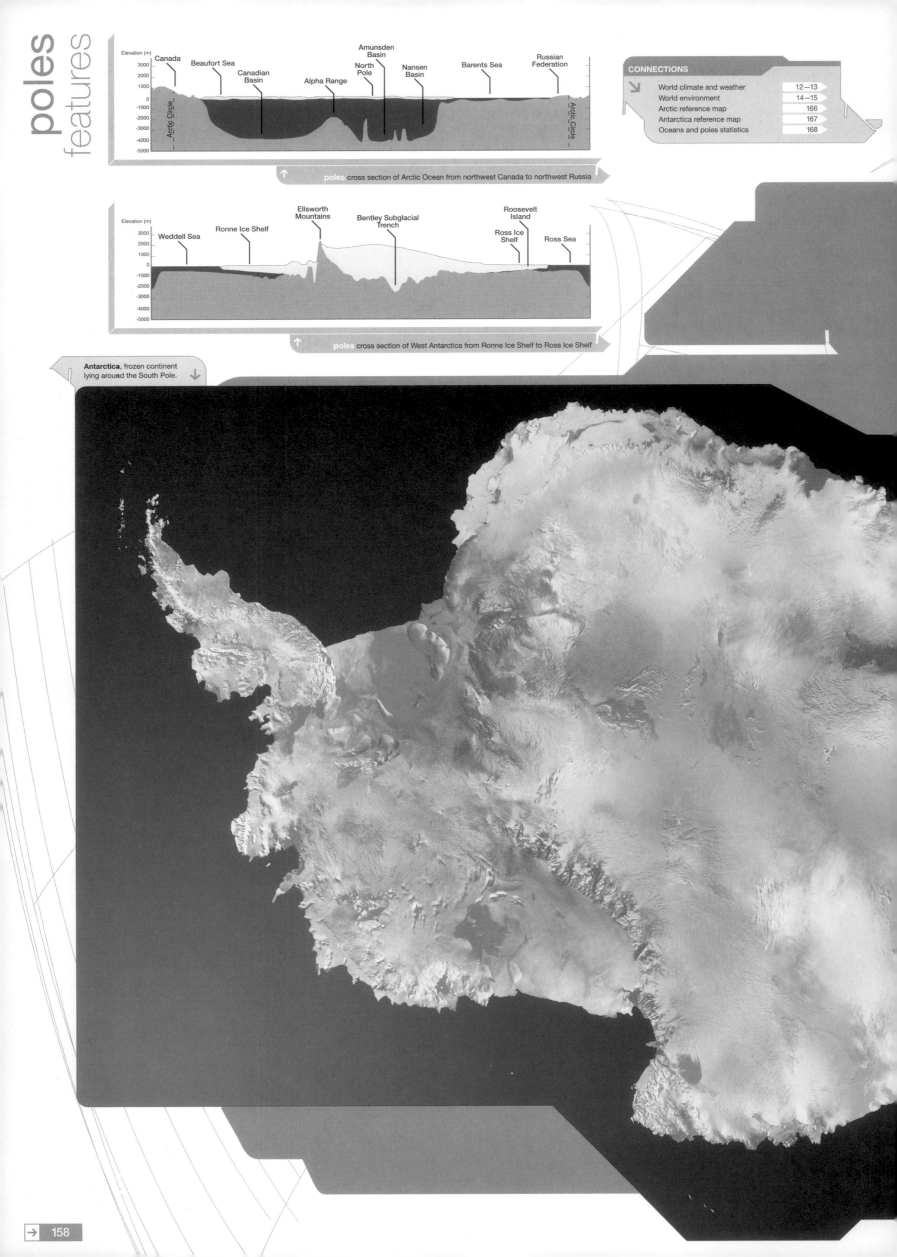

Dark blue area shows the **ozone hole** over Antarctica, September 2001.

February 2000 / Antarctica

September 2000 / Antarctica

February 2000 / Arctic Ocean

September 2000 / Arctic Ocean

<=12   16   24   32   40   48   56   64   72   80   88   >=95
Sea ice concentration (percentage)

Ice floes are pushed together forming an **ice pressure ridge**, Arctic Ocean.

Nentsy herders' winter camp, Russian Federation.

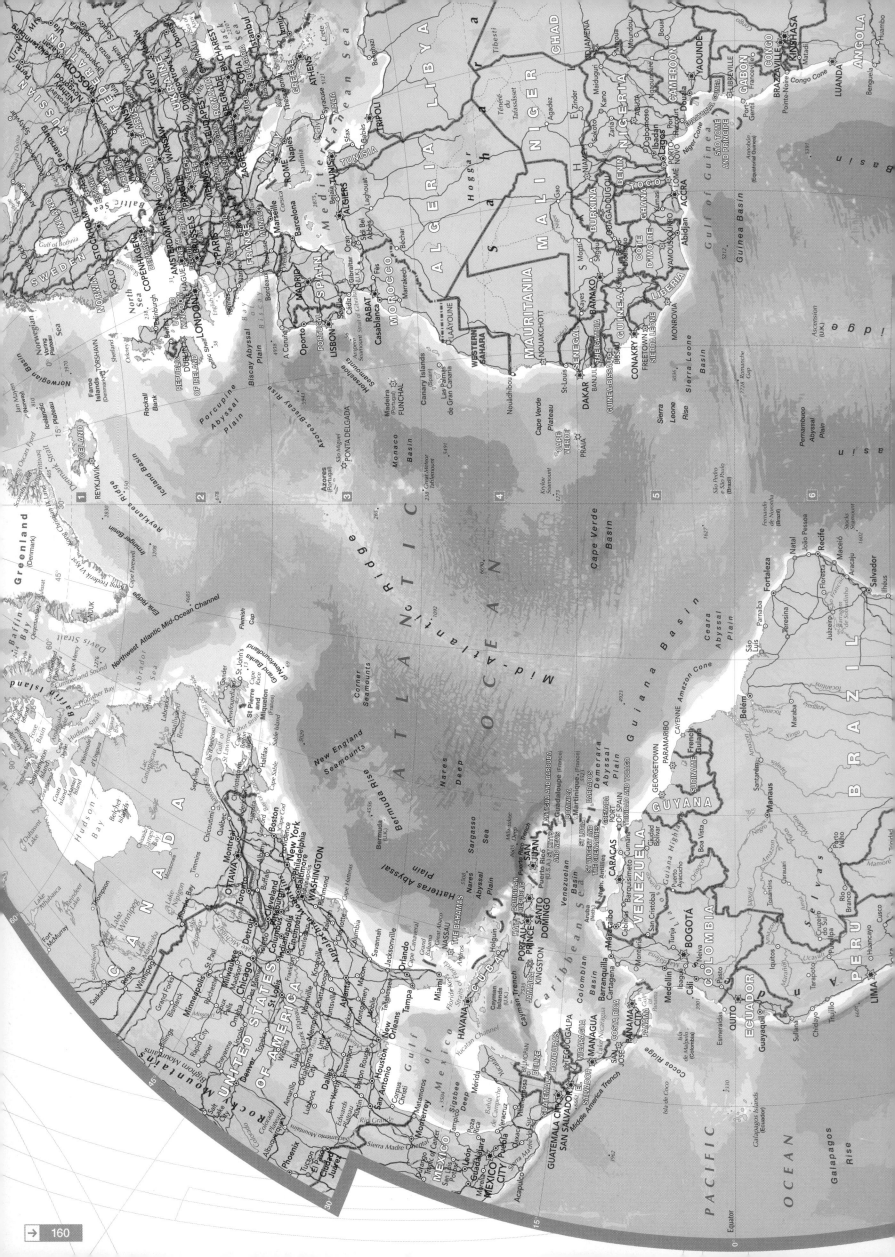

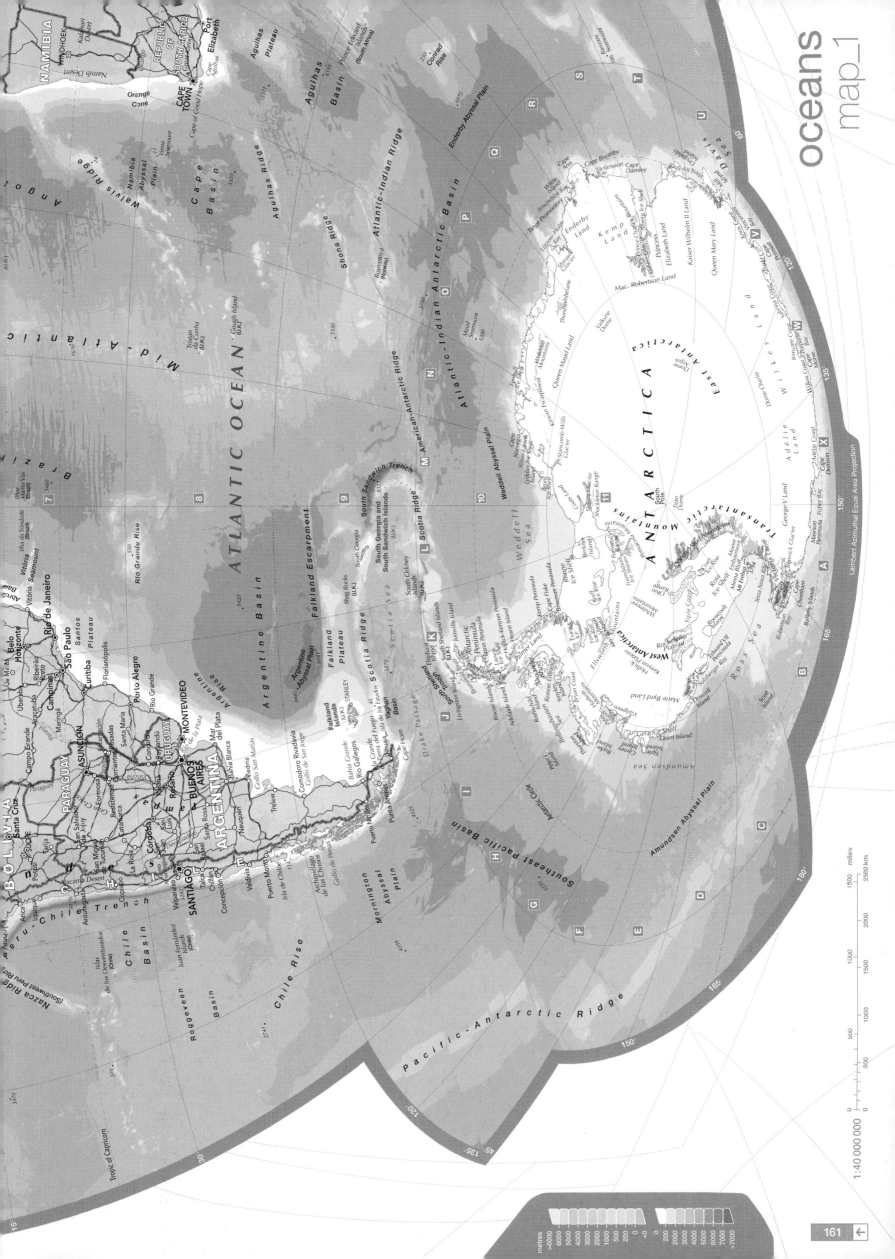

NAMIBIA

WINDHOEK

REPUBLIC
OF
SOUTH AFRICA

Port
Elizabeth

CAPE TOWN

Cape of Good Hope

Cape Agulhas

Namib Desert

Kalahari Desert

Orange
Cone

Agulhas
Plateau

Prince Edward
Islands
(South Africa)

Conrad
Rise

Agulhas
Basin

Agulhas Ridge

Cape
Basin

Namibia
Abyssal
Plain

Walvis Ridge

Angola

Atlantic-Indian Ridge

Atlantic-Indian-Antarctic Basin

Shona Ridge

Bouvetøya
(Norway)

Enderby Abyssal Plain

S

R

Q

P

O

N

American-Antarctic Ridge

Cape
Ann

Cape Boothby

Cape
Darnley

Enderby
Land

Kemp
Land

Mac. Robertson Land

Princess
Elizabeth Land

Kaiser Wilhelm II Land

Queen Mary Land

Queen Maud Land

Wohlthat
Mountains

T

U

V

W

Wilkes Land

East Antarctica

ANTARCTICA

ATLANTIC OCEAN

Mid-Atlantic Ridge

Brazil

Ilhas Martin Vas
(Brazil)

Ilha da Trindade
(Brazil)

7

8

9

10

11

Vitória
Seamount

Abrol

Rio de Janeiro

São Paulo

Santos
Plateau

Curitiba

Florianópolis

Porto Alegre

Rio Grande

Rio Grande Rise

Argentine
Basin

Falkland Escarpment

South Sandwich Trench

South Georgia

South Georgia and
South Sandwich Islands
(U.K.)

South Orkney
Islands
(U.K.)

Scotia Ridge

Weddell Abyssal Plain

Weddell
Sea

M

L

K

Transantarctic Mountains

South
Pole

Titan
Dome

Adélie
Land

Cape
Denison

X

Lambert Azimuthal Equal Area Projection

BOLIVIA

PARAGUAY

ASUNCIÓN

Santa Cruz

SUCRE

Campo Grande

URUGUAY

MONTEVIDEO

BUENOS
AIRES

ARGENTINA

Rosario

Córdoba

Mar del Plata

Bahía Blanca

Golfo San Matías

Golfo San Jorge

Comodoro Rivadavia

Trelew

Puerto Madryn

Rawson

Tierra del Fuego

Cape Horn

Drake Passage

Falkland
Islands
(U.K.)

STANLEY

Falkland
Plateau

Argentine
Abyssal Plain

Argentine
Rise

Yaghan
Basin

Scotia Sea

South Shetland Islands

Antarctic
Peninsula

Palmer Land

West Antarctica

Marie Byrd Land

Ellsworth Mountains

Ross Sea

Ross
Ice Shelf

Mt Erebus

A

B

C

D

E

F

G

H

I

J

Southeast Pacific Basin

Mornington
Abyssal
Plain

Antarctic Circle

Amundsen Abyssal Plain

Amundsen Sea

SANTIAGO

Valparaíso

Concepción

Chillán

Talca

Andes

CHILE

Atacama Desert

Antofagasta

Iquique

Arica

Peru-Chile Trench

Chile
Basin

Chile Rise

Roggeveen
Basin

Nazca Ridge
(Southwest Pacific Ridge)

Juan Fernández Islands
(Chile)

Islas de los Desventurados
(Chile)

Pacific-Antarctic Ridge

Tropic of Capricorn

15

30

45

60

120

135

150

165

180

1:40 000 000

0   500   1000   1500   2000   2500 km

0   500   1000   1500   miles

metres
>6000
6000
5000
4000
3000
2000
1000
500
200
0
0
200
2000
3000
4000
5000
6000
7000
>7000

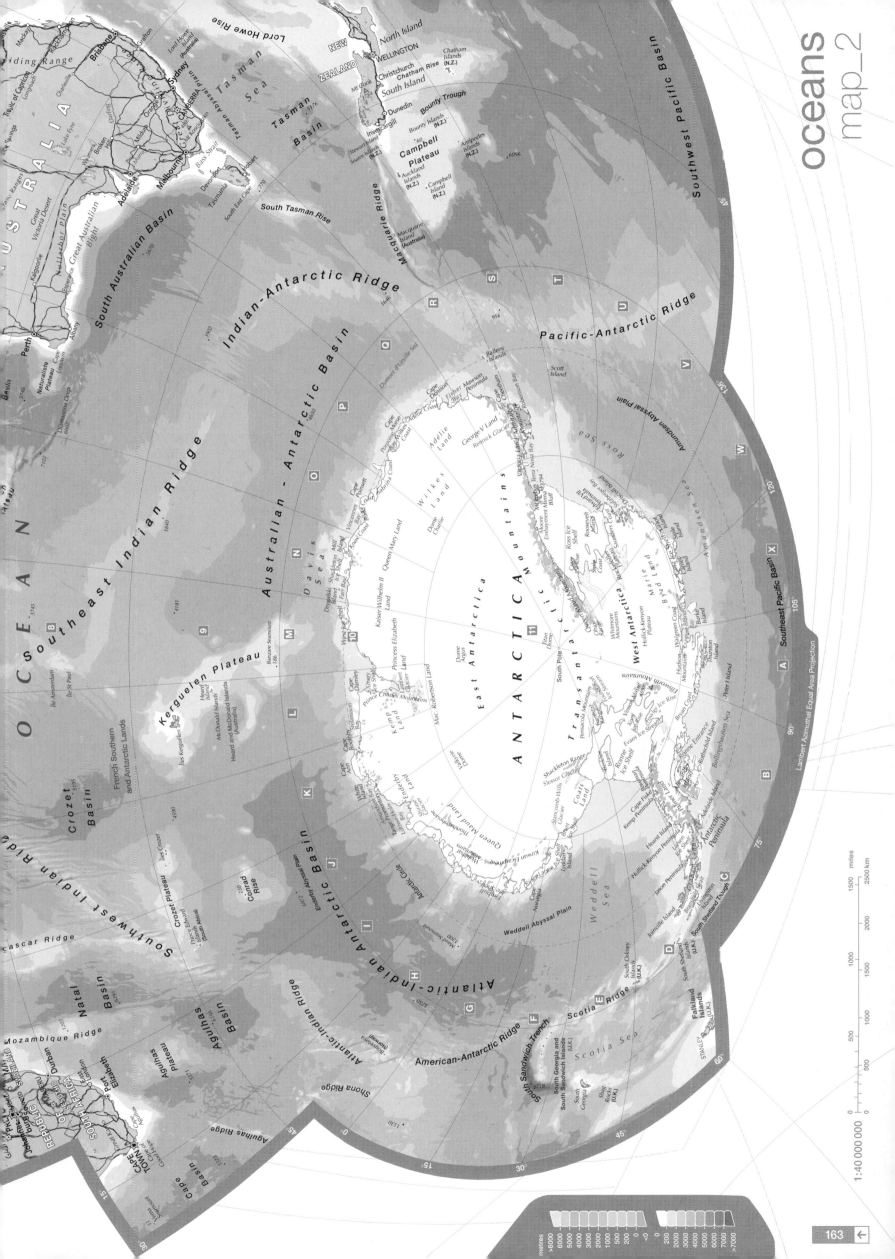

AUSTRALIA

Tropic of Capricorn

Brisbane

Lord Howe Rise

Sydney

CANBERRA

Melbourne

Adelaide

Tasman Sea

Tasman Basin

NEW ZEALAND

North Island

WELLINGTON

Christchurch

Chatham Rise (N.Z.)

Chatham Islands (N.Z.)

South Island

Mt Cook

Dunedin

Invercargill

Stewart Island

Bounty Trough

Bounty Islands (N.Z.)

Antipodes Islands (N.Z.)

Campbell Plateau

Auckland Islands (N.Z.)

Campbell Island (N.Z.)

Southwest Pacific Basin

South Australian Basin

South Tasman Rise

Macquarie Ridge

Macquarie Island (Australia)

Indian-Antarctic Ridge

Pacific-Antarctic Ridge

Ballery Islands

Scott Island

Amundsen Abyssal Plain

OCEAN

Southeast Indian Ridge

Naturaliste Plateau

Perth

Australian - Antarctic Basin

Dumont d'Urville Sea

Cape Denison

Fisher Masson Peninsula

Cape Adare

Robertson Bay

Ross Sea

Adélie Land

George V Land

Rennick Glacier

Victoria Land

Terra Nova Bay

Kerguelen Plateau

Banzare Seamount

Davis Sea

Wilkes Land

Dome Charlie

Mt Erebus

Ross Ice Shelf

Roosevelt Island

Marie Byrd Land

French Southern and Antarctic Lands

Îles Kerguelen

Heard Island

McDonald Islands

Heard and McDonald Islands (Australia)

Kaiser Wilhelm II Land

Queen Mary Land

East Antarctica

ANTARCTICA

Mountains

Dome Argus

South Pole

West Antarctica

Hollick-Kenyon Plateau

Whitmore Mountains

Ellsworth Mountains

Crozet Basin

Crozet Plateau

Île Crozet

Mac. Robertson Land

Prince Charles Mountains

Kemp Land

Lambert Glacier

Transantarctic

Shackleton Range

Coats Land

Southwest Indian Ridge

Conrad Rise

Enderby Abyssal Plain

Enderby Land

Queen Maud Land

Thorshavnheiane Mountains

Slessor Glacier

Ronne Ice Shelf

Filchner Ice Shelf

Bellingshausen Sea

Antarctic Peninsula

Natal Basin

Mozambique Ridge

Atlantic-Indian Antarctic Basin

Atlantic-Indian Ridge

Antarctic Circle

Weddell Sea

Weddell Abyssal Plain

Peter I Island

SOUTH AFRICA

Agulhas Basin

Agulhas Plateau

Cape Basin

Port Elizabeth

Durban

Agulhas Ridge

Shona Ridge

American-Antarctic Ridge

South Sandwich Trench

Scotia Ridge

Scotia Sea

South Georgia and South Sandwich Islands (U.K.)

South Georgia (U.K.)

Falkland Islands (U.K.)

STANLEY

South Orkney Islands

South Shetland Islands

Joinville Island

1:40 000 000

Lambert Azimuthal Equal Area Projection

miles

km

metres
>6000
6000
5000
4000
3000
2000
1000
500
200
0
>0
0
200
2000
3000
4000
5000
6000
7000
>7000

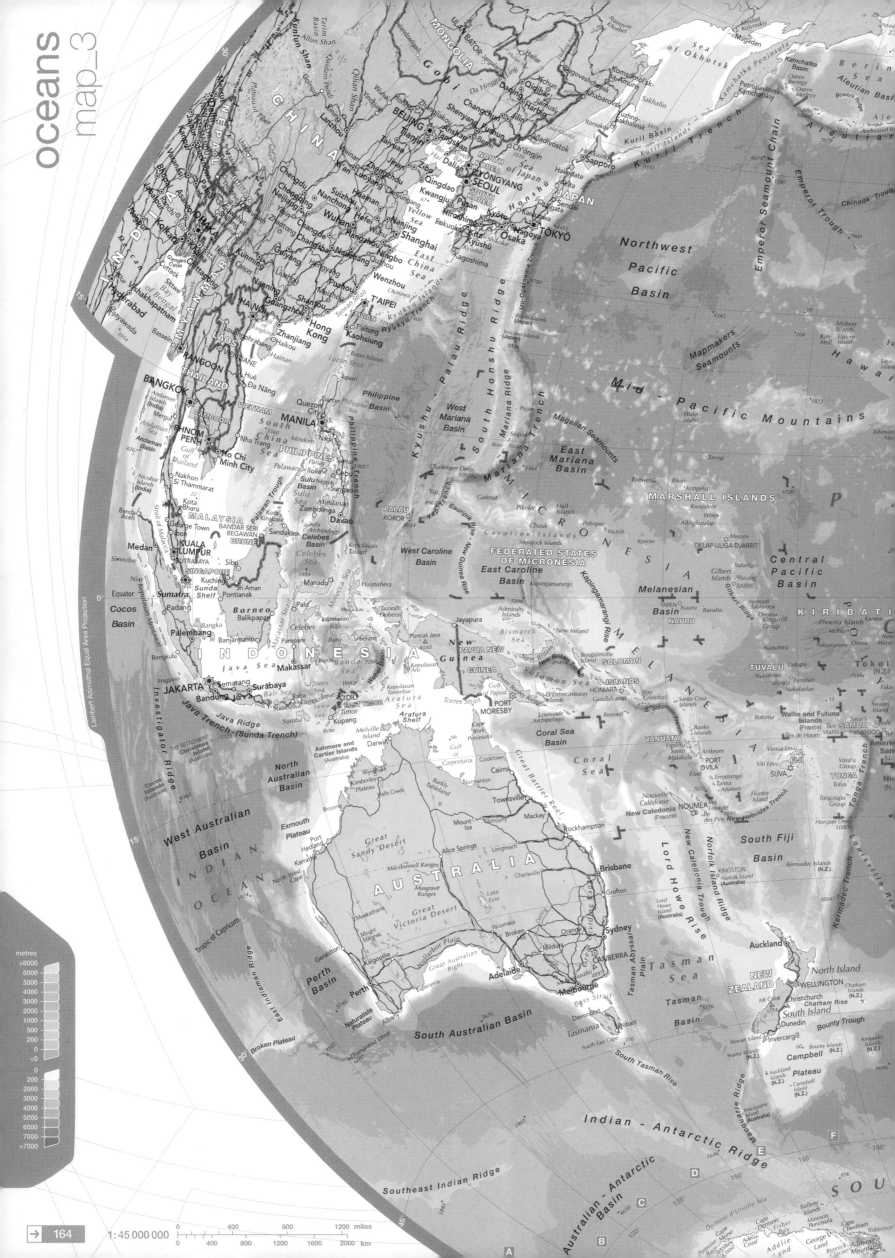

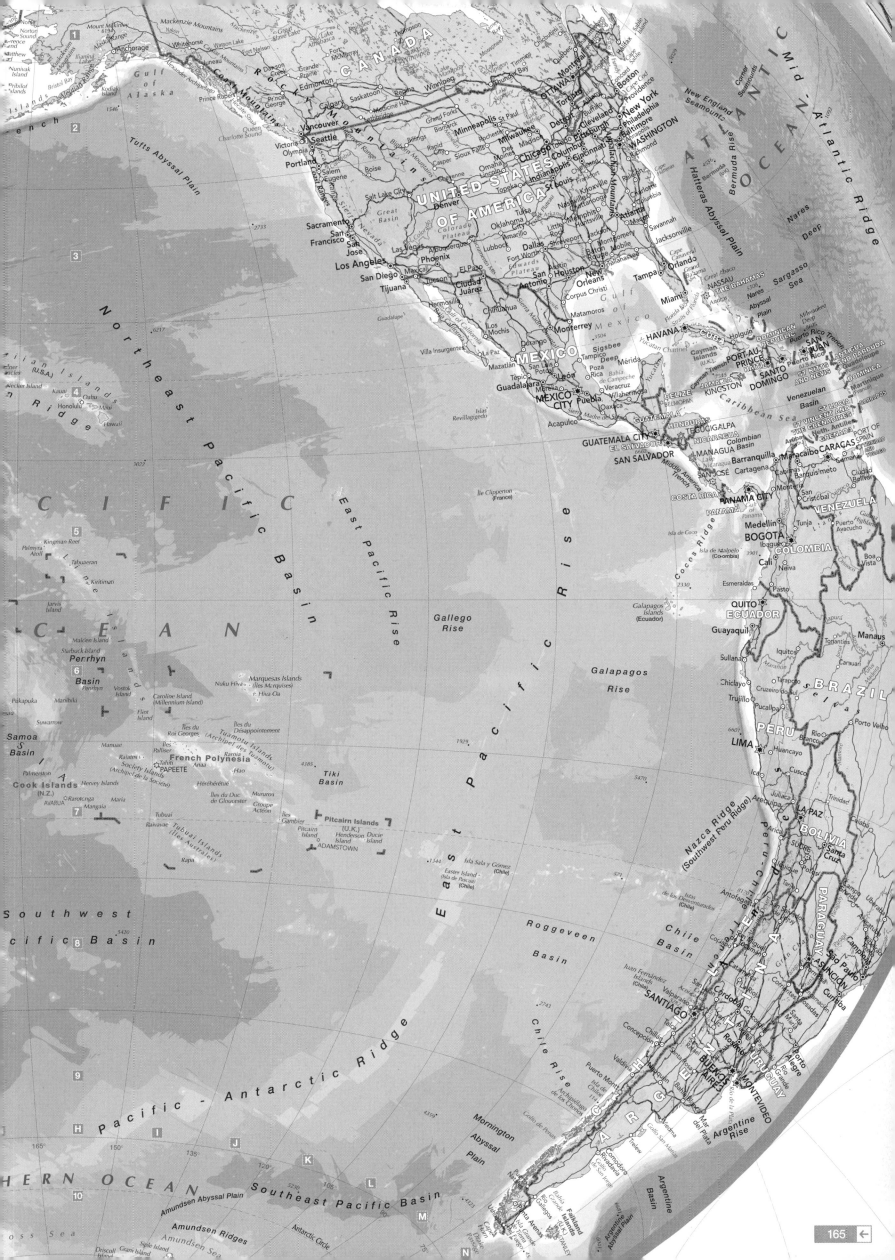

1:26 000 000

metres
>6000
6000
5000
4000
3000
2000
1000
500
0
0
500
1000
2000
3000
4000
5000
6000
7000
>7000

Polar Stereographic Projection

0   200   400   600   800   1000 miles
0 200 400 600 800 1000 1200 1400 1600 km

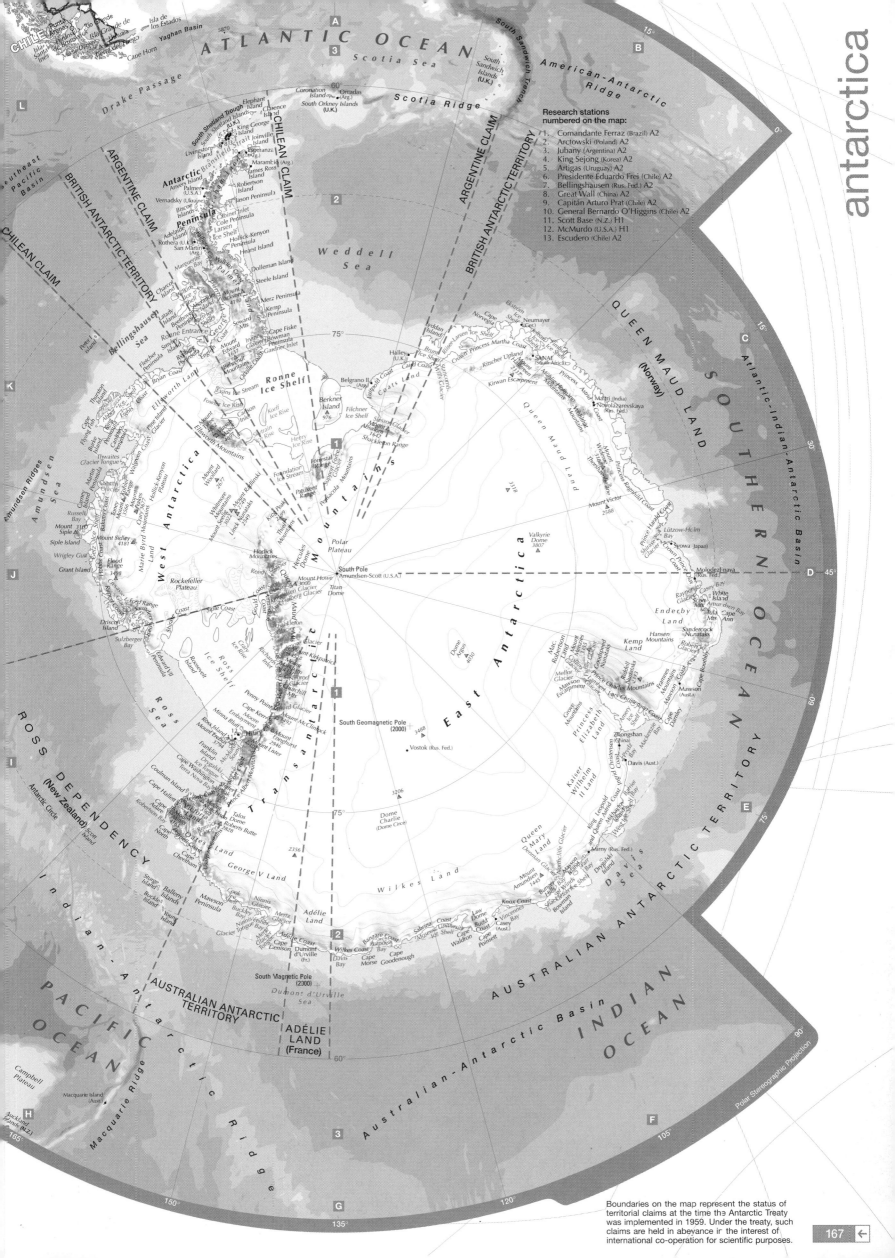

**Research stations
numbered on the map:**

1. Comandante Ferraz (Brazil) A2
2. Arctowski (Poland) A2
3. Jubany (Argentina) A2
4. King Sejong (Korea) A2
5. Artigas (Uruguay) A2
6. Presidente Eduardo Frei (Chile) A2
7. Bellingshausen (Rus. Fed.) A2
8. Great Wall (China) A2
9. Capitán Arturo Prat (Chile) A2
10. General Bernardo O'Higgins (Chile) A2
11. Scott Base (N.Z.) H1
12. McMurdo (U.S.A.) H1
13. Escudero (Chile) A2

Boundaries on the map represent the status of
territorial claims at the time the Antarctic Treaty
was implemented in 1959. Under the treaty, such
claims are held in abeyance in the interest of
international co-operation for scientific purposes.

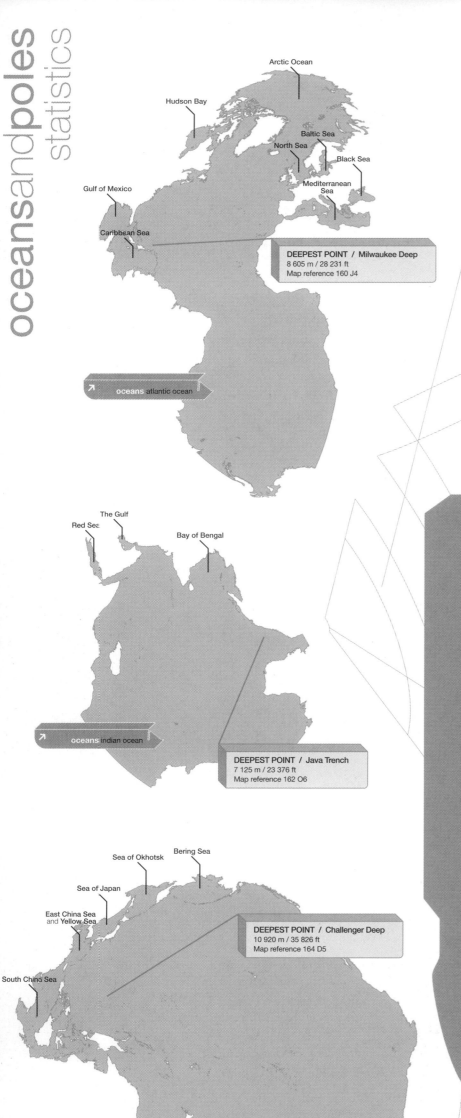

Arctic Ocean

Hudson Bay

Baltic Sea

North Sea

Black Sea

Mediterranean Sea

Gulf of Mexico

Caribbean Sea

DEEPEST POINT / Milwaukee Deep
8 605 m / 28 231 ft
Map reference 160 J4

oceans atlantic ocean

The Gulf

Red Sea

Bay of Bengal

oceans indian ocean

DEEPEST POINT / Java Trench
7 125 m / 23 376 ft
Map reference 162 O6

Sea of Okhotsk

Bering Sea

Sea of Japan

East China Sea and Yellow Sea

DEEPEST POINT / Challenger Deep
10 920 m / 35 826 ft
Map reference 164 D5

South China Sea

oceans pacific ocean

ANTARCTICA		
HIGHEST MOUNTAINS	metres	feet
Vinson Massif	4 897	16 066
Mt Tyree	4 852	15 918
Mt Kirkpatrick	4 528	14 855
Mt Markham	4 351	14 275
Mt Jackson	4 190	13 747
Mt Sidley	4 181	13 717
AREA	sq km	sq miles
Total land area (excluding ice shelves)	12 093 000	4 669 292
Ice shelves	1 559 000	601 954
Exposed rock	49 000	18 920
HEIGHTS	metres	feet
Lowest bedrock elevation (Bentley Subglacial Trench)	-2 496	-8 189
Maximum ice thickness (Astrolabe Subglacial Basin)	4 776	15 669
Mean ice thickness (including ice shelves)	1 859	6 099
VOLUME	cubic km	cubic miles
Ice sheet (including ice shelves)	25 400 000	10 160 000
CLIMATE	°C	°F
Lowest screen temperature (Vostok Station, 21st July 1983)	-89.2	-128.6
Coldest place – Annual mean (Plateau Station)	-56.6	-69.9

ATLANTIC OCEAN	area sq km	area sq miles	maximum depth metres	feet
Atlantic Ocean	86 557 000	33 420 000	8 605	28 231
Arctic Ocean	9 485 000	3 662 000	5 450	17 880
Caribbean Sea	2 512 000	970 000	7 680	25 196
Mediterranean Sea	2 510 000	969 000	5 121	16 800
Gulf of Mexico	1 544 000	596 000	3 504	11 495
Hudson Bay	1 233 000	476 000	259	849
North Sea	575 000	222 000	661	2 168
Black Sea	508 000	196 000	2 245	7 365
Baltic Sea	382 000	147 000	460	1 509

INDIAN OCEAN	area sq km	area sq miles	maximum depth metres	feet
Indian Ocean	73 427 000	28 350 000	7 125	23 376
Bay of Benga	2 172 000	839 000	4 500	14 763
Red Sea	453 000	175 000	3 040	9 973
The Gulf	238 000	92 000	73	239

PACIFIC OCEAN	area sq km	area sq miles	maximum depth metres	feet
Pacific Ocean	166 241 000	64 186 000	10 920	35 826
South China Sea	2 590 000	1 000 000	5 514	18 090
Bering Sea	2 261 000	873 000	4 150	13 615
Sea of Okhotsk (Okhotskoye More)	1 392 000	537 000	3 363	11 033
East China Sea (Dong Hai) and Yellow Sea (Huang Hai)	1 202 000	464 000	2 717	8 913
Sea of Japan (East Sea)	1 013 000	391 000	3 743	12 280

Aurora borealis (northern lights), Alaska, USA

Vortex cloud patterns, Isla Socorro, Pacific Ocean

Larsen Ice Shelf, Antarctica

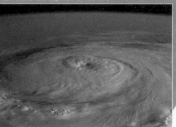

Hurricane Elena, Gulf of Mexico

introduction to the index

The index includes all names shown on the reference maps in the atlas. Each entry includes the country or geographical area in which the feature is located, a page number and an alphanumeric reference. Additional entry details and aspects of the index are explained below.

Name forms
The names policy in this atlas is generally to use local name forms which are officially recognized by the governments of the countries concerned. Rules established by the Permanent Committee on Geographical Names for British Official Use (PCGN) are applied to the conversion of non-roman alphabet names, for example in the Russian Federation, into the roman alphabet used in English.

However, English conventional name forms are used for the most well-known places for which such a form is in common use. In these cases, the local form is included in brackets on the map and appears as a cross-reference in the index. Other alternative names, such as well-known historical names or those in other languages, may also be included in brackets on the map and as cross-references in the index. All country names and those for international physical features appear in their English forms. Names appear in full in the index, although they may appear in abbreviated form on the maps.

Referencing
Names are referenced by page number and by grid reference. The grid reference relates to the alphanumeric values which appear in the margin of each map. These reflect the graticule on the map – the letter relates to longitude divisions, the number to latitude divisions.

Names are generally referenced to the largest scale map page on which they appear. For large geographical features, including countries, the reference is to the largest scale map on which the feature appears in its entirety, or on which the majority of it appears.

Rivers are referenced to their lowest downstream point – either their mouth or their confluence with another river. The river name will generally be positioned as close to this point as possible.

Alternative names
Alternative names appear as cross-references and refer the user to the index entry for the form of the name used on the map.

For rivers with multiple names - for example those which flow through several countries - all alternative name forms are included within the main index entries, with details of the countries in which each form applies.

Administrative qualifiers
Administrative divisions are included in entries to differentiate duplicate names - entries of exactly the same name and feature type within the one country - where these division names are shown on the maps. In such cases, duplicate names are alphabetized in the order of the administrative division names.

Additional qualifiers are included for names within selected geographical areas, to indicate more clearly their location.

Descriptors
Entries, other than those for towns and cities, include a descriptor indicating the type of geographical feature. Descriptors are not included where the type of feature is implicit in the name itself, unless there is a town or city of exactly the same name.

Insets
Where relevant, the index clearly indicates [inset] if a feature appears on an inset map.

Alphabetical order
The Icelandic characters Þ and þ are transliterated and alphabetized as 'Th' and 'th'. The German character ß is alphabetized as 'ss'. Names beginning with Mac or Mc are alphabetized exactly as they appear. The terms Saint, Sainte, etc. are abbreviated to St, Ste, etc. but alphabetized as if in the full form.

Numerical entries
Entries beginning with numerals appear at the beginning of the index, in numerical order. Elsewhere, numerals are alphabetized before 'a'.

Permuted terms
Names beginning with generic geographical terms are permuted - the descriptive term is placed after, and the index alphabetized by, the main part of the name. For example, Mount Everest is indexed as Everest, Mount; Lake Superior as Superior, Lake. This policy is applied to all languages. Permuting has not been applied to names of towns, cities or administrative divisions beginning with such geographical terms. These remain in their full form, for example, Lake Isabella, USA.

Gazetteer entries and connections
Selected entries have been extended to include gazetteer-style information. Important geographical facts which relate specifically to the entry are included within the entry in coloured type.

Entries for features which also appear on, or which have a topical link to, the thematic pages of the atlas include a reference to those pages.

abbreviations

admin. dist.	administrative district	IA	Iowa	plat.	plateau
admin. div.	administrative division	ID	Idaho	P.N.G.	Papua New Guinea
admin. reg.	administrative region	IL	Illinois	Port.	Portugal
Afgh.	Afghanistan	imp. l.	impermanent lake	pref.	prefecture
AK	Alaska	IN	Indiana	prov.	province
AL	Alabama	Indon.	Indonesia	pt	point
Alg.	Algeria	Kazakh.	Kazakhstan	Qld	Queensland
AR	Arkansas	KS	Kansas	Que.	Québec
Arg.	Argentina	KY	Kentucky	r.	river
aut. comm.	autonomous community	Kyrg.	Kyrgyzstan	reg.	region
aut. div.	autonomous division	l.	lake	res.	reserve
aut. reg.	autonomous region	LA	Louisiana	resr	reservoir
aut. rep.	autonomous republic	lag.	lagoon	RI	Rhode Island
AZ	Arizona	Lith.	Lithuania	Rus. Fed.	Russian Federation
Azer.	Azerbaijan	Lux.	Luxembourg	S.	South, Southern
b.	bay	MA	Massachusetts	S.A.	South Australia
Bangl.	Bangladesh	Madag.	Madagascar	salt l.	salt lake
B.C.	British Columbia	Man.	Manitoba	Sask.	Saskatchewan
Bol.	Bolivia	MD	Maryland	SC	South Carolina
Bos.-Herz.	Bosnia-Herzegovina	ME	Maine	SD	South Dakota
Bulg.	Bulgaria	Mex.	Mexico	sea chan.	sea channel
c.	cape	MI	Michigan	Sing.	Singapore
CA	California	MN	Minnesota	Switz.	Switzerland
Cent. Afr. Rep.	Central African Republic	MO	Missouri	Tajik.	Tajikistan
CO	Colorado	Moz.	Mozambique	Tanz.	Tanzania
Col.	Colombia	MS	Mississippi	Tas.	Tasmania
CT	Connecticut	MT	Montana	terr.	territory
Czech Rep.	Czech Republic	mt.	mountain	Thai.	Thailand
DC	District of Columbia	mts	mountains	TN	Tennessee
DE	Delaware	N.	North, Northern	Trin. and Tob.	Trinidad and Tobago
Dem. Rep. Congo	Democratic Republic of Congo	nat. park	national park	Turkm.	Turkmenistan
depr.	depression	N.B.	New Brunswick	TX	Texas
dept	department	NC	North Carolina	U.A.E.	United Arab Emirates
des.	desert	ND	North Dakota	U.K.	United Kingdom
Dom. Rep.	Dominican Republic	NE	Nebraska	Ukr.	Ukraine
E.	East, Eastern	Neth.	Netherlands	U.S.A.	United States of America
Equat. Guinea	Equatorial Guinea	NH	New Hampshire	UT	Utah
esc.	escarpment	NJ	New Jersey	Uzbek.	Uzbekistan
est.	estuary	NM	New Mexico	VA	Virginia
Eth.	Ethiopia	N.S.	Nova Scotia	Venez.	Venezuela
Fin.	Finland	N.S.W.	New South Wales	Vic.	Victoria
FL	Florida	N.T.	Northern Territory	vol.	volcano
for.	forest	NV	Nevada	vol. crater	volcanic crater
Fr. Guiana	French Guiana	N.W.T.	Northwest Territories	VT	Vermont
F.Y.R.O.M.	Former Yugoslav Republic of Macedonia	NY	New York	W.	West, Western
g.	gulf	N.Z.	New Zealand	WA	Washington
GA	Georgia	OH	Ohio	W.A.	Western Australia
Guat.	Guatemala	OK	Oklahoma	WI	Wisconsin
HI	Hawaii	OR	Oregon	WV	West Virginia
H.K.	Hong Kong	PA	Pennsylvania	WY	Wyoming
Hond.	Honduras	P.E.I.	Prince Edward Island	Y.T.	Yukon Territory
i.	island	pen.	peninsula	Yugo.	Yugoslavia

↓ 1

1st Cataract rapids Egypt 89 G3
2nd Cataract rapids Sudan 89 F4
3rd Cataract rapids Sudan 89 F5
5th Cataract rapids Sudan 89 G5
4th Cataract rapids Sudan 89 G5
9 de Julio Arg. 152 E3
25 de Mayo Buenos Aires Arg. 152 E3
25 de Mayo La Pampa Arg. 152 D4
25 de Mayo Mendoza Arg. 152 C3
26 Bakı Komissarı Azer. 79 G3
70 Mile House Canada 122 F5
100 Mile House Canada 122 F5
150 Mile House Canada 122 F4

↓ A

Aabenraa Denmark see Åbenrå
Aachen Germany 36 C3
Aalborg Denmark see Ålborg
Aalen Germany 36 E4
Aalesund Norway see Ålesund
Aaley Lebanon see 'Āley
Aalst Belgium 39 F1
Aanaar Fin. see Inari
Äänekoski Fin. 32 G3
Aarau Switz. 39 H3
Aarberg Switz. 39 G3
Aarhus Denmark see Århus
Aarlen Belgium see Arlon
Aarschot Belgium 39 F1
Aasiaat Greenland 121 N3
Aath Belgium see Ath
Aavasaksa Fin. 32 F2
Aba China 66 B1
Aba Dem. Rep. Congo 96 A4
Aba Nigeria 93 G4
Abā ad Dūd Saudi Arabia 89 J3
Abā al Afan oasis Saudi Arabia 76 E6
Abacaxis r. Brazil 147 G6
Abadan Iran see Ābādān
Ābādān Iran 80 B4
Ābādeh Iran 80 C4
Ābādeh Ṭashk Iran 80 C4
Abadla Alg. 90 E3
Abádszalók Hungary 37 J5
Abaetetuba Brazil 150 B2
Abagnar Qi China see Xilinhot
Abai Para. 149 G6
Abaiang atoll Kiribati 164 F5
A Baiuca Spain 42 B1
Abaji Nigeria 93 G3
Abajo Peak U.S.A. 137 H3
Abakaliki Nigeria 93 H4
Abakan Rus. Fed. 62 E1
Abala Congo 94 B5
Abala Niger 93 F2
Abalak Niger 93 G2
Abana Turkey 78 C2
Abancay Peru 148 B3
Abanga r. Gabon 94 A5
Abarqū Iran 80 C4
Abarshahr Iran see Neyshābūr
Abashiri Japan 64 F3
Abashiri-wan b. Japan 64 F3
Abasula waterhole Kenya 96 C5
Abau P.N.G. 106 D3
Abaya, Lake Eth. 96 C3
Abaya Hāyk' Eth. see Abaya, Lake
Ābay Wenz r. Eth./Sudan 76 B7 see Blue Nile
Abaza Rus. Fed. 62 E1
Abba Cent. Afr. Rep. 94 B3
Abbadia San Salvatore Italy 44 C3
Abbāsābād Iran 80 D3
Abbasanta Sardinia Italy 45 B4
Abbatis Villa France see Abbeville
Abbe, Lake Djibouti/Eth. 96 D2
Abbeville France 38 D1
Abbeville GA U.S.A. 129 C6
Abbeville LA U.S.A. 133 C6
Abbeville SC U.S.A. 129 C5
Abbey Canada 123 I5
Abbeyfeale Rep. of Ireland 35 B5
Abbiategrasso Italy 44 B2
Abborrträsk Sweden 32 E2
Abbot Ice Shelf Antarctica 167 K2
Abbotsford Canada 134 B2
Abbotsford U.S.A. 132 D2
Abbott NM U.S.A. 135 F5
Abbott VA U.S.A. 130 C5
Abbott WV U.S.A. 130 C4
Abbottabad Pak. 81 H3
'Abd al 'Azīz, Jabal hill Syria 79 E3
'Abd al Kūrī i. Yemen 76 E7
'Abd Allah, Khawr sea chan Iraq/Kuwait 79 G5
Abd al Ma'asīr well Saudi Arabia 77 D4
Ābdānān Iran 80 A3
Abdollāhābād Iran 80 D2
Abdulino Rus. Fed. 29 J5
Abéché Chad 88 D6
Abejukolo Nigeria 93 G4
Abelbod well Mali 93 E1
Abellinum Italy see Avellino
Abel Tasman National Park N.Z. 113 C3
Abengourou Côte d'Ivoire 92 E4
Abenójar Spain 42 D3
Åbenrå Denmark 33 C5
Abensberg Germany 36 E4
Abeokuta Nigeria 93 F4
Abera Eth. 96 B3
Aberaeron U.K. 35 D5
Abercorn Zambia see Mbala
Aberdare U.K. 35 E6
Aberdare National Park Kenya 96 C5
Aberdaron U.K. 35 D5
Aberdaugleddau U.K. see Milford Haven
Aberdeen Australia 112 D4
Aberdeen Hong Kong China 67 [inset]
Aberdeen S. Africa 98 E7
Aberdeen U.K. 34 E3
Aberdeen MD U.S.A. 131 E4
Aberdeen MS U.S.A. 129 A5
Aberdeen SD U.S.A. 132 B2
Aberdeen WA U.S.A. 134 B3
Aberdeen Lake Canada 123 L1
Aberfeldy U.K. 34 E3
Aberfoyle U.K. 34 D3
Abergavenny U.K. 35 E6
Abergwaun U.K. see Fishguard
Aberhonddu U.K. see Brecon
Abermaw U.K. see Barmouth
Abertawe U.K. see Swansea
Aberteifi U.K. see Cardigan
Aberystwyth U.K. 35 D5
Abeshr Chad see Abéché
Abez' Rus. Fed. 28 L2
Abhā Saudi Arabia 89 I5
Abhar Iran 80 B2
Abhar Rūd r. Iran 80 B3
Abia state Nigeria 93 G4
Abiad, Bahr el r. Sudan/Uganda 96 B2 see White Nile
Ābiata Hāyk' l. Eth. 96 C3
Ab-i-Bazuft r. Iran 80 B4
Abibe, Serranía de mts Col. 146 B2

▶Abidjan Côte d'Ivoire 92 D4
Former capital of Côte d'Ivoire. 4th most populous city in Africa.
africa 86–87
world 16–17

Ab-i-Istada l. Afgh. 81 G3
Abijatta-Shalla National Park Eth. 96 C3
Ab-i-Kavīr salt flat Iran 80 D3
Abilene KS U.S.A. 132 B4
Abilene TX U.S.A. 133 B5
Abingdon U.S.A. 130 B5
Abington U.S.A. 131 H2
Abington Reef Australia 111 G3
Abinsk Rus. Fed. 29 F7
Ab-i-Panja r. Afgh./Tajik. see Pyandzh
Ab-i-Safed r. Afgh. 81 F2
Abiseo, Parque Nacional nat. park Peru 148 A1
Abisko nationalpark nat. park Sweden 32 E1
Abitibi r. Canada 124 D3
Abitibi, Lake Canada 124 D3
Āb Naft r. Iraq 79 F4
Abnūb Egypt 89 F3
Åbo Fin. see Turku
Abohar India 74 B3
Aboisso Côte d'Ivoire 92 E4
Aboke Sudan 96 B2
Abomey Benin 93 F4
Abongabong, Gunung mt. Indon. 58 B1
Abong Mbang Cameroon 93 I5
Abou Déia Chad 94 C2
Abou Goulem Chad 88 D6
Abqaiq Saudi Arabia 76 D4
Abra, Lago del l. Arg. 152 E5
Abraka Nigeria 93 G4
Abra Pampa Arg. 148 D5
'Abri Sudan 89 F4
Abrolhos Bank sea feature S. Atlantic Ocean 161 L7
Abrud Romania 46 C1
Abruzzi admin. reg. Italy see Abruzzo
Abruzzo admin. reg. Italy 44 D3
Abruzzo, Parco Nazionale d' nat. park Italy 44 D4
'Abs Yemen 89 I5
Absalom, Mount Antarctica 167 B1
Absaroka Range mts U.S.A. 134 E3
Absecon U.S.A. 131 F4
Abşeron Yarımadası pen. Azer. 79 G2
Abtar, Jabal al hills Syria 77 C2
Abū ad Ḍuhūr Syria 77 C2
Abū al Ḥusayn, Qā' imp. l. Jordan 77 D3
Abū 'Alī i. Saudi Arabia 80 B5
Abū al Jirab i. U.A.E. 80 C5
Abū 'Āmūd, Wādī watercourse Jordan 77 C4
Abū 'Arīsh Saudi Arabia 89 I5
Abū Ballāṣ hill Egypt 89 E3
Abu Deleiq Sudan 89 G6

▶Abu Dhabi U.A.E. 80 C5
Capital of the United Arab Emirates.

Abu Gabra Sudan 94 E2
Abu Gubeiha Sudan 96 A2
Abū Ḥafnah, Wādī watercourse Jordan 77 D3
Abū Ḥallūfah, Jabal hill Jordan 77 C4
Abu Hamed Sudan 89 G5
Abu Haraz Sudan 89 G5
Abu Hashim Sudan 89 G5
Abu Higar Sudan 89 G6

▶Abuja Nigeria 93 G3
Capital of Nigeria.

Abū Kamāl Syria 79 E4
Abū Kammāsh Libya 88 A1
Abu La'ot watercourse Sudan 89 F6
Abū Latt Island Saudi Arabia 89 I5
Abū Madd, Ra's hd Saudi Arabia 89 H3
Abu Matariq Sudan 94 E2
Abu Mena tourist site Egypt 78 B5
Abu Mena tourist site Egypt 89 F2
Abumombazi Dem. Rep. Congo 94 D4
Abū Mūsá i. The Gulf 80 C5
Abū Mūsá, Jazīreh-ye i. The Gulf see Abu Musa
Abunã r. Bol. 148 D2
Abunã Brazil 148 D2
Abunai Brazil 146 E5
Abune Yosēf mt. Eth. 96 C1
Abū Nā'im well Libya 88 C2
Abū Nujaym Libya 88 B2
Abū Qīr, Khalīj b. Egypt 78 B5
Abū Qurīn Libya 88 B2
Abū Rawthah, Jabal mt. Egypt 77 B5
Aburo mt. Dem. Rep. Congo 96 A4
Abu Road India 74 B4
Abū Rubayq Saudi Arabia 89 H4
Abū Rujmayn, Jabal mts Syria 77 D2
Abū Sawādah well Saudi Arabia 80 B5
Abu Shagara, Ras pt Sudan 89 H4
Abu Simbel Temple tourist site Egypt 89 F4
Abū Şukhayr Iraq 79 F5
Abū Sunbul Egypt 89 F4
Abū Tabaq well Sudan 76 A5
Abū Ṭarfā', Wādī watercourse Egypt 77 A5
Abut Head N.Z. 113 B3
Abū Ṭuyūr, Jabal mt. Egypt 89 G3
Abū 'Uwayqilah well Egypt 77 B4
Abuye Meda mt. Eth. 96 C2
Abu Zabad Sudan 89 F6
Abū Ẓabī U.A.E. see Abu Dhabi
Abū Zanīmah Egypt 89 G2
Abwong Sudan 96 B2
Åby Sweden 33 E4
Abyad Sudan 89 E6
Abyaḍ, Jabal al mts Syria 77 C2
Abyār al Hakīm well Libya 88 D2
Abyār an Nakhīlan well Libya 88 D2
Abydos Australia 108 B5
Abyei Sudan 94 F2
Abyssinia country Africa see Ethiopia
Acacias Col. 146 C4
Acadia prov. Canada see Nova Scotia
Acadia National Park U.S.A. 131 I1
Açailândia Brazil 150 C3
Acamarachi mt. Chile see Pili, Cerro
Acampamento de Caça do Mucusso Angola 95 D9
Acandí Col. 146 B2
Acaponeta Mex. 126 E7
Acapulco Mex. 138 E5
Acapulco de Juárez Mex. see Acapulco
Acará Brazil 150 B2
Acará r. Brazil 150 B2
Acará Mirí r. Brazil 150 B2
Acaraú Brazil 150 D2
Acaraú r. Brazil 150 D2
Acaray, Represa de resr Para. 149 G6
Acarí Peru 148 B3
Acarí r. Peru 148 B3
Acari, Serra hills Brazil/Guyana 147 G4
Acarigua Venez. 146 D2
Acatlan Mex. 138 E5
Accho Israel see 'Akko
Accomac U.S.A. 128 E4
Accomack U.S.A. see Accomac

▶Accra Ghana 93 E4
Capital of Ghana.

Aceguá Brazil 152 G2
Aceh admin. dist. Indon. 58 B1
Achacachi Bol. 148 C4
Achaguas Venez. 146 D3
Achalpur India 74 C5
Achampet India 72 C2
Achan Rus. Fed. 64 D2
Achanta India 73 D2
Achayvayam Rus. Fed. 27 R3
Acheh admin. dist. Indon. see Aceh
Achemelmel well Mali 91 F5
Achemmim well Mauritania 92 D1
Acheng China 64 A3
Achern Germany 36 D4
Achhota India 72 D1
Achikulak Rus. Fed. 79 F1
Achill Island Rep. of Ireland 35 A5
Achim Germany 36 D2
Achin admin. dist. Indon. see Aceh
Achinsk Rus. Fed. 27 J4
Achit Rus. Fed. 28 K4
Achkhoy-Martan Rus. Fed. 79 F2
Achnasheen U.K. 34 D3
Aci Castello Sicily Italy 45 E6
Acıgöl l. Turkey 78 B3
Acıpayam Turkey 78 B3
Acireale Sicily Italy 45 E6
Ackerman U.S.A. 129 A5
Acklins Island Bahamas 127 L7
Acobamba Peru 148 B2
Acomayo Cusco Peru 148 C3
Acomayo Huánuco Peru 148 A2

▶Aconcagua, Cerro mt. Arg. 152 C3
Highest mountain in South America.
southamerica 142–143

Acopiara Brazil 150 E3
Acora Peru 148 C3
A Coruña Spain 42 B1
Acostambo Peru 148 B3
Acquapendente Italy 44 C3
Acqui Terme Italy 44 B2
Acragas Sicily Italy see Agrigento
Acraman, Lake salt flat Australia 109 F8
Acre r. Brazil 148 D2
Acre state Brazil 148 C2
Acre Israel see 'Akko
Acri Italy 45 F5
Actéon, Groupe is Fr. Polynesia 165 I7
Acton Canada 130 C2
Acton U.S.A. 136 C4
Açuã r. Brazil 149 D1
Acunum Acusio France see Montélimar
Açurizal Brazil 149 F3
Ada Ghana 93 F4
Ada OH U.S.A. 130 B3
Ada OK U.S.A. 133 B5
Ada Yugo. 46 B2
Ādaba Eth. 96 C3
Adabazar Turkey see Sakarya
Adaf, Djebel mts Alg. 91 H5
Adaja r. Spain 42 D2
Adak U.S.A. 120 B4
Adak Island U.S.A. 120 B4
Adalia Turkey see Antalya
Adam Oman 76 F5
Adam, Mount Falkland Is 153 F7
Adamaoua prov. Cameroon 93 I4
Adamas Greece 47 D6
Adamawa state Nigeria 93 H3
Adamclisi Romania 46 E2
Adamello mt. Italy 44 C1
Adams MA U.S.A. 131 G2
Adams NY U.S.A. 131 E2
Adam's Bridge sea feature India/Sri Lanka 72 C4
Adams Center U.S.A. 131 E2
Adams Lake Canada 122 G5
Adams Mountain U.S.A. 122 D4
Adam's Peak Sri Lanka 72 D5
Adams Peak U.S.A. 136 B2

▶Adamstown Pitcairn Is 165 J7
Capital of the Pitcairn Islands.

'Adan Yemen see Aden
Adana Turkey 78 C3
Adana prov. Turkey 77 B1
Adana Yemen see Aden
'Adan aṣ Ṣughra Yemen 96 E1
Adang, Teluk b. Indon. 59 G3
Adani Nigeria 93 G4
Adapazari Turkey see Sakarya
Adare Rep. of Ireland 35 B5
Adare, Cape Antarctica 167 H2
Adaut Indon. 108 E2
Adavale Australia 111 F5
Adban Afgh. 81 G2
Adda r. Italy 44 B2
Aḍ Ḍab'ah Egypt 41 H5
Ad Dabbah Sudan see Ed Debba
Ad Dafīnah Saudi Arabia 89 I4
Ad Daghghārah Iraq 79 F4
Ad Dahnā' des. Saudi Arabia 76 D5
Ad Dakhla W. Sahara 90 B5
Ad Damir Sudan see Ed Damer
Ad Dammām Saudi Arabia see Dammam
Addanki India 72 C3
Ad Daqahlīyah governorate Egypt 78 B5
Ad Dār al Ḥamrā' Saudi Arabia 89 H3
Ad Darb Saudi Arabia 89 I5
Addatigala India 73 D2
Ad Dawḥah Qatar see Doha
Ad Dawr plain Syria 77 C2
Ad Dibdibah plain Saudi Arabia 80 A5
Ad Dir'īyah Saudi Arabia 76 D5

▶Addis Ababa Eth. 96 C2
Capital of Ethiopia.

Addison U.S.A. 131 E2
Ad Dīwānīyah Iraq 79 F5
Ad Dīwānīyah governorate Iraq see Al Qādisīyah
Addo Elephant National Park S. Africa 98 E7
Addoo Atoll Maldives see Addu Atoll
Addu Atoll Maldives 71 D12
Ad Duwayd well Saudi Arabia 89 I2
Ad Duwaym Sudan see Ed Dueim
Adel U.S.A. 132 C3

▶Adelaide Australia 112 A4
State capital of South Australia.

Adelaide Bahamas 129 D7
Adelaide Island Antarctica 167 L2
Adelaide River Australia 110 B2
Adelebsen Germany 36 D3
Adele Island Australia 108 C3
Adélie Coast Antarctica 167 G2
Adélie Land reg. Antarctica 167 G2
Aden Yemen 76 C7
Aden, Gulf of Somalia/Yemen 96 E2
Aderbissinat Niger 93 G2
Aderno Sicily Italy see Adrano
Adesar India 74 A5
Adhámas Greece see Adamas
Adhan, Jabal mt. U.A.E. 80 D5
Adh Dhayd U.A.E. 80 C5
'Adhfā' well Saudi Arabia 79 E5
'Ādhirīyāt, Jibāl al mts Jordan 77 C4
Adi i. Indon. 57 H6
Ādī Ārk'ay Eth. 89 H6
Adícora Venez. 146 D2
'Adid Umm Inderab well Sudan 89 F6
Adige r. Italy 44 D2
Ādīgrat Eth. 89 H6
Adıgüzel Barajı resr Turkey 78 B3
Adi Keyih Eritrea 89 H6
Adi Kwala Eritrea 89 H6
Adilabad India 72 C2
Adilanga Uganda 96 B4
Adin U.S.A. 134 B4
Adīrī Libya 88 B3
Adirondack Mountains U.S.A. 131 F1
Ādīs Ālem Eth. 68 B6
Ādīs Zemen Eth. 96 C1
Adi Ugri Eritrea see Mendefera
Adıyaman Turkey 79 D3
Adjud Romania 46 E1
Adjumani Uganda 96 A4
Adlavik Islands Canada 125 J2
Admiralty Inlet Canada 121 K2
Admiralty Island U.S.A. 120 F4
Admiralty Island National Monument - Kootznoowoo Wilderness nat. park U.S.A. 120 F4
Admiralty Islands P.N.G. 57 K6
Admiralty Mountains Antarctica 164 F10
Ādo Eth. 96 E3
Ado-Ekiti Nigeria 93 G4
Adok Sudan 96 A2
Adolfo Gonzáles Chaves Arg. 152 E4
Adolfsström Sweden 32 E2
Adonara i. Indon. 108 C2
Adoni India 72 C3
Adour r. France 38 C5
Adra India 75 E5
Adra Spain 42 E4
Adra r. Spain 42 E4
Adramyttium Turkey see Edremit
Adramyttium, Gulf of Turkey see Edremit Körfezi
Adrano Sicily Italy 45 E6
Adrar Alg. 91 E4
Adrar mts Alg. 91 G4
Adrar hills Mali see Ifôghas, Adrar des
Adrar admin. reg. Mauritania 90 C5
Adraskand r. Afgh. 81 E3
Adré Chad 88 D6
Adrian MI U.S.A. 130 A3
Adrian TX U.S.A. 133 A5
Adrianople Turkey see Edirne
Adrianopolis Turkey see Edirne
Adriatic Sea Europe 44 D2
Adua Eth. see Ādwa
Adunara i. Indon. see Adonara
Adur India 72 C4
Adusa Dem. Rep. Congo 94 F4
Adutiškis Lith. 33 G5
Aduwa Eth. see Ādwa
Adverse Well Australia 108 C5
Ādwa Eth. 89 H6
Adwufia Ghana 92 E4
Adycha r. Rus. Fed. 27 N3
Adygeysk Rus. Fed. 79 D1
Adyk Rus. Fed. 29 H7
Adzhiyan Turkm. 80 C2
Adzopé Côte d'Ivoire 92 E4
Adz'va r. Rus. Fed. 28 L2
Adz'vavom Rus. Fed. 28 K2
Aegean Sea Greece/Turkey 47 D5
Aegina i. Greece see Aigina
Aegviidu Estonia 33 G4
Aegyptus country Africa see Egypt
Aela Jordan see Al 'Aqabah
Aelana Jordan see Al 'Aqabah
Aelia Capitolina Israel/West Bank see Jerusalem
Aenus Turkey see Enez
Ærø i. Denmark 36 E1
Aesernia Italy see Isernia
A Estrada Spain 42 B1
Afabet Eritrea 89 H5
Afal watercourse Saudi Arabia see 'Ifāl, Wādī
Afanas'yevo Rus. Fed. 28 J4
Afándou Greece see Afantou
Afantou Greece 47 F6
Afar admin. reg. Eth. 96 D1
Afar Depression Eritrea/Eth. 89 I6
Affreville Alg. see Khemis Miliana
Afghānestān country Asia see Afghanistan
▶Afghanistan country Asia 81 F3
asia 52–53, 82
Afgooye Somalia 96 E4
'Afīf Saudi Arabia 89 I4
Afikpo Nigeria 93 G4
Afiun Karahissar Turkey see Afyon
Åfjord Norway 32 C3
Aflou Alg. 91 F2
Afmadow Somalia 96 D4
Afognak Island U.S.A. 120 D4
Afojjar well Mauritania 92 B1
A Fonsagrada Spain 42 C1
Afragola Italy 45 E4
Afrânio Brazil 150 D4
Āfrēra Terara vol. Eth. 96 D1
Āfrēra YeChe'ew Hāyk' l. Eth. 96 D1
Africa Nova country Africa see Tunisia
'Afrīn Syria 77 C1
'Afrīn, Nahr r. Syria/Turkey 77 C1
Afşin Turkey 78 D3
Afsluitdijk barrage Neth. 36 B2
Aftol well Eth. 96 E3
Afton U.S.A. 134 E4
Aftoût Faï depr. Mauritania 92 B1
Afuá Brazil 150 B2
'Afula Israel 77 B3
Afyon Turkey 78 B3
Afyonkarahisar Turkey see Afyon
Aga-Buryat Autonomous Okrug admin. div. Rus. Fed. see Aginskiy Buryatskiy Avtonomnyy Okrug
Agadem well Niger 93 I1
Agadès Niger see Agadez
Agadez Niger 93 G1
Agadez dept Niger 93 H1
Agadir Morocco 90 C3
Agadyr' Kazakh. 70 D2
Agaie Nigeria 93 G3
Agalega Islands Mauritius 162 K6
Agana Guam see Hagåtña
Agar India 74 C5
Agārak well Niger 93 G1
Agâraktem well Mali 90 D5
Āgaro Eth. 96 C3
Agartala India 75 F5
Agashi India 72 B2
Agate Canada 124 D3
Agathe France see Agde
Agathonisi i. Greece 47 E6
Agatti i. India 72 B4
Agbor Bojiboji Nigeria 93 G4
Agboville Côte d'Ivoire 92 D4
Ağcabädi Azer. 79 F2
Ağdam Azer. 79 F3
Ağdaş Azer. 79 F2
Agdash Azer. see Ağdaş
Agde France 39 E5
Agdzhabedi Azer. see Ağcabädi
Agedabia Libya see Ajdābiyā
Agen France 38 D4
Agenebode Nigeria 93 G4
Āgere Maryam Eth. 96 C3
Aggeneys S. Africa 98 C6
Aggershus county Norway see Akershus
Aggteleki nat. park Hungary 37 J4
Aghezzaf well Mali 93 E1
Aghil Pass China/Jammu and Kashmir 74 C1
Aghireşu Romania 46 C1
Aghouâvil des. Mauritania 92 D1
Aghrījīt well Mauritania 92 C1
Aghzoumal, Sabkhat salt pan W. Sahara 90 B4
Agia Greece 47 C5
Agia Eirinis, Akra pt Greece 47 D5
Agia Marina Greece 47 E6
Agiasos Greece 47 E5
Agia Vervara Greece 47 D7
Agigea Romania 46 F2
Agighiol Romania 46 F2
Agiguan i. N. Mariana Is see Aguijan
Ağın Turkey 79 D3
Aginskiy Buryatskiy Avtonomnyy Okrug admin. div. Rus. Fed. 63 I1
Aginskoye Rus. Fed. 63 I1
Aginum France see Agen
Agios Dimitrios Greece 47 C6
Agios Efstratios Greece 47 D5
Agios Efstratios i. Greece 47 D5
Agios Fokas, Akra pt Greece 47 E5
Agios Georgios i. Greece 47 C6
Agios Ioannis, Akra pt Greece 47 D7
Agios Kirykos Greece 47 E6
Agios Nikolaos Greece 47 D7
Agios Paraskevi Greece 47 E5
Agios Petros Greece 47 C6
Agiou Orous, Kolpos b. Greece 47 C4
Agirwat Hills Sudan 89 G5
Agly r. France 39 E5
Agnantero Greece 47 B5
Agnew Australia 109 C7
Agnibilékrou Côte d'Ivoire 92 E4
Agnita Romania 46 D2
Agniye-Afanas'yevsk Rus. Fed. 64 D2
Agno r. Italy 44 C2
Agnone Italy 44 E4
Ago-Are Nigeria 93 F3
Agounni Jefal well Mali 92 E1
Agous-n-Ehsel well Mali 93 F1
Agout r. France 38 D5
Agra India 74 C4
Agrakhanskiy Poluostrov pen. Rus. Fed. 79 F2
Agram Croatia see Zagreb
Agreda Spain 43 F2
Agri r. Italy 45 F4
Ağrı Turkey 79 E3
Agria Gramvousa i. Greece 47 C7
Ağrı Dağı mt. Turkey see Ararat, Mount
Agrigan i. N. Mariana Is see Agrihan
Agrigento Sicily Italy 45 D6
Agrigentum Sicily Italy see Agrigento
Agrihan i. N. Mariana Is 57 K2
Agrinio Greece 47 B5
Agropoli Italy 45 E4
Agryz Rus. Fed. 28 J4
Ågskaret Norway 32 D2
Ağstafa Azer. 79 F2
Ağsu Azer. 79 G2
Agua Blanca Arg. 152 D4
Agua Clara Bol. 148 D3
Água Clara Brazil 149 G5
Aguaclara Col. 146 C3
Aguadilla Puerto Rico 139 K5
Aguado Cecilio Arg. 152 D5
Aguadulce Panama 139 H7
Agua Escondida Arg. 152 C4
Agua Fria r. U.S.A. 137 F5
Aguanaval r. Mex. 126 F7
Aguanga U.S.A. 136 D5
Aguanus r. Canada 125 I3
Aguapeí Brazil 149 F4
Aguapeí r. Brazil 149 H5
Aguapeí, Serra hills Brazil 149 F4
Agua Prieta Mex. 135 E7
Aguaragüe, Cordillera de mts Bol. 149 E5
Aguaray Arg. 149 E5
A Guardia Spain 42 B2
Aguaro-Guariquito, Parque Nacional nat. park Venez. 146 E2
Aguas r. Spain 43 F4
Águas Belas Brazil 150 E4
Aguascalientes Mex. 126 F7
Águas Formosas Brazil 151 D6
Aguasvivas r. Spain 43 F2
Água Verde r. Brazil 149 F3
Agudo Spain 42 D3
Águeda Port. 42 B2
Agueda r. Port./Spain 42 C2
Aguelal Niger 93 H1
Aguelhok Mali 93 F1
Aguemour, Oued watercourse Alg. 91 F4
Aguessis well Niger 91 H6
Aguié Niger 93 G2
Aguijan i. N. Mariana Is 57 K3
Aguila mt. Spain 43 F2
Aguila U.S.A. 135 D6
Aguilar de Campóo Spain 42 D1
Águilas Spain 43 F4

▶Agulhas, Cape S. Africa 98 D7
Most southerly point of Africa.

Agulhas Basin sea feature Indian Ocean 163 I9
Agulhas Negras mt. Brazil 151 C7
Agulhas Plateau sea feature Indian Ocean 163 I8
Agulhas Ridge sea feature S. Atlantic Ocean 161 O8
Aguntum Italy see San Candido
Ağva Turkey 78 B2
Agvali Rus. Fed. 79 F2
Agwarra Nigeria 93 G3
Agwei r. Sudan 96 B3
Ahaggar plat. Alg. see Hoggar
Ahar Iran 80 A2
Ahaura N.Z. 113 B3
Ahaus Germany 36 C2
Ahigal Spain 42 C2
Ahillo mt. Spain 42 D4
Ahioma P.N.G. 111 G1
Ahipara Bay N.Z. 113 C1
Ahiri India 72 D2
Ahklun Mountains U.S.A. 120 C4
Ahlat Turkey 79 E3
Ahmadabad India 74 B5
Aḥmadābād Iran 81 E3
Aḥmad al Bāqir, Jabal mt. Jordan 77 B5
Ahmadnagar India 72 B2
Ahmadpur India 72 C2
Ahmadpur East Pak. 81 G4
Ahmadpur Sial Pak. 81 G4
Ahmar Mountains Eth. 96 D2
Ahmedabad India see Ahmadabad
Ahmednagar India see Ahmadnagar
Ahmetli Turkey 47 E5
Ahoada Nigeria 93 G4
Ahome Mex. 126 E6
Ahore India 74 B4
Ahram Iran 80 B4
Ahraura India 75 D4
Ahrensburg Germany 36 E2
Ahtme Estonia 33 G4
Āhū Iran 80 B4
Ahun France 38 E3
Ahuriri r. N.Z. 113 B4
Ahvāz Iran 80 B4
Ahvenanmaa is Fin. see Åland Islands
Ahwa India 72 B1
Aḥwar Yemen 76 D7
Ahwāz Iran see Ahvāz
Ai r. China 65 A4
Ai-Ais Namibia 98 C5
Ai-Ais Hot Springs and Fish River Canyon Park nature res. Namibia 98 C5
Aichach Germany 36 E4
Aidin Turkm. 80 C2
Aigiali Greece 47 D6
Aigialousa Cyprus 77 B2
Aigina Greece 47 C6
Aigina i. Greece 47 C6
Aiginio Greece 46 C4
Aigio Greece 47 C5
Aigle Switz. 39 G3
Aigle de Chambeyron mt. France 39 G4
Aigoual, Mont mt. France 39 E4
Aiguá Uruguay 152 G3
Aigües Tortes i Estany de St Maurici, Parque Nacional d' nat. park Spain 43 G1
Aiguille de Scolette mt. France/Italy 39 G4
Aiguilles d'Arves mts France 39 G4
Aiguille Verte mt. France 39 G4
Aigurande France 38 D3
Aihua China see Yunxian
Aihui China see Heihe
Aija Peru 148 A2
Aijal India see Aizawl
Aiken U.S.A. 129 C5
Ailao Shan mts China 66 B3
Aileron Australia 110 C4
Ailigandi Panama 146 B2
Ailing China 67 D3
Ailinglapalap atoll Marshall Is 164 F6
Ailsa Craig i. U.K. 34 D4
Aimogasta Arg. 152 D2
Aimorés, Serra dos hills Brazil 151 D6
Ain r. France 39 F4
Ainaži Latvia 33 G4
Aïn Beïda Alg. 91 G2
Aïn Beni Mathar Morocco 90 E2
'Aïn Ben Tili Mauritania 90 C4
Aïn Bessem Alg. 43 H4
Aïn Biré well Mauritania 92 C1
Aïn Boucif Alg. 43 H5
Aïn Defla Alg. 91 F1
Aïn Deheb Alg. 91 F2
Aïn Draham Tunisia 45 B6
Aïn el Hadjadj well Alg. 91 F3
'Aïn el Hadjadj well Alg. 91 G4
Aïn el Hadjel Alg. 43 H5
Aïn Galakka spring Chad 88 C5
Aïn Mdila well Alg. 91 G2
Aïn-M'Lila Alg. 91 G1
Ainos nat. park Greece 47 B5
Aïn Oussera Alg. 91 F2
Aïn Salah Alg. see In Salah
Aïn Sefra Alg. 91 E2
Ainsworth U.S.A. 132 B3
Aintab Turkey see Gaziantep
Aïn Taya Alg. 43 H4
Aïn Tédélès Alg. 43 G5
Aïn Temouchent Alg. 91 E2
Aïn Ti-m Misaou well Alg. 91 F5
Aipe Col. 146 C4
Aiquile Bol. 148 D4
Air i. Indon. 59 D2
Airão Brazil 147 F5
Airbangis Indon. 58 B2
Airdrie Canada 134 D2
Aire r. France 39 F2
Aire-sur-l'Adour France 38 C5
Airhitam r. Indon. 59 E3
Airhitam, Teluk b. Indon. 59 E3
Airlie Beach Australia 111 G4
Airolo Switz. 39 H3
Airpanas Indon. 57 G7
Air Ronge Canada 123 J4
Aisatung Mountain Myanmar 60 A3
Aisch r. Germany 36 E4
Aisén admin. reg. Chile 153 B6
Aishihik Canada 122 B2
Aishihik Lake Canada 122 B2
Aisími Greece see Aisymi
Aisne r. France 39 E2
Aïssa, Djebel mt. Alg. 91 E2
Aisymi Greece 46 D4
Aitana mt. Spain 43 F3
Aitape P.N.G. 57 J6
Aït Benhaddou tourist site Morocco 90 D3
Aitkin U.S.A. 132 C2
Aiud Romania 46 C1
Aivadzh Tajik. 81 G2
Aiviekste r. Latvia 33 G4
Aix France see Aix-en-Provence
Aix r. France 39 F4
Aix-en-Othe France 39 E2
Aix-en-Provence France 39 F5
Aixe-sur-Vienne France 38 D4
Aix-la-Chapelle Germany see Aachen
Aix-les-Bains France 39 F4
Āīy Ādī Eth. 89 H6
Aiyiáli Greece see Aigiali
Aíyina i. Greece see Aigina
Aiyínion Greece see Aiginio
Aíyion Greece see Aigio
Aizawl India 75 G5
Aizenay France 38 C3
Aizkraukle Latvia 33 G4
Aizpute Latvia 33 F4
Aizu-wakamatsu Japan 65 D5
Ajaccio Corsica France 31 G5
Ajaccio, Golfe d' b. Corsica France 44 B4
Ajaigarh India 74 D4
Ajajú r. Col. 146 C4
Ajanta India 72 B1
Ajanta Range hills India see Sahyadriparvat Range
Ajasse Nigeria 93 G3
Ajax Canada 130 D2
Ajayameru India see Ajmer
Ajban U.A.E. 80 C5
Ajdābiyā Libya 88 D2
Ajdovščina Slovenia 44 D2
a-Jiddét des. Oman see Ḥarāsīs, Jiddat al
Ajka Hungary 37 H5
'Ajlūn Jordan 77 B3
'Ajmah, Jabal al mts Egypt 77 B5
Ajman U.A.E. 80 C5
Ajmer India 74 B4
Ajmer-Merwara India see Ajmer
Ajo U.S.A. 137 F5
Ajra India 72 B2
Akabira Japan 64 E4
Akabli Alg. 91 F4
Akaboun well Mali 93 F1
Akademii Nauk, Khrebet mt. Tajik. see Akademiyai Fanho, Qatorkŭhi
Akademiyai Fanho, Qatorkŭhi mt. Tajik. 81 G2
Akagera National Park Rwanda 96 A5
Āk'ak'ī Beseka Eth. 96 C2
Akalkot India 72 C2
Akama, Akra c. Cyprus see Arnauti, Cape
Akamagaseki Japan see Shimonoseki
Akampka Nigeria 93 H4
Akan National Park Japan 64 F4
Akarkar well Niger 93 G2
Akarnanika mts Greece 47 B5
Akaroa N.Z. 113 C3

Akasha Sudan 89 F4
'Akāshat Iraq 79 D4
Äkäsjokisuu Fin. 32 F2
Akbarābād Iran 80 C4
Akbarpur Uttar Pradesh India 74 D4
Akbarpur Uttar Pradesh India 75 D4
Akbaytal Tajik. 81 H2
Akbaytal Pass Tajik. 81 H2
Akbou Alg. 43 I4
Akbulak Rus. Fed. 29 J6
Akçadağ Turkey 79 D3
Akçakale Turkey 79 D3
Akçakertikbeli Geçidi pass Turkey 47 F5
Akçakoca Turkey 78 B2
Akçali Dağları mt. Turkey 78 C3
Akçalı Dağları mts Turkey 77 A1
Akçaova Turkey 47 E6
Akçay r. Turkey 47 F6
Akchâr reg. Mauritania 90 B6
Akdağ mt. Turkey 47 F5
Akdağlar mts Turkey 78 B3
Akdağmadeni Turkey 78 C3
Akdere Turkey 77 A1
Akelamo Indon. 57 G5
Akelo Sudan 96 B3
Åkersberga Sweden 33 E4
Akershus county Norway 33 C3
Åkerstrømmen Norway 33 C3
Aketi Dem. Rep. Congo 94 D4
Akgyr Erezi hills Turkm. see Akkyr, Gory
Akhalk'alak'i Georgia 79 E2
Akhal Oblast admin. div. Turkm. see Akhal'skaya Oblast'
Akhal'skaya Oblast' admin. div. Turkm. 81 D2
Akhalts'ikhe Georgia 79 E2
Akhḑar, Al Jabal al mts Libya 88 D2
Akhḑar, Jabal mts Oman 76 F5
Akheloy Bulg. 46 E3
Akhisar Turkey 78 A3
Akhmīm Egypt 89 F3
Akhnoor Jammu and Kashmir 74 B2
Akhsu Azer. see Ağsu
Akhta Armenia see Hrazdan
Akhtarīn Syria 77 C1
Akhtubinsk Rus. Fed. 29 H6
Akhty Rus. Fed. 79 F2
Akhtyrka Ukr. see Okhtyrka
Aki Japan 65 C6
Akiéni Gabon 94 B5
Akimiski Island Canada 124 D2
Akıncılar Turkey see Selçuk
Akishma r. Rus. Fed. 64 C1
Akita Japan 65 E5
Akjoujt Mauritania 92 B1
Akka Morocco 90 C3
Akkajaure l. Sweden 32 E2
Akkerman Ukr. see Bilhorod-Dnistrovs'kyy
'Akko Israel 77 B3
Akkol' Kazakh. 26 H4
Akkol' Atyrauskaya Oblast' Kazakh. 29 I7
Akköy Aydın Turkey 78 A3
Akköy Denizli Turkey 47 F6
Akkul' Kazakh. see Akkol'
Akkuş Turkey 78 D2
Akkyr, Gory hills Turkm. 80 C1
Akkystau Kazakh. 29 I7
Aklavik Canada 120 F3
Aklera India 74 C4
Ak-Mechet Kazakh. see Kyzylorda
Akmeņrags pt Latvia 33 F4
Akmeqit China 74 C1
Akmola Kazakh. see Astana
Akmolinsk Kazakh. see Astana
Akniste Latvia 33 G4
Aknoul Morocco 90 E2
Akō Japan 65 C6
Akobo Sudan 96 B3
Akobo Wenz r. Eth./Sudan 96 B3
Akodia India 74 C5
Akola Maharashtra India 72 B2
Akola Maharashtra India 72 C1
Akom II Cameroon 93 H5
Akonolinga Cameroon 93 I5
Akop Sudan 94 F2
Akordat Eritrea 89 H6
Akören Turkey 78 C3
Akot India 74 C5
Akouménaye Fr. Guiana 147 H4
Akoupé Côte d'Ivoire 92 E4
Akpatok Island Canada 121 M3
Akraifnio Greece 47 C5
Akranes Iceland 32 [inset]
Akrathos, Akra pt Greece 47 D4
Akréréb Niger 93 H1
Akritas, Akra pt Greece 47 B6
Akron CO U.S.A. 132 A3
Akron OH U.S.A. 130 C3
Akrotirion Bay Cyprus 77 A2
Akrotiriou, Kolpos b. Cyprus see Akrotirion Bay
Akrotiri Sovereign Base Area military base Cyprus 77 A2

▶Aksai Chin terr. Asia 74 C2
Disputed territory (China/India).

Aksakal Turkey 47 F4
Aksakovo Bulg. 46 E3
Aksaray Turkey 78 C3
Aksay Kazakh. 29 J6
Aksay Rus. Fed. 29 F7
Akşehir Turkey 78 B3
Akşehir Gölü l. Turkey 78 B3
Akseki Turkey 78 B3
Aksenovo Rus. Fed. 29 J5
Aks-e Rostam r. Iran 80 C4
Akshiganak Kazakh. 70 B2
Akshukur Kazakh. 79 G2
Aksu China 70 F3
Aksu Kazakh. 29 J6
Aksu r. Tajik. see Oksu
Aksu r. Turkey 78 B3
Āksum Eth. 89 H6
Aktag mt. China 75 E1
Aktash Uzbek. 81 F2
Aktau Kazakh. 79 G2
Aktepe Turkey 77 C1
Aktobe Kazakh. 26 F4
Aktogay Kazakh. 70 E2
Aktsyabrski Belarus 29 D5
Aktyubinsk Kazakh. see Aktobe
Aktyubinskaya Oblast' admin. div. Kazakh. 29 K6
Aktyubinsk Oblast admin. div. Kazakh. see Aktyubinskaya Oblast'
Akujärvi Fin. 32 G1
Akula Dem. Rep. Congo 94 D4
Akulivik Canada 121 L3
Akumadan Ghana 93 E4
Akune Japan 65 B6
Akur mt. Uganda 96 B4
Akure Nigeria 93 G4
Akureyri Iceland 32 [inset]
Akwa Ibom state Nigeria 93 G4
Akwanga Nigeria 93 H3
Akyab Myanmar see Sittwe
Akyatan Gölü salt l. Turkey 77 B1
Akzhaykyn, Ozero salt l. Kazakh. 70 C3
Ål Norway 33 C3
Ala Italy 44 C2
'Alā, Jabal al hills Syria 77 C2
Alabama r. U.S.A. 129 B6
Alabama state U.S.A. 129 B5
Alabaster U.S.A. 129 B5
Al 'Abṭīyah well Iraq 79 F5
Al Abyaḑ Libya 88 B3
Al Abyār Libya 88 D2
Alaca Turkey 78 C2
Alacahan Turkey 79 D3
Alaçam Turkey 78 C2
Alaçam Dağları mts Turkey 47 F5
Alacant Spain see Alicante-Alicant
Alaçatı Turkey 47 E5
Alacrán, Arrecife reef Mex. 127 I7
Al Adabīyah Egypt 77 A5
Aladag mt. Bulg. 46 D4
Aladağ Turkey 78 C3
Ala Dag mt. Turkey 79 E3
Ala Dağlar mts Turkey 79 E3
Ala Dağları mts Turkey 78 C3
Al 'Adam Libya 88 D2
Alaejos Spain 42 D2
Alagapuram India 72 C4
Alagir Rus. Fed. 29 H8
Alagoas state Brazil 150 E4
Alagoinhas Brazil 150 E5
Alagón Spain 43 F2
Alagón r. Spain 42 C3
Alahanpanjang Indon. 58 C3
Alahärmä Fin. 32 F3
Al Aḩmadī Kuwait 79 G5
Alaid, Ostrov i. Rus. Fed. see Atlasova, Ostrov
Alaior Spain 43 I3
Alai Range mts Asia 70 D4
Alaivān Iran 80 C3
Al Ajām Saudi Arabia 80 B5
Alajärvi Fin. 32 F3
Al 'Ajrūd Egypt 77 A4
Al 'Ajrūd well Egypt 77 B4
Alajuela Costa Rica 139 H6
Alakanuk U.S.A. 120 C3
Alaknanda r. India 74 C3
Alakol', Ozero salt l. Kazakh. 70 F2
Ala Kul salt l. Kazakh. see Alakol', Ozero
Alakurtti Rus. Fed. 32 H2
Al 'Alamayn Egypt 89 F2
Alalaú r. Brazil 147 F5
Al 'Alayyah Saudi Arabia 89 I5
Alama Somalia 96 D3
Al 'Amādīyah Iraq 79 E3
Alamagan i. N. Mariana Is 57 K2
Alamaguan i. N. Mariana Is see Alamagan
Al 'Amār Saudi Arabia 89 J3
Al 'Amārah Iraq 79 F5
'Alam ar Rūm, Ra's pt Egypt 89 E2
'Alāmarvdasht watercourse Iran 80 C4
Al Amghar waterhole Iraq 79 F5
Al 'Āmirīyah Egypt 78 B5
Alamito Creek r. U.S.A. 135 F7
Alamo U.S.A. 128 A5
Alamo Dam U.S.A. 137 F4
Alamogordo U.S.A. 135 F6
Alamo Heights U.S.A. 133 B6
Alamos Mex. 135 E8
Alamos r. Mex. 126 F6
Alamos, Sierra mts Mex. 135 E8
Alamosa U.S.A. 135 F5
Alamosa Creek r. U.S.A. 135 F6
Alampur India 72 C3
Al 'Anad Yemen 96 E1
Alanäs Sweden 32 D2
Al Anbār governorate Iraq 79 E4
Aland India 72 C2
Aland r. Iran 80 A2
Åland is Fin. see Åland Islands
Åland Islands Fin. 33 E3
Ålands Hav sea chan. Fin./Sweden 33 E4
Alandur India 72 D3
Alanganlang, Tanjung pt Indon. 59 G3
Alang Besar i. Indon. 58 C2
Alange, Embalse de resr Spain 42 C3
Alanggantang i. Indon. 58 D3
Alanya Turkey 78 C3
'Alā' od Dīn Iran 80 C4
Alapaha r. U.S.A. 129 C6
Alaplı Turkey 29 D8
Alappuzha India see Alleppey
Al 'Aqabah Jordan 78 C5
Al 'Aqīq Saudi Arabia 89 I4
Al 'Arabīyah as Sa'ūdīyah country Asia see Saudi Arabia
Alarcón, Embalse de resr Spain 43 E3
Al Arin Saudi Arabia 89 I5
Al 'Arīsh Egypt 89 G2
Al Arṭāwīyah Saudi Arabia 76 D4
Alas Indon. 59 G5
Alas, Selat sea chan. Indon. 59 G5
Alaşehir Turkey 78 B3
Alashiya country Asia see Cyprus
Al Ashmūnayn Egypt 89 F3
Al 'Āshūrīyah well Iraq 89 I2
▶Alaska state U.S.A. 120 D3
northamerica 118–119
Alaska, Gulf of U.S.A. 120 E4
Alaska Highway Canada/U.S.A. 122 A2
Alaska Peninsula U.S.A. 120 C4
Alaska Range mts U.S.A. 120 E3
Al 'Assāfīyah Saudi Arabia 89 H2
Alassio Italy 44 B2
Älät Azer. 79 G3
Alat Uzbek. 81 E2
Alatau Shankou pass China/Kazakh. see Dzungarian Gate
Al Atwā' well Saudi Arabia 89 I2
Alatyr' Rus. Fed. 29 H5
Alatyr' r. Rus. Fed. 29 H5
Alausí Ecuador 146 B5
Alaverdi Armenia 79 F2
Ala-Vuokki Fin. 32 H2
Alavus Fin. 32 F3
Alawoona Australia 112 B4
Alaykel' Kyrg. see Alaykuu
Alaykuu Kyrg. 81 H1
Alay Kyrka Toosu mts Asia see Alai Range
Al 'Ayn U.A.E. 80 C5
Alayskiy Khrebet mts Asia see Alai Range
Alazani r. Azer./Georgia 79 F2
Alazeya r. Rus. Fed. 27 P2
Al 'Azīzīyah Iraq 79 F4

▶Al 'Azīzīyah Libya 88 B1
Highest recorded shade temperature in the world.
world 12–13

Alba Italy 44 B2
Al Ba'ā'ith Saudi Arabia 89 I3
Al Bāb Syria 77 C1
Albacete Spain 43 F3
Al Badā'i' Saudi Arabia 89 H3
Alba de Tormes Spain 42 D2
Al Bādiyah al Janūbīyah hill Iraq 79 F5
Ålbæk Denmark 33 C4
Ålbæk Bugt b. Denmark 33 C4
Al Baḩr al Aḩmar governorate Egypt 77 A5
Al Bahrayn country Asia see Bahrain
Alba Iulia Romania 46 C1
Al Bajā' well U.A.E. 80 B5
Al Bakhrā well Saudi Arabia 80 A5
Al Bakkī Libya 88 B3
Albalate de Arzobispo Spain 43 F2
Albanel, Lac l. Canada 125 F3
▶Albania country Europe 46 A4
europe 24–25, 48
Albany Australia 109 B8
Albany r. Canada 124 D2
Albany GA U.S.A. 129 B6
Albany MO U.S.A. 132 C3

▶Albany NY U.S.A. 131 G2
State capital of New York.

Albany OH U.S.A. 130 B4
Albany OR U.S.A. 134 B3
Albany TX U.S.A. 133 B5
Albany Downs Australia 111 G5
Albardão do João Maria coastal area Brazil 152 G3
Al Bardī Libya 88 E2
Al Başrah governorate Iraq 79 F5
Al Baṭḩa' marsh Iraq 79 F5
Al Bāṭinah admin. reg. Oman 80 D5
Al Bāṭinah i. Saudi Arabia 80 B5
Albatross Bay Australia 111 E2
Al Bawīṭī Egypt 89 F2
Al Bayḑā' Libya 88 D1
Al Bayḑā' Yemen 76 D7
Albemarle U.S.A. 128 C5
Albemarle Sound sea chan. U.S.A. 128 D5
Albenga Italy 44 B2
Alberche r. Spain 42 D3
Alberdi Para. 149 F6
Alberga watercourse Australia 110 C5
Albert Australia 112 C4
Albert France 39 E2
Albert, Lake Australia 112 A4
Albert, Lake Dem. Rep. Congo/Uganda 96 A4
Albert, Parc National nat. park Dem. Rep. Congo see Virunga, Parc National des
Alberta prov. Canada 123 H4
Albertirsa Hungary 37 I5
Albert Kanaal canal Belgium 36 B3
Albert Lea U.S.A. 132 C3
Albert Nile r. Sudan/Uganda 96 B4
Alberto de Agostini, Parque Nacional nat. park Chile 153 C8
Albertville Dem. Rep. Congo see Kalémié
Albertville France 39 G4
Albertville U.S.A. 129 B5
Albi France 38 E5
Albia U.S.A. 132 C3
Al Bi'ār Saudi Arabia 89 H4
Al Biḑah des. Saudi Arabia 80 B5
Albignasego Italy 44 C2
Albina Suriname 147 H3
Albion CA U.S.A. 136 A2
Albion IN U.S.A. 128 B3
Albion MI U.S.A. 130 A2
Albion NE U.S.A. 132 B3
Albion NY U.S.A. 130 D2
Albion PA U.S.A. 130 C3
Al Bi'r Saudi Arabia 89 H2
Al Birk Saudi Arabia 89 I5
Al Birkah Saudi Arabia 89 I4
Alborán, Isla de i. Spain 42 E5
Ålborg Denmark 33 C4
Ålborg Bugt b. Denmark 33 C4
Alborz, Reshteh-ye mts Iran see Elburz Mountains
Albota Romania 46 D2
Albox Spain 43 E4
Albro Australia 111 F4
Albstadt Germany 36 D4
Al Budayyi Bahrain 80 B5
Albufeira Port. 42 B4
Al Buḩayrah governorate Egypt 78 B5
Al Bukayrīyah Saudi Arabia 89 I3
Albula Alpen mts Switz. 39 H3
Albuquerque U.S.A. 135 F6
Al Buraymī Oman 76 F5
Albury Australia 112 C5
Al Buşayrah Syria 79 E4
Al Buşayṭā' plain Saudi Arabia 89 H2
Al Buşayyah Iraq 79 F5
Al Bushūk well Saudi Arabia 89 J2
Al Buwī well Oman 76 F6
Alca Peru 148 B3
Alcácer do Sal Port. 42 B3
Alcáçovas r. Port. 42 B3
Alcalá de Chivert Spain 43 G2
Alcalá de Guadaira Spain 42 D4
Alcalá de Henares Spain 42 E2
Alcalá de los Gazules Spain 42 D4
Alcalá la Real Spain 42 E4
Alcalde, Punta pt Chile 152 C2
Alcamo Sicily Italy 45 D6
Alcanadre r. Spain 43 G2
Alcañiz Spain 43 F2
Alcântara Brazil 150 C2
Alcántara Spain 42 C3
Alcántara, Embalse de resr Spain 42 C3
Alcántara II, Embalse de resr Spain 42 C3
Alcantara Lake Canada 123 I2
Alcantarilla Spain 43 F4
Alcaraz Spain 43 E3
Alcaraz, Sierra de mts Spain 43 E3
Alcaria Ruiva hill Port. 42 C4
Alcarrache r. Port./Spain 42 C3
Alcaudete Spain 42 D4
Alcázar de San Juan Spain 42 E3
Alcazarquivir Morocco see Ksar el Kebir
Alchevs'k Ukr. 29 F6
Alcira Arg. 152 D3
Alcira Spain see Alzira
Alcobaça Brazil 151 E6
Alconchel Spain 42 C3
Alcora Spain 43 F2
Alcorneo r. Port./Spain 42 C3
Alcoy-Alcoi Spain 43 F3
Alcubierre, Sierra de mts Spain 43 F2
Alcúdia Spain 43 H3
Aldabra Atoll Seychelles 97 E7
▶Aldabra Islands is Seychelles 97 E7
africa 86–87
Aldama Mex. 135 F7
Aldan Rus. Fed. 27 M4
Aldan r. Rus. Fed. 27 M3
Aldeburgh U.K. 35 G5
Aldeia Velha Brazil 150 B4
Aldeia Viçosa Angola 95 B7
Alder Creek U.S.A. 131 F2
Alderney i. Channel Is 38 B2
Aldershot U.K. 35 F6
Alderson U.S.A. 130 C5
Aldie Eth. 96 D3
Aleg Mauritania 92 B1
Alegre Brazil 151 D7
Alegrete Brazil 152 G2
Alegros Mountain U.S.A. 135 E6
Alejandro Korn Arg. 152 F3
Alekhovshchina Rus. Fed. 28 E3
Aleksandra Bekovicha-Cherkassogo, Zaliv b. Kazakh. 79 G2
Aleksandriya Ukr. see Oleksandriya
Aleksandropol Armenia see Gyumri
Aleksandrov Rus. Fed. 28 F4
Aleksandrov Gay Rus. Fed. 29 I6
Aleksandrovka Rus. Fed. 29 J5
Aleksandrovo Bulg. 46 D3
Aleksandrovsk Rus. Fed. 28 K4
Aleksandrovsk Ukr. see Zaporizhzhya
Aleksandrovskiy Rus. Fed. see Aleksandrovsk
Aleksandrovskoye Stavropol'skiy Kray Rus. Fed. 29 G7
Aleksandrovskoye Stavropol'skiy Kray Rus. Fed. 29 H7
Aleksandrovsk-Sakhalinskiy Rus. Fed. 64 E2
Aleksandrów Kujawski Poland 37 I2
Aleksandry, Zemlya i. Rus. Fed. 26 E1
Alekseyevka Kazakh. see Akkol'
Alekseyevka Belgorodskaya Oblast' Rus. Fed. 29 F6
Alekseyevka Belgorodskaya Oblast' Rus. Fed. 29 F6
Alekseyevskaya Rus. Fed. 29 G6
Aleksin Rus. Fed. 29 F5
Aleksinac Yugo. 46 B3
Alèmbé Gabon 94 A5
'Alem Ketema Eth. 96 C2
'Alem Maya Eth. 96 D2
Além Paraíba Brazil 151 D7
Ålen Norway 32 C3
Alençon France 38 D2
Alenquer Brazil 147 H5
Alenuihaha Channel U.S.A. 135 [inset] Z1
Alep Syria see Aleppo
Alépé Côte d'Ivoire 92 E4
Aleppo Syria 78 D3
Aler r. India 72 C2
Alert Canada 121 M1
Alerta Peru 148 C2
Alès France 39 F4
Aleşd Romania 31 J4
Aleshki Ukr. see Tsyurupyns'k
Aleşkirt Turkey see Eleşkirt
Alessandria Italy 44 B2
Alessio Albania see Lezhë
Ålesund Norway 32 B3
Aletschhorn mt. Switz. 39 G3
Aleutian Basin sea feature Bering Sea 164 F2
Aleutian Islands U.S.A. 120 B4
Aleutian Range mts U.S.A. 120 D4
Aleutian Trench sea feature N. Pacific Ocean 164 G2
Alevina, Mys c. Rus. Fed. 27 P4
Alevişik Turkey see Samandağı
Alexander, Mount Australia 110 D2
Alexander Archipelago is U.S.A. 120 F4
Alexander Bay S. Africa 98 C6
Alexander City U.S.A. 129 B5
Alexander Island Antarctica 167 L2
Alexandra Australia 112 C5
Alexandra r. Australia 111 D3
Alexandra N.Z. 113 B4
Alexandra, Cape S. Georgia 153 [inset]
Alexandra Channel India 73 G3
Alexandra Falls Canada 123 G2
Alexandra Land i. Rus. Fed. see Aleksandry, Zemlya
Alexandreia Greece 46 C4
Alexandretta Turkey see İskenderun
Alexandria Afgh. see Ghaznī

▶Alexandria Egypt 89 F2
5th most populous city in Africa.
world 16–17

Alexandria Romania 46 D3
Alexandria Turkm. see Mary
Alexandria KY U.S.A. 130 A4
Alexandria LA U.S.A. 133 C6
Alexandria VA U.S.A. 131 E4
Alexandria Arachoton Afgh. see Kandahār
Alexandria Areion Afgh. see Herāt
Alexandria Bay U.S.A. 131 F1
Alexandria Prophthasia Afgh. see Farāh
Alexandrina, Lake Australia 112 A4
Alexandroupoli Greece 46 D4
Alexis r. Canada 125 J2
'Āley Lebanon 77 B3
Aleyak Iran 80 D2
Aleysk Rus. Fed. 26 I4
Alfambra r. Spain 43 F2
Alfaro Spain 43 F1
Alfarràs Spain 43 G2
Al Farūq reg. Saudi Arabia 80 B5
Al Farwānīyah Kuwait 76 D4
Al Farwānīyah Kuwait 79 F5
Al Fas Morocco see Fès
Al Fashn Egypt 78 B5
Alfatar Bulg. 46 E3
Al Fatḩah Iraq 79 E4
Al Fāw Iraq 79 G5
Al Fayyūm Egypt 89 F2
Al Fayyūm governorate Egypt 78 B5
Alfeios r. Greece 47 B6
Alfeld (Leine) Germany 36 D3
Alfenas Brazil 151 C7
Alfios r. Greece see Alfeios
Alföld plain Hungary 37 J5
Alford U.K. 34 E3
Alfred U.S.A. 131 H2
Alfred and Marie Range hills Australia 109 D6
Alfta Sweden 33 E3
Al Fujayrah U.A.E. see Fujairah
Al Fuqahā' Libya 88 C3
Al Furāt r. Iraq/Syria 76 C3 see Euphrates
Algabas Kazakh. 29 J6
Algar Spain 42 D4
Ålgård Norway 33 B4
Algarrobal Chile 152 C2
Algarrobo del Aguilla Arg. 152 D4
Algarve reg. Port. 42 B4
Algeciras Spain 42 D4
Algemesí Spain 43 F3
Algena Eritrea 89 H5
Alger Alg. see Algiers
Alger U.S.A. 130 A1

▶Algeria country Africa 91 F4
2nd largest country in Africa.
africa 86–87, 100

Al Gharbīyah governorate Egypt 78 B5
Al Ghawr plain Jordan/West Bank 77 B4
Al Ghayḑah Yemen 76 E6
Alghero Sardinia Italy 45 B4
Al Ghurdaqah Egypt 89 G3
Al Ghuwayr well Qatar 80 B5
Al Ghwaybiyah Saudi Arabia 76 D4

▶Algiers Alg. 91 F1
Capital of Algeria.

Alginet Spain 43 F3
Algodón r. Peru 146 D5
Algodor r. Spain 42 D3
Algoma U.S.A. 132 E2
Algona U.S.A. 132 C3
Algonac U.S.A. 130 B2
Algonquin Park Canada 124 E4
Algorta (Guecho) Spain 42 E1
Älgsjö Sweden 32 E2
Alguerao Moz. see Hacufera
Algueirão-Mem Martins Port. 42 B3
Al Habakah well Saudi Arabia 79 E5
Al Ḩabbānīyah Iraq 79 E4
Al Ḩadaqah well Saudi Arabia 79 F5
Al Ḩadd Bahrain 80 B5
Al Hadhālīl plat. Saudi Arabia 89 I2
Al Ḩadīthah Iraq 79 E4
Al Ḩafar well Saudi Arabia 89 I2
Al Ḩaffah Syria 77 C2
Al Haggounia W. Sahara 90 B4
Al Ḩā'ir Saudi Arabia 80 A5
Al Ḩajar al Gharbī mts Oman 76 F5
Al Ḩajar ash Sharqī mts Oman 76 F5
Alhama r. Spain 43 F1
Al Ḩamād plain Asia 76 B3
Al Ḩamādah al Ḩamrā' plat. Libya 88 A2
Alhama de Granada Spain 42 E4
Alhama de Murcia Spain 91 E1
Alhamilla, Sierra hills Spain 43 E4
Al Ḩammām Egypt 89 F2
Al Ḩammām well Iraq 79 E5
Al Ḩamrā' Saudi Arabia 89 H4
Al Ḩanīsh al Kabīr i. Yemen 89 I6
Al Haniyah esc. Iraq 79 F5
Al Ḩaqū Saudi Arabia 89 I5
Al Ḩarrah Egypt 89 F2
Al Ḩarūj al Aswad hills Libya 88 C3
Al Ḩasakah Syria 79 E3
Al Ḩāshimīyah Iraq 79 F4
Al Ḩatīfah plain Saudi Arabia 80 A5
Al Ḩawi salt pan Saudi Arabia 77 D5
Al Ḩawīyah Saudi Arabia 89 I4
Al Ḩawjā' Saudi Arabia 89 H2
Al Ḩayy Iraq 79 F4
Al Ḩazm Saudi Arabia 77 C5
Al Ḩazm al-Jawf Yemen 76 C6
Al Ḩibāk des. Saudi Arabia 76 E6
Al Ḩillah governorate Iraq see Bābil
Al Ḩillah Saudi Arabia 76 D5
Al Ḩimārah well Saudi Arabia 80 B5
Al Hindīyah Iraq 79 F4
Al Ḩinnāh Saudi Arabia 80 B5
Al Ḩinw mt. Saudi Arabia 89 H2
Al Ḩismā plain Saudi Arabia 77 B5
Al Ḩişn Jordan 77 B3
Al Ḩişn Yemen 96 E1
Al Hoceima Morocco 90 E2
Al Ḩudaydah Yemen see Hodeidah
Al Ḩudūd ash Shamālīyah prov. Saudi Arabia 79 E5
Al Ḩufayrah well Saudi Arabia 80 B5
Al Ḩufrah reg. Saudi Arabia 89 H2
Al Hufūf Saudi Arabia 76 D4
Al Ḩūj hills Saudi Arabia 79 E5
Al Ḩulayq al Kabīr hills Libya 88 C3
Al Ḩunayy Saudi Arabia 80 B5
Al Ḩuwayyiţ Saudi Arabia 89 I3
Al Ḩuwayz Syria 77 C2
Ali China 74 C2
'Alīābād Hormozgan Iran 80 C4
'Alīābād Khorāsan Iran 81 D3
'Alīābād Khorāsan Iran 81 E4
'Alīābād Kordestān Iran 80 A3
'Alīābād Qom Iran 80 B3
'Alīābād, Kūh-e mt. Iran 80 B3
Aliağa Turkey 78 A3
Aliakmonas r. Greece 47 C4
Aliakmonas, Limni l. Greece 47 B4
Aliartos Greece 47 C5
Alibag India 72 B2
Äli Bayramlı Azer. 79 G3
Alibey Adası i. Turkey 47 E5
Alibunar Yugo. 46 B2
Alicante-Alicant Spain 43 F3
Alice U.S.A. 133 B7
Alice, Punta pt Italy 45 F5
Alice Arm Canada 122 D4
Alice Springs Australia 110 C4
Alice Town Bahamas 129 D7
Aliceville U.S.A. 129 A5
Alichur Tajik. 81 H2
Alichur r. Tajik. 81 H2
Alichuri Janubī, Qatorkŭhi mts Tajik. 81 H2
Alicudi, Isola i. Isole Lipari Italy 45 E5
Al 'Idwah well Saudi Arabia 89 I3
Aliero Nigeria 93 G2
Alife Italy 44 E4
Aligarh India 74 C4
Alīgūdarz Iran 80 B3
Alihe China 63 K1
Alījūq, Kūh-e mt. Iran 80 B4
'Alī Kheyl Afgh. 81 G3
Al Ikhwān is Yemen 76 E7
Alima r. Congo 94 C5
Al Imārāt al 'Arabīyah at Muttaḩidah country Asia see United Arab Emirates
Alimia i. Greece 47 E6
Alindao Cent. Afr. Rep. 94 D3
Alinghar r. Afgh. 81 G3
Alingsås Sweden 33 D4
Alintale well Eth. 96 D3
Aliova r. Turkey 78 B3
Alipur Pak. 81 G4
Alipur Duar India 75 F4
Aliquippa U.S.A. 130 C3
Alirajpur India 74 B5
Ali Sabieh Djibouti 96 D2
Al 'Īsāwīyah Saudi Arabia 89 H2
Al Iskandarīyah Egypt see Alexandria
Al Iskandarīyah governorate Egypt 78 B5
Aliskerovo Rus. Fed. 27 Q3
Al Ismā'īlīyah Egypt 89 G2
Aliste r. Spain 42 C2
Aliveri Greece 47 D5
Alix Canada 123 H4
Aliyaha r. Ukr. 46 F2
Al Jafr Jordan 78 D5
Al Jāfūrah des. Saudi Arabia 76 E4
Al Jaghbūb Libya 88 E2
Al Jahrah Kuwait 79 F5
Al Jamalīyah Qatar 80 B5
Al Jarāwī well Saudi Arabia 77 D4
Al Jawf Libya 88 D3
Al Jawf Saudi Arabia 89 H2
Al Jawf prov. Saudi Arabia 77 D5
Al Jawlān hills Syria see Golan
Al Jawsh Libya 88 A1
Al Jaza'ir Alg. see Algiers
Alj Beyk Iran 80 C2
Aljezur Port. 42 B4
Al Jībān reg. Saudi Arabia 80 B5
Al Jithāmīyah Saudi Arabia 89 I3
Al Jīzah Egypt see Giza
Al Jīzah governorate Egypt 78 B5
Al Jubayl Saudi Arabia 76 D4
Al Jubayl hills Saudi Arabia 80 A5
Al Jubaylah Saudi Arabia 80 A5
Aljucén r. Spain 42 C3
Al Jufra Oasis Libya 88 B2
Al Jumūm Saudi Arabia 89 H4
Al Junaynah Saudi Arabia 89 I4
Al Jurayd i. Saudi Arabia 80 B5
Al Juwayf depr. Syria 77 C3
Al Kahfah Saudi Arabia 89 I3
Alkali Flat salt flat NV U.S.A. 136 C1
Alkali Flat salt flat NV U.S.A. 136 E1
Alkaliya r. Ukr. 46 G2
Alkamari Niger 93 I2
Al Karak Jordan 78 C5
Al Kāẓimīyah Iraq 79 F4
Al Khābūrah Oman 76 F5
Al Khadrā' well Saudi Arabia 79 E5
Al Khafaq well Saudi Arabia 80 A5
Al Khalf Saudi Arabia 89 I3
Al Khalīl West Bank see Hebron
Al Khāliş Iraq 79 F4
Al Khārijah Egypt 89 F3
Al Kharrārah Qatar 80 B5
Al Khaşab Oman 76 F4
Al Khasfah well Oman 76 E6
Al Khāşirah Saudi Arabia 89 I4
Al-Khatam reg. U.A.E. 80 C5
Al Khawr Qatar 80 B5
Al Khişah well Saudi Arabia 80 B5
Al Khizāmī well Saudi Arabia 80 B5
Al Khobar Saudi Arabia 80 B5
Al Khubrah Saudi Arabia 80 B5
Al Khufrah Libya 88 D3
Al Khufrah Oasis Libya 88 D3
Al Khums Libya 88 B1
Al Khunfah sand area Saudi Arabia 89 H2
Al Khunn Saudi Arabia 76 D5
Al Khuwayr Qatar 80 B5
Al Kifl Iraq 79 F4
Al Kir'ānah Qatar 80 B5
Alkmaar Neth. 36 B2
Al Kūfah Iraq 79 F4
Al Kumayt Iraq 79 F4
Al Kūt Iraq 79 F4
Al Kuwayt country Asia see Kuwait
Al Kuwayt Kuwait see Kuwait
Al Labbah plain Saudi Arabia 89 I2
Allada Benin 93 F4
Al Lādhiqīyah Syria see Latakia
Al Lādhiqīyah governorate Syria 77 B2
Allagadda India 72 C3
Allahabad India 75 D4
Al Lajā lava field Syria 77 C3
Allakh-Yun' Rus. Fed. 27 N3
Allanmyo Myanmar 60 A4
'Allāqī, Wādī al watercourse Egypt 89 G4
Allariz Spain 42 C1
Alldays S. Africa 99 F4
Allegheny r. U.S.A. 130 D3
Allegheny Mountains U.S.A. 130 B5
Allegheny Reservoir U.S.A. 130 D3
Allen, Lough l. Rep. of Ireland 35 B4
Allen, Mount U.S.A. 112 A2
Allendale U.S.A. 129 C5
Allende Coahuila Mex. 133 A6
Allende Nuevo León Mex. 126 F6
Allenford Canada 130 C1
Allenstein Poland see Olsztyn
Allensville U.S.A. 130 B4
Allentown U.S.A. 131 F3
Alleppey India 72 C4
Aller r. Germany 36 D2
Alliance NE U.S.A. 134 G4
Alliance OH U.S.A. 130 C3
Al Lībīyah country Africa see Libya
Allier r. France 39 E3
Al Liftyah well Iraq 79 E5
Alligator Point Australia 111 E3
Al Līhābah well Saudi Arabia 80 A5
Allikher India 72 C2
Allinge-Sandvig Denmark 33 D5
Al Lişāfah well Saudi Arabia 80 A5
Al Lisān pen. Jordan 77 B4
Allison U.S.A. 132 C3
Alliston Canada 130 D1
Al Līth Saudi Arabia 89 I4
Al Liwā' oasis U.A.E. 76 E5
Allonnes Pays de la Loire France 38 D3
Allora Australia 111 H6
Allschwil Switz. 39 G3
Al Luḩayyah Yemen 89 I5
Allur India 72 D3
Alluru Kottapatnam India 72 D3
Al Lussuf well Iraq 79 E5
Alma Canada 125 G3
Alma KS U.S.A. 132 B4
Alma MI U.S.A. 130 A2
Alma NE U.S.A. 132 B3
Al Ma'ānīyah Iraq 79 E5
Alma-Ata Kazakh. see Almaty
Almacelles Spain 43 G2
Almada Port. 42 B3
Al Madāfi' plat. Saudi Arabia 77 C5
Al Ma'danīyāt well Iraq 79 F5
Almaden Australia 111 F3
Almadén Spain 42 D3
Al Madīnah Saudi Arabia see Medina
Al Mafraq Jordan 78 D4
Al Maḩāriq Egypt 89 F3
Al Mahbas W. Sahara 90 C4
Al Maḩmūdīyah Iraq 79 F4
Al Maḩwīt Yemen 76 C6
Al Majma'ah Saudi Arabia 76 D4
Almājului, Munţii mts Romania 46 C2
Al Maks al Baḩrī Egypt 89 F3
Al Malsūnīyah reg. Saudi Arabia 80 B5
Al Manāmah Bahrain see Manama
Almanor, Lake U.S.A. 136 B1
Almansa Spain 43 F3
Al Manşūrah Egypt 89 F2
Almanzor mt. Spain 42 D2
Almanzora r. Spain 43 F4
Al Ma'qil Iraq 79 F5
Almār Afgh. 81 F3
Almar r. Spain 42 D2
Al Mariyyah U.A.E. 76 E5
Al Marj Libya 88 D1
Almas, Rio das r. Brazil 150 B5
Al Matmarfag W. Sahara 90 B4

▶Almaty Kazakh. 70 E3
Former capital of Kazakhstan.

Al Mayādīn Syria 79 E4
Almazán Spain 43 E2
Almeida Port. 42 C2
Almeirim Brazil 147 H5
Almeirim Port. 42 B3
Almelo Neth. 36 C2
Almenara Brazil 151 D6
Almenara Spain 43 F3
Almenara, Sierra de hills Spain 43 F4
Almendra, Embalse de resr Spain 42 C2
Almendralejo Spain 42 C3
Almere Neth. 36 B2
Almería Spain 43 E4
Almería, Golfo de b. Spain 43 E4
Al'metievsk Rus. Fed. see Al'met'yevsk
Al'met'yevsk Rus. Fed. 28 J5
Älmhult Sweden 33 D4
Al Midhnab Saudi Arabia 89 J3
Al Miḩrāḑ reg. Saudi Arabia 76 E5
Almina, Punta pt Spain 42 D5
Al Mindak Saudi Arabia 89 I4
Al Minyā Egypt 89 F2
Al Minyā governorate Egypt 78 B5
Al-Mirfa U.A.E. 80 C5
Almirós Greece see Almyros
Al Mish'āb Saudi Arabia 76 D4
Al Mismīyah Syria 77 C3
Almodôvar Port. 42 B4
Almodóvar del Campo Spain 42 D3
Almont U.S.A. 130 B2
Almonte Spain 42 C4
Almonte r. Spain 42 C3
Almora India 74 C3
Almoradí Spain 43 F3
Almorox Spain 42 D2
Al Mota well Niger 93 G2
Almoustarat Mali 93 F1
Al Mu'ayzīlah hill Saudi Arabia 77 D5
Al Mubarrez Saudi Arabia 76 D4
Al Muḑairib Oman 76 F5
Al Mudawwarah Jordan 78 D5
Al Muharraq Bahrain 80 B5
Al Muḩtaṭab depr. Saudi Arabia 77 C5
Al Mukallā Yemen see Mukalla
Al Mukhā Yemen see Mocha
Al Mukhaylī Libya 88 D1
Almuñécar Spain 42 E4
Al Muqdādīyah Iraq 79 F4
Al Mūrītānīyah country Africa see Mauritania
Al Murūt well Saudi Arabia 79 D5
Al Musannāh ridge Saudi Arabia 80 A4
Al Musayjīd Saudi Arabia 89 H3
Al Muthannā governorate Iraq 79 F5
Al Muwaylih Saudi Arabia 89 G3

Almyropotamos Greece **47** D5
Almyros Greece **47** C5
Almyrou, Ormos b. Greece **47** D7
Alness U.K. **34** D3
Alnwick U.K. **34** F4

▶**Alofi** Niue **107** I3
Capital of Niue.
oceania 104–105, 114

Aloi Uganda **96** B4
Aloja Latvia **33** G4
Along India **75** G3
Alonnisos i. Greece **47** C5
Alor i. Indon. **57** F7
Alor, Kepulauan is Indon. **57** F7
Alor, Selat sea chan. Indon. **108** C2
Álora Spain **42** D4
Alor Setar Malaysia **58** C1
Alor Star Malaysia see Alor Setar
Alosno Spain **42** C4
Alost Belgium see Aalst
Alot India **74** B5
Alota Bol. **148** D5
Alotau P.N.G. **107** E3
Aloysius, Mount Australia **109** E6
Alpachiri Arg. **152** E4
Alpagut Turkey **47** F5
Alpena U.S.A. **132** F2
Alpercatas, Serra das hills Brazil **150** C3
Alpha Australia **111** F4
Alpha Ridge sea feature Arctic Ocean **166** A1
Alpine AZ U.S.A. **137** H5
Alpine CA U.S.A. **137** D5
Alpine TX U.S.A. **133** A6
Alpine WY U.S.A. **134** E4
Alpine National Park Australia **112** C5
▶**Alps** mts Europe **39** G4
europe 24–25
Al Qā' Saudi Arabia **89** I4
Al Qa'āmīyāt reg. Saudi Arabia **68** C5
Al Qaddāḥīyah Libya **88** B2
Al Qādisīyah governorate Iraq **79** F5
Al Qadmūs Syria **77** C2
Al Qaffāy i. U.A.E. **80** C5
Al Qāhirah Egypt see Cairo
Al Qāhirah governorate Egypt **78** B5
Al Qā'īyah Saudi Arabia **89** I3
Al Qal'a Beni Hammad tourist site Alg. **91** G2
Al Qalībah Saudi Arabia **89** H2
Al Qāmishlī Syria **79** E3
Al Qanṭarah Egypt **77** A4
Al Qar'ah well Saudi Arabia **76** D4
Al Qar'ah lava field Syria **77** C3
Al Qaryatayn Syria **78** D4
Al Qaṣr Egypt **89** F3
Al Qaṣr Saudi Arabia **89** I3
Al Qaṣṣ Abū Sa'īd plat. Egypt **89** E3
Al Qaṭīf Saudi Arabia **80** B5
Al Qaṭn Yemen **76** D6
Al Qaṭrānah Jordan **78** D5
Al Qaṭrūn Libya **88** B3
Al Qayṣūmah Saudi Arabia **76** D4
Al Qāyṣūmah well Saudi Arabia **89** I2
Al Qumur country Africa see Comoros
Al Qunayṭirah Syria **78** C4
Al Qunayṭirah governorate Syria **77** B3
Al Qunfidhah Saudi Arabia **89** I5
Al Qurayn Saudi Arabia **89** I3
Al Qurayyah U.A.E. **80** D5
Al Qurayyāt Saudi Arabia **89** H2
Al Qurnah Iraq **79** F5
Al Quṣayr Egypt **89** G3
Al Quwārah Saudi Arabia **89** I3
Al Quwayrah Jordan **78** C5
Alrar Est Alg. **91** H3
Alroy Downs Australia **110** D3
Alsace admin. reg. France **39** G2
Alsace, Plaine d' valley France **39** G3
Al Samha U.A.E. **80** C5
Al Samīt well Iraq **79** E5
Alsask Canada **123** I5
Alsek r. U.S.A. **122** B3
Alsfeld Germany **36** D3
Alston U.K. **34** E4
Alsuku Nigeria **93** H4
Alsunga Latvia **33** F4
Alta Norway **32** F1
Altaelva r. Norway **32** F1
Alta Floresta Brazil **149** F2
Alta Gracia Arg. **152** D2
Altai Mountains Asia **69** G2
Altamaha r. U.S.A. **129** C6
Altamira Amazonas Brazil **146** E4
Altamira Pará Brazil **147** H5
Altamira Col. **146** C4
Altamira, Cuevas de tourist site Spain **42** D1
Altamira, Sierra de mts Spain **42** D3
Altamonte Springs City U.S.A. **129** C6
Altamura Italy **45** F4
Altapirire Venez. **147** E2
Altar Mex. **135** E7
Altar r. Mex. **135** E7
Altar, Desierto de des. Mex. **135** D6
Altavista U.S.A. **130** D5
Altay China **70** G2
Altay Mongolia **62** F2
Altay, Respublika aut. rep. Rus. Fed. **70** G1
Altay Kray admin. div. Rus. Fed. see Altayskiy Kray
Altay Republic aut. rep. Rus Fed. see Altay, Respublika
Altayskiy Khrebet mts Asia see Altai Mountains
Altayskiy Kray admin. div. Rus. Fed. **62** C1
Altdorf Switz. **39** H3
Altea Spain **43** F3
Alteidet Norway **32** F1
Altenburg Germany **37** F3
Altenqoke China **75** G1
Alter do Chão Brazil **147** H5
Alter do Chão Port. **42** C3
Altevatnet l. Norway **32** E1
Altin Köprü Iraq **79** F4
Altınoluk Turkey **47** E5
Altınova Turkey **47** E5
Altıntözü Turkey **77** C1
Altıntaş Turkey **78** B3
▶**Altiplano** plain Bol. **148** C4
southamerica 142–143
Altnaharra U.K. **34** D2
Alto Araguaia Brazil **151** A6
Alto Chicapa Angola **95** C7
Alto Cruz mt. Spain **43** E2
Alto de Cabezas mt. Spain **42** E1
Alto de Covelo pass Spain **42** C1
Alto del Moncayo mt. Spain **43** F2
Alto de Pencoso hills Arg. **152** D3
Alto Douro Wine Region tourist site Port. **42** C2
Alto Garças Brazil **151** A6
Alto Ligonha Moz. **99** H2
Alto Molócuè Moz. **99** H2
Alton U.K. **35** F6
Alton IL U.S.A. **132** D4
Alton MO U.S.A. **133** D4
Alton NH U.S.A. **131** H2
Altona Canada **122** F3
Alto Nevado mt. Chile **153** E6
Altoona U.S.A. **130** D3
Alto Parnaíba Brazil **150** C4
Alto Purús r. Peru **148** C2
Alto Río Senguerr Arg. **153** C6
Altos Brazil **150** D3
Altos de Chacaya Chile **148** C4
Altos de Chinchilla mts Spain **43** F3
Altotero mt. Spain **42** E1
Altötting Germany **37** F4
Altun Shan mt. China **70** H4
Altun Shan mts China **70** G4
Alturas U.S.A. **134** B4
Altus U.S.A. **133** B5
Altyn-Topkan Tajik. see Oltintopkan
Alua Moz. **97** C8
Alucra Turkey **79** D2
Al 'Udaylīyah Saudi Arabia **80** B5
Alūksne Latvia **33** G4
Al 'Ulā Saudi Arabia **89** H3
Alūm Iran **80** B3
Alum Bridge U.S.A. **130** C4
Alum Creek Lake U.S.A. **130** B3
Alunda Sweden **33** E3
Alupka Ukr. **78** C1
Al 'Uqaylah Libya **88** C2
Al 'Uqaylah Saudi Arabia see An Nabk
Al 'Uqayr Saudi Arabia **80** B5
Al Uqṣur Egypt see Luxor
Alur India **72** C3
Al Urayq des. Saudi Arabia **89** H2
Al 'Urdun country Asia see Jordan
Alur Setar Malaysia see Alor Setar
Al Uthaylī Saudi Arabia **89** H2
Aluva India see Alwaye
Al 'Uwaynah well Saudi Arabia **80** B5
Al 'Uwaynāt Libya **88** E4
Al 'Uwaynāt Libya **88** A3
Al 'Uwayqīlah Saudi Arabia **89** I2
Al Uyainah Saudi Arabia **80** A5
Al 'Uyaynah well Saudi Arabia **77** C5
Al 'Uzaym Saudi Arabia **89** I3
Alva r. Port. **42** B2
Alva U.S.A. **133** B4
Alvand, Kūh-e mt. Iran **80** B3
Alvarado U.S.A. **133** B5
Alvarães Brazil **147** E5
Älvdalen Sweden **33** D3
Alvdalen valley Sweden **33** D3
Alvedro airport Spain **42** B1
Alvesta Sweden **33** D4
Alvin U.S.A. **133** C6
Älvsbyn Sweden **32** F2
Al Wafrah Kuwait **79** F5
Al Wajh Saudi Arabia **89** H3
Al Wakrah Qatar **80** B5
Al Wannān Saudi Arabia **80** B5
Al Waqbá well Saudi Arabia **80** A4
Alwar India **74** C4
Al Warī'ah Saudi Arabia **80** A5
Al Wāṭiyah well Egypt **89** E2
Alwaye India **72** C4
Al Widyān plat. Iraq/Saudi Arabia **79** E4
Al Wigh Libya **88** B3
Al Wigh, Ramlat des. Libya **88** C3
Al Wusayl Qatar **80** B5
Al Wusayṭ well Saudi Arabia **89** J2
Alxa Youqi China see Ehen Hudag
Al Yamāmah Saudi Arabia **80** A5
Alyangula Australia **110** D2
Al Yāsāt i. U.A.E. **80** B5
Alytus Lith. **33** G5
Alzey Germany **36** D4
Alzira Spain **43** F3
Amacayacu, Parque Nacional nat. park Col. **146** D5
Åmådalen Sweden **33** D3
Amadeus, Lake salt flat Australia **110** B5
Amadi Sudan **96** A3
Amadjuak Lake Canada **121** L3
Amadora Port. **42** B3
Amadror plain Alg. **91** G4
Amaga Col. **146** C3
Amakusa-nada b. Japan **65** B6
Åmal Sweden **33** D4
Amalaoulaou well Mali **93** F2
Amalat r. Rus. Fed. **63** J1
Amaliada Greece **47** B6
Amalner India **74** B5
Amamapare Indon. **57** I6
Amambaí Brazil **149** G5
Amambaí, Serra de hills Brazil/Para. **149** G5
Amami-Ō-shima i. Japan **63** L6
Amami-shotō is Japan **63** L6
Amamula Dem. Rep. Congo **94** E5
Åmån r. Sweden **33** D3
Amanã, Lago l. Brazil **147** E5
Amanda U.S.A. **130** B4
Amandola Italy **44** D3
Amangel'dy Kazakh. **26** G4
Amankeldi Kazakh. see Amangel'dy
Amantea Italy **45** F5
Amanzimtoti S. Africa **99** F6
Amapá Brazil **147** I4
Amapá state Brazil **147** I4
Amapari r. Brazil **147** I4
Amara Abu Sin Sudan **89** G6
Amaradia r. Romania **46** C2
Amaral Ferrador Brazil **152** G2
Amarante Brazil **150** D3
Amarapura Myanmar **60** B3
Amaravati r. India **72** C4
Amargos r. U.S.A. **137** D4
Amargosa Brazil **150** E5
Amargosa watercourse U.S.A. **135** C5
Amargosa Desert U.S.A. **137** D3
Amargosa Valley U.S.A. **137** D3
Amargura Island Tonga see Fonualei
Amarillo U.S.A. **133** A5
Amarkantak India **75** D5
Amaro, Monte mt. Italy **44** E3
Amarpur India **75** F5
Amasia Turkey see Amasya
Amasine W. Sahara **90** B4
Amasra Turkey **78** C2
Amâssine well Mali **93** F1
Amasya Turkey **78** C2
Amata Australia **110** B5
Amataurá Brazil **146** D5

▶**Amazon** r. S. America **150** A2
Longest river in South America and 2nd in the world.
southamerica 142–143
world 6–7

Amazon, Mouths of the Brazil **150** B1
Amazon, Source of the Peru **148** C3
Amazonas state Brazil **147** E6
Amazonas dept Col. **146** D5
Amazonas dept Peru **146** B6
Amazonas r. S. America see Amazon
Amazonas state Venez. **147** E4
Amazon Cone sea feature S. Atlantic Ocean **160** K5
Amazônia, Parque Nacional nat. park Brazil **147** G6
Āmba Ālagē mt. Eth. **96** C1
Ambad India **72** B2
Amba Farit mt. Eth. **96** C2
Ambahikily Madag. **99** [inset] I4
Ambajogai India **72** C2
Ambala India **74** C3
Ambalangoda Sri Lanka **72** D5
Ambalavao Madag. **99** [inset] J4
Ambam Cameroon **93** H5
Ambanja Madag. **99** [inset] K2
Ambar Iran **81** D4
Ambarchik Rus. Fed. **27** Q3
Ambarès-et-Lagarve France **38** C4
Ambargasta, Salinas de salt pan Arg. **152** D2
Ambasa India **75** F5
Ambasamudram India **72** C4
Ambathala Australia **111** F5
Ambato Ecuador **146** B5
Ambato, Sierra mts Arg. **152** D2
Ambato Boeny Madag. **99** [inset] J3
Ambato Finandrahana Madag. **99** [inset] J4
Ambatolahy Madag. **99** [inset] J4
Ambatolampy Madag. **99** [inset] J3
Ambatomainty Madag. **99** [inset] J3
Ambatondrazaka Madag. **99** [inset] K3
Ambatosia Madag. **99** [inset] K2
Ambejogai India see Ambajogai
Amberg Germany **36** E4
Ambergris Cay i. Belize **138** G5
Ambérieu-en-Bugey France **39** F4
Amberley Canada **130** C1
Ambert France **39** E4
Ambgaon India **72** D1
Ambianum France see Amiens
Ambidédi Mali **92** C2
Ambikapur India **75** D5
Ambilobe Madag. **99** [inset] K2
Ambition, Mount Canada **122** D3
Ambleside U.K. **35** E4
Amblève r. Belgium **39** F1
Ambo India **75** E5
Ambo Peru **148** A2
Amboasary Madag. **99** [inset] J5
Amboasary Gara Madag. **99** [inset] K3
Ambodifotatra Madag. **99** [inset] K3
Ambodiharina Madag. **99** [inset] K4
Ambohidratrimo Madag. **99** [inset] J3
Ambohijanahary Madag. **99** [inset] K3
Ambohimahasoa Madag. **99** [inset] J4
Ambohimanga, Royal Hill of tourist site Madag. **99** [inset] J3
Ambohipaky Madag. **99** [inset] J3
Ambohitra mt. Madag. **99** [inset] K2
Ambohitralanana Madag. **99** [inset] K2
Amboina Indon. see Ambon
Amboise France **38** D3
Ambon Indon. **57** G6
Ambon i. Indon. **57** G6
Amboró, Parque Nacional nat. park Bol. **149** D4
Amboseli National Park Kenya **96** C5
Ambositra Madag. **99** [inset] J4
Ambovombe Madag. **99** [inset] J5
Amboy U.S.A. **137** E4
Ambre, Cap d' c. Madag. see Bobaomby, Tanjona
Ambrim i. Vanuatu see Ambrym
Ambriz Angola **95** B6
Ambrizete Angola see N'zeto
Ambrosio Brazil **146** D5
Ambrym i. Vanuatu **107** F3
Ambunten Indon. **59** F4
Amchitka Island U.S.A. **120** A4
Åmdals Verk Norway **33** C4
Am-Dam Chad **88** D6
Amded, Oued watercourse Alg. **91** F5
Amderma Rus. Fed. **28** L1
Amdillis well Mali **93** E1
Am Djéména Chad **88** C6
Amdo China **75** F2
Ameca Mex. **126** F7
Amedamit mt. Eth. **96** C2
Ameghino Arg. **152** E3
Ameland i. Neth. **36** B2
Amelia Court House U.S.A. **130** E5
Amellu India **74** D4
Amendolara Italy **45** F5
Amenia U.S.A. **131** G3
American, North Fork r. U.S.A. **136** B2
American-Antarctic Ridge sea feature S. Atlantic Ocean **161** M9
American Falls U.S.A. **134** D4
American Falls Reservoir U.S.A. **134** D4
American Fork U.S.A. **137** G1

▶**American Samoa** terr. S. Pacific Ocean **107** I3
United States Unincorporated Territory.
oceania 104–105, 114

Americus U.S.A. **129** B5
Amersfoort Neth. **36** B2
Amery Canada **123** M3
Amery Ice Shelf Antarctica **167** E2
Ames U.S.A. **132** C3
Amesbury U.S.A. **131** H2
Amet India **74** B4
Amethi India **75** D4
Amfilochia Greece **47** B5
Amfissa Greece **47** C5
Amga Rus. Fed. **27** N3
Amga Rus. Fed. **64** D3
Amguema Rus. Fed. **27** S3
Amguid Alg. **91** G4
Amgun' r. Rus. Fed. **64** D1
Amhara admin. reg. Eth. **96** C2
Amherst Canada **125** H4
Amherst MA U.S.A. **131** G2
Amherst OH U.S.A. **130** B3
Amherst VA U.S.A. **130** D5
Amherstburg Canada **130** B2
Amherstdale U.S.A. **130** C5
Amherst Island Canada **131** E1
Amherstview Canada **131** E1
Amida Turkey see Diyarbakır
Amidon U.S.A. **132** A2
Amiens France **38** E2
'Amīj, Wādī watercourse Iraq **79** E4
Amik Ovası marsh Turkey **78** D3
Amilly France **39** E3
'Amīnābād Iran **80** C4
Amindhaion Greece see Amyntaio
Amindivi i. India see Amini
Amindivi Islands India **72** B4
Amini i. India **72** B4
Aminuis Namibia **98** C4
Amipshahr India **74** C3
Amīrābād Eṣfahān Iran **80** B3
Amīrābād Īlām Iran **80** A3
Amirabad Iran see Fūlād Maïalleh
Amirante Islands Seychelles **162** K6
Amirante Trench sea feature Indian Ocean **162** K6
Amisk Lake Canada **123** K4
Amistad, Represa de resr Mex./U.S.A. see Amistad Reservoir
Amistad Reservoir Mex./U.S.A. **126** F6
Amisus Turkey see Samsun
Amite U.S.A. **133** D6
Amite Creek r. U.S.A. **133** D6
Amla India **74** C5
Amlekhganj Nepal **75** E4
Åmli Norway **33** C4
Amlia Island U.S.A. **120** B4
Amlwch U.K. **35** D5
'Amm Adam Sudan **89** H5

▶**'Ammān** Jordan **78** C5
Capital of Jordan.

Amman Jordan see 'Ammān
Ammanazar Turkm. **80** C2
Ämmänsaari Fin. **28** D2
'Ammār, Tall hill Syria **77** C3
Ammarnäs Sweden **32** E2
Ammaroodinna watercourse Australia **110** C5
Ammassalik Greenland **121** P3
Ammer r. Germany **36** E5
Ammerån r. Sweden **32** E3
Ammersee l. Germany **36** E5
Ammochostos Cyprus see Famagusta
Ammochostos Bay Cyprus **77** B2
Amne Machin Range mts China see A'nyêmaqên Shan
Amnok-kang r. China/N. Korea see Yalu Jiang
Amod India **74** B5
Amo Jiang r. China **66** B4
Amol Iran **80** C2
Amolar Brazil **149** F4
Amoliani i. Greece **47** C4
Amontada Brazil **150** E2
Amor mt. Spain **42** D3
Amorebieta Spain **43** E1
Amorgos i. Greece **47** D6
Amory U.S.A. **129** A5
Amos Canada **124** E3
Åmot Norway **33** B4
Amotape, Cerros de mts Peru **146** A6
Åmotfors Sweden **33** D4
Amourj Mauritania **92** D1
Amoy China see Xiamen
Ampah Indon. **59** F3
Ampanefena Madag. **99** [inset] K2
Ampani India **73** D2
Ampanihy Madag. **99** [inset] J5
Ampanotoamaizina Madag. **99** [inset] K3
Amparafaka, Tanjona pt Madag. **99** [inset] J2
Amparai Sri Lanka **72** D5
Ampasimanolotra Madag. **99** [inset] K3
Amper r. Germany **36** E4
Amper Nigeria **93** H3
Ampere Seamount sea feature N. Atlantic Ocean **160** N3
Amphitrite Group is Paracel Is **56** D2
Ampisikinana Madag. **99** [inset] K2
Ampitsikinana Madag. see Ampisikinana
Amposta Spain **43** G2
Amqui Canada **125** H3
Amrabad India **72** C2
Amraoti India see Amravati
Amravati India **72** C1
Amreli India **74** A5
Am Rijā' Yemen **96** E1
Amritsar India **74** B3
Amroha India **74** C3
Amrum i. Germany **36** D1
Åmsele Sweden **32** E2
Amstelveen Neth. **36** B2

▶**Amsterdam** Neth. **36** B2
Official capital of the Netherlands.
europe 48
world 8–9

Amsterdam S. Africa **99** F5
Amsterdam NY U.S.A. **131** F2
Amsterdam OH U.S.A. **130** C3
Amsterdam, Île i. Indian Ocean **163** M8
Amstetten Austria **37** G4
Am Timan Chad **94** D2
Amū r. Col. **146** C4
Amu Co l. China **75** F2
Amu Darya r. Asia see Amudar'ya
Amudar'ya r. Asia **81** E1
Amudaryo r. Asia see Amudar'ya
Amund Ringnes Island Canada **121** J2
Amundsen, Mount Antarctica **167** F2
Amundsen Abyssal Plain sea feature Southern Ocean **163** W10
Amundsen Basin sea feature Arctic Ocean **166** H1
Amundsen Bay Antarctica **167** D2
Amundsen Coast Antarctica **167** J1
Amundsen Glacier Antarctica **167** I1
Amundsen Gulf Canada **120** G2
Amundsen Ridges sea feature Southern Ocean **165** J10
Amundsen-Scott research station Antarctica **167** C1
Amundsen Sea Antarctica **167** K2
Amuntai Indon. **59** F3
Amur r. Rus. Fed. **64** B3
also known as Heilong Jiang (China)
'Amur, Wadi watercourse Sudan **89** G5
Amur Oblast admin. div. Rus. Fed. see Amurskaya Oblast'
Amurrio Spain **38** B5
Amursk Rus. Fed. **64** D2
Amurskaya Oblast' admin. div. Rus. Fed. **64** B1
Amurskiy liman strait Rus. Fed. **64** E1
Amurzet Rus. Fed. **64** B3
Amvrakikos Kolpos b. Greece **47** B5
Amyderya r. Asia see Amudar'ya
Amyntaio Greece **46** B4
Amzacea Romania **46** F3
Amzérakad well Mali **93** F1
Am-Zoer Chad **88** D6
Ana r. Turkey **46** E4
Anaa atoll Fr. Polynesia **165** I7
Anabanua Indon. **57** F6
Anabar r. Rus. Fed. **27** L2
Anacapa Islands U.S.A. **136** C4
Anaco Venez. **147** E2
Anacortes U.S.A. **134** B2
Anadarko U.S.A. **133** B5
Anadolu Dağları mts Turkey **79** D2
Anadyr' Rus. Fed. **27** R3
Anadyr' r. Rus. Fed. **27** R3
Anadyr, Gulf of Rus. Fed. see Anadyrskiy Zaliv
Anadyrskiy Zaliv b. Rus. Fed. **27** S3
Anafi Greece **47** D6
Anafi i. Greece **47** D6
Anagé Brazil **150** D5
Anagni Italy **44** D4
Anagnia Italy see Anagni
'Ānah Iraq **79** E4
Anaheim U.S.A. **136** D5
Anahim Lake Canada **122** E4
Anáhuac Mex. **126** F6
Anahuac U.S.A. **133** C6
Anaimalai Hills India **72** C4
Anai Mudi Peak India **72** C4
Anaiteum i. Vanuatu see Anatom
Anajás Brazil **150** B2
Anajás, Ilha i. Brazil **150** B2
Anajatuba Brazil **150** C2
Anakao Madag. **99** [inset] I4
Anakapalle India **73** D2
Anakie Australia **111** F4
Analalava Madag. **99** [inset] J2
Analavelona mts Madag. **99** [inset] I4
Anamã Brazil **147** F5
Anambas, Kepulauan is Indon. **58** D2
Anambra state Nigeria **93** G4
Anamu r. Brazil **147** G4
Anamur Turkey **78** C3
Anan Japan **65** C6
Anand India **74** B5
Anandapur India **75** E5
Anandpur India **74** C3
Anandpur r. India **75** E5
Ananes i. Greece **47** D6
Anantapur India **72** C3
Anantnag Jammu and Kashmir **74** B2
Anant Peth India **74** C4
Ananyev Ukr. see Anan'yiv
Anan'yiv Ukr. **29** D7
Anapa Rus. Fed. **29** F7
Anápolis Brazil **149** H4
Anapú r. Brazil **147** I5
Anār Fin. see Inari
Anār Iran **80** C4
Anārak Iran **80** C3
Anarbar r. Iran **80** B3
Anardara Afgh. **81** E3
Ånäset Sweden **32** F2
Anatahan i. N. Mariana Is **57** K2
Anatajan i. N. Mariana Is see Anatahan
Anatolia reg. Turkey **78** C3
Anatoliki Makedonia kai Thraki admin. reg. Greece **46** D4
Anatom i. Vanuatu **107** F4
Añatuya Arg. **152** E2
Anauá r. Brazil **147** F4
Anavilhanas, Arquipélago das is Brazil **147** F5
Anaypazari Turkey see Gülnar
Anaz mts Saudi Arabia **77** C5
Anbyon N. Korea **65** A5
Ancares, Serra dos mts Spain **42** C1
Ancash dept Peru **148** A2
Ancaster Canada **130** D2
Ancasti, Sierra mts Arg. **152** D2
Ancenis France **38** C3
Anchán Arg. **153** D5
Anchang China see Anxian
Anchau Nigeria **93** H3
Anchodaya Bol. **148** C3
Anchorage U.S.A. **120** E3
Anchorage Reefs P.N.G. **111** G1
Anchor Bay U.S.A. **130** B2
Anchuthengu India see Anjengo
An Cóbh Rep. of Ireland see Cóbh
Ancón Peru **148** A2
Ancona Italy **44** D3
Ancud Chile **153** B5
Ancud, Golfo de g. Chile **153** B5
Ancyra Turkey see Ankara
Anda Heilong. China see Daqing
Anda Heilong. China **64** A3
Andacollo Chile **152** C2
Andahuaylas Peru **148** B3
Andal India **75** E5
Andalgalá Arg. **152** D1
Åndalsnes Norway **32** B3
Andalucía aut. comm. Spain **42** D4
Andalusia aut. comm. Spain see Andalucía
Andalusia U.S.A. **129** B6
Andām, Wādī r. Oman **76** F5
Andaman and Nicobar Islands union terr. Andaman & Nicobar Is India **73** G4
Andaman Basin sea feature Indian Ocean **162** N5
Andaman Islands India **73** G3
Andaman Sea Indian Ocean **61** A6
Andaman Strait India **73** G3
Andamooka Australia **112** A3
Andapa Madag. **99** [inset] K2
Andarāb Afgh. **81** G3
Andarob Tajik. **81** G2
Andeg Rus. Fed. **28** J2
Andegavum France see Angers
Andenes Norway **32** E1
Andéramboukane Mali **93** F2
Ånderdalen Nasjonalpark nat. park Norway **32** E1
Andermatt Switz. **39** H3
Andernos-les-Bains France **38** C4
Anderob Tajik. see Andarob
Anderson r. Canada **120** G3
Anderson AK U.S.A. **166** A2
Anderson CA U.S.A. **136** A1
Anderson IN U.S.A. **132** E3
Anderson MO U.S.A. **133** C4
Anderson SC U.S.A. **129** C5
Andes Col. **146** C3
▶**Andes** mts S. America **146** B5
southamerica 144–145
Andévalo, Sierra de hills Spain **42** C4
Andfjorden sea chan. Norway **32** E1
Andhíparos i. Greece see Antiparos
Andhra Pradesh state India **72** C2
Andía, Sierra de mts Spain **43** F1
Andijon Uzbek. see Andizhan
Andikíra Greece see Antikyra
Andikíthira i. Greece see Antikythira
Andilamena Madag. **99** [inset] K3
Andilanatoby Madag. **99** [inset] K3
Andīmeshk Iran **80** B3
Andímilos i. Greece see Antimilos
Andípaxoi i. Greece see Antipaxoi
Andípsara i. Greece see Antipsara
Andir He r. China **75** D1
Andırın Turkey **78** D3
Andiyskoye Koysu r. Rus. Fed. **79** F2
Andiyur India **72** C4
Andizhan Uzbek. **70** D3
Andkhui r. Afgh. **81** F2
Andkhvoy Afgh. **81** F2
Andoany Madag. **99** [inset] K2
Andoas Peru **146** B5
Andoas Nuevo Ecuador **146** B5
Andohajango Madag. **99** [inset] K2
Andol India **72** C2
Andong China see Dandong
Andong S. Korea **65** B5
Andoom Australia **111** E2
▶**Andorra** country Europe **43** G1
europe 24–25, 48
Andorra Spain **43** F2

▶**Andorra la Vella** Andorra **43** G1
Capital of Andorra.

Andorra la Vieja Andorra see Andorra la Vella
Andover U.K. **35** F6
Andover MA U.S.A. **131** H2
Andover NH U.S.A. **131** H2
Andover NY U.S.A. **130** E2
Andover OH U.S.A. **130** C3
Andøya i. Norway **32** D1
Andrade U.S.A. **137** E5
Andradina Brazil **149** H5
Andramy Madag. **99** [inset] J3
Andranomavo Madag. **99** [inset] J3
Andranomena Madag. **99** [inset] J3
Andranopasy Madag. **99** [inset] I4
Andranovondronina Madag. **99** [inset] K2
Andranovory Madag. **99** [inset] J4
Andreanof Islands U.S.A. **120** B4
Andreapol' Rus. Fed. **28** E4
André Félix, Parc National de nat. park Cent. Afr. Rep. **94** D2
Andrew Canada **123** H4
Andrews U.S.A. **133** A5
Andreyevka Rus. Fed. **29** I5
Andria Italy **44** F4
Andriba Madag. **99** [inset] J3
Andringitra mts Madag. **99** [inset] J4
Androka Madag. **99** [inset] J5
Andronа reg. Madag. **99** [inset] K2
Andropov Rus. Fed. see Rybinsk
Andros i. Bahamas **129** D7
Andros Greece **47** D6
Andros i. Greece **47** D6
Androscoggin r. U.S.A. **131** I2
Andros Town Bahamas **129** D7
Andrott i. India **72** B4
Andrushevka Ukr. see Andrushivka
Andrushivka Ukr. **29** D6
Andrychów Poland **37** I4
Andselv Norway **32** E1
Andsnes Norway **32** F1
Andújar Spain **42** D3
Andulo Angola **95** C7
Anec, Lake salt flat Australia **109** E5
Anecón Grande mt. Arg. **153** C5
Anéfis Mali **93** F1
Anéfis well Mali **93** E1
Anegada i. Virgin Is (U.K.) **139** L5
Anegada, Bahía b. Arg. **152** E5
Anegada Passage Virgin Is (U.K.) **139** L5
Anegam U.S.A. **137** F5
Aného Togo **93** F4
Aneityum i. Vanuatu see Anatom
'Aneiza, Jabal hill Iraq see 'Unayzah, Jabal
Anekal India **72** C3
Añelo Arg. **152** C4
Anemourion tourist site Turkey **77** A1
Anesbaraka well Alg. **91** G6
Anet France **38** D2
Anetchom, Île i. Vanuatu see Anatom
Aneto mt. Spain **43** G1
Aney Niger **93** I1
Aneytioum, Île i. Vanuatu see Anatom
Anfile Bay Eritrea **89** I6
Anfu China **67** E3
Angadippuram India **72** C4
Angadoka, Lohatanjona hd Madag. **99** [inset] J2
Angalarri r. Australia **110** B2
Angamma, Falaise d' esc. Chad **88** C5
Angamos, Punta pt Chile **148** C5

▶**Angara** r. Rus. Fed. **27** J4
Part of the Yenisey-Angara-Selenga, 3rd longest river in Asia.
asia 50–51

Angarsk Rus. Fed. **62** G1
Angas Downs Australia **110** C5
Angas Range hills Australia **108** E5
Angaston Australia **112** A4
Angaur i. Palau **57** H4
Ånge Sweden **33** D3
Ángel, Salto waterfall Venez. see Angel Falls
Angel de la Guarda, Isla i. Mex. **135** D7

▶**Angel Falls** Venez. **147** F3
Highest waterfall in the world.
southamerica 154

Ängelholm Sweden **33** D4
Angellala Creek r. Australia **111** F5
Angelo r. Australia **108** B5
Angels Camp U.S.A. **136** B2
Ängereb Wenz r. Eth. **96** C1
Ångermanälven r. Sweden **32** E3
Angermünde Germany **37** G2
Angers France **38** C3
Angical Brazil **150** C4
Angikuni Lake Canada **123** L2
Angkor tourist site Cambodia **61** C5
Anglesey i. U.K. **35** D5
Angleton U.S.A. **133** C6
Anglin r. France **38** D3
Anglo-Egyptian Sudan country Africa see Sudan
Angmagssalik Greenland see Ammassalik
Ang Mo Kio Sing. **58** [inset]
Ango Dem. Rep. Congo **94** E3
Angoche Moz. **99** H3
Angohrān Iran **80** D5
Angol Chile **152** B4
▶**Angola** country Africa **95** C7
africa 86–87, 100
Angola IN U.S.A. **132** E3
Angola NY U.S.A. **130** D2
Angola Basin sea feature S. Atlantic Ocean **160** N7
Angonia, Planalto de plat. Moz. **97** B8
Angora Turkey see Ankara
Angoulême France **38** D4
Angren Uzbek. **70** D3
Ang Thong Thai. **61** C5
Angu Dem. Rep. Congo **94** E4
Angualasto Arg. **152** C2

▶**Anguilla** terr. West Indies **139** L5
United Kingdom Overseas Territory.
northamerica 118–119, 140

Anguilla Cays is Bahamas **129** D8
Anguille, Cape Canada **125** J4
Angurugu Australia **110** D2
Anholt i. Denmark **33** C4
Anhua China **67** D2
Anhui prov. China **67** F1
Anhumas Brazil **151** A6
Anhwei prov. China see Anhui
Aniak U.S.A. **120** D3
Aniakchak National Monument and Preserve nat. park U.S.A. **120** D4
Ánidhros i. Greece see Anydro
Anié Togo **93** F4
Anie, Pic d' mt. France **38** C5
Animas r. U.S.A. **135** E5
Anina Romania **46** B2
Anıtlı Turkey **77** A1
Aniva Rus. Fed. **64** E3
Aniva, Mys c. Rus. Fed. **64** E3
Aniva, Zaliv b. Rus. Fed. **64** E3
Anivorano Avaratra Madag. **99** [inset] K2
Anjad India **74** B5
Anjafy mt. Madag. **99** [inset] J3
Anjalankoski Fin. **33** G3
Anjangaon India **74** C5
Anjar India **74** A5
Anjengo India **72** C4
Anji China **67** F2
Anji India **72** C1
Anjiang China see Qianyang
Anjir Avand Iran **80** C3
Anjou, Val d' valley France **38** C3
Anjouan i. Comoros see Nzwani
Anjozorobe Madag. **99** [inset] J3
Anjŭ N. Korea **63** L4
Anka Nigeria **93** G2
Ankaboa, Tanjona pt Madag. **99** [inset] I4
Ankang China **67** D1

▶**Ankara** Turkey **78** C3
Capital of Turkey.

Ankaratra mts Madag. **99** [inset] J3
Ankatafa Madag. **99** [inset] K2
Ankavandra Madag. **99** [inset] J3
Ankazoabo Madag. **99** [inset] J4
Ankazobe Madag. **99** [inset] J3
Ankeny U.S.A. **132** C3
Ankerika Madag. **99** [inset] J2
An Khê Vietnam **61** E5
Ankiliabo Madag. **99** [inset] I4
Anklam Germany **37** F2
Ankleshwar India **74** B5
Anklesvar India see Ankleshwar
Ankofa mt. Madag. **99** [inset] K3
Ankogel mt. Austria **37** F5
Ankola India **72** B3
Ankpa Nigeria **93** G4
Anloga Ghana **93** F4
Anlong China **66** C3
Ânlong Vêng Cambodia **61** D5
Anlu China **67** E2
Anmoore U.S.A. **130** C4

An Muileann gCearr Rep. of Ireland see Mullingar
Anmyŏn-do i. S. Korea 65 A5
Ann, Cape Antarctica 167 D2
Ann, Cape U.S.A. 131 H2
Anna Rus. Fed. 29 G6
Anna, Lake U.S.A. 130 E4
Annaba Alg. 91 G1
Annaberg-Buchholtz Germany 37 F3
An Nabk Saudi Arabia 77 C4
An Nabk Syria 78 D4
Annai Guyana 147 G4
An Najaf Iraq 79 F5
An Najaf governorate Iraq 79 E5
Annalee r. Rep. of Ireland see
Annam reg. Vietnam 60 D4
Annam Highlands mts Laos/Vietnam 60 D4
Annan U.K. 34 E4
Annan r. U.K. 34 E4
'Annān, Wādī al watercourse Syria 77 D2
Annandale U.S.A. 131 E4
Anna Plains Australia 108 C4
▶Annapolis U.S.A. 131 E4
State capital of Maryland.
▶Annapolis Royal Canada 125 H4
▶Annapurna I mt. Nepal 75 D3
10th highest mountain in the world and in Asia.
asia 50-51
world 6-7
Annapurna II mt. Nepal 75 E3
Ann Arbor U.S.A. 130 B2
Anna Regina Guyana 147 G3
An Nás Rep. of Ireland see Naas
An Nashū, Wādī watercourse Libya 88 B3
An Nāşiriyah Iraq 79 F5
An Nawfalīyah Libya 88 C2
Annean, Lake salt flat Australia 109 B6
Anne Arundel Town U.S.A. see Annapolis
Annecy France 39 G4
Annecy, Lake c. d' l. France 39 G4
Annecy-le-Vieux France 39 G4
Anne Marie Lake Canada 125 I2
Annette Island U.S.A. 122 C4
Annie r. Australia 111 I3
An Nimārah Syria 78 D4
An Nimāş Saudi Arabia 89 I5
Anning China 66 B3
Anning He r. China 66 B3
Anniston U.S.A. 129 B5
Annobón i. Equat. Guinea 93 G6
Annonay France 39 F4
An Nu'ayrīyah Saudi Arabia 76 D4
An Nu'mānīyah Iraq 79 F4
An Nuqay'ah Qatar 80 D5
An Nuşayrīyah, Jabal mts Syria 77 C2
Annville U.S.A. 130 E4
Anogeia Greece 47 D7
Anori Brazil 146 F5
Anorontany, Tanjona hd Madag. 99 [inset] I2
Anosibe An'Ala Madag. 99 [inset] K3
Anou I-n-Atei well Alg. 91 G3
Ânou Mellene well Mali 93 F1
Anou-n-Bidek well Alg. 91 G6
Ano Viannos Greece 47 D7
Anóyia Greece see Anogeia
Anpu China 67 D4
Anpu Gang b. China 67 D4
Anqing China 67 F2
Anren China 67 E3
Ansbach Germany 39 I2
Anserma Col. 146 C3
Anshan China 63 K3
Anshun China 66 E3
Anshunchang China 66 B2
Ansina Uruguay 152 G2
An Sirhān, Wādī watercourse Saudi Arabia 89 H3
Ansjö Sweden 32 E3
Anson U.S.A. 133 B5
Anson Bay Australia 110 B2
Ansongo Mali 93 F2
Ansted U.S.A. 130 E4
Anstruther U.K. 34 E3
Anta India 74 C4
Anta Peru 148 B3
Antabamba Peru 148 B3
Antakya Turkey 78 D3
Antalaha Madag. 99 [inset] K2
Antalya Turkey 78 B3
Antalya Körfezi g. Turkey 78 B3
Antanambao Manampotsy Madag. 99 [inset] K3
Antanambe Madag. 99 [inset] K3
▶Antananarivo Madag. 99 [inset] J3
Capital of Madagascar.
Antananarivo prov. Madag. 99 [inset] J3
Antanifotsy Madag. 99 [inset] J3
Antanimora Atsimo Madag. 99 [inset] J5
An tAonach Rep. of Ireland see Nenagh
▶Antarctica 163 H6
Most southerly and coldest continent, and the continent with the highest average elevation.
poles 158-159, 168
Antarctic Peninsula Antarctica 167 L2
Antaritarika Madag. 99 [inset] J5
Antelope Range mts U.S.A. 137 D6
Antequera Spain 42 D4
Anthony KS U.S.A. 132 B4
Anthony NM U.S.A. 135 F6
Anthony Lagoon Australia 110 C3
Anti Atlas mts Morocco 90 C3
Antibes France 39 G5
Anticosti, Île d' i. Canada 125 I3
Anticosti Island Canada see Anticosti, Île d'
Antifer, Cap d' c. France 38 D2
Antigo U.S.A. 130 A3
Antigonish Canada 125 I4
Antigua i. Antigua and Barbuda 139 L5
Antigua country West Indies see Antigua and Barbuda
▶Antigua and Barbuda country West Indies 139 L5
northamerica 118-119, 140
Antikyra Greece 47 C5
Antikythira i. Greece 47 C7
Antikythiro, Steno sea chan. Greece 47 C7
Anti Lebanon mts Lebanon/Syria see Sharqī, Jabal ash
Antilla Arg. 152 C2
Antilla Cuba 127 K7
Antimilos i. Greece 47 D6
Antimony U.S.A. 137 G2
An tInbhear Mór Rep. of Ireland see Arklow
Antioch Turkey see Antakya
Antioch U.S.A. 136 B2

Antiocheia ad Cragum tourist site Turkey 77 A1
Antiochia Turkey see Antakya
Antioquia Col. 146 C3
Antioquia dept Col. 146 C3
Antiparos i. Greece 47 D6
Antipaxoi i. Greece 47 B5
Antipodes Islands N.Z. 107 G6
Antissa i. Greece 47 E6
Antium Italy see Anzio
Antlers U.S.A. 133 C5
An t-Ob U.K. see Leverburgh
Antofagasta Chile 148 C5
Antofagasta admin. reg. Chile 148 C5
Antonhibe Madag. 99 [inset] J2
Antonio de Biedma Arg. 153 D6
António Enes Moz. see Angoche
Antônio Lemos Brazil 150 B2
Antrim U.K. 35 C4
Antrim Hills U.K. 34 C3
Antrim Plateau Australia 108 E4
Antrodoco Italy 44 E3
Antsalova Madag. 99 [inset] J3
Antsambalahy Madag. 99 [inset] K2
Antseranana Madag. see Antsirañana
Antsirabe Madag. 99 [inset] K3
Antsirabe Avaratra Madag. 99 [inset] K2
Antsirañana Madag. 99 [inset] K2
Antsirañana prov. Madag. 99 [inset] K2
Antsla Estonia 28 O4
Antsohihy Madag. 99 [inset] J2
Antsohimbondrona Madag. 99 [inset] K2
Antsondrodava Madag. 99 [inset] J3
Anttis Sweden 28 N3
Antu China see Songjiang
An Tuc Vietnam see An Khê
Antuco Chile 152 C4
Antuco, Volcán vol. Chile 152 C4
Antwerp Belgium 36 B3
Antwerp U.S.A. 131 F1
An Uaimh Rep. of Ireland see Navan
Anuc, Lac l. Canada 125 F1
Anuchino Rus. Fed. 64 D4
Anueque, Sierra mts Arg. 153 C5
Anugul India 73 E1
Anupgarh India 74 B3
Anuppur India 74 D5
Anuradhapura Sri Lanka 72 D4
Anvers Belgium see Antwerp
Anvers Island Antarctica 167 L2
Anvil Range mts Canada 122 C2
Anxi China 70 H4
Anxian China 66 C2
Anxiang China 67 E2
Anxious Bay Australia 109 F8
Anxur Italy see Terracina
Anyang Guangxi China see Du'an
Anyang Henan China 63 I4
Anyang S. Korea 65 A5
Anydro i. Greece 47 D6
A'nyêmaqên Shan mts China 66 A1
Anyi China 67 E2
Anykščiai Lith. 33 G5
Anyuan China 67 E3
Anyue China 66 D2
Anyuy r. Rus. Fed. 64 D2
Anyuysk Rus. Fed. 27 Q3
Anzac Alta Canada 123 I3
Anzac B.C. Canada 122 F4
Anzhero-Sudzhensk Rus. Fed. 27 I4
Anzi Dem. Rep. Congo 94 D5
Anzio Italy 44 E4
Aoba i. Vanuatu 107 F3
Aob Luang National Park Thai. 60 B4
Aoga-shima i. Japan 65 D6
Aomen China see Macau
Aomori Japan 64 E4
Aoos r. Greece 47 B4
Aoraki N.Z. see Mount Cook
Aoraki mt. N.Z. see Cook, Mount
Aôral, Phnum mt. Cambodia 61 D5
Aorangi mt. N.Z. see Cook, Mount
Aosta Italy 44 A2
Aotearoa country Oceania see New Zealand
Aouderas Niger 93 H1
Aoufist W. Sahara 90 B4
Aouinet bel Egra well Alg. 90 D4
Aouk, Bahr r. Cent. Afr. Rep./Chad 94 C2
Aoukâlé r. Cent. Afr. Rep./Chad 94 C2
Aoukâr reg. Mali/Mauritania 90 C5
Aoukenek well Mali 93 F1
Aoulef Alg. 91 F4
Aoulime, Jbel mt. Morocco 90 C3
Aourou Mali 92 C2
Aoxi China see Le'an
Aoyang China see Shanggao
Aozou Chad 88 C4
Apa r. Brazil 149 F5
Apac Uganda 96 B4
Apache U.S.A. 133 C5
Apache Junction U.S.A. 137 G5
Apahida Romania 46 C1
Apalachee Bay U.S.A. 129 B6
Apalachicola U.S.A. 129 B6
Apalachicola r. U.S.A. 129 B6
Apamea Turkey see Dinar
Apaporis r. Col. 146 D5
Apar, Teluk b. Indon. 59 G3
Aparecida do Tabuado Brazil 149 H5
Aparima r. N.Z. see Riverton
Aparri Phil. 57 F2
Apatin Yugo. 46 A2
Apatity Rus. Fed. 32 I2
Apatou Fr. Guiana 147 H3
Apatzingán Mex. 126 F8
Ape Latvia 33 G4
Apeldoorn Neth. 36 B2
Apennines mts Italy 31 G4
Apere r. Bol. 148 B3
Apex Mountain Canada 122 B2
Aphrodite's Birthplace tourist site Cyprus 77 A2
Api Dem. Rep. Congo 94 E4
Api mt. Nepal 74 D3
▶Apia Samoa 107 H3
Capital of Samoa.
Apiacas, Serra dos hills Brazil 149 F2
Apiaí Brazil 151 B8
Apiaú, Serra do mts Brazil 147 F4
Apio Solomon Is 107 F2
Apiti N.Z. 113 C2
Apizaco Peru 148 B3
Apo, Mount vol. Phil. 57 G4
Apodi Brazil 150 B3
Apodi, Chapada do Brazil 150 B3
Apoera Suriname 147 G3
Apolda Germany 37 E3
Apollinopolis Magna Egypt see Idfū
Apollonia Bulg. see Sozopol
Apollonia Greece 47 D6
Apolo Bol. 148 C3
Apopka U.S.A. 129 C6
Aporé Brazil 150 C5
Aporema Brazil 147 I4
Apostle Islands U.S.A. 130 A2
Apostolens Tommelfinger mt. Greenland 121 O3

Apostolos Andreas, Cape Cyprus 77 B2
Apoteri Guyana 147 G3
Appalachia U.S.A. 130 B5
Appalachian Mountains U.S.A. 130 D4
Appalla i. Fiji see Kabara
Appennino Abruzzese mts Italy 44 D3
Appennino Lucano mts Italy 45 E4
Appennino Napoletano mts Italy 44 C3
Appiano sulla Strada del Vino Italy 44 C1
Applecross U.K. 34 D3
Appleton MN U.S.A. 132 B2
Appleton WI U.S.A. 130 C2
Apple Valley U.S.A. 136 D4
Appomattox U.S.A. 130 D5
Aprilia Italy 44 D4
Apsheronsk Rus. Fed. 29 F7
Apsheronsk Rus. Fed. see Apsheronsk
Apsheronsk Rus. Fed. see Abşeron Yarımadası
Apsley Canada 130 D1
Apt France 39 G5
Apucarana Brazil 149 H5
Apucarana, Serra da hills Brazil 149 H5
Apulum Romania see Alba Iulia
Apure state Venez. 146 D3
Apure r. Venez. 146 E3
Apurímac dept Peru 148 B3
Apurímac r. Peru 148 B3
Apurito Venez. 146 E3
Aq''a Georgia see Sokhumi
'Aqaba Jordan see Al 'Aqabah
Aqaba, Gulf of Asia 77 B5
'Aqabah, Wādī al watercourse Egypt 77 A4
Aqadyr Kazakh. see Agadyr'
Āqchah Afgh. 81 F2
Aq Chai r. Iran 79 F3
Aqdā Iran 80 C3
Aqdoghmish r. Iran 80 A2
Aqiq Sudan 89 H3
Aqköl Kazakh. see Akkol
Aqköl Atyrauskaya Oblast' Kazakh. see Akkol'
Aqmola Kazakh. see Astana
Āq Qal'eh Iran 80 C2
Aqqikkol Hu salt l. China 70 G4
'Aqrah hill Iraq 79 F3
'Aqran hill Saudi Arabia 77 D4
Aqsay Kazakh. see Aksay
Aqsayqin Hit terr. Asia see Aksai Chin
Aqshuqyr Kazakh. see Akshukur
Aqtaü Kazakh. see Aktau
Aqtöbe Kazakh. see Aktobe
Aqtöbe Oblysy admin. div. Kazakh. see Aktyubinskaya Oblast'
Aquae Grani Germany see Aachen
Aquae Gratianae France see Aix-les-Bains
Aquae Sextiae France see Aix-en-Provence
Aquae Statiellae Italy see Acqui Terme
Aquarius Mountains U.S.A. 137 F4
Aquarius Plateau U.S.A. 137 G2
Aquaviva delle Fonti Italy 44 F4
Aquidabánmi r. Para. 149 F5
Aquidauana Brazil 149 G5
Aquidauana r. Brazil 149 G4
Aquiles Mex. 135 F7
Aquin Haiti 139 J5
Aquincum Hungary see Budapest
Aquiry r. Brazil see Acre
Aquisgranum Germany see Aachen
Aquitaine admin. reg. France 38 C4
Aqzhaygyn Köli salt l. Kazakh. see Akzhaykyn, Ozero
Ara India 75 E4
Ara r. Spain 43 G1
Āra Ārba mt. Eth. 96 D3
Arab, Bahr el watercourse Sudan 94 E3
'Arab, Khalīj al b. Egypt 89 F2
Ara Bacalle well Eth. 96 D3
'Arabah, Wādī watercourse Egypt 77 A5
'Arabah, Wādī al watercourse Israel/Jordan 77 B5
Arabelo Venez. 147 F3
Arabian Basin sea feature Indian Ocean 162 L5
Arabian Gulf Asia see The Gulf
Arabian Peninsula Asia 76 C4
Arabian Sea Indian Ocean 68 G5
Ara Bonel Eth. 96 D3
Arabopó Venez. 147 F3
Araç Turkey 78 C2
Araça r. Brazil 146 F4
Aracaju Brazil 150 E4
Aracanguy, Montes de hills Para. 149 G6
Aracati Brazil 150 D5
Aracatu Brazil 150 D5
Araçatuba Brazil 149 H5
Aracena Spain 42 C4
Aracena, Sierra de hills Spain 42 C4
Arachthos r. Greece 47 B5
Aračinovo Macedonia 46 B3
Aracoiaba Brazil 150 B3
Aracruz Brazil 151 D6
Araçuaí Brazil 150 D4
Araçuaí r. Brazil 151 D6
'Arad Israel 77 B4
Arad Romania 46 B1
Arada Chad 88 D6
Arādān Iran 80 C3
Aradeib, Wadi watercourse Sudan 88 D6
Arafura Sea Australia/Indon. 106 C2
Arafura Shelf sea feature Australia/Indon. 164 C6
Aragarças Brazil 150 C5
Aragón aut. comm. Spain 43 C3
Aragón r. Spain 43 C2
Aragoncillo mt. Spain 43 E2
Aragua state Venez. 146 E2
Araguacema Brazil 150 B4
Aragua de Barcelona Venez. 147 E2
Aragua de Maturín Venez. 147 E2
Araguaia r. Brazil 149 H1
Araguaia, Parque Nacional de nat. park Brazil 150 B4
Araguaiana Brazil 149 H3
Araguari Brazil 150 B3
Araguapiche, Punta pt Venez. 147 F2
Araguari r. Brazil 147 I4
Araguari r. Brazil 150 B3
Araguatins Brazil 150 B3
Arai Japan 65 D5
Araioses Brazil 150 D2
Arak Alg. 91 F3
Arāk Iran 80 B3
Arak Syria 77 D2
Arakaka Guyana 147 G2
Arakan state Myanmar 60 A3
Arakan Yoma mts Myanmar 60 A3
Arakhthos r. Greece see Arachthos
Arakkonam India 72 C3
Aral Kazakh. see Aral'sk
Aral Tajik. see Vose

▶Aral Sea salt l. Kazakh./Uzbek. 70 B2
2nd largest lake in Asia and 6th in the world.
asia 50-51
world 6-7
Aral'sk Kazakh. 70 B2
Aral'skoye More salt l. Kazakh./Uzbek. see Aral Sea
Aralsor, Ozero l. Kazakh. 29 I6
Aralsor, Ozero salt l. Kazakh. 29 J6
Aral Tengizi salt l. Kazakh./Uzbek. see Aral Sea
Aramac Australia 111 F4
Aramac Creek watercourse Australia 111 F4
Aramah plat. Saudi Arabia 80 A5
Arame Brazil 150 C3
Aramia r. P.N.G. 57 J7
Aran r. India 72 C2
Arancibia Arg. 152 C2
Aranda de Duero Spain 42 E2
Arandelovac Yugo. 46 B2
Arandis Namibia 98 B4
Arang India 75 D5
Aranjuez Spain 42 E2
Aranos Namibia 98 C5
Aransas Pass U.S.A. 133 B7
Arantangi India 72 C4
Aranyaprathet Thai. 61 C5
Arao Japan 65 B6
Araouane Mali 92 E1
Arapaho U.S.A. 132 E1
Arapahoe U.S.A. 132 B3
Arapgir Turkey 79 D3
Arapiraca Brazil 150 E4
Arapis, Akra pt Greece 47 D4
Arapkir Turkey see Arapgir
Arapongas Brazil 149 H5
Arapsun Turkey see Gülşehir
'Ar'ar Saudi Arabia 79 E5
'Ar'ar, Wādī watercourse Iraq/Saudi Arabia 79 E5
Arara r. Brazil 147 F5
Araracuara Col. 146 C5
Araracuara, Cerros de hills Col. 146 C5
Araranguá Brazil 151 B9
Araraquara Brazil 149 H5
Araras Amazonas Brazil 148 C2
Araras Pará Brazil 147 H6
Ararás Brazil 148 C2
Araras, Açude resr Brazil 150 D3
Araras, Serra das mts Brazil 151 A6
Araras, Serra das mts Brazil 151 A8
Ararat Armenia 79 F3
Ararat Australia 112 B5
Ararat, Mount Turkey 79 F3
Araripe, Chapada do hills Brazil 150 D3
Araripina Brazil 150 D3
Aras Turkey 79 F3
Aras r. Turkey 79 F3
Aratāne well Mauritania 92 C1
Arataú r. Brazil 150 B2
Aratürük China see Yiwu
Arauá r. Brazil 147 F6
Arauá r. Brazil 147 F6
Arauca Col. 146 D3
Arauca dept Col. 146 D3
Arauca r. Venez. 146 E3
Arauco Chile 152 C4
Arauquita Col. 146 D3
Araure Venez. 146 D2
Aravaipa Creek watercourse U.S.A. 137 G5
Aravalli Range mts India 74 B4
Aravete Estonia 33 G4
Araviana r. Spain 43 E2
Arawale National Reserve nature res. Kenya 96 D5
Araxá Brazil 151 C6
Araxos, Akra pt Greece 47 B5
Araya, Península de pen. Venez. 147 E2
Arayıt Dağı m. Turkey 78 B3
Araz r. Azer. 79 G2
Arba r. Spain 43 F2
Arbailu Iraq see Arbīl
Ārba Minch Eth. 96 D3
Arbela Iraq see Arbīl
Arbil Iraq 79 F3
Arbil governorate Iraq 79 E4
Arboga Sweden 33 I4
Arboletes Col. 146 B2
Arbon Switz. 39 I3
Arborfield Canada 123 K4
Arborg Canada 123 L5
Arbroath U.K. 34 E3
Arbu Lut, Dasht-e des. Afgh. 81 E4
Arc r. France 39 G4
Arcachon France 38 C4
Arcachon, Bassin d' inlet France 38 C4
Arcadia LA U.S.A. 133 C5
Arcadia U.S.A. 129 C7
Arcadia U.S.A. 130 A4
Arcanum U.S.A. 130 A4
Arcata U.S.A. 134 A4
Arc Dome mt. U.S.A. 136 D2
Arcelia Mex. 138 D5
Archangel Rus. Fed. 28 G2
Archangel Oblast admin. div. Rus. Fed. see Arkhangel'skaya Oblast'
Archar r. Bulg. 46 C3
Archbold U.S.A. 130 B3
Archena Spain 43 F3
Archer r. Australia 111 F2
Archer Bend National Park Australia 111 F2
Arches National Park U.S.A. 137 H2
Archidona Spain 42 D4
Archie Creek r. Australia 110 D3
Archman Turkm. 80 C2
Arcipelago di La Maddalena, Parco Nazionale dell' nat. park Sardinia Italy 44 C4
Arco Italy 44 C2
Arco U.S.A. 134 D4
Arcos de Jalón Spain 43 E2
Arcos de la Frontera Spain 42 D4
Arcos de Valdevez Port. 42 B2
Arcot India 72 C3
Arcoverde Brazil 150 E4
Arctic Bay Canada 121 K2
Arctic Institute Islands Rus. Fed. see Arkticheskogo Instituta, Ostrova
Arctic Mid-Ocean Ridge sea feature Arctic Ocean 166 H1
▶Arctic Ocean 166
poles 158-159, 168
Arctic Red r. Canada 122 C1
Arctic Red River Canada see Tsiigehtchic
Arctowski research station Antarctica 167 A2
Arda r. Bulg. 46 D4
Ardabīl Iran 80 A2
Ardahan Turkey 79 E2

Ardak Iran 81 D2
Ardakān Fārs Iran 80 C4
Ardakān Yazd Iran 80 C3
Ardal Norway 33 B3
Ardalstangen Norway 33 B3
Ardas r. Greece 46 E4
Ardatov Nizhegorodskaya Oblast' Rus. Fed. 28 I4
Ardatov Respublika Mordoviya Rus. Fed. 29 H5
Ardèche r. France 39 F4
Ardee Rep. of Ireland 35 C5
Ardennes plat. Belgium 39 F2
Ardentes France 38 D3
Ardestān Iran 80 C3
Ardila r. Port. 42 C3
Ardlethan Australia 112 C4
Ardmore Australia 110 C4
Ardmore U.S.A. 133 B5
Ardnamurchan, Point of U.K. 34 C3
Ardon Rus. Fed. 79 G2
Ardrossan Australia 112 A4
Ardrossan U.K. 34 D4
Ards Peninsula U.K. 35 D4
Ardvasar U.K. 34 D3
Åre Sweden 32 I3
Arebi Dem. Rep. Congo 94 E4
Aregua Para. 149 F6
Areia Branca Brazil 150 E3
Arel Belgium see Arlon
Arelas France see Arles
Arelate France see Arles
Arena, Point U.S.A. 136 A2
Arenal, Campo del Arg. 152 C1
Arenal, Puerto del pass Spain 43 E4
Arenápolis Brazil 149 F3
Arenas, Punta de pt Arg. 153 C8
Arendal Norway 33 C4
Arendsee (Altmark) Germany 36 E2
Areopoli Greece 47 B6
Areponapuchi Mex. 135 F8
Arequipa Peru 148 C4
Arequipa dept Peru 148 B3
Arere Brazil 147 H5
Arévalo Spain 42 D2
Arezzo Italy 44 C3
'Arfajah well Saudi Arabia 79 D5
Arfara Greece 47 C6
Arga r. Spain 43 F1
Argadargada Australia 110 C4
Argalasti Greece 47 C5
Arganda Spain 42 E2
Argelès-Gazost France 38 C5
Argens r. France 39 G5
Argenta Italy 44 C2
Argentan France 38 C2
Argentat France 38 D2
Argentera, Cima dell' mt. Italy 44 A2
▶Argentina country S. America 152 C3
2nd largest country in South America and 8th in the world. 3rd most populous country in South America.
southamerica 144-145, 154
world 8-9
Argentine Abyssal Plain sea feature S. Atlantic Ocean 161 K9
Argentine Basin sea feature S. Atlantic Ocean 161 L8
Argentine Republic country S. America see Argentina
Argentine Rise sea feature S. Atlantic Ocean 161 K8
Argentino, Lago l. Arg. 153 B7
Argenton r. France 38 C2
Argentoratum France see Strasbourg
Argentré France 38 C2
Argeş r. Romania 46 E2
Argeşel r. Romania 46 D2
Arghandab r. Afgh. 81 F4
Arghastan r. Afgh. 81 F4
Argolikos Kolpos b. Greece 47 C6
Argos Greece 47 C6
Argos Orestiko Greece 47 B4
Argostoli Greece 47 B5
Argun' r. China/Rus. Fed. 63 K1
Argun r. Georgia/Rus. Fed. 79 F2
Argun Rus. Fed. 79 F2
Argungu Nigeria 93 G3
Argus Range mts U.S.A. 136 D3
Argyle Canada 124 D2
Argyle, Lake Australia 110 E3
Argyrokastron Albania see G rokastë
Ar Horqin Qi China see Tianshan
Århus Denmark 33 C4
Ariake-ko b. Japan 65 B6
Ariamsvlei Namibia 98 B6
Ariano Irpino Italy 44 E4
Arias Arg. 152 E3
Ari Atoll Maldives 71 D11
Aribi r. Venez. 147 F3
Aribinda Burkina 93 E2
Arica Chile 148 C5
Arica Col. 146 D5
Aricagua Venez. 146 D2
Arid, Cape Australia 109 C8
Aridaia Greece 46 C4
Arieş r. Romania 46 C1
Arih Syria 78 D3
Arihā West Bank see Jericho
Arikaree r. U.S.A. 132 A3
Arilje Yugo. 46 B3
Ariminum Italy see Rimini
Arimu Mine Guyana 147 G3
Arinagour U.K. 34 C3
Arinos Mato Grosso Brazil 149 G3
Arinos Minas Gerais Brazil 150 B5
Arinos r. Brazil 149 G3
Ariogala Lith. 33 F5
Aripuanã Brazil 149 F2
Aripuanã r. Brazil 147 F6
Ariquemes Brazil 148 C2
Arisaig U.K. 34 D3
Arisaig, Sound of sea chan. U.K. 34 D3
Aristazábal, Cabo c. Arg. 153 D6
Aritwala Pak. 81 H4
Arivonimamo Madag. 99 [inset] J3
Ariyalur India 72 C4
Arizaro, Salar de salt flat Arg. 148 D6
Arizona Arg. 152 D4
Arizona state U.S.A. 137 G4
'Arjah Saudi Arabia 89 I5
Arjäng Sweden 33 D4
Arjasa Indon. 59 F5
Arjeplog Sweden 32 J3
Arjona Col. 146 C2
Arjona Spain 42 D4
Arjuni India 75 D5
Arkadak Rus. Fed. 29 H6
Arkadelphia U.S.A. 133 C5
Arkagala Rus. Fed. 27 Q3
Arkalgud India 72 C3
Arkalyk Kazakh. 26 E2
Arkansas r. U.S.A. 135 F5
Arkansas state U.S.A. 127 H4

Arkansas City U.S.A. 132 B4
Arkata China 75 G2
Arkatag Shan mts China 75 F1
Arkenu, Jabal mt. Libya 88 E4
Arkhangel'sk Rus. Fed. see Archangel
Arkhangel'skaya Oblast' admin. div. Rus. Fed. 28 G3
Arkhangel'skoye Rus. Fed. 28 K5
Arkhara Rus. Fed. 64 B2
Arkhara r. Rus. Fed. 64 B2
Arkhipovka Rus. Fed. 64 C4
Arki i. Greece 47 E6
Arklow Rep. of Ireland 35 C5
Arkoi i. Greece 47 E6
Arkona, Kap c. Germany 37 F1
Arkonam India see Arakkonam
Arkösund Sweden 33 E4
▶Arktichesky, Mys i. Rus. Fed. 27 J1
Most northerly point of Asia.
Arkticheskogo Instituta, Ostrova is Rus. Fed. 27 I2
Arkul' Rus. Fed. 28 I4
Arlanc France 39 E4
Arlang, Gora m. Turkm. 80 C2
Arlanza r. Spain 42 D1
Arlanzón r. Spain 42 D1
Arles France 39 F5
Arli Burkina 93 F3
Arlington NY U.S.A. 131 G3
Arlington OH U.S.A. 130 B3
Arlington OR U.S.A. 134 B3
Arlington TX U.S.A. 131 E4
Arlington Heights U.S.A. 132 B3
Arlit Niger 93 G1
Arlon Belgium 39 F2
Arltunga Australia 110 C4
Arm r. Canada 123 J5
Armadale Australia 109 B8
Armageddon tourist site Israel see Tel Megiddo
Armagh U.K. 35 C4
Armançon r. France 39 E3
Armant Egypt 89 G3
Armathia i. Greece 47 E7
Armavir Armenia 79 G7
▶Armenia country Asia 79 F2
asia 52-53, 82
Armenia Col. 146 C3
Armenia Mex. 126 F8
Armi, Capo dell' c. Italy 45 E6
Armidale Australia 112 D3
Armit Lake Canada 123 N1
Armori India 72 C1
Armstrong r. Australia 110 B3
Armstrong Arg. 152 E3
Armstrong Canada 124 D3
Armur r. Rus. Fed. 64 D3
Armur India 72 C1
Armutçuk Dağı m. Turkey 78 A3
Armutlu Turkey 47 F4
Armutova Turkey see Gömeç
Armyans'k Ukr. 29 E7
Armyanskaya S.S.R. country Asia see Armenia
Arna Greece 47 C6
Arnaç France 38 C2
Arnaia Greece 47 C4
Arnaoutis, Cape Cyprus see Arnauti, Cape
Arnarfjörður inlet Iceland 32 [inset]
Arnaud r. Canada 121 M4
Arnauti, Cape Cyprus 77 A2
Arnay-le-Duc France 39 F3
Arnedo Spain 43 E1
Arneiroz Brazil 150 D3
Arnemark Sweden 32 F2
Arnett U.S.A. 133 B4
Arnhem Neth. 36 B3
Arnhem, Cape Australia 110 D2
Arnhem Land reg. Australia 110 C2
Arnissa Greece 46 C4
Arno r. Italy 44 C3
Arno Bay Australia 109 G8
Arnoia r. Spain 42 B1
Arnold MD U.S.A. 131 E4
Arnold MO U.S.A. 132 D4
Arnold's Cove Canada 125 K4
Arnoldstein Austria 37 F5
Arnon r. France 38 E3
Arnon r. Jordan see Mawjib, Wādī al
Arnøya i. Norway 32 L1
Arnoya r. Spain see Arnoia
Arnprior Canada 124 F4
Arnsberg Germany 36 D3
Arnstadt Germany 37 E3
Aro r. Venez. 147 E3
Aroab Namibia 98 C5
Aroania mt. Greece 47 C6
Aroánia Canada 124 C3
Arolsen Germany 36 D3
Aron r. France 38 E3
Aron India 74 C4
Arona Italy 44 B2
Arorae i. Kiribati 107 G2
Arore i. Kiribati see Arorae
Arosa, Ría de est. Spain see Arousa, Ría de
Arossi i. Solomon Is see San Cristobal
Arouca Port. 42 B2
Arouelli well Chad 88 D5
Arousa, Ría de est. Spain 42 B1
Arpa r. Armenia/Turkey 79 G3
Arpaçay Turkey 79 E2
Arpaçakarlar Turkey 77 B1
Arpajon-sur-Cère France 38 E4
Arqalyq Kazakh. see Arkalyk
Arquata del Tronto Italy 44 D3
Arquipélago dos Açores is N. Atlantic Ocean see Azores
Arra r. Pak. 81 F5
Arrabury Australia 111 E5
Ar Radīsiyah Baḥrī Egypt 89 G3
Arrah India see Ara
Ar Raḥḥālīyah Iraq 79 F4
Arraias r. Brazil 150 A4
Arraias, Serra de hills Brazil 150 C5
Arraiolos Port. 42 C3
Ar Ramādī Iraq 79 F4
Ar Ramthā Jordan 77 C3
Arran i. U.K. 34 D4
Ar Raqqah Syria 79 D3
Ar Raqqah governorate Syria 77 D1
Ar Raqqah i. Eth. 96 D3
Archer Bend National Park Australia 111 F2
Arras France 39 E1
Arrasate Spain 43 E1
Ar-Rass Saudi Arabia 89 I3
Arrats r. France 38 D4
Ar Rawḍ well Saudi Arabia 79 E5
Ar Rawḍah Saudi Arabia 89 H5
Ar Rayyān Qatar 80 B5
Arrecifal Col. 146 D4
Arrecife Canary Is 90 B3
Arrecifes Arg. 152 E3
Arrée, Monts d' hills France 38 A2
Arretium Italy see Arezzo
Arriagá Mex. 138 D5
Arribeños Arg. 152 E3
Ar Rifā'ī Iraq 79 F5
Ar Riḥāb salt flat Iraq 79 F5
Ar Riyāḍ Saudi Arabia see Riyadh
Ar Riyāḍ prov. Saudi Arabia 80 A5
Arroio Grande Brazil 152 G3
Arros r. France 38 C5
Arrou r. France 39 E3

Arrow, Lough l. Rep. of Ireland 35 B4
Arrowsmith, Mount N.Z. 113 B3
Arroyo de la Luz Spain 42 C3
Arroyo Grande U.S.A. 136 B4
Ar Rubay'iyah Saudi Arabia 89 J3
Arruda Brazil 149 F3
Ar Rumaythā Bahrain 80 B5
Ar Rumaythah Iraq 79 F5
Ar Ruq'ī well Saudi Arabia 80 A4
Ar Ruşāfah Syria 77 D2
Ar Ruşayfah Jordan 77 C3
Ar Rustāq Oman 76 F5
Ar Ruţbah Iraq 79 E4
Ar Ruwaybāt well Libya 88 C3
Års Denmark 33 C4
Ars Iran 80 A2
Ärsarybaba Erezi hills Turkm. see Irsarybaba, Gory
Arsenajān Iran 80 C4
Arseno Lake Canada 123 H1
Arsen'yev Rus. Fed. 64 C3
Arsikere India 72 C3
Arsk Rus. Fed. 28 I4
Arta Greece 47 B5
Artashat Armenia 79 F3
Arteaga Mex. 138 D5
Artem Rus. Fed. 64 C4
Artemisa Cuba 129 C8
Artemivs'k Ukr. 29 F6
Artemovsk Ukr. see Artemivs'k
Artenay France 38 D2
Artesa de Segre Spain 43 G2
Artesia AZ U.S.A. 137 H5
Artesia NM U.S.A. 135 F6
Arthur Canada 130 C2
Arthur NE U.S.A. 132 A3
Arthur TN U.S.A. 130 B5
Arthur, Lake U.S.A. 130 C3
Arthur's Pass National Park N.Z. 113 B3
Arthur's Town Bahamas 129 E7
Artigas research station Antarctica 167 A2
Artigas Uruguay 152 F2
Art'ik Armenia 79 E2
Artillery Lake Canada 123 I2
Artisia Botswana 99 E5
Artos Dağı mt. Turkey 79 E3
Artova Turkey 78 D2
Artrutx, Cap d' c. Spain 43 H3
Artsakh aut. reg. Azer. see Dağlıq Qarabağ
Artsiz Ukr. see Artsyz
Artsyz Ukr. 29 D7
Artur de Paiva Angola see Kuvango
Artux China 70 E4
Artvin Turkey 79 E2
Artyk Turkm. 81 D2
Aru Dem. Rep. Congo 96 A4
Aru, Kepulauan is Indon. 57 H7
Arua Uganda 96 A4
Aruanã Brazil 149 H3
▶Aruba terr. West Indies 146 D1
Self-governing Netherlands Territory.
northamerica 118–119, 140
Arudy France 38 C5
Arun r. Nepal 75 E4
Arunachal Pradesh state India 75 G4
Aruppukkottai India 72 C4
Arusha Tanz. 96 C5
Arusha admin. reg. Tanz. 97 C5
Arusha National Park Tanz. 96 C5
Arut r. Indon. 59 E3
Aruwimi r. Dem. Rep. Congo 94 D4
Arvayheer Mongolia 62 G2
Arvi India 72 C1
Arviat Canada 123 M2
Arvidsjaur Sweden 32 E2
Arvika Sweden 33 D4
Årviksand Norway 32 F1
Arvonia U.S.A. 130 D5
Arwād i. Syria 77 B2
Aryanah Tunisia see L'Ariana
Arys' Kazakh. 70 C3
Arzamas Rus. Fed. 28 G5
Arzanah i. U.A.E. 80 C5
Arzew Alg. 91 E2
Arzgir Rus. Fed. 29 H7
Arzúa Spain 42 B1
Aš Czech Rep. 36 F3
Asa waterhole Kenya 96 C5
Åsa Sweden 33 D4
Asaba Nigeria 93 G4
Asad, Buḩayrat al resr Syria 79 D3
Asadābād Afgh. 81 G3
Asadābād Hamadān Iran 80 B3
Asadābād Khorāsan Iran 81 D3
Asagny, Parc National d' nat. park Côte d'Ivoire 92 D4
Asahan r. Indon. 58 B2
Asahi-dake vol. Japan 64 E4
Asahi-gawa r. Japan 65 C6
Asahikawa Japan 64 E4
Āsalē l. Eth. 89 I6
Asālem Iran 80 B2
Asama-yama vol. Japan 65 D5
Asankranguaa Ghana 93 E4
Asan-man b. S. Korea 65 A5
Asansol India 75 E5
Asanwenso Ghana 92 E4
Āsayita Eth. 96 D2
Asbestos Mountains S. Africa 98 D6
Āsbe Teferi Eth. 96 D2
Asbury Park U.S.A. 131 F3
Ascalon Israel see Ashqelon
Ascea Italy 45 E4
Ascensión Bol. 149 E3
Ascensión Mex. 135 F7
▶Ascension i. S. Atlantic Ocean 160 N6
Dependency of St Helena.
Aschaffenburg Germany 36 D4
Aschersleben Germany 36 E3
Asciano Italy 44 C3
Ascoli Piceno Italy 44 D3
Ascotán Chile 148 C5
Ascotán, Salar de salt flat Chile 148 C5
Asculum Italy see Ascoli Piceno
Asculum Picenum Italy see Ascoli Piceno
Ascutney U.S.A. 131 G2
Åse Norway 32 D1
Āseb Eritrea see Assab
Asedjrad plat. Alg. 91 F4
Āsela Eth. 96 C3
Åsele Sweden 32 E2
Asenovgrad Bulg. 46 D3
Åseral Norway 33 B4
Asfāk Iran 80 D3
Aşfar, Jabal al mt. Jordan 77 C3
Aşfar, Tall al hill Syria 77 C3
Ásgarður Iceland 32 [inset]
Asha Rus. Fed. 28 K5
Ashanti admin. reg. Ghana 93 E4
Asharat Saudi Arabia 76 D4
Ashbourne U.K. 35 F5
Ashburton watercourse Australia 109 A5
Ashburton N.Z. 113 B3
Ashburton Range hills Australia 110 C3
Ashcroft Canada 134 B2
Ashdod Israel 77 B4
Ashdown U.S.A. 133 C5
Asheboro U.S.A. 128 D5
Ashern Canada 123 L5
Asheville U.S.A. 128 C5
Asheweig r. Canada 124 C2
Ashford Australia 112 D3
Ashford U.K. 35 G6
Ash Fork U.S.A. 137 F4
▶Ashgabat Turkm. 80 D2
Capital of Turkmenistan.
Ashington U.K. 34 F4
Ashizuri-misaki pt Japan 65 C6
Ashizuri-Uwakai National Park Japan 65 C6
Ashkazar Iran 80 C4
Ashkelon Israel see Ashqelon
Ashkhabad Turkm. see Ashgabat
Ashkhabadskaya Oblast' admin. div. Turkm. see Akhal'skaya Oblast'
Ashkīdah Libya 88 B3
Ashland KS U.S.A. 132 B4
Ashland KY U.S.A. 130 B4
Ashland NE U.S.A. 132 B3
Ashland NH U.S.A. 131 H2
Ashland OH U.S.A. 130 B3
Ashland OR U.S.A. 134 B4
Ashland VA U.S.A. 130 E5
Ashland WI U.S.A. 132 D2
Ashley MI U.S.A. 130 A2
Ashley ND U.S.A. 132 B2
Ashley OH U.S.A. 130 B3
▶Ashmore and Cartier Islands terr. Australia 108 C3
Australian External Territory.
oceania 114
Ashmore Reef Australia 108 C3
Ashmyany Belarus 29 C5
Ashoknagar India 74 C4
Ashqelon Israel 77 B4
Ash Sha'ār Saudi Arabia 89 I5
Ash Shabakah Iraq 79 E5
Ash Shabb well Egypt 89 F4
Ash Shaddādah Syria 79 E3
Ash Shafa Saudi Arabia 89 I4
Ash Sham Syria see Damascus
Ash Sha'm U.A.E. 80 D5
Ash Shanāfiyah Iraq 79 F5
Ash Shaqiq well Saudi Arabia 89 I2
Ash Sha'rā' Saudi Arabia 89 J3
Ash Sharawrah Saudi Arabia 76 D6
Ash Shāriqah U.A.E. see Sharjah
Ash Sharqāţ Iraq 79 E4
Ash Sharqīyah governorate Egypt 78 B5
Ash Sharqīyah prov. Saudi Arabia 80 B5
Ash Shaţrah Iraq 79 F5
Ash Shawbak Jordan 78 C5
Ash Shaykh 'Uthman Yemen 76 C7
Ash Shiblīyāt hill Saudi Arabia 77 C5
Ash Shiḩr Yemen 76 D7
Ash Shināş Oman 80 D5
Ash Shu'āybah Saudi Arabia 89 I3
Ash Shu'bah Saudi Arabia 89 J2
Ash Shumlūl Saudi Arabia 80 A5
Ash Shuqayq Saudi Arabia 89 I5
Ash Shurayf Saudi Arabia see Khaybar
Ash Shuwayrif Libya 88 B2
Ashta Madhya Pradesh India 74 C5
Ashta Maharashtra India 72 B2
Ashtabula U.S.A. 130 C3
Ashtarak Armenia 79 F2
Ashti Maharashtra India 72 B2
Ashti Maharashtra India 72 C2
Ashti Maharashtra India 74 C5
Ashton U.S.A. 134 E3
Ashuanipi r. Canada 125 H2
Ashuanipi Lake Canada 125 H2
Ashur Iraq see Ash Sharqāţ
Ashusuu pass Kyrg. 81 H1
Ashville U.S.A. 130 D3
'Āşī r. Lebanon/Syria see Orontes
'Āşī, Nahr al r. Asia 77 C1
Asifabad India 72 C2
Asika India 73 E2
Asikkala Fin. 33 G3
Asillo Peru 148 C3
Asimi Greece 47 D7
Asinara, Golfo dell' b. Sardinia Italy 44 B4
Asinara, Isola i. Sardinia Italy 44 B4
Asind India 74 B4
Asino Rus. Fed. 27 I4
Asipovichy Belarus 29 D5
Asīr prov. Saudi Arabia 89 I4
'Asīr reg. Saudi Arabia 76 C5
Asisium Italy see Assisi
Aşkale Turkey 79 E3
Asker Norway 33 C4
Askersund Sweden 33 D4
Askim Norway 33 C4
Askino Rus. Fed. 28 K4
Askio mt. Greece 47 B4
Askira Nigeria 93 I3
Askiz Rus. Fed. 62 E1
Askola Fin. 33 G3
Askot India 74 D3
Aşlāndūz Iran 80 A2
Asmar Afgh. 74 A2
▶Asmara Eritrea 89 H6
Capital of Eritrea.
Āsmera Eritrea see Asmara
Åsnen l. Sweden 33 D4
As Neves Spain 42 B1
Asoenangka Brazil 147 G4
Aso-Kuju National Park Japan 65 B6
Asopos r. Greece 47 C5
Asopos r. Greece 47 C6
Āsosa Eth. 96 B2
Asoteriba, Jebel mt. Sudan 89 H4
Aspang-Markt Austria 37 H5
Asparukhovo Bulg. 46 E3
Aspås Sweden 32 D3
Aspe Spain 43 F3
Aspeå Sweden 32 E3
Aspen U.S.A. 134 F5
Aspermont U.S.A. 133 A5
Aspiring, Mount N.Z. 113 B4
As Pontes de García Rodríguez Spain 42 C1
Asprokavos, Akra pt Greece 47 B5
Aspromonte, Parco Nazionale dell' nat. park Italy 45 E5
Asprovalta Greece 46 C4
Aspur India 74 B5
Asquith Canada 123 J4
Assa Morocco 90 C3
As Sa'an Syria 78 D4
Assab Eritrea 89 I6
Assaba admin. reg. Mauritania 92 C1
As Sabsab well Saudi Arabia 80 B5
Aş Şafā lava field Syria 77 C3
Aş Şafāqīs Tunisia see Sfax
Aş Şaff Egypt 89 F2
Aş Şāfī Jordan 78 C5
As Safirah Syria 77 C1
Aş Şahāf Saudi Arabia 80 B5
Aş Şaḩrā' al Gharbīyah des. Egypt see Western Desert
Aş Şaḩrā' ash Sharqīyah des. Egypt see Eastern desert
Assake-Audan, Vpadina depr. Uzbek. 70 A3
'Assal, Lac l. Djibouti see Assal, Lake
▶Assal, Lake l. Djibouti 96 D2
Lowest point in Africa.
africa 84–85
As Salamiyah Saudi Arabia 80 A5
Aş Şāliḩīyah Egypt 78 C5
Aş Şāliḩīyah Syria 79 E4
As Sallūm Egypt 78 A5
As Salmān Iraq 79 F5
As Salţ Jordan 78 C4
Assam state India 75 F4
Assamakka Niger 93 G1
As Samāwah Iraq 79 F5
Assaq watercourse W. Sahara 90 B4
As Sarīr reg. Libya 88 D3
Assemini Sardinia Italy 45 B5
Assen Neth. 36 C2
As Sidrah Libya 88 C2
Assigny, Lac l. Canada 125 H2
As Sikak Saudi Arabia 80 B5
Assiniboia Canada 134 F2
Assiniboine r. Canada 134 H2
Assiniboine, Mount Canada 134 D2
Assinica, Lac l. Canada 124 F3
Assis Brazil 149 H5
Assisi Italy 44 D3
Assomada Cape Verde 92 [inset]
Assouf Mellene watercourse Alg. 91 F4
Aş Şubayḩīyah Kuwait 79 F5
As Subaykhah Saudi Arabia 89 I5
Aş Şufayrī well Saudi Arabia 79 F5
As Sukhnah Syria 79 D4
As Sulaymānīyah Iraq 79 F4
As Sulaymānīyah governorate Iraq 79 F4
As Sulaymī Saudi Arabia 89 I3
As Sulayyil Saudi Arabia 76 D5
Aş Şulb reg. Saudi Arabia 80 B5
Aş Şummān plat. Saudi Arabia 80 A5
As Sūq Saudi Arabia 89 I4
As Sūrīyah country Asia see Syria
Aş Şuwar Syria 79 E4
As Suwaydā' Syria 78 D4
As Suwaydā' governorate Syria 77 C3
As Suwayḩ Oman 76 F5
Aş Şuwayrah Iraq 79 F4
As Suways Egypt see Suez
As Suways governorate Egypt 77 A5
Asta r. Norway 33 C3
Astacus Turkey see Kocaeli
Astaffort France 38 D4
Astakida i. Greece 47 E7
Astakos Greece 47 B5
Astalu Island Pak. see Astola Island
▶Astana Kazakh. 26 H4
Capital of Kazakhstan.
Astaneh Iran 80 B2
Astara Azer. 79 G3
Āstārā Iran 80 B2
Asterabad Iran see Gorgān
Asti Italy 44 B2
Astica Arg. 152 D2
Astillero Peru 148 C3
Astin Tag mts China see Altun Shan
Astipálaia i. Greece see Astypalaia
Astola Island Pak. 81 E5
Astor Jammu and Kashmir 74 B2
Astor r. Pak. 74 B2
Astorga Spain 42 C1
Astoria U.S.A. 134 B3
Astra Arg. 153 D6
Astrabad Iran see Gorgān
Astrakhan' Rus. Fed. 29 I7
Astrakhan' Bazar Azer. see Cälilabad
Astrakhan Oblast admin. div. Rus. Fed. see Astrakhanskaya Oblast'
Astrakhanskaya Oblast' admin. div. Rus. Fed. 29 H7
Astravyets Belarus 33 G5
Astrida Rwanda see Butare
Astrolabe, Récifs de l' reef New Caledonia 107 F3
Astros Greece 47 C6
Asturias airport Spain 42 C1
Asturias aut. comm. Spain 42 C1
Asturica Augusta Spain see Astorga
Astypalaia Greece 47 E6
Astypalaia i. Greece 47 E6
Asunción Bol. 148 D2
Asunción r. Mex. 135 D7
Asunción i. N. Mariana Is 57 K2
▶Asunción Para. 149 F6
Capital of Paraguay.
Asvyeya Belarus 33 H4
Aswa r. Uganda 96 A4
Aswad Oman 80 D5
Aswān Egypt 89 G3
Aswan Dam Egypt 89 G3
Asyūţ Egypt 89 F3
Ata i. Tonga 107 H4
Atabapo r. Col./Venez. 146 E3
Atacama admin. reg. Chile 152 C1
Atacama, Desierto de des. Chile see Atacama Desert
Atacama, Salar de salt flat Chile 148 C5
▶Atacama Desert Chile 152 C1
Driest place in the world.
southamerica 144–145
world 12–13
Ataco Col. 146 C4
Atafu atoll Tokelau 107 H2
Atafu i. Tokelau 164 G6
Atakent Turkey 77 B1
Atakor mts Alg. 91 G5
Atakpamé Togo 93 F4
Atalaia Brazil 150 F4
Atalaia hill Port. 42 B3
Atalaia do Norte Brazil 146 D6
Atalaya Madre de Dios Peru 148 C3
Atalaya Ucayali Peru 148 B2
Atamisqui Arg. 152 E2
Ataniya Turkey see Adana
Atapupu Indon. 108 D2
'Ataq Yemen 76 D7
Atâr Mauritania 90 B5
Ataran r. Myanmar 61 B4
Atascadero U.S.A. 136 B4
Atascosa watercourse U.S.A. 133 B6
Atasu Kazakh. 70 D2
Atatürk Milli Parkı nat. park Turkey 47 F6
Atauro, Ilha de i. East Timor 57 G7
Atáviros mt. Greece see Attavyros
Atayurt Turkey 77 A1
Atbara Sudan 89 G5
Atbara r. Sudan 89 G5
Atbasar Kazakh. 26 G4
Atchison U.S.A. 132 C4
Atebubu Ghana 93 E4
Ateca Spain 43 F2
Ateransk Kazakh. see Atyrau
Aterno r. Italy 44 D3
Āteshān Iran 80 C3
Āteshkhāneh, Kūh-e hill Afgh. 81 E3
Ath Belgium 39 E1
Athabasca r. Canada 123 I3
Athabasca, Lake Canada 123 I3
Athagarh India 73 E1
Athboy Rep. of Ireland 35 C5
Athenae Greece see Athens
Athenry Rep. of Ireland 35 B5
Athens Canada 131 F1
▶Athens Greece 47 C6
Capital of Greece.
Athens AL U.S.A. 128 B5
Athens GA U.S.A. 129 C5
Athens OH U.S.A. 130 B4
Athens TN U.S.A. 128 B5
Athens TX U.S.A. 133 C5
Atherton Australia 111 F3
Athi r. Kenya 96 C5
Athina Greece see Athens
Athínai Greece see Athens
Athi River Kenya 96 C5
Athlone Rep. of Ireland 35 C5
Athnā', Wādī al watercourse Jordan 77 D3
Athni India 72 B2
Athol N.Z. 113 B4
Athol U.S.A. 131 G2
Athos mt. Greece 47 D4
Ath Thamad Egypt 89 G2
Ath Tharthār, Wādī r. Iraq 79 E4
Ath Thāyat mt. Saudi Arabia 77 C5
Athy Rep. of Ireland 35 C5
Ati Chad 88 C6
Ati, Jabal mts Libya 88 B4
Aţīābād Iran 81 D3
Atiak Uganda 96 B4
Ati Ardébé Chad 88 C6
Atico Peru 148 B4
Atiedo Sudan 94 E3
Atikameg Canada 123 H4
Atikameg r. Canada 124 D2
Atik Lake Canada 123 M4
Atikokan Canada 124 B3
Atikonak Lake Canada 125 H2
Atina Italy 44 D4
Atirampattinam India 72 C4
Atjeh admin. dist. Indon. see Aceh
Atka Rus. Fed. 27 P3
Atka U.S.A. 120 B4
Atka Island U.S.A. 120 B4
Atkarsk Rus. Fed. 29 H6
▶Atlanta GA U.S.A. 129 B5
State capital of Georgia.
Atlanta TX U.S.A. 133 C5
Atlantı Turkey 78 C3
Atlantic U.S.A. 132 C3
Atlantic City U.S.A. 131 F4
Atlantic-Indian-Antarctic Basin sea feature S. Atlantic Ocean 161 N10
Atlantic-Indian Ridge sea feature S. Atlantic Ocean 163 G9
Atlántico dept Col. 146 C2
▶Atlantic Ocean 160 K3
2nd largest ocean in the world.
oceans 156–157, 168
Atlas Méditerranéen mts Alg. see Atlas Tellien
Atlas Mountains Africa 90 D3
Atlasova, Ostrov i. Rus. Fed. 27 P4
Atlas Saharien mts Alg. 91 F2
Atlas Tellien mts Alg. 91 F2
Atlin Canada 122 C3
Atlin Lake Canada 122 C3
'Atlit Israel 77 B3
Atlixco Mex. 126 G8
Atmakur Andhra Pradesh India 72 C3
Atmakur Andhra Pradesh India 72 C3
Atmore U.S.A. 129 B6
Atna Norway 33 C3
Atner India 74 C5
Atnur India 72 C2
Atocha Bol. 148 D5
Atoka U.S.A. 133 B5
Atome Angola 95 B7
Atonyia W. Sahara 90 C4
Atouat mt. Laos 61 D4
Atpadi India 72 B2
Atqasuk U.S.A. 120 D2
Atrai r. India 75 F4
Atrak, Rūd-e r. Iran/Turkm. 80 C2
Ātran r. Sweden 33 D4
Atranh India 74 C4
Atrato r. Col. 146 B2
Atrek r. Iran/Turkm. 80 C2
Atri Italy 44 D3
Atropatene country Asia see Azerbaijan
Atsiki Greece 47 D5
Atsion U.S.A. 131 F4
Aţ Ţaff reg. U.A.E. 80 C5
Aţ Ţafilah Jordan 78 C5
Aţ Ţā'if Saudi Arabia 89 I4
Attalea Turkey see Antalya
Attalia Turkey see Antalya
At Ta'mīm governorate Iraq 79 E4
At Tamīmī Libya 88 D1
Attapu Laos 61 D5
Attar, Oued el watercourse Alg. 91 G2
Attavyros mt. Greece 47 E6
Attawapiskat Canada 124 D2
Attawapiskat r. Canada 124 D2
Attawapiskat Lake Canada 124 C2
Aţ Ţawīl mts Saudi Arabia 79 D5
At Taysīyah plat. Saudi Arabia 89 I2
Aţ Ţayyibah Jordan 78 C7
Attendorn Germany 36 C3
Attersee l. Austria 37 F5
Attica IN U.S.A. 132 E3
Attica NY U.S.A. 130 D2
Attica OH U.S.A. 130 B3
Attikamagen Lake Canada 125 H2
Attiki admin. reg. Greece 47 C6
At Tin, Ra's pt Libya 88 D1
Attleboro U.S.A. 131 H3
Attock City Pak. 81 H3
Attopeu Laos see Attapu
Attu Greenland 121 N3
Aţ Ţubayq reg. Saudi Arabia 89 H2
▶Attu Island U.S.A. 164 F2
Most westerly point of North America.
Attunga Australia 112 D3
At Tūnisīyah country Africa see Tunisia
Aţ Ţūr Egypt 89 G2
Attur Tamil Nadu India 72 C4
Attur Tamil Nadu India 72 C4
At Turbah Yemen 96 D1
Atuel r. Arg. 152 D4
Åtvidaberg Sweden 33 D4
Atwari Bangl. 75 F4
Atwater U.S.A. 136 B3
Atwood U.S.A. 132 A4
Atyrau Kazakh. 29 I7
Atyrau Oblast admin. div. Kazakh. see Atyrauskaya Oblast'
Atyraū Oblysy admin. div. Kazakh. see Atyrauskaya Oblast'
Atyrauskaya Oblast' admin. div. Kazakh. 29 I7
Auati-Paraná r. Brazil 146 E5
Aubagne France 39 F5
Aube r. France 39 F2
Aubenas France 39 F4
Aubergenville France 38 D2
Aubigny-sur-Nère France 39 E3
Auboué France 39 F2
Aubrey Cliffs mts U.S.A. 137 F4
Aubry Lake Canada 120 G3
Auburn r. Australia 111 G5
Auburn AL U.S.A. 129 B5
Auburn CA U.S.A. 136 B2
Auburn IN U.S.A. 132 E3
Auburn MA U.S.A. 131 H2
Auburn ME U.S.A. 131 H1
Auburn MI U.S.A. 130 A2
Auburn NE U.S.A. 132 C3
Auburn NY U.S.A. 131 E2
Auburn WA U.S.A. 134 B3
Auburn Range hills Australia 111 G5
Aubusson France 38 E4
Auca Mahuida, Sierra de mt. Arg. 152 C4
Auce Latvia 33 F4
Auch France 38 D5
Auche Myanmar 60 B2
Auchi Nigeria 93 G4
▶Auckland N.Z. 113 C2
5th most populous city in Oceania.
Auckland Islands N.Z. 164 F9
Aude r. France 38 E5
Auden Canada 124 C3
Audenarde Belgium see Oudenaarde
Audierne, Baie d' b. France 38 A3
Audincourt France 39 G3
Audo Range mts Eth. 96 D3
Audru Estonia 33 G4
Audruicq France 38 E1
Audubon U.S.A. 132 C3
Aue Germany 37 F3
Aue r. Germany 36 D2
Auerbach in der Oberpfalz Germany 36 E4
Augathella Australia 111 F5
Augrabies Falls National Park S. Africa 98 D6
Augsburg Germany 36 E4
Augšlīgatne Latvia 33 G4
Augšzemes Augstiene hills Latvia 33 G4
Augusta Australia 109 A8
Augusta Sicily Italy 45 E6
Augusta GA U.S.A. 129 C5
Augusta KS U.S.A. 132 B4
Augusta KY U.S.A. 130 A4
▶Augusta ME U.S.A. 131 I1
State capital of Maine.
Augusta WV U.S.A. 130 D4
Augusta, Golfo di b. Sicily Italy 45 E6
Augusta Auscorum France see Auch
Augusta Taurinorum Italy see Turin
Augusta Treverorum Germany see Trier
Augusta Victoria Chile 148 C6
Augusta Vindelicorum Germany see Augsburg
Augustin Cadazzi Col. 146 C2
Augustine Island U.S.A. 120 D4
Augusto Cardosa Moz. see Metangula
Augustodunum France see Autun
Augusto Severo Brazil 150 E3
Augustus Island Australia 108 D3
Aukštaitijos nacionalinis parkas nat. park Lith. 33 G5
Auktsjaur Sweden 32 E2
Aulavik National Park Canada 121 H2
Auld, Lake salt flat Australia 108 C5
Auliye Ata Kazakh. see Taraz
Aulla Italy 44 B2
Aulnoye-Aymeries France 39 E1
Aulon Albania see Vlorë
Ault France 38 D1
Aumale France 38 D2
Aumance r. France 39 E3
Auna Nigeria 93 G3
Aungban Myanmar 60 B3
Auning Denmark 33 C4
Auob watercourse Namibia/S. Africa 98 D5
Aupaluk Canada 125 G1
Aur i. Malaysia 58 D2
Aura Fin. 33 F3
Aurad India 72 C2
Auraiya India 74 C4
Aurangabad Bihar India 75 E4
Aurangabad Maharashtra India 72 B2
Auray France 38 B3
Aure Norway 32 C3
Aurich Germany 36 C2
Aurigny i. Channel Is see Alderney
Aurillac France 38 E4
Aurino r. Italy 44 C1
Auron r. France 39 E3
Auronzo di Cadore Italy 44 D1
Aurora CO U.S.A. 134 F5
Aurora IL U.S.A. 132 D3
Aurora IN U.S.A. 130 A4
Aurora MO U.S.A. 132 C4
Aurora NE U.S.A. 132 B3
Aurora OH U.S.A. 130 C3
Aurora UT U.S.A. 137 G2
Aurora Island Vanuatu see Maéwo
Aurukun Australia 111 E2
Aurunci, Monti mts Italy 44 D4
Aus Namibia 98 C5
Au Sable r. U.S.A. 130 B1
Ausable Forks U.S.A. 131 G1
Au Sable Point U.S.A. 130 B1
Auschwitz Poland see Oświęcim
Aust-Agder county Norway 33 C4
Austertana Norway 32 H1
Austin MN U.S.A. 132 C3
Austin NV U.S.A. 136 D2
▶Austin TX U.S.A. 133 B6
State capital of Texas.
Austin, Lake salt flat Australia 109 B6
Austral Downs Australia 110 D4
Australes, Îles is Fr. Polynesia see Tubuai Islands
▶Australia country Oceania 106 B4
Largest country in Oceania and 6th in the world. Most populous country in Oceania.
oceania 104–105, 114
world 8–9
Australian-Antarctic Basin sea feature Indian Ocean 163 N9
Australian Antarctic Territory Antarctica 167 G2
Australian Capital Territory admin. div. Australia 106 D5
Australind Australia 109 A8
▶Austria country Europe 37 F5
europe 24–25, 48
Austrumkursas Augstiene hills Latvia 33 F4
Austvågøy i. Norway 32 D1
Autazes Brazil 147 G5
Auterive France 38 D5
Autesiodorum France see Auxerre
Authie r. France 38 D1
Autlán Mex. 126 F8
Autti Fin. 32 G2
Autun France 39 F3
Auvergne admin. reg. France 39 E4
Auvergne, Monts d' mts France 39 E4
Auvézère r. France 38 D4
Auxerre France 39 E3
Auxonne France 39 F3
Auyan Tepuí plat. Venez. 147 F3
Auyuittuq National Park Reserve Canada 121 M3
Auzoue r. France 38 D4
Ava Myanmar 60 A3
Ava MO U.S.A. 132 C4
Ava NY U.S.A. 131 F2
Availles-Limouzine France 38 D3
Avallon France 39 E3
Avalon U.S.A. 136 C5
Avalon Peninsula Canada 125 K4
Avān Iran 80 A2
Avanashi India 72 C4
Avanganna mt. Guyana 147 G3
Avanigadda India 72 D2
Avanos Turkey 41 I4
Avaré Brazil 149 H5
Avaricum France see Bourges
Avarskoye Koysu r. Rus. Fed. 79 F2
▶Avarua Cook Is 165 H7
Capital of the Cook Islands, on Rarotonga island.
Avaträsk Sweden 32 E2
Avawatz Mountains U.S.A. 137 D4
Ave r. Port. 42 B2
Aveiro Brazil 147 H5
Aveiro Port. 42 B2
Aveiro admin. dist. Port. 42 B2
Aveiro, Ria de est. Port. 42 B2
Āvej Iran 80 B3
Avellaneda Arg. 152 F2
Avellino Italy 45 E4
Avenal U.S.A. 136 B3
Avenio France see Avignon
Averøya i. Norway 32 B3
Aversa Italy 44 E4
Aves is West Indies see Las Aves, Islas
Avesnes-sur-Helpe France 39 E1
Avesta Sweden 33 E3
Aveyron r. France 38 D4
Avezzano Italy 44 D3
Avgo i. Kythira Greece 47 C6
Avgo i. Greece 47 D7
Aviá Terai Arg. 152 E1
Aviemore U.K. 34 E3
Avigliano Italy 45 E4
Avignon France 39 F5
Ávila Spain 42 D2
Ávila, Sierra de mts Spain 42 D2
Avilés Spain 42 D1
Avión mt. Spain 42 B1
Avis Port. 42 C3
Avisio r. Italy 44 C1
Avize France 39 F2
Avlemonas Greece 47 C6
Avlida Greece 47 C5
Avlona Albania see Vlorë
Avnyugskiy Rus. Fed. 28 H3
Avoca Australia 112 B5
Avoca r. Australia 112 B4
Avoca IA U.S.A. 132 C3
Avoca NY U.S.A. 131 E2
Avola Sicily Italy 45 E6
Avon r. Australia 109 B7
Avon r. England U.K. 35 E5
Avon r. England U.K. 35 E6
Avon r. England U.K. 35 F6
Avon U.S.A. 130 E2
Avondale U.S.A. 137 F5
Avon Downs Australia 111 F4
Avonmore r. Rep. of Ireland 35 C5
Avon Park U.S.A. 129 C7
Avram Iancu Romania 46 B1
Avranches France 38 C2
Avre r. France 39 E2
Avrig Romania 46 D2
Avrillé France 38 C3
Avsuyu Turkey 77 C1
Avuavu Solomon Is 107 F2
Avveel Fin. see Ivalo
Avvil Fin. see Ivalo
A'waj r. Syria 77 B3
Awaji-shima i. Japan 65 C6
Awakino N.Z. 113 C2
Awālī Bahrain 80 B5
Awang Indon. 59 G5
Awanui N.Z. 113 C1
Awarawar, Tanjung pt Indon. 59 F4
Awarē Eth. 96 E2
Awarua Point N.Z. 113 B4
Āwasa Eth. 96 C3
Āwash Eth. 96 D2
Āwash r. Eth. 96 D2
Awa-shima i. Japan 65 D5
Āwash National Park Eth. 96 C2
Āwash Shet' r. Eth. 96 C3
Awatere r. N.Z. 113 C3
Awbārī Libya 88 B3
'Awdah well Saudi Arabia 76 E5
'Awdah, Hawr al imp. l. Iraq 79 F5
Aw Dheegle Somalia 96 E4
Awdiinle Somalia 96 D4
Awe, Loch l. U.K. 34 D3
Aweil Sudan 94 E3
Awgu Nigeria 93 G4
Awka Nigeria 93 G4
Awlitis watercourse W. Sahara 90 B4
Awry Lake Canada 123 H2
Awserd W. Sahara 90 B5
Axe r. U.K. 35 E6
Axel Heiberg Glacier Antarctica 167 I1
Axel Heiberg Island Canada 121 J2
Axim Ghana 93 E4
Axinim Brazil 147 G6
Axios r. Greece 46 C4
Axum Eth. see Āksum
Ayachi, Jbel mt. Morocco 90 D2
Ayacucho Arg. 152 F4
Ayacucho Peru 148 B3
Ayacucho dept Peru 148 B3
Ayadaw Myanmar 60 A3
Ayagoz Kazakh. 70 F2
Ayaguz Kazakh. see Ayagoz
Ayakagytma, Vpadina depr. Uzbek. 81 F1
Ayakkum Hu salt l. China 70 G4
Ayaköz Kazakh. see Ayagoz
Ayamé Côte d'Ivoire 92 E4
Ayamiken Equat. Guinea 93 H5
Ayamonte Spain 42 C4
Ayan Rus. Fed. 27 N4
Ayancık Turkey 78 C2
Ayang N. Korea 65 A5
Ayangba Nigeria 93 G4
Ayanka Rus. Fed. 27 Q3
Ayapel, Serranía de mts Col. 146 C3
Ayaş Turkey 78 C2
Ayaviri Peru 148 C3
Ayayei Eth. 89 H6
Āybak Afgh. 81 G2
Aydar r. Ukr. 29 F6
Aydarkul', Ozero l. Uzbek. 81 F1
Aydın Turkey 78 A3
Aydın prov. Turkey 47 F6
Aydıncık Turkey 77 A1
Aydın Dağları mts Turkey 78 A3
Ayeat, Gora hill Kazakh. 70 C2
Ayedo mt. Spain 43 E1
Āyelu Terara vol. Eth. 96 D2
Ayem Gabon 94 A5
Ayer U.S.A. 131 H2
Ayers Rock hill Australia see Uluru
Ayeyarwady r. Myanmar see Irrawaddy
Ayiá Greece see Agia
Ayiásos Greece see Agiasos
Ayila Ri'gyü mts China 74 C2
Áyios Dhimítrios Greece see Agios Dimitrios

Áyios Evstrátios i. Greece see Agios Efstratios
Áyios Nikólaos Greece see Agios Nikolaos
Áyios Yeóryios i. Greece see Agios Georgios
Aykhal Rus. Fed. 27 L3
Aylesbury N.Z. 113 C3
Aylesbury U.K. 35 F6
Aylett U.S.A. 131 E5
Ayllón, Sierra de mts Spain 42 E2
Aylmer Canada 130 C2
Aylmer Lake Canada 123 I1
Ayna Peru 148 B3
'Ayn al 'Abd Libya 88 C2
'Ayn al 'Abd well Saudi Arabia 80 B4
'Ayn al Bayḍā' well Syria 77 C2
'Ayn al Furṭājah well Egypt 77 B5
'Ayn al Ghazāl spring Libya 88 E4
'Ayn al Maqfī spring Egypt 89 F3
'Ayn 'Āmūr spring Egypt 89 F3
'Ayn Dāllah spring Egypt 89 E3
Ayní Tajik. 81 G2
'Aynīn well Saudi Arabia 89 I4
'Ayn Tabaghbugh spring Egypt 89 E2
'Ayn Tumayrah spring Egypt 89 E2
'Ayn Zaytūn Egypt 78 A5
Ayod Sudan 68 B6
Ayon, Ostrov i. Rus. Fed. 27 Q3
Ayora Spain 43 F3
Ayorou Niger 93 F2
Ayos Cameroon 93 I5
'Ayoûn 'Abd el Mâlek well Mauritania 90 D4
'Ayoûn el 'Atroûs Mauritania 92 C1
Ayr Australia 111 F3
Ayr U.K. 34 D4
Ayr r. U.K. 34 D4
Ayrancı Turkey 78 C3
Ayrancılar Turkey 47 E5
Ayre, Point of Isle of Man 35 D4
Āysha Eth. 96 D2
Ayteke Bi Kazakh. 70 B2
Aytos Bulg. 46 E3
Aytoska Reka r. Bulg. 46 E3
Ayuthia Thai. see Ayutthaya
Ayutthaya Thai. 61 C5
Ayvacık Turkey 78 A3
Ayvadzh Tajik. see Aivadzh
Ayvalık Turkey 78 A3
Azak Rus. Fed. see Azov
Azambuja Port. 42 B3
Azamgarh India 75 D4
Azaouâd reg. Mali 93 E1
Azaouagh, Vallée de watercourse Mali/Niger 93 F1
Azapa Chile 148 C4
Azar watercourse Niger 93 G1
Azaran Iran see Hashtrud
Azărbayjan country Asia see Azerbaijan
Āzarbāyjān-e Gharbī prov. Iran 80 A2
Āzarbāyjān-e Sharqī prov. Iran 80 A2
Azare Nigeria 93 H3
A'zāz Syria 77 C1
Azbine mts Niger see L'Aïr, Massif de
Azdavay Turkey 78 C2
Azélik well Niger 93 H1
Azemmour Morocco 90 C2
▶Azerbaijan country Asia 79 G2
asia 52–53, 82
Azerbaydzhanskaya S.S.R. country Asia see Azerbaijan
Azergues r. France 39 F4
Āzezo Eth. 96 C1
Azilal Morocco 90 D2
Azingo Gabon 94 A5
'Azīzābād Iran 81 D4
Azizbekov Armenia see Vayk'
Aziziye Turkey see Pınarbaşı
Aznakayevo Rus. Fed. 28 J5
Aznalcóllar Spain 42 C4
Azogues Ecuador 146 B5
Azopol'ye Rus. Fed. 28 H2

▶Azores terr. N. Atlantic Ocean 160 M3
Autonomous Region of Portugal.
europe 24–25, 48

Azores-Biscay Rise sea feature N. Atlantic Ocean 160 M3
Azotus Israel see Ashdod
Azov Rus. Fed. 29 F7
Azov, Sea of Rus. Fed./Ukr. 29 F7
Azovs'ke More sea Rus. Fed./Ukr. see Azov, Sea of
Azovskoye More sea Rus. Fed./Ukr. see Azov, Sea of
Azraq, Bahr el r. Eth./Sudan 89 G6 see Blue Nile
Azrou Morocco 90 D2
Azrou, Oued watercourse Alg. 91 G5
Aztec U.S.A. 135 E5
Azuaga Spain 42 D3
Azuay prov. Ecuador 146 B5
Azúcar r. Chile 152 C1
Azuer r. Spain 42 E3
Azuero, Península de pen. Panama 139 H7
Azufre, Cerro del mt. Chile 152 C1
Azul Arg. 152 F4
Azul, Cordillera mts Peru 148 B2
Azul, Serra hills Brazil 149 G3
Azum, Wadi watercourse Sudan 88 D6
Azuma-san vol. Japan 65 E5
Azurduy Bol. 149 D5
'Azza Gaza see Gaza
Az Zabadānī Syria 78 D4
Az Zabīrah well Saudi Arabia 89 I3
Az Ẓafīrī reg. Iraq 79 E5
Az Ẓahrān Saudi Arabia see Dhahran
Az Zallāf, Wādī watercourse Libya 88 B3
Az Zallāq Bahrain 80 B5
Azzano Decimo Italy 44 D2
Az Zaqāzīq Egypt 89 F2
Az Zarbah Syria 77 C1
Az Zarqā' Jordan 78 D4
Az Zāwiyah Libya 88 B1
Azzeffâl hills Mauritania/W. Sahara 90 B5
Azzel Matti, Sebkha salt pan Alg. 91 F4
Az Zintān Libya 88 B2
Az Zubayr Iraq 79 F5
Az Zuhrah Yemen 89 I6
Az Zuqur i. Yemen 76 C7
Az Zuwaytīnah Libya 88 D2

↓ B

Baa Indon. 57 F8
Baai r. Indon. 59 G2
Ba'albek Lebanon 77 C2
Ba'al Ḥazor mt. West Bank 77 B4
Baardheere Somalia 96 D4
Bab India 74 C4
Baba mt. Bulg. 46 C3
Bābā, Kūh-e mts Afgh. 81 G3
Baba Burnu pt Turkey 47 E5
Babaçulândia Brazil 150 C3
Babadağ mt. Azer. 79 G2
Babadag Romania 46 F2
Baba Dağ mt. Turkey 47 F6
Babadagului, Podişul plat. Romania 46 F2
Babadaykhan Turkm. 81 E2
Babadurmaz Turkm. 81 D2
Babaeski Turkey 78 A2
Babahoyo Ecuador 146 B5
Babai r. Nepal 75 D3
Bābā Kalān Iran 80 B4
Babakourimigana well Niger 93 H2
Bāb al Mandab strait Africa/Asia 96 D1
Bab al Mandab, Cape Yemen see Bāb al Mandab, Ra's
Bāb al Mandab, Ra's c. Yemen 96 D1
Babana Indon. 56 E6
Babanki Cameroon 93 H4
Babanusa Sudan 94 E2
Babao China 66 C4
Babar i. Indon. 57 G7
Babar, Kepulauan is Indon. 57 G7
Babat Indon. 59 F4
Babati Tanz. 97 B6
Babau Indon. 108 C2
Babayevo Rus. Fed. 28 E4
Babayurt Rus. Fed. 79 F2
Babeldaob i. Palau 57 H4
Babelthuap i. Palau see Babeldaob
Băbeni Romania 46 D2
Baberu India 74 D4
Bab Ezzouar Alg. 43 H4
Babi, Pulau i. Indon. 58 B2
Babia Góra mt. Poland 37 I4
Babian Jiang r. Yunnan China 62 G7
Babian Jiang r. Yunnan China 66 B4
Bābil governorate Iraq 79 F4
Babīlē Eth. 96 D2
Babine r. Canada 122 E4
Babine Lake Canada 122 E4
Babine Range mts Canada 122 E4
Babinga Dem. Rep. Congo 95 C5
Babo Indon. 57 H6
Bābol Iran 80 C2
Bābol Sar Iran 80 C2
Babonā r. Brazil 146 E6
Babongo Cameroon 93 I4
Baboon Point S. Africa 98 C7
Baboua Cent. Afr. Rep. 94 B3
Babruysk Belarus 29 D5
Babstovo Rus. Fed. 64 C2
Babtai Lith. 33 F5
Babu China see Hezhou
Babuna Planina mts Macedonia 46 B4
Babusar Pass Pak. 81 H3
Babushkin Rus. Fed. 62 H1
Babušnica Yugo. 46 C3
Babuyan i. Phil. 57 F2
Babuyan Channel Phil. 57 F2
Babuyan Islands Phil. 57 F2
Babylon tourist site Iraq 79 F4
Bač Yugo. 46 A2
Bacaadweyn Somalia 96 E3
Bacaba r. Brazil 146 D5
Bacabal Maranhão Brazil 150 C3
Bacabal Pará Brazil 147 G6
Bacajá r. Brazil 147 I5
Bacan i. Indon. 57 G6
Bacanora Mex. 135 E7
Bacău Romania 46 E1
Baccarat France 39 G2
Baccaro Point Canada 125 H5
Bacchiglione r. Italy 44 D2
Băc Giang Vietnam 60 D3
Bachaquero Venez. 146 D2
Bach Ice Shelf Antarctica 167 L2
Bachiniva Mex. 135 F7
Bach Long Vi, Đao i. Vietnam 60 D3
Bachu China 70 E4
Bachuma Eth. 96 C3
Back r. Australia 111 E3
Back r. Canada 123 M1
Bačka Palanka Yugo. 46 A2
Bačka Topola Yugo. 46 A2
Backbone Mountain U.S.A. 130 D4
Backbone Ranges mts Canada 122 D2
Backe Sweden 32 E3
Bäckefors Sweden 33 D4
Bäckhammar Sweden 33 D4
Backnang Germany 36 D4
Backstairs Passage Australia 112 A4
Bac Lac Vietnam 60 D3
Bac Liêu Vietnam 61 D6
Băc Ninh Vietnam 60 D3
Bacoachi Mex. 135 E7
Bacoachi watercourse Mex. 135 E7
Bacobampo Mex. 135 E8
Bacolod Phil. 57 F3
Băc Quang Vietnam 60 D3
Bactra Afgh. see Balkh
Bacuri Brazil 150 C2
Bad r. U.S.A. 132 A2
Bada China see Xilin
Bada mt. Eth. 96 C3
Bada i. Myanmar 61 B6
Badagara India 72 B4
Badain Jaran Shamo des. China 70 J3
Badajós Amazonas Brazil 147 F5
Badajós Pará Brazil 150 C2
Badajós, Lago l. Brazil 147 F5
Badajoz Spain 42 C3
Badakhshān prov. Afgh. 81 G2
Badakhshan aut. rep. Tajik. see Kŭhistoni Badakhshon
Badakhshoni Kŭhī aut. rep. Tajik. see Kŭhistoni Badakhshon
Badami India 72 B3
Badanah Saudi Arabia 89 I2
Badaojiang China see Baishan
Badarinath mts India see Badrinath Peaks
Badarpur India 75 G4
Badas, Kepulauan is Indon. 59 D2
Badaun India see Budaun
Bad Aussee Austria 37 F5
Bad Axe U.S.A. 130 B2
Bad Bergzabern Germany 36 C4
Bad Berka Germany 36 E3
Bad Berleburg Germany 36 D3
Bad Bevensen Germany 36 E2
Baddeck Canada 125 I4
Badderen Norway 32 F1
Baddo r. Pak. 81 F4
Bad Doberan Germany 36 E1
Badéguichéri Niger 93 G2
Bademli Turkey see Aladağ
Bademli Geçidi pass Turkey 78 B3
Bad Ems Germany 36 C3
Baden Austria 37 H4
Baden Switz. 36 D5
Baden-Baden Germany 36 D4
Baden-Württemberg land Germany 36 D4
Bad Freienwalde Germany 37 G2
Badger Canada 125 K3
Bādghīs prov. Afgh. 81 E3
Bad Harzburg Germany 36 E3
Bad Hersfeld Germany 36 D3
Bad Hofgastein Austria 37 F5
Bad Homburg vor der Höhe Germany 36 D3
Badi r. Guinea 92 B3
Badia Polesine Italy 44 C2
Badigeru Swamp Sudan 96 B3
Badin Pak. 81 G5
Bad Ischl Austria 37 F5
Bādiyat ash Shām Asia see Syrian Desert
Badje-Sohppar Sweden see Övre Soppero
Bad Kissingen Germany 36 E3
Bad Königsdorff Poland see Jastrzębie-Zdrój
Bad Kreuznach Germany 36 C4
Bad Krozingen Germany 36 C5
Badlands reg. U.S.A. 132 A3
Badlands National Park U.S.A. 132 A3
Bad Langensalza Germany 36 E3
Bad Lauterberg im Harz Germany 36 E3
Bad Liebenwerda Germany 37 F3
Bad Lippspringe Germany 36 D3
Bad Mergentheim Germany 36 D4
Badnawar India 74 B5
Bad Neuenahr-Ahrweiler Germany 36 C3
Bad Neustadt an der Saale Germany 36 E3
Badong China 67 D2
Ba Đông Vietnam 61 D6
Badou Togo 93 F4
Bad Reichenhall Germany 37 F5
Badr Ḥunayn Saudi Arabia 89 H4
Badrinath Peaks India 74 C3
Bad Säckingen Germany 36 C5
Bad Salzuflen Germany 36 D2
Bad Salzungen Germany 36 E3
Bad Schwartau Germany 36 E2
Bad Segeberg Germany 36 E2
Badu China 67 F3
Badu Island Australia 57 J8
Badulla Sri Lanka 72 D5
Badvel India 72 C3
Bad Waldsee Germany 36 D5
Bad Windsheim Germany 36 E4
Badzhal'skiy Khrebet mts Rus. Fed. 64 C2
Bad Zwischenahn Germany 36 D2
Bae Colwyn U.K. see Colwyn Bay
Bæir Iceland 32 [inset]
Baena Spain 42 D4
Baeza Ecuador 146 B5
Baeza Spain 42 E4
Bafang Cameroon 93 H4
Bafatá Guinea-Bissau 92 B2
Baffa Pak. 74 B2
Baffin Bay sea Canada/Greenland 121 M2

▶Baffin Island Canada 121 M3
2nd largest island in North America and 5th in the world.
northamerica 116–117
world 6–7

Bafia Cameroon 93 H4
Bafilo Togo 93 F3
Bafing r. Guinea/Mali 92 C2
Bafing Makana Mali 92 C2
Bafoulabé Mali 92 C2
Bafoussam Cameroon 93 H4
Bāfq Iran 80 C4
Bafra Turkey 78 C2
Bafra Burnu pt Turkey 78 C2
Bāft Iran 80 D4
Bafwasende Dem. Rep. Congo 94 E4
Baga Nigeria 93 I2
Bagà Spain 43 G1
Bagaha India 75 E4
Bagahak hill Sabah Malaysia 59 G1
Bagalkot India 72 B2
Bagamoyo Tanz. 97 C6
Bagan China 66 A1
Bagan Datoh Malaysia see Bagan Datuk
Bagan Datuk Malaysia 58 C2
Bagani Namibia 98 D3
Bagansiapiapi Indon. 58 C2
Bağarası Turkey 47 E6
Bagaré well Niger 93 G2
Bagaroua Niger 93 G2
Bagata Dem. Rep. Congo 95 C5
Bagazán Peru 146 C6
Bagbag Sudan 89 F6
Bagé Brazil 152 G2
Bagepalli India 72 C3
Bageshwar India 74 C3
Bagevadi India 72 C2
Baggs U.S.A. 134 F4
Bagh India 74 B5
Baghak Pak. 81 F4
Baghbaghū Iran 81 E3
Baghdad Iraq see Baghdād

▶Baghdād Iraq 79 F4
Capital of Iraq.

Bāgh-e Bābū'īyeh Iran 80 D4
Bagheria Sicily Italy 45 D5
Bāghīn Iran 80 D4
Baghlān Afgh. 81 G2
Baghlān prov. Afgh. 81 G3
Bağırsak Deresi r. Syria/Turkey see Sājūr, Nahr
Bagley U.S.A. 132 C2
Baglung Nepal 75 D3
Bagn Norway 33 C3
Bagnara Calabra Italy 45 E5
Bagnères-de-Bigorre France 38 D5
Bagnères-de-Luchon France 38 D5
Bagno di Romagna Italy 44 C3
Bagnolo Mella Italy 44 C2
Bagnols-sur-Cèze France 39 F4
Bagnuiti r. Nepal 75 E4
Bago Myanmar see Pegu
Bago admin. div. Myanmar see Pegu
Bagoé r. Côte d'Ivoire/Mali 92 D2
Bagong China see Sansui
Bagrationovsk Rus. Fed. 37 J1
Bagrax China see Bohu
Bagrax Hu l. China see Bosten Hu
Bagre Brazil 150 B2
Bagua Peru 146 B6
Bagudo Nigeria 93 G3
Bagzane, Monts mts Niger 93 H1
Bahadurgarh India 74 C3
Bahāmabād Iran see Rafsanjān
▶Bahamas, The country West Indies 129 E7
northamerica 118–119, 140
Baharampur India 75 F4
Bahardipur Pak. 81 G5
Bahariya Oasis Egypt 89 F3
Bahau r. Indon. 59 G2
Bahau Malaysia 58 C2
Bahaur Indon. 59 F3
Bahawalnagar Pak. 81 H4
Bahawalpur Pak. 81 G4
Bahçe Adana Turkey 77 B1
Bahçe Turkey 78 D3
Ba He r. China 66 C2
Bäherden Turkm. see Bakherden
Baheri India 74 C3
Bahi Tanz. 97 B6
Bahia Brazil see Salvador
Bahia state Brazil 150 D5
Bahía Asunción Mex. 135 D8
Bahía Blanca Arg. 152 E4
Bahía Bustamante Arg. 153 D6
Bahía Kino Mex. 135 E7
Bahía Laura Arg. 153 D7
Bahía Negra Para. 149 F5
Bahía San Blas Arg. 152 E5
Bahía Tortugas Mex. 135 D8
Bahir Dar Eth. 96 C2
Bahmanshīr, Khowr-e r. Iran 80 B4
Bahraich India 75 D4
▶Bahrain country Asia 80 B5
asia 52–53, 82
Bahrain, Gulf of Asia 80 B5
Bahrāmābād Iran 80 B2
Bahrāmjerd Iran 80 D4
Bahr el Jebel state Sudan 96 A3
Bahrīyah, Wāḥāt al oasis Egypt see Bahariya Oasis
Bahror India 74 C4
Bahuaja-Sonene, Parque Nacional nat. park Peru 148 C3
Bāhū Kālāt Iran 81 E5
Baia Romania 46 F2
Baia de Aramă Romania 46 C2
Baia dos Tigres Angola 95 A9
Baia Farta Angola 95 B8
Baia Mare Romania 31 J4
Baião Brazil 150 B2
Baiazeh Iran 80 C3
Baïbeli well Chad 88 D5
Baïbokoum Chad 94 B3
Baicheng Henan China see Xiping
Baicheng Jilin China 63 K2
Băicoi Romania 46 D2
Baidoa Somalia see Baydhabo
Baidoi Co l. China 75 E2
Baidu China 67 F3
Baie-aux-Feuilles Canada see Tasiujaq
Baie-Comeau Canada 125 G3
Baie-du-Poste Canada see Mistissini
Baie-Johan-Beetz Canada 125 I3
Baie-St-Paul Canada 125 G4
Baie-Trinite Canada 125 H3
Baie Verte Canada 125 J3
Baiguan China see Shangyu
Baiguo China 67 E2
Baigura mt. Spain 43 F1
Baihanchang China 66 A3
Baihar India 74 D5
Baihe Jilin China 64 B4
Baihe Shaanxi China 67 D1
Bai He r. China 67 E1
Baiji Iraq see Bayjī
Baijnath Himachal Pradesh India 74 C2
Baijnath Uttaranchal India 74 C3

▶Baikal, Lake Rus. Fed. 27 K4
Deepest lake in the world and in Asia. 3rd largest lake in Asia and 9th in the world.
asia 50–51
world 6–7

Baikunthpur India 75 D5
Bailanhe Shuiku resr China 67 E2
Baile Átha Cliath Rep. of Ireland see Dublin
Baile Átha Luain Rep. of Ireland see Athlone
Băile Govora Romania 46 D2
Băile Herculane Romania 46 C2
Bailén Spain 42 E3
Băile Olănești Romania 46 D2
Băilești Romania 46 C2
Băileștilor, Câmpia plain Romania 46 C2
Băile Tușnad Romania 46 D1
Bailey Range hills Australia 109 C7
Bailicun China 67 D3
Bailique Brazil 147 I4
Baillie r. Canada 123 J1
Bailong Jiang r. China 66 C1
Baima Qinghai China 66 B1
Baima Xizang China see Baxoi
Bainang China 70 G6
Bainbridge GA U.S.A. 129 B6
Bainbridge NY U.S.A. 131 F2
Bainbridge OH U.S.A. 130 B4
Bain-de-Bretagne France 38 C3
Bainduru India 72 B3
Baingoin China 75 F3
Baini China see Yuqing
Baiona Spain 42 B1
Baiqên China 66 B1
Baiquan China 64 A3
Bā'ir Jordan 77 C4
Bā'ir, Wādī watercourse Jordan/Saudi Arabia 77 C4
Bairab Co l. China 75 D2
Bairagnia India 75 E4
Baird U.S.A. 133 B5
Baird, Mount Canada 122 C1
Baird Mountains U.S.A. 120 D3

▶Bairiki Kiribati 164 F5
Capital of Kiribati, on Tarawa atoll.

Bairin Youqi China see Daban
Bairnsdale Australia 112 C5
Bais France 38 C2
Baïse r. France 38 D4
Baisha Chongqing China 66 C2
Baisha Hainan China 67 D5
Baisha Jiangxi China 67 E3
Baisha Sichuan China 66 D2
Baishan Guangxi China see Mashan
Baishan Jilin China 64 A4
Baishan Jilin China 64 A4
Baishui Jiang r. China 66 C1
Băișoara Romania 46 C1
Baisogala Lith. 33 F5
Baitadi Nepal 74 D3
Bai Thương Vietnam 60 D4
Baixa da Banheira Port. 42 B3
Baixi China see Yibin
Baixo-Longa Angola 95 C8
Baiyashi China see Dong'an
Baiyin China 62 G4
Baiyü China 66 A2
Baiyuda Desert Sudan 89 G5
Baja Hungary 46 A1
Baja California pen. Mex. 126 C5
Baja California state Mex. 135 D7
Baja California Sur state Mex. 135 D8
Bajan Mex. 133 A7
Bajang Nepal 74 D3
Bajau i. Indon. 59 D2
Bajawa Indon. 57 F7
Baj Baj India 75 F5
Bājgīrān Iran 80 D2
Bājil Yemen 89 I6
Bajina Bašta Yugo. 46 A3
Bajitpur Bangl. 75 F4
Bajmok Yugo. 46 A2
Bajna India 74 B5
Bajo Baudó Col. 146 B3
Bajo Caracoles Arg. 153 C6
Bajoga Nigeria 93 H3
Bajo Grande Arg. 153 C6
Bajo Hondo Arg. 152 D2
Bajrakot India 75 E5
Bajram Curri Albania 46 B3
Bakaba Chad 94 C3
Bakala Cent. Afr. Rep. 94 D3
Bakaly Rus. Fed. 28 J5
Bakau Gambia 92 A2
Bakayan, Gunung mt. Indon. 59 G2
Bakel Senegal 92 B2
Baker CA U.S.A. 135 C6
Baker LA U.S.A. 133 D6
Baker MT U.S.A. 134 F3
Baker OR U.S.A. 134 C3
Baker WV U.S.A. 130 D4
Baker, Mount vol. U.S.A. 134 B2
Baker Butte mt. U.S.A. 137 G4

▶Baker Island N. Pacific Ocean 107 H1
United States Unincorporated Territory.
oceania 104–105, 114

Baker Lake salt flat Australia 109 D6
Baker Lake Canada 123 M1
Baker Lake l. Canada 123 M1
Baker's Dozen Islands Canada 124 E1
Bakersfield U.S.A. 136 C4
Bakhā Oman 80 D5
Bakharden Turkm. see Bakherden
Bakhardok Turkm. 81 D2
Bākharz mts Iran 81 E3
Bakherden Turkm. 80 D2
Bakhirevo Rus. Fed. 64 B2
Bakhmach Ukr. 29 E6
Bakhmut Ukr. see Artemivs'k
Bakhta Rus. Fed. 27 I3
Bākhtarān Iran see Kermānshāh
Bākhtarān prov. Iran see Kermānshāh
Bakhtegan, Daryācheh-ye l. Iran 80 C4
Bakhtiyarpur India 75 E4
Bakhuis Gebergte mts Suriname 147 G3
Bakı Azer. see Baku
Baki well Chad 88 D5
Bakır r. Turkey 47 E5
Bakırköy Turkey 78 B2
Bakkaflói b. Iceland 32 [inset]
Bakloh India 74 B2
Bako Côte d'Ivoire 92 D3
Bako Eth. 96 C2
Bako National Park Sarawak Malaysia 59 E2
Bakool admin. reg. Somalia 96 D4
Bakouma Cent. Afr. Rep. 94 D3
Bakoumba Gabon 94 B5
Bakoy r. Mali 92 C2
Baksan Rus. Fed. 29 G8

▶Baku Azer. 79 G2
Capital of Azerbaijan.

Bakung i. Indon. 58 D2
Bakuriani Georgia 79 E2
Bakutis Coast Antarctica 167 J2
Baky Azer. see Baku
Baky Uyandino r. Rus. Fed. 27 O3
Balâ Turkey 78 C3
Bala U.K. 35 E5
Bala, Cerros de mts Bol. 148 C3
Balabac i. Phil. 56 E4
Balabac Strait Malaysia/Phil. 59 G1
Balābād, Gardaneh-ye pass Iran 80 C3
Balabalangan, Kepulauan atolls Indon. 59 G3
Bălăceanu Romania 46 E2
Bălăcița Romania 46 C2
Balad Iraq 79 F4
Bālā Deh Iran 80 B4
Baladeh Iran 80 B2
Balaghat India 74 D5
Balaghat Range hills India 72 B2
Balaguer Spain 43 G2
Bālā Ḥowz Iran 80 D4
Balaiberkuak Indon. 59 E3
Balaikarangan Indon. 59 E2
Balaipungut Indon. 58 C2
Balairiam Indon. 59 E3
Balaïtous mt. France 38 C5
Balaka Malawi 97 B8
Balakän Azer. 79 F2
Balakhna Rus. Fed. 28 G4
Balaklava Australia 112 A4
Balaklava Ukr. 78 C1
Balakleya Ukr. see Balakliya
Balakliya Ukr. 29 F6
Balakovo Rus. Fed. 29 H5
Balama Moz. 97 C8
Balambangan i. Sabah Malaysia 59 G1
Bālā Morghāb Afgh. 81 E3
Balan India 74 A4
Bălan Romania 46 D1
Balanda Rus. Fed. see Kalininsk
Balan Dağı hill Turkey 47 F6
Balangala Dem. Rep. Congo 94 C4
Balangir India 73 D1
Balangoda Sri Lanka 72 D5
Balapur India 72 C1
Balarampur India 75 E5
Balashi Rus. Fed. 29 I6
Balashov Rus. Fed. 29 G6
Balassagyarmat Hungary 37 I4
Balaton, Lake Hungary 37 H5
Balatonboglár Hungary 37 H5
Balatonfüred Hungary 37 H5
Balauring Indon. 108 C2
Balazote Spain 43 E3
Balbina Brazil 147 G5
Balbina, Represa de resr Brazil 147 G5
Balcad Somalia 96 E4
Balcanoona Australia 112 A3
Balcarce Arg. 152 F4
Balchik Bulg. 46 F3
Balclutha N.Z. 113 B4
Bald Knob AR U.S.A. 133 D5
Bald Knob WV U.S.A. 130 C5
Bald Mountain U.S.A. 137 E3
Baldock Lake Canada 123 L3
Baldwin U.S.A. 129 C6
Baldwinsville U.S.A. 131 E2
Baldwinville U.S.A. 131 G2
Baldy Mount Canada 134 C2
Baldy Mountain Canada 134 G2
Baldy Peak U.S.A. 137 H5
Bale Indon. 58 C3
Bâle Switz. see Basel
Baléa Mali 92 C2
Baleares, Islas is Spain see Balearic Islands
Baleares Insulae is Spain see Balearic Islands
Balearic Islands Spain 43 G3
Balears, Illes is Spain see Balearic Islands
Baleh r. Sarawak Malaysia 59 F2
Baleia, Ponta da pt Brazil 151 E6
Baleines, Pointe des pt France 38 C3
Bale Mountains National Park Eth. 96 C3
Băleni Romania 46 D2
Baleshwar India 75 E5
Balestrand Norway 33 B3
Baléyara Niger 93 F2
Balezino Rus. Fed. 28 J4
Balfe's Creek Australia 111 F4
Balfour Canada 122 G5
Balfour Downs Australia 108 C5
Balgo Australia 108 D5
Bālḥaf Yemen 76 D7
Balho Djibouti 96 D1
Bali India 74 B4
▶Bali i. Indon. 59 F5
asia 52–53
Bali prov. Indon. 59 F5
Bali, Selat sea chan. Indon. 59 F5
Baliapal India 75 E5
Bali Barat National Park Indon. 59 F5
Balichak India 75 E5
Balige Indon. 58 B2
Baliguda India 73 D1
Balıkesir Turkey 78 A3
Balıkesir prov. Turkey 47 F5
Balık Gölü l. Turkey 79 E3
Balīkh r. Syria/Turkey 79 D4
Balıklıçeşme Turkey 47 E4
Balikpapan Indon. 59 G3
Balikpapan, Teluk b. Indon. 59 G3
Balimila Reservoir India 73 D2
Balimo P.N.G. 57 J7
Balingen Germany 36 D4
Balingian Sarawak Malaysia 59 F2
Balingian r. Sarawak Malaysia 59 F2
Balintang Channel Phil. 57 F2
Bali Sea Indon. 59 F4
Balitondo Cent. Afr. Rep. 94 D3
Baljurshī Saudi Arabia 89 I5
Balkan Mountains Bulg./Yugo. 46 C3
Balkan Oblast admin. div. Turkm. see Balkanskaya Oblast'
Balkanskaya Oblast' admin. div. Turkm. 80 C1
Balkh Afgh. 81 F2
Balkh prov. Afgh. 81 F2
Balkhab r. Afgh. 81 F2
Balkhash Kazakh. 70 D2

▶Balkhash, Lake Kazakh. 70 D2
4th largest lake in Asia.
asia 50–51

Balkhash, Ozero Kazakh. see Balkhash, Lake
Balkuduk Kazakh. 29 H7
Balla Bangl. 75 F4
Balla Balla Zimbabwe see Mbalabala
Ballachulish U.K. 34 D3
Balladonia Australia 109 C8
Ballaghaderreen Rep. of Ireland 35 B5
Ballangen Norway 32 E1
Ballantrae U.K. 34 D4
Ballarat Australia 112 B5
Ballard, Lake salt flat Australia 109 C7
Ballarpur India 72 C2
Ballater U.K. 34 E3
Ballé Mali 92 C2
Ballena, Punta pt Chile 152 C1
Balleny Islands Antarctica 167 H2
Ballia India 75 E4
Ballina Australia 111 H6
Ballina Rep. of Ireland 35 B4
Ballinasloe Rep. of Ireland 35 B5
Ballineen Rep. of Ireland 35 B6
Ballinger U.S.A. 133 B6
Ballinrobe Rep. of Ireland 35 B5
Ballsh Albania 46 A4
Ballston Spa U.S.A. 131 G2
Ballybunnion Rep. of Ireland 35 B5
Ballycastle Rep. of Ireland 35 B4
Ballycastle U.K. 34 C4
Ballyhaunis Rep. of Ireland 35 B5
Ballymena U.K. 34 C4
Ballymoney U.K. 34 C4
Ballyshannon Rep. of Ireland 35 B4
Balmaceda Aisén Chile 153 C6
Balmaceda Antofagasta Chile 148 C6
Balmaseda Spain 42 E1
Balmazújváros Hungary 37 J5
Balmer India see Barmer
Balmertown Canada 123 M5
Balnearia Arg. 152 E2
Balochistan prov. Pak. 81 F4
Balod India 72 D1
Baloda Bazar India 75 D5
Balok, Teluk b. Indon. 59 D3
Balombo Angola 95 B8
Balonne r. Australia 111 G6
Balotra India 74 B4
Balpahari Reservoir India 75 E4
Balpyk Bi Kazakh. 70 E3
Balqash Kazakh. see Balkhash
Balqash Köli l. Kazakh. see Balkhash, Lake
Balrampur India 75 D4
Balranald Australia 112 B4
Balș Romania 46 D2
Balsam Lake Canada 130 D1
Balsapuerto Peru 146 B6
Balsareny Spain 43 G2
Balsas Brazil 150 C3
Balsas, Rio das r. Brazil 150 C3
Bålsta Sweden 33 E4
Balta Ukr. 29 D7
Baltay Rus. Fed. 29 H5
Bălți Moldova 29 C7
Baltic Sea g. Europe 33 E5
Balṭīm Egypt 89 F2
Baltimore Rep. of Ireland 35 B6
Baltimore MD U.S.A. 131 E4
Baltimore OH U.S.A. 130 B4
Baltinglass Rep. of Ireland 35 C5
Baltistan reg. Jammu and Kashmir 74 B2
Baltiysk Rus. Fed. 37 I1
Baltoro Glacier Jammu and Kashmir 74 C2
Baluarte Brazil 150 D4
Baluch Ab well Iran 81 D4
Balūchestān va Sīstān prov. Iran 81 E5
Balui r. Sarawak Malaysia 59 F2
Balumundam Indon. 58 B2
Baluran, Gunung mt. Indon. 59 F3
Baluran National Park Indon. 59 F4
Balurghat India 75 F4
Balvatnet l. Norway 32 D2
Balvi Latvia 33 G4
Balya Turkey 78 A3
Balykchy Kyrg. 62 B3
Balykshi Kazakh. 29 I7
Balyqshy Kazakh. see Balykshi
Balzar Ecuador 146 B5
Bam Iran 80 D4
Bām Iran 80 D2
Bama China 66 C3
Bama Nigeria 93 I3
Bamaga Australia 111 E1
Bamaji Lake Canada 124 B3

▶Bamako Mali 92 D2
Capital of Mali.

Bamba r. Cent. Afr. Rep. 94 C3
Bamba Dem. Rep. Congo 95 C6
Bamba Mali 93 E1
Bambama Congo 94 B5
Bambangando Angola 95 D9
Bambari Cent. Afr. Rep. 94 D3
Bamberg Germany 36 E4
Bamberg U.S.A. 129 C5
Bambesi Eth. 96 B2
Bambey Senegal 92 A2
Bambili Dem. Rep. Congo 94 E4
Bambio Cent. Afr. Rep. 94 C4
Bamboi Ghana 93 E3
Bamboo Creek Australia 108 C5
Bambou well Mali 93 E1
Bambouk reg. Mali 92 C2
Bambouti Cent. Afr. Rep. 94 E3
Bambudi Eth. 96 B2
Bambuí Brazil 151 C7
Bamda China 66 A2
Bāmdezh Iran 80 B4
Bamenda Cameroon 93 H4
Bamendjing, Lac de l. Cameroon 93 H4
Bamfield Canada 122 E5
Bami Turkm. 80 D2
Bāmīān Afgh. 81 F3
Bāmīān prov. Afgh. 81 F3
Bamiantong China see Muling
Bamingui Cent. Afr. Rep. 94 D3
Bamingui r. Cent. Afr. Rep. 94 C2
Bamingui-Bangoran pref. Cent. Afr. Rep. 94 D2
Bamingui-Bangoran, Parc National du nat. park Cent. Afr. Rep. 94 C2
Bamiyan r. Afgh. 81 F3
Bammo well Niger 93 H2
Bamor India 74 C4
Bam Posht, Kūh-e mts Iran 81 E5
Bampūr Iran 81 E5
Bampūr watercourse Iran 81 D5
Bamrūd Iran 81 E3
Bamy Turkm. see Bami
Ban Burkina 93 E2
Banaba i. Kiribati 164 F6
Banabuiu, Açude resr Brazil 150 E3
Bañados del Atuel marsh Arg. 152 D4
Bañados del Izozog swamp Bol. 149 E4

Bañados de Otuquis *marsh* Bol. **149** F4
Banalia Dem. Rep. Congo **94** E4
Banamba Mali **92** D2
Banan China **66** C2
Banana Australia **111** G5
Bananal, Ilha do *i.* Brazil **150** B4
Bananga India **73** E2
Banankoro Guinea **92** C3
Banapur India **73** E2
Banarlı Turkey **46** E4
Banas *r.* India **74** B4
Banas, Ra's *pt* Egypt **89** G4
Banaz Turkey **78** B3
Ban Ban Laos **60** C4
Banbar China **75** F2
Banbridge U.K. **35** C4
Ban Bua Yai Thai. **61** C5
Banbury U.K. **35** F5
Banca Romania **46** E1
Banc d'Arguin, Parc National du
  nat. park Mauritania **90** A5
Banchory U.K. **34** G3
Bancroft Canada **124** E4
Bancroft Zambia *see* Chililabombwe
Band India **74** B4
Banda Dem. Rep. Congo **94** E3
Banda *Madhya Pradesh* India **74** D4
Banda *Uttar Pradesh* India **74** D4
Banda, Kepulauan *is* Indon. **57** G6
Banda Aceh Indon. **58** A1
Banda Banda, Mount Australia **112** E3
Bandahara, Gunung *mt.* Indon. **58** B2
Bandai-Asahi National Park Japan
  65 D5
Bandama *r.* Côte d'Ivoire **92** C4
Bandama Blanc *r.* Côte d'Ivoire **92** D3
Bandān Iran **81** E4
Bandān Kūh *mts* Iran **81** E4
Bandar India *see* Machilipatnam
Bandar Abbas Iran *see* Bandar-e 'Abbās
Bandaragung Indon. **58** D4
Bandarban Bangl. **75** G5
Bandar-e 'Abbās Iran **80** D5
Bandar-e Anzalī Iran **80** C5
Bandar-e Chārak Iran **80** C5
Bandar-e Deylam Iran **80** C5
Bandar-e Emām Khomeynī Iran **80** B4
Bandar-e Lengeh Iran **80** C5
Bandar-e Magām Iran **80** C5
Bandar-e Ma'shur Iran **80** B4
Bandar-e Moghūyeh Iran **80** C5
Bandar-e Pahlavī Iran *see*
  Bandar-e Anzalī
Bandar-e Shāh Iran *see*
  Bandar-e Torkeman
Bandar-e Shāhpūr Iran *see*
  Bandar-e Emām Khomeynī
Bandar-e Torkeman Iran **80** D2
Bandar Lampung Indon. **58** D4
Bandarpunch *mt.* India **74** C3

▶ Bandar Seri Begawan Brunei **59** F1
  Capital of Brunei.

Banda Sea Indon. **57** H7
Bandeirante Brazil **150** B5
Bandeiras, Pico de *mt.* Brazil **151** D7
Bandera Arg. **152** E2
Bandera U.S.A. **133** B6
Banderas, Mex. **135** F7
Bandhi Pak. **81** G5
Bandhogarh India **74** D5
Bandi *r.* India **74** B4
Bandia *r.* India **72** D2
Bandiagara Mali **92** C3
Bandiagara, Falaise de *esc.* Mali **92** E2
Band-i-Amir *r.* Afgh. **81** F2
Band-i-Baba *mts* Afgh. **81** E3
Bandikui India **74** C4
Bandini Iran **81** F3
Bandipur Jammu and Kashmir **74** B2
Bandipur National Park India **72** C4
Bandırma Turkey **78** B3
Band-i-Turkestan *mts* Afgh. **81** F3
Bandjarmasin Indon. *see* Banjarmasin
Bandjer *pass* Yugo. **46** B2
Bandon Rep. of Ireland **35** B6
Bandon *r.* Rep. of Ireland **35** B6
Ban Don Thai. *see* Surat Thani
Bandon U.S.A. **134** A4
Ban Don, Ao *b.* Thai. **61** B6
Band Qīr Iran **80** B4
Bandula Moz. **99** D3
Bandundu Dem. Rep. Congo **94** B4
Bandundu *prov.* Dem. Rep. Congo **95** C6
Bandung Indon. **58** D4
Bandya Australia **109** C7
Băneasa Romania **46** E2
Băneasa Romania **46** E2
Bāneh Iran **80** B3
Banera India **74** E4
Bañeres Spain **43** F3
Banff Canada **134** D2
Banff U.K. **34** G3
Banff National Park Canada **123** G5
Banfora Burkina **92** C3
Bang Cent. Afr. Rep. **94** B3
Banga Dem. Rep. Congo **95** D6
Bangall Creek *watercourse* Australia
  111 F4
Bangalore India **72** C3
Banganapalle India **72** C3
Banganga *r.* India **74** B4
Bangaon India **75** F5
Bangar Brunei **59** F1
Bangara *r.* Bangl. **75** F5
Bangarapet India **72** C3
Bangassou Cent. Afr. Rep. **94** D3
Bangdag Co *salt l.* China **75** D2
Bangfai, Xé *r.* Laos **60** D4
Banggai Indon. **57** F6
Banggai, Kepulauan *is* Indon. **57** F6
Banggi *i.* Sabah Malaysia **59** G1
Banghāzī Libya *see* Benghazi
Banghiang, Xé *r.* Laos **60** D4
Bangka *i.* Indon. **58** D3
Bangka, Selat *sea chan.* Indon. **58** D3
Bangkalan Indon. **58** E4
Bangkaru *i.* Indon. **58** B2
Bangkinang Indon. **58** C2
Bangko Indon. **58** C3
Bangkog Co *salt l.* China **75** F3

▶ Bangkok Thai. **61** C5
  Capital of Thailand.

Bangkok, Bight of *b.* Thai. **61** C5
Bangkor China **75** E3
Bangla *state* India *see* West Bengal

▶ Bangladesh *country* Asia **75** F5
  8th most populous country in the world.
  asia **52–53**, **82**
  world **16–17**

Bang Lang Reservoir Thai. **58** C1
Bangma Shan *mts* China **66** A4
Ban Mun Nak Thai. **61** C4
Bangolo Côte d'Ivoire **92** D4
Bangong Co *salt l.*
  China/Jammu and Kashmir **74** C2
Bangor *Gwynedd, Wales* U.K. **35** D5

Bangor *Northern Ireland* U.K. **35** D4
Bangor *ME* U.S.A. **127** M3
Bangor *PA* U.S.A. **131** F3
Bangriposi India **75** E5
Bangsalsepulun Indon. **59** G3
Bang Saphan Yai Thai. **61** B6
Bangu Dem. Rep. Congo **95** D7

▶ Bangui Cent. Afr. Rep. **94** C3
  Capital of Central African Republic.

Bangui Phil. **67** G5
Bangula Malawi **97** B9
Bangunpurba Indon. **58** B2
Banguru Dem. Rep. Congo **94** E4
Bangweulu, Lake Zambia **95** F7
Banhã Egypt **89** G4
Banhine, Parque Nacional de *nat. park*
  Moz. **99** D3
Ban Houayxay Laos **60** C3
Ban Houei Sai Laos *see* Ban Houayxay
Bani Burkina **93** E2
Bani Cent. Afr. Rep. **94** D3
Bani Dom. Rep. **139** J5
Bani *r.* Mali **92** D2
Bani, Jbel *ridge* Morocco **90** C3
Bani-Bangou Niger **93** F2
Bania Cent. Afr. Rep. **94** C3
Banifing *r.* Mali **92** D2
Banifing *r.* Mali **92** D2
Banihal Pass and Tunnel
  Jammu and Kashmir **74** B2
Banikoara Benin **93** F3
Banī Mazār Egypt **78** D5
Banī Suwayf Egypt **78** D5
Banī Suwayf *governorate* Egypt **78** D5
Banī Thawr Saudi Arabia **89** I5
Banitsa Bulg. **46** C3
Banī Walīd Libya **88** E2
Bāniyās Syria **78** C3
Banja Luka Bos.-Herz. **44** F7
Banjar India **74** D3
Banjarbaru Indon. **59** F3
Banjarmasin Indon. **59** F3
Banjes, Liqeni *resr* Albania **46** B4

▶ Banjul Gambia **92** A2
  Capital of The Gambia.

Banka India **75** F4
Banka Banka Australia **110** C3
Bankapur India **72** B3
Ban Khao Yoi Thai. **61** B5
Banki India **73** F1
Bankim Cameroon **93** H4
Banko, Massif de *mt.* Guinea **92** C3
Bankobankoang *i.* Indon. **59** G4
Bankol India **72** B2
Bankon Guinea **92** C3
Ban Lamduan Thai. **61** C5
Bankura India **75** E5
Bankya Bulg. **46** C3
Bankya Bulg. **46** C3
Ban Loc Romania **46** E2
Ban Mae Mo Thai. **60** B3
Banmauk Myanmar **60** A2
Bann *r.* U.K. **35** C4
Ban Na San Thai. **61** B6
Ban Napè Laos **60** D4
Ban Phaeng Thai. **60** D4
Ban Phai Thai. **61** C4
Ban Phon Laos **61** D5
Banphot Phisai Thai. **61** B5
Ban Pong Thai. **61** B5
Banqiao China **66** C3
Ban Saraphi Thai. **60** B3
Ban Sawi Thai. **61** B6
Bansgaon India **75** E4
Bansi *Rajasthan* India **74** C4
Bansi *Uttar Pradesh* India **74** C4
Bansi *Uttar Pradesh* India **75** D4
Banská Bystrica Slovakia **37** I4
Banská Štiavnica Slovakia **37** I4
Bansko Bulg. **46** C4
Bansloi *r.* India **75** E4
Ban Sut Ta Thai. **60** B4
Banswada India **72** C2
Banswara India **74** B5
Bantè Benin **93** F4
Ban Tha Kham Thai. **61** B6
Ban Tha Song Yang Thai. **60** B4
Banthat *mts* Cambodia *see*
  Cardamom Range
Ban Tha Tako Thai. **61** C5
Ban Tha Tum Thai. **61** C5
Ban Thung Luang Thai. **61** B5
Bantry Rep. of Ireland **35** B6
Bantry Bay Rep. of Ireland **35** B6
Bantul Indon. **59** E4
Bantva India **74** A5
Bantval India **72** B3
Banyak, Pulau-pulau *is* Indon. **58** B2
Banyo Cameroon **93** H4
Banyoles Spain **43** H1
Banyuwangi Indon. **58** E4
Banzare Coast Antarctica **167** G2
Banzare Seamount *sea feature*
  Indian Ocean **163** M9
Banzart Tunisia *see* Bizerte
Banzyville Dem. Rep. Congo *see*
  Mobayi-Mbongo
Bao, Embalse del *resr* Spain *see*
  Vao, Embalse de
Bao, Ouadi *watercourse* Chad **88** D5
Baochang China *see* Taibus Qi
Baocheng China **66** C1
Baoding China **63** I4
Baofeng China **67** E1
Baoji *Shaanxi* China **66** C1
Baoji *Shaanxi* China **66** C1
Baokang China **67** D2
Bao Lôc Vietnam **61** D6
Baoqing China **64** C3
Baoro Cent. Afr. Rep. **94** C3
Baoshan *Shanghai* China **67** G2
Baoshan *Yunnan* China **66** A3
Baotou China **63** I3
Baoulé *r.* Mali **92** D2
Baoulé *r.* Mali **92** D2
Baoxing China **66** B4
Baoying China **67** F1
Baoyou China *see* Ledong
Bap India **74** B4
Bapatla India **73** D3
Bapaume France **39** E1
Bapu China *see* Meigu
Baqarah Saudi Arabia **89** I4

Baqiu China *see* Xiajiang
Baqrān Saudi Arabia **89** I4
Ba'qūbah Iraq **79** F4
Bar Yugo. **46** A3
Bara Nigeria **93** H3
Bara Issa *r.* Mali **92** C3
Bara Sudan **89** F6
Bara *well* Sudan **89** F6
Baraawe Somalia **96** E4
Barabai Indon. **59** F3
Bara Banki India **74** D4
Barabaum India **75** E5
Baraboo U.S.A. **132** D3
Baraboulé Burkina **93** E2
Baracaldo Spain *see* Barakaldo
Baracoa Cuba **127** L7
Baradá, Nahr *r.* Syria **77** C3
Baradero Arg. **152** E3
Băragănului, Câmpia *plain* Romania
  46 E2
Baragoi Kenya **96** C4
Baragua, Sierra de *mts* Venez. **146** D2
Barahona Dom. Rep. **139** J5
Barail Range *mts* India **75** G4
Barak Afgh. **81** G2
Barak *r.* India **75** H4
Baraka *watercourse* Eritrea/Sudan **89** H5
Barakaldo Spain **42** E1
Baraki Barak Afgh. **81** G3
Barakot India **75** E5
Baralaba Australia **111** G5
Bara Lacha Pass India **74** C2
Baramanni Guyana **147** G3
Baramati India **72** B2
Barameiya Sudan **89** H5
Baramula Jammu and Kashmir **74** B2
Baran India **74** C4
Baran *r.* Pak. **81** G5
Bārān, Kūh-e *mts* Iran **81** E3
Baranavichy Belarus **29** C5
Barang, Dasht-i *des.* Afgh. **81** E3
Baranikha Rus. Fed. **27** Q3
Baranis Egypt **89** G4
Baranof Island U.S.A. **120** C3
Baranovichi Belarus *see* Baranavichy
Baranowicze Belarus *see* Baranavichy
Barão de Melgaço Brazil **149** G6
Baraolt Romania **46** D1
Baraqueville France **38** E4
Barararil *r.* Brazil **149** F1
Barat Daya, Kepulauan *is* Indon. **57** G7
Baratta Australia **112** A4
Barauaná, Serra *mts* Brazil **147** F4
Baraut India **74** C3
Barbacena *Minas Gerais* Brazil **151** D7
Barbacena Pará Brazil **149** H4
▶ Barbados *country* West Indies **147** G1
  northamerica **118–119**, **140**
Barbar, Jabal *mt.* Egypt **77** A5
Barbara Lake Canada **122** D4
Barbastro Spain **43** G1
Barbate de Franco Spain **42** D4
Bárbele Latvia **33** N8
Barbezieux-St-Hilaire France **38** D4
Barbigha India **75** F4
Barbosa Col. **146** C2
Barbour Bay Canada **123** M2
Barbours U.S.A. **131** E3
Barbourville U.S.A. **130** D5
Barbuda *i.* Antigua and Barbuda **139** L5
Barcaldine Australia **111** F4
Barce Libya *see* Al Marj
Barcellona Pozzo di Gotto *Sicily* Italy
  45 F5
Barcelona Spain **43** H2
Barcelona Venez. **147** F2
Barcelonnette France **39** G4
Barcelos Brazil **147** F5
Barcelos Brazil **147** F5
Barcin Poland **37** H2
Barcino Spain *see* Barcelona
Barclayville Liberia **92** C4
Barcoo *watercourse* Australia **111** E5
Barcoo Creek *watercourse* Australia *see*
  Cooper Creek
Barcoo National Park Australia *see*
  Welford National Park
Barcs Hungary **44** F2
Bárðà Azer. **79** F2
Bardai Chad **88** D5
Ban Phon Thai. **61** B5
Bardardale Somalia **96** E3
Bárðarbunga *mt.* Iceland **32** [inset]
Bardas Blancas Arg. **152** C5
Bardaskan Iran **80** D3
Bardawīl, Sabkhat al *lag.* Egypt **77** A4
Barddhaman India **75** F5
Bardejov Slovakia **37** J4
Bardera Somalia *see* Baardheere
Bard Shah Iran **80** B3
Bardsir Iran **80** D4
Bardstown U.S.A. **128** B4
Barduli Italy *see* Barletta
Bardwell U.S.A. **128** A4
Bareh Eth. **96** D3
Bareilly India **74** D3
Bareli India **74** C5
Barengapara India **75** F4
Barents Island Svalbard *see* Barentsøya
Barentsburg Svalbard **26** B2
Barentsøya *i.* Svalbard **26** C2
Barents Sea Arctic Ocean **26** D2
Barentu Eritrea **89** H6
Bareo Sarawak Malaysia **59** F2
Barfleur, Pointe de *pt* France **38** C2
Barga China **75** D3
Bargaal Somalia **96** F2
Bārgāh Iran **80** D5
Bargë Eth. **96** D3
Bargi India **74** C4
Bargırı Turkey *see* Muradiye
Bargteheide Germany **36** F2
Barguna Bangl. **75** F5
Bargur India **72** C4
Barh India **70** G6
Barhaj India **75** F4
Barhalganj India **75** D4
Barharwa India **75** E4
Bari Dem. Rep. Congo **94** D4
Bari India **74** C4
Bari Italy **44** F4
Bari *admin. reg.* Somalia **96** F2
Barika Alg. **91** H1
Barikot Afgh. **74** A2
Barikot Nepal **75** D3
Barima *r.* Guyana **147** G2
Barinas Venez. **146** D2
Barinas *state* Venez. **146** D2
Baringa Dem. Rep. Congo **94** D4
Baringo, Lake Kenya **96** C4
Baripada India **75** E5
Bariri Brazil **149** H5
Bari Sadri India **74** B4
Barisal Bangl. **75** F5
Barisal *admin. div.* Bangl. **75** F5
Barisan, Pegunungan *mts* Indon. **58** C3
Barito *r.* Indon. **59** F3
Baritu, Parque Nacional *nat. park* Arg.
  152 D2
Barium Italy *see* Bari
Barjols France **39** G5
Barjūj, Wādī *watercourse* Libya **88** D3
Barkam China **66** B2
Barkan, Ra's-e *pt* Iran **80** B4
Barkava Latvia **33** G4

Barkerville Canada **122** F4
Barkéwol el Abiod Mauritania **92** B1
Barkhan Pak. **81** G4
Barki Saraiya India **75** E4
Barkley, Lake U.S.A. **128** B4
Barkley Sound *inlet* Canada **134** A2
Barkol China **70** H3
Barkot India **74** D4
Barkly East S. Africa **99** I6
Barkly Tableland *reg.* Australia **110** C3
Barkly West S. Africa **99** G5
Barlad Romania **46** E1
Bârlad *r.* Romania **46** E2
Bar-le-Duc France **39** F2
Barlee, Lake *salt flat* Australia **109** B7
Barlee Range *hills* Australia **108** A5
Barletta Italy **44** G4
Barlinek Poland **37** G2
Barlow Canada **122** B2
Barlow Lake Canada **123** K2
Barmedman Australia **112** C4
Barmen-Elberfeld Germany *see*
  Wuppertal
Barmer India **74** A4
Barm Fīrūz, Kūh-e *mt.* Iran **79** G5
Barmouth U.K. **35** D5
Barnagar India **74** B5
Barnala India **74** B5
Barnard Castle U.K. **34** F4
Barnato Australia **112** C3
Barnaul Rus. Fed. **62** C1
Barnegat U.S.A. **131** H4
Barnegat Bay U.S.A. **131** H4
Barnes Icecap Canada **121** L2
Barnesville *GA* U.S.A. **129** C5
Barnesville *MN* U.S.A. **132** D2
Barnet U.S.A. **131** G1
Barneveld Neth. *see* Barneveld
Barney Top *mt.* U.S.A. **137** G3
Barnhart U.S.A. **133** A6
Barnsley U.K. **35** F5
Barnstable U.S.A. **131** H3
Barnstaple U.K. **35** D6
Barnstaple Bay U.K. *see* Bideford Bay
Barnwell U.S.A. **129** C5
Baro Nigeria **93** G3
Baroda *Gujarat* India *see* Vadodara
Baroda *Madhya Pradesh* India **74** C4
Baroghil Pass Afgh. **81** H2
Barong China **66** A2
Barons *Range hills* Australia **108** D6
Baroua Cent. Afr. Rep. **94** D3
Baro Wenz *r.* Eth. **96** B2
Barpeta India **75** F4
Bar Pla Soi Thai. *see* Chon Buri
Barqah, Jabal *mt.* Egypt **77** B5
Barques, Point Aux U.S.A. **130** D1
Barquisimeto Venez. **146** D2
Barra *i.* U.K. **34** C3
Barracão do Barreto Brazil **149** G5
Barrackville U.S.A. **130** E4
Barra do Bugres Brazil **149** F3
Barra do Corda Brazil **150** D4
Barra do Cuanza Angola **95** B7
Barra do Garças Brazil **149** H3
Barrado Mendes Brazil **150** D4
Barra do São Manuel Brazil **149** F1
Barra Falsa, Ponta da *pt* Moz. **99** D4
Barraigh *i.* U.K. *see* Barra
Barrāmiyah Egypt **89** G4
Barranca Peru **148** F2
Barranca *r.* Arg. **152** C4
Barrancas *Barinas* Venez. **146** D2
Barrancas *Monagas* Venez. **147** F2
Barranco de Loba Col. **146** C2
Barranqueras Arg. **152** E3
Barranquilla *Atlántico* Col. **146** C1
Barranquilla *Guaviare* Col. **146** C4
Barranquita Peru **146** C6
Barras Brazil **150** D3
Barrax Spain **43** E3
Barreal Arg. **152** C2
Barre des Écrins *mt.* France **39** G4
Barreiras Brazil **150** C5
Barreirinha Brazil **147** G5
Barreirinhas Brazil **150** D2
Barreiro *r.* Brazil **149** D2
Barren India **73** G3
Barren Islands U.S.A. **120** D4
Barrett, Mount Australia **108** D4
Barrhead Canada **123** H4
Barrie Canada **130** D1
Barrier Bay Antarctica **167** E2
Barrière Canada **122** F5
Barrier Range *hills* Australia **112** A3
Barrington Canada **125** H5
Barrington, Mount Australia **112** E4
Barrington Lake Canada **123** K3
Barrington Tops National Park
  Australia **112** E4
Barringun Australia **112** C3
Barro Alto Brazil **149** H3
Barrow *r.* Rep. of Ireland **35** E5
Barrow Arg. **152** E4
Barrow U.S.A. **120** C2
Barrow, Point U.S.A. **120** D2
Barrow Creek Australia **110** C4
Barrow-in-Furness U.K. **35** E4
Barrow Island Australia **108** A5
Barrow Range *hills* Australia **110** A5
Barrow Strait Canada **121** I2
Barr Smith Range *hills* Australia **109** C6
Barry U.K. **35** E6
Barrydale S. Africa **98** D7
Barry Islands Canada **123** I1
Barry Mountains Australia **112** C5
Barrys Bay Canada **124** F5
Barsalogo Burkina **93** E2
Barsalpur India **74** B3
Barsbüttel Germany *see* Barsbüttel
Barshi India *see* Barsi
Barsi India **72** C2
Barstow U.S.A. **136** D4
Barth Germany **37** F1
Bartica Guyana **147** G2
Bartın Turkey **78** D2
Bartle Frere, Mount Australia **111** F3
Bartlesville U.S.A. **133** B4
Bartlett U.S.A. **132** D3
Bartlett Reservoir U.S.A. **137** G5
Barton U.S.A. **131** G1
Bartow U.S.A. **129** C7
Barú, Volcán *vol.* Panama **139** H7
Baruipur India **75** F5
Barumun *r.* Indon. **58** B2
Baruni India **75** F4
Barus Indon. **58** B3
Baruth Germany **37** F2
Baruun Urt Mongolia **63** L3
Baruva India **73** D2
Barwa India **75** E5
Barwah *Gujarat* India **74** A5
Barwala *Haryana* India **74** B3
Barwani India **74** B5
Barwa Sagar India **74** C4
Barwice Poland **37** H2
Bath Canada **131** E1

Barwon *r.* Australia **111** F6
Barycz *r.* Poland **37** H3
Barygaza India *see* Bharuch
Barysaw Belarus **29** D5
Barysh Rus. Fed. **29** J5
Basaga Turkm. **81** F2
Bāsa'īdū Iran **80** D5
Basail Arg. **152** E1
Basaka India **75** F4
Basankusu Dem. Rep. Congo **94** C4
Basantpur India **75** F4
Basarabeasca Moldova **46** F1
Basarabi Romania **46** F2
Basargechar Armenia *see* Vardenis
Basavilbaso Arg. **152** F3
Basco Phil. **67** G3
Bascuñán, Cabo *c.* Chile **152** C2
Bascuñana, Sierra *mts* Spain **43** F3
Basel Switz. **39** H3
Basel-Mulhouse *airport* France **39** H3
Basentello *r.* Italy **45** F4
Basento *r.* Italy **45** F4
Bashākerd, Kūhhā-ye *mts* Iran **80** D5
Bashan China *see* Chongren
Bashanta Rus. Fed. *see* Gorodovikovsk
Bashaw Canada **123** H4
Bāshī Iran **80** C4
Bashi Channel Taiwan **67** G4
Bashimuke Dem. Rep. Congo **95** E6
Bashkiria *aut. rep.* Rus. Fed. *see*
  Bashkortostan, Respublika
Bashkirskaya A.S.S.R. *aut. rep.* Rus. Fed.
  see Bashkortostan, Respublika
Bashkortostan, Respublika *aut. rep.*
  Rus. Fed. **28** K5
Bashmakovo Rus. Fed. **29** G5
Bāsht Iran **80** C4
Bashtanka Ukr. **29** E7
Basi India **75** E5
Basia India **75** E5
Basilaki Island P.N.G. **111** L3
Basilan *i.* Phil. **57** F4
Basildon U.K. **35** G6
Basile, Pico *mt.* Equat. Guinea **93** H4
Basilicata *admin. reg.* Italy **45** F4
Basin U.S.A. **134** F3
Basingstoke U.K. **35** F6
Basin Lake Canada **123** J4
Bāsira *r.* Iraq **79** F4
Basirhat India **75** F5
Basīt, Ra's al *pt* Syria **77** C2
Başkale Turkey **79** F3
Baskatong, Réservoir Canada **124** F5
Baskerville, Cape Australia **108** C4
Başkomutan Milli Parkı *nat. park*
  Turkey **78** B3
Baskunchak, Ozero *l.* Rus. Fed. **29** J6
Basle Switz. *see* Basel
Basmat India **72** C2
Basoko Dem. Rep. Congo **94** D4
Basoda India **74** C4
Basoko Dem. Rep. Congo **94** D4
Basotu Tanz. **97** B6
Basque Country *aut. comm.* Spain *see*
  País Vasco
Basra Iraq **79** F5
Bassano Canada **123** H5
Bassano del Grappa Italy **44** C2
Bassar Togo **93** F3
Bassas da India *reef* Indian Ocean
  162 J7
Bassas de Pedro Padua Bank
  sea feature India **72** B3
Bassawa Côte d'Ivoire **92** D3
Bassein Myanmar **60** A4
Bassein *r.* Myanmar **61** A4
Basse-Kotto *pref.* Cent. Afr. Rep. **94** D3
Basse-Normandie *admin. reg.* France
  38 C2
Basse Santa Su Gambia **92** B3

▶ Basse-Terre Guadeloupe **139** L5
  Capital of Guadeloupe.

▶ Basseterre St Kitts and Nevis **139** L5
  Capital of St Kitts and Nevis.

Bassett *NE* U.S.A. **132** D3
Bassett *VA* U.S.A. **130** D5
Bassikounou Mauritania **92** C2
Bassila Benin **93** F3
Basso, Plateau de Chad **88** D5
Bass Strait Australia **112** C5
Basswood Lake Canada **124** B3
Båstad Sweden **33** D4
Bastak Iran **80** D5
Bastānābād Iran **80** A2
Basti India **75** E4
Bastia *Corsica* France **39** H5
Bastia Italy **44** D3
Bastian U.S.A. **130** D5
Bastogne Belgium **39** F1
Bastrop *TX* U.S.A. **133** B6
Bastuträsk Sweden **32** F2
Basu, Tanjung *pt* Indon. **58** D3
Basul *r.* Pak. **81** F5
Basuo China *see* Dongfang
Basutoland *country* Africa *see* Lesotho
Bas-Zaïre *prov.* Dem. Rep. Congo *see*
  Bas-Congo
Bat *mt.* Croatia **44** F3
Bata Equat. Guinea **93** H5
Batabanó, Golfo de *b.* Cuba **127** J7
Batac Phil. **67** G5
Batagay Rus. Fed. **27** N3
Batagay-Alyta Rus. Fed. **27** N3
Bataguaçu Brazil **149** G5
Batak Bulg. **46** C3
Batakan Indon. **59** F3
Batala India **74** B3
Batalha Brazil **150** D3
Batalha Port. **42** B3
Batam Indon. **58** C2
Batama Dem. Rep. Congo **94** E4
Batamay Rus. Fed. **27** N3
Batan *i.* Phil. **67** G3
Batang China **66** A2
Batangafo Cent. Afr. Rep. **94** C3
Batang Ali National Park *Sarawak*
  Malaysia **59** F2
Batangas Phil. **57** F3
Batangtoru Indon. **58** B2
Batan Islands Phil. **57** F1
Batavia Indon. *see* Jakarta
Batavia *NY* U.S.A. **130** F2
Batavia *OH* U.S.A. **130** A4
Bataysk Rus. Fed. **29** F7
Batchawana Mountain Canada **124** C4
Bātdâmbâng Cambodia **61** C5
Bateemeucica, Gunung *mt.* Indon.
  58 A1
Batéké, Plateaux Congo **94** B5
Bāteng Norway **32** G1
Batesburg U.S.A. **129** C5
Bates Range *hills* Australia **109** C6
Batesville *AR* U.S.A. **133** D5
Batesville *MS* U.S.A. **133** D5
Batetskiy Rus. Fed. **28** D4
Bath Canada **131** E1

Bath U.K. **35** E6
Bath *ME* U.S.A. **131** I2
Bath *NY* U.S.A. **131** E2
Bath *PA* U.S.A. **131** E3
Batha *pref.* Chad **88** C6
Bathawatercourse Chad **88** C6
Bathinda India **74** B3
Bathurst Australia **112** D4
Bathurst Canada **125** H4
Bathurst Gambia *see* Banjul
Bathurst, Cape Canada **120** G2
Bathurst Inlet Canada **123** I1
Bathurst Inlet *inlet* Canada **123** I1
Bathurst Island Australia **110** B1
Bathurst Island Canada **121** J2
Bati Eth. **96** D2
Batié Burkina **92** E3
Bati Mentese Dağları *mts* Turkey **47** O5
Bâtin, Wādī al *watercourse* Asia **79** F5
Bati Toroslar *mts* Turkey **78** B3
Batken Kyrg. **70** D4
Batken *admin. div.* Kyrg. **81** G2
Batkes Indon. **108** E1
Bâţlaq-e Gavkhūnī *marsh* Iran **80** C3
Batman Turkey **79** F3
Batna Alg. **91** G2
Batoçina Yugo. **46** B2
Batok, Bukit Sing. **58** [inset]

▶ Baton Rouge U.S.A. **127** H5
  State capital of Louisiana.

Batopilas Mex. **135** F8
Batoue Jammu and Kashmir **74** B2
Batouri Cameroon **93** I4
Batra' *tourist site* Jordan *see* Petra
Batra', Jabal al *mt.* Jordan **77** B5
Ba Tri Vietnam **61** D6
Batroûn Lebanon **77** B2
Bâtsfjord Norway **32** H1
Battambang Cambodia *see* Bâtdâmbâng
Batti India **74** B3
Batticaloa Sri Lanka **72** D5
Batti Malv *i.* India **73** G4
Battipaglia Italy **44** E4
Battle *r.* Canada **123** I4
Battle Creek *r.* Australia **110** B2
Battle Creek U.S.A. **132** E3
Battleford Canada **123** I4
Battle Mountain U.S.A. **136** D1
Battura Glacier Jammu and Kashmir
  74 B1
Batu *mt.* Eth. **96** C3
Batu, Bukit *mt.* Sarawak Malaysia **59** F2
Batu, Pulau-pulau *is* Indon. **58** B3
Batu Bora, Bukit *mt.* Sarawak Malaysia
  59 F2
Batudaka *i.* Indon. **57** F6
Batu Gajah Malaysia **58** C2
Batulanteh *mt.* Indon. **108** B2
Batulicin Indon. **59** G3
Batulingmebang, Gunung *mt.* Indon.
  59 F2
Batum Georgia *see* Bat'umi
Bat'umi Georgia **79** F2
Batumonga Indon. **58** C3
Batu Pahat Malaysia **58** C2
Baturaja Indon. **58** C3
Batys Qazaqstan Oblysy *admin. div.*
  Kazakh. *see* Zapadnyy Kazakhstan
Batz, Île de *i.* France **38** B2
Bau *r.* Brazil **149** G1
Bau *Sarawak* Malaysia **59** E2
Baubau Indon. **57** F7
Baucau East Timor India *see* Baucau
Bauchi Nigeria **93** H3
Bauchi *state* Nigeria **93** H3
Bauda India **73** E1
Baudette U.S.A. **132** C1
Baudo, Serranía de *mts* Col. **146** B3
Baudouinville Dem. Rep. Congo *see* Moba
Bauer, *well* Eth. **96** E3
Baugé France **38** D3
Baukau East Timor *see* Baucau
Bauld, Cape Canada **125** K4
Baunei *Sardinia* Italy **45** B4
Bauru Brazil **149** H5
Bauska Latvia **33** G4
Bautzen Germany **37** G3
Bavaria *land* Germany *see* Bayern
Bavda India **72** B2
Baviaanskloofberg *mts* S. Africa **98** E7
Bavispe *r.* Mex. **135** F7
Bavla India **74** B5
Bavly Rus. Fed. **28** J5
Bawal India **74** C3
Bawan Indon. **59** E3
Baw Baw National Park Australia
  112 C5
Bawdwin Myanmar **60** B3
Bawean *i.* Indon. **59** F4
Bawku Ghana **93** E3
Bawlake Myanmar **60** B4
Bawolung China **66** B2
Baxian China *see* Banan
Baxley U.S.A. **129** C5
Baxoi China **66** A2
Bay *admin. reg.* Somalia **96** D4
Baya *r.* Côte d'Ivoire **92** E4
Bayad Alg. **45** B7
Bayamo Cuba **127** K7
Bayan China **64** A3
Bayan Indon. **59** G5
Bayana India **74** C4
Bayang, Pegunungan *mts* Indon. **59** E2
Bayanga-Didi Cent. Afr. Rep. **94** B3
Bayan Gol China *see* Dengkou
Bayan Har Shan *mts* China **70** H4
Bayan Har Shankou *pass* China **66** A1
Bayanhongor Mongolia **62** G2
Bayano, Lago *l.* Panama **146** D2
Bayan Obo China **63** H3
Bayan UI China **63** J3
Bayard *NE* U.S.A. **132** C3
Bayard *WV* U.S.A. **130** D4
Bayat Turkey **78** C3
Bayāz Iran **80** D4
Bay Bulls Canada **125** K4
Bayburt Turkey **79** E2
Baychunas Kazakh. **29** J7
Bay City *MI* U.S.A. **130** D2
Bay City *TX* U.S.A. **133** B6
Baydaratskaya Guba Rus. Fed. **26** G3
Baydhabo Somalia **96** D4
Bayelsa *state* Nigeria **93** H3
Bayerischer Wald *mts* Germany **37** F4
Bayerischer Wald *nat. park* Germany
  37 F4
Bayern *land* Germany **36** E4
Bayer Wald, Nationalpark *nat. park*
  Germany **37** F4
Bayeux France **38** D2
Bayfield Canada **130** E2
Bayındır Turkey **78** A3
Bay Islands Hond. *see* La Bahía, Islas de
Bayingoin China **75** G3
Bayji Iraq **79** E4
Bay Minette U.S.A. **129** B6
Baikal, Lake

Baykal-Amur Magistral Rus. Fed. 64 B1
Baykal Range mts Rus. Fed. see Baykal'skiy Khrebet
Baykal'sk Rus. Fed. 62 G1
Baykal'skiy Khrebet mts Rus. Fed. 63 H1
Baykan Turkey 79 E3
Baykibashevo Rus. Fed. 28 K5
Baykit Rus. Fed. 27 J3
Baykonur Kazakh. 70 B2
Baykonyr Kazakh. see Baykonur
Bay Minette U.S.A. 129 B6
Bayombong Phil. 57 F2
Bayona Spain see Baiona
Bayonne France 38 C5
Bayóvar Peru 146 A6
Bay Port U.S.A. 130 B2
Bayqongyr Kazakh. see Baykonur
Bayramaly Turkm. 81 E2
Bayramiç Turkey 78 A3
Bayreuth Germany 36 E4
Bayrūt Lebanon see Beirut
Baysh watercourse Saudi Arabia 89 I5
Bayshonas Kazakh. see Baychunas
Bay Springs U.S.A. 129 A6
Baysun Uzbek. 81 F2
Bayt Lahm West Bank see Bethlehem
Baytown U.S.A. 133 C6
Bayunglincir Indon. 58 C3
Bay View N.Z. 113 D2
Bayy al Kabīr, Wādī watercourse Libya 88 B2
Baza Spain 43 E4
Baza, Sierra de mts Spain 43 E4
Bazarchulan Kazakh. 29 I6
Bazardyuzi, Gora mt. Azer./Rus. Fed. 79 F2
Bāzār-e Māsāl Iran 80 B2
Bazarnyy Karabulak Rus. Fed. 29 H5
Bazarshulan Kazakh. see Bazarchulan
Bazartobe Kazakh. 29 I6
Bazaruto, Ilha do i. Moz. 99 G4
Bazas France 38 C4
Bazdar Pak. 81 F5
Bazhong China 66 C2
Baziwehn Liberia 92 C3
Bazmān Iran 81 E5
Bazmān, Kūh-e mt. Iran 81 E4
Bcharre Lebanon 77 C2
Be r. Vietnam 61 D6
Bé, Nossi i. Madag. see Bé, Nosy
Bé, Nosy i. Madag. 99 [inset] K2
Beach City U.S.A. 130 C3
Beachport Australia 112 B5
Beachy Head U.K. 35 G6
Beacon Australia 109 B7
Beacon U.S.A. 131 G3
Beaconsfield Australia 112 C6
Beagle, Canal sea chan. Arg. 153 C8
Beagle Bank reef Australia 108 C3
Beagle Bay Australia 108 C4
Beagle Gulf Australia 110 B2
Bealanana Madag. 99 [inset] K2
Béal an Átha Rep. of Ireland see Ballina
Béal Átha na Sluaighe Rep. of Ireland see Ballinasloe
Beampingaratra mts Madag. 99 [inset] J5
Beandrarezona Madag. 99 [inset] K2
Bear r. U.S.A. 134 D4
Bearalváhki Norway see Berlevåg
Bear Creek Canada 122 B1
Beardmore Glacier Antarctica 167 H1
Beardmore Reservoir Australia 111 G5
Beardstown U.S.A. 132 D3
Bear Island Arctic Ocean see Bjørnøya
Bear Island Canada 124 D2
Bear Island Rep. of Ireland 35 B6
Bear Lake Canada 123 L4
Bear Lake U.S.A. 134 E4
Bearma r. India 74 C4
Bearpaw Mountains U.S.A. 134 E2
Bearskin Lake Canada 124 B2
Beas r. India 74 B3
Beasain Spain 43 E1
Beata, Cabo c. Dom. Rep. 139 J5
Beata, Isla i. Dom. Rep. 139 J5
Beatrice U.S.A. 132 B3
Beatrice Zimbabwe 99 F3
Beatrice, Cape Australia 110 D2
Beatton r. Canada 122 F3
Beatty U.S.A. 137 D3
Beattyville Canada 124 E3
Beattyville U.S.A. 130 B5
Beaucaire France 39 F5
Beauchene Island Falkland Is 153 F8
Beaufort Sabah Malaysia 59 F1
Beaufort NC U.S.A. 129 D5
Beaufort SC U.S.A. 129 C5
Beaufort Castle tourist site Lebanon 77 B3
Beaufort Island Hong Kong China 67 [inset]
Beaufort Sea Canada/U.S.A. 120 G2
Beaufort West S. Africa 98 D7
Beaulieu-sur-Dordogne France 38 D4
Beauly U.K. 34 D3
Beauly r. U.K. 34 D3
Beaumont Belgium 39 F1
Beaumont N.Z. 113 B4
Beaumont CA U.S.A. 136 D5
Beaumont MS U.S.A. 129 A6
Beaumont TX U.S.A. 133 C6
Beaumont-de-Lomagne France 38 D5
Beaumont-le-Roger France 38 D2
Beaune France 39 F3
Beauraing Belgium 39 F1
Beauséjour Canada 123 L5
Beauvais France 38 E2
Beauval Canada 123 J4
Beaver r. Alta/Sask. Canada 123 J4
Beaver r. Ont. Canada 124 C2
Beaver r. Y.T. Canada 122 C2
Beaver r. Y.T. Canada 122 E3
Beaver U.S.A. 137 F2
Beaver r. OK U.S.A. 133 A4
Beaver r. UT U.S.A. 137 F2
Beaver Creek Canada 122 A2
Beaver Creek r. MT U.S.A. 134 F2
Beaver Creek r. ND U.S.A. 132 A2
Beaver Creek r. NE U.S.A. 132 B3
Beaver Dam KY U.S.A. 128 B4
Beaver Dam WI U.S.A. 132 D3
Beaver Falls U.S.A. 130 C3
Beaverhead r. U.S.A. 134 D3
Beaverhead Mountains U.S.A. 134 D3
Beaverhill Lake Canada 123 H4
Beaver Hill Lake Canada 123 M4
Beaver Island U.S.A. 132 E2
Beaverlodge Canada 122 G4
Beaver Run Reservoir U.S.A. 130 D3
Beaverton MI U.S.A. 130 A2
Beaverton OR U.S.A. 134 B3
Beawar India 74 B4
Beazley Arg. 152 D3
Bebedouro Brazil 149 H5
Bebra Germany 36 D3
Bêca China 66 A2
Beccles U.K. 35 G5
Bečej Yugo. 46 B2
Becerreá Spain 42 C1
Becerrero hill Spain 42 D4
Béchar Alg. 90 E3
Becharof Lake U.S.A. 120 D4
Bechevinka Rus. Fed. 28 F4
Bechuanaland country Africa see Botswana
Beçin Turkey 47 E6
Beckley U.S.A. 130 C5
Becky Peak U.S.A. 137 E2
Bečva r. Czech Rep. 37 H4
Beda Hāyk' l. Eth. 96 D2
Bédarieux France 39 E5
Bedeau Alg. see Ras el Ma
Bedelē Eth. 96 C2
Bedford Canada 125 I4
Bedford U.K. 35 F5
Bedford IN U.S.A. 128 B4
Bedford NY U.S.A. 131 G3
Bedford PA U.S.A. 130 D3
Bedford VA U.S.A. 130 D5
Bedford, Cape Australia 111 F2
Bedford Downs Australia 108 D4
Bedford Heights U.S.A. 130 C3
Bedi India 74 A5
Bedingong Indon. 58 D3
Bednja r. Croatia 44 F1
Bednodem'yanovsk Rus. Fed. 29 G5
Bedok Sing. 58 [inset]
Bedok, Sungai r. Sing. 58 [inset]
Bedok Jetty Sing. 58 [inset]
Bedok Reservoir Sing. 58 [inset]
Bedouaram well Niger 93 I2
Bedourie Australia 111 D5
Bedrock U.S.A. 137 H2
Beechal Creek watercourse Australia 111 F5
Beech Fork Lake U.S.A. 130 B4
Beechy Canada 123 J5
Beelitz Germany 37 F2
Beenleigh Australia 111 H5
Beer Somalia 96 E2
Beersheba Israel 77 B4
Beer Sheva watercourse Israel 77 B4
Beeskow Germany 37 G2
Beetaloo Australia 110 C3
Beethoven Peninsula Antarctica 167 L2
Beeville U.S.A. 133 B6
Befale Dem. Rep. Congo 94 D4
Befandriana Atsimo Madag. 99 [inset] I4
Befandriana Avaratra Madag. 99 [inset] K2
Befori Dem. Rep. Congo 94 D4
Befotaka Madag. 99 [inset] J4
Bega Australia 112 D5
Bega r. Romania 46 B2
Begamganj Bangl. 75 F5
Begari r. Pak. 81 G4
Begicheva, Ostrov i. Rus. Fed. see Bol'shoy Begichev, Ostrov
Begun India 74 B4
Begusarai India 75 E4
Behābād Iran 81 D3
Béhague, Pointe pt Fr. Guiana 147 I3
Behbehān Iran 80 B4
Beheira governorate Egypt see Al Buḩayrah
Behm Canal sea chan. U.S.A. 122 D4
Behrendt Mountains Antarctica 167 L2
Behshahr Iran 80 C2
Behsūd Afgh. 81 F3
Bei'an China 64 A2
Beiba China 66 C1
Beibei China 66 C2
Beichuan China 66 C2
Beida Libya see Al Bayḑā'
Beigang Taiwan see Peikang
Beihai China 67 D4
Bei Jiang r. China 67 E4
▶Beijing China 63 J4
Capital of China.
asia 82
world 16–17
Beijing municipality China 63 J3
Beilen Neth. 36 C2
Beiliu China 67 D4
Béinamar Chad 94 B2
Beinn Mhòr hill U.K. 34 C3
Beinn na Faoghlia i. U.K. see Benbecula
Beira Moz. 99 G3
Beira prov. Moz. see Sofala
Beiru r. China 67 E1
▶Beirut Lebanon 77 B3
Capital of Lebanon.
Beiseker Canada 123 H5
Beitbridge Zimbabwe 99 F4
Beiuş Romania 46 C1
Beja Port. 42 C3
Beja admin. dist. Port. 42 B4
Béja Tunisia 91 H1
Bejaïa Alg. 91 G1
Béjar Spain 42 D2
Bejestān Iran 80 D3
Beji r. Pak. 81 G4
Béka Est Cameroon 93 I4
Béka Nord Cameroon 93 I3
Bekapaika Madag. 99 [inset] J3
Bekasi Indon. 59 D4
Bekdash Turkm. 79 H2
Beke Dem. Rep. Congo 95 E7
Békés Hungary 37 J5
Békéscsaba Hungary 37 J5
Beketovskaya Rus. Fed. 28 F3
Bekily Madag. 99 [inset] J5
Bekopaka Madag. 99 [inset] J3
Bekoropoka-Antongo Madag. 99 [inset] I4
Bekovo Rus. Fed. 29 G5
Bekwai Ghana 93 E4
Bekyem Ghana 93 E4
Bela Bihar India 75 E4
Bela Uttar Pradesh India 75 D4
Bela Pak. 81 F5
Belab r. Pak. 81 G4
Bela-Bela S. Africa 99 F5
Bélabo Cameroon 93 I4
Bela Crkva Yugo. 46 B2
Belaga Sarawak Malaysia 59 F2
Bel Air U.S.A. 131 E4
Belalcázar Spain 42 D3
Belangiran Indon. 59 E3
Bela Palanka Yugo. 46 C3
Belapur India 72 B2
▶Belarus country Europe 31 K2
europe 24–25, 48
Belasica mts Bulg./Macedonia 46 C4
Belasitsa mts Bulg./Macedonia see Belasica
Belau country N. Pacific Ocean see Palau
Bela Vista Amazonas Brazil 146 E4
Bela Vista Mato Grosso do Sul Brazil 149 F5
Bela Vista Moz. 99 G5
Bela Vista de Goiás Brazil 149 H4
Belawan Indon. 58 B2
Belaya mt. Eth. 76 B7
Belaya r. Rus. Fed. 27 R3
Belaya Glina Rus. Fed. 29 G7
Belaya Kalitva Rus. Fed. 29 G6
Belaya Kholunitsa Rus. Fed. 28 I4
Belayan r. Indon. 59 G3
Belayan, Gunung mt. Indon. 59 F2
Belaya Tserkva Ukr. see Bila Tserkva
Belbédji Niger 93 G2
Bełchatów Poland 37 I3
Belcher U.S.A. 130 B5
Belcher Islands Canada 124 E1
Belchiragh Afgh. 81 F3
Beldanga India 75 F5
Belden U.S.A. 136 B1
Beldibi Turkey 47 F6
Beleapani reef India see Cherbaniani Reef
Belebey Rus. Fed. 29 J5
Beled Hungary 37 H5
Beledweyne Somalia 96 E3
Belek Turkm. 80 C2
Bélèl Cameroon 93 I4
Belel Nigeria 93 I3
Belém Brazil 150 B2
Belén Arg. 152 D1
Belén Para. 149 F5
Belen Turkey 78 D3
Belen U.S.A. 135 F6
Belén, Cuchilla de hills Uruguay 152 F2
Belene Bulg. 46 D3
Bélep, Îles is New Caledonia 107 F3
Belesar, Embalse de resr Spain 42 C1
Belev Rus. Fed. 29 F5
Belevi Turkey 47 E5
Belfast N.Z. 113 C3
▶Belfast U.K. 35 D4
Capital of Northern Ireland.
Belfast U.S.A. 131 I1
Bēlfodiyo Eth. 96 B2
Belford U.K. 34 F4
Belfort France 39 G3
Belgaum India 72 B3
Belgian Congo country Africa see Congo, Democratic Republic of
België country Europe see Belgium
Belgique country Europe see Belgium
▶Belgium country Europe 36 B3
europe 24–25, 48
Belgorod Rus. Fed. 29 F6
Belgorod-Dnestrovskyy Ukr. see Bilhorod-Dnistrovs'kyy
Belgorod Oblast admin. div. Rus. Fed. see Belgorodskaya Oblast'
Belgorodskaya Oblast' admin. div. Rus. Fed. 29 F6
Belgrade ME U.S.A. 131 I1
Belgrade MT U.S.A. 134 E3
▶Belgrade Yugo. 46 B2
Capital of Yugoslavia.
Belgrano II research station Antarctica 167 A1
Belhirane Alg. 91 G3
Béli Guinea-Bissau 92 B3
Beli Nigeria 93 H4
Belice r. Sicily Italy 45 D6
Beliliou i. Palau see Peleliu
Beli Lom r. Bulg. 46 E3
Beli Manastir Croatia 44 G2
Belington U.S.A. 130 D4
Belingwe Zimbabwe see Mberengwa
Belinskiy Rus. Fed. 29 G5
Belint Romania 46 B2
Belinyu Indon. 58 D3
Beli Timok r. Yugo. 46 C2
Belitung i. Indon. 59 E3
Belize Angola 95 B6
▶Belize Belize 138 G5
Former capital of Belize.
▶Belize country Central America 138 G5
northamerica 118–119, 140
Bélizon Fr. Guiana 147 H3
Beljak Austria see Villach
Beljanica mt. Yugo. 46 B2
Bel'kovskiy, Ostrov i. Rus. Fed. 27 N2
Bell Australia 111 G5
Bell r. Australia 112 D4
Bell r. Canada 124 E3
Bella Bella Canada 122 D4
Bellac France 38 D3
Bella Coola Canada 122 E4
Bella Coola r. Canada 122 E4
Bellaire MI U.S.A. 128 B2
Bellaire TX U.S.A. 133 C6
Bellaria Italy 44 D2
Bellary India 72 C3
Bella Unión Uruguay 152 F2
Bella Vista Corrientes Arg. 152 F2
Bella Vista Santa Cruz Arg. 153 C7
Bella Vista Bol. 149 E3
Bella Vista Para. 149 F5
Bellavista Peru 146 C5
Bell Cay reef Australia 111 G4
Belle U.S.A. 130 C4
Belledonne mts France 39 F4
Bellefontaine U.S.A. 130 B3
Belle Fourche U.S.A. 134 G3
Belle Fourche r. U.S.A. 134 G3
Bellegarde-sur-Valserine France 39 F3
Belle Glade U.S.A. 129 C7
Belle-Île i. France 38 B3
Belle Isle i. Canada 125 K3
Belle Isle, Strait of Canada 125 J3
Bellemont U.S.A. 137 G4
Belleville Canada 131 E1
Belleville France 39 F3
Belleville U.S.A. 132 B4
Bellevue NE U.S.A. 132 C3
Bellevue OH U.S.A. 130 B3
Bellevue WA U.S.A. 134 B3
Belley France 39 F4
Bellin Canada see Kangirsuk
Bellingen Australia 112 E3
Bellingham U.K. 34 E4
Bellingham U.S.A. 134 B2
Bellingshausen research station Antarctica 167 A2
Bellingshausen Sea Antarctica 167 L2
Bellinzona Switz. 39 H3
Bello Col. 146 C3
Bellows Falls U.S.A. 131 G2
Bellpat Pak. 81 G4
Belluno Italy 44 D1
Belluru India 72 C3
Bell Ville Arg. 152 E3
Bellville S. Africa 98 C7
Bellville U.S.A. 130 B3
Bellwood U.S.A. 130 D3
Belly r. Canada 123 H5
Bélmez Spain 42 D3
Belmont Australia 112 D4
Belmont U.S.A. 130 D2
Belmonte Brazil 151 E5
Belmonte Port. 42 C2
Belmont-sur-Rance France 39 E5
▶Belmopan Belize 138 G5
Capital of Belize.
Belmore Creek r. Australia 111 E3
Belmullet Rep. of Ireland 35 B4
Belo Madag. 99 [inset] J4
Beloe More sea Rus. Fed. see White Sea
Belogorsk Rus. Fed. 64 B2
Belogradchik Bulg. 46 C3
Beloha Madag. 99 [inset] J5
Belo Horizonte Brazil 151 D6
Beloit U.S.A. 132 B4
Belo Jardim Brazil 150 E4
Belo Monte Pará Brazil 147 I5
Belo Monte Piauí Brazil see Batalha
Belomorsk Rus. Fed. 28 E2
Belonia India 75 F5
Belorado Spain 42 E1
Belorechensk Rus. Fed. 29 F7
Belorechenskaya Rus. Fed. see Belorechensk
Belören Adıyaman Turkey 78 D3
Belören Turkey 78 C3
Beloretsk Rus. Fed. 26 F4
Belorussia country Europe see Belarus
Belorusskaya S.S.R. country Europe see Belarus
Beloslav Bulg. 46 E3
Belostok Poland see Białystok
Belot, Lac l. Canada 122 E1
Belotintsi Bulg. 46 C3
Belo Tsiribihina Madag. 99 [inset] J3
Belovo Bulg. 46 D3
Beloye, Ozero l. Rus. Fed. 28 F3
Beloye More sea Rus. Fed. see White Sea
Belozersk Rus. Fed. 28 F3
Belpre U.S.A. 130 C4
Belted Range mts U.S.A. 137 D3
Belterra Brazil 147 H5
Belton MO U.S.A. 132 C4
Belton TX U.S.A. 133 B6
Bel'ts' Moldova see Bălţi
Bel'tsy Moldova see Bălţi
Belukha, Gora mt. Kazakh./Rus. Fed. 70 G2
Belur India 72 B3
Belush'ye Rus. Fed. 28 H2
Belva U.S.A. 130 C4
Belvès France 38 D4
Belvidere IL U.S.A. 132 D3
Belvidere NJ U.S.A. 131 F3
Belyando r. Australia 111 F4
Belyando Crossing Australia 111 F4
Belyayevka Ukr. see Bilyayivka
Belyy Rus. Fed. 28 E5
Belyy, Ostrov i. Rus. Fed. 26 H2
Belyy Yar Rus. Fed. 27 I4
Belzig Germany 37 F2
Belzoni U.S.A. 133 D5
Bełżyce Poland 37 K3
Bemaraha, Plateau du Madag. 99 [inset] J3
Bembe Angola 95 B6
Bembèrèkè Benin 93 F3
Bembibre Spain 42 C1
Bemidji U.S.A. 132 C2
Béna Burkina 92 D2
Bena Dibele Dem. Rep. Congo 95 D6
Benagin Indon. 59 F3
Ben Alder mt. U.K. 34 D3
Benalla Australia 112 C5
Benalmádena Spain 42 D4
Ben 'Amîra well Mauritania 90 B5
Benares India see Varanasi
Ben Arous Tunisia 91 H1
Benavente Spain 42 D1
Benavides Bol. 148 D3
Benbecula i. U.K. 34 C3
Ben Boyd National Park Australia 112 D5
Benbury hill Rep. of Ireland 35 B5
Bend U.S.A. 134 B3
Bendearg mt. S. Africa 99 E6
Bendela Dem. Rep. Congo 94 C5
Bender Moldova see Tighina
Bender-Bayla Somalia 96 F2
Bendery Moldova see Tighina
Bendigo Australia 112 C5
Bēne Latvia 33 F4
Bene Moz. 97 B8
Benedict, Mount Canada 125 J2
Beneditinos Brazil 150 D3
Benedito Leite Brazil 150 C3
Bénéna Mali 92 D2
Benenitra Madag. 99 [inset] J4
Benešov Czech Rep. 37 G4
Benevento Italy 44 E4
Beneventum Italy see Benevento
Beng, Nam r. Laos 60 C4
Bengal, Bay of sea Indian Ocean 73 F2
Bengamisa Dem. Rep. Congo 94 E4
Bengbis Cameroon 93 I5
Bengbu China 67 F1
Benghazi Libya 88 D1
Benghisa Point Malta 45 E7
Bengkalis Indon. 58 C2
Bengkalis i. Indon. 58 C2
Bengkayang Indon. 59 E2
Bengkulu Indon. 58 C3
Bengkulu prov. Indon. 58 C3
Bengo Angola 95 C9
Bengo prov. Angola 95 B7
Bengtsfors Sweden 33 D4
Benguela Angola 95 B8
Benguela prov. Angola 95 B8
Ben Guerdane Tunisia 91 H2
Benguerir Morocco 90 D2
Benha Egypt see Banhā
Ben Hope hill U.K. 34 D2
Beni dept Bol. 148 D3
Beni r. Bol. 148 D2
Beni Dem. Rep. Congo 94 F4
Beni Nepal 75 D3
Beni-Abbès Alg. 90 E3
Benicarló Spain 43 G2
Benicasim Spain 43 G2
Benidorm Spain 43 F3
Beni Dourso well Niger 88 B4
Benifaió Spain 43 F3
Benifayo Spain see Benifaió
Benigánim Spain 43 F3
Beni Guil reg. Morocco 90 E2
Beni Mellal Morocco 90 D2
▶Benin country Africa 93 F3
africa 86–87, 100
Benin r. Nigeria 93 G4
Benin, Bight of g. Africa 93 F4
Benin City Nigeria 93 G4
Beni-Ounif Alg. 91 E3
Beni-Saf Alg. 91 E2
Benishangul admin. reg. Eth. 96 B2
Benisheikh Nigeria 93 I3
Benissa Spain 43 G3
Beni Suef Egypt see Banī Suwayf
Beni Suef governorate Egypt see Banī Suwayf
Benithora r. India 72 C2
Benito r. Equat. Guinea see Mbini
Benito Juárez Arg. 152 F4
Benjamin U.S.A. 133 B5
Benjamin, Isla i. Chile 153 B6
Benjamin Hill Mex. 135 E7
Benjamin Zorrillo Arg. 152 D4
Benjina Indon. 57 H7
Benkelman U.S.A. 132 A3
Benkovac Croatia 44 E2
Ben Lawers mt. U.K. 34 D3
Ben Lomond mt. Australia 112 D3
Ben Lomond hill U.K. 34 D3
Ben Lomond National Park Australia 112 C6
Ben Macdui mt. U.K. 34 E3
Ben Mahidi Alg. 45 A6
Benmara Australia 110 D3
Ben More hill U.K. 34 C3
Ben More mt. U.K. 34 D3
Benmore, Lake N.Z. 113 B4
Ben More Assynt hill U.K. 34 D2
Bennett Canada 122 C3
Bennett, Lake salt flat Australia 110 B4
Bennetta, Ostrov i. Rus. Fed. 27 O2
Bennett Island Rus. Fed. see Bennetta, Ostrov
Bennettsville U.S.A. 129 D5
Ben Nevis mt. U.K. 34 D3
Bennington NH U.S.A. 131 H2
Bennington VT U.S.A. 131 G2
Bénoué r. Cameroon 93 I3
Bénoy Chad 94 C2
Ben Rinnes hill U.K. 34 E3
Bensheim Germany 36 D4
Ben Slimane Morocco 90 D2
Benson AZ U.S.A. 135 E7
Benson MN U.S.A. 132 C2
Bensonville Liberia 92 C4
Bens Run U.S.A. 130 C4
Bent Iran 81 D5
Benta Seberang Malaysia 58 C1
Benteng Indon. 57 F7
Bentiaba Angola 95 B8
Bentinck Island Myanmar 61 E6
Bentiu Sudan 94 F2
Bent Jbail Lebanon 77 B3
Bentley Canada 123 H4
Bentleyville U.S.A. 130 C3
Benton AR U.S.A. 133 C5
Benton CA U.S.A. 136 C3
Benton IL U.S.A. 128 A4
Benton KY U.S.A. 128 A4
Benton MO U.S.A. 132 D4
Bentong Malaysia see Bentung
Benton Harbor U.S.A. 132 E3
Bentonville U.S.A. 133 C4
Bên Tre Vietnam 61 D6
Bentuang Karimun National Park Indon. 59 F2
Bentung Malaysia 58 C2
Benua i. Indon. 59 D2
Benuamartinus Indon. 59 F2
Benue r. Nigeria 93 G4
Benue state Nigeria 93 H4
Benum, Gunung mt. Malaysia 58 C2
Benwa Zambia 95 E7
Benwood U.S.A. 130 C3
Benxi China 63 K3
Ben Zireg Alg. 90 E3
Beograd Yugo. see Belgrade
Beohari India 75 D4
Béoumi Côte d'Ivoire 92 D4
Bepagut, Gunung mt. Indon. 58 C4
Bepian Jiang r. China 66 C3
Beppu Japan 65 B6
Bequia i. St Vincent 147 F1
Bequimão Brazil 150 C2
Bera Bangl. 75 F4
Berach r. India 74 B4
Beramanja Madag. 99 [inset] K2
Berane Yugo. 46 A3
Bérard, Lac l. Canada 125 G1
Berasia India 74 C5
Berastagi Indon. 58 B2
Berat Albania 46 A4
Beratus, Gunung mt. Indon. 59 G3
Berau r. Indon. 59 G2
Berau, Teluk b. Indon. 57 H6
Beravina Madag. 99 [inset] J3
Berbak National Park Indon. 58 D3
Berber Sudan 89 G5
Berbera Somalia 96 E2
Berbérati Cent. Afr. Rep. 94 B3
Bercel Hungary 37 I5
Berceto Italy 44 B2
Berchi-Guélé well Chad 88 C5
Berchtesgaden, Nationalpark nat. park Germany 37 F5
Berck France 38 D1
Berdichev Ukr. see Berdychiv
Berdigestyakh Rus. Fed. 27 M3
Berdsk Rus. Fed. 26 I4
Berdyans'k Ukr. 29 F7
Berdychiv Ukr. 29 D6
Berea KY U.S.A. 130 A5
Berea OH U.S.A. 130 C3
Beregovo Ukr. see Berehove
Berehove Ukr. 31 J3
Bereina P.N.G. 57 K7
Bereketa Madag. 99 [inset] J4
Berekum Ghana 92 E4
Berenguela Bol. 148 C4
Berenice Libya see Benghazi
Berens r. Canada 123 L4
Berens River Canada 123 L4
Berenty Madag. 99 [inset] J4
Beresford U.S.A. 132 B3
Bereşti Romania 46 E1
Berettyó r. Hungary 37 J5
Berettyóújfalu Hungary 37 J5
Berevo Madag. 99 [inset] J3
Berevo-Ranobe Madag. 99 [inset] J3
Bereza Belarus see Byaroza
Berezino Belarus see Byerazino
Berezivka Ukr. 29 D7
Berezne Ukr. 29 C6
Bereznik Rus. Fed. 28 G3
Berezniki Rus. Fed. 28 K4
Berezovka Rus. Fed. 28 K4
Berezovka Ukr. see Berezivka
Berezovyy Rus. Fed. 64 C2
Berezyne Ukr. 46 F1
Berga Spain 43 G1
Bergama Turkey 78 A3
Bergamo Italy 44 B2
Bergantes r. Spain 43 F2
Bergby Sweden 33 E3
Bergen Mecklenburg-Vorpommern Germany 37 F1
Bergen Niedersachsen Germany 36 D2
Bergen Norway 33 B3
Bergen U.S.A. 130 E2
Bergen op Zoom Neth. 36 B3
Bergerac France 38 D4
Bergheim (Erft) Germany 36 C3
Bergisch Gladbach Germany 36 C3
Bergland Namibia 98 C4
Bergnäs Sweden 32 E2
Bergnäsviken Sweden 32 E2
Bergomum Italy see Bergamo
Bergsjö Sweden 33 E3
Berhala, Selat sea chan. Indon. 58 C3
Berhampur India see Baharampur
Berheci r. Romania 46 E1
Berikat, Tanjung pt Indon. 59 D3
Beringa, Ostrov i. Rus. Fed. 27 Q4
Beringen Belgium 39 F1
Beringovskiy Rus. Fed. 27 R3
Bering Sea N. Pacific Ocean 164 F2
Bering Strait Rus. Fed./U.S.A. 120 C3
Berja Spain 42 E4
Berkåk Norway 32 C3
Berkane Morocco 90 E2
Berkel r. Neth. 36 C2
Berkeley r. Australia 108 D3
Berkeley U.S.A. 136 A3
Berkeley Springs U.S.A. 130 D4
Berkner Island Antarctica 167 A1
Berkovitsa Bulg. 46 C3
Berkshire Hills U.S.A. 131 G2
Berlevåg Norway 32 H1
▶Berlin Germany 37 F2
Capital of Germany.
Berlin MD U.S.A. 131 F4
Berlin NH U.S.A. 131 H1
Berlin NJ U.S.A. 131 F4
Berlin OH U.S.A. 130 C3
Berlin PA U.S.A. 130 D4
Berlişte Romania 46 B2
Berme Turkm. 80 D2
Bermeja, Punta pt Arg. 152 E5
Bermejillo Mex. 126 F6
Bermejo r. Arg. 152 D3
Bermejo r. Arg./Bol. 149 F6
Bermejo Bol. 149 D5
Bermeo Spain 43 E1
▶Bermuda terr. N. Atlantic Ocean 127 N5
United Kingdom Overseas Territory.
northamerica 118–119, 140
Bermuda Rise sea feature N. Atlantic Ocean 160 J4
▶Bern Switz. 39 G3
Capital of Switzerland.
Bernalda Italy 45 F4
Bernardo O'Higgins, Parque Nacional nat. park Chile 153 B7
Bernau Germany 37 F2
Bernau am Chiemsee Germany 37 F5
Bernay France 38 D2
Bernburg (Saale) Germany 36 E3
Berndorf Austria 37 H5
Berne Switz. see Bern
Berne U.S.A. 130 A3
Berner Alpen mts Switz. 39 G3
Berneray i. U.K. 34 C3
Bernese Alps mts Switz. see Berner Alpen
Bernesga r. Spain 42 D1
Bernier Island Australia 109 A6
Bernina Pass Switz. 39 I3
Berninches mt. Spain 43 E2
Bernstadt U.S.A. 130 A5
Beroea Greece see Veroia
Beroea Syria see Aleppo
Beroroha Madag. 99 [inset] J4
Beroun Czech Rep. 37 G4
Berounka r. Czech Rep. 37 G4
Berovina Madag. see Beravina
Berovo Macedonia 46 C4
Berre, Étang de lag. France 39 F5
Berrechid Morocco 90 D2
Berri Australia 112 B4
Berriane Alg. 91 F2
Berridale Australia 112 D5
Berrouaghia Alg. 91 F1
Berry reg. France 38 D3
Berry Creek r. Canada 123 I5
Berryessa, Lake U.S.A. 136 A2
Berry Head U.K. 35 E6
Berry Islands Bahamas 129 D7
Berryville U.S.A. 130 E4
Bersenbrück Germany 36 C2
Berté, Lac l. Canada 125 G3
Bertinho Brazil 150 B2
Bertolínia Brazil 150 D3
Bertoua Cameroon 93 I4
Beru atoll Kiribati 107 G2
Beruri Brazil 147 F5
Beruwala Sri Lanka 72 C5
Berwick-upon-Tweed U.K. 34 E4
Berytus Lebanon see Beirut
Berzasca Romania 46 B2
Bērzaune Latvia 33 G4
Bès r. France 39 E4
Besalampy Madag. 99 [inset] J3
Besalú Spain 43 H1
Besançon France 39 G3
Besar i. Indon. 108 C2
Besar, Gunung mt. Indon. 59 F3
Besbre r. France 39 E3
Beshariq Uzbek. see Besharyk
Besharyk Uzbek. 81 G1
Beshkent Uzbek. 81 F2
Beshneh Iran 80 C4
Besikama Indon. 108 D2
Beşiri Turkey 79 E3
Beskid Niski hills Poland 37 J4
Beskid Sądecki mts Poland 37 J4
Beskra Alg. see Biskra
Beslan Rus. Fed. 29 H8
Besna Kobila mt. Yugo. 46 C3
Besnard Lake Canada 123 J4
Besni Turkey 79 D3
Besor watercourse Israel 77 B4
Beşparmak Dağları mts Cyprus see Pentadaktylos Range
Bessao Chad 94 B3
Bessarabka Moldova see Basarabeasca
Bessaye, Gora mt. Kazakh. 70 C3
Bessemer U.S.A. 132 D2
Besshoky, Gora hill Kazakh. 79 H1
Bessines-sur-Gartempe France 38 D3
Bessonovka Rus. Fed. 29 H5
Bessou, Mont de hill France 38 E4
Beswick Australia 110 C2
Betafo Madag. 99 [inset] J3
Betanzos Bol. 148 D4
Betanzos Spain 42 B1
Bétaré Oya Cameroon 93 I4
Bete Hor Eth. 96 C2
Bétérou Benin 93 F3
Betet i. Indon. 58 D3
Beth, Oued r. Morocco 90 D2
Bethanie Namibia 98 C5
Bethany U.S.A. 132 C3
Bethari Nepal 75 D4
Bethel AK U.S.A. 120 C3
Bethel ME U.S.A. 131 H1
Bethel OH U.S.A. 130 A4
Bethesda MD U.S.A. 131 E4
Bethesda OH U.S.A. 130 C3
Bethlehem S. Africa 99 F6
Bethlehem U.S.A. 131 F3
Bethlehem West Bank 77 B4
Béthune France 39 E1
Betioky Madag. 99 [inset] J4
Betiri, Gunung mt. Indon. 59 F5
Bet Lehem West Bank see Bethlehem
Betma India 74 B5
Betong Thai. 61 C7
Betoota Australia 111 E5
Bétou Congo 94 C4
Betpak-Dala plain Kazakh. 70 D2
Betrandraka Madag. 99 [inset] J3
Betroka Madag. 99 [inset] J4
Bet She'an Israel 77 B3
Betsiamites r. Canada 125 G3
Betsiboka r. Madag. 99 [inset] J2
Betsie, Point U.S.A. 128 B2
Bettiah India 75 E4
Betul India 74 C5
Betwa r. India 74 C4
Betws-y-coed U.K. 35 E5
Béu Angola 95 B6
Beulah U.S.A. 132 A2
Beuthen Poland see Bytom
Beuvron r. France 38 D3
Beverley U.K. 35 F5
Beverly MA U.S.A. 131 H2
Beverly OH U.S.A. 130 C4
Beverly Hills U.S.A. 136 C4
Beverungen Germany 36 D3
Beyağaç Turkey 47 F6
Beyazköy Turkey 46 E4
Beyce Turkey see Orhaneli
Beydağ Turkey 47 F5
Bey Dağları mts Turkey 78 B3
Beykoz Turkey 78 B2
Beyla Guinea 92 C3
Beylagan Azer. see Beyläqan
Beyläqan Azer. 79 F3
Beylul Eritrea 89 I6
Beyneu Kazakh. 70 A2
Beypazarı Turkey 78 B2
Beypınarı Turkey 79 D3
Beypore India 72 B4
Beyra Somalia 96 E3
Beyram Iran 80 C5
Beyrouth Lebanon see Beirut
Beyşehir Turkey 78 B3
Beyşehir Gölü l. Turkey 78 B3
Beytüşşebap Turkey 79 E3
Bezameh Iran 80 D3
Bezbozhnik Rus. Fed. 28 I4

Bezdan Yugo. 46 A2
Bezenjān Iran 80 D4
Bezhanitsy Rus. Fed. 31 L1
Bezhetsk Rus. Fed. 31 N1
Béziers France 39 E5
Bezmein Turkm. see Byuzmeyin
Bezwada India see Vijayawada
Bhabhar India 74 A4
Bhabra India 74 A4
Bhabua India 75 D4
Bhadar r. India 74 A5
Bhadarwah Jammu and Kashmir 74 B2
Bhadgaon Nepal see Bhaktapur
Bhadohi India 75 D4
Bhadra India 74 B3
Bhadrachalam India 72 D2
Bhadrachalam Road Station India see
   Kottagudem
Bhadrakh India 75 E5
Bhadra Reservoir India 72 B3
Bhadravati India 72 B3
Bhag Pak. 81 F4
Bhagalpur India 75 E4
Bhagirathi r. India 75 F5
Bhainsa India 72 C2
Bhainsdehi India 74 C5
Bhairab Bazar Bangl. 75 F4
Bhairawa Nepal 75 D4
Bhairawaha Nepal see Bhairawa
Bhairi Hol mt. Pak. 81 F5
Bhakkar Pak. 81 H4
Bhaktapur Nepal 75 D4
Bhalki India 72 C2
Bhalwal Pak. 81 H3
Bhamgarh India 74 C5
Bhamo Myanmar 60 B1
Bhandara India 74 C5
Bhander India 74 C4
Bhanjanagar India 73 E2
Bhanpura India 74 C4
Bhanrer Range hills India 74 C5
Bharat country Asia see India
Bharatpur India 72 B3
Bharatpur Nepal 75 E4
Bhareli r. India 75 F5
Bharthana India 74 C4
Bharuch India 74 B5
Bhatapara India 75 D5
Bhatarsaigh i. U.K. see Vatersay
Bhatghar Lake India 72 B3
Bhatinda India see Bathinda
Bhatnair India see Hanumangarh
Bhatpara India 75 F5
Bhaun Gharibwal Pak. 81 H3
Bhavani India 72 C4
Bhavani r. India 72 C4
Bhavani Sagar l. India 72 C4
Bhavnagar India 74 B5
Bhawana Pak. 81 H4
Bhawanipatna India 73 D2
Bhearnaraigh, Eilean i. U.K. see
   Berneray
Bheemavaram India see Bhimavaram
Bhera Pak. 81 H3
Bheri r. Nepal 75 D3
Bhilai India 75 D5
Bhildi India 74 B4
Bhilwara India 74 B4
Bhima r. India 72 C2
Bhimavaram India 72 D2
Bhimbar Pak. 74 B2
Bhimnagar India 75 E4
Bhimphedi Nepal 75 E4
Bhind India 74 C4
Bhinga India 75 D4
Bhinmal India 74 B4
Bhiwandi India 72 B2
Bhiwani India 74 C3
Bhogat India 74 A5
Bhojpur Nepal 75 E4
Bhola Bangl. 75 F5
Bhongaon India 74 C4
Bhongir India 72 C2
Bhongweni S. Africa 99 F6
Bhopal India 74 C5
Bhopalpatnam India 72 D2
Bhor India 72 B2
Bhrigukaccha India see Bharuch
Bhuban India 73 E1
Bhubaneshwar India 73 E1
Bhubaneswar India see Bhubaneshwar
Bhuban Hills India 75 G4
Bhuj India 74 A5
Bhumiphol Dam Thai. 60 B4
Bhusawal India 74 B5
► Bhutan country Asia 75 F4
asia 52–53, 82
Bhuttewala India 74 A4
Biá r. Brazil 146 E5
Bia, Monts mts Dem. Rep. Congo 95 E7
Bia, Phou mt. Laos 60 C4
Biabān mts Iran 80 D5
Biafra, Bight of g. Africa see
   Benin, Bight of
Biak i. Indon. 57 I6
Biała r. Poland 37 J3
Biała Piska Poland 37 K2
Biała Podlaska Poland 37 J2
Białobrzegi Poland 37 J3
Białogard Poland 37 G2
Biały Bór Poland 37 H2
Białystok Poland 37 K2
Bianco Italy 45 F5
Bianga Cent. Afr. Rep. 94 D3
Biankouma Côte d'Ivoire 92 D4
Bianouan Côte d'Ivoire 92 D4
Biaora India 74 C5
Biärjmand Iran 80 C2
Biarritz France 39 C5
Bi'är Tabräk well Saudi Arabia 80 A5
Biasca Switz. 39 H3
Bibā Egypt 89 F2
Bibai Japan 64 F4
Bibala Angola 95 B8
Bibas Egypt 89 F2
Bibbenluke Australia 112 D5
Bibbiena Italy 44 D3
Bibiani Ghana 93 E4
Bibiyana r. Bangl. 75 F4
Biblos Lebanon see Jbail
Bicheng China see Bishan
Bicheno Australia 112 C6
Bichevaya Rus. Fed. 64 C3
Bichi r. Rus. Fed. 64 C2
Bickerton Island Australia 110 D2
Bicuari, Parque Nacional do nat. park
   Angola 95 B8
Bid India 72 B2
Bida Nigeria 93 G4
Bidache France 38 C5
Bidar India 72 C2
Bidasar India 74 B4
Biddeford U.S.A. 131 H2
Bideford U.K. 35 D6
Bideford Bay U.K. 35 D6
Bidjovagge Norway 32 F1
Bidkhan, Küh-e mt. Iran 80 D4
Bidokht Iran 81 D3
Bidon 5 tourist site Alg. 91 F5
Bidzhan Rus. Fed. 64 B3
Bidzhar r. Rus. Fed. 64 C3
Bié Angola see Kuito
Bié prov. Angola 95 C8

Biebrza r. Poland 37 K2
Biebrzański Park Narodowy nat. park
   Poland 37 K2
Biedenkopf Germany 36 D3
Biel Switz. 39 G3
Bielefeld Germany 36 D2
Biella Italy 44 B2
Bielsko-Biała Poland 37 I4
Bielsk Podlaski Poland 37 K2
Bién Hoa Vietnam 61 D6
Bienne Switz. see Biel
Bienne r. France 39 F3
Bienvenida hill Spain 42 C3
Bienville, Lac l. Canada 125 F2
Bierbank Australia 111 F5
Bierutów Poland 37 H3
Biesiesvlei S. Africa 98 E5
Bièvre Belgium 39 F2
Biferno r. Italy 44 E4
Bifoun Gabon 94 A5
Big r. U.S.A. 136 D4
Biga Turkey 47 L4
Biga r. Turkey 47 L4
Bigadiç Turkey 78 B3
Biga Yarımadası pen. Turkey 47 L5
Bingen am Rhein Germany 36 C5
Big Bear Lake U.S.A. 136 D4
Big Belt Mountains U.S.A. 134 E3
Big Bend National Park U.S.A. 133 A6
Big Black r. U.S.A. 133 D5
Big Blue r. U.S.A. 132 B4
Big Canyon watercourse U.S.A. 133 A6
Biger Nuur salt l. Mongolia 70 I2
Big Fork r. U.S.A. 132 C1
Biggar Canada 134 F1
Biggar U.K. 34 E4
Biggar, Lac l. Canada 124 F1
Bigge Island Australia 108 D3
Biggenden Australia 111 H5
Bigger, Mount Canada 122 A2
Biggleswade U.K. 35 F5
Big Hole r. U.S.A. 134 D3
Bighorn r. U.S.A. 134 F3
Bighorn Mountains U.S.A. 134 F3
Big Island i. Nunavut Canada 121 L3
Big Island i. N.W.T. Canada 123 G2
Big Island i. N.W.T. Canada 130 D3
Big Kalzas Lake Canada 122 C2
Big Lake U.S.A. 133 A6
Big Lake l. U.S.A. 128 C2
Big Muddy Creek r. U.S.A. 134 F2
Big Otter r. U.S.A. 130 D5
Big Pine U.S.A. 136 D3
Big Pine Peak U.S.A. 136 C4
Big Rapids U.S.A. 132 E3
Big River Canada 123 J4
Big Salmon Canada 122 C2
Big Salmon r. Canada 122 C2
Big Sand Lake Canada 123 L3
Big Sandy watercourse U.S.A. 137 F4
Big Sandy Creek r. U.S.A. 134 G5
Big Sioux r. U.S.A. 132 B3
Big Smokey Valley U.S.A. 136 D2
Big Spring U.S.A. 133 A5
Big Stone Canada 123 I5
Big Sur U.S.A. 136 B3
Big Timber U.S.A. 134 E3
Big Trout Lake Canada 124 B2
Big Trout Lake l. Canada 124 B2
Big Valley Canada 123 H4
Big Water U.S.A. 137 G3
Bihać Bos.-Herz. 44 F2
Bihar state India 75 E4
Bihariganj India 75 F4
Bihar Sharif India 75 E4
Bihor, Vârful mt. Romania 46 C1
Bihpuriagaon India 75 G4
Bijagós, Arquipélago dos is
   Guinea-Bissau 92 A3
Bijainagar India 74 C4
Bijaipur India 74 C4
Bijapur India 75 E2
Bijarpur India 72 D2
Bijawar India 74 C4
Bijbehara Jammu and Kashmir 74 B2
Bijeljina Bos.-Herz. 46 A2
Bijelolasica mt. Croatia 44 F2
Bijelo Polje Yugo. 46 A3
Bijie China 66 C3
Bijni India 75 F4
Bijnor India 74 C3
Bijolia India 74 B4
Bijrän well Saudi Arabia 80 B5
Bijrän, Khashm hill Saudi Arabia 76 E5
Bikampur India 74 B3
Bikaner India 74 B3
Bikin Rus. Fed. 64 C3
Bikin r. Rus. Fed. 64 C3
Bikini atoll Marshall Is 164 F5
Bikori Sudan 96 B2
Bikoro Dem. Rep. Congo 94 C4
Bikou China 66 C1
Bikramganj India 75 E4
Bilanga Burkina 93 E3
Bilara India 74 B4
Bilari India 74 C3
Bilaspur Chhattisgarh India 75 D5
Bilaspur Himachal Pradesh India 74 C3
Bilasuvar Azer. 79 G3
Bila Tserkva Ukr. 29 D6
Bilauktaung Range mts Myanmar/Thai.
   61 B5
Bilbao Spain 42 E1
Bilbays Egypt 78 B5
Bilbo Spain see Bilbao
Bildudalur Iceland 32 [inset]
Bileća Bos.-Herz. 44 G3
Bilecik Turkey 78 C2
Bilesha Plain Kenya 96 D4
Biłgoraj Poland 31 J3
Bilharamulo Tanz. 96 A5
Bilhaur India 74 C4
Bilhorod-Dnistrovs'kyy Ukr. 29 D7
Bili Chad 94 C2
Bili r. Dem. Rep. Congo 94 D3
Bilibino Rus. Fed. 27 Q3
Bilibiza Moz. 97 E5
Bilin Myanmar 60 B4
Bilisht Albania 46 B4
Bilis Qooqaani Somalia 96 D4
Billabalong Australia 109 A6
Billabong Creek r. Australia see
   Moulamein Creek
Billère France 38 C5
Bilibilina Australia 108 E3
Billiluna Australia 108 E4
Billings U.S.A. 134 E3
Billiton i. Indon. see Belitung
Bill of Portland hd U.K. 35 E6
Billund airport Denmark 33 C5
Bill Williams r. U.S.A. 137 E4
Bill Williams Mountain U.S.A. 137 F4
Bilma Niger 93 I1
Bilo Eth. 96 C2
Biloela Australia 111 G5
Bilohir"ya Ukr. 29 D6
Biloku Guyana 147 G4
Biloli India 72 C2
Bilovods'k Ukr. 29 F6
Biloxi U.S.A. 133 D6
Bilpa Morea Claypan salt flat Australia
   111 D5

Biltine Chad 88 D6
Biltine pref. Chad 88 D6
Bilugyun Island Myanmar 61 B4
Bilyayivka Ukr. 29 D7
Bima r. Dem. Rep. Congo 94 E4
Bima Indon. 108 B2
Bimbe Angola 95 B7
Bimbila Ghana 93 F3
Bimini Islands Bahamas 129 D7
Bimlipatam India 73 D2
Bina-Etawa India 74 C4
Binaija, Gunung mt. Indon. 57 G6
Binalūd, Küh-e mts Iran 81 D2
Binatang Sarawak Malaysia 59 E2
Binboğa Daği mt. Turkey 78 D3
Binchuan China 66 B3
Bindki India 74 D4
Bindu Dem. Rep. Congo 95 B4
Bindura Zimbabwe 99 F3
Binefar Spain 43 G2
Binga Zimbabwe 99 E3
Binga, Monte mt. Moz. 99 G3
Bingara Australia 112 D3
Bing Bong Australia 110 D2
Bingham U.S.A. 128 F2
Binghamton U.S.A. 131 F2
Bin Ghanimah, Jabal hills Libya 88 B3
Bingmei China see Congjiang
Bingöl Turkey 79 E3
Bingöl Daği mt. Turkey 79 E3
Bingxi China see Yushan
Bingzhongluo China 66 A2
Binh Son Vietnam 61 E5
Bini Erda well Chad 88 C4
Binika India 73 D5
Binjai Indon. 58 B2
Binna, Raas pt Somalia 96 F1
Binnaway Australia 112 D3
Binpur India 75 E5
Bintan i. Indon. 58 D2
Bintang, Bukit mts Malaysia 58 C1
Bintuhan Indon. 58 C4
Bintulu Sarawak Malaysia 59 F2
Binxian Heilong. China 64 A3
Binxian Shaanxi China 66 D1
Binyang China 67 D4
Bin-Yauri Nigeria 93 F3
Binzhou Guangxi China see Binyang
Binzhou Heilong. China see Binxian
Binzhou Shandong China 67 D4
Biobio admin. reg. Chile 152 B5
Biobío r. Chile 152 B5
Bioco i. Equat. Guinea 93 H5
Biograd na Moru Croatia 44 F2
Biogradska Gora nat. park Yugo. 46 A3
Bioko i. Equat. Guinea see Bioco
Bir India see Bid
Bira Rus. Fed. 64 C2
Bira r. Rus. Fed. 64 C2
Bi'r Abū Daraj well Egypt 77 A5
Bi'r Abū Garad well Sudan 89 F5
Bi'r Abū Hashīm well Egypt 89 G4
Bi'r Abū Husayn well Egypt 89 F4
Bi'r Abū Jady oasis Syria 77 D1
Bi'r Abū Minqār well Egypt 89 F3
Bi'r ad Damar well Libya 88 D3
Bi'r ad Duwaydār well Egypt 77 A4
Bi'r ad Dhakar well Libya 88 D3
Bir Aïdiat well Mauritania 90 C4
Biräk Libya 88 B3
Birakan Rus. Fed. 64 B2
Bi'r al Atbaq well Saudi Arabia 89 H3
Bi'r al 'Awadī well Egypt 89 H4
Bi'r al Fātiyah well Libya 88 B2
Bi'r al Ghanam well Libya 88 B1
Bi'r al Ḥalbā well Syria 77 D1
Bi'r al Ḥaymūr well Egypt 89 G4
Bi'r al Ḥisw well Saudi Arabia 89 I3
Bi'r al Ikhwän well Libya 88 B2
Bi'r al Jadīd well Libya 88 B3
Bi'r al Jāhilīyah well Saudi Arabia 89 I4
Bi'r al Khamsah well Egypt 78 A5
Bi'r al Māliḥah well Egypt 89 F3
Bi'r al Mashī well Saudi Arabia 89 H3
Bi'r al Mastūtah well Libya 88 D3
Bi'r al Mulūsī Iraq 79 E4
Bi'r al Mushayqiq well Libya 88 A2
Bi'r al Muwaylih well Libya 88 B2
Bi'r al Qatrānī well Egypt 89 E2
Bi'r al Qurr well Saudi Arabia 89 I3
Bi'r 'Amräne well Mauritania 90 C5
Birandozero Rus. Fed. 28 F3
Bi'r an Nuss well Egypt 89 E2
Bir Anzarane W. Sahara 90 B5
Birao Cent. Afr. Rep. 94 D2
Bir Aouine well Tunisia 91 H2
Bi'r ar 'Alaqah well Libya 88 B2
Bi'r ar 'Arja well Egypt 89 F2
Bi'r ar Rābiyah well Egypt 78 A5
Bi'r ar Rummānah well Egypt 77 A4
Biratnagar Nepal 75 E4
Bi'r aş Şarfāwī well Libya 88 D2
Bi'r 'Azīz well Saudi Arabia 76 E5
Birecik Turkey 79 D3
Bi'r el Arbi well Syria 77 C2
Bi'r Baydā' well Egypt 77 B4
Bi'r Bayli well Egypt 89 F2
Bir Bel Guerdâne well Mauritania 90 C4
Bir Ben Takoul well Alg. 91 E4
Bir Bidi well Sudan 89 E5
Bi'r Bū Athlah well Libya 88 A3
Bi'r Bū Raḥah well Libya 88 A3
Birch r. Canada 123 H3
Bir Chali well Mali 90 D5
Birch Hills Canada 123 J4
Birchip Australia 112 B4
Birch Lake N.W.T. Canada 123 G2
Birch Lake l. Sask. Canada 123 I4
Birch Mountains Canada 123 H3
Birch River Canada 123 K4
Birch River U.S.A. 130 C4
Bircot Eth. 96 D3
Bir Di Sudan 94 F3
Bir Dolmane well Alg. 91 F3
Birdsboro U.S.A. 131 F3
Birdseye U.S.A. 137 G2
Birdsville Australia 111 D5
Birdum r. Australia 110 C2
Birecik Turkey 79 D3
Bir ed Deheb well Alg. 90 E4
Bir el Ghoralia well Tunisia 91 H4
Bir El Hadjaj well Alg. 91 E4
Birendranagar Nepal see Surkhet
Bir en Natrûn well Sudan 89 E5
Bir en Nugeim well Sudan 89 G5
Bir es Smeha well Alg. 91 G3
Bireun Indon. 58 B1
Bi'r Fâdil well Saudi Arabia 76 D5
Bi'r Fajr well Saudi Arabia 89 H2
Bir Furawiya well Sudan 88 D6
Bir Gandouz W. Sahara 90 B5
Birhan mt. Eth. 96 C2
Bi'r Haraqi well Saudi Arabia 89 H4
Bi'r Ḥasanah well Egypt 77 A4
Bi'r Ḥatab well Sudan 89 G2
Bi'r Ḥayzān well Saudi Arabia 89 H3
Bi'r Hismet 'Umar well Egypt 89 G3
Bi'r Ḥudurī well Saudi Arabia 89 I4
Bir Huwait well Sudan 89 G4
Bi'r Ibn Ḥirmās Saudi Arabia see Al Bi'r
Birigüi Brazil 149 H5

Birin, Col de pass Alg. 43 H5
Birin Cent. Afr. Rep. 94 D3
Bi'r Istabl well Egypt 89 E2
Birjand Iran 81 D3
Birkat al Ḥamrā well Saudi Arabia 89 I2
Birkat Zubālah waterhole Saudi Arabia
   79 E5
Birkeland Norway 33 C4
Birkenhead U.K. 35 E5
Birkirkara Malta 45 E7
Bi'r Khurbah hills Saudi Arabia 76 C6
Bi'r Khurbah well Saudi Arabia 89 H3
Bi'r Khuwärah well Saudi Arabia 89 I4
Bi'r Kiau well Sudan 89 G4
Birkim Iraq 79 F3
Birkirkara Malta 45 E7
Birlad Romania see Bârlad
Bi'r Lahfän well Egypt 77 A4
Bir Lahmar W. Sahara 90 C4
Birlik Kazakh. see Brlik
Bi'r Majal well Egypt 89 G4
Bi'r Misāha well Egypt 89 E4
Birmingham U.K. 35 F5
Birmingham U.S.A. 129 B5
Bi'r Mogreïn Mauritania 90 C4
Bi'r Mujayfil well Saudi Arabia 77 B5
Bi'r Murrah well Egypt 89 G4
Bi'r Nāhid oasis Egypt 89 F2
Bi'r Nasif Saudi Arabia 89 I4
Birni Benin 93 F3
Birnie i. Kiribati 107 H2
Birin-Gaouré Niger 93 F2
Birnin-Gwari Nigeria 93 G3
Birnin-Kebbi Nigeria 93 G2
Birnin Konni Niger 93 F2
Birnin Kudu Nigeria 93 H3
Birniwa Nigeria 93 H2
Birobidzhan Rus. Fed. 64 C2
Biröne well Mali 90 E5
Birpur India 75 E4
Bi'r Qasir as Sirr well Egypt 78 A5
Bi'r Qulayb well Egypt 89 G3
Birr Rep. of Ireland 35 D5
Bi'r Rawd Sālim well Egypt 77 A4
Birrindudu Australia 110 B3
Bi'r Roumi well Alg. 91 G2
Bi'r Sābil Iraq 79 F3
Bi'r Şahra' well Egypt 89 F4
Bi'r Salala well Sudan 89 G4
Birsay U.K. 34 E2
Bi'r Shalatayn well Egypt 89 G4
Birsk Rus. Fed. 28 J5
Bi'r Tābah Egypt 77 B4
Bi'r Tānjidar well Libya 88 D2
Bi'r Thäl well Egypt 77 A5
Birthday Mountain Australia 111 E2
Birtle Canada 123 K5
Biru China 75 G3
Bi'r 'Udayb well Egypt 77 A5
Bi'r Umm al Gharānīq Libya 88 D2
Bi'r Umm Missä well Saudi Arabia
   89 I3
Bi'r 'Unjät well Egypt 89 G4
Birur India 72 B3
Biruxiong China see Biru
Biryusa r. Rus. Fed. 64 C2
Bi'r Webeb well Libya 88 B3
Bi'r Wurshah well Saudi Arabia 89 I4
Birzai Lith. 33 N4
Bir Zar well Tunisia 91 H3
Bisalpur India 74 C3
Bisau India 74 B3
Biscarrosse France 38 C4
Biscarrosse et de Parentis, Étang de l.
   France 38 C4
Biscay, Bay of sea France/Spain 30 C4
Biscay Abyssal Plain sea feature
   N. Atlantic Ocean 160 N3
Biscayne National Park U.S.A. 129 C7
Bischofshofen Austria 37 F5
Bischofswerda Germany 37 G3
Biscoe Islands Antarctica 167 K4
Biscotasing Canada 124 D4
Bīsert' r. Rus. Fed. 28 K4
Biševo i. Croatia 44 E3
Bishan China 66 C3
Bishbek Kyrg. see Bishkek

► Bishkek Kyrg. 62 A3
Capital of Kyrgyzstan.

Bishnupur India 75 E5
Bisho S. Africa 99 E7
Bishop U.S.A. 136 D3
Bishop Auckland U.K. 35 F4
Bishop's Stortford U.K. 35 G6
Bishopville U.S.A. 129 D5
Bishrī, Jabal hills Syria 79 D4
Bishti i Pallës pt Albania 46 A4
Bishui Heilong. China 63 K1
Bishui Henan China see Biyang
Bisinaca Col. 146 D3
Biskra Alg. 91 G2
Biskupiec Poland 37 J2

► Bismarck U.S.A. 134 C3
State capital of North Dakota.

Bismarck Archipelago is P.N.G. 57 K6
Bismarck Sea P.N.G. 57 K6
Bismil Turkey 79 E3
Bison U.S.A. 132 B2
Bīsotūn Iran 80 A3
Bispgården Sweden 32 E3
Bissa, Djebel mt. Alg. 43 G4
Bissamcuttak India 73 D2

► Bissau Guinea-Bissau 92 B3
Capital of Guinea-Bissau.

Bissaula Nigeria 93 H4
Bissett Canada 123 M5
Bissikrima Guinea 92 C3
Bissorã Guinea-Bissau 92 B3
Bistcho Lake Canada 122 G3
Bistra mt. Macedonia 46 B4
Bistra r. Romania 46 C2
Bistret Romania 46 C3
Bistrita Romania 46 D1
Bistrita r. Romania 46 E1
Bistrita Lacul l. Romania 46 E1
Bistrita r. Romania 46 E1
Biswan India 74 D4
Bisztynek Poland 37 J1
Bitam Gabon 94 A4
Bitata Eth. 96 C3
Bitburg Germany 36 C4
Bitche France 39 G2
Bitik Kazakh. 29 I6
Bitkine Chad 94 F3
Bitlis Turkey 79 E3
Bitola Macedonia 46 B4
Bitolj Macedonia see Bitola
Bitonto Italy 44 F4
Biträn, Jabal hill Saudi Arabia 76 D5
Bitra Par reef India 72 B4
Bitter Creek r. UT U.S.A. 137 H1
Bitter Creek r. WY U.S.A. 134 E4

Bitterfontein S. Africa 98 C6
Bitterroot r. U.S.A. 134 D3
Bitterroot Range mts U.S.A. 134 D3
Bitterwater U.S.A. 136 B3
Bittou Burkina 93 E3
Bituca Brazil 150 A4
Biu Nigeria 93 I3
Biula Angola 95 D7
Biwa-ko l. Japan 65 C6
Biyang China 67 D1
Biy K'obē Eth. 96 D2
Biyo Ado well Eth. 96 E2
Biysk Rus. Fed. 62 D1
Bizana S. Africa 99 D7
Bizerta Tunisia see Bizerte
Bizerte Tunisia 44 C6
Bīzhanābād Iran 80 D5

► Bjargtangar hd Iceland 32 [inset]
Most westerly point of Europe.

Bjärna Sweden 32 E3
Bjärnum Norway 46 A3
Bjelašnica mts Bos.-Herz. 44 G3
Bjelovar Croatia 44 F2
Bjerkvik Norway 32 E1
Bjöllånes Norway 32 D2
Björbo Sweden 33 D3
Bjørkelangen Norway 33 C4
Björkfjället mts Sweden 32 E2
Björkliden Sweden 32 E1
Björkö i. Sweden 32 F3
Björksele Sweden 32 E2
Bjorli Norway 33 C3
Björna Sweden 32 E3
Bjørnafjorden b. Norway 33 B3
Björneborg Fin. see Pori
Bjørneborg Fin. see Pori
Bjørnfjell Norway 32 E1

► Bjørnøya i. Arctic Ocean 26 B2
Part of Norway.

Bjørnstad Norway 32 H1
Bjurholm Sweden 32 E3
Bjuröklubb pt Sweden 32 F2
Bjursås Sweden 33 D3
Bla Mali 92 D3
Blace Kosovo, Srbija Yugo. 46 B3
Blace Srbija Yugo. 46 B3
Blachownia Poland 37 I3
Black r. Canada 123 L5
Black r. AR U.S.A. 127 I4
Black r. AR U.S.A. 133 D5
Black r. AZ U.S.A. 137 G5
Black r. MI U.S.A. 130 D1
Black r. WI U.S.A. 132 C3
Blackall Australia 111 F5
Blackbear r. Canada 124 C2
Blackbull Australia 111 E3
Blackburn U.K. 35 E5
Blackburn, Mount U.S.A. 122 A2
Black Butte mt. U.S.A. 136 B2
Black Butte Lake U.S.A. 136 B2
Black Canyon gorge U.S.A. 137 E4
Black Canyon of the Gunnison
   National Park U.S.A. 135 F5
Black Creek watercourse U.S.A. 137 H4
Blackdown Tableland National Park
   Australia 111 F4
Blackfoot U.S.A. 134 D4
Black Foot r. U.S.A. 134 D3
Black Forest mts Germany 36 D5
Black Hills SD U.S.A. 126 F3
Black Hills SD U.S.A. 134 F3
Black Island Canada 123 L5
Black Lake Canada 123 J3
Black Lake l. Canada 123 J3
Black Mesa ridge U.S.A. 137 G3
Black Mountain U.S.A. 130 D5
Black Mountains hills U.K. 35 E6
Black Mountains U.S.A. 137 G2
Black Nossob watercourse Namibia
   98 C4
Black Pagoda India see Konarka
Blackpool U.K. 35 E5
Black River r. U.S.A. 131 F1
Black River r. Vietnam 60 D3
Black River Falls U.S.A. 132 D2
Black Rock hill Jordan see
   'Unäb, Jabal al
Black Rock Desert U.S.A. 134 C4
Blacksburg U.S.A. 130 C5
Black Sea Asia/Europe 29 F5
Blackshear U.S.A. 129 C6
Blacksod Bay Rep. of Ireland 35 A4
Black Springs U.S.A. 136 C2
Blackstone r. N.W.T. Canada 122 D1
Blackstone r. Y.T. Canada 122 B1
Blackstone U.S.A. 130 D5
Black Sugarloaf mt. Australia 112 D3
Black Volta r. Africa 92 E3
   also known as Mouhoun
Blackwater Australia 111 G4
Blackwater watercourse Australia
   111 F4
Blackwater r. Canada 122 E2
Blackwater r. Rep. of Ireland 35 C5
Blackwater r. U.S.A. 131 E5
Blackwater watercourse U.S.A. 133 A5
Blackwater Lake Canada 122 F2
Blackwood r. Australia 109 A8
Blackwood National Park Australia
   111 F4
Bladensburg National Park Australia
   111 E4
Blåfjellshatten mt. Norway 32 D3
Blagodarnyy Rus. Fed. 29 G7
Blagoevgrad Bulg. 46 C3
Blagoveshchensk Amurskaya Oblast'
   Rus. Fed. 28 K5
Blagoveshchensk Rus. Fed. 28 K5
Blaikiston, Mount Canada 123 H5
Blain France 38 C3
Blain U.S.A. 133 B3
Blaine Lake Canada 123 J4
Blair U.S.A. 132 B3
Blair Athol Australia 111 F4
Blair Atholl U.K. 34 E3
Blairgowrie U.K. 34 E3
Blairs U.S.A. 130 D5
Blairsden U.S.A. 136 B2
Blairsville U.S.A. 128 C5
Błaj Romania 46 C1
Blakang Mati, Pulau i. Sing. see Sentosa
Blakely U.S.A. 129 B6
Blakeslee U.S.A. 131 F3
Blama Sierra Leone 92 C4
Blambangan, Semenanjung pen. Indon.
   59 F5

► Blanc, Mont mt. France/Italy 39 G4
5th highest mountain in Europe.
europe 22–23

Blanca, Bahía b. Arg. 152 C4
Blanca, Cordillera mts Peru 148 A2
Blanca, Sierra mt. U.S.A. 133 F6
Blanca Peak U.S.A. 135 F5
Blanche, Cape Australia 109 F8
Blanche, Lake salt flat S.A. Australia
   111 D6
Blanche, Lake salt flat W.A. Australia
   108 C5
Blanchester U.S.A. 130 B4
Blanchetown Australia 112 A4

Blanco r. Arg. 152 C2
Blanco r. Bol. 149 F6
Blanco r. Peru 146 C6
Blanco r. Spain 42 D4
Blanco, Cape U.S.A. 134 A4
Blanc-Sablon Canada 125 J3
Bland r. Australia 112 C4
Bland U.S.A. 130 C5
Blanda r. Iceland 32 [inset]
Blandford Forum U.K. 35 E6
Blanding U.S.A. 137 H3
Blanes Spain 43 H2
Blangkejeren Indon. 58 B2
Blangpidie Indon. 58 B2
Blangy-sur-Bresle France 38 D2
Blanice r. Czech Rep. 37 H4
Blanquefort France 38 D4
Blanquilla, Isla i. Venez. 147 E2
Blansko Czech Rep. 37 H4
Blantyre Malawi 97 F5
Blarney Rep. of Ireland 35 B6
Blåsjø l. Norway 33 B4
Blaskavlen mt. Norway 33 B3
Błaszki Poland 37 I3
Blatná Czech Rep. 37 H4
Blattniksele Sweden 32 E2
Blaubeuren Germany 36 D5
Blåvands Huk pt Denmark 33 C5
Blavet r. France 38 B3
Blayeul Sommet mt. France 39 G4
Blayney Australia 112 C4
Blaze, Point Australia 110 B2
Blega Indon. 59 F5
Blekinge county Sweden 33 D4
Blenheim Canada 130 C2
Blenheim N.Z. 113 D5
Blenheim Palace tourist site U.K. 35 F6
Bletchley U.K. 35 F6
Bleus, Monts mts Dem. Rep. Congo
   96 A4
Blida Alg. 91 F1
Bligh Water b. Fiji 107 G3
Blind River Canada 124 D4
Blinman Australia 111 D6
Bliss U.S.A. 134 D4
Blissfield MI U.S.A. 130 B3
Blissfield OH U.S.A. 130 D3
Blitar Indon. 59 F5
Block Island i. U.S.A. 131 H3
   131 H3
Block Island Sound sea chan. U.S.A.
   131 H3
Bloemfontein S. Africa 99 E6
Bloemhof Dam S. Africa 98 E5
Blois France 38 D3
Blönduós Iceland 32 [inset]
Blöndulón l. Iceland 32 [inset]
Blongas Indon. 59 G5
Blonie Poland 37 J2
Bloods Range mts Australia 110 B5
Bloodsworth Island U.S.A. 131 E4
Bloodvein r. Canada 123 L5
Bloody Foreland pt Rep. of Ireland 34 A1
Bloomer U.S.A. 132 C2
Bloomfield IN U.S.A. 128 B4
Bloomfield IN U.S.A. 128 B4
Bloomfield MN U.S.A. 135 F5
Blooming Prairie U.S.A. 132 C3
Bloomington IL U.S.A. 132 D3
Bloomington IN U.S.A. 128 B4
Bloomington MN U.S.A. 132 C3
Bloomsburg U.S.A. 131 E3
Bloomsbury Australia 111 G4
Blora Indon. 59 F4
Blossburg U.S.A. 131 E3
Blosseville Kyst coastal area Greenland
   121 Q3
Blountstown U.S.A. 129 B6
Bludenz Austria 36 D5
Bluch r. U.S.A. 133 C5
Blue watercourse U.S.A. 137 H5
Blue Bell Knoll mt. U.S.A. 137 G2
Blue Earth r. U.S.A. 132 C3
Blue Earth r. U.S.A. 132 C2
Bluefield U.S.A. 130 C5
Bluefields Nicaragua 139 H6
Blue Knob hill U.S.A. 130 D3
Blue Lagoon National Park Zambia
   95 E5
Blue Mountain Canada 125 J3
Blue Mountain India 75 G5
Blue Mountains Australia 112 C4
Blue Mountains U.S.A. 134 C3
Blue Mountains National Park Australia
   112 D4
Blue Nile r. Eth./Sudan 89 G6
   also known as Äbay Wenz (Ethiopia),
   Azraq, Bahr el (Sudan)
Blue Stack Mountains hills Sudan 96 B2
Bluenose Lake Canada 120 H3
Blue Rapids U.S.A. 132 B4
Blue Ridge GA U.S.A. 128 C5
Blue Ridge VA U.S.A. 130 D5
Blue Ridge mts U.S.A. 130 C5
Blue River Canada 122 G4
Blue Stack Mountains hills
   Rep. of Ireland 34 B4
Bluestone Lake U.S.A. 130 C5
Bluff N.Z. 113 B4
Bluff U.S.A. 137 H3
Bluffdale U.S.A. 137 G1
Bluff Face Range hills Australia 108 B5
Bluff Island Hong Kong China 67 [inset]
Bluff Knoll mt. Australia 109 B8
Bluffton IN U.S.A. 128 B3
Bluffton OH U.S.A. 130 B3
Blumberg Germany 36 D5
Blumenau Brazil 151 B8
Blyth r. Australia 110 C2
Blythe U.S.A. 137 E5
Blytheville U.S.A. 127 I4
Bo Sierra Leone 92 C4
Boac Phil. 57 F3
Boa Esperança Brazil 147 F4
Boa Esperança, Açude resr Brazil 150 D3
Boa Hora Brazil 148 D2
Bo'ai China 66 C4
Boali Cent. Afr. Rep. 94 C3
Boa Nova Brazil 150 D5
Boardman U.S.A. 130 C3
Boatman Australia 111 F4
Boa Viagem Brazil 150 D3
Blakang Mati, Pulau i. Sing. see Sentosa
Boa Vista Amazonas Brazil 146 C6
Boa Vista Amazonas Brazil 147 F5
Boa Vista Pará Brazil 147 H5
Boa Vista Roraima Brazil 147 F4
Boa Vista i. Cape Verde 92 [inset]
Bobai China 67 D4
Bobaomby, Tanjona c. Madag.
   99 [inset] K4
Bobbili India 73 D2
Bobbio Italy 44 B2
Bobcaygeon Canada 130 D1
Bobigny France 39 E2
Bobo-Dioulasso Burkina 92 D3
Bobolice Poland 37 H2
Bobonong Botswana 99 F4
Boborás Spain 42 B2
Bobotov Kuk mt. Yugo. see Durmitor
Bóbr r. Poland 37 G3
Bobriki Rus. Fed. see Novomoskovsk
Bobrinets Ukr. see Bobrynets'
Bobrov Rus. Fed. 29 G5
Bobrovitsa Ukr. see Bobrovytsya

Bobrovytsya Ukr. 29 D6
Bobruysk Belarus see Babruysk
Bobrynets' Ukr. 29 E6
Bobs Lake Canada 131 E1
Bobso China 66 B1
Bobuk Sudan 96 B2
Bobures Venez. 146 D2
Boby mt. Madag. 99 [inset] J4
Boca de la Travesía Arg. 152 D5
Boca del Pao Venez. 147 E2
Boca de Macareo Venez. 147 F2
Boca de Uracoa Venez. 147 F2
Boca do Acre Brazil 148 D2
Boca do Curuquetê Brazil 148 D2
Boca do Jari Brazil 147 I5
Boca do Moaco Brazil 148 C1
Bocaiúva Brazil 151 D6
Bocaiúva do Sul Brazil 151 B8
Boca Mavaca Venez. 147 E4
Bocanda Côte d'Ivoire 92 D4
Bocaranga Cent. Afr. Rep. 94 B3
Boca Raton U.S.A. 129 C7
Bocas del Toro Panama 139 H7
Bochinche Venez. 147 F3
Bochnia Poland 37 J4
Bocholt Germany 36 C3
Bochum Germany 36 C3
Bochum S. Africa 99 F4
Bockenem Germany 36 E2
Bocoio Angola 95 B8
Bocşa Romania 46 B2
Boda Cent. Afr. Rep. 94 C3
Böda Sweden 33 E4
Bodallin Australia 109 B7
Bodaybo Rus. Fed. 27 L4
Bode r. Germany 36 E3
Bodega Head U.S.A. 136 A2
Bodélé reg. Chad 88 C5
Boden Sweden 32 F2
Bodensee l. Germany/Switz. see Constance, Lake
Bode-Sadu Nigeria 93 G3
Bodhan India 72 C2
Bodh Gaya India 75 E4
Bodie U.S.A. 136 C2
Bodinayakkanur India 72 C4
Bodión r. Spain 42 C3
Bodmin U.K. 35 D6
Bodø Norway 32 D2
Bodocó Brazil 150 E3
Bodoquena Brazil 149 F5
Bodoquena, Serra da hills Brazil 149 F5
Bodoukpa Cent. Afr. Rep. 94 C3
Bodrog r. Hungary 37 J4
Bodrum Turkey 78 A3
Bodsjö Sweden 32 D3
Bódva r. Hungary 37 J4
Bodva r. Slovakia 37 J4
Boechout Belgium 36 B3
Boedo r. Spain 42 D1
Boende Dem. Rep. Congo 94 D5
Boerne U.S.A. 133 B6
Boeuf r. U.S.A. 133 D6
Boftsa Norway 32 H1
Bogale Myanmar 61 A4
Bogale r. Myanmar 61 A5
Bogalusa U.S.A. 133 D6
Bogan r. Australia 112 C3
Bogandé Burkina 93 E2
Bogan Gate Australia 112 C4
Bogangolo Cent. Afr. Rep. 94 C3
Boğazlıyan Turkey 78 C3
Bogbonga Dem. Rep. Congo 94 C4
Bogcang Zangbo r. China 75 E3
Bogda Feng mt. China 70 G3
Bogdan mt. Bulg. 46 D3
Bogdanci Macedonia 46 C4
Bogda Shan mts China 70 G3
Bogen Norway 32 E1
Boggabilla Australia 111 G6
Boggeragh Mountains hills Rep. of Ireland 35 B5
Boghar Alg. 43 H5
Boghari Alg. see Ksar el Boukhari
Bogia P.N.G. 57 J6
Bogie r. Australia 111 F4
Bogodukhov Ukr. see Bohodukhiv
Bogol Manya Eth. 96 D3
Bogong, Mount Australia 112 C5
Bogor Indon. 59 D4
Bogoroditsk Rus. Fed. 29 F5
Bogorodskoye Khabarovskiy Kray Rus. Fed. 64 E1
Bogorodskoye Kirovskaya Oblast' Rus. Fed. 28 I4
Bogoslof Island U.S.A. 120 C4

▶Bogotá Col. 146 C3
Capital of Colombia and 5th most populous city in South America.
world 16–17

Bogotol Rus. Fed. 27 I4
Bogoyavlenskoye Rus. Fed. see Pervomayskiy
Bogra Bangl. 75 F4
Boguchany Rus. Fed. 27 J4
Boguchar Rus. Fed. 29 G6
Bogué Mauritania 92 B1
Boh r. Indon. 59 F2
Bo Hai g. China 63 J4
Bohain-en-Vermandois France 39 E2
Bohai Wan b. China 63 J4
Bohemia reg. Czech Rep. 37 G3
Bohemia Downs Australia 108 D4
Bohemian Forest mts Germany see Böhmer Wald
Bohicon Benin 93 F4
Bohlokong S. Africa 99 F6
Böhmen reg. Czech Rep. see Bohemia
Böhmer Wald mts Germany 37 F4
Bohodukhiv Ukr. 29 E6
Bohol i. Phil. 57 F4
Bohol Sea Phil. 57 F4
Bohu China 70 G3
Boiaçu Brazil 147 F5
Boigu Island Australia 57 J7
Boila Moz. 99 H3
Boileau, Cape Australia 108 C4
Boim Brazil 147 H5
Boinu r. Myanmar 60 A3
Boiro Spain 42 B1
Bois r. Brazil 149 H4
Bois, Lac des l. Canada 122 E1
Bois de Sioux r. U.S.A. 132 B2

▶Boise U.S.A. 134 C4
State capital of Idaho.

Boise r. U.S.A. 134 C4
Boise City U.S.A. 135 G5
Boissevain Canada 123 K5
Boite r. Italy 44 D1
Boitumelong S. Africa 98 E5
Boizenburg Germany 36 E2
Bojano Italy 44 E4
Bojeador, Cape Phil. 67 G5
Bojnik Yugo. 46 B3
Bojnūrd Iran 80 D2
Bojonegoro Indon. 59 E4
Bojuru Brazil 152 H2
Bokada Dem. Rep. Congo 94 C3
Bokadaban Feng mt. China 75 F1
Bokajan India 75 G4
Bokaro India 75 E5
Bokatola Dem. Rep. Congo 94 C5
Boké Guinea 92 B3
Bokhara r. Australia 112 C3
Boknafjorden sea chan. Norway 33 B4
Boko Congo 95 B6
Boko Dem. Rep. Congo 95 C6
Bokoko Dem. Rep. Congo 94 E3
Bokolo Gabon 94 A5
Bokoro Chad 88 C6
Bokote Dem. Rep. Congo 94 C5
Bokote Dem. Rep. Congo 94 D5
Bokovskaya Rus. Fed. 29 G6
Bokpyin Myanmar 61 B6
Bokspits S. Africa 98 D5
Boktor Rus. Fed. 64 D2
Bokungu Dem. Rep. Congo 94 D5
Bokurdak Turkm. see Bakhardok
Bokwankusu Dem. Rep. Congo 94 D5
Bol Chad 88 B6
Bola, Bahr watercourse Chad 94 C2
Bolaiti Dem. Rep. Congo 94 E5
Bolama Guinea-Bissau 92 B3
Bolan r. Pak. 81 F4
Bolanda, Jebel mt. Sudan 94 E3
Bolaños de Calatrava Spain 42 E3
Bolan Pass Pak. 81 F4
Bolbec France 38 D2
Boldaji Iran 80 B4
Boldu Romania 46 E2
Bole China 70 F3
Bole Ghana 93 E3
Boleko Dem. Rep. Congo 94 C5
Bolesławiec Poland 37 G3
Bolgar Rus. Fed. 28 I5
Bolgatanga Ghana 93 E3
Bolgrad Ukr. see Bolhrad
Bolhrad Ukr. 29 D7
Boli China 64 B3
Boli Sudan 94 F3
Bolia Dem. Rep. Congo 94 C5
Boliden Sweden 32 F2
Bolintin-Vale Romania 46 D2
Bolívar Antioquia Col. 146 B3
Bolívar Cauca Col. 146 B4
Bolívar dept Col. 146 C2
Bolívar prov. Ecuador 146 B5
Bolívar Peru 148 A1
Bolivar MO U.S.A. 132 C4
Bolivar NY U.S.A. 130 D2
Bolivar TN U.S.A. 128 A5
Bolívar state Venez. 147 F3

▶Bolivia country S. America 148 D4
5th largest country in South America.
southamerica 144–145, 154
world 14–15

Boljevac Yugo. 46 B3
Bolkhov Rus. Fed. 29 F5
Bolków Poland 37 H3
Bollène France 39 F4
Bollnäs Sweden 33 E3
Bollon Australia 111 F6
Bollstabruk Sweden 32 E3
Bolmen l. Sweden 33 D4
Bolnisi Georgia 79 F2
Bolobo Dem. Rep. Congo 94 C5
Bologna Italy 44 C2
Bolognesi Peru 148 B2
Bologoye Rus. Fed. 28 E4
Bolomba Dem. Rep. Congo 94 C4
Bolombo r. Dem. Rep. Congo 94 D4
Bolon' Rus. Fed. see Achan
Bolondo Equat. Guinea 93 H5
Bolovens, Phouphieng plat. Laos 61 D5
Bolozo Congo 94 B4
Bolpur India 75 E5
Bolsa, Cerro mt. Arg. 152 C2
Bolsena, Lago di l. Italy 44 C3
Bol'shakovo Rus. Fed. 33 F5
Bol'shaya Chernigovka Rus. Fed. 29 I5
Bol'shaya Glushitsa Rus. Fed. 29 I5
Bol'shaya Imandra, Ozero l. Rus. Fed. 28 E2
Bol'shaya Kokshaga r. Rus. Fed. 28 H4
Bol'shaya Rogovaya r. Rus. Fed. 28 L2
Bol'shaya Synya r. Rus. Fed. 28 K2
Bol'shaya Usa Rus. Fed. 28 J4
Bol'sheretsk Rus. Fed. 27 P4
Bol'shevik, Ostrov i. Rus. Fed. 27 K2
Bol'shezemel'skaya Tundra lowland Rus. Fed. 28 J2
Bol'shiye Chirki Rus. Fed. 28 H3
Bol'shiye Kozly Rus. Fed. 28 F2
Bol'shiye Peshnyye, Ostrova is Kazakh. 29 I7
Bol'shoy Aluy r. Rus. Fed. 27 P3
Bol'shoy Anyuy r. Rus. Fed. 27 Q3
Bol'shoy Begichev, Ostrov i. Rus. Fed. 27 L2
Bol'shoy Berezovyy, Ostrov i. Rus. Fed. 33 H3
Bol'shoye Murashkino Rus. Fed. 28 H5
Bol'shoy Irgiz r. Rus. Fed. 29 H6
Bol'shoy Kamen' Rus. Fed. 64 C4
Bol'shoy Kavkaz mts Asia/Europe see Caucasus
Bol'shoy Lyakhovskiy, Ostrov i. Rus. Fed. 27 O2
Bol'shoy Porog Rus. Fed. 27 J3
Bol'shoy Tokmak Kyrg. see Tokmak
Bol'shoy Tokmak Ukr. see Tokmak
Bol'shoy Uzen' r. Kazakh./Rus. Fed. 29 I6
Bol'shoy Zelenchuk r. Rus. Fed. 79 E1
Bolsward Neth. 36 B2
Bolton Canada 130 D2
Bolton U.K. 35 E5
Bolu Turkey 78 B2
Bolungarvík Iceland 32 [inset]
Boluntay China 75 G1
Boluo China 67 E4
Bolus Head Rep. of Ireland 35 A6
Bolvadin Turkey 78 B3
Bolyarovo Bulg. 46 E3
Bolzano Italy 44 C1
Boma Dem. Rep. Congo 95 B6
Bomaderry Australia 112 D4
Bomai China 66 A2
Bombala Australia 112 D5
Bombarral Port. 42 B3
Bombay India see Mumbai
Bombay Beach U.S.A. 137 E5
Bomberai, Semenanjung pen. Indon. 57 H6
Bomberai Peninsula Indon. see Bomberai, Semenanjung
Bombo r. Dem. Rep. Congo 95 B5
Bom Comércio Brazil 148 D2
Bomdila India 75 G4
Bomi China 62 F6
Bomili Dem. Rep. Congo 94 E4
Bom Jardim Brazil 148 D2
Bom Jesus Piauí Brazil 150 C4
Bom Jesus Rio Grande do Sul Brazil 151 B9
Bom Jesus da Gurgueia, Serra do hills Brazil 150 D4
Bom Jesus da Lapa Brazil 150 D5
Bom Jesus do Itabapoana Brazil 151 D7
Bømlo i. Norway 33 B4
Bomokandi r. Dem. Rep. Congo 94 E4
Bom Retiro Brazil 151 B8
Bon, Cap c. Tunisia 91 H1
Bona Alg. see Annaba
Bona, Mount U.S.A. 122 A2
Bonāb Iran 80 A2
Bon Air U.S.A. 130 E5
Bonaire i. Neth. Antilles 146 D1
Bonandolok Indon. 58 B2
Bonanza Nicaragua 139 H6
Bonaparte Archipelago is Australia 110 A2
Bonaparte Lake Canada 134 B2
Bonasse Trin. and Tob. 147 F2
Bonavista Canada 121 N5
Bonavista Bay Canada 125 K3
Bondo Équateur Dem. Rep. Congo 94 D5
Bondo Orientale Dem. Rep. Congo 94 D4
Bondoukou Côte d'Ivoire 92 E3
Bondoukui Burkina 92 E3
Bondowoso Indon. 59 F4
Bondyuzhskiy Rus. Fed. see Mendeleyevsk
Bône Alg. see Annaba
Bone, Teluk b. Indon. 57 F7
Bonerate, Kepulauan is Indon. 57 F7

▶Bonete, Cerro mt. Arg. 152 C1
3rd highest mountain in South America.

Bonfinópolis de Minas Brazil 151 C6
Bonga Eth. 96 C3
Bongaigaon India 75 F4
Bongandanga Dem. Rep. Congo 94 D4
Bongani S. Africa 98 D6
Bongba China 75 D2
Bong Co l. China 75 F3
Bongo, Massif des mts Cent. Afr. Rep. 94 D2
Bongo, Serra do mts Angola 95 B7
Bongolava mts Madag. 99 [inset] J3
Bongor Chad 94 B2
Bongouanou Côte d'Ivoire 92 D4
Bông Sơn Vietnam 61 E5
Bönhamn Sweden 32 E3
Boni Mali 93 E2
Bonifacio Corsica France 31 G5
Bonifacio, Bocche di strait France/Italy see Bonifacio, Strait of
Bonifacio, Bouches de strait France/Italy see Bonifacio, Strait of
Bonifacio, Strait of France/Italy 44 B4
Boni National Reserve nature res. Kenya 96 D5

▶Bonin Islands N. Pacific Ocean 54 G4
Part of Japan.

Bonito Brazil 149 F5

▶Bonn Germany 36 C3
Former capital of Germany.

Bonna Germany see Bonn
Bonnat France 38 D3
Bonners Ferry U.S.A. 134 C2
Bonnet, Lac du resr Canada 123 M5
Bonnet Plume r. Canada 122 C1
Bonneval France 38 D2
Bonneville France 39 G3
Bonnie Rock Australia 109 B7
Bonnyville Canada 123 I4
Bonom Mhai mt. Vietnam 61 D6
Bononia Italy see Bologna
Bonorva Sardinia Italy 45 B4
Bonoua Côte d'Ivoire 92 E4
Bonsall U.S.A. 136 D5
Bonthe Sierra Leone 92 B4
Bontoc Phil. 57 F2
Bontosunggu Indon. 57 E7
Bontrug S. Africa 98 E7
Bonvouloir Islands P.N.G. 111 G1
Bonyhád Hungary 44 G1
Boo Sweden 33 E4
Boodie Boodie Range hills Australia 109 C6
Book Cliffs ridge U.S.A. 137 H2
Booker U.S.A. 133 A4
Boola Guinea 92 C3
Booligal Australia 112 C4
Boologooro Australia 109 A6
Boomi Australia 112 D3
Boone IA U.S.A. 132 C3
Boone NC U.S.A. 128 C4
Boone Lake U.S.A. 130 B5
Boones Mill U.S.A. 130 D5
Booneville AR U.S.A. 133 C5
Booneville KY U.S.A. 130 B5
Booneville MS U.S.A. 128 A5
Boonsboro U.S.A. 130 E4
Böön Tsagaan Nuur salt l. Mongolia 70 I2
Boonville CA U.S.A. 136 A2
Boonville IN U.S.A. 128 B4
Boonville MO U.S.A. 132 C4
Boopi r. Bol. 148 D3
Boorabin National Park Australia 109 C7
Boorama Somalia 96 D2
Booroorban Australia 112 C4
Boorowa Australia 112 D4
Boosaaso Somalia 96 F2
Boothbay Harbor U.S.A. 131 I2
Boothby, Cape Antarctica 167 D2
Boothia, Gulf of Canada 121 K3
Boothia Peninsula Canada 121 J2
Booué Gabon 94 A5
Bopolu Liberia 92 C4
Boppard Germany 36 C3
Boqê China 75 F3
Boqueirão Brazil 152 G2
Boqueirão, Serra do hills Brazil 150 C5
Bor Rus. Fed. 28 H4
Bor Sudan 96 A3
Bor Turkey 78 C3
Bor Yugo. 46 C2
Boragi waterhole Kenya 96 C5
Borah Peak U.S.A. 134 D3
Boraraigh i. U.K. see Boreray
Borås Sweden 33 D4
Borasambar India 73 D1
Borāzjān Iran 80 B4
Borba Brazil 147 G6
Borba Port. 42 C3
Borbollón, Embalse del resr Spain 42 C2
Borborema, Planalto da plat. Brazil 150 E3
Borcea, Braţul watercourse Romania 46 E2
Borchalo Georgia see Marneuli
Borchgrevink Coast Antarctica 167 H2
Borçka Turkey 79 E2
Bor Dağı mt. Turkey 47 F6
Bordeaux France 38 C4
Bordein Sudan 89 G6
Borden Canada 125 I4
Borden Island Canada 121 H2
Borden Peninsula Canada 121 K2
Bordentown U.S.A. 131 F3
Border Ranges National Park Australia 112 E3
Bordertown Australia 112 B5
Borðeyri Iceland 32 [inset]
Bordj Bou Arréridj Alg. 91 G1
Bordj Bounaama Alg. 43 G5
Bordj Flye Ste-Marie Alg. 90 E4
Bordj Messaouda Alg. 91 H3
Bordj Mokhtar Alg. 91 F5
Bordj Omar Driss Alg. see Bordj Omer Driss
Bordj Omer Driss Alg. 91 G3
Borðoy i. Faroe Is 34 [inset]
Boré Mali 92 E2
Boreas Abyssal Plain sea feature Arctic Ocean 166 H1
Borensberg Sweden 33 D4
Boreray i. U.K. 34 B3
Borgå Fin. see Porvoo
Borgarfjörður Iceland 32 [inset]
Borgarnes Iceland 32 [inset]
Børgefjell Nasjonalpark nat. park Norway 32 D2
Borger U.S.A. 133 A5
Borgholm Sweden 33 E4
Borgo Corsica France 44 B3
Borgo a Mozzano Italy 44 C3
Borgomanero Italy 44 B2
Borgo San Dalmazzo Italy 44 A2
Borgo San Lorenzo Italy 44 C3
Borgosesia Italy 44 B2
Borgo Val di Taro Italy 44 B2
Borgo Valsugana Italy 44 C1
Borgsjåbrotet mt. Norway 33 C3
Bori India 72 C1
Bori r. India 74 B5
Borino Bulg. 46 D4
Borisoglebsk Rus. Fed. 29 G6
Borisov Belarus see Barysaw
Borisovka Rus. Fed. 29 F6
Borispol' Ukr. see Boryspil'
Bo River Post Sudan 94 E3
Boriziny Madag. 99 [inset] J2
Borja mts Bos.-Herz. 44 F2
Borja Peru 146 B6
Borjas Blancas Spain see Les Borges Blanques
Borj Bourguiba Tunisia 91 H2
Borken Germany 36 C3
Borkenes Norway 32 E1
Borkou-Ennedi-Tibesti pref. Chad 88 C5
Borkovskaya Rus. Fed. 28 I2
Borkum Germany 36 C2
Borkum i. Germany 36 C2
Borlänge Sweden 33 D3
Borlaug Norway 33 B3
Borlu Turkey 78 B3
Borna Germany 37 F3
Born-Berge hill Germany 36 E3
Borne Alg. 91 G4

▶Borneo i. Asia 59 F2
Largest island in Asia and 3rd in the world.
asia 50–51
world 6–7

Bornes mts France 39 G4
Bornholm i. Denmark 33 D5
Bornholmsgattet strait Denmark/Sweden 33 D5
Borno state Nigeria 93 I3
Bornova Turkey 78 A3
Borobudur tourist site Indon. 59 E4
Borodino Rus. Fed. 166 F2
Borodinskoye Rus. Fed. 33 H3
Borohoro Shan mts China 70 F3
Boromo Burkina 92 E3
Boron Mali 92 D2
Borovan Bulg. 46 C3
Borovichi Rus. Fed. 28 E4
Borovo Selo Croatia 44 G2
Borovoy Rus. Fed. 28 J3
Borovskoy Kazakh. 26 G4
Borroloola Australia 110 D3
Børsa Norway 32 C3
Borşa Romania 31 K4
Borsad India 74 B5
Børselv Norway 32 G1
Borshchiv Ukr. 29 C6
Borshchovochnyy Khrebet mts Rus. Fed. 63 H2
Borsippa tourist site Iraq 79 F4
Bortala China see Bole
Bort-les-Orgues France 39 E4
Borūjen Iran 80 B4
Borūjerd Iran 80 B3
Borushtitsa Bulg. 46 D3
Boryspil' Ukr. 31 L3
Borzna Ukr. 29 E6
Borzya Rus. Fed. 27 L4
Bosa Sardinia Italy 45 B4
Bosanska Dubica Bos.-Herz. 44 F2
Bosanska Gradiška Bos.-Herz. 44 F2
Bosanska Kostajnica Bos.-Herz. 44 F2
Bosanska Krupa Bos.-Herz. 44 F2
Bosanski Brod Bos.-Herz. 44 G2
Bosanski Novi Bos.-Herz. 44 F2
Bosanski Petrovac Bos.-Herz. 44 F2
Bosanski Šamac Bos.-Herz. 44 G2
Boscawen U.S.A. 131 H2
Boscawen Island Tonga see Niuatoputopu
Bosch Arg. 152 F4
Bose China 66 C4
Boshnyakovo Rus. Fed. 64 E2
Boshruyeh Iran 80 D3
Bosilegrad Yugo. 46 C3
Bosiljgrad Yugo. see Bosilegrad
Boskovice Czech Rep. 37 H4
Bosna r. Bos.-Herz. 44 G2
Bosna hills Bulg. 46 E3
Bosna i Hercegovina country Europe see Bosnia-Herzegovina
Bosna Saray Bos.-Herz. see Sarajevo
▶Bosnia-Herzegovina country Europe 44 F2
europe 24–25, 48
Boso Dem. Rep. Congo 94 D4
Bosobolo Dem. Rep. Congo 94 C3
Bōsō-hantō pen. Japan 65 E6
Bososama Dem. Rep. Congo 94 D3
▶Bosporus strait Turkey 46 F4
europe 24–25
Bosque Spain 42 B1
Bossaga Turkm. see Basaga
Bossangoa Cent. Afr. Rep. 94 C3
Bossembélé Cent. Afr. Rep. 94 C3
Bossemptélé Cent. Afr. Rep. see Bossentélé
Bossentélé Cent. Afr. Rep. 94 C3
Bossier City U.S.A. 133 C5
Bossiesvlei Namibia 98 C5
Bossut, Cape Australia 108 C4
Bostan China 75 E1
Bostān Iran 80 A4
Bosten Hu l. China 70 G3
Boston U.K. 35 F5

▶Boston U.S.A. 131 H2
State capital of Massachusetts.

Boston Mountains U.S.A. 133 C5
Bosut r. Croatia 46 A2
Boswell U.S.A. 130 D3
Botad India 74 A5
Botata Liberia 92 C4
Boteå Sweden 32 E3
Boteti r. Botswana 98 E4
Botev mt. Bulg. 46 D3
Botevgrad Bulg. 46 C3
Bothell U.S.A. 134 B3
Bothnia, Gulf of Fin./Sweden 32 E3
Bothwell Australia 112 C6
Bothwell Canada 130 C2
Boticas Port. 42 C2
Botin mt. Bos.-Herz. 44 G3
Botlikh Rus. Fed. 79 F2
Botoşani Romania 31 K4
Bô Trach Vietnam 60 D4
Botro Côte d'Ivoire 92 D4
Botshabelo S. Africa 99 E6
Botsmark Sweden 32 F2
▶Botswana country Africa 98 D4
africa 86–87, 100
Bottenviken g. Fin./Sweden 32 F2
Bottineau U.S.A. 134 G2
Bottrop Germany 36 C3
Botucatu Brazil 149 H5
Bouaflé Côte d'Ivoire 92 D4
Bouaké Côte d'Ivoire 92 D4
Boualem Alg. 91 F2
Bouandougou Côte d'Ivoire 92 D3
Bouanga Congo 94 C5
Bouar Cent. Afr. Rep. 94 B3
Bou Arada Tunisia 45 B6
Bouârfa Morocco 91 E2
Bou Aroua Alg. 91 G2
Bouba Ndjida, Parc National de nat. park Cameroon 93 I3
Boû Bleï'îne well Mauritania 92 C1
Boubout well Alg. 90 D4
Bouca Cent. Afr. Rep. 94 C3
Boucaut Bay Australia 110 C2
Bouctouche Canada 125 H4
Boû Djébéha well Mali 93 E1
Boudoua Cent. Afr. Rep. 94 C3
Bouenza admin. reg. Congo 95 B6
Bouenza r. Congo 94 B6
Bougainville, Cape Australia 108 D3
Bougainville Island P.N.G. 107 E2
Boughessa Mali 93 F1
Bougie Alg. see Bejaïa
Bougoumen Chad 94 B2
Bougouni Mali 92 D3
Bougtob Alg. 91 F2
Boû Guendoûz well Mali 92 D1
Bougzoul Alg. 43 H5
Bouillon Belgium 39 F2
Bouira Alg. 91 F1
Bou Izakarn Morocco 90 C3
Boujdour W. Sahara 90 B4
Boukoumbé Benin 93 F3
Boulder Australia 109 C7
Boulder CO U.S.A. 134 F4
Boulder MT U.S.A. 134 D3
Boulder UT U.S.A. 137 G3
Boulder Canyon gorge U.S.A. 137 E3
Boulder City U.S.A. 137 E4
Boulemane Morocco 90 D2
Boulemane Morocco 90 D2
Boulevard U.S.A. 137 D5
Boulhaut Morocco see Ben Slimane
Boulia Australia 111 D4
Boulogne France see Boulogne-sur-Mer
Boulogne r. France 38 C3
Boulogne-Billancourt France 38 E2
Boulogne-sur-Mer France 38 D1
Boulou r. Cent. Afr. Rep. 94 E3
Boulouba Cent. Afr. Rep. 94 D3
Bouloupari New Caledonia 107 F4
Boulsa Burkina 93 E2
Boultoum Niger 93 H2
Boumango Gabon 94 B5
Boumba r. Cameroon 94 B4
Boumbé I r. Cent. Afr. Rep. 94 B3
Boumerdes Alg. 91 F1
Bouna Côte d'Ivoire 92 E3
Bou Naceur, Jbel mt. Morocco 90 E2
Boû Nâga Mauritania 92 B1
Boundary U.S.A. 122 A1
Boundary Peak U.S.A. 136 C3
Boundiali Côte d'Ivoire 92 D3
Boung r. Vietnam 61 E4
Boungou r. Cent. Afr. Rep. 94 D3
Bountiful U.S.A. 134 E4
Bounty Islands N.Z. 107 G6
Bounty Trough sea feature S. Pacific Ocean 164 F9
Bourail New Caledonia 107 F4
Bourbince r. France 39 F3
Bourbon-Lancy France 39 E3
Bourbonne-les-Bains France 39 F3
Bourem Mali 93 E1
Bouressa Mali see Boughessa
Bourganeuf France 38 D4
Bourg-en-Bresse France 39 F3
Bourges France 38 E3
Bourgneuf, Baie de b. France 38 B3
Bourgogne admin. reg. France 39 F3
Bourgoin-Jallieu France 39 F4
Bourg-St-Andéol France 39 F4
Bourg-St-Maurice France 39 G4
Bourke Australia 111 F6
Bournemouth U.K. 35 F6
Bouroum-Bouroum Burkina 92 E3
Bourtoutou Chad 94 D2
Bourzanga Burkina 93 E2
Bou Saâda Alg. 91 G2
Bou Salem Tunisia 45 B6
Bouse U.S.A. 137 E5
Bouse Wash watercourse U.S.A. 137 E4
Boussé Burkina 93 E2
Bousso Chad 94 C2
Boû Tezâya well Mauritania 92 C1
Boutilimit Mauritania 92 B1
Boutougou Fara Senegal 92 B2

▶Bouvetøya terr. S. Atlantic Ocean 161 O9
Dependency of Norway.

Boven Kapuas Mountains Indon./Malaysia see Kapuas Hulu, Pegunungan
Bow r. Australia 108 E4
Bow r. Alta Canada 123 I5
Bow r. Alta Canada 134 E2
Bowa China see Muli
Bowbells U.S.A. 132 A1
Bowden U.S.A. 130 D4
Bowen Arg. 152 D3
Bowen Australia 111 G4
Bowen r. Australia 111 F4
Bowen, Mount Australia 112 D5
Bowen Downs Australia 111 F4
Bowers Ridge sea feature Bering Sea 164 F2
Bowie AZ U.S.A. 137 H5
Bowie TX U.S.A. 133 B5
Bow Island Canada 123 I5
Bowkan Iran 80 A2
Bowling Green KY U.S.A. 128 B4
Bowling Green MO U.S.A. 132 D4
Bowling Green OH U.S.A. 130 B3
Bowling Green VA U.S.A. 131 E4
Bowling Green Bay National Park Australia 111 F3
Bowman U.S.A. 134 G3
Bowman Island Antarctica 167 F2
Bowman Peninsula Antarctica 167 L2
Bown Somalia 96 D2
Bowo Sichuan China see Bomai
Bowo Xizang China see Bomi
Bowser Lake Canada 122 D3
Box Elder U.S.A. 132 A2
Box Elder r. U.S.A. 134 G3
Boxholm Sweden 33 D4
Boxtel Neth. 36 B3
Boyabat Turkey 78 C2
Boyaca dept Col. 146 C3
Boyalık Turkey see Çiçekdağı
Boyana tourist site Bulg. 46 C3
Boyang China 67 F2
Boyd Lagoon salt flat Australia 109 D6
Boyd Lake Canada 123 K2
Boydton U.S.A. 130 D5
Boyer r. U.S.A. 132 C3
Boyera Dem. Rep. Congo 94 C5
Boyertown U.S.A. 131 F3
Boykins U.S.A. 131 E5
Boyle Canada 123 H4
Boyle Rep. of Ireland 35 B5
Boyne r. Qld Australia 111 G4
Boyne r. Qld Australia 111 G5
Boyne r. Rep. of Ireland 35 C5
Boyni Qara Afgh. 81 F2
Boyo Cent. Afr. Rep. 94 D3
Boyoma, Chutes waterfall Dem. Rep. Congo see Boyoma Falls
Boyoma Falls Dem. Rep. Congo 94 E4
Boysun Uzbek. see Baysun
Boyuibe Bol. 149 E5
Boyup Brook Australia 109 B8
Bozashy Tübegi pen. Kazakh. see Buzachi, Poluostrov
Bozburun Turkey 78 B3

▶Bozcaada i. Turkey 78 A3
Most westerly point of Asia.

Bozdağ mt. Turkey 47 E5
Bozdağ mt. Turkey 77 C1
Boz Dağları mts Turkey 78 A3
Bozdoğan Turkey 78 B3
Bozeman U.S.A. 134 E3
Bozen Italy see Bolzano
Bozhou China 67 E1
Bozkır Turkey 78 C3
Bozouls France 39 E4
Bozoum Cent. Afr. Rep. 94 C3
Bozova Turkey 79 D3
Bozovici Romania 46 C2
Bozqūsh, Kūh-e mts Iran 80 A2
Bozüyük Turkey 78 B3
Bozyazı Turkey 77 A1
Bra Italy 44 A2
Brač i. Croatia 44 F3
Bracara Port. see Braga
Bracciano Italy 44 D3
Bracciano, Lago di l. Italy 44 D3
Bracebridge Canada 124 E4
Bräcke Sweden 32 D3
Brackettville U.S.A. 133 A6
Bračk Kanal sea chan. Croatia 44 F3
Bracknell U.K. 35 F6
Brad Romania 46 C1
Bradano r. Italy 45 F4
Bradenton U.S.A. 129 C7
Bradford U.K. 35 F5
Bradford PA U.S.A. 130 D3
Bradford VT U.S.A. 131 G2
Bradshaw U.S.A. 130 C5
Brady U.S.A. 133 B6
Braemar U.K. 34 E3
Braga Port. 42 B2
Braga admin. dist. Port. 42 B2
Bragado Arg. 152 E3
Bragança Brazil 150 C2
Bragança Port. 42 C2
Bragança admin. dist. Port. 42 C2
Brahmakund India 60 B2
Brahmanbaria Bangl. 75 F5
Brahmani r. India 73 E1
Brahmapur India 73 E2
Brahmaputra r. China/India 75 F4
also known as Dihang (India) or Yarlung Zangbo (China)
Brăila Romania 46 E2
Brăilei, Insula Mare a i. Romania 46 E2
Braine France 39 E2
Brainerd U.S.A. 132 C2
Braintree U.K. 35 G6
Braithwaite Point Australia 110 C1
Braives Belgium 39 F1
Brake (Unterweser) Germany 36 D2
Brâkna admin. reg. Mauritania 92 B1
Brakwater Namibia 98 C4
Bralorne Canada 122 F5
Bramhapuri India 72 C1
Bramming Denmark 33 C5
Brampton Canada 130 D2
Brampton U.K. 34 E4
Bramsche Germany 36 D2
Bramsöfjärden l. Sweden 33 E3
Brancaleone Italy 45 F6
Branch Canada 125 K4
Branco r. Mato Grosso Brazil 149 E2
Branco r. Roraima Brazil 147 F5
Brandberg mt. Namibia 98 B4
Brändbo Sweden 33 E3
Brandbu Norway 33 C3
Brande Denmark 33 C5
Brandenburg Germany 37 F2
Brandenburg land Germany 37 F2
Brandenburg U.S.A. 128 B4
Brändö Fin. 33 F3
Brandon Canada 134 H2
Brandon MS U.S.A. 133 D5
Brandon SD U.S.A. 132 B3
Brandon VT U.S.A. 131 G2
Brandon Head Rep. of Ireland 35 A5
Brandonville U.S.A. 130 D4
Brandvlei S. Africa 98 D6
Brandvoll Norway 32 E1
Brani, Pulau i. Sing. 58 [inset]
Braniewo Poland 37 I1
Brännberg Sweden 32 F2
Brannenburg Germany 36 F5
Bransfield Strait Antarctica 167 L2
Brantas r. Indon. 59 F4
Brantford Canada 130 C2
Brantôme France 38 D4
Brás Brazil 147 G5
Brasaljce Yugo. 46 B3
Bras d'Or Lake Canada 125 I4
Brasil country S. America see Brazil
Brasil, Planalto do plat. Brazil 151 D6
Brasileia Brazil 148 C2

▶Brasília Brazil 149 I3
Capital of Brazil.
southamerica 154

Brasília de Minas Brazil 151 C6
Brasília Legal Brazil 147 H5
Braslav Belarus see Braslaw
Braslaw Belarus 31 K2
Braşov Romania 46 D2
Brassey, Banjaran mts Sabah Malaysia 59 G1
Brassey Range hills Australia 109 C6
Bratan mt. Bulg. 46 D3

▶Bratislava Slovakia 37 H4
Capital of Slovakia.

Bratsk Rus. Fed. 27 K4
Bratskoye Vodokhranilishche resr Rus. Fed. 27 K4
Brattleboro U.S.A. 131 G2
Brattmon Sweden 33 D3
Brattvåg Norway 32 B3
Bratunac Bos.-Herz. 46 A2
Braunau am Inn Austria 37 F4
Braunschweig Germany 36 E2
Brava i. Cape Verde 92 [inset]
Brave U.S.A. 130 C4
Bråviken inlet Sweden 33 E4
Bravo, Cerro mt. Bol. 148 D4
Bravo del Norte, Río r. Mex. 133 B7
Bravo del Norte, Río r. Mex./U.S.A. see Rio Grande
Brawley U.S.A. 137 E5
Bray Rep. of Ireland 35 C5
Braye r. France 38 D3
Bray-sur-Seine France 39 E2
Brazeau r. Canada 123 H4

►Brazil country S. America **150** B4
Largest country in South America and
5th in the world. Most populous country
in South America and 5th in the world.
southamerica **144–145, 154**
world **8–9, 14–15, 16–17**

Brazil Basin sea feature S. Atlantic Ocean
160 M7
Brazos r. U.S.A. **133** C6

►Brazzaville Congo **95** B3
Capital of Congo.

Brčko Bos.-Herz. **44** G2
Brda r. Poland **37** I2
Brdy hills Czech Rep. **37** F4
Bré Rep. of Ireland see Bray
Breaksea Sound inlet N.Z. **113** A4
Breaksea Spit Australia **111** H5
Bream Bay N.Z. **113** E1
Breas Chile **152** C1
Breaza Romania **46** D2
Brebes Indon. **59** E4
Brechin U.K. **34** E3
Brecht Belgium **36** B3
Breckenridge CO U.S.A. **134** F5
Breckenridge MN U.S.A. **132** B2
Breckenridge TX U.S.A. **133** B5
Brecknock, Peninsula pen. Chile **153** B8
Brecon U.K. **35** E6
Brecon Beacons reg. U.K. **35** E6
Brecon Beacons National Park U.K.
35 E6
Breda Neth. **36** B3
Bredasdorp S. Africa **98** C7
Bredviken Sweden **32** G2
Breginica r. Macedonia **46** B4
Bregenz Austria **36** D5
Bregovo Bulg. **46** C3
Bréhal France **38** C2
Breiðafjörður Iceland **32** [inset]
Breiðdalsvík Iceland **32** [inset]
Breil-sur-Roya France **39** H5
Breivikeidet Norway **32** E1
Brejo r. Brazil **150** D4
Brejo da Porta Brazil **150** C4
Brekstad Norway **32** C3
Bremen Germany **36** D2
Bremen GA U.S.A. **129** B5
Bremen OH U.S.A. **130** D4
Bremer Bay Australia **109** B8
Bremerhaven Germany **36** D2
Bremer Range hills Australia **109** C8
Bremersdorp see Manzini
Bremervörde Germany **36** D2
Bren r. Poland **37** J3
Brenham U.S.A. **133** B6
Brenna Norway **32** D2
Brennero Italy **44** C1
Brennero, Passo di pass Austria/Italy
see Brenner Pass
Brennerpaß pass Austria/Italy see
Brenner Pass
Brenner Pass Austria/Italy **36** E5
Breno Italy **44** C2
Brenta r. Italy **44** C2
Brenta, Gruppo di mts Italy **44** C1
Brentwood U.K. **35** G6
Brenzone Italy **44** C2
Brescia Italy **44** C2
Breslau Germany see Wrocław
Bresle r. France **38** D1
Brésolles, Lac l. Canada **125** G2
Bressanone Italy **44** C1
Bressay i. U.K. **34** F1
Bressuire France **38** C3
Brest Belarus **31** J2
Brest France **38** A2
Brest-Litovsk Belarus see Brest
Brestovac Rus. Fed. **46** D3
Bretagne admin. reg. France **38** B2
Brețcu Romania **46** F1
Breteuil Haute-Normandie France **38** D2
Breteuil Picardie France **38** E2
Breton Canada **123** H4
Breton Sound b. U.S.A. **129** A6
Brett, Cape N.Z. **113** E1
Bretten Germany **36** D4
Breu r. Brazil/Peru **148** C2
Breueh, Pulau i. Indon. **58** A1
Brevard U.S.A. **128** C5
Breves Brazil **150** B2
Brewarrina Australia **112** C3
Brewster NE U.S.A. **132** B3
Brewster OH U.S.A. **130** C3
Brewster WA U.S.A. **134** C2
Brewster, Kap c. Greenland see
Kangikajik
Brewton U.S.A. **129** B6
Breytovo Rus. Fed. **28** F4
Brezhnev Rus. Fed. see
Naberezhnyye Chelny
Brežice Slovenia **44** F2
Breznik Bulg. **46** C3
Breznitsa Bulg. **46** C4
Brezno Slovakia **37** I4
Brezovo Bulg. **46** D3
Brezovo Polje hill Croatia **44** F2
Bria Cent. Afr. Rep. **94** D3
Briakan Rus. Fed. **64** C1
Briançon France **39** G4
Brian Head mt. U.S.A. **137** F3
Briare France **39** E3
Briceni Moldova **29** C6
Brichany Moldova see Briceni
Bridgehampton U.S.A. **131** G3
Bridgeport AL U.S.A. **133** E5
Bridgeport CA U.S.A. **136** C2
Bridgeport CT U.S.A. **131** I3
Bridgeport MI U.S.A. **130** D2
Bridgeport NE U.S.A. **134** G4
Bridgeport TX U.S.A. **133** B5
Bridger Peak U.S.A. **134** F4
Bridgeton U.S.A. **131** F4
Bridgetown Australia **109** B8

►Bridgetown Barbados **147** G1
Capital of Barbados.

Bridgetown Canada **125** I4
Bridgeville U.S.A. **131** F4
Bridgewater Australia **112** C6
Bridgewater MA U.S.A. **131** H3
Bridgewater NY U.S.A. **131** F2
Bridgewater VA U.S.A. **130** D4
Bridgton U.S.A. **131** H1
Bridgwater U.K. **35** E6
Bridgwater Bay U.K. **35** E6
Brie reg. France **39** E2
Briec France **38** B2
Brie-Comte-Robert France **39** E2
Brienne-le-Château France **39** F2
Brienzer See l. Switz. **39** G3
Briery Knob mt. U.S.A. **130** C4
Brig Switz. **39** G3
Brigham City U.S.A. **134** E4
Brighton Canada **130** E1
Brighton U.K. **35** F6

Brighton CO U.S.A. **134** F5
Brighton MI U.S.A. **130** B2
Brighton NY U.S.A. **130** E2
Brighton WV U.S.A. **130** B4
Brighton Downs Australia **111** E4
Brignoles France **39** G5
Brikama Gambia **92** A2
Brilon Germany **36** D3
Brindisi Italy **45** H4
Brinkley U.S.A. **133** D5
Brionne France **38** D2
Brioude France **39** E4
Brisay Canada **125** G2

►Brisbane Australia **111** H5
State capital of Queensland and 3rd
most populous city in Oceania.

Brisighella Italy **44** C2
Bristol U.K. **35** E6
Bristol CT U.S.A. **131** I3
Bristol FL U.S.A. **129** B6
Bristol NH U.S.A. **131** H2
Bristol RI U.S.A. **131** I3
Bristol TN U.S.A. **130** B5
Bristol VT U.S.A. **131** I1
Bristol Bay U.S.A. **120** C4
Bristol Channel est. U.K. **35** D6
Bristol Lake U.S.A. **137** E4
Bristol Mountains U.S.A. **137** E4
Britannia Island New Caledonia see Maré
British Antarctic Territory Antarctica
167 L2
British Columbia prov. Canada **122** F5
British Empire Range mts Canada
121 K1
British Guiana country S. America see
Guyana
British Honduras country
Central America see Belize

►British Indian Ocean Territory terr.
Indian Ocean **162** L4
United Kingdom Overseas Territory.
asia **52–53, 82**

British Solomon Islands country
S. Pacific Ocean see Solomon Islands
Brito Godins Angola see Kiwaba N'zogi
Brits S. Africa **99** E5
Britstown S. Africa **98** D6
Brittany admin. reg. France see Bretagne
Brittany reg. France **38** B2
Britton U.S.A. **132** B2
Brive-la-Gaillarde France **38** D4
Briviesca Spain **42** E1
Brixia Italy see Brescia
Brlik Kazakh. **70** D3
Broach India see Bharuch
Broad r. U.S.A. **129** C5
Broad Arrow Australia **109** C7
Broadback r. Canada **124** E3
Broad Bay U.K. **34** C2
Broadford U.K. **34** D3
Broad Law mt. U.K. **34** E4
Broadmere Australia **110** C3
Broad Sound sea chan. Australia
111 G4
Broadsound Range hills Australia
111 G4
Broadus U.S.A. **134** F3
Broadway U.S.A. **130** D4
Broadwood N.Z. **113** C1
Broby Sweden **33** D4
Brochet Canada **123** K3
Brocken mt. Germany **36** E3
Brockman, Mount Australia **108** B5
Brockport NY U.S.A. **130** E2
Brockport PA U.S.A. **130** D3
Brockton U.S.A. **131** H2
Brockville Canada **131** F1
Brockway U.S.A. **130** D3
Brod Macedonia **46** B4
Broderick Falls Kenya see Webuye
Brodeur Peninsula Canada **121** K2
Brodhead U.S.A. **130** A5
Brodheadsville U.S.A. **131** F3
Brodick U.K. **34** D4
Brodnica Poland **37** I2
Brody Ukr. **29** C6
Brok r. Poland **37** J2
Broken Arrow U.S.A. **133** C4
Broken Bow NE U.S.A. **132** B3
Broken Bow OK U.S.A. **133** C5
Broken Bow Reservoir U.S.A. **133** C5
Brokenhead r. Canada **123** L5
Broken Hill Australia **112** B3
Broken Hill Zambia see Kabwe
Broken Plateau sea feature
Indian Ocean **163** N8
Brokopondo Suriname **147** H3
Brokopondo Stuwmeer resr Suriname
see Professor van Blommestein Meer
Bromberg Poland see Bydgoszcz
Bromo Tengger Semeru National Park
Indon. **59** F4
Brønderslev Denmark **33** C4
Brong-Ahafo admin. reg. Ghana **93** G4
Brønnøysund Norway **32** D2
Bronson U.S.A. **132** C3
Bronte Sicily Italy **45** E6
Brooke's Point Phil. **56** E4
Brookfield U.S.A. **132** C4
Brookhaven U.S.A. **127** H5
Brookings OR U.S.A. **134** A4
Brookings SD U.S.A. **132** B2
Brookline U.S.A. **131** H2
Brooklyn Center U.S.A. **132** C2
Brooklyn Park U.S.A. **132** C2
Brookneal U.S.A. **130** D5
Brooks Canada **134** E2
Brooks U.S.A. **131** I1
Brooks Brook Canada **122** C2
Brooks Range mts U.S.A. **120** E3
Brooksville FL U.S.A. **129** D6
Brooksville KY U.S.A. **130** A4
Brookton Australia **109** B8
Brookville U.S.A. **130** D3
Broom, Loch inlet U.K. **34** D3
Broome Australia **108** C4
Broomehill Australia **109** B8
Broons France **38** B2
Brora r. U.K. **34** E2
Brøstadbotn Norway **32** E1
Brosville U.S.A. **130** D5
Brothers U.S.A. **134** B4
Brou France **38** D2
Broughton Island Canada see
Qikiqtarjuaq
Broulkou well Chad **88** C3
Brovary Ukr. **29** D6
Brown City U.S.A. **130** B2
Brown Creek r. Australia **111** B3
Browne Range hills Australia **109** D6
Brownfield U.S.A. **133** A5
Brown Mountain U.S.A. **136** D4
Brownstown U.S.A. **128** D4
Brownsville PA U.S.A. **130** D3
Brownsville TN U.S.A. **128** A5
Brownsville TX U.S.A. **133** B7
Brownsweg Suriname **147** H3
Brownwood U.S.A. **133** B6
Browse Island Australia **108** C3
Brozas Spain **42** C3

Bruay-la-Bussière France **39** E1
Bruce U.S.A. **132** C2
Bruce Rock Australia **109** B7
Bruchsal Germany **36** D4
Bruck an der Leitha Austria **37** H4
Bruck an der Mur Austria **37** G5
Bruges Belgium see Brugge
Brugge Belgium **36** A3
Bruin KY U.S.A. **130** D4
Bruin PA U.S.A. **130** D3
Bruin Point mt. U.S.A. **137** G2
Bruint India **66** A2
Brukkaros Namibia **98** C5
Brûlé Canada **122** G4
Brûlé, Lac l. Canada **125** I2
Brumado Brazil **150** D5
Brumer Islands P.N.G. **111** G1
Brú Na Bóinne tourist site
Rep. of Ireland **35** F4
Brundisium Italy see Brindisi
Bruneau U.S.A. **134** D4
►Brunei country Asia **59** F1
asia **52–53, 82**
Brunei Brunei see Bandar Seri Begawan
Brunei Bay Malaysia **59** F1
Brunette Downs Australia **110** C3
Brunflo Sweden **32** D3
Brunico Italy **44** C1
Brünn Czech Rep. see Brno
Brunna Sweden **33** D4
Brunner, Lake N.Z. **113** B3
Bruno Canada **134** F1
Brunsbüttel Germany **36** D2
Brunswick Germany see Braunschweig
Brunswick GA U.S.A. **129** C6
Brunswick ME U.S.A. **131** I2
Brunswick MO U.S.A. **132** C4
Brunswick NY U.S.A. **130** E3
Brunswick OK U.S.A. **132** B4
Brunswick SD U.S.A. **134** G4
Brunswick TX U.S.A. **133** B6
Brunswick WY U.S.A. **134** F5
Brunswick Bay Australia **108** D3
Brunswick Junction Australia **109** A8
Brunswick Lake Canada **124** D3
Brunswick, Península de pen. Chile
153 C8
Bruntál Czech Rep. **37** H4
Brunt Ice Shelf Antarctica **167** B2
Bruny Island Australia **112** C6
Brus Yugo. **46** B3
Brush U.S.A. **134** G4
Brusque Brazil **151** B8
Brussel Belgium see Brussels
►Brussels Belgium **39** F1
Capital of Belgium.
europe **48**
Brusy Poland **37** H2
Bruthen Australia **112** C6
Bruxelles Belgium see Brussels
Bruyères France **39** G2
Bruzual Venez. **146** D2
Bryan OH U.S.A. **130** A3
Bryan TX U.S.A. **133** B6
Bryan, Mount Australia **112** A4
Bryan Coast Antarctica **167** L2
Bryansk Rus. Fed. **29** E5
Bryanskaya Oblast' admin. div.
Rus. Fed. **29** E5
Bryansk Oblast admin. div. Rus. Fed.
see Bryanskaya Oblast'
Bryanskoye Rus. Fed. **79** F1
Bryant Pond U.S.A. **131** H1
Bryce Canyon National Park U.S.A.
137 F3
Bryce Mountains U.S.A. **137** H5
Bryne Norway **33** A4
Bryukhovetskaya Rus. Fed. **29** F7
Brzava r. Yugo. **46** B2
Brzeg Poland **37** H3
Brzeg Dolny Poland **37** H3
Brześć nad Bugiem Belarus see Brest
Brzozów Poland **37** K4
Bua Angola **95** B6
Bu'aale Somalia **96** D4
Buala Solomon Is. **107** E2
Buandougou Côte d'Ivoire see
Bouandougou
Buatan Indon. **58** C2
Bū Athlah well Libya **88** D2
Bu'ayj well Saudi Arabia **80** B5
Bu'ayrāt al Ḥasūn Libya **88** B2
Bubanza Burundi **94** F5
Bubi r. Zimbabwe **99** F4
Būbiyān Island Kuwait **79** G5
Buca Turkey **47** E5
Bucak Turkey **78** B3
Bucaramanga Col. **146** C3
Buccaneer Archipelago is Australia
108 C4
Buchan Indon. **58** C2
Buchan Australia **112** D5
Buchanan Liberia **92** A4
Buchanan U.S.A. **130** D5
Buchanan, Lake salt flat Australia
111 F4
Buchan Gulf Canada **121** L2
Buchans Canada **125** J3

►Bucharest Romania **46** E2
Capital of Romania.

Buchen (Odenwald) Germany **36** D4
Bucholz in der Nordheide Germany
36 D2
Buchon, Point U.S.A. **136** B4
Bucin, Pasul pass Romania **46** D1
Bückeburg Germany **36** D2
Buckeye U.S.A. **137** F5
Buckhannon U.S.A. **130** C4
Buckhannon r. U.S.A. **130** D4
Buckhaven U.K. **34** E3
Buckie U.K. **34** F3
Buckingham U.K. **35** F5
Buckingham PA U.S.A. **131** F3
Buckingham VA U.S.A. **130** D5
Buckland U.S.A. **120** C3
Buckland Tableland reg. Australia
111 G5
Buckleboo Australia **109** G8
Buckle Island Antarctica **167** H2
Buckley watercourse Australia **110** D4
Buckley Bay Antarctica **167** G2
Buckskin Mountains U.S.A. **137** F4
Bucksport U.S.A. **131** I1
Bučovice Czech Rep. **37** H4
București Romania see Bucharest
Bucyrus U.S.A. **130** D3
Bud Norway **32** B3
Buda, Illa de i. Spain **43** G2
Buda-Kashalyova Belarus **31** L2
Budalin Myanmar **60** A3

►Budapest Hungary **37** I5
Capital of Hungary.

Budaun India **74** C3
Bud Bud Somalia **96** E3
Budd Coast Antarctica **167** F2
Buddi Eth. **96** E3
Buddusò Sardinia Italy **45** B4
Bude U.K. **35** D6
Budennovsk Rus. Fed. **29** H7
Buderim Australia **111** H5
Budeşti Romania **46** E2
Budiyah, Jabal hills Egypt **77** A5
Budogoshch' Rus. Fed. **28** E4
Budoni Sardinia Italy **45** B4
Budongquan China **75** G2

Büdszentmihály Hungary see
Tiszavasvári
Budva Yugo. **46** A3
Budwang National Park Australia
112 D4
Budweis Czech Rep. see
České Budějovice
Buea Cameroon **93** H4
Buěch r. France **39** F4
Buellton U.S.A. **136** B4
Buena Esperanza Arg. **152** D3
Buenaventura Col. **146** B3
Buenaventura Mex. **135** F7
Buena Vista Bol. **148** E4
Buena Vista i. N. Mariana Is. see Tinian
Buena Vista CO U.S.A. **134** F5
Buena Vista VA U.S.A. **130** D5
Buendia, Embalse de resr Spain **43** E3
Buenga r. Angola **95** B6
Buengas Angola **95** B6
Buenópolis Brazil **151** B2

►Buenos Aires Arg. **152** E4
Capital of Argentina. 2nd most populous
city in South America.
southamerica **154**
world **16–17**

Buenos Aires prov. Arg. **152** E4
Buenos Aires Amazonas Col. **146** D5
Buenos Aires Guaviare Col. **146** C4
Buenos Aires, Lago l. Arg./Chile
153 B6
Buen Pasto Arg. **153** C6
Buen Tiempo, Cabo c. Arg. **153** C7
Buerarema Brazil **150** E5
Buesaco Col. **146** B4
Bueu Spain **42** B1
Bufalo Mex. **135** F8
Buffalo r. Canada **123** H2
Buffalo MO U.S.A. **132** C4
Buffalo NY U.S.A. **130** E2
Buffalo OK U.S.A. **132** B4
Buffalo SD U.S.A. **134** G3
Buffalo TX U.S.A. **133** B6
Buffalo WY U.S.A. **134** G3
Buffalo r. U.S.A. **133** A5
Buffalo Head Hills Canada **123** G3
Buffalo Head Prairie Canada **123** G3
Buffalo Hump mt. U.S.A. **134** D3
Buffalo Lake Alta Canada **123** H4
Buffalo Lake N.W.T. Canada **123** H2
Buffalo Narrows Canada **123** I4
Buffalo Range Zimbabwe **99** F4
Buffels watercourse S. Africa **98** C6
Buffels Drift S. Africa **99** F6
Buford U.S.A. **129** B5
Buftea Romania **46** E2
Bug r. Poland **37** K3
Buga Col. **146** B4
Bugala Island Uganda **96** A4
Bugana Nigeria **93** G3
Bugarach, Pic de mt. France **38** E5
Bugeat France **38** D4
Bugel, Tanjung pt Indon. **59** E4
Bugojno Bos.-Herz. **44** F2
Bugrino Rus. Fed. **28** I1
Bugsuk i. Phil. **56** E4
Bugul'ma Rus. Fed. **28** J5
Bügür China see Luntai
Buguruslan Rus. Fed. **29** J5
Bühäbäd Iran **80** D4
Buharkent Turkey **47** F6
Buhera Zimbabwe **99** F3
Buhoro Flats plain Tanz. **97** B7
Buhu r. Tanz. **97** B6
Buhuşi Romania **46** E1
Buick Canada **122** F3
Builth Wells U.K. **35** E5
Buin P.N.G. **107** F2
Bui National Park Ghana **93** E3
Buinsk Rus. Fed. **28** J5
Bu'in Zahra Iran **80** B3
Buir Nur l. Mongolia **63** J2
Buitepos Namibia **98** C4
Bujalance Spain **42** D4
Bujanovac Yugo. **46** B3
Bujoru Romania **46** D3

►Bujumbura Burundi **94** F5
Capital of Burundi.

Buk Poland **37** H2
Bukachacha Rus. Fed. **63** J1
Buka Island P.N.G. **107** E2
Bukavu Dem. Rep. Congo **95** E7
Bukedi Dem. Rep. Congo **94** F5
Bukene Tanz. **97** B6
Bukeya Dem. Rep. Congo **95** E7
Bukhara Uzbek. **81** F2
Bukhara Oblast admin. div. Uzbek. see
Bukharskaya Oblast'
Bukharskaya Oblast' admin. div. Uzbek.
81 E1
Bukhoro Uzbek. see Bukhara
Bukhoro Wiloyati admin. div. Uzbek. see
Bukharskaya Oblast'
Bukima Tanz. **96** A4
Bukit Baka Bukit Raya National Park
Indon. **59** F3
Bukit Timah Sing. **58** [inset]
Bukit Timah hill Sing. **58** [inset]
Bukittinggi Indon. **58** C3
Bükk mts Hungary **37** J4
Bükki nat. park Hungary **37** J4
Bükkszérc Hungary **37** J5
Bukoba Tanz. **96** A5
Bukowo, Jezioro lag. Poland **37** H1
Bukrane Indon. **108** E1
Bükres Mex. see Bucharest
Buku, Tanjung pt Indon. **58** D3
Bukum, Pulau i. Sing. **58** [inset]
Būl, Küh-e mt. Iran **80** C4
Bula Indon. **57** H6
Bülach Switz. **39** H3
Bulancak Turkey **79** D2
Bulandshahr India **74** C3
Bulanık Turkey **79** D3
Bulava Rus. Fed. **64** E2
Bulawayo Zimbabwe **99** F4
Buldan Turkey **78** B3
Buldana India **72** C1
Buldibuyo Peru **148** A2
Buldir Island U.S.A. **120** A4
Bulei well Eth. **96** E3
Bulembu Swaziland **99** F5
Bulgan Mongolia **62** G2
Bulgar Rus. Fed. see Bolgar

►Bulgaria country Europe **46** D3
europe **24–25, 48**

Bŭlgarska country Europe see Bulgaria
Bulkley Ranges mts Canada **122** D4
Bullaque r. Spain **42** D3
Bullas Spain **43** F3
Bulle Switz. **39** G3
Bullen r. Canada **123** K1
Buller r. N.Z. **113** B3
Bulleringa National Park Australia
111 E3

Bullfinch Australia **109** B7
Bullhead City U.S.A. **137** E4
Bullion Mountains **137** D4
Bullo r. Australia **110** B2
Bulloo watercourse Australia **111** E6
Bulloo Downs Australia **111** E6
Bulloo Lake salt flat Australia **111** E6
Bull Shoals Lake U.S.A. **133** C4
Bulman Australia **110** C2
Bulman Gorge Australia **110** C2
Bulmer Lake Canada **122** F2
Buloh, Pulau i. Sing. **58** [inset]
Bulolo P.N.G. **57** K7
Bulqizë Albania **46** B4
Bulu, Gunung mt. Indon. **59** G3
Buluk well Kenya **96** C3
Bulukumba Indon. **57** F7
Bulun Rus. Fed. **27** N2
Bulungu Bandundu Dem. Rep. Congo
95 C6
Bulungu Kasai Occidental
Dem. Rep. Congo **95** D6
Bulungur Uzbek. **81** F2
Bumba Bandundu Dem. Rep. Congo
95 C6
Bumba Équateur Dem. Rep. Congo **94** D4
Bumbah, Khalīj b. Libya **88** D1
Bumbeşti-Jiu Romania **46** C2
Bumhkāng Myanmar **60** B2
Bumpha Bum mt. Myanmar **60** B2
Buna Dem. Rep. Congo **95** C5
Buna Kenya **96** C4
Bunazi Tanz. **96** A5
Bunbury Australia **109** A8
Bunclody Rep. of Ireland **35** C5
Buncrana Rep. of Ireland **34** C4
Bunda Tanz. **96** B5
Bundaberg Australia **111** H5
Bundaleer Australia **111** F6
Bundi India **74** B4
Bundibugyo Uganda **96** A4
Bundjalung National Park Australia
112 D3
Bundoran Rep. of Ireland **35** B4
Bundu India **75** D5
Bunduqiya Sudan **96** A3
Bunë r. Albania/Yugo. **46** A4
Bunga r. Nigeria **93** G3
Bungalaut, Selat sea chan. Indon. **58** B3
Bungendore Australia **112** D4
Bunger Hills Antarctica **167** F2
Bungil Creek r. Australia **111** G5
Bungle Bungle National Park Australia
see Purnululu National Park
Bungo Angola **95** B6
Bungo-suidō sea chan. Japan **65** C6
Bunguran, Kepulauan is Indon. see
Natuna, Kepulauan
Bunguran, Pulau i. Indon. see
Natuna Besar
Bunia Dem. Rep. Congo **96** A4
Buningonia well Australia **109** C7
Bunji Jammu and Kashmir **74** B2
Bunker France see Bordeaux
Bunker Group atolls Australia **111** H4
Bunkie U.S.A. **133** D6
Bunnell U.S.A. **129** D6
Buñol Spain **43** F4
Buntok Indon. **59** F3
Buntokecil Indon. **59** F3
Bununu Nigeria **93** H3
Bunya Mountains National Park
Australia **111** G5
Būnyan Turkey **78** C3
Bunyu i. Indon. **59** G2
Bunza Nigeria **93** G3
Buonconvento Italy **44** C3
Buôn Mê Thuột Vietnam **61** E5
Buorkhaya, Guba b. Rus. Fed. **27** N2
Bup r. China **75** D4
Buqaya Saudi Arabia see Abqaiq
Buqayq Egypt **77** A4
Bu'in Zahrā Iran **80** B3
Bura Kenya **96** C5
Burakin Australia **109** B7
Buram Sudan **94** D2
Burang China **62** C5
Burao Somalia **96** E2
Burao Dem. Rep. Congo **94** C5
Buraydah Saudi Arabia **89** I3
Brayevo Rus. Fed. **28** J5
Burbach Germany **36** D3
Burbank U.S.A. **136** C4
Burcher Australia **112** C4
Burdalyk Turkm. **81** F2
Burdekin r. Australia **111** F3
Burdekin Falls Australia **111** F4
Burdigala France see Bordeaux
Burdur Turkey **78** B3
Burdwan India see Barddhaman
Burë Eth. **96** C2
Bure r. U.K. **35** G5
Bureinskiy Khrebet mts Rus. Fed. **64** C2
Bureiqa well Sudan **89** F5
Bureya r. Rus. Fed. **64** C2
Bureya-Pristan' Rus. Fed. **64** C2
Bureya Range mts Rus. Fed. see
Bureinskiy Khrebet
Burgas Bulg. **46** F3
Burgaw U.S.A. **129** E5
Burg bei Magdeburg Germany **36** E2
Burgdorf Germany **36** E2
Burgdorf Switz. **39** G3
Burgeo Canada **125** J4
Burgersdorp S. Africa **99** E6
Burgersfort S. Africa **99** F5
Burgess U.S.A. **131** F5
Burget Tuyur waterhole Sudan **89** E4
Burghausen Germany **37** F4
Burgin China **70** I2
Burgos Mex. **133** B7
Burgos Spain **42** E1
Burgsvik Sweden **33** E4
Burhabalanga r. India **75** E5
Burhan Budai Shan mts China **70** H4
Burhaniye Turkey **47** E5
Burhanpur India **74** C5
Burhar-Dhanpuri India **75** D5
Burhi Gandak r. India **75** E4
Buriat-Mongol Republic aut. rep.
Rus. Fed. see Buryatiya, Respublika
Buriram Thai. **61** C5
Burin Canada **125** K4
Buriram Thai. **61** C5
Buriti Brazil **150** D2
Buriti r. Brazil **149** H3
Buriti Alegre Brazil **149** H4
Buriti Bravo Brazil **150** D3
Buritirama Brazil **150** D5
Buritis Brazil **150** C5
Burjassot Spain **43** F3
Burjuk India **75** E4
Burkburnett U.S.A. **133** B5
Burke Island Antarctica **167** K2
Burke watercourse Australia **111** D4
Burketown Australia **111** D3
Burkeville U.S.A. **130** D5
Burkhala Rus. Fed. **27** O3

Burk's Falls Canada **124** E4
Burla Rus. Fed. **34** D4
Burlin Kazakh. **29** J6
Burlington Canada **130** F2
Burlington CO U.S.A. **134** G5
Burlington IA U.S.A. **132** D3
Burlington KS U.S.A. **132** C4
Burlington NC U.S.A. **128** D4
Burlington VT U.S.A. **131** G1
Burly Rus. Fed. **28** K5
Burma country Asia see Myanmar
Burnaby Canada **122** F5
Burnet U.S.A. **133** B6
Burnett r. Australia **111** H5
Burney U.S.A. **134** B4
Burney, Monte vol. Chile **153** B8
Burnham U.S.A. **131** I1
Burnie Australia **112** C6
Burning Springs U.S.A. **130** B5
Burns U.S.A. **134** C4
Burns r. Canada **123** I1
Burns Junction U.S.A. **134** C4
Burnside r. Canada **123** I1
Burnside, Lake salt flat Australia **109** C6
Burns Lake Canada **122** E4
Burnsville U.S.A. **130** C4
Burnt r. U.S.A. **134** D3
Burnt Lake Canada see Brûlé, Lac
Burntwood r. Canada **123** L4
Burntwood Lake Canada **123** K4
Burog Co l. China **75** G3
Burovoy Uzbek. **81** E1
Burqin China **70** G2
Burqu' Jordan **77** D3
Burra Australia **112** A4
Burra r. U.K. **34** F1
Burrel Albania **46** B4
Burrel U.S.A. **136** C3
Burren reg. Rep. of Ireland **35** B5
Burren Junction Australia **112** D3
Burriana Spain **43** F3
Burro, Serranías del mts Mex. **126** D3
Burr Oak Reservoir U.S.A. **130** B4
Burruyacú Arg. **152** D1
Bursa Turkey **78** B2
Bursa prov. Turkey **47** F4
Bür Safājah Egypt **89** G3
Bür Sa'īd Egypt see Port Said
Bür Sa'īd governorate Egypt **77** A4
Bursinskoye Vodokhranilishche resr
Rus. Fed. **29** J5
Bür Sudan Sudan see Port Sudan
Burt Lake U.S.A. **130** C1
Burton, Lac l. Canada **124** E2
Burton upon Trent U.K. **35** F5
Burträsk Sweden **32** F2
Burtundy Australia **112** B4
Burt Well Australia **110** C4
Buru i. Indon. **57** G6
Burük, Wādī al watercourse Egypt **77** A4
Burullus, Lake lag. Egypt **78** B5
Burultokay China see Fuhai
Burūn, Ra's pt Egypt **77** A4
►Burundi country Africa **95** F5
africa **86–87, 100**
Burunniy Rus. Fed. see Tsagan Aman
Burwash Landing Canada **122** B2
Burwell Rep. of Ireland **35** B5
Burwell U.S.A. **132** B3
Buryatia, Respublika aut. rep.
Rus. Fed. see
Buryatiya, Respublika aut. rep.
Rus. Fed. **63** I1
Buryatskaya A.S.S.R.
aut. rep. Rus. Fed. see
Buryatiya, Respublika
Buryn' Ukr. **29** E6
Burynshyk Kazakh. **29** I7
Bury St Edmunds U.K. **35** G5
Burzil Pass Jammu and Kashmir **74** B2
Busalla Italy **44** B2
Busan S. Korea see Pusan
Busanga Dem. Rep. Congo **94** D5
Busca Italy **44** A2
Buseire Syria see Al Buşayrah
Büsherehr Iran **80** B4
Büsherehr prov. Iran **80** B4
Bushenyi Uganda **96** A5
Bushire Iran see Büshehr
Bushkill U.S.A. **131** F3
Busia Kenya **96** B4
Busing, Pulau i. Sing. **58** [inset]
Businga Dem. Rep. Congo **94** C4
Busira r. Dem. Rep. Congo **94** C5
Buskerud county Norway **33** C3
Busselton Australia **109** A8
Busko-Zdrój Poland **37** J3
Buşteni Romania **46** E2
Bustillos, Lago l. Mex. **135** F7
Busto Arsizio Italy **44** B2
Büsum Germany **36** D1
Busu Modanda Dem. Rep. Congo **94** C4
Buta Dem. Rep. Congo **94** C4
Butajira Eth. **96** C2
Butan Bulg. **46** C3
Butang Group is Thai. **61** B7
Butare Rwanda **94** F5
Butaritari atoll Kiribati **164** F6
Bute i. U.K. **34** D4
Butembo Dem. Rep. Congo **94** E4
Butha Buthe Lesotho **99** F6
Buthidaung Myanmar **73** G1
Butiaba Uganda **96** A4
Butler AL U.S.A. **129** A5
Butler GA U.S.A. **129** B5
Butler IN U.S.A. **130** A3
Butler KY U.S.A. **130** A4
Butler MO U.S.A. **132** C4
Butler PA U.S.A. **130** D3
Buton i. Indon. **57** F6
Butrint, Liqeni i U.S.A. Albania **47** B5
Buttahatchee r. U.S.A. **129** A5
Butte U.S.A. **134** E3
Butterworth Malaysia **58** C1
Buttes, Sierra mt. U.S.A. **136** C2
Butt of Lewis hd U.K. **34** C2
Button Bay Canada **123** M3
Buttonwillow U.S.A. **136** C4
Butuan U.S.A. **57** F6
Buturlinovka Rus. Fed. **29** G6
Butwal Nepal **75** D4
Butzbach Germany **36** D3
Bützow Germany **36** E1
Buulobarde Somalia **96** E4
Buulohotha Somalia **96** E4
Buur Gaabo Somalia **96** D5
Buurhakaba Somalia **96** E4
Buvuma Island Uganda **96** A4
Buwārah, Jabal mt. Saudi Arabia **77** B5
Buwāṭah, Jabal mt. Saudi Arabia **89** H3
Buxar India **75** E4
Buxtehude Germany **36** D2
Buxton U.K. **35** F5
Buy Rus. Fed. **28** G4
Buy r. Rus. Fed. **28** K4
Buynaksk Rus. Fed. **79** F2
Buyo Côte d'Ivoire **92** B4
Buyo, Lac de l. Côte d'Ivoire **92** B4
Buyuan Jiang r. China **66** B4
Büyükada i. Turkey **47** F4
Büyük Egri Dağ mt. Turkey **77** A1
Büyükkarıştıran Turkey **46** E4

Büyükmenderes r. Turkey 78 A3
Buzachi, Poluostrov pen. Kazakh. 29 I7
Buzançais France 38 D3
Buzău Romania 46 E2
Buzău r. Romania 46 E2
Buzău r. Romania 46 E2
Buzaymah oasis Libya 88 D3
Buzdyak Rus. Fed. 28 J5
Búzi Moz. 99 G3
Búzi r. Moz. 99 G3
Buziaş Romania 46 B2
Büzmeyin Turkm. see Byuzmeyin
Buzuluk Rus. Fed. 29 J5
Buzuluk r. Rus. Fed. 29 G6
Buzzards Bay U.S.A. 131 H3
Bwagaoia P.N.G. 107 E3
Bwasiaiai P.N.G. 111 G1
Bwindi Impenetrable National Park Uganda 96 A5
Byakar Bhutan see Jakar
Byala Bulg. 46 D3
Byala Bulg. 46 E3
Byala Slatina Bulg. 46 C3
Byalynichy Belarus 29 D5
Byarezina r. Belarus 31 L2
Byaroza Belarus 29 C5
Byblos tourist site Lebanon 77 B2
Byczyna Poland 37 I3
Bydgoszcz Poland 37 I2
Byel'ki Belarus 33 G5
Byelorussia country Europe see Belarus
Byerazino Belarus 29 D5
Byers U.S.A. 134 F5
Byesville U.S.A. 130 C4
Byfield Australia 111 G4
Byfield National Park Australia 111 G4
Bygdeå Sweden 32 F2
Byglandsfjord Norway 33 B4
Bykhaw Belarus 29 D5
Bykhov Belarus see Bykhaw
Bykle Norway 33 B4
Bykovskiy Rus. Fed. 27 M2
Bylas U.S.A. 137 G5
Bylot Island Canada 121 L2
Bynoe r. Australia 111 E3
Byramgore Reef India 72 A4
Byrd Glacier Antarctica 167 H1
Byrkjelo Norway 33 B3
Byrock Australia 112 C3
Byron Island Kiribati see Nikunau
Byrranga, Gory mts Rus. Fed. 166 E2
Byske Sweden 32 F2
Byskeälven r. Sweden 32 F2
Byssa r. Rus. Fed. 64 B1
Bystrá mt. Slovakia 37 I4
Bystřice nad Pernštejnem Czech Rep. 37 H4
Bystryy Tanyp r. Rus. Fed. 28 J5
Bystrzyca r. Poland 37 H3
Bytantay r. Rus. Fed. 27 N3
Bytča Slovakia 37 I4
Bytom Poland 37 I3
Bytów Poland 37 H1
Byurgyutli Turkm. 80 C2
Byuzmeyin Turkm. 80 D2
Byxelkrok Sweden 33 E4
Byzantium Turkey see İstanbul
Bzura r. Poland 37 J2

↓ C

Ca, Sông r. Vietnam 60 D4
Caacupé Para. 149 F6
Caaguazú Para. 149 F6
Caaguazú, Cordillera de hills Para. 149 G6
Caála Angola 95 B8
Caapiranga Brazil 147 F5
Caapucú Para. 149 F6
Caarapó Brazil 151 A7
Caazapá Para. 149 F6
Cabaçal r. Brazil 149 F3
Caballas Peru 148 B3
Caballo mt. Spain 42 E4
Caballococha Peru 146 D5
Cabana Ancash Peru 148 A2
Cabana Ayacucho Peru 148 B3
Cabanaconde Peru 148 C3
Cabañaquinta Spain 42 D1
Cabanatuan Phil. 57 F2
Cabanères hill France 38 D5
Cabano Canada 125 G4
Čabar Croatia 44 E2
Cabdul Qaadir Somalia 96 D2
Cabeceiras Brazil 150 C5
Cabeço Rainha mt. Port. 42 C3
Cabedelo Brazil 150 F3
Cabeza del Buey Arg. 153 C5
Cabeza del Buey Spain 42 D3
Cabeza de Vaca, Punta pt Chile 152 C1
Cabezas Bol. 149 E4
Cabezo Gordo hill Spain 42 C4
Cabimas Venez. 146 D2
Cabinda Angola 95 B6
Cabinda prov. Angola 95 B6
Cabinet Inlet Antarctica 167 L2
Cabinet Mountains U.S.A. 134 D2
Cabistra Turkey see Ereğli
Cabo Brazil 150 F4
Cabo Blanco Arg. 153 D6
Cabo Delgado prov. Moz. 97 C8
Cabo Frio Brazil 151 D7
Cabonga, Réservoir Canada 124 E4
Cabool U.S.A. 132 C4
Caboolture Australia 111 H5
Cabo Orange, Parque Nacional de nat. park Brazil 147 I4
Cabo Pantoja Peru 146 C5
Cabora Bassa, Lake resr Moz. 99 F2
Cabo Raso Arg. 153 D6
Caborca Mex. 135 D7
Cabot Strait Canada 125 I4
Cabo Verde country N. Atlantic Ocean see Cape Verde
Cabo Verde, Ilhas do is N. Atlantic Ocean 92 [inset]
Cabo Yubi Morocco see Tarfaya
Cabra Spain 42 D4
Cabra r. Spain 42 D4
Cabral, Serra do mts Brazil 151 C6
Cabras Sardinia Italy 45 B5
Cabred Arg. 152 F2
Cabrela r. Port. 42 B3
Cabrera i. Spain 43 H3
Cabri Canada 123 I5
Cabriel r. Spain 43 F3
Cabrobó Brazil 150 E4
Cabruta Venez. 146 E3
Čabulja mt. Bos.-Herz. 44 F3
Caçador Brazil 151 B8
Cacagoin China see Qagca
Čačak Yugo. 46 B3
Cacao Fr. Guiana 147 H3
Caçapava do Sul Brazil 151 A9
Cacapon r. U.S.A. 130 D4
Cácares Col. 146 C3
Caccia, Capo c. Sardinia Italy 45 B4
Cacém Port. 42 B3
Cáceres Brazil 149 F4
Cáceres Spain 42 C3
Cache r. U.S.A. 133 D4
Cacheau r. Guinea-Bissau 92 A2
Cache Creek Canada 122 F5
Cache Creek r. U.S.A. 136 B2
Cache la Poudre r. U.S.A. 134 F4
Cacheu Guinea-Bissau 92 A2
Cachi Arg. 152 D1
Cachi, Nevados de mts Arg. 148 D6
Cachimbo Brazil 150 A4
Cachimbo, Serra do hills Brazil 150 A4
Cachingues Angola 95 C8
Cáchira Col. 146 C3
Cachoeira Alta Brazil 149 H4
Cachoeira do Arari Brazil 150 B2
Cachoeira do Sul Brazil 151 A9
Cachoeiro de Itapemirim Brazil 151 D7
Cachos, Punta de pt Chile 152 C1
Cachuela Esperanza Bol. 148 D2
Cacine Guinea-Bissau 92 B3
Caciporé, Cabo c. Brazil 147 I4
Cacolo Angola 95 C7
Caconda Angola 95 B8
Cacongo Angola 95 B6
Cactus U.S.A. 133 A4
Caçu Brazil 149 H4
Cacuaco Angola 95 B7
Cacula Angola 95 B8
Caculama Angola 95 C7
Caculé Brazil 150 D5
Cacuso Angola 95 B7
Cadale Somalia 96 E4
Čadca Slovakia 37 I4
Caddabassa i. Eth. 96 D2
Caddo Lake U.S.A. 133 C5
Cadell r. Australia 110 C2
Cadell Creek watercourse Australia 111 E4
Cadenberge Germany 36 D2
Cadereyta Mex. 126 F6
Cadí, Serra de mts Spain 43 G1
Cadibarrawirracanna, Lake salt flat Australia 110 C6
Cadillac Canada 123 J5
Cadillac U.S.A. 132 E2
Cádiz Spain 42 C4
Cadiz CA U.S.A. 137 E4
Cadiz KY U.S.A. 128 B4
Cadiz OH U.S.A. 130 C3
Cádiz, Bahía de b. Spain 42 C4
Cádiz, Golfo de g. Spain 42 C4
Cadiz Lake U.S.A. 137 E4
Cadomin Canada 123 G4
Caen France 38 C2
Caerdydd U.K. see Cardiff
Caere Italy see Cerveteri
Caerfyrddin U.K. see Carmarthen
Caergybi U.K. see Holyhead
Caernarfon U.K. 35 D5
Caernarfon Bay U.K. 35 D5
Caernarfon Castle tourist site U.K. 35 D5
Caernarvon U.K. see Caernarfon
Caesaraugusta Spain see Zaragoza
Caesarea Alg. see Cherchell
Caesarea tourist site Israel 77 B3
Caesarea Cappadociae Turkey see Kayseri
Caesarea Philippi Syria see Bāniyās
Caesarodunum France see Tours
Caesaromagus U.K. see Chelmsford
Cafayate Arg. 152 D1
Caffa Ukr. see Feodosiya
Cafuini r. Brazil 147 G4
Cagayan de Oro Phil. 57 F4
Cagli Italy 44 D3
Cagliari Sardinia Italy 45 B5
Cagliari, Golfo di b. Sardinia Italy 45 B5
Cagnes-sur-Mer France 39 G5
Caguán r. Col. 146 C5
Cahaba r. U.S.A. 129 B5
Cahama Angola 95 B9
Caha Mountains hills Rep. of Ireland 35 B6
Cahersiveen Rep. of Ireland 35 A6
Cahir Rep. of Ireland 35 C5
Cahirciveen Rep. of Ireland see Cahersiveen
Cahore Point Rep. of Ireland 35 C5
Cahors France 38 D4
Cahul Moldova 29 D7
Caia Moz. 99 G3
Caia r. Port. 42 C3
Caia, Barragem do resr Port. 42 C3
Caiabis, Serra dos hills Brazil 149 F3
Caianda Angola 95 D7
Caiapó, Serra do mts Brazil 149 G4
Caiapônia Brazil 149 H4
Caiaza Angola 95 D7
Cai Bâu, Đao i. Vietnam 60 D3
Cai Be Vietnam 61 D6
Caicara Venez. 147 E3
Caicó Brazil 150 E3
Caicos Islands Turks and Caicos Is 127 L7
Caidian China 67 E2
Caidu China see Shangcai
Caifuche Angola 95 D7
Caiguna Australia 109 D8
Cailloma Peru 148 C3
Caimodorro mt. Spain 43 F2
Căineni Romania 46 D2
Caineville U.S.A. 137 G2
Cainnyigoin China 66 B1
Cains Store U.S.A. 130 A5
Caipe Arg. 148 C6
Caird Coast Antarctica 167 B1
Cairngorm Mountains U.K. 34 E3
Cairns Australia 111 F3
Cairnsmore of Carsphairn hill U.K. 34 D4
Cairns Section Australia see Great Barrier Reef Marine Park (Cairns Section)

►Cairo Egypt 89 F2
Capital of Egypt and most populous city in Africa.
world 16–17

Cairo U.S.A. 128 A4
Cairo, Monte mt. Italy 44 D4
Cairo Montenotte Italy 44 B2
Caisleán an Bharraigh Rep. of Ireland see Castlebar
Caistor U.K. 35 F5
Caiundo Angola 95 C8
Caiwarro Australia 111 F6
Caixi China 67 F3
Caiyuanzhen China see Shengsi
Caiza Bol. 148 D5
Caizi Hu l. China 67 F2
Cajabamba Peru 148 A1
Cajamarca Peru 148 A1
Cajamarca dept Peru 146 B6
Cajapió Brazil 150 C2
Cajarc France 38 D4
Cajatambo Peru 148 A2
Cajàzeiras Brazil 150 E3
Čajniče Bos.-Herz. 46 A3
Cajuata Bol. 148 D4
Caka'lho China see Yanjing
Čakovec Croatia 44 F1
Çal Denizli Turkey 78 B3
Çal Turkey see Çukurca
Cala r. Spain 42 C4
Calabar Nigeria 93 H4
Calabozo Venez. 146 E2
Calabria admin. reg. Italy 45 F5
Calabria, Parco Nazionale della nat. park Italy 45 F5
Calacoto Bol. 148 C4
Calaf Spain 43 G2
Calafat Romania 46 C3
Calafate Arg. 153 B7
Cala Figuera, Cap de c. Spain 43 H3
Calagurris Spain see Calahorra
Calahorra Spain 43 F1
Calai Angola 95 C9
Calais France 38 D1
Calais U.S.A. 128 G2
Calalasteo, Sierra de mts Arg. 152 D1
Calama Brazil 149 E2
Calama Chile 148 C5
Calamajué Mex. 135 D7
Calamar Col. 146 C2
Calamarca Bol. 148 C4
Calamian Group is Phil. 57 E3
Calamocha Spain 43 F2
Călan Romania 46 C2
Calanaque Brazil 147 E5
Calañas Spain 42 C4
Calanda Spain 43 F2
Calandula Angola 95 C7
Calang Indon. 58 A1
Calanscio Sand Sea des. Libya 88 D2
Calapan Phil. 57 F3
Calar Alta mt. Spain 43 E4
Călărași Romania 46 E2
Calatafimi Sicily Italy 45 D6
Calatayud Spain 43 F2
Calau Germany 37 F3
Calavà, Capo c. Sicily Italy 45 E5
Calayan i. Phil. 57 F2
Calbayog Phil. 57 F3
Calca Peru 148 C3
Calcasieu r. U.S.A. 133 C6
Calcasieu Lake U.S.A. 133 C6
Calchaquí Arg. 152 E2
Calçoene Brazil 147 I4
Calcutta India see Kolkata
Căldăraru Romania 46 D2
Caldas dept Col. 146 C3
Caldas da Rainha Port. 42 B3
Caldas Novas Brazil 149 H4
Caldeirão Brazil 148 D2
Calder r. Canada 123 G1
Caldera Chile 152 C1
Caldervale Australia 111 F5
Caldwell ID U.S.A. 134 C4
Caldwell KS U.S.A. 132 B4
Caldwell OH U.S.A. 130 C4
Caldwell TX U.S.A. 133 B6
Caledon Canada 130 D2
Caledon r. Lesotho/S. Africa 99 E6
Caledon S. Africa 98 C7
Caledon Bay Australia 110 D2
Caledonia admin. div. U.K. see Scotland
Caledonia U.S.A. 130 E2
Calella Spain 43 H2
Calen Australia 111 G4
Calenzana Corsica France 44 B3
Calera U.S.A. 129 B5
Calera y Chozas Spain 42 D3
Caleta el Cobre Chile 148 C6
Caleta Josefina Chile 153 C8
Caleta Lobos Chile 148 C5
Caleta Pabellón de Pica Chile 148 C5
Caleufú Arg. 152 D3
Calexico U.S.A. 137 E5
Calf of Man i. Isle of Man 35 D4
Calgary Canada 134 D2
Cali Col. 146 B4
Calicut India 72 B4
Caliente U.S.A. 137 E3
►California state U.S.A. 136 B3
world 10–11
California, Gulf of Mex. 135 D7
California Aqueduct U.S.A. 136 C4
California Aqueduct canal U.S.A. 136 B3
Californian Delta U.S.A. 136 B2
Călilabad Azer. 79 G3
Călimănești Romania 46 D2
Calistoga U.S.A. 136 A2
Calitri Italy 45 E4
Calkiní Mex. 127 H7
Callabonna, Lake salt flat Australia 111 E6
Callabonna Creek watercourse Australia 111 E6
Callac France 38 B2
Callaghan U.S.A. 130 C5
Callaghan, Mount U.S.A. 136 D2
Callan Rep. of Ireland 35 C5
Callander Canada 124 E4
Callander U.K. 34 D3
Callands U.S.A. 130 D5
Callao Peru 148 A3
Callao U.S.A. 137 F2
Callicoon U.S.A. 131 F3
Calling Lake Canada 123 H4
Calliope Australia 111 G5
Callipolis Turkey see Gallipoli
Callyharra Springs Australia 109 A6
Calmar Canada 123 H4
Calmar U.S.A. 132 D3
Călmățui r. Romania 46 D3
Călniștea r. Romania 46 D2
Calore r. Italy 44 E4
Čalovo Slovakia see Veľký Meder
Calpe Spain 43 G3
Calstock Canada 124 C3
Caltagirone Sicily Italy 45 E6
Caltanissetta Sicily Italy 45 E6
Calucinga Angola 95 C7
Caluire-et-Cuire France 39 F4
Calulo Angola 95 B7
Calunda Angola 95 D8
Calunga Angola 95 C9
Caluquembe Angola 95 B8
Caluula Somalia 96 F2
Calvert r. Australia 110 D3
Calvert Hills Australia 110 D3
Calvert Island Canada 122 D5
Calvert Range hills Australia 109 C5
Calvi Corsica France 31 G5
Calvinia S. Africa 98 C6
Calvitero mt. Spain 42 D2
Calvo, Monte mt. Italy 31 H5
Cam r. U.K. 35 G5
Camabatela Angola 95 B7
Camaçari Brazil 150 E5
Camache Reservoir U.S.A. 136 B2
Camachigama r. Canada 124 E4
Camacho Mex. 126 F7
Camacuio Angola 95 B8
Camacupa Angola 95 C8
Camaguán Venez. 146 E2
Camagüey Cuba 127 K7
Camagüey, Archipiélago de is Cuba 127 K7
Camah, Gunung mt. Malaysia 58 C1
Camaiú r. Brazil 147 G6
Çamalan Turkey see Gülek
Camana Peru 148 B4
Camaná r. Peru 148 B4
Camanongue Angola 95 D7
Camapuã Brazil 151 A6
Camaquã Brazil 152 H2
Camaquã r. Brazil 152 H2
Camarão Brazil 146 D4
Camararé r. Brazil 149 F3
Camargo Bol. 148 D5
Camargo Mex. 126 G6
Camarillo U.S.A. 136 C4
Camariñas Spain 42 B1
Camarones Arg. 153 D6
Camarones, Bahía b. Arg. 153 D6
Camas r. U.S.A. 134 D4
Camas Creek r. U.S.A. 134 D4
Ca Mau Vietnam 61 D6
Camaxilo Angola 95 C7
Cambara Brazil 149 F4
Cambay India see Khambhat
Cambay, Gulf of India see Khambhat, Gulf of
►Cambodia country Asia 61 D5
asia 52–53, 82
Cambrai Australia 112 A4
Cambrai France 39 E1
Cambre Spain 42 B1
Cambria admin. div. U.K. see Wales
Cambria U.S.A. 136 B4
Cambrian Mountains hills U.K. 35 E5
Cambridge Canada 130 C2
Cambridge N.Z. 113 C2
Cambridge U.K. 35 G5
Cambridge IL U.S.A. 132 D3
Cambridge MA U.S.A. 131 H2
Cambridge MD U.S.A. 131 E4
Cambridge MN U.S.A. 132 C2
Cambridge NY U.S.A. 131 G2
Cambridge OH U.S.A. 130 C3
Cambridge Bay Canada 121 I3
Cambridge Springs U.S.A. 130 C3
Cambrien, Lac l. Canada 125 G1
Cambrils Spain 43 G2
Cambulo Angola 95 D7
Cam Co l. China 75 D2
Camden AL U.S.A. 129 B5
Camden AR U.S.A. 133 C5
Camden ME U.S.A. 131 I1
Camden NJ U.S.A. 131 F4
Camden NY U.S.A. 131 F2
Camden OH U.S.A. 130 A4
Camden SC U.S.A. 129 C5
Camdenton U.S.A. 132 C4
Cameia Angola 95 D7
Cameia, Parque Nacional da nat. park Angola 95 D7
Cameron AZ U.S.A. 137 G4
Cameron LA U.S.A. 133 C6
Cameron MO U.S.A. 132 C4
Cameron TX U.S.A. 133 B6
Cameron WV U.S.A. 130 C4
Cameron Highlands Malaysia 58 C1
Cameron Highlands mts Malaysia 58 C1
Cameron Hills Canada 122 G3
Cameron Island Canada 121 I2
Cameron Park U.S.A. 136 B2
►Cameroon country Africa 94 A3
africa 86–87, 100
Caméroun country Africa see Cameroon
Cameroun, Mont vol. Cameroon 93 H4
Cametá Brazil 150 B2
Camfield r. Australia 110 B3
Çamiçi Gölü l. Turkey 78 A3
Camiguin i. Phil. 57 F2
Camilla U.S.A. 129 B6
Camiranga Brazil 150 C2
Camiri Bol. 149 E5
Camisea Peru 148 B2
Camisea r. Peru 148 B2
Camissombo Angola 95 D7
Cammarata, Monte mt. Sicily Italy 45 D6
Cammin Poland see Kamień Pomorski
Camocim Brazil 150 D2
Camooweal Australia 110 D3
Camooweal Caves National Park Australia 110 D4
Camopi Brazil 147 H4
Camorta i. India 73 G4
Campagna Italy 45 E4
Campana, Isla i. Chile 153 B7
Campanário Mato Grosso do Sul Brazil 149 G5
Campanário Minas Gerais Brazil 151 D6
Campanella, Punta pt Italy 45 E4
Campania admin. reg. Italy 44 E4
Campanquiz, Cerro hills Peru 146 B6
Campaspe r. Australia 111 F4
Campbell U.S.A. 130 C3
Campbell, Cape N.Z. 113 C3
Campbell Island Myanmar 61 B6
Campbell Island N.Z. 164 F9
Campbell Lake Canada 123 J2
Campbell Plateau sea feature S. Pacific Ocean 164 F9
Campbell Range hills Australia 108 D3
Campbell River Canada 122 E5
Campbellton Canada 125 H4
Campbelltown Australia 112 D4
Campbell Town Australia 112 C6
Campbeltown U.K. 34 D4
Camp Creek U.S.A. 130 C5
Campeche Mex. 127 H8
Campeche, Bahía de g. Mex. 127 H8
Câmpeni Romania 46 C1
Camperdown Australia 112 B5
Câmpia Turzii Romania 46 C1
Campiglia Marittima Italy 44 C3
Campillos Spain 42 D4
Campina Brazil 150 B3
Câmpina Romania 46 D2
Campinaçu Brazil 150 B5
Campina Grande Brazil 150 F3
Campinas Brazil 149 I5
Campina Verde Brazil 149 H4
Campo Cameroon 93 H5
Campo r. Cameroon see Ntem
Campoalegre Col. 146 C4
Campobasso Italy 44 E4
Campo Belo Brazil 151 C7
Campo de Criptana Spain 42 E3
Campo de Diauarum Brazil 150 A4
Campodolcino Italy 44 B1
Campo Erê Brazil 151 A8
Campo Esperanza Para. 149 F5
Campo Florido Brazil 149 H4
Campo Formoso Brazil 150 D4
Campo Gallo Arg. 152 E1
Campo Grande Amazonas Brazil 149 F2
Campo Grande Mato Grosso do Sul Brazil 151 A7
Campo Largo Brazil 151 B8
Campo Maior Brazil 150 D3
Campo Maior Port. 42 C3
Campomarino Italy 44 E4
Campo Mourão Brazil 149 G6
Campo Novo Brazil 151 A8
Campos Brazil 151 D7
Campos Belos Brazil 150 C5
Campos del Puerto Spain 43 H3
Campo Serio Peru 146 C5
Campos Sales Brazil 150 D3
Campo Tencia mt. Switz. 39 H3
Campo Troco Col. 146 D3
Camp Point U.S.A. 124 B5
Camprodon Spain 43 H1
Campton U.S.A. 130 B5
Câmpulung Romania 46 D2
Campuya Peru 146 C5
Campuya r. Peru 146 C5
Camp Verde U.S.A. 137 G4
Cam Ranh Vietnam 61 E6
Camrose Canada 123 H4
Camsell Range mts Canada 122 F2
Camulodunum U.K. see Colchester
Çan Turkey 78 A2
Canaan r. Canada 125 H4
Canaan U.S.A. 131 G2
Canacona India 72 B3

►Canada country N. America 120 G3
Largest country in North America and 2nd in the world. 3rd most populous country in North America.
northamerica 118–119, 140
world 8–9

Canada Basin sea feature Arctic Ocean 166 A1
Cañada Honda Arg. 152 C2
Canadian U.S.A. 133 A5
Canadian r. U.S.A. 135 G6
Canadian Abyssal Plain sea feature Arctic Ocean 166 A1
Cañadón de las Vacas Arg. 153 C7
Cañadón Grande, Sierra mts Arg. 153 C6
Canaima, Parque Nacional nat. park Venez. 147 F3
Canajoharie U.S.A. 131 F2
Çanakkale Turkey 78 A2
Çanakkale prov. Turkey 47 E4
Çanakkale Boğazı strait Turkey see Dardanelles
Canal Flats Canada 134 D2
Canals Spain 43 F3
Canal Winchester U.S.A. 130 B4
Canamari Brazil 148 C2
Canandaigua U.S.A. 131 E2
Cananea Mex. 135 E7
Cananéia Brazil 151 C8
Canapiare, Cerro hill Col. 146 D4
Cañar Ecuador 146 B5
Cañar prov. Ecuador 146 B5
Canarana Brazil 150 A5
Canarias, Islas is N. Atlantic Ocean see Canary Islands
Canarias, Islas terr. N. Atlantic Ocean see Canary Islands
Canary Islands N. Atlantic Ocean 90 A3

►Canary Islands terr. N. Atlantic Ocean 90 A3
Autonomous Community of Spain.
africa 86–87, 100

Canastota U.S.A. 131 F2
Canastra, Serra da mts Brazil 151 C6
Canaveral, Cape U.S.A. 129 C6
Canavieiras Brazil 150 E5

►Canberra Australia 112 D4
Capital of Australia.
oceania 114

Canby U.S.A. 134 B4
Canchyuaya, Cerros de hills Peru 146 C6
Cancún Mex. 127 I7
Çandar Turkey see Kastamonu
Candarave Peru 148 C4
Candás Spain 42 D1
Candé France 38 C3
Candeias r. Brazil 149 E2
Candelaria Arg. 152 D1
Candelaria Mex. 138 F5
Candelaria Venez. 147 E3
Candelaro r. Italy 44 E4
Candeleda Spain 42 D2
Candia Greece see Iraklion
Çandır Turkey 78 C2
Candle Lake Canada 123 J4
Candle Lake l. Canada 123 J4
Candlewood, Lake U.S.A. 131 G3
Cando U.S.A. 132 B1
Cândrelu, Vârful mt. Romania 46 C2
Cane r. Australia 108 A5
Canea Greece see Chania
Canelli Italy 44 B2
Canelones Uruguay 152 F3
Caney U.S.A. 132 C4
Caney r. U.S.A. 132 C4
Cangallo Peru 148 B3
Cangamba Angola 95 C8
Cangandala Angola 95 C7
Cangandala, Parque Nacional de nat. park Angola 95 C7
Çangarâfa Mauritania 92 B1
Cangas Spain 42 B1
Cangas del Narcea Spain 42 C1
Cangola Angola 95 B7
Cangombe Angola 95 D8
Canguçu Brazil 152 G2
Canguçu, Serra do hills Brazil 152 G2
Cangzhou China 63 J4
Caniapiscau Canada 125 G2
Caniapiscau r. Canada 125 G1
Caniapiscau, Lac l. Canada 125 G2
Canicattì Sicily Italy 45 D6
Canigou, Pic du mt. France 38 E5
Canim Lake Canada 122 F5
Canindé Ceará Brazil 150 E3
Canindé Pará Brazil 150 C2
Canindé r. Brazil 150 D3
Canino Italy 44 C3
Canisteo r. U.S.A. 130 E2
Canisteo Peninsula Antarctica 167 K2
Canister Falls Guyana 147 G3
Cañitas de Felipe Pescador Mex. 126 F7
Çankırı Turkey 78 C2
Cankuzo Burundi 96 A5
Canna i. U.K. 34 C3
Cannanore India 72 B4
Cannanore Islands India 72 B4
Cannes France 39 G5
Cannich U.K. 34 D3
Cannonball r. U.S.A. 132 A2
Cannon Beach U.S.A. 134 B3
Cannonsburg U.S.A. 130 B4
Cann River Australia 112 D5
Canoas Brazil 151 B9
Canoeiros Brazil 151 C6
Canoe Lake Canada 123 I4
Canoe Lake l. Canada 123 I4
Canoinhas Brazil 151 B8
Canon City U.S.A. 135 F5
Cañon Largo watercourse U.S.A. 135 F5
Canoochia r. U.S.A. 129 C6
Canoona Australia 111 G4
Canora Canada 134 G2
Caño Riecito Venez. 146 D3
Canosa di Puglia Italy 44 F4
Canouan i. St Vincent 147 F1
Canowindra Australia 112 D4
Cansado W. Sahara 90 A5
Canso Canada 125 I4
Canso, Strait of Canada 125 I4
Canta Peru 148 A2
Cantabria aut. comm. Spain 42 D1
Cantabrian Mountains Spain see Cantábrica, Cordillera
Cantabrian Sea Spain see Cantábrico, Mar
Cantábrica, Cordillera mts Spain 42 D1
Cantábrico, Mar sea Spain 42 C1
Cantagalo Brazil 147 G6
Cantalejo Spain 42 E2
Cantanhede Port. 42 B2
Canterras hill Spain 43 E3
Canterbury U.K. 35 G6
Canterbury Bight b. N.Z. 113 B4
►Canterbury Plains plain South I. N.Z. 113 B3
oceania 104–105
Cân Thơ Vietnam 61 D6
Cantil U.S.A. 136 D4
Cantillana Spain 42 D4
Canto do Buriti Brazil 150 D4
Canton China see Guangzhou
Canton GA U.S.A. 129 B5
Canton IL U.S.A. 132 D3
Canton MO U.S.A. 132 D3
Canton MS U.S.A. 127 I5
Canton NY U.S.A. 131 F1
Canton OH U.S.A. 130 C3
Canton PA U.S.A. 131 E3
Canton SD U.S.A. 132 B3
Canton TX U.S.A. 133 C5
Cantù Italy 44 B2
Cantu, Serra do hills Brazil 151 B8
Cantuaria U.K. see Canterbury
Cañuelas Arg. 152 F3
Canumã Amazonas Brazil 147 F6
Canumã Amazonas Brazil 147 G6
Canunda National Park Australia 112 B5
Canusium Italy see Canosa di Puglia
Canutama Brazil 147 E6
Cany-Barville France 38 D2
Cànyoles r. Spain 43 F3
Canyon Canada 122 B2
Canyon U.S.A. 133 A5
Canyon Creek r. U.S.A. 136 B2
Canyondam U.S.A. 136 B1
Canyon de Chelly National Monument nat. park U.S.A. 137 H3
Canyon Ferry Lake U.S.A. 134 E3
Canyonlands National Park U.S.A. 137 H2
Canyon Ranges mts Canada 122 E2
Canzar Angola 95 D6
Cao Bằng Vietnam 60 D3
Caocheng China see Caoxian
Caohe China see Qichun
Caojiahe China see Qichun
Caojian China 66 A3
Cao Nguyên Đắc Lắc plat. Vietnam 61 E5
Caorle Italy 44 D2
Caoxian China 67 E1
Caozhou China see Heze
Capaccio Italy 45 E4
Capaci Sicily Italy 45 D5
Capaia Angola 95 D7
Çapakçur Turkey see Bingöl
Capana Brazil 146 D5
Capanaparo r. Venez. 146 E3
Capanema Brazil 150 C2
Capanne, Monte mt. Italy 44 C3
Capão Bonito Brazil 149 H6
Caparo r. Venez. 146 D3
Căpățânii, Munții mts Romania 46 C2
Cap-aux-Meules Canada 125 I4
Capbreton France 38 C5
Cap-de-la-Madeleine Canada 128 E2
Capdenac-Gare France 38 E4
Capdepera Spain 43 H3
Cape r. Australia 111 F4
Cape Arid National Park Australia 109 C8
Cape Barren Island Australia 112 D6
Cape Basin sea feature S. Atlantic Ocean 161 O8
Cape Borda Australia 109 G8
Cape Breton Highlands National Park Canada 125 I4
Cape Breton Island Canada 125 I4
Cape Charles Canada 125 K2
Cape Charles U.S.A. 131 E5
Cape Coast Ghana 93 E4
Cape Coast Castle Ghana see Cape Coast
Cape Cod Bay U.S.A. 131 H3
Cape Coral U.S.A. 129 C7
Cape Crawford Australia 110 C3
Cape Dorset Canada 121 L3
Cape Fear r. U.S.A. 129 D5
Cape George Canada 125 I4
Cape Girardeau U.S.A. 127 I4
Cape Juby Morocco see Tarfaya
Cape Krusenstern National Monument nat. park U.S.A. 120 C3
Capel Australia 109 A8
Cape Le Grand National Park Australia 109 C8
Capelinha Brazil 151 D6
Capella Australia 111 G4
Capelle aan de IJssel Neth. 36 B3
Capelongo Angola see Kuvango
Cape May U.S.A. 131 F4
Cape May Court House U.S.A. 131 F4
Cape May Point U.S.A. 131 F4
Cape Melville National Park Australia 111 F2
Capenda-Camulemba Angola 95 C7
Cape Palmerston National Park Australia 111 G4
Cape Range National Park Australia 108 A5
Cape St George Canada 125 J3

►Cape Town S. Africa 98 C7
Legislative capital of South Africa.
world 8–9

Cape Tribulation National Park Australia 111 F2
Cape Upstart National Park Australia 111 F3
►Cape Verde country N. Atlantic Ocean 92 [inset]
africa 86–87, 100
Cape Verde Basin sea feature N. Atlantic Ocean 160 L5
Cape Verde Plateau sea feature N. Atlantic Ocean 160 L4
Cape Vincent U.S.A. 131 E1
Cape Yakataga U.S.A. 122 A2
Cape York Peninsula Australia 111 E2
Cap-Haïtien Haiti 127 L8
Capibara Venez. 146 E4
Capim Brazil 150 C2
Capim r. Brazil 150 B2
Capinota Bol. 148 D4
Capitán Arturo Prat research station Antarctica 167 A2
Capitari Brazil 147 F6

►Capitol Hill N. Mariana Is 57 K2
Capital of the Northern Mariana Islands, on Saipan.

Capitol Reef National Park U.S.A. 137 G2
Capivari r. Brazil 150 E5
Capixaba Brazil 150 D4
Čapljina Bos.-Herz. 44 F3
Capoche r. Moz./Zambia 97 B8
Capo d'Orlando Sicily Italy 45 E5
Capoeira Brazil 147 G6
Capoeiras, Cachoeira das waterfall Brazil 147 G6
Capoterra Sardinia Italy 45 B5
Capraia, Isola di i. Italy 44 B3
Caprera, Isola i. Sardinia Italy 44 B4
Capri, Isola di i. Italy 45 E4
Capricorn Channel Australia 111 G4
Capricorn Group atolls Australia 111 H4

Capricorn Section Australia see Great Barrier Reef Marine Park (Capricorn Section)
Caprivi admin. reg. Namibia 98 D3
Caprivi Game Park nature res. Namibia 98 D3
Caprivi Strip reg. Namibia 98 D3
Capsa Tunisia see Gafsa
Captain Cook U.S.A. 135 [inset] Z2
Captieux France 38 C4
Capuna Angola 95 C8
Caqueta dept Col. 146 C4
Caquetá r. Col. 146 D5
Cáqueza Col. 146 C3
Carabaya, Cordillera de mts Peru 148 C3
Carabobo state Venez. 146 E2
Caracal Romania 46 D2
Caracarai Brazil 147 F4

▶Caracas Venez. 146 E2
Capital of Venezuela.

Caracol Piauí Brazil 150 D4
Caracol Rondônia Brazil 149 D2
Caracollo Bol. 148 D4
Caragabal Australia 112 C4
Carahue Chile 152 B4
Carajás Brazil 150 B3
Carajás, Serra dos hills Brazil 147 I6
Carales Sardinia Italy see Cagliari
Caralis Sardinia Italy see Cagliari
Caramulo mt. Port. 42 B2
Caranavi Bol. 148 D4
Carandaiti Bol. 149 E5
Carandazal Brazil 149 F4
Caransebeş Romania 46 C2
Carapajó Brazil 150 B2
Cara Paraná r. Col. 146 C5
Carapeguá Para. 149 F6
Carapelle r. Italy 44 E4
Caraquet Canada 125 H4
Caráquez Ecuador 146 A5
Carare r. Col. 146 C3
Caraşova Romania 46 B2
Caratasca, Laguna lag. Hond. 139 H5
Caratinga Brazil 151 D6
Carauté r. Col. 146 D5
Carauari Brazil 146 E6
Caraúbas Brazil 150 E3
Caraunâ mt. Brazil see Grande, Serra
Caravaca de la Cruz Spain 43 F3
Caravelas Brazil 151 E6
Caraveli Peru 148 B3
Carballiño Spain 42 B1
Carballo Spain 42 B1
Carberry Canada 123 L5
Carbó Mex. 135 E7
Carbon, Cap c. Alg. 43 F5
Carbonara, Capo c. Sardinia Italy 45 B5
Carbondale CO U.S.A. 134 F5
Carbondale IL U.S.A. 128 A4
Carbondale PA U.S.A. 131 F3
Carbonear Canada 121 N5
Carboneras Spain 43 F4
Carbonero El Mayor Spain 42 D2
Carbonia Sardinia Italy 45 B5
Carbonita Brazil 151 D6
Carbonne France 38 D5
Carcajou Canada 123 G3
Carcajou r. Canada 122 D[illegible]
Carcaliu Romania 46 F2
Carcassonne France 38 E5
Carcastillo Spain 43 F1
Carchi prov. Ecuador 146 B4
Carcross Canada 122 C2
Cardamomes, Chaîne des mts Cambodia see Cardamom Range
Cardamom Mountains Cambodia see Cardamom Range
Cardamom Range mts Cambodia 61 C5
Cardamom Hills India 72 C4
Cardeña Spain 42 D3
Cárdenas Cuba 129 C8
Cárdenas Mex. 126 G7
Cárdenas Mex. 138 F5
Cardenyabba watercourse Australia 112 B3
Çardi Turkey see Harmancık
Cardiel, Lago l. Arg. 153 C7

▶Cardiff U.K. 35 E6
Capital of Wales.

Cardiff U.S.A. 131 E4
Cardigan U.K. 35 D5
Cardigan Bay U.K. 35 D5
Cardinal Canada 131 F1
Cardinal Lake Canada 122 G3
Cardington U.S.A. 130 B3
Cardona Uruguay 152 F3
Cardoner r. Spain 43 G2
Cardoso Brazil 149 H5
Cardoso, Ilha do i. Brazil 151 C8
Cardrona N.Z. 113 B4
Cardston Canada 123 H5
Cardwell Australia 111 F3
Carega, Cima mt. Italy 44 C2
Carei Romania 31 J4
Careiro Brazil 147 G5
Careiro do Castanho Brazil 147 F5
Carén Chile 152 C2
Carentan France 38 C2
Carey U.S.A. 130 B3
Carey, Lake salt flat Australia 109 C7
Carey Downs Australia 109 A6
Carey Lake Canada 123 K2
Cargados Carajos Islands Mauritius 162 K7
Carhaix-Plouguer France 38 B2
Carhuamayo Peru 148 A2
Carhué Arg. 152 E4
Cariacica Brazil 151 D7
Cariamanga Ecuador 146 B6
Cariango Angola 95 B7
Cariati Italy 45 F5
Caribbean Sea N. Atlantic Ocean 139 H5
Cariboo Mountains Canada 122 F4
Caribou r. Man. Canada 123 M3
Caribou r. N.W.T. Canada 122 E2
Caribou U.S.A. 128 F2
Caribou Islands Canada 123 H2
Caribou Mountains Canada 123 H3
Carichic Mex. 135 F8
Carignan France 39 F2
Carinda Australia 112 C3
Cariñena Spain 43 F2
Carinhanha Brazil 150 D5
Carinhanha r. Brazil 150 D5
Caripande Angola 95 D8
Caripaé Brazil 150 C4
Caripe Venez. 147 F2
Caripito Venez. 147 F2
Cariris Novos, Serra dos hills Brazil 150 D3
Caris r. Venez. 147 F2
Carlabhagh U.K. see Carloway
Carleton U.S.A. 130 B2
Carleton, Mount Canada 125 H4
Carleton Place Canada 124 E4
Carletonville S. Africa 99 E5
Carlin U.S.A. 137 D1
Carlinville U.S.A. 132 D4
Carlisle U.K. 34 E4
Carlisle KY U.S.A. 130 A4
Carlisle NY U.S.A. 131 F2
Carlisle PA U.S.A. 131 E3
Carlisle Lakes salt flat Australia 109 D7
Carlos Casares Arg. 152 E3
Carlos Chagas Brazil 151 D6
Carlos Tejedor Arg. 152 E3
Carlow Rep. of Ireland 35 C5
Carloway U.K. 34 C2
Carlsbad Czech Rep. see Karlovy Vary
Carlsbad CA U.S.A. 136 D5
Carlsbad NM U.S.A. 135 F6
Carlsbad Caverns National Park U.S.A. 135 F6
Carlsberg Ridge sea feature Indian Ocean 162 K5
Carlson Inlet Antarctica 167 L1
Carlton U.S.A. 132 C2
Carlyle Canada 134 G2
Carlyle Lake U.S.A. 128 A4
Carmacks Canada 122 B2
Carmagnola Italy 44 A2
Carman Canada 123 L5
Carmana Iran see Kermān
Carmarthen U.K. 35 D6
Carmarthen Bay U.K. 35 D6
Carmaux France 38 E4
Carmel U.S.A. 128 B4
Carmel, Mount Israel 77 B3
Carmel-by-the-Sea U.S.A. 136 B3
Carmel Head U.K. 35 D5
Carmelita Guat. 138 F5
Carmelo Uruguay 152 F3
Carmen Col. 146 C2
Carmen r. Mex. 135 F7
Carmen Uruguay 152 F3
Carmen Alto Chile 148 C5
Carmen del Paraná Para. 149 F6
Carmen de Patagones Arg. 152 E5
Carmi U.S.A. 128 A4
Carmila Australia 111 G4
Carmona Angola see Uíge
Carmona Spain 42 D4
Carnamah Australia 109 A7
Carnarvon Australia 109 A6
Carnarvon S. Africa 98 D6
Carnarvon National Park Australia 111 F5
Carnarvon Range hills Australia 109 C6
Carnarvon Range mts Australia 111 G5
Carnegie Australia 109 C6
Carnegie, Lake salt flat Australia 109 C6
Carn Eighe mt. U.K. 34 D3
Carnes Australia 110 C6
Carnesville U.S.A. 133 F5
Carney Island Antarctica 167 J2
Car Nicobar i. India 73 G4
Carnikava Latvia 33 G4
Carnot Cent. Afr. Rep. 94 B3
Carnot Bay Australia 108 C4
Carnoustie U.K. 34 E3
Carnsore Point Rep. of Ireland 35 C5
Caro U.S.A. 130 B2
Caroaebe r. Brazil 147 F4
Caroch mt. Spain see El Caroche
Carola Cay reef Australia 111 H3
Carolina Brazil 150 C3
Caroline Canada 134 D1
Caroline Island Kiribati 165 H6
Caroline Islands N. Pacific Ocean 57 J4
Caroline Peak N.Z. 113 A4
Carondelet Ecuador 146 B4
Caroni r. Venez. 147 F2
Carora Venez. 146 D2
Carpathian Mountains Europe 37 I4
Carpații mts Europe see Carpathian Mountains
Carpații Meridionali mts Romania see Transylvanian Alps
Carpentaria, Gulf of Australia 110 D2
Carpentras France 39 F4
Carpi Italy 44 C2
Carpina Brazil 150 F3
Cărpiniș Romania 46 B2
Carpinteria U.S.A. 136 C4
Carquefou France 38 C3
Carraig na Siuire Rep. of Ireland see Carrick-on-Suir
Carraipía Col. 146 C2
Carrantuohill mt. Rep. of Ireland 35 B6
Carrara Italy 44 C2
Carrasco, Parque Nacional nat. park Bol. 148 D4
Carrazeda de Ansiães Port. 42 C2
Carr Boyd Range hills Australia 108 E4
Carrbridge U.K. 34 E3
Carregal do Sal Port. 42 C2
Carriacou i. Grenada 147 F1
Carrickmacross Rep. of Ireland 35 C5
Carrick-on-Shannon Rep. of Ireland 35 B5
Carrick-on-Suir Rep. of Ireland 35 C5
Carrieton Australia 112 A4
Carrillo Mex. 133 A7
Carrington U.S.A. 132 B2
Carrión r. Spain 42 D1
Carrión de los Condes Spain 42 D1
Carrizal Bajo Chile 152 C2
Carrizo U.S.A. 137 G4
Carrizo Creek r. U.S.A. 133 A4
Carrizo Creek watercourse AZ U.S.A. 137 G5
Carrizo Creek watercourse CA U.S.A. 137 E5
Carrizo Plain National Monument nat. park U.S.A. 136 C4
Carrizo Springs U.S.A. 133 B6
Carrizo Wash watercourse U.S.A. 137 H4
Carrizozo U.S.A. 135 F6
Carroll U.S.A. 132 C3
Carrollton AL U.S.A. 129 A5
Carrollton GA U.S.A. 129 B5
Carrollton IL U.S.A. 132 D4
Carrollton KY U.S.A. 128 B4
Carrollton MO U.S.A. 132 C4
Carrollton MS U.S.A. 133 D5
Carrolltown U.S.A. 130 D3
Carron r. Australia 111 E3
Carron r. U.K. 34 D3
Carrot r. Canada 123 K4
Carrot River Canada 123 K4
Carrsville U.S.A. 131 E5
Carruthersville U.S.A. 133 D4
Çarşamba Turkey 78 D2
Carson r. Australia 108 D3
Carson U.S.A. 132 A2
Carson r. U.S.A. 136 C2
Carson City MI U.S.A. 130 A2

▶Carson City NV U.S.A. 136 C2
State capital of Nevada.

Carson Lake U.S.A. 136 C2
Carson Sink l. U.S.A. 136 C2
Carsonville U.S.A. 130 B2
Carstensz-top mt. Indon. see Jaya, Puncak
Carswell Lake Canada 123 I3
Cartagena Chile 152 C3
Cartagena Col. 146 C2
Cartagena Spain 43 F4
Cartago Col. 146 C3
Cartago Costa Rica 139 H7
Cártama Spain 42 D4
Cartaxo Port. 42 B3
Carteret Group is P.N.G. see Kilinailau Islands
Carteret Island Solomon Is see Malaita
Cartersville U.S.A. 129 B5
Carthage tourist site Tunisia 91 H1
Carthage IL U.S.A. 132 D3
Carthage MO U.S.A. 132 C4
Carthage NC U.S.A. 128 D5
Carthage NY U.S.A. 131 F2
Carthage TN U.S.A. 128 B4
Carthage TX U.S.A. 133 C5
Carthago tourist site Tunisia see Carthage
Carthago Nova Spain see Cartagena
Cartier Island Australia 108 C3
Cartwright Man. Canada 123 L5
Cartwright Nfld. and Lab. Canada 125 J2
Caruachi Venez. 147 F2
Caruarú Brazil 150 F4
Caruçambaba Brazil 150 B2
Cărunta, Vârful mt. Romania 46 E1
Carúpano Venez. 147 F2
Carutapera Brazil 150 C2
Carvalho Brazil 147 I5
Carver U.S.A. 130 B5
Carvin France 39 E1
Carvoeiro Brazil 147 F5
Carvoeiro, Cabo c. Port. 42 B3
Cary U.S.A. 128 D5
Caryapundy Swamp Australia 111 E6
Casabindo, Cerro de mt. Arg. 148 D5
Casablanca Chile 152 C3
▶Casablanca Morocco 90 D2
world 16–17
Casa Branca Brazil 149 I5
Casa de Janos Mex. 135 E7
Casa de Piedra, Embalse resr Arg. 152 D4
Casa Grande U.S.A. 137 G5
Casale Monferrato Italy 44 B2
Casalins Arg. 152 F4
Casalmaggiore Italy 44 C2
Casalpusterlengo Italy 44 B2
Casalvasco Brazil 149 E3
Casamance r. Senegal 92 A2
Casanare dept Col. 146 D3
Casanare r. Col. 146 D3
Casas Grandes Mex. 135 F7
Casas Grandes r. Mex. 135 F7
Casas-Ibáñez Spain 43 F3
Casbas Arg. 152 E4
Casca Brazil 151 A9
Cascada de Bassaseachic, Parque Nacional nat. park Mex. 135 E7
Cascade Australia 109 C8
Cascade r. N.Z. 113 B4
Cascade IA U.S.A. 132 D3
Cascade ID U.S.A. 134 C3
Cascade Range mts Canada/U.S.A. 120 G5
Cascade Reservoir U.S.A. 134 C3
Cascais Port. 42 B3
Cascapédia r. Canada 125 H3
Cascavel Ceará Brazil 150 E3
Cascavel Paraná Brazil 151 A8
Casco Bay U.S.A. 131 I2
Caserta Italy 44 E4
Caseville U.S.A. 130 B2
Casey research station Antarctica 167 F2
Casey Bay Antarctica 167 D2
Caseyr, Raas c. Somalia 96 F2
Cashel Rep. of Ireland 35 C5
Cashmere Australia 111 G5
Casigua Falcón Venez. 146 D2
Casigua Zulia Venez. 146 C2
Casilda Arg. 152 E3
Casimcea Romania 46 F2
Casimcea r. Romania 46 F2
Casino Australia 111 H6
Casinos Spain 43 F3
Čáslav Czech Rep. 37 G4
Casma Peru 148 A2
Casnewydd U.K. see Newport
Casoli Italy 44 E3
Caspe Spain 43 F2
Casper U.S.A. 134 F4
Caspian Lowland Kazakh./Rus. Fed. 29 H7

▶Caspian Sea Asia/Europe 68 C2
Largest lake in the world and in Asia/Europe. Lowest point in Europe.
europe 22–23
asia 50–51
world 6–7

Cass r. U.S.A. 130 B2
Cassacatiza Moz. 97 B8
Cassai Angola 95 D7
Cassamba Angola 95 D8
Cassano allo Ionio Italy 45 F5
Cassara Brazil 149 E3
Cass City U.S.A. 130 B2
Casselman Canada 124 F4
Casselton U.S.A. 132 B2
Cassiar Mountains Canada 122 D3
Cassilândia Brazil 149 H4
Cassilis Australia 112 D4
Cassinga Angola 95 C8
Cassino Brazil 152 G3
Cassino Italy 44 D4
Cassongue Angola 95 B7
Cassopolis U.S.A. 132 E3
Cassville U.S.A. 133 C4
Castanhal Amazonas Brazil 147 F6
Castanhal Pará Brazil 150 C2
Castanheira de Pêra Port. 42 B2
Castanho Brazil 149 E1
Castaño Nuevo Arg. 152 C2
Castaños Mex. 126 F6
Castejón, Montes de mts Spain 43 F2
Castel di Sangro Italy 44 E4
Castelfiorentino Italy 44 C3
Castelfranco Emilia Italy 44 C2
Castelfranco Veneto Italy 44 C2
Casteljaloux France 38 D4
Castellammare, Golfo di b. Sicily Italy 45 D5
Castellammare di Stabia Italy 45 E4
Castellane France 39 G5
Castellaneta Italy 45 F4
Castellanos mt. Spain 43 E3
Castell de Ferro Spain 42 E4
Castelli Buenos Aires Arg. 152 F4
Castelli Chaco Arg. 152 E1
Castell-nedd U.K. see Neath
Castelló de la Plana Spain 43 F3
Castellón de la Plana Spain see Castelló de la Plana
Castelnaudary France 38 D5
Castelnau-de-Médoc France 38 C4
Castelnovo ne'Monti Italy 44 C2
Castelo Branco Port. 42 C3
Castelo Branco admin. dist. Port. 42 C2
Castelo de Vide Port. 42 C3
Castelo do Piauí Brazil 150 D3
Castèl San Pietro Terme Italy 44 C2
Castelsardo Sardinia Italy 44 B4
Castelsarrasin France 38 D4
Castelvetrano Sicily Italy 45 D6
Castèl Volturno Italy 44 D4
Casterton Australia 112 B5
Castets France 38 C5
Castiglione dei Pepoli Italy 44 C2
Castiglione del Lago Italy 44 D3
Castiglione della Pescaia Italy 44 C3
Castile U.S.A. 130 D2
Castilla Chile 152 C1
Castilla Peru 146 A6
Castilla - La Mancha aut. comm. Spain 42 E3
Castilla y León aut. comm. Spain 43 D2
Castillejo Venez. 147 F3
Castilletes Col. 146 D2
Castillo, Pampa del hills Arg. 153 C6
Castillos, Lago de l. Uruguay 152 G3
Castlebar Rep. of Ireland 35 B5
Castleblayney Rep. of Ireland 35 C4
Castle Dale U.S.A. 137 G2
Castle Dome Mountains U.S.A. 137 E5
Castle Douglas U.K. 34 E4
Castlegar Canada 134 C2
Castleisland Rep. of Ireland 35 B5
Castlemaine Australia 112 C5
Castle Mountain U.S.A. 136 B4
Castle Peak hill Hong Kong China 67 [inset]
Castle Peak Bay Hong Kong China 67 [inset]
Castlepoint N.Z. 113 D3
Castlepollard Rep. of Ireland 35 C5
Castlerea Rep. of Ireland 35 B5
Castlereagh r. Australia 112 C3
Castle Rock CO U.S.A. 134 F5
Castle Rock WA U.S.A. 134 B3
Castor Canada 123 I4
Castor, Rivière du r. Canada 124 E2
Castor Creek r. U.S.A. 133 C6
Castra Regina Germany see Regensburg
Castres France 38 E5
Castricum Neth. 36 B2

▶Castries St Lucia 139 L6
Capital of St Lucia.

Castro Brazil 151 B8
Castro Chile 153 B5
Castro Alves Brazil 150 E5
Castro del Río Spain 42 D4
Castro Marim Port. 42 C4
Castro-Urdiales Spain 42 E1
Castro Verde Port. 42 B4
Castrovillari Italy 45 F5
Castroville U.S.A. 136 B3
Castrovirreyna Peru 148 B3
Castuera Spain 42 D3
Çat Turkey 79 E3
Catacaos Peru 146 A6
Çatak Turkey 79 E3
Catalão Brazil 149 I4
Çatalca Turkey 46 F4
Çatalca Yarımadası pen. Turkey 46 F4
Catalina U.S.A. 137 G5
Catalonia aut. comm. Spain see Cataluña
Cataluña aut. comm. Spain 43 G2
Catalunya aut. comm. Spain see Cataluña
Catamarca Arg. 152 D2
Catamarca prov. Arg. 152 D1
Catambia Moz. see Catandica
Catana Sicily Italy see Catania
Catandica Moz. 99 G3
Catanduanes i. Phil. 57 F3
Catanduva Brazil 149 H5
Catanduvas Brazil 151 A8
Catania Sicily Italy 45 E6
Catania, Golfo di g. Sicily Italy 45 E6
Catán Lil Arg. 152 C4
Catanzaro Italy 45 F5
Cataract Creek watercourse U.S.A. 137 F3
Catarina Brazil 150 E3
Catarina U.S.A. 133 B6
Catarman Phil. 57 F3
Catastrophe, Cape Australia 109 F8
Catata Nova Angola 95 B8
Catatumbo Bari nat. park Col. 146 C2
Catavi Bol. 148 D4
Catawba r. U.S.A. 129 C5
Catawissa U.S.A. 131 E3
Cat Ba, Đao i. Vietnam 60 D3
Catengue Angola 95 B8
Catete Angola 95 B7
Catete r. Brazil 147 H6
Cathedral City U.S.A. 137 D5
Catherine, Mount U.S.A. 137 F2
Catheys Valley U.S.A. 136 B3
Catió Guinea-Bissau 92 B3
Catisimiña Venez. 147 F3
Cat Island Bahamas 129 E7
Catoche, Cabo c. Mex. 127 I7
Cato Island and Bank Australia 111 H4
Catolé do Rocha Brazil 150 E3
Catolo Angola 95 C7
Catota Angola 95 C8
Catoute mt. Spain 42 C1
Catria, Monte mt. Italy 44 D3
Catriló Arg. 152 E4
Catrimani Brazil 147 F4
Catrimani r. Brazil 147 F4
Catskill U.S.A. 131 G2
Catskill Mountains U.S.A. 131 F2
Cattolica Italy 44 D3
Catúa Arg. 148 D5
Catuane Moz. 99 G5
Catur Moz. 97 B8
Cauaxi r. Brazil 150 B2
Cauayan Phil. 57 F4
Caubvick, Mount Canada 125 I1
Cauca dept Col. 146 B4
Cauca r. Col. 146 C2
Caucaia Brazil 150 E3
Caucasia Col. 146 C3
▶Caucasus mts Asia/Europe 79 E2
europe 22–23
Caucete Arg. 152 C2
Cauchari, Salar de salt flat Arg. 148 D5
Cauchon Lake Canada 123 L4
Caudete Spain 43 F3
Caudry France 39 E1
Caulnes France 38 B2
Cauno Angola 95 C9
Cauquenes Chile 152 B3
Caura r. Venez. 147 E3
Caurés r. Brazil 147 F5
Căușeni Moldova 46 F1
Caussade France 38 D4
Cautário r. Brazil 149 D3
Caution, Cape Canada 122 E5
Cávado r. Port. 42 B2
Cavaglià Italy 44 B2
Cavaillon France 39 F5
Cavalcante Goiás Brazil 150 C5
Cavalcante Rondônia Brazil 149 E2
Cavalier U.S.A. 132 B1
Cavalleria, Cap de c. Spain 43 I2
Cavally r. Côte d'Ivoire 92 D4
Cavan Rep. of Ireland 35 C5
Çavdır Turkey 78 B3
Cavera, Serra do hills Brazil 152 G2
Cavernoso, Serra do mts Brazil 151 A8
Cave Run Lake U.S.A. 130 B4
Caviana, Ilha i. Brazil 150 B1
Cavo, Monte hill Italy 44 D4
Cavongo Angola 95 C8
Çavuşçu Turkey 78 B3
Cawnpore India see Kanpur
Cawood U.S.A. 130 B5
Caxias Amazonas Brazil 146 D6
Caxias Maranhão Brazil 150 D3
Caxias do Sul Brazil 151 B9
Caxito Angola 95 B7
Caxiuana, Baía de l. Brazil 147 I5
Çay Turkey 78 B3
Cayambe-Coca, Parque Nacional nat. park Ecuador 146 B5
Çaybaşı Turkey see Çayeli
Cayce U.S.A. 129 C5
Çaycuma Turkey 78 C2
Çayeli Turkey 79 E2

▶Cayenne Fr. Guiana 147 H3
Capital of French Guiana.

Çaygören Barajı resr Turkey 47 F5
Çayhan Turkey 78 C3
Çayırhan Turkey 78 B2
Caylus France 38 D4
Cayman Brac i. Cayman Is 127 K8

▶Cayman Islands terr. West Indies 127 J8
United Kingdom Overseas Territory.
northamerica 118–119, 140

Cayman Trench sea feature Caribbean Sea 160 I4
Cay Sal i. Bahamas 129 C8
Cayuga Canada 130 D2
Cayuga Heights U.S.A. 131 E2
Cayuga Lake U.S.A. 131 E2
Cazage Angola 95 D7
Cazaje Angola see Cazage
Cazalla de la Sierra Spain 42 D4
Căzănești Romania 46 E2
Caza Pava Arg. 152 F2
Cazaux et de Sanguinet, Étang de l. France 38 C4
Cazé China 75 E3
Cazenovia U.S.A. 131 F2
Cazères France 38 D5
Cazombo Angola 95 D7
Cazorla Spain 42 E4
Cazula Moz. 99 G2
Cea r. Spain 42 D1
Ceadâr-Lunga Moldova see Ciadîr-Lunga
Ceanannus Mór Rep. of Ireland see Kells
Ceará Brazil see Fortaleza
Ceará state Brazil 150 E3
Ceara Abyssal Plain sea feature S. Atlantic Ocean 160 L5
Ceatharlach Rep. of Ireland see Carlow
Ceballos Mex. 126 F6
Cebollar Arg. 152 D2
Cebreros Spain 42 D2
Cebu Phil. 57 F3
Cebu i. Phil. 57 F3
Ceccano Italy 44 D4
Cecil Plains Australia 111 G5
Cecil Rhodes, Mount Australia 109 C6
Cecina Italy 44 C3
Cecina r. Italy 44 C3
Ceclavín Spain 42 C3
Cedar r. MI U.S.A. 132 E3
Cedar r. ND U.S.A. 132 A2
Cedar r. NE U.S.A. 132 B3
Cedar Bluff U.S.A. 130 C5
Cedar City U.S.A. 137 F3
Cedar Creek Reservoir U.S.A. 133 B5
Cedar Falls U.S.A. 132 C3
Cedar Grove CA U.S.A. 136 C3
Cedar Grove IN U.S.A. 130 A4
Cedar Grove WV U.S.A. 130 C4
Cedar Island U.S.A. 131 F5
Cedar Lake Canada 123 K4
Cedar Point U.S.A. 130 B3
Cedar Rapids U.S.A. 132 D3
Cedar Ridge U.S.A. 137 G3
Cedar Run U.S.A. 131 F4
Cedar Springs Canada 130 B2
Cedegolo Italy 44 C1
Cedeira Spain 42 B1
Cedro Brazil 150 E3
Cedros, Isla i. Mex. 135 D7
Ceduna Australia 109 F8
Cée Spain 42 B1
Ceelbuur Somalia 96 E3
Ceel Dhaab Somalia 96 E2
Ceeldheere Somalia 96 E4
Ceel Gaal Bari Somalia 96 F2
Ceel Gaal Woqooyi Galbeed Somalia 96 D2
Ceel Huur Somalia 96 F3
Ceel Walaaq well Somalia 96 D4
Ceerigaabo Somalia 96 E2
Cefalù Sicily Italy 45 E5
Cega r. Spain 42 D2
Cegléd Hungary 37 I5
Çeğné China 75 G2
Ceheng China 66 C3
Ceira r. Port. 42 B2
Çekerek Turkey 78 C2
Celano Italy 44 D3
Celaya Mex. 126 F7
Célé r. France 38 D4

▶Celebes i. Indon. 57 F6
4th largest island in Asia.
asia 50–51

Celebes Basin sea feature Pacific Ocean 164 C5
Celebes Sea Indon./Phil. 57 F5
Celendín Peru 146 B6
Celina OH U.S.A. 130 A3
Celina TN U.S.A. 128 B4
Celje Slovenia 44 E1
Cella Spain 43 F2
Celldömölk Hungary 37 H5
Celle Germany 36 E2
Celles-sur-Belle France 38 C3
Cellina r. Italy 44 D1
Celone r. Italy 44 E4
Celovec Austria see Klagenfurt
Celtic Sea Rep. of Ireland/U.K. 35 C6
Celtic Shelf sea feature N. Atlantic Ocean 160 N2
Cempi, Teluk b. Indon. 59 G5
Cenajo, Embalse del resr Spain 43 F3
Cenderawasih, Teluk b. Indon. 57 I6
Cenei Romania 46 B2
Cenis, Col du Mont pass France 39 G4
Ceno r. Italy 44 C2
Cenon France 38 C4
Čenta Yugo. 46 B2
Centane S. Africa see Kentani
Centennial Wash watercourse U.S.A. 137 F5
Center ND U.S.A. 132 A2
Center NE U.S.A. 132 B3
Center TX U.S.A. 133 C6
Centereach U.S.A. 131 G3
Center Hill Lake resr U.S.A. 128 B5
Center Point U.S.A. 129 B5
Centerville AL U.S.A. 129 B5
Centerville IA U.S.A. 132 C3
Centerville MO U.S.A. 132 D4
Centerville OH U.S.A. 130 B4
Centerville TX U.S.A. 133 C6
Centerville WV U.S.A. 130 C4
Cento Italy 44 C2
Centrafricaine, République country Africa see Central African Republic
Central admin. dist. Botswana 98 E4
Central Brazil 150 D4
Central Chile 148 C5
Central admin. reg. Ghana 93 E4
Central prov. Kenya 96 C5
Central admin. reg. Malawi 97 B8
Central prov. Zambia 95 F8
Central, Cordillera mts Bol. 148 D4
Central, Cordillera mts Col. 146 B4
Central, Cordillera mts Peru 148 A2
Central African Empire country Africa see Central African Republic
▶Central African Republic country Africa 94 C3
africa 86–87, 100
Central Brahui Range mts Pak. 81 F4
Central Butte Canada 123 J5
Central City IA U.S.A. 132 D3
Central City NE U.S.A. 132 B3
Central City PA U.S.A. 130 D3
Central Falls U.S.A. 131 H3
Centralia IL U.S.A. 128 A4
Centralia WA U.S.A. 134 B3
Central Islip U.S.A. 131 G3
Central Kalahari Game Reserve nature res. Botswana 98 D4
Central Kara Rise sea feature Arctic Ocean 166 F1
Central Makran Range mts Pak. 81 F5
Central Mount Stuart Australia 110 C4
Central Mount Wedge Australia 110 B4
Central Pacific Basin sea feature Pacific Ocean 164 F5
Central Provinces state India see Madhya Pradesh
Central Range mts P.N.G. 57 J6
Central Russian Upland hills Rus. Fed. 29 F5
Central Section Australia see Great Barrier Reef Marine Park (Central Section)
Central Siberian Plateau Rus. Fed. 27 L3
Central Sikhote-Alin tourist site Rus. Fed. 64 D3
Central Square U.S.A. 131 E2
Centre prov. Cameroon 93 H4
Centre admin. reg. France 38 D3
Centre U.S.A. 129 B5
Centreville MD U.S.A. 131 E4
Centreville VA U.S.A. 130 E4
Cenxi China 67 D4
Ceos i. Greece see Kea
Céou r. France 38 D4
Cephaloedium Sicily Italy see Cefalù
Cephalonia i. Greece 47 B5
Čepin Croatia 44 G2
Ceprano Italy 44 D4
Cepu Indon. 59 E4
Cer hills Yugo. 46 A2
Ceram i. Indon. see Seram
Ceram Sea Indon. see Seram Sea
Cerbat Mountains U.S.A. 137 E4
Cerbol r. Spain see Servol
Cercal hill Port. 42 B4
Čerchov mt. Czech Rep. 37 F4
Cère r. France 38 D4
Cerea Italy 44 C2
Cereales Arg. 152 E4
Ceres Arg. 152 E2
Ceres S. Africa 98 C7
Ceres U.S.A. 136 B3
Céret France 39 E5
Cereté Col. 146 C2
Cerignola Italy 44 E4
Cerigo i. Greece see Kythira
Çerikli Turkey 78 C3
Cêringgolêb China see Dongco
Çerkeş Turkey 78 C2
Çerkezköy Turkey 46 F4
Cerknica Slovenia 44 E2
Cermei Romania 46 B1
Çermik Turkey 79 D3
Cerna Romania 46 F2
Cerna r. Romania 46 C2
Cerna r. Romania 46 C2
Cerna r. Romania 46 D2
Cernat Romania 46 E2
Cernăuţi Ukr. see Chernivtsi
Cernavodă Romania 46 F2
Cernay France 39 G3
Cerralvo Mex. 133 B7
Cerralvo, Isla i. Mex. 126 E7
Cërrik Albania 46 A4
Cerrillos Arg. 148 D6
Cerritos Mex. 126 F7
Cerro Azul Brazil 151 B8
Cerro Azul Mex. 126 G7
Cerro de Pasco Peru 148 A2
Cerro Las Nopaleras mt. Mex. 133 A7
Cerro Manantiales Chile 153 C8
Cerrón mt. Spain 42 E4
Cerrón, Cerro mt. Venez. 146 D2
Cerros Colorados, Embalse resr Arg. 152 C4
Cerros de Amotape, Parque Nacional nat. park Peru 146 A5
Certeju de Sus Romania 46 C2
Cervantes Australia 109 A7
Cervantes, Cerro mt. Arg. 153 B7
Cervaro r. Italy 44 E4
Cervati, Monte mt. Italy 45 E4
Cervenia Romania 46 D3
Cervera Spain 43 G2
Cervera de Pisuerga Spain 42 D1
Cerveteri Italy 44 D4
Cervia Italy 44 D2
Cervialto, Monte mt. Italy 45 E4
Cervignano del Friuli Italy 44 D2
Cervina, Punta mt. Italy 44 C1
Cervione Corsica France 31 G5
Cervo Spain 42 C1
César dept Col. 146 C2
César r. Col. 146 C2
Cesarò Sicily Italy 45 E6
Cesena Italy 44 D2
Cesenatico Italy 44 D2
Cēsis Latvia 33 G4
Česká Lípa Czech Rep. 37 G3
Česká Republika country Europe see Czech Republic
České Budějovice Czech Rep. 37 G4
Českomoravská Vysočina hills Czech Rep. 37 G4
Český Krumlov Czech Rep. 37 G4
Český Les mts Czech Rep./Germany 37 F4
Český Těšín Czech Rep. 37 I4
Česma r. Croatia 44 F2
Çeşme Turkey 78 A3
Cessnock Australia 112 D4
Cesson-Sévigné France 38 C2
Cestas France 38 C4
Cestos r. Liberia 92 C4
Cesuras Spain 42 B1
Cetate Romania 46 C2
Cetatea Albă Ukr. see Bilhorod-Dnistrovs'kyy
Cetina r. Croatia 44 F3
Cetinje Yugo. 46 A3
Cetraro Italy 45 E5

▶Ceuta N. Africa 42 D5
Spanish Territory.
africa 100

Ceva-i-Ra reef Fiji 107 G4
Cévennes mts France 39 E5
Cévennes, Parc National des nat. park France 39 E4
Cevizlik Turkey see Maçka
Ceyhan Turkey 78 C3
Ceyhan r. Turkey 78 C3
Ceyhan Boğazı r. mouth Turkey 77 B1
Ceylanpınar Turkey 79 D3
Ceylon country Asia see Sri Lanka
Cèze r. France 39 F4

Chaacha Turkm. **81** E2
Châbahâr Iran **81** E5
Chablais *mts* France **39** G3
Chablis France **39** E3
Chabre *ridge* France **39** F4
Chabroi *i.* New Caledonia *see* Lifou
Chabyêr Caka *salt l.* China **75** D3
Chaca Chile **148** C4
Chacabuco Arg. **152** E3
Chacarilla Bol. **148** D4
Chachapoyas Peru **146** B6
Chachaura-Binaganj India **74** C4
Châche Turkm. *see* Chaacha
Chachoengsao Thai. **61** C5
Chaco *prov.* Arg. **152** E1
Chaco Boreal *reg.* Para. **149** F5
Chaco Culture National Historical
  Park *nat. park* U.S.A. **135** F4
Chacorão, Cachoeira da *waterfall* Brazil
  147 G6
Chacra de Piros Peru **148** B2

▶ **Chad** *country* Africa **88** C6
5th largest country in Africa.
africa 86–87, 100

▶ **Chad, Lake** Africa **93** B6
4th largest lake in Africa.
africa 84–85
world 14–15

Chadaasan Mongolia **62** G2
Chadan Rus. Fed. **27** J4
Chadileo *r.* Arg. **152** D4
Chadron U.S.A. **134** C4
Chadyr-Lunga Moldova *see* Ciadîr-Lunga
Chae Hom Thai. **60** B3
Chaek Kyrg. **70** D3
Chaeryŏng N. Korea **65** A5
Chae Son National Park Thai. **60** B4
Chaffee U.S.A. **132** C4
Chaffers, Isla *i.* Chile **153** B6
Chagai Pak. **81** F4
Chagai Hills Afgh./Pak. **81** E4
Chagdo Kangri *mt.* China **75** E2
Chaghā Khūr *mt.* Iran **80** C4
Chaghcharān Afgh. **81** F3
Chagny France **39** F3
Chagos Archipelago *is* Indian Ocean
  162 L6
Chagos-Laccadive Ridge *sea feature*
  Indian Ocean **162** L6
Chagos Trench *sea feature*
  Indian Ocean **162** L6
Chagoyan Rus. Fed. **64** B1
Chagres, Parque Nacional *nat. park*
  Panama **146** B2
Chaguanas Trin. and Tob. **147** F2
Chaguaramas Venez. **146** E2
Chagyl Turkm. **80** C1
Chagyllyshor, Vpadina *depr.* Turkm.
  79 H2
Chaha *r.* Ukr. **46** F2
Chahah Burjal Afgh. **81** E4
Chaharbagh Afgh. **81** G3
Chahah Bahar *i.* Afgh. **81** G3
Chāhār Mahāll va Bakhtīārī *prov.* Iran
  80 B3
Chah Baba *well* Iran **80** C3
Chāh Bahār, Khalīj-e *b.* Iran **81** E5
Chāh-e Bābā *well* Iran **80** D3
Chāh-e Gonbad *well* Iran **80** D3
Chāh-e Kavīr *well* Iran **80** D3
Chāh-e Khorāsān *well* Iran **80** C3
Chāh-e Malek *well* Iran **80** C3
Chāh-e Mīrzā *well* Iran **80** C3
Chāh-e Mūjān *well* Iran **80** C3
Chāh-e Nūklok *well* Iran **80** C3
Chāh-e Pansu *well* Iran **80** C3
Chāh-e Qeyşar *well* Iran **80** C4
Chāh-e Qobād *well* Iran **80** C4
Chāh-e Raḥmān *well* Iran **81** D4
Chāh-e Shūr *well* Iran **80** C3
Chāh-e Tūni *well* Iran **80** C4
Chāh Haji Abdulla *well* Iran **80** C3
Chāh Ḥaqq Iran **80** C4
Chāh-i-Ab Afgh. **81** G2
Chāh Pās *well* Iran **80** C3
Chāh Ru'i *well* Iran **81** D4
Chāh Sandan Pak. **81** F4
Chai *r.* China **66** A4
Chaibasa India **75** E5
Chaigneau, Lac *l.* Canada **125** H2
Chaillu, Massif du *mts* Gabon **94** A5
Chainat Thai. **61** C5
Chainjoin Co *l.* China **75** E2
Chaitén Chile **153** B6
Chai Wan *Hong Kong* China **67** [inset]
Chaiya Thai. **61** B6
Chaiyaphum Thai. **61** C5
Chajari Arg. **152** E2
Chakai India **75** E4
Chakar *r.* Pak. **81** H4
Chake Chake Tanz. **97** C6
Chākhānsūr Afgh. **81** E4
Chakia India **75** D4
Chak Jhumra Pak. **81** H4
Chakradharpur India **75** E5
Chakulia India **75** E5
Chakwal Pak. **81** H3
Chala Peru **148** C4
Chala Tanz. **97** A6
Chala France **38** C4
Chalais France **38** C4
Chalap Dalan *mts* Afgh. **81** F3
Chalatenango El Salvador **138** G6
Chalāua Moz. **99** D5
Chalaxung China **66** A1
Chalbi Desert Kenya **96** C3
Chalcedon Turkey *see* Kadıköy
Chaleur Bay *inlet* Canada **125** H3
Chaleurs, Baie de *inlet* Canada *see*
  Chaleur Bay
Chalia *r.* Arg. **153** C7
Chaling China **67** G3
Chalinze Tanz. **97** C6
Chalisgaon India **72** B1
Chalkar *salt l.* Kazakh. *see*
  Shalkar, Ozero
Chalki Greece **47** L6
Chalki *i.* Greece **47** L6
Chalkida Greece **47** J5
Chalkatós India **72** C3
Challans France **38** C3
Challapata Bol. **148** D4

▶ **Challenger Deep** *sea feature*
  N. Pacific Ocean **164** D5
Deepest point in the world (Mariana
Trench).
oceans 156–157, 168

Challis U.S.A. **134** D3
Chalmette U.S.A. **133** D6
Chal'mny-Varre Rus. Fed. **28** F2
Châlons-en-Champagne France **39** E2
Châlons-sur-Marne France *see*
  Châlons-en-Champagne
Chalon-sur-Saône France **39** F3
Chalt Jammu and Kashmir **74** C1
Chālūs Iran **80** B2
Cham Germany **37** N5
Cham U.S.A. **135** F4
Chama *r.* U.S.A. **135** F5
Chamamba Tanz. **97** B6

Chaman Pak. **81** F4
Chaman Bid Iran **80** D2
Chamao, Khao *mt.* Thai. **61** C5
Chamba India **74** C2
Chamba Tanz. **97** C7
Chambal *r.* India **74** C4
Chambeaux, Lac *l.* Canada **125** G2
Chamberlain *r.* Australia **108** D4
Chamberlain Canada **123** J5
Chamberlain U.S.A. **132** B3
Chamberlain Lake U.S.A. **128** F2
Chambers U.S.A. **137** H4
Chambersburg U.S.A. **130** E4
Chambéry France **39** G4
Chambeshi Zambia **97** A7
Chambeshi *r.* Zambia **97** A8
Chambi, Jebel *mt.* Tunisia **40** D7
Chambira *r.* Peru **146** C6
Chamdo China *see* Qamdo
Chamechaude *mt.* France **39** G4
Châmi *well* Mauritania **90** B5
Chamical Arg. **152** C3
Chamili *i.* Greece **47** E7
Ch'amo Hāyk' *l.* Eth. **96** C3
Chamoli India *see* Gopeshwar
Chamonix-Mont-Blanc France **39** G4
Chamouse, Montagne de *mt.* France
  39 F4
Champa India **75** D5
Champagne-Ardenne *admin. reg.*
  France **39** E2
Champagnole France **39** F3
Champagny Islands Australia **108** D3
Champaign U.S.A. **132** D3
Champaquí, Cerro *mt.* Arg. **152** D2
Champara *mt.* Peru **148** C2
Champasak Laos **61** D5
Champdoré, Lac *l.* Canada **125** H2
Champion Canada **123** H5
Champlain *NY* U.S.A. **128** F2
Champlain *VA* U.S.A. **131** E4
Champlain, Lake Canada/U.S.A. **128** E2
Champlitte France **39** F3
Champotón Mex. **127** H8
Chamrajnagar India **72** C4
Cham Siyāh Iran **80** B4
Chamusca Port. **42** C2
Chamzinka Rus. Fed. **29** H5
Chan, Ko *i.* Thai. **61** B6
Chana Thai. **61** C7
Chanak Turkey *see* Çanakkale
Chañar Arg. **152** C4
Chañaral Chile **152** C1
Chañarán Iran **81** E2
Chança *r.* Port./Spain *see* Chanza
Chanco Chile **152** B3
Chanda India *see* Chandrapur
Chandalar *r.* U.S.A. **120** D3
Chandausi India **74** D3
Chandbali India **73** E1
Chandeleur Islands U.S.A. **129** A6
Chanderi India **74** C4
Chandia India **74** C3
Chandigarh India **74** C3
Chandil India **75** E5
Chandler Canada **125** H3
Chandler U.S.A. **137** G5
Chandless *r.* Brazil **148** C1
Chandpur Bangl. **75** F5
Chandpur India **74** C3
Chandragiri India **72** C3
Chandrapur Bangl. *see* Chandpur
Chandur India **72** C1
Chandvad India **72** B1
Chandyr *r.* Turkm. **80** D2
Chang, Ko *i.* Thai. **61** C5
Changane *r.* Moz. **99** C5
Changara Moz. **99** G3
Changbai China **65** B4
Changbai Shan *mts* China/N. Korea
  64 A4
Changchow *Fujian* China *see* Zhangzhou
Changchow *Jiangsu* China *see*
  Changzhou
Changchun China **64** A4
Changde China **67** D2
Changfeng China **67** F1
Changge China **67** G1
Chang-gap *pt* S. Korea **65** B5
Changgo China **75** E3
Chang Hu *l.* China **67** G2
Changhua Taiwan **67** I3
Changhua Jiang *r.* China **67** D5
Changhŭng S. Korea **65** A6
Chang Jiang *r.* China **66** G2 *see* Yangtze
Changjin-gang *r.* N. Korea **65** A4
Changkiang China *see* Zhanjiang
Changle China **67** F3
Changleng China *see* Xinjian
Changlun Jammu and Kashmir **74** C2
Changning *Hunan* China **67** E3
Changning *Jiangxi* China *see* Xunwu
Changnyŏn N. Korea **65** A5
Ch'ang-pai Shan *mts* China/N. Korea
  see Changbai Shan
Changpu China *see* Suining
Changsan-got *pt* N. Korea **65** A5
Changsha China **67** G2
Changshan China **67** H2
Changshou China **66** E2
Changshoujie China **67** G2
Changshu China **67** I2
Changtai China **67** F3
Changteh China *see* Changde
Changting *Fujian* China **67** H3
Changting *Heilong.* China **64** B3
Changtu China **64** A4
Ch'angwŏn S. Korea **65** B6
Changxing China **67** I2
Changyang China **67** F2
Changyŏn N. Korea **65** A5
Changzhi China **63** I4
Changzhou China **67** H2
Chanḥ, Nevado de *mt.* Arg. **148** D6
Chania Greece **47** D7
Chanion, Kolpos *b.* Greece **47** D7
Channel Islands English Chan. **38** B2
Channel Islands U.S.A. **136** C5
Channel Islands National Park U.S.A.
  136 C4
Channel Rock *i.* Bahamas **129** D8
Channel Tunnel France/U.K. **38** D1
Chantada Spain **42** C1
Chantal'sky *mt.* Rus. Fed. **27** R3
Chanthaburi Thai. **61** C5
Chantilly France **39** E2
Chantonnay France **38** C3
Chanumla India **73** D4
Chany, Ozero *salt l.* Rus. Fed. **26** H4
Chanza *r.* Port./Spain **42** C4
Chao Peru **148** A2
Chaohu China **67** H2
Chao Hu *l.* China **67** H2
Chaoloy China **67** F1
Chao Phraya *r.* Thai. **61** C5
Chaouèn Morocco **90** D7
Chaoyang *Guangdong* China **67** H4
Chaoyang *Heilong.* China *see* Jiayin
Chaoyang *Jilin* China *see* Huinan
Chaoyang *Liaoning* China **63** K3
Chaozhou China **67** H4

Chapada Diamantina, Parque Nacional
  nat. park Brazil **150** D5
Chapada dos Guimarães Brazil **149** G3
Chapada dos Veadeiros, Parque
  Nacional da *nat. park* Brazil **150** C5
Chapadão do Sul Brazil **151** A6
Chapadinha Brazil **150** D2
Chapais Canada **125** F3
Chapak Guzar Afgh. **81** F2
Chapala, Laguna de *l.* Mex. **126** F7
Chapare *r.* Bol. **148** D3
Chaparral Col. **146** C4
Chapayev Kazakh. **26** F4
Chapayevsk Rus. Fed. **29** J5
Chapecó Brazil **151** A8
Chapecó *r.* Brazil **151** A8
Chapleau Canada **124** D4
Chaplin Canada **123** J5
Chaplino Rus. Fed. **27** S3
Chaplygin Rus. Fed. **29** H5
Chapman, Mount *hill* U.S.A. **129** B5
Chapmanville U.S.A. **130** D4
Chappell U.S.A. **132** A3
Chappell Islands Australia **112** C6
Chapri Pass Afgh. **81** F3
Charadai Arg. **152** E2
Charagua Bol. **149** E4
Charana Bol. **148** C4
Charapita Col. **146** C5
Charata Arg. **152** E1
Charcas Mex. **138** D4
Char Chu *r.* China **75** G3
Charcot Island Antarctica **167** L2
Chard Canada **123** I4
Chard U.K. **35** E6
Chardara, Step' *plain* Kazakh. **70** C3
Chardon U.S.A. **130** C3
Chardzhev Turkm. **81** F2
Chardzhou Turkm. *see* Chardzhev
Chardzhouskaya Oblast' *admin. div.*
  Turkm. *see* Lebapskaya Oblast'
Charente *r.* France **38** C4
Charg Iran **80** C4
Chari *r.* Cameroon/Chad **94** B1
Chari-Baguirmi *pref.* Chad **94** C2
Chārīkār Afgh. **81** G3
Charikot Nepal **75** F4
Chariton U.S.A. **132** E3
Chariton *r.* U.S.A. **132** C4
Chärjew Turkm. *see* Chardzhev
Charkayuvom Rus. Fed. **28** J2
Charkhari India **74** C4
Charkhi Dadri India **74** C3
Charkhlik China *see* Ruoqiang
Charleroi Belgium **39** E4
Charles, Cape U.S.A. **131** F5
Charlesbourg Canada **125** G4
Charles City *IA* U.S.A. **132** E3
Charles City *VA* U.S.A. **131** E5
Charles de Gaulle *airport* France **39** E2
Charles Lake Canada **123** I3
Charles Point Australia **110** E3
Charleston N.Z. **113** B3
Charleston *IL* U.S.A. **128** A4
Charleston *SC* U.S.A. **129** D5

▶ **Charleston** *WV* U.S.A. **130** C4
State capital of West Virginia.

Charleston Peak U.S.A. **137** E3
Charlestown *NH* U.S.A. **131** G2
Charlestown *RI* U.S.A. **131** H3
Charles Town U.S.A. **130** E4
Charleville Australia **111** F5
Charleville *Rep. of Ireland see* Rathluirc
Charleville-Mézières France **39** E2
Charlevoix U.S.A. **132** C1
Charley *r.* U.S.A. **122** A1
Charlie Lake Canada **122** F3
Charlotte *MI* U.S.A. **130** A2
Charlotte *NC* U.S.A. **128** C5

▶ **Charlotte Amalie** Virgin Is (U.S.A.)
  139 L5
Capital of the U.S. Virgin Islands.

Charlotte Bank *sea feature* S. China Sea
  59 D1
Charlotte Lake Canada **122** E4
Charlottesville U.S.A. **130** D4

▶ **Charlottetown** Canada **125** I4
Provincial capital of Prince Edward Island.

Charlotteville Trin. and Tob. **147** F2
Charlton Australia **112** B6
Charlton Island Canada **124** E2
Charmes France **39** G2
Charnley *r.* Australia **108** D4
Charron Lake Canada **123** M4
Charsadda Pak. **81** G3
Charshanga Turkm. **81** F2
Charters U.S.A. **130** B4
Charters Towers Australia **111** F4
Chartres France **38** D2
Chas India **75** D5
Châs *mt.* Port. **42** D2
Chaschuil Arg. **152** C1
Chascomús Arg. **152** E3
Chase Canada **122** G5
Chase City U.S.A. **130** D5
Chashkent Turkm. **81** G2
Chashmeh-ye Safid *spring* Iran **80** D3
Chashmeh-ye Shotoran *well* Iran **80** C3
Chashniki Belarus **29** D5
Chasia *reg.* Greece **47** J5
Chasico Arg. **153** D5
Chaska U.S.A. **132** E2
Chaslands Mistake *c.* N.Z. **113** B4
Chasŏng N. Korea **64** F4
Chassezac *r.* France **39** F4
Chassiron, Pointe de *pt* France **38** C3
Chastab, Kūh-e *mts* Iran **80** C3
Chastyye Rus. Fed. **28** J4
Chasuta Peru **146** B6
Chât Iran **80** D2
Chatang China *see* Zhanang
Château-Arnoux France **39** F4
Châteaubriant France **38** C3
Château-Chinon France **39** F3
Château-du-Loir France **38** E3
Château-Gontier France **38** C3
Châteauguay Canada **125** G1
Châteauguay, Lac *l.* Canada **125** G1
Châteaulin France **38** B2
Châteauneuf-en-Thymerais France
  38 D2
Châteauneuf-sur-Loire France **38** E3
Château-Renault France **38** D3
Châteauroux France **38** D3
Château-Salins France **39** G2
Château-Thierry France **39** E2
Châtelaillon-Plage France **38** C3
Châtelet Belgium **39** F1
Châtelguyon France **38** D3
Châtenois France **39** F2
Chatfield U.S.A. **132** E3
Chatham *MA* U.S.A. **131** I3
Chatham *NY* U.S.A. **131** G2
Chatham *VA* U.S.A. **130** D5
Chatham, Isla *i.* Chile **153** B7
Chatham Island Samoa *see* Savai'i

Chatham Island S. Pacific Ocean
  107 H6
Chatham Islands S. Pacific Ocean
  107 H6
Chatham Rise *sea feature*
  S. Pacific Ocean **164** G8
Chatham Sound *sea chan.* Canada
  122 D4
Chatham Strait U.S.A. **122** C3
Châtillon-sur-Indre France **38** D3
Châtillon-sur-Seine France **39** F3
Chatom U.S.A. **129** A6
Chatra India **75** E4
Chatra Nepal **75** E4
Chatsu India **74** C4
Chatsworth Australia **111** E4
Chatsworth U.S.A. **129** B5
Chatsworth Zimbabwe **99** F3
Chattagam Bangl. *see* Chittagong
Chattahoochee U.S.A. **129** B6
Chattahoochee *r.* U.S.A. **129** B6
Chattanooga U.S.A. **128** C5
Chatturat Thai. **61** C5
Châu Đôc Vietnam **61** D6
Chauffailles France **39** F3
Chauhtan India **74** B4
Chauk Myanmar **60** A3
Chaukan Pass Afgh. **81** D5
Chaukhamba *mts* India *see*
  Badrinath Peaks
Chaumont France **39** F2
Chauncey U.S.A. **130** D4
Chaungwabyin Myanmar **61** B5
Chaunskaya Guba *b.* Rus. Fed. **27** S3
Chauny France **39** E2
Chau Phu Vietnam *see* Châu Đôc
Chaurai India **74** C5
Chausey, Îles *is* France **38** C2
Chausy Belarus *see* Chavusy
Chauvigny France **38** D3
Chauvin Canada **123** I4
Chavakachcheri Sri Lanka **72** D4
Chaval Brazil **150** D2
Chavan'ga Rus. Fed. **28** F2
Chavār Iran **80** B3
Chaves Brazil **150** B2
Chaves Port. **42** C2
Chaves Valdivia Peru **146** B6
Chavusy Belarus **29** F5
Chawai *r.* Pak. **81** F4
Chāy *r.* Vietnam **60** D2
Chayatyn, Khrebet *ridge* Rus. Fed.
  64 D1
Chayevo Rus. Fed. **28** H4
Chaykovskiy Rus. Fed. **28** J4
Chazhegovo Rus. Fed. **28** J3
Chazón Arg. **152** E3
Chazy U.S.A. **131** G1
Cheat *r.* U.S.A. **130** C4
Cheb Czech Rep. **37** M4
Cheboksary Rus. Fed. **28** H4
Cheboygan U.S.A. **132** C1
Chechen *i.* Rus. Fed. **79** H1
Chechenia *aut. rep.* Rus. Fed. *see*
  Chechenskaya Respublika
Chechenskaya Respublika *aut. rep.*
  Rus. Fed. **79** F2
Chechnia *aut. rep.* Rus. Fed. *see*
  Chechenskaya Respublika
Chechnya *aut. rep.* Rus. Fed. *see*
  Chechenskaya Respublika
Chech'ŏn S. Korea **65** B5
Checotah U.S.A. **133** C5
Cheduba Myanmar **60** A4
Cheduba Island Myanmar **60** A4
Cheduba Strait Myanmar **60** A4
Chée *r.* France **39** E2
Cheektowaga U.S.A. **130** D2
Cheepash *r.* Canada **124** E3
Cheepie Australia **111** E5
Cheetham, Cape Antarctica **167** H2
Cheffadène *well* Niger **93** H2
Chefoo China *see* Yantai
Chefornak U.S.A. **120** C4
Chegdomyn Rus. Fed. **64** C2
Chegga Mauritania **90** D4
Cheggué *watercourse* Mauritania **92** C1
Chegguet Ti-n-Kerkâz *des.* Mauritania
  92 D1
Chegutu Zimbabwe **99** F3
Chehalis U.S.A. **134** C3
Chehariz *tourist site* Iraq **79** G4
Chehel Chashmeh, Kūh-e *hill* Iran **80** A3
Chehel Dokhtarān, Kūh-e *mt.* Iran **81** E4
Chehell'āyeh *well* Iran **80** D4
Cheikria *well* Iran **80** D4
Cheju S. Korea **65** A6
Cheju-do *i.* S. Korea **65** A6
Cheju-haehyŏp *sea chan.* S. Korea **65** A6
Chek Chue *Hong Kong* China *see* Stanley
Chekiang *prov.* China *see* Zhejiang
Chek Lap Kok *i. Hong Kong* China
  see Ngong Shuen Chau
Chekshino Rus. Fed. **28** G4
Chela, Serra da *mts* Angola **95** B9
Chelan U.S.A. **134** C3
Chelan, Lake U.S.A. **134** C2
Cheleken Turkm. **80** C2
Chelforó Arg. **152** C5
Chélif, Oued *r.* Alg. **43** G4
Chélia, Djebel *mt.* Alg. **54** B7
Chelkar Kazakh. **70** C2
Chełm Poland **31** J3
Chelmer *r.* U.K. **35** H6
Chełmno Poland **37** I2
Chelmsford U.K. **35** H6
Chełmża Poland **37** I2
Chelsea U.S.A. **130** A2
Cheltenham U.K. **35** E6
Chelva Spain **43** F3
Chelyabinsk Rus. Fed. **26** G4
Chelyan U.S.A. **130** C4
Chelyuskin Rus. Fed. **27** K2
Chelyaba Morocco **90** C2
Chembe Zambia **95** F7
Chemchām, Sebkhet *salt flat* Mauritania
  90 B5
Chem Co *l.* China **74** C2
Chemenibit Turkm. **81** E3
Chemillé France **38** C3
Chemmis Egypt *see* Akhmīm
Chemnitz Germany **37** F3
Chemulpo S. Korea *see* Inch'ŏn
Chemult U.S.A. **134** C4
Chemung *r.* U.S.A. **131** E3
Chenab *r.* India/Pak. **74** B3
Chenachane Alg. **90** D4
Chenachane, Oued *watercourse* Alg.
  90 D4
Chendir *r.* Turkm. *see* Chandyr
Cheney U.S.A. **134** D3
Cheney Reservoir U.S.A. **132** D4
Chengalpattu India **72** C3
Chengam India **72** C3
Chengbihe Shuiku *resr* China **66** C3
Chengchow China *see* Zhengzhou
Chengde China **63** J3
Chengdu China **66** C2
Chenggong China **66** B3

Chenghai China **67** F4
Cheng Hai *l.* China **66** B3
Chengjiang China *see* Taihe
Chengkou China **67** F2
Chengmai China **67** D5
Chengshou China *see* Yingshan
Chengtu China *see* Chengdu
Chengxian China *see* Fuquan
Chengxiang *Chongqing* China *see* Wuxi
Chengxiang *Jiangxi* China *see* Quannan
Chengxiang *Sichuan* China *see* Mianning
Chengzhong China *see* Ningming
Chennai China *see* Fuchuan
Chenstokhov Poland *see* Częstochowa
Chenting, Tanjong *pt* Sing. **58** [inset]
Chenxi China **67** F3
Chenyang China *see* Chenxi
Chenying China *see* Wannian
Chenzhou China **67** E3
Cheom Ksan Cambodia *see*
  Chŏâm Khsant
Chepelare Bulg. **46** D4
Chepén Peru **148** A1
Chepes Arg. **152** D2
Chepo Panama **146** B1
Chepstow U.K. **35** E6
Cheptsa *r.* Rus. Fed. **28** I4
Chera *state* India *see* Kerala
Cherangany Hills Kenya **96** B4
Cheraw U.S.A. **129** D5
Cherbaniani Reef India **72** A3
Cherbourg France **38** C2
Cherchell Alg. **43** H4
Cherchen China *see* Qiemo
Cherdakly Rus. Fed. **29** I5
Cherdyn' Rus. Fed. **28** K3
Chère *r.* France **38** C3
Cherepanovo Rus. Fed. **26** J4
Cherekha *r.* Rus. Fed. **33** H4
Cheremkhovo Rus. Fed. **62** G1
Cheremshany Rus. Fed. **64** C3
Cheremukhovka Rus. Fed. **28** I4
Cherepovets Rus. Fed. **28** H4
Cherevkovo Rus. Fed. **28** I3
Chergui, Chott ech *imp. l.* Alg. **91** E2
Chéria Alg. **91** G2
Cherial India **72** C2
Cheriton U.S.A. **131** F5
Cheriyam *i.* India **72** B4
Cherkasy Ukr. *see* Cherkasy
Cherkasy Ukr. **29** F6
Cherkessk Rus. Fed. **29** G7
Cherla India **72** D2
Chermenze Angola **95** D8
Chermoz Rus. Fed. **28** K4
Chernaya Rus. Fed. **28** K1
Chernaya *r.* Rus. Fed. **28** K1
Chernevo Rus. Fed. **33** H4
Chernigov Ukr. *see* Chernihiv
Chernigovka Rus. Fed. **64** C3
Chernihiv Ukr. **29** D6
Cherni Lom *r.* Bulg. **46** D3
Chernivtsi Ukr. **29** E6
Cherni Vrŭkh *mt.* Bulg. **46** C3
Chernivtsi Ukr. *see* Chernivtsi
Chernobyl' Ukr. *see* Chornobyl'
Chernogorsk Rus. Fed. **62** G2
Chernoostrovskoye Rus. Fed. **27** I3
Chernoye More *sea* Asia/Europe *see*
  Black Sea
Chernushka Rus. Fed. **28** K4
Chernyakhiv Ukr. **29** F6
Chernyakhovsk Rus. Fed. **37** J1
Chernyanka Rus. Fed. **29** G6
Chernyayevo Rus. Fed. **64** A1
Chernyshevsk Rus. Fed. **63** J1
Chernyshkovskiy Rus. Fed. **29** G6
Chernyy Irtysh *r.* China/Kazakh. *see*
  Ertix He
Chernyy Otrog Rus. Fed. **29** J6
Chernyy Porog Rus. Fed. **28** F3
Chernyy Rynok Rus. Fed. *see* Kochubey
Chernyy Yar Rus. Fed. **29** H6
Cherokee *IA* U.S.A. **132** C3
Cherokee *OK* U.S.A. **133** C4
Cherokees, Lake o' the U.S.A. **133** C4

▶ **Cherrapunji** India **75** F4
Highest recorded annual rainfall in the
world.
world 12–13

Cherry Creek *r.* U.S.A. **132** A2
Cherry Creek Mountains U.S.A. **137** E1
Cherry Hill U.S.A. **131** F4
Cherry Lake U.S.A. **136** C2
Cherry Valley Canada **131** E2
Cherskiy Rus. Fed. **27** Q3
Cherskogo, Khrebet *mts* Rus. Fed.
  27 O3
Chersonisos Methano *pen.* Greece **47** J6
Cherthala India *see* Shertally
Chertkov Ukr. *see* Chortkiv
Chertkovo Rus. Fed. **29** G6
Cherven Bryag Bulg. **46** C3
Chervonoarmiys'k Ukr. *see*
  Krasnoarmiys'k
Chervonograd Ukr. *see* Chervonohrad
Chervonohrad Ukr. **29** C6
Chervonozavods'ke Ukr. **29** EE
Chervyen' Belarus **29** D5
Cherykaw Belarus **31** L2
Chesaning U.S.A. **130** A2
Chesapeake U.S.A. **131** E5
Chesapeake Bay U.S.A. **131** E4
Cheshme Vtoroy Turkm. **81** E3
Cheshskaya Guba *b.* Rus. Fed. **28** H2
Chesht-e Sharīf Afgh. **81** E3
Chesnokovka Rus. Fed. *see* Novoaltaysk
Chester Canada **125** H4
Chester U.K. **35** E5
Chester *CA* U.S.A. **136** B1
Chester *IL* U.S.A. **132** D4
Chester *MT* U.S.A. **134** F2
Chester *OH* U.S.A. **130** C4
Chester *PA* U.S.A. **131** F4
Chester *SC* U.S.A. **129** D5
Chester *VA* U.S.A. **130** E5
Chesterfield U.K. **35** F5
Chesterfield, Îles *is* New Caledonia
  107 F3
Chesterfield Inlet Canada **123** N2
Chesterfield Inlet *inlet* Canada **123** M2
Chesterton U.S.A. **131** F5
Chestnut Ridge U.S.A. **130** F4
Chesuncook Lake U.S.A. **128** F2
Chéticamp Canada **125** I4
Chetlat *i.* India **72** B4
Chetopa U.S.A. **133** C4
Chetumal Mex. **138** G5
Chetwynd Canada **122** F4
Cheung Chau *Hong Kong* China **67** [inset]
Chevelon Creek *r.* U.S.A. **137** H4
Cheviot N.Z. **113** C3
Cheviot Hills U.K. **34** E3
Cheviot Range *hills* Australia **111** E5
Chevreulx *r.* Canada **125** F2

Che'w Bahir *salt l.* Eth. **96** C3
Chewelah U.S.A. **134** C2
Cheyenne OK U.S.A. **133** B5

▶ **Cheyenne** *WY* U.S.A. **134** F4
State capital of Wyoming.

Cheyenne *r.* U.S.A. **132** C2
Cheyenne Wells U.S.A. **134** G5
Cheyne Bay Australia **109** B8
Cheyur India **72** C3
Cheyyar *r.* India **72** C3
Chezacut Canada **122** E4
Chhabra India **74** C4
Chhapar India **74** C4
Chhapra India **75** E4
Chhata India **74** C4
Chhatak Bangl. **75** F4
Chhatarpur *Jharkhand* India **75** E4
Chhatarpur *Madhya Pradesh* India **74** C4
Chhatrapur India **73** E2
Chhattisgarh *state* India **75** D5
Chhay Arêng, Stœng *r.* Cambodia **61** C6
Chhibramau India **74** C4
Chhindwara India **74** C5
Chhota Chhindwara India **74** C5
Chhota Udepur India **74** C5
Chhukha Bhutan **75** F4
Chiai Taiwan **67** I3
Ch'iak-san National Park S. Korea
  65 B5
Chiang Dao Thai. **60** B3
Chiange Angola **95** B8
Chiang Kham Thai. **60** C3
Chiang Khan Thai. **60** C3
Chiang Mai Thai. **60** B3
Chiang Rai Thai. **60** B3
Chiani *r.* Italy **44** D3
Chiapa Mex. **138** F5
Chiapas *state* Mex. **138** F5
Chiat'ura Georgia **79** F2
Chiautla Mex. **138** E5
Chiavari Italy **44** B2
Chiavenna Italy **44** B1
Chiba Japan **65** E6
Chibemba Angola **95** B8
Chibi China **67** G2
Chibia Angola **95** B8
Chibizovka Rus. Fed. *see* Zherdevka
Chibougamau Canada **125** F3
Chibougamau, Lac *l.* Canada **125** F3
Chibu-Sangaku National Park Japan
  65 D5
Chibuto Moz. **99** G5
Chibuzhang Hu *l.* China **70** H5
Chicacole India *see* Srikakulam

▶ **Chicago** U.S.A. **132** E3
4th most populous city in North America.
world 16–17

Chicala Angola **95** C7
Chicapa *r.* Angola **95** D6
Chic-Chocs, Monts *mts* Canada **125** H3
Chicha *well* Chad **88** C7
Chichagof Island U.S.A. **120** F4
Chichak *r.* Pak. **81** F5
Chicheng China *see* Pengxi
Chichester U.K. **35** F6
Chichester Range *mts* Australia **108** B5
Chichgarh India **72** D1
Chichibu Japan **65** D6
Chichibu-Tama National Park Japan
  65 D6
Chichiriviche Venez. **146** D2
Chicholi India **74** C5
Chickahominy *r.* U.S.A. **131** E5
Chickasawhay *r.* U.S.A. **129** A6
Chickasha U.S.A. **133** D5
Chiclayo Peru **146** C6
Chico *r. Chubut* Arg. **153** C5
Chico *r. Chubut* Arg. **153** C6
Chico *r. Santa Cruz* Arg. **153** C5
Chico U.S.A. **136** B2
Chicoa Moz. **99** D5
Chicomo Moz. **99** G5
Chiconono Moz. **99** G5
Chicopee U.S.A. **131** G2
Chicoutimi Canada **125** G3
Chicualacuala Moz. **99** F4
Chicuma Angola **95** B8
Chidambaram India **72** C4
Chido China **75** G3
Chiede Angola **95** C9
Chiefland U.S.A. **129** C5
Chiemsee *l.* Germany **37** F5
Chiengi Zambia **95** F7
Chiengmai Thai. *see* Chiang Mai
Chienti *r.* Italy **44** E3
Chieo Lan Reservoir Thai. **61** B6
Chieri Italy **44** B2
Chiers *r.* France **39** F2
Chiese *r.* Italy **44** C2
Chieti Italy **44** F3
Chifeng China **63** K3
Chifre, Serra do *mts* Brazil **151** D6
Chiganak Kazakh. **70** D2
Chiginagak, Mount *vol.* U.S.A. **120** D4
Chignik U.S.A. **120** D4
Chigorodó Col. **146** B3
Chigu China **75** G3
Chiguboo Moz. **99** G3
Chigu Co *l.* China **70** H6
Chihli, Gulf of China *see* Bo Hai
Chihuahua Mex. **135** F7
Chihuahua *state* Mex. **133** A7
Chiili Kazakh. **70** C3
Chikalda India **74** C5
Chikan China **67** D4
Chikaskia *r.* U.S.A. **132** B4
Chik Ballapur India **72** C3
Chikhali Kalan Parasia India **74** C5
Chikhli India **72** C1
Chikmagalur India **72** B3
Chikodi India **72** B2
Chikodi Road India **72** B2
Chikwa Zambia **97** B7
Chikwawa Malawi **97** B9
Chila Angola **95** B8
Chilanko *r.* Canada **122** E4
Chilanko Forks Canada **122** E4
Chilas Jammu and Kashmir **74** B2
Chilaw Sri Lanka **72** C5
Chilcaya Chile **148** C4
Chilcotin *r.* Canada **122** E5
Childers Australia **111** H5
Childress U.S.A. **133** B5

▶ **Chile** *country* S. America **152** B6
southamerica 144–145, 154

Chile Basin *sea feature* S. Pacific Ocean
  165 M8
Chile Chico Chile **153** C6
Chilecito Arg. **152** D2
Chilengue, Serra do *mts* Angola **95** B8
Chile Rise *sea feature* S. Pacific Ocean
  165 M8
Chilete Peru **148** A1
Chilia-Nouă Ukr. *see* Kiliya
Chilika Lake India **73** E2
Chililabombwe Zambia **95** E8

Chiliomodi Greece **47** C6
Chilko *r.* Canada **122** E5
Chilko Lake Canada **122** E5
Chilkoot Trail National Historic Site *nat. park* U.S.A. **120** F4
Chillán Chile **152** B4
Chillar Arg. **152** F4
Chillicothe *MO* U.S.A. **132** C4
Chillicothe *OH* U.S.A. **130** B4
Chilliculco Peru **148** C3
Chilliwack Canada **134** B2
Chil'mamedkum, Peski *des.* Turkm. **80** C1
Chilmari Bangl. **75** F4
Chiloé, Isla de *i.* Chile **153** B5
Chiloé, Isla Grande de *i.* Chile *see* Chiloé, Isla de
Chilombo Angola **95** D8
Chilonga Zambia **95** F7
Chiloquin U.S.A. **134** B4
Chilpancingo Mex. **138** E5
Chiltern Australia **112** C5
Chiltern Hills U.K. **35** F6
Chilton U.S.A. **132** C2
Chiluage Angola **95** D7
Chilubi Zambia **95** F7
Chilung Taiwan **67** G3
Chilung Pass Jammu and Kashmir **74** C2
Chilwa, Lake Malawi **97** B8
Chimala Tanz. **97** B7
Chimaltenango Guat. **138** H6
Chimanimani Zimbabwe **99** G3
Chi Ma Wan *Hong Kong* China **67** [inset]
Chimba Zambia **97** A7
Chimbas Arg. **152** C2
Chimbay Uzbek. **76** F1
Chimborazo *mt.* Ecuador **146** B5
Chimborazo *prov.* Ecuador **146** B5
Chimbote Peru **148** A2
Chimboy Uzbek. *see* Chimbay
Chimian Pak. **81** H3
Chimishliya Moldova *see* Cimişlia
Chimkent Kazakh. *see* Shymkent
Chimoio Moz. **99** G3
Chimorra *hill* Spain **42** D3
Chimpay Arg. **152** C3
Chimtargha, Qullai *mt.* Tajik. **81** G2
Chimtorga, Gora *mt.* Tajik. *see* Chimtargha, Qullai
Chin *state* Myanmar **60** A3

►**China** *country* Asia **62** D2
Most populous country in the world and in Asia. 2nd largest country in Asia and 4th largest in the world.
asia 52–53, 82
world 8–9, 16–17

China Mex. **133** B7
China, Republic of *country* Asia *see* Taiwan
China Bakir *r.* Myanmar *see* To
Chinandega Nicaragua **133** G6
China Point U.S.A. **136** C5
Chinati Peak U.S.A. **135** F7
Chincha Alta Peru **148** A3
Chinchilla Australia **111** G5
Chincholi India **72** C3
Chinchorro, Banco *sea feature* Mex. **127** I8
Chincolco Chile **152** C3
Chincoteague U.S.A. **131** F5
Chincoteague Bay U.S.A. **131** F5
Chinde Moz. **99** H3
Chin-do *i.* S. Korea **65** A6
Chindu China **70** I1
Chindwin *r.* Myanmar **60** A3
Chineni Jammu and Kashmir **74** B2
Chinese Turkestan *aut. reg.* China *see* Xinjiang Uygur Zizhiqu
Chingaza, Parque Nacional *nat. park* Col. **146** C3
Chinghai *prov.* China *see* Qinghai
Chingirlau Kazakh. **29** J6
Chingleput India *see* Chengalpattu
Chingola Zambia **95** B8
Chinguar Angola **95** C8
Chinguetti Mauritania **90** B5
Chinguil Chad **94** C2
Chinhoyi Zimbabwe **99** F3
Chini India *see* Kalpa
Chining China *see* Jining
Chiniot Pak. **81** H4
Chinipas Mex. **135** E8
Chinit, Stœng *r.* Cambodia **61** D5
Chinko *r.* Cent. Afr. Rep. **94** D3
Chinle U.S.A. **137** H3
Chinle Valley U.S.A. **137** H3
Chinmen Taiwan **67** F3
Chinmen Tao *i.* Taiwan **67** F3
Chinna Ganjam India **72** D2
Chinnamp'o N. Korea *see* Namp'o
Chinna Salem India **72** C4
Chinnur India **72** C2
Chino Japan **65** E6
Chino Creek *watercourse* U.S.A. **137** F4
Chinon France **38** D3
Chinook U.S.A. **134** E2
Chinook Trough *sea feature* N. Pacific Ocean **164** G3
Chino Valley U.S.A. **137** F4
Chinsali Zambia **97** B7
Chintalnar India **72** D2
Chintamani India **72** C3
Chinteni Romania **46** C1
Chinú Col. **146** C2
Chinyama Litapi Zambia **95** D8
Chin'yavoryk Rus. Fed. **28** J3
Chioco Moz. **99** D3
Chioggia Italy **44** D2
Chiona Tanz. **97** B6
Chios Greece **47** E5
Chios *i.* Greece **47** D5
Chios Strait Greece **47** E5
Chipanga Moz. **99** G3
Chipata Zambia **97** B8
Chipchihua, Sierra de *mts* Arg. **153** C5
Chipindo Angola **95** B8
Chipinga Zimbabwe *see* Chipinge
Chipinge Zimbabwe **99** G4
Chipiona Spain **42** C4
Chipley U.S.A. **129** D6
Chiplun India **72** B3
Chipola Angola **95** C8
Chippenham U.K. **35** E6
Chipperone, Monte *mt.* Moz. **99** G3
Chippewa *r.* U.S.A. **132** C2
Chippewa, Lake U.S.A. **132** D2
Chippewa Falls U.S.A. **132** C2
Chipping Norton U.K. **35** F6
Chipundu Zambia **95** F7
Chipuriro Zimbabwe *see* Guruve
Chipurupalle *Andhra Pradesh* India **73** D2
Chipurupalle *Andhra Pradesh* India **73** D2
Chiquian Peru **148** A2
Chiquinquira Col. **146** C3
Chiquitirca Peru **148** B3
Chiquita, Mar *l.* Arg. **152** D2
Chiquitos, Llanos de *plain* Bol. **149** E4
Chiquitos Jesuit Missions *tourist site* Brazil **149** E4

Chir *r.* Rus. Fed. **29** G6
Chirada India **72** D3
Chirala India **72** D3
Chiramba Moz. **99** G3
Chirambirá, Punta *pt* Col. **146** B3
Chiras Afgh. **81** F3
Chirchik Uzbek. **70** C3
Chiredzi Zimbabwe **99** F4
Chirfa Niger **88** E4
Chirgua *r.* Venez. **146** E2
Chiricahua Peak U.S.A. **135** E7
Chiriguaná Col. **146** C2
Chirikof Island U.S.A. **120** D4
Chiriquí, Golfo de *b.* Panama **139** H7
Chiriquí, Laguna de *b.* Panama **139** H7
Chiri-san *mt.* S. Korea **65** A6
Chiri-san National Park S. Korea **65** A6
Chirnside U.K. **34** E4
Chirpan Bulg. **46** D3
Chirripo *mt.* Costa Rica **139** H7
Chirundu Zimbabwe **99** F3
Chirûyeh Iran **80** C5
Chisamba Zambia **95** F8
Chisana U.S.A. **122** A2
Chisana *r.* U.S.A. **122** A2
Chisasa Zambia **95** E8
Chisasibi Canada **124** E2
Chisekesi Zambia **95** E9
Chiselet Romania **46** E2
Chisenga Malawi **97** B7
Chishima-retto *is* Rus. Fed. *see* Kuril Islands
Chishmy Rus. Fed. **28** J5
Chisholm Canada **123** H4
Chisholm U.S.A. **131** H1
Chishtian Mandi Pak. **81** H4
Chishui China **66** C2
Chishui He *r.* China **66** C2
Chisimaio Somalia *see* Kismaayo

►**Chişinău** Moldova **29** D7
Capital of Moldova.

Chişineu-Criş Romania **46** B1
Chişone *r.* Italy **44** A2
Chistopol' Rus. Fed. **28** I5
Chita Col. **146** C4
Chita Rus. Fed. **27** L4
Chita Tanz. **97** B7
Chitado Angola **95** B9
Chitaldrug India *see* Chitradurga
Chitalwana India **74** B4
Chita Oblast *admin. div.* Rus. Fed. *see* Chitinskaya Oblast'
Chitato Angola **95** D6
Chitek Lake Canada **123** J4
Chitek Lake *l.* Canada **123** L4
Chitembo Angola **95** C8
Chitinskaya Oblast' *admin. div.* Rus. Fed. **63** J1
Chitipa Malawi **97** B7
Chitobe Moz. **99** D3
Chitokoloki Zambia **95** D8
Chitongo Zambia **95** E9
Chitor India *see* Chittaurgarh
Chitose Japan **64** F4
Chitradurga India **72** C3
Chitrakut India **74** D4
Chitral Pak. **81** G3
Chitral *r.* Pak. **81** G3
Chitravati *r.* India **72** C3
Chitré Panama **139** H7
Chittrod India **74** D4
Chittagong Bangl. **75** F5
Chittagong *admin. div.* Bangl. **75** F5
Chittaranjan India **75** E5
Chittaurgarh India **74** B4
Chittoor India **72** C3
Chittorgarh India *see* Chittaurgarh
Chittur India **72** C4
Chitungulu Zambia **97** B8
Chitungwiza Zimbabwe **99** F3
Chiu Lung *Hong Kong* China *see* Kowloon
Chiume Angola **95** D8
Chiúre Novo Moz. **97** C8
Chiusa Sclafani *Sicily* Italy **45** D6
Chiúta Moz. **99** G2
Chiva Spain **43** F3
Chivasso Italy **44** A2
Chivato, Punta *pt* Mex. **135** E8
Chivay Peru **148** C3
Chive Bol. **148** C3
Chivhu Zimbabwe **99** F3
Chivilcoy Arg. **152** F3
Chiyirchik, Pereval *pass* Kyrg. *see* Ashusuu
Chizarira Hills Zimbabwe **99** F3
Chizarira National Park Zimbabwe **99** F3
Chizha Vtoraya Kazakh. **29** I6
Chkalov Rus. Fed. *see* Orenburg
Chkalovsk Rus. Fed. **28** I4
Chkalovskaya Oblast' *admin. div.* Rus. Fed. *see* Orenburgskaya Oblast'
Chlef Alg. *see* Ech Chélif
Chlumec nad Cidlinou Czech Rep. **37** G3
Chmielnik Poland **37** J3
Choa Chu Kang Sing. **58** [inset]
Choa Chu Kang *hill* Sing. **58** [inset]
Choâm Khsant Cambodia **61** D5
Chobe *admin. dist.* Botswana **98** E3
Chobe National Park Botswana **98** E3
Chocianów Poland **37** G2
Chociwel Poland **37** G2
Choco *dept* Col. **146** B3
Chocolate Mountains U.S.A. **137** E5
Chocontá Col. **146** C3
Choctawhatchee *r.* U.S.A. **129** B6
Chodavaram India **73** D2
Chodecz Poland **37** I2
Cho-do *i.* N. Korea **65** A5
Chodzież Poland **37** H2
Choele Choel Arg. **152** D4
Chofombo Moz. **97** A8
Chogo Lungma Glacier Jammu and Kashmir **74** B2
Chogori Feng *mt.* China/Jammu and Kashmir *see* K2
Chograyskoye Vodokhranilishche *resr* Rus. Fed. **29** H7
Choiceland Canada **123** C4
Choique Arg. **152** C4
Choiseul *i.* Solomon Is **107** E2
Choiseul Sound *sea chan.* Falkland Is **153** F7
Chojna Poland **37** G2
Chojnice Poland **37** H2
Chojnów Poland **37** G2
Chōkai-san *vol.* Japan **65** E5
Chok'ē Mountains Eth. **96** C2
Choksum China **75** E3
Chokue Moz. *see* Chókwé
Chokurdakh Rus. Fed. **27** O2
Chókwé Moz. **99** G4
Cho La *pass* China **66** A2
Cholame U.S.A. **136** C4
Cholame Creek *r.* U.S.A. **136** C4
Chola Shan *mts* China **66** A1
Cholet France **38** D3
Choluteca Hond. **138** G6
Choma Zambia **95** E9
Chomo Ganggar *mt.* China **75** F3
Chomo Lhari *mt.* Bhutan **75** F4

Chomo Yummo *mt.* China/India **75** F4
Chomun India **74** B4
Chomutov Czech Rep. **37** F3
Chona *r.* Rus. Fed. **27** K3
Chon Buri Thai. **61** C5
Chone Ecuador **146** A5
Chong'an China *see* Wuyishan
Ch'ŏngch'ŏn-gang *r.* N. Korea **65** A5
Chonggye China *see* Qonggyai
Ch'ŏngjin N. Korea **64** B4
Ch'ŏngju N. Korea **65** A4
Ch'ŏngju S. Korea **65** B5
Chongkü China **66** A2
Chonglong China *see* Zizhong
Chongming Dao *i.* China **67** G2
Chongoroi Angola **95** B8
Ch'ŏngp'yŏng N. Korea **65** A5
Chongqing *Chongqing* China **66** C2
Chongqing *Sichuan* China *see* Chongzhou
Chongqing *municipality* China **66** C2
Chongren China **67** G3
Chŏngŭp S. Korea **65** A6
Chongwe Zambia **95** F8
Chongyang China **67** G2
Chongyang Xi *r.* China **67** F3
Chongyi China **67** G3
Chongzhou China **66** B2
Chongzuo China **66** C4
Chŏnju S. Korea **65** A6
Chon Thanh Vietnam **61** D6

►**Cho Oyu** *mt.* China/Nepal **75** E3
6th highest mountain in the world and in Asia.
asia 50–51
world 6–7

Chopan India **75** D4
Chopda India **74** D5
Cho Phuoc Hai Vietnam **61** D6
Choptank *r.* U.S.A. **131** E4
Choquecamata Bol. **148** D4
Chor Pak. **81** G5
Chora Greece **47** B6
Chorley U.K. **35** E5
Chornobyl' Ukr. **29** D6
Chornomors'ke Ukr. **29** E7
Chortkiv Ukr. **29** C6
Ch'ŏrwŏn S. Korea **65** A5
Chorzele Poland **37** J2
Ch'osan N. Korea **65** A4
Chōshi Japan **65** F6
Choshuenco, Volcán *vol.* Chile **152** B4
Chos Malal Arg. **152** C4
Chosmes Arg. **152** C3
Choszczno Poland **37** G2
Chota Peru **146** B5
Choteau U.S.A. **134** D3
Chotila India **74** A5
Choûm Mauritania **90** B5
Chowchilla U.S.A. **136** B3
Chowghat India **72** B4
Chowilla Regional Reserve *nature res.* Australia **112** B5
Chown, Mount Canada **122** G4
Choya Arg. **152** C3
Choybalsan Mongolia **63** I2
Choyr Mongolia **68** I7
Chozi Zambia **97** B7
Chreïrik *well* Mauritania **90** B5
Chriby *hills* Czech Rep. **37** H4
Christchurch U.K. **35** F6
Christchurch N.Z. **113** C6
Christian *r.* Canada **123** I3
Christiana S. Africa **98** G4
Christian, Cape Canada **166** K2
Christiana Norway *see* Oslo
Christiansburg U.S.A. **130** C5
Christianshåb Greenland *see* Qasigiannguit
Christie Bay Canada **123** I2
Christina *r.* Canada **123** I3
Christina, Mount N.Z. **113** B4
Christmas Creek Australia **108** D4
Christmas Creek *r.* Australia **108** D4

►**Christmas Island** *terr.* Indian Ocean **55** C8
Australian External Territory.
asia 82

Christopher, Lake *salt flat* Australia **109** D6
Christos Greece **47** E6
Chrudim Czech Rep. **37** G4
Chrysi *i.* Greece **47** D7
Chrysochou Bay Cyprus **77** A2
Chrysochous, Kolpos *b.* Cyprus *see* Chrysochou Bay
Chrysoupoli Greece **46** D4
Chu Kazakh. *see* Shu
Chu *r.* Kazakh. **70** C3
Chuadanga Bangl. **75** F5
Chuansha China **66** A2
Chubalung China **66** A2
Chubarovka Ukr. *see* Polohy
Chubbuck U.S.A. **134** D4
Chubut *prov.* Arg. **153** C5
Chubut *r.* Arg. **153** C5
Chuckhono Rus. Fed. **29** G5
Chuckwalla Mountains U.S.A. **137** E5
Chudovo Rus. Fed. **28** D7
Chudskoye, Ozero *l.* Estonia/Rus. Fed. *see* Peipus, Lake
Chugach Mountains U.S.A. **120** D3
Chūgoku-sanchi *mts* Japan **65** C6
Chūgênsumdo China *see* Jigzhi
Chuguchak China *see* Tacheng
Chuguyev Ukr. *see* Chuhuyiv
Chuguyevka Rus. Fed. **64** C3
Chuhai China *see* Zhuhai
Chuhuyiv Ukr. **29** F6
Chuka Kenya **96** D4
Chukai Malaysia *see* Cukai
Chukchagirskoye, Ozero *l.* Rus. Fed. **64** D1
Chukchi Abyssal Plain *sea feature* Arctic Ocean **166** N1
Chukchi Peninsula Rus. Fed. *see* Chukotskiy Poluostrov
Chukchi Plateau *sea feature* Arctic Ocean **166** B1
Chukchi Sea Rus. Fed./U.S.A. **120** B3
Chukhloma Rus. Fed. **28** I4
Chukotskiy, Mys *c.* Rus. Fed. **27** S3
Chukotskiy Poluostrov *pen.* Rus. Fed. **27** S3
Chulaktau Kazakh. *see* Karatau
Chulasa Rus. Fed. **28** H2
Chula Vista U.S.A. **136** E5
Chulucanas Peru **146** A6
Chulung Pass Pak. **74** D2
Chulym Rus. Fed. **69** G1
Chumba Eth. **96** C3
Chumbicha Arg. **152** C3
Chumda China **66** A1
Chumerna *mt.* Bulg. **46** D3
Chumikan Rus. Fed. **27** N4
Chum Phae Thai. **61** B6
Chumphon Thai. **61** B6
Chum Saeng Thai. **61** C5
Chuna *r.* Rus. Fed. **27** J4
Chuña Huasi Arg. **152** D2
Chun'an China **67** G2
Ch'unch'ŏn S. Korea **65** A5

Chunga Zambia **95** E8
Chung-hua Jen-min Kung-ho-kuo *country* Asia *see* China
Chung-hua Min-kuo *country* Asia *see* Taiwan
Ch'ungju S. Korea **65** A5
Chungking China *see* Chongqing
Chungu *r.* Tanz. **97** C7
Chungyang Shanmo *mts* Taiwan **67** G4
Chunhua China **64** B4
Chunxi China *see* Gaochun
Chunya *r.* Rus. Fed. **27** J3
Chunya Tanz. **97** B7
Chunya *r.* Rus. Fed. **28** J3
Chuōr Phnum Dângrêk *mts* Cambodia/Thai. **61** D5
Chuosijia China *see* Guanyinqiao
Chupa Rus. Fed. **28** C2
Chúplú Iran **80** A2
Chuquicamata Chile **148** C5
Chuquisaca *dept* Bol. **149** D5
Chuqung China *see* Chindu
Chur *r.* Rus. Fed. **28** J4
Chur Switz. **39** H3
Churachandpur India **75** G4
Churapcha Rus. Fed. **27** N3
Chūrān Iran **80** C5
Churayevo Rus. Fed. **28** J5
Church Hill *MD* U.S.A. **131** F4
Church Hill *TN* U.S.A. **130** B5
Churchill Canada **123** M3
Churchill *r.* *Man.* Canada **123** M3
Churchill *r.* *Nfld. and Lab.* Canada **125** I2
Churchill, Cape Canada **123** M3
Churchill Falls Canada **125** I2
Churchill Lake Canada **123** I4
Churchill Mountains Antarctica **167** H1
Churchville U.S.A. **130** D4
Churia Ghati Hills Nepal **75** E4
Churu India **74** B3
Churuguara Venez. **146** D2
Churov Rus. Fed. **28** H4
Chusovaya *r.* Rus. Fed. **28** K4
Chusovoy Rus. Fed. **28** K4
Chust Ukr. *see* Khust
Chutung Taiwan **67** G3
Chuy Uruguay **152** G3
Chu Yang Sin *mt.* Vietnam **61** E5
Chuzhou China **67** F1
Chymyshliya Moldova *see* Cimişlia
Chyulu Range *mts* Kenya **96** C5
Ciacova Romania **46** B2
Ciadâr-Lunga Moldova *see* Ciadir-Lunga
Ciadîr-Lunga Moldova **46** F1
Ciamis Indon. **59** D4
Ciampino *airport* Italy **44** D4
Cianjur Indon. **59** D4
Cianorte Brazil **149** G5
Cibatu Indon. **59** D4
Cibecue U.S.A. **137** G4
Cibitoke Burundi **94** F5
Ci Buni *r.* Indon. **59** D4
Cibuta, Sierra *mt.* Mex. **135** E7
Ciçarija *mts* Croatia **44** D2
Çiçekdağı Turkey **78** C3
Çiçekli *İçel* Turkey **77** B1
Çiçekli *Manisa* Turkey **47** F5
Cícero Dantas Brazil **150** E4
Cićevac Yugo. **46** B3
Cidacos *r.* Spain **43** F1
Cide Turkey **78** C2
Cidlina *r.* Czech Rep. **37** G3
Ciechanów Poland **37** J2
Ciechanowiec Poland **37** K2
Ciechocinek Poland **37** I2
Ciego de Avila Cuba **127** K7
Ciénaga Col. **146** C2
Ciénagas del Catatumbo *nat. park* Venez. **146** D2
Cienfuegos Cuba **127** J7
Cíes, Illas *is* Spain **42** B1
Cieszyn Poland **37** I4
Cieza Spain **43** F3
Cifuentes Spain **43** E2
Cigüela *r.* Spain **42** E3
Cihanbeyli Turkey **78** C3
Cihuatlán Mex. **126** F8
Cijara, Embalse de *resr* Spain **42** D3
Çikes, Maja e *mt.* Albania **47** A4
Cikobia *i.* Fiji **107** H3
Cilacap Indon. **59** D4
Cilangkahan Indon. **58** D4
Çıldır Turkey **79** E2
Çıldır Gölü *l.* Turkey **79** E2
Cileduğ Indon. **59** E4
Cilento e del Vallo di Diano, Parco Nazionale del *nat. park* Italy **45** F4
Cili China **67** F2
Cilician Gates *pass* Turkey *see* Gülek Boğazı
Cill Airne Rep. of Ireland *see* Killarney
Cill Chainnigh Rep. of Ireland *see* Kilkenny
Cill Mhantáin Rep. of Ireland *see* Wicklow
Cilo Dağı *mt.* Turkey **79** F3
Çiloy Adası *i.* Azer. **79** G2
Cima U.S.A. **137** E4
Cimahi Indon. **59** D4
Cimişlia Moldova **46** F1
Cimone, Monte *mt.* Italy **44** C2
Cîmpeni Romania *see* Câmpeni
Cîmpia Turzii Romania *see* Câmpia Turzii
Cîmpina Romania *see* Câmpina
Cîmpulung Romania *see* Câmpulung
Çınar Turkey **79** E3
Çinarcık Turkey **46** F4
Cinaruco *r.* Venez. **146** E2
Cinaruco-Capanaparo, Parque Nacional *nat. park* Venez. **146** E2
Cinca *r.* Spain **43** G2
Cincar *mt.* Bos.-Herz. **44** F3
Cincinnati U.S.A. **130** A4
Cincinnatus U.S.A. **131** F2
Cinco de Outubro Angola *see* Xá-Muteba
Çine Turkey **78** B3
Çine *r.* Turkey **47** E6
Ciney Belgium **39** F1
Cinfães Port. **42** B2
Cingoli Italy **44** D3
Cinque Island India **73** G4
Cintalapa Mex. **138** F5
Cinto, Monte *mt.* France **31** G5
Cintruénigo Spain **43** F1

Cinzas *r.* Brazil **149** H5
Ciolpani Romania **46** E2
Ciovo *i.* Croatia **44** F3
Cipatuja Indon. **59** F4
Ciping China *see* Jinggangshan
Cipolletti Arg. **152** D4
Circeo, Parco Nazionale del *nat. park* Italy **44** D4
Circle *AK* U.S.A. **120** D3
Circle *MT* U.S.A. **134** F3
Circleville *OH* U.S.A. **130** D4
Circleville *UT* U.S.A. **137** G2
Cirebon Indon. **59** D4
Cirencester U.K. **35** F6
Cirenaica *tourist site* Libya *see* Cyrene
Cirò Marina Italy **45** F5
Ciron *r.* France **38** D4
Cirta Alg. *see* Constantine
Cisco U.S.A. **133** D5
Cisnădie Romania **46** D2
Cisterna di Latina Italy **44** D4
Cistierna Spain **42** D1
Città di Castello Italy **44** D3
Cittadella Italy **44** D2
Cittanova Italy **45** F5
City of Derry *airport* U.K. **34** C4
Ciucaş, Vârful *mt.* Romania **46** D2
Ciudad Acuña Mex. **126** F6
Ciudad Altamirano Mex. **138** D5
Ciudad Bolívar Venez. **147** F2
Ciudad Camargo Mex. **135** F8
Ciudad Constitución Mex. **126** D6
Ciudad del Carmen Mex. **127** H8
Ciudad del Este Para. **149** G6
Ciudad de Valles Mex. **126** G7
Ciudad Delicias Mex. **135** F7
Ciudad Guayana Venez. **147** F2
Ciudad Guzmán Mex. **138** H5
Ciudad Ixtepec Mex. **138** E5
Ciudad Juárez Mex. **135** F7
Ciudad Mante Mex. **126** G7
Ciudad Mier Mex. **133** B7
Ciudad Obregón Mex. **135** E8
Ciudad Piar Venez. **147** F3
Ciudad Real Spain **42** E3
Ciudad Río Bravo Mex. **126** G6
Ciudad Rodrigo Spain **42** C2
Ciudad Victoria Mex. **126** G7
Ciudadela de Menorca Spain **43** H2
Cividale del Friuli Italy **44** D2
Civa Burnu *pt* Turkey **78** D2
Civita Castellana Italy **44** D3
Civitanova Marche Italy **44** D3
Civitavecchia Italy **44** C3
Civitella Roveto Italy **44** D3
Civray France **38** D3
Çivril Turkey **78** B3
Cixi China **67** G2
Cizre Turkey **79** E3
Clackamas *r.* U.S.A. **134** B3
Clacton-on-Sea U.K. **35** G6
Clain *r.* France **38** D3
Claire, Lake Canada **123** H3
Clair Engle Lake *resr* U.S.A. **134** B4
Claise *r.* France **38** D3
Clan Alpine Mountains U.S.A. **136** D2
Clanwilliam S. Africa **98** C7
Clara *r.* Australia **110** C3
Clara Island Myanmar **61** B6
Clara Rep. of Ireland **35** D5
Claraville Australia **111** E3
Clare *N.S.W.* Australia **112** A4
Clare *S.A.* Australia **112** A4
Clare *r.* Rep. of Ireland **35** B5
Clare U.S.A. **130** A2
Clare Island Rep. of Ireland **35** A5
Claremont U.S.A. **131** G2
Claremont Isles Australia **111** E2
Claremore U.S.A. **133** C4
Claremorris Rep. of Ireland **35** B5
Clarence *r.* Australia **112** F2
Clarence N.Z. **113** C6
Clarence, Isla *i.* Chile **153** C8
Clarence Island Antarctica **167** A2
Clarence Strait U.S.A. **122** C3
Clarence Town Bahamas **129** E8
Clarendon *AR* U.S.A. **133** D5
Clarendon *PA* U.S.A. **130** D3
Clarendon *TX* U.S.A. **133** B5
Clareville Canada **125** K3
Clarinda U.S.A. **132** C3
Clarington U.S.A. **130** C4
Clarion *IA* U.S.A. **132** C3
Clarion *PA* U.S.A. **128** D3
Clarion *r.* U.S.A. **130** D3
Clark U.S.A. **132** B2
Clark, Mount Canada **122** F1
Clarkdale U.S.A. **137** F4
Clarke *r.* Australia **111** F3
Clarkebury S. Africa **99** F6
Clarke Range *mts* Australia **111** F4
Clarke's Head Canada **125** K3
Clark Fork U.S.A. **134** C2
Clark Fork *r.* *MT* U.S.A. **134** C2
Clark Mountain U.S.A. **137** E4
Clarksburg U.S.A. **130** D4
Clarksdale U.S.A. **127** H5
Clarkston U.S.A. **134** C3
Clarksville *AR* U.S.A. **133** D5
Clarksville *TN* U.S.A. **128** B4
Clarksville *TX* U.S.A. **133** D5
Claro *r.* *Goiás* Brazil **149** H4
Claro *r.* *Mato Grosso* Brazil **149** H3
Claude U.S.A. **133** A5
Cláudio Brazil **151** C7
Claveria Phil. **67** G5
Clavering Ø *i.* Greenland **121** Q2
Claxton U.S.A. **129** D5
Clay U.S.A. **130** C4
Clayburg U.S.A. **131** G1
Clay Center *KS* U.S.A. **132** B4
Clay Center *NE* U.S.A. **132** B3
Clayhole Wash *watercourse* U.S.A. **137** F3
Claymont U.S.A. **131** F4
Claypool U.S.A. **137** G5
Clay Springs U.S.A. **137** G4
Clayton *DE* U.S.A. **131** F4
Clayton *GA* U.S.A. **129** D5
Clayton *NM* U.S.A. **135** G5
Clayton *NY* U.S.A. **131** F1
Claytor Lake U.S.A. **130** C5
Clear, Cape Rep. of Ireland **35** B6
Clearco U.S.A. **130** C4
Clear Creek Canada **130** C4
Clear Creek *r.* U.S.A. **137** G4
Clear Creek *r.* U.S.A. **137** G4
Clearfield *PA* U.S.A. **130** D3
Clearfield *UT* U.S.A. **134** E4
Clear Fork Brazos *r.* U.S.A. **133** B5
Clear Hills Canada **122** G3
Clear Island Rep. of Ireland **35** B6
Clear Lake *IA* U.S.A. **132** C3
Clear Lake *SD* U.S.A. **132** B2
Clear Lake *l.* *CA* U.S.A. **136** A2
Clear Lake *l.* *UT* U.S.A. **137** G2
Clearlake Oaks U.S.A. **136** B2
Clearmont U.S.A. **134** F3
Clearwater Canada **122** G4
Clearwater *r.* Canada **123** I3

Clearwater *r.* *ID* U.S.A. **134** C3
Clearwater *r.* *MN* U.S.A. **132** B2
Clearwater Lake Canada **123** K4
Clearwater Mountains U.S.A. **134** D3
Cleburne U.S.A. **133** B5
Cle Elum U.S.A. **134** B3
Clejani Romania **46** D2
Clément *r.* Fr. Guiana **147** H4
Clementi Sing. **58** [inset]
Clemson U.S.A. **129** D5
Clendenin U.S.A. **130** C4
Clendening Lake U.S.A. **130** B2
Clerf Lux. *see* Clervaux
Clerke Reef Australia **108** B4
Clermont Australia **111** F4
Clermont France **39** F2
Clermont U.S.A. **129** C6
Clermont-en-Argonne France **39** F2
Clermont-Ferrand France **39** E4
Clermont-l'Hérault France **39** E5
Clervaux Lux. **39** F4
Cles Italy **44** C1
Cleve Australia **109** G3
Cleveland *r.* Canada **123** O1
Cleveland *GA* U.S.A. **129** C5
Cleveland *MS* U.S.A. **133** D5
Cleveland *OH* U.S.A. **130** B3
Cleveland *TN* U.S.A. **128** B5
Cleveland *TX* U.S.A. **133** C6
Cleveland, Cape Australia **111** F3
Cleveland, Mount U.S.A. **134** D2
Cleveland Peninsula U.S.A. **122** C4
Cleves Germany *see* Kleve
Clew Bay Rep. of Ireland **35** B5
Clewiston U.S.A. **129** C7
Clifden Rep. of Ireland **35** B5
Cliffdale *r.* Australia **110** D3
Clifftop U.S.A. **130** C4
Clifton Australia **111** G5
Clifton U.S.A. **137** H5
Clifton Beach Australia **111** F3
Clifton Forge U.S.A. **130** D5
Clifton Hills Australia **110** C5
Climax Canada **123** I5
Clinch *r.* U.S.A. **130** B5
Clinch Mountain *mts* U.S.A. **130** B5
Clinchport U.S.A. **130** B5
Cline River Canada **123** G4
Clint U.S.A. **135** F5
Clinton Canada **130** C2
Clinton *IA* U.S.A. **132** D3
Clinton *LA* U.S.A. **133** D6
Clinton *ME* U.S.A. **131** I1
Clinton *MI* U.S.A. **130** B2
Clinton *MO* U.S.A. **132** C4
Clinton *MS* U.S.A. **133** D5
Clinton *NC* U.S.A. **128** E5
Clinton *OK* U.S.A. **133** B5
Clinton-Colden Lake Canada **123** J1
Clinton Creek Canada **122** A1
Clintwood U.S.A. **130** B5
Clio U.S.A. **130** B2

►**Clipperton, Île** *terr.* N. Pacific Ocean **165** K5
French Overseas Territory. Most easterly point of Oceania.
oceania 114

Clishham *hill* U.K. **34** C3
Clisson France **38** C3
Clitheroe U.K. **35** E5
Clive Lake Canada **122** G2
Clonakilty Rep. of Ireland **35** B6
Clonagh Australia **111** E4
Cloncurry Australia **111** E4
Cloncurry *r.* Australia **111** E3
Clones Rep. of Ireland **35** C4
Clonmel Rep. of Ireland **35** C5
Cloppenburg Germany **36** D2
Cloquet U.S.A. **132** C2
Cloquet *r.* U.S.A. **132** C2
Clorinda Arg. **152** F1
Cloud Peak *WY* U.S.A. **126** E3
Cloud Peak *WY* U.S.A. **134** F3
Cloudy Bay N.Z. **113** C3
Clova Canada **124** F3
Cloverdale U.S.A. **136** B2
Clovis *CA* U.S.A. **136** C3
Clovis *NM* U.S.A. **135** G5
Cloyes-sur-le-Loir France **38** D3
Cloyne Canada **131** E1
Cluain Meala Rep. of Ireland *see* Clonmel
Cluanie, Loch *l.* U.K. **34** D3
Cluff Lake Mine Canada **123** I3
Cluny Australia **111** D5
Cluj-Napoca Romania **46** C1
Cluny Australia **111** D5
Cluny France **39** G3
Cluses France **39** G3
Cluster Springs U.S.A. **130** D5
Clut Lake Canada **123** G1
Clyde Canada **123** H4
Clyde *r.* U.K. **34** D4
Clyde U.S.A. **131** E2
Clyde, Firth of *est.* U.K. **34** D4
Clydebank U.K. **34** D4
Clyde River Canada **121** M2
Clymer U.S.A. **130** D3
Cnossus *tourist site* Greece *see* Knossos
Côa *r.* Port. **42** C2
Coachella U.S.A. **137** E5
Coachella Canal U.S.A. **137** D5
Coahoma U.S.A. **133** B5
Coahuila *state* Mex. **133** C7
Coal *r.* Canada **122** E3
Coalgate U.S.A. **133** B5
Coal Harbour Canada **122** E5
Coalinga U.S.A. **136** B3
Coalport U.S.A. **130** D3
Coal River Canada **122** E3
Coal Valley U.S.A. **137** E3
Coalville U.S.A. **134** E4
Coari Brazil **147** F5
Coari *r.* Brazil **147** F6
Coari, Lago *l.* Brazil **147** F5
Coarsegold U.S.A. **136** C3
Coast *admin. reg.* Tanz. *see* Pwani
Coastal Plain U.S.A. **129** E6
Coast Mountains Canada **122** E4
Coast Ranges *mts* U.S.A. **136** A1
Coatesville U.S.A. **131** F4
Coats Island Canada **121** K3
Coats Land *reg.* Antarctica **167** A1
Coatzacoalcos Mex. **138** D5
Cobadin Romania **46** F2
Cobán Guat. **138** F5
Cobar Australia **112** C3
Cóbh Rep. of Ireland **35** B6
Cobham *r.* Canada **123** M4
Cobija Bol. **148** C2
Coblenz Germany *see* Koblenz
Cobleskill U.S.A. **131** F2
Cobourg Canada **130** D2
Cobourg Peninsula Australia **110** C1
Cobquecura Chile **152** B4
Cobra Australia **109** B6
Cobram Australia **112** C4
Côbuè Moz. **97** B8
Coburg Germany **36** E3
Coburg Island Canada **121** L2
Coca Spain **42** D2
Cocal Brazil **150** D2
Cocalinho Brazil **150** B5
Cocanada India *see* Kakinada
Cocentaina Spain **43** F3

Cochabamba Bol. 148 D4
Cochabamba dept Bol. 148 D4
Cochamó Chile 153 B5
Coche, Isla i. Venez. 147 F2
Cochem Germany 36 C3
Co Chiên, Sông r. mouth Vietnam 61 D6
Cochin India 72 C4
Cochin reg. Vietnam 61 D6
Cochran U.S.A. 129 C5
Cochrane Alta Canada 123 H5
Cochrane Ont. Canada 124 D3
Cochrane r. Canada 123 K3
Cochrane Chile 153 B6
Cochrane, Lago l. Arg./Chile 153 B6
Cochranton U.S.A. 130 C3
Cockranville U.S.A. 131 F4
Cockburn Australia 112 B4
Cockburn Town Bahamas 129 E7
Cockburn Town Turks and Caicos Is see Grand Turk
Cocklebiddy Australia 109 D8
Cockscomb mt. S. Africa 98 E7
Coco r. Hond./Nicaragua 139 H6
Coco, Isla de i. N. Pacific Ocean 138 G7
Cocobeach Gabon 94 A4
Coco Channel India 73 G3
Coconino Plateau U.S.A. 137 F4
Cocopara National Park Australia 112 C4
Cocorná Col. 146 C3
Cocos Brazil 150 C5
Cocos Basin sea feature Indian Ocean 162 N5

▶Cocos Islands terr. Indian Ocean 55 B8
Australian External Territory.
asia 82

Cocos Ridge sea feature N. Pacific Ocean 165 M5
Cod, Cape U.S.A. 131 H3
Codajás Brazil 147 F5
Codera, Cabo c. Venez. 147 E2
Coderre Canada 123 J5
Codfish Island N.Z. 113 A4
Codigoro Italy 44 D2
Cod Island Canada 125 I1
Codlea Romania 46 D2
Codó Brazil 150 D3
Codogno Italy 44 B2
Codol airport Spain 43 G3
Codroipo Italy 44 D2
Cody U.S.A. 134 E3
Coeburn U.S.A. 130 B5
Coelho Neto Brazil 150 D3
Coen Australia 111 E2
Coen r. Australia 111 E2
Coeroeni r. Suriname 147 G4
Coesfeld Germany 36 C3
Coeur d'Alene U.S.A. 134 C3
Coffee Bay S. Africa 99 F6
Coffee Creek Canada 122 B2
Coffeyville U.S.A. 132 C4
Coffin Bay Australia 109 F8
Coffin Bay National Park Australia 109 F8
Coffin Bay Peninsula Australia 109 F8
Coffs Harbour Australia 112 E3
Cogâlniceanu airport Romania see Kogălniceanu
Cogealac Romania 46 F2
Coghinas r. Sardinia Italy 45 B4
Cognac France 38 C4
Cogo Equat. Guinea 93 H5
Cogolin France 39 G5
Coguno Moz. 99 G5
Cohocton r. U.S.A. 131 E2
Cohoes U.S.A. 131 G2
Cohuna Australia 112 C4
Coiba, Isla i. Panama 139 H7
Coihaique Chile 153 B6
Coihaique Alto Chile 153 C6
Coimbatore India 72 C4
Coimbra Port. 42 B2
Coimbra admin. dist. Port. 42 B2
Coín Spain 42 D4
Coipasa, Salar de salt flat Bol. 148 C4
Coire Switz. see Chur
Cojasca Romania 46 D2
Cojata Peru 148 C3
Cojedes state Venez. 146 D2
Cojudo Blanco, Cerro mt. Arg. 153 C6
Colac Australia 112 B5
Colair Lake India see Kolleru Lake
Colares Brazil 150 B2
Colatina Brazil 151 D6
Colborne Canada 130 E2
Colby U.S.A. 132 A4
Colca r. Peru 148 B3
Colchester U.K. 35 G6
Colchester U.S.A. 131 G3
Cold Bay U.S.A. 120 C4
Cold Lake Canada 123 I4
Cold Lake l. Canada 123 I4
Cold Springs U.S.A. 136 D2
Coldstream U.K. 34 E4
Coldwater Canada 130 D1
Coldwater KS U.S.A. 132 B4
Coldwater MI U.S.A. 132 E3
Coldwater Creek r. U.S.A. 133 A4
Colebrook U.S.A. 128 F2
Coleman r. Australia 111 E2
Coleman MI U.S.A. 130 A2
Coleman TX U.S.A. 133 B6
Çölemerik Turkey see Hakkâri
Colenso S. Africa 99 F6
Colentina r. Romania 46 D2
Cole Peninsula Antarctica 167 L2
Coleraine U.K. 34 C4
Coleroon r. India 72 C4
Coles, Punta de pt Peru 148 C4
Coles Bay Australia 112 D6
Colesberg S. Africa 98 E6
Coleville U.S.A. 136 C2
Colfax CA U.S.A. 136 B2
Colfax LA U.S.A. 133 C6
Colfax WA U.S.A. 134 C3
Colhué Huapí, Lago l. Arg. 153 C6
Colibași Romania 46 D2
Coligny S. Africa 99 E5
Colima Mex. 126 F8
Colima, Nevado de vol. Mex. 126 F8
Colinas Brazil 150 C3
Coll i. U.K. 34 C3
Collado Bajo mt. Spain 43 F2
Collado Villalba Spain 42 E2
Collahuasi Chile 148 C5
Collalto mt. Austria/Italy 36 F5
Collarenebri Australia 112 D3
Collecchio Italy 44 C2
Colle di Val d'Elsa Italy 44 C3
College Corner U.S.A. 130 A4
College Hill U.S.A. 130 A4
College Park U.S.A. 129 B5
College Station U.S.A. 133 B6
Collerina Australia 112 C3
Collesalvetti Italy 44 C3
Collie Australia 109 B8
Collier Bay Australia 108 D4
Collier Range National Park Australia 109 B6
Collierville U.S.A. 133 D5
Collingwood Canada 130 C1
Collingwood N.Z. 113 C3
Collins U.S.A. 133 D6
Collins Glacier Antarctica 167 E2
Collinsville Australia 111 F4
Collinsville U.S.A. 130 D5
Collipulli Chile 152 B4
Collmberg hill Germany 37 F3
Collooney Rep. of Ireland 35 B4
Colmar France 39 G2
Colmena Arg. 152 E2
Colmenar de Oreja Spain 42 E2
Cologne Germany 36 C3
Colomb-Béchar Alg. see Béchar
Colombia Col. 146 C4
Colombia Mex. 133 B7

▶Colombia country S. America 146 C4
2nd most populous and 4th largest country in South America.
southamerica 144–145, 154

Colombian Basin sea feature S. Atlantic Ocean 160 I5

▶Colombo Sri Lanka 72 C5
Former capital of Sri Lanka.

Colomiers France 38 D5
Colón Buenos Aires Arg. 152 E3
Colón Entre Ríos Arg. 152 F3
Colón Panama 146 B2
Colonelganj India 75 D4
Colonet, Cabo c. Mex. 135 C7
Colonia Arg. 152 E1
Colonia Micronesia 57 I4
Colonia Agrippina Germany see Cologne
Colonia del Sacramento Uruguay 152 F3
Colonia Dora Arg. 152 E2
Colonia Emilio Mitre Arg. 152 D4
Colonia Julia Fenestris Italy see Fano
Colonia Las Heras Arg. 153 C6
Colonial Heights U.S.A. 130 E5
Colonia Suiza Uruguay 152 F3
Colonna, Capo c. Italy 45 F5
Colonsay i. U.K. 34 C3
Colorado r. La Rioja Arg. 152 D2
Colorado r. San Juan Arg. 152 C2
Colorado r. Arg. 152 E4
Colorado r. Mex./U.S.A. 135 D7
Colorado r. U.S.A. 133 B6
Colorado state U.S.A. 134 F5
Colorado City U.S.A. 133 A5
Colorado Desert U.S.A. 137 D5
Colorado National Monument nat. park U.S.A. 137 H2
Colorado Plateau U.S.A. 137 H3
Colorado River Aqueduct canal U.S.A. 137 E4
Colorados, Cerro mt. Arg. 152 C1
Colorado Springs U.S.A. 134 F5
Colotlán Mex. 138 D4
Colquechaca Bol. 148 D4
Colquiri Bol. 148 D4
Colton NY U.S.A. 131 F1
Colton UT U.S.A. 137 G2
Columbia KY U.S.A. 128 B4
Columbia LA U.S.A. 133 C5
Columbia MD U.S.A. 131 E4
Columbia MO U.S.A. 132 C4
Columbia MS U.S.A. 133 D6
Columbia NJ U.S.A. 131 F3
Columbia PA U.S.A. 131 E3

▶Columbia SC U.S.A. 129 C5
State capital of South Carolina.

Columbia TN U.S.A. 128 B5
Columbia r. U.S.A. 134 B3
Columbia, Mount Canada 122 G4
Columbia, Sierra mts Mex. 135 D7
Columbia Falls U.S.A. 134 D2
Columbia Mountains Canada 122 F4
Columbia Plateau U.S.A. 134 C3
Columbretes, Islas is Spain 43 G3
Columbus GA U.S.A. 129 B5
Columbus IN U.S.A. 128 B4
Columbus KS U.S.A. 132 C4
Columbus MS U.S.A. 129 A5
Columbus MT U.S.A. 134 E3
Columbus NC U.S.A. 128 C5
Columbus NE U.S.A. 132 B3

▶Columbus OH U.S.A. 130 B4
State capital of Ohio.

Columbus PA U.S.A. 130 D3
Columbus TX U.S.A. 133 B6
Columbus WI U.S.A. 132 D3
Columbus Grove U.S.A. 130 A3
Columbus Salt Marsh U.S.A. 136 C2
Colunga Spain 42 D1
Colusa U.S.A. 136 A2
Colville N.Z. 113 C2
Colville U.S.A. 134 C2
Colville r. U.S.A. 120 D2
Colville Channel N.Z. 113 C2
Colville Lake Canada 122 E1
Colwyn Bay U.K. 35 E5
Comacchio Italy 44 D2
Comacchio, Valli di lag. Italy 44 D2
Comai China 75 F3
Comalcalco Mex. 138 F5
Comallo Arg. 152 C5
Comana Romania 46 E2
Comanche U.S.A. 133 B6
Comandante Ferraz research station Antarctica 167 A2
Comandante Fontana Arg. 152 F1
Comandante Luis Piedra Buena Arg. 153 C7
Comandante Salas Arg. 152 C3
Comănești Romania 46 E1
Comarnic Romania 46 D2
Combahee r. U.S.A. 129 C5
Combarbalá Chile 152 C2
Combermere Bay Myanmar 60 A4
Combol i. Indon. 58 C2
Combourg France 38 C2
Comet r. Australia 111 G4
Comfort U.S.A. 133 B6
Comilla Bangl. 75 F5
Comino i. Malta see Kemmuna
Comino, Capo c. Sardinia Italy 45 B4
Comiso Sicily Italy 45 E6
Comitán de Domínguez Mex. 138 F5
Commentry France 39 E3
Committee Bay Canada 121 K3
Commonwealth Territory admin. div. Australia see Jervis Bay Territory
Como Italy 44 B2
Como, Lake Italy 44 B2
Como Chamling l. China 75 F3
Comodoro Rivadavia Arg. 153 D6
Comoé r. Côte d'Ivoire see Komoé
Comores country Africa see Comoros
Comorin, Cape India 72 C4
▶Comoros country Africa 97 D7
africa 86–87, 100
Comox Canada 122 E5
Compiègne France 39 E2
Compostela Mex. 126 F7
Compton U.S.A. 136 C5
Comrat Moldova 29 D7
Comino, Sông r. Vietnam 60 D4
Cona China 75 F4

▶Conakry Guinea 92 B3
Capital of Guinea.

Conambo Ecuador 146 B5
Conambo r. Ecuador 146 B5
Cona Niyeo Arg. 153 D5
Conay Chile 152 C2
Concarneau France 38 B3
Conceição Amazonas Brazil 147 F5
Conceição Mato Grosso Brazil 149 F1
Conceição Paraíba Brazil 150 E3
Conceição Roraima Brazil 147 F4
Conceição da Barra Brazil 151 E6
Conceição do Araguaia Brazil 150 B4
Conceição do Coité Brazil 150 E4
Conceição do Mato Dentro Brazil 151 D6
Conceição do Maú Brazil 147 G4
Concepción Corrientes Arg. 152 F2
Concepción Tucumán Arg. 152 D1
Concepción Beni Bol. 148 D2
Concepción Santa Cruz Bol. 149 E4
Concepción Chile 152 B4
Concepción Mex. 126 F7
Concepción r. Mex. 135 D7
Concepción Panama 139 H7
Concepción Para. 149 F5
Concepción, Canal sea chan. Chile 153 B7
Concepción, Punta pt Mex. 135 E8
Concepción del Uruguay Arg. 152 F3
Conception, Point U.S.A. 136 B4
Concesio Italy 44 C2
Concession Zimbabwe 99 F3
Conches-en-Ouche France 38 D2
Conchi Chile 148 C5
Concho Mex. 135 F8
Concho U.S.A. 137 H4
Concho r. U.S.A. 133 B6
Conchos r. Chihuahua Mex. 135 F7
Conchos r. Nuevo León/Tamaulipas Mex. 126 G7
Concord CA U.S.A. 136 A3
Concord NC U.S.A. 128 C5

▶Concord NH U.S.A. 131 H2
State capital of New Hampshire.

Concord PA U.S.A. 130 E3
Concord VA U.S.A. 130 D5
Concordia Arg. 152 F2
Concórdia Amazonas Brazil 146 E6
Concórdia Santa Catarina Brazil 151 A8
Concordia Col. 146 C4
Concordia Peru 146 C6
Concordia U.S.A. 132 B4
Concord Peak Afgh. 81 H2
Con Cuông Vietnam 60 D4
Conda Angola 95 B7
Condamine Australia 111 G5
Condamine r. Australia 111 G5
Conde Brazil 150 E4
Condé-sur-Noireau France 38 C2
Condeúba Brazil 150 D5
Condobolin Australia 112 C4
Condoe Moz. 99 G3
Condom France 38 D5
Condon U.S.A. 134 B3
Condor, Cordillera del mts Ecuador/Peru 146 B6
Conejos Mex. 133 A7
Conejos U.S.A. 135 F5
Conemaugh r. U.S.A. 130 D3
Conero, Monte hill Italy 44 D3
Conestogo Lake Canada 130 C2
Conesville U.S.A. 130 C3
Coney Island Sing. see Serangoon, Pulau
Coney Island U.S.A. 131 G3
Conflict Group is P.N.G. 107 E3
Confluence U.S.A. 130 D4
Confoederatio Helvetica country Europe see Switzerland
Confolens France 38 D3
Confusion Range mts U.S.A. 137 F2
Confuso r. Para. 149 F6
Congdü China see Nyalam
Conghua China 67 E4
Congjiang China 67 D3
▶Congo country Africa 94 B5
africa 86–87, 100

▶Congo r. Congo/Dem. Rep. Congo 95 B6
2nd longest river in Africa and 8th in the world.
africa 84–85
world 6–7

Congo (Brazzaville) country Africa see Congo
Congo (Kinshasa) country Africa see Congo, Democratic Republic of

▶Congo, Democratic Republic of country Africa 94 D5
3rd largest and 4th most populous country in Africa.
africa 86–87, 100

Congo, Republic of country Africa see Congo
Congo Basin Dem. Rep. Congo 94 D5
Congo Cone sea feature S. Atlantic Ocean 160 O6
Congo Free State country Africa see Congo, Democratic Republic of
Congress U.S.A. 137 F4
Conguillo, Parque Nacional nat. park Chile 152 C4
Cónico, Cerro mt. Arg. 153 C5
Conil de la Frontera Spain 42 C4
Coniston Australia 110 C4
Coniston U.K. 35 E4
Conjuboy Australia 111 F3
Conklin Canada 123 I4
Conlara r. Arg. 152 D3
Conn, Lough l. Rep. of Ireland 35 B4
Connacht reg. Rep. of Ireland see Connaught
Connaught reg. Rep. of Ireland 35 B5
Conneaut U.S.A. 130 C3
Conneaut Lake U.S.A. 130 C3
Conneautville U.S.A. 130 C3
Connecticut r. U.S.A. 131 G3
Connecticut state U.S.A. 131 G3
Connel U.K. 34 D3
Connemara Australia 111 E5
Connemara reg. Rep. of Ireland 35 B5
Connemara National Park Rep. of Ireland 35 B5
Connersville U.S.A. 128 B4
Connolly, Mount Canada 122 C2
Connors Range hills Australia 111 G4
Cononaco Ecuador 146 C5
Conquista Bol. 148 D2
Conrad U.S.A. 134 E2
Conrad Rise sea feature Indian Ocean 163 J9
Conroe U.S.A. 133 C6
Conroe, Lake U.S.A. 133 C6
Conselheiro Lafaiete Brazil 151 D7
Conselheiro Pena Brazil 151 D6
Conselice Italy 44 C2
Consett U.K. 34 F4
Côn Sơn i. Vietnam 61 D6
Consort Canada 123 I4
Constance Germany see Konstanz
Constance, Lake Germany/Switz. 39 H3
Constância dos Baetas Brazil 147 F6
Constanța Romania 46 F2
Constanța airport Romania see Kogălniceanu
Constantia tourist site Cyprus see Salamis
Constantia Germany see Konstanz
Constantina Spain 42 D4
Constantine Alg. 91 G1
Constantine, Cape U.S.A. 120 D4
Constantinople Turkey see İstanbul
Consuelo Australia 111 G5
Consul Canada 123 I5
Consul r. Canada 123 K1
Contamana Peru 148 B1
Contas r. Brazil 150 E5
Contoocook r. U.S.A. 131 H2
Contratacion Col. 146 C3
Contreras, Embalse de resr Spain 43 F3
Contreras, Isla i. Chile 153 B7
Contres France 38 D3
Contwoyto Lake Canada 123 I1
Convención Col. 146 C2
Convent U.S.A. 133 D6
Conway AR U.S.A. 133 C5
Conway KY U.S.A. 130 A5
Conway NC U.S.A. 131 E5
Conway NH U.S.A. 131 H2
Conway SC U.S.A. 129 D5
Conway, Cape Australia 111 G4
Conway National Park Australia 111 G4
Coober Pedy Australia 110 C6
Cooch Behar India see Koch Bihar
Cook Australia 109 E7
Cook, Bahía de b. Chile 153 C8
Cook, Cape Canada 122 E5
Cook, Mount Canada/U.S.A. 122 B2

▶Cook, Mount N.Z. 113 B3
Highest mountain in New Zealand.
oceania 114

Cookes Peak U.S.A. 135 F6
Cookeville U.S.A. 128 B4
Cookhouse S. Africa 98 E7
Cook Ice Shelf Antarctica 167 H2
Cook Inlet sea chan. U.S.A. 120 D3

▶Cook Islands terr. S. Pacific Ocean 165 H7
Self-governing New Zealand Territory.
oceania 104–105, 114

Cooks Passage Australia 111 F2
Cookstown U.K. 35 C4
Cook Strait N.Z. 113 C3
Cooktown Australia 111 F2
Coolabah Australia 112 C3
Coolah Australia 112 D3
Coolamon Australia 112 C4
Coolgardie Australia 109 C7
Coolimba Australia 109 A7
Cooloola National Park Australia 111 H5
Coolum Beach Australia 111 H5
Cooma Australia 112 D5
Coombah Australia 112 B4
Coonabarabran Australia 112 D3
Coonalpyn Australia 112 A4
Coondapoor India see Kundapura
Coongan r. Australia 108 B5
Coongoola Australia 111 F5
Coon Rapids U.S.A. 132 C2
Cooper r. Australia 110 C2
Cooper Creek watercourse Australia 111 D6
Coopersburg U.S.A. 131 F3
Coopers Mills U.S.A. 131 I1
Cooper's Town Bahamas 129 D7
Cooperstown ND U.S.A. 132 B2
Cooperstown NY U.S.A. 131 F2
Coopracambra National Park Australia 112 D5
Coorabie Australia 109 F7
Coorong National Park Australia 112 A5
Coorow Australia 109 B7
Cooroy Australia 111 H5
Coosa r. U.S.A. 129 B5
Coos Bay U.S.A. 134 A4
Cootamundra Australia 112 D4
Cooum r. India 72 D3
Copahue, Volcán vol. Chile 152 C4
Copala Mex. 138 E5
Copal Urcu Peru 146 C5
Cope, Cabo c. Spain 43 F4

▶Copenhagen Denmark 33 D5
Capital of Denmark.

Copere Bol. 149 E4
Copetonas Arg. 152 E4
Cô Pi, Phou mt. Laos/Vietnam 60 D4
Copiapó Chile 152 C1
Copiapo, Volcán vol. Chile 152 C1
Copley Australia 112 A3
Coporaque Peru 148 C3
Coppename r. Suriname 147 G3
Copperbelt prov. Zambia 95 E8
Copperfield r. Australia 111 E3
Copper Harbor U.S.A. 132 E2
Coppermine Canada see Kugluktuk
Coppermine r. Canada 123 H1
Copperton S. Africa 98 D6
Copșa Mică Romania 46 D1
Coqên China 75 E3
Coquilhatville Dem. Rep. Congo see Mbandaka
Coquimbo Chile 152 C2
Coquimbo admin. reg. Chile 152 C2
Coquitlam Canada 122 F5
Corabia Romania 46 D3
Coração de Jesus Brazil 151 C6
Coracesium Turkey see Alanya
Coracora Peru 148 B3
Coral Bay Australia 108 A5
Coral Harbour Canada 121 K3
Coral Sea S. Pacific Ocean 107 E3
Coral Sea Basin S. Pacific Ocean 164 E6

▶Coral Sea Islands Territory terr. Australia 107 E3
Australian External Territory.
oceania 104–105, 114

Corangamite, Lake Australia 112 B5
Coraopolis U.S.A. 130 C3
Corbett National Park India 74 C3
Corbie France 39 E2
Corbin U.S.A. 130 A5
Corbones r. Spain 42 D4
Corby U.K. 35 F5
Corcaigh Rep. of Ireland see Cork
Córcoles r. Spain 43 E3
Corcoran U.S.A. 136 C3
Corcovado Arg. 153 C5
Corcovado, Golfo de sea chan. Chile 153 B5
Corcyra i. Greece see Corfu
Cordele U.S.A. 129 C6
Cordelia U.S.A. 136 A2
Cordell U.S.A. 133 B5
Cordillera Azul, Parque Nacional nat. park Peru 148 A1
Cordillera de los Picachos, Parque Nacional nat. park Col. 146 C4
Cordillo Downs Australia 111 E5
Córdoba Córdoba Arg. 152 D2
Córdoba Río Negro Arg. 152 C5
Córdoba prov. Arg. 152 E3
Córdoba dept Col. 146 C2
Córdoba Mex. 133 A7
Córdoba Mex. 126 G8
Córdoba Spain 42 D4
Córdoba, Sierras de mts Arg. 152 D3
Cordova Spain see Córdoba
Cordova U.S.A. 120 E3
Corduba Spain see Córdoba
Corella r. Australia 111 E3
Corella Lake salt flat Australia 110 C3
Corfield Australia 111 E4
Corfu i. Greece 47 A5
Coria Spain 42 C3
Corigliano, Golfo di b. Italy 45 F5
Corigliano Calabro Italy 45 F5
Coringa Islands Australia 111 G3
Corinium U.K. see Cirencester
Corinne Canada 123 J5
Corinth Greece 47 C6
Corinth U.S.A. 128 A5
Corinth, Gulf of sea chan. Greece 47 C5
Corinth Canal Greece 47 C6
Corinthus Greece see Corinth
Corinto Brazil 151 C6
Corixa Grande r. Bol./Brazil 149 F4
Corixinha r. Brazil 149 F4
Cork Rep. of Ireland 35 B6
Corlay France 38 B2
Corleone Sicily Italy 45 D6
Çorlu Turkey 78 A2
Çorlu r. Turkey 46 E4
Cormorant Canada 123 K4
Cormorant Lake Canada 123 K4
Cornacchia, Monte mt. Italy 44 E4
Cornelia U.S.A. 133 F5
Cornélio Procópio Brazil 149 H5
Corneliskondre Suriname 147 G3
Cornell U.S.A. 132 D2
Cornellà de Llobregat Spain 43 H2
Corner Brook Canada 125 J3
Corner Seamounts sea feature N. Atlantic Ocean 160 K3
Corneto Italy see Tarquinia
Cornetto mt. Italy 44 C2
Cornettsville U.S.A. 130 B5
Cornia r. Italy 44 C3
Corning AR U.S.A. 133 D4
Corning CA U.S.A. 136 A2
Corning IA U.S.A. 132 C3
Corning NY U.S.A. 131 E2
Corning OH U.S.A. 130 B4
Cornish watercourse Australia 111 F4
Cornish, Estrada b. Chile 153 B6
Corn Islands Nicaragua see Maíz, Islas del
Corno, Monte mt. Italy 44 D3
Cornwall Canada 125 F4
Cornwall U.S.A. 131 E3
Cornwallis Island Canada 121 J2
Cornwall Island Canada 121 J2
Coro Venez. 146 D2
Coroaci Brazil 151 D6
Coroatá Brazil 150 C3
Corocoro Bol. 148 C4
Corocoro, Isla i. Venez. 147 F2
Coroico Bol. 148 D4
Coromandel Brazil 151 C6
Coromandel Coast India 72 D4
Coromandel Peninsula N.Z. 113 C2
Coromandel Range hills N.Z. 113 C2
Corona CA U.S.A. 136 D5
Corona NM U.S.A. 135 F6
Coronado, Bahía de b. Costa Rica 139 H7
Coronation Canada 123 I4
Coronation Gulf Canada 121 H3
Coronation Island S. Atlantic Ocean 167 A2
Coronda Arg. 152 E2
Coronel Brandsen Arg. 152 F3
Coronel Dorrego Arg. 152 E4
Coronel Fabriciano Brazil 151 D6
Coronel Francisco Sosa Arg. 152 D5
Coronel Moldes Arg. 152 D1
Coronel Oviedo Para. 149 F6
Coronel Portillo Peru 146 B5
Coronel Pringles Arg. 152 E4
Coronel Sapucaia Brazil 149 G5
Coronel Suárez Arg. 152 E4
Coronel Vidal Arg. 152 F4
Çorovodë Albania 46 B4
Corowa Australia 112 C4
Corpen Aike Arg. 153 C7
Corpus Christi U.S.A. 133 B7
Corque Bol. 148 D4
Corral Chile 152 B4
Corral de Almaguer Spain 42 E3
Corral de Cantos mt. Spain 42 D3
Corrasi, Punta mt. Sardinia Italy 45 B4
Corrente Brazil 150 C4
Corrente r. Bahia Brazil 150 D5
Corrente r. Minas Gerais Brazil 149 H4
Correntes Brazil 151 A6
Correntes r. Brazil 149 G4
Correntina Brazil 150 C5
Correntina r. Brazil see Éguas
Corrèze France 38 D4
Corrèze r. France 38 D4
Corrib, Lough l. Rep. of Ireland 35 B5
Corrientes Arg. 152 F1
Corrientes prov. Arg. 152 F2
Corrientes r. Arg. 152 F2
Corrientes r. Peru 146 C5
Corrientes, Cabo c. Arg. 152 F4
Corrientes, Cabo c. Col. 146 B3
Corrientes, Cabo c. Mex. 126 E7
Corrigan U.S.A. 133 C6
Corrigin Australia 109 B8
Corriverton Guyana 147 G3
Corrubedo, Cabo c. Spain 42 B1
Corry U.S.A. 130 D3
Corse admin. reg. France 44 B3
Corse i. France see Corsica
Corse, Cap c. Corsica France 39 H5
Corsica i. France 44 B4
Corsicana U.S.A. 133 B5
Corsico, Baie de b. Gabon 94 A4
Corte Corsica France 31 G5
Cortegana Spain 42 C4
Cortes Spain 43 F2
Cortés, Sea of g. Mex. see California, Gulf of
Cortez U.S.A. 135 E5
Cortina d'Ampezzo Italy 44 D1
Cortland U.S.A. 131 E2
Cortona Italy 44 C3
Corubal r. Guinea-Bissau 92 B3
Coruche Port. 42 B3
Çoruh Turkey see Artvin
Çoruh r. Turkey 79 E2
Çorum Turkey 78 C2
Corumbá Brazil 149 F4
Corumbá r. Brazil 149 H4
Corumbá de Goiás Brazil 149 H3
Corumbaíba Brazil 149 H4
Corund Romania 46 D1
Corunna Canada 130 B2
Corunna Spain see A Coruña
Corunna U.S.A. 130 A2
Coruripe Brazil 150 E4
Corvallis U.S.A. 134 B3
Corwen U.K. 35 E5
Corydon IA U.S.A. 132 C3
Corydon IN U.S.A. 128 B4
Coryville U.S.A. 130 D3
Cos i. Greece see Kos
Cosalá Mex. 126 E7
Coscaya Chile 148 C4
Cosentia Italy see Cosenza
Cosenza Italy 45 F5
Coșereni Romania 46 E2
Coshocton U.S.A. 130 C3
Cosmoledo Atoll Seychelles 97 E7
Cosne-Cours-sur-Loire France 39 E3
Cosquín Arg. 152 D2
Costa Brazil 150 D3
Costa Blanca coastal area Spain 43 F3
Costa Brava coastal area Spain 43 H2
Costache Negri Romania 46 E2
Costa de la Luz coastal area Spain 42 C4
Costa del Azahar coastal area Spain 43 F3
Costa del Sol coastal area Spain 42 D4
Costa Dorada coastal area Spain 43 H2
Costa Marques Brazil 149 D3
Costa Rica Brazil 151 A6
▶Costa Rica country Central America 139 H6
northamerica 118–119, 140
Costa Rica Mex. 126 E7
Costa Verde coastal area Spain 42 C1
Costermansville Dem. Rep. Congo see Bukavu
Costești Romania 46 D2
Costești Romania 46 E1
Costigan Lake Canada 123 J3
Coșuștea r. Romania 46 C2
Cotabato Phil. 57 F4
Cotacajes r. Bol. 148 D4
Cotahuasi Peru 148 B3
Cotaxé r. Brazil 151 D6
Coteau des Prairies slope U.S.A. 132 B2
Coteau du Missouri slope ND U.S.A. 132 A1
Coteau du Missouri slope SD U.S.A. 132 A2
Côte d'Azur coastal area France 39 G5
▶Côte d'Ivoire country Africa 92 D4
africa 86–87, 100
world 16–17
Côte Française de Somalis country Africa see Djibouti
Cotegipe Brazil 150 C4
Cotentin pen. France 38 C2
Côtes de Meuse ridge France 39 F2
Cotiaeum Turkey see Kütahya
Cotiella mt. Spain 43 G1
Cotingo r. Brazil 147 F4
Cotmeana r. Romania 46 D2
Cotonou Benin 93 F4
Cotopaxi prov. Ecuador 146 B5
Cotopaxi, Volcán vol. Ecuador 146 B5
Cotswold Hills U.K. 35 E6
Cottage Grove U.S.A. 134 B4
Cottbus Germany 37 G3
Cotteliar r. India 72 D4
Cottian Alps mts France/Italy 39 G4
Cottica Suriname 147 H4
Cottiennes, Alpes mts France/Italy see Cottian Alps
Cottonbush Creek watercourse Australia 111 D4
Cottonwood AZ U.S.A. 137 F4
Cottonwood CA U.S.A. 136 A1
Cottonwood r. KS U.S.A. 132 B4
Cottonwood r. MN U.S.A. 132 C2
Cottonwood Creek watercourse U.S.A. 135 G7
Cottonwood Falls U.S.A. 132 B4
Cottonwood Wash watercourse U.S.A. 137 G4
Cotulla U.S.A. 133 B6
Couchman Range hills Australia 108 D3
Coudersport U.S.A. 130 D3
Coudres, Île aux i. Canada 128 F2
Couëdic, Cape de Australia 109 G9
Couëron France 38 C3
Couesnon r. France 38 C2
Couiza France 38 E5
Coulee Dam U.S.A. 134 C3
Coulman Island Antarctica 167 H2
Coulogne France 38 D1
Coulommiers France 39 E2
Coulonge r. Canada 124 E4
Coulterville U.S.A. 136 B3
Council U.S.A. 134 C3
Council Bluffs U.S.A. 132 C3
Council Grove U.S.A. 132 B4
Coupeville U.S.A. 134 B2
Courageous Lake Canada 123 I1
Courantyne r. Guyana 147 G3
Courland Lagoon b. Lith./Rus. Fed. 31 J2
Cournon-d'Auvergne France 39 E4
Coursan France 39 E5
Courtenay Canada 134 A2
Courtland U.S.A. 131 E5
Courtrai Belgium see Kortrijk
Coushatta U.S.A. 133 C5
Coutances France 38 C2
Coutinho Moz. see Ulongue
Coutras France 38 C4
Coutts Canada 123 I5
Couvin Belgium 39 F1
Couzeix France 38 D4
Covaleda Spain 43 E2
Covasna Romania 46 E2
Cove Fort U.S.A. 137 F2
Cove Mountains hills U.S.A. 130 D4
Covendo Bol. 148 D3
Coventry U.K. 35 F5
Covesville U.S.A. 130 D5
Covilhã Port. 42 C2
Covington GA U.S.A. 129 C5
Covington IN U.S.A. 128 B3
Covington KY U.S.A. 130 A4
Covington LA U.S.A. 133 D6
Covington OH U.S.A. 130 A3
Covington TN U.S.A. 133 D5
Covington VA U.S.A. 130 C5
Cowan, Lake salt flat Australia 109 C7
Cowcowing Lakes salt flat Australia 109 B7
Cowdenbeath U.K. 34 E3
Cowell Australia 109 G8
Cowen U.S.A. 130 C4
Cowes Australia 112 C5
Cowley Australia 111 F5
Cowlitz r. U.S.A. 134 B3
Cowpasture r. U.S.A. 130 D5
Cowra Australia 112 D4
Cox r. Australia 110 C2
Coxen Hole Hond. see Roatán
Coxilha de Santana hills Brazil/Uruguay 152 G2
Coxilha Grande hills Brazil 151 A9
Coxim Brazil 151 A6
Coxim r. Brazil 151 A6
Coxsackie U.S.A. 131 G2
Cox's Bazar Bangl. 75 F5
Coyah Guinea 92 B3
Coy Aike Arg. 153 C7
Coyame Mex. 135 F7
Coyote Lake U.S.A. 137 D4
Coyote Peak hill U.S.A. 137 E5
Cozie, Alpi mts France/Italy see Cottian Alps
Cozumel Mex. 127 I7
Cozumel, Isla de i. Mex. 127 I7
Cozzo del Pellegrino mt. Italy 45 F5

Crab Orchard U.S.A. **130** A5
Cracovia Poland *see* Kraków
Cracow Australia **111** G5
Cracow Poland *see* Kraków
Cradle Mountain Lake St Clair National Park Australia **112** C6
Cradock Australia **112** A3
Cradock S. Africa **98** E7
Craig *AK* U.S.A. **122** C4
Craig *CO* U.S.A. **134** F4
Craigieburn Australia **112** C5
Craignure U.K. **34** D3
Craigsville U.S.A. **130** C4
Crailsheim Germany **36** E4
Craiova Romania **46** C2
Cramlington U.K. **34** F4
Cranberry Junction Canada **122** D4
Cranberry Lake U.S.A. **131** F1
Cranberry Portage Canada **123** K4
Cranbourne Australia **112** C5
Cranbrook Canada **134** D2
Crandon U.S.A. **132** D2
Crane *OR* U.S.A. **134** C4
Crane *TX* U.S.A. **133** A6
Cranston *KY* U.S.A. **130** B4
Cranston *RI* U.S.A. **131** H3
Cranz Rus. Fed. *see* Zelenogradsk
Craolândia Brazil **150** C3
Craon France **38** C3
Crary Ice Rise Antarctica **167** I1
Crary Mountains Antarctica **167** J1
Crater Lake National Park U.S.A. **134** B4
Craters of the Moon National Monument *nat. park* U.S.A. **134** D4
Crateús Brazil **150** D3
Crato Brazil **150** E3
Crato Port. **42** C3
Cravari *r.* Brazil **149** F3
Cravo Norte Col. **146** D3
Crawford U.S.A. **132** A3
Crawford Range *hills* Australia **110** C4
Crawfordsville U.S.A. **128** B3
Crawfordville U.S.A. **129** B6
Crawley U.K. **35** F6
Crazy Mountains U.S.A. **134** E3
Crean Lake Canada **123** J4
Crécy-en-Ponthieu France **38** D1
Crediton U.K. **35** E6
Cree *r.* Canada **123** J3
Creede U.S.A. **135** F5
Creel Mex. **135** F8
Cree Lake Canada **123** J3
Creil France **39** E2
Crema Italy **44** B2
Cremona Canada **123** H5
Cremona Italy **44** C2
Crepori *r.* Brazil **147** G6
Crépy-en-Valois France **39** E2
Cres Croatia **44** E2
Cres *i.* Croatia **44** E2
Crescent City U.S.A. **134** A4
Crescent Group *is* Paracel Is **56** D2
Crescent Junction U.S.A. **137** H2
Crescent Valley U.S.A. **137** D1
Crespo Arg. **152** E3
Cresswell *watercourse* Australia **110** C3
Cresswell Downs Australia **110** C3
Crest France **39** F4
Crest Hill *Hong Kong* China **67** [inset]
Crestline U.S.A. **130** B3
Creston Canada **123** G5
Creston *IA* U.S.A. **132** C3
Creston *WY* U.S.A. **134** F4
Crestview U.S.A. **129** B6
Creta *i.* Greece *see* Crete
Crêt de la Neige *mt.* France **39** F3
Crete *i.* Greece **47** D7
Crêt Monniot *mt.* France **39** G3
Creus, Cap de *c.* Spain **43** H1
Creuse *r.* France **38** D3
Crevasse Valley Glacier Antarctica **167** J1
Crevillente Spain **43** F3
Crewe U.K. **35** E5
Crewe U.S.A. **130** D5
Crianlarich U.K. **34** D3
Criccieth U.K. **35** D5
Criciúma Brazil **151** B9
Cricovu Sărat *r.* Romania **46** E2
Crieff U.K. **34** E3
Criffell *hill* U.K. **34** E4
Crillon, Mount U.S.A. **122** B3
Crimea *pen.* Ukr. **29** E7
Crișan Romania **46** F2
Crisfield U.S.A. **131** F5
Cristal, Monts de *mts* Equat. Guinea/Gabon **93** H5
Cristalândia Brazil **150** B4
Cristalina Brazil **149** I4
Cristalino *r.* Brazil **149** G2
Cristalino *r.* Brazil *see* Mariembero
Cristino Castro Brazil **150** C4
Cristuru Secuiesc Romania **46** D1
Crișul Alb *r.* Romania **46** B1
Crișul Negru *r.* Romania **46** B1
Crișurilor, Câmpia *plain* Romania **46** B1
Criterion *mt.* Peru **148** B3
Crivitz Germany **36** E2
Crixás Brazil **150** B5
Crixás Açu *r.* Brazil **150** B5
Crixás Mirim *r.* Brazil **150** B5
Crna *r.* Macedonia **46** B4
Crna Glava *mt.* Yugo. **46** A3
Crna Gora *mts* Macedonia/Yugo. **46** B3
Crna Gora *aut. rep.* Yugo. **46** A3
Crni Drim *r.* Macedonia **46** B4
Crni Timok *r.* Yugo. **46** C3
Črni vrh *mt.* Slovenia **44** E1
Crni Vrh *mt.* Yugo. **31** J4
Črnomelj Slovenia **44** E2
Croajingolong National Park Australia **112** D5
▶Croatia *country* Europe **44** E2
europe 24–25, 48
Crocco, Monte *mt.* Italy **45** F5
Crocker, Banjaran *mts* Malaysia **59** F1
Crocker Range National Park *Sabah* Malaysia **59** G1
Crockett U.S.A. **133** C6
Croghan U.S.A. **131** F2
Croisette, Cap *c.* France **39** F5
Croisic, Pointe de *pt* France **38** B3
Croisilles France **39** E1
Croker, Cape Australia **110** C1
Croker Island Australia **110** C1
Cromarty U.K. **34** D3
Cromer U.K. **35** G5
Cromwell N.Z. **113** B4
Crooked *r.* U.S.A. **134** B3
Crooked Creek U.S.A. **122** A1
Crooked Harbour *b. Hong Kong* China **67** [inset]
Crooked Island Bahamas **129** E8
Crooked Island *Hong Kong* China **67** [inset]
Crooked Island Passage Bahamas **129** E8
Crooked River Canada **123** K4
Crookston U.S.A. **132** B2
Crooksville U.S.A. **130** B4
Crookwell Australia **112** D4
Crosby U.K. **35** E5
Crosby *MN* U.S.A. **132** C2
Crosby *ND* U.S.A. **132** A1
Crosbyton U.S.A. **133** A5
Cross *r.* Nigeria **93** H4
Cross Bay Canada **123** M2
Cross City U.S.A. **129** C6
Crosse, Île-à-la- Canada **123** J4
Crossett U.S.A. **133** C5
Cross Fell *hill* U.K. **35** E4
Crossfield Canada **123** H5
Cross Lake Canada **123** L4
Cross Lake *l.* Canada **123** L4
Cross River *state* Nigeria **93** H4
Cross Sound *sea chan.* U.S.A. **122** B3
Croswell U.S.A. **130** B2
Crotch Lake Canada **131** E1
Croton Italy *see* Crotone
Crotone Italy **45** F5
Crow Agency U.S.A. **134** F3
Crowdy Bay National Park Australia **112** E3
Crowell U.S.A. **133** B5
Crowley U.S.A. **133** C6
Crowley, Lake U.S.A. **136** C3
Crown Point *IN* U.S.A. **132** E3
Crownpoint U.S.A. **135** E6
Crown Point *NY* U.S.A. **131** G2
Crown Prince Olav Coast Antarctica **167** D2
Crown Princess Martha Coast Antarctica **167** B1
Crowsnest Pass Canada **134** D2
Crowsnest Pass *pass* Canada **123** H5
Crow Wing *r.* U.S.A. **132** C2
Croydon Australia **111** E3
Crozet U.S.A. **130** D4
Crozet, Îles *is* Indian Ocean **163** K9
Crozet Basin *sea feature* Indian Ocean **163** L8
Crozet Plateau *sea feature* Indian Ocean **163** J8
Crozon France **38** A2
Crucero Peru **148** C3
Cruces, Punta *pt* Col. **146** B3
Crum U.S.A. **130** B5
Cruz *mt.* Spain **43** E3
Cruz Venez. **147** E2
Cruz, Cabo *c.* Cuba **127** K8
Cruz Alta Brazil **151** A9
Cruz del Eje Arg. **152** D2
Cruzeiro Brazil **151** C7
Cruzeiro do Sul Brazil **148** B1
Crvenka Yugo. **46** A2
Cry Lake Canada **122** D3
Crysdale, Mount Canada **122** F4
Crystal Brook Australia **112** A4
Crystal City Canada **132** B1
Crystal City *MO* U.S.A. **132** D4
Crystal City *TX* U.S.A. **133** B6
Crystal Falls U.S.A. **132** D2
Crystal River U.S.A. **129** C6
Cserhát *hills* Hungary **37** I5
Csongrád Hungary **37** J5
Csorna Hungary **37** H5
Csorvás Hungary **37** J5
Csóványos *hill* Hungary **37** I5
Csurgó Hungary **44** F1
Ctesiphon *tourist site* Iraq **79** F4
Cua *r.* Spain **42** C1
Cu'a Đinh An *r. mouth* Vietnam **61** D6
Cuadrada, Sierra *hills* Arg. **153** C6
Cuale Angola **95** C7
Cualedro Spain **42** C2
Cuamato Angola **95** B9
Cuamba Moz. **97** C8
Cuando *r.* Angola/Zambia **95** D9
Cuando Cubango *prov.* Angola **95** C8
Cuangar Angola **95** C9
Cuango *Cuando Cubango* Angola **95** C8
Cuango *Lunda Norte* Angola **95** C7
Cuango *Uíge* Angola **95** C6
Cuango *r.* Angola **95** C6
Cuanza *r.* Angola **95** B7
Cuanza Norte *prov.* Angola **95** B7
Cuanza Sul *prov.* Angola **95** B7
Cuareim *r.* Uruguay **152** F2
Cuarto *r.* Arg. **152** E3
Cuatir *r.* Angola **95** C9
Cuatro Ciénegas Mex. **126** F6
Cuauhtémoc Mex. **135** F7
Cuba Port. **42** C3
Cuba *NY* U.S.A. **130** D2
Cuba *OH* U.S.A. **130** B4
▶Cuba *country* West Indies **127** J7
5th largest island and 5th most populous country in North America.
northamerica 118–119, 140
Cubal Angola **95** B8
Cubal *r.* Angola **95** B7
Cubango *r.* Angola/Namibia **95** D9
Cubara Col. **146** C3
Cub Hills Canada **123** J4
Cubillas *r.* Spain **42** E4
Çubuk Turkey **78** C2
Cucao Chile **153** B5
Cucapa, Sierra *mts* Mex. **137** E5
Cuchi Angola **95** C8
Cuchilla Grande *hills* Uruguay **152** G3
Cuchilla Grande Inferior *hills* Uruguay **152** F3
Cuchillo-Có Arg. **152** D4
Cucuí Brazil **146** E4
Cucumbi Angola **95** C7
Cucurrupí Col. **146** B3
Cúcuta Col. **146** C3
Cucutas *hill* Spain **43** F2
Cuddalore India **72** C4
Cuddapah India **72** C3
Cuddeback Lake U.S.A. **136** D4
Cudillero Spain **42** C1
Cue Australia **109** B6
Cuebe *r.* Angola **95** C8
Cueio *r.* Angola **95** D8
Cuéllar Spain **42** D2
Cuemba Angola **95** C8
Cuenca Ecuador **146** B5
Cuenca Spain **43** E2
Cuenca, Serranía de *mts* Spain **43** E2
Cuernavaca Mex. **126** G8
Cuero U.S.A. **133** B6
Cuers France **39** G5
Cuervos Mex. **137** E5
Cuevo Bol. **149** E5
Cugir Romania **46** C2
Cugir *r.* Romania **46** C2
Cuglieri *Sardinia* Italy **45** B4
Cugnaux France **38** D5
Cugo *r.* Angola **95** C6
Cuiabá Brazil **149** F3
Cuiabá *r.* Brazil **149** F4
Cuihua China *see* Daguan
Cuijiang China *see* Ninghua
Cuilcagh *hill* Rep. of Ireland/U.K. **35** C4
Cuillin Hills U.K. **34** C3
Cuillin Sound *sea chan.* U.K. **34** C3
Cuilo Angola **95** C7
Cuilo-Futa Angola **95** B6
Cuiluan China **64** B3
Cuito *r.* Angola **95** D9
Cuito Cuanavale Angola **95** C8
Cuiuni *r.* Brazil **147** F5
Cuivre *r.* U.S.A. **132** D4
Cujmir Romania **46** C2
Cukai Malaysia **58** C1
Çukë Albania **47** B5
Çukurca Turkey **79** E3
Çukurova *plat.* Turkey **77** B1
Cu Lao Cham *i.* Vietnam **61** E5
Cu Lao Re *i.* Vietnam **61** E5
Cu Lao Thu *i.* Vietnam **61** E6
Culbertson U.S.A. **134** F2
Culcairn Australia **112** C4
Culebras Peru **148** A2
Culfa Azer. **79** F3
Culiacán Mex. **126** E7
Culion *i.* Phil. **57** E3
Cúllar-Baza Spain **43** E4
Cullen Point Australia **111** E1
Cullera Spain **43** F3
Cullman U.S.A. **133** E5
Cul Mor *hill* U.K. **34** D2
Culpeper U.S.A. **130** E4
Culuene *r.* Brazil **150** A4
Culver, Point Australia **109** D8
Culverden N.Z. **113** C3
Cumaná Venez. **147** E2
Cumbal, Nevado de *vol.* Col. **146** B4
Cumberland *KY* U.S.A. **130** B5
Cumberland *MD* U.S.A. **130** D4
Cumberland *OH* U.S.A. **130** C4
Cumberland *VA* U.S.A. **130** D5
Cumberland *r.* U.S.A. **130** B5
Cumberland Bay S. Georgia **153** [inset]
Cumberland House Canada **123** K4
Cumberland Islands Australia **111** G4
Cumberland Mountain *mts* U.S.A. **130** B5
Cumberland Peninsula Canada **121** M3
Cumberland Plateau U.S.A. **128** B5
Cumberland Sound *sea chan.* Canada **121** M3
Cumbernauld U.K. **34** E4
Cumbre Alta *mt.* Spain **42** D3
Cumbre Negro *mt.* Arg. **153** C6
Cumbres de Majalca, Parque Nacional *nat. park* Mex. **135** F7
Cumbum India **72** C3
Cuminá Brazil **147** G5
Cuminapanema *r.* Brazil **147** H5
Cummins Australia **109** F8
Cummins Range *hills* Australia **108** D4
Cumnock U.K. **34** D4
Cumpas Mex. **135** E7
Çumra Turkey **78** C3
Cunani Brazil **147** I4
Cuñaré Col. **146** C4
Cunderdin Australia **109** B7
Cundinamarca *dept* Col. **146** C3
Cunene *prov.* Angola **95** B9
Cunene *r.* Angola **95** A9
Cuneo Italy **44** A2
Cung Son Vietnam **61** E5
Cunhinga Angola **95** C8
Cunnamulla Australia **111** F6
Cunshamayo Peru **148** B1
Cununa *mt.* Romania **46** C1
Čuokkarašša *mt.* Norway **32** G1
Cuorgnè Italy **44** A2
Cupar U.K. **34** E3
Ćuprija Yugo. **46** B3
Curaça Brazil **147** F6
Curaçá Brazil **150** E4
Curaçá *r.* Brazil **146** D6
Curaçao *i.* Neth. Antilles **146** D1
Curacautín Chile **152** C4
Curacó *r.* Arg. **152** D4
Curaculo Angola **95** B8
Curahuara de Carangas Bol. **148** C4
Curanilahue Chile **152** B4
Curaray *r.* Ecuador **146** C5
Curatabaca Venez. **147** F3
Curaya *r.* Arg. **152** F2
Curdlawidny Lagoon *salt flat* Australia **109** G7
Curé *r.* Col. **146** D5
Cure *r.* France **39** E3
Curia Switz. *see* Chur
Curicó Chile **152** C3
Curicuriari, Serra *hill* Brazil **146** E5
Curieuriari *r.* Brazil **146** E5
Curimata Brazil **150** C4
Curiplaya Col. **146** C4
Curitiba Brazil **151** B8
Curitibanos Brazil **151** B8
Curnamona Australia **112** A3
Curoca *r.* Angola **95** A8
Currais Novos Brazil **150** E3
Curralinho Brazil **150** B2
Curralulla *watercourse* Australia **110** C5
Currawilla Australia **111** E5
Currawinya National Park Australia **111** F6
Current *r.* U.S.A. **132** D4
Currie Australia **112** B5
Currie U.S.A. **137** E1
Currituck U.S.A. **131** E5
Curtea de Argeș Romania **46** D2
Curtici Romania **46** B1
Curtis Channel Australia **111** H5
Curtis Island Australia **111** G4
Curtis Island N.Z. **107** H5
Curuá Brazil **147** H5
Curuá *r.* Brazil **147** H6
Curuaés *r.* Brazil **150** A3
Curuapanema *r.* Brazil **147** H5
Curuá Una *r.* Brazil **147** H5
Curuçá Brazil **150** C2
Curup Indon. **58** C3
Curupira Brazil **147** F5
Curupira, Serra *mts* Brazil/Venez. **147** E4
Cururú Bol. **149** E3
Cururu *r.* Brazil **149** F1
Cururupu Brazil **150** C2
Curutú, Cerro *mt.* Venez. **147** F3
Curuzú Cuatiá Arg. **152** F2
Curvelo Brazil **151** C6
Cusco Peru **148** C3
Cusco *dept* Peru **148** B3
Cushendun U.K. **34** C4
Cusset France **39** E3
Cusseta U.S.A. **129** B5
Custer *MT* U.S.A. **134** F3
Custer *SD* U.S.A. **132** A3
Cutato Angola **95** C8
Cut Bank U.S.A. **134** D2
Cut Bank Creek *r.* U.S.A. **134** D2
Cuthbert U.S.A. **129** B6
Cuthbertson Falls Australia **110** C2
Cutler U.S.A. **136** C3
Cut Off U.S.A. **133** D6
Cutral-Co Arg. **152** C4
Cutro Italy **45** F5
Cuttaburra Creek *r.* Australia **111** F6
Cuttack India **73** E1
Cuvelai Angola **95** B8
Cuvette *admin. reg.* Congo **94** B5
Cuvette Ouest *admin. reg.* Congo **94** B4
Cuxhaven Germany **36** D2
Cuya Chile **148** C4
Cuyama U.S.A. **136** C4
Cuyama *r.* U.S.A. **136** B4
Cuyo Islands Phil. **57** F3
Cuyuni *r.* Guyana **147** G3
Cuzco Peru *see* Cusco
Cuzco *San Martín* Peru **148** A1
Cuzna *r.* Spain **42** D3
Cyclades *is* Greece **47** D6
Cydonia Greece *see* Chania
Cymru *admin. div.* U.K. *see* Wales
Cynthiana U.S.A. **130** A4
Cypress Hills Canada **134** E2
▶Cyprus *country* Asia **76** A2
asia 52–53, 82
Cyprus *i.* Asia **77** A2
Cyrenaica *reg.* Libya **88** D3
Cyrene *tourist site* Libya **88** D1
Cythera *i.* Greece *see* Kythira
Czaplinek Poland **37** H2
Czar Canada **123** I4
Czarna *r.* Poland **37** I3
Czarna *r.* Poland **37** J3
Czarna Struga *r.* Poland **37** I2
Czarne Poland **37** H2
Czarnków Poland **37** H2
▶Czechoslovakia
Divided in 1993 into the Czech Republic and Slovakia.
Czechowice-Dziedzice Poland **37** I4
▶Czech Republic *country* Europe **37** G4
europe 24–25, 48
Czempiń Poland **37** H2
Czernowitz Ukr. *see* Chernivtsi
Czersk Poland **37** H2
Czerwieńsk Poland **37** G2
Częstochowa Poland **37** I3
Człopa Poland **37** H2
Człuchów Poland **37** H2

↓ D

Đa, Sông *r.* Vietnam *see* Black River
Da'an China **64** A3
Ḍabāb, Jabal aḍ *mt.* Jordan **77** B4
Dabaga Tanz. **97** B7
Dabajuro Venez. **146** D2
Dabakala Côte d'Ivoire **92** D3
Daban China **63** J3
Dabao China **66** B2
Dabas Hungary **37** I5
Daba Shan *mts* China **67** D1
Dabba China *see* Daocheng
Dabeiba Col. **146** B3
Dabein Myanmar **60** B4
Dabhoi India **74** B5
Dabhol India **72** B2
Ḍab'ī, Wādī aḍ *watercourse* Jordan **77** C4
Dąbie, Jezioro *l.* Poland **37** G2
Dabie Shan *mts* China **67** E2
Dabl, Wādī *watercourse* Saudi Arabia **77** C5
Daboh India **74** C4
Dabola Guinea **92** C3
Dabou Côte d'Ivoire **92** D4
Daboya Ghana **93** E3
Dabra India **74** C4
Dąbrowa Górnicza Poland **37** I3
Dąbrowa Tarnowska Poland **37** J3
Dabsan Hu *salt l.* China **75** G1
Dabu China **67** F3
Dăbuleni Romania **46** D3
Dacca Bangl. *see* Dhaka
Dachau Germany **36** E4
Dachepalle India **72** C2
Dadaj, Jezioro *l.* Poland **37** J2
Dadanawa Guyana **147** G4
Daday Turkey **78** C2
Daddato Djibouti **96** D1
Dade City U.S.A. **129** C6
Dadhar Pak. **81** F4
Dādkān Iran **81** E5
Dadong China *see* Donggang
Dadou *r.* France **38** D5
Dadra *Dadra* India **72** B1
Dadra *Maharashtra* India *see* Achalpur
Dadra and Nagar Haveli *union terr.* India **72** B1
Dadu Pak. **81** F5
Dadu He *r.* China **66** B2
Đa Dung *r.* Vietnam **61** D6
Daedalus Reef Saudi Arabia **89** H3
Daet Phil. **57** F3
Dafang China **66** C3
Dafeng China **67** G1
Dafla Hills India **75** G4
Dafnoudi, Akra *pt* Greece **47** B5
Dafoe *r.* Canada **123** M4
Dafra Chad **94** C2
Daga Medo Eth. **96** D3
Dagana Senegal **92** B1
Daga Post Sudan **96** B2
Dagash Sudan **89** G5
Dagcanglhamo China **66** B1
Dagda Latvia **33** G4
Dagestan, Respublika *aut. rep.* Rus. Fed. **79** F2
Dagestanskaya A.S.S.R. *aut. rep.* Rus. Fed. *see* Dagestan, Respublika
Daghestan *aut. rep.* Rus. Fed. *see* Dagestan, Respublika
Dağlıq Qarabağ *aut. reg.* Azer. **79** F3
Daglung China **75** F3
Dagmersellen Switz. **39** G3
Dagö *i.* Estonia *see* Hiiumaa
Dagon Myanmar *see* Rangoon
Dagrag Zangbo *r.* China **75** E3
Daguan China **66** B3
Daguéla Chad **94** C2
Daguokui Shan *hill* China **64** B3
Dagupan Phil. **57** F2
Dagxoi *Sichuan* China *see* Sowa
Dagxoi *Sichuan* China *see* Yidun
Dagzê China **75** F3
Dagzê Co *salt l.* China **75** E3
Dagzhuka China **75** F3
Dahabān Saudi Arabia **89** H4
Dahadinni *r.* Canada **122** E2
Dahalach, Isole *is* Eritrea *see* Dahlak Archipelago
Dahana *des.* Saudi Arabia *see* Ad Dahnā'
Dahanu India **72** B2
Dahe China *see* Ziyuan
Daheiding Shan *mt.* China **64** B3
Dahei Shan *mts* China **64** A4
Daheng China **67** F3
Dahezhen China **64** C3
Da Hinggan Ling *mts* China **63** J3
Dahlak Archipelago *is* Eritrea **89** I6
Dahlak Marine National Park Eritrea **89** I5
Daḥl al Furayy *well* Saudi Arabia **80** A5
Dahlem Germany **36** C3
Dahlia Zimbabwe **99** E3
Daḥl Iftākh *well* Saudi Arabia **80** A5
Dahmani Tunisia **91** H2
Dahme Germany **37** F3
Dahod India **74** B5
Dahomey *country* Africa *see* Benin
Dahongliutan Aksai Chin **74** C2
Dahra Senegal *see* Dara
Dahūk Iraq **79** E3
Dahūk *governorate* Iraq **79** E3
Daik Indon. **58** D3
Daikanvik Sweden **32** E2
Daik-u Myanmar **60** B4
Dailekh Nepal **75** D3
Dailey U.S.A. **130** D4
Daim Iran **81** D3
Daimanji-san *hill* Japan **65** C5
Daimiel Spain **42** E3
Daingerfield U.S.A. **133** C5
Dainkog China **66** A1
Daintree Australia **111** F3
Daintree National Park Australia **111** F3
Daireaux Arg. **152** E4
Dairen China *see* Dalian
Dai-sen *vol.* Japan **65** C6
Daisen-Oki National Park Japan **65** C6
Daisetsu-zan National Park Japan **64** E4
Daiyun Shan *mts* China **67** F3
Dajarra Australia **111** D4
Dajie China *see* Jiangchuan
Dajin Chuan *r.* China **66** B2
Da Juh China **75** G1
▶Dakar Senegal **92** A2
Capital of Senegal.
Dakhal, Wādī ad *watercourse* Egypt **77** A5
Dākhilah, Wāḥāt ad *oasis* Egypt *see* Dakhla Oasis
Dakhin Shahbazpur Island Bangl. **75** F5
Dakhla W. Sahara *see* Ad Dakhla
Dakhla Oasis Egypt **89** F3
Dakhlet Nouâdhibou *admin. reg.* Mauritania **90** A5
Dakingari Nigeria **93** G3
Dak Kon Vietnam **61** D5
Đak Nghe *r.* Vietnam **61** D5
Dakoank India **73** G5
Dakol'ka *r.* Belarus **29** D5
Dakor India **74** B5
Dakoro Niger **93** G2
Dakota City *IA* U.S.A. **132** C3
Dakota City *NE* U.S.A. **132** B3
Đakovica Yugo. **46** B3
Đakovo Croatia **44** G2
Dala Angola **95** D7
Dalaba Guinea **92** B3
Dalai China *see* Da'an
Dalain Hob China **70** J3
Dālakī Iran **80** B4
Dālakī, Rūd-e *r.* Iran **80** B4
Dalälven *r.* Sweden **33** E3
Dalaman Turkey **78** B3
Dalaman *r.* Turkey **78** B3
Dalandzadgad Mongolia **62** G3
Dalarna *county* Sweden **33** D3
Dalarna *reg.* Sweden **33** D3
Dalat *Sarawak* Malaysia **59** E2
Đa Lat Vietnam **61** E6
Dalatando Angola *see* N'dalatando
Dalbandin Pak. **81** F4
Dalbeg Australia **111** F4
Dalbosjön *l.* Sweden **33** D4
Dalby Australia **111** G5
Dalcahue Chile **153** B5
Dale *Hordaland* Norway **33** B3
Dale *Sogn og Fjordane* Norway **33** B3
Dale City U.S.A. **131** E4
Dale Hollow Lake U.S.A. **132** E4
Daletme Myanmar **60** A3
Dalfors Sweden **33** D3
Dalhart U.S.A. **133** A4
Dalhousie Canada **125** H3
Dalhousie, Cape Canada **120** G2
Dali *Shaanxi* China **67** D1
Dali *Yunnan* China **66** B3
Dalian China **63** K4
Daliang China *see* Shunde
Daliang Shan *mts* China **66** B2
Dalizi China **64** A4
Dalj Croatia **44** G2
Dalkola India **75** E4
Dallas U.S.A. **133** B5
Dalles City U.S.A. *see* The Dalles
Dall Island U.S.A. **122** C4
Dallol Bosso *watercourse* Mali/Niger **93** F2
Dalmā *i.* U.A.E. **80** C5
Dalmally U.K. **34** D3
Dalman India **74** D4
Dalmas, Lac *l.* Canada **125** G2
Dalmatia *reg.* Croatia **44** E2
Dalmellington U.K. **34** D4
Dal'negorsk Rus. Fed. **64** D3
Dal'nerechensk Rus. Fed. **64** C3
Dal'niye Zelentsy Rus. Fed. **28** F1
Dalny China *see* Dalian
Daloa Côte d'Ivoire **92** D4
▶Dalol Eth. **89** I6
Highest recorded annual mean temperature in the world.
world 12–13
Dalou Shan *mts* China **66** C3
Dalqān *well* Saudi Arabia **76** D5
Dalrymple, Lake Australia **111** F4
Dalrymple, Mount Australia **111** G4
Daltenganj India **75** E4
Dalton Canada **124** C3
Dalton *GA* U.S.A. **129** B5
Dalton *MA* U.S.A. **131** G2
Dalton *OH* U.S.A. **130** C3
Dalton *PA* U.S.A. **131** F3
Daltonganj India *see* Daltenganj
Daludalu Indon. **58** C2
Daluo Shan *mt.* China **67** E4
Dalupiri *i.* Phil. **67** G5
Dalvík Iceland **32** [inset]
Dalwallinu Australia **109** B7
Dalwhinnie U.K. **34** D3
Daly *r.* Australia **110** B2
Daly City U.S.A. **136** A3
Daly River Australia **110** B2
Daly Waters Australia **110** C3
Damagaram Takaya Niger **93** H2
Daman India **72** B1
Daman and Diu *union terr.* India **72** A1
Damāne *well* Mauritania **92** B1
Dāmaneh Iran **80** B3
Damanhūr Egypt **89** F2
Damant Lake Canada **123** J2
Damão India *see* Daman
Damar *i.* Indon. **57** G7
Damara Cent. Afr. Rep. **94** C3
Damaraland *reg.* Namibia **98** C4
Damariscotta Lake U.S.A. **131** I1
Damas Syria *see* Damascus
Damasak Nigeria **93** I2
▶Damascus Syria **78** D4
Capital of Syria.
Damascus *MD* U.S.A. **131** E4
Damascus *VA* U.S.A. **130** C5
Damaturu Nigeria **93** H3
Damāvand Iran **80** C3
Damāvand, Qolleh-ye *mt.* Iran **80** C3
Damba Angola **95** B6
Dambai Ghana **93** F3
Dambatta Nigeria **93** H2
Damboa Nigeria **93** I3
Dâmbovița *r.* Romania **46** D2
Damghan Iran **80** C2
Damietta Egypt *see* Dumyāṭ
Daming Shan *mt.* China **67** D4
Damjong China **75** G2
Dammam Saudi Arabia **76** E4
Dammastock *mt.* Switz. **39** H3
Damme Germany **36** D2
Damoh India **74** C5
Damongo Ghana **93** E3
Damour Lebanon **77** B3
Dampar, Tasik *l.* Malaysia **58** C2
Dampier Australia **108** B5
Dampier Archipelago *is* Australia **108** B5
Dampier Island P.N.G. *see* Karkar Island
Dampier Land *reg.* Australia **108** C4
Dampierre-sur-Salon France **39** F3
Dampier Strait P.N.G. **106** D2
Dampir, Selat *sea chan.* Indon. **57** H6
Dampit Indon. **59** F5
Damqog Zangbo *r.* China *see* Maquan He
Dam Qu *r.* China **75** G2
Dâmrei, Chuŏr Phnum *mts* Cambodia **61** D6
Damxoi China *see* Comai
Damxung China **70** H5
Dan *r.* U.S.A. **128** D4
Dana Nepal **75** D3
Danakil *reg.* Eritrea/Eth. *see* Denakil
Danané Côte d'Ivoire **92** C4
Đa Năng Vietnam **61** E4
Đa Nang, Vinh *b.* Vietnam **61** E4
Danata Turkm. **80** C2
Danba China **66** B2
Danbury *CT* U.S.A. **131** G3
Danbury *NH* U.S.A. **131** H2
Danby U.S.A. **131** G2
Danby Lake U.S.A. **137** E4
Dancheng China *see* Xiangshan
Dande *r.* Angola **95** B7
Dande Eth. **96** C3
Dandel'dhura Nepal **74** D3
Dandeli India **72** B3
Dandong China **65** A4
Daneborg Greenland **121** Q2
Daneți Romania **46** D3
Dänew Turkm. *see* Dyanev
Danfeng *Shaanxi* China **67** D1
Danfeng *Yunnan* China *see* Shizong
Dangan Liedao *i.* China **67** E4
Dangara Tajik. *see* Danghara
Dangbizhen Rus. Fed. **64** B3
Dangchang China **66** C1
Dange Angola **95** B6
Danger Point S. Africa **98** C7
Dangé-St-Romain France **38** D3
Danghara Tajik. **81** G2
Dangila Eth. **76** B7
Dangla Shan *mts* China *see* Tanggula Shan
Dan Gorayo Somalia **96** F2
Dangori India **75** G4
Dangqên China **75** F3
Dangshan China **67** F1
Dangtu China **67** F2
Dan-Gulbi Nigeria **93** G3
Dangur Eth. **96** B2
Dangur Mountains Eth. **96** B2
Dangyang China **67** D2
Daniel's Harbour Canada **125** J3
Danielson U.S.A. **131** H3
Danilov Rus. Fed. **28** G4
Danilovgrad Yugo. **46** A3
Danilovka Rus. Fed. **29** H6
Danilovskaya Vozvyshennost' *hills* Rus. Fed. **28** F4
Dänizkänarı Azer. **79** G2
Danjiang China *see* Leishan
Danjiangkou China **67** D1
Danjiangkou Shuiku *resr* China **67** D1
Danjo-guntō *is* Japan **65** B6
Dankov Rus. Fed. **29** F5
Danlí Hond. **138** G6
Dannebrog Ø *i.* Greenland *see* Qillak
Dannenberg (Elbe) Germany **36** E2
Dannet *well* Niger **93** G1
Dannevirke N.Z. **113** D3
Dan Sai Thai. **60** C4
Danshui Taiwan *see* Tanshui
Dansville U.S.A. **130** E2
Danta India **74** B4
Dantewara India **72** D2
Dantu China **67** F1
▶Danube *r.* Europe **36** E4
2nd longest river in Europe.
Also spelt Donau (Austria/Germany) or Duna (Hungary) or Dunaj (Slovakia) or Dunărea (Romania) or Dunav (Bulgaria/Croatia/Yugoslavia) or Dunay (Ukraine).
europe 22–23
Danube Delta Romania **46** F2
Danubyu Myanmar **60** A4
Danumparai Indon. **59** F2
Danville *AR* U.S.A. **133** C5
Danville *IL* U.S.A. **132** E3
Danville *KY* U.S.A. **130** A5
Danville *OH* U.S.A. **130** B3
Danville *VA* U.S.A. **130** D5
Danville *VT* U.S.A. **131** G1
Danxian China *see* Danzhou
Danyang China **67** F2
Danzhai China **66** C3
Danzhou *Guangxi* China **67** D3
Danzhou *Hainan* China **67** D5
Danzig Poland *see* Gdańsk
Danzig, Gulf of Poland/Rus. Fed. *see* Gdańsk, Gulf of
Dão *r.* Port. **42** B2
Daocheng China **66** B2
Daojiang China *see* Daoxian
Dao Tay Sa *is* S. China Sea *see* Paracel Islands
Dao Timmi Niger **88** B4
Daoud Alg. *see* Aïn Beïda
Daoudi *well* Mauritania **92** D2
Daoukro Côte d'Ivoire **92** E4
Daoxian China **67** D3
Daozhen China **66** C2
Dapaong Togo **93** F3
Dapchi Nigeria **93** H2
Dapeng Wan *b. Hong Kong* China *see* Mirs Bay
Daphabum *mt.* India **60** B2
Daphne U.S.A. **129** B6
Dapingdi China *see* Yanbian
Daqahlīya *governorate* Egypt *see* Ad Daqahlīyah
Da Qaidam Zhen China **70** I4
Daqiao China **66** B3
Daqing China **64** A3
Daqiu China **67** F3
Daqq-e Patargān *salt flat* Iran **81** E3
Daqq-e-Tundi, Dasht-e *imp. l.* Afgh. **81** E3
Daqu Shan *i.* China **67** G2
Dara Senegal **92** B2
Dar'ā Syria **78** D4
Dar'ā *governorate* Syria **77** C3
Daraá *r.* Brazil **147** E5
Dārāb Iran **80** C4
Daraina Madag. **99** [inset] K2
Daraj Libya **88** A2
Dārān Iran **80** B3
Đa Răng, Sông *r.* Vietnam **61** E5
Darasun Rus. Fed. **63** I1
Daraut-Kurgan Kyrg. *see* Daroot-Korgan
Đaravica *mt.* Yugo. **46** B3
Darazo Nigeria **93** H3
Darband Iran **80** D4
Darband Uzbek. *see* Derbent
Darband, Kūh-e *mt.* Iran **80** D4
Darb-e Behesht Iran **80** D4
Darbėnai Lith. **33** F4
Darbhanga India **75** E4
Darcang China **66** A1
Dar Chabanne Tunisia **45** C6
D'Arcy Canada **122** F5
Darda Croatia **44** G2
Dardanelle U.S.A. **136** C2
Dardanelle, Lake U.S.A. **133** C5
Dardanelles *str.* Turkey **78** A2
Dardo China *see* Kangding
Dar el Beida Morocco *see* Casablanca
Darende Turkey **78** D3
▶Dar es Salaam Tanz. **97** C6
Former capital of Tanzania.

Dārestān Iran **80** C4
Darfo Boario Terme Italy **44** C2
Dargai Pak. **81** G3
Darganata Turkm. **81** E1
Dargaville N.Z. **113** C1
Darhan Mongolia **62** H2
Darıca Turkey **46** F4
Darien *CT* U.S.A. **131** G3
Darién, Golfo del Col. **146** B2
Darién, Parque Nacional de *nat. park* Panama **146** B2
Darién, Serranía del *mts* Panama **146** B2
Dar'inskoye Kazakh. **29** I6
Darjeeling India **75** F4
Darjeeling India *see* Darjeeling
Dārkhovin Iran **80** C4
Darlag China **66** A1

▶Darling *r.* Australia **112** B4
2nd longest river in Oceania. Part of the longest (Murray-Darling).
oceania **102–103**

Darling Downs *hills* Australia **111** G5
Darling Range *hills* Australia **109** A8
Darlington U.K. **35** F4
Darlington India **129** D5
Darlington Point Australia **112** C4
Darlot, Lake *salt flat* Australia **109** C6
Darłowo Poland **37** H1
Därmänești Romania **46** E1
Darmstadt Germany **36** D4
Darna *r.* India **72** C1
Darnah Libya **88** D1
Darnick Australia **112** B4
Darnley, Cape Antarctica **167** E2
Darnley Bay Canada **120** G3
Daroca Spain **43** F2
Daroot-Korgan Kyrg. **81** H2
Darovskoy Rus. Fed. **28** H4
Dar Pahn Iran **80** D5
Darragueira Arg. **152** E4
Darreh Bid Iran **80** D3
Darreh Gaz Iran **81** D2
Darreh-ye Bāhābād Iran **80** C4
Darreh-ye Shekārī *r.* Afgh. **81** G3
Darro *watercourse* Eth. **96** D3
Darsa *r.* Iran **76** E7
Darsi India **72** C3
Darß *pen.* Germany **37** F1
Darßer Ort *c.* Germany **37** F1
Darta Turkm. **80** D1
Dartford U.K. **35** H6
Dartmoor *hills* U.K. **35** D6
Dartmoor National Park U.K. **35** E6
Dartmouth Canada **125** I4
Dartmouth U.K. **35** E6
Dartmouth Reservoir Australia **112** C5
Daru P.N.G. **57** J7
Daru *waterhole* Sudan **89** G5
Daruba Indon. **57** G5
Daruvar Croatia **44** F2
Darvaza Turkm. **81** D1
Darvoz, Qatorkŭhi *mts* Tajik. **81** G2
Darwendale Zimbabwe **99** F3
Darwha India **72** C1

▶Darwin Australia **110** B2
Capital of Northern Territory.

Darwin Falkland Is **153** F7
Darwin, Canal *sea chan.* Chile **153** B6
Darwin, Monte *mt.* Chile **153** C8
Darya Khan Pak. **81** G4
Dar"yoi Amu *r.* Asia *see* Amudar'ya
Dar"yoi Sir *r.* Asia *see* Syrdar'ya
Därzin Iran **80** D4
Dās *i.* U.A.E. **80** C5
Dasada India **74** A5
Dashhowuz Turkm. *see* Dashhowuz
Dashkesan Azer. *see* Daşkäsän
Dashkhovuz Turkm. **76** F1
Dashkhovuz Oblast *admin. div.* Turkm.
  see Dashkhovuzskaya Oblast'
Dashkhovuzskaya Oblast' *admin. div.*
  Turkm. **80** D1
Dashköpri Turkm. *see* Tashkepri
Dashoguz Turkm. *see* Dashhowuz
Dasht Iran **80** D2
Dasht *r.* Pak. **81** E5
Dasht-e Bar Iran **80** D4
Dasht-e Palang *r.* Iran **80** C4
Dashtiari Iran **81** E5
Daska Pak. **81** H4
Daşkäsän Azer. **79** F2
Dasongshu China **66** C3
Daspar *mt.* Pak. **81** H3
Dassa Benin **93** F4
Da Suifen He *r.* China **64** C4
Dasuya India **74** B3
Datadian Indon. **59** F2
Datça Turkey **78** A3
Daté Japan **64** G4
Date Creek *watercourse* U.S.A. **137** F5
Dateland U.S.A. **137** F5
Datha India **74** B5
Datia India **74** C4
Datian China **67** F3
Datian Ding *mt.* China **67** D4
Datong *Fujian* China *see* Tong'an
Datong *Shanxi* China **63** I3
Datta Rus. Fed. **64** D2
Datu *i.* Indon. **59** E2
Datu, Tanjung *c.* Indon./Malaysia **59** E2
Datu Piang Phil. **57** G5
Daudkandi Bangl. **75** F5
Daud Khel Pak. **81** G3
Daudnagar India **75** E4
Daudzeva Latvia **33** G4
Daugai Lith. **33** G5
Daugava *r.* Latvia **33** G4
Daugavpils Latvia **33** G5
Daulatabad Iran *see* Malāyer
Daulatpur Bangl. **75** F5
Daule Ecuador **146** B5
Daun Germany **36** C3
Daund India **72** B2
Daung Kyun *i.* Myanmar **61** B5
Daungyu *r.* Myanmar **60** A3
Dauphin Canada **134** C2
Dauphiné *reg.* France **39** F4
Dauphiné, Alpes du *mts* France **39** F4
Dauphin Island U.S.A. **129** H4
Dauphin Lake Canada **123** L5
Daura Nigeria **93** H2
Daurie Creek *r.* Australia **109** A6
Dausa India **74** C4
Dău Tiếng, Hồ *resr* Vietnam **61** D6
Dăvăçi Azer. **79** G2
Davangere India **72** B3
Davao Phil. **57** G4
Davao Gulf Phil. **57** G4
Dāvarān Iran **80** D4
Dāvar Panāh Iran **81** E5
Davenport *IA* U.S.A. **132** D3
Davenport *WA* U.S.A. **134** C3
Davenport Downs Australia **111** E5
Davenport Range *hills* Australia **110** C4
Daveyton S. Africa **99** F5
David Panama **139** H7
David City U.S.A. **132** B3
Davidson Canada **134** F2
Davidson, Mount Australia **110** B4

Davie Ridge *sea feature* Indian Ocean
  162 J6
Davis *research station* Antarctica **167** E2
Davis *i.* Myanmar *see* Than Kyun
Davis *CA* U.S.A. **136** B2
Davis *WV* U.S.A. **130** D4
Davis, Mount Australia **112** B2
Davis Dam U.S.A. **137** E4
Davis Inlet Canada **125** I2
Davison U.S.A. **130** D2
Davis Sea Antarctica **167** F2
Davis Strait Canada/Greenland **121** N3
Davlekanovo Rus. Fed. **28** J5
Davos Switz. **39** H3
Davy U.S.A. **130** C5
Davy Lake Canada **123** I3
Dawa Co *l.* China **75** E3
Dawa Wenz *r.* Eth. **96** E3
Dawaxung China **75** E3
Dawê China **66** B2
Dawei Myanmar *see* Tavoy
Dawei *b.* Myanmar *see* Tavoy
Dawera *i.* Indon. **108** E1
Dawqah Oman **76** E6
Dawqah Saudi Arabia **89** I5
Dawson *r.* Australia **111** G5
Dawson Canada **122** B1
Dawson *GA* U.S.A. **129** B6
Dawson *ND* U.S.A. **132** B2
Dawson, Isla *i.* Chile **153** C8
Dawson Creek Canada **122** F4
Dawson Inlet Canada **123** M2
Dawson Range *mts* Canada **122** A2
Dawsons Landing Canada **122** E5
Dawu *Hubei* China **67** E2
Dawu *Qinghai* China *see* Maqên
Dawu *Sichuan* China **66** B2
Dawu Taiwan *see* Tawu
Dawukou China *see* Shizuishan
Dawu Shan *hill* China **67** E2
Dax France **38** C5
Daxian China *see* Dazhou
Daxiang Ling *mts* China **66** B2
Daxin China **66** C4
Daxing *Yunnan* China *see* Ninglang
Daxing *Yunnan* China *see* Lüchun
Daxue China *see* Wencheng
Daxue Shan *mts* China **66** B2
Dayan China *see* Lijiang
Dayao China **66** B3
Dayao Shan *mts* China **67** D4
Dâyat an Nahârât *well* Mali **92** E1
Daye China **67** E2
Daying Jiang *r.* China *see* Guanyun
Daylesford Australia **112** C5
Dayong China **67** E2
Dayr Abū Sa'īd Jordan **77** B3
Dayr az Zawr Syria **79** E4
Dayr Ḩāfir Syria **77** C1
Daysland Canada **123** H4
Dayton *OH* U.S.A. **130** A4
Dayton *TN* U.S.A. **128** B5
Dayton *TX* U.S.A. **133** E6
Dayton *WA* U.S.A. **134** C3
Daytona Beach U.S.A. **129** C6
Dayu China **67** E3
Dayu Indon. **59** F3
Dayu Ling *mts* China **67** E3
Da Yunhe *canal* China **67** F1
Dayyina *i.* U.A.E. **80** C5
Dazhe China *see* Pingyuan
Dazhongji China *see* Dafeng
Dazhou China **66** C2
Dazhou Dao *i.* China **67** D5
Dazhu China **66** C2
Dazu China *see* Dafeng
Dazu Rock Carvings *tourist site* China
  66 C2
De Aar S. Africa **98** E6
Deadman's Cay Bahamas **129** E8
Dead Mountains U.S.A. **137** E4

▶Dead Sea *salt l.* Asia **76** B3
Lowest point in the world and in As a.

Deakin Australia **109** E7
Deal U.K. **35** I6
Dean *r.* Canada **122** E4
De'an China **67** E2
Deán Funes Arg. **152** D2
Deanuvuotna *inlet* Norway *see*
  Tanafjorden
Dearborn U.S.A. **130** D2
Dease *r.* B.C. Canada **122** D3
Dease *r.* N.W.T. Canada **122** H1
Dease Arm *b.* Canada **122** F1
Dease Lake Canada **122** D3
Dease Lake *l.* Canada **122** D3
Dease Strait Canada **121** I3
Death Valley U.S.A. **136** D3

▶Death Valley *depr.* U.S.A. **136** D3
Lowest point in the Americas.
northamerica **116–117**
world **14–15**

Death Valley Junction U.S.A. **137** D3
Death Valley National Park U.S.A.
  136 D3
Deaver U.S.A. **134** E3
Debak *Sarawak* Malaysia **59** E2
Debao China **66** C4
Debar Macedonia **46** B4
Debark Eth. **96** C1
Debden Canada **123** J4
Debelt Canada **125** I4
Debesy Rus. Fed. **28** J4
Debica Poland **37** J3
De Biesbosch, Nationaal Park *nat. park*
  Neth. **36** B3
Debila Alg. **91** G2
Debin Rus. Fed. **27** P3
Dęblin Poland **37** J3
Dębno Poland **37** G2
Dębo, Lac *l.* Mali **92** D3
Deborah East, Lake *salt flat* Australia
  109 B7
Deborah West, Lake *salt flat* Australia
  109 B7
Debre Birhan Eth. **96** C2
Debrecen Hungary **37** J5
Debre Markos Eth. **96** C2
Debre Tabor Eth. **96** C2
Debre Werk' Eth. **96** C2
Debre Zeyit Eth. **96** C2
Debrzno Poland **37** H2
Dečani Yugo. *see* Dečani
Decatur *AL* U.S.A. **133** E5
Decatur *GA* U.S.A. **129** B5
Decatur *IL* U.S.A. **128** F4
Decatur *IN* U.S.A. **130** C3
Decatur *TX* U.S.A. **133** B5
Decazeville France **38** E4

▶Deccan *plat.* India **72** C2
Plateau making up most of southern and central India.

Deception *watercourse* Botswana **98** E4
Deception Bay Australia **111** H5

Dechang China **66** B3
Decheng China *see* Deqing
Decize France **39** F3
Decorah U.S.A. **132** D3
Dedap i. Indon. *see* Penyu, Pulau-pulau
Dedegöl Dağları *mts* Turkey **78** B3
Dedop'listsqaro Georgia **79** F2
Dedovichi Rus. Fed. **28** F4
Dedu China **64** A2
Dedza Malawi **97** B8
Dee *r.* England/Wales U.K. **35** E5
Dee *r.* Scotland U.K. **34** F3
Deeg India **74** C4
Deep Bay Hong Kong China **67** [inset]
Deep Creek Lake U.S.A. **130** D4
Deep Creek Range *mts* U.S.A. **137** F2
Deep River Canada **124** E4
Deep River U.S.A. **131** G3
Deering, Mount Australia **109** E6
Deer Island U.S.A. **120** B4
Deer Island *ME* U.S.A. **131** I1
Deer Lake *Nfld. and Lab.* Canada
  125 J3
Deer Lake *Ont.* Canada **123** M4
Deer Lake *l.* Canada **123** M4
Deer Lodge U.S.A. **134** E3
Deer Park U.S.A. **134** C3
Deesa India *see* Disa
Defeng China *see* Liping
Defensores del Chaco, Parque
  Nacional *nat. park* Para. **149** E5
Defiance U.S.A. **130** A3
Defiance Plateau U.S.A. **137** H4
De Funiak Springs U.S.A. **129** B6
Degana India **74** C4
Degano *r.* Italy **44** D1
Degeh Bur Eth. **96** D2
Dégelis Canada **125** G4
Degema Nigeria **93** G4
Degerfors Sweden **33** D4
Dégh *r.* Pak. **81** H4
Degirmenlik Cyprus *see* Kythrea
Değirmenlik *r.* Turkey **47** F5
Değirmenlik Cyprus *see* Kythrea
De Grey *r.* Australia **108** B5
De Grey *r.* Australia **108** B5
Dehaj Iran **80** D4
Dehalak Deset *i.* Eritrea **89** I6
Deh Bakri Iran **80** D4
Deh Barez Iran *see* Fāryāb
Deh-Dasht Iran **80** B4
Dehdez Iran **80** C4
Dehej India **74** B5
Deh-e Khalīfeh Iran **80** B4
Deh-e Kohneh Iran **80** B4
Dehgāh Iran **80** C4
Deh Golān Iran **80** B3
Dehgolān Iran **80** B3
Dehi Afgh. **81** F3
Dehküyeh Iran **80** C5
Dehlorān Iran **80** A3
De Hoge Veluwe, Nationaal Park
  nat. park Neth. **36** C2
Dehqonobod Uzbek. *see* Dekhkanabad
Dehra Dun India **74** C3
Dehri India **75** E4
Deh Shū Afgh. **81** E4
Dehua China **67** F3
Dehui China **64** A3
Deim Zubeir Sudan **94** E3
Deinze Belgium **39** E1
Deir el Qamar Lebanon **77** B3
Deir-ez-Zor Syria *see* Dayr az Zawr
Dej Romania **31** J4
Dejë, Mal *mt.* Albania **46** B4
Deji China *see* Rinbung
Dejiang China **66** D2
Deka Drum Zimbabwe **99** E3
De Kalb *IL* U.S.A. **132** D3
De Kalb *TX* U.S.A. **133** C5
De-Kastri Rus. Fed. **27** O4
Dekemhare Eritrea **89** H6
Dekese Dem. Rep. Congo **94** D5
Dekhkanabad Uzbek. **81** F2
Dékoa Cent. Afr. Rep. **94** C3
Delaki Indon. **108** D2
Delami Sudan **96** A2
De Land U.S.A. **129** C6
Delano U.S.A. **136** C4
Delano Peak U.S.A. **137** F2

▶Delap-Uliga-Djarrit Marshall Is **164** F5
Capital of the Marshall Islands, on Majuro atoll.

Delārām Afgh. **81** E3
Delareyville S. Africa **98** E5
Delarof Islands U.S.A. **120** B4
Delaronde Lake Canada **123** J4
Delaware U.S.A. **130** B3
Delaware *r. KS* U.S.A. **132** C4
Delaware *r. NJ/PA* U.S.A. **131** F4
Delaware *state* U.S.A. **131** H4
Delaware, East Branch *r.* U.S.A. **131** F3
Delaware, West Branch *r.* U.S.A.
  131 F3
Delaware Bay U.S.A. **131** F4
Delaware City U.S.A. **131** H4
Delay *r.* Canada **125** G1
Delbarton U.S.A. **130** B5
Del Bonita Canada **123** H5
Delčevo Macedonia **46** C4
Delegate Australia **112** D6
Delémont Switz. **39** H3
Delevan U.S.A. **136** A2
Delft Neth. **36** B2
Delft Island Sri Lanka **72** C4
Delfzijl Neth. **36** C2
Delgado, Cabo *c.* Moz. **97** D7
Delgo Sudan **89** F4
Delhi Canada **130** C2
Delhi China **70** I4

▶Delhi India **74** C3
world **16–17**

Delhi *LA* U.S.A. **133** D5
Delhi *NY* U.S.A. **131** F2
Deli *i.* Indon. **58** D4
Deli *r.* Turkey **79** E3
Delice *r.* Turkey **78** C2
Délices Fr. Guiana **147** H3
Delijān Iran **80** C3
Déline Canada **122** F1
Delingha China *see* Delhi
Delisle Canada **123** J5
Delitzsch Germany **37** F3
Dellys Alg. **91** F1
Del Mar U.S.A. **136** D5
Delmenhorst Germany **36** D2
Delmont U.S.A. **132** D3
Delmore Downs Australia **110** C4
Delnice Croatia **44** F2
De-Longa, Ostrova *is* Rus. Fed. *see*
  De-Longa, Ostrova
Delong Canada **66** C4
De Long Islands Rus. Fed. *see*
  De-Longa, Ostrova
De Long Mountains U.S.A. **120** C3
De Long Strait Rus. Fed. *see*
  Longa, Proliv

Deloraine Australia **112** C6
Deloraine Canada **123** K5
Delphi *tourist site* Greece **47** C5
Delphi U.S.A. **128** C3
Delphos U.S.A. **130** A3
Delray Beach U.S.A. **129** C7
Del Rio Mex. **135** E7
Del Rio U.S.A. **133** A6
Delsbo Sweden **33** J3
Delta state Nigeria **93** G4
Delta *CO* U.S.A. **135** G5
Delta *OH* U.S.A. **130** A3
Delta *UT* U.S.A. **137** F2
Delta Amacuro state Venez. **147** F2
Delta du Saloum, Parc National du
  nat. park Senegal **92** A2
Delta Junction U.S.A. **120** D3
Delvada India **74** A1
Delvinë Albania **46** B5
Dema *r.* Rus. Fed. **29** J5
Demavend *mt.* Iran *see*
  Damāvand, Qolleh-ye
Demba Dem. Rep. Congo **95** D6
Dembia Cent. Afr. Rep. **94** C3
Dembi Dolo Eth. **96** B2
Demerara Guyana *see* Georgetown
Demerara Abyssal Plain *sea feature*
  S. Atlantic Ocean **160** K5
Demidov Rus. Fed. **31** L2
Deming U.S.A. **135** F6
Demini *r.* Brazil **147** F4
Demini, Serras do *mts* Brazil **147** F4
Demirci Turkey **78** B3
Demir Hisar Macedonia **46** B4
Demirköprü Baraji *resr* Turkey **78** B3
Demirköy Turkey **46** E4
Demirler *r.* Turkey **47** F5
Demmin Germany **37** F2
Democracia Brazil **147** F6
Demopolis U.S.A. **129** B5
Dempo, Gunung *vol.* Indon. **58** C4
Dempster Highway Canada **122** B1
Dêmqog *Jammu and Kashmir* **74** C2
Dem'yanovo Rus. Fed. **28** J3
Denakil *reg.* Eritrea/Eth. **89** I6
Denali *mt.* U.S.A. *see* McKinley, Mount
Denan Eth. **96** C2
Denau Uzbek. **81** F2
Denbigh Canada **124** E4
Denbigh U.K. **35** D5
Den Bosch Neth. *see* 's-Hertogenbosch
Den Burg Neth. **36** B2
Den Chai Thai. **60** C4
Dendang Indon. **59** D3
Dendâra Mauritania **92** D1
Dendermonde Belgium **39** E1
Dendi *mt.* Eth. **76** D7
Deneral Janković Yugo. **46** B3
Denezhkin Kamen', Gora *mt.* Rus. Fed.
  28 K3
Dengas Niger **93** H2
Denge Nigeria **93** G2
Dengfeng China **67** E3
Dêngka China *see* Tewo
Dêngkagoin China *see* Tewo
Dêngqên China **75** G3
Dengta China **67** E2
Denguiro Cent. Afr. Rep. **94** D3
Dengxian China *see* Dengzhou
Dengzhou China **67** E1
Den Haag Neth. *see* The Hague
Den Helder Neth. **36** B2
Denholm Canada **123** I4
Denia Spain **43** G4
Denial Bay Australia **109** F8
Deniliquin Australia **112** C3
Denison *IA* U.S.A. **132** C3
Denison *TX* U.S.A. **133** B5
Denison, Cape Antarctica **167** G2
Denison Plains Australia **108** E4
Denizli Turkey **78** B3
Denizli *prov.* Turkey **47** F6
Denman Australia **112** D4
Denman Glacier Antarctica **167** F2
Denmark Australia **109** B8

▶Denmark *country* Europe **33** C5
europe **24–25, 48**

Denmark Strait Greenland/Iceland
  121 Q3
Dennison U.S.A. **130** C3
Dennisville U.S.A. **131** F4
Denow U.S.A. *see* Denau
Denpasar Indon. **59** F5
Denton *MD* U.S.A. **131** H4
Denton *TX* U.S.A. **133** B5
D'Entrecasteaux, Point Australia **109** A8
D'Entrecasteaux, Récifs *reef*
  New Caledonia **107** F3
D'Entrecasteaux Islands P.N.G. **107** F2
D'Entrecasteaux National Park
  Australia **109** A8
Dents du Midi *mt.* Switz. **39** G3

▶Denver U.S.A. **134** F4
State capital of Colorado.

Denys *r.* Canada **124** E2
Deoband India **74** C3
Deobhog India **73** D2
Deogarh *Orissa* India **75** E5
Deogarh *Rajasthan* India **74** B4
Deogarh India **75** E4
Deoghar India **75** F4
Deoli India **72** C1
Dêols France **38** D3
Deori India **74** C5
Deoria India **75** E4
Deosai, Plains of *Jammu and Kashmir*
  74 B2
Depalpur India **74** B5
De Pas, Rivière *r.* Canada **125** H2
Depew U.S.A. **130** E2
Deposit U.S.A. **131** F2
Depsang Point *hill Aksai Chin* **74** C2
Deputatskiy Rus. Fed. **27** N3
Dêqên *Xizang* China **75** G3
Dêqên *Xizang* China *see* Dagzê
Deqing *Guangdong* China **67** D4
Deqing *Zhejiang* China **67** G2
De Queen U.S.A. **133** C5
Dera *r.* China **133** C5
Der, Lac du *r.* France **39** F2
Dera Bugti Pak. **81** G4
Dera Ghazi Khan Pak. **81** G4
Deraheib *reg.* Sudan **89** H5
Dera Ismail Khan Pak. **81** G4
Derawar Fort Pak. **81** H4
Derbent Rus. Fed. **29** I8
Derbesiye Turkey *see* Şenyurt
Derby Australia **108** C4
Derby U.K. **35** F5
Derby *CT* U.S.A. **131** G3
Derby *KS* U.S.A. **132** B4
Dere/cke Hungary **37** J5
Derecske Hungary **37** J5
Derg, Lough *l.* Rep. of Ireland **35** B5
Dergachi Rus. Fed. **29** J6

Derik Turkey **79** E3
Derinkuyu Turkey **78** C3
Derkali *well* Kenya **96** D4
Derna Libya *see* Darnah
Derry U.K. *see* Londonderry
Derry U.S.A. **131** H2
Derryveagh Mountains *hills*
  Rep. of Ireland **34** B4
Dêrub China *see* Rutög
Derudeb Sudan **89** H5
Derventa Bos.-Herz. **44** G2
Derwent *r. Derbyshire, England* U.K. **35** F5
Derwent *r. England* U.K. **35** F5
Derweze Turkm. *see* Darvaza
Derzhavino Rus. Fed. **29** J5
Derzhavinsk Kazakh. **26** F1
Derzhavinskiy Kazakh. *see* Derzhavinsk
Desaguadero *r.* Arg. **152** C3
Desaguadero *r.* Bol. **148** E7
Désappointement, Îles du *is*
  Fr. Polynesia **165** K6
Desatoya Mountains U.S.A. **136** D2
Descalvado Brazil **149** F3
Descartes France **38** D3
Deschambault Lake Canada **123** K4
Deschambault Lake *l.* Canada **123** K4
Desē Eth. **96** C2
Deseada Chile **153** D6
Deseado Arg. **153** D6
Deseado *r.* Arg. **153** D6
Desemboque Mex. **135** D7
Deseret Peak U.S.A. **137** F1
Desert Canal Pak. **81** G4
Desert Center U.S.A. **137** E5
Desert View U.S.A. **137** G3
Deshler U.S.A. **130** B3
Deshnok India **74** B4
Desiderio Tello *arg.* Chile **152** D2
Desierto de Sechura *des.* Peru **146** A6
Deskati Greece **47** B5
De Smet U.S.A. **132** B2

▶Des Moines *IA* U.S.A. **132** C3
State capital of Iowa.

Des Moines *NM* U.S.A. **132** A4
Des Moines *r.* U.S.A. **132** C3
Desna *r.* Rus. Fed./Ukr. **29** D6
Desnaţui *r.* Romania **31** M2
Desnogorsk Rus. Fed. **31** M2
Desnudo, Cerro *mt.* Arg. **153** C6
Desolación, Isla *i.* Chile **153** B8
Despotovac Yugo. **46** B2
Dessau Germany **37** F3
Dessye Eth. *see* Desē
Destruction Bay Canada **122** A2
Desvres France **38** D1
Deta Romania **46** B2
Detah Canada **123** I2
Dete Zimbabwe **99** E3
Deti Jon *r.* Albania/Greece **47** A4
Detinja *r.* Yugo. **46** B3
Detmold Germany **36** D3
De Tour Village U.S.A. **132** F2
Detroit U.S.A. **130** D2
Detroit Lakes U.S.A. **132** C2
Detva Slovakia **37** I4
Deua National Park Australia **112** D4
Deurne Neth. **36** C3
Deutschland *country* Europe *see*
  Germany
Deutschlandsberg Austria **37** G5
Deva Romania **46** C2
Deva U.K. *see* Chester
Devana U.K. *see* Aberdeen
Devanhalli India **72** C2
Devarkonda India **72** C2
Deve Bair *pass* Macedonia *see*
  Velbŭzhdki Prokhod
Devecser Hungary **37** H5
Deveron *r.* U.K. **34** F3
Devesel Romania **46** C2
Devét Skal *hill* Czech Rep. **37** H4
Devgadh Bariya India **74** B5
Devghar India *see* Deoghar
Devikot India **74** A4
Devil's Gate *pass* U.S.A. **136** C2
Devil's Lake Canada **123** K4
Devil's Lake *l.* U.S.A. **133** A6
Devil's Paw *mt.* U.S.A. **122** C3
Devil's Point Bahamas **129** E7
Devil's Thumb *mt.* Canada/U.S.A.
  122 C3
Devine U.S.A. **133** B6
Devine U.S.A. **133** B6
Devizes U.K. **35** F6
Devli India **74** B5
Devnya Bulg. **46** E3
Devoll *r.* Albania **46** B4
Devon Island Canada **121** J2
Devonport Australia **112** C6
Devrek Turkey **78** B2
Devrez *r.* Turkey **78** C2
Devrukh India **72** B2
Dewa, Tanjung *pt* Indon. **58** A2
Dewakang Besar *i.* Indon. **59** G4
Dewangani Bangl. **75** F4
Dewangiri Bhutan **75** F4
Dewas India **74** C5
Dewèrek, Nationaal Park
  nat. park Neth. **36** C2
Dewele Eth. **96** D2
De Witt *AR* U.S.A. **133** D5
De Witt *IA* U.S.A. **132** D3
Dexing China **67** F3
Dexter *MO* U.S.A. **133** D4
Dexter *NM* U.S.A. **135** F6
Dexter *NY* U.S.A. **131** E1
Deyang China **66** C2
Dey-Dey, Lake *salt flat* Australia **110** B6
Deyhuk Iran **80** D3
Deynau Turkm. *see* Dyanev
Deyong, Tanjung *pt* Indon. **57** 7
Dêyŭ *Qu r.* China **75** G3
Deyyer Iran **80** B5
Dez *r.* Iran **80** B3
Dezadeash Canada **122** B2
Dezfūl Iran **80** B3

▶Dezhneva, Mys *c.* Rus. Fed. **120** B3
Most easterly point of Asia.

Dezhou *Shandong* China **63** J4
Dezhou *Sichuan* China *see* Dechang
Dezh Shāhpūr Iran *see* Marīvān
Dhading Nepal **75** E4
Dhahab, Wādī adh *r.* Syria **77** B3
Dhāhiriya West Bank **77** B4
Dhahran Saudi Arabia **80** C5

▶Dhaka Bangl. **75** F5
Capital of Bangladesh and 5th most populous city in Asia.
world **16–17**

Dhaka *admin. div.* Bangl. **75** F5
Dhaleswari *r.* Bangl. **75** F5
Dhaleswari *r.* India **75** G4
Dhalgaon India **72** B2
Dhamār Yemen **76** C7
Dhamnod India **74** B5
Dhamtari India **72** D1
Dhanbad India **75** E5
Dhandhuka India **74** B5
Dhang Range *mts* Nepal **74** D3
Dhangarhi Nepal **74** D3
Dhankuta Nepal **75** F4
Dhar India **74** C5
Dhar Adrar *hills* Mauritania **90** B6
Dharampur India **72** B1
Dharan Bazar Nepal **75** E4
Dharapuram India **72** C3
Dhari India **74** C5
Dharmanagar India **75** G4
Dharmapuri India **72** C3
Dharmavaram India **72** C3
Dharmjaygarh India **75** D5
Dharmkot India **74** B3
Dharoor *watercourse* Somalia **96** E2
Dhar Oualâta *hills* Mauritania **92** D1
Dhar Tîchît *hills* Mauritania **92** C1
Dharug National Park Australia **112** D4
Dharur India **72** C2
Dharwad India **72** B3
Dharwar India *see* Dharwad
Dhasa India **74** C4
Dhasan *r.* India **74** C4

▶Dhaulagiri *mt.* Nepal **75** D3
7th highest mountain in the world and in Asia.
asia **50–51**
world **6–7**

Dhaulpur India **74** D4
Dhaurahra India **74** D4
Dhawlagiri *mt.* Nepal *see* Dhaulagiri
Dhebar Lake India **74** B4
Dhekelia Sovereign Base Area
  military base Cyprus **77** A2
Dhekiajuli India **75** G4
Dhenkanal India **73** E1
Dheskáti Greece *see* Deskati
Dhiafánion Greece *see* Diafani
Dhībān Jordan **77** B4
Dhidhimótikhon Greece *see*
  Didymoteicho
Dhing India **75** G4
Dhī Qār *governorate* Iraq **79** F5
Dhirwāh, Wādī adh *watercourse* Jordan
  77 C4
Dhodhekánisos *is* Greece *see*
  Dodecanese
Dhokós *i.* Greece *see* Dokos
Dhola India **74** A5
Dholka India **74** B5
Dhomokós Greece *see* Domokos
Dhone India **72** C3
Dhoomadheere Somalia **96** E3
Dhoraji India **74** A5
Dhori India **74** A5
Dhragonádha *i.* Greece *see* Dragonada
Dhragónisos *i.* Greece *see* Dragonisi
Dhrangadhra India **74** A5
Dhrol India **74** A5
Dhrosia Greece *see* Drosia
Dhubāb Yemen **96** D1
Dhubri India *see* Dhuburi
Dhuburi India **75** F4
Dhule India **72** B1
Dhulian India **75** F4
Dhunche Nepal **75** E4
Dhuudo Somalia **96** E3
Dhuusa Marreeb Somalia **96** E3
Dytiki Ellás *admin. reg.* Greece *see*
  Dytiki Ellas
Dhytiki Makedhonía *admin. reg.* Greece
  see Dytiki Makedonia
Dia *i.* Greece **47** D7
Diablo, Mount U.S.A. **136** B3
Diablo Range *mts* U.S.A. **136** B3
Diaca Moz. **97** C7
Diafani Greece **47** E7
Diafarabé Mali **92** D2
Diaka *r.* Mali **92** D2
Dialakoto Senegal **92** B2
Diallassagou Mali **92** E2
Diamante Arg. **152** E3
Diamante Italy **45** F5
Diamantina *watercourse* Australia
  111 D5
Diamantina Brazil **147** F6
Diamantina, Chapada *plat.* Brazil
  150 D5
Diamantina Deep *sea feature*
  Indian Ocean **163** N8
Diamantina Gates National Park
  Australia **111** E4
Diamantina Lakes Austral a **111** E4
Diamantino *Mato Grosso* Brazil **151** A6
Diamantino *Mato Grosso* Brazil **151** A6
Diamond Harbour India **75** F5
Diamond Islets Australia **111** G3
Diamond Peak U.S.A. **137** E2
Diamondville U.S.A. **134** E4
Diamou Mali **92** C2
Diamougnelé Senegal **92** B2
Dianbai China **67** D4
Dianbu China *see* Feidong
Diancang Shan *mt.* China **66** B3
Dian Chi *l.* China **66** B3
Diandioumé Mali **92** C2
Diane Bank *sea feature* Australia
  111 G2
Diangounté Kamara Mali **92** C2
Diani *r.* Guinea **92** C4
Diano Marina Italy **44** B3
Dianópolis Brazil **150** C4
Dianra Côte d'Ivoire **92** C3
Diapaga Burkina **93** F3
Diaporioi *i.* Greece *see* D'S
Diarizos *r.* Cyprus **77** A2
Diatifère Guinea **92** C3
Diavolo, Mount India **73** G3
Diaz Point Namibia **98** B5
Dibā al Ḩişn U.A.E. **80** D5
Dibang *r.* India *see* Dingba Qu
Dibaya Dem. Rep. Congo **95** D6
Dibbis Sudan **88** D3
Dibella *well* Niger **93** I1
Dibeng S. Africa **98** D5
Diblê Eth. **96** D2
Dibrugarh India **75** G4
Dibula Col. **146** C2
Dickens U.S.A. **133** A5
Dickinson U.S.A. **134** G3
Dickson U.S.A. **128** B5
Dicle *r.* Turkey **79** E3 *see* Tigris
Dida Galgalu *reg.* Kenya **96** C3
Didiéni Mali **92** C2
Dido *waterhole* Kenya **96** D3
Didsbury Canada **134** F2
Didwana India **74** C4
Didymoteicho Greece **46** E4
Dīdžiasalis Lith. **33** G4
Die France **39** F4

Diébougou Burkina 92 E3
Dieburg Germany 36 D4
Diedenhofen France see Thionville
Diefenbaker, Lake Canada 123 I5
Diège r. France 38 E4
Diego de Almagro, Isla i. Chile 153 B7
Diégo Suarez Madag. see Antsirañana
Diégrâga well Mauritania 92 C2
Diéké Guinea 92 C4
Diekirch Lux. 39 G2
Diéma Mali 92 C2
Diên Châu Vietnam 60 D4
Diepholz Germany 36 D2
Dieppe France 38 D2
Dierks U.S.A. 133 C5
Di'er Songhua Jiang r. China 64 A3
Dietikon Switz. 39 H3
Diffa Niger 93 I2
Diffa dept Niger 93 I1
Dig well Eth. 96 E3
Diga Diga well Niger 93 F2
Digapahandi India 73 E2
Digba Dem. Rep. Congo 94 E3
Digboi India 75 G4
Digby Canada 127 M3
Digerbergen hill Sweden 33 D3
Digerberget hill Sweden 33 D3
Diggi India 74 B4
Diglur India 72 C2
Digne-les-Bains France 39 G4
Digoin France 39 E3
Digras India 72 C1
Digri Pak. 81 G5
Digul r. Indon. 57 I7
Digya National Park Ghana 93 E4
Dihang r. India 75 G3 see Brahmaputra
Diinsoor Somalia 96 D4
Dijlah, Nahr r. Iraq/Syria 79 F4 see Tigris
Dijon France 39 F3
Dik Chad 94 C2
Dikanäs Sweden 32 E2
Diken India 74 B4
Dikhil Djibouti 96 D2
Dikho r. India 75 G4
Dikili Turkey 47 E5
Diksal India 72 B2
Dikson Rus. Fed. 26 I2
Dikwa Nigeria 93 I2
Dīla Eth. 96 C3
Dilaram Iran 80 D4
Dilek Yarımadası Milli Parkı nat. park Turkey 47 E6
Dili Dem. Rep. Congo 94 E4

▶Dili East Timor 57 G7
Capital of East Timor.

Dilia watercourse Niger 93 I2
Dilijan Armenia 79 F2
Di Linh Vietnam 61 E6
Dilizhan Armenia see Dilijan
Dillenburg Germany 36 D3
Dilley U.S.A. 133 B6
Dilli Mali 92 D2
Dilling Sudan 89 F6
Dillingen an der Donau Germany 36 E4
Dillingham U.S.A. 120 D4
Dillon r. Canada 123 I4
Dillon MT U.S.A. 134 D3
Dillon SC U.S.A. 129 D5
Dillsburg U.S.A. 131 E3
Dillwyn U.S.A. 130 D5
Dilolo Dem. Rep. Congo 95 D7
Dilos i. Greece 47 D6
Diltāwa Iraq 79 F4
Dimapur India 75 G4
Dimashq Syria see Damascus
Dimashq governorate Syria 77 C3
Dimbelenge Dem. Rep. Congo 95 D6
Dimbokro Côte d'Ivoire 92 D4
Dimboola Australia 112 B5
Dimbulah Australia 111 F3
Dimitrovgrad Bulg. 46 D3
Dimitrovgrad Rus. Fed. 29 I5
Dimitrovgrad Yugo. 46 C3
Dimitrovo Bulg. see Pernik
Dimmitt U.S.A. 133 A5
Dimona Israel 77 B4
Dinagat i. Phil. 57 G3
Dinajpur Bangl. 75 F4
Dinan France 38 B2
Dinanagar India 74 B2
Dinangourou Mali 93 E2
Dinant Belgium 39 F1
Dinapur India 75 E4
Dinar Turkey 78 B3
Dīnār, Kūh-e mt. Iran 80 B4
Dinara mt. Bos.-Herz. 44 F2
Dinara Planina mts Bos.-Herz./Croatia see Dinaric Alps
Dinard France 38 B2
Dinaric Alps mts Bos.-Herz./Croatia 44 F2
Dinas well Kenya 96 C4
Dinbych U.K. see Denbigh
Dinbych-y-Pysgod U.K. see Tenby
Dinder r. Sudan 89 G6
Dinder National Park Sudan 89 G6
Dindigul India 72 C4
Dindima Nigeria 93 H3
Dindiza Moz. 99 G4
Dindori India 74 D5
Dinga Dem. Rep. Congo 95 C6
Dinga Pak. 81 H3
Dingba Qu r. India 75 G4
Dingbujie China 67 E2
Dingla Nepal 75 E4
Dingle Rep. of Ireland 35 A5
Dingle Bay Rep. of Ireland 35 A5
Dingnan China 67 E3
Dingo Australia 111 G4
Dingolfing Germany 37 F4
Dingping China see Linshui
Dingras Phil. 67 G5
Dingwall Canada 125 I4
Dingwall U.K. 34 D3
Dingyuan China 67 F1
Dinhata India 75 F4
Dinh Lâp Vietnam 60 D3
Dinkel r. Neth. 36 C2
Dinkelsbühl Germany 36 E4
Dinngyê China 75 E3
Dinokwe Botswana 99 E4
Dinosaur U.S.A. 137 H1
Dinosaur National Monument nat. park U.S.A. 137 H1
Dintiteladas Indon. 58 D4
Dinwiddie U.S.A. 130 E5
Dioïla Mali 92 D2
Diois, Massif du mts France 39 F4
Dion r. Guinea 92 C3
Dionísio Cerqueira Brazil 151 A8
Dioscurias Georgia see Sokhumi
Diospolis Magna tourist site Egypt see Thebes
Dioumara Mali 92 C2
Dioundiou Niger 93 F2
Dioura Mali 92 D2
Diourbel Senegal 92 A2
Dipalpur Pak. 74 B3
Dipayal Nepal 74 D3
Diphu India 75 G4
Dipkarpaz Cyprus see Rizokarpason
Diplo Pak. 81 G5
Dipolog Phil. 57 F4
Dipperu National Park Australia 111 G4
Dipu China see Anji
Dir Pak. 81 G3
Dirah U.A.E. 80 C5
Dirang India 75 G4
Diré Mali 92 E1
Direction, Cape Australia 111 E2
Dirē Dawa Eth. 96 D2
Dirfys mts Greece 47 C5
Dirhami Estonia 33 F4
Dirico Angola 95 D9
Dirillo r. Sicily Italy 45 E6
Dirk Hartog Island Australia 109 A6
Dirkou Niger 93 I1
Dirranbandi Australia 111 G6
Dirs Saudi Arabia 89 I5
Dirschau Poland see Tczew
Dirty Devil r. U.S.A. 137 G3
Disa India 74 B4
Disang r. India 75 G4
Disappointment, Cape S. Georgia 153 [inset]
Disappointment, Cape U.S.A. 134 A3
Disappointment, Lake salt flat Australia 108 C5
Disappointment Lake Canada 125 I2
Discovery Bay Australia 112 B5
Disentis Muster Switz. 39 H3
Disgrazia, Monte mt. Italy 44 B1
Dishnā Egypt 89 G3
Disko i. Greenland see Qeqertarsuaq
Disko Bugt b. Greenland see Qeqertarsuup Tunua
Dismal Lakes Canada 123 G1
Dispur India 75 F4
Disputanta U.S.A. 131 E5
Disraëli Canada 125 G4
Diss U.K. 35 G5
Dissān Island Saudi Arabia 89 I5
Distrito Federal admin. dist. Brazil 149 I3
Distrito Federal admin. dist. Venez. 146 E2
Dittaino r. Sicily Italy 45 E6
Diu India 72 A1
Dīvān Darreh Iran 80 A3
Divehi country Indian Ocean see Maldives
Divénié Congo 94 B5
Dives r. France 38 C2
Divichi Azer. see Däväçi
Divide Mountain U.S.A. 122 A2
Divinópolis Brazil 151 C7
Divisor, Sierra de mts Peru see Ultraoriental, Cordillera
Divjaka nat. park Albania 46 A4
Divnoye Rus. Fed. 29 G7
Divo Côte d'Ivoire 92 D4
Divor r. Port. 42 B3
Divounia i. Greece 47 E7
Divriği Turkey 79 D3
Divuma Dem. Rep. Congo 95 D7
Diwaniyah Iraq see Ad Dīwānīyah
Dixcove Ghana 93 E4
Dixmont U.S.A. 131 I1
Dixon CA U.S.A. 136 B2
Dixon IL U.S.A. 132 D3
Dixon Entrance sea chan. Canada/U.S.A. 120 F4
Dixonville Canada 123 G3
Diyadin Turkey 79 E3
Diyālā governorate Iraq 79 F4
Diyālá, Nahr r. Iraq 79 F4
Diyarbakır Turkey 79 E3
Diyodar India 74 A4
Diz Pak. 81 E5
Dizak Iran see Dāvar Panāh
Dizangué Cameroon 93 H5
Diz Chah Iran 80 C3
Dize Turkey see Yüksekova
Dizney U.S.A. 130 B5
Dja r. Cameroon 93 I5
Djado Niger 88 B4
Djado, Plateau du Niger 88 B4
Djakarta Indon. see Jakarta
Djakovica Yugo. see Đakovica
Djamâa Alg. 91 G2
Djamba Dem. Rep. Congo 95 D7
Djambala Congo 94 B5
Djampie Dem. Rep. Congo 94 C5
Djampiel Cameroon 94 B3
Djanet Alg. 91 H4
Djebr mt. Alg. 91 F4
Djébrène Chad 94 C2
Djédaa Chad 88 C6
Djedid well Alg. 91 E4
Djelfa Alg. 91 F2
Djéma Cent. Afr. Rep. 94 E3
Djèmber Chad 94 C2
Djeneral Janković Yugo. see Đeneral Janković
Djenné Mali 92 D2
Djerdap nat. park Yugo. 46 C2
Djermaya Chad 88 B6
Djia Dem. Rep. Congo 94 D5
Djibo Burkina 93 E2
Djiborosso Côte d'Ivoire 92 D3
▶Djibouti country Africa 96 D2
africa 86–87, 100

▶Djibouti Djibouti 96 D2
Capital of Djibouti.

Djidjelli Alg. see Jijel
Djiguéni Mauritania 92 C2
Djolu Dem. Rep. Congo 94 D4
Djombo Kibbit Chad 88 C6
Djoua r. Congo/Gabon 94 B4
Djoubissi Cent. Afr. Rep. 94 D3
Djougou Benin 93 F3
Djoum Cameroon 93 I5
Djugu Dem. Rep. Congo 96 A4
Djuma Dem. Rep. Congo 95 C6
Djúpivogur Iceland 121 R3
Djurås Sweden 33 D3
Djurdjura National Park Alg. 43 I4
Djurö nationalpark nat. park Sweden 33 D4
Dlairi India 74 B3
Dmitriya Lapteva, Proliv sea chan. Rus. Fed. 27 O2
Dmitriyev-L'govskiy Rus. Fed. 29 E5
Dmitriyevsk Ukr. see Makiyivka
Dmitrov Rus. Fed. 28 F4
Dmytriyevs'k Ukr. see Makiyivka
Dnepr r. Rus. Fed. 29 D5 see Dnieper
Dneprodzerzhinsk Ukr. see Dniprodzerzhyns'k
Dnepropetrovsk Ukr. see Dnipropetrovs'k
Dneprorudnoye Ukr. see Dniprorudne
Dnestrovsc Moldova 46 F1

▶Dnieper r. Europe 29 D6
3rd longest river in Europe.
Also spelt Dnepr (Rus. Fed.) or Dnipro (Ukraine) or Dnyapro (Belarus).
europe 22–23

Dniester r. Moldova 31 L4
Dniester r. Ukr. 29 C6
also spelt Dnister (Ukraine) or Nistru (Moldova)
Dnipro r. Ukr. 29 D6 see Dnieper
Dniprodzerzhyns'k Ukr. 29 E6
Dnipropetrovs'k Ukr. 29 E6
Dniprorudne Ukr. 29 E7
Dnister r. Ukr. 29 C6 see Dniester
Dnistrov'ky Lyman l. Ukr. 46 G1
Dno Rus. Fed. 28 D4
Dnyapro r. Belarus 29 D6 see Dnieper
Doa Moz. 99 G3
Doabi Mekh-i-Zarin Afgh. 81 F3
Doaktown Canada 125 H4
Doangdoangan Besar i. Indon. 59 G4
Doangdoangan Kecil i. Indon. 59 G4
Doany Madag. 99 [inset] K2
Doba Chad 94 C2
Doba China see Toiba
Dobbs, Cape Canada 123 O1
Dobele Latvia 33 F4
Döbeln Germany 37 F3
Doberai, Jazirah pen. Indon. 57 H6
Doberai Peninsula Indon. see Doberai, Jazirah
Döbern Germany 37 G3
Dobiegniew Poland 37 G2
Doblas Arg. 152 D4
Dobo Indon. 57 H7
Doboj Bos.-Herz. 44 G2
Do Borji Iran 80 C4
Dobre Miasto Poland 37 J2
Dobreşti Romania 46 C1
Dobrich Bulg. 46 E3
Dobrinka Rus. Fed. 29 G5
Dobroteşti Romania 46 D2
Dobroye Rus. Fed. 29 F5
Dobruchi Rus. Fed. 33 G4
Dobrudzhansko Plato plat. Bulg. 46 E3
Dobrush Belarus 29 D5
Dobryanka Rus. Fed. 28 K4
Dobskie, Jezioro l. Poland 37 J1
Dobzha China 75 F3
Doce r. Brazil 151 E6
Do China Qala Afgh. 81 G4
Doctor Hicks Range hills Australia 109 D7
Doctor Petru Groza Romania see Ştei
Doda Tanz. 97 C6
Dod Ballapur India 72 C3
Dodecanese is Greece 47 E7
Dodekanisos is Greece see Dodecanese
Dodge City U.S.A. 132 A4
Dodgeville U.S.A. 132 D3
Dodman Point U.K. 35 D6
Dodola Eth. 96 C3

▶Dodoma Tanz. 97 B6
Capital of Tanzania.

Dodoma admin. reg. Tanz. 97 B6
Dodori National Reserve nature res. Kenya 96 D5
Doetinchem Neth. 36 C3
Dofa Indon. 57 G6
Doftana r. Romania 46 D2
Dog r. Canada 124 B3
Dogai Coring salt l. China 70 G5
Dogaicoring Qangco salt l. China 75 F2
Doğanbey Aydın Turkey 47 E6
Doğanbey İzmir Turkey 47 E5
Doğanşehir Turkey 79 D3
Dog Creek Canada 122 F5
Doghārūn Iran 81 E3
Dog Lake Ont. Canada 124 C3
Dog Lake Ont. Canada 132 D1
Dōgo i. Japan 65 C5
Dogoble well Somalia 96 E2
Dogondoutchi Niger 93 G2
Dogoumbo Chad 94 C2
Dōgo-yama mt. Japan 65 C6
Dog Rocks is Bahamas 129 D7
Doğubeyazıt Turkey 79 F3
Doğu Menteşe Dağları mts Turkey 78 B3

▶Doha Qatar 80 B5
Capital of Qatar.

Dohad India see Dahod
Dohazari Bangl. 75 G5
Doi i. Fiji 107 H4
Doi Inthanon National Park Thai. 60 B4
Doi Luang National Park Thai. 60 B4
Doilungdêqên China 75 F3
Doïranis, Limni l. Greece/Macedonia see Dojran, Lake
Doire U.K. see Londonderry
Doisanagar India 75 E5
Dois Irmãos, Serra dos hills Brazil 150 D4
Dojran, Lake Greece/Macedonia 46 C4
Dojransko Ezero l. Greece/Macedonia see Dojran, Lake
Doka Sudan 89 G6
Dokali Iran 80 C3
Dokhara, Dunes de des. Alg. 91 G2
Dokkum Neth. 36 B2
Dokos i. Greece 47 C6
Dokri Pak. 81 G5
Dokshukino Rus. Fed. see Nartkala
Dokshytsy Belarus 33 G5
Doksy Czech Rep. 37 G3
Dokuchayevs'k Ukr. 29 F7
Dolak, Pulau i. Indon. 57 I7
Dolavón Arg. 153 D5
Dolbeau Canada 125 F3
Dol-de-Bretagne France 38 C2
Dole France 39 F3
Dolgellau U.K. 35 E5
Dolgiy, Ostrov i. Rus. Fed. 28 K1
Dolgoye Rus. Fed. 29 F5
Dolinsk Rus. Fed. 64 E3
Dolisie Congo see Loubomo
Doljevac Yugo. 46 B3
Dolleman Island Antarctica 167 L2
Dolni Chiflik Bulg. 46 E3
Dolni Dŭbnik Bulg. 46 D3
Dolno Kamartsi Bulg. 46 C3
Dolno Levski Bulg. 46 D3
Dolný Kubín Slovakia 37 I4
Dolomites mts Italy 44 C2
Dolomiti mts Italy see Dolomites
Dolomiti Bellunesi, Parco Nazionale delle nat. park Italy 44 C1
Dolomitiche, Alpi mts Italy see Dolomites
Dolo Odo Eth. 96 D3
Dolores Arg. 152 F4
Dolores Uruguay 152 F3
Dolores r. U.S.A. 137 H2
Dolphin, Cape Falkland Is 153 F7
Dolphin and Union Strait Canada 120 H3
Đô Lương Vietnam 60 D4
Dolyna Ukr. 31 J3
Dom, Gunung mt. Indon. 57 I6
Domanic Turkey 78 B3
Domartang China see Banbar
Domažlice Czech Rep. 37 F4
Domba China 75 G2
Dombås Norway 33 C3
Dombe Moz. 99 G3
Dombe Grande Angola 95 B8
Dombóvár Hungary 44 G1
Dombrau Poland see Dąbrowa Górnicza
Dombrovitsa Ukr. see Dubrovytsya
Dombrowa Poland see Dąbrowa Górnicza
Domda China see Qingshuihe
Dome Argus ice feature Antarctica 167 E1
Dome Charlie ice feature Antarctica 167 F2
Dome Circe ice feature Antarctica see Dome Charlie
Domel Island Myanmar see Letsok-aw Kyun
Dome Rock Mountains U.S.A. 137 E5
Domeyko Chile 152 C2
Dom Feliciano Brazil 152 G2
Domfront France 38 C2
▶Dominica country West Indies 139 L5
northamerica 118–119, 140
Dominicana, República country West Indies see Dominican Republic
▶Dominican Republic country West Indies 139 J5
northamerica 118–119, 140
Dominion, Cape Canada 121 L3
Domiongo Dem. Rep. Congo 95 D6
Domka Bhutan 75 F4
Domneşti Romania 46 D2
Domneşti Romania 46 D2
Domo Eth. 96 E3
Domodossola Italy 44 B1
Domokos Greece 47 C5
Domoni Comoros 97 E8
Dom Pedrito Brazil 152 G2
Dom Pedro Brazil 150 C3
Dompu Indon. 59 G5
Domula China 75 D2
Domuyo, Volcán vol. Arg. 152 C4
Domžale Slovenia 44 E1
Don r. India 72 C2

▶Don r. Rus. Fed. 29 F7
5th longest river in Europe.
europe 22–23

Don r. U.K. 34 E3
Don, Xé r. Laos 61 D5
Donadeu Arg. 152 E1
Donald Australia 112 B5
Donaldsonville U.S.A. 133 D6
Donalnes, Cerro mt. Chile 152 C1
Donalsonville U.S.A. 129 B6
Doñana, Parque Nacional de nat. park Spain 42 C4
Donau r. Austria/Germany 36 G4 see Danube
Donaueschingen Germany 36 D5
Donauwörth Germany 36 E4
Don Benito Spain 42 D3
Doncaster U.K. 35 F5
Dondo Angola 95 B7
Dondo Moz. 99 G3
Dondra Head Sri Lanka 72 D5
Donegal Rep. of Ireland 35 B4
Donegal Bay Rep. of Ireland 35 B4
Donets'k Ukr. 29 F7
Dønfoss Norway 33 C3
Donga r. Cameroon/Nigeria 93 H3
Donga Nigeria 93 H4
Dong'an China 67 D3
Dongara Australia 109 A7
Dongargarh India 74 D5
Dongbo China see Mêdog
Dongchuan Yunnan China 66 B3
Dongchuan Yunnan China see Yao'an
Dongco China 75 E2
Dong Co l. China 75 E2
Dongfang China 67 D5
Dongfanghong China 64 C3
Dongfeng China 64 A4
Donggala Indon. 57 E6
Donggang China 65 A5
Donggou China see Donggang
Donggu China 67 E3
Dongguan China 67 E4
Đông Ha Vietnam 60 D4
Donghai China 67 F1
Dong Hai sea N. Pacific Ocean see East China Sea
Donghai Dao i. China 67 D4
Dong He r. China 66 C2
Đông Hôi Vietnam 60 D4
Dong Jiang r. China 67 E4
Dongjiang Reservoir China 67 E2
Dongjingcheng China 64 B3
Dongkait, Tanjung pt Indon. 59 G3
Dongkou China 67 D3
Donglan China 66 C3
Dongmen China see Luocheng
Dongning China 64 B3
Dongo Angola 95 B8
Dongo Italy 44 B1
Dongobesh Tanz. 97 B6
Dongola Sudan 89 F5
Dongotona Mountains Sudan 96 B3
Dongou Congo 94 C4
Dong Phraya Fai mts Thai. 61 C4
Dong Phraya Yen esc. Thai. 61 C5
Dongping Guangdong China 67 E4
Dongping Hunan China see Anhua
Dongpo China see Meishan
Dongqiao China 75 F3
Dongshan Fujian China 67 F4
Dongshan Jiangsu China see Jiangning
Dongshan Jiangxi China see Shangyou
Dongshao China 67 E3
Dongsha Qundao is China 63 J7
Dongsheng China 63 I4
Dongshuan China see Tangdan
Dongtai China 67 G1
Dongtai r. China 67 G1
Dongting Hu l. China 67 E2
Donguena Angola 95 B9
Donguila Gabon 94 A4
Dong Ujimqin Qi China see Uliastai
Donguxung Zangbo r. China 75 E3
Dongxiang China see Xuanhan
Dongyang China 67 G2
Dongying China 63 J4
Dongzhi China 67 F2
Doniphan U.S.A. 133 D4
Donjek r. Canada 122 A2
Donji Miholjac Croatia 44 G2
Donji Vakuf Bos.-Herz. 44 F2
Donji Zemunik Croatia 44 E2
Donmanick Islands Bangl. 75 F5
Dønna i. Norway 32 D2
Donnelly Canada 123 G4
Donnellys Crossing N.Z. 113 C1
Donner Pass U.S.A. 136 B2
Donnersberg hill Germany 36 C4
Donnybrook Australia 109 A8
Donostia - San Sebastián Spain 43 F1
Donoussa Greece 47 D6
Donoussa i. Greece 47 D6
Donskoye Rus. Fed. 29 G7
Donthami r. Myanmar 60 B4
Doomadgee Australia 110 D3
Door Peninsula U.S.A. 128 B2
Dooxo Nugaaleed valley Somalia 96 F2
Do Qu r. China 66 B2
Dor watercourse Afgh. 81 E4
Dora, Lake salt flat Australia 108 C5
Do Rāhak Iran 80 B5
Dorah Pass Pak. 81 G2
Doramarkog China 66 A1
Doran Lake Canada 123 I2
Dora Riparia r. Italy 44 A2
D'Orbigny Bol. 149 E5
Dorbod China see Taikang
Đorče Petrov Macedonia 46 B3
Dorchester U.K. 35 E6
Dordabis Namibia 98 C4
Dordogne r. France 39 C4
Dordrecht Neth. 36 B3
Dordrecht S. Africa 99 E6
Doré Lake Canada 123 J4
Doré Lake l. Canada 123 J4
Dores do Indaiá Brazil 151 C6
Dorey Mali 93 E2
Dorgali Sardinia Italy 45 B4
Dori r. Afgh. 81 F4
Dori Burkina 93 E2
Doring r. S. Africa 98 C6
Dorisvale Australia 110 B2
Dormaa-Ahenkro Ghana 92 E4
Dormans France 39 E2
Dornakal India 72 D2
Dornbirn Austria 36 D5
Dornoch U.K. 34 D3
Doro Mali 93 E1
Dorog Hungary 37 I5
Dorohoi Romania 31 K4
Dorokhsh Iran 81 D3
Döröö Nuur salt l. Mongolia 62 E2
Dorostol Bulg. see Silistra
Dorotea Sweden 32 E2
Dorowa Zimbabwe 99 F3
Dorpat Estonia see Tartu
Dorre Island Australia 109 A6
Dorrigo Australia 112 E3
Dorris U.S.A. 134 B4
Dorsale Camerounaise slope Cameroon/Nigeria 93 H4
Dorset and East Devon Coast tourist site U.K. 35 E6
Dorsoidong Co l. China 75 F2
Dortmund Germany 36 C3
Dorton U.S.A. 130 B5
Dörtyol Turkey 78 D3
Doruma Dem. Rep. Congo 94 E3
Dorūneh Iran 80 D3
Dorylaeum Turkey see Eskişehir
Do Sārī Iran 80 D4
Dos Bahías, Cabo c. Arg. 153 D6
Doshakh, Koh-i- mt. Afgh. 81 E3
Dos Hermanas Spain 42 D4
Đo Son Vietnam 60 D3
Dospat Bulg. 46 D4
Dos Pozos Arg. 153 D5
Dosse r. Germany 37 F2
Dosso Niger 93 F2
Dosso dept Niger 93 F2
Dossor Kazakh. 29 J7
Dothan U.S.A. 129 B6
Douai France 39 E1
Douako Guinea 92 C3
Douala Cameroon 93 H4
Douarnenez France 38 A2
Douarnenez, Baie de b. France 38 A2
Double Headed Shot Cays is Bahamas 129 C8
Double Island Hong Kong China 67 [inset]
Double Mountain Fork r. U.S.A. 133 A5
Double Peak U.S.A. 136 C4
Double Point Australia 111 F3
Double Springs U.S.A. 129 B5
Doubs r. France/Switz. 39 F3
Doubtful Sound inlet N.Z. 113 A4
Doubtless Bay N.Z. 113 C1
Doué-la-Fontaine France 38 C3
Douentza Mali 92 E2
Dougga tourist site Tunisia 91 H1

▶Douglas Isle of Man 35 D4
Capital of the Isle of Man.

Douglas S. Africa 98 D6
Douglas AZ U.S.A. 135 E7
Douglas GA U.S.A. 129 C6
Douglas WY U.S.A. 134 F4
Douglas Apsley National Park Australia 112 D6
Douglas Channel Canada 122 D4
Douglas Creek watercourse Australia 110 D6
Douglas Creek r. U.S.A. 137 H1
Douglas Reef i. Japan see Okino-Tori-shima
Dougoulé well Niger 93 H2
Douhi Chad 88 C5
Douhudi China see Gong'an
Doukato, Akra pt Greece 47 B5
Doulaincourt-Saucourt France 39 F2
Douliu Taiwan see Touliu
Doullens France 38 E1
Doumè Benin 93 F3
Doumé Cameroon 93 I4
Doumé r. Cameroon 93 I4
Doumen China 67 E4
Douna Mali 93 E2
Doupovské Hory mts Czech Rep. 37 F3
Dourada, Serra mts Brazil 150 B5
Dourados Brazil 151 A7
Dourados r. Brazil 151 A7
Dourbali Chad 94 C2
Dourdou r. France 39 E4
Dourdoura Chad 94 C2
Douro r. Port. 42 C2
also known as Duero (Spain)
Douro Internacional, Parque Natural do nature res. Port. 42 C2
Doushi China see Gong'an
Doushui Shuiku resr China 67 E3
Douve r. France 38 C2
Douz Tunisia 91 H2
Douze r. France 38 C5
Douziat Chad 88 C6
Dove r. U.K. 35 F5
Dove Brook Canada 125 J2
Dove Creek U.S.A. 137 H3
Dover U.K. 35 G6

▶Dover DE U.S.A. 131 F4
State capital of Delaware.

Dover NH U.S.A. 131 H2
Dover NJ U.S.A. 131 F3
Dover OH U.S.A. 130 C3
Dover, Strait of France/U.K. 38 D1
Dover-Foxcroft U.S.A. 128 F2
Dover Plains U.S.A. 131 G3
Dovey r. U.K. see Dyfi
Dovnsklint cliff Denmark 36 E1
Dovrefjell mts Norway 33 C3
Dovrefjell Nasjonalpark nat. park Norway 33 C3
Dow, Lake Botswana see Xau, Lake
Dowa Malawi 97 B8
Dowgha'i Iran 81 D2
Dowi, Tanjung pt Indon. 58 B2
Dowlatābād Afgh. 81 F2
Dowlatābād Fārs Iran 80 B4
Dowlatābād Khorāsan Iran 80 D2
Dowlatābād Khorāsan Iran 81 E2
Dowl at Yār Afgh. 81 F3
Dowl at Yār Afgh. 81 F3
Downey U.S.A. 136 C5
Downham Market U.K. 35 G5
Downieville U.S.A. 136 B2
Downpatrick U.K. 35 D4
Downs U.S.A. 132 B4
Downsville U.S.A. 131 F2
Dow Rūd Iran 80 B3
Dow Sar Iran 80 B3
Dowshī Afgh. 81 G3
Doyle U.S.A. 136 B1
Doyles Canada 125 J4
Doyrentsi Bulg. 46 D3
Dozdān r. Iran 80 D5
Dōzen is Japan 65 C5
Dozois, Réservoir Canada 124 E4
Drâa, Oued watercourse Morocco 90 C3
Drachten Neth. 36 C2
Dragalina Romania 46 E2
Dragan l. Sweden 32 D2
Drăgăneşti-Olt Romania 46 D2
Drăgăneşti-Vlaşca Romania 46 D2
Drăgăşani Romania 46 D2
Dragoman Bulg. 46 C3
Dragonada i. Greece 47 E7
Dragones Arg. 149 E5
Dragonisi i. Greece 47 D6
Dragon's Mouths strait Trin. and Tob./Venez. 147 F2
Dragør Denmark 33 D5
Dragsfjärd Fin. 33 F3
Draguignan France 39 G5
Drăguşeni Romania 46 E2
Drahichyn Belarus 29 C5
Drakensberg mts Lesotho/S. Africa 99 F6
Drakensberg mts S. Africa 99 F5
Drake Passage S. Atlantic Ocean 161 J9
Drakes Bay U.S.A. 136 A3
Drakulya r. Ukr. 46 F2
Drama Greece 46 D4
Drammen Norway 33 C4
Drang, Prêk r. Cambodia 61 D5
Drangedal Norway 33 C4
Drangme Chhu r. Bhutan 75 F4
Dranov, Lacul l. Romania 46 F2
Dranske Germany 37 F1
Draper, Mount U.S.A. 122 B3
Drapsaca Afgh. see Kondūz
Dras Jammu and Kashmir 74 B2
Drau r. Austria 37 G5
Drava r. Europe 31 I4
Dráva r. Hungary 44 G2
Dravinja r. Slovenia 44 E1
Dravograd Slovenia 44 E1
Drawa r. Poland 37 G2
Drawieński Park Narodowy nat. park Poland 37 G2
Drawno Poland 37 G2
Drawsko, Jezioro l. Poland 37 H2
Drayton Valley Canada 123 H4
Drebber Germany 36 D2
Dreistelzberge hill Germany 36 D3
Drenovets Bulg. 46 C3
Drepano, Akra pt Greece 47 C5
Dresden Canada 130 B2
Dresden Germany 37 F3
Dresden U.S.A. 128 A4
Dreux France 38 D2
Drevsjø Norway 33 D3
Drewryville U.S.A. 131 E5
Drezdenko Poland 37 G2
Driftwood U.S.A. 130 D3
Driggs U.S.A. 134 E4
Drin r. Albania 46 A3
Drina r. Bos.-Herz./Yugo. 44 G2
Drincea r. Romania 46 C2
Drini i Zi r. Albania 46 B3
Drinit, Gjiri i b. Albania 46 A4
Drino r. Albania 47 B4
Driscoll Island Antarctica 167 J1
Drissa Belarus see Vyerkhnyadzvinsk
Drniš Croatia 44 F3
Drobeta - Turnu Severin Romania 46 C2
Drochtersen Germany 36 D2
Drogheda Rep. of Ireland 35 C5
Drogichin Belarus see Drahichyn
Drogobych Ukr. see Drohobych
Drohiczyn Poland 37 K2
Drohobych Ukr. 31 J3
Droichead Átha Rep. of Ireland see Drogheda
Droitwich U.K. 35 E5
Dronne r. France 38 C4
Dronning Ingrid Land reg. Greenland 121 O3
Dronning Louise Land reg. Greenland 121 Q2
Dropt r. France 38 C4
Drosh Pak. 81 G3
Drosia Greece 47 C5
Drowning r. Canada 124 C3
Druk-Yul country Asia see Bhutan
Drumheller Canada 134 D2
Drummond, Lake U.S.A. 131 E5
Drummond Island Kiribati see McKean
Drummond Range hills Australia 111 F5
Drummondville Canada 125 F4
Drummore U.K. 35 D4
Drumnadrochit U.K. 34 D3
Druskieniki Lith. see Druskininkai
Druskininkai Lith. 31 K2
Druya Belarus 33 G5
Druzhina Rus. Fed. 27 O3
Drwęca r. Poland 37 I2
Dry r. Australia 110 C2
Dryanovo Bulg. 46 D3
Dryazhno Rus. Fed. 33 H4
Dryberry Lake Canada 132 C1
Dry Cimarron r. U.S.A. 132 A4
Dryden Canada 124 A3
Dryden U.S.A. 131 E2
Dry Fork r. U.S.A. 134 F4
Drygalski Ice Tongue Antarctica 167 H1
Drygalski Island Antarctica 167 F2
Dry Lake U.S.A. 137 E3
Dry Ridge U.S.A. 130 A4
Drysdale r. Australia 110 A2
Drysdale River National Park Australia 108 D3
Dry Tortugas is U.S.A. 129 C7
Drzewica Poland 37 J3
Dschang Cameroon 93 H4
Dua r. Dem. Rep. Congo 94 D4
Dūāb r. Iran 80 B3
Du'an China 66 D4
Duaringa Australia 111 G4
Duarte, Pico mt. Dom. Rep. 127 L8
Ḑubā Saudi Arabia 89 G3
Dubai U.A.E. 80 C5
Dubawnt r. Canada 123 L2
Dubawnt Lake Canada 123 K2
Dubayy U.A.E. see Dubai
Dubbagh, Jabal ad mt. Saudi Arabia 89 G3
Dubbo Australia 112 D4
Dube r. Liberia 92 D4
Dübendorf Switz. 39 H3

▶Dublin Rep. of Ireland 35 C5
Capital of the Republic of Ireland.

Dublin GA U.S.A. 129 C5
Dublin VA U.S.A. 130 C5
Dubna Rus. Fed. 28 F4
Dubnica nad Váhom Slovakia 37 I4
Dubno Ukr. 29 C6
Dubois U.S.A. 134 D3
Du Bois U.S.A. 130 D3
Dubovka Rus. Fed. 29 H6
Dübrar Pass Azer. 79 G2
Dubréka Guinea 92 B3
Dubris U.K. see Dover
Dubrovnik Croatia 44 G3
Dubrovytsya Ukr. 29 C6
Dubuque U.S.A. 132 D3
Duc de Gloucester, Îles du is Fr. Polynesia 165 I7
Ducey France 38 C2
Duchateau Entrance sea chan. P.N.G. 111 H1
Ducherow Germany 37 F2
Duchesne U.S.A. 137 G1

Duchesne r. U.S.A. 137 H1
Duchess Australia 111 D4
Duchess Canada 123 I5
Ducie Island Pitcairn Is 165 J7
Duck r. U.S.A. 128 B4
Duck Bay Canada 134 G1
Duck Creek r. Australia 108 B5
Duckwater U.S.A. 137 E2
Duckwater Peak U.S.A. 137 E2
Đuc Trong Vietnam 61 E6
Duda r. Col. 146 C4
Duderstadt Germany 36 E3
Dudhi India 75 D4
Dudinka Rus. Fed. 27 I3
Dudley U.K. 35 E5
Dudleyville U.S.A. 137 G5
Dudna r. India 72 C2
Duékoué Côte d'Ivoire 92 D4
Duen, Bukit vol. Indon. 58 C3
Duerė Brazil 150 B4
Duerna r. Spain 42 D1
Duero r. Spain 43 D2
also known as Douro (Portugal)
Duffer Peak U.S.A. 134 C4
Duffield U.S.A. 130 B5
Duff Islands Solomon Is 107 F2
Duffreboy, Lac l. Canada 125 G1
Dufftown U.K. 34 E3
Dufourspitze mt. Italy/Switz. 44 A2
Dufrost Canada 123 L5
Dugab Uzbek. 81 F2
Duga Resa Croatia 44 E2
Duga-Zapadnaya, Mys c. Rus. Fed. 27 O4
Dughdash mts Saudi Arabia 77 C5
Dughoba Uzbek. see Dugab
Dugi Otok i. Croatia 44 E2
Dugo Selo Croatia 44 F2
Düğüncübaşı Turkey 46 E4
Dugway U.S.A. 137 F1
Du He r. China 67 D1
Duhūn Tārsū mts Chad/Libya 88 C4
Duida-Marahuaca, Parque Nacional nat. park Venez. 147 E4
Duifken Point Australia 111 E2
Duisburg Germany 36 C3
Duitama Col. 146 C3
Dujiangyan China 66 B2
Dukān Dam Iraq 79 F4
Dukat mt. Yugo. 46 C3
Dukathole S. Africa 99 E6
Dukat i Ri Albania 47 A4
Duke Island U.S.A. 122 D4
Duke of Clarence atoll Tokelau see Nukunonu
Duke of York atoll Tokelau see Atafu
Duk Fadiat Sudan 96 A3
Duk Faiwil Sudan 96 A3
Dukhān Qatar 80 B5
Dukhnah Saudi Arabia 89 I3
Duki Rus. Fed. 64 C2
Duki r. Rus. Fed. 64 C2
Dukku Nigeria 93 H3
Dukou China see Panzhihua
Dūkštas Lith. 33 G5
Dulan China 70 I4
Dulawan Phil. see Datu Piang
Dulce r. Arg. 152 E2
Dulce r. Spain 43 E2
Dulce U.S.A. 135 F5
Dulce Nombre de Culmí Hond. 139 G5
Dulcinea Chile 152 C1
Dulgalakh r. Rus. Fec. 27 N3
Dŭlgopol Bulg. 46 E3
Dulhunty r. Australia 111 E1
Dulishi Hu salt l. China 75 D2
Dulit, Pegunungan mts Sarawak Malaysia 59 F2
Duliu Jiang r. China 66 D3
Dullabchara India 75 G4
Dülmen Germany 36 C3
Dulovo Bulg. 46 E3
Duluth U.S.A. 132 C2
Dūmā Syria 77 C3
Dumago Bone National Park Indon. 57 F5
Dumaguete Phil. 57 F4
Dumai Indon. 58 C2
Dumaran i. Phil. 57 F3
Dumaresq r. Australia 112 D3
Dumas AR U.S.A. 133 D5
Dumas TX U.S.A. 133 A5
Dumayr Syria 78 D4
Dumayr, Jabal mts Syria 77 C3
Dumbarton U.K. 34 D4
Dumbéa New Caledonia 107 F4
Dumbo Cameroon 93 H4
Dumbrăveni Romania 46 E2
Dumbrăvița Romania 46 D2
Dumdum i. Indon. 59 D2
Dumfries U.K. 34 E4
Dumka India 75 E4
Dummagudem India 72 D2
Dummerstorf Germany 37 F2
Dumoine r. Canada 124 E4
Dumont d'Urville research station Antarctica 167 G2
Dumont d'Urville Sea Antarctica 167 G2
Dumraon India 75 E4
Dumyāṭ Egypt 89 F2
Dumyāṭ governorate Egypt 78 B5
Duna r. Hungary 37 G4 see Danube
Dünaburg Latvia see Daugavpils
Dunaföldvár Hungary 37 I5
Dunaj r. Slovakia 37 G4 see Danube
Dunajec r. Poland 37 J3
Dunajská Streda Slovakia 37 H5
Dunakeszi Hungary 37 I5
Dunany Point Rep. of Ireland 35 C5
Dunărea r. Romania 46 B2 see Danube
Dunaújváros Hungary 37 I5
Dunav r. Bulg./Croatia/Yugo. 46 B2 see Danube
Dunavtsi Bulg. 46 C3
Dunay r. Ukr. 46 B2 see Danube
Dunay, Ostrova is Rus. Fed. 27 M2
Dunback N.Z. 113 B4
Dunbar Australia 111 E3
Dunbar U.S.A. 130 D4
Dunbeath U.K. 34 E2
Duncan AZ U.S.A. 135 E6
Duncan OK U.S.A. 133 B5
Duncan, Cape Canada 124 D2
Duncan Lake Canada 123 H2
Duncannon U.S.A. 131 E3
Duncan Passage India 73 G4
Duncansby Head U.K. 34 E2
Dundaga Latvia 33 F4
Dundalk Rep. of Ireland 35 C4
Dundalk U.S.A. 131 E4
Dundalk Bay Rep. of Ireland 35 C5
Dundas Canada 130 D2
Dundas Greenland 121 M2
Dundas, Lake salt flat Australia 109 C8
Dundas Island Canada 122 D4
Dundas Strait Australia 110 B1
Dún Dealgan Rep. of Ireland see Dundalk
Dundee S. Africa 99 F6
Dundee U.K. 34 E3
Dundee U.S.A. 131 E2
Dundrum Bay U.K. 35 D4
Dundwa Range mts India/Nepal 75 D4
Dune, Lac l. Canada 125 F1
Dunedin N.Z. 113 B4
Dunfermline U.K. 34 E3
Dungannon U.K. 35 C4
Dún Garbhán Rep. of Ireland see Dungarvan
Dungargarh India 74 B3
Dungarpur India 74 B5
Dungarvan Rep. of Ireland 35 C5
Dung Co l. China 75 F3
Dungeness hd U.K. 35 G6
Dungeness, Punta pt Arg. 153 C8
Dungu Dem. Rep. Congo 94 F4
Dungun Malaysia 58 C1
Dungunab Sudan 68 B4
Dunhou China see Ji'an
Dunhua China 64 B4
Dunhuang China 70 H3
Dunkeld Australia 111 G5
Dunkeld U.K. 34 E3
Dunkirk France 38 E1
Dunkirk U.S.A. 130 D2
Dunkwa Ghana 93 E4
Dún Laoghaire Rep. of Ireland 35 C5
Dunlap U.S.A. 128 B5
Dunluce tourist site U.K. 34 C4
Dunmanway Rep. of Ireland 35 B6
Dunmarra Australia 110 C3
Dunmore PA U.S.A. 131 F3
Dunmore WV U.S.A. 130 D4
Dunmore Town Bahamas 129 D7
Dunn U.S.A. 128 D5
Dunnet Head U.K. 34 E2
Dunnigan U.S.A. 136 B2
Dunning U.S.A. 132 A3
Dunnville Canada 130 D2
Dunolly Australia 112 B5
Dunphy U.S.A. 137 D1
Duns U.K. 34 E4
Dunsmuir U.S.A. 134 B4
Dunstan Mountains N.Z. 113 B4
Duntroon N.Z. 113 B4
Dunvegan U.K. 34 C3
Dunvegan Lake Canada 123 J2
Dunyapur Pak. 81 G4
Duobukur r. China 64 A2
Dupang Ling mts China 67 D3
Duperré Alg. see Aïn Defla
Dupnitsa Bulg. 46 C3
Dupree U.S.A. 132 A2
Duque de Bragança Angola see Calandula
Duque de York, Isla i. Chile 153 B7
Dura r. Eth. 96 C2
Durack r. Australia 110 A2
Durack Range hills Australia 108 D4
Dura Europos Syria see Aş Şāliḩīyah
Durağan Turkey 78 C2
Durance r. France 39 F5
Durand U.S.A. 130 B2
Duranes hill Spain 42 D3
Durango Mex. 126 F7
Durango state Mex. 133 A7
Durango Spain 43 E1
Durango U.S.A. 135 F5
Durankulak Bulg. 46 F3
Durant MS U.S.A. 133 D5
Durant OK U.S.A. 133 B5
Duratón r. Spain 42 D2
Durazno Arg. 152 C2
Durazno Uruguay 152 F3
Durazzo Albania see Durrës
Durban S. Africa 99 F6
Durban-Corbières France 39 E5
Durbin U.S.A. 130 D4
Durbuy Belgium 39 F1
Dúrcal Spain 42 E4
Đurđevac Croatia 44 F1
Durdura, Raas pt Somalia 96 F2
Düren Germany 36 C3
Düren Iran 80 D3
Duren, Kūh-e mt. Iran 80 D3
Durg India 75 D5
Durgapur Bangl. 75 F4
Durgapur India 75 E5
Durham Canada 130 C1
Durham U.K. 35 F4
Durham CA U.S.A. 136 B2
Durham NC U.S.A. 128 D5
Durham NH U.S.A. 131 H2
Durham Downs Australia 111 E5
Durhi well Eth. 96 D3
Duri Indon. 58 C2
Durlas Rep. of Ireland see Thurles
Durleşti Moldova 29 D7
Durmitor mt. Yugo. 46 A3
Durmitor nat. park Yugo. 46 A3
Durness U.K. 34 D2
Durocortorum France see Reims
Durostorum Bulg. see Silistra
Durovernum U.K. see Canterbury
Durrës Albania 46 A4
Dursey Island Rep. of Ireland 35 A6
Dursunbey Turkey 78 B3
Durtal France 38 C3
Duru r. Dem. Rep. Congo 94 F4
Dürüh Iran 81 E3
Durukhsi Somalia 96 E2
Durusu Gölü l. Turkey 46 F4
Durūz, Jabal ad mt. Syria 77 C3
D'Urville, Tanjung pt Indon. 57 I6
D'Urville Island N.Z. 113 C3
Durzab Afgh. 81 F3
Dushak Turkm. 81 D2
Dushan China 66 C3
▶Dushanbe Tajik. 81 G2
Capital of Tajikistan.
Dushore U.S.A. 131 E3
Düsseldorf Germany 36 C3
Dusti Tajik. 81 G2
Dustlik Uzbek. 81 G1
Dusty U.S.A. 134 C3
Dutch East Indies country Asia see Indonesia
Dutch Guiana country S. America see Suriname
Dutch Mountain U.S.A. 137 F1
Dutch West Indies terr. West Indies see Netherlands Antilles
Dutsan-Wai Nigeria 93 H3
Dutse Nigeria 93 H3
Dutsin-Ma Nigeria 93 G2
Dutton r. Australia 111 E4
Dutton Canada 130 C2
Dutton, Mount U.S.A. 137 F2
Duval Canada 134 F2
Duved Sweden 32 D3
Duvert, Lac l. Canada 125 G1
Duvno Bos.-Herz. see Tomislavgrad
Duweihin well Saudi Arabia 80 B5
Duweihin, Khor b. Saudi Arabia/U.A.E. 80 B5
Duwin Iraq 79 F3
Duyinzeik Myanmar 60 B4
Duyun China 66 C3
Duzab Pak. 81 E5
Düzce Turkey 78 B2
Duzdab Iran see Zāhedān
Dve Mogili Bulg. 46 D3
Dvinsk Latvia see Daugavpils
Dvinskaya Guba g. Rus. Fed. 28 F2
Dvor Croatia 44 F2
Dwangwa Malawi 97 B8
Dwarka India 74 A5
Dwarsberg S. Africa 99 E5
Dwellingup Australia 109 B8
Dwingelderveld, Nationaal Park nat. park Neth. 36 C2
Dyanev Turkm. 81 E2
Dyankovo Bulg. 46 E3
Dyat'kovo Rus. Fed. 29 E5
Dyce U.K. 34 E3
Dyer, Cape Canada 121 M3
Dyersburg U.S.A. 128 A4
Dyfi r. U.K. 35 E5
Dyje r. Austria/Czech Rep. 37 H4
▶Dykh-Tau, Gora mt. Rus. Fed. 29 G8
2nd highest mountain in Europe.
europe 22–23
Dylewska Góra hill Poland 37 I2
Dynevor Downs Australia 111 F6
Dyrrhachium Albania see Durrës
Dysart Australia 111 G4
Dytiki Ellas admin. reg. Greece 47 B5
Dytiki Makedonia admin. reg. Greece 47 B4
Dyuendyu Rus. Fed. 27 N3
Dyulino Bulg. 46 E3
Dyurtyuli Rus. Fed. 28 J5
Dyviziya Ukr. 46 F2
Dzamïn Üüd Mongolia 63 I3
Dzanga-Ndoki, Parc National de nat. park Cameroon 94 B4
▶Dzaoudzi Mayotte 97 E8
Capital of Mayotte.
Dzaudzhikau Rus. Fed. see Vladikavkaz
Dzavhan Gol r. Mongolia 70 H2
Džbán mts Czech Rep. 37 F3
Dzerzhinsk Belarus see Dzyarzhynsk
Dzerzhinsk Rus. Fed. 28 G4
Dzhagdy, Khrebet mts Rus. Fed. 27 M4
Dzhaki-Unakhta Yakbyyana, Khrebet mts Rus. Fed. 64 C2
Dzhalalabad Azer. see Cälilabad
Dzhalal-Abad Kyrg. see Jalal-Abad
Dzhaltyr Kazakh. see Zhaltyr
Dzhambeyty Kazakh. see Zhympity
Dzhambul Kazakh. see Taraz
Dzhangala Kazakh. 29 I6
Dzhangel'dy Uzbek. 81 E1
Dzhankel'dy Uzbek. see Dzhangel'dy
Dzhankoy Ukr. 29 E7
Dzhanybek Kazakh. 29 H6
Dzharkent Kazakh. see Zharkent
Dzharkurgan Uzbek. 81 F2
Dzhebel Turkm. 80 C2
Dzhelondi Tajik. see Dzhilandy
Dzhetygara Kazakh. see Zhitikara
Dzhezkazgan Kazakh. see Zhezkazgan
Dzhigirbent Turkm. 81 E1
Dzhilandy Tajik. 81 H2
Dzhingil'dy Uzbek. see Dzhangel'dy
Dzhirgatal' Tajik. see Jirgatol
Dzhizak Uzbek. 81 F1
Dzhizak Oblast admin. div. Uzbek. see Dzhizakskaya Oblast'
Dzhizakskaya Oblast' admin. div. Uzbek. 81 F1
Dzhokhar Ghala Rus. Fed. see Groznyy
Dzhubga Rus. Fed. 79 D1
Dzhu-Dzhu-Klu Turkm. 81 E2
Dzhugdzhur, Khrebet mts Rus. Fed. 27 N4
Dzhul'fa Azer. see Culfa
Dzhuma Uzbek. 81 F2
Dzhungarskiy Alatau, Khrebet mts China/Kazakh. 70 E3
Dzhusaly Kazakh. 70 B2
Działdowo Poland 37 J2
Dzierżoniów Poland 37 H3
Dzioua Alg. 91 G2
Dzodze Ghana 93 F4
Dzungarian Basin China see Junggar Pendi
Dzungarian Gate pass China/Kazakh. 70 F2
Dzuunmod Mongolia 63 H2
Dzyarzhynsk Belarus 29 C5

↓ E

Eabamet Lake Canada 124 C3
Eads U.S.A. 132 A4
Eagar U.S.A. 137 H4
Eagle r. Canada 125 J2
Eagle U.S.A. 122 A1
Eagle Cap mt. U.S.A. 134 C3
Eagle Crags mt. U.S.A. 136 D4
Eagle Creek r. Canada 123 J4
Eagle Lake CA U.S.A. 136 B1
Eagle Lake ME U.S.A. 128 F2
Eagle Mountain U.S.A. 132 D2
Eagle Pass U.S.A. 133 A6
Eagle Peak U.S.A. 135 F7
Eagle Plain Canada 120 F3
Eagle Rock U.S.A. 130 D5
Eaglesham Canada 122 G4
Eagle Village U.S.A. 122 A1
Eap i. Micronesia see Yap
Earaheedy Australia 109 C6
Ear Falls Canada 124 A3
Earlimart U.S.A. 136 C4
Earn r. U.K. 34 E3
Earp U.S.A. 137 E4
Earth U.S.A. 133 A5
East Alligator r. Australia 110 C2
East Antarctica reg. Antarctica 167 F1
East Ararat U.S.A. 131 F3
East Aurora U.S.A. 130 D2
East Baines r. Australia 110 B2
East Bay inlet U.S.A. 129 B6
East Bengal country Asia see Bangladesh
Eastbourne U.K. 35 G6
East Brady U.S.A. 130 D3
East Branch U.S.A. 131 F3
East Cape N.Z. 113 D2
East Cape Rus. Fed. see Dezhneva, Mys
East Carbon City U.S.A. 137 G2
East Caroline Basin sea feature N. Pacific Ocean 164 D5
East China Sea N. Pacific Ocean 63 L5
East Coast Bays N.Z. 113 C2
East Dereham U.K. 35 G5
Eastend Canada 123 I5
▶Easter Island S. Pacific Ocean 165 K7
Part of Chile.
Eastern admin. reg. Ghana 93 E4
Eastern prov. Kenya 96 C5
Eastern prov. Sierra Leone 92 C3
Eastern prov. Zambia 97 A8
Eastern Cape prov. S. Africa 99 E6
Eastern Desert Egypt 89 G3
Eastern Equatoria state Sudan 96 B3
Eastern Ghats mts India 72 C4
▶Eastern Island U.S.A. 164 G4
Most northerly point of Oceania.
Eastern Nara canal Pak. 81 G5
Eastern Samoa terr. S. Pacific Ocean see American Samoa
Eastern Sayan Mountains Rus. Fed. see Vostochnyy Sayan
Eastern Taurus plat. Turkey see Güneydoğu Toroslar
Eastern Transvaal prov. S. Africa see Mpumalanga
Easterville Canada 123 L4
East Falkland i. Falkland Is 153 F8
East Frisian Islands Germany 36 C2
East Grand Forks U.S.A. 132 B2
East Hampton U.S.A. 131 G3
East Hartford U.S.A. 131 G3
East Indiaman Ridge sea feature Indian Ocean 162 N7
East Island P.N.G. 111 H1
East Jamaica U.S.A. 131 G2
East Kilbride U.K. 34 D4
East Lamma Channel Hong Kong China 67 [inset]
Eastland U.S.A. 133 B5
East Lansing U.S.A. 130 A2
Eastleigh U.K. 35 F6
East Linton U.K. 34 E4
East Liverpool U.S.A. 130 C3
East London S. Africa 99 E7
Eastmain Canada 124 E2
Eastmain r. Canada 125 E2
East Mariana Basin sea feature N. Pacific Ocean 164 E5
East Middlebury U.S.A. 131 G2
East Millinocket U.S.A. 128 F2
East Naples U.S.A. 129 C7
Easton CA U.S.A. 136 C3
Easton MD U.S.A. 131 E4
Easton PA U.S.A. 131 F3
East Pacific Rise sea feature N. Pacific Ocean 165 K4
East Pakistan country Asia see Bangladesh
East Park Reservoir U.S.A. 136 A2
East Point Canada 125 I4
East Range mts U.S.A. 136 D1
East Retford U.K. see Retford
East Ridge U.S.A. 128 B5
East St Louis U.S.A. 127 H4
East Sea N. Pacific Ocean see Japan, Sea of
East Shoal Lake Canada 123 L5
East Siberian Sea Rus. Fed. 27 O2
East Side Canal r. U.S.A. 136 C4
East Tavaputs Plateau U.S.A. 137 H2
▶East Timor country Asia 108 D2
asia 52–53, 82
East Tons r. India 75 E4
East Verde r. U.S.A. 137 G4
East Walker r. U.S.A. 136 C2
East York Canada 130 D2
Eaton CO U.S.A. 134 F4
Eaton OH U.S.A. 130 A4
Eatonia Canada 123 I5
Eaton Rapids U.S.A. 130 A2
Eatonton U.S.A. 129 C5
Eau Claire U.S.A. 132 D2
Eauripik atoll Micronesia 57 J4
Eauripik Rise - New Guinea Rise sea feature N. Pacific Ocean 164 D5
Eaurypyg atoll Micronesia see Eauripik
Eauze France 38 D5
Ebagoola Australia 111 E2
Eban Nigeria 93 G3
Ebano Mex. 126 G7
Ebebiyin Equat. Guinea 93 H5
Ebeltoft Denmark 33 C4
Ebenerde Namibia 98 C5
Ebensburg U.S.A. 130 D3
Ebensee Austria 37 F5
Eberswalde-Finow Germany 37 F2
Ebetsu Japan 64 E4
Ebian China 66 B2
Ebi Nor salt l. China see Ebinur Hu
Ebinur Hu salt l. China 70 F3
Ebla tourist site Syria 77 C2
Ebnat-Kappel Switz. 39 H3
Ebola r. Dem. Rep. Congo 94 D4
Ebolowa Cameroon 93 H5
Ebony Namibia 98 B4
Ebonyi state Nigeria 93 H4
Ebre r. Spain see Ebro
Ebro r. Spain 43 G2
Ebro, Embalse del resr Spain 42 E1
Eburacum U.K. see York
Ebusus i. Spain see Ibiza
Ecbatana Iran see Hamadān
Eccles U.S.A. 130 C5
Eceabat Turkey 47 E4
Echarri-Aranaz Spain 43 E1
Ech Chélif Alg. 91 F1
Ech Cherita, Sebkhet salt pan Tunisia 45 C7
Echeng China see Ezhou
Echinos Greece 46 D4
Echmiadzin Armenia see Ejmiatsin
Echo Bay N.W.T. Canada 120 H3
Echo Bay N.W.T. Canada 123 G1
Echo Cliffs esc. U.S.A. 137 G3
Echoing r. Canada 123 M4
Echternach Lux. 39 G2
Echuca Australia 112 C5
Écija Spain 42 D4
Ečka Yugo. 46 B2
Eckernförde Germany 36 D1
Eckerö Fin. 33 E3
Eckman U.S.A. 130 C5
Eclipse Sound sea chan. Canada 121 K2
Écrins, Parc National des nat. park France 39 G4
▶Ecuador country S. America 146 B5
southamerica 144–145, 154
Ed Eritrea 89 I6
Ed Sweden 33 C4
Eday i. U.K. 34 E2
Ed Da'ein Sudan 94 E2
Ed Dair, Jebel mt. Sudan 89 F6
Ed Damazin Sudan 96 B2
Ed Damer Sudan 89 G5
Ed Debba Sudan 89 F5
Eddeki well Chad 88 C5
Eddies Cove Canada 125 J3
Ed Dueim Sudan 89 G6
Eddystone Point Australia 112 D6
Eddyville U.S.A. 128 A4
Ede Neth. 36 B2
Edéa Cameroon 93 H5
Edehon Lake Canada 123 L2
Edéia Brazil 149 H4
Eden Australia 112 D5
Eden r. U.K. 34 E4
Eden NC U.S.A. 130 D5
Eden TX U.S.A. 133 B6
Edenburg S. Africa 98 E6
Edendale N.Z. 113 B4
Edenderry Rep. of Ireland 35 C5
Edenhope Australia 112 B5
Edenton U.S.A. 128 D4
Eder r. Germany 36 D3
Edessa Greece 46 C4
Edessa Turkey see Şanlıurfa
Edevik Sweden 32 D3
Edfu Egypt see Idfū
Edgar Ranges hills Australia 108 C4
Edgartown U.S.A. 131 H3
Edgecumbe Island Solomon Is see Utupua
Edgefield U.S.A. 129 C5
Edge Island Svalbard see Edgeøya
Edgeøya i. Svalbard 26 C2
Edgerton Canada 123 I4
Edgerton U.S.A. 130 E5
Edgewood U.S.A. 131 E4
Édhessa Greece see Edessa
Édîkel well Niger 93 G1
Edina U.S.A. 132 C3
Edinboro U.S.A. 130 C3
Edinburg TX U.S.A. 133 B7
Edinburg VA U.S.A. 130 D4
▶Edinburgh U.K. 34 E4
Capital of Scotland.
Edincik Turkey 47 E4
Edingeni Malawi 97 B8
Edirne Turkey 78 A2
Edirne prov. Turkey 46 E4
Edisto r. U.S.A. 129 C5
Edith, Mount U.S.A. 134 E3
Edithburgh Australia 112 A4
Edjeleh Libya 88 A3
Édjérir watercourse Mali 93 F1
Edjudina Australia 109 C7
Edmond U.S.A. 133 B5
Edmonds U.S.A. 134 B3
▶Edmonton Canada 123 H4
Provincial capital of Alberta.
Edmund Lake Canada 123 M4
Edmundston Canada 125 G4
Edna U.S.A. 133 B6
Edo Japan see Tōkyō
Edo state Nigeria 93 G4
Edolo Italy 44 C1
Edom reg. Israel/Jordan 77 B4
Edremit Turkey 78 A3
Edremit Körfezi b. Turkey 78 A3
Edsbro Sweden 33 E4
Edsbyn Sweden 33 D3
Edsele Sweden 32 E3
Edson Canada 123 G4
Eduardo Castex Arg. 152 D3
Eduni, Mount Canada 122 D1
Edward r. Australia 111 E2
Edward, Lake Dem. Rep. Congo/Uganda 94 F5
Edward, Mount Antarctica 167 L1
Edwardesabad Pak. see Bannu
Edwards U.S.A. 131 F1
Edwards Plateau U.S.A. 133 A6
Edwardsville U.S.A. 132 D4
Edward VII Peninsula Antarctica 167 I
Edziza, Mount Canada 122 D3
Edzo Canada see Rae-Edzo
Eel r. U.S.A. 136 A1
Eel, South Fork r. U.S.A. 136 A1
Eesti country Europe see Estonia
Éfaté i. Vanuatu 107 F3
Efes tourist site Turkey see Ephesus
Effingham U.S.A. 128 A4
Efsus Turkey see Afşin
Ega r. Spain 43 F1
Egadi, Isole is Sicily Italy 45 C5
Egadi Islands Sicily Italy see Egadi, Isole
Egan Range mts U.S.A. 137 E2
Egbe Nigeria 93 G3
Egedesminde Greenland see Aasiaat
Eger r. Germany 36 F3
Eger Hungary 37 J5
Egersund Norway 33 B4
Egerton, Mount Australia 109 B6
Eggenfelden Germany 37 F4
Egg Harbor City U.S.A. 131 F4
Egg Lake Canada 123 J4
Egilsstaðir Iceland 32 [inset]
Eğin Turkey see Kemaliye
Eginbah Australia 108 B5
Eğirdir Turkey 78 B3
Eğirdir Gölü l. Turkey 78 B3
Égletons France 38 E4
Eglinton Island Canada 121 H2
Eglisau Switz. 39 H3
Egmont, Cape N.Z. 113 C2
Egmont, Mount vol. N.Z. see Taranaki, Mount
Egmont National Park N.Z. 113 C2
Egua Col. 146 E3
Éguas r. Brazil 150 C5
Egvekinot Rus. Fed. 27 S3
▶Egypt country Africa 89 F2
2nd most populous country in Africa.
africa 86–87, 100
Ehcel well Mali see Agous-n-Ehsel
Ehen Hudag China 70 J4
Ehingen (Donau) Germany 36 D4
Ehrenberg U.S.A. 137 E5
Ehrenberg Range hills Australia 110 B4
Eibar Spain 43 E1
Eibergen Neth. 36 C2
Eichstätt Germany 36 E4
Eide Norway 32 B3
Eider r. Germany 36 D1
Eidfjord Norway 33 B3
Eiði Faroe Is 34 [inset]
Eidsvåg Norway 32 C3
Eidsvold Australia 111 G5
Eidsvoll Norway 33 C3
Eifel hills Germany 36 C3
Eigg i. U.K. 34 C3
Eight Degree Channel India/Maldives 72 B5
Eights Coast Antarctica 167 K2
Eighty Mile Beach Australia 108 C4
Eilat Israel 77 B5
Eildon, Lake Australia 112 C5
Eileen Lake Canada 123 J2
Eilenburg Germany 37 F3
Eilerts de Haan Gebergte mts Suriname 147 G4
Einasleigh Australia 111 F3
Einasleigh r. Australia 111 E3
Einbeck Germany 36 D3
Eindhoven Neth. 36 B3
Einsiedeln Switz. 39 H3
Éire country Europe see Ireland, Republic of
Eirik Ridge sea feature N. Atlantic Ocean 160 L2
Eiriosgaigh i. U.K. see Eriskay
Eiru r. Brazil 146 D6
Eirunepé Brazil 146 D6
Eisberg hill Germany 36 D3
Eiseb watercourse Namibia 98 D3
Eisenach Germany 36 E3
Eisenerz Austria 37 G5
Eisenerzer Alpen mts Austria 37 G5
Eisenhüttenstadt Germany 37 G2
Eisenstadt Austria 37 H5
Eišiškės Lith. 33 G5
Eisleben Lutherstadt Germany 36 E3
Eitape P.N.G. see Aitape
Eivissa Spain see Ibiza
Eivissa i. Spain see Ibiza
Ejea de los Caballeros Spain 43 F1
Ejeda Madag. 99 [inset] J5
Ejin Qi China see Dalain Hob
Ej Jill, Sebkhet salt flat Mauritania 90 B5
Ejmiadzin Armenia see Ejmiatsin
Ejmiatsin Armenia 79 F2
Ejura Ghana 93 E4
Ekalaka U.S.A. 134 F3
Ekang Nigeria 93 H4
Ékata Gabon 94 B4
Ekenäs Fin. 33 F4
Ekenäs Sweden 33 D4
Ekenäs skärgårds Nationalpark nat. park Fin. 33 F4
Ekerem Turkm. see Okarem
Eket Nigeria 93 G4
Eketahuna N.Z. 113 C3
Ekhinos Greece see Echinos
Ekhmîm Egypt see Akhmîm
Ekibastuz Kazakh. 26 H4
Ekimchan Rus. Fed. 64 C
Ekiti state Nigeria 93 G4
Ekoli Dem. Rep. Congo 94 E5
Ekonda Rus. Fed. 27 K3
Ekondo Titi Cameroon 93 H4
Ekostrovskaya Imandra, Ozero l. Rus. Fed. 32 I2
Ekouamou Congo 94 C4
Ekpoma Nigeria 93 G4
Ekşere Turkey see Gündoğmuş
Ekshärad Sweden 33 D3
Eksjö Sweden 33 D4
Eksteenfontein S. Africa 98 C6
Ekström Ice Shelf Antarctica 167 B2
Ekträsk Sweden 32 E2
Ekwan r. Canada 124 D2
El Aaiún W. Sahara see Laâyoune
Elafonisos i. Greece 47 C6
Elafonisou, Steno sea chan. Greece 47 C6
Elaia, Cape Cyprus 77 B2
El Aiadia well Sudan 89 G5
El 'Alamein Egypt see Al 'Alamayn
El Alamo Mex. 135 C7
El Alia Alg. 91 G2
El Alia Tunisia 45 B6
El Alto Peru 146 A6
Elands r. S. Africa 99 F5
El Aouinet Alg. 45 A7
El Arahal Spain 42 D4
El Araïche Morocco see Larache
El Aricha Alg. 91 E2
Elasa i. Greece 47 E7
El Ashmûnein Egypt see Al Ashmūnayn
El Asnam Alg. see Ech Chélif
Elassona Greece 47 C5
El Astillero Spain 42 E1
El 'Aṭf reg. W. Sahara 90 B5
Elati mt. Greece 47 B5
Elato atoll Micronesia 57 K4
Elazığ Turkey 79 D3
Elba, Isola d' i. Italy 44 C3
El Bahret el Ahmar governorate Egypt see Al Baḩr al Aḩmar
El'ban Rus. Fed. 64 D2
El Banco Col. 146 C2
El Bânoûn well Mauritania 92 D1
El Barco de Ávila Spain 42 D2
El Barco de Valdeorras Spain see O Barco
El Barreal salt l. Mex. 135 F7
El Barun Sudan 96 B2
Elbasan Albania 46 B4
Elbaşı Turkey 78 C3
El Bauga Sudan 89 G5
El Baúl Venez. 146 D2
El Bayadh Alg. 91 F2
Elbe r. Germany 37 D2
also known as Labe (Czech Republic)
'Elb el Fçâl des. Mauritania 92 C1
El Beqa'a valley Lebanon 77 C2
El Berié well Mauritania 92 C1
Elberta U.S.A. 137 G2
Elberton U.S.A. 129 C5
El Beru Hagia Somalia 96 D4
Elbeuf France 38 D2
Elbeyli Turkey 77 C1
El Beyyed well Mauritania 90 C5
El Beyyed well Mauritania 92 C1
Elbing Poland see Elbląg
Elbistan Turkey 78 D3
Elbląg Poland 37 I1
Elbląski, Kanał canal Poland 37 I
El Bolsón Arg. 153 C5
El Borma Tunisia 91 H3
El Boulaïda Alg. see Blida
Elbow Lake U.S.A. 132 B2
▶Elbrus mt. Rus. Fed. 29 G8
Highest mountain in Europe.
europe 22–23
El Buheyrat state Sudan 94 F3
El Buitre mt. Spain 43 F3
El Burgo de Osma Spain 42 E2
Elburz Mountains Iran 80 B2
El Cain Arg. 153 C5
El Cajon U.S.A. 136 D5
El Callao Venez. 147 F3
El Campo U.S.A. 133 B6
El Canton Venez. 146 D2
El Capulín r. Mex. 133 A7
El Carmelo Venez. 146 D2
El Carmen Beni Bol. 149 E3
El Carmen Santa Cruz Bol. 149 F4
El Carmen Ecuador 146 B5
El Caroche mt. Spain 43 F3
El Centro U.S.A. 137 E5
El Cerro Bol. 149 E4
El Chaparro Venez. 147 E2
Elche-Elx Spain 43 F3
El Chichonal vol. Mex. 138 F5
El Chilicote Mex. 135 F7
Elcho Island Australia 110 C1
El Coca Ecuador see Puerto Francisco de Orellana
El Cocuy, Parque Nacional nat. park Col. 146 C3
El Collado hill Spain 42 D3
El Contador, Puerto de pass Spain 43 E4
El Cuy Arg. 152 C4
Elda Spain 43 F3
Elde r. Germany 36 E2
El Debb well Eth. 96 D3
El Desemboque Mex. 135 D7
El Diamante Mex. 133 A6
El Difícil Col. 146 C2
El'dikan Rus. Fed. 27 N3
El Diviso Col. 146 B4
El Djezair Alg. see Algiers
El Doctor Mex. 135 D7
Eldon U.S.A. 132 C4
Eldorado Arg. 152 G1
El Dorado Col. 146 D4
El Dorado AR U.S.A. 133 C5
El Dorado KS U.S.A. 132 B4
Eldorado U.S.A. 133 A6
El Dorado Venez. 147 F3
Eldorado Mountains U.S.A. 137 E4
Eldoret Kenya 96 B4
Eldridge, Mount U.S.A. 122 A1
Elea, Cape Cyprus see Elaia, Cape
Eleanor U.S.A. 130 C4
Electric Peak U.S.A. 134 E3
El Eglab plat. Alg. 90 D4
El 'Ein well Sudan 89 F5
Eleja Latvia 33 F4
El Ejido Spain 43 E4
Elek Hungary 37 J5
Elek r. Rus. Fed. see Ilek
Elektrėnai Lith. 33 G5
Elele Nigeria 93 G4
▶Elemi Triangle terr. Africa 96 B3
Disputed territory (Ethiopia/Kenya/Sudan) administered by Kenya.
Elena Bulg. 46 D3
El Encanto Col. 146 C5
El Encinal Mex. 137 D5
Elephanta Caves tourist site India 72 B2
Elephant Butte Reservoir U.S.A. 135 F6
Elephant Island Antarctica 167 A2
Eleşkirt Turkey 79 E3
Eleuthera i. Bahamas 129 D7

Eleven Point r. U.S.A. 133 D4
El Fahs Tunisia 45 B6
El Faiyûm Egypt see Al Fayyūm
El Faiyûm governorate Egypt see Al Fayyūm
El Faouar Tunisia 91 H2
El Fasher Sudan 88 E6
El Ferrol Spain see Ferrol
El Ferrol del Caudillo Spain see Ferrol
El Fud Eth. 96 D3
El Fuerte Mex. 126 E6
Elgå Norway 33 C3
Elgal waterhole Kenya 96 C4
El Gçaib well Mali 90 D5
El Geili Sudan 89 G6
El Geneina Sudan 88 D6
El Geteina Sudan 89 G6
El Gezira state Sudan 89 G6
El Ghaba Sudan 89 F5
El Ghalla, Wadi watercourse Sudan 94 C2
El Ghàllaouîya well Mauritania 90 C5
El Gheddiya Mauritania 92 C1
El Ghor plain Jordan/West Bank see Al Ghawr
Elgin U.K. 34 E3
Elgin IL U.S.A. 132 D3
Elgin NV U.S.A. 137 E3
Elgin OR U.S.A. 134 C3
Elgin TX U.S.A. 133 B6
Elgin Down Australia 111 F4
El'ginskiy Rus. Fed. 27 O3
El Gir well Sudan 89 F5
El Giza Egypt see Giza
El Giza governorate Egypt see Al Jīzah
El Goléa Alg. 91 F3
El Golfo de Santa Clara Mex. 135 D7
Elgon, Mount Uganda 96 B4
Elgoras, Gora hill Rus. Fed. 32 H1
El Guante Mex. 135 F7
El Guetar Tunisia 91 H2
El Guettâra well Mali 90 D5
El Hamma Tunisia 91 H2
El Hammâmi reg. Mauritania 90 C5
El Hank reg. Alg. 90 D4
El Hank esc. Mauritania 90 C5
El Haouaria Tunisia 45 C6
El Hawata Sudan 89 G6
El Hierro i. Canary Is 90 A4
El Hilla Sudan 89 E6
El Homr Alg. 91 F3
El Homra Sudan 89 F6
El Houeïtat well Mauritania 92 C1
El Huecu Arg. 152 C4
Eli well Niger 93 H2
Eliase Indon. 108 E2
Elias García Angola 95 D7
Elichpur India see Achalpur
Elila Dem. Rep. Congo 94 C4
Elila r. Dem. Rep. Congo 94 C4
Elim U.S.A. 120 C3
Elimberrum France see Auch
Elin Pelin Bulg. 46 C3
Eliozondo Spain 43 F1
Elipa Dem. Rep. Congo 94 C4
Elisabetha Dem. Rep. Congo 94 D4
Élisabethville Dem. Rep. Congo see Lubumbashi
Eliseu Martins Brazil 150 D4
El Iskandarîya Egypt see Alexandria
El Iskandarîya governorate Egypt see Al Iskandarîyah
Elista Rus. Fed. 29 H7
Elizabeth U.S.A. 131 F3
Elizabeth, Mount Australia 108 D4
Elizabeth City U.S.A. 128 E4
Elizabeth Creek r. Australia 110 D3
Elizabeth Islands U.S.A. 131 H3
Elizabeth Reef Australia 107 E4
Elizabethton KY U.S.A. 128 B4
Elizabethtown NC U.S.A. 129 D5
Elizabethtown NY U.S.A. 131 G1
Elizabethville U.S.A. 131 E3
Elizavety, Mys c. Rus. Fed. 27 O4
El Jadida Morocco 90 C2
El Jebelein Sudan 89 G6
El Jem Tunisia 91 H2
Elk r. Canada 123 H5
Ełk Poland 37 K2
Ełk r. Poland 37 K2
Elk r. MD U.S.A. 131 F4
Elk r. TN U.S.A. 128 B5
El Kaa Lebanon see Qaa
El Kab Sudan 89 G5
Elkader U.S.A. 132 D3
El Kala Alg. 45 B6
El Kamlin Sudan 89 G6
El Karabi Sudan 89 G5
Elk City U.S.A. 133 B5
Elk Creek U.S.A. 136 A2
Elkedra Australia 110 C4
El Kelaâ des Srarhna Morocco 90 D2
El Kerë Eth. 96 D3
Elkford Canada 123 H5
Elk Grove U.S.A. 136 B2
El Khalil West Bank see Hebron
El Khandaq Sudan 89 F5
El Khârga Egypt see Al Khārijah
Elkhart IN U.S.A. 132 C3
Elkhart KS U.S.A. 132 A4
El Khartum Sudan see Khartoum
El Khenachich esc. Mali 90 D5
El Khnàchîch esc. Mali see El Khnàchîch
Elkhorn U.S.A. 132 D3
Elkhorn r. U.S.A. 132 B3
Elkhovo Bulg. 46 E3
Elki Turkey see Beytüşşebap
Elkin U.S.A. 128 C4
Elkins U.S.A. 130 D4
Elk Island National Park Canada 123 H4
Elk Lake Canada 124 D4
Elkland U.S.A. 131 F3
Elko Canada 123 H5
Elko U.S.A. 134 D4
El K'oran Eth. 96 D4
Elk Point Canada 123 I4
Elk Point U.S.A. 132 B3
Elk River U.S.A. 132 C2
El Ksaib Ounane well Mali see El Gçaib
El Ksour Tunisia 45 B7
Elk Springs U.S.A. 137 H1
Elkton MD U.S.A. 131 F4
Elkton VA U.S.A. 130 D4
Elkview U.S.A. 130 D4
El Lagowa Sudan 94 F2
Ellas country Europe see Greece
Ellavalla Australia 109 A6
Ellaville U.S.A. 129 B5
Ellef Ringnes Island Canada 121 I2
El Lëh Eth. 96 C4
El Lein well Kenya 96 D5
Elléloyé well Chad 88 C5
Ellen, Mount U.S.A. 137 G2
Ellenabad India 74 C3
Ellenboro U.S.A. 130 E4
Ellendale DE U.S.A. 131 F4
Ellendale ND U.S.A. 132 B2
Ellensburg U.S.A. 134 C3
Ellenville U.S.A. 131 H3
Ellesmere, Lake N.Z. 113 C3
►Ellesmere Island Canada 121 K2
4th largest island in North America and 10th in the world.
northamerica 116–117
world 6–7

Ellesmere Port U.K. 35 E5
Ellice r. Canada 121 K1
Ellice Island atoll Tuvalu see Funafuti
Ellice Islands country S. Pacific Ocean see Tuvalu
Ellicottville U.S.A. 130 D2
Elliot Australia 110 C3
Elliot S. Africa 99 E6
Elliot, Mount Australia 111 F3
Elliot Knob mt. U.S.A. 130 D4
Elliot Lake Canada 124 D4
Ellis U.S.A. 132 B4
Ellisras S. Africa 99 E4
Elliston Australia 109 F8
Elliston U.S.A. 130 C5
Ellon U.K. 34 E3
Ellora Caves tourist site India 72 B1
Ellsworth KS U.S.A. 132 B4
Ellsworth ME U.S.A. 128 G2
Ellsworth WI U.S.A. 132 C2
Ellsworth Mountains Antarctica 167 L1
Ellwangen (Jagst) Germany 36 E4
El Mahia reg. Mali 90 E5
El Maitén Arg. 153 C5
Elmalı Turkey 78 B3
El Malpais National Monument nat. park U.S.A. 135 F5
El Mango Venez. 146 E4
El Mansûra Egypt see Al Manşūrah
El Manteco Venez. 147 F3
El Manzla Morocco 42 D5
El Marsa Alg. 43 G4
El Marsa Tunisia 45 D6
El Medo Eth. 96 D3
El Meghaïer Alg. 91 G2
El Melemm Sudan 94 F2
El Melhes well Mauritania 92 C1
El Mesellemiya Sudan 89 G6
El Messir well Chad 88 C4
El Miamo Venez. 147 F3
El Mîna Lebanon 77 B2
El Minya governorate Egypt see Al Minyā
Elmira Canada 130 D2
Elmira U.S.A. 131 G2
El Moïnane well Mauritania 92 C1
Elmore Australia 112 C5
El Morro nat. Arg. 152 D3
El Mrâîfîg well Mauritania 92 C2
El Mraïti well Mali 93 E1
El Mugrón mt. Spain 43 F3
El Mzereïb well Mali 90 D4
Elne France 39 E5
El Oasis Mex. 137 E5
El Obeid Sudan 89 F6
El Odaiya Sudan 89 F6
El Oro prov. Ecuador 146 B5
El Oro Mex. 126 F7
Elos Greece 47 C7
El Oued Alg. 91 G2
Eloy U.S.A. 137 G5
El Palmar Venez. 147 F2
El Pao Bolívar Venez. 147 F2
El Pao Cojedes Venez. 146 D2
El Paso IL U.S.A. 132 D3
El Paso KS U.S.A. see Derby
El Paso TX U.S.A. 135 F7
El Peñón Arg. 152 C3
El Perelló Spain 43 G3
Elphinstone i. Myanmar see Thayawthadangyi Kyun
El Picacho mt. Hond. 138 G6
El Pinalón, Cerro mt. Guat. 138 G5
El Pino, Sierra mts Mex. 133 A6
El Pintado Arg. 149 E6
El Pluma Arg. 153 C6
El Pocito Bol. 149 E3
El Porvenir Col. 146 D3
El Porvenir Mex. 135 F7
El Porvenir Panama 146 B2
El Prat de Llobregat Spain 43 H2
El Qâhira Egypt see Cairo
El Qâhira governorate Egypt see Al Qāhirah
El Quds Israel/West Bank see Jerusalem
El Qasimiye r. Lebanon 77 B3
El Quebrachal Arg. 152 D1
El Real Panama 146 B2
El Reno U.S.A. 133 B5
El Rey, Parque Nacional nat. park Arg. 149 D6
El Rosario watercourse Mex. 135 D7
Elrose Canada 123 I5
Elsa Canada 122 C2
Elsa r. Italy 44 C3
El Sahuaro Mex. 135 E7
El Salado Arg. 153 D7
El Salado Mex. 126 E7
El Salto Mex. 126 E7
►El Salvador country Central America 138 G6
northamerica 118–119, 140
El Salvador Chile 152 C1
Elsen Nur l. China 75 G2
El Serrat Andorra 43 G1
Elsinore Denmark see Helsingør
Elsinore CA U.S.A. 136 D5
Elsinore UT U.S.A. 137 F2
Elsinore Lake U.S.A. 136 D5
El Sosneado Arg. 152 C3
Elsterwerda Germany 37 F3
El Sueco Mex. 135 F7
El Suweis Egypt see Suez
El Suweis governorate Egypt see Al Suways
El Tama, Parque Nacional nat. park Venez. 146 C3
El Tarf Alg. 91 H1
El Teleno mt. Spain 42 C2
El Tigre Venez. 147 F2
El Tocuyo Venez. 146 D2
El'ton Rus. Fed. 29 H6
El'ton, Ozero l. Rus. Fed. 29 H6
El Toro Chile 152 C2
El Totumo Venez. 146 C2
El Tunal Arg. 152 D1
El Tuparro, Parque Nacional nat. park Col. 146 D3
El Turbio Chile 153 B7
El Uqsur Egypt see Luxor
Eluru India 72 D2
Elva Estonia 28 C3
Elvas Port. 42 C3
Elven France 38 B3
El Vendrell Spain 43 G2
Elverum Norway 32 H1
El Viejo mt. Col. 146 C3
Elvire r. Australia 108 E4
Elvo r. Italy 44 B2
El Wak Kenya 96 D4
Elwood IN U.S.A. 132 C3
Elwood NE U.S.A. 132 B3
Elwood NJ U.S.A. 131 F4
El Wuz Sudan 89 F6
Ely U.K. 35 G6
Ely MN U.S.A. 132 D1
Ely NV U.S.A. 137 E2
El Yagual Venez. 146 D3
El Yibo well Kenya 96 C3
Elyria U.S.A. 130 D3
Elysburg U.S.A. 131 F3
El Zagâzîg Egypt see Az Zaqāzīq
Emâm Qoli Iran 81 D2
Emámrúd Iran 80 C2
Emâm Sâheb Afgh. 81 G2

Emâm Taqi Iran 81 D2
Emas, Parque Nacional das nat. park Brazil 149 G4
Emba Kazakh. 70 A2
Emba r. Kazakh. 70 A2
Embalenhle S. Africa 99 F5
Embarcación Arg. 149 D5
Embarras Portage Canada 123 I3
Embi Kazakh. see Emba
Embira r. Brazil see Envira
Êmbonas Greece see Emponas
Embocação, Represa de resr Brazil 149 I4
Emborion Greece see Emporeio
Embu Kenya 96 C5
Embundo Angola 95 C9
Emden Germany 36 C2
Emecik Turkey 47 E6
Emei China see Emeishan
Emei Shan mt. China 66 B2
Emeishan China 66 B2
Emerald Australia 111 G4
Emeril Canada 125 I2
Emerson Canada 123 L5
Emerson U.S.A. 130 B4
Emery U.S.A. 137 G2
Emesa Syria see Homs
Emet Turkey 78 B3
Emigrant Gap U.S.A. 136 B2
Emigrant Pass U.S.A. 137 D1
Emigrant Valley U.S.A. 137 E3
eMijondini S. Africa 99 F5
Emile r. Canada 123 G2
Emiliano Zapata Mex. 138 F5
Emilia-Romagna admin. reg. Italy 44 C2
Emine, Nos pt Bulg. 46 E3
Eminska Planina hills Bulg. 46 E3
Emirdağ Turkey 78 B3
Emir Dağı mt. Turkey 78 B3
Emlenton U.S.A. 130 D3
Emmaboda Sweden 33 D4
Emmahaven Indon. see Telukbayur
Emmaste Estonia 33 F4
Emmaus U.S.A. 131 F3
Emmeloord Neth. 36 C2
Emmen Neth. 36 C2
Emmen Switz. 39 H3
Emmendingen Germany 36 C4
Emmerich Germany 36 C3
Emmet Australia 111 F5
Emmetsburg U.S.A. 132 C3
Emmiganuru India 72 C3
Emmitsburg U.S.A. 131 E4
Emo Canada 124 A3
Emőd Hungary 37 J5
Emona Slovenia see Ljubljana
Emory U.S.A. 133 C5
Emory Peak U.S.A. 133 A6
Empada Guinea-Bissau 92 B3
Empalme Mex. 135 D5
Empedrado Arg. 152 F1
Emperor Seamount Chain sea feature N. Pacific Ocean 164 H2
Emperor Trough sea feature N. Pacific Ocean 164 F2
Empexa, Salar de salt flat Bol. 148 C5
Empoli Italy 44 C3
Emponas Greece see Emua
Emporeio Greece 47 D6
Emporia KS U.S.A. 132 B4
Emporia VA U.S.A. 130 E5
Emporium U.S.A. 130 D3
Empress Canada 123 I5
Empress Mine Zimbabwe 99 F3
Empty Quarter des. Saudi Arabia see Rub' al Khālī
'Emrânî Iran 81 D3
Ems r. Germany 36 C2
Ems-Jade-Kanal canal Germany 36 C2
Emumägi hill Estonia 33 G4
Emzinoni S. Africa 99 F5
Enafors Sweden 32 C3
Enamuna Brazil 147 F3
Enard Bay U.K. 34 D2
Encanadé mt. Spain 43 G4
Encantadas, Serra das hills Brazil 152 G2
Encarnación Mex. 126 F7
Encarnación Para. 152 G1
Enchi Ghana 92 C4
Encinas mt. Spain 42 C3
Encinitas U.S.A. 136 D5
Encino U.S.A. 135 F6
Encón Arg. 152 D3
Encontrados Venez. 146 C2
Encs Hungary 37 J4
Endau Malaysia 58 C2
Endau r. Malaysia 58 C2
Endeavour Strait Australia 111 E1
Endeh Indon. 57 I7
Enderbury i. Kiribati 107 H2
Enderby Canada 122 G5
Enderby Abyssal Plain sea feature Indian Ocean 163 J9
Enderby Land reg. Antarctica 167 D2
Endicott Mountains U.S.A. 120 D3
Endimari r. Brazil 148 D1
Endom Cameroon 93 I5
Endwell U.S.A. 131 E2
Ene r. Peru 148 B2
Eneabba Australia 109 A7
Enemutu Brazil 147 G3
Energía Arg. 153 D5
Enewetak atoll Marshall Is 164 F4
Enez Turkey 47 E4
Enfidaville Tunisia 45 C6
Enfield U.S.A. 128 D4
Engan Norway 32 C3
Engaño, Río de los r. Col. see Yari
Engelhard U.S.A. 128 E5
Engel's Rus. Fed. 29 H6
Engerdal Norway 33 C3
Enggano i. Indon. 58 C4
Enghershatu mt. Eritrea 89 H5
Engineer Canada 122 C3
Engkilili Sarawak Malaysia 59 E2
England admin. div. U.K. 35 F5
Englee Canada 125 K3
Englehart Canada 124 E4
Englewood FL U.S.A. 129 C7
Englewood OH U.S.A. 130 A4
English r. Canada 123 M5
English U.S.A. 132 C4
English Bazar India see Ingraj Bazar
English Channel France/U.K. 30 D3
English Coast Antarctica 167 L2
Engozero Rus. Fed. 28 D2
Engstingen Germany 36 D4
Engures ezers l. Latvia 33 F4
Enguri r. Georgia 79 E2
Enhlalakahle S. Africa 99 F5
Enid U.S.A. 133 B4
Enipefs r. Greece 47 C5
eNjesuthi mt. Lesotho 99 I4
Enkan, Mys pt Rus. Fed. 27 O4
Enkeldoorn Zimbabwe see Chivhu
Enkhuizen Neth. 36 C2
Enköping Sweden 33 E4
Enle China see Zhenyuan
Enna Sicily Italy 45 E6
Ennadai Lake Canada 123 K2
En Nahud Sudan 89 F6
E-n-Nassamé well Niger 93 H2
Enné, Ouadi watercourse Chad 88 C6

Ennedi, Massif mts Chad 88 D5
Enneri Achelouma watercourse Niger 91 I5
Enneri Maro watercourse Chad 88 C5
Enneri Yebigué watercourse Chad 88 C4
Enngonia Australia 111 F6
Ennis Rep. of Ireland 35 C5
Ennis MT U.S.A. 134 E3
Ennis TX U.S.A. 133 C5
Enniscorthy Rep. of Ireland 35 C5
Enniskillen U.K. 35 B5
Enn Nâqoûra Lebanon 77 B3
Enns Austria 37 G4
Enns r. Austria 37 G4
Eno Fin. 32 H3
Enoch U.S.A. 137 F3
Enonkoski Fin. 33 H3
Enontekiö Fin. 32 F1
Enoree r. U.S.A. 129 C5
Enping China 67 E4
Enschede Neth. 36 C2
Ensenada Arg. 153 F5
Ensenada Mex. 135 B5
Ensenada de Utria nat. park Col. 146 B3
Enshi China 67 D2
Ensley U.S.A. 129 B6
Enterprise Canada 123 G2
Enterprise U.S.A. 129 C6
Entrance Canada 122 G4
Entrepeñas, Embalse de resr Spain 43 E2
Entre Rios prov. Arg. 152 F3
Entre Rios Bahia Brazil 150 E4
Entre Rios Pará Brazil 147 H6
Entre Rios Moz. see Malema
Entre Rios de Minas Brazil 151 C7
Entroncamento Port. 42 B3
Entuba Zimbabwe 99 E3
Enugu Nigeria 93 H4
Enugu state Nigeria 93 G4
Enurmino Rus. Fed. 27 S3
Envigado Col. 146 C2
Envira Brazil 148 C1
Envira r. Brazil 148 C1
Enying Hungary 37 I5
Eo r. Spain 42 C1
Eochaill Rep. of Ireland see Youghal
Eooa i. Tonga see Eua
Epe Nigeria 93 F4
Épéna Congo 94 C2
Épernay France 39 E2
Ephesus tourist site Turkey 47 E6
Ephraim U.S.A. 137 G2
Ephrata U.S.A. 131 E3
Ephrata WA U.S.A. 134 C3
Epi i. Vanuatu 107 G3
Épila Spain 43 E2
Épinal France 39 G2
Epirus admin. reg. Greece see Ipeiros
Episkopi Cyprus 77 A2
Episkopi Bay Cyprus 77 A2
Episkopis, Kolpos b. Cyprus see Episkopi Bay
Epping U.K. 35 G6
Epping U.S.A. 131 H2
Epping Forest National Park Australia 111 F4
Eppynt, Mynydd hills U.K. 35 E5
Epsom U.K. 35 F6
Epte r. France 38 D2
Epu-pel Arg. 152 D4
Epuyén Arg. 152 D4
Eqlid Iran 80 D4
Équateur prov. Dem. Rep. Congo 94 D4
►Equatorial Guinea country Africa 93 H5
africa 86–87, 100
Equeipa Venez. 147 F3
Era r. Italy 44 C3
Eraclea Italy 44 D2
Erakurri mt. Spain 43 F1
Erandol India 72 B1
Erawan National Park Thai. 61 B5
Erba, Jebel mt. Sudan 89 H4
Erbaa Turkey 78 D2
Erbendorf Germany 36 F4
Erbeskopf hill Germany 36 C4
Ercan airport Cyprus 77 A2
Erçek Turkey 79 E3
Erciş Turkey 79 E3
Erciyes Dağı mt. Turkey 78 C3
Erd Hungary 37 I5
Erdaobaihe China see Baihe
Erdaogou China 75 G2
Erdao Jiang r. China 64 A4
Erdek Turkey 78 A2
Erdemli Turkey 78 C3
Erding Germany 36 F4
Erdniyevskiy Rus. Fed. 29 H7
Erdre r. France 38 C3
Eré Peru 146 C5
Erebato r. Venez. 147 E3
Erebus, Mount vol. Antarctica 167 H1
Erech tourist site Iraq 79 F5
Erechim Brazil 151 A8
Ereentsav Mongolia 63 J2
Ereğli Turkey 78 B2
Ereğli Turkey 78 B2
Erego Moz. see Errego
Erei, Monti mts Sicily Italy 45 E6
Ereikoussa i. Greece 47 A5
Erementaū Kazakh. see Yereymentau
Erenhot China 63 I3
Erenik r. Yugo. 46 B3
Eresk Iran 80 D3
Eresma r. Spain 42 D2
Eresos Greece 47 D5
Eretria Greece 47 C5
Erevan Armenia see Yerevan
Erfoud Morocco 90 D3
Erft r. Germany 36 C3
Ergani Turkey 79 D3
Erg Azennezal des. Alg. 91 H4
Erg Bourarhet des. Alg. 91 H4
'Erg Chech des. Alg./Mali 90 D4
'Erg d' Amer des. Alg. 91 H4
Erg du Djourab des. Chad 88 C5
Erg du Ténéré des. Niger 93 H1
Ergene r. Turkey 78 A2
Erg Iguidi des. Alg./Mauritania 90 D4
'Erg Issaouane des. Alg. 91 H4
Erg Kilian des. Alg. 91 H4
Erg Tassedjefit des. Alg. 91 G5
Ergun He r. China/Rus. Fed. see Argun'
Ergun Qi China 63 K2
Er Hai l. China 66 B3
Eria r. Spain 42 C1
Erie KS U.S.A. 133 C4
Erie PA U.S.A. 130 C2
Erie, Lake Canada/U.S.A. 130 C2
'Erîgât reg. Mali 92 D1
Erik Eriksenstretet sea chan. Svalbard 26 C2
Erikoússi i. Greece see Ereikoussa
Eriksdale Canada 123 L5
Erimo-misaki c. Japan 64 G4
Eriskay i. U.K. 34 A3
Eritrea Greece see Erythres

Erithropótamos r. Greece see Erydropotamos
►Eritrea country Africa 89 H6
africa 86–87, 100
Erkech-Tam Kyrg. 81 H2
Erkner Germany 37 F2
Erlangen Germany 36 E4
Erlangping China 67 D1
Erlong Shan mt. China 64 B4
Erlanger U.S.A. 130 B5
Erlong r. Rep. of Ireland 35 C5
Ermelo S. Africa 99 F5
Ermenek Turkey 78 C3
Ermenek r. Turkey 77 A1
Ermil Sudan 89 E6
Ermont Egypt see Armant
Ermoupoli Greece 47 D6
Ernakulam India 72 C4
Erne r. Rep. of Ireland/U.K. 35 B4
Ernée r. France 38 C2
Ernest Giles Range hills Australia 109 C6
Ernest Sound sea chan. U.S.A. 122 C4
Erode India 72 C4
Eromanga Australia 111 E5
Erongo admin. reg. Namibia 98 B4
Erqu China see Zhouzhi
Errabiddy Hills Australia 109 A6
Er Rachidia Morocco 90 D3
Er Rahad Sudan 89 F6
Erramala Hills India 72 C3
Er Raoui des. Alg. 90 D3
Er Renk Sudan 96 B2
Errego Moz. 99 H3
Errinundra National Park Australia 112 D5
Erris Head Rep. of Ireland 35 A4
Er Rogel Sudan 89 G5
Erromango i. Vanuatu 107 F3
Erronan i. Vanuatu see Futuna
Er Roseires Sudan 96 B2
Er Rua'at Sudan 89 G6
Erseké Albania 47 B4
Ersekë Albania see Erseke
Erskine U.S.A. 132 C2
Ertil' Rus. Fed. 29 G6
Ertis r. Kazakh./Rus. Fed. see Irtysh
Ertix He r. China/Kazakh. 70 D2
Eruh Turkey 79 E3
Erufu Nigeria 93 G3
Eruwa Nigeria 93 F4
Erval Brazil 152 G3
Erve r. France 38 C2
Erwitte Germany 36 D3
Erwood Canada 123 K5
Erxleben Germany 36 E2
Erzgebirge mts Czech Rep./Germany 37 F3
Erzhan China 64 A2
Erzincan Turkey 79 D3
Erzurum Turkey 79 E3
Esa-ala P.N.G. 107 I2
Esan-misaki pt Japan 64 F4
Esbjerg Denmark 33 C4
Esbo Fin. see Espoo
Escada Brazil 150 F4
Escalante r. U.S.A. 137 G3
Escalante Desert U.S.A. 137 F3
Escalón Mex. 126 F5
Escalon U.S.A. 136 B3
Escambia r. U.S.A. 129 B6
Escanaba U.S.A. 132 E2
Escárcega Mex. 127 H8
Escàrdena, Puerto de pass Spain 43 F2
Escatrón Spain 43 F2
Escaut r. Belgium 39 E1
Esch-sur-Alzette Lux. 39 F2
Eschwege Germany 36 E3
Eschweiler Germany 36 C3
Escoma Bol. 148 C3
Escondido r. Mex. 133 A6
Escondido U.S.A. 136 D5
Escudilla mt. U.S.A. 137 H5
Escuinapa Mex. 126 E7
Escuintla Guat. 138 F6
Escusa mt. Spain 42 D2
Esèka Cameroon 93 H5
Ese-Khayya Rus. Fed. 27 N3
Eşen Turkey 47 F4
Esenguly Turkm. 80 C2
Esenköy Turkey 46 F4
Esenyurt Turkey 46 F4
Esera r. Spain 43 G1
Eşfahân prov. Iran 80 C3
Esfandak Iran 81 E5
Esfarâyen, Reshteh-ye mts Iran 81 D2
Esfideh Iran 81 D3
Esgueva r. Spain 42 D2
Eshan China 66 B3
Eshkamesh Afgh. 81 G2
Eshowe S. Africa 99 G6
Esikhawini S. Africa 99 G6
Esil Kazakh. see Yesil'
Esil r. Kazakh./Rus. Fed. see Ishim
Esino r. Italy 44 D3
Esk r. Australia 112 C5
Esk r. U.K. 34 E4
Esker Canada 125 H2
Eskifjördur Iceland 32 [inset]
Eskilstuna Sweden 33 E4
Eskimo Lakes Canada 120 F3
Eskimo Point Canada see Arviat
Eski Mosul Iraq 79 E3
Eskipazar Turkey 78 C2
Eskişehir Turkey 78 B3
Esla r. Spain 42 C2
Esla, Embalse de resr Spain see Ricobayo, Embalse de
Eslâmâbâd-e Gharb Iran 80 A3
Eslâmshahr Iran 80 C3
Esler Dağı mt. Turkey 47 F5
Eslöv Sweden 33 D5
Eşme Turkey 78 B3
Esmä'íl-ye Soflá Iran 80 D4
Eşme Turkey 78 B3
Esmeralda Cuba 129 D8
Esmeralda, Isla i. Chile 153 B7
Esmeraldas Ecuador 146 B4
Esmeraldas prov. Ecuador 146 B4
Esmont U.S.A. 130 D5
Espakeh Iran 81 E5
Espalha r. Brazil see São Francisco
Espalion France 39 E4
Espalmador, Isla i. Spain see S'Espalmador
España country Europe see Spain
Espanola Canada 124 D4
Espanola U.S.A. 135 F4
Esparto U.S.A. 136 A2
Espelette France 38 C5
Esperance Australia 109 C8
Esperance Bay Australia 109 C8
Esperantinópolis Brazil 150 D3
Esperanza research station Antarctica 167 A2
Esperanza Santa Cruz Arg. 153 C7
Esperanza Santa Fé Arg. 152 E2
Esperanza Mex. 135 E8
Esperanza Peru 148 C2
Espichel, Cabo c. Port. 42 B3
Espiel Spain 42 D3
Espigão, Serra do mts Brazil 151 B8
Espinazo Mex. 133 A7
Espinhaço, Serra do mts Brazil 151 D6
Espinheira Angola 95 B9

Espinheira hill Port. 42 C3
Espinho Port. 42 B2
Espinilho, Serra do hills Brazil 151 A9
Espino Venez. 147 E2
Espinosa Brazil 150 D5
Espinosa de los Monteros Spain 42 E1
Espírito Santo Brazil see Vila Velha
Espírito Santo state Brazil 151 D6
Espíritu Santo Bol. 148 D4
Espíritu Santo i. Vanuatu 107 F3
Espíritu Santo, Isla i. Mex. 138 B4
Esplanada Brazil 150 E4
Espoo Fin. 33 G3
Espuña mt. Spain 43 F4
Espungabera Moz. 99 G4
Esquel Arg. 153 C5
Esquina Arg. 152 F2
Esrange Sweden 32 F2
Essaouira Morocco 90 C3
Essé Cameroon 93 H4
Es Semara W. Sahara 90 C3
►Essen Germany 36 C3
5th most populous city in Europe.
world 16–17
Essendon, Mount Australia 109 C6
Essex Canada 130 B2
Essex CA U.S.A. 137 E4
Essex NY U.S.A. 131 G1
Essex Junction U.S.A. 131 G1
Esslingen am Neckar Germany 36 D4
Esso Rus. Fed. 27 P4
Essonne r. France 38 E2
Estats, Pic d' mt. France/Spain 43 G1
Estcourt S. Africa 99 F6
Este Italy 44 C2
Esteban de Urízar Arg. 149 D5
Esteli Nicaragua 138 G6
Estella Spain 43 F1
Estena r. Spain 42 D3
Estepa Spain 42 D4
Estepona Spain 42 D4
Esternay France 39 E2
Esterhazy Canada 123 K5
Estero Bay U.S.A. 136 B4
Esteros Para. 149 E5
Estes Park U.S.A. 134 F4
Estevan Canada 123 K5
Estherville U.S.A. 132 C3
Estill U.S.A. 129 C5
Estiva r. Brazil 150 D4
Eston Canada 123 I5
►Estonia country Europe 33 G4
europe 30–31
Estonskaya S.S.R. country Europe see Estonia
Estreito Brazil 152 H2
Estrela, Serra da mts Port. 42 C2
Estrela mt. Spain 42 D3
Estrella, Punta pt Mex. 135 D7
Estrella, Sierra mts U.S.A. 137 F5
Estremadura reg. Port. 42 B3
Estremoz Port. 42 C3
Estrondo, Serra hills Brazil 150 B4
Estuaire prov. Gabon 94 A4
Estún Iran 80 B3
Esztergom Hungary 37 I5
Etadunna Australia 110 D5
Etah India 74 C3
Étain France 39 F2
Etamamiou Canada 125 J3
Étampes France 38 E2
Étaples France 38 E1
Etawah Rajasthan India 74 C3
Etawah Uttar Pradesh India 74 C4
Etelä-Suomi prov. Fin. 33 G3
eThandakukhanya S. Africa 99 G5
Ethel watercourse Australia 109 D6
Ethelbert Canada 123 K5
Ethel Creek Australia 108 C4
E'Thembini S. Africa 98 D6
Etheridge r. Australia 111 E3
►Ethiopia country Africa 96 C2
3rd most populous country in Africa.
africa 86–87, 100
Ethiopian Highlands mts Eth. 96 C2
Etili Turkey 47 E5
Etimesğut Turkey 78 C3
Etna r. Norway 33 C3
Etna, Mount vol. Sicily Italy 45 E6
Etne Norway 33 C3
Etobicoke Canada 130 D2
Etolin Island U.S.A. 122 C3
Etorofu-tö i. Rus. Fed. see Iturup, Ostrov
Etosha National Park Namibia 98 B3
Etosha Pan salt pan Namibia 98 C3
Etoumbi Congo 94 B4
Etowah r. U.S.A. 133 C5
Etropole Bulg. 46 D3
Ettelbruck Lux. 39 G2
Ettumanur India 72 C4
Etxarri-Aranatz Spain see Echarri-Aranaz
Etzicom Coulee r. Canada 123 I5
Eua i. Tonga 107 H4
Eubank U.S.A. 130 A5
Euboea i. Greece see Evvoia
Eucla Australia 109 E7
Euclid U.S.A. 130 C3
Euclides da Cunha Brazil 150 E4
Eucumbene, Lake Australia 112 C5
Eudora U.S.A. 133 D5
Eudunda Australia 112 A4
Eufaula AL U.S.A. 129 B6
Eufaula Lake resr U.S.A. 133 C5
Eugene U.S.A. 134 B3
Eugenia, Punta pt Mex. 135 D8
Eugowra Australia 112 C4
Eulo Australia 111 F6
Eungella National Park Australia 111 G4
Eunice LA U.S.A. 133 C6
Eunice NM U.S.A. 133 A5
►Euphrates r. Asia 76 C3
Longest river in western Asia. Also known as Al Furāt (Iraq/Syria) or Firat (Turkey).
Eura Fin. 33 F3
Eure r. France 38 D2
Eureka CA U.S.A. 134 A4
Eureka KS U.S.A. 132 B4
Eureka MT U.S.A. 134 D2
Eureka NV U.S.A. 137 E2
Eureka OH U.S.A. 130 D4
Eureka SD U.S.A. 132 B2
Eureka UT U.S.A. 137 F2

Eureka Springs U.S.A. 133 C4
Eureka Valley U.S.A. 136 D3
Eurinilla watercourse Australia 112 B3
Euriowie Australia 112 B3
Euroa Australia 112 C5
Europa, Île i. Indian Ocean 162 J7
Europa, Picos de mts Spain 42 D1
Europa, Punta de pt Spain see
  Europa Point
Europa Point Gibraltar 42 D4
Eustis U.S.A. 129 C6
Eutaw U.S.A. 129 B5
Eutsuk Lake Canada 122 E4
Evale Angola 95 B9
Evans, Lac l. Canada 124 E3
Evansburg Canada 123 H4
Evans City U.S.A. 130 E3
Evans Ice Stream Antarctica 167 L1
Evanston IL U.S.A. 132 E3
Evanston WY U.S.A. 134 E4
Evansville IN U.S.A. 132 B4
Evansville WI U.S.A. 134 F4
Eva Perón Arg. see La Plata
Eva Perón prov. Arg. see La Pampa
Evaton S. Africa 99 E5
Evaz Iran 80 C5
Evening Shade U.S.A. 133 D4
Evensk Rus. Fed. 31 P3
Everard, Lake salt flat Australia 109 F7
Everard, Mount Australia 110 C4
Everek Turkey see Develi

▶Everest, Mount China/Nepal 75 E4
  Highest mountain in the world and in Asia.
  asia 50–51
  world 6–7

Everett PA U.S.A. 130 D3
Everett WA U.S.A. 134 B3
▶Everglades swamp U.S.A. 129 C7
  world 14–15
Everglades National Park U.S.A.
  129 C7
Evergreen U.S.A. 129 B6
Everman, Volcán vol. Mex. 126 D8
Everson U.S.A. 134 B2
Evertsberg Sweden 33 D3
Evesham U.K. 35 F5
Évian-les-Bains France 39 G3
Evijärvi Fin. 32 E3
Evinayong Equat. Guinea 93 H5
Evington U.S.A. 130 D5
Evinos r. Greece 47 B5
Evje Norway 33 B4
Evolène Switz. 39 G3
Évora Port. 42 C3
Évora admin. dist. Port. 42 C3
Evoron, Ozero l. Rus. Fed. 64 D2
Evosmo Greece 46 C4
Evowghlī Iran 80 B2
Évreux France 38 D2
Évron France 38 D2
Evros r. Greece/Turkey 46 E4
Evrotas r. Greece 47 C6
Évry France 39 E2
Evvoia i. Greece 47 D5
Ewan Australia 111 F4
Ewaso Ngiro r. Kenya 96 D4
Ewasi, Lake salt l. Tanz. 96 B5
Ewawadi r. Myanmar see Irrawaddy
Eyeberry Lake Canada 123 I2
Eyelenoborsk Rus. Fed. 28 L2
Eyemouth U.K. 34 F4
Eyjafjallajökull ice cap Iceland 32 [inset]
Eyjafjörður inlet Iceland 32 [inset]
Eyl Somalia 96 F3
Eylau Rus. Fed. see Bagrationovsk
Eymet France 38 D4
Eymir Turkey 47 F6
Eymoutiers France 38 D4
Eyre r. France 38 D4
Eyre (South), Lake salt flat Australia 110 D6

▶Eyre, Lake salt flat Australia 110 D6
  Largest lake in Oceania and lowest point.
  oceania 102–103

Eyre Creek watercourse Australia
  110 D5
Eyre Mountains N.Z. 113 B7
Eyre Peninsula Australia 109 F8
Eyrieux r. France 39 F4
Eysturoy i. Faroe Is 34 [inset]
Eyuku waterhole Kenya 96 C5
Eyvānaki Iran 80 C3
Ezakheni S. Africa 99 F6
Ezel U.S.A. 130 D5
Ezequiel Ramos Mexía, Embalse resr
  Arg. 152 C4
Ezernieki Latvia 33 G4
Ezhou China 67 G2
Ezine Turkey 78 A3
Ezinepazar Turkey 78 D2
Ezo i. Japan see Hokkaidō
Ezousa r. Cyprus 77 A2
Ezra's Tomb tourist site Iraq 79 F3

Faadhippolhu Atoll Maldives 72 35
Fabens U.S.A. 135 F7
Faber, Mount Sing. 58 [inset]
Faber Lake Canada 123 G2
Fåborg Denmark 33 C5
Fabriano Italy 44 D3
Facatativá Col. 146 C3

Fachi Niger 93 H1
Factoryville U.S.A. 131 F3
Fada Chad 88 D5
Fada-Ngourma Burkina 93 F2
Fadnoun, Plateau du Alg. 91 H4
Faenza Italy 44 C2
Færingehavn Greenland see
  Kangerluarsoruseq
Færoerne terr. N. Atlantic Ocean see
  Faroe Islands
Faeroes terr. N. Atlantic Ocean see
  Faroe Islands
Fafa r. Cent. Afr. Rep. 94 C3
Fafanlap Indon. 57 H6
Fafe Port. 42 B2
Fafen Shet' watercourse Eth. 96 E3
Fāgāraş Romania 46 D2

▶Fagatogo American Samoa 107 H3
  Capital of American Samoa.

Fagersta Sweden 33 D4
Făget Romania 46 C2
Fagnano, Lago l. Arg./Chile 153 C8
Fagne reg. Belgium 39 F1
Fagochia well Niger 93 H1
Faguibine, Lac l. Mali 92 D1
Fagurhólsmýri Iceland 32 [inset]
Fagwir Sudan 96 A3
Fahlīān, Rūdkhāneh-ye watercourse
  Iran 80 B4
Fahraj Iran 80 E4
Fā'id Egypt 77 A4
Fairbanks U.S.A. 120 E3
Fairborn U.S.A. 130 A4
Fairbury U.S.A. 132 C3
Fairfax U.S.A. 131 G1
Fairfield CA U.S.A. 136 A2
Fairfield IA U.S.A. 132 C3
Fairfield IL U.S.A. 128 A3
Fairfield OH U.S.A. 130 A4
Fairfield TX U.S.A. 133 B6
Fairgrove U.S.A. 130 D2
Fair Haven U.S.A. 131 G2
Fair Hill U.S.A. 131 F4
Fair Head U.K. 34 C2
Fairlee U.S.A. 131 H2
Fairmont MN U.S.A. 132 C3
Fairmont WV U.S.A. 130 C4
Fairmont Hot Springs Canada 123 H5
Fairplay U.S.A. 134 F5
Fairplay, Mount U.S.A. 122 A2
Fairview Australia 111 F4
Fairview Canada 122 G3
Fairview KY U.S.A. 130 B4
Fairview OK U.S.A. 133 B4
Fairview PA U.S.A. 130 F2
Fairview Park Hong Kong China 67 [inset]
Fairweather, Mount Canada/U.S.A.
  120 F1
Fais i. Micronesia 57 J4
Faisalabad Pak. 81 H4
Faizabad Afgh. see Feyzābād
Faizabad India 75 D4
Fajr, Wādī watercourse Saudi Arabia
  89 H2
Fakaofo atoll Tokelau 164 G6
Fakenham U.K. 35 G5
Fakfak Indon. 57 H6
Fakhrabad Iran 80 D5
Fakiragram India 75 F4
Fakiyska Reka r. Bulg. 46 E3
Fakse Denmark 33 D5
Fakse Bugt b. Denmark 33 D5
Falaba Sierra Leone 92 C3
Falagountou Burkina 93 F2
Falaise France 38 C2
Falaise Lake Canada 123 G2
Falakata India 75 F4
Falam Myanmar 60 A1
Falavarjan Iran 80 B3
Fălciu Romania 46 F1
Falcón state Venez. 146 D2
Falconara Marittima Italy 44 D3
Falcone, Capo del c. Sardinia Italy
  44 C4
Falcon Island Tonga see Fonuafo'ou
Falcon Lake Canada 123 M5
Falcon Lake l. Mex./U.S.A. 133 B7
Falelima Samoa 107 H3
Falémé r. Mali/Senegal 92 B2
Falerii Italy see Civita Castellana
Falfurrias U.S.A. 133 B7
Falher Canada 123 G4
Falkenberg Germany 37 F3
Falkenberg Sweden 33 D4
Falkensee Germany 37 F2
Falkirk U.K. 34 E4

▶Falkland Islands terr.
  S. Atlantic Ocean 153 F7
  United Kingdom Overseas Territory.
  southamerica 144–145, 154

Falkland Plateau sea feature
  S. Atlantic Ocean 161 K9
Falkland Sound sea chan. Falkland Is
  153 E8
Falkner Arg. 152 D5
Falköping Sweden 33 D4
Fall r. U.S.A. 132 C4
Fallieres Coast Antarctica 167 L2
Fallon U.S.A. 136 C2
Fall River U.S.A. 131 H3
Fall River Pass U.S.A. 134 F4
Falls City U.S.A. 132 C3
Falls Creek U.S.A. 133 D3
Falmouth U.K. 35 D6
Falmouth KY U.S.A. 130 C4
Falmouth MA U.S.A. 131 H3
Falmouth ME U.S.A. 130 E4
Falou Mali 92 D2
False r. Canada 125 F2
False Bay S. Africa 98 C7
False Point India 75 E1
Falso Cabo de Hornos c. Chile 153 C8
Fălticeni Romania 31 K4
Falun Sweden 33 D3
Falzarego, Passo di pass Italy 44 D1
Famagusta Cyprus 77 A2
Famagusta Bay Cyprus see
  Ammochostos Bay
Famatina, Sierra de mts Arg. 152 C2
Famenin Iran 80 B3
Fame Range hills Australia 109 C6
Family Well Australia 108 D5
Fana Mali 92 D2
Fanandrana Madag. 99 [inset] K3
Fanchang China 67 G2
Fandriana Madag. 99 [inset] J4
Fangak Sudan 96 A2
Fangcheng Guangxi China see
  Fangchenggang
Fangcheng Henan China 67 F1
Fangchenggang China 67 D4
Fangdou Shan mts China 67 F2
Fangshan Taiwan 67 F4
Fangxian China 67 D1

Fangzheng China 64 B3
Fani i Vogël r. Albania 46 A4
Fankuai China 66 D2
Fankuaidian China see Fankuai
Fanling Hong Kong China 67 [inset]
Fannrem Norway 32 C3
Fannūj Iran 81 D5
Fanø i. Denmark 33 B5
Fanouaile i. Tonga see Fonualei
Fanshan China 67 G3
Fan Si Pan mt. Vietnam 60 C3
Fanum Fortunae Italy see Fano
Farab Turkm. see Farap
Faradje Dem. Rep. Congo 94 F4
Faradofay Madag. see Tôlañaro
Farafangana Madag. 99 [inset] J4
Farafenni Gambia 92 B2
Farāfirah, Wāḥāt al Egypt see Farafra
  Oasis
Farafra Oasis Egypt 89 F3
Farāgheh Iran 80 C4
Farāh Afgh. 81 E3
Farāh prov. Afgh. 81 E3
Farahābād Iran see Khezerābād
Farah Rūd watercourse Afgh. 81 E4
Farakhulm Afgh. 81 H2
Farallon de Medinilla i. N. Mariana Is
  57 K2
Farallon de Pajaros vol. N. Mariana Is
  57 J1
Farallones de Cali, Parque Nacional
  nat. park Col. 146 B3
Faramuti i. Sudan 94 E2
Faranah Guinea 92 C3
Faraoani Romania 46 E1
Far'aoun well Mauritania 92 B1
Farap Turkm. 81 E2
Farāsān, Jazā'ir is Saudi Arabia 89 I5
Faratsiho Madag. 99 [inset] J3
Faraulep atoll Micronesia 57 J5
Fardes r. Spain 42 E4
Farewell, Cape Greenland 121 O3
Farewell, Cape N.Z. 113 C3
Farewell Spit N.Z. 113 C3
Färgelanda Sweden 33 D4
Farghona Uzbek. see Fergana
Farghona Wiloyati admin. div. Uzbek.
  see Ferganskaya Oblast'
Fargo U.S.A. 132 D2
Faribault U.S.A. 132 C2
Faribault, Lac l. Canada 125 G1
Faridabad India 74 C3
Faridkot India 74 C3
Faridpur Bangl. 75 F5
Faridpur India 74 C3
Fārīg r. Iran 81 D2
Farīgh, Wādī al watercourse Libya 88 C2
Farīmān Iran 81 D3
Farinha r. Brazil 150 C3
Farish Uzbek. 81 F1
Färjestaden Sweden 33 E4
Farkadhon Greece 47 C5
Farkhar Afgh. see Farkhato
Farkhato Afgh. 81 H2
Farkhor Tajik. 81 G2
Farmahin Iran 80 B3
Farmer City U.S.A. 132 D3
Farmer Island Canada 124 D1
Farmerville U.S.A. 133 C5
Farmington ME U.S.A. 131 H1
Farmington MO U.S.A. 132 C4
Farmington NH U.S.A. 131 H2
Farmington NM U.S.A. 135 I3
Farmington UT U.S.A. 134 E4
Farmington Hills U.S.A. 130 D2
Farmville U.S.A. 130 D5
Farne Islands U.K. 34 F4
Farnham U.K. 35 F6
Farnham, Lake salt flat Australia 109 D6
Farnham, Mount Canada 123 G5
Far North Section Australia see
  Great Barrier Reef Marine Park
  (Far North Section)
Faro Brazil 147 G5
Faro r. Cameroon 93 I3
Faro Canada 122 C2
Faro Port. 42 C4
Faro admin. dist. Port. 42 B4
Fårö i. Sweden 33 E4
Faro, Serra do mts Spain 42 C1
Faroe-Iceland Ridge sea feature
  Arctic Ocean 166 I2

▶Faroe Islands terr. N. Atlantic Ocean
  34 [inset]
  Self-governing Danish Territory.
  europe 24–25, 48

Fårösund Sweden 33 E4
Farquhar Atoll i. Seychelles 97 F7
Farquhar Islands Seychelles 97 F7
Farquharson Tableland hills Australia
  109 C6
Farrandsville U.S.A. 130 E3
Farrars Creek watercourse Australia
  111 E5
Farrāshband Iran 80 C4
Farr Bay Antarctica 167 E2
Farrokhī Iran 81 D3
Farrukhabad India see Fatehgarh
Fārs prov. Iran 80 C4
Farsakh Iran 80 C4
Farsala Greece 47 C5
Farson U.S.A. 134 F4
Farsund Norway 33 B4
Fārtāq, Ra's pt Yemen 77 H6
Fartura, Serra da mts Brazil 151 A8
Farvel, Kap c. Greenland see
  Farewell, Cape
Farwell U.S.A. 133 A5
Fāryāb prov. Afgh. 81 F2
Fāryāb Hormozgan Iran 80 D5
Fāryāb Kermān Iran 80 D4
Fasā Iran 80 D4
Fasano Italy 45 F4
Faşikan Geçidi pass Turkey 77 A1
Fasil Ghebbi and Gonder Monuments
  tourist site Eth. 96 C1
Fastiv Ukr. 29 D6
Fastov Ukr. see Fastiv
Fatehabad India 74 B3
Fatehgarh Madhya Pradesh India 74 C4
Fatehgarh Uttar Pradesh India 74 C4
Fatehnagar India 74 B4
Fatehpur Rajasthan India 74 B4
Fatehpur Uttar Pradesh India 74 C4
Fatehpur Sikri India 74 C4
Fathābād Iran 80 D4
Fathai Sudan 96 A2
Fati, Lac l. Mali 92 D1
Fatick Senegal 92 A2
Fattoilep atoll Micronesia see Faraulep
Fatuma Dem. Rep. Congo 95 F4
Faulkton U.S.A. 132 C2
Fauquier Canada 122 G5
Fauresmith S. Africa 98 E6
Fauske Norway 32 D2
Favalto, Monte mt. Italy 44 D3
Favignana Sicily Italy 45 D6
Favignana, Isola i. Sicily Italy 45 D6
Fawcett Canada 123 H4
Fawn r. Canada 124 D3
Fawwārah Saudi Arabia 89 I3

Faxaflói b. Iceland 32 [inset]
Faxälven r. Sweden 32 E3
Ferlo, Vallée du watercourse Senegal
  92 B2
Faya Chad 88 C5
Fayaoué New Caledonia 107 F4
Fayette MO U.S.A. 132 H2
Fayette MS U.S.A. 133 D6
Fayette OH U.S.A. 130 A3
Fayetteville AR U.S.A. 133 C4
Fayetteville NC U.S.A. 128 E5
Fayetteville NY U.S.A. 131 E2
Fayetteville PA U.S.A. 130 E4
Fayetteville TN U.S.A. 128 B5
Fayetteville WV U.S.A. 130 C4
Faylakah i. Kuwait 79 G5
Fayrān well Egypt 77 A5
Fayrān, Wādī watercourse Egypt 77 A5
Fayu i. Micronesia 77 B5
Fazair al Mazhūmah watercourse
  Saudi Arabia 77 C5
Fazao Malfakassa, Parc National de
  nat. park Togo 93 F3
Fazeï well Niger 93 H1
Fazilka India 74 B3
Fazran, Jabal hill Saudi Arabia 76 C4
Fderīk Mauritania 90 B5
Fead Group is P.N.G. see
  Nuguria Islands
Feale r. Rep. of Ireland 35 B5
Fear, Cape U.S.A. 129 D5
Feather r. U.S.A. 136 C2
Feather, North Fork r. U.S.A. 136 C2
Featherston N.Z. 113 C3
Fécamp France 38 D2
Federación Bosna i Hercegovina
  aut. div. Bos.-Herz. 44 G2
Federal Arg. 152 F2
Federal Capital Territory admin. div.
  Nigeria 93 G3
Federal District admin. dist. Brazil see
  Distrito Federal
Federal District admin. dist. Venez. see
  Distrito Federal
Federalsburg U.S.A. 131 F4
Federated Malay States country Asia
  see Malaysia
Federation of Bosnia and Herzegovina
  aut. div. Bos.-Herz. see
  Federacija Bosna i Hercegovina
Fedorov Kazakh. see Fedorovka
Fedorovka Kazakh. 29 I6
Fehet Lake Canada 123 M1
Fehmarn i. Germany 36 E1
Fehmarn Belt strait Denmark/Germany
  33 C5
Fehmarnbelt strait Denmark/Germany see
  Fehmarn Belt
Feia, Lagoa lag. Brazil 151 D7
Feidong China 67 F2
Feijó Brazil 148 C2
Feilding N.Z. 113 C3
Feio r. Brazil see Aguapeí
Feira Zambia see Luangwa
Feira de Santana Brazil 150 E5
Feira do Monte Spain 42 C1
Feixi China 67 F2
Feixian China 67 G1
Fejaj, Chott el salt l. Tunisia 91 H2
Fejø i. Denmark 36 E1
Feke Turkey 77 B1
Felanitx Spain 43 H3
Feldberg mt. Germany 39 G3
Feldkirch Austria 39 G3
Feldkirchen in Kärnten Austria 37 G5
Feliciano r. Arg. 152 F2
Felicity U.S.A. 130 A4
Felidhu Atoll Maldives 71 D11
Felixlândia Brazil 151 C6
Felixstowe U.K. 35 G6
Felletin France 38 E4
Fellowsville U.S.A. 130 D4
Felsberg Germany 36 D3
Felsina Italy see Bologna
Femeas r. Brazil 150 C5
Femer Bælt strait Denmark/Germany see
  Fehmarn Belt
Femminamorta, Monte mt. Italy 45 F5
Femundsmarka Nasjonalpark nat. park
  Norway 33 D3
Fenelon Falls Canada 130 D1
Fener Burnu hd Turkey 77 B1
Fénérive Madag. see
  Fenoarivo Atsinanana
Fengari mt. Greece 46 D4
Fengcheng Fujian China see Yongding
Fengcheng Guangdong China see
  Xinfeng
Fengcheng Guangxi China see Fengshan
Fengcheng Jiangxi China 67 G2
Fengcheng Liaoning China 65 A4
Fengdu China 66 C2
Fenggang Fujian China see Shaxian
Fenggang Guizhou China 66 C3
Fenggang Jiangxi China see Yihuang
Fenggeling China 66 C1
Fenghua China 67 G2
Fenghuang China 67 D3
Fengjiaba China see Wangcang
Fengjie China 67 D2
Fengkai China 67 E3
Fenglin Taiwan 67 F4
Fengning China 65 A2
Fengqing China 66 C4
Fengqiu China 67 F1
Fengshan Fujian China see Luoyuan
Fengshan Guangxi China 66 C3
Fengshan Hubei China see Luotian
Fengshan Yunnan China see Fengqing
Fengshuba Shuiku resr China 67 E3
Fengtai China 67 F1
Fengxian Jiangsu China 67 F1
Fengxian Shaanxi China 66 D1
Fengxian Shanghai China 67 G2
Fengxiang Heilong. China see Luobei
Fengxiang Yunnan China see Lincang
Fengyang China 67 F1
Fengyi China see Zheng'an
Fengyi Sichuan China see Maoxian
Fengyüan Taiwan 67 F4
Fengzhen China 63 I3
Feni Bangl. 75 F5
Feni Islands P.N.G. 107 E2
Fenny r. Bangl./India 75 F5
Fenton U.S.A. 130 B2
Fenwick U.S.A. 130 C4
Fenyi China 67 F3
Feodosiya Ukr. 78 C1
Fer, Cap de c. Alg. 91 G1
Féraï Greece see Feres
Ferdows Iran 80 D3
Fère-Champenoise France 39 F2
Fère-en-Tardenois France 39 E2
Feres Greece 46 E4
Fergana Uzbek. 81 G1
Fergana Oblast admin. div. Uzbek. see
  Ferganskaya Oblast'
Ferganskaya Oblast' admin. div. Uzbek.
  81 G1
Fergus Canada 130 C2
Fergus Falls U.S.A. 132 B2
Ferguson Lake Canada 123 L2
Fergusson Island P.N.G. 107 E2
Fériana Tunisia 91 H2
Ferjukot Iceland 32 [inset]
Ferkessédougou Côte d'Ivoire 92 D3

Ferlach Austria 37 G5
Fermont Canada 125 H2
Fermoselle Spain 42 C2
Fermoy Rep. of Ireland 35 B5
Fernandina Beach U.S.A. 129 C6
Fernandina, Isla i. Galápagos
  Ecuador see Narborough, Isla
Fernando de Magallanes, Parque
  Nacional nat. park Chile 153 B8
Fernando de Noronha i. Braz 161 LE
Fernandópolis Brazil 149 H5
Fernando Póo i. Equat. Guinea see
  Bioco
Fernão Veloso Moz. 97 D8
Fernie Canada 122 H5
Fernie Australia 111 F6
Fernley U.S.A. 136 C2
Ferns Rep. of Ireland 35 C5
Feroze Haryana India 74 C3
Ferozepur Haryana India 74 B3
Ferozepore India see Firozpur
Ferrara Italy 44 C2
Ferrato, Capo c. Sardinia Italy 45 B5
Ferreira do Alentejo Port. 42 C4
Ferreira-Gomes Brazil 147 I4
Ferrellsburg U.S.A. 130 D5
Ferreñafe Peru 148 B5
Ferriday U.S.A. 133 D6
Ferro r. Brazil 151 B6
Ferrol Spain 42 B1
Ferron U.S.A. 137 G2
Ferrum U.S.A. 130 C5
Ferryland Canada 125 K4
Ferryville Tunisia see Menzel Bourguiba
Fertö-tavi r. nat. park Hungary 37 H5
Fès Morocco 90 D2
Feshi Dem. Rep. Congo 95 C6
Fessenden U.S.A. 132 B2
Fété Bowé Senegal 92 B2
Fetesti Romania 46 E2
Fetești-Gară Romania 46 E2
Fethiye Turkey see Yazihan
Fethiye Muğla Turkey 78 B3
Fetisovo Kazakh. 79 H2
Fetlar i. U.K. 34 F1
Fevral'sk Rus. Fed. 64 B1
Feyzābād Afgh. 81 H2
Fez Morocco see Fès
Fiambalá Arg. 152 C1
Fian Ghana 93 D2
Fianarantsoa Madag. 99 [inset] J4
Fianarantsoa prov. Madag. 99 [inset] J4
Fianga Chad 93 H3
Ficalho hill Port. 42 C4
Fiche Eth. 76 B8
Fidenza Italy 44 C2
Fidjedt Norway 33 B4
Fidlův Kopec hill Czech Rep. 37 H4
Field U.S.A. 130 B5
Field Island Australia 110 C3
Fieni Romania 46 D2
Fier Albania 46 A4
Fierzes, Liqeni i resr Albania 46 B3
Fife Ness pt U.K. 34 E3
Fifth Cataract rapids Sudan see
  5th Cataract
Fifth Meridian Canada 123 H3
Figari, Capo c. Sardinia Italy 44 B4
Figeac France 38 E4
Figueira r. Arg. 152 F2
Figueira da Foz Port. 42 B2
Figueras Spain see Figueres
Figueres Spain 43 H1
Figuig Morocco 91 E2
Figuil Cameroon 93 I3

▶Fiji country S. Pacific Ocean 107 G3
  4th most populous and 5th largest
  country in Oceania.
  oceania 104–105, 114

Fik' Eth. 96 E3
Filabusi Zimbabwe 99 F4
Filadelfia Italy 45 F5
Filadelfia Para. 149 E5
Fiľakovo Slovakia 37 I4
Filamana Mali 92 D3
Filchner Ice Shelf Antarctica 167 A1
Filey U.K. 35 F4
Filiaşi Romania 46 C2
Filiates Greece 47 B5
Filiatra Greece 47 B6
Filibe Bulg. see Plovdiv
Filicudi, Isola i. Isole Lipari Italy 45 E5
Filingué Niger 93 F2
Filiouri r. Greece 46 D4
Filipinas country Asia see Philippines
Filippiada Greece 47 B5
Filippoi tourist site Greece 46 D4
Filipstad Sweden 33 D4
Filian Norway 32 C3
Fillmore CA U.S.A. 136 D4
Fillmore UT U.S.A. 137 F2
Filtu Eth. 96 E3
Fimbull Ice Shelf Antarctica 167 B2
Finale Ligure Italy 44 B2
Fincastle U.S.A. 130 D5
Finch'a'ā Häyk' l. Eth. 96 E2
Findhorn r. U.K. 34 E3
Findik Turkey 79 E3
Findlay U.S.A. 130 D3
Fine U.S.A. 131 F1
Finger Lake Canada 123 M4
Finger Lakes U.S.A. 131 E3
Fingoè Moz. 97 A8
Finiels, Sommet de mt. France 39 F4
Finike Turkey 78 B3
Finike Körfezi b. Turkey 78 B3
Finisterre Spain see Fisterra
Finisterre, Cabo c. Spain see
  Finisterre, Cape
Finisterre, Cape Spain 42 B1
Finke Australia 110 C5
Finke watercourse Australia 110 C5
Finke Flood Flats lowland Australia
  110 C5
Finke Gorge National Park Australia
  110 C5
Finland country Europe 32 G3
  europe 24–25, 48
Finland, Gulf of Europe 33 G3
Finlay r. Canada 122 E3
Finlay, Mount Canada 122 E3
Finlay Forks Canada 122 F4
Finley Australia 112 B5
Finley U.S.A. 132 B2
Finn r. Rep. of Ireland 34 C1
Finne ridge Germany 36 E3
Finnigan, Mount Australia 111 F3
Finniss, Cape Australia 109 F8
Finnmark county Norway 32 G1
Finnmarksvidda reg. Norway 32 F1
Finnskog Norway 33 D3
Finnsnes Norway 32 E1
Finschhafen P.N.G. 106 F2
Finspång Sweden 33 D4
Finsteraarhorn mt. Switz. 39 H3
Finsterwalde Germany 37 F3
Finucane Range hills Australia 111 E4
Fiora r. Italy 44 C3
Fiordland National Park N.Z. 113 A4
Fiorenzuola d'Arda Italy 44 C2
Firat r. Turkey 76 B2 see Euphrates
Firavahana Madag. 99 [inset] J3
Firebaugh U.S.A. 136 C3
Firedrake Lake Canada 123 J2

Firenze Italy see Florence
Fireside Canada 122 E3
Firesteel Creek r. U.S.A. 132 B3
Firīña Venez. 147 E3
Firk, Sha'ib watercourse Iraq 79 F5
Firkachi well Niger 93 I2
Firmat Arg. 152 E2
Firminy France 39 F4
Firovo Rus. Fed. 31 M1
Firozabad India 74 C4
Firozpur Haryana India 74 C3
Firozpur Punjab India 74 B3
First Cataract rapids Egypt see
  1st Cataract
First Three Mile Opening sea chan.
  Australia 111 F2
Firūzābād Iran 80 D2
Firūzeh Iran 80 D2
Firūzkūh Iran 80 C2
Fischbachau Germany 37 E5
Fischersbrunn Namibia 98 B5
Fish watercourse Namibia 98 C6
Fish r. S. Africa 98 D6
Fisher Australia 109 E7
Fisher Bay Antarctica 167 G2
Fisher Glacier Antarctica 167 E1
Fisher Strait Canada 121 K3
Fishersville U.S.A. 130 D4
Fishguard U.K. 35 D6
Fishing Creek U.S.A. 131 E4
Fishing Lake Canada 123 M4
Fish Lake Canada 122 F2
Fish Point U.S.A. 130 D2
Fishponds Hong Kong China 67 [inset]
Fiskå Norway 33 B3
Fiske, Cape Antarctica 167 L2
Fiskebol Norway 32 D1
Fiskenæsset Greenland see
  Qeqertarsuatsiaat
Fismes France 39 E2
Fisterra Spain 42 B1
Fisterra, Cabo Spain see
  Finisterre, Cape
Fitampito Madag. 99 [inset] J4
Fitchburg MA U.S.A. 131 H2
Fitchburg WI U.S.A. 132 D3
Fitchville U.S.A. 130 D3
Fitjar Norway 33 B4
Fitri, Lac l. Chad 88 C6
Fitzcarrald Peru 148 B2
Fitzgerald River National Park Australia
  109 B8
Fitz Hugh Sound sea chan. Canada
  122 D5
Fitzmaurice r. Australia 110 B2
Fitz Roy Arg. 153 C6
Fitzroy r. Qld Australia 111 F4
Fitzroy r. W.A. Australia 110 A3
Fitzroy Crossing Australia 110 A3
Fiume Croatia see Rijeka
Five Points U.S.A. 136 B3
Fivizzano Italy 44 C2
Fizi Dem. Rep. Congo 95 F4
Fizuli Azer. see Füzuli
Fjällsjöäs Sweden 32 E3
Fjellbu Norway 32 E1
Fjerritslev Denmark 33 C4
Flå Norway 33 C3
Flaga Iceland 32 [inset]
Flagstaff U.S.A. 137 G4
Flagstaff Lake U.S.A. 128 F2
Flaherty Island Canada 124 E1
Flåm Norway 33 B3
Flambeau r. U.S.A. 132 D2
Flamborough Head U.K. 35 F4
Fläming hills Germany 37 F3
Flaming Gorge Reservoir U.S.A.
  134 E4
Flannagan Lake U.S.A. 130 B5
Flannan Isles U.K. 34 C2
Flåsjön l. Sweden 32 C3
Flat r. Canada 122 E2
Flat U.S.A. 126 C3
Flathead Lake U.S.A. 134 D3
Flatiron mt. U.S.A. 134 D3
Flat Island S. China Sea 56 F3
Flat Lick U.S.A. 130 D5
Flattery, Cape Australia 111 F2
Flattery, Cape U.S.A. 134 A2
Flat Top mt. Canada 122 B2
Flatwillow Creek r. U.S.A. 134 F3
Flatwoods KY U.S.A. 130 B4
Flatwoods WV U.S.A. 130 C4
Fleetwood U.K. 35 E5
Fleetwood U.S.A. 131 F3
Flekkefjord Norway 33 B4
Flemingsburg U.S.A. 130 B4
Flemington U.S.A. 131 F3
Flemish Cap sea feature
  N. Atlantic Ocean 160 L2
Flen Sweden 33 E4
Flensborg Fjord inlet Denmark/Germany
  33 C5
Flensburg Germany 36 D1
Flensburger Förde inlet
  Denmark/Germany see Flensborg Fjord
Flers France 38 C2
Flesherton Canada 130 C1
Fletcher Lake Canada 123 I2
Fletcher Peninsula Antarctica 167 L2
Fleurance France 38 D5
Fleur de Lys Canada 125 J3
Fleur-de-May, Lac l. Canada 125 I3
Fleury-les-Aubrais France 38 D3
Flinders r. Australia 111 E3
Flinders Chase National Park Australia
  109 G8
Flinders Group National Park Australia
  111 F2
Flinders Island Australia 112 D5
Flinders Passage Australia 111 E3
Flinders Ranges mts Australia 112 A4
Flinders Ranges National Park
  Australia 112 A3
Flinders Reefs Australia 111 F3
Flin Flon Canada 123 K4
Flint U.K. 35 E5
Flint U.S.A. 130 B2
Flint r. GA U.S.A. 129 B6
Flint r. MI U.S.A. 130 D2
Flint Island Kiribati 165 H6
Flintstone U.S.A. 130 D4
Flisa Norway 33 D3
Flisa r. Norway 33 D3

▶Flissingskiy, Mys c. Rus. Fed. 26 G2
  Most easterly point of Europe.

Flix Spain 43 G2
Flöha Germany 37 F3
Flood Range mts Antarctica 167 J1
Flora r. Australia 110 B2
Florac France 39 F4
Florala U.S.A. 129 B6
Flora Reef Australia 111 F3
Floraville Australia 111 E3
Flor de Punga Peru 146 C6
Florence Italy 44 C2
Florence AL U.S.A. 128 B5
Florence AZ U.S.A. 137 G5
Florence KY U.S.A. 130 A4
Florence OR U.S.A. 134 A4
Florence SC U.S.A. 129 D5
Florence Junction U.S.A. 137 G5
Florencia Arg. 152 F2
Florencia Col. 146 C3
Florentia Italy see Florence

Florentino Ameghino Arg. 153 D5
Florentino Ameghino, Embalse resr Arg. 153 D5
Flores Brazil 150 D3
Flores Guat. 138 G5
Flores i. Indon. 57 F7
Florescência Brazil 148 C2
Flores de Goiás Brazil 150 C5
Flores Sea Indon. 57 E7
Floresta Brazil 150 E4
Floresville U.S.A. 133 B6
Floriano Brazil 150 D3
Floriano Peixoto Brazil 148 D2
Florianópolis Brazil 151 B8
Florida Bol. 149 E4
Florida Chile 152 B4
Florida Uruguay 152 F3
▶Florida state U.S.A. 129 C6
northamerica 118–119
Florida, Straits of Bahamas/U.S.A. 129 C8
Florida Bay U.S.A. 129 C7
Florida Keys is U.S.A. 129 C7
Florida Negra Arg. 153 D7
Floridia Sicily Italy 45 E6
Florin U.S.A. 136 B2
Florina Greece 46 B4
Florø Norway 33 B3
Flour Lake Canada 125 H2
Floyd U.S.A. 130 C5
Floyd, Mount U.S.A. 137 F4
Floydada U.S.A. 133 A5
Fluchthorn mt. Austria/Switz. 39 I3
Flums Switz. 39 H3
Flushing Neth. see Vlissingen
Flushing U.S.A. 130 C3
Fluvià r. Spain 43 H1
Fly r. P.N.G. 57 J7
Flying Fish, Cape Antarctica 167 K2
Foam Lake Canada 123 K5
Foča Bos.-Herz. 44 G3
Foça Turkey 78 A3
Focșani Romania 46 E2
Fodé Cent. Afr. Rep. 94 D3
Foelsche r. Australia 110 D2
Fogang China 67 E4
Fogelsville U.S.A. 131 F3
Foggâret el Arab Alg. 91 F4
Foggia Italy 44 E4
Foglia r. Italy 44 D3
Föglö Fin. 33 F3
Fogo i. Cape Verde 92 [inset]
Fogo Island Canada 125 K3
Föhr i. Germany 36 D1
Foinaven hill U.K. 34 D2
Foix France 38 D5
Fokku Nigeria 93 G3
Folarskarnuten mt. Norway 33 B3
Folda sea chan. Norway 32 D2
Foldereid Norway 32 D2
Folegandros Greece 47 D6
Folegandros i. Greece 47 D6
Foley Botswana 99 E4
Foley U.S.A. 129 B6
Foleyet Canada 124 D3
Foligno Italy 44 D3
Folkestone U.K. 35 G6
Folkston U.S.A. 129 C6
Folldal Norway 33 C3
Föllinge Sweden 32 D3
Follonica Italy 44 C3
Folsom U.S.A. 130 C4
Folsom Lake U.S.A. 136 B2
Fomboni Comoros 97 D8
Fomin Rus. Fed. 29 G7
Fominskoye Rus. Fed. 28 G4
Fonda U.S.A. 131 F2
Fond-du-Lac Canada 123 J3
Fond du Lac r. Canada 123 J3
Fond du Lac U.S.A. 132 D3
Fonde U.S.A. 130 B5
Fondevila Spain 42 B2
Fondi Italy 44 D4
Fon Going ridge Guinea 92 C3
Fonni Sardinia Italy 45 B4
Fonsagrada Spain see A Fonsagrada
Fonseca, Golfo do b. Central America 138 G6
Fontainebleau France 39 E2
Fontanges Canada 125 G2
Fontas Canada 122 F3
Fontas r. Canada 122 F3
Fonte Boa Brazil 147 E5
Fonte do Pau-d'Agua Brazil 149 F3
Fontenay-le-Comte France 38 C3
Fonteneau, Lac l. Canada 125 I3
Fontur pt Iceland 32 [inset]
Fonuafo'ou i. Tonga 107 H4
Fonuafu'u i. Tonga see Fonuafo'ou
Fonualei i. Tonga 107 H3
Fonyód Hungary 37 H5
Foochow China see Fuzhou
Foping China 66 D1
Foraker, Mount U.S.A. 120 D3
Forat Iran 80 C3
Foraulep atoll Micronesia see Faraulep
Forbes Australia 112 D4
Forbesganj India 75 E4
Forchheim Germany 36 E4
Ford r. U.S.A. 132 E2
Ford City CA U.S.A. 136 C4
Ford City PA U.S.A. 130 D3
Førde Norway 33 B3
Forde Lake Canada 123 L2
Ford Range mts Antarctica 167 J1
Fords Bridge Australia 112 C3
Fordyce U.S.A. 133 C5
Forécariah Guinea 92 B3
Forel, Mont mt. Greenland 121 P3
Foremost Canada 123 I5
Foresight Mountain Canada 122 E4
Forest Canada 130 C2
Forest MS U.S.A. 133 D5
Forest OH U.S.A. 130 B3
Forest VA U.S.A. 130 D5
Forestburg Canada 123 H4
Forest City U.S.A. 131 F3
Forest Creek r. Australia 111 E3
Forest Lakes U.S.A. 137 G4
Forest Park U.S.A. 129 B5
Forest Ranch U.S.A. 136 B2
Forestville Canada 125 G3
Forestville U.S.A. 130 B2
Forêt Dense de Dzanga-Sangha, Réserve Spéciale de res. Cameroon 94 B4
Forêt des Deux Balé nat. park Burkina 92 E3
Forfar U.K. 34 E3
Forges-les-Eaux France 38 D2
Forillon, Parc National de nat. park Canada 125 H3
Forish Uzbek. see Farish
Forks U.S.A. 134 A3
Forksville U.S.A. 131 E3
Fork Union U.S.A. 130 D5
Forlì Italy 44 D2
Forman U.S.A. 132 B2
Formentera i. Spain 43 G3
Formentor, Cap de c. Spain 43 H3
Formerie France 38 D2
Former Yugoslav Republic of Macedonia country Europe see Macedonia
Formia Italy 44 D4
Formiga Brazil 151 C7
Formosa Arg. 152 F1
Formosa prov. Arg. 149 F6
Formosa country Asia see Taiwan
Formosa Brazil 150 C5
Formosa, Serra hills Brazil 149 G3
Formosa do Rio Preto Brazil 150 C4
Formosa Strait China/Taiwan see Taiwan Strait
Formoso Brazil 150 B4
Formoso r. Bahia Brazil 150 C5
Formoso r. Tocantins Brazil 150 B4
Fornos Moz. 99 G4
Forolshogna mt. Norway 32 C3
Forres U.K. 34 E3
Forrest Australia 109 E7
Forrest r. Australia 108 E3
Forrestal Range mts Antarctica 167 A1
Forrest City U.S.A. 127 H4
Forrest Lakes salt flat Australia 109 E7
Forsand Norway 33 B4
Forsayth Australia 111 E3
Forsbakken Norway 32 E1
Forssa Fin. 33 F3
Forst Germany 37 G3
Forsyth GA U.S.A. 129 C5
Forsyth MO U.S.A. 133 C4
Forsyth MT U.S.A. 134 F3
Forsyth Range hills Australia 111 E4
Fort Abbas Pak. 81 H4
Fort Albany Canada 124 D2
Fortaleza Pando Bol. 148 D2
Fortaleza Pando Bol. 148 D3
Fortaleza Brazil 150 E2
Fortaleza de Santa Teresa Uruguay 152 G3
Fort Archambault Chad see Sarh
Fort Ashby U.S.A. 130 D4
Fort Assiniboine Canada 123 H4
Fort Augustus U.K. 34 D3
Fort Babine Canada 122 E4
Fort Beaufort S. Africa 99 E7
Fort Benton U.S.A. 134 E3
Fort Brabant Canada see Tuktoyaktuk
Fort Bragg U.S.A. 136 A2
Fort Carillon U.S.A. see Ticonderoga
Fort Carnot Madag. see Ikongo
Fort Charlet Alg. see Djanet
Fort Chimo Canada see Kuujjuaq
Fort Chipewyan Canada 123 I3
Fort Collins U.S.A. 134 F4
Fort-Coulonge Canada 124 E4
Fort Crampel Cent. Afr. Rep. see Kaga Bandoro
Fort-Dauphin Madag. see Tôlañaro
Fort Davis U.S.A. 133 A6
▶Fort-de-France Martinique 139 L6
Capital of Martinique.
Fort de Kock Indon. see Bukittinggi
Fort de Polignac Alg. see Illizi
Fort Deposit U.S.A. 129 B5
Fort Dodge U.S.A. 132 C3
Fort Duchesne U.S.A. 137 H1
Forte, Monte hill Sardinia Italy 45 B4
Fort Edward U.S.A. 131 G2
Forte Nordeste Angola 95 D6
Fort Erie Canada 130 D2
Fortescue r. Australia 108 B5
Forte Veneza Brazil 147 H6
Fort Flatters Alg. see Bordj Omer Driss
Fort Foureau Cameroon see Kousséri
Fort Franklin Canada see Déljne
Fort Gardel Alg. see Zaouatallaz
Fort Garland U.S.A. 135 F5
Fort Gay U.S.A. 130 B4
Fort George Canada see Chisasibi
Fort Good Hope Canada 122 D1
Fort Gouraud Mauritania see Fdérik
Forth r. U.K. 34 E3
Forth, Firth of est. U.K. 34 E3
Fort Hall Kenya see Muranga
Fort Hertz Myanmar see Putao
Fortification Range mts U.S.A. 137 E2
Fortín Aroma Para. 149 E5
Fortín Ávalos Sánchez Para. 149 E5
Fortín Boquerón Para. 149 F5
Fortín Carlos Antonio López Para. 149 F5
Fortín Coronel Bogado Para. 149 F5
Fortín Coronel Eugenio Garay Para. 149 E5
Fortín Galpón Para. 149 F4
Fortín General Caballero Para. 149 F6
Fortín General Diaz Para. 149 E5
Fortín General Mendoza Para. 149 E5
Fortín Infante Rivarola Para. 149 E5
Fortín Juan de Zalazar Para. 149 F5
Fortín Lavalle Arg. 152 E1
Fortín Leonardo Britos Para. 149 E5
Fortín Linares Para. 149 E5
Fortín Madrejón Para. 149 F5
Fortín May Alberto Gardel Para. 149 E5
Fortín Nueva Asunción Para. 149 E5
Fortín Pilcomayo Arg. 149 E5
Fortín Presidente Ayala Para. 149 F5
Fortín Ravelo Bol. 149 E4
Fortín Suárez Arana Bol. 149 E4
Fortín Teniente Juan Echauri López Para. 149 E5
Fortín Teniente Mountania Para. 149 F5
Fortín Teniente Primero H. Mendoza Para. 149 F4
Fortín Teniente Rojas Silva Para. 149 E6
Fort Jameson Zambia see Chipata
Fort Johnston Malawi see Mangochi
Fort Kent U.S.A. 128 F2
Fort Lamy Chad see Ndjamena
Fort Laperrine Alg. see Tamanrasset
Fort Lauderdale U.S.A. 129 C7
Fort Liard Canada 122 F2
Fort Mackay Canada 123 I3
Fort Macleod Canada 134 D2
Fort Madison U.S.A. 124 B5
Fort Manning Malawi see Mchinji
Fort McMurray Canada 123 I3
Fort McPherson Canada 120 F3
Fort Myers U.S.A. 129 C7
Fort Nelson Canada 122 F3
Fort Nelson r. Canada 122 F3
Fort Norman Canada see Tulita
Fort Orange U.S.A. see Albany
Fortore r. Italy 44 E4
Fort Payne U.S.A. 133 E5
Fort Peck Reservoir U.S.A. 134 F3
Fort Pierce U.S.A. 129 C7
Fort Pierre U.S.A. 132 A2
Fort Portal Uganda 96 A4
Fort Providence Canada 123 G2
Fort Qu'Appelle Canada 134 G2
Fort Randall U.S.A. see Cold Bay
Fort Recovery U.S.A. 130 A3
Fort Resolution Canada 123 H2
Fortrose N.Z. 113 B4
Fort Rosebery Zambia see Mansa
Fort Rousset Congo see Owando
Fort Rupert Canada see Waskaganish
Fort St James Canada 122 E4
Fort St John Canada 122 F3
Fort Sandeman Pak. see Zhob
Fort Saskatchewan Canada 123 H4
Fort Scott U.S.A. 132 C4
Fort Severn Canada 124 C1
Fort-Shevchenko Kazakh. 79 G1
Fort Simpson Canada 122 F2
Fort Smith Canada 123 H2
Fort Smith U.S.A. 133 C5
Fort Stockton U.S.A. 133 A6
Fort Sumner U.S.A. 135 F6
Fort Trinquet Mauritania see Bîr Mogreïn
Fortune Bay Canada 125 K4
Fort Valley U.S.A. 129 C5
Fort Vermilion Canada 123 G3
Fort Victoria Zimbabwe see Masvingo
Fort Walton U.S.A. see Fort Walton Beach
Fort Walton Beach U.S.A. 129 B6
Fort Ware Canada see Ware
Fort Wayne U.S.A. 132 E3
Fort Wellington Guyana 147 G3
Fort White Myanmar 60 A3
Fort William U.K. 34 D3
Fort Worth U.S.A. 133 B5
Fort Yates U.S.A. 132 A2
Fortymile r. Canada/U.S.A. 122 A1
Forty Mile Scrub National Park Australia 111 F3
Fort Yukon U.S.A. 120 E3
Forum Iulii France see Fréjus
Forūr, Jazīreh-ye i. Iran 80 C5
Forvik Norway 32 D2
Foshan China 67 E4
Foskvallen Sweden 33 D3
Fosna pen. Norway 32 C3
Foso Ghana 93 E4
Foss Iceland 32 [inset]
Fossano Italy 44 A2
Fosshóll Iceland 32 [inset]
Fossil U.S.A. 134 B3
Fossil Downs Australia 108 D4
Fossombrone Italy 44 D3
Fos-sur-Mer France 39 F5
Foster Australia 112 C5
Foster Bugt b. Greenland 121 Q2
Foster Lakes Canada 123 J3
Fostoria U.S.A. 130 B3
Fotadrevo Madag. 99 [inset] J5
Fotuna i. Vanuatu see Futuna
Fouesnant France 38 A3
Fougamou Gabon 94 A5
Fougères France 38 C2
Foula i. U.K. 34 E1
Foulamôri Guinea 92 B2
Foul Bay Egypt 89 G4
Foulenzem Gabon 94 A5
Foulness Point U.K. 35 G6
Foul Point Sri Lanka 72 D4
Foumbot Cameroon 93 H4
Foum Zguid Morocco 90 D3
Foundation Ice Stream glacier Antarctica 167 L1
Founougo Benin 93 F3
Fountains Abbey tourist site U.K. 35 F4
Four, Pointe de pt Alg. 43 H4
Fourchambault France 39 E3
Fourches, Mont des hill France 39 F2
Four Corners U.S.A. 136 D4
Four Mountains, Islands of the U.S.A. 120 C4
Fournoi Greece 47 E6
Fournoi i. Greece 47 E6
Fouta Djallon reg. Guinea 92 B3
Foveaux Strait N.Z. 113 A4
Fowler CO U.S.A. 135 F5
Fowler IN U.S.A. 128 B3
Fowler MI U.S.A. 130 A2
Fowler Ice Rise Antarctica 167 L1
Fowlerville U.S.A. 130 A2
Fox r. U.S.A. 132 D3
Foxas Spain 42 B1
Fox Creek Canada 123 G4
Foxe Basin g. Canada 121 L3
Foxe Channel Canada 121 K3
Foxen l. Sweden 33 C4
Foxe Peninsula Canada 121 L3
Fox Glacier N.Z. 113 B3
Fox Islands U.S.A. 120 C4
Fox Lake Canada 123 H3
Fox Mountain Canada 122 C2
Foxton N.Z. 113 C3
Fox Valley Canada 123 I5
Foyle r. Rep. of Ireland/U.K. 34 C4
Foyle, Lough b. Rep. of Ireland/U.K. 34 C4
Foz Spain 42 C1
Foz de Areia, Represa de resr Brazil 151 B8
Foz de Gregório Brazil 146 D6
Foz do Copeá Brazil 147 F5
Foz do Cunene Angola 95 A9
Foz do Iguaçu Brazil 151 A8
Foz do Jutaí Brazil 146 E5
Foz do Mamoriá Brazil 146 E5
Foz do Riosinho Brazil 148 C1
Frackville U.S.A. 131 E3
Fraga Arg. 152 D3
Fraga Spain 43 G2
Fraile Muerto Uruguay 152 G3
Frakes, Mount Antarctica 167 K1
Framingham U.S.A. 131 H2
Framnes Mountains Antarctica 167 E2
Franca Brazil 149 I5
Français, Récif des reef New Caledonia 107 F3
Francavilla Fontana Italy 45 F4
▶France country Europe 38 E3
3rd largest and 4th most populous country in Europe.
europe 24–25, 48
France, Île de i. Greenland 121 R2
Frances Australia 112 B5
Frances r. Canada 122 D2
Frances Lake Canada 122 D2
Frances Lake l. Canada 122 D2
Franceville Gabon 94 B5
Franche-Comté admin. reg. France 39 G3
Francis Canada 123 K5
Francis atoll Kiribati see Beru
Francisco de Orellana Ecuador see Puerto Francisco de Orellana
Francisco de Orellana Peru 146 C5
Francisco I. Madero Mex. 133 A7
Francisco Meeks Arg. 152 F4
Francisco Sá Brazil 151 D6
Francisco Zarco Mex. 135 C6
Francistown Botswana 99 E4
Francofonte Sicily Italy 45 E6
François Lake Canada 122 E4
Francois Peron National Park Australia 109 A6
Francs Peak U.S.A. 134 E4
Frankenberg (Eder) Germany 36 D3
Frankenmuth U.S.A. 130 B2
Frankford Canada 130 E1
Frankfort IN U.S.A. 132 E3
▶Frankfort KY U.S.A. 130 A4
State capital of Kentucky.
Frankfort OH U.S.A. 130 B4
Frankfurt am Main Germany 36 D3
Frankfurt an der Oder Germany 37 G2
Frank Hann National Park Australia 109 C8
Frankin Lake U.S.A. 137 E1
Fränkische Alb hills Germany 36 E4
Fränkische Schweiz reg. Germany 36 E4
Frankland, Cape Australia 112 C5
Franklin GA U.S.A. 133 E5
Franklin IN U.S.A. 128 B4
Franklin LA U.S.A. 133 D6
Franklin MA U.S.A. 131 H2
Franklin NC U.S.A. 128 C5
Franklin NE U.S.A. 132 B3
Franklin NH U.S.A. 131 H2
Franklin NJ U.S.A. 131 F3
Franklin OH U.S.A. 130 A4
Franklin PA U.S.A. 130 D3
Franklin TN U.S.A. 128 B5
Franklin TX U.S.A. 133 B6
Franklin VA U.S.A. 131 E5
Franklin WV U.S.A. 130 D4
Franklin D. Roosevelt Lake U.S.A. 126 C2
Franklin Furnace U.S.A. 130 B4
Franklin-Gordon National Park Australia 112 C6
Franklin Island Antarctica 167 H1
Franklin Lake Canada 123 M1
Franklin Mountains Canada 122 F2
Franklin Strait Canada 121 J2
Franklinton U.S.A. 133 D6
Franklinville U.S.A. 130 D2
Frankrike Sweden 32 D3
Frankston Australia 112 C5
Fransfontein Namibia 98 B4
Fränsta Sweden 33 E3
Frantsa-Iosifa, Zemlya is Rus. Fed. 26 F2
Franz Canada 124 C3
Franz Josef Glacier N.Z. 113 B3
Franz Josef Land is Rus. Fed. see Frantsa-Iosifa, Zemlya
Frascati Italy 44 D4
Fraser r. B.C. Canada 134 B2
Fraser r. Nfld. and Lab. Canada 125 I1
Fraser, Mount Australia 109 B6
Fraserburg S. Africa 98 D6
Fraserburgh U.K. 34 E3
Fraserdale Canada 124 D3
Fraser Island Australia 111 H5
Fraser Island National Park Australia 111 H5
Fraser Lake Canada 122 E4
Fraser National Park Australia 112 C5
Fraser Plateau Canada 122 E4
Fraser Range Australia 109 C8
Fraser Range hills Australia 109 C8
Frasertown N.Z. 113 D2
Frătești Romania 46 D3
Frauenfeld Switz. 39 H3
Fray Bentos Uruguay 152 F3
Fray Marcos Uruguay 152 G3
Frederica U.S.A. 131 F4
Fredericia Denmark 33 C5
Frederick MD U.S.A. 130 E4
Frederick OK U.S.A. 133 B5
Frederick Hills Australia 110 C2
Frederick Reef Australia 111 H4
Fredericksburg TX U.S.A. 133 B6
Fredericksburg VA U.S.A. 130 E4
Frederick Sound sea chan. U.S.A. 122 C3
Fredericktown MO U.S.A. 132 D4
Fredericktown OH U.S.A. 130 B3
▶Fredericton Canada 125 H4
Provincial capital of New Brunswick.
Fredericton airport Canada 128 G2
Frederikshåb Greenland see Paamiut
Frederikshavn Denmark 33 C4
Frederiksværk Denmark 33 D5
Fredonia AZ U.S.A. 137 F3
Fredonia KS U.S.A. 132 C4
Fredonia NY U.S.A. 130 D2
Fredrika Sweden 32 E2
Fredriksberg Sweden 33 D3
Fredrikshamn Fin. see Hamina
Fredrikstad Norway 33 C4
Freehold U.S.A. 131 F3
Freeland U.S.A. 131 F3
Freeling, Mount Australia 110 C4
Freeling Heights hill Australia 111 D6
Freels, Cape Canada 125 K3
Freeman U.S.A. 132 B3
Freeport IL U.S.A. 132 D3
Freeport ME U.S.A. 131 H2
Freeport PA U.S.A. 130 D3
Freeport TX U.S.A. 133 C6
Freeport City Bahamas 129 D7
Freer U.S.A. 133 B7
Free State prov. S. Africa 99 E6
▶Freetown Sierra Leone 92 B3
Capital of Sierra Leone.
Freewood Acres U.S.A. 131 F3
Fregenal de la Sierra Spain 42 C3
Fregon Australia 110 C5
Fréhel, Cap c. France 38 B2
Freiberg Germany 37 F3
Freiburg Switz. see Fribourg
Freiburg im Breisgau Germany 36 C4
Freising Germany 36 E4
Freistadt Austria 37 G4
Freital Germany 37 F3
Freixo de Espada à Cinta Port. 42 C2
Fréjus France 39 G5
Frekhaug Norway 33 B3
Fremantle Australia 109 A8
Fremont CA U.S.A. 136 B3
Fremont NE U.S.A. 132 B3
Fremont OH U.S.A. 130 B3
Fremont r. U.S.A. 137 G2
Fremont Junction U.S.A. 137 G2
Frenchburg U.S.A. 130 B5
French Congo country Africa see Congo
French Creek r. U.S.A. 130 D3
▶French Guiana terr. S. America 147 H4
French Overseas Department.
southamerica 144–145, 154
French Guinea country Africa see Guinea
Frenchman r. U.S.A. 134 F2
Frenchman Creek r. U.S.A. 132 A3
Frenchman Lake U.S.A. 136 B2
French Pass N.Z. 113 C3
▶French Polynesia terr. S. Pacific Ocean 165 I7
French Overseas Territory.
oceania 104–105, 114
French Somaliland country Africa see Djibouti
▶French Southern and Antarctic Lands terr. Indian Ocean 163 L8
French Overseas Territory.
asia 52–53, 82
French Sudan country Africa see Mali
French Territory of the Afars and Issas country Africa see Djibouti
Frenchtown U.S.A. 131 F3
Frenda Alg. 91 F2
Fresco r. Brazil 147 I6
Fresco Côte d'Ivoire 92 D4
Fresnillo Mex. 126 F7
Fresno U.S.A. 136 C3
Fresno r. U.S.A. 136 B3
Fressel, Lac l. Canada 125 F2
Freu, Cap des c. Spain 43 H3
Freudenstadt Germany 36 D4
Frew watercourse Australia 110 C4
Frewsburg U.S.A. 130 D2
Freycinet Estuary inlet Australia 109 A6
Freycinet Peninsula Australia 112 D6
Freyming-Merlebach France 39 G2
Freyre Arg. 152 E2
Freyung Germany 37 F4
Fria Guinea 92 B3
Fria, Cape Namibia 98 B3
Friant U.S.A. 136 C3
Friant-Kern Canal U.S.A. 136 C4
Frias Arg. 152 D2
Fribourg Switz. 39 G3
Frick Switz. 39 H3
Friday Harbor U.S.A. 134 B2
Friedberg Germany 36 E4
Friedens U.S.A. 130 D3
Friedland Germany 37 F2
Friedland Rus. Fed. see Pravdinsk
Friedrichshafen Germany 36 D5
Friend U.S.A. 132 B3
Friendly Islands country S. Pacific Ocean see Tonga
Friesach Austria 37 G5
Friesack Germany 37 F2
Friesoythe Germany 36 C2
Frio r. TX U.S.A. 133 B6
Frio r. TX U.S.A. 133 B6
Frio watercourse U.S.A. 133 A5
Friol Spain 42 C1
Frisco Mountain U.S.A. 137 F2
Frissell, Mount U.S.A. 131 G2
Friuli - Venezia Giulia admin. reg. Italy 44 D1
Frobisher Bay Canada see Iqaluit
Frobisher Bay b. Canada 121 M3
Frobisher Lake Canada 123 I3
Frohavet b. Norway 32 C3
Frohburg Germany 37 F3
Frohnleiten Austria 37 G5
Frolovo Rus. Fed. 29 G6
Frome watercourse Australia 110 D6
Frome U.K. 35 E6
Frome, Lake salt flat Australia 112 A3
Fromveur, Passage du strait France 38 A2
Fronteira Port. 42 C3
Fronteiras Brazil 150 D3
Frontera Coahuila Mex. 133 A7
Frontera Mex. 138 F5
Fronteras Mex. 135 E7
Frontignan France 39 E5
Front Royal U.S.A. 130 D4
Frosinone Italy 44 D4
Frostburg U.S.A. 130 D4
Frøya i. Norway 32 C3
Føroyar terr. N. Atlantic Ocean see Faroe Islands
Fruges France 38 E1
Fruita U.S.A. 137 H2
Fruitland MD U.S.A. 131 F4
Fruitland UT U.S.A. 137 G1
Frunze Kyrg. 81 G1
Frunze Kyrg. see Bishkek
Frunzenskoye Kyrg. see Frunze
Frusino Italy see Frosinone
Fruska Gora nat. park Yugo. 46 A2
Frutuoso Brazil 149 E3
Frýdek-Místek Czech Rep. 37 I4
Fryeburg U.S.A. 131 H1
Fu'an China 67 F3
Fucheng China see Fengyang
Fuchuan China 67 D3
Fuchun Jiang r. China 67 G2
Fude China 67 F3
Fuding China 67 G3
Fudua waterhole Kenya 96 C5
Fuengirola Spain 42 D4
Fuenlabrada Spain 42 E2
Fuente Albilla, Cerro de mt. Spain 43 F3
Fuente de Cantos Spain 42 C3
Fuente Obejuna Spain 42 D3
Fuentesaúco Spain 42 D2
Fuentes de Ebro Spain 43 F2
Fuerte Olimpo Para. 149 F5
Fuerteventura i. Canary Is 90 B3
Fuga i. Phil. 67 G5
Fugloy i. Faroe Is 34 [inset]
Fuglstad Norway 32 D2
Fugou China 67 E1
Fuhai China 70 G2
Fujairah U.A.E. 80 D5
Fujeira U.A.E. see Fujairah
Fuji China see Luxian
Fuji Japan 65 D6
Fujian prov. China 67 F3
Fu Jiang r. China 66 C2
Fuji-Hakone-Izu National Park Japan 65 D6
Fujin China 64 B3
Fujinomiya Japan 65 D6
Fuji-san vol. Japan 65 D6
Fukagawa Japan 64 E4
Fūkah Egypt 78 A5
Fukien prov. China see Fujian
Fukuchiyama Japan 65 C6
Fukue Japan 65 B6
Fukue-jima i. Japan 65 B6
Fukui Japan 65 D5
Fukuoka Japan 65 B6
Fukushima Japan 65 E5
Fūl, Jabal hill Egypt 77 A5
Fulacunda Guinea-Bissau 92 B3
Fūlād Maïalleh Iran 80 C2
Fulchhari Bangl. 75 F4
Fulda Germany 36 D3
Fulda r. Germany 36 D3
Fule China 66 C3
Fuli China see Jixian
Fuliji China 67 F1
Fulin China see Hanyuan
Fuling China 66 C2
Fulitun China see Jixian
Fullerton U.S.A. 132 B3
Fullerton, Cape Canada 123 N2
Fulnek Czech Rep. 37 H4
Fulton KY U.S.A. 128 A4
Fulton MO U.S.A. 132 D4
Fulton MS U.S.A. 129 A5
Fulton NY U.S.A. 131 E2
Fulunäs Sweden 33 D3
Fumay France 39 F2
Fumel France 38 D4
Fumin China 66 B3
Funabashi Japan 65 D6
Funafuti atoll Tuvalu 107 G2
Funan China see Fusui
Funäsdalen Sweden 33 D3
▶Funchal Madeira 90 A2
Capital of Madeira.
Fundación Col. 146 C2
Fundão Brazil 151 D6
Fundão Port. 42 C2
Fundi Italy see Fondi
Fundición Mex. 135 E8
Fundo das Figuerias Cape Verde 92 [inset]
Fundulea Romania 46 E2
Fundy, Bay of g. Canada 125 H4
Fünen i. Denmark see Fyn
Funeral Peak U.S.A. 137 D3
Fünfkirchen Hungary see Pécs
Funhalouro Moz. 99 G4
Funing Jiangsu China 67 F1
Funing Yunnan China 66 C4
Funiu Shan mts China 67 D1
Funsi Ghana 93 E3
Funtua Nigeria 93 G3
Funzie U.K. 34 F1
Fuqing China 67 F3
Fuquan China 66 C3
Furancungo Moz. 97 B8
Furano Japan 64 E4
Fūrgun, Kūh-e mt. Iran 80 D5
Furmanov Rus. Fed. 28 G4
Furmanovo Kazakh. see Zhalpaktal
Furnas, Represa resr Brazil 151 C7
Furneaux Group is Australia 112 D6
Furnes Belgium see Veurne
Fürstenau Germany 36 C2
Fürstenberg Germany 37 F2
Fürstenfeld Austria 37 H5
Fürstenfeldbruck Germany 36 E4
Fürstenwalde Germany 37 G2
Fürth Germany 36 E4
Furth im Wald Germany 37 F4
Furudal Sweden 33 D3
Furukawa Japan 65 E5
Fury and Hecla Strait Canada 121 K3
Fusagasugá Col. 146 C3
Fusan S. Korea see Pusan
Fushun Liaoning China 63 K3
Fushun Sichuan China 66 C2
Fusong China 64 A4
Fusui China 66 C4
Fu Tau Pun Chau i. Hong Kong China 67 [inset]
Futog Yugo. 46 A2
Futuna i. Vanuatu 107 G3
Futuna Islands is Wallis and Futuna Is see Hoorn, Îles de
Futun Xi r. China 67 F3
Fuwayriṭ Qatar 80 B5
Fuxian China see Wafangdian
Fuxin China 63 K3
Fuxing China see Wangmo
Fuxinzhen China see Fuxin
Fuyang Anhui China 67 E1
Fuyang Guangxi China see Fuchuan
Fuyang Zhejiang China 67 F2
Fuying Dao i. China 67 G3
Fuyu Heilong. China 63 K2
Fuyu Jilin China see Songyuan
Fuyu Jilin China 64 A3
Fuyuan Heilong. China 64 C2
Fuyuan Yunnan China 66 C3
Fuyun China 70 G2
Füzesabony Hungary 37 J5
Füzesgyarmat Hungary 37 J5
Fuzhou Fujian China 67 F3
Fuzhou Jiangxi China see Linchuan
Füzuli Azer. 79 F3
Fwamba Dem. Rep. Congo 95 D6
Fyn county Denmark 33 C5
Fyn i. Denmark 33 C5
Fyne, Loch inlet U.K. 34 D4
Fyresvatn l. Norway 33 C4
F.Y.R.O.M. (Former Yugoslav Republic of Macedonia) country Europe see Macedonia

↓ G

Gaâfour Tunisia 45 B6
Gaalkacyo Somalia 96 E3
Gaat r. Sarawak Malaysia 59 F2
Gabakly Turkm. see Kabakly
Gabangab well Eth. 96 E3
Gabas r. France 38 C5
Gabbs Valley Range mts U.S.A. 136 C2
Gabd Pak. 81 E5
Gabela Angola 95 B7
Gaberones Botswana see Gaborone
Gabès Tunisia 91 H2
Gabès, Golfe de g. Tunisia 91 H2
Gabès, Gulf of Tunisia see Gabès, Golfe de
Gabgaba, Wadi watercourse Sudan 89 G4
▶Gabon country Africa 94 A5
africa 86–87,100
Gabon, Estuaire du est. Gabon 94 A4
▶Gaborone Botswana 98 E5
Capital of Botswana.
Gabou Senegal 92 B2
Gabriel y Galán, Embalse de resr Spain 42 C2
Gābrīk Iran 80 D5
Gābrīk watercourse Iran 80 D5
Gabrovnitsa Bulg. 46 C3
Gabrovo Bulg. 46 D3
Gabú Guinea-Bissau 92 B2
Gabuli vol. Eth. 89 I6
Gacé France 38 D2
Gacko Bos.-Herz. 44 G3
Gadag India 72 B3
Gadaisu P.N.G. 111 G1
Gäddede Sweden 32 D2
Gadê China 66 A1
Gades Spain see Cádiz
Gadhada India 74 A5
Gadhra India 72 A1
Gadsden U.S.A. 129 B5
Gadwal India 72 C2
Gadyach Ukr. see Hadyach
Gadyn Turkm. 81 E2
Gadzi Cent. Afr. Rep. 94 C3
Gæi'dnuvuop'pi Norway 32 F1
Găești Romania 46 D2
Gaeta Italy 44 D4
Gaeta, Golfo di g. Italy 44 D4
Gafanha da Nazaré Port. 42 B2
Gaferut i. Micronesia 57 K4
Gafsa Tunisia 91 H2
Gagal Chad 94 B2
Gagarin Rus. Fed. 28 E5
Gagarin Uzbek. 81 G1
Gagere watercourse Nigeria 93 G2
Gagliano del Capo Italy 45 G5
Gagnoa Côte d'Ivoire 92 D4
Gagnon Canada 125 G3
Gago Coutinho Angola see Lumbala N'guimbo
Gagra Georgia 79 E2
Gaiab watercourse Namibia 98 C6
Gaibandha Bangl. 75 F4
Gail r. Austria 37 F5
Gaillac France 38 D5
Gaillimh Rep. of Ireland see Galway
Gaillon France 38 D2
Gaindaingoinkor China see Lhünzhub
Gaindainqoinkor China see Lhünzhub
Gainesboro U.S.A. 133 E4
Gainesville FL U.S.A. 129 C6
Gainesville GA U.S.A. 133 F5
Gainesville MO U.S.A. 133 C4
Gainesville TX U.S.A. 133 B5
Gainsborough U.K. 35 F5
Gairdner r. Australia 109 B8
Gairdner, Lake salt flat Australia 109 F7
Gairloch U.K. 34 D3
Gairo Tanz. 97 C6
Gaja r. Hungary 37 I5
Gajah Hutan, Bukit hill Malaysia 58 C1
Gaji r. Nigeria 93 H3
Gajol India 75 F4
Gajos well Kenya 96 C4

Gakarosa mt. S. Africa 98 D5
Gakem Nigeria 93 H4
Gakuch Jammu and Kashmir 74 B1
Gala China 75 F3
Galán, Cerro mt. Arg. 152 D1
Galana r. Kenya 96 D5
Galand Iran 80 C2
Galangue Angola 95 C8
Galanta Slovakia 37 H4
Galápagos, Islas see Galapagos Islands

▶Galapagos Islands Pacific Ocean 165 L6
Part of Ecuador. Most westerly point of South America.
southamerica 144–145

Galapagos Rise sea feature Pacific Ocean 165 L6
Galashiels U.K. 34 E4
Galata Bulg. 46 E3
Galați Romania 46 F2
Galatista Greece 47 C4
Galatone Italy 45 G4
Galax U.S.A. 130 C5
Galaymor Turkm. see Kala-I-Mor
Galdhøpiggen mt. Norway 33 C3
Galeana Mex. 135 F7
Galegu Sudan 89 G6
Galena AK U.S.A. 120 D3
Galena IL U.S.A. 132 D3
Galena MD U.S.A. 131 F4
Galena MO U.S.A. 133 C4
Galena Bay Canada 122 G5
Galera, Punta pt Chile 152 B5
Galera, Punta pt Ecuador 146 A4
Galeras vol. Col. 146 B4
Galesburg U.S.A. 132 D3
Galeshewe S. Africa 98 E6
Galeton U.S.A. 130 E3
Galga r. Hungary 37 I5
Galguduud admin. reg. Somalia 96 E3
Gal Hareeri Somalia 96 E3
Galich Rus. Fed. 28 G4
Galichskaya Vozvyshennost' hills Rus. Fed. 28 G4
Galicia aut. comm. Spain 42 C1
Galičica nat. park Macedonia 46 B4
Galilee, Sea of l. Israel 77 B3
Galissas Greece 47 D6
Galiuro Mountains U.S.A. 137 G5
Galiwinku Australia 110 C2
Gallabat Sudan 89 H6
Gallatin MO U.S.A. 132 C4
Gallatin TN U.S.A. 128 B4
Gallatin r. U.S.A. 134 E3
Galle Sri Lanka 72 D5
Gállego r. Spain 43 F2
Gallego Rise sea feature Pacific Ocean 165 K6
Gallegos r. Arg. 153 C7
Gallegos, Cabo c. Chile 153 B6
Gallia country Europe see France

▶Gallinas, Punta pt Col. 146 D1
Most northerly point of South America.

Gallipoli Italy 45 G4
Gallipoli Turkey 78 A2
Gallipolis U.S.A. 130 B4
Gällivare Sweden 32 F2
Gallo r. Spain 43 E2
Gällö Sweden 32 D3
Gallo, Capo c. Sicily Italy 45 D5
Gallup KY U.S.A. 130 B4
Gallup NM U.S.A. 135 E6
Gallur Spain 43 F2
Gallura reg. Sardinia Italy 44 B4
Gallyaaral Uzbek. 81 F1
Galma watercourse Nigeria 93 G3
Galoya Sri Lanka 72 D4
Gal Oya National Park Sri Lanka 72 D5
Gal Shiikh Somalia 96 E2
Galt U.S.A. 136 B2
Gal Tardo Somalia 96 E4
Galtat Zemmour W. Sahara 90 B4
Galtee Mountains hills Rep. of Ireland 35 B5
Galtymore hill Rep. of Ireland 35 B5
Galūgāh, Kūh-e mts Iran 80 C4
Galūgāh-e Āsīyeh Iran 81 D3
Galunggung, Gunung vol. Indon. 59 E4
Galveston U.S.A. 133 C6
Galveston Bay U.S.A. 133 C6
Galvez Arg. 152 E3
Galwa Nepal 75 D3
Galway Rep. of Ireland 35 B5
Galway Bay Rep. of Ireland 35 B5
Gâm r. Vietnam 60 D3
Gamaches France 38 D2
Gamalakhe S. Africa 99 F6
Gámas Fin. see Kaamanen
Gamawa Nigeria 93 H2
Gamba China 75 F3
Gambēla Eth. 96 B2
Gambēla admin. reg. Eth. 96 B3
Gambēla National Park Eth. 96 B3
Gambell U.S.A. 27 S3
Gambia r. Gambia 92 A2
▶Gambia, The country Africa 92 A2
africa 86–87, 100
Gambie r. Senegal 92 B2
Gambier, Îles is Fr. Polynesia 165 J7
Gambier Islands Australia 109 G8
Gambo Canada 125 K3
Gamboma Congo 94 B5
Gamboola Australia 111 E3
Gamboula Cent. Afr. Rep. 94 B3
Gamda China see Zamtang
Gamlakarleby Fin. see Kokkola
Gamleby Sweden 33 E4
Gammams well Sudan 89 G5
Gammelstaden Sweden 32 F2
Gammon Ranges National Park Australia 112 A3
Gamova, Mys pt Rus. Fed. 64 B4
Gampaha Sri Lanka 72 D5
Gampola Sri Lanka 72 D5
Gamshadzai Kūh mts Iran 81 E4
Gamtog China 66 A2
Gamud mt. Eth. 96 C3
Gan r. China 64 A2
Gana China see Gengda
Ganado U.S.A. 137 H4
Gananoque Canada 131 E1
Ganāveh Iran 80 B4
Gäncä Azer. 79 F2
Gand Belgium see Ghent
Ganda Angola 95 B8
Gandadiwata, Bukit mt. Indon. 56 E6
Gandai India 74 D5
Gandajika Dem. Rep. Congo 95 D6
Gándara Spain 42 B1
Gandarbal Jammu and Kashmir 74 B2
Gandari Mountain Pak. 81 G4
Gandava Pak. 81 F4
Gander Canada 125 K3
Gander r. Nfld. and Lab. Canada 121 N5
Gander r. Nfld. and Lab. Canada 125 K3
Gandesa Spain 43 G2
Gandevi India 72 B1
Gandhidham India 74 A5
Gandhinagar India 74 B5
Gandhi Sagar resr India 74 B4
Gandi, Wadi watercourse Sudan 94 E2
Gandía Spain 43 F3
Gand-i-Zureh plain Afgh. 81 E4
Gandomān Iran 80 B4
Gandu Brazil 150 E5
Gandvik Norway 32 H1
Gandzha Azer. see Gäncä
Gâneb well Mauritania 92 C1
Ganga r. Bangl./India see Ganges
Ganga Nigeria 93 G3
Ganga r. Sri Lanka 72 D5
Gangakher India 72 C2
Gangán Arg. 153 C5
Gangán, Pampa de plain Arg. 153 C5
Ganganagar India 74 B3
Gangapur Maharashtra India 72 B2
Gangapur Rajasthan India 74 B4
Gangapur Rajasthan India 74 C4
Gangara Niger 93 H2
Gangavali r. India 72 B3
Gangaw Myanmar 60 A3
Gangawati India 72 C3
Gangaw Range mts Myanmar 60 B3
Gangca China 70 J4
Gangdhar India 74 B5
Gangdisê Shan mts China 70 F5
Ganges r. Bangl./India 74 F5
Ganges France 39 E5
▶Ganges, Mouths of the Bangl./India 75 F5
asia 82
Ganges Cone sea feature Indian Ocean 162 M4
Gangi Sicily Italy 45 E6
Ganglota Liberia 92 C4
Gangra Turkey see Çankırı
Gangtok India 75 F4
Gangu China 66 C1
Ganiakali Guinea 92 C3
Ganjam India 71 G8
Gan Jiang r. China 67 F2
Ganluo China 66 B2
Gannat France 39 E3
Gannett Peak U.S.A. 134 E4
Gänserndorf Austria 37 H4
Ganshui China 66 C2
Gansu prov. China 70 I3
Gantamaa Somalia 96 D4
Gantheaume Point Australia 108 C4
Gant'iadi Georgia 79 E2
Ganting China see Huxian
Gantsevichi Belarus see Hantsavichy
Ganxian China 67 E3
Ganye Nigeria 93 I3
Ganyushkino Kazakh. 29 I7
Ganzhe China see Minhou
Ganzhou China 67 E3
Ganzi Sudan 96 A3
Gao Mali 93 E1
Gao admin. reg. Mali 93 F1
Gao'an China 67 E2
Gaocheng China see Litang
Gaochun China 67 F2
Gaocun China see Mayang
Gaohebu China 67 F2
Gaojian China 67 G2
Gaoleshan China see Xianfeng
Gaoliangjian China see Hongze
Gaoligong Shan mts China 66 A3
Gaoling China 67 D1
Gaomutang China 67 D3
Gaotangling China see Wangcheng
Gaoua Burkina 92 E3
Gaoxiong Taiwan see Kaohsiung
Gaoyou China 67 F1
Gaoyou Hu l. China 67 F1
Gaozhou China 67 D4
Gap France 39 G4
Gapuwiyak Australia 110 C2
Gaqoi China 75 D3
Gar China 70 F5
Gar Pak. 81 E5
Gar' r. Rus. Fed. 64 B1
Garaa Tebourt well Tunisia 91 H3
Garabekevyul Turkm. 81 F2
Garabil Belentligi hills Turkm. see Karabil', Vozvyshennost'
Garabinzam Congo 94 B4
Garabogazköl Aylagy b. Turkm. see Kara-Bogaz-Gol, Zaliv
Garabogazköl Bogazy sea chan. Turkm. see Kara-Bogaz-Gol, Proliv
Garacad Somalia 96 F3
Garadag Somalia 96 E2
Gara Ekar hill Alg. 91 G6
Garagoa Col. 146 C3
Garagum des. Kazakh. see Karakum Desert
Garagum des. Turkm. see Karakum Desert
Garah Australia 112 D3
Garalo Mali 92 D3
Garamätnyyaz Turkm. see Karamet-Niyaz
Garamba r. Dem. Rep. Congo 94 F4
Garanhuns Brazil 150 E4
Garapu Brazil 150 A5
Garar, Plaine de plain Chad 94 D2
Garba Cent. Afr. Rep. 94 D2
Garbahaarey Somalia 96 D4
Garba Tula Kenya 96 C4
Garberville U.S.A. 136 A1
Garbo China see Lhozhag
Garbosh, Kūh-e mt. Iran 80 B3
Garbsen Germany 36 D2
Garcia Sola, Embalse de resr Spain 42 D3
Gard r. France 39 F5
Garda Italy 44 C2
Garda, Lake Italy 44 C2
Gardabani Georgia 79 F2
Gârda de Sus Romania 46 C1
Gardelegen Germany 36 E2
Garden City U.S.A. 132 A4
Garden Hill Canada 123 M4
Garden Mountain U.S.A. 130 C5
Gardermoen airport Norway 33 C3
Gardinas Belarus see Hrodna
Gardiner U.S.A. 131 I1
Gardiner Range hills Australia 110 B3
Gardiners Island U.S.A. 131 G3
Gardīz Afgh. 81 G3
Gardner atoll Micronesia see Faraulep
Gardner U.S.A. 131 H2
Gardner Inlet Antarctica 167 L1
Gardner Island Kiribati see Nikumaroro
Gardner Pinnacles is U.S.A. 165 G4
Gardno, Jezioro lag. Poland 37 H1
Gárdony Hungary 37 I5
Gardsjönäs Sweden 32 E2
Gardslösa Sweden 33 E4
Gáregasnjárga Fin. see Karigasniemi
Gares Spain see Puente la Reina
Garešnica Croatia 44 F2
Garet El Djenoun mt. Alg. 91 G4
Gare Tigre Fr. Guiana 147 H3
Garfield U.S.A. 135 F5
Gargáligas r. Spain 42 D3
Gargano, Parco Nazionale del nat. park Italy 44 E4
Gargantua, Cape Canada 124 C4
Gargunsa China see Gar
Gargždai Lith. 33 F5
Garhakota India 74 C5
Garhbeta India 75 E5
Garhchiroli India 72 D1
Garhi India 74 B5
Garhi Khairo Pak. 81 F4
Garhi Malehra India 74 C4
Garhmuktesar India 74 C3
Garhshankar India 74 C3
Garibaldi Brazil 151 B9
Garibaldi Canada 134 B2
Gariep Dam resr S. Africa 98 E6
Garies S. Africa 98 C6
Garissa Kenya 96 C5
Garkalne Latvia 33 G4
Garkung Caka l. China 75 E2
Garland U.S.A. 133 B5
Garliava Lith. 33 F5
Gârliciu Romania 46 F2
Garlin France 38 C5
Garm Tajik. see Gharm
Garmab Afgh. 81 F3
Garmdasht Iran 80 B4
Garmeh Iran 80 D2
Garmī Iran 80 B2
Garmisch-Partenkirchen Germany 36 E5
Garmo, Qullai mt. Tajik. 81 G2
Garmsar Iran 80 C3
Garner U.S.A. 132 C3
Garnett U.S.A. 132 C4
Garnpung Lake imp. l. Australia 112 B4
Garo Hills India 75 F4
Garonne r. France 38 C4
Garoowe Somalia 96 F2
Garoth India 74 B4
Garou, Lac l. Mali 93 E1
Garoua Cameroon 93 I3
Garoua Boulai Cameroon 94 B3
Garqêntang China see Sog
Garrison KY U.S.A. 130 B4
Garrison ND U.S.A. 132 A2
Garrucha Spain 43 F4
Garrygala Turkm. 80 D2
Garry Lake Canada 123 K1
Garsen Kenya 96 D5
Garshy Turkm. see Karshi
Garsila Sudan 88 D6
Gartar China see Qianning
Gartempe r. France 38 D3
Gartog China see Markam
Gartok China see Garyarsa
Garut Indon. 59 D4
Garwa India 75 D4
Garwolin Poland 37 J3
Gar Xincun China 70 F5
Gary IN U.S.A. 132 E3
Gary WV U.S.A. 130 C5
Garyarsa China 74 D3
Garyi China 66 A2
Garyū-zan mt. Japan 65 C6
Garza Arg. 152 E2
Gar Zangbo r. China 74 C2
Garzê China 66 A2
Garzón Col. 146 C4
Gasan-Kuli Turkm. see Esenguly
Gascogne reg. France see Gascony
Gascogne, Golfe de g. France/Spain see Gascony, Gulf of
Gascony reg. France 38 C5
Gascony, Gulf of France/Spain 38 B5
Gascoyne r. Australia 109 A6
Gascoyne, Mount Australia 109 B6
Gascoyne Junction Australia 109 A6
Gascuña, Golfo de g. France/Spain see Gascony, Gulf of
Gasherbrum mt. Jammu and Kashmir 74 C2
Gasht Iran 81 E5
Gashua Nigeria 93 H2
Gaspar, Selat sea chan. Indon. 59 D3
Gaspé Canada 125 H3
Gaspé, Cap c. Canada 125 H3
Gaspé, Péninsule de pen. Canada 125 H3
Gassan Burkina 92 E2
Gassan vol. Japan 65 E5
Gassane Senegal 92 B2
Gassaway U.S.A. 130 C4
Gassol Nigeria 93 H3
Gasteiz Spain see Vitoria-Gasteiz
Gastello Rus. Fed. 64 E2
Gaston, Lake U.S.A. 130 E5
Gastonia U.S.A. 128 C5
Gastouni Greece 47 B6
Gastre Arg. 153 C5
Gata, Cabo de c. Spain 43 E4
Gata, Cape Cyprus 77 A2
Gata, Sierra de mts Spain 42 C2
Gatagara r. Canada 122 E3
Gătaia Romania 46 B2
Gatas, Akra c. Cyprus see Gata, Cape
Gatchina Rus. Fed. 28 D4
Gateshead U.K. 34 F4
Gates of the Arctic National Park and Preserve U.S.A. 120 D3
Gatesville U.S.A. 133 B6
Gateway U.S.A. 137 H2
Gatico Chile 148 C5
Gatineau Canada 124 F4
Gatineau r. Canada 124 F4
Gatong China see Jomda
Gatooma Zimbabwe see Kadoma
Gatton Australia 111 H5
Gatvand Iran 80 B3
Gatwick airport U.K. 35 F6
Gaúcha do Norte Brazil 150 A5
Gaud-i-Zirreh depr. Afgh. 81 E4
Gauer Lake Canada 123 L3
Gauhati India see Guwahati
Gauja r. Latvia 33 G4
Gaujas nacionālais parks nat. park Latvia 33 G4
Gaul country Europe see France
Gaula r. Norway 32 C3
Gauley Bridge U.S.A. 130 C4
Gaupne Norway 33 B3
Gaurdak Turkm. see Govurdak
Gaurela India 75 D5
Gauribidanur India 72 C3
Gaurnadi Bangl. 75 F5
Gauteng prov. S. Africa 99 F5
Gavà Spain 43 H2
Gavarr Armenia see Kamo
Gavāter Iran 81 E5
Gāvbandī Iran 80 C5
Gāvbūs, Kūh-e mts Iran 80 C5
Gavdopoula i. Greece 47 D7

▶Gavdos i. Greece 47 D7
Most southerly point of Europe.

Gave r. France 38 C5
Gāveh Rūd r. Iran 80 A3
Gavião r. Brazil 150 D5
Gavião Port. 42 C3
Gävle Sweden 33 E3
Gävleborg county Sweden 33 D3
Gävlebukten b. Sweden 33 E3
Gavrilov-Yam Rus. Fed. 28 F4
Gavrio Greece 47 D6
Gawai Myanmar 60 B2
Gawan India 75 E4
Gawat well Libya 88 B3
Gawilgarh Hills India 74 C5
Gawler Australia 112 A4
Gawler Ranges hills Australia 109 F8
Gäwür watercourse Turkm. see Gyaur
Gaya r. China 64 B4
Gaya India 75 E4
Gaya i. Sabah Malaysia 59 G1
Gaya Niger 93 F3
Gaya, Pulau i. Sabah Malaysia 59 G1
Gayam Indon. 59 F4
G'Aydat al Jhoucha ridge W. Sahara 90 C4
Gayéri Burkina 93 F2
Gaylord U.S.A. 132 E2
Gayndah Australia 111 G5
Gayny Rus. Fed. 28 J3
Gaysin Ukr. see Haysyn
Gayutino Rus. Fed. 28 F4
Gaz Iran 80 D5

▶Gaza terr. Asia 77 B4
Semi-autonomous region.
asia 82

▶Gaza Gaza 77 B4
Capital of Gaza.

Gaza prov. Moz. 99 G4
Gaz-Achak Turkm. 76 G1
Gazandzhyk Turkm. 80 C2
Gazawa Cameroon 93 I3
Gaziantep Turkey 78 D3
Gazīk Iran 81 E3
Gazimağusa Cyprus see Famagusta
Gazipaşa Turkey 78 C3
Gazli Uzbek. 81 E1
Gazojak Turkm. see Gaz-Achak
Gbaaka Liberia 92 D4
Gbarnga Liberia 92 C4
Gbatala Liberia 92 C4
Gbérouboué Benin 93 F3
Gboko Nigeria 93 H4
Gbwado Dem. Rep. Congo 94 D4
Gdańsk Poland 37 I1
Gdańsk, Gulf of Poland/Rus. Fed. 37 I1
Gdańska, Zatoka g. Poland/Rus. Fed. see Gdańsk, Gulf of
Gdingen Poland see Gdynia
Gdov Rus. Fed. 28 C4
Gdyel Alg. 43 F5
Gdynia Poland 37 I1
Gearhart Mountain U.S.A. 134 B4
Gebe i. Indon. 57 G5
Gebeit Sudan 89 H5
Gebeit Mine Sudan 89 H4
Gebre Guracha Eth. 96 C2
Gebze Turkey 46 F4
Gech'a Eth. 96 B3
Gecheng China see Chengkou
Gedaref Sudan 89 G6
Gedaref state Sudan 89 G6
Gediz r. Turkey 78 A3
Gedlegubē Eth. 96 E3
Gēdo Eth. 96 C2
Gedo admin. reg. Somalia 96 D4
Gedong, Tanjong pt Sing. 58 [inset]
Gedser Denmark 33 C5
Geel Belgium 36 B3
Geelong Australia 112 C5
Geelvink Channel Australia 109 A7
Geesthacht Germany 36 E2
Gēgē r. Lith. 33 F5
Gê'gyai China 70 F5
Ge Hu l. China 67 F2
Geidam Nigeria 93 H2
Geiersberg hill Germany 36 D4
Geikie r. Canada 123 K3
Geilo Norway 33 C3
Geiselhöring Germany 37 F4
Geislingen an der Steige Germany 36 D4
Geita Tanz. 96 B5
Gejiu China 66 B4
Gel r. Sudan 96 A3
Gel watercourse Sudan 94 F2
Gela Sicily Italy 45 E6
Gela r. Sicily Italy 45 E6
Gela, Golfo di g. Sicily Italy 45 E6
Geladaindong mt. China 75 F2
Geladī Eth. 96 E3
Gelam i. Indon. 59 E3
Geldern Germany 36 C3
Gelembe Turkey 47 E5
Gelemso Eth. 96 D2
Gelendzhik Rus. Fed. 29 F7
Gelephu Bhutan 75 F4
Gelibolu Turkey see Gallipoli
Gelibolu Yarımadası pen. Turkey 47 E4
Gelibolu Yarımadası Tarihi Milli Parkı nat. park Turkey 47 E4
Gelidonya Burnu pt Turkey see Yardımcı Burnu
Gelincik Dağı mt. Turkey 78 B3
Gelinsoor Somalia 96 E3
Gelmord Iran 80 D3
Gelnica Slovakia 37 J4
Gemas Malaysia 58 C2
Gembu Nigeria 93 H4
Gemena Dem. Rep. Congo 94 C4
Gemerek Turkey 78 D3
Gemlik Turkey 78 B2
Gemlik Körfezi b. Turkey 46 F4
Gemlufall Iceland 32 [inset]
Gemona del Friuli Italy 44 D1
Gémozac France 38 C4
Gemsbok National Park Botswana 98 D5
Genal r. Spain 42 D4
Genalē Wenz r. Eth. 96 D3
General Acha Arg. 152 D4
General Alvear Buenos Aires Arg. 152 E4
General Alvear Mendoza Arg. 152 D3
General Artigas Para. 149 F6
General Belgrano Arg. 152 F3
General Bernardo O'Higgins research station Antarctica 167 A2

▶General Carrera, Lago l. Arg./Chile 153 B6
Deepest lake in South America.

General Conesa Arg. 152 D5
General Freire Angola see Muxaluando
General José de San Martín Arg. 152 F1
General Juan Madariaga Arg. 152 F4
General Lagos Chile 148 C4
General La Madrid Arg. 152 E4
General Machado Angola see Camacupa
General Martín Miguel de Güemes Arg. 148 D6
General Paz Arg. 152 F1
General Pico Arg. 152 E3
General Pinto Arg. 152 E3
General Roca Arg. 152 D4
General Santos Phil. 57 G4
General Terán Mex. 133 B7
General Toshevo Bulg. 46 F3
General Trias Mex. 135 F7
General Villegas Arg. 152 E3
Genesee U.S.A. 130 E3
Genesee r. U.S.A. 130 E2
Geneseo U.S.A. 130 E2
Genet Eth. 96 C2
Geneva Switz. 39 G3
Geneva AL U.S.A. 129 B6
Geneva NE U.S.A. 132 B3
Geneva NY U.S.A. 131 E2
Geneva OH U.S.A. 130 C3
Geneva, Lake France/Switz. 39 G3
Genève Switz. see Geneva
Genf Switz. see Geneva
Gengda China 66 B1
Gengenbach Germany 36 D4
Genglou China 67 E4
Geni r. Sudan 96 B3
Genil r. Spain 42 D4
Genk Belgium 39 F1
Gennargentu, Monti del mts Sardinia Italy 45 B5
Genoa Australia 112 D5
Genoa Italy 44 B2
Genoa, Gulf of Italy 44 B2
Genova Italy see Genoa
Genteng Indon. 59 D4
Genteng i. Indon. 59 F4
Genthin Germany 36 F2
Genua Italy see Genoa
Genzano di Roma Italy 44 D4
Geoagiu r. Romania 46 C1
Geographe Bay Australia 109 A8
Geographical Society Ø i. Greenland 121 Q2
Georga, Zemlya i. Rus. Fed. 26 E1
George r. Canada 125 H1
George S. Africa 98 D7
George, Lake Australia 112 D4
George, Lake FL U.S.A. 129 C6
George, Lake NY U.S.A. 131 G2
George Land i. Rus. Fed. see Georga, Zemlya
Georges Mills U.S.A. 131 G2
George Sound inlet N.Z. 113 A4
Georgetown Australia 111 E3
George Town Australia 112 C6
George Town Bahamas 129 E8
Georgetown Canada 130 D2

▶George Town Cayman Is 139 H5
Capital of the Cayman Islands.

Georgetown Gambia 92 B2

▶Georgetown Guyana 147 G3
Capital of Guyana.

George Town Malaysia 58 C1
Georgetown DE U.S.A. 131 F4
Georgetown GA U.S.A. 129 B6
Georgetown KY U.S.A. 130 A4
Georgetown OH U.S.A. 130 B4
Georgetown SC U.S.A. 129 D5
Georgetown TX U.S.A. 133 B6
George VI Sound sea chan. Antarctica 167 L2
George V Land reg. Antarctica 167 H2
George West U.S.A. 133 B6
▶Georgia country Asia 79 E2
asia 52–53, 82
Georgia state U.S.A. 129 C5
Georgia, Strait of Canada 122 E5
Georgian Bay Canada 130 C1
Georgian Bay Islands National Park Canada 130 D1
Georgi Dimitrov, Yazovir resr Bulg. see Koprinka, Yazovir
Georgina watercourse Australia 110 D5
Georgi Traykov Bulg. see Dolni Chiflik
Georgiu-Dezh Rus. Fed. see Liski
Georgiyevka Kazakh. 70 F2
Georgiyevsk Rus. Fed. 29 G7
Georgiyevskoye Rus. Fed. 28 H4
Gera Germany 36 F3
Gerakarou Greece 46 C4
Geraki Greece 47 C6
Geraki, Akra pt Greece 47 B6
Geral de Goiás, Serra hills Brazil 150 C4
Geraldine N.Z. 113 B4
Geral do Paraná, Serra hills Brazil 149 I3
Geraldton Australia 109 A7
Geraneia mts Greece 47 C6
Gerar watercourse Israel 77 B4
Gerāsh Iran 80 C5
Gerber U.S.A. 136 A1
Gercüş Turkey 79 E3
Gerdauen Rus. Fed. see Zheleznodorozhnyy
Gerede Turkey 78 C2
Gerede r. Turkey 78 C2
Gereshk Afgh. 81 F4
Geretsried Germany 36 E5
Gergovie tourist site France 39 E4
Gerik Malaysia 58 C1
Gerimenj Iran 81 D3
Gerlach U.S.A. 136 C1
Gerlachovský štít mt. Slovakia 37 J4
Gerlospaß pass Austria 36 F5
Germania country Europe see Germany
Germanicea Turkey see Kahramanmaraş
Germansen Landing Canada 122 E4
German South-West Africa country Africa see Namibia
Germantown U.S.A. 133 D5

▶Germany country Europe 36 E3
2nd most populous country in Europe.
europe 24–25, 48

Germencik Turkey 47 E6
Gernika-Lumo Spain 43 E1
Gerolstein Germany 36 C3
Gerolzhofen Germany 36 E4
Gerona Spain see Girona
Gerrit Denys is P.N.G. see Lihir Group
Gers r. France 38 D4
Gersoppa India 72 B3
Géryville Alg. see El Bayadh
Gêrzê China 70 F5
Gerze Turkey 78 C2
Geschriebenstein hill Austria 37 H5
Gesoriacum France see Boulogne-sur-Mer
Gessler Arg. 152 E2
Geta Fin. 33 E3
Getafe Spain 42 E2
Getcheh, Kūh-e hills Iran 80 C3
Gete r. Belgium 39 F1
Getic, Podișul plat. Romania 46 C2
Gettysburg PA U.S.A. 131 E4
Gettysburg SD U.S.A. 132 B2
Gettysburg National Military Park nat. park U.S.A. 131 E4
Getu He r. China 66 C3
Getúlio Vargas Brazil 151 A8
Getz Ice Shelf Antarctica 167 J2
Geumapang r. Indon. 58 B2
Geureudong, Gunung vol. Indon. 58 B1
Gevān-e Ţāleb Khānī Iran 81 D5
Gevaş Turkey 79 E3
Gevgelija Macedonia 46 C4
Gevrai India 72 B2
Gevrey-Chambertin France 39 F3
Gex France 39 G3
Gey Iran see Nīkshahr
Geyikli Turkey 47 E5
Geylang Sing. 58 [inset]
Geylang r. Sing. 58 [inset]
Geyserville U.S.A. 136 A2
Geyve Turkey 78 B2
Ghaap Plateau S. Africa 98 D5
Ghabeish Sudan 89 E6
Ghadaf, Wādī al watercourse Iraq 79 E4
Ghadaf, Wādī al watercourse Jordan 77 C4
Ghadamès Libya see Ghadāmis
Ghadāmis Libya 88 A2
Ghaddūwah Libya 88 B3
Ghaem Shahr Iran 80 C2
Ghaggar, Dry Bed of watercourse Pak. 81 H4
Ghaghara r. India 75 E4
Ghaghra India 75 E5
Ghalkarteniz, Solonchak salt marsh Kazakh. 70 B2
Ghallamane reg. Mauritania 90 C5
Ghallaorol Uzbek. see Gallyaaral
▶Ghana country Africa 93 E3
africa 86–87, 100
Ghanādah, Rās pt U.A.E. 80 C5
Ghanliala India 74 B4
Ghantwar India 72 A1
Ghanwā Saudi Arabia 80 B5
Ghanzi Botswana 98 D4
Ghanzi admin. dist. Botswana 98 D4
Ghap'an Armenia see Kapan
Gharandal Jordan 77 B4
Gharbīya governorate Egypt see Al Gharbīyah
Ghardaïa Alg. 91 F2
Ghardimaou Tunisia 45 B6
Ghar el Melh Tunisia 45 C6
Ghārib, Jabal mt. Egypt 89 G2
Gharm Tajik. 81 G2
Gharo Pak. 81 F5
Gharyān Libya 88 B1
Gharz, Wādī al watercourse Syria 77 C3
Ghāt Libya 88 A3
Ghatampur India 74 D4
Ghatgan India 75 E5
Ghatol India 74 B5
Ghatsila India 75 E5
Ghauspur Pak. 81 G4
Ghawdex i. Malta see Gozo
Ghazal, Bahr el watercourse Chad 88 C6
Ghazal, Bahr el r. Sudan 96 A2
Ghazaouet Alg. 91 E2
Ghaziabad India 74 C3
Ghazipur India 75 D4
Ghazira, Ghubbat al inlet Oman 80 D5
Ghazna Afgh. see Ghaznī
Ghaznī Afgh. 81 G3
Ghaznī prov. Afgh. 81 F3
Ghazni r. Afgh. 81 F3
Ghazzālah Saudi Arabia 89 I3
Ghemeis, Ras pt U.A.E. 80 B5
Ghent Belgium 39 E1
Ghent U.S.A. 130 C5
Gheorghe Gheorghiu-Dej Romania see Onești
Gheorgheni Romania 46 D1
Ghijduwon Uzbek. see Gizhduvan
Ghīnah, Wādī al watercourse Saudi Arabia 77 D4
Ghioroiu Romania 46 C2
Ghisonaccia Corsica France 31 G5
Ghizao Afgh. 81 F3
Ghizar Jammu and Kashmir 74 B1
Ghod India 72 B2
Ghod r. India 72 B2
Gholvad India 72 B1
Ghorak Afgh. 81 F3
Ghorband r. Afgh. 81 G3
Ghost Lake Canada 123 H2
Ghotaru India 74 A4
Ghotki Pak. 81 G5
Ghowr prov. Afgh. 81 F3
Ghuari r. India 75 E4
Ghudamis Libya see Ghadāmis
Ghugus India 72 C2
Ghulam Mohammed Barrage Pak. 81 G5
Ghurayfah hill Saudi Arabia 77 C4
Ghūrī Iran 80 C4
Ghurian Afgh. 81 E3
Ghuzayyil, Sabkhat salt marsh Libya 88 C2
Ghuzor Uzbek. see Guzar
Gia Đinh Vietnam 61 D6
Giaginskaya Rus. Fed. 79 E1
Gialias r. Cyprus 77 A2
Giang r. Vietnam 60 D4
Gia Nghia Vietnam 61 D5
Giannitsa Greece 46 C4
Giannutri, Isola di i. Italy 44 C3
Giant's Causeway lava field U.K. 34 C4
Giant Sequoia National Monument nat. park U.S.A. 136 C3
Gianysada i. Greece 47 E7
Giarmata Romania 46 B2
Giarre Sicily Italy 45 E6
Gibarrayo hill Spain 42 D4
Gibb r. Australia 108 D3
Gibb River Australia 108 D4
Gibeon Namibia 98 C5
Gibraleón Spain 42 C4

▶Gibraltar Europe 42 D4
United Kingdom Overseas Territory.
europe 24–25, 48

▶Gibraltar, Strait of Morocco/Spain 42 C5
europe 24–25
Gibraltar Range National Park Australia 112 E3
Gibson Australia 109 C8
Gibson Desert Australia 110 A5
Gibsons Canada 122 F5
Gichgeniyn Nuruu mts Mongolia 62 E2
Gīdamī Eth. 96 B2
Gidda Eth. 96 B2
Giddalur India 72 C3
Giddi, Gebel el hill Egypt see Jiddī, Jabal al
Giddings U.S.A. 133 B6
Giddi Pass hill Egypt see Jiddī, Jabal al
Gideälven r. Sweden 32 E3
Gīdolē Eth. 96 C3
Gien France 39 E3
Giesecke Isfjord inlet Greenland see Kangerlussuaq
Gießen Germany 36 D3
Gīfan Iran 80 D2
Gifhorn Germany 36 E2
Gift Lake Canada 123 H4
Gifu Japan 65 D6
Gigant Rus. Fed. 29 G7
Gigante Col. 146 C4
Gigha i. U.K. 34 D4
Ghighera Romania 46 C3
Giglio, Isola del i. Italy 44 C3
Gijón-Xixón Spain 42 D1
Gila r. U.S.A. 137 E5
Gila Bend U.S.A. 137 F5
Gila Bend Mountains U.S.A. 137 F5
Gila Mountains U.S.A. 137 E5
Gīlān prov. Iran 80 B2
Gilău Romania 46 C1
Gilāzi Azer. 79 G2
Gilbert r. Australia 111 E3
Gilbert AZ U.S.A. 137 G5
Gilbert WV U.S.A. 130 C5
Gilbert Islands Kiribati 164 F5
Gilbert Islands country Pacific Ocean see Kiribati
Gilbert Ridge sea feature Pacific Ocean 164 F5
Gilbert River Australia 111 E3
Gilbués Brazil 150 C4
Gilé Moz. 99 H3
Giles Creek r. Australia 110 B3
Giles Meteorological Station Australia 109 E6
Gilf Kebir Plateau Egypt see Jilf al Kabīr, Haḑabat al
Gilgandra Australia 112 D3
Gil Gil Creek r. Australia 112 D3
Gilgit Jammu and Kashmir 74 B2

Gilgit r. Jammu and Kashmir 74 B2
Gilgunnia Australia 112 C4
Gilimanuk Indon. 59 F5
Gılındire Turkey see Aydıncık
Gillam Canada 123 M3
Gillen watercourse Australia 110 C4
Gillen, Lake salt flat Australia 109 D6
Gilles, Lake salt flat Australia 109 G8
Gillett U.S.A. 131 E3
Gillette U.S.A. 134 F3
Gilliat Australia 111 E4
Gillingham U.K. 35 G6
Gilman U.S.A. 132 E3
Gilmer U.S.A. 133 C5
Gilort r. Romania 46 C2
Gilroy U.S.A. 136 B3
Giluwe, Mount P.N.G. 57 J7
Gīmbī Eth. 96 B2
Gimo Sweden 33 E3
Gimont France 38 D5
Ginda Eritrea 89 H6
Gindie Australia 111 G4
Ginebra, Laguna l. Bol. 148 D3
Gingee India 72 C3
Gin Gin Australia 111 G5
Gingin Australia 109 A7
Gīnīr Eth. 96 D3
Ginzo de Limia Spain see Xinzo de Limia
Gioia, Golfo di b. Italy 45 E5
Gioia del Colle Italy 45 F4
Gioura i. Greece 47 D5
Gipouloux r. Canada 124 F2
Gippsland reg. Australia 112 C5
Girab India 74 A4
Gīrān Rīg mt. Iran 81 D4
Girard U.S.A. 130 C3
Girardin, Lac l. Canada 125 H1
Girdar Dhor r. Pak. 81 F5
Girdi Iran 81 E4
Giresun Turkey 79 D2
Girgenti Sicily Italy see Agrigento
Giri r. Dem. Rep. Congo 94 C4
Giridih India 75 E4
Girna r. India 74 B5
Gir National Park India 74 A5
Girne Cyprus see Kyrenia
Giromagny France 39 G3
Girón Ecuador 146 B5
Giron Sweden see Kiruna
Girona Spain 43 H2
Gironde est. France 38 C4
Girou r. France 38 D5
Giruá Brazil 151 A9
Girvan U.K. 34 D4
Girvas Rus. Fed. 28 E3
Gisborne N.Z. 113 D2
Gisenyi Rwanda 94 F5
Gislaved Sweden 33 D4
Gisors France 38 D2
Gissar Tajik. see Hisor
Gissar Range mts Tajik./Uzbek. 81 F2
Gissarskiy Khrebet mts Tajik./Uzbek. see Gissar Range
Gitarama Rwanda 94 F5
Gitega Burundi 94 F5
Giuba r. Somalia see Jubba
Giubega Romania 46 C2
Giulianova Italy 44 D3
Giurgiu Romania 46 D3
Givar Iran 80 D2
Give Denmark 33 C5
Givors France 39 F4
Giyani S. Africa 99 F4
Giyon Eth. 96 C2
Giza Egypt 89 F2
▶Giza Pyramids tourist site Egypt 89 F2
africa 86–87
Gīzeh Rūd r. Iran 80 A3
Gizhduvan Uzbek. 81 F1
Gizhiga Rus. Fed. 27 Q3
Gizo Solomon Is 107 E2
Giżycko Poland 37 J1
Gjalicë e Lumës, Mal mt. Albania 46 B3
Gjerde Norway 33 B3
Gjirokastër Albania 47 B4
Gjoa Haven Canada 121 J3
Gjögur Iceland 32 [inset]
Gjøra Norway 32 C3
Gjøvik Norway 33 C3
Gjuhëzës, Kepi i pt Albania 47 A4
Glace Bay Canada 125 J4
Glacier Bay U.S.A. 122 C3
Glacier Bay National Park and Preserve U.S.A. 120 F4
Glacier National Park Canada 122 G5
Glacier National Park U.S.A. 134 D2
Glacier Peak vol. U.S.A. 134 B2
Glade Spring U.S.A. 130 C5
Gladstone Qld Australia 111 G4
Gladstone S.A. Australia 112 A4
Gladstone Canada 123 L5
Gladstone U.S.A. 130 D5
Gladwin U.S.A. 130 A2
Gladys U.S.A. 130 D5
Gladys Lake Canada 122 C3
Glamis U.S.A. 137 E5
Glamoč Bos.-Herz. 44 F2
Glan r. Austria 37 G5
Glan r. Germany 36 C4
Glan l. Sweden 33 D4
Glarner Alpen mts Switz. 39 H3
Glarus Switz. 39 H3
Glasfjorden l. Sweden 33 D4
Glasgow U.K. 34 D4
Glasgow KY U.S.A. 128 B4
Glasgow MT U.S.A. 134 F2
Glasgow VA U.S.A. 130 D5
Glaslyn Canada 123 I4
Glassboro U.S.A. 131 F4
Glass Mountain U.S.A. 136 C3
Glauchau Germany 37 F3
Glavacioc r. Romania 46 D2
Glavan Bulg. 46 E3
Glăvăneşti Romania 46 E1
Glavinitsa Bulg. 46 E3
Glavnik Yugo. 46 B3
Glazoué Benin 93 F4
Glazov Rus. Fed. 28 J4
Glazunovka Rus. Fed. 29 F5
Gleichen Canada 123 H5
Gleisdorf Austria 37 G5
Gleiwitz Poland see Gliwice
Glen Sweden 32 D3
Glen U.S.A. 131 H1
Glen Allen U.S.A. 130 E5
Glénan, Îles de is France 38 B3
Glenavy N.Z. 113 B4
Glenboro Canada 123 L5
Glen Burnie U.S.A. 131 E4
Glen Canyon gorge U.S.A. 137 G3
Glen Canyon Dam U.S.A. 137 G3
Glencoe KY U.S.A. 130 A4
Glencoe MN U.S.A. 132 C2
Glen Cove U.S.A. 131 G3
Glendale AZ U.S.A. 137 F5
Glendale CA U.S.A. 136 C4
Glendale UT U.S.A. 137 F3
Glendale Lake U.S.A. 130 D3
Glendambo Australia 109 F7
Glendive U.S.A. 134 F3
Glendon Canada 123 I4
Glendo Reservoir U.S.A. 134 F4
Glenelg r. Australia 112 B5
Glenfinnan U.K. 34 D3
Glengarry Range hills Australia 109 B6
Glengyle Australia 111 D5
Glen Innes Australia 111 G6
Glenlyon Peak Canada 122 C2
Glen More valley U.K. 34 D3
Glenmorgan Australia 111 G5
Glenn U.S.A. 136 A2
Glennallen U.S.A. 120 E3
Glennie U.S.A. 130 B1
Glenns U.S.A. 131 E5
Glenns Ferry U.S.A. 134 D4
Glenora Canada 122 D3
Glenore Australia 111 E3
Glenormiston Australia 110 D4
Glen Rock U.S.A. 131 E4
Glen Rogers U.S.A. 130 C5
Glen Rose U.S.A. 133 B5
Glenrothes U.K. 34 E3
Glenroy Australia 108 D4
Glens Falls U.S.A. 131 G2
Glenties Rep. of Ireland 34 B4
Glenveagh National Park Rep. of Ireland 34 C4
Glenville U.S.A. 130 C4
Glen Wilton U.S.A. 130 D5
Glenwood AR U.S.A. 133 C5
Glenwood IA U.S.A. 132 C3
Glenwood MN U.S.A. 132 C2
Glenwood WV U.S.A. 130 B4
Glenwood Springs U.S.A. 134 F5
Glevum U.K. see Gloucester
Glina r. Bos.-Herz./Croatia 44 F2
Glina Croatia 44 F2
Glittertinden mt. Norway 33 C3
Gliwice Poland 37 I3
Globe U.S.A. 137 G5
Glodeanu-Sărat Romania 46 E2
Glodeni Romania 46 D1
Glogau Poland see Głogów
Gloggnitz Austria 37 G5
Glogovac Yugo. 46 B3
Głogów Poland 37 H3
Głogówek Poland 37 H3
Glomfjord Norway 32 D2
Glomma r. Norway 33 C4
Glommersträsk Sweden 32 E2
Glória Brazil 150 E4
Glorieuses, Îles is Indian Ocean 97 E7
Glorioso Islands Indian Ocean see Glorieuses, Îles
Gloucester Australia 112 D3
Gloucester U.K. 35 E6
Gloucester MA U.S.A. 131 H2
Gloucester VA U.S.A. 131 E5
Gloucester Island Australia 111 G4
Gloucester Point U.S.A. 131 E5
Gloversville U.S.A. 131 F2
Glovertown Canada 125 K3
Glöwen Germany 36 F2
Głowno Poland 37 I3
Głubczyce Poland 37 H3
Glubinnoye Rus. Fed. 64 C3
Glubokiy Rus. Fed. 29 G6
Glubokoye Belarus see Hlybokaye
Glubokoye Kazakh. 70 F1
Glücksburg (Ostsee) Germany 36 D1
Glückstadt Germany 36 D2
Gluggarnir hill Faroe Is 34 [inset]
Glukhov Ukr. see Hlukhiv
Gmünd Austria 37 G4
Gmunden Austria 37 F5
Gnadenhutten U.S.A. 130 C3
Gnarp Sweden 33 E3
Gnesen Poland see Gniezno
Gniew Poland 37 I2
Gniezno Poland 37 H2
Gnisvärd Sweden 33 E4
Gnjilane Yugo. 46 B3
Gnowangerup Australia 109 B8
Gnows Nest Range hills Australia 109 B7
Goa state India 72 B3
Goageb Namibia 98 C5
Goalpara India 75 F4
Goaso Ghana 93 E4
Goat Fell hill U.K. 34 D4
Goba Eth. 96 D3
Gobabis Namibia 98 C4
Gobannium U.K. see Abergavenny
Gobas Namibia 98 C5
Gobernador Crespo Arg. 152 E2
Gobernador Duval Arg. 152 D4
Gobernador Gregores Arg. 153 C7
Gobernador Mayer Arg. 153 C7
Gobernador Virasoro Arg. 152 F2
Gobi des. China/Mongolia 70 K3
Gobi Desert China/Mongolia see Gobi
Göblberg hill Austria 37 F4
Gobō Japan 65 C6
Goch Germany 36 C3
Gochas Namibia 98 C5
Go Công Vietnam 61 D6
Godagari Bangl. 75 F4
Godavari r. India 72 D2
Godavari, Mouths of the India 69 G5
Godbout r. Canada 125 H3
Godda India 75 E4
Godē Eth. 96 D3
Godeal hill Port. 42 B3
Godech Bulg. 46 C3
Goderich Canada 130 C2
Goderville France 38 D2
Godhavn Greenland see Qeqertarsuaq
Godhra India 74 B5
Godinlabe Somalia 96 E3
Gödöllő Hungary 37 I5
Gods r. Canada 123 M3
Gods Lake Canada 123 M4
God's Mercy, Bay of Canada 123 O2
Godthåb Greenland see Nuuk
Godučohkka mt. Sweden 32 E1
Godwin-Austen, Mount China/Jammu and Kashmir see K2
Goedgegun Swaziland see Nhlangano
Goéland, Lac au l. Canada 127 K2
Goélands, Lac aux l. Canada 125 I2
Goes Neth. 36 A3
Goffstown U.S.A. 131 H2
Gogama Canada 124 D4
Gogebic Range hills U.S.A. 132 D2
Gogland, Ostrov i. Rus. Fed. 33 G3
Gogounou Benin 93 F3
Gogra India see Ghaghra
Gogra r. India see Ghaghara
Gogrial Sudan 94 F2
Gogunda India 74 B4
Gohad India 74 C4
Gohana India 74 C3
Goharganj India 74 C5
Goiana Brazil 150 F3
Goianésia Brazil 149 H3
Goiânia Brazil 149 H3
Goianinha Brazil 150 F3
Goiás Brazil 149 H3
Goiás state Brazil 149 H4
Goincang China 66 B1
Goio-Erê Brazil 151 A8
Goito Italy 44 C2
Gojeb Wenz r. Eth. 96 C3
Gojra Pak. 81 H4
Gokak India 72 B2
Gokarn India 72 B3
Gökçeada i. Turkey 78 A2
Gökçedağ Turkey 78 B3
Gökçen Turkey 47 E5
Gökçeören Turkey 47 F5
Gökdere r. Turkey 77 A1
Gökirmak r. Turkey 78 C2
Goklenkuy, Solonchak salt l. Turkm. 80 D1
Gökova Turkey see Ula
Gökova Körfezi b. Turkey 78 A3
Gokprosh Hills Pak. 81 E5
Göksun Turkey 78 D3
Göksu Nehri r. Turkey 78 C3
Gokteik Myanmar 60 B3
Göktepe Turkey 77 A1
Gokwe Zimbabwe 99 F3
Gol Norway 33 C3
Gola India 74 D3
Golaghat India 75 G4
Golakganj India 75 F4
Golan hills Syria 77 B3
Golbāf Iran 80 D4
Golbahār Afgh. 81 G3
Gölbaşı Turkey 78 D3
Golconda India 72 C2
Golconda U.S.A. 134 C4
Gölcük Turkey see Etili
Gölcük Turkey 78 B2
Gölcük r. Turkey 47 F5
Golczewo Poland 37 G2
Gold U.S.A. 130 E3
Gołdap Poland 37 K1
Gołdapa r. Poland 37 J1
Gold Beach U.S.A. 134 A4
Goldberg Germany 36 F2
Gold Coast country Africa see Ghana
Gold Coast Australia 111 H6
Gold Coast coastal area Ghana 93 E4
Golden Canada 134 C2
Golden Bay N.Z. 113 C3
Goldendale U.S.A. 134 B3
Golden Hinde mt. Canada 134 A2
Golden Meadow U.S.A. 133 D6
Golden Valley Zimbabwe 99 F3
Goldfield U.S.A. 136 D3
Gold River Canada 122 E5
Goldsboro U.S.A. 128 D5
Goldsworthy Australia 108 B5
Goldthwaite U.S.A. 133 B6
Goldvein U.S.A. 130 E4
Göle Turkey 79 E2
Goleniów Poland 37 G2
Golestān Afgh. 81 E3
Golestān prov. Iran 80 C2
Goleta U.S.A. 136 C4
Golfo di Orosei Gennargentu e Asinara, Parco Nazionale del nat. park Sardinia Italy 45 B4
Gölgeli Dağları mts Turkey 78 B3
Goliad U.S.A. 133 B6
Golija nat. park Yugo. 46 B3
Golija Planina mts Yugo. 46 B3
Golingka China see Gongbo'gyamda
Gölköy Turkey 79 D2
Gölmarmara Turkey 47 E5
Golmberg hill Germany 37 F2
Golmud China 70 H4
Golmud He r. China 75 G1
Golodnaya Step' plain Uzbek. 81 F1
Golpāyegān Iran 80 B3
Golspie U.K. 34 E3
Golub-Dobrzyń Poland 37 I2
Golungo Alto Angola 95 B7
Gol Vardeh Iran 81 E3
Golweyn Somalia 96 E4
Golyama Syutkya mt. Bulg. 46 D4
Golyam Perelik mt. Bulg. 46 D4
Golyam Persenk mt. Bulg. 46 D4
Goma Dem. Rep. Congo 94 F5
Goma Uganda 96 A5
Gomang Co salt l. China 75 F3
Gomati r. India 74 D4
Gombak, Bukit hill Sing. 58 [inset]
Gombari Dem. Rep. Congo 94 F4
Gombe Nigeria 93 H3
Gombe state Nigeria 93 H3
Gombe r. Tanz. 97 A6
Gombi Nigeria 93 I3
Gombroon Iran see Bandar-e 'Abbās
Gömeç Turkey 47 E5
Gomel' Belarus see Homyel'
Gómez Palacio Mex. 126 F6
Gomīshān Iran 80 C2
Gomo China 75 E2
Gomo Co salt l. China 75 E2
Gonabad Iran see Jūymand
Gonaïves Haiti 127 L8
Gonarezhou National Park Zimbabwe 99 F4
Gonbad-e Kavus Iran 80 C2
Gonda India 75 D4
Gondal India 74 A5
Gonda Libah well Eth. 96 E2
Gondar Col. 146 C5
Gondar Eth. see Gonder
Gonder Eth. 96 C1
Gondey Chad 94 C2
Gondia India 74 D5
Gönen Turkey 78 A2
Gönen r. Turkey 47 E4
Gonfreville-l'Orcher France 38 D2
Gong'an China 67 E2
Gongbalou China see Gamba
Gongbo'gyamda China 75 G3
Gonggar China 75 F3
Gongga Shan mt. China 66 B2
Gonghe China 70 J4
Gongjiang China see Yudu
Gongliu China 26 I5
Gongola r. Nigeria 93 I3
Gongolgon Australia 112 C3
Gongoué Gabon 94 A5
Gongquan China see Gongxian
Gongshan China 66 A3
Gongtang China see Damxung
Gongwang Shan mts China 66 B3
Gongxian Henan China see Gongyi
Gongxian Sichuan China 66 C2
Gongyi China 67 E1
Gongzhuling China 64 A4
Goniądz Poland 37 K2
Goniri Nigeria 93 I3
Gonjo China 66 A2
Gonjog China 75 E3
Gonnesa Sardinia Italy 45 B5
Gonnoi Greece 47 C5
Gonzáles Mex. 126 G7
Gonzales CA U.S.A. 136 B3
Gonzales TX U.S.A. 133 B6
González Moreno Arg. 152 E3
Gonzalo Vásquez Panama 146 B2
Goochland U.S.A. 130 E5
Goodenough, Cape Antarctica 167 G2
Goodenough Island P.N.G. 107 E2
Gooderham Canada 130 D1
Good Hope, Cape of S. Africa 98 C7
Goodland U.S.A. 132 A4
Goodooga Australia 112 C3
Goodparla Australia 110 C2
Goodspeed Nunataks nunataks Antarctica 167 E2
Goodwood r. Canada 125 G2
Goole U.K. 35 F5
Goolgowi Australia 112 C4
Goomalling Australia 109 B7
Goombalie Australia 112 C3
Goomeri Australia 111 H5
Goonda Moz. 99 G3
Goondiwindi Australia 111 G6
Goongarrie National Park Australia 109 C7
Goonyella Australia 111 F4
Goorly, Lake salt flat Australia 109 B7
Goose r. Canada 125 I2
Goose r. U.S.A. 132 B2
Goose Bay Canada see Happy Valley - Goose Bay
Goose Creek U.S.A. 129 C5
Goose Creek r. U.S.A. 134 D4
Goose Green Falkland Is 153 F7
Goose Lake U.S.A. 134 B4
Goose Lake Canal r. U.S.A. 136 C4
Gooty India 72 C3
Gopalganj Bangl. 75 F5
Gopalganj India 75 E4
Gopeshwar India 74 C3
Gopichettipalayam India 72 C4
Gopiganj India 75 D4
Göppingen Germany 36 D4
Góra Poland 37 H3
Goradiz Azer. see Horadiz
Goragorskiy Rus. Fed. 79 F2
Góra Kalwaria Poland 37 J3
Gorakhpur India 75 D4
Goražde Bos.-Herz. 46 A3
Gorczański Park Narodowy nat. park Poland 37 J4
Gorda, Sierra mts Spain 42 D4
Gördalen Sweden 33 D3
Gördes Turkey 78 B3
Gordon r. Canada 123 O1
Gordon U.S.A. 132 A3
Gordon, Lake Australia 112 C6
Gordon Downs Australia 108 E4
Gordon Lake Canada 123 H2
Gordonsville U.S.A. 130 D4
Gordonvale Australia 111 F3
Goré Chad 94 C3
Gorē Eth. 96 B2
Gore N.Z. 113 B4
Gore U.S.A. 130 D4
Gore Point U.S.A. 120 D4
Gorey Rep. of Ireland 35 C5
Gorg Iran 81 D4
Gorgān Iran 80 C2
Gorgan Bay Iran 80 C2
Gorge Range hills Australia 108 B5
Gorgol admin. reg. Mauritania 92 B1
Gorgona, Isola di i. Italy 44 B3
Gorgora Eth. 96 C1
Gorgoram Nigeria 93 H2
Gorham U.S.A. 131 H1
Gori Georgia 79 F2
Gorinchem Neth. 36 B3
Goris Armenia 79 F3
Goritsy Rus. Fed. 28 F4
Gorizia Italy 44 D2
Gorkhā Nepal 75 E4
Gorki Belarus see Horki
Gor'kiy Rus. Fed. see Nizhniy Novgorod
Gor'kovskaya Oblast' admin. div. Rus. Fed. see Nizhegorodskaya Oblast'
Gor'kovskoye Vodokhranilishche resr Rus. Fed. 28 G4
Gorlice Poland 37 J4
Görlitz Germany 37 G3
Gorlovka Ukr. see Horlivka
Gormi India 74 C4
Gorna Dzhumaya Bulg. see Blagoevgrad
Gorna Oryakhovitsa Bulg. 46 D3
Gorni Dŭbnik Bulg. 46 D3
Gornja Radgona Slovenia 44 E1
Gornji Matejevac Yugo. 46 B3
Gornji Milanovac Yugo. 46 B2
Gornji Vakuf Bos.-Herz. 44 F3
Gorno-Altaysk Rus. Fed. 62 D1
Gorno-Altayskaya Avtonomnaya Oblast' aut. rep. Rus. Fed. see Altay, Respublika
Gorno-Badakhshan aut. rep. Tajik. see Kŭhistoni Badakhshon
Gornotrakiyska Nizina lowland Bulg. 46 D3
Gornozavodsk Permskaya Oblast' Rus. Fed. 28 K4
Gornozavodsk Sakhalinskaya Oblast' Rus. Fed. 64 E3
Gornyak Rus. Fed. 26 I4
Gornyy Rus. Fed. 64 D2
Gornyy Altay aut. rep. Rus. Fed. see Altay, Respublika
Gornyy Badakhshan aut. rep. Tajik. see Kŭhistoni Badakhshon
Goro Eth. 96 D3
Goro i. Fiji see Koro
Goroch'an mt. Eth. 96 C2
Gorodets Rus. Fed. 28 G4
Gorodishche Penzenskaya Oblast' Rus. Fed. 29 H5
Gorodishche Volgogradskaya Oblast' Rus. Fed. 29 H6
Gorodok Belarus see Haradok
Gorodok Ukr. see Horodok
Gorodovikovsk Rus. Fed. 29 G7
Goroka P.N.G. 57 K7
Goroke Australia 112 B5
Gorokhovets Rus. Fed. 28 G4
Gorom Gorom Burkina 93 E2
Gorong, Kepulauan is Indon. 57 H6
Gorongosa Moz. 99 G3
Gorongosa mt. Moz. 99 G3
Gorongosa, Parque Nacional de nat. park Moz. 99 G3
Gorontalo Indon. 57 F5
Goroubi watercourse Niger 93 F2
Gorouol r. Burkina/Niger 93 F2
Gorshechnoye Rus. Fed. 29 F6
Gór Stołowych, Park Narodowy nat. park Poland 37 H3
Goru, Vârful mt. Romania 46 E2
Gorumna Island Rep. of Ireland 35 B5
Goryachiy Klyuch Rus. Fed. 29 F7
Gorzów Wielkopolski Poland 37 G2
Gosainthan mt. China see Xixabangma Feng
Goschen Strait P.N.G. 111 G1
Goshen CA U.S.A. 136 C3
Goshen IN U.S.A. 132 E3
Goshen NH U.S.A. 131 G2
Goshen VA U.S.A. 130 D5
Goshogawara Japan 64 E4
Goslar Germany 36 E3
Gospić Croatia 44 E2
Gossas Senegal 92 A2
Gosse watercourse Australia 110 C3
Gossi Mali 93 E2
Gossinga Sudan 94 E2
Gostivar Macedonia 46 B4
Gostyń Poland 37 H3
Gostynin Poland 37 I2
Gosu China 66 A1
Gota Eth. 96 D2
Götaälven r. Sweden 33 C4
Göteborg Sweden see Gothenburg
Gotel Mountains Cameroon/Nigeria 93 H4
Götene Sweden 33 D4
Gotenhafen Poland see Gdynia
Gotha Germany 36 E3
Gothem Sweden 33 E4
Gothenburg Sweden 33 C4
Gothenburg U.S.A. 132 A3
Gothèye Niger 93 F2
Gotland i. Sweden 33 E4
Gotō-rettō is Japan 65 B6
Gotse Delchev Bulg. 46 C4
Gotska Sandön Sweden 33 E4
Gotska Sandön i. Sweden 33 E4
Gōtsu Japan 65 C6
Gottero, Monte mt. Italy 44 B2
Göttingen Germany 36 D3
Gottne Sweden 32 E3
Gott Peak Canada 134 B2
Gottwaldow Czech Rep. see Zlín
Gotval'd Ukr. see Zmiyiv
Gouako Cent. Afr. Rep. 94 D3
Gouda Neth. 36 B2
Goudiri Senegal 92 B2
Goudoumaria Niger 93 H2
Goûgaram Niger 93 G1
▶Gough Island S. Atlantic Ocean 161 N8
Dependency of St Helena.
Gouin, Réservoir Canada 125 F3
Goulburn Australia 112 D4
Goulburn Islands Australia 110 C1
Goulburn River National Park Australia 112 D4
Gould Coast Antarctica 167 J1
Goulféy Cameroon 88 B6
Goulia Côte d'Ivoire 92 D3
Goulou atoll Micronesia see Ngulu
Goumbou Mali 92 D2
Gouna Cameroon 93 I3
Goundam Mali 92 E1
Goundi Chad 94 C2
Gounou-Gaya Chad 94 B2
Gouraya Alg. 43 G4
Gouraye Mauritania 92 B2
Gourcy Burkina 93 E2
Gourdon France 38 D4
Gouré Niger 93 H2
Gourin France 38 B2
Gouripur Bangl. 75 F4
Gourma-Rharous Mali 93 E1
Gourmeur well Chad 88 D5
Gournay-en-Bray France 38 D2
Gouro Chad 88 C5
Goûr Oulad Ahmed reg. Mali 90 D5
Gourouro well Chad 88 D5
Gouveia Port. 42 C2
Gouverneur U.S.A. 131 F1
Gove, Barragem do resr Angola 95 B8
Govedartsi Bulg. 46 C3
Govena, Mys hd Rus. Fed. 27 Q4
Governador Valadares Brazil 151 D6
Governor's Harbour Bahamas 129 D7
Govĭ Altayn Nuruu mts Mongolia 62 F3
Govind Ballash Pant Sagar resr India 75 D4
Govindgarh India 75 D4
Govind Sagar resr India 74 C3
Govurdak Turkm. 81 F2
Gowanda U.S.A. 130 D2
Gowan Range hills Australia 111 F5
Gowd-e Aḥmar Iran 80 C4
Gowdeh, Rūd-e watercourse Iran 80 C5
Gowd-e Hasht Tekkeh waterhole Iran 80 D3
Gowmal Kalay Afgh. 81 G3
Gowurdak Turkm. see Govurdak
Goya Arg. 152 F2
Göyçay Azer. 79 F2
Goyder r. Australia 110 C2
Goyder watercourse Australia 110 C5
Goymatdag hills Turkm. see Koymatdag, Gory
Göynük Turkey 79 E3
Göynük Turkey 78 B2
Gözareh Afgh. 81 E3
Goz-Beïda Chad 88 D6
Gözcüler Turkey 77 B1
Gozha Co salt l. China 70 F5
Gozo i. Malta 45 E6
Goz Regeb Sudan 89 G5
Graaf-Reinet S. Africa 98 E7
Grabia r. Poland 37 I3
Grabo Côte d'Ivoire 92 D4
Grabovica Yugo. 46 C2
Grabow Germany 36 E2
Grabowa r. Poland 37 H1
Gračac Croatia 44 E2
Gračanica Bos.-Herz. 44 G2
Gracefield Canada 124 F4
Gracemere Australia 111 G4
Grachevka Rus. Fed. 29 J5
Gradačac Bos.-Herz. 44 G2
Gradaús Brazil 150 B3
Gradaús, Serra dos hills Brazil 150 B4
Gradets Bulg. 46 E3
Gradignan France 38 C4
Gradishte hill Bulg. 46 E3
Gradiška Bos.-Herz. see Bosanska Gradiška
Gradište Croatia 44 G2
Grădiştea Romania 46 E2
Grado Italy 44 D2
Grado Spain 42 C1
Grady U.S.A. 133 A5
Gräfenhainichen Germany 37 F3
Gräftåvallen Sweden 32 D3
Grafton Australia 111 H6
Grafton ND U.S.A. 132 B1
Grafton WV U.S.A. 130 C4
Grafton, Cape Australia 111 F3
Grafton, Mount U.S.A. 137 E2
Grafton Passage Australia 111 F3
Graham NC U.S.A. 128 D4
Graham TX U.S.A. 133 B5
Graham, Mount U.S.A. 137 H5
Graham Bell Island Rus. Fed. see Greem-Bell, Ostrov
Graham Island Canada 122 C4
Graham Land reg. Antarctica 167 L2
Grahamstown S. Africa 99 E7
Grajagan Indon. 59 F5
Grajaú Brazil 150 C3
Grajaú r. Brazil 150 C2
Grajewo Poland 37 K2
Gram Denmark 33 C5
Gramada mt. Yugo. 46 C3
Gramat France 38 D4
Gramatikovo Bulg. 46 E3
Grammichele Sicily Italy 45 E6
Grammos mt. Greece 47 B4
Gramoz, Mal mt. Albania/Greece 47 B4
Grampian U.S.A. 130 D3
Grampian Mountains U.K. 34 D3
Grampians, The mts Australia 112 B5
Grampians National Park Australia 112 B5
Gramsh Albania 46 B4
Gran Hungary see Esztergom
Granada Col. 146 C4
Granada Nicaragua 138 G6
Granada Spain 42 E4
Gran Altiplanicie Central plain Arg. 153 C7
Gran Baja San Julián valley Arg. 153 C7
Gran Bajo depr. Arg. 153 D6
Gran Bajo Salitroso salt flat Arg. 152 D4
Granby U.S.A. 134 F4
Gran Canaria i. Canary Is 90 B4
Gran Chaco reg. Arg./Para. 149 E6
Grand r. MO U.S.A. 132 E3
Grand r. SD U.S.A. 132 A2
Grandas de Salime Spain 42 C1
Grand Atlas mts Morocco see Haut Atlas
Grand Bahama i. Bahamas 129 D7
Grand Bank Canada 125 K4
Grand Banks of Newfoundland sea feature N. Atlantic Ocean 160 K3
Grand-Bassam Côte d'Ivoire 92 E4
Grand Bay Canada 125 H4
Grand Bend Canada 130 C2
Grand Canal China see Da Yunhe
Grand Canal Rep. of Ireland 35 C5
Grand Canary i. Canary Is see Gran Canaria
Grand Canyon U.S.A. 137 F3
▶Grand Canyon gorge U.S.A. 137 F3
northamerica 118–119
Grand Canyon National Park U.S.A. 137 F3
Grand Canyon - Parashant National Monument nat. park U.S.A. 137 F3
Grand Cayman i. Cayman Is 127 J8
Grand Combin mt. Switz. 39 G4
Grande r. Arg. 152 C4
Grande r. Santa Cruz Bol. 149 E4
Grande r. Santa Cruz Bol. 149 E4
Grande r. Bahia Brazil 150 D4
Grande r. São Paulo Brazil 151 B7
Grande r. Nicaragua 139 H6
Grande, Bahía b. Arg. 153 C7
Grande, Ciénaga lag. Col. 146 C2
Grande, Serra hills Brazil 149 E2
Grande, Serra mt. Brazil 147 F4
Grande Cache Canada 122 G4
Grande Comore i. Comoros see Njazidja
Grande Leyre r. France 38 C4
Grande Prairie Canada 122 G4
Grand Erg de Bilma des. Niger 93 I1
Grand Erg Occidental des. Alg. 91 E3
Grand Erg Oriental des. Alg. 91 G3
Grande-Rivière Canada 125 H3
Grande Ronde r. U.S.A. 134 C3
Grandes, Salinas salt marsh Arg. 148 D5
Grande Terre i. Mayotte 97 E8
Grande Tête de l'Obiou mt. France 39 F4
Grande-Vallée Canada 125 H3
Grand Falls N.B. Canada 125 H4
Grand Falls Nfld. and Lab. Canada 121 N5
Grand Forks Canada 122 G5
Grand Forks U.S.A. 132 B2
Grand Gorge U.S.A. 131 F2
Grand Haven U.S.A. 132 E3
Grandin, Lac l. Canada 122 G1
Grand Island U.S.A. 132 B3
Grand Isle U.S.A. 127 H6
Grand Junction U.S.A. 137 H2
Grand-Lahou Côte d'Ivoire 92 D4
Grand Lake N.B. Canada 125 H4
Grand Lake Nfld. and Lab. Canada 125 I2
Grand Lake Nfld. and Lab. Canada 125 J3
Grand Lake U.S.A. 133 C6
Grand Lake St Marys U.S.A. 130 A3
Grand Manan Island Canada 125 H4
Grand Marais MI U.S.A. 132 E2
Grand Marais MN U.S.A. 132 D2
Grand-Mère Canada 125 F4
Grândola Port. 42 B3
Grândola, Serra de mts Port. 42 B3
Grand Passage New Caledonia 107 F3
Grand Rapids Canada 123 L4
Grand Rapids MI U.S.A. 132 E3
Grand Rapids MN U.S.A. 132 C2
Grand Récif de Cook reef New Caledonia 107 F3
Grand Récif du Sud reef New Caledonia 107 F4
Grand St Bernard, Col du pass Italy/Switz. see Great St Bernard Pass
Grand Santi Fr. Guiana 147 H3
Grand Teton mt. U.S.A. 134 E4
Grand Teton National Park U.S.A. 134 E4
▶Grand Turk Turks and Caicos Is 127 L7
Capital of the Turks and Caicos Islands.
Grand Wash watercourse U.S.A. 137 E3
Grand Wash Cliffs mts U.S.A. 137 E4
Grañén Spain 43 F2
Granger U.S.A. 134 E4
Grängesberg Sweden 33 D3
Grangeville U.S.A. 134 C3
Granhult Sweden 32 F2
Granisle Canada 122 E4
Granite Falls U.S.A. 132 C2
Granite Mountains CA U.S.A. 137 E4
Granite Mountains CA U.S.A. 137 E5
Granite Peak MT U.S.A. 134 E3
Granite Peak UT U.S.A. 137 F1
Granitola, Capo c. Sicily Italy 45 D6
Granja Brazil 150 D2
Gran Laguna Salada l. Arg. 153 D6
Gran Morelos Mex. 135 F7
Granollers Spain 43 H2
Gran Pajonal plain Peru 148 B2
Gran Paradiso mt. Italy 44 A2
Gran Paradiso, Parco Nazionale del nat. park Italy 44 A2
Gran Pilastro mt. Austria/Italy 36 E5
Gran San Bernardo, Colle del pass Italy/Switz. see Great St Bernard Pass
Gran Sasso d'Italia mts Italy 44 D3
Gran Sasso e Monti della Laga, Parco Nazionale del nat. park Italy 44 D3
Gransee Germany 37 F2
Grant U.S.A. 132 A3
Grant, Mount U.S.A. 136 D2
Grantham U.K. 35 F5
Grant Island Antarctica 167 J2
Grantown-on-Spey U.K. 34 E3
Grant Range mts U.S.A. 137 E2
Grants U.S.A. 135 F6
Grantsburg U.S.A. 132 C2
Grants Pass U.S.A. 134 B4
Grantsville U.S.A. 137 F1
Granville Canada 122 B2
Granville France 38 C2
Granville AZ U.S.A. 137 H5
Granville NY U.S.A. 131 G2
Granville Lake Canada 123 K3
Granvin Norway 33 B3
Grão Mogol Brazil 151 D6
Gras, Lac de l. Canada 123 I1
Graskop S. Africa 99 F5
Gräsö i. Sweden 33 E3
Grasplatz Namibia 98 B5
Grass r. Canada 123 L4
Grasse France 39 G5
Grass Lake U.S.A. 130 A2
Grasslands National Park Canada 123 J5
Grass Patch Australia 109 C8
Grassrange U.S.A. 134 E3
Grass Valley U.S.A. 136 B2
Grassy Australia 112 C6
Grästorp Sweden 33 D4
Gratkorn Austria 37 G5
Graudenz Poland see Grudziądz
Graulhet France 38 D5
Graus Spain 43 G1
Gravatá Brazil 150 F4
Gravataí Brazil 151 B9
Grave, Pointe de pt France 38 C4
Gravelbourg Canada 123 J5
Gravenhurst Canada 124 E4
Grave Peak U.S.A. 134 D3

Gravesend Australia 112 D3
Gravina in Puglia Italy 45 F4
Gravina Island U.S.A. 122 D4
Gray France 39 F3
Gray KY U.S.A. 130 A5
Gray ME U.S.A. 131 H2
Gray Lake Canada 123 I2
Grayling r. Canada 122 E3
Grayling U.S.A. 132 E2
Grays Lake U.S.A. 134 E4
Grayville U.S.A. 128 B4
Graz Austria 37 G5
Grdelica Yugo. 46 C3
Greasy Lake Canada 122 F2
Great Abaco i. Bahamas 129 D7
Great Australian Bight g. Australia 109 E8
Great Bahama Bank sea feature Bahamas 129 D7
Great Barrier Island N.Z. 113 C2
▶Great Barrier Reef Australia 111 F1
oceania 104–105
oceans 156–157
Great Barrier Reef Marine Park (Cairns Section) Australia 111 F3
Great Barrier Reef Marine Park (Capricorn Section) Australia 111 G4
Great Barrier Reef Marine Park (Central Section) Australia 111 G3
Great Barrier Reef Marine Park (Far North Section) Australia 111 F2
Great Barrington U.S.A. 131 G2
Great Basalt Wall National Park Australia 111 F3
Great Basin U.S.A. 137 D2
Great Basin National Park U.S.A. 137 E2
Great Bear r. Canada 122 E1

▶Great Bear Lake Canada 122 G1
4th largest lake in North America and 8th in the world.
northamerica 116–117
world 6–7

Great Belt sea chan. Denmark 33 C5
Great Bend KS U.S.A. 132 B4
Great Bend PA U.S.A. 131 F3
Great Bitter Lake Egypt 89 G2
Great Blasket Island Rep. of Ireland 35 A5

▶Great Britain i. U.K. 35 E4
Largest island in Europe and 8th in the world.
europe 22–23
world 6–7

Great Coco Island Cocos Is 61 A5
Great Dividing Range mts Australia 111 F3
Great Driffield U.K. 35 F4
Great Eastern Erg des. Alg. see Grand Erg Oriental
Great Egg Harbor Inlet U.S.A. 131 F4
Greater Antilles is Caribbean Sea 127 J7
Greater Khingan Mountains China see Da Hinggan Ling
Greater Tunb i. The Gulf 80 C5
Great Exuma i. Bahamas 129 E8
Great Falls U.S.A. 134 E3
Great Fish r. S. Africa 99 E7
Great Gandak r. India 75 E4
Great Inagua i. Bahamas 127 L7
Great Karoo plat. S. Africa 98 D7
Great Kei r. S. Africa 99 F7
Great Lake Australia 112 C6

▶Great Lakes Canada/U.S.A. 124
Consist of Lakes Erie, Huron, Michigan, Ontario and Superior.

Great Meteor Tablemount sea feature N. Atlantic Ocean 160 M4
Great Miami r. U.S.A. 130 A4
Great Namaqualand reg. Namibia 98 C5
Great Nicobar i. India 73 G5
Great North East Channel Australia/P.N.G. 57 J7
Great Oasis, The Egypt 89 F3
Great Ouse r. U.K. 35 G5
Great Oyster Bay Australia 112 D6
Great Palm Island Australia 111 F3
Great Plain of the Koukdjuak Canada 121 L3
Great Plains U.S.A. 132 A3
Great Point U.S.A. 131 H3
Great Rift Valley Africa 96 B5
Great Ruaha r. Tanz. 97 C6
Great Sacandaga Lake U.S.A. 131 F2
Great St Bernard Pass Italy/Switz. 39 G4
▶Great Salt Lake UT U.S.A. 134 D4
northamerica 116–117
Great Salt Lake Desert U.S.A. 137 F1
Great Sand Dunes National Park U.S.A. 135 F5
Great Sand Hills Canada 123 I5
Great Sand Sea des. Egypt/Libya 88 E2
Great Sandy Desert Australia 110 A4
Great Sandy Island Australia see Fraser Island
Great Sea Reef Fiji 107 G3

▶Great Slave Lake Canada 123 H2
Deepest and 5th largest lake in North America.
northamerica 116–117

Great Smoky Mountains U.S.A. 128 B5
Great Smoky Mountains National Park U.S.A. 128 C5
Great Snow Mountain Canada 122 E3
Great South Bay U.S.A. 131 G3
Great Victoria Desert Australia 110 B6
Great Wall research station Antarctica 167 A2
▶Great Wall tourist site China 63 J3
asia 52–53
Great Western Erg des. Alg. see Grand Erg Occidental
Great West Torres Islands Myanmar 61 B6
Great Yarmouth U.K. 35 G5
Great Zab r. Iraq see Zāb al Kabīr, Nahr az
Great Zimbabwe National Monument tourist site Zimbabwe 99 F4
Grebbestad Sweden 33 C4
Grebenkovskiy Ukr. see Hrebinka
Grebyonka Ukr. see Hrebinka
Greci, Vârful hill Romania 46 F2
Greco, Cape Cyprus see Greko, Cape
Greco, Monte mt. Italy 44 D4
Gredos, Sierra de mts Spain 42 D2
Greec Chile 153 C8
▶Greece country Europe 47 B5
europe 24–25, 48
Greece U.S.A. 130 E2
Greeley U.S.A. 134 F4
Greely Center U.S.A. 132 B3
Greem-Bell, Ostrov i. Rus. Fed. 26 G1
Green r. Canada 127 M2
Green r. KY U.S.A. 128 B4
Green r. ND U.S.A. 132 A2
Green r. WY U.S.A. 137 H2
Green Bay U.S.A. 132 D2
Green Bay b. U.S.A. 132 E2
Greencastle U.S.A. 130 E4
Green Cove Springs U.S.A. 129 C6
Greendale IN U.S.A. 130 A4
Greendale KY U.S.A. 130 A4
Greene U.S.A. 131 F2
Greeneville U.S.A. 128 C4
Greenfield CA U.S.A. 136 B3
Greenfield IN U.S.A. 128 B4
Greenfield MA U.S.A. 131 G2
Greenfield MO U.S.A. 132 C4
Greenfield OH U.S.A. 130 B4
Green Head Australia 109 A7
Greenhill Island Australia 110 C1
Green Island Taiwan see Lü Tao
Green Islands P.N.G. 107 E2
Green Lake Canada 123 J4
Green Lake U.S.A. 132 D3

▶Greenland terr. N. America 121 O2
Self-governing Danish Territory. Largest island in the world and in North America.
northamerica 116–117, 118–119, 140
world 6–7

Greenland Fracture Zone sea feature Arctic Ocean 166 I1
Greenland Sea Greenland/Svalbard 166 I1
Green Mountains U.S.A. 131 G1
Greenock U.K. 34 D4
Greenough Australia 109 A7
Greenough r. Australia 109 A7
Greenport U.S.A. 131 G3
Green River U.S.A. 134 E4
Greensboro AL U.S.A. 129 B5
Greensboro MD U.S.A. 131 F4
Greensboro NC U.S.A. 128 D4
Greensburg IN U.S.A. 128 B4
Greensburg KS U.S.A. 132 B4
Greensburg KY U.S.A. 128 B4
Greensburg LA U.S.A. 133 D6
Greensburg PA U.S.A. 130 D3
Greens Peak U.S.A. 137 H4
Greenup IL U.S.A. 128 A4
Greenup KY U.S.A. 130 B4
Greenvale Australia 111 F3
Green Valley U.S.A. 135 E7
Greenville Canada 122 D4
Greenville Liberia 92 C4
Greenville AL U.S.A. 129 B6
Greenville CA U.S.A. 136 B1
Greenville ME U.S.A. 128 F2
Greenville MO U.S.A. 132 D4
Greenville MS U.S.A. 127 H5
Greenville NC U.S.A. 128 D5
Greenville OH U.S.A. 130 A3
Greenville PA U.S.A. 130 C3
Greenville SC U.S.A. 129 C5
Greenville TX U.S.A. 133 B5
Greenwich CT U.S.A. 131 G3
Greenwich OH U.S.A. 130 B3
Greenwood AR U.S.A. 133 C5
Greenwood MS U.S.A. 133 D5
Greenwood SC U.S.A. 129 C5
Greer U.S.A. 128 C5
Gregório r. Brazil 148 C1
Gregory r. Australia 110 D3
Gregory MI U.S.A. 130 A2
Gregory SD U.S.A. 132 B3
Gregory, Lake salt flat S.A. Australia 110 D6
Gregory, Lake salt flat W.A. Australia 109 B6
Gregory, Lake salt flat W.A. Australia 110 A4
Gregory Downs Australia 110 D3
Gregory National Park Australia 110 B3
Gregory Range hills Qld Australia 111 E3
Gregory Range hills W.A. Australia 108 C5
Greifswald Germany 37 F1
Greifswalder Bodden b. Germany 37 F1
Greifswalder Oie i. Germany 37 F1
Greiz Germany 36 F3
Greko, Cape Cyprus 77 B2
Gremikha Rus. Fed. 28 F1
Gremyachinsk Permskaya Oblast' Rus. Fed. 28 K4
Gremyachinsk Respublika Buryatiya Rus. Fed. 63 H1
Grenå Denmark 33 C4
Grenada U.S.A. 133 D5
▶Grenada country West Indies 147 F1
northamerica 118–119, 140
Grenade France 38 D5
Grenade-sur-l'Adour France 38 C5
Grenchen Switz. 39 G3
Grenen spit Denmark 33 C4
Grenfell Australia 112 D4
Grenfell Canada 123 K5
Grenoble France 39 F4
Grense-Jakobselv Norway 32 H1
Grenville Grenada 147 F1
Grenville, Cape Australia 111 E1
Grenville Island Fiji see Rotuma
Greshak Pak. 81 F5
Gresham U.S.A. 134 B3
Gresik Indon. 59 F4
Gressåmoen Nasjonalpark nat. park Norway 32 D2
Gretna LA U.S.A. 133 D6
Gretna VA U.S.A. 130 D5
Grevelingen sea chan. Neth. 36 A3
Greven Germany 36 C2
Grevena Greece 47 B4
Grevenbroich Germany 36 C3
Grevenmacher Lux. 39 G2
Grevesmühlen Germany 36 E2
Grey r. Canada 125 J4
Grey r. N.Z. 113 B3
Grey, Cape Australia 110 D2
Greybull U.S.A. 134 E3
Greybull r. U.S.A. 134 E3
Grey Hunter Peak Canada 122 C2
Grey Islands Canada 125 K3
Greylock, Mount U.S.A. 131 G2
Greymouth N.Z. 113 B3
Grey Range hills Australia 111 E6
Grey's Plains Australia 109 A6
Greystone Zimbabwe 99 F4
Greytown S. Africa 99 F6
Gria, Akra pt Greece 47 D6
Gribanovskiy Rus. Fed. 29 G6
Gribingui r. Cent. Afr. Rep. 94 C2
Gridley U.S.A. 136 B2
Griffin U.S.A. 129 B5
Griffith Australia 112 C4
Griffithsville U.S.A. 130 C4
Grigan i. N. Mariana Is see Agrihan
Grignols France 38 C4
Grik Malaysia see Gerik
Grimari Cent. Afr. Rep. 94 D3
Grimma Germany 37 F3
Grimmen Germany 37 F1
Grimsby Canada 130 D2
Grimsby U.K. 35 F5
Grímsey i. Iceland 32 [inset]
Grimshaw Canada 123 G3
Grímsstaðir Iceland 32 [inset]
Grimstad Norway 33 C4
Grindavík Iceland 32 [inset]
Grindsted Denmark 33 C5
Grindul Chituc spit Romania 46 F2
Grindușu, Vârful mt. Romania 46 E1
Grinnell Peninsula Canada 121 J2
Griquatown S. Africa 98 D6
Grise Fiord Canada 121 K2
Grishino Ukr. see Krasnoarmiys'k
Grisik Indon. 58 C3
Grisolles France 38 D5
Grisslehamn Sweden 33 E3
Gritley U.K. 34 E2
Grizim well Alg. 90 E4
Grizzly Bear Mountain Canada 122 F1
Grmeč mts Bos.-Herz. 44 F2
Grobbendonk Belgium 36 B3
Grobiņa Latvia 33 F4
Groblersdal S. Africa 99 F5
Groblershoop S. Africa 98 D6
Gröbming Austria 37 F5
Grodekovo Rus. Fed. 64 B3
Grodków Poland 37 H3
Grodno Belarus see Hrodna
Grodzisk Wielkopolski Poland 37 H2
Gröf Iceland 32 [inset]
Groganville Australia 111 F3
Groix, Île de i. France 38 B3
Grójec Poland 37 J3
Grombalia Tunisia 45 C6
Gronau (Westfalen) Germany 36 C2
Grong Norway 32 D2
Groningen Neth. 36 C2
Groningen Suriname 147 H3
Grønland terr. N. America see Greenland
Groote Eylandt i. Australia 110 D2
Grootfontein Namibia 98 C3
Groot Karas Berg plat. Namibia 98 C5
Groot Letaba r. S. Africa 99 F4
Groot Swartberge mts S. Africa 98 D7
Grootvloer salt pan S. Africa 98 D6
Groot Winterberg mt. S. Africa 99 E7
Gros Morne National Park Canada 125 J3
Grosne r. France 39 F3
Gross Barmen Namibia 98 C4
Großenhain Germany 37 F3
Großenkneten Germany 36 D2
Großer Arber mt. Germany 37 F4
Grösser Bösenstein mt. Austria 37 G5
Grosser Priel mt. Austria 37 G5
Großer Rachel mt. Germany 37 F4
Grosser Speikkofel mt. Austria 37 F5
Grosser Speikkogel mt. Austria 37 G5
Grosseto Italy 44 C3
Groß-Gerau Germany 36 D4
Großglockner mt. Austria 37 F5
Großräschen Germany 37 G3
Groß Schönebeck Germany 37 F2
Gross Ums Namibia 98 C4
Großvenediger mt. Austria 37 F5
Grosuplje Slovenia 44 E2
Gros Ventre Range mts U.S.A. 134 E4
Groswater Bay Canada 125 J2
Groton NY U.S.A. 131 E2
Groton SD U.S.A. 132 B2
Grottoes U.S.A. 130 D4
Grouard Mission Canada 123 G4
Grouin, Pointe du pt France 38 C2
Groumania Côte d'Ivoire 92 E4
Grove U.S.A. 133 C4
Grove City OH U.S.A. 130 B4
Grove City PA U.S.A. 130 C3
Grove Hill U.S.A. 129 B6
Grövelsjön Sweden 33 D3
Grove Mountains Antarctica 167 E2
Grover Beach U.S.A. 136 B4
Groveton NH U.S.A. 131 H1
Groveton TX U.S.A. 133 C6
Grovfjord Norway 32 E1
Groznyy Rus. Fed. 29 H8
Grubišno Polje Croatia 44 F2
Grudovo Bulg. see Sredets
Grudziądz Poland 37 I2
Grums Sweden 33 D4
Grünau Namibia 98 C5
Grünberg Poland see Zielona Góra
Grundforsen Sweden 33 D3
Grundsuna Sweden 32 E3
Grundy U.S.A. 130 B5
Gruver U.S.A. 133 A4
Gruzinskaya S.S.R. country Asia see Georgia
Gryazi Rus. Fed. 29 F5
Gryazovets Rus. Fed. 28 G4
Gryböw Poland 37 J4
Gryfice Poland 37 G2
Gryfino Poland 37 G2
Gryfów Śląski Poland 37 G3
Gryllefjord Norway 32 E1
Grytviken S. Georgia 153 [inset]
Gua India 75 E5
Guà r. Italy 44 C2
Guacanayabo, Golfo de b. Cuba 127 K7
Guacharía r. Col. 146 D3
Guaçu Brazil 151 A7
Guadaira r. Spain 42 C4
Guadajira r. Spain 42 C3
Guadajoz r. Spain 42 D4
Guadalajara Mex. 126 F7
Guadalajara Spain 42 E2
Guadalaviar r. Spain 43 F2
Guadalcacín, Embalse de resr Spain 42 D4
Guadalcanal i. Solomon Is 107 F2
Guadalcanal Spain 42 D3
Guadalén r. Spain 42 E3
Guadales Arg. 152 D3
Guadalhorce, Embalse de resr Spain 42 D4
Guadalimar r. Spain 42 E4
Guadalmez r. Spain 42 D3
Guadalope r. Spain 43 F2
Guadalquivir r. Spain 42 C4
Guadalupe Brazil 150 D3
Guadalupe Mex. 133 A7
Guadalupe i. Mex. 126 C6
Guadalupe watercourse Mex. 135 C6
Guadalupe Peru 148 A1
Guadalupe Spain 42 D3
Guadalupe U.S.A. 136 B4
Guadalupe r. TX U.S.A. 133 B6
Guadalupe r. TX U.S.A. 133 B6
Guadalupe, Sierra de mts Spain 42 D3
Guadalupe Mountains National Park U.S.A. 135 F7
Guadalupe Victoria Baja California Mex. 137 E5
Guadalupe Victoria Mex. 126 F7
Guadamez r. Spain 42 D3
Guadarrama r. Spain 42 D3
Guadarrama Venez. 146 D2
Guadarrama, Puerto de pass Spain 42 D2
Guadarrama, Sierra de mts Spain 42 D2
Guadazaón r. Spain 43 F3

▶Guadeloupe terr. West Indies 139 L5
French Overseas Department.
northamerica 118–119, 140

Guadeloupe Passage Caribbean Sea 139 L5
Guadiana r. Port./Spain 42 C4
Guadiana Menor r. Spain 42 E4
Guadiaro r. Spain 42 D4
Guadiato r. Spain 42 D4
Guadiela r. Spain 43 E2
Guadiervas r. Spain 42 D2
Guadix Spain 42 E4
Guafo, Isla i. Chile 153 B5
Guaiba Brazil 151 B9
Guaicuras Brazil 149 F5
Guaillabamba r. Ecuador 146 B4
Guaina Venez. 147 F3
Guainia dept Col. 146 D4
Guainía r. Col./Venez. 146 E4
Guaiquinima, Cerro mt. Venez. 147 F3
Guaira Brazil 151 A8
Guajará Mirim Brazil 148 D2
Guaje, Laguna de l. Mex. 133 A6
Guaje, Llano de plain Mex. 133 A7
Guajira dept Col. 146 C2
Gualala U.S.A. 136 A2
Gualaquiza Ecuador 146 B5
Gualdo Tadino Italy 44 D3
Gualeguay Arg. 152 F3
Gualeguay r. Arg. 152 F3
Gualeguaychu Arg. 152 F3
Gualicho, Salina salt flat Arg. 152 D5
Gualjaina Arg. 153 C5
Guallatiri vol. Chile 148 C4

▶Guam terr. N. Pacific Ocean 57 J3
United States Unincorporated Territory.
oceania 104–105, 114

Guamini Arg. 152 E4
Guampí, Sierra de mts Venez. 147 E3
Guamúchil Mex. 126 E6
Guan r. China 67 F1
Guanabara Brazil 148 C2
Guanajay Cuba 129 C8
Guanajuato Mex. 126 F7
Guanambi Brazil 150 D5
Guanare Venez. 146 D2
Guanare Viejo r. Venez. 146 E2
Guanarito Venez. 146 D2
Guanarito r. Venez. 146 D2
Guanay Bol. 148 D3
Guandacol Arg. 152 C2
Guandaokou China 67 D1
Guandu China 67 E3
Guane Cuba 127 J7
Guang'an China 66 C2
Guangchang China 67 F3
Guangde China 67 F2
Guangdong prov. China 67 E4
Guangfeng China 67 F2
Guanghai China 67 E4
Guanghan China 66 C2
Guanghua China see Laohekou
Guangmao Shan mt. China 66 B3
Guangming China see Xide
Guangming Ding mt. China 67 F2
Guangnan China 66 C4
Guangning China 67 E4
Guangshui China 67 E2
Guangxi aut. reg. China see Guangxi Zhuangzu Zizhiqu
Guangxi Zhuangzu Zizhiqu aut. reg. China 67 D4
Guangyuan China 66 C1
Guangze China 67 F3
Guangzhou China 67 E4
Guanhães Brazil 151 D6
Guanling China 66 C3
Guanmian Shan mts China 67 D2
Guanpo China 67 D1
Guansuo China see Guanling
Guanta Venez. 147 E2
Guantánamo Cuba 127 K7
Guanxian China see Dujiangyan
Guanyang China 67 D3
Guanyinqiao China 66 B2
Guanyun China 67 F1
Guapay r. Bol. see Grande
Guapé Brazil 151 C7
Guaporé r. Bol./Brazil 149 D2
Guaporé Brazil 151 B9
Guaporé state Brazil see Rondônia
Guaqui Bol. 148 C4
Guará r. Brazil 150 C5
Guara, Sierra de mts Spain 43 F1
Guarabira Brazil 150 F3
Guaranda Ecuador 146 B5
Guarapari Brazil 151 D7
Guarapuava Brazil 151 B8
Guaratinga Brazil 151 E6
Guaratuba Brazil 151 B8
Guarayos Bol. 148 C3
Guarda Port. 42 C2
Guarda admin. dist. Port. 42 C2
Guardafui, Cape Somalia see Caseyr, Raas
Guardal r. Spain 43 E4
Guardatinajas Venez. 146 E2
Guardia Escolta Arg. 152 E2
Guardo Spain 42 D1
Guardunha, Serra da mts Port. 42 C3
Guareña Spain 42 C3
Guariba r. Brazil 149 E1
Guárico state Venez. 146 E2
Guarrojo r. Col. 146 D3
Guasdualito Venez. 146 D3
Guasuba r. India 75 F5

▶Guatemala country Central America 138 F5
4th most populous country in Central and North America.
northamerica 118–119, 140

▶Guatemala City Guat. 138 F6
Capital of Guatemala.

Guatimozin Arg. 152 E3
Guatrache Arg. 152 E4
Guatrochi Arg. 153 D5
Guaviare dept Col. 146 D4
Guaviare r. Col. 146 E3
Guayabal Col. 146 D3
Guayaguas, Sierra da mts Arg. 152 D2
Guayapo, Serranía mts Venez. 146 E3
Guayaquil Ecuador 146 B5
Guayaquil, Golfo de g. Ecuador 146 A5
Guayaramerín Bol. 148 D2
Guayas prov. Ecuador 146 A5
Guayatayoc, Lago de imp. l. Arg. 148 D5
Guaymas Mex. 135 E8
Guayquiraró r. Arg. 152 F2
Guba Eth. 96 B2
Gubakha Rus. Fed. 26 F4
Guban plain Somalia 96 E2
Gubbi India 72 C3
Gubbio Italy 44 D3
Gubdor Rus. Fed. 28 K3
Guben Germany 37 G3
Gübene Bulg. 46 D3
Gubin Poland 37 G3
Gubio Nigeria 93 I2
Gubkin Rus. Fed. 29 F6
Gucheng China 67 D1
Gudalur India 72 C4
Gudar, Sierra de mts Spain 43 F2
Gudari India 73 D2
Gudaut'a Georgia 79 E2
Gudbrandsdalen valley Norway 33 C3
Guddu Barrage Pak. 81 G4
Gudermes Rus. Fed. 79 F2
Gudi Nigeria 93 H3
Gudivada India 72 D2
Gudiyattam India 72 C3
Gudri r. Pak. 81 E5
Güdül Turkey 78 C2
Gudur Andhra Pradesh India 72 C3
Gudur Andhra Pradesh India 72 C3
Gudvangen Norway 33 B3
Gudzhal r. Rus. Fed. 64 C2
Guè, Rivière du r. Canada 125 G1
Guéckédou Guinea 92 C3
Guelb er Rîchât hill Mauritania 90 C5
Guélengdeng Chad 94 B2
Guelma Alg. 91 G1
Guelmine Morocco 90 C3
Guelph Canada 130 C2
Guendour well Mauritania 90 C6
Guènt Paté Senegal 92 B2
Guer France 38 B3
Guéra pref. Chad 94 C2
Guéra, Massif du mts Chad 94 C2
Guérande France 38 B3
Guerara Alg. 91 G2
Guérard, Lac l. Canada 125 H1
Guercif Morocco 90 E2
Guéré watercourse Chad 88 C5
Guéréda Chad 88 D6
Guerende Libya 88 D4
Guéret France 38 D3
Guernica Spain see Gernika-Lumo

▶Guernsey terr. Channel Is 35 E7
United Kingdom Crown Dependency.
europe 24–25, 48

Guernsey U.S.A. 134 F4
Guérou Mauritania 92 C1
Guerrero Mex. 133 A6
Guerrero Negro Mex. 135 D8
Guers, Lac l. Canada 125 H1
Guerzim Alg. 91 E3
Gueugnon France 39 F3
Guéyo Côte d'Ivoire 92 D4
Gufu China see Xingshan
Gugë mt. Eth. 96 C3
Gügerd, Kūh-e mts Iran 80 C3
Guglieri Arg. 152 E2
Guguan i. N. Mariana Is 57 K2
Gugu Mountains Eth. 96 C2
Guhakolak, Tanjung pt Indon. 58 D4
Guhe China 67 F2
Gūh Kūh mt. Iran 80 D5
Guhuai China see Pingyu
Guiana Basin sea feature N. Atlantic Ocean 160 K5
Guiana Highlands mts S. America 147 E3
Guichen France 38 C3
Guichi China 67 F2
Guichón Uruguay 152 F3
Guidan-Roumji Niger 93 G2
Guidari Chad 94 C2
Guider Cameroon 93 I3
Guidiguir Niger 93 H2
Guidimaka admin. reg. Mauritania 92 B2
Guiding China 66 C3
Guidong China 67 E3
Guidonia-Montecelio Italy 44 D4
Guier, Lac de l. Senegal 92 B1
Guietsou Gabon 94 A5
Guigang China 67 D4
Guiglo Côte d'Ivoire 92 D4
Gui Jiang r. China 67 D4
Guiji Shan mts China 67 G2
Guijuelo Spain 42 D2
Guildford U.K. 35 F6
Guilherand France 39 F4
Guilherme Capelo Angola see Cacongo
Guilin China 67 D3
Guillaume-Delisle, Lac l. Canada 121 L4
Guillaumes France 39 G4
Guillestre France 39 G4
Guimarães Brazil 150 C2
Guimarães Port. 42 B2
▶Guinea country Africa 92 C3
africa 86–87, 100
Guinea, Gulf of Africa 93 G5
Guinea Basin sea feature N. Atlantic Ocean 160 N5
▶Guinea-Bissau country Africa 92 B2
africa 86–87, 100
Guinea-Conakry country Africa see Guinea
Guinea Ecuatorial country Africa see Equatorial Guinea
Guiné-Bissau country Africa see Guinea-Bissau
Guinée country Africa see Guinea
Guinée-Forestière admin. reg. Guinea 92 C3
Guinée-Maritime admin. reg. Guinea 92 B3
Güines Cuba 129 C8
Guines France 38 D1
Guingamp France 38 B2
Guinguinéo Senegal 92 B2
Guipavas France 38 A2
Guiping China 67 D4
Guiratinga Brazil 151 A6
Güiria Venez. 147 F2
Guise France 39 E2
Guissefa well Mali 93 F1
Guitiriz Spain 42 C1
Guiuan Phil. 57 G3
Guivi hill Fin. 32 G1
Guixi China see Dianjiang
Guiyang Guizhou China 66 C3
Guiyang Hunan China 67 E3
Guizhou prov. China 66 C3
Guizi China 67 D4
Gujan-Mestras France 38 C4
Gujarat state India 74 B5
Gujar Khan Pak. 81 H3
Gujba Nigeria 93 H3
Gujerat state India see Gujarat
Gujranwala Pak. 74 B2
Gujrat Pak. 74 B2
Gukovo Rus. Fed. 29 F6
Gulabgarh Jammu and Kashmir 74 C2
Gulabie Uzbek. 70 A3
Gülbahçe Turkey 47 E5
Gulbarga India 72 C2
Gulbene Latvia 33 G4
Gul'cha Kyrg. see Gülchö
Gülchö Kyrg. 70 D3
Gülek Turkey 78 C3
Gülek Boğazı pass Turkey 78 C3
Gulfport U.S.A. 129 A6
Gulf Shores U.S.A. 129 B6
Gulgong Australia 112 D4
Gulian China 63 K1
Gulin China 66 C3
Gulistan Pak. 81 F4
Gulistan Uzbek. 81 G1
Gulistan Uzbek. see Gulistan
Gulja China see Yining
Gul Kach Pak. 81 G4
Gull r. Canada 124 B3
Gullbrå Norway 33 B3
Gullhorna fjärd b. Fin. 33 F4
Gull Lake Canada 134 E2
Gullspång Sweden 33 D4
Gullträsk Sweden 32 F2
Güllük Turkey 47 E6
Güllük Körfezi b. Turkey 78 A3
Gulmarg Jammu and Kashmir 74 B2
Gülnar Turkey 78 C3
Gülpınar Turkey 47 E5
Gulrip'shi Georgia 79 E2
Gülşehir Turkey 78 C3
Gulû China see Xincai
Gulu Uganda 96 B4
Gülübovo Bulg. 46 D3
Gulumba Gana Nigeria 93 I3
Gulwe Tanz. 97 C6
Gulyantsi Bulg. 46 D3
Gulyayevskiye Koshki, Ostrova is Rus. Fed. 28 J1
Gumal r. Pak. 81 G4
Gumare Botswana 98 D3
Gumbinnen Rus. Fed. see Gusev
Gumbiri mt. Sudan 96 A3
Gumdag Turkm. 80 C2
Gumel Nigeria 93 H2
Gümgüm Turkey see Varto
Gumla India 75 E5
Gummersbach Germany 36 C3
Gumpang r. Indon. 58 B1
Gumsi Nigeria 93 H2
Gümüşhane Turkey 79 D2
Gümüşsuyu Turkey 47 E5
Guna India 74 C4
Gunan China see Qijiang
Guna Terara mt. Eth. 96 C2
Gund r. Tajik. 81 G2
Gundagai Australia 112 D4
Gundji Dem. Rep. Congo 94 D4
Gundlakamma r. India 72 D3
Gundlupet India 72 C4
Gündoğmuş Turkey 78 C3
Güneşli Turkey 47 F5
Güney Turkey 47 F5
Güneydoğu Toroslar plat. Turkey 107 D3
Gunglilap Myanmar 60 B2
Gungu Dem. Rep. Congo 95 C6
Gungue Angola 95 B8
Gunib Rus. Fed. 79 F2
Gunisao r. Canada 123 L4
Gunja Croatia 44 G2
Gunnarn Sweden 32 E2
Gunnbjørn Fjeld nunatak Greenland 121 Q3
Gunnedah Australia 112 D3
Gunnison CO U.S.A. 135 F5
Gunnison UT U.S.A. 137 G2
Gunnison r. U.S.A. 137 H2
Gunong Ayer Sarawak Malaysia see Gunung Ayer
Güns Hungary see Kőszeg
Gunt r. Tajik. see Gund
Guntakal India 72 C3
Guntur India 72 D2
Gununa Australia 110 D3
Gunung Ayer Sarawak Malaysia 59 E2
Gunung Gading National Park Sarawak Malaysia 59 E2
Gunung Leuser National Park Indon. 58 B2
Gunung Mulu National Park Sarawak Malaysia 59 F1
Gunung Palung National Park Indon. 59 E3
Gunung Rinjani National Park Indon. 59 G5
Gunungsitoli Indon. 58 B2
Gunungtua Indon. 58 B2
Gunupur India 73 D2
Günyüzü Turkey 78 B3
Gunza Angola see Porto Amboim
Günzburg Germany 36 E4
Gunzenhausen Germany 36 E4
Guo He r. China 67 E1
Guo He r. China 67 F1
Guoluezhen China see Lingbao
Guoyang China 67 F1
Guozhen China see Baoji
Gupis Jammu and Kashmir 74 B1
Gurais Jammu and Kashmir 74 B2
Gura Portiței sea chan. Romania 46 F2
Gurara r. Nigeria 93 G3
Gura Teghii Romania 46 E2
Gurba r. Dem. Rep. Congo 94 E4
Gurbantünggüt Shamo des. China 70 G3
Gurdim Iran 81 E5
Gurdon U.S.A. 133 C5
Güre Turkey 78 B3
Gürgān Azer. 80 B1
Gurgan Iran see Gorgān
Gurgaon India 74 C3
Gurgei, Jebel mt. Sudan 88 E6
Gurghiu r. Romania 46 D1
Gurghiului, Munții mts Romania 46 D1
Gurgueia r. Brazil 150 D3
Gurha India 74 A4
Guri, Embalse de resr Venez. 147 F3
Gurig National Park Australia 110 C1
Gurktaler Alpen mts Austria 37 F5
Gurmatkal India 72 C2
Guro Moz. 99 G3
Gürpınar Turkey 79 E3
Gurramkonda India 72 C3
Gürsu Turkey 47 F4
Guruè Moz. 99 H2
Gürün Turkey 78 D3
Gurupá Brazil 147 I5
Gurupá, Ilha Grande de i. Brazil 147 I5
Gurupi Brazil 150 B4
Gurupi r. Brazil 150 C2
Gurupi, Cabo c. Brazil 150 C2
Gurupi, Serra do hills Brazil 150 B3
Guru Sikhar mt. India 74 B4
Guruve Zimbabwe 99 F3
Guruwe Zimbabwe see Guruve
Gur'yev Kazakh. see Atyrau
Gur'yevsk Rus. Fed. 33 F5
Gur'yevskaya Oblast' admin. div. Kazakh. see Atyrauskaya Oblast'
Gusau Nigeria 93 G2
Gusev Rus. Fed. 37 K1
Gushgy Turkm. 81 E3
Gushgy r. Turkm. 81 E2
Gushi China 67 E1
Gushiegu Ghana 93 E3
Gusinoozersk Rus. Fed. 27 K4
Guskara India 75 E5
Gus'-Khrustal'nyy Rus. Fed. 28 G5
Guspini Sardinia Italy 45 B5
Güssing Austria 37 H5
Gustavo Sotelo Mex. 135 D7
Gustavus U.S.A. 122 C3
Gustine U.S.A. 136 B3
Güstrow Germany 37 F2
Gütersloh Germany 36 D3
Guthrie AZ U.S.A. 137 H5
Guthrie KY U.S.A. 128 B4
Guthrie OK U.S.A. 133 B5
Guthrie TX U.S.A. 133 A5
Gutian Fujian China 67 F3
Gutian Fujian China 67 F3
Gutian Shuiku resr China 67 F3
Gutiérrez Bol. 149 E4
Guttenberg U.S.A. 132 D3
Gutu Zimbabwe 99 F3
Guvertfjället mts Sweden 32 E2
Guwahati India 75 F4
Guwēr Iraq 79 E3
Guwlumayak Turkm. see Kuuli-Mayak
▶Guyana country S. America 147 G3
southamerica 144–145, 154
Guyane Française terr. S. America see French Guiana
Guyang China see Guzhang
Guyenne reg. France 38 C4
Guy Fawkes River National Park Australia 112 E3
Guyi China see Sanjiang
Guymon U.S.A. 133 A4
Güyom Iran 80 C4
Guyong China see Jiangle
Guyra Australia 112 D3
Guysborough Canada 125 I4

Guyu Zimbabwe **99** F4
Guzar Uzbek. **81** F2
Güzelhisar Barajı *resr* Turkey **47** E5
Güzeloluk Turkey **77** B1
Güzelyurt Cyprus *see* Morfou
Guzhang China **67** F1
Guzhou China *see* Rongjiang
Guzmán Mex. **135** F7
Guzmán, Lago de *l.* Mex. **126** E5
Gvardeysk Rus. Fed. **37** J1
Gvasyugi Rus. Fed. **64** D3
Gwa Myanmar **60** A4
Gwada Nigeria **93** G3
Gwadabawa Nigeria **93** G2
Gwadar Pak. **81** E5
Gwadar West Bay Pak. **81** E5
Gwador Pak. *see* Gwadar
Gwaii Haanas National Park Reserve
  Canada **122** D4
Gwalior India **74** C4
Gwanda Zimbabwe **99** F4
Gwarzo Nigeria **93** G3
Gwatar Bay Pak. **81** E5
Gwayi Zimbabwe **99** E3
Gwayi *r.* Zimbabwe **99** E3
Gwda *r.* Poland **37** H2
Gweebarra Bay Rep. of Ireland **34** B4
Gweedore Rep. of Ireland **34** D4
Gwelo Zimbabwe *see* Gweru
Gweru Zimbabwe **99** F3
Gweta Botswana **99** E4
Gwoza Nigeria **93** I3
Gwydir *r.* Australia **112** D3
Gyablung China **75** G3
Gyaca China **75** G3
Gyagartang China **66** B1
Gya'gya China *see* Saga
Gyaijêpozhanggê China *see* Zhidoi
Gyai Qu *r.* China **75** G3
Gyaisi China *see* Jiulong
Gyali *i.* Greece **47** L6
Gyamotang China *see* Dêngqên
Gyamug China **74** D2
Gyandzha Azer. *see* Gäncä
Gyangkar China *see* Dinngyê
Gyangnyi Caka *salt l.* China **75** E2
Gyangrang China **75** E3
Gyangtse China *see* Gyangzê
Gyangzê China **75** F3
Gyaring Co *l.* China **70** G5
Gyaring Hu *l.* China **70** I5
Gyaros Greece **47** D6
Gyaros *i.* Greece **47** D6
Gyaur *watercourse* Turkm. **80** C2
Gyaurs Turkm. *see* Sakhra
Gydan, Khrebet *mts* Rus. Fed. *see*
  Kolymskiy, Khrebet
Gydan Peninsula Rus. Fed. **26** H2
Gydanskiy Poluostrovl Rus. Fed. *see*
  Gydan Peninsula
Gyêgu China *see* Yushu
Gyêsar Co *l.* China **75** E3
Gyêwa China **75** E3
Gyimda China **75** G3
Gyirong *Xizang* China **75** E3
Gyirong *Xizang* China **75** E3
Gyitang China **66** A2
Gyixong China *see* Gonggar
Gyiza China **75** G2
Gyldenløve Fjord *inlet* Greenland *see*
  Umiiviip Kangertiva
Gyljen Sweden **32** F2
Gympie Australia **111** H5
Gyobingauk Myanmar **60** A4
Gyomaendrőd Hungary **37** J5
Gyöngyös Hungary **37** I5
Győr Hungary **37** H5
Győrszentmárton Hungary *see*
  Pannonhalma
Gypsum Point Canada **123** H2
Gypsumville Canada **123** L5
Gytheio Greece **47** C6
Gyula Hungary **37** J5
Gyulafehérvár Romania *see* Alba Iulia
Gyümai China *see* Darlag
Gyumri Armenia **79** E2
Gyurgen Bair *hill* Turkey **46** E4
Gyzylarbat Turkm. **80** D2
Gyzyletrek Turkm. **80** C2
Gyzylsuw Turkm. *see* Kizyl-Su
Gzhatsk Rus. Fed. *see* Gagarin

↓ H

Ha Bhutan **75** F4
Häädemeeste Estonia **33** G4
Haanja Estonia **33** G4
Ha'ano *i.* Tonga **107** I3
Ha'apai Group *is* Tonga **107** H3
Haapajärvi Fin. **28** C3
Haapavesi Fin. **32** G2
Haapsalu Estonia **28** B4
Ha 'Arava *watercourse* Israel/Jordan *see*
  'Arabah, Wādī al
Haarlem Neth. **36** C3
Haarlem S. Africa **98** D7
Haarstrang *ridge* Germany **36** C3
Haaway Somalia **96** D4
Hab *r.* Pak. **81** F5
Habahe China **70** G2
Habai Group *is* Tonga *see* Ha'apai Group
Habana Cuba *see* Havana
Habarōn *well* Saudi Arabia **76** E5
Habaswein Kenya **96** C4
Habay Canada **122** G4
Habbān Yemen **68** G7
Habbāniyah, Hawr al *l.* Iraq **79** E4
Habiganj Bangl. **75** F4
Habo Sweden **33** D4
Habra India **75** F5
Hacha Col. **146** C5
Hachijō-jima *i.* Japan **65** D6
Hachiman Japan **65** D6
Hachiōji Japan **65** D6
Hacıbektaş Turkey **78** D2
Hacıköy Turkey *see* Çekerek
Hacıpaşa Turkey **77** C3
Hacı Zeynalabdin Azer. **79** G2
Hack, Mount Australia **112** A3
Hackberry U.S.A. **137** F4
Hacker Valley U.S.A. **130** C4
Hackettstown U.S.A. **131** F3
Ha Côi Vietnam **60** D2
Hacufera Moz. **99** G4
Hadagalli India **72** B3
Ḥadāriba, Râs *pt* Sudan **89** H4
Hadd, Ouad el *well* Mali **92** E1
Haddad, Ouadi *watercourse* Chad **88** C6
Haddington U.K. **34** F4
Hadejia Nigeria **93** H3
Hadejia *watercourse* Nigeria **93** I2
Ḥadera *r.* Israel **77** B3
Haderslev Denmark **33** C5
Hadgaon India **72** C2
Hadhdhunmathi Atoll Maldives **71** D11
Ḥadī, Jabal al *mts* Jordan **77** C4
Hadım Turkey **78** C3

Hadjer Momou *mt.* Chad **88** D5
Ḥadraj, Wādī *watercourse* Saudi Arabia
  77 C4
Ḥaḍramawt, Wādī *watercourse* Yemen
  76 D6
Hadranum Sicily Italy *see* Adrano
Hadrian's Wall *tourist site* U.K. **34** D4
Hadrumetum Tunisia *see* Sousse
Hadseløy *i.* Norway **32** D1
Hadsund Denmark **33** G4
Hadyach Ukr. **29** E6
Haedo, Cuchilla de *hills* Uruguay **152** F3
Haeju N. Korea **65** A5
Haeju-man *b.* N. Korea **65** A5
Haena U.S.A. **135** [inset] Y1
Hafar al 'Atk *well* Saudi Arabia **80** A5
Hafar al Bāṭin Saudi Arabia **80** A5
Hafford Canada **123** J4
Hafik Turkey **78** D2
Ḥafīrah, Qā' al *depr.* Jordan **77** C4
Hafirat al 'Aydā Saudi Arabia **89** H3
Hafit, Jabal *mt.* U.A.E. **80** C5
Haflong India **75** G4
Haft Gel Iran **80** B4
Haftvān Iran **80** C5
Haga Myanmar *see* Haka
Hag Abdullah Sudan **89** G6
Hagari *r.* India **72** C3
Hagar Nish Plateau Eritrea **89** H5

▶Hagåtña Guam **57** J3
  Capital of Guam.

Hagen Germany **36** C3
Hagenow Germany **36** E2
Hägere Hiywet Eth. **96** C2
Hagerstown U.S.A. **130** E4
Hagetmau France **38** C5
Häggenås Sweden **32** D3
Haggin, Mount U.S.A. **134** D3
Hagi Japan **65** B6
Ha Giang Vietnam **60** D2
Ha Giao, Sông *r.* Vietnam **61** E4
Hag's Head Rep. of Ireland **35** B5
Hague U.S.A. **131** G2
Haguenau France **39** G2
Hahajima-rettō *is* Japan **54** G4
Hai Tanz. **96** C5
Hai'an China **67** G1
Haib *watercourse* Namibia **98** C4
Haicheng China *see* Haifeng
Haidargarh India **74** D4
Hai Duong Vietnam **60** D3
Haifa Israel **77** B3
Haifa, Bay of Israel **77** B3
Haifeng China **67** F4
Haikakan *country* Asia *see* Armenia
Haikang China *see* Leizhou
Haikou China **67** F4
Hā'il Saudi Arabia **89** I3
Hailakandi India **75** G4
Hailar China **63** J2
Hailey U.S.A. **134** D4
Haileybury Canada **124** E4
Hailin China **64** B3
Hailong China *see* Meihekou
Hailun China **64** A3
Hailuoto *i.* Fin. **32** G2
Haimen China **67** G1
Hainan *i.* China **67** D5
Hai-nang Myanmar **60** B3
Hainan Strait China **67** D5
Hainaut *reg.* France **39** C4
Haindi Liberia **92** C4
Haines U.S.A. **120** C4
Haines City U.S.A. **129** C6
Haines Junction Canada **122** B2
Haines Road Canada **122** B2
Hainich *ridge* Germany **36** E3
Hainleite *ridge* Germany **36** E3
Hai Phong Vietnam **60** D3
Haiphong Vietnam *see* Hai Phong
Haiqing China **64** C3
Haitan Dao *i.* China **67** F3

▶Haiti *country* West Indies **139** J5
  northamerica **118–119**, **140**

Haiwee Reservoir U.S.A. **136** D3
Haiya Sudan **89** H5
Haiyaf *l.* Sudan **94** E2
Haiyan China **67** G2
Haiyang China *see* Sanmen
Haiyou China *see* Sanmen
Ḥāj 'Ali Qoli, Kavīr-e *salt l.* Iran **80** C3
Hajdar, Oued el *well* Mali **92** E1
Hajdúböszörmény Hungary **37** J5
Hajeb El Ayoun Tunisia **45** B7
Hajhir *r.* Yemen **68** D5
Hajipur India **75** E4
Ḥajjah Yemen **76** D6
Ḥājjīābād *Fārs* Iran **80** C4
Ḥājjīābād *Golestān* Iran **80** D4
Ḥājjīābād *Hormozgan* Iran **80** C4
Hajo India **75** F4
Haka Myanmar **60** A3
Hakha Myanmar *see* Haka
Hakkipa, Har *hill* Israel **77** B4
Ḥakkāri Turkey **79** F3
Hakkas Sweden **32** F2
Hakken-zan *mt.* Japan **65** C6
Hako-dake *mt.* Japan **64** E3
Hakodate Japan **64** E4
Hakos Mountains Namibia **98** C2
Hakseen Pan *salt pan* S. Africa **98** D5
Haku-san National Park Japan **65** D5
Hal Belgium *see* Halle
Hala Pak. **81** F5
Ḥalā', Jabal al *mt.* Jordan **77** B4
Ḥalab Syria *see* Aleppo
Ḥalab *governorate* Syria **77** C1
Halabja Iraq **79** F4
Halach Turkm. *see* Khalach
Halahai China **64** A3
Halaib Sudan **89** H4

▶Halaib Triangle *terr.* Egypt/Sudan **89** G4
  Disputed territory (Egypt/Sudan)
  administered by Sudan.

Ḥalānīyāt, Juzur al *is* Oman **76** F6
Ḥalat 'Ammār Saudi Arabia **89** H2
Halawa U.S.A. **135** [inset] Z1
Halban Mongolia **62** F2
Halberstadt Germany **36** E3
Halcon, Mount Phil. **57** F3
Halden Norway **33** G7
Haldensleben Germany **36** E2
Haldi *r.* India **75** F5
Haldia India **75** F5
Haldibari India **75** F4
Haldwani India **74** C3
Hale *watercourse* Australia **110** C5
Hale U.S.A. **130** B1
Hale, Mount Australia **109** B6
Haleakala National Park U.S.A.
  135 [inset] Z1
Halenia U.S.A. *see* Dead Sea
Haleparki Deresi *r.* Syria/Turkey *see*
  Quwayq, Nahr

Half Assini Ghana **92** E4
Halfeti Turkey **79** D3
Halfmoon Bay N.Z. **113** B4
Halfway *r.* Canada **122** F3
Halfway U.S.A. **130** E4
Haliburton Highlands *hills* Canada
  124 E4
Halicarnassus Turkey *see* Bodrum

▶Halifax Canada **125** I4
  Provincial capital of Nova Scotia.

Halifax U.K. **35** F5
Halifax *NC* U.S.A. **128** D4
Halifax *VA* U.S.A. **130** E5
Halilulik Indon. **108** D2
Ḥalīmah *mt.* Lebanon/Syria **77** C2
Halimun National Park Indon. **59** D4
Ḥaliyā *well* Yemen **76** D6
Ḥaliyal India **72** B3
Hall U.S.A. **130** A5
Hälla Sweden **32** E3
Halland *county* Sweden **33** D4
Halla-san *mt.* S. Korea **65** A6
Halla-san National Park S. Korea **65** A6
Hall Beach Canada **121** K3
Halle Belgium **39** E4
Halle (Saale) Germany **36** E3
Hällefors Sweden **33** D4
Hälleforsnäs Sweden **33** E4
Hallein Austria **37** F5
Hallen Sweden **32** D3
Hallett, Cape Antarctica **167** H2
Hallettsville U.S.A. **133** B6
Hälleviksstrand Sweden **33** C4
Halley *research station* Antarctica
  167 B1
Hallgren, Mount Antarctica **167** H2
Halliday Lake Canada **123** I2
Halligen *is* Germany **36** C1
Hallingdal *valley* Norway **33** C3
Hallingskarvet *mts* Norway **33** C3
Hall in Tirol Austria **36** E5
Hall Islands Micronesia **164** C5
Hallock U.S.A. **132** B1
Hall Peninsula Canada **121** M3
Hallsberg Sweden **33** D4
Halls Creek Australia **110** A3
Hallstavik Sweden **33** E3
Hallviken Sweden **32** E3
Hallyŏ Haesang National Park S. Korea
  65 B6
Halmahera *i.* Indon. **57** G5
Halmstad Sweden **33** D4
Halol India **74** B5
Haloze *reg.* Slovenia **44** E1
Hals Denmark **33** C4
Hal Saflieni Hypogeum *tourist site*
  Malta **45** C7
Hälsingborg Sweden *see* Helsingborg
Halsua Fin. **32** G3
Hälül *i.* Qatar **80** C5
Halvad India **74** A5
Halvmåneøya *i.* Svalbard **26** C2
Ham France **39** C4
Ham, Oued el *r.* Alg. **43** I5
Hamada Japan **65** C6
Hamada du Drâa *plat.* Alg. **90** C3
Hamâda El Haricha *des.* Mali **90** D5
Hamadān Iran **80** B3
Hamadān *prov.* Iran **80** B3
Hamada Tounassine *des.* Alg. **90** D4
Hamaguir Alg. **90** D3
Ḥamāh Syria **78** D4
Ḥamāh *governorate* Syria **77** C2
Hamamatsu Japan **65** D6
Hamapega *hill* Spain **42** D3
Hamar Iceland **32** [inset]
Hamar Norway **33** G3
Hamaroy Norway **32** D1
Hamaroy *i.* Norway **32** D1
Ḥamāṭah, Jabal *mt.* Egypt **89** G3
Hambantota Sri Lanka **72** D5
Hambleton U.S.A. **130** D4
Hamburg Germany **36** D2
Hamburg *AR* U.S.A. **133** D5
Hamburg *IA* U.S.A. **132** C3
Hamburg *NY* U.S.A. **130** D2
Hamburg *PA* U.S.A. **131** F3
Hamburgisches Wattenmeer,
  Nationalpark *nat. park* Germany **36** D2
Hamd, Wādī al *watercourse*
  Saudi Arabia **89** H4
Ḥamdah Saudi Arabia **89** I5
Ḥamdānah Saudi Arabia **89** I5
Hamden U.S.A. **131** G3
Hamdibey Turkey **47** L5
Häme *reg.* Fin. **33** G3
Hämeenkangas *moorland* Fin. **33** F3
Hämeenkyrö Fin. **33** F3
Hämeenlinna Fin. **33** G3
HaMelaḥ, Yam *salt l.* Asia *see* Dead Sea
Hamelin Australia **109** A6
Hamelin Pool *b.* Australia **109** A6
Hameln Germany **36** D2
Hamero Hadad Eth. **96** D3
Hamersley Australia **108** B5
Hamersley Lakes *salt flat* Australia
  109 B7
Hamersley Range *mts* Australia **108** B5
Hamgyŏng-sanmaek *mts* N. Korea
  64 B4
Hamhŭng N. Korea **65** A5
Hami China **70** H3
Hamid Iran **80** B4
Hamid Sudan **89** F4
Hamidiye Turkey **46** E4
Hamilton *Qld* Australia **111** E4
Hamilton *S.A.* Australia **110** C5
Hamilton *Vic.* Australia **112** B5
Hamilton *watercourse Qld* Australia
  111 E4
Hamilton *watercourse S.A.* Australia
  110 C5

▶Hamilton Bermuda **127** N5
  Capital of Bermuda.

Hamilton Canada **130** D2
Hamilton *r.* Canada *see* Churchill
Hamilton N.Z. **113** C2
Hamilton U.K. **34** E5
Hamilton *AL* U.S.A. **129** B5
Hamilton *MT* U.S.A. **134** D3
Hamilton *NY* U.S.A. **131** F2
Hamilton *TX* U.S.A. **133** B6
Hamilton, Mount *CA* U.S.A. **136** B3
Hamilton, Mount *NV* U.S.A. **137** E2
Hamilton City U.S.A. **136** A2
Hamilton Downs Australia **110** C4
Hamilton Mountain U.S.A. **131** F2
Hamilton Sound *sea chan.* Canada
  125 K3
Hamim, Wādī al *watercourse* Libya
  88 D2
Hamina Fin. **33** G3
Ḥamīr, Wādī al *watercourse* Saudi Arabia
  79 E5
Ḥamīrah Saudi Arabia **80** B5
Ḥamīrpur *Himachal Pradesh* India **74** C3
Hamirpur *Uttar Pradesh* India **74** D4
Hamitabat Turkey *see* Isparta
Hamlet U.S.A. **129** D5
Hamley Bridge Australia **112** A4
Hamlin *PA* U.S.A. **131** F3
Hamlin *TX* U.S.A. **133** A5

Ham Luông, Sông *r. mouth* Vietnam
  61 D5
Hamm Germany **36** C3
Hammada du Drâa *plat.* Alg. **90** C3
Hammâdat Tingharat *des.* Libya **88** A2
Hammam al 'Alīl Iraq **79** E3
Hammamet Tunisia **45** C6
Hammamet, Golfe de *g.* Tunisia **91** H1
Ḥammār, Hawr al *imp. l.* Iraq **79** F5
Hammarstrand Sweden **32** E3
Hammelburg Germany **36** D3
Hammerdal Sweden **32** D3
Hammerfest Norway **32** F1
Hammond *IN* U.S.A. **132** E3
Hammond *LA* U.S.A. **137** I5
Hammondsport U.S.A. **131** E2
Hammonton U.S.A. **131** F4
Ham Ninh Vietnam **61** D6
Hamorton N.Z. **113** B4
Hampden N.Z. **113** C2
Håmpjåkk Sweden **32** F2
Hampstead U.S.A. **131** I4
Hampton Canada **125** H4
Hampton *AR* U.S.A. **133** C5
Hampton *IA* U.S.A. **132** E3
Hampton *NH* U.S.A. **131** H2
Hampton *VA* U.S.A. **131** E5
Hampton Bays U.S.A. **131** G3
Hampton Tableland *reg.* Australia
  109 D8
Hamra esh Sheikh Sudan **89** E6
Hamrīn, Jabal *hills* Iraq **79** F4
Hams Fork *r.* U.S.A. **134** F4
Ham Tân Vietnam **61** D5
Hamta Pass India **74** C2
Hāmūn-e-Chah Gheybi *salt pan* Iran
  81 E4
Hāmūn-e Jaz Mūrīān *salt marsh* Iran
  81 D5
Hāmūn Helmand *salt flat* Afgh./Iran
  81 E4
Hamun-i-Lora *dry lake* Pak. **81** F4
Hamun-i-Mashkel *salt flat* Pak. **81** E4
Hāmūn Pu *marsh* Afgh. **81** E4
Hamur Turkey **79** E3
Hamwic U.K. *see* Southampton
Ḥanā *r.* Czech Rep. **37** H4
Hana U.S.A. **135** [inset] Z1
Hanahai *watercourse* Botswana/Namibia
  98 D4
Hanakpınar Turkey *see* Çınar
Ḥanak Saudi Arabia **89** H3
Hanamaki Japan **64** F5
Hanang *mt.* Tanz. **97** B6
Hanapepe U.S.A. **135** [inset] Y1
Hanau Germany **36** D3
Hanchuan China **67** G2
Hancock *MD* U.S.A. **130** D4
Hancock *MI* U.S.A. **132** D6
Hancock *NY* U.S.A. **131** F3
Handan China **63** I4
Handeni Tanz. **97** C6
Handlová Slovakia **37** I4
HaNegev *reg.* Israel *see* Negev
Haneqarot *watercourse* Israel **77** B4
Hanerau-Hademarschen Germany
  36 D1
Hanfeng China *see* Kaixian
Hanford U.S.A. **136** C3
Hangal India **72** B3
Hangan Myanmar **61** B5
Hangayn Nuruu *mts* Mongolia **62** F2
Hangchow China *see* Hangzhou
Hangchuan China *see* Guangze
Hanggin Houqi China *see* Xamba
Hango Fin. *see* Hanko
Hangu Pak. **81** G3
Hangzhou China **67** G2
Hangzhou Wan *b.* China **67** G2
Hani Turkey **79** E3
Han Jiang *r.* China **67** F4
Hanko Fin. **33** F4
Hanksville U.S.A. **137** G2
Hanle *Jammu and Kashmir* **74** C2
Hanley Canada **123** J5
Hanmer Springs N.Z. **113** C3
Hann *r.* W.A. Australia **111** F2
Hann *r.* W.A. Australia **108** D4
Hann, Mount Australia **108** D4
Hanna Canada **134** E2
Hannagan Meadow U.S.A. **137** H5
Hannah Bay Canada **124** D3
Hannibal *MO* U.S.A. **127** H4
Hannibal *NY* U.S.A. **131** E2
Hannik *well* Sudan **89** G5
Hannover Germany **36** D2
Hannoversch Münden Germany **36** D3
Hann Range *mts* Australia **110** C4
Hanöbukten *b.* Sweden **33** D5

▶Ha Nôi Vietnam **60** D3
  Capital of Vietnam.

Hanover Canada **130** C1
Hanover Germany *see* Hannover
Hanover S. Africa **98** E6
Hanover *NH* U.S.A. **131** G3
Hanover *PA* U.S.A. **131** E4
Hanover *VA* U.S.A. **130** E5
Hanover, Isla *i.* Chile **153** B7
Hansen Mountains Antarctica **167** D2
Hanshou China **67** F2
Han Shui *r.* China **67** E2
Hansi India **74** C3
Hansnes Norway **32** E1
Hanson *watercourse* Australia **110** C4
Hansonville U.S.A. **130** D5
Hanstholm Denmark **33** C4
Hantsavichy Belarus **29** C5
Hanumana India **74** D4
Hanumangarh India **74** B3
Hanuy Gol *r.* Mongolia **70** J2
Hanyang China *see* Caidian
Hanyin China **67** D1
Hanyuan *Gansu* China *see* Xihe
Hanyuan *Sichuan* China **66** B2
Hao *atoll* Fr. Polynesia **165** I7
Haora India **75** F5
Haoud el Hamra Alg. **91** G2
Houza W. Sahara **90** C4
Haparanda skärgård nationalpark
  nat. park Sweden **32** F2
Happy Valley - Goose Bay Canada
  125 J3
Hapsu N. Korea **64** B4
Hapur India **74** C3
Ḥaql Saudi Arabia **89** G4
Hara Alol *mt.* Djibouti **96** D2
Ḥaraḍ *well* Saudi Arabia **89** I5
Ḥaraḍ Yemen **89** I5
Ḥaraḍ, Jabal al *mt.* Jordan **77** B5
Ḥaraḍh Saudi Arabia **76** D5
Haradok Belarus **29** F5
Harads Sweden **32** F2
Haraiya India **75** D4
Haramachi Japan **65** F5
Haramukh *mt.* Jammu and Kashmir
  74 B2
Ḥarapa Road Pak. **81** H4

Harare Zimbabwe **99** F3
  Capital of Zimbabwe.

Ḥarāsīs, Jiddat al *des.* Oman **76** F6
Ḥarāt Iran **80** C4
Harat Island Eritrea **89** H5
Haraym *well* Saudi Arabia **76** E6
Haraz-Djombo Chad **88** D6
Haraze-Mangueigne Chad **94** D2
Harbel Liberia **92** C4
Harbin China **64** A3
Harboi Hills Pak. **81** F4
Harbor Beach U.S.A. **130** B2
Harbour Breton Canada **125** K4
Har Khas India **74** C5
Harda India **74** C5
Hardangerfjorden *sea chan.* Norway
  33 B4
Hardangervidda Nasjonalpark *nat. park*
  Norway **33** B3
Hardap *admin. reg.* Namibia **98** C5
Hardap Dam Namibia **98** C5
Hardbakke Norway **33** B3
Harden, Bukit *mt.* Indon. **59** F1
Hardenberg Neth. **36** D2
Harderwijk Neth. **36** C2
Hardeveld *mts* S. Africa **98** C6
Hardin *IL* U.S.A. **132** F4
Hardin *MT* U.S.A. **134** F3
Harding *r.* Australia **108** B5
Harding S. Africa **99** F6
Harding Range *hills* W.A. Australia
  108 D4
Harding Range *hills* W.A. Australia
  108 B6
Hardoi India **74** D4
Hardwar India *see* Haridwar
Hardwick U.S.A. **131** G1
Hardy U.S.A. **133** D4
Hardy, Peninsula *pen.* Chile **153** C8
Hare Bay Canada **125** K3
Hareid Norway **32** D3
Hare Indian *r.* Canada **122** D1
Haren (Ems) Germany **36** C2
Hārer Eth. **96** D2
Harf el Mreffit *mt.* Lebanon **77** B3
Hargeisa Somalia *see* Hargeysa
Hargele Somalia **96** D3
Hargeysa Somalia **96** E2
Harghita, Munṭii *mts* Romania **46** D1
Harghita-Mādāraş, Vârful *mt.* Romania
  46 D1
Harhal Dağlari *mts* Turkey **79** E3
Har Hu *l.* China **70** I4
Harib Yemen **76** D6
Haribomo, Lac *l.* Mali **93** E1
Haridwar India **74** C3
Harif, Har *mt.* Israel **77** B4
Harihar India **72** B3
Harihari N.Z. **113** B3
Harij India **74** A5
Harī kurk *sea chan.* Estonia **33** F4
Ḥārim Syria **77** C1
Ḥarīr, Wādī adh *r.* Syria **77** C3
Hari Rūd *r.* Afgh./Iran **81** D2
Härjåsjön Sweden **33** D3
Härjedalen *reg.* Sweden **33** D3
Härkan *r.* Sweden **32** D3
Harlan U.S.A. **130** B5
Harlem U.S.A. **134** E2
Harlingen Neth. **36** B2
Harlingen U.S.A. **133** B7
Harlow U.K. **35** G6
Harlowton U.S.A. **134** E3
Harman U.S.A. **130** D4
Harmancık Turkey **78** D3
Harmil *i.* Eritrea **89** I5
Harnahalli India **72** B3
Harnai India **72** B2
Harnai Pak. **81** F4
Harney Basin U.S.A. **134** C4
Harney Lake U.S.A. **134** C3
Härnösand Sweden **33** E3
Har Nur China **63** K2
Har Nuur *l.* Mongolia **62** E2
Haro Spain **43** E1
Haroldswick U.K. **34** F1
Harp Lake Canada **125** J2
Harrai India **74** C5
Harran Turkey **79** E3
Harney *r.* Australia **108** D4
Harper Liberia **92** D4
Harper U.S.A. **132** B4
Harper, Mount U.S.A. **122** A1
Harper Lake U.S.A. **136** D4
Harpers Ferry U.S.A. **131** E4

▶Harrisburg *PA* U.S.A. **131** E3
  State capital of Pennsylvania.

Harrisburg *SD* U.S.A. **132** B3

Harbin China **64** A3
Harricana *r.* Canada **124** F3
Harriman U.S.A. **131** F3
Harrington Australia **112** E3
Harrington U.S.A. **131** H4
Harris *reg.* U.K. **34** C3
Harris, Lake *salt flat* Australia **109** F7
Harris, Sound of *sea chan.* U.K. **34** C3
Harrison *AR* U.S.A. **133** C4
Harrison *MI* U.S.A. **130** A1
Harrison *NE* U.S.A. **132** A3
Harrison *OH* U.S.A. **130** A4
Harrison, Cape Canada **125** J2
Harrison Bay U.S.A. **120** D2
Harrisonburg U.S.A. **130** E4
Harrison Lake Canada **122** F5
Harrisonville U.S.A. **132** C4
Harriston Canada **130** C2
Harrisville U.S.A. **131** F1
Harrodsburg U.S.A. **130** A5
Harrogate U.K. **35** F5
Harrowsmith Canada **131** E1
Harry S. Truman Reservoir U.S.A.
  132 C4
Harsa Sweden **33** D3
Hârșeşti Romania **46** D2
Harsin Iran **80** B3
Harsiṭ *r.* Turkey **79** D2
Hârșova Romania **46** D2
Harstad Norway **32** E1
Harsud India **74** C5
Harsvik Norway **32** C3
Hart U.S.A. **132** D5
Hart *r.* Canada **122** B1
Hart, Lake *salt flat* Australia **109** G7
Hartbees *watercourse* S. Africa **98** D5
Hartberg Austria **37** G5
Harteigan *mt.* Norway **33** B3
Hartford *CT* U.S.A. **131** G3
  State capital of Connecticut.

Hartford *SD* U.S.A. **132** B3
Hartford City U.S.A. **128** B3

Hârtibaciu *r.* Romania **46** D2
Hartland Point U.K. **35** D6
Hartlepool U.K. **35** F4
Hartley U.S.A. **135** G6
Hartley Zimbabwe *see* Chegutu
Hartley Bay Canada **122** D4
Hartola Fin. **33** G3
Harts *r.* S. Africa **98** E4
Hartselle U.S.A. **129** B5
Hartshorne U.S.A. **133** C5
Harts Range Australia **110** C4
Harts Range *mts* Australia **110** C4
Hartsville U.S.A. **129** C5
Hartville *MO* U.S.A. **132** E4
Hartville *OH* U.S.A. **130** E3
Hartwell U.S.A. **129** C5
Hartz Mountains National Park
  Australia **112** C6
Har Us Nuur *l.* Mongolia **62** E2
Harut *watercourse* Afgh. **81** E4
Harūz-e Bālā Iran **80** D4
Harvey Canada **125** H4
Harvey U.S.A. **132** A2
Harwich U.K. **35** G6
Harwich Port U.S.A. **131** H3
Haryana *state* India **74** C3
Harz *hills* Germany **36** E3
Harz *park* Germany **36** E3
Har Zin Israel **77** B4
Ḥaṣāh, Wādī al *watercourse* Jordan
  77 B4
Ḥaṣāh, Wādī al *watercourse*
  Jordan/Saudi Arabia **77** C4
Hasan Dağı *mts* Turkey **78** C3
Hasan Guli Turkm. *see* Esenguly
Hasankeyf Turkey **79** E3
Hasanparti India **72** C2
Hasanur India **72** C4
Hasbaïya Lebanon **77** B3
Hasbani *r.* Lebanon **78** C4
Hasdo *r.* India **75** D5
Haselünne Germany **36** C2
HaSharon *plain* Israel *see* Sharon, Plain of
Hashtgerd Iran **80** B3
Hashtpar Iran **80** B2
Hashtrud Iran **80** A2
Hasić Bos.-Herz. *see* Srnice
Hasilpur Pak. **81** H4
Haskell U.S.A. **133** B5
Hasle Denmark **33** F5
Haslemere U.K. **35** F6
Ḥaşmuşi Mare *mt.* Romania **46** D1
Ḥasş, Jabal al *hills* Syria **77** C1
Hassa Turkey **77** C1
Hassan India **72** C3
Hassayampa *watercourse* U.S.A. **137** F5
Hasselt Belgium **39** F4
Hassi Aridal *well* W. Sahara **90** B4
Hassi Bedjedjene *well* Alg. **91** G3
Hassi Bel Guebbour *well* Alg. **91** G3
Hassi Bou Bernous *well* Alg. **90** D4
Hassi Bourahla *well* Alg. **91** H4
Hassi Chebbaba *well* Alg. **91** F3
Hassi Dalaa Alg. **91** F2
Hassi Doumas *well* W. Sahara **90** B5
Hassi el Ahmar *well* Alg. **91** F3
Hassi el Krenig *well* Alg. **91** G3
Hassi Fahl *well* Alg. **91** F3
Hassi Habadra *well* Alg. **91** F3
Hassi Inifel *well* Libya **88** A2
Hassi I-n-Akeouet *well* Alg. **91** H4
Hassi I-n-Belrem *well* Alg. **91** F4
Hassi Inifel Alg. **91** F3
Hassi Khanem *well* Alg. **91** F3
Hassi Mdakene *well* Alg. **90** D3
Hassi Messaoud Alg. **91** G2
Hassi Mseguuem *well* Alg. **91** G3
Hassi Nebka *well* Alg. **91** F3
Hassi Ntsel *well* Alg. **91** G4
Hassi Sebbakh *well* Alg. **91** G3
Hassi Tabelbalet *well* Alg. **91** H3
Hassi Tiguentourine *well* Alg. **91** H3
Hassi Ti-n-Fouchaye *well* Alg. **91** H3
Hässleholm Sweden **33** D4
Hastings Australia **112** B4
Hastings Canada **130** E1
Hastings N.Z. **113** C2
Hastings U.K. **35** G6
Hastings *MI* U.S.A. **132** D2
Hastings *MN* U.S.A. **132** C2
Hastings *NE* U.S.A. **132** B3
Hasvik Norway **32** F1
Ḥasy Ḥaghe *well* Libya **88** A3
Hata India **75** D4
Hatay Turkey *see* Antakya
Hatay *prov.* Turkey **77** C1
Hatch U.S.A. **137** J5
Hatches Creek Australia **110** C4
Hatchie *r.* U.S.A. **128** A5
Hateg Romania **46** C2
Hatfield Australia **112** B4
Hatgal Mongolia **62** J1
Hat Head National Park Australia **112** E3
Hathras India **74** C4
Hatia Bangl. **75** F5
Hatia Nepal **75** F4
Ḥāṭibah, Ra's *pt* Saudi Arabia **89** H4
Ha Tien Vietnam **61** D5
Ha Tinh Vietnam **60** D3
Hato Corozal Col. **146** D2
Hato Hud East Timor *see* Hatudo
Hato la Vergareña Venez. **147** F3
Hatra Iraq **79** E4
Hatta India **74** C4
Hattah Australia **112** B4
Hatteras, Cape U.S.A. **128** E5
Hatteras Abyssal Plain *sea feature*
  S. Atlantic Ocean **160** J4
Hattfjelldal Norway **32** D2
Hatti *r.* India **73** D2
Hattiesburg U.S.A. **129** A6
Hatton, Gunung *hill* Sabah Malaysia
  59 G1
Hattras Passage Myanmar **61** B5
Hattula Fin. **33** G3
Hatudo East Timor **108** D2
Hatvan Hungary **37** I5
Hat Yai Thai. **61** C7
Haud *reg.* Eth. **96** E2
Haugesund Norway **33** B4
Hau Giang, Sông *r.* Vietnam **61** D6
Haukeligrend Norway **33** B4
Haukipudas Fin. **32** G2
Haukivesi *l.* Fin. **33** H3
Haultain *r.* Canada **123** J4
Haungpa Myanmar **60** A1
Hauraki Gulf N.Z. **113** C2
Hausach Germany **36** D4
Haut, Isle au *i.* U.S.A. **128** F2
Haut-Congo *prov.* Dem. Rep. Congo *see*
  Orientale
Hautefort France **38** D4
Haute-Guinée *admin. reg.* Guinea **92** C3
Haute-Kotto *pref.* Cent. Afr. Rep. **94** D3
Haute-Normandie *admin. reg.* France
  38 D2
Hauteurs de la Gâtine *reg.* France **38** C3
Haute-Volta *country* Africa *see* Burkina
Haut-Folin *hill* France **39** F3
Haut-Mbomou *pref.* Cent. Afr. Rep. **94** D3
Haut-Ogooué *prov.* Gabon **94** B5

Hauts Plateaux Alg. **91** E2
Haut-Zaïre *prov.* Dem. Rep. Congo *see* Orientale
Hauvo Fin. *see* **Nagu**
Hauzenberg Germany **37** F4

▶**Havana** Cuba **129** C8
Capital of Cuba.

Havana U.S.A. **132** D3
Havant U.K. **35** F6
Havasu, Lake U.S.A. **137** E4
Havel *r.* Germany **37** E2
Haveli Pak. **81** H4
Havelian Pak. **81** H3
Havelock Canada **130** E1
Havelock N.Z. **113** C3
Havelock Swaziland *see* **Bulembu**
Havelock U.S.A. **129** D5
Havelock Falls Australia **110** C2
Havelock Island India **73** G4
Havelock North N.Z. **113** D2
Haverfordwest U.K. **35** D6
Haverhill U.K. **35** G5
Haverhill U.S.A. **131** H2
Haveri India **72** B3
Haverö Sweden **33** D3
Havlíčkův Brod Czech Rep. **37** G4
Havøysund Norway **32** G1
Havran Turkey **47** E5
Havre U.S.A. **134** E2
Havre Aubert, Île du *i.* Canada **125** I4
Havre de Grace U.S.A. **131** E4
Havre Rock *i.* N.Z. **107** H5
Havre-St-Pierre Canada **125** I3
Havsa Turkey **46** E4
Havza Turkey **78** C2
Hawaii *i.* U.S.A. **135** [inset] Z1
Hawaii *state* U.S.A. **135** [inset] Z2
Hawaiian Islands N. Pacific Ocean **165** G4
Hawaiian Ridge *sea feature* N. Pacific Ocean **165** G4
Hawaii Volcanoes National Park U.S.A. **135** [inset] Z2
Ḩawallī Kuwait **79** G5
Ḩawar *i.* The Gulf *see* **Huwār**
Hawea, Lake N.Z. **113** B4
Hawera N.Z. **113** C2
Hawes U.K. **35** E4
Hawesville U.S.A. **128** B4
Hawick U.K. **34** E4
Ḩawīzah, Hawr al *imp. l.* Iraq **79** F5
Hawkdun Range *mts* N.Z. **113** B4
Hawke Bay N.Z. **113** D2
Hawker Australia **112** A5
Hawkers Gate Australia **112** B3
Hawkes Bay Canada **125** J3
Hawkins Peak U.S.A. **137** F3
Hawler Iraq *see* **Arbīl**
Hawley U.S.A. **131** F3
Hawng Luk Myanmar **60** B3
Ḩawrān, Wādī *watercourse* Iraq **79** E4
Ḩawşal *hills* Saudi Arabia **77** B5
Hawthorne U.S.A. **136** C2
Hay Australia **112** C4
Hay *watercourse* Australia **110** D5
Hay *r.* Canada **123** H2
Hayachine-san *mt.* Japan **65** E5
Haydān, Wādī al *r.* Jordan **77** B4
Haydarābad Iran **80** A2
Hayes *r.* Canada **123** M3
Hayes Creek Australia **110** B2
Hayes Halvø *pen.* Greenland **121** M2
Ḩayf Yemen **76** E7
Hayfield Reservoir U.S.A. **137** E5
Ḩayl Oman **80** D5
Ḩayl, Wādī *watercourse* Syria **77** C3
Haymā' Oman **76** F6
Haymana Turkey **78** C3
Haymarket U.S.A. **130** E4
Hayotboshi Toghi *mt.* Uzbek. *see* **Khayatbashi, Gora**
Hayrabolu Turkey **78** A2
Hay River Canada **123** H2
Hay River Reserve Canada **123** H2
Hays U.S.A. **132** B4
Haysah, Sabkhat al *salt pan* Libya **88** B2
Haysi U.S.A. **130** B5
Haysyn Ukr. **29** D6
Ḩayṭān, Jabal *hill* Egypt **77** A4
Hayward *CA* U.S.A. **136** A3
Hayward *WI* U.S.A. **132** D2
Haywards Heath U.K. **35** F6
Hazard U.S.A. **130** B5
Hazaribag India **75** E5
Hazaribagh Range *mts* India **75** D5
Hazār Masjed, Kūh-e *mts* Iran **81** D2
Hazebrouck France **39** E1
Hazelton Canada **122** E4
Hazen U.S.A. **132** A2
Hazen Strait Canada **121** H2
Hazlehurst *GA* U.S.A. **129** C6
Hazlehurst *MS* U.S.A. **133** D6
Hazleton U.S.A. **131** F3
Hazlett, Lake *salt flat* Australia **108** E5
Hazrat Sultan Afgh. **81** F2
Hazro Pak. **81** H3
H. Bouchard Arg. **152** E3
Headingly Australia **110** D4
Head of Bight *b.* Australia **109** E7
Healdsburg U.S.A. **136** A2

▶**Heard and McDonald Islands** *terr.* Indian Ocean **163** L9
Australian External Territory.
asia **82**

Heard Island Indian Ocean **163** L9
Hearne U.S.A. **133** B6
Hearne Lake Canada **123** H2
Hearst Canada **124** D3
Hearst Island Antarctica **167** L2
Heart *r.* U.S.A. **132** A2
Heath *r.* Bol./Peru **148** C3
Heathcote Australia **112** C5
Heathfield U.K. **35** G6
Heathrow *airport* U.K. **35** F6
Heathsville U.S.A. **131** E5
Heavener U.S.A. **133** C5
Hebbronville U.S.A. **133** B7
Hebei *prov.* China **63** J4
Hebel Australia **111** F6
Heber U.S.A. **137** G4
Heber City U.S.A. **137** G1
Heber Springs U.S.A. **133** C5
Hebi China **63** I4
Hebron Canada **125** I1
Hebron U.S.A. **132** B3
Hebron West Bank **77** B4
Hebros *r.* Greece/Turkey *see* **Evros**
Heby Sweden **33** E4
Hecate Strait Canada **122** D4
Hecheng *Jiangxi* China *see* **Zixi**
Hecheng *Zhejiang* China *see* **Qingtian**
Hechi China **66** D3
Hechingen Germany **36** D4
Hechuan *Chongqing* China **66** C2
Hechuan *Jiangxi* China *see* **Yongxing**
Hedberg Sweden **32** E2
Hede China *see* **Sheyang**
Hédé France **38** C2
Hede Sweden **33** D3
Hedemora Sweden **33** D3
Hedenäset Sweden **32** F2
Hede Shuiku *resr* China **67** D4
Hedesunda Sweden **33** E3
He Devil Mountain U.S.A. **134** C3
Hedmark *county* Norway **33** C3
Heerenveen Neth. **36** B2
Heerhugowaard Neth. **36** B2
Heerlen Neth. **36** B3
Ḩefa Israel *see* **Haifa**
Hefei China **67** F2
Hefeng China **67** D2
Heflin U.S.A. **129** B5
Hegang China **64** B3
Heiban Sudan **96** A2
Heidan *r.* Jordan *see* **Haydān, Wādī al**
Heide Germany **36** D4
Heidelberg Germany **36** D4
Heihe China **64** A2
Heilbronn Germany **36** D4
Heiligenbeil Rus. Fed. *see* **Mamonovo**
Heiligenhafen Germany **36** E1
Hei Ling Chau *i. Hong Kong* China **67** [inset]
Heilongjiang *prov.* China **64** B3
Heilong Jiang *r.* China **64** B3
also known as Amur (Rus. Fed.)
Heilungkiang *prov.* China *see* **Heilongjiang**
Heinävesi Fin. **32** H3
Heinola Fin. **33** G3
Heinz Bay Myanmar **61** B5
Heinze Islands Myanmar **61** B5
Heishi Beihu *l.* China **75** D2
Heishui China **66** B1
Heisker Islands U.K. *see* **Monach Islands**
Hejaz *reg.* Saudi Arabia *see* **Hijaz**
Hejiang China **66** C2
He Jiang *r.* China **67** D4
Hekimhan Turkey **79** D3
Hekla *vol.* Iceland **32** [inset]
Hekou *Gansu* China **37** F5
Hekou *Hubei* China **67** E2
Hekou *Jiangxi* China *see* **Yanshan**
Hekou *Sichuan* China *see* **Yajiang**
Hekou *Yunnan* China **66** B4
Hel Poland **37** I1
Helagsfjället *mt.* Sweden **32** D3
Helem India **75** G4
Helen *i.* Palau **57** H5
Helena *AR* U.S.A. **133** D5

▶**Helena** *MT* U.S.A. **134** D3
State capital of Montana.

Helena *OH* U.S.A. **130** B3
Helen Reef Palau **57** H5
Helensburgh U.K. **34** D3
Helen Springs Australia **110** C3
Helenwood U.S.A. **130** A5
Helgoland *i.* Germany **36** C1
Helgoländer Bucht *b.* Germany **36** D1
Heligoland *i.* Germany *see* **Helgoland**
Heligoland Bight *b.* Germany *see* **Helgoländer Bucht**
Helixi China *see* **Ningguo**
Hella Iceland **32** [inset]
Hellas *country* Europe *see* **Greece**
Helleh *r.* Iran **80** B4
Hellespont *strait* Turkey *see* **Dardanelles**
Hellevoetsluis Neth. **36** B3
Hellhole Gorge National Park Australia **111** F5
Helligskogen Norway **32** F1
Hellín Spain **43** F3
Hells Canyon *gorge* U.S.A. **134** C3
Hell-Ville Madag. *see* **Andoany**
Helm U.S.A. **136** B3
Helmand *prov.* Afgh. **81** E4
Helmand *r.* Afgh. **81** E4
Helmantica Spain *see* **Salamanca**
Helme *r.* Germany **36** E3
Helmeringhausen Namibia **98** C5
Helmond Neth. **36** B3
Helmsdale U.K. **34** E2
Helmsdale *r.* U.K. **34** E2
Helmsley U.K. **35** F4
Helmstedt Germany **36** E2
Helodrano Antongila *b.* Madag. **99** [inset] K2
Helong China **64** B4
Helper U.S.A. **137** G2
Helsingborg Sweden **33** D4
Helsingfors Fin. *see* **Helsinki**
Helsingør Denmark **33** D4

▶**Helsinki** Fin. **33** G3
Capital of Finland.

Helston U.K. **35** D6
Heltermaa Estonia **33** F4
Helvacı Turkey **47** E5
Helvetic Republic *country* Europe *see* **Switzerland**
Helvetinjärven kansallispuisto *nat. park* Fin. **33** F3
Ḩelwân Egypt *see* **Ḩulwān**
Hemel Hempstead U.K. **35** F6
Hemet U.S.A. **136** D5
Hemmoor Germany **36** D2
Hemnesberget Norway **32** D2
Hemphill U.S.A. **133** C6
Hempstead U.S.A. **133** B6
Hemse Sweden **33** E4
Hemsedal Norway **33** C3
Hemsedal *valley* Norway **33** C3
Henan China **66** B1
Henan *prov.* China **67** E1
Henares *r.* Spain **42** E2
Henashi-zaki *pt* Japan **64** D4
Henbury Australia **110** C5
Hendawashi Tanz. **97** B5
Henderson *KY* U.S.A. **128** B4
Henderson *NC* U.S.A. **128** D4
Henderson *NV* U.S.A. **137** E3
Henderson *NY* U.S.A. **131** E2
Henderson *TN* U.S.A. **128** A5
Henderson *TX* U.S.A. **133** C5
Henderson Island Pitcairn Is **165** J7
Hendersonville U.S.A. **128** B4
Hendorābī *i.* Iran **80** C5
Hengch'un Taiwan **67** G4
Hengdong China **67** E3
Hengduan Shan *mts* China **66** A2
Hengelo Neth. **36** C2
Hengnan China *see* **Hengyang**
Hengshan *Heilong.* China **64** B3
Hengshan *Hunan* China **67** E3
Heng Shan *mt.* China **67** E3
Hengshui China *see* **Chongyi**
Hengxian China **67** D4
Hengyang *Hunan* China **67** E3
Hengyang *Hunan* China **67** E3
Hengzhou China *see* **Hengxian**
Henley N.Z. **113** B4
Henlopen, Cape U.S.A. **131** F4
Hennebont France **38** B3
Hennef (Sieg) Germany **36** C3
Hennessey U.S.A. **133** B4
Hennigsdorf Berlin Germany **37** F2
Henniker U.S.A. **131** H2
Henrietta U.S.A. **133** B5
Henrietta Maria, Cape Canada **124** D2
Henrique de Carvalho Angola *see* **Saurimo**
Henry, Cape U.S.A. **131** E5
Henryetta U.S.A. **133** C5
Henry Ice Rise Antarctica **167** L1
Henry Kater, Cape Canada **121** M3
Henry Mountains U.S.A. **137** G2
Hensall Canada **130** C2
Henshaw, Lake U.S.A. **137** D5
Hentiesbaai Namibia **98** B4
Henzada Myanmar **60** A4
Heping *Guizhou* China *see* **Huishui**
Heping *Guizhou* China *see* **Yanhe**
Hepo China *see* **Jiexi**
Heppner U.S.A. **134** C3
Hepu China **67** D4
Heqing *Guangdong* China **67** E4
Heqing *Yunnan* China **66** B3
Heraclea Turkey *see* **Ereğli**
Heraclea Pontica Turkey *see* **Ereğli**
Heraklion Greece *see* **Iraklion**
Herald Cays *atolls* Australia **111** G3
Herāt Afgh. **81** E3
Herāt *prov.* Afgh. **81** E3
Hérault *r.* France **39** E5
Herbert *r.* Australia **111** F3
Herbert *watercourse* Australia **110** D3
Herbert Canada **134** F2
Herbert Downs Australia **110** D4
Herbert River Falls National Park Australia **111** F3
Herbert Wash *salt flat* Australia **109** D6
Herbignac France **38** B3
Herbstein Germany **36** D3
Herceg-Novi Yugo. **44** G3
Hercules Dome *ice feature* Antarctica **167** K1
Hereford U.K. **35** E5
Hereford U.S.A. **133** A5
Héréhérétué *atoll* Fr. Polynesia **165** I7
Herford Germany **36** D2
Héricourt France **39** G3
Herington U.S.A. **132** B4
Herisau Switz. **39** H3
Herkimer U.S.A. **131** F2
Hermagor Austria **37** F5
Herma Ness *hd* U.K. **34** F1
Hermann U.S.A. **132** D4
Hermel Lebanon **77** C2
Hermidale Australia **112** C3
Hermitage *MO* U.S.A. **132** C4
Hermitage *PA* U.S.A. **130** C3
Hermitage Bay Canada **125** J4
Hermite, Islas *is* Chile **153** D8
Hermit Islands P.N.G. **57** K6
Hermon, Mount Lebanon/Syria **77** B3
Hermonthis Egypt *see* **Armant**
Hermopolis Magna Egypt *see* **Al Ashmūnayn**
Hermosillo Mex. **135** E7
Hernád *r.* Hungary **37** J5
also spelt Hornád (Slovakia)
Hernandarias Para. **149** G6
Hernando U.S.A. **133** D5
Hernani Spain **43** F1
Herndon *CA* U.S.A. **136** C3
Herndon *WV* U.S.A. **130** C5
Herne Germany **36** C3
Herning Denmark **33** C4
Heroica Nogales Mex. *see* **Nogales**
▶**Heron Island** *i.* Australia **111** G4
oceania **102–103**
Hérouville-St-Clair France **38** C2
Herowābād Iran *see* **Khalkhāl**
Herrenberg Germany **36** D4
Herrera del Duque Spain **42** D3
Herrin U.S.A. **128** A4
Herrljunga Sweden **33** D4
Herrvik Sweden **33** E4
Hers *r.* France **38** D5
Hershey U.S.A. **131** E3
Hertford U.K. **35** F6
Hertford U.S.A. **128** D4
Hervey Bay Australia **111** H5
Hervey Islands Cook Is **165** H7
Herzberg Germany **37** F3
Herzliyya Israel **77** B3
Herzogenburg Austria **37** G4
Ḩesār Iran **80** B4
Ḩeşar Iran **80** B3
Hesdin France **38** E1
Heshan China **67** D4
Heshengqiao China **67** E2
Hesperia U.S.A. **136** D4
Hesquiat Canada **122** E5
Hess *r.* Canada **122** C1
Hesse *land* Germany *see* **Hessen**
Hesselberg *hill* Germany **36** E4
Hessen *land* Germany **36** D3
Hestvika Norway **32** C3
Het *r.* Laos **60** D3
Hetch Hetchy Aqueduct *canal* U.S.A. **136** A3
Hettinger U.S.A. **132** A2
Hettstedt Germany **36** E3
Heung Kong Tsai *Hong Kong* China *see* **Aberdeen**
Heves Hungary **37** J5
Ḩevron West Bank *see* **Hebron**
Hewlett U.S.A. **130** E5
Hexenkopf *mt.* Austria **36** E5
Hexham U.K. **34** E4
Heydebreck Poland *see* **Kędzierzyn-Koźle**
Heygali *well* Eth. **96** E3
Heyuan China **67** E4
Heywood Australia **112** B5
Heze China **63** J4
Hezhang China **66** C3
Hezhou China **67** D3
Hezuozhen China **66** B1
Hialeah U.S.A. **129** C7
Hiawatha U.S.A. **132** C4
Hibbing U.S.A. **132** C2
Hibbs, Point Australia **112** C6
Hibernia Reef Australia **108** C3
Hīchān Iran **81** E5
Hickman U.S.A. **128** A4
Hickory U.S.A. **128** C5
Hicks Bay N.Z. **113** D2
Hicksville *NY* U.S.A. **131** G3
Hicksville *OH* U.S.A. **130** A3
Hico U.S.A. **133** B5
Hidaka-sanmyaku *mts* Japan **64** E4
Hidalgo Mex. **133** B7
Hidalgo del Parral Mex. **126** E6
Hidasnémeti Hungary **37** J4
Hidrolândia Brazil **149** H4
Hierosolyma Israel/West Bank *see* **Jerusalem**
Higashi-suidō *sea chan.* Japan **65** B6
Higgins Bay U.S.A. **131** F2
Higgins Lake U.S.A. **130** A1
High Atlas *mts* Morocco *see* **Haut Atlas**
High Desert U.S.A. **134** B4
High Island *i. Hong Kong* China **67** [inset]
High Island U.S.A. **133** C6
High Island Reservoir *Hong Kong* China **67** [inset]
Highland U.S.A. **131** G3
Highland Peak *CA* U.S.A. **136** C2
Highland Peak *NV* U.S.A. **137** E3
Highland Springs U.S.A. **131** E5
High Level Canada **123** G3
High Level Canal India **73** E1
Highline Canal U.S.A. **137** E5
Highmore U.S.A. **132** B2
High Point U.S.A. **128** D5
High Prairie Canada **123** G4
High River Canada **134** D2
Highrock Lake Canada **123** K4
High Springs U.S.A. **129** C6
High Tatra *mts* Poland/Slovakia *see* **Tatra Mountains**
Hightstown U.S.A. **131** F3
High Wycombe U.K. **35** F6
Higüey Dom. Rep. **139** K5
Hihifo Tonga **107** H3
Hiidenportin kansallispuisto *nat. park* Fin. **32** H3
Hiiraan Somalia **96** E3
Hiiraan *admin. reg.* Somalia **96** E3
Hiiumaa *i.* Estonia **33** F4
Ḩijānah, Buḩayrat al *imp. l.* Syria **77** C3
Hijaz *reg.* Saudi Arabia **89** H3
Ḩikmah, Ra's al *pt* Egypt **89** E2
Hikone Japan **65** D6
Hikurangi *mt.* N.Z. **113** D2
Hilāl, Jabal *hill* Egypt **77** A4
Hilaritos Chile **148** C5
Hilary Coast Antarctica **167** H1
Hildale U.S.A. **137** F3
Hildburghausen Germany **36** E3
Hildesheim Germany **36** D2
Hili Bangl. **75** F4
Hillah Iraq **79** F4
Hill City U.S.A. **132** B4
Hill Creek *r.* U.S.A. **137** H2
Hillerød Denmark **33** D5
Hillerstorp Sweden **33** D4
Hillesheim Germany **36** C3
Hillgrove Australia **111** F3
Hill Island Lake Canada **123** I2
Hillsboro *IL* U.S.A. **132** D4
Hillsboro *ND* U.S.A. **132** B2
Hillsboro *NH* U.S.A. **131** H2
Hillsboro *OH* U.S.A. **130** B4
Hillsboro *TX* U.S.A. **133** B5
Hillsborough Grenada **147** F1
Hillsborough, Cape Australia **111** G4
Hillsdale *MI* U.S.A. **130** A3
Hillsdale *NY* U.S.A. **131** G2
Hillside Australia **108** B5
Hillsport Canada **124** C3
Hillston Australia **112** C4
Hillsville U.S.A. **130** C5
Hillswick U.K. **34** F1
Hilo U.S.A. **135** [inset] Z2
Hilton Australia **111** D4
Hilton U.S.A. **130** E2
Hilton Head Island U.S.A. **129** C5
Hilvan Turkey **79** D3
Hilversum Neth. **36** B2
Himachal Pradesh *state* India **74** C3
Ḩimā Ḑarīyah, Jabal *mt.* Saudi Arabia **89** I3
▶**Himalaya** *mts* Asia **74** C2
asia **52–53**
world **6–7**
Himalchuli *mt.* Nepal **75** E3
Himanka Fin. **32** F2
Himarë Albania **47** A4
Himatnagar India **74** B5
Himeji Japan **65** C6
Himi Japan **65** D5
Himora Eth. **89** H6
Ḩimş Syria *see* **Homs**
Ḩimş *governorate* Syria **77** D2
Ḩimş, Baḩrat *resr* Syria *see* **Qaţţīnah, Buḩayrat**
Hinako *i.* Indon. **58** B2
Hinchinbrook Island Australia **111** F3
Hinckley *MN* U.S.A. **132** C2
Hinckley *UT* U.S.A. **137** F2
Hinckley Reservoir U.S.A. **131** F2
Hind, Wādī al *watercourse* Saudi Arabia **77** B5
Hinda Congo **95** B6
Hindaun India **74** C4
Hindelang Germany **36** E5
Hindenburg Poland *see* **Zabrze**
Hindman U.S.A. **130** B5
Hindmarsh, Lake *dry lake* Australia **112** B5
Hindola India **73** E1
Hindoli India **74** B4
Hindoria India **74** C5
Hindri *r.* India **72** C3
Hindu Kush *mts* Afgh./Pak. **81** F3
Hindupur India **72** C3
Hines Creek Canada **122** G3
Hinesville U.S.A. **129** C6
Hinganghat India **72** C1
Hingol *r.* Pak. **81** F5
Hingol *r.* Pak. *see* **Girdar Dhor**
Hınıs Turkey **79** E3
Hinnøya *i.* Norway **32** D1
Hinojedo *mt.* Spain **43** E2
Hino-misaki *pt* Japan **65** C6
Hinsdale U.S.A. **131** G2
Hinterzarten Germany **36** D5
Hinthada Myanmar *see* **Henzada**
Hinton *KY* U.S.A. **130** A4
Hinton *WV* U.S.A. **130** C5
Hiort *i.* U.K. *see* **Hirta**
Hipólito Mex. **133** A7
Hipponium Italy *see* **Vibo Valentia**
Hippo Regius Alg. *see* **Annaba**
Hippo Zarytus Tunisia *see* **Bizerte**
Hirabit Dağ *mt.* Turkey **79** F3
Hirado Japan **65** B6
Hirafok Alg. **91** G5
Hirakud Reservoir India **75** D5
Hiraman *watercourse* Kenya **96** C5
Hiré-Watta Côte d'Ivoire **92** D4
Hiriyur India **72** C3
Hirosaki Japan **64** E4
Hiroshima Japan **65** C6
Hirschaid Germany **36** E4
Hirschberg Germany **36** E3
Hirschberg Poland *see* **Jelenia Góra**
Hirsingue France **39** G3
Hirson France **39** F2
Hîrşova Romania *see* **Hârşova**
Hirta *i.* U.K. **34** B3
Hirtshals Denmark **33** C4
Hisar India **74** B3
Hisar, Koh-i- *mts* Afgh. **81** F3
Hisarcık Turkey **47** F5
Hisarköy Turkey *see* **Domaniç**
Hisarönü Turkey **78** C2
Hisarönü Körfezi *b.* Turkey **47** E6
Ḩisb, Sha'īb *watercourse* Iraq **79** F5
Hisor Tajik. **81** G2
Hisor Tizmasi *mts* Tajik./Uzbek. *see* **Gissar Range**
Hispalis Spain *see* **Seville**
Hispania *country* Europe *see* **Spain**

▶**Hispaniola** *i.* Caribbean Sea **127** L7
Consists of the Dominican Republic and Haiti.

Hispur Glacier Jammu and Kashmir **74** B1
Hissar India *see* **Hisar**
Hisua India **75** E4
Hīt Iraq **79** E4
Hitachi Japan **65** E5
Hitachinaka Japan **65** E5
Hitoyoshi Japan **65** B6
Hitra *i.* Norway **32** C3
Hiva Oa *i.* Fr. Polynesia **165** I6
Hixon Canada **122** F4
Hixson Cay *reef* Australia **111** H4
Hiyon *watercourse* Israel **77** B4
Hizan Turkey **79** E3
Hjallerup Denmark **33** C4
Hjälmaren *l.* Sweden **33** D4
Hjelle Norway **33** B3
Hjelmeland Norway **33** B4
Hjerkinn Norway **33** C3
Hjo Sweden **33** D4
Hjørring Denmark **33** C4
Hjuvik Sweden **33** C4
Hka, Nam *r.* Myanmar **60** B3
Hkakabo Razi *mt.* Myanmar **60** B1
Hkok *r.* Myanmar **60** B3
Hkring Bum *mt.* Myanmar **60** B2
Hlabisa S. Africa **99** F6
Hlaing *r.* Myanmar **60** B4
Hlako Kangri *mt.* China *see* **Lhagoi Kangri**
Hlinsko Czech Rep. **37** G4
Hlohlowane S. Africa **99** E6
Hlohovec Slovakia **37** H4
Hlotse Lesotho **99** F6
Hlučín Czech Rep. **37** I4
Hlukhiv Ukr. **29** E6
Hlung-Tan Myanmar **60** B3
Hlybokaye Belarus **31** K2
Hnilec *r.* Slovakia **37** J4
Hnúšťa Slovakia **37** I4
Ho Ghana **93** F4
Hoa Binh Vietnam **60** D3
Hoachanas Namibia **98** C4
Hoang Liên Son *mts* Vietnam **60** C3
Hoang Sa *is* S. China Sea *see* **Paracel Islands**
Hoanib *watercourse* Namibia **98** B3
Hoarusib *watercourse* Namibia **98** B3

▶**Hobart** Australia **112** C6
State capital of Tasmania.

Hobart U.S.A. **133** B5
Hobbs U.S.A. **135** G6
Hobbs Coast Antarctica **167** J1
Hobe Sound U.S.A. **129** C7
Hobot Xar Qi China *see* **Xin Bulag**
Hobro Denmark **33** C4
Hoburg Sweden **33** E4
Hoburgen *pt* Sweden **33** E4
Hobyo Somalia **96** F3
Hochfeiler *mt.* Austria/Italy *see* **Gran Pilastro**
Hochfeld Namibia **98** C4
Hochgall *mt.* Austria/Italy *see* **Collalto**
Hochgolling *mt.* Austria **37** F5
Hochharz *nat. park* Germany **36** E3
Hô Chi Minh Vietnam *see* **Ho Chi Minh City**
Ho Chi Minh City Vietnam **61** D6
Hochschwab *mt.* Austria **37** G5
Hochtor *mt.* Austria **37** G5
Hocking *r.* U.S.A. **130** C4
Hodal India **74** C4
Hodda *mt.* Somalia **96** F2
Hodeidah Yemen **76** C7
Hodgesville U.S.A. **130** C4
Hodgson Downs Australia **110** C2
Hodh Ech Chargui *admin. reg.* Mauritania **92** D1
Hodh El Gharbi *admin. reg.* Mauritania **92** C1
Hódmezővásárhely Hungary **46** B1
Hodmo *watercourse* Somalia **96** E2
Hodna, Chott el *salt l.* Alg. **91** G2
Hodonín Czech Rep. **37** H4
Hoek van Holland Neth. *see* **Hook of Holland**
Hoeryŏng N. Korea **64** B4
Hof Germany **36** E3
Hoffman Mountain U.S.A. **131** G2
Hofmeyr S. Africa **98** E6
Höfn Iceland **32** [inset]
Hofors Sweden **33** E3
Hofsjökull *ice cap* Iceland **32** [inset]
Hōfu Japan **65** B6
Hofūf Saudi Arabia *see* **Al Hufūf**
Höganäs Sweden **33** D4
Hoganthulla Creek *r.* Australia **111** F5
Hogg, Mount Canada **122** C2
Hoggar *plat.* Alg. **91** G5
Hog Island U.S.A. **131** F5
Högsby Sweden **33** E4
Høgste Breakulen *mt.* Norway **33** B3
Hőgyész Hungary **37** I5
Hoh *r.* U.S.A. **134** A3
Hohenems Austria **36** D5
Hohenloher Ebene *plain* Germany **36** D4
Hohensalza Poland *see* **Inowrocław**
Hoher Dachstein *mt.* Austria **37** F5
Hoher Göll *mt.* Austria/Germany **37** F5
Hohe Rhön *mts* Germany **36** D3
Hohe Tauern *mts* Austria **37** F5
Hohe Tauern, Nationalpark *nat. park* Austria **37** F5
Hohe Venn *moorland* Belgium **39** G1
Hohhot China **63** I3
Hoh Xil Hu *salt l.* China **75** F2
Hoh Xil Shan *mts* China **70** G4
Hội An Vietnam **61** E5
Hoima Uganda **96** A4
Hoisington U.S.A. **132** B4
Hôi Xuân Vietnam **60** D3
Hojagala Turkm. *see* **Khodzha-Kala**
Hojai India **75** G4
Hojambaz Turkm. *see* **Khodzhambaz**
Hökensås *hills* Sweden **33** D4
Hokitika N.Z. **113** B3
Hokkaidō *i.* Japan **64** E4
Hokksund Norway **33** C4
Hokmābād Iran **80** D2
Hoktemberyan Armenia **79** F2
Hol *Buskerud* Norway **33** C3
Hol *Nordland* Norway **32** E1
Hola Kenya **96** C5
Holalkere India **72** C3
Holanda Bol. **148** D3
Holbæk Denmark **33** C5
Holberg Canada **122** D5
Holbrook Australia **112** C4
Holbrook U.S.A. **137** G4
Holden Canada **123** H4
Holden U.S.A. **137** F2
Holdenville U.S.A. **133** B5
Holdich Arg. **153** C6
Holdrege U.S.A. **132** B3
Hole Narsipur India **72** C3
Holgate U.S.A. **130** A3
Holguín Cuba **127** K7
Holíč Slovakia **37** H4
Hollabrunn Austria **37** H4
Holland *country* Europe *see* **Netherlands**
Holland *MI* U.S.A. **132** E3
Holland *NY* U.S.A. **130** D2
Hollandale U.S.A. **133** D5
Hollandia Indon. *see* **Jayapura**
Hollands Diep *est.* Neth. **36** B3
Hollick-Kenyon Peninsula Antarctica **167** L2
Hollick-Kenyon Plateau Antarctica **167** K1
Hollis U.S.A. **133** B5
Hollister U.S.A. **136** B3
Hollola Fin. **33** G3
Hollum Neth. **36** B2
Holly U.S.A. **130** B2
Holly Springs U.S.A. **128** A5
Hollywood U.S.A. **129** C7
Holm Norway **32** D2
Holman Canada **120** H2
Holmes Reef Australia **111** F3
Holmgard Rus. Fed. *see* **Velikiy Novgorod**
Holmön *i.* Sweden **32** F3
Holmsund Sweden **32** F3
Holmudden *pt* Sweden **33** E4
Holod *r.* Romania **46** C1
Ḩolon Israel **77** B3
Holoog Namibia **98** C5
Holothuria Banks *reef* Australia **108** D3
Holroyd *r.* Australia **111** E2
Holstebro Denmark **33** C4
Holstein U.S.A. **132** C3
Holsteinsborg Greenland *see* **Sisimiut**
Holston *r.* U.S.A. **130** B5
Holston Lake U.S.A. **130** C5
Holt U.S.A. **130** A2
Holton U.S.A. **132** C4
Holtville U.S.A. **137** E5
Holtwood U.S.A. **131** E4
Holyhead U.K. **35** D5
Holy Island *England* U.K. **34** F4
Holy Island *Wales* U.K. **35** D5
Holyoke *CO* U.S.A. **134** G4
Holyoke *MA* U.S.A. **131** G2
Holy See Europe *see* **Vatican City**
Holzkirchen Germany **36** E5
Holzminden Germany **36** D3
Homa Bay Kenya **96** B5
Homalin Myanmar **60** A2
Homathko *r.* Canada **122** E5
Homāyūnshahr Iran *see* **Khomeynīshahr**
Homberg (Efze) Germany **36** D3
Hombori Mali **93** E2
Hombre Muerto, Salar del *salt flat* Arg. **152** D1
Home Bay Canada **121** M3
Home Hill Australia **111** F3
Homer *AK* U.S.A. **120** D4
Homer *LA* U.S.A. **133** C5
Homer *MI* U.S.A. **130** A2
Homer City U.S.A. **130** D3
Homerville U.S.A. **129** C6
Homestead Australia **111** F4
Homestead U.S.A. **129** C7
Homewood U.S.A. **129** B5
Hommelvik Norway **32** C3
Homnabad India **72** C2
Homocea Romania **46** E1
Homodji *well* Niger **93** I1
Homoine Moz. **99** G4
Homs Libya *see* **Al Khums**
Homs Syria **78** D4
Homyel' Belarus **29** D5
Honaker U.S.A. **130** C5
Honan *prov.* China *see* **Henan**
Honavar India **72** B3
Hon Bai Canh *i.* Vietnam **61** D6
Hon Chông Vietnam **61** D6
Hon Chuôi *i.* Vietnam **61** D6
Honda Col. **146** C3
Honda India **75** E5
Hondeklipbaai S. Africa **98** C6
Hondo *NM* U.S.A. **135** F6
Hondo *TX* U.S.A. **133** B6

▶**Honduras** *country* Central America **138** G6
5th largest country in Central and North America.
northamerica **118–119, 140**

Hønefoss Norway **33** C3
Honesdale U.S.A. **131** F3
Honey Brook U.S.A. **131** F3
Honey Lake U.S.A. **136** B1
Honfleur France **38** D2
Hong'an China **67** E2
Hongch'ŏn S. Korea **65** A5
Hông Gai Vietnam **60** D3
Honghai Wan *b.* China **67** E4
Honghe China **66** B4
Hong He *r.* China **67** E1
Honghu China **67** E2
Hong Hu *l.* China **67** E2
Hongjiang *Hunan* China **67** D3
Hongjiang *Sichuan* China *see* **Wangcang**
▶**Hong Kong** *Hong Kong* China **67** [inset]
asia **52–53, 82**
world **16–17**
Hong Kong *special admin. reg.* China **67** [inset]
Hong Kong Harbour *sea chan. Hong Kong* China **67** [inset]
Hong Kong Island *Hong Kong* China **67** [inset]
Hông Ngư Vietnam **61** D5
Hongqiao China *see* **Qidong**
Hongqizhen China *see* **Tongshi**
Hongshan China **66** A2
Hongshui He *r.* China **66** D4
Honguedo, Détroit d' *sea chan.* Canada **125** H3
Hongwŏn N. Korea **65** A4
Hongyuan China **66** B1
Hongze China **67** F1
Hongze Hu *l.* China **67** F1

▶**Honiara** Solomon Is **107** E2
Capital of the Solomon Islands.

Honiton U.K. **35** E6
Honjō Japan **65** E5
Honkajoki Fin. **33** F3
Hon Khoai *i.* Vietnam **61** D6
Hon Mê *i.* Vietnam **60** D4
Hon Minh Hoa *i.* Vietnam **61** D6
Honnali India **72** B3
Honningsvåg Norway **32** G1
Honokaa U.S.A. **135** [inset] Z1

▶**Honolulu** U.S.A. **135** [inset] Z1
State capital of Hawaii.

Hon Rai *i.* Vietnam **61** D6

▶**Honshū** *i.* Japan **65** C6
3rd largest island in Asia and 7th in the world.
asia **50–51**
world **6–7**

Honwad India **72** B2
Hood *r.* Canada **123** I1
Hood, Mount *vol.* U.S.A. **134** B3
Hood Point Australia **109** B8
Hood River U.S.A. **134** B3
Hoogeveen Neth. **36** C2
Hoogezand-Sappemeer Neth. **36** C2
Hooghly *r. mouth* India *see* **Hugli**
Hooker U.S.A. **132** A4
Hook Head Rep. of Ireland **35** C5
Hook of Holland Neth. **36** B3
Hook Reef Australia **111** G3
Hoonah U.S.A. **122** C3
Hooper Bay U.S.A. **120** C3
Hooper Island U.S.A. **131** E4
Hoopstad S. Africa **98** E5
Hoorn Neth. **36** B2
Hoorn, Îles de *is* Wallis and Futuna Is **107** H3
Hoorn Islands Wallis and Futuna Is *see* **Hoorn, Îles de**
Hoover Dam U.S.A. **137** E3
Hoover Memorial Reservoir U.S.A. **130** B3
Hóp *lag.* Iceland **32** [inset]
Hopa Turkey **79** E2
Hope Canada **134** B2
Hope U.S.A. **133** C5
Hope, Lake *salt flat* Australia **109** C8
Hope, Point U.S.A. **166** B2
Hopedale Canada **125** I2
Hopei *prov.* China *see* **Hebei**

Hope Mountains Canada **125** I2
Hopen *i.* Svalbard **26** C2
Hope Saddle *pass* N.Z. **113** C3
Hopes Advance, Cap Canada **121** M3
Hopes Advance Bay Canada *see* Aupaluk
Hopetoun *Vic.* Australia **112** B4
Hopetoun *W.A.* Australia **109** C8
Hopetown S. Africa **98** E6
Hope Valley U.S.A. **131** H3
Hopewell U.S.A. **131** E5
Hopewell Islands Canada **124** E1
Hopkins *r.* Australia **112** B5
Hopkins, Lake *salt flat* Australia **110** B5
Hopland U.S.A. **136** A2
Hopong Myanmar **60** B3
Hor China **75** D3
Horadiz Azer. **79** F3
Horasan Turkey **79** E2
Horažďovice Czech Rep. **37** F4
Horb am Neckar Germany **36** D4
Hörby Sweden **33** C5
Horcajo de Santiago Spain **42** E3
Horcón *hill* Spain **42** D3
Horda Norway **33** B4
Hordaland *county* Norway **33** B3
Horezu Romania **46** C2
Horgo Mongolia **70** I2
Horgoš Yugo. **46** A1
Horia Romania **46** F2

▶ **Horizon Deep** *sea feature*
S. Pacific Ocean **164** G7
2nd deepest point in the world (Tonga Trench).

Horki Belarus **29** D5
Horlick Mountains Antarctica **167** K1
Horlivka Ukr. **29** F6
Hormak Iran **81** E4
Hormoz, Küh-e *mt.* Iran **80** C5
Hormozgan *prov.* Iran **80** D5
Hormūd-e Bāgh Iran **80** C5
Hormuz, Strait of Iran/Oman **80** D5
Horn Austria **37** G4
Horn *r.* Canada **123** G2
Horn *c.* Iceland **32** [inset]

▶ **Horn, Cape** Chile **153** D8
Most southerly point of South America.

Hornád *r.* Slovakia **37** J4
also spelt Hernád (Hungary)
Hornavan *l.* Sweden **32** E3
Hornbrook U.S.A. **134** B4
Horndal Sweden **33** E3
Horne, Îles de *is* Wallis and Futuna Is *see* Hoorn, Îles d'
Hörnefors Sweden **32** E3
Hornell U.S.A. **130** E3
Hornepayne Canada **124** C3
Hornindal Norway **33** B3
Hornkranz Namibia **98** C4
Horn Mountains Canada **122** F4
Hornos, Cabo de *c.* Chile *see* Horn, Cape
Hornos, Parque Nacional de *nat. park* Chile **153** D8
Hornoy-le-Bourg France **38** D2
Horn Peak Canada **122** D4
Hornsea U.K. **35** F5
Hornslandet *pen.* Sweden **33** E3
Hornslet Denmark **33** C4
Horodnya Ukr. **29** D6
Horodok Ukr. **29** C6
Horodok Ukr. **31** J3
Horoshiri-dake *mt.* Japan **64** E4
Horqin Youyi Qianqi China *see* Ulanhot
Horqueta Para. **149** F5
Horred Sweden **33** D4
Horru China **75** F3
Horse Creek *r.* U.S.A. **134** F4
Horsefly Canada **122** F4
Horseheads U.S.A. **131** E3
Horsens Denmark **33** C5
Horseshoe Bend Australia **110** C5
Horseshoe Seamounts *sea feature* N. Atlantic Ocean **160** M3
Horsham Australia **112** B5
Horsham U.K. **35** F6
Horten Norway **33** C4
Hortobágyi *nat. park* Hungary **37** J5
Horton *r.* Canada **120** G3
Horwood Lake Canada **124** D3
Ho Sai Hu *l.* China **75** G2
Hosa'ina Eth. **96** C3
Hosdurga India **72** C3
Hose, Pegunungan *mts* Sarawak Malaysia **59** E2
Hosenofu *well* Libya **88** D4
Hoseynīyeh Iran **80** B4
Hoshab Pak. **81** E5
Hoshangabad India **74** C5
Hoshiarpur India **74** B3
Hoskins P.N.G. **107** K2
Hospet India **72** C3
Hosséré Vokre *mt.* Cameroon **93** I3
Hoste, Isla *i.* Chile **153** C8
Hosur India **72** C3
Hotahudo East Timor *see* Hatudo
Hotan China **70** D4
Hotazel S. Africa **98** D5
Hot Creek *r.* U.S.A. **137** D2
Hot Creek Range *mts* U.S.A. **137** D2
Hotham *r.* Australia **109** B8
Hotham, Cape Australia **110** B2
Hoting Sweden **32** E2
Hot Springs *AR* U.S.A. **133** C5
Hot Springs *NM* U.S.A. *see* Truth or Consequences
Hot Springs *SD* U.S.A. **134** G4
Hottah Lake Canada **123** G1
Hottentots Point Namibia **98** B5
Houaïlou New Caledonia **107** F4
Houdan France **38** D2
Houffalize Belgium **39** F1
Hougang Sing. **58** [inset]
Houghton *MI* U.S.A. **132** D2
Houghton *NY* U.S.A. **131** E3
Houghton Lake U.S.A. **130** C1
Houie Moc, Phou *mt.* Laos **60** C3
Houlton U.S.A. **128** G2
Houma China **63** I4
Houma U.S.A. **127** D4
Houmen China **67** C4
Houmt Souk Tunisia **91** H2
Houndé Burkina **92** E3
Hourtin et de Carcans, Étang d' *l.* France **38** C4
Housatonic *r.* U.S.A. **131** G3
House Range *mts* U.S.A. **137** F2
Housesteads *tourist site* U.K. **34** E4
Houston Canada **122** E4
Houston *MO* U.S.A. **132** E4
Houston *TX* U.S.A. **133** D6
Houtman Abrolhos *is* Australia **109** A7
Hov Denmark **33** C4
Hov Norway **33** C3
Hova Sweden **33** D4
Hovd Mongolia **63** E2
Hoveyzeh Iran **79** G5
Hovmantorp Sweden **33** D4
Hövsgöl Nuur *l.* Mongolia **62** G1
Howa, Ouadi *watercourse* Chad/Sudan **88** D4
Howar, Wadi *watercourse* Sudan **88** E5
Howard Australia **111** H5

Howard *KS* U.S.A. **132** B4
Howard *SD* U.S.A. **132** B4
Howard Island Australia **110** C2
Howe, Cape Australia **112** D5
Howe, Mount Antarctica **167** J1
Howell U.S.A. **130** B2
Howes U.S.A. **134** F3
Howick S. Africa **99** F6
Howland U.S.A. **128** F2

▶ **Howland Island** N. Pacific Ocean **107** H1
United States Unincorporated Territory.
oceania 104–105, 114

Howlong Australia **112** C4
Howrah India *see* Haora
Howz *well* Iran **80** D4
Howz-e Panj Iran **80** D4
Howz-e Panj *waterhole* Iran **80** C3
Howz-i-Khan *well* Iran **80** D3
Howz i-Mīan i-Tak Iran **80** C3
Hoxie U.S.A. **132** A4
Höxter Germany **36** D3
Hoy *i.* U.K. **34** E2
Høyanger Norway **33** B3
Hoyerswerda Germany **37** G3
Høylandet Norway **32** D2
Höytiäinen *l.* Fin. **32** H3
Hozat Turkey **79** E3
Hpa-an Myanmar *see* Pa-an
Hradec Králové Czech Rep. **37** G3
Hradiště *hill* Czech Rep. **37** F3
Hrasnica Bos.-Herz. **44** H3
Hraun Iceland **32** [inset]
Hraun *slope* Iceland **32** [inset]
Hrazdan Armenia **79** F2
Hrazený *hill* Czech Rep. **37** G3
Hrebinka Ukr. **29** D6
Hrodna Belarus **31** J2
Hron *r.* Slovakia **37** I5
Hrvatska *country* Europe *see* Croatia
Hrvatska Kostajnica Croatia **44** F2
Hsenwi Myanmar **60** B2
Hsiang Chang *i.* Hong Kong China *see* Hong Kong Island
Hsiang Kang *Hong Kong* China *see* Hong Kong
Hsi-hseng Myanmar **60** B3
Hsin, Nam *r.* Myanmar **60** B3
Hsin-chia-p'o *country* Asia *see* Singapore
Hsinchu Taiwan **67** F3
Hsinking China *see* Changchun
Hsinying Taiwan **67** F4
Hsipaw Myanmar **60** B3
Hsi-sha Ch'un-tao *is* S. China Sea *see* Paracel Islands
Hsüyü'p'ing Yü *i.* Taiwan **67** F4
Hsüeh Shan *mt.* Taiwan **67** F3
Hua'an China **67** F3
Huab *watercourse* Namibia **98** B4
Huacaraje Bol. **149** E3
Huacaya Bol. **149** E5
Huacheng China **67** F3
Huachinera Mex. **135** F7
Huacho Peru **148** A3
Huachón Peru **148** A2
Huachuan China **64** C3
Huacrachuco Peru **148** A2
Huacullani Peru **148** C4
Huade China **63** I3
Huadian China **64** A4
Huadu China **67** F3
Huafeng China *see* Hua'an
Huai'an *Jiangsu* China **67** F1
Huaibei China **67** F1
Huaibin China **67** F1
Huaicheng China *see* Huaiji
Huaide China *see* Gongzhuling
Huaidian China *see* Shenqiu
Huai He *r.* China **67** F1
Huaihua China **67** D3
Huaiji China **67** E4
Huai Luang *r.* Thai. **60** C4
Huainan China **67** F2
Huaining China **67** F2
Huaiyang China **67** E1
Huaiyin *Jiangsu* China **67** F1
Huaiyin *Jiangsu* China **67** F1
Huaiyuan *Anhui* China **67** F1
Huaiyuan *Guangxi* China **67** D3
Huajuápan de León Mex. **138** C5
Huaki Indon. **57** G7
Hualahuises Mex. **133** B7
Hualapai Peak U.S.A. **137** F4
Hualfin Arg. **152** D1
Hualien Taiwan **67** F3
Hualla Peru **148** B3
Huallaga *r.* Peru **146** C6
Huamachuco Peru **148** A1
Huamani Peru **148** B3
Huambo *r.* Angola **95** B8
Huambo *prov.* Angola **95** B8
Huanan China **64** C3
Huancabamba *r.* Peru **146** B6
Huancache, Sierra *mts* Arg. **153** C5
Huancavelica Peru **148** B3
Huancavelica *dept* Peru **148** A2
Huancayo Peru **148** B3
Huangcaoba China *see* Xingyi
Huangchuan China **67** E1
Huanggang China **67** F2
Huang He *r.* China *see* Yellow River
Huangjiajian China **67** G1
Huangliu China **67** D5
Huanglongsi China *see* Kaifeng
Huangmao Jian *mt.* China **67** F3
Huangmei China **67** F2
Huangnihe China **64** A4
Huangpi China **67** E2
Huangping China **66** C3
Huangqi China **67** F3
Huangshan China **67** F2
Huang Shan *mts* China **67** F2
Huangshi China **67** F2
Huangtu Gaoyuan *plat.* China **63** H4
Huangyan China **70** J4
Huangyuan China **63** H4
Huangzhou China *see* Huanggang
Huanjiang China **67** D3
Huanren China **64** A4
Huanshan China *see* Yuhuan
Huanta Peru **148** B3
Huánuco Peru **148** A2
Huanuni Bol. **148** D4
Huaping China **66** B3
Huap'ing Yü *i.* Taiwan **67** F3
Huar Bol. **148** D4
Huaral Peru **148** A3
Huaráz Peru **148** A2
Huarmey Peru **148** A3
Huarochiri Peru **148** A3
Huaron Peru **148** A2
Huasaga *r.* Peru **146** C5
Huascarán, Parque Nacional *nat. park* Peru **148** A2
Huasco Chile **152** C2
Hua Shan *mt.* China **67** D1
Huatabampo Mex. **126** E6
Huaxian *Guangdong* China *see* Huadu
Huaxian *Shaanxi* China **67** D1
Huayang China *see* Jixi
Huayin China **67** D1
Huayllay Peru **148** A2
Huaylas Peru **148** A2

Huayuan *Hubei* China *see* Xiaochang
Huayuan *Hunan* China **67** D2
Huazangsi China *see* Tianzhu
Huazhou China **67** D4
Hubbard, Mount Canada/U.S.A. **122** B2
Hubbard, Pointe *pt* Canada **125** H1
Hubbard Lake U.S.A. **132** D2
Hubei *prov.* China **67** E2
Hubli India **72** B3
Huça'l Arg. **152** D4
Huddersfield U.K. **35** F5
Huddinge Sweden **33** E4
Hudiksvall Sweden **33** E3
Hudson *MD* U.S.A. **131** E4
Hudson *MI* U.S.A. **130** A3
Hudson *NY* U.S.A. **131** G3
Hudson *r.* U.S.A. **131** G3
Hudson, Baie d' *sea* Canada *see* Hudson Bay
Hudson, Détroit d' *strait* Canada *see* Hudson Strait
Hudson Bay *sea* Canada **123** K4
Hudson Bay Canada **121** K4
Hudson Falls U.S.A. **131** G2
Hudson Island Tuvalu *see* Nanumaga
Hudson Mountains Antarctica **163** A10
Hudson's Hope Canada **122** F3
Hudson Strait Canada **121** L3
Huế Vietnam **61** D4
Huebra *r.* Spain **42** C3
Huehuetenango Guat. **138** F5
Huedin Romania **46** C1
Huehuetenango Guat. **138** F5
Huelma Spain **42** E4
Huelva Spain **42** C4
Huelva *r.* Spain **42** C4
Huentelauquén Chile **152** C2
Huércal-Overa Spain **43** F4
Huerfano *r.* U.S.A. **135** F4
Huerva *r.* Spain **43** F2
Huesca Spain **43** F1
Huéscar Spain **43** E3
Huete Spain **43** E3
Hueytown U.S.A. **129** B5
Hugeilig *l.* Sudan **89** G6
Hugh *watercourse* Australia **110** C5
Hughenden Australia **111** F4
Hughes Australia **109** E7
Hughes *r.* Canada **123** L3
Hughesville *MD* U.S.A. **131** E4
Hughesville *PA* U.S.A. **131** E3
Hughson U.S.A. **136** B3
Hugli *r.* India **75** F5
Hugli-Chunchura India **75** F5
Hugo *CO* U.S.A. **132** A4
Hugo *OK* U.S.A. **133** C5
Hugoton U.S.A. **132** A4
Huhehot China *see* Hohhot
Huhhot China *see* Hohhot
Huhucunya Venez. **147** A3
Huhudi S. Africa **98** E5
Huhus Fin. **32** H3
Hui'an China **67** F3
Hui'anbao China **67** F3
Huiarau Range *mts* N.Z. **113** D4
Huib-Hoch Plateau Namibia **98** C5
Huichang China **67** F3
Huicheng *Anhui* China *see* Shexian
Huicheng *Guangdong* China *see* Huilai
Huich'ŏn N. Korea **65** A4
Huidong China **67** F4
Huifa *r.* China **64** A4
Huiji *r.* China **67** F1
Huila *prov.* Angola **95** B8
Huila *dept* Col. **146** C4
Huila, Nevado de *vol.* Col. **146** C4
Huilai China **67** F4
Huili China **66** B3
Huila Plateau Angola **95** B8
Huilong China *see* Qidong
Huimanguillo Mex. **138** F5
Huimin China **67** F1
Huinahuaca Arg. **148** D1
Huinan *Shanghai* China *see* Nanhui
Huinca Renancó Arg. **152** D3
Huishui China **66** E3
Huiten Nur *l.* China **75** F2
Huitong China **67** D3
Huittinen Fin. **33** F3
Huixian China **66** C1
Huixtla Mex. **138** F5
Huiyang China *see* Huizhou
Huize China **66** B3
Huizhou China **67** E4
Hujirt Mongolia **62** G2
Hukawng Valley Myanmar **60** B2
Hukou China **67** F2
Hukuntsi Botswana **98** D4
Hulan China **64** A3
Hulan China **64** A3
Hulayfah Saudi Arabia **89** I3
Hulayhah *well* Syria **77** D2
Huliao China *see* Dabu
Hulin China **64** C3
Hull Canada **124** F1
Hull U.K. *see* Kingston upon Hull
Hull Island Kiribati *see* Orona
Hulst Neth. **36** E2
Hultsfred Sweden **33** D4
Hulun China *see* Hailar
Hulun Nur *l.* China **63** J2
Hulwān Egypt **89** F2
Huma China **64** A2
Huma *r.* China **64** A2
Humaitá Bol. **148** D2
Humaitá Brazil **149** E1
Humaitá Para. **149** F6
Humay Peru **148** B3
Humbe Angola **95** B9
Humber, Mouth of the U.K. **35** G5
Humberside *airport* U.K. **35** F5
Humberstone Chile **148** C5
Humberto de Campos Brazil **150** D2
Humboldt Canada **134** F1
Humboldt *AZ* U.S.A. **137** G4
Humboldt *NV* U.S.A. **136** C1
Humboldt *TN* U.S.A. **128** A5
Humboldt *r.* U.S.A. **136** C1
Humboldt, Mont *mt.* New Caledonia **107** F4
Humboldt Bay U.S.A. **134** A4
Humboldt Gletscher *glacier* Greenland *see* Sermersuaq
Humbolt Salt Marsh U.S.A. **136** D2
Hume *r.* Canada **122** D1
Humeburn Australia **111** F5
Humeda *plain* Arg. **152** E4
Humenné Slovakia **37** J4
Hume Reservoir Australia **112** C4
Humos, Cabo *c.* Chile **152** B3
Humpata Angola **95** B8
Humphreys, Mount U.S.A. **136** D3
Humphreys Peak U.S.A. **137** G4
Humpolec Czech Rep. **37** G4
Humppila Fin. **33** F3
Humpty Doo Australia **110** B2
Hūn Libya **88** B2
Húnaflói *b.* Iceland **32** [inset]
Hunan *prov.* China **67** D3
Hunchun China **64** B4
Hundorp Norway **33** C3
Hundred U.S.A. **130** E4

Hunedoara Romania **46** C2
Hünfeld Germany **36** D3
▶ **Hungary** *country* Europe **31** I4
europe 24–25, 48
Hungerford Australia **111** F6
Hungerford U.K. **35** F6
Hung Fa Leng *hill* Hong Kong China **67** [inset]
Hüngnam N. Korea **65** A5
Hung Shui Kiu Hong Kong China **67** [inset]
Hungund India **72** C2
Hunjiang China *see* Baishan
Hun Jiang *r.* China **64** B4
Hunsrück *hills* Germany **39** H1
Hunstanton U.K. **35** G5
Hunsur India **72** C3
Hunte *r.* Germany **36** D2
Hunter *r.* Australia **112** D4
Hunter Island Australia **112** C6
Hunter Island Canada **122** D5
Hunter Islands S. Pacific Ocean **107** G4
Hunter Islands Australia **112** C6
Hunter's Bay Myanmar **60** A4
Huntingdon U.K. **35** F5
Huntingdon *PA* U.S.A. **130** E3
Huntington *IN* U.S.A. **130** C3
Huntington *UT* U.S.A. **137** G2
Huntington *WV* U.S.A. **130** B4
Huntington Beach U.S.A. **136** C5
Huntington Creek *r.* U.S.A. **137** E1
Huntly N.Z. **113** E3
Huntly U.K. **34** E1
Huntsville Canada **124** E4
Huntsville *AL* U.S.A. **129** B5
Huntsville *TX* U.S.A. **133** C6
Hunucmá Mex. **138** F4
Hunyani *r.* Moz./Zimbabwe *see* Manyame
Hunza Jammu and Kashmir **74** B1
Hunza *reg.* Jammu and Kashmir **74** B1
Hunza *r.* Pak. **74** B2
Huoer China *see* Hor
Huolongmen China **64** A2
Huoshan China **67** F2
Huo Shan *mt.* China **67** F1
Huoshao Tao *i.* Taiwan *see* Lü Tao
Huotsais *waterhole* Namibia **98** D3
Hupeh *prov.* China *see* Hubei
Hupnik *r.* Turkey **77** C1
Hür Iran **80** D4
Ḩurayḏīn, Wādī *watercourse* Egypt **77** A4
Huraymilā Saudi Arabia **80** A5
Hurbanovo Slovakia **37** I5
Hurd, Cape Canada **124** D4
Hurd Island Kiribati *see* Arorae
Hurdiyo Somalia **96** F2
Hurghada Egypt *see* Al Ghurdaqah
Huri *mt.* Kenya **96** C3
Huriel France **39** I3
Hurley U.S.A. **131** F3
Hurlock U.S.A. **131** F4
Huron *CA* U.S.A. **136** B3
Huron *SD* U.S.A. **132** B2

▶ **Huron, Lake** Canada/U.S.A. **130** B1
2nd largest lake in North America and 4th in the world.
northamerica 116–117
world 6–7

Hurricane U.S.A. **137** F3
Hurricane Flats *sea feature* Bahamas **129** D8
Hurtado Chile **152** C2
Hurung, Gunung *mt.* Indon. **59** F2
Hurunui *r.* N.Z. **113** C3
Hurup Denmark **33** C4
Husain Nika Pak. **81** G4
Húsavík Iceland **32** [inset]
Húsavík Iceland **32** [inset]
Huseyinabad Turkey *see* Alaca
Hushan *Zhejiang* China *see* Wuyi
Hushan *Zhejiang* China *see* Cixi
Husheib Sudan **89** G6
Huşi Romania **46** F1
Huskvarna Sweden **33** D4
Husn Jordan *see* Al Ḩişn
Husn Āl 'Abr Yemen **76** D6
Husnes Norway **33** B4
Hussainabad India **75** E4
Hustopeče Czech Rep. **37** H4
Husum Germany **36** D1
Husvik S. Georgia **153** I8
Hutag Mongolia **62** G2
Hutanopan Indon. **58** B2
Hūtak Iran **80** D4
Hutchinson *KS* U.S.A. **132** B4
Hutchinson *MN* U.S.A. **132** C2
Hutch Mountain U.S.A. **137** G4
Hutou China **64** C3
Huttah Kulkyne National Park Australia **112** B4
Hutton, Mount Australia **111** G5
Hutton Range *hills* Australia **109** C6
Huvadhu Atoll Maldives **71** D11
Hüvär *i.* The Gulf **80** B5
Hüvek Turkey *see* Bozova
Hüvián, Küh-e *mts* Iran **81** D5
Huwär *i.* The Gulf **80** B5
Huxi China **67** E3
Huxian China **67** D1
Huy Belgium **39** F1
Hūzgān Iran **80** B4
Huzhen China **67** G2
Huzhou China **67** G2
Hvalnes Iceland **32** [inset]
Hvalpsund Denmark **33** C4
Hvannadalshnúkur *vol.* Iceland **32** [inset]
Hvar *i.* Croatia **44** A4
Hvardíys'ke Ukr. **29** E7
Hvarski Kanal *sea chan.* Croatia **44** F3
Hveragerði Iceland **32** [inset]
Hvide Sande Denmark **33** C4
Hvíta *r.* Iceland **32** [inset]
Hvitárvatn *l.* Iceland **32** [inset]
Hwange Zimbabwe **99** C5
Hwange National Park Zimbabwe **99** C5
Hwang Ho *r.* China *see* Yellow River
Hwangju N. Korea **65** A5
Hwedza Zimbabwe **99** D5
Hwlffordd U.K. *see* Haverfordwest
Hyannis *MA* U.S.A. **131** H3
Hyannis *NE* U.S.A. **132** B3
Hyargas Nuur *salt l.* Mongolia **62** G2
Hyco Lake U.S.A. **130** E4
Hyden Australia **109** B8
Hyden U.S.A. **130** B5
Hyderabad India **72** C2
Hyderabad Pak. **81** G5
Hydra *i.* Greece *see* Ydra
Hydra *i.* Slovenia **44** D1
Hyères France **39** I5
Hyères, Îles d' *is* France **39** G5
Hyesan N. Korea **65** B4
Hyland *r.* Canada **122** D2
Hyland Post Canada **122** D3
Hyllekrog *i.* Denmark **36** E1
Hyltebruk Sweden **33** D4

Hyndman U.S.A. **130** D4
Hyndman Peak U.S.A. **134** D4
Hyōno-sen *mt.* Japan **65** C6
Hyrcania Iran *see* Gorgān
Hyrra Banda Cent. Afr. Rep. *see* Ira Banda
Hyrynsalmi Fin. **32** H2
Hysham U.S.A. **134** F3
Hyūga Japan **65** B6
Hyvinkää Fin. **33** G3

↓ I

Iaciara Brazil **150** C5
Iaco *r.* Brazil **148** C2
Iaçu Brazil **150** D5
Iadera Croatia *see* Zadar
Iaeger U.S.A. **130** C5
Iakora Madag. **99** [inset] J4
Ialomiţa *r.* Romania **46** E2
Ialomiţa, Balta *marsh* Romania **46** E2
Ialpug *r.* Moldova **46** F2
Ianca Romania **46** E2
Ian Calder Lake Canada **123** L1
Iancu Jianu Romania **46** C2
Iara *r.* Romania **46** D2
Iarauarune, Serra *mts* Brazil **147** F4
Iargara Moldova **46** F1
Iaşi Romania **31** K4
Iasmos Greece **46** D4
Iba Phil. **57** F3
Ibadan Nigeria **93** F3
Ibagué Col. **146** C3
Ibanda Uganda **94** D4
Ibañeta, Puerto de *pass* Spain **43** F1
Ibanga *Kasai Occidental* Dem. Rep. Congo **95** D6
Ibanga *Sud-Kivu* Dem. Rep. Congo **94** C5
Ibapah U.S.A. **137** F1
Ibar *r.* Yugo. **46** B2
Ibarra Ecuador **146** B4
Ibarreta Arg. **152** F1
Ibb Yemen **76** C7
Ibba *watercourse* Sudan **94** F3
Ibbenbüren Germany **36** C2
Ibdeqqene *watercourse* Mali **93** F1
Iberá, Esteros del *marsh* Arg. **152** F2
Iberá, Lago *l.* Arg. **152** F2
Iberia Rus. Fed. **28** J4

▶ **Iberian Peninsula** **42**
Consists of Portugal, Spain and Gibraltar.

Iberville, Lac d' *l.* Canada **125** G3
Ibestad Norway **32** F1
Ibeto Nigeria **93** G3
Ibi Indon. **58** B1
Ibi Nigeria **93** H3
Ibi Spain **43** F3
Ibiá Brazil **151** C6
Ibiapaba, Serra da *hills* Brazil **150** D2
Ibias *r.* Spain **42** C1
Ibicaraí Brazil **151** D6
Ibicuí *r.* Brazil **152** F2
Ibicuí *r.* Brazil **152** F2
Ibina *r.* Dem. Rep. Congo **94** F4
Ibitiara Brazil **150** D5
Ibiza Spain **43** G3
Ibiza *i.* Spain **43** G3
Iblei, Monti *mts* Sicily Italy **45** E6
Iblis Burnu *pt* Turkey **47** F6
Ibn Hādī Saudi Arabia **89** I5
Ibotirama Brazil **150** D5
Iboundji, Mont *hill* Gabon **94** A5
Ibrā' Oman **76** F5
Ibra, Wadi *watercourse* Sudan **94** E2
Ibri Oman **76** F5
Icá *r.* Brazil **146** E5
Ica Peru **148** B3
Ica *dept* Peru **148** B3
Icabarú Venez. **147** F3
Içana Brazil **146** E4
Içana *r.* Brazil **146** E4
Icaraí Brazil **150** D3
Icaria *i.* Greece *see* Ikaria
Icatu Brazil **150** C2
Iceberg Canyon *gorge* U.S.A. **137** E3

▶ **Iceland** *country* Europe **32** [inset]
2nd largest island in Europe.
europe 22–23, 24–25, 48

Iceland Basin *sea feature* N. Atlantic Ocean **160** M2
Icelandic Plateau *sea feature* N. Atlantic Ocean **160** N1
Ichakaranji India **72** B2
Ichchapuram India **73** E2
Ichifusa-yama *mt.* Japan **65** B6
Ichilo *r.* Bol. **149** E4
Ichinoseki Japan **65** F5
Ichinskiy, Vulkan *vol.* Rus. Fed. **54** H1
Ichkeria *aut. rep.* Rus. Fed. *see* Chechenskaya Respublika
Ichkeul National Park Tunisia **45** B6
Ich'ŏn S. Korea **65** A5
Ichuña Peru **148** B4
Içikler Turkey **47** F5
Icó Brazil **150** E3
Icosium Alg. *see* Algiers
Iconium Turkey *see* Konya
Iculisma France *see* Angoulême
Icy Strait U.S.A. **122** C3
Idabel U.S.A. **133** C5
Idah Nigeria **93** G4
Idaho *state* U.S.A. **134** D3
Idaho City U.S.A. **134** D3
Idaho Falls U.S.A. **134** E3
Idalia National Park Australia **111** F5
Idar India **74** B5
Idar-Oberstein Germany **36** C4
Iday *well* Niger **93** H2
Iddan Somalia **96** F3
Idd el Asoda *well* Sudan **89** F6
Idd el Chanam Sudan **94** E2
Idd esh Shurak *well* Sudan **89** F5
Idefjorden *inlet* Norway/Sweden **33** C4
Ideriyn Gol *r.* Mongolia **70** J2
Idfū Egypt **89** G3
Idhān Awbārī *des.* Libya **88** A3
Idhān Murzūq *des.* Libya **88** B3
Idhra *i.* Greece *see* Ydra
Ídhras, Kólpos *sea chan.* Greece *see* Ydras, Kolpos
Idi Amin Dada, Lake Dem. Rep. Congo/Uganda *see* Edward, Lake
Idice *r.* Italy **44** C1
Idini Mauritania **92** B3
Idkū Egypt **78** B5
Idlib *governorate* Syria **77** C2
Idlib Syria **77** C2
Idra *i.* Greece *see* Ydra
Idracowra Australia **110** C5
Idre Sweden **33** D3
Idrija Slovenia **44** E1
Idrijca *r.* Slovenia **44** D1
Idstein Germany **36** D3
Idugala Tanz. **97** B6
Idukki India **72** C4
Idutywa S. Africa **99** F7
Idzhevan Armenia *see* Ijevan
Iecava Latvia **33** G4
Iecava *r.* Latvia **33** F4

Ieper Belgium **39** E1
Ierapetra Greece **47** D7
Ierissou, Kolpos *b.* Greece **47** C4
Iesi Tanz. **97** C7
'Ifal, Wādī *watercourse* Saudi Arabia **89** G2
Ifalik *atoll* Micronesia **57** J4
Ifanadiana Madag. **99** [inset] J4
Ifanirea Madag. **99** [inset] J4
Ife Nigeria **93** G4
Ifenat Chad **88** C6
Iferouâne Niger **93** H1
Ifetesene *mt.* Alg. **91** G4
Iffley Australia **111** E3
Ifjord Norway **32** G1
Ifôghas, Adrar des *hills* Mali **93** F1
Iforas, Adrar des *hills* Mali *see* Ifôghas, Adrar des
Ifrane Morocco **90** D2
Ifume Dem. Rep. Congo **94** D5
Ifunda Tanz. **97** B7
Igan *r.* Sarawak Malaysia **59** E2
Igan *r.* Sarawak Malaysia **59** E2
Igarapé Miri Brazil **150** B2
Igarka Rus. Fed. **27** I3
Igatpuri India **72** B2
Igbetti Nigeria **93** F3
Igboho Nigeria **93** F3
Iğdır Turkey **79** G3
Iggesund Sweden **33** E3
Iglesia Arg. **152** C2
Iglesias *Sardinia* Italy **45** B5
Igli Alg. **90** E3
Iglino Rus. Fed. **28** K5
Igloolik Canada **121** K3
Iglulgaarjuk Canada *see* Chesterfield Inlet
Ignace Canada **123** B4
Ignacio Zaragoza Mex. **135** F7
Ignalina Lith. **33** G5
Iğneada Turkey **78** A2
Iğneada Burnu *pt* Turkey **78** A2
Igoma Tanz. **97** B6
Igombe *r.* Tanz. **97** A6
Igorevskaya Rus. Fed. **31** M2
Igoumenitsa Greece **47** B5
Igra Rus. Fed. **28** J4
Igrim Rus. Fed. **26** J3
Iguaçu *r.* Brazil **148** C5
Iguaçu, Parque Nacional do *nat. park* Brazil **151** A8
Iguaçu Falls Arg./Brazil *see* Iguaçu Falls
Iguaje, Mesa de *hills* Col. **146** C4
Iguala Mex. **138** D5
Igualada Spain **43** G2
Iguape Brazil **151** C8
Iguatemi Brazil **151** A7
Iguatemi *r.* Brazil **151** A7
Iguatu Brazil **150** E3
Iguazú, Cataratas do *waterfall* Arg./Brazil *see* Iguaçu Falls
Iguazú, Parque Nacional del *nat. park* Arg. **152** G1
Iguéla Gabon **94** A5
Iguetti, Sebkhet *salt flat* Mauritania **90** C4
Igunga Tanz. **97** B6
Iguobazuwa Nigeria **93** G4
Igusule Tanz. **97** B5
Iguvium Italy *see* Gubbio
Iharaña Madag. **99** [inset] K2
Ihavandhippolhu Atoll Maldives **72** B5
Ihirène, Oued *watercourse* Alg. **91** G5
Ihosy Madag. **99** [inset] J4
Iide-san *mt.* Japan **65** D5
Iijoki *r.* Fin. **32** G2
Iisalmi Fin. **32** G3
Iijäfene *des.* Mauritania **90** C5
Iijara Kenya **96** D5
Iijebu-Ode Nigeria **93** F4
Iijevan Armenia **79** F2
IJmuiden Neth. **36** B2
IJnâouene *well* Mauritania **92** D3
Iijoubbâne *des.* Mali **90** D5
IJssel *r.* Neth. **36** F2
IJsselmeer *l.* Neth. **36** B2
Iijuí Brazil **151** A9
Iijuí *r.* Brazil **151** A8
Ikaahuk Canada *see* Sachs Harbour
Ikaalinen Fin. **33** F3
Ikageleng S. Africa **99** E5
Ikageng S. Africa **99** H4
Ikahavo *hill* Madag. **99** [inset] J3
Ikare Nigeria **93** G4
Ikaria *i.* Greece **47** E6
Ikast Denmark **33** C4
Ikeja Nigeria **93** F4
Ikela Dem. Rep. Congo **94** C5
Ikelemba *r.* Dem. Rep. Congo **94** C4
Ikelenge Zambia **95** E7
Ikengo Dem. Rep. Congo **94** C4
Ikéngue Gabon **94** A5
Ikere Nigeria **93** G4
Ikerre Nigeria *see* Ikere
Ikhtiman Bulg. **46** C3
Iki *i.* Japan **65** B6
Iki-Burul Rus. Fed. **29** H7
Ikimba, Lake Tanz. **96** A5
Ikire Nigeria **93** G4
Ikla Estonia **33** G4
Ikom Nigeria **93** H4
Ikoma Tanz. **96** B5
Ikongo Madag. **99** [inset] J4
Ikopa *r.* Madag. **99** [inset] J3
Ikot Ekpene Nigeria **93** G4
Ikouhaouene, Adrar *mt.* Alg. **91** H4
Iksan S. Korea **65** H4
Ikungu Tanz. **97** B6
Ila Nigeria **93** G3
Ilaferh, Oued *watercourse* Alg. **91** G4
Ilagala Tanz. **97** A6
Ilagan Phil. **57** F2
Ilaisamis Kenya **96** B5
Ilaka Atsinanana Madag. **99** [inset] J4
Ilām Iran **80** A3
Ilam Nepal **75** F4
Ilan Taiwan **67** F3
Ilanz Switz. **39** H3
Ilave Peru **148** C4
Iława Poland **37** I2
Ilazärän, Küh-e *mt.* Iran **80** D4
Ile *r.* China/Kazakh. **70** E3
Île-à-la-Crosse, Lac *l.* Canada **123** J4
Île-de-France *admin. reg.* France **39** E2
Ileje Tanz. **97** B7
Ilek Kazakh. **28** J6
Ilek *r.* Rus. Fed. **29** J6
Ilen *r.* Rep. of Ireland **35** B6
Ileret Kenya **96** C4
Ilesa Nigeria *see* Ilesha
Ileťa *r.* Rus. Fed. **28** I5
Ileza Rus. Fed. **28** J3
Ilford Canada **123** M3
Ilfracombe Australia **111** F4
Ilfracombe U.K. **35** D6
Ilgaz Turkey **78** C2

Ilgaz Dağları mts Turkey 78 C2
Ilgın Turkey 78 B3
Ilhabela Brazil 151 C7
Ilha Grande Brazil 147 E5
Ilha Grande, Represa resr Brazil 151 A7
Ilha Solteíra, Represa resr Brazil 149 H5
Ílhavo Port. 42 B2
Ilhéus Brazil 150 E5
Ili Kazakh. see Kapchagay
Ilia Romania 46 C2
Iliamna Lake U.S.A. 120 D4
İliç Turkey 79 D3
Il'ich Kazakh. 81 G1
Il'ichevsk Azer. see Şärur
Ilici Spain see Elche-Elx
Iligan Phil. 57 F4
Ilimananngip Nunaa i. Greenland 121 Q2
Ilimpeya r. Rus. Fed. 27 K3
Il'inskiy Permskaya Oblast' Rus. Fed. 28 J4
Il'inskiy Sakhalinskaya Oblast' Rus. Fed. 64 E3
Il'insko-Podomskoye Rus. Fed. 28 H3
Iliomar East Timor 108 D2
Ilion U.S.A. 131 F2
Ilirska Bistrica Slovenia 44 E2
Ilium tourist site Turkey see Troy
Iliysk Kazakh. see Kapchagay
Ilkal India 72 C3
Ill r. France 39 G2
Illapel Chile 152 C2
Illapel r. Chile 152 C2
Ille r. France 38 C2
Illela Nigeria 93 G2
Iller r. Germany 36 D4
Illertissen Germany 36 E4
Illescas Spain 42 E2
Illimani, Nevado de mt. Bol. 148 D4
Illinois r. U.S.A. 132 D4
Illinois state U.S.A. 132 D4
Illizi Alg. 91 H4
Illueca Spain 43 F2
Ilm r. Germany 36 E3
Il'men', Ozero l. Rus. Fed. 28 D4
Ilmenau Germany 36 E3
Ilo Peru 148 C4
Ilobu Nigeria 93 G4
Iloilo Phil. 57 F3
Ilomantsi Fin. 28 D3
Ilorin Nigeria 93 G3
Ilova r. Croatia 44 F2
Ilovatka Rus. Fed. 29 H6
Ilovik i. Croatia 44 E2
Ilovlya Rus. Fed. 29 G6
Ilovlya r. Rus. Fed. 29 G6
Iłowa Poland 37 G3
Il'pyrskiy Rus. Fed. 27 Q3
Il'pyrskoye Rus. Fed. see Il'pyrskiy
Ilūkste Latvia 33 G5
Ilulissat Greenland 121 N3
Ilunde Tanz. 97 B6
Ilva i. Italy see Elba, Isola d'
Ilych r. Rus. Fed. 28 K3
Iłżanka r. Poland 37 J3
Imabari Japan 65 C6
Imaichi Japan 65 D5
Imala Moz. 97 C8
Imām al Ḩamzah Iraq 79 F5
Imam-baba Turkm. 81 E2
İmamoğlu Turkey 78 C3
Iman Rus. Fed. see Dal'nerechensk
Iman r. Rus. Fed. 64 C3
Imari Japan 65 B6
Imata Peru 148 C3
Imataca, Serranía de mts Venez. 147 F3
Imatra Fin. 33 H3
Imbabura prov. Ecuador 146 B4
Imbaimadai Guyana 147 F3
Imbituba Brazil 151 B9
imeni 26 Bakinskikh Komissarov Azer. see 26 Bakı Komissarı
imeni 26 Bakinskikh Komissarov Turkm. 80 C2
imeni C. A. Niyazova Turkm. 81 E2
imeni Chapayevka Turkm. see imeni C. A. Niyazova
imeni Gastello Rus. Fed. 27 O3
imeni Kalinina Tajik. 81 H2
imeni Kerbabayeva Turkm. 81 E2
imeni Petra Stuchki Latvia see Aizkraukle
imeni Poliny Osipenko Rus. Fed. 64 D1
Imeri, Serra mts Brazil 147 E4
Imese Dem. Rep. Congo 94 C4
Īmī Eth. 96 D3
Imishli Azer. see İmişli
İmişli Azer. 79 G3
Imit Jammu and Kashmir 74 B1
Imja-do i. S. Korea 65 A6
Imjin-gang r. N. Korea/S. Korea 65 A5
Imlay City U.S.A. 130 B2
Imlili W. Sahara 90 B5
Immokalee U.S.A. 129 C7
Imo state Nigeria 93 G4
Imola Italy 44 C2
Imotski Croatia 44 F3
Imperatriz Brazil 150 C3
Imperia Italy 44 B3
Imperial U.S.A. 132 A3
Imperial Dam U.S.A. 137 E5
Imperial Valley plain U.S.A. 137 E5
Imperieuse Reef Australia 108 B4
Impfondo Congo 94 C4
Imphal India 75 G4
İmralı Adası i. Turkey 46 F4
İmroz Turkey 78 A2
İmroz i. Turkey see Gökçeada
ımrun Turkey see Pütürge
Imst Austria 36 E5
Imtān Syria 77 C3
Imuris Mex. 135 E7
In r. Rus. Fed. 64 C2
I-n-Abangharit well Niger 93 G1
In Afaleleh well Alg. 91 H5
Inago Moz. 99 H2
Inahuaya Peru 148 B1
Inajá Brazil 150 E4
Inaja, Serra do hills Brazil 149 H2
I-n-Akhmed well Mali 93 E1
I-n-Alchi well Mali 93 E1
I-n-Aleï well Mali 93 E1
Inambari Peru 148 C3
Inambari r. Peru 148 C3
I-n-Ameddé well Mali 92 D1
In Aménas Alg. 91 H3
In Amguel Alg. 91 G5
Inangahua Junction N.Z. 113 B3
Inanwatan Indon. 57 H6
Iñapari Peru 148 C2
Inari Fin. 32 G1
Inarijärvi l. Fin. 32 G1
Inarijoki r. Fin./Norway 32 G1
I-n-Arouinat well Niger 93 G1
I-n-Atankarer well Mali 93 F1
Inauini r. Brazil 148 D2
I-n Azaoua well Alg. 91 G4
In-Azaoua well Alg. 91 G5
I-n-Azaoua watercourse Niger 91 G5
In Azar well Libya 88 C3
In Azâwah well Libya 88 A3
I-n-Azerraf well Mali 93 F1
In Belbel Alg. 91 F4
Inca Spain 43 H3
Inca de Oro Chile 152 C1
Ince Burun pt Turkey 78 C2
İncheh Iran 80 D2
Inchiri admin. reg. Mauritania 90 B5
Inch'ŏn S. Korea 65 A5
Inchope Moz. 99 G3
I-n-Choumaguene well Mali 93 F1
Incirli Turkey see Karasu
Incomati r. Moz. 99 G5
Incudine, Monte mt. Corsica France 44 B4
Indalsälven r. Sweden 32 E3
Indalstø Norway 33 B3
Indargarh Madhya Pradesh India 74 C4
Indargarh Rajasthan India 74 C4
Inda Silasē Eth. 89 H6
Indawgyi, Lake Myanmar 60 B2
Indé Mex. 126 E6
I-n-Délimane well Mali 93 F2
Independence CA U.S.A. 136 C3
Independence IA U.S.A. 132 D3
Independence KS U.S.A. 132 C4
Independence KY U.S.A. 130 A4
Independence MO U.S.A. 132 C4
Independence VA U.S.A. 130 C5
Independence Fjord inlet Greenland 121 Q1
Independence Mountains U.S.A. 134 C4
Independencia Bol. 148 D4
Independenta Romania 46 E2
Independenta Romania 46 E2
Independenta Romania 46 F3
Inder, Ozero salt l. Kazakh. 29 I6
Inderborskiy Kazakh. 26 F5
Indi India 72 C2

▶India country Asia 71 E7
2nd most populous country in the world and in Asia. 3rd largest country in Asia and 7th in the world.
asia 52–53, 82
world 8–9, 16–17

Indiana U.S.A. 130 D3
Indiana state U.S.A. 132 E3
Indian-Antarctic Ridge sea feature Indian Ocean 163 O9

▶Indianapolis U.S.A. 128 B4
State capital of Indiana.

Indian Cabins Canada 123 G3
Indian Desert India/Pak. see Thar Desert
Indian Fields U.S.A. 130 B5
Indian Harbour Canada 125 J2
Indian Lake U.S.A. 131 F2
Indian Lake l. NY U.S.A. 131 F2
Indian Lake l. OH U.S.A. 130 B3
Indian Lake l. PA U.S.A. 130 D3

▶Indian Ocean 162 L7
3rd largest ocean in the world.
oceans 156–157, 168

Indianola IA U.S.A. 132 C3
Indianola MS U.S.A. 127 H5
Indian Peak U.S.A. 137 F2
Indian Springs U.S.A. 137 E3
Indian Wells U.S.A. 137 G4
Indiaroba Brazil 150 E4
Indibir Eth. 96 C2
Indiga Rus. Fed. 28 I2
Indigirka r. Rus. Fed. 27 O2
Indigskaya Guba b. Rus. Fed. 28 I2
Inđija Yugo. 46 B2
Indin Lake Canada 123 H1
Indio U.S.A. 137 D5
Indispensable Reefs Solomon Is 107 F3
Indo-China reg. Asia 56 C2

▶Indonesia country Asia 56 D7
4th most populous country in the world and 3rd in Asia.
asia 52–53, 82
world 16–17

Indore India 74 B5
Indragiri r. Indon. 58 C3
Indramayu Indon. 59 E4
Indramayu, Tanjung pt Indon. 56 C7
Indrapura, Gunung vol. Indon. see Kerinci, Gunung
Indrapura, Tanjung pt Indon. 58 C3
Indravati r. India 72 D2
Indre r. France 38 D3
Indulkana Australia 110 C5
Indur India see Nizamabad
Indurti India 72 C2
Indus r. China/Pakistan 70 C7
Indus, Mouths of the Pak. 81 F5
Indus Cone sea feature Indian Ocean 162 L4
Indzhe Voyvoda Bulg. 46 E3
In Ebeggi well Alg. 91 G5
İnebolu Turkey 78 C2
I-n-Échaï well Mali 90 E5
İnegöl Turkey 78 B2
In Ekker Alg. 91 G4
Ineu Romania 46 B1
Inevi Turkey see Cihanbeyli
Inez U.S.A. 130 B5
In Ezzane well Alg. 91 H5
Infantes Spain see Villanueva de los Infantes
Infernao, Cachoeira waterfall Brazil 149 E2
Infiernillo, Presa resr Mex. 126 F8
Ing, Mae Nam r. Thai. 60 C3
Inga Dem. Rep. Congo 95 B6
Ingå Fin. 33 G3
Ingabu Myanmar 60 A4
Ingal Niger 93 G1
Ingallanna watercourse Australia 110 C4
Ingalls, Mount U.S.A. 136 B2
Inganda Dem. Rep. Congo 94 D5
Ingelstad Sweden 33 D4
Ingende Dem. Rep. Congo 94 C5
Ingeniero Guillermo Nueva Juárez Arg. 149 E5
Ingeniero Jacobacci Arg. 152 C5
Ingenika r. Canada 122 E3
Ingenio r. Peru 148 B3
Ingersoll Canada 130 C2
Ingessana Hills Sudan 96 B2
Ingezi Zimbabwe see Ngezi
Ingham Australia 111 F3
Ingichka Uzbek. 81 F2
Inglefield Land reg. Greenland 121 L2
Inglewood Qld Australia 111 G6
Inglewood Vic. Australia 112 B5
Inglewood U.S.A. 136 C5
Ingoka Pum mt. Myanmar 60 B2
Ingolstadt Germany 36 E4
Ingomar Australia 110 C6
Ingraj Bazar India 75 F4
Ingray Lake Canada 123 G1
Ingrid Christensen Coast Antarctica 167 E2
I-n-Guezzam Alg. 91 G6
I-n-Guita well Mali 93 F2
Ingulets Ukr. see Inhulets'
Ingulsvatn Norway 32 D2
Ingushetia aut. rep. Rus. Fed. see Ingushetiya, Respublika
Ingushetiya, Respublika aut. rep. Rus. Fed. 29 H8
Ingush Republic aut. rep. Rus. Fed. see Ingushetiya, Respublika
Ingwe Zambia 95 E8
Inhaca, Peninsula pen. Moz. 99 G5
Inhafenga Moz. 99 G4
Inhambane Moz. 99 G4
Inhambane prov. Moz. 99 G4
Inhambupe Brazil 150 E4
Inhamitanga Moz. 99 G3
Inhapim Brazil 151 D6
Inharrime Moz. 99 G5
Inhassoro Moz. 99 G4
Inhaúmas Brazil 150 C5
I-n-Hihaou, Adrar hills Alg. 91 F5
Inhulets' Ukr. 29 E7
Iniesta Spain 43 F3
Inírida r. Col. 146 E4
Inis Rep. of Ireland see Ennis
Inis Córthaidh Rep. of Ireland see Enniscorthy
Inishbofin i. Rep. of Ireland 35 A5
Inishmore i. Rep. of Ireland 35 B5
Inishmurray i. Rep. of Ireland 35 B4
Inishowen pen. Rep. of Ireland 34 C4
Injibara Eth. 96 C2
Injune Australia 111 G5
I-n-Kerchef well Mali 92 D1
Inkerman Australia 111 E3
Inklin Canada 122 C3
Inklin r. Canada 122 C3
Inland Kaikoura Range mts N.Z. 113 C3
Inland Sea Japan see Seto-naikai
Inlet U.S.A. 131 F2
I-n-Milach well Mali 93 E1
Inn r. Europe 36 E5
Innaanganeq c. Greenland 121 M2
Innamincka Australia 111 E5
Innamincka Regional Reserve nature res. Australia 111 E5
Inner Mongolia aut. reg. China see Nei Mongol Zizhiqu
Inner Sound sea chan. U.K. 34 D3
Innes National Park Australia 112 A4
Innisfail Australia 111 F3
Innisfail Canada 123 H4
Innokent'yevka Rus. Fed. 64 B2
Innsbruck Austria 36 E5
Innuksuak r. Canada 124 E1
Inny r. Rep. of Ireland 35 C5
Inocência Brazil 149 H4
Inongo Dem. Rep. Congo 94 C5
Inoni Congo 94 B5
İnönü Turkey 78 B3
Inosu Col. 146 D1
Inoucdjouac Canada see Inukjuak
Inovec mt. Slovakia 37 I4
Inowrocław Poland 37 I2
Inquisivi Bol. 148 D4
In Salah Alg. 91 F4

▶Inscription, Cape Australia 109 A6
Most westerly point of Oceania.

Insein Myanmar 60 B4
Ińsko Poland 37 G2
In Sokki, Oued watercourse Alg. 91 F3
Insterburg Rus. Fed. see Chernyakhovsk
Însurăţei Romania 46 E2
Insiza r. Zimbabwe 99 E3
Inta Rus. Fed. 28 L2
I-n-Tadéra well Niger 91 H5
I-n-Tadrof well Niger 93 H1
In Takoufi, Oued watercourse Alg. 91 G4
I-n-Tassit well Mali 93 F1
I-n-Tebezas Mali 93 F1
I-n-Téguift well Mali 93 F1
I-n-Telli well Mali 93 F1
I-n-Témegui well Mali 93 F1
İntepe Turkey 47 E4
Interamna Italy see Teramo
Interlaken Switz. 39 G3
International Falls U.S.A. 132 C1
Interview Island India 73 G3
Întorsura Buzăului Romania 46 E2
I-n-Touft well Mali 93 F1
Intracoastal Waterway canal U.S.A. 133 C6
Inubō-zaki pt Japan 65 E6
Inukjuak Canada 124 E1
Inuvik Canada 120 F3
Inuya r. Peru 148 B2
In'va r. Rus. Fed. 28 K4
Inveraray U.K. 34 D3
Invercargill N.Z. 113 B4
Inverell Australia 112 D3
Inverleigh Australia 111 E3
Inverness Canada 125 I4
Inverness U.K. 34 D3
Inverness CA U.S.A. 136 A2
Inverness FL U.S.A. 129 C6
Inverurie U.K. 34 E3
Inverway Australia 110 B3
Investigator Channel Myanmar 61 B5
Investigator Group is Australia 109 F8
Investigator Ridge sea feature Indian Ocean 162 N6
Investigator Strait Australia 109 G8
Inwood U.S.A. 130 D4
Inya Rus. Fed. 27 I4
Inyanga Zimbabwe see Nyanga
Inyanga Mountains Zimbabwe 99 G3
Inyanga National Park Zimbabwe see Nyanga National Park
Inyangani mt. Zimbabwe 99 G3
Inyati Zimbabwe see Nyathi
Inyazura Zimbabwe see Nyazura
Inyokern U.S.A. 136 D4
Inyo Mountains U.S.A. 136 C3
Inyonga Tanz. 97 B6
Inza Rus. Fed. 29 H5
Inzhavino Rus. Fed. 29 G5
Ioannina Greece 47 B5
Ioanninon, Limni l. Greece 47 B5
Iōf di Montasio mt. Italy 44 D1
Iokanga r. Rus. Fed. 28 F2
Iola U.S.A. 132 C4
Iolotan' Turkm. see Yeloten
Iona Angola 95 B9
Iona i. U.K. 34 C3
Iona, Parque Nacional do nat. park Angola 95 B9
Iona Abbey tourist site U.K. 34 C3
Ione U.S.A. 136 D2
Ioneşti Romania 46 D2
Ionia U.S.A. 132 E3
Ionian Islands admin. reg. Greece see Ionioi Nisoi
Ionian Islands is Greece 47 B5
Ionian Sea Greece/Italy 47 A5
Ionioi Nisoi admin. reg. Greece 47 A5
Iony, Ostrov i. Rus. Fed. 27 O4
Iori r. Georgia 79 F2
Ios Greece 47 D6
Ios i. Greece 47 D6
Iouîk Mauritania 90 A6
Iowa r. U.S.A. 132 D3
Iowa state U.S.A. 132 C3
Iowa City U.S.A. 132 D3
Iowa Falls U.S.A. 132 C3
Ipanema Brazil 151 D6
Ipanema r. Brazil 150 E4
Iparía Peru 148 B2
Ipatinga Brazil 151 D6
Ipatovo Rus. Fed. 29 G7
Ipeiros admin. reg. Greece 47 B5
Ipel' r. Slovakia 37 I5
Ipelegeng S. Africa 98 E5
Ipiales Col. 146 B4
Ipiaú Brazil 150 E5
Ipirá Brazil 150 E5
Ipiranga Amazonas Brazil 146 D5
Ipiranga Amazonas Brazil 147 F6
Ipiros admin. reg. Greece see Ipeiros
Ipixuna Brazil 148 B1
Ipixuna r. Amazonas Brazil 147 F6
Ipixuna r. Amazonas Brazil 148 B1
Ipoh Malaysia 58 C1
Ipoly r. Hungary/Slovakia 37 I5
Iporá Brazil 149 H4
Ippy Cent. Afr. Rep. 94 D3
Ipsala Turkey 46 E4
Ipswich Australia 111 H5
Ipswich U.K. 35 G5
Ipswich U.S.A. 132 B2
Ipu Brazil 150 D3
Ipuh Indon. 58 C3
Ipupiara Brazil 150 D4

▶Iqaluit Canada 121 M3
Territorial capital of Nunavut.

Iquê r. Brazil 149 F3
Iquique Chile 148 C5
Iquiri r. Brazil see Ituxi
Iquitos Peru 146 C5
Ira Banda Cent. Afr. Rep. 94 D3
Iracoubo Fr. Guiana 147 H3
Irakleia Greece 46 C4
Irakleia i. Greece 47 D6
Irakleio Greece see Iraklion
Irakleiou, Kolpos b. Greece 47 D7
Iráklia i. Greece see Irakleia
Iraklion Greece 47 D7
Irala Para. 149 G6
Iramaia Brazil 150 D5
▶Iran country Asia 80 C4
asia 52–53, 82
Iran, Pegunungan mts Indon. 59 F2
Īrānshāh Iran 80 A2
Īrānshahr Iran 81 E5
Irapuato Mex. 126 F7
▶Iraq country Asia 79 E4
asia 52–53, 82
Irarrarene reg. Alg. 91 G4
Irataparu r. Brazil 147 H5
Irati Brazil 151 B8
Irati r. Spain 43 F1
Irayel' Rus. Fed. 28 J2
Irazu, Volcán vol. Costa Rica 139 H7
Irbes šaurums sea chan. Estonia/Latvia see Irbe Strait
Irbe Strait Estonia/Latvia 33 F4
Irbe väin sea chan. Estonia/Latvia see Irbe Strait
Irbid Jordan 78 C4
Irbil Iraq see Arbīl
Irbit Rus. Fed. 166 F3
Irebu Dem. Rep. Congo 94 C5
Irecê Brazil 150 D4
Iregua r. Spain 43 E1

▶Ireland i. Europe 35 B5
4th largest island in Europe.
europe 22–23

▶Ireland, Republic of country Europe 35 C5
europe 24–25, 48
Irene Arg. 152 E4
Ireng r. Guyana/Venez. 147 G4
Irgiz Kazakh. 70 B2
Irgiz r. Kazakh. 70 B2
Irharhar, Oued watercourse Alg. 91 G3
Irharhar, Oued watercourse Alg. 91 G5
Irherm Morocco 90 C3
Irhil M'Goun mt. Morocco 90 D3
Iri S. Korea see Iksan
Irian, Teluk b. Indon. see Cenderawasih, Teluk
Iriba Chad 88 D6
Iricoumé, Serra hills Brazil 147 G4
Īrī Dāgh mt. Iran 80 A2
Iringa Tanz. 97 B6
Iringa admin. reg. Tanz. 97 B7
Iriri r. Brazil 147 H5
Iriri Novo r. Brazil 150 A4
Irish Free State country Europe see Ireland, Republic of
Irish Sea Rep. of Ireland/U.K. 35 D5
Irituia Brazil 150 C2
'Irj well Saudi Arabia 80 B5
Irkeshtam Kyrg. see Erkech-Tam
Irkutsk Rus. Fed. 62 G1
Irkutskaya Oblast' admin. div. Rus. Fed. 62 G1
Irkutsk Oblast admin. div. Rus. Fed. see Irkutskaya Oblast'
Irmak Turkey 78 C3
Irminger Basin sea feature N. Atlantic Ocean 160 L2
Irminio r. Sicily Italy 45 E6
Irmo U.S.A. 129 C5
Irnijärvi l. Fin. 32 H2
Iro, Lac l. Chad 94 C2
Iroise, Mer d' g. France 38 A2
Iron Baron Australia 112 A4
Irondequoit U.S.A. 130 E2
Iron Knob Australia 112 A4
Iron Mountain U.S.A. 132 D2
Iron Mountain mt. U.S.A. 137 F3
Iron Range National Park Australia 111 E2
Iron River U.S.A. 132 D2
Ironton MO U.S.A. 132 D4
Ironton OH U.S.A. 130 B4
Ironwood U.S.A. 132 D2
Iroquois Canada 131 F1
Iroquois Falls Canada 124 D3
Irosin Phil. 57 F3
Irpen' Ukr. see Irpin'
Irpin' Ukr. 29 D6
'Irq al Ḩarūrī des. Saudi Arabia 80 A5
'Irq al Mazhūr des. Saudi Arabia 89 I3
'Irq Banbān des. Saudi Arabia 80 A5
'Irq Jahām des. Saudi Arabia 80 A5
Irrawaddy admin. div. Myanmar 60 A4
Irrawaddy r. Myanmar 60 A5
Irrawaddy, Mouths of the Myanmar 61 A5
Irsarybaba, Gory hills Turkm. 80 C1
Irshad Pass Afgh./Pak. 81 H2
Irta Rus. Fed. 28 I3

▶Irtysh r. Kazakh./Rus. Fed. 26 G3
5th longest river in Asia and 10th in the world. Part of the 2nd longest river in Asia (Ob'-Irtysh).
asia 50–51
world 6–7

Irumu Dem. Rep. Congo 94 F4
Irún Spain 43 F1
Iruña Spain see Pamplona
Irvine U.K. 34 D4
Irvine U.S.A. 130 B5
Irvine Glacier Antarctica 167 L2
Irving U.S.A. 133 B5
Irwin r. Australia 109 A7
Isa Nigeria 93 G2
'Īsá, Ra's pt Yemen 89 I6
Isaac r. Australia 111 G4
Isaac Lake Canada 122 F4
Isabela Phil. 57 F4
Isabelia, Cordillera mts Nicaragua 139 G6
Isabella Lake U.S.A. 136 C4
Isaccea Romania 46 F2
Isachenko, Ostrov i. Rus. Fed. 27 I2
Isachsen, Cape Canada 121 I2
Ísafjarðardjúp est. Iceland 32 [inset]
Ísafjörður Iceland 32 [inset]
Isagarh India 74 C4
Isai Kalat Pak. 81 F5
Isà Khel Pak. 81 G3
Isakogorka Rus. Fed. 28 G2
Işalniţa Romania 46 C2
Isana r. Col. 146 D4
Isanga Dem. Rep. Congo 94 D5
Isangano National Park Zambia 97 A7
Isaouane-n-Tifernine des. Alg. 91 G4
Isar r. Germany 37 F4
Isbister U.K. 34 F1
Iscayachi Bol. 148 D5
Ischia, Isola d' i. Italy 45 D4
Ise Japan 65 D6
Isefjord b. Denmark 33 C5
Iseke Tanz. 97 B6
Isel r. Austria 37 F5
Isengi Dem. Rep. Congo 94 E4
Iseo, Lago d' l. Italy 44 C2
Isère r. France 39 F4
Isère, Pointe pt Fr. Guiana 147 H3
Iserlohn Germany 36 C3
Isernia Italy 44 E4
Ise-shima National Park Japan 65 D6
Ise-wan b. Japan 65 D6
Iseyin Nigeria 93 F4
Isfahan Iran see Eşfahān
Isfana Kyrg. 81 G2
Isfandaqeh Iran see Sangū'īyeh
Isfara Tajik. 81 G1
Isherton Guyana 147 G4
Ishikari-wan b. Japan 64 E4
Ishim r. Kazakh./Rus. Fed. 26 H4
Ishim Rus. Fed. 26 G4
Ishinomaki Japan 65 E5
Ishkoshim Tajik. 81 G2
Ishkuman Jammu and Kashmir 74 B1
Ishurdi Bangl. 75 F4
Isiboro r. Bol. 148 D3
Isiboro Sécure, Parque Nacional nat. park Bol. 148 D4
Isigny-sur-Mer France 38 C2
Isil'kul' Rus. Fed. 26 H4
Isimbira Tanz. 97 B6
Isinliví Ecuador 146 B5
Isiolo Kenya 96 C4
Isiro Dem. Rep. Congo 94 E4
Isisford Australia 111 F5
Iskabad Canal Afgh. 81 F2
İskele Cyprus see Trikomon
İskenderun Turkey 78 D3
İskenderun Körfezi b. Turkey 78 C3
İskilip Turkey 78 C2
Iskine Kazakh. 29 J7
Iskitim Rus. Fed. 26 I4
Iskŭr r. Bulg. 46 D3
Iskŭr, Yazovir resr Bulg. 46 C3
Iskushuban Somalia 96 F2
Iskut r. Canada 122 D3
Isla de Salamanca, Parque Nacional nat. park Col. 146 C2
Isla Gorge National Park Australia 111 G5
İslahiye Turkey 78 D3
Islamabad Jammu and Kashmir see Anantnag

▶Islamabad Pak. 81 H3
Capital of Pakistan.

Isla Magdalena, Parque Nacional nat. park Chile 153 B6
Islamkot Pak. 81 G5
Islampur India 75 E4
Island country Europe see Iceland
Island Lagoon salt flat Australia 109 G7
Island Lake Canada 123 M4
Island Magee pen. U.K. 34 D4
Island Pond U.S.A. 131 H1
Islas Baleares aut. comm. Spain 43 H3
Islay i. U.K. 34 C4
Islaz Romania 46 D3
Isle r. France 38 C4

▶Isle of Man i. Irish Sea 35 D4
United Kingdom Crown Dependency.
europe 48

Isle Royale National Park U.S.A. 132 D2
Isluga, Parque Nacional nat. park Chile 148 C4
Ismail Ukr. see Izmayil
Ismâ'ilîya Egypt see Al Ismā'īlīyah
Ismā'īlīyah governorate Egypt 77 A4
Ismailly Azer. see İsmayıllı
İsmayıllı Azer. 79 G2
Isnā Egypt 89 G3
Isoanala Madag. 99 [inset] J4
Isojoki Fin. 33 F3
Isoka Zambia 97 B7
Isokylä Fin. 32 G2
Isokyrö Fin. 32 F3
Isola del Liri Italy 44 D4
Isola di Capo Rizzuto Italy 45 F5
Isonzo r. Italy 44 D2
Isopa Tanz. 97 A7
Isorana Madag. 99 [inset] J4
Iso-Syöte hill Fin. 32 G2
Ispahan Iran see Eşfahān
Isparta Turkey 78 B3
Isperikh Bulg. 46 E3
Ispica Sicily Italy 45 E6
İspir Turkey 79 E2
Ispisar Tajik. see Khŭjand
▶Israel country Asia 77 B4
asia 52–53, 82
Israelite Bay Australia 109 C8
Isra'īl country Asia see Israel
Issa Croatia see Vis
Issa r. Rus. Fed. 33 H4
Issano Guyana 147 G3
Issia Côte d'Ivoire 92 D4
Issin tourist site Iraq 79 F5
Issoire France 39 E4
Issoudun France 38 D3
Issuna Tanz. 97 B6
Is-sur-Tille France 39 F3
Issyk-Kul' Kyrg. see Balykchy
Issyk-Kul', Ozero salt l. Kyrg. see Ysyk-Köl
Iştablāt tourist site Iraq 79 E4

▶İstanbul Turkey 78 B2
2nd most populous city in Europe.

İstanbul prov. Turkey 46 F4
İstanbul Boğazı strait Turkey see Bosporus
İsten dombja hill Hungary 37 H5
Istgāh-e Eznā Iran 80 B3
Isthilart Arg. 152 F2
Istiaia Greece 47 C5
Istik r. Tajik. 81 H2
Istmina Col. 146 B3
Istokpoga, Lake U.S.A. 129 C7
Istres France 39 F5
Istria pen. Croatia 44 D2
Istria Romania 46 F2
Istriţa, Dealul hill Romania 46 E2
Isuela r. Spain 43 F2
Iswaripur Bangl. 75 F5
Itabaianinha Brazil 150 E4
Itaberaba Brazil 150 D5
Itaberaí Brazil 149 H4
Itabira Brazil 151 D6
Itaboca Brazil 147 F6
Itabuna Brazil 150 E5
Itacaiuna r. Brazil 150 B3
Itacajá Brazil 150 C4
Itacarambi Brazil 150 C5
Itacaré Brazil 150 E5
Itacoatiara Brazil 147 G5
Itacuaí r. Brazil 146 D6
Itaetê Brazil 150 D5
Itagmatana Iran see Hamadān
Itaguaçu Brazil 151 D6
Itahuania Peru 148 C3
Itaí Brazil 149 H5
Itaim r. Brazil 150 D3
Itaiópolis Brazil 151 B8
Itaipu, Represa de resr Brazil 151 A8
Itäisen Suomenlahden kansallispuisto nat. park Fin. 33 G3
Itaituba Brazil 147 G6
Itajaí Brazil 151 B8
Itajubá Brazil 151 C7
Itaki India 75 E5
Italia country Europe see Italy

▶Italy country Europe 44 D3
5th most populous country in Europe.
europe 24–25, 48

Itamaracá, Ilha de i. Brazil 150 F3
Itamaraju Brazil 151 E6
Itamarandiba Brazil 151 D6
Itambé Brazil 150 D5
Itambé, Pico de mt. Brazil 151 D6
Itami airport Japan 65 D6
Itampolo Madag. 99 [inset] I5
Itanagar India 75 G4
Itanguari r. Brazil 150 C5
Itanhaém Brazil 149 I6
Itanhauã r. Brazil 147 F6
Itanhém r. Brazil 151 E6
Itany r. Fr. Guiana/Suriname 147 H4
Itaobím Brazil 151 D6
Itapaci Brazil 149 H3
Itapajipe Brazil 149 H4
Itaparaná r. Brazil 147 F6
Itaparica, Represa de resr Brazil 150 E4
Itapebi Brazil 151 E5
Itapebí Uruguay 152 F2
Itapemirim Brazil 151 D7
Itaperuna Brazil 151 D7
Itapetinga Brazil 150 D5
Itapetininga Brazil 149 H5
Itapeva Brazil 149 H5
Itapeva, Lago l. Brazil 151 B9
Itapi r. Brazil 147 G5
Itapicuru Brazil 150 D4
Itapicuru r. Brazil 150 C2
Itapicuru r. Brazil 150 E4
Itapicuru, Serra de hills Brazil 150 C3
Itapicuru Mirim Brazil 150 C2
Itapicuru Mirim r. Brazil 150 E4
Itapipoca Brazil 150 E2
Itapira Brazil 151 C7
Itapiranga Brazil 147 G5
Itaporanga Brazil 149 H5
Itapuranga Brazil 149 H3
Itaqui Brazil 152 F2
Itararé Brazil 149 H6
Itarsi India 74 C5
Itä-Suomi prov. Fin. 32 H3
Itatinga Brazil 149 H5
Itatuba Brazil 147 F6
Itatupã Brazil 147 I5
Itaueira r. Brazil 150 D3
Itaúna Amazonas Brazil 147 E5
Itaúna Minas Gerais Brazil 151 C7
Itbayat i. Phil. 57 F1
Itchen Lake Canada 123 H1
Ite Peru 148 C4
Itea Greece 47 C5
Itebero Dem. Rep. Congo 94 F5
Itende Tanz. 97 B6
Itezhi-Tezhi Dam Zambia 95 E8
Ithaca Greece see Ithaki
Ithaca i. Greece see Ithaki
Ithaca MI U.S.A. 130 A2
Ithaca NY U.S.A. 131 E2
Ithaki Greece 47 B5
Ithaki i. Greece 47 B5
Ithakis, Steno sea chan. Greece 47 B5
Ith Hils ridge Germany 36 D2
Itigi Tanz. 97 B6
Itilleq Greenland 121 N3
Itimbiri r. Dem. Rep. Congo 94 D4
Itinga Brazil 151 D6
Itiquira Brazil 151 A6
Itiquira r. Brazil 149 F4
Itiúba Brazil 150 E4
Itiúba, Serra de hills Brazil 150 E4
Itiyura r. Arg. 149 E5
Itkhari India 75 E4
Itō Japan 65 D6
Itoculo Moz. 99 I2
Itoigawa Japan 65 D5
Itoko Dem. Rep. Congo 94 D5
Iton r. France 38 D2
Itongafeno mt. Madag. 99 [inset] J4
Ittiri Sardinia Italy 45 B4
Ittoqqortoormiit Greenland 121 Q2
Itu Brazil 149 I5
Itu Nigeria 93 G4
Itu Abu Island S. China Sea 56 D3
Ituaçu Brazil 150 D5
Ituberá Brazil 150 E5
Ituí r. Brazil 146 D6
Ituiutaba Brazil 149 H4
Itula Dem. Rep. Congo 94 E5
Itumba Tanz. 97 B6
Itumbiara Brazil 149 H4
Itumbiara, Barragem resr Brazil 149 H4
Itungi Port Malawi 97 B7
Ituni Guyana 147 G3
Itupiranga Brazil 150 B3
Iturama Brazil 149 H4
Iturbe Para. 149 F6
Ituri r. Dem. Rep. Congo 94 E4
Iturup, Ostrov i. Rus. Fed. 54 G2
Ituverava Brazil 149 I5
Ituxi r. Brazil 148 D1
Ituzaingo Arg. 152 F1
Ityopia country Africa see Ethiopia
Itzehoe Germany 36 D2
Iuaretê Brazil 146 D4
Iuka U.S.A. 128 A5
Iul'tin Rus. Fed. 27 S3
Iuluti Moz. 99 H2
Iutica Brazil 146 D4
Ivaí r. Brazil 149 G5
Ivakoany mt. Madag. 99 [inset] J4
Ivalo Fin. 32 G1
Ivalojoki r. Fin. 32 G1
Ivanava Belarus 29 C5
Ivanec Croatia 44 F1
Ivangorod Rus. Fed. 33 H4
Ivangrad Yugo. see Berane
Ivanhoe N.S.W. Australia 112 C4
Ivanhoe W.A. Australia 108 E3
Ivanhoe U.S.A. 132 B2
Ivanhoe Lake Canada 123 J2

Ivanić-Grad Croatia **44** F2
Ivanjica Yugo. **46** B3
Ivankiv Ukr. **29** D6
Ivankovtsy Rus. Fed. **64** C2
Ivano-Frankivs'k Ukr. **29** C6
Ivano-Frankovsk Ukr. *see* Ivano-Frankivs'k
Ivanovka *Amurskaya Oblast* Rus. Fed. **64** A2
Ivanovka *Orenburgskaya Oblast'* Rus. Fed. **29** J5
Ivanovo Belarus *see* Ivanava
Ivanovo *tourist site* Bulg. **46** D3
Ivanovo Rus. Fed. **28** G4
Ivanovo Oblast *admin. div.* Rus. Fed. *see* Ivanovskaya Oblast'
Ivanovskaya Oblast' *admir. div.* Rus. Fed. **28** G4
Ivanpah Lake U.S.A. **137** E4
Ivanščica *mts* Croatia **44** E1
Ivanski Bulg. **46** E3
Ivantsevichi Belarus *see* Ivatsevichy
Ivato Madag. **99** [inset] J4
Ivatsevichy Belarus **29** C5
Ivaylovgrad Bulg. **46** E4
Ivaylovgrad, Yazovir *resr* Bulg. **46** D4
Ivdel' Rus. Fed. **26** G3
Iveşti Romania **46** E2
Iveşti Romania **46** E1
Ivi, Cap *c.* Alg. **43** G4
Ivindo *r.* Gabon **94** B5
Ivinheima Brazil **151** A7
Iviza *i.* Spain *see* Ibiza
Ivohibe Madag. **99** [inset] J4
Ivor U.S.A. **131** E5
Ivory Coast *country* Africa *see* Côte d'Ivoire
Ivösjön *l.* Sweden **33** D4
Ivrea Italy **39** G4
Ivrindi Turkey **47** E5
Ivris Ugheltekhili *pass* Georgia **79** F2
Ivugivik Canada *see* Ivujivik
Ivujivik Canada **120** F3
Ivuna Tanz. **97** B7
Ivvavik National Park Canada **120** F3
Ivydale U.S.A. **130** C4
Iwaizumi Japan **65** F4
Iwaki Japan **65** E5
Iwakuni Japan **65** C6
Iwamizawa Japan **64** E4
Iwan *r.* Indon. **59** G2
Iwanda Tanz. **97** B7
Iwate-san *vol.* Japan **65** E5
Iwo Nigeria **93** C4
Iwye Belarus **29** C5
Ixiamas Bol. **148** E1
Ixmiquilpán Mex. **126** G7
Ixopo S. Africa **99** H6
Ixtlán Mex. **126** F7
Iya *vol.* Indon. **108** C2
Iya *r.* Rus. Fed. **62** G1
Iyayi Tanz. **97** B7
Iyirmi Altı Bakı Komissarı Azer. *see* 26 Bakı Komissarı
Iyo Japan **65** C6
Iyo-nada *b.* Japan **65** C6
Izabal, Lago de *l.* Guat. **138** G5
Izari-dake *mt.* Japan **64** E4
Izazi Tanz. **97** B6
Izberbash Rus. Fed. **79** F2
Iˇzeh Iran **80** B4
Izgagane *well* Niger **93** H1
Izhevsk Rus. Fed. **28** J4
Izhma *Respublika Komi* Rus. Fed. **28** J2
Izhma *Respublika Komi* Rus. Fed. *see* Sosnogorsk
Izhma *r.* Rus. Fed. **28** J2
Izki Oman **76** F5
Izmail Ukr. *see* Izmayil
Izmayil Ukr. **29** D7
İzmir Turkey **78** A3
İzmir *prov.* Turkey **47** E5
İzmir Körfezi *g.* Turkey **78** A3
İzmit Turkey *see* Kocaeli
İzmit Körfezi *b.* Turkey **78** B2
İznik Gölü *l.* Turkey **78** B2
Iznajar, Embalse de *resr* Spain **42** D4
Iznalloz Spain **42** E4
İznik Gölü *l.* Turkey **78** B2
Izoard, Col d' *pass* France **39** G4
Izobil'noye Rus. Fed. *see* Izobil'nyy
Izobil'nyy Rus. Fed. **28** F6
Izola Slovenia **44** D2
Izozog Santa Cruz Bol. **149** E4
Izra' Syria **77** C3
Iztochni Rodopi *mts* Bulg. **46** D4
Izu-hantō *pen.* Japan **65** E6
Izumo Japan **65** C6

▶Izu-Ogasawara Trench *sea feature*
  N. Pacific Ocean **164** D3
  5th deepest trench in the world.

Izu-shotō *is* Japan **65** D6
Izvestiy Tsentral'nogo Ispolnitel'nogo Komiteta, Ostrova *is* Rus. Fed. **27** I2
Izvestkovyy Rus. Fed. **64** D2
Izvoarele Romania **46** E2
Izyaslav Ukr. **29** D6
Iz"yayu Rus. Fed. **28** K2
Izyum Ukr. **29** F6

 J

Jaama Estonia **33** G4
Jaba *watercourse* Iran **80** D3
Jabalón *r.* Spain **42** D3
Jabalpur India **74** C5
Jabbārah Fara Islands Saudi Arabia **89** I5
Jabbūl, Sabkhat al *salt flat* Syria **77** C2
Jabiru Australia **110** C2
Jablah Syria **77** B2
Jablanica Bos.-Herz. **44** F3
Jablanica *r.* Yugo. **46** B3
Jablonec nad Nisou Czech Rep. **37** O1
Jabłonowo Pomorskie Poland **37** I2
Jaboticabal Brazil **149** H5
Jabuka *i.* Croatia **44** E3
Jabung, Tanjung *pt* Indon. **58** D3
Jaburu Brazil **147** G4
Jabuti Brazil **147** F5
Jaca Spain **43** F1
Jacaré *Mato Grosso* Brazil **150** A5
Jacaré *Rondônia* Brazil **149** D2
Jacaré *r.* Brazil **149** E1
Jacaré *r.* Brazil **150** D4
Jacareacanga Brazil **147** 36
Jacareí Brazil **151** C7
Jacarézinho Brazil **149** H5
Jáchal *r.* Arg. **152** D2
Jaciara Brazil **150** A5
Jacinto Brazil **151** D1
Jaciparaná *r.* Brazil **149** D2
Jack Lee, Lake *resr* U.S.A. **133** C5
Jacksboro *TN* U.S.A. **128** B4
Jacksboro *TX* U.S.A. **133** 35
Jackson Australia **111** G5
Jackson *AL* U.S.A. **129** B6
Jackson *CA* U.S.A. **136** B2
Jackson *GA* U.S.A. **129** C5
Jackson *KY* U.S.A. **130** B5
Jackson *MI* U.S.A. **130** A2

Jackson *MN* U.S.A. **132** C3
Jackson *MO* U.S.A. **132** D4

▶Jackson *MS* U.S.A. **133** D5
  State capital of Mississippi.

Jackson *OH* U.S.A. **130** B4
Jackson *TN* U.S.A. **128** A5
Jackson *WY* U.S.A. **134** E4
Jackson Head N.Z. **113** B6
Jackson Lake U.S.A. **134** E4
Jackson's Arm Canada **125** J3
Jacksonville *AR* U.S.A. **133** C5
Jacksonville *FL* U.S.A. **129** C6
Jacksonville *IL* U.S.A. **127** H4
Jacksonville *NC* U.S.A. **129** D5
Jacksonville *OH* U.S.A. **130** B4
Jacksonville *TX* U.S.A. **131** E6
Jacksonville Beach U.S.A. **129** C6
Jack Wade U.S.A. **122** A1
Jacmel Haiti **139** J5
Jacobabad Pak. **81** G4
Jacobina Brazil **150** D4
Jacob Lake U.S.A. **137** F3
Jacques-Cartier, Détroit de *sea chan.* Canada **125** H3
Jacques Cartier, Mont *mt.* Canada **125** H3
Jacques Cartier Passage Canada *see* Jacques-Cartier, Détroit de
Jacuí *r.* Brazil **151** B9
Jacunda Brazil **150** B3
Jacundá *r.* Brazil **150** B2
Jacupiranga Brazil **151** C18
Jacura Venez. **146** E2
Jadar *r.* Bos.-Herz. **46** A2
Jadar *r.* Yugo. **46** A2
Jadcherla India **73** D2
Jaddangi India **73** D2
Jaddi, Ras *pt* Pak. **81** E5
Jadebusen *b.* Germany **36** D2
Jádova *r.* Croatia **44** E2
Jadovnik *mt.* Bos.-Herz. **44** F2
Jaén Peru **146** B6
Jaén *reg.* Norway **32** B4
Ja'farābad *Ardabil* Iran **80** B2
Ja'farābad *Khorāsan* Iran **80** D2
Jaffa Israel *see* Tel Aviv-Yafo
Jaffa, Cape Australia **112** A5
Jaffna Sri Lanka **72** C4
Jaffrey U.S.A. **131** G2
Jagadhri India **74** C3
Jagalur India **72** C3
Jagdalak Afgh. **81** G3
Jagdalpur India **73** D2
Jagdispur India **75** E4
Jaggang China **74** E2
Jaghin *r.* Iran **80** D5
Jagin *watercourse* Iran **80** D5
Jagodina Yugo. **46** B2
Jagok Tso *salt l.* China *see* Urru Co
Jagsamka China *see* Luding
Jagst *r.* Germany **36** D4
Jagtial India **72** C2
Jaguarão *r.* Brazil/Uruguay **152** G3
Jaguarão Uruguay **152** G3
Jaguarari Brazil **150** D4
Jaguaretama Brazil **150** E3
Jaguariaíva Brazil **149** H6
Jaguaribe Brazil **150** E3
Jaguaruana Brazil **150** E3
Jagüe Arg. **152** C2
Jahanabad India **75** E4
Jahān Dāgh *mt.* Iran **80** B2
Jahmah *well* Iraq **79** F5
Jahrom Iran **80** D4
Jāhyad Iran **81** D5
Jailolo Gilolo *i.* Indon. *see* Halmahera
Jaiña China **148** G4
Jaintiapur Bangl. **75** G4
Jaipur India **74** C4
Jaisalmer India **74** A4
Jaisinghnagar India **75** D5
Jaitaran India **74** C4
Jaitgarh *hill* India **72** C1
Jaitpur India **74** C4
Jajarkot Nepal **75** D3
Jajce Bos.-Herz. **44** F2
Jajnagar *state* India *see* Orissa
Jakar Bhutan **75** F4

▶Jakarta Indon. **59** D4
  Capital of Indonesia.
  world 16–17

Jakharrah Libya **88** D2
Jakin *mt.* Afgh. **81** F4
Jakkalsberg Namibia **98** C3
Jakki Kowr Iran **81** E5
Jakliat India **74** C3
Jakobshavn Greenland *see* Ilulissat
Jakobstad Fin. **32** F3
Jakupica *mts* Macedonia **46** B4
Jalājil Saudi Arabia **80** B5
Jalālābād Afgh. **81** G3
Jalalabad *Punjab* India **74** B3
Jalalabad *Uttar Pradesh* India **74** C3
Jalal-Abad Kyrg. **70** D3
Jalālah al Baḥrīyah, Jabal *plat.* Egypt **78** B5
Jalalpur India **72** B1
Jalandhar India **74** B3
Jalan Kayu Sing. **58** [inset]
Jalapa Mex. **74** B2
Jalapa Enríquez Mex. *see* Jalapa
Jalapur Pak. **74** B2
Jalapur Pirwala Pak. **81** G4
Jalasjärvi Fin. **33** F3
Jalaun India **74** C4
Jalawlā' Iraq **79** G4
Jalbar *r.* Australia **110** C2
Jaldak Afgh. **81** F4
Jaldhaka *r.* Bangl. **75** F4
Jales Brazil **149** H5
Jaleswar India **74** C4
Jaleswar India **75** E5
Jalgaon India **74** B5
Jalibah Iraq **79** F5
Jalingo Nigeria **93** H3
Jallābī Iran **80** B5
Jalna India **72** B2
Jālo Iran **81** F5
Jalón *r.* Spain **43** F2
Jalor India **74** B4
Jalpaiguri India **75** F4
Jalpan Mex. **126** G7
Jalrez Afgh. **81** G3
Jālū Libya **88** D2
Jalūlā Iraq *see* Jalawlā'
Jālū Oasis Libya **88** D2
Jām *r.* Iran **81** E2

▶Jamaica *country* West Indies **139** I5
  northamerica 118–119, 140

Jamaica Channel Haiti/Jamaica **139** I5
Jamalpur Bangl. **75** F4
Jamalpur India **75** F4
Jamanxim *r.* Brazil **147** G6
Jamari Brazil **149** D2
Jamba Angola **95** B5
Jambi Indon. **58** C3
Jamboaye *r.* Indon. **58** B1
Jambongan *i.* Sabah Malaysia **59** G1
Jambu Australia **111** G5
Jambusar India **74** B5
Jamekunte India **72** C3
James *watercourse* Australia **110** D4
James *r.* Canada **123** I1
James *r.* ND/SD U.S.A. **132** B3
James *r.* VA U.S.A. **131** E5
James, Isla *i.* Chile **153** B6
Jamesabad Pak. **81** G5
James Bay Canada **124** D2
James Cistern Bahamas **129** D7
Jameson Land Greenland **121** Q2
Jameson Range *hills* Australia **109** D6
James Peak N.Z. **113** B4
James Ranges *mts* Australia **110** C5
James Ross Island Antarctica **167** A2
James Ross Strait Canada **121** J3
Jamestown Australia **112** A4

▶Jamestown St Helena **160** N7
  Capital of St Helena and Dependencies.

Jamestown *KY* U.S.A. **128** B4
Jamestown *ND* U.S.A. **132** B2
Jamestown *NY* U.S.A. **130** D2
Jamestown *PA* U.S.A. **130** D1
Jamestown *TN* U.S.A. **130** A5
Jamkhandi India **72** B2
Jamkhed India **72** B2
Jammalamadugu India **72** C3
Jammerbugten *b.* Denmark **33** G4
Jammu Jammu and Kashmir **74** B2

▶Jammu and Kashmir *terr.* Asia **74** B2
  Disputed territory (India/Pakistan).
  asia 52–53, 82

Jamnagar India **74** A5
Jamner India **72** B1
Jamni *r.* India **74** C4
Jamno, Jezioro *lag.* Poland **37** H1
Jampang Kulon Indon. **59** D4
Jampur Pak. **81** G4
Jāmsā Fin. **33** G3
Jāmsänkoski Fin. **33** G3
Jamshedpur India **75** E5
Jamtara India **75** E5
Jämtland *county* Sweden **32** D3
Jamui India **75** E4
Jamu Mare Romania **46** B2
Jamuna *r.* Bangl. **75** F4
Jamuna *r.* India **75** E4
Janā *i.* Saudi Arabia **80** B5
Janāb, Wādī al *watercourse* Jordan **77** C4
Janakpur India **75** D5
Janakpur Nepal **75** E4
Janaúba Brazil **150** D5
Janaucú, Ilha *i.* Brazil **147** I4
Jandaq Iran **80** C3
Jandiala India **74** B3
Jandiatuba *r.* Brazil **146** D5
Jandongi Dem. Rep. Congo **94** D4
Jandowae Australia **111** I5
Jándula *r.* Spain **42** D3
Janeiro *r.* Brazil **150** C5
Janesville U.S.A. **132** D3
Jang, Tanjung *pt* Indon. **58** D3
Jangal Iran **81** D3
Jangamo Moz. **99** G5
Jangaon India **72** C2
Jangeldi Uzbek. *see* Dzhangel'dy
Jangipur India **75** F4
Jangngai Ri *mts* China **75** E3
Jangngai Zangbo *r.* China **75** E2
Jäni Beygü Iran **80** B2
Janja Bos.-Herz. **46** A2
Janja *r.* Bos.-Herz. **46** A2
Jankov Kamen *mt.* Yugo. **46** B3

▶Jan Mayen *i.* Arctic Ocean **121** S2
  Part of Norway.

Jan Mayen Fracture Zone *sea feature* Arctic Ocean **166** I2
Jannatābād Iran **81** D3
Jañona *mt.* Spain **42** C2
Janos Mex. **135** E7
Jánoshalma Hungary **46** A1
Jánossomorja Hungary **37** H5
Jansenville S. Africa **98** E7
Jãnua Coeli Brazil **150** B2
Januária Brazil **150** C5
Janūbī, Al Fulayj al *watercourse* Saudi Arabia **80** A4
Janūb Sīnā' *governorate* Egypt **77** A5
Janzar *mt.* Pak. **81** E5
Janzé France **38** C3
Jaora India **74** B5

Japan *country* Asia **65** D6
  9th most populous country in the world.
  asia 52–53, 82
  world 16–17

Japan, Sea of N. Pacific Ocean **65** C5
Japan Alps National Park Japan *see* Chibu-Sangaku National Park
Japan Trench *sea feature* N. Pacific Ocean **164** D3
Japurá *r.* Brazil **147** I5
Japvo Mount India **75** G4
Jaqué Panama **146** D3
Jarābulus Syria **79** D3
Jaraguá Brazil **150** C5
Jaraguá do Sul Brazil **151** B8
Jaraguari Brazil **150** A2
Jaraíz de la Vera Spain **42** D2
Jarama *r.* Spain **42** D2
Jarash Jordan **78** C4
Jaraucu *r.* Brazil **147** H5
Jarboesville U.S.A. *see* Lexington Park
Jardim *Ceará* Brazil **150** E3
Jardim *Mato Grosso do Sul* Brazil **149** F5
Jardín *r.* Spain **43** E3
Jardine River National Park Australia **111** F1
Jargalant Mongolia **63** J2
Jargalant Mongolia *see* Hovd
Jari *r.* Brazil **147** I5
Jaria Jhanjail Bangl. **75** F4
Jarmen Germany **37** F2
Jaro Phil. **57** G3
Jarocin Poland **37** H3
Jaroměř Czech Rep. **37** O3
Jarosław Poland **31** J3
Jarqŭrghon Uzbek. *see* Dzharkurgan
Jarrāḥī *watercourse* Iran **80** B4

Jamaica Channel Haiti/Jamaica **139** I5
Jarratt U.S.A. **130** E5
Jarrettsville U.S.A. **131** E4
Jartai China **62** H4
Jarú Brazil **149** E2
Jarud China *see* Lubei
Järvakandi Estonia **33** G4
Järvenpää Fin. **33** G3

▶Jarvis Island *terr.* N. Pacific Ocean **165** H6
  United States Unincorporated Territory.
  oceania 104–105, 114

Jarwa India **75** D4
Jasdan India **74** A5
Jashpurnagar India **75** E5
Jasień Poland **37** G3
Jāsk Iran **80** D5
Jāsk-e Kohneh Iran **80** D5
Jasliq Uzbek. **70** A3
Jasło Poland **37** J4
Jaśłūnai Lith. **33** G5
Jasmund, Nationalpark *nature res.* Germany **37** F1
Jason Peninsula Antarctica **167** L2
Jasper Canada **122** G4
Jasper *AL* U.S.A. **129** C5
Jasper *AR* U.S.A. **133** C4
Jasper *FL* U.S.A. **129** C6
Jasper *GA* U.S.A. **129** C5
Jasper *IN* U.S.A. **128** B4
Jasper *NY* U.S.A. **130** D2
Jasper *OH* U.S.A. **130** B4
Jasper *TN* U.S.A. **128** C5
Jasper *TX* U.S.A. **133** C6
Jasper National Park Canada **122** G4
Jaşşān Iraq **79** G4
Jassy Romania *see* Iași
Jastarnia Poland **37** I1
Jastrebarsko Croatia **44** E2
Jastrowie Poland **37** H2
Jastrzębie-Zdrój Poland **37** I4
Jászárokszállás Hungary **37** I5
Jászberény Hungary **37** I5
Jataí Brazil **149** H4
Jatapu *r.* Brazil **147** G5
Jatara India **74** C4
Jati Pak. **81** G5
Jatibarang Indon. **59** E4
Játiva Spain *see* Xàtiva
Jatiwangi Indon. **59** E4
Jatobá Brazil **150** A5
Jatoi Pak. **81** G4
Jättendal Sweden **33** E3
Jatuarana Brazil **150** E1
Jaú Brazil **149** H5
Jaú *r.* Brazil **147** F5
Jaú, Parque Nacional do *nat. park* Brazil **147** F5
Jauaperi *r.* Brazil **147** F5
Jaua Sarisariñama, Parque Nacional *nat. park* Venez. **147** E3
Jauja Peru **148** B2
Jaunay-Clan France **38** D3
Jaunpiebalga Latvia **33** G4
Jaunpur India **75** D4
Jauru Brazil **151** A6
Jauru *r.* Brazil **149** F4

▶Java *i.* Indon. **59** D5
  5th largest island in Asia.
  asia 50–51

Javaés *r.* Brazil *see* Formoso
Javaés, Serra dos *hills* Brazil **150** B4
Javalambre, Sierra de *mts* Spain **43** F2
Javand Afgh. **81** F3
Javari *r.* Brazil **146** D6
Java Ridge *sea feature* Indian Ocean **162** O6
Javarthushuu Mongolia **63** I2
Java Sea Indon. **59** E4

▶Java Trench *sea feature* Indian Ocean **162** N6
  Deepest point in the Indian Ocean.
  oceans 156–157, 168

Javier, Isla *i.* Chile **153** B6
Javor *mts* Yugo. **46** B3
Javořice *hill* Czech Rep. **37** G4
Javorie *mt.* Slovakia **37** I4
Javorniky *mts* Slovakia **37** I4
Jävre Sweden **32** F2
Jawa *i.* Indon. *see* Java
Jawa Barat *prov.* Indon. **59** D4
Jawad India **74** C4
Jawai *r.* India **74** B4
Jawa Tengah *prov.* Indon. **59** E4
Jawar India **74** C4
Jawhar India **72** B2
Jawhar Somalia **96** E4
Jawor Poland **37** H3
Jay U.S.A. **133** C4

▶Jaya, Puncak *mt.* Indon. **57** I6
  Highest mountain in Oceania.
  oceania 102–103

Jayakwadi Sagar *l.* India **72** B2
Jayanca Peru **146** B5
Jayanti India **75** F4
Jayapura Indon. **57** J6
Jayb, Wādī al *watercourse* Israel/Jordan **77** B4
Jayfi, Wādī al *watercourse* Egypt **77** B4
Jaynagar *Bihar* India **75** E4
Jaynagar *W. Bengal* India **75** F5
Jaypur India **73** D2
Jayrūd Syria **77** C3
Jayton U.S.A. **133** A5
Jazīrat al Hamrā U.A.E. **80** C5
Jazminal Mex. **133** A7
Jbail Lebanon **77** B2
Jean U.S.A. **137** E4
Jeanerette U.S.A. **133** D6
Jean Marie River Canada **122** F2
Jebäl Bārez, Küh-e *mts* Iran **80** D4
Jebel Libya **88** D1
Jebel Romania **46** B2
Jebel Turkm. *see* Dzhebel
Jebel, Bahr el *r.* Sudan/Uganda **96** A2 *see* White Nile
Jebel Abyad Plateau Sudan **89** F5
Jeberos Peru **146** B6
Jebus Indon. **58** D3
Jedburgh U.K. **34** G4
Jeddore Lake Canada **125** K3
Jedeida Tunisia **45** B6
Jędrzejów Poland **37** J3
Jedwabne Poland **37** K2
Jeetze *r.* Germany **36** E2
Jefferson *IA* U.S.A. **132** C3
Jefferson *OH* U.S.A. **130** E3
Jefferson *TX* U.S.A. **133** C5
Jefferson, Mount U.S.A. **136** D2
Jefferson, Mount *vol.* U.S.A. **134** B3

▶Jefferson City U.S.A. **132** C4
  State capital of Missouri.

Jeffersonton U.S.A. **130** E4
Jeffersonville *IN* U.S.A. **128** B4
Jeffersonville *OH* U.S.A. **130** B4
Jeffrey U.S.A. **130** C5
Jega Nigeria **93** G3
Jehanabad India *see* Jahanabad
Jēkabpils Latvia **33** G4
Jelbart Ice Shelf Antarctica **167** B2
Jelcz-Laskowice Poland **37** H3
Jeldēsa Eth. **96** E3
Jelenia Góra Poland **37** G3
Jelep La *pass* China/India **75** F4
Jelgava Latvia **33** F4
Jellico U.S.A. **130** A5
Jellicoe Canada **124** C3
Jelondī Tajik. *see* Dzhilandy
Jelow Gīr Iran **80** B3
Jemaja *i.* Indon. **58** D2
Jember Indon. **59** F5
Jemma Nigeria **93** H3
Jemmel Tunisia **45** C7
Jemnice Czech Rep. **37** G4
Jempang, Danau *l.* Indon. **59** G3
Jena Germany **36** E3
Jena U.S.A. **133** C6
Jenda Malawi **97** E5
Jendouba Tunisia **91** H1
Jengish Chokusu *mt.* China/Kyrg. *see* Pobeda Peak
Jenin West Bank **77** B3
Jenipapo Brazil **147** F6
Jenkinjones U.S.A. **130** C5
Jenkins U.S.A. **130** B5
Jenkintown U.S.A. **131** F3
Jenne Mali *see* Djenné
Jenner Canada **123** I1
Jennersdorf Austria **37** H5
Jennings *r.* Canada **122** C2
Jennings U.S.A. **133** C6
Jenpeg Canada **123** L4
Jepara Indon. **59** E4
Jeppo Fin. **32** F3
Jequié Brazil **150** D5
Jequitaí Brazil **151** C6
Jequitinhonha Brazil **151** D6
Jequitinhonha *r.* Brazil **151** D6
Jerba, Île de *i.* Tunisia **91** H2
Jerbar Sudan **96** A3
Jereh Iran **79** G5
Jérémie Haiti **139** J5
Jeremoabo Brazil **150** E4
Jerer Shet' *watercourse* Eth. **96** E3
Jerez Mex. **126** F7
Jerez de la Frontera Spain **42** C4
Jerez de los Caballeros Spain **42** C3
Jerfojaur Sweden **32** E2
Jergucat Albania **46** B5
Jericho Australia **111** D4
Jericho West Bank **77** B4
Jerid, Chott el *salt l.* Tunisia **91** H2
Jerijih, Tanjong *pt* Sarawak Malaysia **59** E2
Jerilderie Australia **112** C4
Jermyn U.S.A. **131** F3
Jerome Australia **108** C5
Jerramungup Australia **109** B8

▶Jersey *terr.* Channel Is **38** B2
  United Kingdom Crown Dependency.
  europe 24–25, 48

Jersey City U.S.A. **131** F3
Jerseyville U.S.A. **132** D4
Jerte *r.* Spain **42** D2
Jerumenha Brazil **150** D3

▶Jerusalem Israel/West Bank **77** B4
  Capital of Israel.

Jervis Bay Territory *admin. div.* Australia **107** C2
Jervis Range *hills* Australia **110** C4
Jesenice Slovenia **44** E1
Jesenik Czech Rep. **37** H3
Jesi Italy **44** D3
Jesmond Canada **122** F5
Jesolo Italy **44** D2
Jesselton *Sabah* Malaysia *see* Kota Kinabalu
Jessen Germany **37** F3
Jessheim Norway **33** G3
Jessore Bangl. **75** F5
Jesup U.S.A. **129** C6
Jesús María Arg. **152** D2
Jetalsar India **74** A5
Jethro *tourist site* Saudi Arabia **78** C5
Jetmore U.S.A. **132** B4
Jewett City U.S.A. **131** I3
Jewish Autonomous Oblast *admin. div.* Rus. Fed. *see* Yevreyskaya Avtonomnaya Oblast'
Jeziorak, Jezioro *l.* Poland **37** I2
Jeziorany Poland **37** J2
Jezioro Zegrzyńskie *l.* Poland **37** J2
Jeziorsko, Jezioro *l.* Poland **37** I3
Jezzine Lebanon **77** B3
Jhabua India **74** B5
Jha Jha India **75** E4
Jhajjar India **74** C3
Jhajju India **74** B4
Jhal Pak. **81** F4
Jhalakati Bangl. **75** F5
Jhalawar India **74** C4
Jhalida India **75** E5
Jhalrapatan India **74** C4
Jhang Pak. **81** H4
Jhanjharpur India **75** E4
Jhansi India **74** C4
Jhapa Nepal **75** E4
Jhargram India **75** E5
Jharia India **75** E5
Jharkhand *state* India **75** E5
Jharsuguda India **75** E5
Jhatpat Pak. **81** G4
Jhawani Nepal **75** E4
Jhelum *r.* India/Pak. **81** H3
Jhelum Pak. **81** H3
Jhenaidah Bangl. **75** F5
Jhenaidaha Bangl. *see* Jhenaidah
Jhinjhuvada India **74** A5
Jhudo Pak. **81** G5
Jhumritilaiya India **75** E4
Jhunjhunun India **74** B3
Jhusi India **75** D4
Jiachuan China **66** C1
Jiachuanzhen China *see* Jiachuan
Jiading *Jiangxi* China *see* Xinfeng
Jiading *Shanghai* China **67** G2
Jiahe China **67** B3
Jiajiang China **66** B2
Jialing Jiang *r.* China **66** C2
Jiamusi China **64** D3
Ji'an *Jiangxi* China **67** E3
Ji'an *Jiangxi* China **67** E3
Ji'an *Jilin* China **64** A4
Jianchang China *see* Nancheng
Jianchuan China **66** B3
Jiande China **67** F2
Ji'an Gou China **66** C2
Jiangbei China *see* Yubei
Jiangbiancun China **67** F3
Jiangcheng China **66** B4

Jiangchuan China **66** B3
Jiangdu China **67** F1
Jiange China **66** C2
Jiangjiehe China **66** C3
Jiangjin China **66** C2
Jiangkou *Guangdong* China *see* Fengkai
Jiangkou *Guizhou* China **66** C3
Jiangkou *Shaanxi* China **66** C1
Jiangle China **67** F3
Jiangling China *see* Jingzhou
Jiangluozhen China **66** C1
Jiangmen China **67** F5
Jiangna China *see* Yanshan
Jiangning China **67** F2
Jiangshan China **67** F2
Jiangsi China *see* Dejiang
Jiangsu *prov.* China **67** F1
Jiangxi *prov.* China **67** E3
Jiangxia China *see* Wuchang
Jiangyan China **67** G1
Jiangyong China **67** E3
Jiangyou China **66** C2
Jiangzhesongrong China **75** E3
Jianli China **67** F2
Jianning China **67** F3
Jian'ou China **67** F3
Jianshe China *see* Baiyü
Jianshi China **67** C2
Jianshui China **66** B4
Jianxing China **66** C1
Jianyang *Fujian* China **67** F3
Jianyang *Sichuan* China **66** C2
Jiaochangba China *see* Jiaochang
Jiaocheng China *see* Jiaoling
Jiaohe China **64** A4
Jiaojiang China *see* Taizhou
Jiaokui China *see* Yiliang
Jiaoling China **67** F3
Jiaowei China **67** F3
Jiaozhou China **63** K4
Jiaozuo China **63** I4
Jiasa China **66** B3
Jiashan China *see* Mingguang
Jiashan China *see* Huaqiao
Jia Tsuo La *pass* China **75** E3
Jiaxing China **67** G2
Jiayi Taiwan *see* Chiai
Jiayin China **64** B3
Jiayuguan China **70** I4
Jiazi China **67** F4
Jibūtī *country* Africa *see* Djibouti
Jibuti Djibouti *see* Djibouti
Jičín Czech Rep. **37** G3
Jiddah Saudi Arabia *see* Jeddah
Jiddī, Jabal al *hill* Egypt **89** G2
Jiehkkevarri *mt.* Norway **32** G4
Jieshi China **67** F4
Jieshi Wan *b.* China **67** F4
Jieshou China **67** F3
Jiešjávri *l.* Norway **32** G1
Jiexi China **67** F3
Jieyang China **67** F4
Jieznas Lith. **33** G5
Jigawa *state* Nigeria **93** H2
Jigerbent Turkm. *see* Dzhigirbent
Jiggalong Australia **108** C5
Jiggs U.S.A. **137** E1
Jigzhi China **66** B1
Jihār, Wādī al *watercourse* Syria **77** C2
Jihlava Czech Rep. **37** G4
Jihlava *r.* Czech Rep. **37** H4
Jijel Alg. **91** G1
Jijiga Eth. **96** E3
Jiju China **66** B2
Jilava Romania **46** E2
Jilf al Kabīr, Ḥaḍabat al Egypt **89** E4
Jilga *r.* Afgh. **81** G3
Jilh al 'Ishār *plain* Saudi Arabia **80** A5
Jilib Somalia **96** E4
Jilin China **64** A4
Jilin *prov.* China **64** A4
Jilin Hada Ling *mts* China **64** A4
Jiloca *r.* Spain **43** F2
Jilong Taiwan *see* Chilung
Jima Eth. **96** D3
Jima Ali *well* Eth. **96** E3
Jimbo Tanz. **97** C6
Jimbolia Romania **46** B2
Jimda China *see* Zindo
Jiménez *Chihuahua* Mex. **135** F8
Jiménez *Coahuila* Mex. **133** A6
Jiménez *Tamaulipas* Mex. **126** G7
Jimeta Nigeria **93** I3
Jimi *r.* P.N.G. **57** J6
Jimía, Cerro *mt.* Hond. **138** C7
Jimsar China **70** G3
Jina Romania **46** C2
Jin'an China *see* Songpan
Jinbi China *see* Dayao
Jincheng *Sichuan* China *see* Leibo
Jincheng *Sichuan* China *see* Yilong
Jinchengjiang China *see* Hechi
Jinchuan *Gansu* China *see* Jinchang
Jinchuan *Jiangxi* China *see* Xingan
Jinchuan *Sichuan* China **66** C2
Jind India **74** C3
Jindřichův Hradec Czech Rep. **37** G4
Jin'e China *see* Longchang
Jing *r.* China **67** D1
Jing'an China *see* Doumen
Jingdezhen China **67** F2
Jingdong China **66** B3
Jinggangshan China **67** F3
Jinggang Shan *hill* China **67** E3
Jinggongqiao China **67** F2
Jinggu China **66** B4
Jinghong China **66** B4
Jing Jiang *r.* China **67** G1
Jingmen China **67** E2
Jingpo Hu *resr* China **64** B4
Jingshan China **67** E2
Jingtai China **62** H4
Jingxi China **66** C4
Jingxian China *see* Jingzhou
Jingxin China *see* Yongshan
Jingyan China **66** B2
Jingyu China **62** B4
Jingyuan China **62** I4
Jinhe China **66** B4
Jinhua *Yunnan* China *see* Jianchuan
Jinhua *Zhejiang* China **67** F2
Jining *Nei Mongol* China **63** I3
Jining *Shandong* China **63** J4
Jinja Uganda **96** D4
Jinjiang *Fujian* China **67** F3
Jinjiang *Hainan* China *see* Chengmai
Jinjiang *Yunnan* China **66** B3
Jin Jiang *r.* China **67** E3
Jinka Eth. **96** C3
Jinkouhe China **66** B2
Jinmen Taiwan *see* Chinmen
Jinmu Jiao *pt* China **67** D5
Jinning China **66** B3
Jinotega Nicaragua **138** G6
Jinotepe Nicaragua **138** G6
Jinping *Guizhou* China **67** D3
Jinping *Yunnan* China *see* Jingdong
Jinping *Yunnan* China **66** B4

Jinping Yunnan China see Qiubei
Jinping Shan mts China 66 B3
Jinsen S. Korea see Inch'ŏn
Jinsha China 66 C3
Jinsha Jiang r. China see Yangtze
Jinsha Jiang r. China 66 C2 see Yangtze
Jinshan China see Lufeng
Jinshi Hunan China 67 D2
Jinshi Hunan China see Xinning
Jintan China 67 F2
Jintang China 66 C2
Jintur India 72 C2
Jinxi Jiangxi China 67 F3
Jinxi Liaoning China see Lianshan
Jin Xi r. China 67 F3
Jinxian China 67 F2
Jinxiang China 67 G3
Jinxiu China 67 D3
Jinyang China 66 B3
Jinyun China 67 G2
Jinz, Qa' al salt flat Jordan 77 C4
Jinzhai China 67 E2
Jinzhong China 63 I4
Jinzhou China 63 K3
Jinzhu China see Daocheng
Ji-Paraná Brazil 149 E2
Jiparaná r. Brazil 149 E2
Jipijapa Ecuador 146 A5
Jirā', Wādī watercourse Egypt 77 A5
Jirau Brazil 148 D2
Jirgatol Tajik. 81 G2
Jiri r. India 75 G4
Jirjā Egypt 89 F3
Jiroft Iran 80 D4
Jirriiban Somalia 96 E3
Jishou China 67 D2
Jishui China see Yongfeng
Jisr ash Shughūr Syria 77 C2
Jitian China see Lianshan
Jitra Malaysia 58 C1
Jiu r. Romania 46 C3
Jiuding Shan mt. China 66 B2
Jiugong Shan mt. China 67 E2
Jiujiang Jiangxi China 67 E2
Jiujiang Jiangxi China 67 F2
Jiulian China see Mojiang
Jiuling Shan mts China 67 E2
Jiulong Hong Kong China see Kowloon
Jiulong Sichuan China 66 B2
Jiuquan China 70 I4
Jiutai China 64 A3
Jiuxu China 66 C3
Jiwani Pak. 81 E5
Jixi Anhui China 67 F2
Jixi Heilong. China 64 B3
Jixian China 64 B3
Jīzah, Ahrāmāt al tourist site Egypt see Pyramids of Giza
Jīzān Saudi Arabia 89 I5
Jizera r. Czech Rep. 37 G3
Jizerské Hory mts Czech Rep. 37 G3
Jizō-zaki pt Japan 65 C6
Jizzakh Uzbek. see Dzhizak
Jizzakh Wiloyati admin. div. Uzbek. see Dzhizakskaya Oblast'
Joaçaba Brazil 151 B8
Joal-Fadiout Senegal 92 A2
Joana Peres Brazil 150 B2
João Belo Moz. see Xai-Xai
João de Almeida Angola see Chibia
João Pessoa Brazil 150 F3
João Pinheiro Brazil 151 C6
Joaquin V. González Arg. 152 D1
Job Peak U.S.A. 136 C2
Jockfall Sweden 32 F2
Jocoli Arg. 152 C3
Joda India 75 E5
Jódar Spain 42 E4
Jodhpur India 74 B4
Jodiya India 74 A5
Joensuu Fin. 32 H3
Joesjö Sweden 32 D2
Jōetsu Japan 65 D5
Jofane Moz. 99 G4
Joffre, Mount Canada 123 H5
Jogbani India 75 E4
Jogbura Nepal 74 D3
Jõgeva Estonia 33 G4
Jogighopa India 75 F4
Jogindarnagar India 74 C3
Jogjakarta Indon. see Yogyakarta
Johannesburg S. Africa 99 E5
Johan Peninsula Canada 121 L2
Johilla r. India 74 D5
John Day U.S.A. 134 C3
John Day r. U.S.A. 134 B3
John Day, Middle Fork r. U.S.A. 134 C3
John Day, North Fork r. U.S.A. 134 C3
John d'Or Prairie Canada 123 H3
John F. Kennedy airport U.S.A. 131 G3
John H. Kerr Reservoir U.S.A. 130 D5
John Jay, Mount Canada/U.S.A. 122 D3
Johnny Hoe r. Canada 122 F1
John o'Groats U.K. 34 E2
Johnson U.S.A. 131 G1
Johnsonburg U.S.A. 130 D3
Johnson City NY U.S.A. 131 F2
Johnson City TN U.S.A. 128 C4
Johnson City TX U.S.A. 133 B6
Johnston, Lake salt flat Australia 109 C8
Johnston and Sand Islands N. Pacific Ocean see Johnston Atoll

▶Johnston Atoll N. Pacific Ocean 164 G4
United States Unincorporated Territory.
oceania 104–105, 114

Johnstone Lake Canada see Old Wives Lake
Johnston Range hills Australia 109 B7
Johnstown NY U.S.A. 131 F2
Johnstown OH U.S.A. 130 B3
Johnstown PA U.S.A. 130 D3
Johor state Malaysia 58 C2
Johor, Selat strait Malaysia/Sing. 58 [inset]
Johor, Sungai Malaysia 58 [inset]
Johor Bahru Malaysia 58 C2
Jõhvi Estonia 28 C4
Joigny France 39 E3
Joinville Brazil 151 B8
Joinville France 39 F2
Joinville Island Antarctica 167 A2
Jokiperä Fin. 32 F3
Jokkmokk Sweden 32 E2
Jökulbunga hill Iceland 32 [inset]
Jökulsá á Fjöllum r. Iceland 32 [inset]
Jolarpettai India 72 C3
Joliet U.S.A. 132 D3
Joliet, Lac l. Canada 124 E3
Joliette Canada 125 F4
Jolly Lake Canada 123 H1
Jolo Phil. 57 F4
Jolo i. Phil. 57 F4
Jomard Entrance sea chan. P.N.G. 111 G1
Jombang Indon. 59 F4
Jomda China 66 A2
Jomna Norway 33 C3
Jomsom Nepal 75 D3
Jonāḩ Iran 80 C5
Jonancy U.S.A. 130 B5
Jonava Lith. 33 G5
Jondal Norway 33 E3
Jonê China 66 B1
Jonesboro AR U.S.A. 127 H4
Jonesboro LA U.S.A. 133 C5
Jones Mills U.S.A. 130 D3
Jones Sound sea chan. Canada 121 K2
Jonestown U.S.A. 131 E3
Jonesville LA U.S.A. 133 D6
Jonesville VA U.S.A. 130 B5
Jonglei Sudan 96 A3
Jonglei state Sudan 96 B3
Jonglei Canal Sudan 96 A3
Joniškis Lith. 33 F4
Jonk r. India 75 D5
Jönköping Sweden 33 D4
Jönköping county Sweden 33 D4
Jonquière Canada 125 G3
Jonzac France 38 C4
Joplin U.S.A. 132 C4
Joppa Israel see Tel Aviv-Yafo
Jora India 74 C4
▶Jordan country Asia 77 C4
asia 52–53, 82
Jordan r. Asia 78 C5
Jordan MT U.S.A. 134 F3
Jordan NY U.S.A. 131 E2
Jordan r. U.S.A. 137 F1
Jordet Norway 33 D3
Jorge Montt, Isla i. Chile 153 B7
Jorhat India 75 G4
Jorm Afgh. 81 G2
Jormvattnet Sweden 32 D2
Jörn Sweden 32 F2
Joroinen Fin. 33 G3
Jørpeland Norway 33 B4
Jos Nigeria 93 H3
José Bonifácio Brazil 149 E3
José Cardel Mex. 126 G8
José de San Martín Arg. 153 C6
José Enrique Rodó Uruguay 152 F3
Joselândia Brazil 149 F4
José Pedro Varela Uruguay 152 G3
Joseph, Lac l. Canada 125 H2
Joseph Bonaparte Gulf Australia 110 B2
Joseph City U.S.A. 137 G4
Joshimath India 74 C3
Jōshinetsu-kōgen National Park Japan 65 D5
Joshipur India 75 E5
Joshua Tree U.S.A. 137 D4
Joshua Tree National Park U.S.A. 137 E5
Jos Plateau Nigeria 93 H3
Josselin France 38 B3
Jossund Norway 32 C2
Jostedalsbreen glacier Norway 33 B3
Jostedalsbreen Nasjonalpark nat. park Norway 33 B3
Jotunheimen mts Norway 33 C3
Jotunheimen Nasjonalpark nat. park Norway 33 C3
Jouberton S. Africa 99 E5
Joué-lès-Tours France 38 D3
Joukokylä Fin. 32 G2
Joûnié Lebanon 77 B3
Joussard Canada 123 H4
Joutsa Fin. 33 G3
Joutsijärvi Fin. 32 G2
Jovellanos Cuba 129 C8
Jowai India 75 G4
Jowzjān prov. Afgh. 81 F2
Joy, Mount Canada 122 C2
Joypurhat Bangl. 75 F4
Jrayfiya well W. Sahara 90 B4
Jreïda Mauritania 92 A1
Juan Aldama Mex. 126 F7
Juan de Fuca Strait Canada/U.S.A. 120 G5
Juan de Nova i. Indian Ocean 97 D9
Juan E. Barra Arg. 152 E4
Juan Fernández Islands S. Pacific Ocean 165 M8
Juangriego Venez. 147 F2
Juanjuí Peru 148 A1
Juan Mata Ortíz Mex. 135 E7
Juanshui China see Tongcheng
Juan Stuven, Isla i. Chile 153 B6
Juara Brazil 149 F2
Juaréz Mex. 133 A7
Juárez, Sierra de 135 D7
Juàzeiro Brazil 150 D4
Juàzeiro do Norte Brazil 150 E3
Juazohn Liberia 92 C4
Juba r. Somalia see Jubba
Juba Sudan 96 A3
Jubany research station Antarctica 167 A2
Jubba r. Somalia 96 D5
Jubbada Dhexe admin. reg. Somalia 96 D4
Jubbada Hoose admin. reg. Somalia 96 D4
Jubbah Saudi Arabia 89 I2
Jubbulpore India see Jabalpur
Jubilee Lake salt flat Australia 109 D7
Jubing Nepal 75 E4
Júcar r. Spain 43 F3
Juçara Brazil 149 H3
Juchitán Mex. 138 E5
Jucuruçu Brazil 151 E6
Judaidat al Hamir Iraq 79 E5
Judaydah Syria 79 D4
Judayyidat 'Ar'ar well Iraq 79 E5
Judenburg Austria 37 G5
Judian China 66 A3
Judith r. U.S.A. 134 E3
Judith Gap U.S.A. 134 E3
Juegang China see Rudong
Juego de Bolos mt. Spain 42 E3
Juelsminde Denmark 33 C5
Jufari r. Brazil 147 F5
Jugon-les-Lacs France 38 B2
Jugoslavija country Europe see Yugoslavia
Juigalpa Nicaragua 139 G6
Juillet, Lac l. Canada 125 I2
Juina Brazil 149 F2
Juina r. Brazil 149 F3
Juist i. Germany 36 C2
Juiz de Fora Brazil 151 D7
Jujuhan r. Indon. 58 C3
Jujuy prov. Arg. 148 D5
Julaca Bol. 148 D5
Julesburg U.S.A. 132 A3
Juli Peru 148 C4
Julia Brazil 146 E5
Juliaca Peru 148 C3
Julia Creek Australia 111 E4
Julian U.S.A. 137 D5
Julian, Lac l. Canada 124 E2
Julian Alps mts Slovenia see Julijske Alpe
Julianatop mt. Indon. see Mandala, Puncak
Juliana Top mt. Suriname 147 G4
Julianehåb Greenland see Qaqortoq
Julijske Alpe mts Slovenia 44 D1
Julimes Mex. 135 F7
Júlio de Castilhos Brazil 151 A9
Juliomagus France see Angers
Jullundur India see Jalandhar
Juma Uzbek. see Dzhuma
Jumba Somalia 96 D5
Jumilla Spain 43 F3
Jumla Nepal 75 D3
Jumna r. India see Yamuna
Jump r. U.S.A. 132 D2
Junagadh India 74 A5
Junagarh India 73 D2
Junaynah, Ra's al mt. Egypt 77 A5
Junction TX U.S.A. 133 B6
Junction UT U.S.A. 137 F2
Junction City KS U.S.A. 132 B4
Junction City KY U.S.A. 130 A5
Junction City OR U.S.A. 134 B3
Jundah Australia 111 E5
Jundiaí Brazil 149 I5

▶Juneau U.S.A. 120 F4
State capital of Alaska.

Junee Australia 112 C4
Jūn el Khudr b. Lebanon 77 B3
Jungfrau mt. Switz. 39 G3
Jungfrau-Aletsch-Bietschhorn tourist site Switz. 39 H3
Junggar Pendi basin China 70 G2
Jungshahi Pak. 81 F5
Junguls Sudan 96 B2
Juniata r. U.S.A. 131 E3
Junik Yugo. 46 B3
Junín Arg. 152 E3
Junín Peru 148 A2
Junín dept Peru 148 B2
Junior U.S.A. 130 D4
Juniper Mountains U.S.A. 137 F4
Junipero Serro Peak U.S.A. 136 B3
Junlian China 66 C2
Junnah, Jabal mts Egypt 77 B5
Junnar India 72 B2
Junosuando Sweden 32 F2
Junsele Sweden 32 E3
Junshan Hu l. China 67 F2
Juntura U.S.A. 134 C4
Juntusranta Fin. 32 H2
Junxi China see Datian
Junxian China see Danjiangkou
Ju'nyung China 66 A1
Ju'nyunggoin China see Ju'nyung
Juodupė Lith. 33 G4
Juoksengi Sweden 32 F2
Jupía, Represa resr Brazil 149 H5
Juquiá Brazil 149 I6
Jur r. Sudan 94 F2
Jura mts France/Switz. 39 F4
Jura i. U.K. 34 D3
Jura, Sound of sea chan. U.K. 34 D4
Juradó Col. 146 B3
Jurbarkas Lith. 33 F5
Juremal Brazil 150 D4
Jurf ad Darāwīsh Jordan 77 B4
Jurgurra r. Australia 108 C4
Jurhen Ul Shan mts China 75 F2
Jurien Australia 109 A7
Jurilovca Romania 46 F2
Juruti Velho Brazil 147 G5
Jūrmala Latvia 33 F4
Jurmu Fin. 32 G2
Jurong China 67 F2
Jurong Sing. 58 [inset]
Jurong, Sungai r. Sing. 58 [inset]
Jurong Island reg. Sing. 58 [inset]
Juruá r. Brazil 146 E5
Juruena Brazil 149 F3
Juruena r. Brazil 149 F1
Juruti Brazil 147 G5
Jurva Fin. 32 F3
Jusepín Venez. 147 F2
Jussey France 39 F3
Justice U.S.A. 130 C5
Justo Daract Arg. 152 D3
Jutaí Brazil 146 D6
Jutaí r. Brazil 146 E5
Jüterbog Germany 37 F3
Juti Brazil 151 A7
Jutiapa Guat. 138 G6
Juticalpa Hond. 138 G6
Jutis Sweden 32 E2
Jutland pen. Denmark 33 C4
Juuka Fin. 32 H3
Juva Fin. 33 G3
Juwain Afgh. 81 E4
Jüymand Iran 81 D3
Jüyom Iran 80 C4
Južnoukrajinsk Ukr. see Yuzhnoukrayinsk
Jyväskylä Fin. 33 G3

K

▶K2 mt. China/Jammu and Kashmir 74 C2
2nd highest mountain in the world and in Asia.
asia 50–51
world 6–7

Ka r. Nigeria 93 G3
Kaabong Uganda 96 B4
Kaa-iya, Parque Nacional nat. park Bol. 149 E4
Kaakhka Turkm. see Kaka
Kaamanen Fin. 32 G1
Kaambooni Kenya 96 D5
Kaapstad S. Africa see Cape Town
Kaarina Fin. 33 F3
Kaarta reg. Mali 92 C2
Kaavi Fin. 32 H3
Kaba China see Habahe
Kabaena i. Indon. 57 F7
Kabakly Turkm. 81 E2
Kabala Sierra Leone 92 C3
Kabale Uganda 96 A5
Kabalega Falls National Park Uganda see Murchison Falls National Park
Kabalo Dem. Rep. Congo 95 E6
Kabambare Dem. Rep. Congo 95 E6
Kabanga Dem. Rep. Congo 95 C6
Kabangu Dem. Rep. Congo 95 D7
Kabanjahe Indon. 58 B2
Kabara i. Fiji 107 H3
Kabare Dem. Rep. Congo 94 F5
Kabarega National Park Uganda see Murchison Falls National Park
Kabaung r. Myanmar 60 B4
Kabaw Valley Myanmar 60 A3
Kabba Nigeria 93 G4
Kabbani r. India 72 C3
Kåbdalis Sweden 32 F2
Kabélawa Niger 93 I2
Kaberneeme Estonia 33 G4
Kabertene Alg. 91 F3
Kab-hegy hill Hungary 44 F1
Kabinakagami r. Canada 124 C3
Kabinda Dem. Rep. Congo 95 E6
Kabir r. Syria 77 B2
Kabīrkūh mts Iran 80 A3
Kabirwala Pak. 81 G4
Kabli Estonia 33 G4
Kabneshwar India 74 C5
Kabo Cent. Afr. Rep. 94 C3
Kābol Afgh. see Kābul
Kabompo Zambia 95 E8
Kabompo r. Zambia 95 D8
Kabondo-Dianda Dem. Rep. Congo 95 E7
Kabongo Dem. Rep. Congo 95 E6
Kabosa Island Myanmar 61 B5
Kabou Cent. Afr. Rep. 94 C3
Kabou Togo 93 F3
Kabrousse Senegal 92 A2
Kabūdeh Iran 81 E3
Kabūd Gonbad Iran 81 D2
Kabūd Rāhang Iran 80 B3

▶Kābul Afgh. 81 G3
Capital of Afghanistan.

Kābul prov. Afgh. 81 G3
Kabul r. Afgh. 81 H3
Kabunda Dem. Rep. Congo 95 F8
Kabunduk Indon. 108 B2
Kaburuang i. Indon. 57 G5
Kabushiya Sudan 89 G5
Kabwe Zambia 95 F8
Kačanik Yugo. 46 B3
Kacha Kuh mts Iran/Pak. 81 E4
Kachalinskaya Rus. Fed. 29 H6
Kachchh, Great Rann of marsh India see Kachchh, Rann of
Kachchh, Gulf of India 74 A5
Kachchh, Rann of marsh India 74 A4
Kachh Pak. 81 F4
Kachhola India 74 B4
Kachhwa India 75 D4
Kachia Nigeria 93 G3
Kachin state Myanmar 60 B2
Kachīsī Eth. 96 C2
Kacholola Zambia 97 A8
Kachug Rus. Fed. 62 H1
Kachung Uganda 96 B4
Kaçkar Dağı mt. Turkey 79 E2
Kaczawa r. Poland 37 H3
Kadaingti Myanmar 60 B4
Kadaiyanallur India 72 C4
Kadam mt. Uganda 96 B4
Kadana Chad 88 D6
Kadanai r. Afgh./Pak. 81 F4
Kadan Kyun i. Myanmar 61 B5
Kadapongan i. Indon. 59 F4
Kadarkút Hungary 44 F1
Kadaura India 74 C4
Kadavu i. Fiji 107 G3
Kadavu Passage Fiji 107 G3
Kaddam l. India 72 C2
Kade Ghana 93 E4
Kadgo, Lake salt flat Australia 109 D6
Kadhdhāb, Sinn al esc. Egypt 89 F4
Kādhimain Iraq see Al Kāẓimīyah
Kadiana Mali 92 D3
Kadijica mt. Bulg. see Kadiytsa
Kadıköy Çanakkale Turkey 46 E4
Kadıköy İstanbul Turkey 46 F4
Kadina Australia 112 A4
Kading r. Laos 60 C4
Kadınhanı Turkey 78 C3
Kadiolo Mali 92 D3
Kadiri India 72 C3
Kadirli Turkey 78 D3
Kadiyevka Ukr. see Stakhanov
Kadiytsa mt. Bulg. 46 C4
Kadmat i. India 72 B4
Kado Nigeria 93 H4
Ka-do i. N. Korea 65 A5
Kadoka U.S.A. 132 A3
Kadoma Zimbabwe 99 F3
Kadonkani Myanmar 61 A5
Kadugli Sudan 94 F2
Kaduna Nigeria 93 G3
Kaduna r. Nigeria 93 G3
Kaduna state Nigeria 93 G3
Kadur India 72 C3
Kadusam mt. China/India 66 A2
Kaduy Rus. Fed. 28 F4
Kadyy Rus. Fed. 28 G4
Kadzherom Rus. Fed. 28 J2
Kaechon N. Korea 65 A5
Kaédi Mauritania 92 B1
Kaegudeck Lake Canada 125 K3
Kaélé Cameroon 93 I3
Kaena Point U.S.A. 135 [inset] Y1
Kaeng Krachan National Park Thai. 61 B5
Kaesŏng N. Korea 65 A5
Kafa Ukr. see Feodosiya
Kafakumba Dem. Rep. Congo 95 D7
Kafan Armenia see Kapan
Kafanchan Nigeria 93 H3
Kaffin-Hausa Nigeria 93 H2
Kaffrine Senegal 92 B2
Kafia Kingi Sudan 94 E2
Kafireas, Akra pt Greece 47 D5
Kafireos, Steno sea chan. Greece 47 D6
Kafirnigan Tajik. see Kofarnihon
Kåfjordbotn Norway 32 F1
Kafolo Côte d'Ivoire 92 D3
Kafr ash Shaykh Egypt 89 F2
Kafr ash Shaykh governorate Egypt
78 B5
Kafr el Sheikh governorate Egypt see Kafr ash Shaykh
Kafret Rihama Egypt 78 A5
Kafu r. Uganda 96 B4
Kafue Zambia 95 F8
Kafue r. Zambia 95 F8
Kafue Flats marsh Zambia 95 E8
Kafue National Park Zambia 95 E8
Kaga Bandoro Cent. Afr. Rep. 94 C3
Kagan Uzbek. 81 F2
Kaganovichabad Tajik. see Kolkhozobod
Kaganovichi Pervyye Ukr. see Polis'ke
Kagarlyk Ukr. see Kaharlyk
Kåge Sweden 32 F2
Kagera admin. reg. Tanz. 96 A5
Kagera, Parc National de la nat. park Rwanda see Akagera National Park
Kağızman Turkey 79 E2
Kagmar Sudan 89 F6
Kagologolo Indon. 58 B3
Kagoshima Japan 65 B7
Kagul Moldova see Cahul
Kāhak Iran 80 D2
Kahama Tanz. 97 B5
Kaharlyk Ukr. 29 D6
Kahawero waterhole Namibia 98 B4
Kahayan r. Indon. 59 F3
Kahemba Dem. Rep. Congo 95 C6
Kahla Germany 36 E3
Kahntah Canada 122 F3
Kahnu Iran see Kahnūj
Kahnūj Iran 80 D5
Kahnwia Liberia 92 C4
Kahoka U.S.A. 132 D3
Kahoolawe i. U.S.A. 135 [inset] Z1
Kahramanmaraş Turkey 78 D3
Kahror Pak. 81 G4
Kahta Turkey 79 D3
Kahugish well Iran 80 D3
Kahuku Point U.S.A. 135 [inset] Y1
Kahul, Ozero l. Ukr. 46 F2
Kahulaui i. U.S.A. see Kahoolawe
Kahului U.S.A. 135 [inset] Z1
Kahurangi National Park N.Z. 113 C3
Kahurangi Point N.Z. 113 C3
Kahuta Pak. 81 H3
Kahuzi-Biega, Parc National du nat. park Dem. Rep. Congo 94 E5
Kai, Kepulauan is Indon. 57 H7
Kaia r. Sudan 96 A3
Kaiama Nigeria 93 F3
Kaiapit P.N.G. 57 K7
Kaibab Plateau U.S.A. 137 F3
Kai Besar i. Indon. 57 H7
Kaibito Plateau U.S.A. 137 G3
Kaieteur Falls Guyana 147 G3
Kaifeng Henan China 67 E1
Kaifeng Henan China 67 E1
Kaihua Yunnan China see Wenshan
Kaihua Zhejiang China 67 F2
Kaijiang China 66 C2
Kai Kecil i. Indon. 57 H7
Kai Keung Leng Hong Kong China 67 [inset]
Kaikoura N.Z. 113 C3
Kailahun Sierra Leone 92 C3
Kailas mt. China see Kangrinboqê Feng
Kailas Range mts China see Gangdisê Shan
Kaili China 66 C3
Kailongong waterhole Kenya 96 B3
Kailua U.S.A. 135 [inset] Z1
Kailua Kona U.S.A. 135 [inset] Z2
Kaimana Indon. 57 H6
Kaimanawa Mountains N.Z. 113 C2
Kaimar China 75 G2
Kaimganj India 74 C4
Kaimur Range hills India 74 D4
Kainji Lake National Park Nigeria 93 G3
Kainji Reservoir Nigeria 93 G3
Kaintaragarh India 73 E1
Kaipara Harbour N.Z. 113 C2
Kaiparowits Plateau U.S.A. 137 G3
Kaiping Guangdong China 67 E4
Kaiping Yunnan China see Dêqên
Kaipokok Bay Canada 125 J2
Kaira India see Kheda
Kairala Fin. 32 G2
Kairana India 74 C3
Kairouan Tunisia 91 H2
Kaisepakte Sweden 32 E1
Kaiserslautern Germany 36 C4
Kaiser Wilhelm II Land reg. Antarctica 167 E2
Kaishantun China 64 B4
Kaišiadorys Lith. 33 G5
Kaitaia N.Z. 113 C1
Kaitangata N.Z. 113 B4
Kaitawa N.Z. 113 D2
Kaithal India 74 C3
Kaitong China see Tongyu
Kaitum Sweden 32 F2
Kaitumälven r. Sweden 32 F2
Kaiwatu Indon. 57 G7
Kaiwi Channel U.S.A. 135 [inset] Z1
Kaixian China 67 D2
Kaiyang China 66 C3
Kaiyuan Liaoning China 64 A4
Kaiyuan Yunnan China 66 B4
Kajaani Fin. 32 G2
Kajabbi Australia 111 E4
Kajaki Afgh. 81 F3
Kajang Malaysia 58 C2
Kajdar Iran 81 E5
Kajiado Kenya 96 C5
Kajo Kaji Sudan 96 A4
Kaju Iran 80 A2
Kaka Sudan 96 B2
Kaka Turkm. 81 D2
Kakaban i. Indon. 59 G2
Kakabeka Falls Canada 124 B3
Kakadu National Park Australia 110 C2
Kakagi Lake Canada 124 A3
Kakamas S. Africa 98 D6
Kakamega Kenya 96 B4
Kakana India 73 G4
Kakanj Bos.-Herz. 44 G2
Kakata Liberia 92 C4
Kakching India 75 G4
Kakenge Dem. Rep. Congo 95 D6
Kakesio Tanz. 96 B5
Kakhi Azer. see Qax
Kakhovs'ke Vodoskhovyshche resr Ukr. 29 E7
Kakhul Moldova see Cahul
Kākī Iran 80 B4
Kakinada India 73 D2
Kakinjës, Maja e mt. Albania 46 A3
Kakisa Lake Canada 123 G2
Kakogawa Japan 65 C6
Kakpin Côte d'Ivoire 92 E3
Kakrala India 74 C4
Kakrima r. Guinea 92 B3
Kakshaal-Too mts China/Kyrg. see Kokshaal-Tau
Kakuda Japan 65 E5
Kakuma Kenya 96 B4
Kakus r. Sarawak Malaysia 59 F2
Kakwa r. Canada 122 G4
Kal hill Croatia 44 E2
Kala Nigeria 93 I2
Kala Tanz. 97 A7
Kalaâ Kebira Tunisia 91 H2
Kalaallit Nunaat terr. N. America see Greenland
Kalabagh Pak. 81 G3
Kalabahi Indon. 57 F7
Kalabak mt. Bulg./Greece see Radomir
Kalabáka Greece see Kalampaka
Kalabakan Sabah Malaysia 59 G1
Kalabaydh Togdheer Somalia 96 E2
Kalabaydh Woqooyi Galbeed Somalia 96 D2
Kalabo Zambia 95 D8
Kalach Rus. Fed. 29 G6
Kalacha Dida Kenya 96 C4
Kalach-na-Donu Rus. Fed. 29 G6
Kaladan r. India/Myanmar 73 G1
Kaladar Canada 131 E1
Kaladgi India 72 B2
Kalagwe Myanmar 60 B3
Kalahari Desert Africa 98 D4
Kalahari Gemsbok National Park S. Africa 98 D5
Kalaikhum Tajik. see Qal'aikhum
Kalai-Khumb Tajik. see Qal'aikhum
Kala-I-Mor Turkm. 81 E3
Kalajoki Fin. 32 F2
Kalajoki r. Fin. 32 F2
Kalak Norway 32 G1
Kalakoch hill Bulg. 46 E3
Kalalé Benin 93 F3
Kalam India 72 C1
Kalam Pak. 81 H3
Kalámai Greece see Kalamata
Kalamaria Greece 46 C4
Kalamata Greece 47 C6
Kalamazoo U.S.A. 132 E3
Kalamazoo r. U.S.A. 132 E3
Kalambau i. Indon. 59 F4
Kalamnuri India 72 C2
Kalamos i. Greece 47 B5
Kalampaka Greece 47 B5
Kalana Estonia 33 F4
Kalana Mali 92 C3
Kalanchak Ukr. 29 E7
Kalandula Angola see Calandula
Kalangala Uganda 96 B5
Kalannie Australia 109 B7
Kalanwali India 74 B3
Kalao i. Indon. 57 F7
Kalaotoa i. Indon. 57 F7
Kala Oya r. Sri Lanka 72 C4
Kalapana U.S.A. 135 [inset] Z2
Kalar watercourse Iran 81 E5
Kalār Iraq 79 F4
Kalasin Thai. 61 C4
Kalāt Balūchestān va Sīstān Iran 81 D5
Kalāt Khorāsan Iran see Kabūd Gonbad
Kalat Balochistān Pak. 81 F4
Kalat Balochistān Pak. 81 F5
Kalat, Kūh-e mt. Iran 80 D3
Kalaus r. Rus. Fed. 29 H7
Kalavad India 74 A5
Kalavryta Greece 47 C5
Kälbäcär Azer. 80 A1
Kalbarri Australia 109 A6
Kalbarri National Park Australia 109 A6
Kalbū Iran 81 D3
Kaldırım Turkey 77 B1
Kaldygayty r. Kazakh. 29 J6
Kale Turkey 47 F6
Kalecik Turkey 78 C2
Kalegauk Island Myanmar 61 B5
Kalema Dem. Rep. Congo 95 E6
Kalémié Dem. Rep. Congo 95 F6
Kalemyo Myanmar 60 A3
Kalenoye Kazakh. 29 I6
Kalesija Bos.-Herz. 44 G2
Kalevala Rus. Fed. 32 H2
Kalewa Myanmar 60 A3
Kalgan China see Zhangjiakou
Kalgoorlie Australia 109 C7
Kalguéri Niger 93 H2
Kali Croatia 44 E2
Kali r. India/Nepal 74 D3
Kaliakra, Nos pt Bulg. 46 F3
Kalianda Indon. 58 D4
Kali Gandaki r. Nepal 75 E4
Kaligiri India 72 C3
Kalima Dem. Rep. Congo 94 E5
Kalimantan reg. Indon. 59 E3
Kalimantan Barat prov. Indon. 59 E2
Kalimantan Selatan prov. Indon. 59 F3
Kalimantan Tengah prov. Indon. 59 F3
Kalimantan Timur prov. Indon. 59 G2
Kálimnos i. Greece see Kalymnos
Kalimpang India 75 F4
Kalinadi r. India 72 B3
Kali Nadi r. India 74 D4
Kalinin Rus. Fed. see Tver'
Kaliningrad Rus. Fed. 37 J1
Kaliningrad Oblast admin. div. Rus. Fed. see Kaliningradskaya Oblast'
Kaliningradskaya Oblast' admin. div. Rus. Fed. 37 J1
Kaliningradskiy Zaliv b. Rus. Fed. 37 I1
Kalinino Armenia see Tashir
Kalinino Kostromskaya Oblast' Rus. Fed. 28 G4
Kalinino Permskaya Oblast' Rus. Fed. 28 K4
Kalininsk Rus. Fed. 29 H6
Kalininskaya Rus. Fed. 29 F7
Kalininskaya Oblast' admin. div. Rus. Fed. see Tverskaya Oblast'
Kalinjara India 74 B5
Kalinkavichy Belarus 31 L2
Kalinkovichi Belarus see Kalinkavichy
Kalinovka Kazakh. 29 J6
Kaliro Uganda 96 B4
Kalis Somalia 96 F2
Kalisch Poland see Kalisz
Kalispell U.S.A. 134 D2
Kalisz Poland 37 I3
Kalisz Pomorski Poland 37 G2
Kalitva r. Rus. Fed. 29 G6
Kaliua Tanz. 97 A6
Kalix Sweden 32 F2
Kalixälven r. Sweden 32 F2
Kalkan Turkey 78 B3
Kalkaringi Australia 110 B3
Kalkaska U.S.A. 132 E2
Kalkfeld Namibia 98 C4
Kallakkurichchi India 72 C4
Kallam India 72 C2
Kallang Sing. 58 [inset]
Kallaste Estonia 28 C4
Kallavesi l. Fin. 32 G3
Kållberget Sweden 32 D3
Kallfjärden b. Sweden 32 F2
Kallifoni Greece 47 B5
Kallmet i Madh Albania 46 A4
Kallonis, Kolpos b. Greece 47 E5
Kallsjön l. Sweden 32 D3
Kallur India 72 C2
Kalmar Sweden 33 E4
Kalmar county Sweden 33 E4
Kalmarsund sea chan. Sweden 33 E4
Kalmūkh Qal'eh Iran 80 D2
Kalmunai Sri Lanka 73 D5
Kalmykia aut. rep. Rus. Fed. see Kalmykiya - Khalm'g-Tangch, Respublika
Kalmykiya - Khalm'g-Tangch, Respublika aut. rep. Rus. Fed. 29 H7
Kalmykovo Kazakh. see Taypak
Kalmytskaya Avtonomnaya Oblast' aut. rep. Rus. Fed. see Kalmykiya - Khalm'g-Tangch, Respublika
Kalnai India 75 D5
Kalni r. Bangl. 75 F4
Kalnik mts Croatia 44 F1
Kalocsa Hungary 37 I5
Kaloko Dem. Rep. Congo 95 E6
Kalol Gujarat India 74 B5
Kalol Gujarat India 74 B5
Kaloma Tanz. 97 A6
Kalomo Zambia 95 E9
Kalone Peak Canada 122 E4
Kalopanagiotis Cyprus 77 A2
Kalpa India 74 C3
Kalpeni i. India 72 B4
Kalpetta India 72 C4
Kalpi India 74 C4
Kāl-Shūr, Rūd-e r. Iran 80 D2
Kaltenkirchen Germany 36 D2
Kaltukatjara Australia 110 B5
Kaltungo Nigeria 93 H3
Kalu India 74 B3
Kalu r. India 72 B2
Kaluđerica Yugo. 46 B2
Kaluga Rus. Fed. 29 F5
Kaluga Oblast admin. div. Rus. Fed. see Kaluzhskaya Oblast'
Kalukalukuang i. Indon. 59 G4
Kalulong, Bukit mt. Sarawak Malaysia 59 F2
Kalulushi Zambia 95 F8
Kalumburu Australia 110 A2
Kalundborg Denmark 33 C5
Kalupis Falls Sabah Malaysia 59 G1
Kalur Kot Pak. 81 G3
Kalush Ukr. 29 C6
Kalutara Sri Lanka 72 C5
Kaluzhskaya Oblast' admin. div. Rus. Fed. 31 M2
Kalvåg Norway 33 B3
Kalvan India 72 B1
Kalvarija Lith. 33 F5
Kalvitsa Fin. 33 G3
Kalvola Fin. 33 G3
Kalwakurti India 72 C2
Kalyan India 72 B2
Kalyandurg India 72 C3
Kalyansingapuram India 73 D2
Kalyazin Rus. Fed. 28 F4
Kalymnos Greece 47 E6
Kalymnos i. Greece 47 E6
Kama Dem. Rep. Congo 94 E5
Kama Myanmar 60 A4

▶Kama r. Rus. Fed. 28 J4
4th longest river in Europe.
europe 22–23

Kamaishi Japan 65 E5
Kamakusa Guyana 147 G3
Kamakwie Sierra Leone 92 B3
Kamal Chad 88 C4
Kamalapuram India 72 C3
Kamalia Pak. 81 H4
Kamamaung Myanmar 60 B4
Kaman India 74 C4
Kaman Turkey 78 C3
Kamanjab Namibia 98 B3
Kamarān Yemen 89 I6
Kamarān i. Yemen 76 C6

Kamarang Guyana 147 F3
Kamaran Island Yemen see Kamarān
Kamareddi India 72 C2
Kamares Dytiki Ellas Greece 47 B5
Kamares Sifnos Greece 47 D6
Kamaria Falls Guyana 147 G3
Kamarlu Armenia see Artashat
Kamas U.S.A. 137 G1
Kamashi Uzbek. 81 F2
Kamativi Zimbabwe 99 E3
Kamba Nigeria 93 F3
Kamba Kota Cent. Afr. Rep. 94 C3
Kambalda Australia 109 C7
Kambam India 72 C4
Kambang Indon. 58 C3
Kambangan i. Indon. 59 E5
Kambara i. Fiji see Kabara
Kambarka Rus. Fed. 28 J4
Kambia Sierra Leone 92 B3
Kambing, Pulau i. East Timor see Ataúro, Ilha de
Kambo-san mt. N. Korea see Kwanmo-bong
Kambove Dem. Rep. Congo 95 E7
Kamburovo Bulg. 46 E3
Kambūt Libya 88 E2
Kamchatka r. Rus. Fed. 27 Q4
Kamchatka, Poluostrov pen. Rus. Fed. see Kamchatka Peninsula
Kamchatka Basin sea feature Bering Sea 164 F2
▶Kamchatka Peninsula Rus. Fed. 27 P4
asia 50–51
Kamchatskiy Proliv strait Rus. Fed. 27 Q4
Kamchiya r. Bulg. 46 E3
Kamchiyska Planina hills Bulg. 46 E3
Kamdesh Afgh. 81 G3
Kameia, Parque Nacional de nat. park Angola see Cameia, Parque Nacional da
Kamelik r. Rus. Fed. 29 I5
Kamen Bulg. 46 D3
Kamen', Gory mts Rus. Fed. 27 J3
Kamende Dem. Rep. Congo 95 E6
Kamenets-Podol'skiy Ukr. see Kam"yanets'-Podil's'kyy
Kamenitsa r. Bulg. 46 D3
Kamenjak, Rt pt Croatia 44 D2
Kamenka Kazakh. 29 I6
Kamenka Arkhangel'skaya Oblast' Rus. Fed. 28 H2
Kamenka Leningradskaya Oblast' Rus. Fed. 33 H3
Kamenka Penzenskaya Oblast' Rus. Fed. 29 H5
Kamenka-Bugskaya Ukr. see Kam"yanka-Buz'ka
Kamenka-Strumilovskaya Ukr. see Kam"yanka-Buz'ka
Kamen'-na-Obi Rus. Fed. 26 I4
Kamennogorsk Rus. Fed. 28 D3
Kamennomostskiy Rus. Fed. 29 G7
Kamennoye, Ozero l. Rus. Fed. 32 H2
Kameno Bulg. 46 E3
Kamenongue Angola see Camanongue
Kamen'-Rybolov Rus. Fed. 64 C3
Kamenskiy Rus. Fed. 29 H6
Kamenskoye Rus. Fed. 27 Q3
Kamenskoye Ukr. see Dniprodzerzhyns'k
Kamensk-Shakhtinskiy Rus. Fed. 29 G6
Kamensk-Ural'skiy Rus. Fed. 26 G4
Kamenz Germany 37 G3
Kamet mt. China 74 C3
Kamiah U.S.A. 134 C3
Kamienna r. Poland 37 J3
Kamienna Gora Poland 37 H3
Kamień Pomorski Poland 37 G2
Kamiesberge mts S. Africa 98 C6
Kamieskroon S. Africa 98 C6
Kamileroi Australia 111 E3
Kamina Dem. Rep. Congo 95 E7
Kamina Base Dem. Rep. Congo 95 E7
Kaminak Lake Canada 123 M2
Kaminške in Savinjske Alpe mts Slovenia 44 E1
Kaminuriak Lake Canada see Qamanirjuaq Lake
Kamiros Greece 47 E6
Kamla r. India 75 E4
Kamla r. India 75 G4
Kamloops Canada 134 B2
Kamnik Slovenia 44 E1
Kamo Armenia 79 F2
Kamob Sanha Sudan 89 H5
Kamoke Pak. 74 B3
Kamola Dem. Rep. Congo 95 E6
Kamonanira Tanz. 97 A6
Kamp r. Austria 37 G4
▶Kampala Uganda 96 B4
Capital of Uganda.
Kampar r. Indon. 58 C2
Kampar Malaysia 58 C1
Kamparkiri r. Indon. 58 C2
Kampen Neth. 36 B2
Kampene Dem. Rep. Congo 94 E5
Kamphaeng Phet Thai. 61 B4
Kampi Katoto Tanz. 97 B6
Kampinoski Park Narodowy nat. park Poland 37 J2
Kampli India 72 C3
Kampolombo, Lake Zambia 95 F7
Kâmpóng Cham Cambodia 61 D6
Kâmpóng Chhnăng Cambodia 61 D5
Kâmpóng Khleăng Cambodia 61 D5
Kâmpóng Saôm Cambodia see Sihanoukville
Kâmpóng Spœ Cambodia 61 D6
Kâmpóng Thum Cambodia 61 D5
Kâmpôt Cambodia 61 D6
Kampuchea country Asia see Cambodia
Kamrau, Teluk b. Indon. 57 H6
Kamsack Canada 134 G2
Kamsar Guinea 92 B3
Kamskoye Vodokhranilishche resr Rus. Fed. 28 K4
Kamsuuma Somalia 96 D4
Kamuli Uganda 96 B4
Kamungu Dem. Rep. Congo 95 E6
Kam"yanets'-Podil's'kyy Ukr. 29 C6
Kam"yanka-Buz'ka Ukr. 29 C6
Kam"yans'ke Ukr. 46 F2
Kāmyārān Iran 80 A3
Kamyshin Rus. Fed. 29 H6
Kamyshla Rus. Fed. 29 J5
Kamyzyak Rus. Fed. 29 I7
Kamzar Oman 80 D5
Kan r. Rus. Fed. 27 J4
Kan Sudan 96 A2
Kana, Bukit mt. Sarawak Malaysia 59 F2
Kanaaupscow r. Canada 125 E2
Kanab U.S.A. 137 F3
Kanab Creek r. U.S.A. 137 F3
Kanaga Island U.S.A. 120 E4
Kanaima Falls Guyana 147 F3
Kanairiktok r. Canada 125 J2
Kanakapura India 72 C3
Kanala Greece 47 D6
Kanallaki Greece 47 B5
Kanan Sweden 32 D2
Kananga Dem. Rep. Congo 95 D6
Kanangra-Boyd National Park Australia 112 D4
Kanarak India see Konarka
Kanarraville U.S.A. 137 F3
Kanash Rus. Fed. 28 H5
Kanawha r. U.S.A. 130 B4
Kanazawa Japan 65 D5
Kanbalu Myanmar 60 A3
Kanchanaburi Thai. 61 B5
Kanchanjanga mt. India/Nepal see Kangchenjunga
Kanchipuram India 72 C3
Kandahār Afgh. 81 F4
Kandahār prov. Afgh. 81 F4
Kandalaksha Rus. Fed. 32 I2
Kandalakshskiy Zaliv g. Rus. Fed. 28 E2
Kandang Indon. 58 B2
Kandangan Indon. 59 F3
Kandavu Passage Fiji see Kadavu Passage
Kandé Togo 93 F3
Kandhkot Pak. 81 G4
Kandi Benin 93 F3
Kandiaro Pak. 81 G5
Kandil Bouzou well Niger 93 H2
Kandıra Turkey 78 B2
Kandja Cent. Afr. Rep. 94 D3
Kandla India 74 A5
Kandos Australia 112 D4
Kandreho Madag. 99 [inset] J3
Kandri India 75 D5
Kandrian P.N.G. 106 D2
Kandukur India 72 C3
Kandy Sri Lanka 72 D5
Kandyagash Kazakh. 26 F5
Kane U.S.A. 130 D3
Kane Bassin b. Greenland see Kane Basin
Kane Basin b. Greenland 121 M2
Kaneh watercourse Iran 80 C5
Kanem pref. Chad 88 B6
Kaneohe U.S.A. 135 [inset] Z1
Kanevskaya Rus. Fed. 29 F7
Kang Botswana 98 D4
Kanga r. Bangl. 75 F5
Kangaarsussuaq c. Greenland 121 L2
Kangaba Mali 92 C3
Kangal Turkey 78 D3
Kangalassy Rus. Fed. 27 M3
Kangān Būshehr Iran 80 C5
Kangān Hormozgan Iran 80 D5
Kangandala, Parque Nacional de nat. park Angola see Cangandala, Parque Nacional de
Kangar Malaysia 58 C1
Kangaroo Island Australia 112 A4
Kangaroo Point Australia 111 D3
Kangasala Fin. 33 G3
Kangaslampi Fin. 32 H3
Kangasniemi Fin. 33 G3
Kangāvar Iran 80 A3
Kangayam India 72 C4
▶Kangchenjunga mt. India/Nepal 75 F4
3rd highest mountain in the world and in Asia.
asia 50–51
world 6–7
Kangding China 66 B2
Kangean, Kepulauan is Indon. 59 F4
Kangen r. Sudan 96 B3
Kangerluarsoruseq Greenland 121 N3
Kangerlussuaq Greenland 121 N3
Kangerlussuaq inlet Greenland 121 N2
Kangerlussuaq inlet Greenland 121 N3
Kangersuatsiaq Greenland 121 N2
Kangertittivaq sea chan. Greenland 121 Q2
Kangetet Kenya 96 C4
Kanggye N. Korea 65 A4
Kangikajik c. Greenland 121 Q2
Kangiqsualujjuaq Canada 125 H1
Kangiqsujuaq Canada 121 L3
Kangirsuk Canada 121 L3
Kang Krung National Park Thai. 61 B6
Kangle China see Wanzai
Kanglong China 66 A1
Kangmar China 70 G6
Kangnŭng S. Korea 65 B5
Kango Gabon 94 A4
Kangra India 74 C2
Kangri Karpo Pass China/India 66 A2
Kangrinboqê Feng mt. China 75 D3
Kangsangdobdê China see Xainza
Kangto mt. China/India 75 G4
Kangtog China 75 F2
Kangxian China 66 C1
Kangxiwar China 74 C1
Kangyidaung Myanmar 60 A4
Kanhan r. India 74 C5
Kanhar r. India 75 D4
Kanhargaon India 72 C2
Kani Côte d'Ivoire 92 D3
Kani Myanmar 60 A3
Kaniama Dem. Rep. Congo 95 E6
Kanibadam Tajik. 81 G1
Kanibongan Sabah Malaysia 59 G1
Kanifing Gambia 92 A2
Kanigiri India 72 C3
Kanimekh Uzbek. 81 F1
Kanin, Poluostrov pen. Rus. Fed. 28 H2
Kanin Nos Rus. Fed. 28 G1
Kanin Nos, Mys c. Rus. Fed. 28 G1
Kaniva Australia 112 B5
Kanjiroba mt. Nepal 75 D3
Kanjiža Yugo. 46 B1
Kankaanpää Fin. 33 F3
Kankakee U.S.A. 132 E3
Kankakee r. U.S.A. 132 D3
Kankan Guinea 92 C3
Kanker India 72 D1
Kankesanturai Sri Lanka 72 D4
Kankiya Nigeria 93 G2
Kankossa Mauritania 92 C2
Kanmaw Kyun i. Myanmar 61 B6
Kannauj India 74 C4
Kanniyakumari India 72 C4
Kanniya Kumari c. India see Comorin, Cape
Kannod India 74 C5
Kannonkoski Fin. 32 G3
Kannur India see Cannanore
Kannus Fin. 32 F3
Kano Nigeria 93 H2
Kano r. Nigeria 93 H3
Kano state Nigeria 93 H3
Kanona Zambia 97 A8
Kanonpunt pt S. Africa 98 D7
Kanor India 74 B4
Kanosh U.S.A. 137 F2
Kanovlei Namibia 98 C3
Kanowit Sarawak Malaysia 59 F2
Kanoya Japan 65 B7
Kanpur India 74 D4
Kanpur Pak. 81 G4
Kansai airport Japan 65 C6
Kansanshi Zambia 95 E8
Kansas r. U.S.A. 132 C4
Kansas state U.S.A. 132 B4
Kansas City KS U.S.A. 132 C4
Kansas City MO U.S.A. 132 C4
Kansenia Dem. Rep. Congo 95 E7
Kansk Rus. Fed. 27 J4
Kansu prov. China see Gansu
Kanta mt. Eth. 96 B3
Kantala Fin. 33 G3
Kantang Thai. 61 B7
Kantara hill Cyprus 77 A2
Kantaralak Thai. 61 D5
Kantavu i. Fiji see Kadavu
Kantchari Burkina 93 F2
Kantemirovka Rus. Fed. 29 F6
Kanth India 74 C3
Kanti India 75 E4
Kantilo India 73 E1
Kantishna r. U.S.A. 120 D3
Kanton i. Kiribati 164 G6
Kanturk Rep. of Ireland 35 B5
Kanuku Mountains Guyana 147 G4
Kanur India 72 C3
Kanuwe r. P.N.G. 57 J7
Kanyakubja India see Kannauj
KaNyamazane S. Africa 99 F5
Kanye Botswana 98 E5
Kanyemba Zimbabwe 99 F2
Kao Niger 93 G2
Kao i. Tonga 107 H3
Kaohsiung Taiwan 67 G4
Kaôh Tang i. Cambodia 61 C6
Kaokoveld plat. Namibia 98 B3
Kaolack Senegal 92 A2
Kaoma Zambia 95 E8
Kaouadja Cent. Afr. Rep. 94 D3
Kapaa U.S.A. 135 [inset] Y1
Kapaau U.S.A. 135 [inset] Z1
Kapa Moračka mt. Yugo. 46 A3
Kapan Armenia 79 F3
Kapanga Dem. Rep. Congo 95 D7
Kapatu Zambia 97 A7
Kapchagay Kazakh. 70 E3
Kapchagayskoye Vodokhranilishche resr Kazakh. 70 E3
Kapchorwa Uganda 96 B4
Kap Dan Greenland see Kulusuk
Kapellen Belgium 36 B3
Kapellskär Sweden 33 E4
Kapelskär Sweden see Kapellskär
Kapfenberg Austria 37 G5
Kapıdağı Yarımadası pen. Turkey 46 E4
Kapili r. India 75 F4
Kapingamarangi atoll Micronesia 164 E5
Kapingamarangi Rise sea feature N. Pacific Ocean 164 E5
Kapıorman Dağları mts Turkey 78 B2
Kapiri Mposhi Zambia 95 F8
Kāpīsā prov. Afgh. 81 G3
Kapisillit Greenland 121 N3
Kapiskau r. Canada 124 D2
Kapit Sarawak Malaysia 59 F2
Kapiti Island N.Z. 113 C3
Kapiting Brazil 147 H4
Kapka well Chad 88 D5
Kapka, Massif du mts Chad 88 D6
Kaplankyr, Chink hills Turkm./Uzbek. 80 C1
Kaplice Czech Rep. 37 G4
Kapoe Thai. 61 B6
Kapoeta Sudan 96 B3
Kapos r. Hungary 44 G1
Kaposvár Hungary 44 F1
Kappar Pak. 81 E5
Kappeln Germany 36 D1
Kapran India 74 C4
Kapsabet Kenya 96 B4
Kap Salt Swamp Pak. 81 E5
Kapsan N. Korea 65 B4
Kapsukas Lith. see Marijampolė
Kaptai Bangl. 75 G5
Kapuas r. Indon. 59 E3
Kapuas r. Indon. 59 F3
Kapuas Hulu, Pegunungan mts Indon./Malaysia 59 F2
Kapuriya India 74 B4
Kapurthala India 74 B3
Kapuskasing Canada 124 D3
Kapustin Yar Rus. Fed. 29 H6
Kaputa Zambia 95 F7
Kaputar mt. Australia 112 D3
Kaputir Kenya 96 B4
Kapuvár Hungary 37 H5
Ka Qu r. China 75 G3
Kara r. Rus. Fed. 28 M1
Kara Togo 93 F3
Kara r. Turkey 79 E3
Kara Ada i. Turkey 47 E5
Karaali Turkey 78 C3
Kara Art Pass China 81 H2
Kara-Balta Kyrg. 62 A3
Karabalyk Kazakh. 26 G4
Karabekaul Turkm. see Garabekevyul
Karabiga Turkey 78 A2
Karabil', Vozvyshennost' hills Turkm. 81 E2
Kara-Bogaz-Gol Turkm. see Karabogazkel'
Kara-Bogaz-Gol, Proliv sea chan. Turkm. 79 H2
Kara-Bogaz-Gol, Zaliv b. Turkm. 80 C1
Karabogazkel' Turkm. 79 H2
Karabük Turkey 78 C2
Karaburun Turkey 78 A3
Karabutak Kazakh. 26 G5
Karacabey Turkey 78 B2
Karacadağ mts Turkey 78 C3
Karacaköy Turkey 78 B2
Karacalı Dağ mt. Turkey 79 D3
Karaçal Tepe mt. Turkey 77 A1
Karacasu Turkey 47 F6
Karachayevsk Rus. Fed. 29 G8
Karachev Rus. Fed. 29 E5
▶Karachi Pak. 81 F5
world 16–17
Karaçoban Turkey 79 E3
Karacurun Turkey see Hilvan
Karad India 72 B2
Kara Dağ hill Turkey 47 E4
Kara Dağ mt. Turkey 78 C3
Kara-Dar'ya Uzbek. see Payshanba
Kara Deniz sea Asia/Europe see Black Sea
Karaganda Kazakh. 70 D2
Karagay Rus. Fed. 28 J4
Karagayly Kazakh. 70 E2
Karagez Turkm. 80 C2
Karaginskiy, Ostrov i. Rus. Fed. 27 Q4
Karagiye, Vpadina depr. Kazakh. 79 G2
Karagwe Tanz. 96 A5
Karahalil Turkey 46 E4
Karahasanlı Turkey 78 C3
Karahisar Turkey 47 F6
Karaidel' Rus. Fed. 28 K5
Karaikal India 72 C4
Karaikkudi India 72 C4
Karaj Iran 80 B3
Karak Jordan see Al Karak
Kara-Kala Turkm. see Garrygala
Karakalli Turkey see Özalp
Karakax He r. China 74 D1
Karakax Shan mts China 74 D2
Karakeçi Turkey 79 D3
Karakeçili Turkey 78 C3
Karakelong i. Indon. 57 G5
Karaki China 75 D1
Karaklis Armenia see Vanadzor
Karakoçan Turkey 79 E3
Karakol' Kazakh. 29 J6
Kara-Köl Kyrg. 70 D3
Karakol Kyrg. 62 B3
Karaköprü Turkey see Karaçoban
Karakoram mts Asia 62 B4
Karakoram Pass China/Jammu and Kashmir 70 E4
Karakoram Range mts Asia 69 F3
Kara K'orē Eth. 96 C2
Karakoro r. Mali/Mauritania 92 B2
Karaköse Turkey see Ağrı
Kara Kul' Kyrg. see Kara-Köl
Karakul' Bukharskaya Oblast' Uzbek. 81 E2
Karakul' Bukharskaya Oblast' Uzbek. 81 E2
Karakul', Ozero l. Tajik. see Qarokŭl
Karakulino Rus. Fed. 28 J4
Karakum, Peski des. Kazakh. see Karakum Desert
Karakum Desert Kazakh. 26 F5
Karakum Desert Turkm. 81 E2
Karakumskiy Kanal canal Turkm. 81 E2
Karakurt Turkey 79 E2
Karala Estonia 33 F4
Karalı Turkey 77 C1
Karalundi Australia 109 B6
Karaman Turkey 78 C3
Karaman prov. Turkey 77 A1
Karamanlı Turkey 78 B3
Karamay China 70 F2
Karambar Pass Afgh./Pak. 81 H2
Karamea N.Z. 113 C3
Karamea Bight b. N.Z. 113 B3
Karamet-Niyaz Turkm. 81 F2
Karamian i. Indon. 59 F4
Karamiran China 75 E1
Karamiran Shankou pass China 75 E1
Karamürsel Turkey 46 F4
Karan r. Afgh. 81 G2
Karan state Myanmar see Kayin
Karān i. Saudi Arabia 80 B5
Karang Senegal 92 A2
Karangagung Indon. 58 D3
Karangan Indon. 58 D4
Karangasem Indon. 59 F5
Karangoua r. Congo 94 B4
Karanja India 72 C1
Karanja r. India 72 C2
Karanjia India 75 E5
Karanpura India 74 B3
Karaova Turkey 47 E6
Karapelit Bulg. 46 E3
Karapınar Turkey 78 C3
Karapürçek Turkey 47 F5
Karas admin. reg. Namibia 98 C5
Karaşar Turkey 78 B2
Karasay China 75 D1
Karasburg Namibia 98 C6
Kara Sea Rus. Fed. 26 H2
Karašica r. Croatia 44 G2
Karasica r. Hungary/Romania 44 G2
Kárášjohka Norway 32 G1
Kárášjohka r. Norway 32 G1
Karasjok Norway see Kárášjohka
Karasjokka r. Norway see Kárášjohka
Karasu r. Syria/Turkey 77 C1
Karasu Turkey see Hizan
Karasu Turkey 78 B2
Karasu r. Turkey 79 E3
Karasuk Rus. Fed. 26 H4
Karasulak r. Ukr. 46 F2
Karāt Iran 81 E3
Karataş Turkey 78 C3
Karataş Burnu hd Turkey see Fener Burnu
Karatau Kazakh. 70 D3
Karatau, Khrebet mts Kazakh. 70 C3
Karatayka Rus. Fed. 28 L1
Karathuri Myanmar 61 B6
Karativu i. Sri Lanka 72 C4
Karatj l. Sweden 32 E2
Karatobe Kazakh. 29 J6
Karaton Kazakh. 29 J7
Karaulbazar Uzbek. 81 F2
Karauli India 74 C4
Karaurgan Turkey 79 E2
Karavas Greece 47 C6
Karavastasë, Laguna e lag. Albania 46 A4
Karavi i. Greece 47 C6
Karawa Dem. Rep. Congo 94 D4
Karawang Indon. 59 D4
Karayılan Turkey 77 C1
Karbalā' Iraq 79 F4
Karbalā' governorate Iraq 79 E4
Karcag Hungary 37 J5
Kardam Bulg. 46 F3
Kardamaina Greece 47 E6
Kardeljevo Croatia see Ploče
Kardhaámaina Greece see Kardamaina
Kardhitsa Greece see Karditsa
Kardis Sweden 32 F2
Karditsa Greece 47 B5
Kärdla Estonia 28 B4
Kareeberge mts S. Africa 98 D6
Kareima Sudan 89 F5
Kareli India 74 C5
Karelia aut. rep. Rus. Fed. see Kareliya, Respublika
Kareliya, Respublika aut. rep. Rus. Fed. 32 I3
Karel'skaya A.S.S.R. aut. rep. Rus. Fed. see Kareliya, Respublika
Karel'skiy Bereg coastal area Rus. Fed. 28 E2
Karema Tanz. 97 A6
Karen state Myanmar see Kayin
Karera India 74 C4
Karesuando Sweden 32 F1
Kārevāndar Iran 81 E5
Kargala Rus. Fed. 29 J5
Kargalinskaya Rus. Fed. 79 F2
Kargalinski Rus. Fed. see Kargalinskaya
Kargapazarı Dağları mts Turkey 79 E3
Karghalik China see Yecheng
Kargı Turkey 78 C2
Kargil Jammu and Kashmir 74 C2
Kargilik China see Yecheng
Kargıpınarı Turkey 77 B1
Kargopol' Rus. Fed. 28 F3
Kargūshkī Iran 80 D5
Karhal India 74 C4
Kari Nigeria 93 H3
Kariān Iran 80 D5
Kariba Zimbabwe 99 F3
Kariba, Lake resr Zambia/Zimbabwe 95 E9
Kariba Dam Zambia/Zimbabwe 95 F9
Kariba-yama vol. Japan 64 D4
Karibib Namibia 98 B4
Kariega r. S. Africa 98 D7
Karigasniemi Fin. 32 G1
Karijini National Park Australia 108 B5
Karikari, Cape N.Z. 113 C1
Karīmābād Iran 80 C3
Karimata i. Indon. 59 E3
Karimata, Pulau-pulau is Indon. 59 E3
Karimata, Selat strait Indon. 59 E3
Karimganj India 75 G4
Karim Khanch Iran 80 B3
Karimnagar India 72 C2
Karimun Besar i. Indon. 58 C2
Karimunjawa i. Indon. 59 E4
Karimunjawa, Pulau-pulau is Indon. 59 E4
Karin Somalia 96 E2
Karinainen Fin. 33 F3
Käringsjön Sweden 33 D3
Karis Fin. 33 F3
Karisimbi, Mont vol. Rwanda 94 F5
Káristos Greece see Karystos
Karit Iran 80 D3
Kariyangwe Zimbabwe 99 E3
Karjaa Fin. see Karis
Karjan India 74 B5
Karjat India 72 B2
Karkai r. India 75 E5
Karkal India 72 B3
Karkamb India 72 B2
Karkaralinsk Kazakh. 70 E2
Karkar Island P.N.G. 57 K6
Karkas, Kūh-e mts Iran 80 B3
Karkh Pak. 81 F5
Karkheh, Rūdkhāneh-ye r. Iran 80 A4
Karkinits'ka Zatoka g. Ukr. 29 E7
Karkkila Fin. 33 G3
Kärkölä Fin. 33 G3
Karkonoski Park Narodowy nat. park Czech Rep./Poland see Krkonošský národní park
Karksi-Nuia Estonia 28 C4
Karkūmā, Ra's hd Saudi Arabia 89 H3
Karlino Poland 37 G1
Karlivka Ukr. 29 E6
Karl Marks, Qullai mt. Tajik. 81 H2
Karl-Marx-Stadt Germany see Chemnitz
Karlovac Croatia 44 E2
Karlovka Ukr. see Karlivka
Karlovo Bulg. 46 D3
Karlovy Vary Czech Rep. 37 F3
Karlsberg Sweden 33 D3
Karlsborg Sweden 33 D4
Karlsburg Romania see Alba Iulia
Karlshamn Sweden 33 D4
Karlskoga Sweden 33 D4
Karlskrona Sweden 33 D4
Karlsruhe Germany 36 D4
Karlstad Sweden 33 D4
Karlstadt Germany 36 D4
Karma Niger 93 F2
Karma, Ouadi watercourse Chad 88 C6
Karmala India 72 B2
Karmas Sweden 32 E2
Karmona Spain see Córdoba
Karnabchul', Step' plain Uzbek. 81 F2
Karnafuli Reservoir Bangl. 75 G5
Karnal India 74 C3
Karnali r. Nepal 75 D3
Karnaprayag India 74 C3
Karnataka state India 72 B3
Karnes City U.S.A. 133 B6
Karnobat Bulg. 46 E3
Karodi Pak. 81 F5
Karoi Zimbabwe 99 F3
Karokpi Myanmar 61 B5
Karo La pass China 75 F3
Karong India 75 G4
Karonga Malawi 97 B7
Karonie Australia 109 C7
Karoo National Park S. Africa 98 D7
Karoonda Australia 112 A4
Karor Pak. 81 G4
Karora Eritrea 89 H5
Karossa, Tanjung pt Indon. 108 B2
Karouassa well Mali 93 E1
Karpasia pen. Cyprus 77 B2
Karpas Peninsula Cyprus see Karpasia
Karpathos Greece 47 E7
Karpathos i. Greece 47 E7
Karpathou, Steno sea chan. Greece 47 E6
Karpaty mts Europe see Carpathian Mountains
Karpenisi Greece 47 B5
Karpilovka Belarus see Aktsyabrski
Karpinsk Rus. Fed. 26 G4
Karpogory Rus. Fed. 28 H2
Karratha Australia 108 B5
Karrī Iran 80 B4
Karroo plat. S. Africa see Great Karoo
Karrukh Afgh. 81 E3
Karrychirla Turkm. see imeni Kerbabayeva
Kars Turkey 79 E2
Kärsämäki Fin. 32 G3
Kārsava Latvia 33 G4
Karshi Turkm. 80 C1
Karshi Uzbek. 81 F2
Karshinskaya Step' plain Uzbek. 81 F2
Karşıyaka Balıkesir Turkey 46 F4
Karşıyaka İzmir Turkey 47 E5
Karsiyang India 75 F4
Karskoye More sea Rus. Fed. see Kara Sea
Karstädt Germany 36 E2
Karsun Rus. Fed. 29 H5
Kartal Turkey 78 B2
Kartala vol. Comoros 97 D7
Kartaly Rus. Fed. 26 G4
Karthaus U.S.A. 130 D3
Kartsino, Akra pt Greece 47 D5
Karttula Fin. 32 G3
Kartuzy Poland 37 I1
Karubwe Zambia 95 F8
Karumba Australia 111 E3
Karun, Kūh-e hill Iran 80 B4
Kārūn, Rūd-e r. Iran 80 B4
Karungi Sweden 32 F2
Karungu Kenya 96 B5
Karuni Indon. 108 B2
Karunjie Australia 108 D4
Karup Denmark 33 C4
Karur India 72 C4
Karvetnagar India 72 C3
Karvia Fin. 33 F3
Karviná Czech Rep. 37 I4
Karwar India 72 B3
Karwi India 74 D4
Karyagino Azer. see Füzuli
Karyes Greece 47 D4
Karymskoye Rus. Fed. 27 L4
Karynzharyk, Peski des. Kazakh. 79 H2
Karystos Greece 47 D5
Kaş Turkey 78 B3
Kasa India 72 B2
Kasaba Turkey see Turgutlu
Kasaba Lodge Zambia 97 A7
Kasabonika Canada 124 B2
Kasai r. Dem. Rep. Congo 94 C5
Kasaï r. Dem. Rep. Congo 95 D6
Kasaï, Plateau du Dem. Rep. Congo 95 D6
Kasaï Occidental prov. Dem. Rep. Congo 95 D6
Kasai Oriental prov. Dem. Rep. Congo 95 E6
Kasaji Dem. Rep. Congo 95 D7
Kasama Zambia 97 A7
Kasan Uzbek. 81 F2
Kasane Botswana 98 E3
Kasanga Tanz. 97 A7
Kasangulu Dem. Rep. Congo 95 B6
Kasanka National Park Zambia 95 F8
Kasanza Dem. Rep. Congo 95 C6
Kasar, Ras pt Sudan 89 H5
Kasaragod India 72 B3
Kasatkino Rus. Fed. 64 B2
Kasba Lake Canada 123 K2
Kasba Tadla Morocco 90 D2
Kasbi Uzbek. 81 F2
Kasempa Zambia 95 E8
Kasenga Katanga Dem. Rep. Congo 95 D7
Kasenga Katanga Dem. Rep. Congo 95 F7
Kasenye Dem. Rep. Congo 96 A4
Kasese Dem. Rep. Congo 94 E5
Kasese Uganda 96 A4
Kasevo Rus. Fed. see Neftekamsk
Kasganj India 74 C4
Kasha China see Gonjo
Kasha waterhole Kenya 96 D5
Kashabowie Canada 124 B3
Kāshān Iran 80 B3
Kashechewan Canada 124 D2
Kashgar China see Kashi
Kashi China 70 E4
Kashihara Japan 65 C6
Kashima-nada b. Japan 65 E5
Kashin Rus. Fed. 28 F4
Kashiobwe Dem. Rep. Congo 95 F7
Kashipur India 74 C3
Kashiwazaki Japan 65 D5
Kashkadar'inskaya Oblast' admin. div. Uzbek. 81 F2
Kashkadar'ya r. Uzbek. 81 F2
Kashkadarya Oblast admin. div. Uzbek. see Kashkadar'inskaya Oblast'
Kāshmar Iran 80 D3
Kashmir terr. Asia see Jammu and Kashmir
Kashmir, Vale of valley India 74 B2
Kashmor Pak. 81 G4
Kashmund reg. Afgh. 81 G3
Kashyukulu Dem. Rep. Congo 95 E6
Kasi India see Varanasi
Kasia India 75 D4
Kasimov Rus. Fed. 29 G5
Kasingi Dem. Rep. Congo 94 F4
Kaskaskia r. U.S.A. 128 A4
Kaskattama r. Canada 123 N3
Kaskinen Fin. 33 F3
Kas Klong i. Cambodia see Kŏng, Kaôh
Kaskö Fin. see Kaskinen
Kaslo Canada 123 G5
Kasmere Lake Canada 123 K3
Kasomeno Dem. Rep. Congo 95 F7
Kasongan Indon. 59 F3
Kasongo Dem. Rep. Congo 95 E6
Kasongo-Lunda Dem. Rep. Congo 95 C6
Kasonguele Dem. Rep. Congo 95 E6
Kasos i. Greece 47 E7
Kasou, Steno sea chan. Greece 47 E7
Kaspi Georgia 79 F2
Kaspiy Mangy Oypaty lowland Kazakh./Rus. Fed. see Caspian Lowland
Kaspiysk Rus. Fed. 79 F2
Kaspiyskiy Rus. Fed. see Lagan'
Kaspiyskoye More sea Asia/Europe see Caspian Sea
Kasrawad India 74 B5
Kasrik Turkey see Gürpınar
Kassa Slovakia see Košice
Kassaare laht b. Estonia 33 F4
Kassala Sudan 89 H6
Kassala state Sudan 89 G6
Kassandra pen. Greece 47 C4
Kassandras, Akra pt Greece 47 C5
Kassandras, Kolpos b. Greece 47 C4
Kassandreia Greece 47 C4
Kassel Germany 36 D3
Kasserine Tunisia 91 H2
Kassinga Angola see Cassinga
Kassouloua well Niger 93 H2
Kastamonu Turkey 78 C2
Kastelli Kriti Greece 47 C7
Kastelli Kriti Greece 47 D7
Kastéllion Greece see Kastelli
Kastellorizon i. Greece see Megisti
Kastoria Greece 46 B4
Kastorias, Limni l. Greece 46 B4
Kastornoye Rus. Fed. 29 F6
Kastos i. Greece 47 B5
Kastrakiou, Techniti Limni resr Greece 47 B5
Kastrova Belarus 33 H4
Kastsyukovichy Belarus 29 E5
Kasugai Japan 65 D6
Kasuku Dem. Rep. Congo 94 E5
Kasulu Tanz. 97 A6
Kasumkent Rus. Fed. 79 G2
Kasungu Malawi 97 B8
Kasungu National Park Malawi 97 B8
Kasur Pak. 74 B3
Kataba Zambia 95 E9
Katagum Nigeria 93 H2
Katahdin, Mount U.S.A. 128 F2
Kataklik Jammu and Kashmir 74 C2
Katako-Kombe Dem. Rep. Congo 94 E5
Katakolo, Akra pt Greece 47 B6
Katakwi Uganda 96 B4
Katanda Dem. Rep. Congo 95 D6
Katanga prov. Dem. Rep. Congo 95 E7
Katangi Madhya Pradesh India 74 C5
Katangi Madhya Pradesh India 74 C5
Katangli Rus. Fed. 64 E2
Katanning Australia 109 B8
Kata Pusht Iran 80 B2
Katastari Greece 47 B6
Katavi National Park Tanz. 97 A6
Katawaz Afgh. 81 G3
Katchall i. India 73 G5
Katchamba Togo 93 F3
Katea Dem. Rep. Congo 95 E6
Katerini Greece 47 C4
Katesh Tanz. 97 B6
Kate's Needle mt. Canada/U.S.A. 120 F4
Katete Zambia 97 B8
Katghora India 75 D5
Katha Myanmar 60 B2
Katherine Australia 110 C2
Katherine r. Australia 110 B2
Katherine Gorge National Park Australia see Nitmiluk National Park
Kathi India 74 B5
Kathiawar pen. India 74 A5
Kathīb, Ra's al pt Yemen 89 I6
Kathleen Falls Australia 110 B2
Kathlehong S. Africa 99 F5
▶Kathmandu Nepal 75 E4
Capital of Nepal.
Kathua Jammu and Kashmir 74 B2
Kathua watercourse Kenya 96 C5
Kati Mali 92 C2
Katibas r. Sarawak Malaysia 59 F2
Kati-ér r. Hungary 37 J5
Katihar India 75 E4
Katima Mulilo Namibia 98 E3
Katimik Lake Canada 123 L4
Katiola Côte d'Ivoire 92 D3
Kā Tiritiri o te Moana mts N.Z. see Southern Alps
Katlabukh, Ozero l. Ukr. 46 F2
Katmai National Park and Preserve U.S.A. 120 D4
Katmandu Nepal see Kathmandu
Kato Achaïa Greece 47 B5
Katochi Greece 47 B5
Kato Figaleia Greece 47 B6
Katol India 74 C5
Kåtölandet i. Fin. 32 F3
Katombe Dem. Rep. Congo 95 D6
Katompi Dem. Rep. Congo 95 E6
Katondwe Zambia 95 F8
Kato Nevrokopi Greece 46 C4
Katong Sing. 58 [inset]
Katonga r. Uganda 96 A4
Katoomba Australia 112 D4
Katosan India 74 B5
Kato Tithorea Greece 47 C5
Kåtotjåkka mt. Sweden see Godučohkka
Katowice Poland 37 I3
Katoya India 75 F5
Kātrīnā, Jabal mt. Egypt 89 G2
Katrineholm Sweden 33 E4
Katsepy Madag. 99 [inset] J2

Katsina Nigeria 93 G2
Katsina *state* Nigeria 93 G3
Katsina-Ala Nigeria 93 H4
Kattaqurghon Uzbek. 81 F2
Kattamudda Well Australia 108 D5
Kattaqürghon Uzbek. *see* Kattaqurgan
Kattasang Hills Afgh. 81 F3
Kattavia Greece 47 E7
Kattegat *strait* Denmark/Sweden 33 C4
Kattisavan Sweden 32 J3
Kattowitz Poland *see* Katowice
Katumba Dem. Rep. Congo 95 E6
Katumbi Malawi 97 B7
Katwa India *see* Katoya
Katyk Ukr. *see* Shakhtars'k
Katy Wrocławskie Poland 37 H3
Katyur Turkm. 80 D2
Kauai *i.* U.S.A. 135 [inset] Y1
Kauai Channel U.S.A. 135 [inset] Y1
Kaudom Game Park *nature res.* Namibia 98 D3
Kaufbeuren Germany 36 E5
Kauhajoki Fin. 33 F3
Kauhanevan-Pohjankankaan kansallispuisto *nat. park* Fin. 33 F3
Kauhava Fin. 32 F3
Kaukauna U.S.A. 132 D2
Kaukkwè Hills Myanmar 60 B2
Kaukonen Fin. 32 G2
Kauksi Estonia 33 G4
Kaulinranta Fin. 32 F2
Kaunas Lith. 33 F5
Kaundy, Vpadina *depr.* Kazakh. 79 H2
Kaunia Bangl. 75 F4
Kaura-Namoda Nigeria 93 G2
Kau Sai Chau *i.* Hong Kong China 67 [inset]
Kaushany Moldova *see* Căuşeni
Kaustinen Fin. 32 F3
Kautokeino Norway 32 F1
Kau-ye Kyun *i.* Myanmar 61 B6
Kavadarci Macedonia 46 C4
Kavajë Albania 46 A4
Kavak *Çanakkale* Turkey 46 E4
Kavak Turkey 78 D2
Kavak Dağı *hill* Turkey 47 E5
Kavaklıdere *Manisa* Turkey 47 F5
Kavaklıdere *Muğla* Turkey 47 F6
Kavala Greece 46 D4
Kavalas, Kolpos *b.* Greece 46 D4
Kavali India 72 B4
Kavār Iran 80 C4
Kavaratti India 72 B4
Kavaratti *i.* India 72 B4
Kavarna Bulg. 46 F3
Kavendou, Mont *mt.* Guinea 92 B3
Kaveri *r.* Indon. 59 D3
Kaveripatnam India 72 C3
Kavi India 74 B5
Kavieng P.N.G. 107 F2
Kavir Iran 80 D3
Kavir, Dasht-e *des.* Iran 80 D3
Kavir-i-Namak *salt flat* Iran 80 D3
Kavir Küshk *well* Iran 80 D3
Kavirondo Gulf Kenya *see* Winam Gulf
Kaw Fr. Guiana 147 H3
Kawagoe Japan 65 D6
Kawaihae U.S.A. 135 [inset] Z1
Kawakawa N.Z. 113 C1
Kawambwa Zambia 95 F7
Kawana Zambia 95 E8
Kawardha India 74 D5
Kawartha Lakes Canada 130 D1
Kawasa Dem. Rep. Congo 95 F7
Kawasaki Japan 65 D6
Kawawachikamach Canada 125 H2
Kaweah, Lake U.S.A. 136 C3
Kaweau N.Z. 113 D2
Kawhia N.Z. 113 C2
Kawhia Harbour N.Z. 113 C2
Kawich Peak U.S.A. 137 D3
Kawich Range *mts* U.S.A. 137 D3
Kawkareik Myanmar 61 B4
Kawlin Myanmar 60 A2
Kawludo Myanmar 60 B4
Kawmapyin Myanmar 61 B5
Kawm Umbū Egypt 89 D5
Kawngmeum Myanmar 60 B3
Kawthaung Myanmar 61 B6
Kawthoolei *state* Myanmar *see* Kayin
Kawthule *state* Myanmar *see* Kayin
Kaxgar China *see* Kashi
Kaxgar He *r.* China 70 E4
Kaxtax Shan *mts* China 75 D1
Kaya Burkina 93 E3
Kayacı Dağı *hill* Turkey 47 E5
Kayadibi Turkey 78 D3
Kayambi Myanmar 60 B4
Kayambi Zambia 97 A7
Kayan *r.* Indon. 59 E3
Kayan *r.* Indon. 59 E2
Kayanaza Burundi 94 F5
Kayangel Atoll Palau 57 H4
Kayankulam India 72 C4
Kaydanovo Belarus *see* Dzyarzhynsk
Kayenta U.S.A. 137 H3
Kayes Mali 92 C2
Kayin *state* Myanmar 60 B4
Kaynar Kazakh. 70 E2
Kaynar Turkey 78 D3
Kaynarlı *r.* Turkey 46 E4
Kayoa *i.* Indon. 59 C3
Kayrakkum Tajik. *see* Qayroqqum
Kayrakkumskoye Vodokhranilishche *resr* Tajik. *see* Obanqori Qayroqqum
Kayseri Turkey 78 C3
Kaysersberg France 39 G2
Kayuagung Indon. 58 D3
Kayuyu Dem. Rep. Congo 94 E5
Kayyerkan Rus. Fed. 27 J3
Kazach'ye Rus. Fed. 27 N2
Kazakh Azer. *see* Qazax
Kazakhskaya S.S.R. *country* Asia *see* Kazakhstan
Kazakhskiy Melkosopochnik *plain* Kazakh. 70 D2
Kazakstan *country* Asia *see* Kazakhstan

► Kazakhstan *country* Asia 26 F5
4th largest country in Asia and 9th in the world.
asia 52–53, 82
world 8–9

Kazakhstan Kazakh. *see* Aksay
Kazan *r.* Canada 123 M2
Kazan' Rus. Fed. 28 I5
Kazandzhik Turkm. *see* Gazandzhyk
Kazanje, Mal *mt.* Albania 47 B3
Kazanka *r.* Rus. Fed. 28 I5
Kazanlı Turkey 77 B1
Kazatin Ukr. *see* Kozyatyn

Kazhim Rus. Fed. 28 I3
Kazhmak *r.* Pak. 81 E5
Kazikbeli Geçidi *pass* Turkey 47 F6
Kazi Magomed Azer. *see* Qazımämmäd
Kazimierza Wielka Poland 37 J3
Kazimierz Dolne Poland 37 J3
Kazincbarcika Hungary 37 J4
Kaziranga National Park India 75 G4
Kazlowshchyna Belarus 33 H5
Kaztalovka Kazakh. 29 I6
Kazuma Pan National Park Zimbabwe 98 E3
Kazumba Dem. Rep. Congo 95 D6
Kazungula Zambia 95 E9
Kazuno Japan 65 E4
Kazym *r.* Rus. Fed. 26 G3
Kazymskiy Mys Rus. Fed. 26 G3
Kea Greece 47 D6
Kea *i.* Greece 47 D6
Keaau U.S.A. 135 [inset] Z2
Keahole Point U.S.A. 135 [inset] Z2
Kealia U.S.A. 135 [inset] Y1
Keams Canyon U.S.A. 137 G4
Kéamu *i.* Vanuatu *see* Anatom
Kearney U.S.A. 132 D3
Kearneysville U.S.A. 130 E4
Kearny U.S.A. 137 G5
Keas, Steno *sea chan.* Greece 47 D6
Keban Turkey 79 D3
Keban Baraji *resr* Turkey 79 D3
Kebatu *i.* Indon. 59 J3
Kebbi *state* Nigeria 93 F2
Kébémèr Senegal 92 A2
Kébi *r.* Cameroon 93 I3
Kébi Côte d'Ivoire 92 C3
Kebili Tunisia 91 H2
Kebir, Nahr al *r.* Lebanon/Syria 77 B2
Kebkabiya Sudan 88 E6
K'ebrī Dehar Eth. 96 E3
Kebnekaise *mt.* Sweden 32 E2
Kebumen Indon. 59 E4
Kecel Hungary 37 I5 (?)
K'ech'a Terara *mt.* Eth. 96 C3
Kechika *r.* Canada 122 E3
Keçiborlu Turkey 78 B3
Kecskemét Hungary 37 I5
Kedah *state* Malaysia 58 C1
Kédainiai Lith. 33 F5
Kedarli Passage Fiji *see* Kadavu Passage
Kédédéssé Chad 94 C2
Kedian China 67 D2
Kediri Indon. 59 F4
Kedougou Senegal 92 B2
Kedva *r.* Rus. Fed. 28 J2
Keele *r.* Canada 122 E1
Keele Peak Canada 122 D2
Keeley Lake Canada 123 I4
Keeling Islands *terr.* Indian Ocean *see* Cocos Islands
Keelung Taiwan *see* Chilung
Keenapusan *i.* Phil. 59 G1
Keene *CA* U.S.A. 136 C3
Keene *NH* U.S.A. 131 G2
Keep *r.* Australia 110 E3
Keep River National Park Australia 110 E2
Keer-weer, Cape Australia 111 E2
Keetmanshoop Namibia 98 C5
Keewatin Canada 123 M5
Keewatin U.S.A. 132 C2
Kefallinia *i.* Greece *see* Cephalonia
Kefallonia *i.* Greece *see* Cephalonia
Kefalos Greece 47 E6
Kefamenanu Indon. 57 F7
Kefe Ukr. *see* Feodosiya
Keffi Nigeria 93 G3
Keflavik Iceland 32 [inset]
Kegalla Sri Lanka 72 D5
Kegen Kazakh. 70 E3
Keg River Canada 123 G3
Kegul'ta Rus. Fed. 29 H7
Keheili Sudan 89 G5
Kehl Germany 36 C4
Kehoula *well* Mauritania 92 C1
Kehra Estonia 28 C4
Kehsi Mansam Myanmar 60 B3
Keighley U.K. 35 F5
Keila Estonia 28 C4
Keilak Sudan 94 F2
Keili Sudan 96 B2
Keimoes S. Africa 98 D6
Keïta Niger 93 G2
Keïta, Bahr *r.* Chad 94 C2
Keitele Fin. 32 H3
Keitele *l.* Fin. 32 G3
Keith Australia 111 B5
Keith U.K. 34 E3
Keith Arm *b.* Canada 122 F1
Kejimkujik National Park Canada 125 H4
Kekaha U.S.A. 135 [inset] Y1
Kek-Art Kyrg. *see* Alaykuu
Kékes *mt.* Hungary 37 J5
Kekra Rus. Fed. 27 O4
Kekri India 74 B4
K'elafo Eth. 96 E3
Kelai *atoll* Maldives 72 B5
Kelang Malaysia 58 C1
Kelantan *r.* Malaysia 58 C1
Kelantan *state* Malaysia 58 C1
Kelardasht Iran 80 B2
Kelawar *i.* Indon. 59 E3
Kelberg Germany 36 C4
Keles Uganda 96 B4
Keles *r.* Kazakh. 70 C3
Kelheim Germany 36 E4
Kelibia Tunisia 45 D6
Kelif Turkm. 81 F2
Kelifskiy Uzboy *marsh* Turkm. 81 E2
Keli Mutu *vol.* Indon. 108 C2
Kelkheim (Taunus) Germany 36 C4
Kelkit Turkey 79 D2
Kelkit *r.* Turkey 79 D2
Kéllé Congo 94 B5
Kellerberrin Australia 109 B7
Keller Lake Canada 122 F2
Kellett, Cape Canada 120 G2
Kelliher Canada 123 K5
Kells Rep. of Ireland 35 C5
Kelly Lake Canada 122 F2
Kelly Range *hills* Australia 109 C6
Kelmė Lith. 33 F5
Kelo Chad 94 B2
Kelowna Canada 134 C2
Kelp Head Canada 122 E5
Kelso U.K. 34 F5
Kelso *CA* U.S.A. 137 E4
Kelso *WA* U.S.A. 134 C3
Keluang Malaysia 58 C2
Kelujärvi Fin. 32 G2
Kelvington Canada 123 K4
Kem' *r.* Rus. Fed. 28 E2
Kem' Rus. Fed. 28 E2
Ke Macina Mali *see* Massina
Kemah Turkey 79 D3
Kemal Turkey 46 E4
Kemalpaşa Turkey 47 E5
Kemano Canada 122 E4
Kembolcha Eth. 96 D2
Kemeneshát *hills* Hungary 37 H5
Kemer Turkey 78 B3
Kemer Turkey 47 F5
Kemer Baraji *resr* Turkey 78 B3

Kemerovo Rus. Fed. 27 I4
Kemerovo Oblast *admin. div.* Rus. Fed. *see* Kemerovskaya Oblast'
Kemerovskaya Oblast' *admin. div.* Rus. Fed. 62 D1
Kemi Fin. 32 G2
Kemihaara Fin. 32 H2
Kemijärvi Fin. 32 G2
Kemijärvi *l.* Fin. 32 G2
Kemijoki *r.* Fin. 32 G2
Keminmaa Fin. 32 G2
Kemiö Fin. *see* Kimito
Kemi Turkm. 80 C2
Kemmerer U.S.A. 134 E4
Kemmuna *i.* Malta 45 E6
Kémo *pref.* Cent. Afr. Rep. 94 C3
Kemp, Lake U.S.A. 133 D5
Kempazh *r.* Rus. Fed. 28 L2
Kempele Fin. 32 G2
Kempendyay Rus. Fed. 27 L3
Kempisch Kanaal *canal* Belgium 36 B3
Kemp Land *reg.* Antarctica 167 D2
Kemp Peninsula Antarctica 167 A2
Kempsey Australia 112 E3
Kempt, Lac *l.* Canada 125 H2
Kempten (Allgäu) Germany 36 E5
Kemujan *i.* Indon. 59 E4
Ken *r.* India 74 D4
Kenai U.S.A. 120 D3
Kenai Fiords National Park U.S.A. 120 D4
Kenai Mountains U.S.A. 120 D4
Kenamuke Swamp Sudan 96 B3
Kenansville U.S.A. 128 D5
Kenbridge U.S.A. 130 D5
Kendal Indon. 59 E4
Kendal U.K. 35 E4
Kendall U.S.A. 129 C7
Kendall, Cape Canada 123 O2
Kendari Indon. 57 F6
Kendawangan Indon. 59 E3
Kendawangan *r.* Indon. 59 E3
Kendégué Chad 94 C2
Kendhriki Makedhonia *admin. reg.* Greece *see* Kentriki Makedonia
Kendraparha India 73 D1
Kendua Bangl. 75 F4
Kendujhargarh India 75 E5
Kendyrli-Kayasanskoye, Plato *plat.* Kazakh. 79 H2
Kendyrlisor, Solonchak *salt l.* Kazakh. 79 H2
Kenedy U.S.A. 133 B6
Kenema Sierra Leone 92 C4
Kenepai, Gunung *mt.* Indon. 59 E2
Kenga *r.* Bhutan 75 F4
Kenge Dem. Rep. Congo 95 C6
Kengere Dem. Rep. Congo 95 E7
Keng Hkam Myanmar 60 B3
Kengis Sweden 32 F2
Keng Lap Myanmar 60 C3
Keng Lon Myanmar 60 B3
Keng Tawng Myanmar 60 B3
Kengtung Myanmar 60 B3
Kenhardt S. Africa 98 D6
Kéniéba Mali 92 C2
Kénitra Morocco 90 D2
Kenmare Rep. of Ireland 35 B6
Kenmare U.S.A. 132 A1
Kenmare River *inlet* Rep. of Ireland 35 A6
Kenmaur Zimbabwe 99 F3
Kenn Germany 36 C4
Kennebec U.S.A. 132 B3
Kennebec *r.* U.S.A. 128 F2
Kennebunk U.S.A. 131 H2
Kennedy, Cape U.S.A. *see* Canaveral, Cape
Kennedy Range National Park Australia 109 A6
Kennedy Town Hong Kong China 67 [inset]
Kennedyville U.S.A. 131 F4
Kenner U.S.A. 133 D6
Kennet *r.* U.K. 35 F6
Kenneth Range *hills* Australia 108 B5
Kennett U.S.A. 133 D4
Kennewick U.S.A. 134 C3
Kennicott U.S.A. 122 A2
Kenogami *r.* Canada 124 D3
Keno Hill Canada 122 C2
Kenora Canada 123 M5
Kenosha U.S.A. 132 F3
Kenova U.S.A. 130 B4
Kenozero, Ozero *l.* Rus. Fed. 28 F3
Kent *OH* U.S.A. 130 C3
Kent *TX* U.S.A. 135 F7
Kent *VA* U.S.A. 130 C5
Kent *WA* U.S.A. 134 C3
Kentani S. Africa 99 F7
Kentau Kazakh. 70 C3
Kent Group *is* Australia 112 C5
Kentland U.S.A. 132 E3
Kenton U.S.A. 130 D3
Kent Peninsula Canada 121 I3
Kentucky *r.* U.S.A. 128 B4
Kentucky *state* U.S.A. 130 A5
Kentucky Lake U.S.A. 128 A4
Kentwood U.S.A. 133 D6

► Kenya *country* Africa 96 C4
africa 86–87, 100

Kenya, Mount Kenya 96 C5
2nd highest mountain in Africa.
africa 84–85

Kenyir, Tasik *resr* Malaysia 58 C1
Keokuk U.S.A. 132 C3
Keoladeo National Park India 74 C4
Keowee, Lake *resr* U.S.A. 129 C5
Kepa Rus. Fed. 32 I2
Kepahiang Indon. 58 C3
Kępice Poland 37 H1
Kepina *r.* Rus. Fed. 28 G2
Kępno Poland 37 H3
Keppel Bay Australia 111 G4
Keppel Harbour *sea chan.* Sing. 58 [inset]
Keppel Island Tonga *see* Tafahi
Kepsut Turkey 78 B3
Kerala *state* India 72 B4
Kerang Australia 112 B4
Kerava Fin. 33 G3
Kerba Alg. 43 G4
Kerbau, Tanjung *pt* Indon. 58 C3
Kerbela Iraq *see* Karbalā'
Kerbi *r.* Rus. Fed. 64 D1
Kerch Ukr. 29 F7
Kerchem'ya Rus. Fed. 28 J3
Kere Eth. 96 C3
Kerema P.N.G. 57 K7
Keremeos Canada 123 K4
Kerempe Burun *pt* Turkey 78 C2
Keren Eritrea 89 H6
Kerend Iran 80 A3
Keret' *r.* Rus. Fed. 32 I2
Keret', Ozero *l.* Rus. Fed. 32 I2
Kerewan Gambia 92 A2
Kergeli Turkm. 80 D2
Kerguélen, Îles *is* Indian Ocean 163 L9
Kerguelen Plateau *sea feature* Indian Ocean 163 L9
Kericho Kenya 96 D5
Kerikeri N.Z. 113 C1
Kerimäki Fin. 33 H3

Kerimäki Fin. 33 H3
Kerinci, Danau *l.* Indon. 58 C3
Kerinci, Gunung *vol.* Indon. 58 C3
Kerinci Seblat National Park Indon. 58 C3
Keriya China *see* Yutian
Keriya Shankou *pass* China 75 D2
Kerka *r.* Hungary 37 H5
Kerkenah, Îles *is* Tunisia 91 H2
Kerki Turkm. 81 F2
Kerkichi Turkm. 81 F2
Kerkini Oros *mts* Bulg./Macedonia *see* Belasica
Kerkinitis, Limni *l.* Greece 46 C4
Kérkira *i.* Greece *see* Corfu
Kerkouane *tourist site* Tunisia 91 H1
Kerkyra Greece 47 A5
Kerkyra *i.* Greece *see* Corfu
Kerma Sudan 89 G6
Kermadec Islands S. Pacific Ocean 107 H5

► Kermadec Trench *sea feature* S. Pacific Ocean 164 G8
4th deepest trench in the world.

Kermān Iran 80 D4
Kermān *prov.* Iran 80 D4
Kermān Desert Iran 81 D4
Kermānshāh Iran 80 A3
Kermānshāh *prov.* Iran 80 A3
Kermānshāhān Iran *see* Kermānshāh
Kermine Uzbek. *see* Navoi
Kermit U.S.A. 133 A6
Kern *r.* U.S.A. 136 C3
Kern, South Fork *r.* U.S.A. 136 C3
Kernville U.S.A. 136 C3
Keros *i.* Greece 47 D6
Kérouané Guinea 92 C3
Kerpen Germany 36 C3
Kerr, Cape Antarctica 167 H1
Kerrobert Canada 123 I5
Kerrville U.S.A. 133 B6
Kerry Head *hd* Rep. of Ireland 35 B5
Kerteminde Denmark 33 C5
Kertosono Indon. 59 F4
Kerur India 72 B2
Keryneia Cyprus *see* Kyrenia
Kerzaz Alg. 91 F4
Kerzhenets *r.* Rus. Fed. 28 H4
Kesagami Lake Canada 124 D3
Kesälahti Fin. 33 H3
Keşan Turkey 78 A2
Keşap Turkey 79 D2
Kesarevo Bulg. 46 E3
Kesariya India 75 E4
Kesennuma Japan 65 E5
Keshan China 64 B3
Keshem Afgh. 81 G2
Keshendeh-ye Bala Afgh. 81 F2
Keshod India 74 A5
Keshorai Patan India 74 C4
Keshvar Iran 80 B3
Keskin Turkey 78 C3
Keskozero Rus. Fed. 28 E3
Kesova Gora Rus. Fed. 28 F4
Kesra Tunisia 45 B7
Kestel *Bursa* Turkey 47 F4
Kestel *Bursa* Turkey *see* Gürsu
Kesten'ga Rus. Fed. 32 H2
Kestilä Fin. 32 G2
Keswick U.K. 35 E4
Keswick Dam U.S.A. 136 A1
Ket' *r.* Rus. Fed. 26 J4
Keta Ghana 93 F4
Ket'a *r.* Rus. Fed. 26 J4
Ketapang *Jawa Timur* Indon. 59 F4
Ketapang *Kalimantan Barat* Indon. 59 E3
Ketchikan U.S.A. 122 C4
Kete Krachi Ghana 93 E4
Ketmen', Khrebet *mts* China/Kazakh. 70 F3
Kétou Benin 93 F4
Kętrzyn Poland 37 J1
Kettering U.K. 35 F5
Kettering U.S.A. 130 A4
Kettle *r.* Canada 122 G5
Kettle *r.* U.S.A. 132 C2
Kettle Creek *r.* U.S.A. 131 E3
Kettle Falls U.S.A. 134 C2
Kettleman City U.S.A. 136 C3
Kettle River Range *mts* U.S.A. 134 C2
Ketungau *r.* Indon. 59 E2
Keuka Lake U.S.A. 131 E2
Keumgang, Mount N. Korea *see* Kumgang-san
Keumsang, Mount N. Korea *see* Kumgang-san
Keur Massène Mauritania 92 A1
Keurusselkä *l.* Fin. 33 G3
Keuruu Fin. 33 G3
Kevelaer Germany 36 C3
Kewanee U.S.A. 128 B2
Keweenaw Bay U.S.A. 132 D2
Keweenaw Peninsula U.S.A. 132 D2
Keweenaw Point U.S.A. 132 E2
Keyala Sudan 96 B3
Key Largo U.S.A. 129 C7
Keymir Turkm. *see* Kemir
Keyser U.S.A. 130 E4
Keysers Ridge U.S.A. 130 D4
Keystone Lake *OK* U.S.A. 133 B4
Keystone Lake *PA* U.S.A. 130 D3
Keysville U.S.A. 130 D5
Keytü Iran 80 D3
Keyvy, Vozvyshennost' *hills* Rus. Fed. 28 F2
Key West U.S.A. 129 C7
Kez Rus. Fed. 28 J4
Kezi Zimbabwe 99 F3
Kgalagadi *admin. dist.* Botswana 98 D3
Kgatleng *admin. dist.* Botswana 99 D3
Kgotsong S. Africa 99 D5
Khabarikha Rus. Fed. 28 J2
Khabarovsk Rus. Fed. 64 D2
Khabarovsk Kray *admin. div.* Rus. Fed. 64 D2 *see* Khabarovskiy Kray
Khabarovskiy Kray *admin. div.* Rus. Fed. 64 D2
Khabary Rus. Fed. 28 J2
Khabis Iran *see* Shahdad
Khabody Pass Afgh. 81 E3
Khābūr, Nahr al *r.* Syria 76 C2
Khachmas Azer. *see* Xaçmaz
Khachrod India 74 B5
Khadari *watercourse* Sudan 94 D2
Khā's Banbān *well* Saudi Arabia 80 A5
Khaga India 74 D4
Khagaria India 75 F4
Khagrachari Bangl. 75 F5 *see* Khagrachhari
Khagrachhari Bangl. 75 G5
Khairagarh India 74 D5
Khairpur Pak. 81 H4
Khairpur Pak. 81 H4
Khairwara India 74 B5
Khajuraho India 74 D4
Khakasiya, Respublika *aut. rep.* Rus. Fed. 62 D1
Khakassia *aut. rep.* Rus. Fed. *see* Khakasiya, Respublika
Khakasskaya A.S.S.R. *aut. rep.* Rus. Fed. *see* Khakasiya, Respublika

Khāk-e Jabbar Afgh. 81 G3
Khakhea Botswana 98 D5
Khakir Afgh. 81 F3
Khalach Turkm. 81 F2
Khalatse Jammu and Kashmir 74 C2
Khalidabad Iran 80 D3
Khalilabad India 75 E4
Khalilabad Turkm. 81 E1
Khalkhāl Iran 80 B2
Khálki *i.* Greece *see* Chalki
Khalkis Greece *see* Chalkida
Khallikot India 73 E2
Khal'mer-Yu Rus. Fed. 28 M2
Khalte Nepal 75 E4
Khalturin Rus. Fed. *see* Orlov
Khamar-Daban, Khrebet *mts* Rus. Fed. 27 K4
Khamaria Rus. Fed. 27 K4
Khambhaliya India 74 A5
Khambhat India 74 B5
Khambhat, Gulf of India 72 A2
Khamgaon India 72 B1
Khamir Iran 80 D5
Khami Ruins National Monument *tourist site* Zimbabwe 99 F4
Khamis Mushayt Saudi Arabia 89 I5
Khammam India 72 C2
Khamma *well* Saudi Arabia 80 A5
Khampa Rus. Fed. 27 M3
Khampat Myanmar 60 A3
Khamra Rus. Fed. 54 D1
Khan Afgh. 81 F3
Khan, Nam *r.* Laos 60 B3
Khānābād Afgh. 81 G2
Khanapur *Karnataka* India 72 E3
Khanapur *Maharashtra* India 72 B2
Khān ar Raḩbah Iraq 80 A4
Khanasur Pass Iran/Turkey 79 F3
Khanbalik China *see* Beijing
Khānch Iran 80 A2
Khandala India 72 B2
Khandud Afgh. 81 G2
Khandwa India 74 C5
Khandyga Rus. Fed. 27 N3
Khanewal Pak. 81 H4
Khangah Pak. 81 I4
Khanh Duong Vietnam 61 E5
Khan Hung Vietnam *see* Soc Trăng
Khani Rus. Fed. 27 M4
Khania Greece *see* Chania
Khanka, Lake China/Rus. Fed. 64 D3
Khanka, Ozero *l.* China/Rus. Fed. *see* Khanka, Lake
Khankendi Azer. *see* Xankändi
Khanna India 74 C3
Khannā, Qāʿ *salt pan* Jordan 77 C3
Khannfoussa *hill* Alg. 91 G4
Khanpur Pak. 81 H4
Khān Ruḩābah Iraq *see* Khān ar Raḩbah
Khan Shaykhūn Syria 77 C2
Khansiir, Raas *pt* Somalia 96 E2
Khantau Kazakh. 70 D3
Khantayskoye, Ozero *l.* Rus. Fed. 27 J3
Khantayskoye Vodokhranilishche *resr* Rus. Fed. 62 D1
Khanty-Mansiysk Rus. Fed. 26 G3
Khanty-Mansiyskiy Avtonomnyy Okrug *admin. div.* Rus. Fed. 28 L3
Khanty-Mansy Autonomous Okrug *admin. div.* Rus. Fed. *see* Khanty-Mansiyskiy Avtonomnyy Okrug
Khān Yūnis Gaza 77 B4
Khao Chum Thong Thai. 61 B6
Khaoen Si Nakarin National Park Thai. 61 B5
Khao Laem National Park Thai. 61 B5
Khao Laem Reservoir Thai. 61 B5
Khao Luang National Park Thai. 61 B6
Khao Pu-Khao Ya National Park Thai. 61 B7
Khao Sok National Park Thai. 61 B6
Khao Yai National Park Thai. 61 C5
Khapa India 74 C5
Khapalu Jammu and Kashmir 74 C2
Khapcheranga Rus. Fed. 63 J2
Khaptad National Park Nepal 74 D3
Kharabali Rus. Fed. 29 H7
Kharagauli Georgia 79 F2
Kharagpur *Bihar* India 75 F4
Kharagpur *W. Bengal* India 75 E5
Kharakī Iran 80 D5
Khārān *r.* Iran 80 D5
Kharan Pak. 81 F4
Kharari India *see* Abu Road
Khardi India 72 B2
Khardung La *pass* Jammu and Kashmir 74 C2
Kharga Egypt *see* Al Khārijah
Kharga Oasis Egypt *see* Khārijah, Wāḥāt al
Kharghoda India 74 B5
Khargon India 74 B5
Khari *r.* India 72 B2
Kharian Pak. 74 B2
Khariar India 73 D1
Khari India 72 B2
Kharkhauda India 74 C3
Kharkiv Ukr. 29 F6
Khar'kov Ukr. *see* Kharkiv
Khār Kūh *mt.* Iran 80 D4
Kharlu Rus. Fed. 28 E3
Kharora India 75 D5
Kharovsk Rus. Fed. 28 G4
Kharsawan India 75 D5
Kharsia India 75 D5

Khavast Uzbek. 81 G1
Khavda India 74 A5
Khawak Pass Afgh. 81 G3
Khawsh Saudi Arabia 89 I5
Khayamnadi S. Africa 98 E6
Khayatbashi, Gora *mt.* Uzbek. 81 F1
Khaybar Saudi Arabia 89 H3
Khaydarken Kyrg. 70 D4
Khayelitsha S. Africa 98 C7
Khaypudyrskaya Guba *b.* Rus. Fed. 28 K1
Khê Bo Vietnam 60 B3
Khed *Maharashtra* India 72 B3
Khed *Maharashtra* India 72 B2
Kheda India 74 B5
Khedbrahma India 74 B4
Khedri Iran 81 D3
Khefa Israel *see* Haifa
Khehuene, Ponta *pt* Moz. 99 G4
Khelari India 75 E5
Khemis Anjra Morocco 42 D5
Khemis Miliana Alg. 91 F1
Khemisset Morocco 90 D2
Khemmarat Thai. 61 C3
Khenchela Alg. 91 G1
Khenifra Morocco 42 D5
Khenjan Afgh. 81 G3
Kheralu India 74 B4
Kherämeh Iran 80 D4
Kherrah Iran 80 C5
Khersan *r.* Iran 80 B4
Kherson Ukr. 29 E7
Khe Sanh Vietnam 61 D4
Khesht Iran 80 B4
Kheta *r.* Rus. Fed. 27 K2
Kheyrābād Iran 80 D4
Khezerābād Iran 80 C2
Khiaw, Khao *mt.* Thai. 61 C5
Khibiny *mts* Rus. Fed. 32 I2
Khilchipur India 74 C4
Khiliomódhion Greece *see* Chiliomodi
Khilok Rus. Fed. 27 L4
Khíos *i.* Greece *see* Chios
Khios Strait Greece *see* Chios Strait
Khirbat Isrīyah Syria 77 C2
Khirkiya India 74 C5
Khisarya Bulg. 46 E3
Khitai Pass Aksai Chin 74 D2
Khiytola Rus. Fed. 33 H3
Khlevnoye Rus. Fed. 29 F5
Khlong, Mae *r.* Thai. 61 B4
Khlong Wang Chao National Park Thai. 61 B4
Khlung Thai. 61 C5
Khmel'nik Ukr. *see* Khmil'nyk
Khmel'nitskiy Ukr. *see* Khmel'nyts'kyy
Khmel'nyts'kyy Ukr. 29 E6
Khmer Republic *country* Asia *see* Cambodia
Khmil'nyk Ukr. 29 E6
Khodā Āfarīd *spring* Iran 80 D3
Khodzha Davlet Uzbek. 81 E2
Khodzha-Kala Turkm. 80 D2
Khodzhambaz Turkm. 81 F2
Khodzhaolen Turkm. 80 D2
Khodzhapir'yakh, Gora *mt.* Uzbek. 70 C4
Khodzhavend Azer. *see* Xocavänd
Khodzhent Tajik. *see* Khŭjand
Khodzheyli Uzbek. 76 E1
Khodzhyder *r.* Ukr. 46 F2
Khogali Sudan 94 E3
Khojand Tajik. *see* Khŭjand
Kholapur India 72 C1
Kholm Afgh. 81 F2
Kholm Poland *see* Chełm
Kholm Rus. Fed. 31 L1
Kholmsk Rus. Fed. 64 E3
Kholon Israel *see* Holon
Khomas *admin. reg.* Namibia 98 B2
Khomeyn Iran 80 B3
Khomeynīshahr Iran 80 B3
Khong, Mae Nam *r.* Myanmar *see* Salween
Khonj Iran 80 C5
Khonj, Kūh-e *mts* Iran 80 C5
Khon Kaen Thai. 61 C4
Khonsa India 75 G4
Khonuu Rus. Fed. 27 O3
Khoper *r.* Rus. Fed. 29 G6
Khor Rus. Fed. 64 D3
Khor *r.* Rus. Fed. 64 C3
Khóra Greece *see* Chora
Khorasan *prov.* Iran 80 D3
Khorat Plateau Thai. 60 C4
Khordha India 73 E1
Khoreyver Rus. Fed. 28 K2
Khorinsk Rus. Fed. 63 H1
Khorixas Namibia 98 B3
Khormūj, Kūh-e *mt.* Iran 80 B4
Khorog Tajik. *see* Khorugh
Khorol Rus. Fed. 64 C3
Khorol Ukr. 29 E6
Khorramābād Iran 80 B3
Khorram Darreh Iran 80 B2
Khorramshahr Iran 80 B4
Khorugh Tajik. 81 G2
Khosedayu *r.* Rus. Fed. 28 K2
Khosf Iran 81 D3
Khosheutovo Rus. Fed. 29 H7
Khosravī Iran 80 A4
Khosta Rus. Fed. 79 F2
Khosūyeh Iran 80 D5
Khotan China *see* Hotan
Khouribga Morocco 90 D2
Khowai India 75 F4
Khowos Uzbek. *see* Khavast
Khowrjan Iran 80 D4
Khowrnāq, Kūh-e *mt.* Iran 80 C3
Khowst Iran 80 D3
Khozap'ini, Tba *l.* Georgia 79 E2
Khri *r.* India 75 F4
Khrisoúpolis Greece *see* Chrysoupoli
Khroma *r.* Rus. Fed. 27 O2
Khromtau Kazakh. 26 F4
Khru *r.* India 75 G4
Khrushchev Ukr. *see* Svitlovods'k
Khrysochou Bay Cyprus *see* Chrysochou Bay
Khudat Rus. Fed. *see* Xudat
Khude Hills Pak. 81 G5
Khudian Pak. 74 B3
Khudzhand Tajik. *see* Khŭjand
Khugiana Afgh. *see* Pirzada
Khuff Saudi Arabia 80 B5
Khŭjand Tajik. 81 G1
Khŭjand *admin. div.* Tajik. *see* Leninobod
Khŭjayli Uzbek. *see* Khodzheyli
Khu Khan Thai. 61 D5
Khuldabad India 72 B1
Khulga *r.* Rus. Fed. 28 L2
Khulm *r.* Afgh. 81 F2
Khulna Bangl. 75 F5
Khulna *admin. div.* Bangl. 75 F5
Khunayzir, Jabal al *mts* Syria 77 C2
Khuneiqa *watercourse* Sudan 89 F6
Khŭninshahr Iran *see* Khorramshahr
Khunjerab Pass China/Jammu and Kashmir 74 C1
Khunsar Iran 80 C4
Khunti India 75 E5
Khur Iran 80 D3
Khūr Iran 80 D3
Khurai India 74 C4
Khŭran *sea chan.* Iran 80 C5

Khurayṣ Saudi Arabia 80 B5
Khurd, Koh-i- mt. Afgh. 81 F3
Khureit Sudan 89 E6
Khuria Tank resr India see Maniari Tank
Khurja India 74 C3
Khurmalik Afgh. 81 E3
Khurmuli Rus. Fed. 64 D2
Khurr, Wādī al watercourse Saudi Arabia 79 E5
Khushab Pak. 81 H3
Khushshah, Wādī al watercourse Jordan/Saudi Arabia 77 C5
Khust Ukr. 31 J3
Khutgaon India 72 D1
Khutmīyah, Mamarr al Egypt 77 A4
Khutse Game Reserve nature res. Botswana 98 E4
Khutu r. Rus. Fed. 64 D2
Khuwei Sudan 89 F6
Khuzdar Pak. 81 F5
Khūzestān prov. Iran 80 B4
Khvājeh Iran 80 A2
Khvalynsk Rus. Fed. 29 I5
Khvor Iran 80 C3
Khvord Nārvan Iran 80 D3
Khvormūj Iran 80 B4
Khvosh Maqām Iran 80 A2
Khvoy Iran 80 A2
Khvoynaya Rus. Fed. 28 E4
Khwae Noi r. Thai. 61 B5
Khwahan Afgh. 81 G2
Khwaja Amran mt. Pak. 81 F4
Khwaja-i-Ghar Afgh. 81 G2
Khwaja Muhammad Range mts Afgh. 81 G2
Khyber Pass Afgh./Pak. 81 G3
Kīā'ī Iran 80 D5
Kiama Australia 112 D4
Kiambi Dem. Rep. Congo 95 F6
Kiamichi r. U.S.A. 133 C5
Kiangsi prov. China see Jiangxi
Kiangsu prov. China see Jiangsu
Kiang West National Park Gambia 92 B2
Kianly Turkm. see Darta
Kiantajärvi l. Fin. 32 H2
Kīāseh Iran 80 C2
Kiato Greece 47 C5
Kibaha Tanz. 97 C6
Kibala Angola 95 B6
Kibale Uganda 96 A4
Kibale National Park Uganda 96 A4
Kibali r. Dem. Rep. Congo 94 F4
Kibangou Congo 94 B5
Kibara Tanz. 96 B5
Kibara, Monts mts Dem. Rep. Congo 95 E7
Kibaya Tanz. 97 C6
Kiberashi Tanz. 97 C6
Kiberege Tanz. 97 C6
Kiboga Uganda 96 A4
Kibombo Dem. Rep. Congo 95 E5
Kibondo Tanz. 96 A5
Kibre Mengist Eth. 96 C3
Kibris country Asia see Cyprus
Kibungo Rwanda 96 A5
Kibuye Rwanda 94 F5
Kibwesa Tanz. 97 A6
Kičevo Macedonia 46 B4
Kichi-Kichi well Chad 88 C5
Kichwamba Uganda 96 A5
Kicking Horse Pass Canada 123 G5
Kidal Mali 93 F1
Kidal admin. reg. Mali 93 F1
Kidatu Tanz. 97 C6
Kidderminster U.K. 35 E5
Kidepo Valley National Park Uganda 96 B4
Kidira Senegal 92 B2
Kidmang Jammu and Kashmir 74 C2
Kidnappers, Cape N.Z. 113 D2
Kiel Germany 36 E1
Kiel Canal Germany 36 D1
Kielce Poland 37 J3
Kielder Water resr U.K. 34 E4
Kieler Bucht b. Germany 36 E1
Kieler Förde g. Germany 36 E1
Kiembara Burkina 92 E2
Kienge Dem. Rep. Congo 95 E7

▶Kiev Ukr. 29 D6
Capital of Ukraine.

Kiffa Mauritania 92 C1
Kifisia Greece 47 C5
Kifisos r. Greece 47 C5
Kifrī Iraq 79 F4
Kifwanzondo Dem. Rep. Congo 95 C6

▶Kigali Rwanda 94 F5
Capital of Rwanda.

Kiği Turkey 79 E3
Kiglapait Mountains Canada 125 I1
Kiglikavik Lake Canada 123 H1
Kignan Mali 92 D3
Kigoma Tanz. 97 A6
Kigoma admin. reg. Tanz. 97 A6
Kigwe Tanz. 97 B6
Kihei U.S.A. 135 [inset] Z1
Kihlanki Fin. 32 F2
Kihniö Fin. 33 F3
Kihnu i. Estonia 33 F4
Kiiminki Fin. 32 G2
Kii-sanchi mts Japan 65 C6
Kii-suidō sea chan. Japan 65 C6
Kijungu Well Tanz. 97 C6
Kikerk Lake Canada 123 H1
Kikinda Yugo. 46 B2
Kikki Pak. 81 E5
Kikládhes is Greece see Cyclades
Kiknur Rus. Fed. 28 H4
Kikondja Dem. Rep. Congo 95 E7
Kikori P.N.G. 57 J7
Kikori r. P.N.G. 57 J7
Kikwit Dem. Rep. Congo 95 C6
Kil Sweden 33 D4
Kilafors Sweden 33 E3
Kilakkarai India 72 C4
Kīlan Iran 80 C3
Kilauea U.S.A. 135 [inset] Y1
Kilauea Crater U.S.A. 135 [inset] Z2
Kilboghamn Norway 32 D2
Kilbotn Norway 32 E1
Kilchu N. Korea 65 B4
Kilcock Rep. of Ireland 35 C5
Kilcoy Australia 111 H5
Kildare Rep. of Ireland 35 C5
Kildonan Zimbabwe 99 F3
Kilekale Lake Canada 122 F1
Kilemary Rus. Fed. 28 H4
Kilembe Dem. Rep. Congo 95 C6
Kilgore U.S.A. 133 C5
Kilgour r. Australia 110 C3
Kilia Ukr. see Kiliya
Kilibo Benin 93 F3
Kilifi Kenya 96 C5
Kilik Pass China 74 B1
Kilimanjaro admin. reg. Tanz. 97 C5

▶Kilimanjaro vol. Tanz. 96 C5
Highest mountain in Africa.
africa 84–85, 86–87

Kilimanjaro National Park Tanz. 96 C5
Kilimatinde Tanz. 97 B6
Kilinailau Islands P.N.G. 107 E2
Kilindoni Tanz. 97 C6
Kilingi-Nõmme Estonia 28 C4
Kılıs Turkey 78 D3
Kilis prov. Turkey 77 C1
Kiliya Ukr. 46 F2
Kilkee Rep. of Ireland 35 B5
Kilkenny Rep. of Ireland 35 C5
Kilkis Greece 46 C4
Killala Rep. of Ireland 35 B4
Killaloe Rep. of Ireland 35 B5
Killam Canada 123 I4
Killarney Australia 111 H6
Killarney Canada 124 D4
Killarney Rep. of Ireland 35 B5
Killarney National Park Rep. of Ireland 35 B6
Killary Harbour b. Rep. of Ireland 35 B5
Killeen U.S.A. 133 B6
Killin U.K. 34 D3
Killinek Island Canada see Killiniq Island
Killíni mt. Greece see Kyllini
Killiniq Canada 121 M3
Killiniq Island Canada 121 M3
Killorglin Rep. of Ireland 35 B5
Killybegs Rep. of Ireland 35 B4
Kilmarnock U.K. 34 D4
Kilmarnock U.S.A. 131 E5
Kil'mez' Rus. Fed. 28 I4
Kil'mez' r. Rus. Fed. 28 I4
Kilmore Australia 112 C5
Kilosa Tanz. 97 C6
Kilpisjärvi Fin. 32 F1
Kilpua Fin. 32 G2
Kilrush Rep. of Ireland 35 B5
Kiltan i. India 72 B4
Kilwa Dem. Rep. Congo 95 F7
Kilwa Masoko Tanz. 97 C7
Kilyazi Azer. see Giläzi
Kim Chad 94 B2
Kimambi Tanz. 97 C7
Kimanis, Teluk b. Sabah Malaysia 59 F1
Kimasozero Rus. Fed. 32 H2
Kimasozero, Ozero l. Rus. Fed. 32 H2
Kimba Australia 109 G8
Kimba Congo 94 B5
Kimball U.S.A. 132 A3
Kimbe P.N.G. 106 E2
Kimberley Canada 123 H5
Kimberley S. Africa 98 E6
Kimberley Downs Australia 108 D4
Kimberley Plateau Australia 110 A3
Kimberley Range hills Australia 109 B6
Kimbirila-Sud Côte d'Ivoire 92 D3
Kimch'aek N. Korea 65 B4
Kimch'ŏn S. Korea 65 B5
Kimhae S. Korea 65 B6
Kimi Greece see Kymi
Kimito Fin. 33 F3
Kimje S. Korea 65 A6
Kimmirut Canada 121 M3
Kimolos i. Greece 47 D6
Kimolou-Sifnou, Steno sea chan. Greece 47 D6
Kimovsk Rus. Fed. 29 F5
Kimpanga Dem. Rep. Congo 95 E6
Kimpangu Dem. Rep. Congo 95 B6
Kimparana Mali 92 D2
Kimpese Dem. Rep. Congo 95 B6
Kimpoko Dem. Rep. Congo 95 B6
Kimpoku-san mt. Japan see Kinpoku-san
Kimry Rus. Fed. 31 N1
Kimsquit Canada 122 E4
Kimvula Dem. Rep. Congo 95 B6
Kinabalu, Gunung mt. Sabah Malaysia 59 G1
Kinabalu National Park Sabah Malaysia 59 G1
Kinabatangan r. Sabah Malaysia 59 G1
Kinango Kenya 97 C6
Kinaros i. Greece 47 E6
Kinaskan Lake Canada 122 D3
Kinbasket Lake Canada 122 G4
Kinbirila Côte d'Ivoire see Kimbirila-Sud
Kinbrace U.K. 34 E2
Kincaid Canada 123 J5
Kincardine Canada 130 C1
Kinchang Myanmar 60 B2
Kinchega National Park Australia 112 B4
Kincolith Canada 122 D4
Kinda Dem. Rep. Congo 95 E7
Kindamba Congo 95 B5
Kindat Myanmar 60 A3
Kinde U.S.A. 130 B2
Kindembe Dem. Rep. Congo 95 C6
Kinder U.S.A. 133 C6
Kindersley Canada 134 E2
Kindia Guinea 92 B3
Kindu Dem. Rep. Congo 94 E5
Kinel' Rus. Fed. 29 I5
Kineshma Rus. Fed. 28 G4
King r. N.T. Australia 110 C2
King r. W.A. Australia 108 E3
King and Queen Courthouse U.S.A. 131 E5
Kingaroy Australia 111 G5
King City U.S.A. 136 B3
King Edward r. Australia 108 D3
King Edward Point research station S. Georgia 153 [inset]
Kingfisher U.S.A. 133 B5
King George Bay Falkland Is 153 E7
King George Island Antarctica 167 A2
King George Islands Canada 124 E1
King George VI Falls Guyana 147 F3
Kingimbi Dem. Rep. Congo 95 B6
Kingisepp Rus. Fed. 28 D4
King Island Australia 112 B5
King Island Canada 122 E4
King Island Myanmar see Kadan Kyun
Kingissepa Estonia see Kuressaare
Kinglake National Park Australia 112 C5
King Leopold and Queen Astrid Coast Antarctica 167 E2
King Leopold Range National Park Australia 108 D4
King Leopold Ranges hills Australia 110 A3
Kingman AZ U.S.A. 137 E4
Kingman KS U.S.A. 132 B4

▶Kingman Reef N. Pacific Ocean 165 H5
United States Unincorporated Territory.
oceania 114

King Mountain Canada 122 D3
King Mountain U.S.A. 133 A6
Kingombe Mbali Dem. Rep. Congo 94 E5
King Peak Antarctica 167 L1
King Peninsula Antarctica 167 K2
Kingri Pak. 81 G4
Kings r. U.S.A. 136 B3
Kingsburg U.S.A. 136 C3
Kings Canyon National Park U.S.A. 136 C3
Kingscote Australia 112 A4
King Sejong research station Antarctica 167 A2
Kingsland U.S.A. 129 C6
King's Lynn U.K. 35 G5
Kingsmill Group is Kiribati 107 G2
King Sound b. Australia 108 C4
Kings Peak U.S.A. 134 E4
Kingsport U.S.A. 130 B5
Kingston Australia 112 C6
Kingston Canada 131 E1

▶Kingston Jamaica 139 I5
Capital of Jamaica.

▶Kingston Norfolk I. 164 F7
Capital of Norfolk Island.

Kingston N.Z. 113 B4
Kingston MA U.S.A. 131 H3
Kingston MO U.S.A. 132 C4
Kingston NY U.S.A. 131 F3
Kingston OH U.S.A. 130 B4
Kingston PA U.S.A. 131 F3
Kingston TN U.S.A. 128 B5
Kingston South East Australia 112 A5
Kingston upon Hull U.K. 35 F5

▶Kingstown St Vincent 147 F1
Capital of St Vincent.

Kingstree U.S.A. 129 D5
Kingsville U.S.A. 133 B7
Kingswood U.K. 35 E6
Kington U.K. 35 E5
Kingungi Dem. Rep. Congo 95 C6
Kingussie U.K. 34 D3
King William Island Canada 121 J3
Kingwood TX U.S.A. 133 C6
Kingwood WV U.S.A. 130 D4
Kiniama Dem. Rep. Congo 95 F7
Kınık Turkey 47 E5
Kinkala Congo 95 B6
Kinloch N.Z. 113 B4
Kinlochleven U.K. 34 D3
Kinmen Taiwan see Chinmen
Kinmount Canada 130 D1
Kinna Sweden 33 D4
Kinnarasani r. India 72 D2
Kinnarodden pt Norway 32 G1
Kinnegad Rep. of Ireland 35 C5
Kinneret, Yam l. Israel see Galilee, Sea of
Kinniyai Sri Lanka 72 D4
Kinnula Fin. 32 G3
Kinoje r. Canada 124 D2
Kinoosao Canada 123 K3
Kinpoku-san mt. Japan 65 D5
Kinsale Rep. of Ireland 35 B6
Kinsarvik Norway 33 B3
Kinsele Dem. Rep. Congo 95 C6

▶Kinshasa Dem. Rep. Congo 95 B6
Capital of the Democratic Republic of Congo and 3rd most populous city in Africa.
world 16–17

Kinshasa municipality Dem. Rep. Congo 95 C6
Kinsley U.S.A. 132 B4
Kinston U.S.A. 128 D5
Kintai Lith. 33 F5
Kintampo Ghana 93 E3
Kintata Dem. Rep. Congo 95 B6
Kintinian Guinea 92 C3
Kintop Indon. 59 F3
Kintore Australia 110 B4
Kintore, Mount Australia 110 B5
Kintyre pen. U.K. 34 D4
Kinu Myanmar 60 A3
Kinushseo r. Canada 124 D2
Kinuso Canada 123 H4
Kinwat India 72 C2
Kinyangiri Tanz. 97 B6
Kinyeti mt. Sudan 96 B4
Kiomboi Tanz. 97 B6
Kiowa CO U.S.A. 134 F5
Kiowa KS U.S.A. 132 B4
Kipahigan Lake Canada 123 K4
Kiparissia Greece see Kyparissia
Kipawa, Lac l. Canada 124 E4
Kipelovo Rus. Fed. 28 F4
Kipengere Range mts Tanz. 97 B7
Kipili Tanz. 97 A6
Kipini Kenya 96 D5
Kipling Canada 123 K5
Kipling Station Canada see Kipling
Kiptopeke U.S.A. 131 F5
Kipungo Angola see Quipungo
Kipushi Dem. Rep. Congo 95 E7
Kipushia Dem. Rep. Congo 95 F8
Kirakat India 75 D4
Kirakira Solomon Is 107 F3
Kirandul India 72 D2
Kirané Mali 92 C2
Kiraz Turkey 47 F5
Kirbla Estonia 33 F4
Kirbyville U.S.A. 133 C6
Kirchdorf an der Krems Austria 37 G5
Kirdimi Chad 88 C5
Kirenga r. Rus. Fed. 27 K4
Kirensk Rus. Fed. 27 K4
Kirghizia country Asia see Kyrgyzstan
Kirgiz-Miyaki Rus. Fed. 29 J5
Kirgizskaya S.S.R. country Asia see Kyrgyzstan
Kirgizstan country Asia see Kyrgyzstan
Kiri Dem. Rep. Congo 94 C5
Kiriákion Greece see Kyriaki
▶Kiribati country Pacific Ocean 107 H2
oceania 104–105
Kiridh Somalia 96 E2
Kırıkhan Turkey 78 D3
Kırıkkale Turkey 78 C3
Kirillov Rus. Fed. 28 F4
Kirillovo Rus. Fed. 64 E3
Kirin China see Jilin
Kirin prov. China see Jilin
Kirinyaga mt. Kenya see Kenya, Mount
Kirishi Rus. Fed. 28 E4
Kirishima-Yaku National Park Japan 65 B7
▶Kiritimati i. Kiribati 165 H5
oceania 114
Kiriwina Islands P.N.G. see Trobriand Islands
Kırkağaç Turkey 47 E5
Kirk Bulāg Dāgh mt. Iran 80 A2
Kirkby U.K. 35 E5
Kirkby Stephen U.K. 35 E4
Kirkcaldy U.K. 34 E3
Kirkcudbright U.K. 34 D4
Kirkenær Norway 33 D3
Kirkenes Norway 32 H1
Kirkfield Canada 130 D1
Kirkkonummi Fin. 33 G3
Kirkland U.S.A. 137 F4
Kirkland Lake Canada 124 D3
Kırklareli Turkey 78 A2
Kırklareli prov. Turkey 46 E4
Kırklareli Barajı resr Turkey 46 E4
Kirkpatrick, Mount Antarctica 167 H1
Kirksville U.S.A. 132 C3
Kirkuk Iraq see Kirkūk
Kirkūk Iraq 79 F4
Kirkwall U.K. 34 E2
Kirman Iran see Kermān
Kırmır r. Turkey 78 B2
Kırobası Turkey see Mağara
Kirov Kaluzhskaya Oblast' Rus. Fed. 29 E5
Kirov Kirovskaya Oblast' Rus. Fed. 28 I4
Kirova, Zaliv b. Azer. see Qızılağac Körfäzi
Kirovabad Azer. see Gäncä
Kirovabad Tajik. see Panj
Kirovakan Armenia see Vanadzor
Kirovo Kazakh. 29 J6
Kirovo Ukr. see Kirovohrad
Kirovo Uzbek. see Besharyk
Kirov Oblast admin. div. Rus. Fed. see Kirovskaya Oblast'
Kirovo-Chepetsk Rus. Fed. 28 I4
Kirovo-Chepetskiy Rus. Fed. see Kirovo-Chepetsk
Kirovograd Ukr. see Kirovohrad
Kirovohrad Ukr. 29 E6
Kirovsk Leningradskaya Oblast' Rus. Fed. 28 D4
Kirovsk Murmanskaya Oblast' Rus. Fed. 32 I2
Kirovsk Turkm. see Babadaykhan
Kirovskaya Oblast' admin. div. Rus. Fed. 28 I4
Kirovskiy Kazakh. see Balpyk Bi
Kirovskiy Rus. Fed. 64 C3
Kırpaşa pen. Cyprus see Karpasia
Kirpili Turkm. 80 D2
Kirriemuir U.K. 34 E3
Kirs Rus. Fed. 28 J4
Kirsanov Rus. Fed. 29 G5
Kırşehir Turkey 78 C3
Kirtachi Niger 93 F2
Kirthar National Park Pak. 81 F5
Kirthar Range mts Pak. 81 F5
Kiruna Sweden 32 F2
Kirundo Burundi 94 F5
Kirundu Dem. Rep. Congo 94 E5
Kirwan Escarpment Antarctica 167 B2
Kirya Rus. Fed. 28 H5
Kiryū Japan 65 D5
Kisa Sweden 33 D4
Kisaki Tanz. 97 C6
Kisama, Parque Nacional de nat. park Angola see Quiçama, Parque Nacional do
Kisangani Dem. Rep. Congo 94 E4
Kisar i. Indon. 108 D2
Kisaran Indon. 58 B2
Kisarawe Tanz. 97 C6
Kisbér Hungary 37 I5
Kiselevsk Rus. Fed. 62 D1
Kiseljak Bos.-Herz. 44 G3
Kisel'ovka Rus. Fed. 64 D2
Kishanganj India 75 E4
Kishangarh Rajasthan India 74 A4
Kishangarh Rajasthan India 74 B4
Kishen Ganga r. India/Pak. 74 B2
Kishi Nigeria 93 F3
Kishinev Moldova see Chişinău
Kishiözen r. Kazakh./Rus. Fed. see Malyy Uzen'
Kishiwada Japan 65 C6
Kishkenekol' Kazakh. 26 H4
Kishoreganj Bangl. 75 F4
Kishtwar Jammu and Kashmir 74 B2
Kisigo r. Tanz. 97 B6
Kisii Kenya 96 B5
Kisiju Tanz. 97 C6
Kiska Island U.S.A. 120 A4
Kiskittogisu Lake Canada 123 L4
Kisko Fin. 33 F3
Kiskőrös Hungary 37 I5
Kiskunfélegyháza Hungary 37 I5
Kiskunhalas Hungary 46 A1
Kiskunmajsa Hungary 46 A1
Kiskunsági nat. park Hungary 37 I5
Kislovodsk Rus. Fed. 29 G8
Kismaayo Somalia 96 D5
Kismayu Somalia see Kismaayo
Kisoro Uganda 96 A5
Kispiox Canada 122 E4
Kispiox r. Canada 122 E4
Kisseraing Island Myanmar see Kanmaw Kyun
Kissidougou Guinea 92 C3
Kissimmee U.S.A. 129 C6
Kissimmee r. U.S.A. 129 C7
Kissimmee, Lake U.S.A. 129 C7
Kississing Lake Canada 123 K4
Kissu, Jebel mt. Sudan 88 E4
Kistanje Croatia 44 E3
Kistelek Hungary 46 A1
Kistna r. India see Krishna
Kisújszállás Hungary 37 J5
Kisumu Kenya 96 B5
Kisykkamys Kazakh. see Dzhangala
Kit r. Sudan 96 A3
Kita Mali 92 C2
Kitab Uzbek. 81 F2
Kita-Daitō-jima i. Japan 63 M6
Kitaibaraki Japan 65 E5
Kitakami-gawa r. Japan 65 E5
Kita-Kyūshū Japan 65 B6
Kitale Kenya 96 B4
Kitami Japan 64 E4
Kitanda Dem. Rep. Congo 95 E6
Kitchener Canada 130 C2
Kitchigama r. Canada 124 E3
Kiteba Dem. Rep. Congo 95 E6
Kitee Fin. 32 H3
Kitendwe Dem. Rep. Congo 95 F6
Kitgum Uganda 96 B4
Kíthira i. Greece see Kythira
Kíthnos i. Greece see Kythnos
Kithnou, Stenón sea chan. Greece see Kythnou, Steno
Kiti, Cape Cyprus see Kition, Cape
Kitimat Canada 122 D4
Kitinen r. Fin. 32 G2
Kition, Cape Cyprus 77 A2
Kitiou, Akra c. Cyprus see Kition, Cape
Kitob Uzbek. see Kitab
Kitsa Rus. Fed. 32 I1
Kitscoty Canada 123 I4
Kittanning U.S.A. 130 D3
Kittilä Fin. 32 G2
Kittur India 72 B3
Kitty Hawk U.S.A. 128 E4
Kitui Kenya 96 C5
Kitumbini Tanz. 97 C7
Kitunda Tanz. 97 B6
Kitwanga Canada 122 D4
Kitwe Zambia 95 F8
Kitzbühel Austria 37 F5
Kitzbüheler Alpen mts Austria 37 F5
Kitzingen Germany 36 E4
Kiu Kenya 96 C5
Kiu Lom Dam Thai. 60 B4
Kiunga P.N.G. 57 J7
Kiunga Marine National Reserve nature res. Kenya 96 D5
Kiuruvesi Fin. 32 G3
Kivalo ridge Fin. 32 G2
Kivijärvi Fin. 32 G3
Kivijärvi l. Fin. 32 G3
Kivilompolo Norway 32 F1
Kiviõli Estonia 33 G4
Kivivaara Fin. 32 H3
Kivu, Lake Dem. Rep. Congo/Rwanda 94 F5
Kiwaba N'zogi Angola 95 C7
Kiwai Island P.N.G. 57 J7
Kiwawa Tanz. 97 C7
Kiyāt Saudi Arabia 89 I5
Kiyev Ukr. see Kiev
Kiyevskoye Vodokhranilishche resr Ukr. see Kyyivs'ke Vodoskhovyshche
Kıyıköy Turkey 46 F4
Kizel Rus. Fed. 28 K4
Kizema Rus. Fed. 28 H3
Kizhi, Ostrov i. Rus. Fed. 28 E3
Kızılca Dağ mt. Turkey 78 B3
Kızılcahamam Turkey 78 C2
Kızıldağ mt. Turkey 77 B1
Kızıl Dağı mt. Turkey 79 D3
Kızılırmak r. Turkey 78 C2
Kızılören Turkey 78 C3
Kızıltepe Turkey 79 E3
Kizil"yurt Rus. Fed. 79 F2
Kızkalesi Turkey 77 B1
Kizlyar Rus. Fed. 79 F2
Kizlyarskiy Zaliv b. Rus. Fed. 79 F1
Kizner Rus. Fed. 28 I4
Kizreka Rus. Fed. 32 I2
Kizyl-Arbat Turkm. see Gyzylarbat
Kizyl-Atrek Turkm. see Gyzyletrek
Kizylayak Turkm. 81 F2
Kizyl Jilga Aksai Chin 74 C2
Kizyl-Su Turkm. 80 C2
Kjøllefjord Norway 32 G1
Kladanj Bos.-Herz. 44 G2
Kladno Czech Rep. 37 G3
Kladovo Yugo. 46 C2
Klagan Sabah Malaysia 59 G1
Klagenfurt Austria 37 G5
Klagetoh U.S.A. 137 H4
Klaipėda Lith. 33 F5
Klaksvig Faroe Is see Klaksvík
Klaksvík Faroe Is 34 [inset]
Klamath r. U.S.A. 134 A4
Klamath Falls U.S.A. 134 B4
Klamath Mountains U.S.A. 134 B4
Klampo Indon. 59 G2
Klang Malaysia see Kelang
Klappan r. Canada 122 D3
Klarälven r. Sweden 31 H1
Klaten Indon. 59 E4
Klatovy Czech Rep. 37 F4
Klawer S. Africa 98 C6
Klawock U.S.A. 120 F4
Klazienaveen Neth. 36 C2
Kłecko Poland 37 H2
Kleinegga mt. Norway 33 C3
Kleinmachnow Germany 37 F2
Kleinsee S. Africa 98 C6
Kleitoria Greece 47 C6
Klekovača mt. Bos.-Herz. 44 F2
Klemtu Canada 122 D4
Kleppestø Norway 33 B3
Klerksdorp S. Africa 99 E5
Kletnya Rus. Fed. 29 E5
Kletsk Belarus see Klyetsk
Kletskaya Rus. Fed. 29 G6
Kletskiy Rus. Fed. see Kletskaya
Kleve Germany 36 C3
Klimavichy Belarus 29 D5
Kliment Bulg. 46 E3
Klimovo Rus. Fed. 31 M2
Klin Rus. Fed. 28 F4
Klina Yugo. 46 B3
Klinaklini r. Canada 122 E5
Klingkang, Banjaran mts Indon./Malaysia 59 E2
Klintsy Rus. Fed. 29 E5
Klippan Sweden 33 D4
Klis Croatia 44 F3
Klitmøller Denmark 33 C4
Klitória Greece see Kleitoria
Ključ Bos.-Herz. 44 F2
Kłobuck Poland 37 I3
Kłodawa Poland 37 I2
Kłodzko Poland 37 H3
Klondike r. Canada 122 B1
Klondike Goldrush National Historical Park nat. park U.S.A. 122 C3
Klosterneuburg Austria 37 H4
Klosters Switz. 39 H3
Klötze (Altmark) Germany 36 E2
Kluane r. Canada 122 B2
Kluane Lake Canada 122 B2
Kluane National Park Canada 122 B2
Kluang Malaysia see Keluang
Kluang, Tanjung pt Indon. 59 E3
Kluczbork Poland 37 I3
Klukhori Rus. Fed. see Karachayevsk
Klumpang, Teluk b. Indon. 59 G3
Klungkung Indon. 59 F5
Klupro Pak. 81 G5
Klyavlino Rus. Fed. 29 J5
Klyetsk Belarus 29 C5
▶Klyuchevskaya, Sopka vol. Rus. Fed. 27 Q4
world 10–11
Klyuchi Rus. Fed. 27 Q4
Knaresborough U.K. 35 F4
Knee Lake Canada 123 M4
Knetzgau Germany 36 E4
Kneževi Vinogradi Croatia 44 G2
Knezha Bulg. 46 D3
Knić Yugo. 46 B3
Knife r. U.S.A. 132 A2
Knighton U.K. 35 E5
Knights Landing U.S.A. 136 B2
Knin Croatia 44 F2
Knittelfeld Austria 37 G5
Knivsta Sweden 33 E4
Knizhovnik Bulg. 46 D4
Knjaževac Yugo. 46 C3
Knob Lake Canada see Schefferville
Knockaboy hill Rep. of Ireland 35 B6
Knockmealdown Mountains hills Rep. of Ireland 35 B5
Knokke-Heist Belgium 36 A3
Knosos tourist site Greece see Knossos
Knossós tourist site Greece see Knossos
Knossos tourist site Greece 47 D7
Knox U.S.A. 130 D3
Knox, Cape Canada 122 C4
Knox Coast Antarctica 167 F2
Knoxville GA U.S.A. 129 C5
Knoxville TN U.S.A. 128 C5
Knud Rasmussen Land reg. Greenland 121 M2
Knyazhitsy Rus. Fed. 33 H4
Knysna S. Africa 98 D7
Ko, Gora mt. Rus. Fed. 64 D3
Koani Tanz. 97 C6
Koartac Canada see Quaqtaq
Koba Indon. 59 D3
Kobayashi Japan 65 B7
Kōbe Japan 65 C6
København Denmark see Copenhagen
Kobenni Mauritania 92 C2
Koblenz Germany 36 C3
K'obo Eth. 96 C1
Koboldo Rus. Fed. 64 C1
Kobrin Belarus see Kobryn
Kobroör i. Indon. 57 H7
Kobryn Belarus 29 C5
Kobuk Valley National Park U.S.A. 120 D3
K'obulet'i Georgia 79 E2
Kobyay Rus. Fed. 27 M3
Kocaafşar r. Turkey 47 F4
Koca Dağ mt. Turkey 47 F5
Kocaeli Turkey 78 B2
Kocaeli prov. Turkey 46 F4
Kočani Macedonia 46 C4
Koçarlı Turkey 47 E6
Kocasu r. Turkey 78 B2
Kočeljevo Yugo. 46 A2
Kočevje Slovenia 44 E2
Koch'ang S. Korea 65 A6
Koch Bihar India 75 F4
Kocher r. Germany 36 D4
Kocherinovo Bulg. 46 C3
Kochevo Rus. Fed. 28 J4
Kochi India see Cochin
Kōchi Japan 65 C6
Koçhisar Turkey see Kızıltepe
Kochubey Rus. Fed. 29 H7
Kochylas hill Greece 47 D5
Kock Poland 37 K3
Kod India 72 B3
Kodaikanal India 72 C4
Kodari Nepal 75 E4
Kodarma India 75 E4
Kodiak U.S.A. 120 D4
Kodiak Island U.S.A. 120 D4
Kodinar India 72 B1
Kodino Rus. Fed. 28 F3
Kodiyakkarai India 72 C4
Kodok Sudan 96 B2
Kodori r. Georgia 79 E2
Kodumuru India 72 C3
Kodyma Ukr. 29 D6
Kodzhaele mt. Bulg./Greece 46 D4
Koës Namibia 98 C5
Kofa Mountains U.S.A. 137 F5
Kofarnihon Tajik. 81 G2
Kofarnihon r. Tajik. 81 G2
Koffiefontein S. Africa 98 E6
Kofinas, Oros mt. Greece 47 D7
Köflach Austria 37 G5
Koforidua Ghana 93 E4
Kōfu Japan 65 D6
Kogălniceanu airport Romania 46 F2
Kogaluc r. Canada 124 E1
Kogaluk r. Canada 125 I1
Kögart Kyrg. see Alaykuu
Køge Denmark 33 D5
Kogi state Nigeria 93 G3
Kogon Uzbek. see Kagan
Kogoni Mali 92 D2
Kohat Pak. 81 G3
Kohila Estonia 33 G4
Kohima India 75 G4
Kohkīlūyeh va Būyer Aḥmadī prov. Iran 80 B4
Kohler Range mts Antarctica 167 K2
Kohls Ranch U.S.A. 137 G4
Kohlu Pak. 81 G4
Kohouro well Chad 88 D5
Kohsan Afgh. 81 E3
Kohtla-Järve Estonia 28 C4
Koidern Canada 122 A2
Koigi Estonia 33 G4
Koihoa India 73 G4
Koilkonda India 72 C2
Koin r. Rus. Fed. 28 I3
Koi Sanjaq Iraq 79 F3
Koitere l. Fin. 32 H3
Koivu Fin. 32 G2
Kŏje-do i. S. Korea 65 B6
Kojonup Australia 109 B8
Kok r. Thai. 60 C3
Kokand Uzbek. 81 G1
Kökar Fin. 33 F4
Kök-Art Kyrg. see Alaykuu
Kokcha r. Afgh. 81 G2
Kokchetav Kazakh. see Kokshetau
Kokemäki Fin. 33 F3
Kokerboom Namibia 98 C6
Koki Senegal 92 B2
Kokkina Cyprus 77 A2
Kokkola Fin. 32 F3
Koknese Latvia 33 G4
Koko Nigeria 93 G3
Kokofata Mali 92 C2
Kokolo-Pozo Côte d'Ivoire 92 D4
Kokomo U.S.A. 132 E3
Kokong Botswana 98 D5
Kokoro Benin 93 F3
Kokou mt. Guinea 92 B3
Kokpekti Kazakh. 70 F2
Koksan N. Korea 65 A5
Kokshaal-Tau mts China/Kyrg. 70 E3
Kokshetau Kazakh. 26 G4
Koksoak r. Canada 125 G1
Kokstad S. Africa 99 F6
Koktokay China see Fuyun
Kola Rus. Fed. 32 I1
Kola r. Rus. Fed. 32 I1
Kolab r. India see Sabari
Kolabira India 73 E1
Kolachi r. Pak. 81 F5
Kolaghat India 75 E5
Kolahoi mt. Jammu and Kashmir 74 B2
Kolaka Indon. 57 F6
Kolana Indon. 108 D2
Ko Lanta Thai. 61 B7
Kola Peninsula Rus. Fed. 28 E2
Kolar Chhattisgarh India 72 D2
Kolar Karnataka India 72 C3
Kolaras India 74 C4
Kolar Gold Fields India 72 C3
Kolari Fin. 32 F2
Kolarovgrad Bulg. see Shumen
Kolašin Yugo. 46 A3
Kolayat India 74 B4
Kolberg Poland see Kołobrzeg
Kolbio Kenya 96 D5
Kolda Senegal 92 B2
Kolding Denmark 33 C5
Kole Kasai Oriental Dem. Rep. Congo 94 D5
Kole Orientale Dem. Rep. Congo 94 E4
Koléa Alg. 43 H4
Kolguyev, Ostrov i. Rus. Fed. 28 I1
Kolhan reg. India 75 E5
Kolhapur India 72 B2
Kolhumadulu Atoll Maldives 71 D11
Koliba r. Guinea/Guinea-Bissau 92 B2
Kolikata India see Kolkata
Kolima l. Fin. 32 G3
Kolín Czech Rep. 37 G3
Kolin kansallispuisto nat. park Fin. 32 H3
Kõljala Estonia 33 F4
Kolkasrags pt Latvia 33 F4

▶Kolkata India 75 F5
3rd most populous city in Asia and 7th in the world.
world 16–17

Kolkhozabad Tajik. see Kolkhozobod
Kolkhozobod Tajik. 81 G2
Kollam India see Quilon
Kollegal India 72 C3
Kolleru Lake India 72 D2
Kollo Niger 93 F2
Köln Germany see Cologne
Kolno Poland 37 J2
Koło Poland 37 I2
Kolo Tanz. 97 B6
Kołobrzeg Poland 37 G1
Kologriv Rus. Fed. 28 H4
Kolokani Mali 92 C2
Kolombangara i. Solomon Is 107 E2
Kolomea Ukr. see Kolomyya
Kolomna Rus. Fed. 29 F5
Kolomonyi Dem. Rep. Congo 95 D6
Kołomyja Ukr. see Kolomyya
Kolomyya Ukr. 29 C6
Kolondiéba Mali 92 D3
Kolonedale Indon. 57 F6
Kolonjë Albania 46 A4
Kolonkwane Botswana 98 D5
Kolozero, Ozero l. Rus. Fed. 32 I1
Kolozsvár Romania see Cluj-Napoca
Kolpashevo Rus. Fed. 26 I4
Kol'skiy Poluostrov pen. Rus. Fed. see Kola Peninsula
Kölsvallen Sweden 33 D3
Koltubanovskiy Rus. Fed. 29 I5
Kolubara r. Yugo. 46 B2
Kölük Turkey see Kahta

Koluli Eritrea **89** I6
Kolva *r.* Rus. Fed. **28** K2
Kolva *r.* Rus. Fed. **28** K3
Kolvereid Norway **32** C2
Kolvik Norway **32** G1
Kolvitsa Rus. Fed. **32** I2
Kolwezi Dem. Rep. Congo **95** E7
Kolya *r.* India **72** B2
Kolyma *r.* Rus. Fed. **27** Q3
Kolyma Lowland Rus. Fed. *see* Kolymskaya Nizmennost'
Kolyma Range *mts* Rus. Fed. *see* Kolymskaya, Khrebet
Kolymskaya Nizmennost' *lowland* Rus. Fed. **27** P3
Kolymskiy, Khrebet *mts* Rus. Fed. **27** Q3
Kolymskoye Vodokhranilishche *resr* Rus. Fed. **29** H5
Kolyshley Rus. Fed. **29** H5
Kolyuchinskaya Guba *b.* Rus. Fed. **120** H3
Kom *mt.* Bulg. **46** C3
Komadugu-gana *watercourse* Nigeria **93** I2
Komaga-take *vol.* Japan **64** E4
Komagvær Norway **32** H1
Komandnaya, Gora *mt.* Rus. Fed. **64** D2
Komandorskiye Ostrova *is* Rus. Fed. **27** Q4
Komarnica *r.* Yugo. **46** A3
Komárno Slovakia **37** I5
Komati *r.* Swaziland **99** F5
Komatipoort S. Africa **99** F5
Komatsu Japan **65** D5
Komatsushima Japan **65** C6
Komba Dem. Rep. Congo **94** E4
Komba *i.* Indon. **57** F7
Kombat Namibia **98** C3
Kombe Dem. Rep. Congo **95** E6
Kombe Tanz. **97** C4
Kombissiri Burkina **93** E2
Komering *r.* Indon. **58** D3
Komi, Respublika *aut. rep.* Rus. Fed. **28** I3
Komi A.S.S.R. *aut. rep.* Rus. Fed. *see* Komi, Respublika
Komintern Ukr. *see* Marhanets'
Komi-Permyak Autonomous Okrug *admin. div.* Rus. Fed. *see* Komi-Permyatskiy Avtonomnyy Okrug
Komi-Permyatskiy Avtonomnyy Okrug *admin. div.* Rus. Fed. **28** J3
Komi Republic *aut. rep.* Rus. Fed. *see* Komi, Respublika
Komiža Croatia **44** F3
Komló Hungary **44** G1
Kommunarsk Ukr. *see* Alchevs'k
Kommunizm, Qullai *mt.* Tajik. *see* Garmo, Qullai
Kommunizm, Pik *mt.* Tajik. *see* Garmo, Qullai
Komodo *i.* Indon. **108** B2
Komodo National Park Indon. **57** E7
Komodou Guinea **92** C3
Komoé *r.* Côte d'Ivoire **92** E4
Komono Congo **94** B5
Komoran *i.* Indon. **57** I7
Komotini Greece **46** D4
Kompong Cham Cambodia *see* Kâmpóng Cham
Kompong Chhnang Cambodia *see* Kâmpóng Chhnăng
Kompong Kleang Cambodia *see* Kâmpóng Khleăng
Kompong Som Cambodia *see* Sihanoukville
Kompong Som Bay Cambodia *see* Sihanoukville, Chhâk
Kompong Speu Cambodia *see* Kâmpóng Spœ
Kompong Thom Cambodia *see* Kâmpóng Thum
Komrat Moldova *see* Comrat
Komsomol Atyrauskaya Oblast' Kazakh. *see* Komsomol'skiy
Komsomol Kazakh. *see* Karabalyk
Komsomol Turkm. *see* Komsomol'sk
Komsomolets, Ostrov *i.* Rus. Fed. **27** J1
Komsomolets, Zaliv *b.* Kazakh. **29** J7
Komsomol'sk Turkm. **81** E2
Komsomol's'k Ukr. **29** F6
Komsomol'skiy Kazakh. **29** J7
Komsomol'skiy Rus. Fed. **27** R3
Komsomol'skiy Khanty-Mansiyskiy Avtonomnyy Okrug Rus. Fed. *see* Yugorsk
Komsomol'skiy Respublika Kalmykiya - Khalm'g-Tangch Rus. Fed. **29** H7
Komsomol'skiy Respublika Mordoviya Rus. Fed. **29** H5
Komsomol'sk-na-Amure Rus. Fed. **64** D2
Komuniga Bulg. **46** D4
Kon India **75** D4
Konacık Turkey **77** B1
Konada India **72** D2
Konarak India *see* Konarka
Konarka India **73** E2
Konch India **74** C4
Konchezero Rus. Fed. **28** E3
Kondagaon India **73** D2
Kondapalle India **72** D2
Kondinin Australia **109** B8
Kondinskoye Rus. Fed. *see* Oktyabr'skoye
Kondoa Tanz. **97** D3
Kondol' Rus. Fed. **29** H5
Kondopoga Rus. Fed. **28** F3
Kondrovo Rus. Fed. **28** G4
Kondūz Afgh. **81** G2
Kondūz *prov.* Afgh. **81** G2
Konečka Planina *mts* Macedonia **46** C4
Kong Cameroon **93** I4
Kong Côte d'Ivoire **92** D3
Kông, Kaôh *i.* Cambodia **61** C6
Kông, Tônlé *r.* Cambodia **61** D5
Kong, Xé *r.* Laos **61** D5
Kongbo Cent. Afr. Rep. **94** D3
Kong Christian IX Land reg. Greenland **121** P3
Kong Christian X Land reg. Greenland **121** Q2
Kong Frederik VI Kyst coastal area Greenland **121** O3
Kong Frederik VIII Land reg. Greenland **121** Q2
Kong Frederik IX Land reg. Greenland **121** N3
Kong Karls Land is Svalbard **26** C2
Kongkemul *mt.* Indon. **59** G2
Kongola Namibia **98** C3
Kongolo Dem. Rep. Congo **95** E6
Kong Oscars Fjord inlet Greenland **121** Q2
Kongoussi Burkina **93** E2
Kongsberg Norway **33** B4
Kongsfjord Norway **32** H1
Kongsvinger Norway **33** C3
Kong Wilhelm Land reg. Greenland **121** Q2
Konibodom Tajik. *see* Kanibadam
Koniecpol Poland **37** I3

▶Koror Palau **57** H4
Capital of Palau.

Kösely *r.* Romania **46** B1

Koro Sea *b.* Fiji **107** G3
Körösladány Hungary **37** J5
Korosten' Ukr. **29** D6
Korostyshiv Ukr. **29** D6
Koro Toro Chad **88** D5
Korpilahti Fin. **32** N5
Korpilombolo Sweden **32** F2
Korpivaara Fin. **32** P5
Korpo. **33** F3
Korsakov Rus. Fed. **64** E3
Korshunovo Rus. Fed. **27** K2
Korsnäs Fin. **32** L5
Korsør Denmark **33** C5
Korsze Poland **37** J1
Kortala Sudan **89** F6
Kortesjärvi Fin. **32** M5
Korti Sudan **89** F6
Kortkeros Rus. Fed. **28** I3
Kortrijk Belgium **39** E1
Korucu Turkey **47** L5
Korup, Parc National de *nat. park* Cameroon **93** H4
Korvala Fin. **32** G2
Korwai India **74** C4
Koryakskaya, Sopka *vol.* Rus. Fed. **27** P4
Koryakskiy Khrebet *mts* Rus. Fed. **27** P3
Koryazhma Rus. Fed. **28** H3
Koryŏng S. Korea **65** B6
Korzhun Kazakh. **29** J6
Kos Greece **47** E6
Kos *i.* Greece **47** E6
Kosa Rus. Fed. **28** J4
Kosa *r.* Rus. Fed. **28** J4
Kosan N. Korea **65** A5
Koschagyl Kazakh. **29** J7
Kościan Poland **37** H2
Kościerzyna Poland **37** H1
Kosciusko U.S.A. **133** D5
Kosciusko, Mount Australia *see* Kosciuszko, Mount
Kosciusko Island U.S.A. **122** C3
Kosciuszko, Mount Australia **112** D5
Kosciuszko National Park Australia **112** D5
Kose Estonia **33** G4
Köseçobanlı Turkey **77** A1
Köse Dağı *mt.* Turkey **79** D2
Kosha Sudan **89** F4
Kosh-Agach Rus. Fed. **27** I5
Koshankol' Kazakh. **29** I6
Koshbulakskoye Vodokhranilishche *resr* Turkm. **81** E1
Koshikijima-rettō *is* Japan **65** B7
Koshk Afgh. **81** E3
Koshk-e Kohneh Afgh. **81** E3
Koshki Rus. Fed. **29** K5
Kosi *r.* India **74** C3
Košice Slovakia **37** J4
Kosigi India **72** C3
Kosi Reservoir Nepal **75** E4
Kosjerić Yugo. **46** B2
Kŏsk Turkey **47** F6
Koskhovik Kazakh. *see* Kasan
Kosŏng N. Korea **65** B5
Kosova *prov.* Yugo. *see* Kosovo
Kosovo *prov.* Yugo. **46** B3
Kosovo-Metohija *prov.* Yugo. *see* Kosovo
Kosovo Polje Yugo. **46** B3
Kosovo Polje plain Yugo. **46** B3
Kosovska Mitrovica Yugo. **46** B3
Kosrae *atoll* Micronesia **164** E5
Kossa *well* Mauritania **92** D2
Kossatori *well* Niger **93** I2
Kösseine *hill* Germany **36** E4
Kossol Reef Palau **57** H4
Kossou, Lac de *l.* Côte d'Ivoire **92** D4
Kosta-Khetagurovo Rus. Fed. *see* Nazran'
Kostanay Kazakh. **26** C4
Kostenets Bulg. **46** C3
Kosti Sudan **89** G6
Kostinbrod Bulg. **46** C3
Kostino Rus. Fed. **27** I3
Kostomuksha Rus. Fed. **32** H4
Kostopil' Ukr. **29** E6
Kostopol' Ukr. *see* Kostopil'
Kostroma Rus. Fed. **28** H4
Kostroma *r.* Rus. Fed. **28** H4
Kostroma Oblast *admin. div.* Rus. Fed. *see* Kostromskaya Oblast'
Kostromskaya Oblast' *admin. div.* Rus. Fed. **28** G4
Kostrzyn Poland **37** H2
Kostrzyn *r.* Poland **37** K2
Kostyantynivka Ukr. **29** F6
Kostyukovichi Belarus *see* Kastsyukovichy
Kosubosu Nigeria **93** F3
Kos'yu Rus. Fed. **28** K2
Kos'yu *r.* Rus. Fed. **28** K2
Koszalin Poland **37** H1
Kőszeg Hungary **37** H5
Kota Andhra Pradesh India **72** D3
Kota Chhattisgarh India **75** D5
Kota Rajasthan India **74** B4
Kotaagung Indon. **58** D4
Kota Baharu Malaysia *see* Kota Bharu
Kotabaru Kalimantan Barat Indon. **59** E3
Kotabaru Kalimantan Selatan Indon. **59** G3
Kota Belud Sabah Malaysia **59** G1
Kota Bharu Malaysia **58** C1
Kotabumi Indon. **58** C2
Kot Addu Pak. **81** H4
Kota Kinabalu Sabah Malaysia **59** G1
Kotala Fin. **32** N2
Kotapinang Indon. **58** C2
Kotari *r.* India **74** C4
Kota Tinggi Malaysia **58** C2
Kotawaringin Indon. **58** D4
Kotchandpur Bangl. **75** F5
Kotcho *r.* Canada **122** F3
Kotcho Lake Canada **122** F3
Kot Diji Pak. **81** G5
Kotdwara India **74** D3
Koteabes India **74** C4
Kotel Bulg. **46** E3
Kotel'nich Rus. Fed. **28** I4
Kotel'nikovo Rus. Fed. **29** H7
Kotel'nyy, Ostrov *i.* Rus. Fed. **27** N2
Kotgar India **73** D2
Kotgarh India **74** D3
Kothagudem India *see* Kottagudem
Kothi India **74** D4
Kotiari Naoude Senegal **92** B2
Kotido Uganda **96** B4
Kotka Fin. **33** G3
Kot Kapura India **74** B3
Kotkino Rus. Fed. **28** J2
Kotlas Rus. Fed. **28** H3
Kotli Pak. **81** H3
Kotlik U.S.A. **120** C3
Kotlina Sandomierska *basin* Poland **37** J3
Kotly Rus. Fed. **33** H4
Kótófa Króvá *mt.* Slovakia **37** J4
Koton-Karifi Nigeria **93** G4
Kotorkoshi Nigeria **93** G3

Kotorsko Bos.-Herz. **44** G2
Kotor Varoš Bos.-Herz. **44** G2
Kotouba Côte d'Ivoire **92** E3
Kotovo Rus. Fed. **29** H6
Kotovsk Rus. Fed. **29** G5
Kotovs'k Ukr. **41** M2
Kot Putli India **74** C4
Kotri *r.* India **72** D2
Kotri Pak. **81** G5
Kottagudem India **72** D2
Kottayam India **72** C4
Kottu Sri Lanka *see* Sri Jayewardenepura Kotte
Kotto *r.* Cent. Afr. Rep. **94** D3
Kotturu India **72** C3
Kotu *r.* Rus. Fed. **27** K2
Kotwar Peak India **75** D5
Kotzebue U.S.A. **120** C3
Kotzebue Sound *sea chan.* U.S.A. **120** C3
Kouango Cent. Afr. Rep. **94** D3
Kouba Olanga Chad **88** D5
Koubia Guinea **92** B3
Kouchibouguac National Park Canada **125** I4
Koudougou Burkina **93** E2
Kouéré Burkina **92** E3
Koufonisi *i.* Kriti Greece **47** E7
Koufonisi *i.* Greece **47** D6
Koufos Greece **47** D5
Kougaberge *mts* S. Africa **98** D7
Koui Cent. Afr. Rep. **94** B3
Kouilou *admin. div.* Congo **95** A6
Kouki Cent. Afr. Rep. **94** C3
Koukourou *r.* Cent. Afr. Rep. **94** C3
Koulbo Chad **88** D6
Koulikoro Mali **92** C3
Koulikoro *admin. div.* Mali **92** D3
Kouloudia Chad **88** B6
Koum Cameroon **93** I3
Kouma *r.* Cent. Afr. Rep. **94** C3
Koumac New Caledonia **107** F4
Koumala Australia **111** G4
Koumameygou Gabon **94** A4
Koumbala Cent. Afr. Rep. **94** D3
Koumbia Burkina **92** E3
Koumbia Guinea **92** B3
Koumogo Chad **94** C2
Koundâra Guinea **92** B3
Koundian Mali **92** C3
Koundoumba Burkina **92** D3
Koungheul Senegal **92** B3
Kounoupoi *i.* Greece **47** E6
Kountel *well* Niger **93** H2
Kountze U.S.A. **133** C6
Koupéla Burkina **93** E2
Kouqian China *see* Yongji
Kourou Fr. Guiana **147** H3
Kourou *r.* Greece **47** D4
Koûroudjél Mauritania **92** C1
Kouroussa Guinea **92** C3
Koussanar Guinea **92** B3
Kousséri Cameroon **88** B3
Koussountou Togo **93** F3
Koutiala Mali **92** C3
Kouto Côte d'Ivoire **92** D3
Kouvola Fin. **33** G3
Kouyou *r.* Congo **94** C5
Kovačica Yugo. **46** B2
Kovdor Rus. Fed. **32** H2
Kovdozero Rus. Fed. **32** H2
Kovel' Ukr. **29** C6
Kovernino Rus. Fed. **28** G4
Kovin Yugo. **46** B2
Kovno Lith. *see* Kaunas
Kovriga, Gora *hill* Rus. Fed. **28** I2
Kovrov Rus. Fed. **28** G4
Kovylkino Rus. Fed. **29** G5
Kovzhskoye, Ozero *l.* Rus. Fed. **28** F3
Kowanyama Australia **111** C2
Kowares *waterhole* Namibia **98** B3
Kowloon Hong Kong China **67** [inset]
Kowloon Peak *hill* Hong Kong China **67** [inset]
Kowloon Peninsula Hong Kong China **67** [inset]
Kowr-e-Koja *watercourse* Iran **81** E5
Kōyama-misaki *pt* Japan **65** B6
Kŏyang S. Korea **65** B5
Köyceğiz Turkey **47** F6
Köyceğiz Gölü *l.* Turkey **47** F6
Koygorodok Rus. Fed. **28** J3
Koymatdag, Gory *hills* Turkm. **80** C1
Koynare Bulg. **46** C3
Koyna Reservoir India **72** B2
Koyukuk *r.* U.S.A. **120** C3
Koyulhisar Turkey **79** D2
Kozağacı Turkey *see* Günyüzü
Kozan Turkey **78** D3
Kozani Greece **47** B4
Kozara *mts* Bos.-Herz. **44** G2
Kozara *r.* Bos.-Herz. **44** F3
Kozarska Dubica Bos.-Herz. *see* Bosanska Dubica
Kozel'sk Rus. Fed. **29** G5
Kozen *well* Chad **88** D4
Kozhevnikovo Rus. Fed. **27** L2
Kozhikode India *see* Calicut
Kozhim-Iz, Gora *mt.* Rus. Fed. **28** K3
Kozhva *r.* Rus. Fed. **28** K2
Kozhva *r.* Rus. Fed. **28** K2
Kozhym *r.* Rus. Fed. **28** K2
Kozienice Poland **37** J3
Kozloduy Bulg. **46** C3
Kozluk Bos.-Herz. **46** A2
Koźmin Poland **37** H3
Koznitsa *mt.* Bulg. **46** C3
Koz'modem'yansk Rus. Fed. **28** H4
Kožuchów Poland **37** G3
Kōzu-shima *i.* Japan **65** D6

Kramfors Sweden **32** E3
Krammer est. Neth. **36** B3
Kranidi Greece **47** C6
Kranj Slovenia **44** F1
Kranji Reservoir Sing. **58** [inset]
Krapani Croatia **44** F3
Krapkowice Poland **37** H3
Krasavino Rus. Fed. **28** I3
Krasino Rus. Fed. **26** F2
Kraskino Rus. Fed. **64** B4
Krāslava Latvia **33** G5
Krasnaya Polyana Rus. Fed. **29** G8
Krasnaya Zarya Rus. Fed. **29** F5
Kraśnik Poland **37** K3
Krasnoarmeysk Kazakh. *see* Tayynsha
Krasnoarmeysk Rus. Fed. **29** H6
Krasnoarmiys'k Ukr. **29** F6
Krasnoarmeyskiy Rus. Fed. **27** R3
Krasnoarmiys'k Ukr. **29** F6
Krasnoarmeyskiy Rus. Fed. *see* Krasnoarmiys'k
Krasnoborsk Rus. Fed. **28** I3
Krasnodar Rus. Fed. **29** F7
Krasnodar Kray *admin. div.* Rus. Fed. *see* Krasnodarskiy Kray
Krasnodarskiy Kray *admin. div.* Rus. Fed. **29** F7
Krasnofarfornyy Rus. Fed. **31** L1
Krasnogorodskoye Rus. Fed. **33** H5
Krasnogorsk Rus. Fed. **64** E2
Krasnogorskoye Rus. Fed. **28** J4
Krasnograd Ukr. *see* Krasnohrad
Krasnogvardeysk Uzbek. *see* Bulungur
Krasnogvardeyskoye Rus. Fed. **29** G7
Krasnohrad Ukr. **29** E6
Krasnohvardiys'ke Ukr. **29** E7
Krasnokamensk Rus. Fed. **63** J3
Krasnokamsk Rus. Fed. **28** J4
Krasnoles'ye Rus. Fed. **37** K1
Krasnokholm Rus. Fed. **28** G4
Krasnoostrovskiy Rus. Fed. **33** H3
Krasnoperekops'k Ukr. **29** E7
Krasnopol' Rus. Fed. **64** E2
Krasnopol'ye Rus. Fed. **64** E3
Krasnoselkup Rus. Fed. **26** I3
Krasnosel'kup Rus. Fed. **26** I3
Krasnoslobodsk Rus. Fed. **29** H5
Krasnotur'insk Rus. Fed. **26** G4
Krasnoufimsk Rus. Fed. **28** K4
Krasnousol'skiy Rus. Fed. **28** K5
Krasnovishersk Rus. Fed. **28** K3
Krasnovodsk Turkm. *see* Turkmenbashi
Krasnovodskaya Oblast' *admin. div.* Turkm. *see* Balkanskaya Oblast'
Krasnovodskiy Zaliv *b.* Turkm. **80** C2
Krasnovodskoye Plato *plat.* Turkm. **80** C1
Krasnoyar Kazakh. **29** J6
Krasnoyarovo Rus. Fed. **64** B2
Krasnoyarsk Rus. Fed. **27** J4
Krasnoyarskiy Kray *admin. div.* Rus. Fed. **27** E1
Krasnoyarsk Kray *admin. div.* Rus. Fed. *see* Krasnoyarskiy Kray
Krasnoye Lipetskaya Oblast' Rus. Fed. **29** F5
Krasnoye Respublika Kalmykiya - Khalm'g-Tangch Rus. Fed. *see* Ulan Erge
Krasnoye, Ozero *l.* Rus. Fed. **27** R3
Krasnozatonskiy Rus. Fed. **28** J3
Krasnoznamensk Rus. Fed. **33** F5
Krasnyye Baki Rus. Fed. **28** H4
Krasnyye Barrikady Rus. Fed. **29** H7
Krasnyye Tkachi Rus. Fed. **28** F4
Krasnyy Kamyshanik Rus. Fed. *see* Komsomol'skiy
Krasnyy Kholm Rus. Fed. **28** G4
Krasnyy Kut Rus. Fed. **29** H6
Krasnyy Luch Ukr. **29** F6
Krasnyy Lyman Ukr. **29** F6
Krasnyy Yar Rus. Fed. **29** I7
Krasyliv Ukr. **29** C6
Kratie Cambodia *see* Krâchéh
Kratovo Macedonia **46** C3
Kraulshavn Greenland *see* Nuussuaq
Krâvanh, Chuŏr Phnum *mts* Cambodia *see* Cardamom Range
Kraynovka Rus. Fed. **79** F2
Krechevitsy Rus. Fed. **28** D4
Krefeld Germany **36** C3
Kremastan, Techniti Limni *resr* Greece **47** B5
Kremenchug Ukr. *see* Kremenchuk
Kremenchuk Ukr. **29** E6
Kremenchuts'ka Vodoskhovyshche *resr* Ukr. **29** E6
Kremges Ukr. *see* Svitlovods'k
Kremmling U.S.A. **134** F1
Krems an der Donau Austria **37** H5
Kremsmünster Austria **37** G5
Krenitzin Islands U.S.A. **120** C4
Krepoljin Yugo. **46** B2
Krems an der Donau Austria **37** G5
Kresna Bulg. **46** C3
Kresta, Zaliv *g.* Rus. Fed. **27** S3
Krest-Khal'dzhayy Rus. Fed. **27** N3
Krestovka Rus. Fed. **28** I2
Kresttsy Rus. Fed. **28** G5
Kretinga Lith. **33** F5
Kreuth Germany **37** G5
Kreuzeck Gruppe *mts* Austria **37** F5
Kreuzlingen Switz. **36** D5
Kreuztal Germany **36** C3
Krichev Belarus *see* Krychaw
Krichim Bulg. **46** D3
Krieza Greece **47** D5
Krikellos Greece **47** B5
Krikelos, Akra *pt* Greece **47** E6
Kril'on, Mys *c.* Rus. Fed. **64** E3
Krishna *r.* India **72** D2
Krishna, Mouths of the India **69** G5
Krishnagiri India **72** C3
Krishnai *r.* India **75** F4
Krishnanagar India **75** F5
Krishnaraja Sagara *l.* India **72** C3
Krishnarajpet India **72** C3
Kristdala Sweden **33** E4
Kristiania Norway *see* Oslo
Kristiansand Norway **33** B4
Kristianstad Sweden **33** D4
Kristiansund Norway **32** B3
Kristiinankaupunki Fin. *see* Kristinestad
Kristinehamn Sweden **33** I7
Kristinestad Fin. **33** F3
Kriti *admin. div.* Greece **47** D7
Kriti *i.* Greece **47** D7
Kritsa *r.* Bos.-Herz. **44** G3
Kriva Palanka Macedonia **46** C3
Kriva Reka *r.* Macedonia **46** C3
Křivoklátská Vrchovina *hills* Czech Rep. **37** F4
Krivoy Porog Rus. Fed. **28** F3
Krivoy Rog Ukr. *see* Kryvyy Rih
Krizevci Croatia **44** F1
Krk Bos.-Herz. **46** A2
Krk Croatia **44** F2
Krk *i.* Croatia **44** F2
Krka *r.* Slovenia **44** F2
Krka *r.* Slovenia **44** F3
Krkonošský národní park *nat. park* Czech Rep./Poland **37** G3
Kraljevica Croatia **44** F2
Kraljevo Yugo. **46** B3
Krňova Slovakia **37** J4
Kroknes Greenland **121** S3
Krokom Sweden **32** D3
Króksfjarðarnes Iceland **32** [inset]

Krokstadøra Norway **32** C3
Krolevets' Ukr. **29** E5
Kronach Germany **36** E4
Kronfjell Norway **33** C4
Kronli India **75** G3
Kronoby Fin. **32** E3
Kronotskiy Zaliv *b.* Rus. Fed. **27** Q4
Kronprins Christian Land reg. Greenland **121** Q1
Kronprins Frederik Bjerge nunataks Greenland **121** P3
Kronshtadt Romania *see* Braşov
Kroonstad S. Africa **99** E5
Kropotkin Rus. Fed. **29** G7
Krosno Poland **37** J4
Krosno Odrzańskie Poland **37** G2
Krossen Norway **33** C4
Krotoszyn Poland **37** H3
Kroya Indon. **58** D4
Kršško Slovenia **44** F2
Kruger National Park S. Africa **99** F3
Kruglyakov Rus. Fed. *see* Oktyabr'skiy
Krui Indon. **58** C4
Kruibertein S. Africa **98** E7
Krujë Albania **46** B3
Krumovgrad Bulg. **46** D4
Krungkao Thai. *see* Ayutthaya
Krung Thep Thai. *see* Bangkok
Krupa Bos.-Herz. *see* Bosanska Krupa
Krupa na Uni Bos.-Herz. *see* Bosanska Krupa
Krupina Slovakia **37** I4
Krupki Belarus **29** D5
Kruševac Yugo. **46** B3
Kruševo Macedonia **46** B4
Krušné Hory *mts* Czech Rep. **37** F3
Kruzof Island U.S.A. **122** C3
Krychaw Belarus **29** D5
Kryezi Albania **46** B3
Krylov Seamount *sea feature* N. Atlantic Ocean **160** M4
Krym' *pen.* Ukr. *see* Crimea
Krymsk Rus. Fed. **29** F7
Krymskaya Rus. Fed. *see* Krymsk
Kryms'kyy Pivostriv *pen.* Ukr. *see* Crimea
Krynica Poland **37** J4
Krystynopol Ukr. *see* Chervonohrad
Krytiko Pelagos *sea* Greece **47** D6
Kryvyy Rih Ukr. **29** E7
Krzyż Wielkopolski Poland **37** H2
Ksabi Alg. **91** E3
Ksar el Boukhari Alg. **43** H5
Ksar el Hirane Alg. **91** F2
Ksar el Kebir Morocco **90** D2
Ksar-es-Souk Morocco *see* Er Rachidia
Ksenofontova Rus. Fed. **28** J3
Kshirpai India **75** F5
Ksour, Monts des *mts* Tunisia **91** H2
Ksour Essaf Tunisia **45** C7
Kstovo Rus. Fed. **28** H4
Kü', Jabal al *hill* Saudi Arabia **80** A5
Ku, Wadi el *watercourse* Sudan **89** F3
Kuaidamao China *see* Tonghua
Kuala Belait Brunei **59** F1
Kuala Dungun Malaysia *see* Dungun
Kualajelai Indon. **59** E3
Kuala Kangsar Malaysia **58** C1
Kualakapuas Indon. **59** F3
Kuala Kerai Malaysia **58** C1
Kuala Kinabatangan *r. mouth* Sabah Malaysia **59** G1
Kuala Kubu Baharu Malaysia **58** C2
Kualakurun Indon. **59** F3
Kuala Lipis Malaysia **58** C1

▶Kuala Lumpur Malaysia **58** C2
National capital of Malaysia.

Kualapembuang Indon. **59** F3
Kuala Penyu Sabah Malaysia **59** F1
Kuala Pilah Malaysia **58** C2
Kualapuu U.S.A. **135** [inset] D1
Kualasampit Indon. **59** F3
Kualasimpang Indon. **58** B1
Kuala Terengganu Malaysia **58** C1
Kualatungal Indon. **58** C3
Kuamut Sabah Malaysia **59** G1
Kuandian China **65** B4
Kuangyuan China *see* Yiliang
Kuanshan Taiwan **67** G4
Kuantan Malaysia **58** C2
Kuba Azer. *see* Quba
Kuban' *r.* Rus. Fed. **29** F7
Kubār Syria **79** D4
Kubbum Sudan **89** F3
Kubenskoye, Ozero *l.* Rus. Fed. **28** G4
Kubnya *r.* Rus. Fed. **28** I5
Kubor, Mount P.N.G. **57** J7
Kubrat Bulg. **46** D3
Kubumesaäi Indon. **59** F3
Kučevo Yugo. **46** B2
Kuchaman India **74** B4
Kuchema Rus. Fed. **28** I2
Kuching Sarawak Malaysia **59** E2
Kucing China *see* Kuching
Kucovë Albania **46** A4
Küçükmenderes *r.* Turkey **47** E4
Küçükmenderes *r.* Turkey **47** F5
Kuda India **74** A5
Kudachi India **72** B2
Kudal India **72** B3
Kudat Sabah Malaysia **59** G1
Kudirkos Naumiestis Lith. **33** F5
Kudligi India **72** C3
Kudremukh *mt.* India **72** B3
Kudu Nigeria **93** G4
Kudus Indon. **59** E4
Kudymkar Rus. Fed. **28** J4
Kueishan Tai. *see* Taiwan **67** G3
Kufstein Austria **36** F5
Kugaaruk Canada **121** J3
Kugesi Rus. Fed. **28** I4
Kugka Lhai China **72** D2
Kugluktuk Canada **120** H3
Küh, Ra's-al- *pt* Iran **80** D5
Kühak Iran **81** F5
Kühbonän Iran **80** D4
Kühdasht Iran **80** A3
Kühīn Iran **80** B2
Kühīrī Iran **81** F5
Kuhmo Fin. **32** P4
Kuhmoinen Fin. **33** G3
Kühpāyeh *mt.* Iran **80** D3
Kührän, Küh-e *mt.* Iran **80** D5
Kührang *r.* Iran **80** B3
Kui Buri Thai. **61** B5
Kuitsa Estonia **33** F4
Kui Nua Namibia **98** C5
Kuitin China **67** F3
Kuitsa China *see* Kuytun
Kuivaniemi Fin. **32** M3
Kuivastu Estonia **33** F4
Kujang N. Korea **65** A5
Kuji Japan **64** F4
Kujū-san *vol.* Japan **65** B6

Kukan Rus. Fed. 64 C2
Kukawa Nigeria 93 I2
Kukerin Australia 109 B8
Kukës Albania 46 B3
Kukkola Fin. 32 G2
Kukmor Rus. Fed. 28 I4
Kukshi India 74 B5
Kukup Malaysia 58 C2
Kukurtli Turkm. 81 D2
Kukushtan Rus. Fed. 28 K4
Kūl r. Iran 80 C5
Kula Bulg. 46 C3
Kula Nigeria 93 G4
Kula Turkey 78 B3
Kula Yugo. 46 A2
Kulabu, Gunung mt. Indon. 58 B2
Kulachi Pak. 81 G4
Kulagino Kazakh. 29 I6
Kula Kangri mt. Bhutan 75 F3
Kulal, Mount Kenya 96 C4
Kulandy Kazakh. 70 A2
Kulao r. Pak. 81 F4
Kular Rus. Fed. 27 N2
Kulat, Gunung mt. Indon. 59 G2
Kuldiga Latvia 33 F4
Kuldja China see Yining
Kul'dur Rus. Fed. 64 D3
Kule Botswana 98 D4
Kulebaki Rus. Fed. 28 G5
Kulgera Australia 110 C5
Kuligi Rus. Fed. 28 J4
Kulikovo Rus. Fed. 28 H3
Kulim Malaysia 58 C1
Kulittalai India 72 C4
Kulmbach Germany 36 E3
Kŭlob Tajik. 81 G2
Kulotino Rus. Fed. 28 E4
Kuloy Rus. Fed. 28 G3
Kuloy r. Rus. Fed. 28 G2
Kulp Turkey 79 E3
Kul'sary Kazakh. 26 F5
Kulu Turkey 78 D3
Kulübe Tepe mt. Turkey 78 B3
Kulunda Rus. Fed. 26 H4
Kulundinskaya Step' plain Kazakh./Rus. Fed. 62 D1
Kulundinskoye, Ozero salt l. Rus. Fed. 26 H4
Kulusuk Greenland 121 P3
Kŭlvand Iran 80 C4
Kulwin Australia 112 B4
Kulyab Tajik. see Kŭlob
Kuma r. Rus. Fed. 32 H2
Kuma r. Rus. Fed. 79 F1
Kumagaya Japan 65 D6
Kumai, Teluk b. Indon. 59 E3
Kumaka Guyana 147 G4
Kumamoto Japan 65 B6
Kumano Japan 65 C6
Kumanovo Macedonia 46 E3
Kumasi Ghana 93 E4
Kumayri Armenia see Gyumri
Kumba Cameroon 93 H4
Kumbağ Turkey 46 E4
Kumbakonam India 72 C4
Kumbharli Ghat mt. India 72 B2
Kumbher Nepal 75 D3
Kumbo Cameroon 93 H4
Kum-Dag Turkm. see Gumdag
Kumel well Iran 80 C3
Kumertau Rus. Fed. 29 J5
Kumgang-san mt. N. Korea 65 B5
Kumguri India 75 F4
Kumher India 74 C4
Kumi S. Korea 65 B5
Kumi Uganda 96 B4
Kumla Sweden 33 I4
Kumlinge Fin. 33 G3
Kumlu Turkey 77 C1
Kummerower See l. Germany 37 F2
Kumo Nigeria 93 H3
Kŭmo-do i. S. Korea 65 A6
Kumon Range mts Myanmar 60 B2
Kumphawapi Thai. 60 C3
Kumputunturi hill Fin. 32 G2
Kumta India 72 B3
Kumu Dem. Rep. Congo 94 E4
Kumukahi, Cape U.S.A. 135 [inset] Z2
Kumul China see Hami
Kumund India 73 D1
Kumylzhenskaya Rus. Fed. see Kumylzhenskiy
Kumylzhenskiy Rus. Fed. 29 G6
Kun r. Myanmar 60 B4
Kunar r. Afgh. 81 G3
Kunashir, Ostrov i. Rus. Fec. 64 F3
Kunchaung Myanmar 60 B3
Kunda Dem. Rep. Congo 95 E5
Kunda Estonia 33 G4
Kunda India 75 D4
Kunda-dia-Baze Angola 95 C5
Kundapura India 72 B3
Kundar r. Afgh./Pak. 81 G3
Kundelungu, Parc National de nat. park Dem. Rep. Congo 95 E7
Kundelungu Ouest, Parc National de nat. park Dem. Rep. Congo 95 E7
Kundgol India 72 B3
Kundian Pak. 81 G3
Kundur r. Indon. see Kondūz
Kunduz Afgh. see Kondūz
Kunene admin. reg. Namibia 98 B3
Kunene r. Namibia 95 A9
Künes China see Xinyuan
Kungälv Sweden 33 C4
Kungei Alatau mts Kazakh./Kyrg. 70 D3
Kunggar China see Maizhokunggar
Küngöy Ala-Too mts Kazakh./Kyrg. see Kungei Alatau
Kungrad Uzbek. 76 F1
Kungsbacka Sweden 33 D4
Kungshamn Sweden 33 C4
Kungsör Sweden 33 E4
Kungu Dem. Rep. Congo 94 C4
Kungur mt. China see Kongur Shan
Kungur Rus. Fed. 28 K4
Kungyangon Myanmar 61 A4
Kunhegyes Hungary 37 J5
Kuni r. India 72 C3
Kunié i. New Caledonia see Pins, Île des
Kunigal India 72 C3
Kunimi-dake mt. Japan 65 B6
Kuningaküla Estonia 33 G4
Kuningan Indon. 59 E4
Kunjabar India 73 E1
Kunlavav India 74 A5
Kunlong Myanmar 60 B3
Kunlui r. India/Nepal 75 E4
Kunlun Shan mts China 70 C4
Kunlun Shankou pass China 75 G2
Kunmadaras Hungary 37 J5
Kunming China 66 B3
Kuno r. India 74 C4
Kunsan S. Korea 65 A6
Kunshan China 67 G2
Kunszentmárton Hungary 37 J5
Kuntshankoie Dem. Rep. Congo 94 D5
Kununurra Australia 110 B2
Kunwak r. Canada 123 L2
Kunwari r. India 74 C4

Kun'ya Rus. Fed. 28 D4
Kunyang Henan China see Yexian
Kunyang Yunnan China see Jinning
Kunyang Zhejiang China see Pingyang
Künzelsau Germany 36 D4
Kuocang Shan mts China 67 G2
Kuolayarvi Rus. Fed. 32 H2
Kuopio Fin. 32 G3
Kupa r. Croatia/Slovenia 44 F2
Kupang Indon. 57 F8
Kupiškis Lith. 33 G5
Kuprava Latvia 33 G4
Kupreanof Island U.S.A. 120 F4
Kupreanof Point U.S.A. 120 D4
Kupwara Jammu and Kashmir 74 B2
Kup"yans'k Ukr. 29 F6
Kuqa China 70 F3
Kür r. Azer. 79 G3
Kür r. Georgia 79 F2
Kur r. Rus. Fed. 64 C2
Kura r. Azer./Georgia 79 F2
Kura r. Rus. Fed. 29 G8
Kuragwi Nigeria 93 H3
Kurakh Rus. Fed. 79 F2
Kura kurk sea chan. Estonia/Latvia see Irbe Strait
Kuramā, Ḩarrat lava field Saudi Arabia 89 I3
Kurashiki Japan 65 C6
Kurasia India 75 D5
Kurayn i. Saudi Arabia 80 B5
Kurayoshi Japan 65 C6
Kurban Daği mt. Turkey 46 F4
Kurbin r. China 64 B2
Kurca r. Romania 46 B1
Kurchatov Rus. Fed. 29 E6
Kürdämir Azer. 79 G2
Kür Dili pt Azer. 79 G3
Kurduvadi India 72 B2
Kürdzhali Bulg. 46 D4
Kure Japan 65 C6
Küre Turkey 78 C2
Kure Atoll U.S.A. 164 G4
Kuressaare Estonia 33 F4
Kureyskoye Vodokhranilische resr Rus. Fed. 27 I3
Kurgan Rus. Fed. 26 G4
Kurganinsk Rus. Fed. 29 G7
Kurgannaya Rus. Fed. see Kurganinsk
Kurgantyube Tajik. see Qŭrghonteppa
Kuri India 74 A4
Kuria Muria Islands Oman see Ḩalāniyāt, Juzur al
Kuridala Australia 111 E4
Kurigram Bangl. 75 F4
Kurikka Fin. 32 F3
Kurikoma-yama vol. Japan 65 E5
Kuril Basin sea feature Sea of Okhotsk 164 D2
Kuril Islands Rus. Fed. 64 F3
Kurilovka Rus. Fed. 29 I6
Kuril'sk Rus. Fed. 54 G2
Kuril'skiye Ostrova is Rus. Fed. see Kuril Islands
Kuril Trench sea feature N. Pacific Ocean 164 D3
Kurino Japan 65 F5
Kurlovskiy Rus. Fed. 28 G5
Kurmanayevka Rus. Fed. 29 I5
Kurmuk Sudan 94 B2
Kurnool India 72 C3
Kurobe Japan 65 D5
Kuroiso Japan 65 D5
Kuror, Jebel mt. Sudan 89 F4
Kuro-shima i. Japan 65 B7
Kurow N.Z. 113 B4
Kurram r. Afgh./Pak. 81 G3
Kuršėnai Lith. 33 F4
Kurshskiy Zaliv b. Lith./Rus. Fed. see Courland Lagoon
Kursiši Lith. 33 F4
Kuršių marios b. Lith./Rus. Fed. see Courland Lagoon
Kursk Rus. Fed. 29 F6
Kurskaya Rus. Fed. 29 H7
Kurskaya Oblast' admin. div. Rus. Fed. 29 F6
Kurskiy Zaliv b. Lith./Rus. Fed. see Courland Lagoon
Kursk Oblast admin. div. Rus. Fed. see Kurskaya Oblast'
Kuršumlija Yugo. 46 B3
Kurşunlu Turkey 78 C2
Kurtalan Turkey 79 E3
Kuru Fin. 33 F3
Kurú r. Greece see Kourou
Kuru India 75 E5
Kuru watercourse Sudan 94 E2
Kurucaşile Turkey 78 D2
Kurud India 73 D1
Kurukshetra India 74 C3
Kurukh China see Guiyang
Kuruktag mts China 70 G3
Kuruman S. Africa 98 D5
Kuruman watercourse S. Africa 98 D5
Kurume Japan 65 B6
Kurumkan Rus. Fed. 63 I1
Kurun r. Sudan 96 B3
Kurunegala Sri Lanka 72 D5
Kurupukari Guyana 147 G3
Kurush, Jebel hills Sudan 89 F4
Kur'ya Rus. Fed. 28 K3
Kuryk Kazakh. 79 H2
Kuşadası Turkey 47 L6
Kuşadası Körfezi b. Turkey 78 A3
Kusary Azer. see Qusar
Kusawa Lake Canada 122 B2
Kuşcenneti Milli Parkı nat. park Turkey 47 L5
Kuş Gölü l. Turkey 78 A2
Kushalgarh India 74 B5
Kushalino Rus. Fed. 28 F4
Kushiro Japan 64 F3
Kushiro-Shitsugen National Park Japan 64 F3
Kushka Turkm. see Gushgy
Kushmurun Kazakh. 26 G4
Kushnarenkovo Rus. Fed. 28 J5
Kushtagi India 72 C3
Kushtia Bangl. 75 F5
Kushtih Iran 81 D4
Kushum r. Kazakh. 29 I6
Kuskokwim r. U.S.A. 120 C3
Kuskokwim Bay U.S.A. 120 C4
Kuskokwim Mountains U.S.A. 120 D3
Kuşluyan Turkey see Gölköy
Kusŏng N. Korea 65 A5
Kussharo-ko l. Japan 64 F3
Kustanay Kazakh. see Kostanay
Kustavi Fin. 33 F3
Küstence Romania see Constanţa
Kustia Bangl. see Kushtia
Kut, Ko i. Thai. 61 C6
Kutacane Indon. 58 B2
Kütahya Turkey 78 B3
Kütahya prov. Turkey 47 L5
Kutai National Park Indon. 59 G2
Kut'aisi Georgia 79 F2
Kut-al-Imara Iraq see Al Kūt
Kutan Rus. Fed. 79 F1
Kutaraja Indon. see Banda Aceh
Kutatyat Ţurayf vol. Saudi Arabia 77 D4

Kutch, Gulf of India see Kachchh, Gulf of
Kutch, Rann of marsh India see Kachchh, Rann of
Kut-e Gapu tourist site Iran 79 G4
Kutina Croatia 44 F2
Kutkai Myanmar 60 B3
Kutná Hora Czech Rep. 37 G4
Kutno Poland 37 I2
Kuttanen Sweden 32 F1
Kutubdia Island Bangl. 75 F5
Kutztown U.S.A. 131 F3
Kuujjua r. Canada 121 H2
Kuujjuaq Canada 125 G1
Kuujjuarapik Canada 124 E2
Kuuli-Mayak Turkm. 80 C1
Kuusamo Fin. 32 H2
Kuusankoski Fin. 33 G3
Kuvango Angola 95 C8
Kuvshinovo Rus. Fed. 28 E4
Kuwait country Asia 79 F5
asia 52–53, 82
Kuwait Kuwait 79 F5
Capital of Kuwait.
Kuwait Jun b. Kuwait 79 F5
Küybyshev Kazakh. see Kuybyshevskiy
Kuybyshev Novosibirskaya Oblast' Rus. Fed. 26 H4
Kuybyshev Respublika Tatarstan Rus. Fed. see Bolgar
Kuybyshev Samarskaya Oblast' Rus. Fed. see Samara
Kuybyshev Ukr. see Bilmak
Kuybyshevka-Vostochnaya Rus. Fed. see Belogorsk
Kuybyshevo Kazakh. see Zhyngyldy
Kuybyshevskaya Oblast' admin. div. Rus. Fed. see Samarskaya Oblast'
Kuybyshevskiy Kazakh. 26 G4
Kuybyshevskoye Vodokhranilishche resr Rus. Fed. 28 I5
Kuyeda Rus. Fed. 28 J4
Kuytun China 70 F3
Kuyucak Turkey 47 L6
Kuyuwini r. Guyana 147 G4
Kužiai Lith. 33 F5
Kuznetsk Rus. Fed. 29 H5
Kuznetsovs'k Ukr. 29 C6
Kuzomen' Rus. Fed. 28 F2
Kuzovatovo Rus. Fed. 29 H5
Kvænangen sea chan. Norway 32 F1
Kvaløya i. Norway 32 E1
Kvaløya i. Norway 32 F1
Kvalsund Norway 32 F1
Kvareli Georgia see Qvareli
Kvarnberg Sweden 33 D3
Kvarner g. Croatia 44 E2
Kvarnerić sea chan. Croatia 44 E2
Kvēdarna Lith. 33 F5
Kvenvær Norway 32 C3
Kvichak Bay U.S.A. 120 D4
Kvikkjokk Sweden 32 E2
Kvinesdal Norway 33 B4
Kvitanosi mt. Norway 33 B3
Kvitøya ice feature Svalbard 26 D2
Kvitsøy Norway 33 B4
Kwa r. Dem. Rep. Congo 94 C5
Kwaga Tanz. 97 A6
Kwajalein atoll Marshall Is 164 G5
Kwakoegron Suriname 147 H3
Kwakwani Guyana 147 G3
Kwale Nigeria 93 G4
KwaMashu S. Africa 99 F6
Kwame Danso Ghana 93 E4
Kwamouth Dem. Rep. Congo 94 C5
Kwandang Indon. 57 F5
Kwangchow China see Guangzhou
Kwangju S. Korea 65 A6
Kwango r. Dem. Rep. Congo 95 C5
Kwangsi Chuang Autonomous Region aut. reg. China see Guangxi Zhuangzu Zizhiqu
Kwangsi prov. China see Guangdong
Kwangtung prov. China see Guangdong
Kwangwazi Tanz. 97 C6
Kwania, Lake Uganda 96 B4
Kwanmo-bong mt. N. Korea 64 B4
Kwanobuhle S. Africa 98 E7
Kwanonzame S. Africa 98 E7
Kwanza r. Angola see Cuanza
Kwatinidubu S. Africa 99 F7
Kwazamukucinga S. Africa 98 E7
Kwazamuxolo S. Africa 98 E7
KwaZanele S. Africa 99 I5
Kwazulu-Natal prov. S. Africa 99 F6
Kwekwe Zimbabwe 99 F3
Kweneng admin. dist. Botswana 98 E4
Kwenge r. Dem. Rep. Congo 95 C6
Kwetabohigan r. Canada 124 D3
Kwiambana Nigeria 93 G3
Kwidzyn Poland 37 I2
Kwikila P.N.G. 106 D2
Kwilu r. Angola/Dem. Rep. Congo 95 C5
Kwisa r. Poland 37 G3
Kwitaro r. Guyana 147 G4
Kwoka mt. Indon. 57 H6
Kwoungo, Mont r. Cent. Afr. Rep. 94 D3
Kyabé Chad 94 C2
Kyabra Australia 111 E5
Kyabra watercourse Australia 111 E5
Kyadet Myanmar 60 A3
Kyaiklat Myanmar 61 A4
Kyaikto Myanmar 60 B4
Kya-in Seikkyi Myanmar 61 B4
Kyakhta Rus. Fed. 27 K4
Kyalite Australia 112 A5
Kyancutta Australia 109 F8
Kyangin Irrawaddy Myanmar 60 A4
Kyangin Mandalay Myanmar 60 B4
Kyaukhnyat Myanmar 60 B4
Kyaukkyi Myanmar 60 B4
Kyaukme Myanmar 60 B3
Kyaukpadaung Myanmar 60 A3
Kyaukpyu Myanmar 60 A4
Kyauktan Myanmar 61 B4
Kyaukse Myanmar 60 B3
Kyauktaw Myanmar 73 G1
Kybartai Lith. 33 F5
Kybeyan Range mts Australia 112 D5
Ky Cung, Sông r. Vietnam 60 D3
Kyeintali Myanmar 60 A4
Kyela Tanz. 97 B6
Kyelang India 74 C2
Kyenjojo Uganda 96 A4
Kyeraa Ghana 93 E4
Kyidaunggan Myanmar 60 B4
Kyinderi Bangl. 93 E3
Kyiv Ukr. see Kiev
Kyjov Czech Rep. 37 H4
Kyklades is Greece see Cyclades
Kyle Canada 123 G5
Kyle of Lochalsh U.K. 34 D3
Kyll r. Germany 36 C4
Kyllini mt. Greece 47 C6
Kymi Greece 47 D5
Kymis, Akra pt Greece 47 D5
Kynna r. Norway 33 D3
Kynuna Australia 111 E4

Kyoga, Lake Uganda 96 B4
Kyōga-misaki pt Japan 65 C5
Kyogle Australia 112 E3
Kyondo Myanmar 61 B4
Kyonan Japan 65 D6
Kyŏnggi-man b. S. Korea 65 A5
Kyŏngju S. Korea 65 B6
Kyŏngju National Park S. Korea 65 B6
Kyonpyaw Myanmar 60 A4
Kyōto Japan 65 C6
Kyparissia Greece 47 B6
Kyparissiakos Kolpos b. Greece 47 B6
Kypros country Asia see Cyprus
Kypshak, Ozero salt l. Kazakh. 69 L1
Kyra Panagia i. Greece 47 D5
Kyrenia Cyprus 77 A2
Kyrenia Mountains Cyprus see Pentadaktylos Range
Kyrgyzstan country Asia 70 D3
asia 52–53, 82
Kyrhyzh-Kytay r. Ukr. 46 F2
Kyriaki Greece 47 C5
Kyritz Germany 37 F2
Kyrnychky Ukr. 46 F2
Kytay, Ozero l. Ukr. 46 F2
Kythira Greece 47 C6
Kythira i. Greece 47 C6
Kythnos i. Greece 47 D6
Kythrea, Steno sea chan. Turkey 47 E6
Kythrea Cyprus 77 A2
Kyunglung China 74 D3
Kyungyaung Myanmar 61 B5
Kyunhla Myanmar 60 B4
Kyuquot Canada 122 E5
Kyurdämir Azer. see Kürdämir
Kyūshū i. Japan 65 B7
Kyushu-Palau Ridge sea feature N. Pacific Ocean 164 D4
Kyustendil Bulg. 46 C3
Kywebwe Myanmar 60 B4
Kywong Australia 112 C4
Kyyev Ukr. see Kiev
Kyyiv Ukr. see Kiev
Kyyiv's'ke Vodoskhovyshche resr Ukr. see Kiev
Kyyjärvi Fin. 32 G3
Kyyvesi l. Fin. 33 G3
Kyzan Kazakh. 29 J7
Kyzyl Moldova see Ştefan Vodă
Kyzyl Rus. Fed. 68 H1
Kyzyl-Art, Pereval pass Kyrg./Tajik. 81 H2
Kyzyl-Burun Azer. see Siyäzän
Kyzyl-Kiya Kyrg. see Kyzyl-Kyya
Kyzylkong Kazakh. 70 C2
Kyzyl-Kyya Kyrg. 81 G2
Kyzylorda Kazakh. 70 C3
Kyzyl-Suu r. Kyrg. 81 G2
Kyzylzhar Kazakh. 70 C2
Kzyl-Dzhar Kazakh. see Kyzylzhar
Kzyl-Orda Kazakh. see Kyzylorda
Kzyltu Kazakh. see Kishkenekol'

↓ L

Laage Germany 37 F2
La Almunia de Doña Godina Spain 43 F2
La Angostura, Presa de resr Mex. 138 F5
Laanle well Somalia 96 F2
La Antigua, Salina salt pan Arg. 152 C2
La Araucania admin. reg. Chile 152 B4
Laas Aano Somalia 96 F3
Laascaanood Somalia 96 E2
La Ascensión, Bahía de b. Mex. 127 I4
La Asunción Venez. 147 F2
Laâyoune W. Sahara 90 B4
Capital of Western Sahara.
Lab r. Yugo. 46 B3
Laba r. Rus. Fed. 29 G7
La Babia Mex. 133 A6
La Bahía, Islas de is Hond. 138 G5
La Baie Canada 125 G3
Labala Indon. 57 F7
La Baleine, Grande Rivière de r. Canada 124 E2
La Baleine, Petite Rivière de r. Canada 124 E2
La Baleine, Rivière à r. Canada 125 H1
La Banda Arg. 152 D1
La Bañeza Spain 42 D1
Labang Sarawak Malaysia 59 F2
Labao China see Liujiang
La Barthe-de-Neste France 38 D5
Labasa Fiji 107 I3
La Baule-Escoublac France 38 C3
Labaz, Ozero l. Rus. Fed. 27 J2
Labazhskoye Rus. Fed. 28 J2
Labe r. Czech Rep. 37 G3
also known as Elbe (Germany)
Labé Guinea 92 B3
Labelle Canada 125 F2
La Belle U.S.A. 129 C7
La Bénoué, Parc National de nat. park Cameroon 93 I3
Laberge, Lake Canada 122 C2
La Bernarde, Sommet de mt. France 39 G4
Labi Brunei 59 F1
La Biche r. Canada 122 F3
La Biche, Lac l. Canada 123 H4
Labin Croatia 44 E2
Labinsk Rus. Fed. 29 G7
Labis Malaysia 58 C2
La Bisbal d'Empordà Spain 43 H2
La Biznaga Mex. 135 F6
La Bobia, Sierra de mts Spain 42 C1
La Bodera mt. Spain 43 E2
La Boquilla Mex. 135 F8
Labora Namibia 98 C3
La Boucle du Baoulé, Parc National de nat. park Mali 92 C2
Laboué Lebanon 77 C2
Labouheyre France 38 C4
Laboulaye Arg. 152 D3
Labrador reg. Canada 125 I2
Labrador City Canada 125 H3
Labrador Sea Canada/Greenland 121 N3
Lábrea Brazil 148 D1
La Brea France 38 C4
Labuan Malaysia 59 F1
Labuan i. Malaysia 58 F1
Labuhan Indon. 58 D4
Labuhanbajo Indon. 57 E7
Labuhanbilik Indon. 58 C2
Labuhanhaji Indon. 58 B2
Labuhanmeringgi Indon. 58 D3
Labuhanruku Indon. 58 B2
Labuk r. Sabah Malaysia 59 G1
Labuk, Teluk b. Sabah Malaysia 59 G1
Labuna Indon. 57 G6
Labutta Myanmar 61 A4

Lågen r. Norway 33 C4
Lagh Bogal watercourse Kenya/Somalia 96 D4
Lagh Bor watercourse Kenya/Somalia 96 D4
Lagh Kutulo watercourse Kenya/Somalia 96 D4
Laghmān prov. Afgh. 81 G3
Laghouat Alg. 91 F2
La Gineta Spain 43 F3
Lagkor Co salt l. China 75 E2
La Gloria Col. 146 C2
La Gloria Mex. 133 B7
Lago prov. Moz. see Niassa
Lago Belgrano Arg. 153 B7
Lago Cardiel Arg. 153 C7
Lago da Pedra Brazil 150 D3
Lagodekhi Georgia 79 F2
La Gomera i. Canary Is 90 A3
La Gonâve, Île de i. Haiti 127 L8
Lagong i. Indon. 59 E2
Lago Posadas Arg. 153 C6
Lagos Nigeria 93 F4
Former capital of Nigeria. 2nd most populous city in Africa.
world 16–17
Lagos state Nigeria 93 F4
Lagos Port. 42 B4
Lagos Tanz. 97 C4
Lagos de Moreno Mex. 126 F7
Lago Verde Brazil 149 E2
Lago Viedma Arg. 153 B7
Lagran Spain 43 F1
La Grande r. Canada 125 E2
La Grande U.S.A. 134 D3
La Grande 2, Réservoir Canada 124 E2
La Grande 3, Réservoir Canada 125 F2
La Grande 4, Réservoir Que. Canada 121 L4
La Grande 4, Réservoir Que. Canada 125 F2
La Grande Casse, Pointe de mt. France 39 G4
La Grande-Combe France 39 F4
Lagrange Australia 108 C4
La Grange CA U.S.A. 128 C3
La Grange GA U.S.A. 129 B5
La Grange TX U.S.A. 133 B6
La Gran Sabana plat. Venez. 147 F3
La Grita Venez. 146 D2
La Guajira, Península de pen. Col. 146 D2
La Guardia Arg. 152 D2
La Guardia Chile 152 C1
La Guardia Spain see A Guardia
Laguna Brazil 151 B9
Laguna U.S.A. 135 F6
Laguna, Ilha da i. Brazil 150 B2
Laguna Beach U.S.A. 136 D5
Laguna Dam U.S.A. 137 E5
Laguna Mountains U.S.A. 137 D5
Laguna de Laja, Parque Nacional nat. park Chile 152 C4
Laguna San Rafael, Parque Nacional nat. park Chile 153 B6
Lagunas Peru 146 C6
Lagunas Yema Arg. 149 E6
Lagunillas Bol. 149 E6
Laha China 64 A2
La Habana Cuba see Havana
La Habra U.S.A. 136 D5
Lahad Datu Sabah Malaysia 59 G1
Lahad Datu, Telukan b. Sabah Malaysia 59 G1
La Hague, Cap de c. France 38 C2
Lahar India 74 C4
Laharpur India 74 D4
Lahat Indon. 58 C3
Lahemaa rahvuspark nat. park Estonia 33 G4
La Héve, Cap de c. France 38 D2
Lahewa Indon. 58 B2
Laḩij Yemen 77 B5
Lahn r. Germany 36 C3
Laholm Sweden 33 D4
Laholmsbukten b. Sweden 33 D4
Lahontan Reservoir U.S.A. 136 C2
Lahore Pak. 74 B3
La Horqueta Venez. 146 D3
Lahr (Schwarzwald) Germany 36 C5
Lahri Pak. 81 G4
Lahti Fin. 33 G3
L'Ahzar, Vallée de watercourse Niger 93 F2
Laï Chad 94 C2
Lai'an China 67 F1
Laibach Slovenia see Ljubljana
Laibin China 67 D4
Laifeng China 67 D2
L'Aigle France 38 D2
Laiha Fin. 32 F3
Lai-hka Myanmar 60 B3
Laihia Fin. 32 F3
Laingsburg S. Africa 98 D7
Lainioälven r. Sweden 32 F2
Lainstrz r. Austria 37 I5
Lair U.S.A. 130 C4
L'Aïr, Massif de mts Niger 93 H1
L'Aïr et du Ténéré, Réserve Naturelle Nationale de nature res. Niger 93 H1
Lairg U.K. 34 D2
Lais Indon. 58 C3
Laisälven r. Sweden 32 E2
Laishevo Rus. Fed. 28 I5
La Isla Col. 146 C4
La Isla, Salar de salt flat Chile 152 C1
Laitila Fin. 33 F3
Laivera well Tanz. 97 C6
Laives Italy 44 C1
Laiyang China 63 J4
Lajamanu Australia 110 B3
Lajanurpekhi Georgia see Lajanurpekhi
Lajeado Brazil 151 A9
Lajes Brazil 151 A9
Lajosmizse Hungary 37 I5
La Joya Peru 148 C7
La Joya de los Sachas Ecuador 146 B5
Lajta r. Austria/Hungary 37 H5
La Junta Bol. 149 E3
La Junta Mex. 135 F7
La Junta U.S.A. 135 G5
La Juventud, Isla de i. Cuba 127 J7
Lakadiya India 74 A5
L'Akagera, Parc National de nat. park Rwanda see Akagera National Park
Lakaträsk Sweden 32 F2
Lake KY U.S.A. 130 B5
Lake WY U.S.A. 134 E3
Lake Andes U.S.A. 132 B3
Lake Arthur U.S.A. 133 C6
Lake Cargelligo Australia 112 C4
Lake Chakonipau Canada 125 G1
Lake Charles U.S.A. 133 C6
Lake City CO U.S.A. 135 F5
Lake City FL U.S.A. 129 C6
Lake City MI U.S.A. 130 C2
Lake City SC U.S.A. 129 D5
Lake Clark National Park and Preserve U.S.A. 120 C3
Lake Clear U.S.A. 131 F1
Lake Cowichan Canada 122 E5
Lake District National Park U.K. 35 E4

Lake Eyre National Park Australia 110 D6
Lakefield Australia 111 F2
Lakefield Canada 130 D1
Lakefield National Park Australia 111 F2
Lake Frome Regional Reserve nature res. Australia 112 A3
Lake Gairdner National Park Australia 109 F7
Lake Grace Australia 109 B8
Lake Harbour Canada see Kimmirut
Lake Havasu City U.S.A. 137 E4
Lakehurst U.S.A. 131 F3
Lake Isabella U.S.A. 136 C4
Lake King Australia 109 B8
Lakeland Australia 111 F2
Lakeland FL U.S.A. 129 C7
Lakeland GA U.S.A. 129 C6
Lake Louise Canada 134 C2
Lake Manyara National Park Tanz. 96 B5
Lake Mburo National Park Uganda 96 A5
Lake Mills U.S.A. 132 C3
Lake Nash Australia 110 D4
Lake Paringa N.Z. 113 B3
Lake Placid U.S.A. 131 G1
Lakeport CA U.S.A. 136 A2
Lakeport MI U.S.A. 130 B2
Lake Providence U.S.A. 133 D5
Lake Pukaki N.Z. 113 B4
La Kéran, Parc National de nat. park Togo 93 F3
Lake Range mts U.S.A. 136 C1
Lake River Canada 124 D2
Lakeshore U.S.A. 136 C3
Lakeside U.S.A. 136 D5
Lake Tekapo N.Z. 113 B4
Lake Torrens National Park Australia 110 D6
Lakeview OH U.S.A. 130 B3
Lakeview OR U.S.A. 134 B4
Lake Village U.S.A. 133 D5
Lakeville U.S.A. 132 C2
Lakewood CO U.S.A. 134 F5
Lakewood OH U.S.A. 130 C3
Lakhdenpokh'ya Rus. Fed. 33 H3
Lakheri India 74 C4
Lakhimpur India 74 D4
Lakhipur India 75 G4
Lakhisarai India see Luckeesarai
Lakhish r. Israel 77 B4
Lakhnadon India 74 C5
Lakhpat India 74 A5
Lakhtar India 74 A5
Lakin U.S.A. 132 A4
Lakitusaki r. Canada 124 D2
Lakki Pak. 81 G3
Lakkoma Greece 47 D4
Lakonikos Kolpos b. Greece 47 C6
Lakor i. Indon. 108 E2
Lakota Côte d'Ivoire 92 D4
Lakota U.S.A. 132 E1
Laksefjorden sea chan. Norway 32 G1
Lakselv Norway 32 G1
Lakshadweep is India see Laccadive Islands
Lakshadweep union terr. India 72 B4
Laksham Bangl. 75 F5
Lakshettipet India 72 C2
Lakshmeshwar India 72 B3
Lakshmikantapur India 75 F5
Lalago Tanz. 96 B5
La Laguna Arg. 152 E3
Lala Musa Pak. 74 B2
Lalapanzi Zimbabwe 99 F3
Lalara Gabon 94 A4
Lalaua Moz. 97 C8
L'Albufera l. Spain 43 F3
Laleham Australia 111 G4
Lāleh Zār, Kūh-e mt. Iran 80 D4
Lalganj India 75 E4
Lalgudi India 72 C4
Lālī Iran 80 B3
Lalibela Eth. 96 C1
La Libertad Ecuador 146 A5
La Libertad Guat. 138 F5
La Libertad dept Peru 148 A2
La Ligua Chile 152 C3
Lalin China 64 A3
Lalin r. China 64 A3
Lalín Spain 42 B1
Lalinde France 38 D4
La Línea de la Concepción Spain 42 D4
Lalitpur India 74 C4
Lalitpur Nepal see Patan
Lalmikor Uzbek. see Lyal'mikar
Lalmonirhat Bangl. 75 F4
La Loche Canada 123 I3
La Loche, Lac l. Canada 123 I3
La Loire et de l'Allier, Plaines de plain France 39 E3
La Loma Bol. 148 D5
La Loma Negra, Planicie de plain Arg. 152 D4
La Loupe France 38 D2
La Louvière Belgium 39 F1
Lalpur India 74 A5
Lal'sk Rus. Fed. 28 H3
Lalsot India 74 C4
La Lufira, Lac de retenue de resr Dem. Rep. Congo 95 E7
Lalung La pass China 75 E3
Lama Bangl. 75 G5
La Macarena, Parque Nacional nat. park Col. 146 C4
La Madeleine, Îles de is Canada 125 I4
Lamag Sabah Malaysia 59 G1
La Maiko, Parc National de nat. park Dem. Rep. Congo 94 E5
Lamaing Myanmar 61 B5
La Malbaie Canada 125 G4
La Manche strait France/U.K. see English Channel
La Manga del Mar Menor Spain 43 F4
La Manika, Plateau de Dem. Rep. Congo 95 E7
La Máquina Mex. 135 F7
Lamar CO U.S.A. 135 G5
Lamar MO U.S.A. 132 C4
La Maraoué, Parc National de nat. park Côte d'Ivoire 92 D4
La Marche, Plateaux de France 38 D3
Lamard Iran 80 C5
La Margeride, Monts de mts France 39 E4
Lamarque Arg. 152 D4
La Marque U.S.A. 133 C6
La Martre, Lac l. Canada 123 G2
Lamas r. Turkey 77 B1
La Matanzilla, Pampa de plain Arg. 152 C4
La Mauricie, Parc National de nat. park Canada 125 F4
Lamballe France 38 B2
Lambaréné Gabon 94 A5
Lambayeque Peru 146 B6
Lambayeque dept Peru 146 B6
Lambay Island Rep. of Ireland 35 D5
Lambeng Indon. 59 F3
Lambert, Cape Australia 108 B5
▶Lambert Glacier Antarctica 167 E2
Largest series of glaciers in the world.
Lambert's Bay S. Africa 98 C7
Lambertville U.S.A. 131 F3
Lambeth Canada 130 C2
Lambi India 74 B3
Lambina Australia 110 C5
Lambro r. Italy 44 B2
Lam Chi r. Thai. 61 C5
Lam Chi r. Thai. 61 D5
La Medjerda, Monts de mts Alg. 45 A6
Lamego Port. 42 C2
La Mejorada Peru 148 B3
Lamen Vanuatu 107 F3
Lamèque, Île i. Canada 125 H4
La Merced Arg. 152 D2
La Merced Peru 148 B2
Lameroo Australia 112 B4
La Mesa U.S.A. 136 D5
Lamesa U.S.A. 133 A5
L'Ametlla de Mar Spain 43 G2
Lamezia Italy 45 F5
Lamhar Touil, Sabkhet imp. l. W. Sahara 90 A5
Lamia Greece 47 C5
Lamington National Park Australia 111 H6
Lamma Island Hong Kong China 67 [inset]
Lammerlaw Range mts N.Z. 113 B4
Lammhult Sweden 33 D4
Lammijärv lake channel Estonia/Rus. Fed. 33 G4
Lamoille r. U.S.A. 131 G1
La Moine r. U.S.A. 132 D4
Lamongan Indon. 59 F4
Lamoni U.S.A. 132 C3
Lamont U.S.A. 136 C4
La Montagne d'Ambre, Parc National de nat. park Madag. 99 [inset] K2
La Morita Chihuahua Mex. 135 F7
La Morita Coahuila Mex. 133 A6
Lamotrek atoll Micronesia 57 K4
Lamotte-Beuvron France 38 E3
La Moure U.S.A. 132 B2
Lampa Peru 148 C3
Lampang Thai. 60 B4
Lam Pao Reservoir Thai. 60 C4
Lampasas U.S.A. 133 B6
Lampasas r. U.S.A. 133 B6
Lampazos Mex. 126 F6
Lampedusa, Isola di i. Sicily Italy 45 D7
Lampeter U.K. 35 D5
Lamphun Thai. 60 B4
Lam Plai Mat r. Thai. 61 C5
Lampozhnya Rus. Fed. 28 H2
Lampsacus Turkey see Lâpseki
Lampung prov. Indon. 58 D4
Lampung, Teluk b. Indon. 58 D4
Lam Si Bai r. Thai. 61 D5
Lamta India 74 D5
Lam Tin Hong Kong China 67 [inset]
Lamu Kenya 96 D5
Lamu Myanmar 60 A4
La Muela mt. Spain 43 F3
La Mure France 39 F4
Lana Australia 111 E4
Lana Italy 44 C1
Lanai i. U.S.A. 135 [inset] Z1
Lanai City U.S.A. 135 [inset] Z1
La Nao, Cabo de c. Spain 43 G3
Lanark U.K. 34 E4
Lanas Sabah Malaysia 59 G1
Lanbi Kyun i. Myanmar 61 B6
Lancang China 66 A4
Lancang Jiang r. Xizang/Yunnan China see Mekong
Lancaster U.K. 35 E4
Lancaster CA U.S.A. 136 C4
Lancaster KY U.S.A. 130 A5
Lancaster MO U.S.A. 132 C3
Lancaster NH U.S.A. 131 H1
Lancaster OH U.S.A. 130 B4
Lancaster PA U.S.A. 131 E3
Lancaster SC U.S.A. 129 C5
Lancaster Sound strait Canada 121 K2
Lancelin Australia 109 A7
Lanchow China see Lanzhou
Lanciano Italy 44 E3
Lanco Chile 152 B4
Lancy Switz. 39 G3
Landak r. Indon. 59 E3
Landana Angola see Cacongo
Landau an der Isar Germany 37 F4
Landau in der Pfalz Germany 36 D4
Landeck Austria 36 E5
Lander watercourse Australia 110 B4
Lander U.S.A. 134 E4
Landerneau France 38 A2
Landes reg. France 38 C4
Landes de Lanvaux reg. France 38 B3
Landes du Mené reg. France 38 B2
Landfall Island India 73 G3
Landis Canada 123 I4
Landivisiau France 38 A2
Landless Corner Zambia 95 F8
Landön Sweden 32 D3
Landor Australia 109 B6
Landquart Switz. 39 H3
Landsberg Poland see Gorzów Wielkopolski
Landsberg am Lech Germany 36 E4
Land's End pt U.K. 35 D6
Landshut Germany 36 F4
Landskrona Sweden 33 D5
Lanfeng China see Lankao
Lang, Nam r. Myanmar 60 B2
Lan'ga Co l. China 74 D3
Langai r. India 75 G4
Langao China 67 D1
Langar Badakhshān Afgh. 81 H2
Langar Parvān Afgh. 81 G3
Langar Iran 81 E3
Langdon U.S.A. 132 B1
Langeac France 39 E4
Langeais France 38 D3
Langeland i. Denmark 36 E1
Langelands Bælt strait Denmark 33 C5
Längelmäki Fin. 33 G3
Längelmävesi l. Fin. 28 C3
Langen Germany 36 D2
Langenburg Canada 123 K5
Langenlois Austria 37 G4
Langenthal Switz. 39 G3
Langeoog Germany 36 C2
Langepas Rus. Fed. 26 H3
Langesund Norway 31 G1
Langgapayung Indon. 58 C2
Langgar China 75 G3
Langgöns Germany 36 D3
Langham Canada 123 J4
Langhko Myanmar 60 B3
Langholm U.K. 34 E4
Langjökull ice cap Iceland 32 [inset]
Langkawi i. Malaysia 58 B1
Lang Kha Toek, Khao mt. Thai. 61 B6
Langkon Sabah Malaysia 59 G1
Langley Canada 122 F5
Langley U.S.A. 130 B5
Langlo watercourse Australia 111 F5
Langmusi China see Dagcanglhamo
Langogne France 39 E4
Langon France 38 C4
Langong, Xé r. Laos 61 D4
Langøya i. Norway 32 D1
Langqi China 67 F3
Langreo Spain 42 D1
Langres France 39 F3
Langres, Plateau de France 39 F3
Langsa Indon. 58 B1
Langsa, Teluk b. Indon. 58 B1
Långsele Sweden 32 E3
Langslett Norway 32 F1
Lang Sơn Vietnam 60 D3
Langtang National Park Nepal 75 E3
Langtao Myanmar 60 B2
Långträsk Sweden 32 F2
Langtry U.S.A. 133 A6
Languan China see Lantian
Languedoc-Roussillon admin. reg. France 39 E5
Languiaru r. Brazil see Iquê
Languiñeo Arg. 153 C5
Långvinds bruk Sweden 33 E3
Langwedel Germany 36 D2
Langzhong China 66 C2
Lanigan Canada 123 J5
Lanín, Parque Nacional nat. park Arg. 152 C4
Lanín, Volcán vol. Arg./Chile 152 C4
Lanjak, Bukit mt. Sarawak Malaysia 59 E2
Lanji India 74 D5
Lanka country Asia see Sri Lanka
Lankao China 67 E1
Länkäran Azer. 79 G3
Lanlacuni Bajo Peru 148 C3
Lannemezan France 38 D5
Lannion France 38 B2
Lansdale U.S.A. 131 F3
L'Anse U.S.A. 132 D2
Lansford U.S.A. 131 F3
▶Lansing U.S.A. 130 A2
State capital of Michigan.
Länsi-Suomi prov. Fin. 32 F3
Lansjärv Sweden 32 F2
Lanta, Ko i. Thai. 61 B7
Lantau Island Hong Kong China 67 [inset]
Lantau Peak hill Hong Kong China 67 [inset]
Lanterne r. France 39 G3
Lantian Hunan China see Lianyuan
Lantian Shaanxi China 67 D1
Lanusei Sardinia Italy 45 B5
Lanxi Heilong. China 64 A3
Lanxi Zhejiang China 67 F2
Lanya Sudan 96 A3
Lan Yü i. Taiwan 67 G4
Lanzarote i. Canary Is 90 B3
Lanzhou China 62 G4
Lanzo Torinese Italy 44 A2
Lao, Mae r. Thai. 60 B4
Laoag Phil. 57 F2
Laobie Shan mts China 66 A4
Laobukou China 67 D3
Lao Cai Vietnam 60 C3
Laodicea Syria see Latakia
Laodicea Turkey see Denizli
Laodicea ad Lycum Turkey see Denizli
Laodicea ad Mare Syria see Latakia
Laoheishan China 64 B4
Laohekou China 67 D1
Laojunmiao China see Yumen
La Okapi, Parc National de nat. park Dem. Rep. Congo 94 E4
Lao Ling mts China 64 A4
Laolong China see Longchuan
Laon France 39 E2
La Oroya Peru 148 B2
▶Laos country Asia 60 C4
asia 52–53, 82
Laotougou China 64 B4
Laotuding Shan hill China 64 A4
Laoudi-Ba Côte d'Ivoire 92 E3
Laowohi pass Jammu and Kashmir see Khardung La
Laoye Ling mts China 64 B4
Lapa Brazil 151 B8
Lapachito Arg. 152 F1
Lapai Nigeria 93 G3
Lapalisse France 39 E3
La Palma i. Canary Is 90 A3
La Palma Panama 146 B2
La Palma U.S.A. 137 G5
La Palma del Condado Spain 42 C4
La Paloma Uruguay 152 G3
La Pampa prov. Arg. 152 D4
La Panza Range mts U.S.A. 136 B4
La Paragua Venez. 147 F3
La Paramera, Puerto de pass Spain 42 D2
La Paramera, Sierra de mts Spain 42 D2
La Parata, Pointe de pt Corsica France 44 B4
La Paya, Parque Nacional nat. park Col. 146 C4
La Paz Entre Ríos Arg. 152 F2
La Paz Mendoza Arg. 152 D3
▶La Paz Bol. 148 C4
Official capital of Bolivia.
world 8–9, 14–15
La Paz dept Bol. 148 C3
La Paz Hond. 138 G6
La Paz Mex. 126 D7
La Paz Venez. 146 C2
La Pedrera Col. 146 D5
Lapeer U.S.A. 130 B2
La Pendjari, Parc National de nat. park Benin 93 F3
La Perla Mex. 135 F7
La Pérouse Strait Japan/Rus. Fed. 64 E3
La Pesca Mex. 126 G7
La Pila, Sierra de mts Spain 43 F3
La Pine U.S.A. 134 B4
Lapinlahti Fin. 32 G3
Laplace U.S.A. 133 D6
La Plata Arg. 152 F3
La Plata U.S.A. 132 C3
La Plata, Río de sea chan. Arg./Uruguay 152 F3
La Plaza Spain 42 C1
La Plonge, Lac l. Canada 123 J4
La Pobla de Segur Spain 43 G1
La Pola de Gordón Spain 42 D1
Lapominka Rus. Fed. 28 G2
Laporte U.S.A. 131 E3
Laporte, Mount Canada 122 E2
La Potherie, Lac l. Canada 125 F1
La Poyata Col. 146 C3
Lappajärvi l. Fin. 32 F3
Lappeenranta Fin. 33 H3
Lappi Fin. 33 F3
Lappi prov. Fin. 32 G2
Lappland reg. Europe 32 E2
Laprida Arg. 152 E4
La Pryor U.S.A. 133 B6
Lâpseki Turkey 47 E4
Laptevo Rus. Fed. see Yasnogorsk
Laptev Sea Rus. Fed. 27 M2
Laptevykh, More sea Rus. Fed. see Laptev Sea
Lapua Fin. 32 F3
Lapuanjoki r. Fin. 32 F3
La Puebla Spain see Sa Pobla
La Puebla del Río Spain 42 C4
La Puerta Catamarca Arg. 152 D2
La Puerta Córdoba Arg. 152 E2
La Puerta Venez. 146 D2
La Punilla, Cordillera de mts Chile 152 C2
Lapurdum France see Bayonne
Lapušnik Yugo. 46 B3
Laqiya Arbain well Sudan 89 F4
La Quiaca Arg. 148 D5
L'Aquila Italy 44 D3
Lār Iran 80 C5
Lara state Venez. 146 D2
Laracha Spain 42 B1
Larache Morocco 90 D2
Laragne-Montéglin France 39 F4
Laramie U.S.A. 134 F4
Laramie r. U.S.A. 134 F4
Laramie Mountains U.S.A. 134 F4
Laranda Turkey see Karaman
Laranjal Brazil 147 G6
Laranjeiras do Sul Brazil 151 A8
Larantuka Indon. 57 F7
Larat i. Indon. 57 H7
La Raygat reg. W. Sahara 90 B5
Larba Alg. 43 H4
L'Arbresle France 39 F4
Lärbro Sweden 33 E4
L'Archipélago de Mingan, Réserve du Parc National de nat. park Canada 125 I3
Laredo Spain 42 E1
Laredo U.S.A. 133 B7
La Reforma Mex. 135 E7
La Reina Adelaida, Archipiélago de is Chile 153 B8
La Réole France 38 C4
Largeau Chad see Faya
L'Argentière-la-Bessée France 39 G4
Largo U.S.A. 129 C7
Largs U.K. 34 D4
Lārī Iran 80 A2
L'Ariana Tunisia 91 H1
La Rinconada Spain 42 D4
Larino Italy 44 E4
La Rioja Arg. 152 D2
La Rioja prov. Arg. 152 D2
La Rioja aut. comm. Spain 43 E1
Larisa Greece 47 C5
Larissa Greece see Larisa
Larkana Pak. 81 G5
Lark Harbour Canada 125 J3
Lar Koh mt. Afgh. 81 E3
Lark Passage Australia 111 F2
L'Arli, Parc National de nat. park Burkina 93 F3
Larnaca Cyprus 77 A2
Larne U.K. 34 D4
Larned U.S.A. 132 B4
Laro Cameroon 93 I3
La Robe Noire, Lac de l. Canada 125 I3
La Robla Spain 42 D1
La Roche-en-Ardenne Belgium 39 F1
La Rochefoucauld France 38 D4
La Rochelle France 38 C3
La Roche-sur-Yon France 38 C3
La Roda Spain 43 E3
La Romana Dom. Rep. 139 K5
La Ronge Canada 123 J4
La Ronge, Lac l. Canada 123 J4
La Rosa Mex. 133 A7
La Rosita Mex. 133 A6
Larouco, Serra do mts Spain 42 C2
Larrey Point Australia 108 B4
Larrimah Australia 110 C2
Lars Christensen Coast Antarctica 167 E2
▶Larsen Ice Shelf Antarctica 167 L2
oceans and poles 168
La Rubia Arg. 152 E2
Larvik Norway 33 C4
Lar'yak Rus. Fed. 26 I3
Larzac, Causse du plat. France 39 E4
La Sabana Arg. 152 F1
La Sabana Col. 146 D4
La Sal U.S.A. 137 H2
La Sal Junction U.S.A. 137 H2
La Salle Canada 125 F4
La Salonga Nord, Parc National de nat. park Dem. Rep. Congo 94 D5
La Salonga Sud, Parc National de nat. park Dem. Rep. Congo 94 D5
Las Animas U.S.A. 132 A4
Las Anod Somalia see Laascaanood
La Sauvette hill France 39 G5
Las Aves, Islas is West Indies 146 E2
Las Avispas Arg. 152 E2
Las Avispas Mex. 135 E7
La Savonnière, Lac l. Canada 125 F2
Las Bonitas Venez. 147 E3
Las Breñas Arg. 152 E1
Las Chapas Arg. 153 D5
La Scie Canada 125 K3
Las Conchas Bol. 149 F4
Las Cruces Mex. 135 F7
Las Cruces CA U.S.A. 136 B4
Las Cruces NM U.S.A. 135 F6
La Selle mt. Haiti 139 J5
La Serena Chile 152 C2
La Serena, Embalse de resr Spain 42 D3
Las Esperanças Mex. 133 A7
Las Estancias, Sierra de mts Spain 43 E4
Las Flores Buenos Aires Arg. 152 F4
Las Flores Salta Arg. 149 E6
Lashburn Canada 123 I4
Las Heras Arg. 152 C3
Las Hermosas, Parque Nacional nat. park Col. 146 C4
Lashio Myanmar 60 B3
Lashkar Gāh Afgh. 81 F4
Las Horquetas Arg. 153 C7
Las Juntas Chile 152 C2
Las Lajas Arg. 152 C4
Las Lajitas Venez. 147 E3
Las Lomas Peru 146 A6
Las Lomitas Arg. 149 E6
Las Marismas marsh Spain 42 C4
Las Martinetas Arg. 153 D6
Las Médulas tourist site Spain 42 C1
Las Mercedes Venez. 146 E2
Las Mesteñas Mex. 135 F7
Las Minas Venez. 147 E2
Las Minas, Cerro de mt. Hond. 138 G6
Las Mulatas is Panama see San Blas, Archipiélago de
Las Nieves Mex. 126 E6
La Société, Archipel de Fr. Polynesia see Society Islands
La Solana Spain 42 E3
Las Orquídeas, Parque Nacional nat. park Col. 146 B3
La Souterraine France 38 D3
Las Ovejas Arg. 152 C4
▶Las Palmas de Gran Canaria Canary Is 90 B3
Joint capital of the Canary Islands.
Las Perlas, Archipiélago de is Panama 146 B2
Las Petas Bol. 149 F4
La Spezia Italy 44 B2
Las Piedras Uruguay 152 F3
Las Piedras, Río de r. Peru 148 C3
Las Pipinas Arg. 152 F3
Las Plumas Arg. 153 D5
Laspur Pak. 81 H2
Las Rosas Arg. 152 E3
Las Rozas de Madrid Spain 42 E2
Las Salinas, Pampa de salt pan Arg. 152 D2
Lassen Peak vol. U.S.A. 136 B1
Lassen Volcanic National Park U.S.A. 136 B1
Las Tablas Panama 139 H7
Las Tablas de Daimiel, Parque Nacional de nat. park Spain 42 E3
Lastarria, Parque Nacional de nat. park Chile 153 B6
Last Chance U.S.A. 132 A4
Las Termas Arg. 152 D1
Last Mountain Lake Canada 134 F2
Las Tórtolas, Cerro mt. Chile 152 C2
Lastoursville Gabon 94 B5
Lastovo i. Croatia 44 F3
Lastovski Kanal sea chan. Croatia 44 F3
Las Tres Vírgenes, Volcán vol. Mex. 135 D8
Las Trincheras Venez. 147 E3
Las Tunas Cuba 127 K7
Las Varas Col. 146 D3
Las Varas Mex. 135 F7
Las Varas Venez. 146 D3
Las Varillas Arg. 152 E2
Las Vegas NM U.S.A. 135 F6
Las Vegas NV U.S.A. 137 E3
Las Villuercas mt. Spain 42 D3
Lata Solomon Is 107 F3
La Tabatière Canada 125 J3
Latacunga Ecuador 146 B5
Latady Island Antarctica 167 L2
La Tagua Col. 146 C5
Latakia Syria 78 C4
Latehar India 75 E5
La Teignouse, Passage de strait France 38 B3
Late Island Tonga 107 H3
Latemar mt. Italy 44 C1
La Teste France 38 C4
Latham Australia 109 B7
Lathi India 74 A5
Lātīdān Iran 80 C5
Latina Italy 44 D4
Latisana Italy 44 D2
La Toma Arg. 152 D3
La Tortuga, Isla i. Venez. 147 E2
Latouche Treville, Cape Australia 108 C4
Latouma well Niger 91 I5
La Tour-du-Pin France 39 F4
La Tranquera, Embalse de resr Spain 43 F2
La Tremblade France 38 C4
La Trinité France 39 G5
Latrobe U.S.A. 130 D3
Latronico Italy 45 F4
Lattaquié Syria see Latakia
Latte Island Tonga see Late Island
Lattes France 39 E5
La Tuque Canada 125 F4
Latur India 72 C2
▶Latvia country Europe 33 F4
europe 24–25, 48
Latvija country Europe see Latvia
Latviyskaya S.S.R. country Europe see Latvia
Lau Nigeria 93 H3
Lau r. Sudan 96 A3
Laua r. India 75 E5
Lauban waterhole Namibia 98 D3
Lauca, Parque Nacional nat. park Chile 148 C4
Lauenburg (Elbe) Germany 36 E2
Lauf an der Pegnitz Germany 36 E4
Laufen Germany 37 F5
Laugarbakki Iceland 32 [inset]
Lauge Koch Kyst reg. Greenland 121 M2
Laughland Lake Canada 123 M1
Laughlen, Mount Australia 110 C4
Laughlin Peak U.S.A. 135 F5
Lauhanvuoren kansallispuisto nat. park Fin. 33 F3
Laukaa Fin. 32 G3
Laukuva Lith. 33 F5
Launceston Australia 112 C6
Launceston U.K. 35 D6
Launglon Myanmar 61 B5
Launglon Bok Islands Myanmar 61 B5
La Unión Bol. 149 E3
La Unión Col. 146 B4
La Unión Spain 43 F4
Laura Australia 111 F2
La Urbana Venez. 146 E3
Laurel DE U.S.A. 131 F4
Laurel MS U.S.A. 129 A6
Laurel MT U.S.A. 134 E3
Laureldale U.S.A. 131 F3
Laureles Para. 149 F6
Laurel Hill hills U.S.A. 130 D4
Laurencekirk U.K. 34 E3
Laurens U.S.A. 129 C5
Lauri India 74 D4
Lauria Italy 45 E4
Laurinburg U.S.A. 129 D5
Lauru i. Solomon Is see Choiseul
Lausanne Switz. 39 G3
Laut i. Indon. 59 E1
Laut i. Indon. 59 E3
Laut i. Indon. 59 G3
Laut, Selat sea chan. Indon. 59 F3
Lauta Germany 37 G3
Lautaro Chile 152 B4
Lautaro, Cerro vol. Chile 153 B7
Lautem East Timor 108 D2
Lauterbrunnen Switz. 39 G3
Lautersbach (Hessen) Germany 36 D3
Laut Kecil, Kepulauan is Indon. 59 F4
Lautoka Fiji 107 G3
Lauttawar, Danau l. Indon. 58 B1
Lauvsnes Norway 32 C2
Lauvuskylä Fin. 32 H3
Lauwersmeer l. Neth. 36 C2
Lava r. Rus. Fed. 37 J1
Lava Beds National Monument nat. park U.S.A. 134 B4
Lavaca r. U.S.A. 133 B6
Laval Canada 125 F4
Laval France 38 C2
Lāvān Iran 80 C5
La Vanoise, Massif de mts France 39 G4
La Vanoise, Parc National de nat. park France 39 G4
Lavant r. Austria/Slovenia 37 G5
Lavapié, Punta pt Chile 152 B4
Lāvar Iran 80 B4
Lavara Greece 46 E4
Lavaraty Madag. 99 [inset] J4
Lavardac France 38 D4
Lāvar Meydān salt marsh Iran 80 C4
La Vassako-Bolo, Réserve National Intégral de nature res. Cent. Afr. Rep. 94 C2
Lavaur France 38 D5
Laveaga Peak U.S.A. 136 B3
La Vega Dom. Rep. 127 L8
La Vela, Cabo de c. Col. 146 C1
Lavello Italy 44 E4
La Venada r. Mex. 133 A6
Laveno Italy 44 B2
La Venturosa Col. 146 D3
Laverne U.S.A. 133 B4
Laverton Australia 109 C7
Lavia Fin. 33 F3
La Víbora Mex. 133 A7
La Viña Arg. 152 D1
La Viña Peru 146 B6
Lavina U.S.A. 134 E3
La Virgen, Sierra de mts Spain 43 F2
La Vôge reg. France 39 G2
Lavongai i. P.N.G. see New Hanover
La Voulte-sur-Rhône France 39 F4
Lavras Brazil 151 C7
Lavrio Greece 47 D6
Lavushi-Manda National Park Zambia 97 A8
Lawa r. Liberia 92 C4
Lawa Myanmar 60 B2
Lawagamau r. Canada 124 E3
Lawan India 75 D5
Lawang i. Indon. 59 G5
Law Dome ice feature Antarctica 167 F2
Lawik Reef P.N.G. 111 H1
Lawit, Gunung mt. Indon./Malaysia 59 F2
Lawit, Gunung mt. Malaysia 58 C1
Lawksawk Myanmar 60 B3
Lawn Hill Australia 110 D3
Lawn Hill National Park Australia 110 D3
Lawqah waterhole Saudi Arabia 89 I2
Lawra Ghana 92 E3
Lawrence KS U.S.A. 132 C4
Lawrence MA U.S.A. 131 H2
Lawrenceburg KY U.S.A. 130 A4
Lawrenceburg TN U.S.A. 128 B5
Lawrenceville PA U.S.A. 131 E3
Lawrenceville VA U.S.A. 130 E5
Lawrence Wells, Mount Australia 109 C6
Lawton U.S.A. 133 B5
Lawu, Gunung vol. Indon. 59 E4
Lawz, Jabal al mt. Saudi Arabia 89 G2
Laxå Sweden 33 D4
Laxey S. Africa 98 D5
Lax Kw'alaams Canada 122 D4
Lay r. France 38 C3
Laya r. Rus. Fed. 28 K2
Layar, Tanjung pt Indon. 59 G4
La Yarada Peru 148 C4
Laydennyy, Mys c. Rus. Fed. 28 H1
Layla salt pan Saudi Arabia 77 D4
Layon r. France 38 C3
L'Ayrolle, Étang de lag. France 39 E5
Laysan Island U.S.A. 164 G4
Laytonville U.S.A. 136 A2
Lazarev Rus. Fed. 64 E1
Lazarevac Yugo. 46 B2
Lazarevskoye Rus. Fed. 79 D2
Lázaro Cárdenas Mex. 138 D5
Lazcano Uruguay 152 G3
Lazdijai Lith. 33 F5
Lazio admin. reg. Italy 44 D3
Lazo Arg. 152 F3
Lazo Primorskiy Kray Rus. Fed. 64 C4
Lazo Rus. Fed. 27 N3
La Zorra watercourse Mex. 133 A6
Leader Canada 123 I5
Leaf r. U.S.A. 129 A6
Leaf Bay Canada see Tasiujaq
Leaf Rapids Canada 123 K3
Leakesville U.S.A. 129 A6
Leakey U.S.A. 133 B6
Leaksville U.S.A. see Eden
Leamington Canada 130 B2
Leamington Spa, Royal U.K. 35 F5
Le'an China 67 E3
Leandro N. Alem Arg. 152 G1
Leanja Madag. 99 [inset] J2
L'Eau Claire, Lac à l. Canada 125 F1
Leava Wallis and Futuna Is see Sigave
Leavenworth KS U.S.A. 132 C4
Leavenworth WA U.S.A. 134 B3
Leavitt Peak U.S.A. 136 C2
Łeba Poland 37 H1
Lebach Germany 36 C4
Lébamba Gabon 94 A5
Lebane Yugo. 46 B3
▶Lebanon country Asia 77 B3
asia 52–53, 82
Lebanon IN U.S.A. 132 E3
Lebanon MO U.S.A. 132 C4
Lebanon NH U.S.A. 131 G2
Lebanon OH U.S.A. 130 A4
Lebanon OR U.S.A. 134 B3
Lebanon PA U.S.A. 131 E3
Lebanon TN U.S.A. 128 B4
Lebanon VA U.S.A. 130 B5
Lebap Turkm. 81 E1
Lebap Oblast admin. div. Turkm. see Lebapskaya Oblast'
Lebapskaya Oblast' admin. div. Turkm. 81 E2
Lebda tourist site Libya see Leptis Magna
Lebec U.S.A. 136 C4
Lebedyan' Rus. Fed. 29 F5
Lebel-sur-Quévillon Canada 124 E3
Lebiolali well Eth. 96 E3
Le Blanc France 38 D3
Lebo Dem. Rep. Congo 94 D3
Lębork Poland 37 H1
Le Bourg-d'Oisans France 39 G4
Lebowakgomo S. Africa 99 F5
Lebrija Spain 42 C4
Łebsko, Jezioro lag. Poland 37 H1
Lebu Chile 152 B4
Le Bugue France 38 D4
Lebyazh'ye Kirovskaya Oblast' Rus. Fed. 28 I4
Lebyazh'ye Leningradskaya Oblast' Rus. Fed. 33 H4
Le Caire Egypt see Cairo
Lecce Italy 45 G4
Lecco Italy 44 B2
Lech r. Austria/Germany 36 E5
Lechaina Greece 47 B6
Lechang China 67 E3
Le Chasseron mt. Switz. 39 G3
Lechința r. Romania 46 D1
Lechtaler Alpen mts Austria 36 E5
Leck Germany 36 D1
Lecompte U.S.A. 133 C6
Le Coteau France 39 F3
Le Creusot France 39 F3
Lectoure France 38 D5
Lecumberri Spain 43 F1
Łęczyca Poland 37 I2
Ledang, Gunung mt. Malaysia 58 C2
Ledava r. Slovenia 44 F1
Ledbury U.K. 35 E5
Ledeč nad Sázavou Czech Rep. 37 G4
Ledesma Spain 42 D2
Lediba Dem. Rep. Congo 94 C5
Ledmozero Rus. Fed. 28 E2
Ledong Hainan China 67 D5
Le Dorat France 38 D3
Leduc Canada 123 H4
Le Duffre mt. France 39 F4
Ledyanaya, Gora mt. Rus. Fed. 27 R3
Lee r. Rep. of Ireland 35 B6
Leechburg U.S.A. 130 D3
Leech Lake U.S.A. 132 C2
Leeds U.K. 35 F5
Leek U.K. 35 E5
Leenane Rep. of Ireland 35 B5
Leeper U.S.A. 130 D3
Leer (Ostfriesland) Germany 36 C2
Leesburg FL U.S.A. 129 C6
Leesburg GA U.S.A. 129 B6
Leesburg OH U.S.A. 130 B4
Leesburg VA U.S.A. 130 E4
Lees Summit U.S.A. 132 C4

Lee Steere Range hills Australia 109 C6
Leesville U.S.A. 133 C6
Leesville Lake U.S.A. 130 D5
Leeu-Gamka S. Africa 98 D7
Leeuwarden Neth. 36 B2
Leeuwin, Cape Australia 109 A8
Leeuwin-Naturaliste National Park Australia 109 A8
Lee Vining U.S.A. 136 C3
Leeward Islands Caribbean Sea 139 L5
Le Faouët France 38 B2
Lefedzha r. Bulg. 46 D3
Lefka Cyprus 77 A2
Lefkada Greece 47 B5
Lefkada i. Greece 47 B5
Lefkás Greece see Lefkada
Lefke Cyprus see Lefka
Lefkimmi Greece 47 B5
Lefkoşa Cyprus see Nicosia
Lefkosia Cyprus see Nicosia
Lefroy, Lake salt flat Australia 109 C7
Łeg r. Poland 37 J3
Legaspi Phil. 57 F3
Legé France 38 C3
Legges Tor mt. Australia 112 C6
Leggett U.S.A. 136 A2
Leghorn Italy see Livorno
Legionowo Poland 37 J2
Legnago Italy 44 C2
Legnica Poland 37 H3
Legnone, Monte mt. Italy 44 B1
Le Grau-du-Roi France 39 F5
Leguena Chile 148 C5
Legune Australia 110 B2
Legwe r. Dem. Rep. Congo 94 E4
Leh Jammu and Kashmir 74 C2
Le Havre France 38 D2
Lehighton U.S.A. 131 F3
Lehliu-Gară Romania 46 E2
Lehrte Germany 36 D2
Lehtimäki Fin. 32 F3
Leiah Pak. 81 G4
Leibnitz Austria 37 G5
Leibo China 66 B2
Leicester U.K. 35 F5
Leichhardt r. Australia 111 D3
Leichhardt Falls Australia 111 D3
Leichhardt Range mts Australia 111 F4
Leiden Neth. 36 B2
Leie r. Belgium 39 E1
Leie Estonia 33 G4
Leigh watercourse Australia 112 A3
Leigh N.Z. 113 C2
Leigh Creek Australia 112 A3
Leikanger Norway 33 B3
Leiktho Myanmar 60 B4
Leine r. Germany 36 D2
Leinefelde Germany 36 E3
Leinster Australia 109 C7
Leinster reg. Rep. of Ireland 35 C5
Leinster, Mount Rep. of Ireland 35 C5
Leipojärvi Sweden 32 F2
Leipsic U.S.A. 130 B3
Leipsoi i. Greece 47 E6
Leipzig Germany 37 F3
Leipzig-Halle airport Germany 37 F3
Leira Møre og Romsdal Norway 32 C3
Leira Oppland Norway 33 C3
Leirbotn Norway 32 F1
Leiria Port. 42 B3
Leiria admin. dist. Port. 42 B3
Leirvik Hordaland Norway 30 F1
Leirvik Sogn og Fjordane Norway 33 B3
Leishan China 66 D3
Lei Shui r. China 67 E3
Leisi Estonia 33 F4
Leisler, Mount Australia 110 B4
Leitchfield U.S.A. 128 B4
Leivonmäki Fin. 33 G3
Leiyang China 67 E3
Leizhou China 67 D4
Leizhou Bandao pen. China 67 D4
Leizhou Wan b. China 67 E4
Lek r. Neth. 36 B3
Leka i. Norway 32 C2
Lékana Congo 94 B5
Le Kef Tunisia 91 H1
Lékéti r. Congo 94 B5
Lekhainá Greece see Lechaina
Lekhcheb Mauritania 92 C1
Lekkersing S. Africa 98 C6
Lekoes Norway 32 D1
Lékoni Gabon 94 B5
Lékoumou admin. reg. Congo 94 B5
Leksand Sweden 33 D3
Leksozero, Ozero l. Rus. Fed. 32 H3
Lek'suiri Georgia see Lentekhi
Leksura Georgia see Lentekhi
Leksvik Norway 32 C3
Leland Norway 32 D2
Leland U.S.A. 133 D5
Lelång l. Sweden 33 D4
Le Lavandou France 39 G5
Leleque Arg. 153 C5
Leli China see Tianlin
Lelija mt. Bos.-Herz. 44 G3
Le Locle Switz. 39 G3
Lelogama Indon. 108 C2
Le Lude France 38 D3
Lelydorp Suriname 147 H3
Lelystad Neth. 36 B2
Le Maire, Estrecho de sea chan. Arg. 153 D8
Léman, Lac l. France/Switz. see Geneva, Lake
Le Mans France 38 D2
Le Mars U.S.A. 132 B3
Lemberg mt. Germany 36 D4
Lemberg Ukr. see L'viv
Lembu Indon. 59 G2
Lembubut Indon. 59 G1
Lemdiyya Alg. see Médéa
Le Merlu Rocher mt. France 39 F4
Lemesos Cyprus see Limassol
Lemförde Germany 36 D2
Lemhi Range mts U.S.A. 134 D3
Lemi Fin. 33 G3
Lemmenjoen kansallispuisto nat. park Fin. 32 G1
Lemmon U.S.A. 134 G3
Lemmon, Mount U.S.A. 137 G5
Lemnos i. Greece see Limnos
Lemoncove U.S.A. 136 C3
Le Mont-Dore New Caledonia 107 F4
Le Mont-St-Michel tourist site France 38 C2
Lemoore U.S.A. 136 C3
Lemro r. Myanmar 60 A3
Lemtybozh Rus. Fed. 28 K3
Lemukutan i. Indon. 59 E2
Le Murge hills Italy 44 F4
Le Muy France 39 G5
Lemva r. Rus. Fed. 28 L2
Lemvig Denmark 33 C4
Lem'yu r. Rus. Fed. 28 K3
Lena r. Rus. Fed. 27 M2
Lénakel Vanuatu 107 F3
Lençóis Maranhenses, Parque Nacional dos nat. park Brazil 150 D2
Lenda r. Dem. Rep. Congo 94 F4
Lendava Slovenia 44 F1
Lendeh Iran 80 B4
Lendery Rus. Fed. 28 D3
Lendinara Italy 44 C2
Le Neubourg France 38 D2
Lengbarūt Iran 81 D4
Lenggries Germany 36 E5
Lenglong Ling mts China 70 J4
Lengoué r. Congo 94 C5
Lengshuijiang China 67 D3
Lengshuitan China 67 D3
Lengua de Vaca, Punta pt Chile 152 C2
Lengwe National Park Malawi 97 B9
Lenhovda Sweden 33 D4
Lenin Tajik. 81 G2
Lenin, Qullai mt. Kyrg./Tajik. see Lenin Peak
Lenina, Kanal canal Rus. Fed. 29 H8
Lenina, Pik mt. Kyrg./Tajik. see Lenin Peak
Leninabad Tajik. see Khŭjand
Leninabad Oblast admin. div. Tajik. see Leninobod
Leninakan Armenia see Gyumri
Lenin Atyndagy Choku mt. Kyrg./Tajik. see Lenin Peak
Lenine Ukr. 29 E7
Leningrad Rus. Fed. see St Petersburg
Leningrad Tajik. 81 G2
Leningrad Oblast admin. div. Rus. Fed. see Leningradskaya Oblast'
Leningradskaya Rus. Fed. 29 F7
Leningradskaya Oblast' admin. div. Rus. Fed. 28 E4
Leningradskiy Tajik. see Leningrad
Lenino Ukr. see Lenine
Leninobod Tajik. see Khŭjand
Leninobod admin. div. Tajik. 81 G2
Leninogor Kazakh. see Leninogorsk
Leninogorsk Kazakh. 70 F1
Leninogorsk Rus. Fed. 28 J5
Lenin Peak Kyrg./Tajik. 70 D4
Leninsk Kazakh. see Baykonur
Leninsk Rus. Fed. 29 H6
Leninskiy Rus. Fed. 29 F5
Leninsk-Kuznetskiy Rus. Fed. 27 I4
Leninskoye Kazakh. 29 I6
Leninskoye Kirovskaya Oblast' Rus. Fed. 28 H4
Leninskoye Yevreyskaya Avtonomnaya Oblast' Rus. Fed. 64 C3
Lenkoran' Azer. see Länkäran
Lennard r. Australia 108 D4
Lennox, Isla i. Chile 153 D8
Lenore U.S.A. 130 B5
Lenore Lake Canada 123 J4
Lenox U.S.A. 131 G2
Lens France 30 E3
Lensk Rus. Fed. 27 L3
Lentekhi Georgia 79 E2
Lenti Hungary 37 H5
Lentini Sicily Italy 45 E6
Lentua l. Fin. 32 H2
Lentvaravas Lith. see Lentvaris
Lentvaris Lith. 33 G5
Lenwood U.S.A. 136 D4
Lenya Myanmar 61 B6
Léo Burkina 93 E3
Leoben Austria 37 G5
Leodhais, Eilean i. U.K. see Lewis, Isle of
Leominster U.K. 35 E5
Leominster U.S.A. 131 H2
León Mex. 126 F7
León Nicaragua 138 G6
León Spain 42 D1
Leon r. U.S.A. 133 B6
León, Montes de mts Spain 42 C1
Leonard U.S.A. 133 B5
Leonardo da Vinci airport Italy 44 D4
Leonardtown U.S.A. 131 E4
Leonardville Namibia 98 C4
Leongatha Australia 112 C5
Leonidi Greece 47 C6
Leonidovo Rus. Fed. 64 E2
Leonora Australia 109 C7
Leopold r. Australia 108 D4
Leopold Downs Australia 108 D4
Léopold II, Lac l. Dem. Rep. Congo see Mai-Ndombe, Lac
Leopoldina Brazil 151 D7
Léopoldville Dem. Rep. Congo see Kinshasa
Leoti U.S.A. 132 A4
Leova Moldova 46 F1
Leoville Canada 123 J4
Leovo Moldova see Leova
Le Palais France 38 B3
Lepar i. Indon. 59 D3
Lepel' Belarus see Lyepyel'
Lepenou Greece 47 B5
Lephepe Botswana 98 E4
Leping China 67 F2
Lep'lya r. Rus. Fed. 28 L3
Lepontine, Alpi mts Italy/Switz. 44 B1
Leposavić Yugo. 46 B3
Leppävirta Fin. 32 G3
Lepreau, Point Canada 125 H4
Lepsa Kazakh. see Lepsy
Lepsy Kazakh. 70 E2
Leptis Magna tourist site Libya 88 B1
Leptokarya Greece 47 C4
Le-Puy-en-Velay France 39 E4
Leqceïba Mauritania 92 B1
Léraba r. Burkina/Côte d'Ivoire 92 D3
Lerala Botswana 99 E4
Lercara Friddi Sicily Italy 45 D6
Léré Chad 94 B3
Léré Mali 92 D2
Lere Nigeria 93 H3
Lérida Col. 146 D5
Lérida Spain see Lleida
Lerik Azer. 79 G3
Lerma Spain 42 E1
Lermontovka Rus. Fed. 64 C3
Lerno, Monte mt. Sardinia Italy 45 B4
Leros i. Greece 47 E6
Lerum Sweden 33 D4
Lerwick U.K. 34 F1
Ler Zerai well Sudan 94 E2
Les Agudes mt. Spain 43 H2
Les Borges Blanques Spain 43 G2
Lesbos i. Greece 47 D5
L'Escala Spain 43 H1
Les Cayes Haiti 139 J5
Les Escaldes Andorra 43 G1
Les Escoumins Canada 125 G3
Le Seu d'Urgell Spain 43 G1
Leshan China 66 B2
Les Herbiers France 38 C3
Leshukonskoye Rus. Fed. 28 H2
Lesina, Lago di lag. Italy 44 E4
Lesjöfors Sweden 33 D4
Leskhimstroy Ukr. see Syeverodonets'k
Leskovac Yugo. 46 B3
Leskovik Albania 47 B4
Leslie U.S.A. 130 A2
Les Mées France 39 F4
Les Minquiers is Channel Is 38 B2
Lesneven France 38 A2
Lesnoy Kirovskaya Oblast' Rus. Fed. 28 J4
Lesnoy Murmanskaya Oblast' Rus. Fed. see Umba
Lesnoye Rus. Fed. 28 E4
Lesosibirsk Rus. Fed. 27 J4
▶Lesotho country Africa 99 F6
africa 86–87, 100
Lesozavodsk Rus. Fed. 64 C3
Lesozavodskiy Rus. Fed. 32 I2
Lesparre-Médoc France 38 C4
L'Espérance Rock i. N.Z. 107 H5
Les Pieux France 38 C2
L'Espina mt. Spain 43 G2
Les Ponts-de-Cé France 38 C3
Les Sables-d'Olonne France 38 C3
Lesse r. Belgium 39 F1
Les Sept-Îles is France 38 B2
Lesser Antilles is Caribbean Sea 146 E1
Lesser Caucasus mts Asia 29 G8
Lesser Himalaya mts India/Nepal 74 C3
Lesser Khingan Mountains China see Xiao Hinggan Ling
Lesser Slave Lake Canada 123 H4
Lesser Tunb i. The Gulf 80 C5
L'Est, Île de i. Canada 125 I4
L'Est, Pointe de pt Canada 125 I3
Lestijärvi Fin. 32 G3
Lestijoki r. Fin. 32 F2
Les Triagoz is France 38 B2
Les Trois Rivieres Cent. Afr. Rep. 94 E3
Lesung, Bukit mt. Indon. 59 F2
Les Vans France 39 F4
Lesvos i. Greece see Lesbos
Leszno Poland 37 H3
Le Teil France 39 F4
Le Télégraphe hill France 39 F3
Letenye Hungary 44 F1
Leteri India 74 C4
Letha Range mts Myanmar 60 A3
Lethbridge Alta Canada 134 D2
Lethbridge Nfld. and Lab. Canada 125 K3
Lethem Guyana 147 G4
Le Thillot France 39 G3
Leti i. Indon. 108 D2
Leti, Kepulauan is Indon. 57 G7
Leticia Col. 146 D6
Letlhakane Botswana 98 E4
Letlhakeng Botswana 98 E5
Letnerechenskiy Rus. Fed. 28 E2
Letniy Navolok Rus. Fed. 28 F2
Letpadan Myanmar 60 A4
Le Tréport France 38 D1
Letsbo Sweden 33 D3
Letsok-aw Kyun i. Myanmar 61 B6
Lette Island Tonga see Late Island
Letterkenny Rep. of Ireland 30 C2
Letung Indon. 58 D2
Letwurung Indon. 108 E1
Lëtzebuerg country Europe see Luxembourg
Leu Romania 46 D2
Léua Angola 95 D7
Leucas Greece see Lefkada
Leucate, Étang de l. France 39 E5
Leukas Greece see Lefkada
Leunovo Rus. Fed. 28 G2
Leupp U.S.A. 137 G4
Leura Australia 111 G4
Leuser, Gunung mt. Indon. 58 B2
Leutkirch im Allgäu Germany 36 E5
Leuven Belgium 39 F1
Levadeia Greece 47 C5
Levan Albania 46 A4
Levanger Norway 32 C3
Levante, Riviera di coastal area Italy 44 B2
Levanzo, Isola di i. Sicily Italy 45 D5
Levashi Rus. Fed. 79 F2
Levelland U.S.A. 133 A5
Levens France 39 G5
Lévêque, Cape Australia 108 C4
Leverburgh U.K. 34 C3
Leverkusen Germany 36 C3
Lévézou mts France 39 E4
Levice Slovakia 37 I4
Levidi Greece 47 C6
Levin N.Z. 113 C3
Levitha i. Greece 47 E6
Levittown U.S.A. 131 F3
Levka Bulg. 46 E4
Levkás i. Greece see Lefkada
Levkímmi Greece see Lefkimmi
Levoča Slovakia 37 J4
Levočské vrchy mts Slovakia 37 J4
Levroux France 38 D3
Levski Bulg. 46 D3
Levskigrad Bulg. see Karlovo
Lev Tolstoy Rus. Fed. 29 F5
Levuka Fiji 107 G3
Lewa Indon. 108 B2
Lewe Myanmar 60 B4
Lewes U.K. 35 G6
Lewes U.S.A. 131 F4
Lewin Brzeski Poland 37 H3
Lewis r. U.S.A. 134 B3
Lewis, Isle of i. U.K. 34 C2
Lewis, Lake salt flat Australia 110 C4
Lewisburg OH U.S.A. 130 A4
Lewisburg PA U.S.A. 131 E3
Lewisburg TN U.S.A. 128 B5
Lewisburg WV U.S.A. 130 C5
Lewis Hills Canada 125 J3
Lewis Pass N.Z. 113 C3
Lewisporte Canada 125 K3
Lewis Range hills Australia 108 E5
Lewis Range mts U.S.A. 134 D2
Lewis Smith, Lake U.S.A. 129 B5
Lewiston ID U.S.A. 134 C3
Lewiston ME U.S.A. 131 H1
Lewistown IL U.S.A. 132 D3
Lewistown MT U.S.A. 134 E3
Lewistown PA U.S.A. 130 E3
Lewisville U.S.A. 133 C5
Lewisville, Lake U.S.A. 133 B5
Lewotobi, Gunung vol. Indon. 108 C2
Lexington KY U.S.A. 130 A4
Lexington MI U.S.A. 130 B2
Lexington MO U.S.A. 132 C4
Lexington NC U.S.A. 128 C5
Lexington NE U.S.A. 132 B3
Lexington OH U.S.A. 130 B3
Lexington VA U.S.A. 130 D5
Lexington Park U.S.A. 131 E4
Leyden Neth. see Leiden
Leye China 66 C3
Leyte i. Phil. 57 F3
Lézère r. France 38 D5
Lezhë Albania 46 A4
Lezhi China 66 C2
Lézignan-Corbières France 39 E5
Lezuza Spain 43 E3
L'gov Rus. Fed. 29 E6
Lhagoi Kangri mt. China 75 E3
Lhari China 75 G3
Lharigarbo China see Amdo
Lhasa China 70 H6
Lhasa He r. China 75 F3
Lhasoi China 75 G3
Lhatog China 66 A2
Lhazê Xizang China 70 G6
Lhazê Xizang China 75 F3
Lhokseumawe Indon. 58 B1
Lhorong China 75 G3
▶Lhotse mt. China/Nepal 75 E4
4th highest mountain in the world and in Asia.
world 6–7
Lhozhag China 75 F3
Lhuentse Bhutan 75 F4
Lhünzê China 75 G3
Lhünzhub China 75 F3
Liancheng Fujian China 67 F3
Liancheng Yunnan China see Guangnan
Liancourt Rocks i. N. Pacific Ocean 65 B5
Lianfeng China see Liancheng
Liangaz Hu l. China 67 E2
Liangdang China 66 C1
Liangfeng China 67 D3
Lianghe China 66 A3
Lianghekou Gansu China 66 C1
Lianghekou Sichuan China 66 B2
Liangping China 66 C2
Liangpran, Bukit mt. Indon. 59 F2
Liangshan China see Liangping
Liang Shan mt. Myanmar 60 B2
Liangshi China see Shaodong
Liangwang Shan mts China 66 B3
Liangzhou China see Wuwei
Lianhe China see Qianjiang
Lianhua China 67 E3
Lianhua Shan mts China 67 E4
Lianjiang Guangdong China 67 D4
Lianjiang Jiangxi China see Xingguo
Lianjiangkou China 67 E3
Lian Jiang r. China 60 D2
Lianping China 67 E3
Lianran China see Anning
Lianshan Guangdong China 67 E3
Lianshan Liaoning China 63 K3
Liant, Cape pt Thai. see Samae San, Laem
Liantang China see Nanchang
Lianxian China see Lianzhou
Lianyuan China 67 D3
Lianyungang China 63 J5
Lianzhou Guangdong China 67 E3
Lianzhou Guangxi China see Hepu
Lianzhushan China 64 B3
Liaodong Bandao pen. China 63 K3
Liaodong Wan b. China 63 K3
Liaoning prov. China 64 A4
Liaoyang China 63 K3
Liaoyuan China 64 A4
Liapades Greece 47 A5
Liaqatabad Pak. 81 G3
Liard r. Canada 122 F2
Liard Highway Canada 122 F2
Liard Plateau Canada 122 E2
Liard River Canada 122 E3
Liari Pak. 81 F5
Liat i. Indon. 59 D3
Liathach mt. U.K. 34 D3
Liban country Asia see Lebanon
Liban, Jebel mts Lebanon 77 C2
Libano Col. 146 C3
Libau Latvia see Liepāja
Libby U.S.A. 134 D2
Libenge Dem. Rep. Congo 94 C4
Liberal U.S.A. 132 A4
Liberdade r. Amazonas Brazil 148 C1
Liberdade r. Mato Grosso Brazil 150 A4
Liberec Czech Rep. 37 G3
▶Liberia country Africa 92 C4
africa 86–87, 100
Liberia Costa Rica 139 G6
Libertad Venez. 146 D2
Libertador General San Martín Arg. 149 D5
Liberty AK U.S.A. 122 A1
Liberty IN U.S.A. 130 A4
Liberty KY U.S.A. 130 A5
Liberty ME U.S.A. 131 I1
Liberty MO U.S.A. 132 C4
Liberty NY U.S.A. 131 F3
Libnī, Jabal hill Egypt 77 A4
Libo China 66 C3
Liboi Kenya 96 D4
Libong, Ko i. Thai. 61 B7
Libourne France 38 C4
Libral Well Australia 108 D5
Librazhd Albania 46 B4
Libre, Sierra mts Mex. 135 E7
▶Libreville Gabon 94 A4
Capital of Gabon.
▶Libya country Africa 88 C3
4th largest country in Africa.
africa 86–87, 100
Libyan Desert Egypt/Libya 88 E3
Libyan Plateau Egypt 89 E2
Licantén Chile 152 B3
Licata Sicily Italy 45 D6
Lice Turkey 79 E3
Lichas pen. Greece 47 C5
Licheng Fujian China see Xianyou
Licheng Guangxi China see Lipu
Lichfield U.K. 35 F5
Lichinga Moz. 97 B8
Lichte Germany 36 E3
Lichtenburg S. Africa 99 E5
Lichtenfels Germany 36 E3
Lichuan Hubei China 67 D2
Lichuan Jiangxi China 67 F3
Liciro Moz. 99 H3
Licking r. U.S.A. 130 A4
Lički Osik Croatia 44 E2
Lida Belarus 29 C5
Lidjombo Cent. Afr. Rep. 94 C4
Lidköping Sweden 33 D4
Lidsjöberg Sweden 32 D2
Lidzbark Poland 37 I2
Lidzbark Warmiński Poland 37 J1
Liebenwalde Germany 37 F2
Liebig, Mount Australia 110 B4
Liebling Romania 46 B2
▶Liechtenstein country Europe 39 H3
europe 24–25, 48
Liège Belgium 39 F1
Liegnitz Poland see Legnica
Lieksa Fin. 32 H3
Lielupe r. Latvia 33 G4
Lielvārde Latvia 33 G4
Lienz Austria 37 F5
Liepāja Latvia 33 F4
Liepaya Latvia see Liepāja
Liestal Switz. 39 G3
Liétor Spain 43 F3
Lietuva country Europe see Lithuania
Lièvre r. Canada 124 F4
Liezen Austria 37 G5
Lifanga Dem. Rep. Congo 94 D4
Liffey r. Rep. of Ireland 35 C5
Lifford Rep. of Ireland 34 C4
Liffré France 38 C2
Lifou i. New Caledonia 107 F4
Lifu i. New Caledonia see Lifou
Lifudzin Rus. Fed. see Rudnyy
Lightning Ridge Australia 111 F6
Ligny-en-Barrois France 39 F2
Ligonha r. Moz. 99 H3
Ligonier U.S.A. 130 D3
Ligoúrion Greece see Lygourio
Ligure, Mar sea France/Italy see Ligurian Sea
Liguria admin. reg. Italy 44 B2
Ligurian Sea France/Italy 44 B3
Ligurienne, Mer sea France/Italy see Ligurian Sea
Ligurta U.S.A. 137 E5
Lihir Group is P.N.G. 107 E2
Lihou Reef and Cays Australia 111 G3
Liivi laht b. Estonia/Latvia see Riga, Gulf of
Lijiang Yunnan China 66 B3
Lijiang Yunnan China see Yuanjiang
Lijiazhai China 67 E2
Lika reg. Croatia 44 E2
Likak Iran 80 B4
Likala Dem. Rep. Congo 94 C4
Likasi Dem. Rep. Congo 95 E7
Likati Dem. Rep. Congo 94 D4
Likati r. Dem. Rep. Congo 94 D4
Likely Canada 122 F4
Likhachevo Ukr. see Pervomays'kyy
Likhachyovo Ukr. see Pervomays'kyy
Likhás pen. Greece see Lichas
Likhoslavl' Rus. Fed. 28 E4
Likimi Dem. Rep. Congo 94 D4
Likma India 73 D1
Likoma Island Malawi 97 B8
Likouala admin. reg. Congo 94 C4
Likouala r. Congo 94 C5
Likouala aux Herbes r. Congo 94 C5
Liku Indon. 59 E2
Liku Sarawak Malaysia 59 F1
L'Île-Rousse Corsica France 31 G5
Lilienfeld Austria 37 G4
Lilienthal Germany 36 D2
Liling China 67 E3
Lilla Pak. 81 H3
Lilla Edet Sweden 33 D4
Lilla Luleälven r. Sweden 32 F2
Lillbläiken hill Sweden 32 E2
Lille France 39 E1
Lille Bælt sea chan. Denmark see Little Belt
Lillehammer Norway 33 C3
Lillestrøm Norway 33 C4
Lillington U.S.A. 128 D5
Lillooet Canada 122 F5
Lillooet r. Canada 122 F5
Lillooet Range mts Canada 122 F5
Lilo r. Dem. Rep. Congo 94 E5
Lilong India 75 G4
▶Lilongwe Malawi 97 B8
Capital of Malawi.
Lim r. Yugo. 46 A3
▶Lima Peru 148 A3
Capital of Peru and 4th most populous city in South America.
world 16–17
Lima dept Peru 148 A2
Lima MT U.S.A. 134 D3
Lima NY U.S.A. 130 E2
Lima OH U.S.A. 130 A3
Limaão Brazil 147 F4
Limah Oman 80 D5
Lima Islands China see Wanshan Qundao
Liman Rus. Fed. 29 H7
Limanowa Poland 37 J4
Limari r. Chile 152 C2
Limas Indon. 58 D2
Limassol Cyprus 77 A2
Limavady U.K. 34 C4
Limay r. Arg. 152 D4
Limay Mahuida Arg. 152 D4
Limbang r. Sarawak Malaysia 59 F1
Limbaži Latvia 33 G4
Limbdi India 74 A5
Limbe Cameroon 93 H4
Limbungan Indon. 59 F3
Limbunya Australia 110 B3
Limburg an der Lahn Germany 36 D3
Lim Chu Kang hill Sing. 58 [inset]
Lime Acres S. Africa 98 D6
Limeira Brazil 149 I5
Limenaria Greece 46 D4
Limerick Rep. of Ireland 35 B5
Limfjorden sea chan. Denmark 33 C4
Limia r. Spain 42 B2
Limin Chersonisou Greece 47 D7
Limingen Norway 32 D2
Limingen l. Norway 32 D2
Liminka Fin. 32 G2
Limmen Bight b. Australia 110 D2
Limmen Bight River r. Australia 110 C2
Limni Greece 47 C5
Limnos i. Greece 47 D5
Limoeiro Brazil 150 F3
Limoges France 38 D4
Limón Costa Rica 139 H6
Limon U.S.A. 134 G5
Limonum France see Poitiers
Limoquije Bol. 148 D3
Limousin admin. reg. France 38 D4
Limousin, Plateaux du France 38 D4
Limoux France 38 E5
Limpopo prov. S. Africa 99 F4
Limpopo r. S. Africa/Zimbabwe 99 G5
Limu China 67 D3
Linaälven r. Sweden 32 F2
Līnah Saudi Arabia 79 E5
Linakhamari Rus. Fed. 32 H1
Lin'an Yunnan China see Jianshui
Lin'an Zhejiang China 67 F2
Linapacan i. Phil. 57 E3
Linares Chile 152 C3
Linares Mex. 126 G7
Linares Spain 42 E3
Linas, Monte mt. Sardinia Italy 45 B5
Linau Balui plat. Sarawak Malaysia 59 F2
Lincang China 66 B4
Lincheng Hainan China see Lingao
Lincheng Hunan China see Huitong
Linchuan China 67 F3
Linck Nunataks nunataks Antarctica 167 K1
Lincoln Arg. 152 E3
Lincoln U.K. 35 F5
Lincoln CA U.S.A. 136 B2
Lincoln IL U.S.A. 132 D3
Lincoln ME U.S.A. 127 M2
▶Lincoln NE U.S.A. 132 B3
State capital of Nebraska.
Lincoln City U.S.A. 134 A3
Lincoln Island Paracel Is 56 D2
Lincoln National Park Australia 109 F8
Lincoln Sea Canada/Greenland 121 O1
Lincolnshire Wolds hills U.K. 35 F5
Lindau (Bodensee) Germany 36 D5
Lindeman Group is Australia 111 G4
Linden Canada 123 H5
Linden Guyana 147 G3
Linden AL U.S.A. 129 B5
Linden CA U.S.A. 136 B2
Linden TN U.S.A. 128 B5
Linden TX U.S.A. 133 C5
Lindesberg Sweden 33 D4
Lindhos Greece see Lindos
Lindi r. Dem. Rep. Congo 94 E4
Lindi Tanz. 97 C7
Lindi admin. reg. Tanz. 97 C7
Lindian China 64 A3
Lindisfarne i. U.K. see Holy Island
Lindome Sweden 33 D4
Lindos Greece 47 F6
Lindos, Akra pt Greece 47 F6
Lindsay Canada 130 D1
Lindsborg U.S.A. 132 B4
Lindsdal Sweden 33 E4
Lindside U.S.A. 130 C5
Lindum U.K. see Lincoln
Line Islands S. Pacific Ocean 165 H5
Linfen China 63 I4
Lingamparti India 73 D2
Linganamakki Reservoir India 72 B3
Lingao China 67 D5
Lingbao China 67 D1
Lingbi China 67 F1
Lingcheng Guangxi China see Lingshan
Lingcheng Hainan China see Lingshui
Lingelihle S. Africa 98 E7
Lingen (Ems) Germany 36 C2
Lingga i. Indon. 58 D3
Lingga, Kepulauan is Indon. 58 D3
Linggo Co l. China 75 F2
Lingle U.S.A. 134 F4
Lingomo Dem. Rep. Congo 94 D4
Lingshan China 67 D4
Lingshi Bhutan see Lingzhi
Lingshui China 67 D5
Lingsugur India 72 C2
Lingtai China 66 C1
Linguère Senegal 92 B2
Lingui China 67 D3
Lingxi China see Yongshun
Lingxian China see Yanling
Lingxiang China 67 E2
Lingyun China 66 C3
Lingzhi Bhutan 75 F4
Lingzi Thang Plains l. Aksai Chin 74 C2
Linhai China 67 G2
Linhares Brazil 151 D6
Linh Cam Vietnam 60 D4
Linhe China 63 H3
Linhpa Myanmar 60 A2
Linjiang Fujian China see Shanghang
Linjiang Jilin China 64 A4
Linköping Sweden 33 D4
Linkou China 64 B3
Linkuva Lith. 33 F4
Linli China 67 D2
Linn U.S.A. 132 D4
Linn, Mount U.S.A. 136 A1
Linnansaaren kansallispuisto nat. park Fin. 33 H3
Linnhe, Loch inlet U.K. 34 D3
Linosa, Isola di i. Sicily Italy 45 D7
Linru China see Ruzhou
Lins Brazil 149 H5
Linsan Guinea 92 B3
Linshui China 66 C2
Linta r. Madag. 99 [inset] J5
Linth r. Switz. 39 H3
Linthal Switz. 39 H3
Linton U.S.A. 132 A2
Lintong China 67 D1
Linxi China 63 J3
Linxia China 62 G4
Linxiang China 67 E2
Linyanti r. Botswana/Namibia 98 E3
Linyanti Swamp Namibia 98 D3
Linyi China 63 J4
Linying China 67 E1
Linz Austria 37 G4
Lion, Golfe du g. France 39 E5
Lions, Gulf of France see Lion, Golfe du
Lions Den Zimbabwe 99 F3
Lioua Chad 88 B6
Liouesso Congo 94 B4
Lipari Isole Lipari Italy 45 E5
Lipari, Isola i. Isole Lipari Italy 45 E5
Lipari, Isole is Italy 45 E5
Lipatkain Indon. 58 C2
Liperi Fin. 32 H3
Lipetsk Rus. Fed. 29 F5
Lipetskaya Oblast' admin. div. Rus. Fed. 29 F5
Lipetsk Oblast admin. div. Rus. Fed. see Lipetskaya Oblast'
Lipez, Cordillera de mts Bol. 148 D5
Lipiany Poland 37 G2
Lipin Bor Rus. Fed. 28 F3
Liping China 67 D3
Lipljan Yugo. 46 B3
Lipník nad Bečvou Czech Rep. 37 H4
Lipno Poland 37 I2
Lipno, Vodní nádrž resr Czech Rep. 37 G4
Lipova Romania 46 B1
Lippe r. Germany 36 C3
Lippstadt Germany 36 D3
Lipsko Poland 37 J3
Lipsoi i. Greece see Leipsoi
Lipti Lekh pass Nepal 74 D3
Liptovský Hrádok Slovakia 37 I4
Liptovský Mikuláš Slovakia 37 I4
Liptrap, Cape Australia 112 C5
Lipu China 67 D3
Lipusz Poland 37 H1
Liquiçá East Timor 108 D2
Liquissa East Timor see Liquiçá
Lira Uganda 96 B4
Liranga Congo 94 C5
Liri r. Italy 44 D4
Liri, Jebel el mt. Sudan 96 A2
Lisala Dem. Rep. Congo 94 D4
L'Isalo, Massif de mts Madag. 99 [inset] J4
L'Isalo, Parc National de nat. park Madag. 99 [inset] J4
Lisboa Port. see Lisbon
Lisboa admin. dist. Port. 42 B3
▶Lisbon Port. 42 B3
Capital of Portugal.
Lisbon ME U.S.A. 131 H1
Lisbon ND U.S.A. 132 B2
Lisbon NH U.S.A. 131 H1
Lisbon OH U.S.A. 130 C3
Lisburn U.K. 35 C4
L'Iseran, Col de pass France 39 G4
Lishan China see Lintong
Lishan Taiwan 67 G3
Lishe Jiang r. China 66 B3
Lishi China see Dingnan
Lishu China 64 A4
Lishui Jiangsu China 67 F2
Lishui Zhejiang China 67 F2
Li Shui r. China 67 D2
Lisichansk Ukr. see Lysychans'k
Lisieux France 38 D2
Liskeard U.K. 35 D6
Liski Rus. Fed. 29 F6
L'Isle-Jourdain France 38 D5
L'Isle-sur-la-Sorgue France 39 F5
L'Isle-sur-le-Doubs France 39 G3
Lismore Australia 111 H6
Lismore Rep. of Ireland 35 C5
Lisne Ukr. 46 F1
Liss mt. Saudi Arabia 77 D4
Lissa Croatia see Vis
Lissa Poland see Leszno
Listafjorden b. Norway 33 B4
Lister, Mount Antarctica 167 H1
Listowel Canada 130 C2
Listowel Rep. of Ireland 35 B5
Liswarta r. Poland 37 I3
Lit Sweden 32 D3
Litang Guangxi China 67 D4
Litang Sichuan China 66 B2
Litang Qu r. China 66 B2
Litani r. Fr. Guiana/Suriname 147 H4
Līṭānī r. Lebanon 77 B3
Litchfield CA U.S.A. 136 B1
Litchfield IL U.S.A. 132 D4
Litchfield MI U.S.A. 130 A2
Litchfield MN U.S.A. 132 C2
Litembe Tanz. 97 C7
Lithgow Australia 112 D4
Lithino, Akra pt Greece 47 D7
▶Lithuania country Europe 33 F5
europe 24–25, 48
Litija Slovenia 44 E1
Lititz U.S.A. 131 E3

Litoměřice Czech Rep. 37 G3
Litovel Czech Rep. 37 H4
Litovko Rus. Fed. 64 C3
Litovskaya S.S.R. country Europe see Lithuania
Little r. LA U.S.A. 133 C6
Little r. TX U.S.A. 133 B6
Little Abaco i. Bahamas 129 D7
Little Abitibi r. Canada 124 D3
Little Abitibi Lake Canada 132 F1
Little Aden Yemen see 'Adan as Sughra
Little Andaman i. Incia 73 C4
Little Bahama Bank sea feature Bahamas 129 D7
Little Barrier Island N.Z. 113 C2
Little Belt sea chan. Denmark 33 C5
Little Belt Mountains U.S.A. 134 E3
Little Bighorn r. U.S.A. 134 F3
Little Bitter Lake Egypt 77 A4
Little Blue r. U.S.A. 132 B4
Little Bow r. Canada 123 H5
Little Buffalo r. Canada 123 H2
Little Cayman i. Cayman Is 127 J8
Little Coco Island Cocos Is 61 A5
Little Colorado r. U.S.A. 137 G3
Little Current Canaca 124 D2
Little Current r. Canada 124 C3
Little Desert National Park Australia 112 B5
Little Egg Harbor inlet U.S.A. 131 F4
Little Exuma i. Bahamas 129 E8
Little Falls MN U.S.A. 132 C2
Little Falls NY U.S.A. 131 F2
Littlefield AZ U.S.A. 137 F3
Littlefield TX U.S.A. 133 A5
Little Fork r. U.S.A. 132 C1
Little Fort Canada 122 F5
Little Grand Rapids Canada 123 M4
Little Kanawha r. U.S.A. 130 E4
Little Karoo plat. S. Africa 98 D7
Little Lake U.S.A. 136 D4
Little Mecatina r. Canada 125 I3
Little Mecatina Island Canada see Petit Mécatina, Île du
Little Miami r. U.S.A. 130 A4
Little Minch sea chan. U.K. 34 C3
Little Missouri r. U.S.A. 134 G3
Little Muskingum r. U.S.A. 130 C4
Little Nicobar i. India 73 D5
Little Pamir mts Afgn. 81 H2
Little Powder r. U.S.A. 134 G3
Little Rann marsh India 74 A5
Little Red r. U.S.A. 133 C5
Little River U.S.A. 129 D5

▶Little Rock U.S.A. 133 C5
State capital of Arkansas.

Littlerock U.S.A. 136 D4
Little Sachigo Lake Canada 124 A2
Little Salt Lake U.S.A. 137 F3
Little Sandy Desert Australia 108 C5
Little Sioux r. U.S.A. 132 B3
Little Sitkin Island U.S.A. 120 A4
Little Smoky Canada 132 G4
Little Snake r. U.S.A. 134 F4
Littlestown U.S.A. 131 G4
Little Tibet reg. Jammu and Kashmir see Ladakh
Littleton NH U.S.A. 131 H1
Little Valley U.S.A. 130 C4
Little Valley U.S.A. 130 D2
Little Wabash r. U.S.A. 128 C4
Little White r. U.S.A. 132 A3
Little Wind r. U.S.A. 134 E4
Little Zab r. Iraq see Zāb aş Şaghīr, Nahr az
Littoral prov. Cameroon 93 H4
Litunde Moz. 97 B8
Litvínov Czech Rep. 37 F3
Liuba China 66 C1
Liuchiu i. Taiwan 67 G4
Liuchow China see Liuzhou
Liuhe China 64 A4
Liuheng Dao i. China 67 G2
Liujiachang China 67 D2
Liujiang China 67 F3
Liulin China see Jonê
Liupai China see Tian'e
Liupanshui China see Liangshui
Liupo Moz. 99 H2
Liuwa Plain Zambia 95 D8
Liuwa Plain National Park Zambia 95 D8
Liuyang China 67 E2
Liuyang He r. China 67 E2
Liuzhou China 67 D3
Līvāni Latvia 33 G4
Livanjsko Polje plain Bos.-Herz. 44 F2
Livarot France 38 D2
Livběrze Latvia 33 F4
Live Oak U.S.A. 129 C6
Liveringa Australia 110 A3
Livermore U.S.A. 136 B3
Livermore, Mount U.S.A. 135 F7
Liverpool Australia 112 D4
Liverpool r. Australia 108 F3
Liverpool Canada 125 H4
Liverpool U.K. 35 E5
Liverpool Range mts Australia 112 D3
Livingston Australia 112 D4
Livingston U.K. 34 E4
Livingston AL U.S.A. 136 B3
Livingston CA U.S.A. 136 B3
Livingston KY U.S.A. 130 A5
Livingston MT U.S.A. 134 E3
Livingston TX U.S.A. 133 C6
Livingstone Zambia 95 C6
Livingston, Lake U.S.A. 133 C6
Livingstone Malawi 97 B7
Livingston Island Antarctica 167 L2
Livno Bos.-Herz. 44 F2
Livny Rus. Fed. 29 F5
Livo r. Rus. Fed. 32 H2
Livonia U.S.A. 130 D2
Livorno Italy 44 D3
Livradois, Monts du mts France 39 E4
Livramento do Brumado Brazil 150 D5
Livron-sur-Drôme France 39 F4
Liwā Oman 80 D5
Liwā', Wādī al watercourse Syria 77 C3
Liwale Tanz. 97 C4
Liwiec r. Poland 37 J2
Liwonde Malawi 97 B8
Liwonde National Park Malawi 97 B8
Lixian Gansu China 66 C1
Lixian Hunan China 67 D2
Lixian Sichuan China 66 B2
Lixin China 67 F1
Lixouri Greece 47 B5
Liyang China 67 G2
Liyuan China see Sangzhi
Liz r. Port. 42 B3
Lizarda Brazil 150 C4
Lizard Point U.K. 35 B7
Lizarra Spain see Estella
Liziping China 66 B2
Lizonne r. France 38 D4
Ljig Yugo. 46 B2

▶Ljubljana Slovenia 44 E1
Capital of Slovenia.

Ljubuški Bos.-Herz. 44 F3
Ljugarn Sweden 33 E4
Ljungå Sweden 32 E3
Ljungan r. Sweden 33 E3
Ljungby Sweden 33 D4
Ljungskile Sweden 33 D4
Ljusdal Sweden 33 E3
Ljusnan r. Sweden 33 E3
Ljusne Sweden 33 E3
Ljutomer Slovenia 44 F1
Llagostera Spain 43 H2
Llaima, Volcán vol. Chile 152 C4
Llanbedr U.K. see Lampeter
Llançà Spain 43 H1
Llancanelo, Salina salt flat Arg. 152 C3
Llandeilo U.K. 35 E6
Llandovery U.K. 35 E6
Llandrindod Wells U.K. 35 E5
Llandudno U.K. 35 D5
Llanelli U.K. 35 D6
Llanes Spain 42 D1
Llangurig U.K. 35 E5
Llanidloes U.K. 35 E5
Llano U.S.A. 133 B6
Llano r. U.S.A. 133 B6
Llano Estacado plain U.S.A. 135 C6
Llanos plain Col./Venez. 146 D3
Llanquihue, Lago l. Chile 152 B5
Llansá Spain see Llançà
Llanymddyfri U.K. see Llandovery
Llata Peru 148 A2
Lleida Spain 43 G2
Llerena Spain 42 C3
Llica Bol. 148 D3
Lliria Spain 43 F3
Llobregat r. Spain 43 G2
Llodio Spain 42 E1
Lloret de Mar Spain 43 H2
Llorgara nat. park Albania 47 A4
Lloyd George, Mount Canada 122 E3
Lloyd Lake Canada 123 I3
Lloydminster Canada 123 I4
Lluchmayor Spain see Llucmajor
Llucmajor Spain 43 H3
Llullaillaco, Volcán vol. Chile 148 C6
Lô r. China/Vietnam see Lo
Loa r. Chile 148 C5
Loa U.S.A. 137 G2
Loagan Bunut National Park Sarawak Malaysia 59 F2
Loakulu Indon. 59 G3
Loano Italy 44 B2
Loban' r. Rus. Fed. 28 I4
Lobatse Botswana 98 E5
Lobaye pref. Cent. Afr. Rep. 94 C3
Lobaye r. Cent. Afr. Rep. 94 C4
Lobenberg hill Germany 37 F3
Lobería Arg. 152 F4
Łobez Poland 37 G2
Lobito Angola 95 B8
Loboko Congo 94 C5
Lobón Spain 42 C3
Lobos Arg. 152 E4
Lobos, Cabo c. Mex. 135 D7
Lobos de Afuera, Islas i. Peru 146 A6
Lobos de Tierra, Isla i. Peru 146 A6
Locarno Switz. 39 H3
Lochaline U.K. 34 C4
Loch Baghasdail U.K. see Lochboisdale
Lochboisdale U.K. 34 C3
Lochern National Park Australia 111 E5
Loches France 38 D3
Loch Garman Rep. of Ireland see Wexford
Lochgilphead U.K. 34 D3
Lochinvar National Park Zambia 95 E6
Lochinver U.K. 34 D2
Lochmaddy U.K. 34 C3
Lochnagar mt. U.K. 34 F3
Loch nam Madadh U.K. see Lochmaddy
Łochów Poland 37 J2
Lochranza U.K. 34 D4
Lochsa r. U.S.A. 134 D3
Lochy, Loch l. U.K. 34 D3
Lock Australia 109 F8
Lockeford U.S.A. 136 B2
Lockerbie U.K. 34 E4
Lockhart Australia 112 C4
Lockhart U.S.A. 133 B6
Lockhart River Australia 111 E2
Lock Haven U.S.A. 130 E3
Löcknitz r. Germany 36 F2
Lockport U.S.A. 130 C2
Locminé France 38 B3
Locorotondo Italy 45 F4
Locri Italy 45 F5
Locumba r. Peru 148 C4

▶London U.K. 35 F6
Capital of the United Kingdom and of England. 4th most populous city in Europe.
europe 24–25
world 16–17

London KY U.S.A. 130 A5
London OH U.S.A. 130 B4
London City airport U.K. 35 G6
Londonderry U.K. 34 C4
Londonderry U.S.A. 131 G2
Londonderry, Cape Australia 110 A2
Londonderry, Isla i. Chile 153 C8
Londres Arg. 152 C1
Lone Pine U.S.A. 136 C3
Loneria r. U.S.A. 136 C4
Long Thai. 66 A5
Longa Angola 95 B7
Longa Bengo/Cuanza Sul Angola 95 B7
Longa Cuando Cubango Angola 95 C8
Longa, Proliv sea chan. Rus. Fed. 27 R2
Longagung China 59 F2
Long Akah Sarawak Malaysia 59 F2
Long'an Guangxi China 66 C4
Long'an Sichuan China see Pingwu
Longarone Italy 44 D1
Longavi, Nevado de mt. Chile 152 C4
Long Bay U.S.A. 129 D5
Long Beach CA U.S.A. 136 C5
Long Beach WA U.S.A. 134 A3
Longbia Indon. 59 G2
Longboh Indon. 59 F2
Long Branch U.S.A. 131 G3
Longcheng China 66 C2
Longcheng Anhui China see Xiaoxian
Longcheng Guangdong China see Longmen
Longcheng Jiangxi China see Pengze
Longcheng Yunnan China see Chenggong
Longchuan Guangdong China 67 E3
Longchuan Yunnan China see Nanhua
Longchuan Jiang r. China 66 A4
Long Eaton U.K. 35 F5
Longford Rep. of Ireland 35 C4
Longgang Chongqing China see Dazu
Longgang Guangdong China 67 E4
Longgi r. Indon. 59 G3
Longhope U.K. 34 F2
Longhui China 67 D3
Longhurst, Mount Antarctica 167 H1
Longibau Indon. 59 G2
Longido Tanz. 96 C5
Longiram Indon. 59 F3
Longikis Indon. 59 G3
Longiram Indon. 59 F3

Long Island Bahamas 129 E8
Long Island Canada 124 E2
Long Island India 73 B4
Long Island P.N.G. 57 K7
Long Island U.S.A. 131 G3
Long Island Sound sea chan. U.S.A. 131 G3
Longjiang China 63 K3
Long Jiang r. China 67 D3
Longjin Fujian China see Qingliu
Longjin Jiangxi China see Anyi
Longjuzhai China see Danfeng
Longlac Canada 124 C3
Long Lake l. Canada 124 C3
Long Lake l. U.S.A. 131 F1
Longli China 66 C3
Longlin China 66 C3
Longmeadow U.S.A. 131 G2
Longmen China 67 E4
Longmen China see Longgang
Longmen Shan mts China 66 C1
Longming China 66 C4
Longmont U.S.A. 134 F4
Longnan China 67 F3
Longnawan Indon. 59 F2
Longobucco Italy 45 F5
Longotoma Chile 152 C3
Longpahangai Indon. 59 F2
Long Phu Vietnam 61 D6
Longping China see Luodian
Long Point Canada 130 C2
Long Point pt Man. Canada 123 L4
Long Point pt Ont. Canada 130 C2
Long Point Bay Canada 130 C2
Long Prairie U.S.A. 132 C2
Longpujungan Indon. 59 F2
Longquan Guizhou China see Danzhai
Longquan Guizhou China see Fenggang
Longquan Zhejiang China 67 G3
Longquan Xi r. China 67 G2
Long Range Mountains Nfld. and Lab. Canada 125 J4
Long Range Mountains Nfld. and Lab. Canada 125 J4
Longreach Australia 111 F4
Longriba China 66 B1
Long Ridge U.S.A. 130 A4
Longshan Guizhou China see Longli
Longshan Hunan China 67 D2
Longsheng China 67 D3
Longs Peak U.S.A. 134 F4
Long Teru Sarawak Malaysia 59 F2
Longtian China 67 D2
Longtom Lake Canada 123 G1
Longtown U.K. 34 E4
Longué-Jumelles France 38 C3
Longue-Pointe Canada 125 H3
Longueuil Canada 125 F4
Longuyon France 39 F2
Longvale U.S.A. 136 A2
Long Valley U.S.A. 137 G4
Longview TX U.S.A. 133 C5
Longview WA U.S.A. 134 B3
Longwei Co l. China 75 F3
Longxi China 66 C1
Longxian Guangdong China see Wengyuan
Longxian Shaanxi China 66 C1
Longxin China see Dehua
Long Xuyên Vietnam 61 D6
Longyan China 67 F3

▶Longyearbyen Svalbard 26 B2
Capital of Svalbard.

Longzhen China 64 A2
Longzhou China 66 C4
Longzhouping China see Changyang
Lonigo Italy 44 D2
Lonjsko Polje plain Croatia 44 F2
Lönsboda Sweden 33 D4
Lönsdalen Norway 32 D2
Lons-le-Saunier France 39 F3
Lonton Myanmar 60 B2
Lontra Brazil 150 B3
Lontra r. Brazil 147 H4
Loochoo Islands Japan see Ryukyu Islands
Looking Glass r. U.S.A. 130 A2
Lookout, Cape Canada 124 C2
Lookout, Cape U.S.A. 129 E5
Lookout, Point U.S.A. 130 B1
Lookout Point U.S.A. 109 B8
Loolmalasin vol. crater Tanz. 96 B5
Looma Australia 108 C4
Loon r. Canada 123 H3
Loongana Australia 109 E7
Loon Lake Canada 123 I4
Lop China 74 D1
Lopary Madag. 99 [inset] J4
Lopatina, Gora mt. Rus. Fed. 64 E2
Lopatka, Mys c. Rus. Fed. 27 P4
Lopatka, Mys c. Rus. Fed. 27 P2
Lopatovo Rus. Fed. 33 H4
Lop Buri Thai. 6 1 C4
Lopez Phil. 57 F3
Lop Nur salt l. China 70 H3
Lopori r. Dem. Rep. Congo 94 C4
Lopphavet b. Norway 32 F1
Loppi Fin. 33 G3
Lora r. Afgh. 81 F4
Lora del Río Spain 42 D4
Loralai Pak. 81 G4
Loralai r. Pak. 81 G4
Lorca Spain 43 F4
Lord Howe Atoll Solomon Is see Ontong Java Atoll
Lord Howe Island Australia 107 E5
Lord Howe Rise sea feature S. Pacific Ocean 164 F7
Lordsburg U.S.A. 135 I5
Lord Loughborough Island Myanmar 61 B6
Lorengau P.N.G. 57 K6
Lorena Brazil 151 C7
Lorentz r. Indon. 57 I7
Lorentz National Park Indon. 57 I6
Lorenzo Geyres Uruguay 152 E4
Lorestān prov. Iran 80 B3
Loreto Brazil 150 D3
Loreto Italy 44 E3
Loreto Para. 149 F5
Loreto dept Peru 148 C4
Lorian Swamp Kenya 96 C4
Lorica Col. 146 C2
Lorient France 38 B3
Lorillard r. Canada 123 N1
Lormi India 75 D5
Lorn, Firth of est. U.K. 34 D3
Lorne Australia 111 F4
Loro r. China 75 D3
Loropéni Burkina 92 C3
Lörrach Germany 36 C5
Lorraine Australia 111 D3
Lorraine admin. reg. France 39 G2
Lort r. Australia 109 C8
Lörudden Sweden 33 E3
Los, Îles de is Guinea 92 B3
Losai National Reserve nature res. Kenya 96 C4

Losal India 74 B4
Los Alamítos, Sierra de mt. Mex. 133 A7
Los Alamos CA U.S.A. 136 B4
Los Alamos NM U.S.A. 135 F6
Los Alerces, Parque Nacional nat. park Arg. 153 C5
Los Amores Arg. 152 F2
Los Andes Chile 152 C3
Los Angeles Chile 152 B4

▶Los Angeles U.S.A. 136 C4
3rd most populous city in North America and 6th in the world.
northamerica 118–119
world 16–17

Los Angeles Aqueduct canal U.S.A. 136 C4
Los Antiguos Arg. 153 C6
Los Argallanes, Sierra de hills Spain 42 D3
Los Banos U.S.A. 136 B3
Los Barreros mt. Spain 43 E3
Los Barrios Spain 42 D5
Los Blancos Arg. 149 E5
Los Caballos Mesteños, Llano de plain Mex. 135 F7
Los Canarreos, Archipiélago de is Cuba 127 J7
Los Chonos, Archipiélago de is Chile 153 B6
Los Choros Chile 152 C2
Los Choros, Islas de is Chile 152 C2
Los Cisnes, Lagunas de lakes Arg. 152 F2
Los Corales del Rosario, Parque Nacional nat. park Col. 146 C2
Los Coronados, Islas is Mex. 136 D5
Los Cusis Beni Bol. 148 D3
Los Cusis Beni Bol. 149 D3
Los Desventurados, Islas de is S. Pacific Ocean 165 M7
Los Difuntos, Lago l. Uruguay see Negra, Lago
Los Estados, Isla de i. Arg. 153 D8
Losevo Rus. Fed. 29 G6
Loseya well Tanz. 97 C6
Los Gatos U.S.A. 136 B3
Los Glaciares, Parque Nacional nat. park Arg. 153 B7
Los Hoyos Mex. 135 F7
Los Huemules, Parque Nacional nat. park Arg. 153 B6
Lošinj i. Croatia 44 E2
Los Jardines de la Reina, Archipiélago de is Cuba 127 K7
Los Juríes Arg. 152 E2
Los Lagos Chile 152 B4
Los Lagos admin. reg. Chile 152 B5
Loslau Poland see Wodzisław Śląski
Los Menucos Arg. 152 C5
Los Mexicanos, Lago de l. Mex. 135 F7
Los Mochis Mex. 126 E6
Los Mosquitos, Golfo de b. Panama 139 H7
Los Navalmorales Spain 42 D3
Los Nevados, Parque Nacional nat. park Col. 146 C3
Los Palacios y Villafranca Spain 42 D4
Lospatos East Timor 108 D2
Los Pedroches plat. Spain 42 D3
Los Picos de Europa, Parque Nacional de nat. park Spain 42 D1
Los Ríos prov. Ecuador 146 B5
Los Roques, Islas is Venez. 146 D2
Lossiemouth U.K. 34 F3
Lost Creek U.S.A. 130 B5
Los Taques Venez. 146 D2
Los Teques Venez. 146 D2
Los Telares Arg. 152 D2
Los Testigos is Venez. 147 F2
Lost Hills U.S.A. 136 C4
Los Vientos Chile 148 C6
Los Vilos Chile 152 B3
Los Yébenes Spain 42 D3
Lota Chile 152 B4
Lotagipi Swamp Kenya 96 B3
Lote Norway 33 C3
Loten Norway 33 C3
Loth U.K. 34 E2
Lothagum Hills Sudan 96 B3
Lotikipi Plain Kenya 96 B3
Loto Dem. Rep. Congo 94 D5
Lotoi r. Dem. Rep. Congo 94 C5
Lot's Wife i. Japan see Sōfu-gan
Lotta r. Fin./Rus. Fed. 32 H1
Louang Namtha Laos 60 C2
Louangphrabang Laos see Louang Prabang
Louang Prabang Range mts Laos/Thai. 60 C3
Loubomo Congo 95 B6
Loučná hill Czech Rep. 37 F3
Loudéac France 38 B2
Loudi China 67 D3
Loudon U.S.A. 129 B5
Loudonville U.S.A. 130 D3
Loudun France 38 D3
Louéssé r. Congo 94 B5
Louga Senegal 92 B3
Loughborough U.K. 35 F5
Lougheed Island Canada 121 I2
Loughrea Rep. of Ireland 35 B5
Louhans France 39 F3
Louisa KY U.S.A. 130 B4
Louisa VA U.S.A. 130 E4
Louisburg Canada see Louisbourg
Louise Falls Canada 123 G2
Louise, Lake Canada 123 J4
Louisiade Archipelago is P.N.G. 107 E3
Louisiana U.S.A. 132 C4
Louisiana state U.S.A. 127 H5
Louis Trichardt S. Africa 99 I3
Louisville GA U.S.A. 129 D5
Louisville IL U.S.A. 128 C4
Louisville KY U.S.A. 128 B4
Louisville MS U.S.A. 129 A5
Louisville OH U.S.A. 130 D3
Louisville Ridge sea feature S. Pacific Ocean 164 G8
Loukhi Rus. Fed. 28 E2
Loukoléla Congo 94 B5
Loukouo Congo 94 B5
Loum Cameroon 93 H4
Louny Czech Rep. 37 F3
Loup r. U.S.A. 132 B3
Loup City U.S.A. 132 B3
Loups-Marins, Lacs des lakes Canada 125 F1
Lourdes Canada 125 J3
Lourdes France 38 D5
Lourdes Brazil 147 I4
Lourenço Marques Moz. see Maputo
Lourinhã Port. 42 B3
Lousã Port. 42 B3
Louth Australia 112 C3
Louth U.K. 35 F5
Loutra Greece 47 D6
Loutra Aidipsou Greece 47 C5
Louvain Belgium see Leuven

Louviers France 38 D2
Lövånger Sweden 32 F2
Lovasberény Hungary 37 I5
Lovat' r. Rus. Fed. 28 D4
Lövberga Sweden 32 G3
Lovech Bulg. 46 D3
Loveland U.S.A. 134 F4
Lovell ME U.S.A. 131 H1
Lovell WY U.S.A. 134 E3
Lovelock U.S.A. 136 C1
Lovere Italy 44 C2
Lovers' Leap mt. U.S.A. 130 C5
Lovington U.S.A. 135 G6
Lovozero Rus. Fed. 28 E1
Lovrin Romania 46 B2
Lövstabukten b. Sweden 33 E3
Lôvua Angola 95 D6
Lôvua Angola 95 D5
Lowa Dem. Rep. Congo 94 E5
Lowa r. Dem. Rep. Congo 94 E5
Lowarai Pass Pak. 81 G3
Lowell MA U.S.A. 131 H2
Lowell OR U.S.A. 134 B4
Lowell VT U.S.A. 131 G1
Lowelli Sudan 96 B3
Lower Arrow Lake Canada 122 G5
Lower California pen. Mex. see Baja California
Lower Glenelg National Park Australia 112 B5
Lower Granite Gorge U.S.A. 137 F4
Lower Hutt N.Z. 113 C3
Lower Laberge Canada 122 C2
Lower Lake U.S.A. 136 A1
Lower Lough Erne l. U.K. 35 C4
Lower Peirce Reservoir Sing. 58 [inset]
Lower Red Lake U.S.A. 132 C1
Lower Saxony land Germany see Niedersachsen
Lower Tunguska r. Rus. Fed. see Nizhnyaya Tunguska
Lower Zambezi National Park Zambia 95 F8
Lowestoft U.K. 35 I5
Lowgar prov. Afgh. 81 G3
Łowicz Poland 37 I2
Lowville U.S.A. 131 F2
Loxton Australia 112 A4
Loyalsock Creek r. U.S.A. 131 G3
Loyalton U.S.A. 136 B2
Loyalty Islands New Caledonia see Loyauté, Îles
Loyang China see Luoyang
Loyauté, Îles is New Caledonia 107 F4
Loyev Belarus see Loyew
Loyew Belarus 29 D6
Loyno Rus. Fed. 28 K4
Loyola, Punta pt Arg. 153 C7
Loznica Yugo. 46 A2
Loznitsa Bulg. 46 E3
Lozova Ukr. 29 F5
Lozovaya Ukr. see Lozova
Lozoya Spain 42 D3
Lu'an China 67 F2
Luachimo r. Angola/Dem. Rep. Congo 95 D6

▶Luanda Angola 95 B7
Capital of Angola.

Luanda prov. Angola 95 B7
Luando Angola 95 C7
Luando r. Angola 95 C7
Luang, Khao mt. Thai. 61 B6
Luanginga r. Zambia 95 D8
Luang Nam Tha Laos see Louang Namtha
Luang Prabang Laos see Louangphrabang
Luanguinga r. Angola 95 D8
Luangwa Zambia 95 F8
Luangwa r. Zambia 97 A8
Luanhaizi China 75 G2
Lua Nova Brazil 147 G6
Luanshya Zambia 95 F8
Luanza Dem. Rep. Congo 95 F7
Luao Angola see Luau
Luapula prov. Zambia 95 F7
Luar, Danau l. Indon. 59 F2
Luarca Spain 42 C1
Luashi Dem. Rep. Congo 95 E7
Luatamba Angola 95 D8
Luau Angola 95 D7
Luba Equat. Guinea 93 H5
Lubalo Angola 95 C6
Luban Poland 37 G3
Lubana Latvia 33 G4
Lubānas ezers l. Latvia 33 G4
Lubango Angola 95 B8
Lubao Dem. Rep. Congo 95 E6
Lubartów Poland 31 J3
Lubawa Poland 37 I2
Lübbecke Germany 36 D2
Lübben Germany 37 F3
Lübbenau Germany 37 F3
Lubbock U.S.A. 133 A5
Lübeck Germany 36 E1
Lübecker Bucht b. Germany 36 E1
Lubefu Dem. Rep. Congo 95 E6
Lubei China 63 K3
Lubelska, Wyżyna hills Poland 37 K3
Lüben Poland see Lubin
Lubenka Kazakh. 29 J6
Lubéron, Montagne du ridge France 39 F5
Lubie, Jezioro l. Poland 37 G2
Lubienka r. Poland 37 I2
Lubień Kujawski Poland 37 I2
Lubin Poland 37 H3
Lublin Poland 31 J3
Lubliniec Poland 37 I3
Lubnān country Asia see Lebanon
Lubny Ukr. 29 E5
Lubok Antu Sarawak Malaysia 59 E2
Luboń Poland 37 H2
Lubraniec Poland 37 I2
Lubrín Spain 43 E4
Lübtheen Germany 36 E2
Lubudi Dem. Rep. Congo 95 E6
Lubudi r. Dem. Rep. Congo 95 E6
Lubuklinggau Indon. 58 C3
Lubukpakam Indon. 58 B2
Lubuksikaping Indon. 58 C2
Lubumbashi Dem. Rep. Congo 95 E6
Lubunda Dem. Rep. Congo 95 E6
Lubungu Zambia 95 F8
Lubutu Dem. Rep. Congo 94 E5
Lubwe Zambia 95 F7
Lucala Angola 95 B7
Lucan Canada 130 C2
Lucanas Peru 148 C4
Lučani Yugo. 46 B3
Lucania, Mount Canada 122 A2
Lucapa Angola 95 D6
Lucas Brazil 149 G3
Lucasville U.S.A. 130 B4

Lucca Italy 44 C3
Lucé France 38 D2
Luce Bay U.K. 34 D4
Lucedale U.S.A. 129 A6
Lucena Phil. 57 F3
Lucena Spain 42 D4
Lučenec Slovakia 37 I3
Lucera Italy 44 E4
Lucerna Peru 148 C5
Lucerne Switz. 39 H3
Lucerne Valley China 136 D4
Lucero Mex. 135 F7
Luchegorsk Rus. Fed. 64 C3
Lucheng Guangxi China see Luchuan
Lucheng Sichuan China see Kangding
Lucheringo r. Moz. 97 C7
Lüchow Germany 36 E2
Luchuan China 67 D4
Lüchun China 66 B4
Lucinda Australia 111 F3
Lucira Angola 95 B8
Luciu Romania 46 F2
Łuck Ukr. see Luts'k
Luckau Germany 37 F3
Luckeesarai India 75 E4
Luckenwalde Germany 37 F2
Luckhoff S. Africa 98 E6
Lucknow Canada 130 C2
Lucknow India 74 C4
Luçon France 38 C3
Lücongpo China 67 D2
Lucunga Angola 95 B6
Lucusse Angola 95 D8
Lucy Creek Australia 110 D4
Lüda China see Dalian
Luda Kamchiya r. Bulg. 46 E3
Ludbreg Croatia 44 F1
Lüdenscheid Germany 36 C3
Ludewa Tanz. 97 B7
Ludhiana India 74 C3
Ludian China 66 B3
Luding China 66 B2
Ludington U.S.A. 132 E3
Ludlow U.K. 35 E5
Ludlow CA U.S.A. 137 D4
Ludlow VT U.S.A. 131 G2
Ludogorsko Plato plat. Bulg. 46 E3
Ludowici U.S.A. 129 C6
Ludus Romania 46 D1
Ludvika Sweden 33 D3
Ludwigsburg Germany 36 D4
Ludwigsfelde Germany 37 F2
Ludwigshafen am Rhein Germany 36 D4
Ludwigslust Germany 36 E2
Ludwigsort Rus. Fed. see Ladushkin
Ludza Latvia 33 G4
Luebo Dem. Rep. Congo 95 D6
Lueki r. Dem. Rep. Congo 94 E5
Lueki r. Dem. Rep. Congo 95 E5
Luembe Zambia 97 A8
Luena Angola 95 C7
Luena r. Dem. Rep. Congo 95 E7
Luena r. Zambia 95 D8
Luena Flats plain Zambia 95 D8
Luengue r. Angola 95 D9
Luenha r. Moz./Zimbabwe 99 C3
Luepa Venez. 147 F3
Lüeyang China 66 C1
Lufeng Guangdong China 67 E4
Lufeng Hunan China see Xupu
Lufeng Yunnan China see Lufeng China B3
Lufira r. Dem. Rep. Congo 95 E7
Lufkin U.S.A. 133 C6
Lufu China see Lunan
Lug r. Yugo. 46 B2
Luga Rus. Fed. 28 D4
Lugano Switz. 39 H3
Lugano, Lake Italy/Switz. 44 B2
Lugansk Ukr. see Luhans'k
Luganville Vanuatu 107 F3
Lugdunum France see Lyon
Lugela Moz. 99 H3
Lugela r. Moz. 99 H3
Lugenda r. Moz. 97 C7
Lugg r. U.K. 35 E5
Luggudontsen mt. China 75 F3
Lughaye Somalia 96 D2
Lugo Italy 44 C2
Lugo Spain 42 C1
Lugoj Romania 46 B2
Lugovaya Proleyka Rus. Fed. see Primorsk
Lugovoy Kazakh. 70 D3
Luhanka Fin. 33 G3
Luhans'k Ukr. 29 F6
Luhe China 67 F1
Luhfi, Wādī watercourse Jordan 77 C3
Luhit r. China/India see Zayü Qu
Luhit r. India 75 G4
Luhombero Tanz. 97 C7
Luhua China see Heishui
Luhuo China 66 B2
Luhyny Ukr. 29 D6
Luia Angola 95 D7
Luia r. Angola 95 D6
Luia r. Moz. 99 G3
Luiana Angola 95 D9
Luiana r. Angola 95 D9
Luichow Peninsula China see Leizhou Bandao
Luik Belgium see Liège
Luilaka r. Dem. Rep. Congo 94 D5
Luimneach Rep. of Ireland see Limerick
Luing i. U.K. 34 D3
Luino Italy 44 B2
Luio r. Angola 95 D8
Luiro r. Fin. 32 G2
Luís Echeverría Álvarez Mex. 137 D5
Luís Gomes Brazil 150 E3
Luishia Dem. Rep. Congo 95 E7
Luís L. León, Presa resr Mex. 135 F7
Luitpold Coast Antarctica 167 A1
Luiza Dem. Rep. Congo 95 D6
Luizi Dem. Rep. Congo 95 E7
Luján Arg. 152 F3
Luján de Cuyo Arg. 152 C3
Lujiang China 67 F2
Lukachek Rus. Fed. 64 C1
Lukala Dem. Rep. Congo 95 B6
Lukanga Dem. Rep. Congo 95 E6
Lukanga Swamps Zambia 95 E8
Lukapa Angola see Lucapa
Lukavac Bos.-Herz. 44 G2
Lukenga, Lac l. Dem. Rep. Congo 95 E7
Lukenie r. Dem. Rep. Congo 94 C5
Lukh r. Rus. Fed. 28 G4
Lukhovitsy Rus. Fed. 29 F5
Lüki Bulg. 46 D4
Luk Keng Hong Kong China 67 [inset]
Lukolela Équateur Dem. Rep. Congo 94 C5
Lukolela Kasai Oriental Dem. Rep. Congo 95 E6
Lukou China see Zhuzhou
Lukovac Bos.-Herz. 44 G2
Lukovit Bulg. 46 D3
Luków Poland 37 K3
Lukoyanov Rus. Fed. 29 H5
Lukuga r. Dem. Rep. Congo 95 E6
Lukula Dem. Rep. Congo 95 B6
Lukulu Zambia 95 D8
Lukumburu Tanz. 97 B7
Lukuni Dem. Rep. Congo 94 B5
Lukusashi r. Zambia 95 F8
Lukusuzi National Park Zambia 97 B8

Lula r. Dem. Rep. Congo 94 D5
Luleå Sweden 32 F2
Luleälven r. Sweden 32 F2
Lüleburgaz Turkey 78 A2
Lules Arg. 152 D1
Luliang China 66 B3
Lüliang Shan mts China 63 I4
Luling U.S.A. 133 B6
Lulonga Dem. Rep. Congo 94 C4
Lulonga r. Dem. Rep. Congo 94 C4
Lulu r. Dem. Rep. Congo 94 D4
Luluabourg Dem. Rep. Congo see Kananga
Lülung China 75 E3
Lumachomo China 75 E3
Lumai Angola 95 D8
Lumajang Indon. 59 F5
Lumajangdong Co salt l. China 75 D2
Lümār Iran 79 F4
Lumbala Angola see Lumbala N'guimbo
Lumbala Moxico Angola see Lumbala Kaquengue
Lumbala Kaquengue Angola 95 D8
Lumbala N'guimbo Angola 95 D8
Lumber r. U.S.A. 129 D5
Lumberton U.S.A. 129 D5
Lumbis Indon. 59 G1
Lumbrales Spain 42 C2
Lumding India 75 G4
Lumecha Tanz. 97 B7
Lumezzane Italy 44 C2
Lumi r. P.N.G. 57 J6
Lumijoki Fin. 32 G2
Lumimba Zambia 95 F8
Lumparland Fin. 33 F3
Lumphăt Cambodia 61 D5
Lumpkin U.S.A. 129 B5
Lumsden Canada 134 F2
Lumsden N.Z. 113 B4
Lumut, Gunung mt. Indon. 59 F3
Lumwana Zambia 95 E7
Luna hill Spain 42 D2
Luna r. Spain 42 D1
Lunan China 66 B3
Lunan Lake Canada 123 M1
Lunan Shan mts China 66 B3
Lunavada India 74 B5
Lunayyir, Ḥarrāt lava field Saudi Arabia 89 H3
Luncavăț r. Romania 46 D2
Lund Sweden 33 D5
Lund NV U.S.A. 137 E2
Lund UT U.S.A. 137 F2
Lunda Norte prov. Angola 95 C7
Lundar Canada 123 L5
Lunda Sul prov. Angola 95 C7
Lundazi Zambia 97 B8
Lundi r. Zimbabwe see Runde
Lundy Island U.K. 35 D6
Lune r. U.K. 35 E4
Lüneburg Germany 36 E2
Lunel France 39 G5
Lunenburg U.S.A. 130 D5
Lunéstedt Germany 36 D2
Lunéville France 39 G2
Lunga r. Zambia 95 E8
Lunggar China 75 D3
Lung Kwu Chau i. Hong Kong China 67 [inset]
Lunglei India see Lunglei
Lunglei India 75 G5
Lungmu Co salt l. China 74 D2
Lungnaquilla Mountain Rep. of Ireland 35 C5
Lungro Italy 45 F5
Lungué-Bungo r. Angola 95 D8
Lungwebungu r. Zambia 95 D8
Lunh Nepal 75 D3
Luni r. India 74 A4
Luni r. Pak. 81 G4
Luninets Belarus see Luninyets
Luning U.S.A. 136 D2
Lunino Rus. Fed. 29 H5
Luninyets Belarus 29 C5
Lunkaransar India 74 B3
Lunkha India 74 B3
Lunkho mt. Afgh./Pak. 81 H2
Lunkkaus Fin. 32 G2
Lunsar Sierra Leone 92 B3
Lunsemfwa r. Zambia 95 F8
Luntai China 70 F3
Lunxhërisë, Mali i ridge Albania 47 B4
Lunyuk Indon. 59 G5
Lunzua Zambia 97 A7
Luo r. China 67 E1
Luobei China 64 B3
Luocheng Fujian China see Hui'an
Luocheng Guangxi China 67 D3
Luodian China 66 C3
Luoding China 67 D4
Luodou Sha i. China 67 D4
Luohe r. China 67 E1
Luoma Hu l. China 67 F1
Luoning China 67 D1
Luoping China 66 C3
Luoshan China 67 E1
Luotian China 67 E2
Luoxiao Shan mts China 67 E3
Luoyang Guangdong China see Boluo
Luoyang Henan China 67 E1
Luoyang Zhejiang China see Taishun
Luoyuan China 67 F3
Luozi Dem. Rep. Congo 95 B6
Luozigou China 64 B4
Lupa Market Tanz. 97 B7
Lupane Zimbabwe 99 E3
Lupanshui China see Liupanshui
Lupar r. Sarawak Malaysia 59 E2
L'Upemba, Parc National de nat. park Dem. Rep. Congo 95 E7
Lupeni Romania 46 D1
Lupeni Romania 46 C2
Lupilichi Moz. 99 C7
Lupire Angola 95 C8
Lupiro Tanz. 97 C7
Lupton U.S.A. 137 H4
Luqiao China see Luding
Luqu China 66 B1
Lu Qu r. China see Tao He
Luquan China 66 B3
Luquembo Angola 95 C7
Lūrā Shīrīn Iran 79 F3
Luray U.S.A. 130 F4
Lure France 39 H3
Lure, Sommet de mt. France 39 F4
Lureco r. Moz. 97 C8
Luremo Angola 95 C6
Lurgan U.K. 35 C3
Lürg-e Shotorān salt pan Iran 81 D3
Lurín Peru 148 B3
Luring China see Gêrzê
Lúrio Moz. 97 D8
Lurio r. Moz. 97 D8
Lusahunga Tanz. 96 A5
Lusaka Zambia 95 F8
Capital of Zambia.
Lusaka prov. Zambia 95 F8
Lusambo Dem. Rep. Congo 95 E6
Lusancay Islands and Reefs P.N.G. 107 E2
Luseland Canada 134 E1

Lusenga Plain National Park Zambia 95 F7
Lusewa Tanz. 97 C7
Lush, Mount Australia 108 D4
Lushi China 67 D1
Lushnjë Albania 46 A4
Lüshun China 67 G1
Lusi r. Indon. 59 E4
Lusignan France 38 D3
Lusikisiki S. Africa 99 F6
Lusiwasi Zambia 97 A8
Lusk U.S.A. 134 F4
Luso Angola see Luena
Lussac-les-Châteaux France 38 D3
Lussusso Angola 95 B7
Lut, Bahrat salt l. Asia see Dead Sea
Lut, Dasht-e des. Iran 80 D3
Lü Tao i. Taiwan 67 G3
Lutetia France see Paris
Lüt-e Zangī Aḥmad des. Iran 81 D4
Luther Lake Canada 130 C2
Luthersburg U.S.A. 130 D3
Lutherstadt Wittenberg Germany 37 F3
Lütjenburg Germany 36 E1
Luton U.K. 35 G6
Lutong Sarawak Malaysia 56 D5
Lutope r. Zimbabwe 99 F3
Lutselk'e Canada 123 I2
Lutshi Dem. Rep. Congo 95 E6
Luts'k Ukr. 29 C6
Lutterworth U.K. 35 F5
Lutto Dem. Rep. Congo 94 C4
Lutynia r. Poland 37 H2
Lutz U.S.A. 129 C6
Lutynia U.S.A. 129 C6
Lützelsachsen-Nette nat. park Germany/Neth. 36 B3
Lützow-Holm Bay Antarctica 167 C2
Lutzputs S. Africa 98 D6
Lutzville S. Africa 98 C6
Luumäki Fin. 33 G3
Luuq Somalia 96 D4
Luverne AL U.S.A. 129 B6
Luverne MN U.S.A. 132 B3
Luvo Dem. Rep. Congo 95 B6
Luvua r. Dem. Rep. Congo 95 E6
Luvuei Angola 95 D8
Luvuvhu r. S. Africa 99 F4
Luwegu r. Tanz. 97 C7
Luwero Uganda 96 B4
Luwingu Zambia 95 F7
Luwuk Indon. 57 F6
►Luxembourg country Europe 36 B4
europe 24–25, 48
Luxembourg Lux. 39 G2
Capital of Luxembourg.
Luxembourg country Europe see Luxembourg
Luxeuil-les-Bains France 39 G3
Luxi Hunan China 67 D3
Luxi Yunnan China 66 A3
Luxi Yunnan China 66 B3
Luxian China 66 C2
Luxor Egypt 89 G3
Luy de France r. France 38 C4
Luyi China 67 E1
Luyuan China see Gaoling
Luza Rus. Fed. 28 H3
Luza r. Rus. Fed. 28 H3
Luzern Switz. see Lucerne
Luzhai China 67 D3
Luzhou China 66 C3
Luziânia Brazil 149 I4
Luzilândia Brazil 150 D2
Lužnice r. Czech Rep. 37 G4
Luzon i. Phil. 57 F2
Luzon Strait Phil. 57 F1
Luzy France 39 E3
Luzzi Italy 45 F5
L'viv Ukr. 29 C6
Lvov Ukr. see L'viv
L'vov Ukr. see L'viv
Lwów Poland 37 H2
Lwówek Poland 37 H2
Lyady Rus. Fed. 28 D4
Lyakhavichy Belarus 29 C5
Lyakhovichi Belarus see Lyakhavichy
Lyakhovskiye Ostrova is Rus. Fed. 27 O2
Lyallpur Pak. see Faisalabad
Lyal'mikar Uzbek. 81 F2
Lyapin r. Rus. Fed. 28 L3
Lyaskovets Bulg. 46 D3
Lybster U.K. 34 E2
Lyck Poland see Elk
Lycksele Sweden 32 E2
Lycopolis Egypt see Asyūţ
Lydda Israel see Lod
Lyddan Island Antarctica 167 B2
Lydenburg S. Africa 99 F5
Lydia reg. Turkey 47 L5
Łydynia r. Poland 37 J2
Lyel'chytsy Belarus 29 D6
Lyell, Mount U.S.A. 136 D3
Lyepyel' Belarus 31 L2
Lygourio Greece 47 D6
Lyman Ukr. 46 F2
Lyman U.S.A. 134 E4
Lyme Bay U.K. 35 E6
Lymington U.K. 35 F6
Łyna r. Poland 37 J1
Lynch U.S.A. 130 B5
Lynchburg U.S.A. 130 D5
Lynches r. U.S.A. 129 D5
Lynd r. Australia 111 E3
Lyndhurst Qld Australia 111 F3
Lyndhurst S.A. Australia 112 A3
Lyndon Australia 108 A5
Lyndon U.S.A. 132 C4
Lyndonville U.S.A. 131 G1
Lyngdal Norway 33 B4
Lyngen sea chan. Norway 32 F1
Lyngseidet Norway 32 F1
Lynher Reef Australia 108 C3
Lynn IN U.S.A. 130 A3
Lynn MA U.S.A. 131 H2
Lynn Canal sea chan. U.S.A. 122 C3
Lynndyl U.S.A. 137 F2
Lynn Lake Canada 123 K3
Lynton U.K. 35 E6
Lyntupy Belarus 33 G5
Lynx Lake Canada 123 J2
Lyon France 39 F4
Lyon Mountain U.S.A. 131 G1
Lyonnais, Monts du hills France 39 F4
Lyons Australia 109 F2
Lyons France see Lyon
Lyons GA U.S.A. 129 C5
Lyons KS U.S.A. 132 B4
Lyons NY U.S.A. 131 E2
Lyons Falls U.S.A. 131 F2
Lyozna Belarus 29 E5
Lyra Reef P.N.G. 107 E2
Lysá hora mt. Czech Rep. 37 I4
Lysekil Sweden 33 C4
Łysica hill Poland 37 J3
Lyskovo Rus. Fed. 28 H4
Lys'va Rus. Fed. 28 L4
Lysychans'k Ukr. 29 F6
Lytham St Anne's U.K. 35 E5
Lytton Canada 134 B2
Lyuban' Rus. Fed. 28 D4
Lyubim Rus. Fed. 28 G4

Lyubimets Bulg. 46 E4
Lyubotin Ukr. see Lyubotyn
Lyubotyn Ukr. 29 E6
Lyubytino Rus. Fed. 28 E4
Lyudinovo Rus. Fed. 29 E5
Lyudvinovo Rus. Fed. 29 E5
Lyulyakovo Bulg. 46 E3
Lyzha r. Rus. Fed. 28 K2

↓ M

Ma r. Myanmar 60 B3
Ma, Nam r. Laos 60 C3
Ma, Sông r. Vietnam 60 D4
Maale Maldives see Male
Maalhosmadulu Atoll Maldives 72 B3
Maamba Zambia 95 E9
Ma'an Jordan 78 C5
Maaninka Fin. 32 G3
Maaninkavaara Fin. 32 H2
Maanselkä Fin. 32 H3
Ma'anshan China 67 F2
Maardu Estonia 33 G4
Maarianhamina Fin. see Mariehamn
Ma'arrat an Nu'mān Syria 78 D4
Maas r. Neth. 36 B3
also spelt Meuse (Belgium/France)
Maas-Schwalm-Nette nat. park Germany/Neth. 36 B3
Maastricht Neth. 36 B3
Maatsuyker Group is Australia 112 C6
Maba Dem. Rep. Congo 94 F4
Maba, Ouadi watercourse Chad 88 D6
Mabalane Moz. 99 G4
Mabana Dem. Rep. Congo 94 F4
Mabanda Gabon 94 A5
Mabaruma Guyana 147 G2
Mabating Zambia 95 E9
Mabein Myanmar 60 B3
Mabel Creek Australia 110 C6
Mabel Downs Australia 108 D4
Mabella Australia 124 B3
Maberly Canada 131 E1
Mabian China 66 B2
Mablethorpe U.K. 35 G5
Mabote Moz. 99 G4
Mabou Canada 125 I4
Mabrouk well Mali 93 E1
Maʻbūs Yūsuf oasis Libya 88 D3
Macá, Monte mt. Chile 153 B6
Macadam Plains Australia 109 B6
Macadam Range hills Australia 110 B2
Macaé Brazil 151 E3
Macaíba Brazil 150 F3
Macajuba Brazil 150 D5
Macaloge Moz. 97 B8
MacAlpine Lake Canada 123 K1
Macamic Canada 124 E4
Macandze Moz. 99 G4
Macao China see Macau
Macao China see Macau
Macapá Amapá Brazil 147 I4
Macapá Amazonas Brazil 148 D2
Macará Ecuador 146 B5
Macarani Brazil 150 D5
Macarena, Cordillera mts Col. 146 C4
Macas Ecuador 146 B5
Maçãs r. Port./Spain 42 C2
Macassar Indon. see Makassar
Macassar Strait Indon. 56 E6
Macau Brazil 150 E3
Macau China 67 E4
Macaú r. Brazil 148 C2
Macaúba Brazil 150 B4
Macaúbas Brazil 150 D5
Macauley Island N.Z. 107 H5
Macayari Col. 146 C4
Macclenny U.S.A. 129 C6
Macclesfield U.K. 35 E5
Macclesfield Bank sea feature S. China Sea 56 E2
MacDiarmid Canada 124 B3
Macdonald, Lake salt flat Australia 110 B4
MacDonald Lake Canada 123 M4
Macdonnell Ranges mts Australia 110 B4
Macedo de Cavaleiros Port. 42 C2
Macedon country Europe see Macedonia
►Macedonia country Europe 46 C4
europe 24–25, 48
Maceió Brazil 150 E3
Maceio, Ponta da pt Brazil 150 E3
Macenta Guinea 92 C4
Macerata Italy 44 D3
Macfarlane, Lake salt flat Australia 109 G8
Macgillycuddy's Reeks mts Rep. of Ireland 35 B6
Mach Pak. 81 F4
Macha Rus. Fed. 27 L3
Machacamarca Bol. 148 D4
Machachi Ecuador 146 B5
Machadinho r. Brazil 149 E2
Machai Zambia 95 E9
Machaila Moz. 99 G4
Machakos Kenya 96 C5
Machala Ecuador 146 B5
Machali China see Madoi
Machanga Moz. 99 G4
Machar Marshes Sudan 96 B2
Machattie, Lake salt flat Australia 111 D5
Machaze Moz. see Chitobe
Machecoul France 38 C3
Macheng China 67 E2
Macherla India 72 C2
Machhlishahr India 75 D4
Machias ME U.S.A. 128 G2
Machias NY U.S.A. 130 D2
Machico Madeira 90 A2
Machilipatnam India 72 D2
Machiques Venez. 146 C2
Machiwara India see Machhiwara
Mâch Kowr Iran 81 E5
Macho, Arroyo del watercourse U.S.A. 135 F6
►Machupicchu tourist site Peru 148 B3
southamerica 154
Machupo r. Bol. 149 D3
Machynlleth U.K. 35 E5
Macia Moz. 99 G5
Macias Nguema i. Equat. Guinea see Bioco
Măcin Romania 46 F2
Macintyre r. Australia 112 D3
Macizo de Tocate mts Peru 148 B3
Maçka Turkey 79 D2
Mackay Australia 111 G4
Mackay U.S.A. 134 D3
Mackay, Lake salt flat Australia 110 B4
MacKay Lake Canada 123 I2
Mackenzie r. Australia 111 G4
Mackenzie Canada 134 D3
Mackenzie r. Canada 122 E2
Mackenzie Guyana see Linden
Mackenzie atoll Micronesia see Ulithi
Mackenzie Bay Antarctica 167 E2
Mackenzie Bay Canada 120 F3
Mackenzie Highway Canada 123 G2
Mackenzie King Island Canada 121 H2
Mackenzie Mountains Canada 122 C1

►Mackenzie-Peace-Finlay r. Canada 122 G2
2nd longest river in North America.
northamerica 116–117
Mackillop, Lake salt flat Australia see Yamma Yamma, Lake
Mackinaw r. U.S.A. 132 D3
Macklin Canada 123 I4
Macksville Australia 112 E3
Mackunda Creek watercourse Australia 111 E4
Maclean Australia 112 E3
Maclear S. Africa 99 F6
MacLeod Canada see Fort Macleod
MacLeod, Lake imp. l. Australia 109 A6
Macmillan r. Canada 122 C2
Macmillan Pass Canada 122 D2
Maçobere Moz. 99 F4
Macocola Angola 95 C6
Mâcon France 39 F3
Macomb U.S.A. 132 C3
Macomer Sardinia Italy 45 B4
Macon GA U.S.A. 129 C5
Macon MO U.S.A. 132 C4
Macon MS U.S.A. 129 A5
Macon OH U.S.A. 130 B4
Macon, Bayou r. U.S.A. 133 D6
Macondo Angola 95 D8
Macossa Moz. 99 G3
Macotera Spain 42 D2
Macoun Lake Canada 123 K3
Macovane Moz. 99 G4
Macquarie r. N.S.W. Australia 112 C3
Macquarie r. Tas. Australia 112 C6
►Macquarie Island S. Pacific Ocean 164 E9
Part of Australia. Most southerly point of Oceania.
Macquarie Marshes Australia 112 C3
Macquarie Mountain Australia 112 D4
Macquarie Ridge sea feature S. Pacific Ocean 164 E9
MacRitchie Reservoir Sing. 58 [inset]
Mac. Robertson Land reg. Antarctica 167 E2
Macroom Rep. of Ireland 35 C6
Macuira, Parque Nacional nat. park Col. 146 D1
Macuje Col. 146 C4
Macumba watercourse Australia 110 D5
Macuspana Mex. 138 F5
Macusani Peru 148 C3
Macuze Moz. 99 H3
►Madagascar country Africa 99 [inset] J4
Largest island in Africa and 4th in the world.
africa 84–85, 86–87, 100
world 6–7
Madagascar Basin sea feature Indian Ocean 162 K7
Madagascar Ridge sea feature Indian Ocean 163 J8
Madagali Nigeria 93 I3
Madā'in Şāliḥ Saudi Arabia 89 H3
Madama well Chad 88 C5
Madan Bulg. 46 D4
Madana well Chad 88 C5
Madanapalle India 72 C3
Madang P.N.G. 57 K7
Madaoua Niger 93 G2
Madaripur Bangl. 75 F5
Madau Turkm. 80 C2
Madaw Turkm. see Madau
Madawaska r. Canada 124 E4
Madaya Myanmar 60 B3
Madalena, Isola i. Sardinia Italy 44 B4
Madded India 72 D2
Maddur India 72 C3
Madeir Sudan 94 F3
►Madeira r. Brazil 147 G5
4th longest river in South America.
southamerica 142–143
►Madeira terr. N. Atlantic Ocean 90 A2
Autonomous Region of Portugal.
africa 86–87, 100
Madeira, Arquipélago da terr. N. Atlantic Ocean see Madeira
Madeira, Arquipélago da is Port. 90 A2
Madeirinha r. Brazil 149 E2
Madel Ouèï Chad 94 C2
Maden Turkey 79 D3
Madera Mex. 135 F7
Madera U.S.A. 136 B3
Madgaon India 72 B3
Madhavpur India 74 A5
Madhepura India 75 E4
Madhubani India 75 E4
Madhugiri India 72 C3
Madhya Pradesh state India 74 C5
Madibogo S. Africa 98 E5
Madikeri India 72 B3
Madill U.S.A. 133 B5
Madimba Angola 95 B6
Madimba Dem. Rep. Congo 95 B6
Madīnat ath Thawrah Syria 77 D2
Madingo-Kayes Congo 95 A6
Madingou Congo 95 B6
Madingrin Cameroon 94 B2
Madini r. Bol. 148 D3
Madīrovalo Madag. 99 [inset] J3
Madison FL U.S.A. 129 C6
Madison GA U.S.A. 129 C5
Madison IN U.S.A. 130 B4
Madison NE U.S.A. 132 C3
Madison OH U.S.A. 130 C3
Madison SD U.S.A. 132 B3
Madison VA U.S.A. 130 D4
►Madison WI U.S.A. 132 D3
State capital of Wisconsin.
Madison WV U.S.A. 130 C4
Madison r. U.S.A. 126 D2
Madison Heights U.S.A. 130 D5
Madisonville KY U.S.A. 128 B4
Madisonville TX U.S.A. 133 C6
Madita Indon. 59 E4
Madiun Indon. 59 E4
Madjingo Gabon 94 B4
Madley, Mount Australia 109 C6
Mado Dem. Rep. Congo 96 A4
Madoc Canada 130 E1
Mado Gashi Kenya 96 C4
Madoi China 70 I5
Madona Latvia 33 G4
Madonie mts Sicily Italy 45 D6
Madra Dağı mts Turkey 47 L5
Madrakah, Ra's c. Oman 77 H6
Madras India see Chennai
Madras state India see Tamil Nadu

Madras U.S.A. 134 B3
Madre, Laguna lag. Mex. 126 G6
Madre, Laguna lag. U.S.A. 133 B7
Madre de Dios dept Peru 148 C2
Madre de Dios, Isla i. Chile 153 B7
Madre del Sur, Sierra mts Mex. 138 D5
Madre Occidental, Sierra mts Mex. 126 E6
Madre Oriental, Sierra mts Mex. 126 F6
Madrès, Pic de mt. France 38 E5
►Madrid Spain 42 E2
Capital of Spain.
Madrid aut. comm. Spain 42 E2
Madridejos Spain 42 E3
Madrona, Sierra mts Spain 42 D3
Madruga Cuba 129 C8
Madugula India 72 D2
Madura Australia 109 D7
Madura i. Indon. 59 F4
Madura, Selat sea chan. Indon. 59 F4
Madurai India 72 C4
Madurantakam India 72 C3
Madvār, Kūh-e mt. Iran 80 C4
Madwas India 75 D4
Madzhalis Rus. Fed. 29 H8
Madzwadzido Zimbabwe 99 F3
Madziwa Mine Zimbabwe 99 F3
Maebashi Japan 65 D5
Mae Hong Son Thai. 60 B4
Maella Spain 43 G2
Mae Ping National Park Thai. 60 B4
Mae Ramat Thai. 60 B4
Mae Rim Thai. 60 B4
Maes Howe tourist site U.K. 34 D2
Maestra, Sierra mts Cuba 127 K8
Mae Sot Thai. 61 B4
Maestra, Sierra mts Cuba 127 K8
Mae Suai Thai. 60 B4
Maéwo i. Vanuatu 107 F3
Mae Wong National Park Thai. 61 B5
Mae Yom National Park Thai. 60 C4
Mafeking Canada 123 K4
Mafeking S. Africa see Mafikeng
Mafeteng Lesotho 99 E6
Mafia Channel Tanz. 97 C7
Mafia Island Tanz. 97 C7
Mafikeng S. Africa 98 E5
Mafinga Tanz. 97 B7
Mafra Brazil 151 B8
Mafra Port. 42 A3
Mafraq Jordan see Al Mafraq
Mafungabusi Plateau Zimbabwe 99 F3
Magacela hill Spain 42 D3
Magadan Rus. Fed. 27 P4
Magadi Kenya 96 C5
Magallanes Chile see Punta Arenas
Magallanes y Antártica Chilena admin. reg. Chile 153 B8
Magangué Col. 146 C2
Mağara Turkey 78 C3
Magaria Niger 93 H2
Magarida P.N.G. 111 G1
Magas Iran see Zāboli
Magas Rus. Fed. 79 F2
Magazine Mountain U.S.A. 133 C5
Magburaka Sierra Leone 92 C3
Magdagachi Rus. Fed. 64 A1
Magdalena Bol. 149 D3
Magdalena dept Col. 146 C2
Magdalena r. Col. 146 C2
Magdalena Mex. 135 E7
Magdalena r. Mex. 135 E7
Magdalena, Bahía b. Col. 146 B3
Magdalena, Isla i. Chile 153 B6
Magdalena, Gunung mt. Sabah Malaysia 59 G1
Magdeburg Germany 36 E2
Magdelaine Cays atoll Australia 111 G3
Magee U.S.A. 133 D6
Magelang Indon. 59 E4
Magellan, Strait of Chile 153 C8
Magellan Seamounts sea feature N. Pacific Ocean 164 E4
Magenta, Lake salt flat Australia 109 B8
Mageroya i. Norway 32 G1
Maggia r. Switz. 39 H3
Maggiorasca, Monte mt. Italy 44 B2
Maggiore, Lake Italy 44 B2
Maghāghah Egypt 89 F2
Maghama Mauritania 92 B2
Maghārah, Jabal hill Egypt 77 A4
Maghera U.K. 34 C3
Maghnia Alg. 91 E2
Maghor Afgh. 81 E3
Maghull U.K. 35 E5
Magina mt. Spain 42 E3
Magistral'nyy Rus. Fed. 27 L4
Maglaj Bos.-Herz. 44 G2
Maglavit Romania 46 C2
Maglie Italy 45 H4
Magna U.S.A. 137 G5
Magnetic Island Australia 111 F3
Magnetic Passage Australia 111 F3
Magnitogorsk Rus. Fed. 26 F4
Magnolia U.S.A. 133 C5
Magnor Norway 33 C4
Magny-en-Vexin France 38 D2
Mago Rus. Fed. 27 O4
Màgoé Moz. 99 F2
Magog Canada 125 F4
Mago National Park Eth. 96 C3
Magosa Cyprus see Famagusta
Magoye Zambia 95 E9
Magpie r. Ont. Canada 124 C4
Magpie r. Que. Canada 125 I3
Magpie, Lac l. Canada 125 I3
Magpie-Ouest r. Canada 125 H3
Magrath Canada 123 H5
Magre r. Spain 43 F3
Magrur, Wadi watercourse Sudan 89 E5
Magta' Lahjar Mauritania 92 B1
Magu Tanz. 96 B5
Magu, Khrebet mts Rus. Fed. 64 D1
Maguan China 66 C4
Maguarinho, Cabo c. Brazil 150 B2
Magude Moz. 99 G5
Magumeri Nigeria 93 I2
Magura Bangl. 75 F5
Mägüri, Vârful mt. Romania 46 F2
Maguse Lake Canada 123 M2
Magwa Myanmar see Magwe
Magway admin. div. Myanmar see Magwe
Magwe Myanmar 60 A3
Magwe admin. div. Myanmar 60 A3
Magweggana watercourse Botswana 98 D3
Magyarkanizsa Yugo. see Kanjiža
Magyar Köztársaság country Europe see Hungary
Magyichaung Myanmar 79 G1
Mahābād Iran 80 A2
Mahabaleshwar India 72 B2
Mahabe Madag. 99 [inset] J4
Mahabharat Range mts Nepal 75 E4
Mahabo Toliara Madag. 99 [inset] J4
Mahad India 72 B2
Mahadday Weyne Somalia 96 E4
Mahadeo Hills India 74 C5
Mahaffey U.S.A. 130 D3
Mahagi Dem. Rep. Congo 96 A4
Mahagi Port Dem. Rep. Congo 96 A4

Mahajan India **74** B3
Mahajanga Madag. **99** [inset] J2
Mahajanga *prov.* Madag. **99** [inset] J3
Mahakam *r.* Indon. **59** G3
Mahalapye Botswana **99** E4
Mahale Mountain National Park Tanz. **97** A6
Mahalevona Madag. **99** [inset] K2
Mahallāt Iran **80** B3
Maham India **74** C3
Māhān Iran **80** D4
Mahanadi *r.* India **73** E1
Mahanoro Madag. **99** [inset] K3
Maharajganj *Bihar* India **75** E4
Maharajganj *Uttar Pradesh* India **75** D4
Maharajpur India **74** C4
Maharashtra *state* India **72** B2
Mahārlū, Daryācheh-ye *salt l.* Iran **80** C4
Maha Sarakham Thai. **61** C4
Mahatalaky Madag. **99** [inset] J5
Maḥaṭṭat Ḍab'ah Jordan **77** C4
Mahavavy *r.* Madag. **99** [inset] J2
Mahaweli Ganga *r.* Sri Lanka **72** D4
Mahazoma Madag. **99** [inset] J3
Mahbub Sudan **89** F6
Mahbubabad India **72** D2
Mahbubnagar India **72** C2
Mahd adh Dhahab Saudi Arabia **89** I4
Maḥḍah Oman **80** C5
Mahdia Alg. **91** F2
Mahdia Guyana **147** G3
Mahdia Tunisia **91** H2
Mahe India **72** B4
Mahé *i.* Seychelles **162** K6
Mahendragarh India **74** C3
Mahendragiri *mt.* India **73** E2
Mahenge Tanz. **97** C7
Mahesana India **74** B5
Mahgawan India **74** C4
Mahi *r.* India **74** B5
Māhī *watercourse* Iran **81** D4
Mahia Peninsula N.Z. **113** D2
Mahilyow Belarus **29** D5
Mahim India **72** B2
Mahina Mali **92** C2
Mahmudabad India **74** D4
Maḥmūd-e 'Erāqī Afgh. **81** G3
Mahmudiye Turkey **47** E5
Mahnomen U.S.A. **132** B2
Mahoba India **74** C4
Maholi India **74** D4
Mahón Spain **43** I3
Mahongo Game Park *nature res.* Namibia **98** D3
Mahony Lake Canada **122** E1
Mahou Mali **92** D2
Mahrauni India **74** C4
Mähren *reg.* Czech Rep. *see* **Moravia**
Mahrès Tunisia **91** H2
Māhrūd Iran **81** E3
Mahsana India *see* **Mahesana**
Mahur India **72** C2
Mahuva India **74** A5
Mahwa India **74** C4
Mahya Dağı *mt.* Turkey **46** E4
Mahyār Iran **80** B3
Maia American Samoa **107** I3
Maia Port. **42** B2
Maiaia Moz. *see* **Nacala**
Maibang India **75** G4
Maicao Col. **146** C2
Maicasagi *r.* Canada **124** E3
Maicasagi, Lac *l.* Canada **124** E3
Maîche France **39** G3
Maici *r.* Brazil **147** F6
Maicuru *r.* Brazil **147** H5
Maidstone Canada **123** I4
Maidstone U.K. **35** G6
Maiduguri Nigeria **93** I3
Maiella, Parco Nazionale della *nat. park* Italy **44** E3
Maigmó *mt.* Spain **43** F3
Mai Gudo *mt.* Eth. **96** C3
Maihar India **74** D4
Maijdi Bangl. **75** F5
Maiji Shan *mt.* China **66** C1
Maikala Range *hills* India **74** D5
Maiko *r.* Dem. Rep. Congo **94** E4
Mailan Hill *mt.* India **75** D5
Mailani India **74** D3
Maïlao Chad **94** B2
Mailsi Pak. **81** H4
Ma'in *tourist site* Yemen **76** C6
Mainaguri India **75** F4
Main Brook Canada **125** K3
Mainburg Germany **36** E4
Maindargi India **72** C2
Mai-Ndombe, Lac *l.* Dem. Rep. Congo **94** C5
Maine *state* U.S.A. **131** I1
Maine, Gulf of U.S.A. **131** I2
Mainé Hanari, Cerro *hill* Col. **146** C5
Maïné-Soroa Niger **93** I2
Maingkwan Myanmar **60** B2
Maingy Island Myanmar **61** B5
Mainkung China **66** A2
Mainland *i.* *Orkney, Scotland* U.K. **34** E2
Mainland *i.* *Shetland, Scotland* U.K. **34** F1
Mainling China **75** G3
Mainoru Australia **110** C2
Mainpat *reg.* India **75** D5
Mainpuri India **74** C4
Main Range National Park Australia **111** H6
Maintenon France **38** D2
Maintirano Madag. **99** [inset] J3
Mainua Fin. **32** G2
Mainz Germany **36** D3
Maio *i.* Cape Verde **92** [inset]
Maipó, Volcán *vol.* Chile **152** C3
Maipú *Buenos Aires* Arg. **152** F4
Maipú *Mendoza* Arg. **152** C3
Maiquetía Venez. **146** E2
Maiqu Zangbo *r.* China **75** E3
Mairi Brazil **150** D4
Maishal Island Bangl. **75** F5
Maitencillo Chile **152** C2
Maitengwe Botswana **99** E4
Maithon India **75** E5
Maitland *N.S.W.* Australia **112** D4
Maitland *S.A.* Australia **112** A4
Maitland, Banjaran *mts Sabah* Malaysia **59** G1
Maitri *research station* Antarctica **167** C2
Maiwo *i.* Vanuatu *see* **Maéwo**
Maíz, Islas del *is* Nicaragua **139** H6
Maizhokunggar China **75** F3
Maizuru Japan **65** C6
Maja Jezercë *mt.* Albania **46** A3
Majalgaon India **72** C2
Majari *r.* Brazil **147** F4
Majdanpek Yugo. **46** B2
Majene Indon. **56** E6
Majevica *mts* Bos.-Herz. **44** G2
Majhgawan India **74** D4
Majholi India **74** C5
Majiang *Guangxi* China **67** D4
Majiang *Guizhou* China **66** C3
Major, Puig *mt.* Spain **43** H3
Majorca *i.* Spain **43** H3
Majuli Island India **75** G4
Majunga Madag. *see* **Mahajanga**
Majuro *atoll* Marshall Is **164** F5
Majwemasweu S. Africa **99** E6
Maka Senegal **92** B2
Makabana Congo **94** B5
Makak Cameroon **93** H5
Makale Indon. **57** E6

▶**Makalu** *mt.* China/Nepal **75** E4
5th highest mountain in the world and in Asia.
asia **50–51**
world **6–7**

Makalu Barun National Park Nepal **75** E4
Makamba Burundi **95** F6
Makanchi Kazakh. **70** F2
Makanjila Malawi **97** B8
Makanya Tanz. **97** C6
Makanza Dem. Rep. Congo **94** C4
Makaraingo Madag. **99** [inset] J3
Makari Cameroon **93** I2
Makari Mountain National Park Tanz. *see* **Mahale Mountain National Park**
Makarov Rus. Fed. **64** E2
Makarov Basin *sea feature* Arctic Ocean **166** B1
Makarska Croatia **44** F3
Makar'ye Rus. Fed. **28** I4
Makassar Indon. **56** E7
Makassar, Selat Indon. *see* **Macassar Strait**
Makassar Strait Indon. *see* **Macassar Strait**
Makat Kazakh. **26** F5
Makatini Flats *lowland* S. Africa **99** G5
Makaw Myanmar **60** B2
Makay, Massif du *mts* Madag. **99** [inset] J4
Makedonija *country* Europe *see* **Macedonia**
Makeni Sierra Leone **92** B3
Makete Tanz. **97** B7
Makeyevka Ukr. *see* **Makiyivka**
Makgadikgadi *salt pan* Botswana **98** E4
Makgadikgadi Pans National Park Botswana **98** E4
Makhachkala Rus. Fed. **29** H8
Makhambet Kazakh. **29** I7
Makharadze Georgia *see* **Ozurget'i**
Makhfar al Ḥammām Syria **79** D4
Makhmal Turkm. **81** E2
Makhtal India **72** C2
Makian *vol.* Indon. **57** G5
Makindu Kenya **96** C5
Makinsk Kazakh. **26** H4
Makira *i.* Solomon Is *see* **San Cristobal**
Makiyivka Ukr. **29** F6
Makkah Saudi Arabia *see* **Mecca**
Makkovik, Cape Canada **125** J2
Makljen *pass* Bos.-Herz. **44** F3
Makó Hungary **46** B1
Makoa, Serra *hills* Brazil **147** G4
Makokou Gabon **94** B4
Makonde Plateau Tanz. **97** C7
Makongolosi Tanz. **97** B7
Makopong Botswana **98** D5
Makoro Dem. Rep. Congo **94** F4
Makotipoko Congo **94** C5
Makoua Congo **94** B5
Maków Mazowiecki Poland **37** J2
Makra *i.* Greece **47** D6
Makrakomi Greece **47** C5
Makran *reg.* Iran/Pak. **81** E5
Makrana India **74** B4
Makran Coast Range *mts* Pak. *see* **Talar-i-Band**
Makronisi *i.* Greece **47** D6
Maksatikha Rus. Fed. **31** M1
Maksi India **74** C5
Maksimovka Rus. Fed. **64** D3
Maksotag Iran **81** E4
Maksudangarh India **74** C5
Makthar Tunisia **45** B7
Mākū Iran **80** A2
Makum India **75** G4
Makumbako Tanz. **97** B7
Makunduchi Tanz. **97** C6
Makung Taiwan **67** F4
Makunguwiro Tanz. **97** C7
Makunudhoo *i.* Maldives **72** B5
Makurazaki Japan **65** B7
Makurdi Nigeria **93** H4
Makuungo Somalia **96** D4
Makuyuni Tanz. **96** C5
Mal India **75** F4
Mala Peru **148** A3
Mala Rep. of Ireland *see* **Mallow**
Mala *i.* Solomon Is *see* **Malaita**
Mala, Punta *pt* Panama **139** H7
Malabar Coast India **72** B3

▶**Malabo** Equat. Guinea **93** H5
Capital of Equatorial Guinea.

Malaca Spain *see* **Málaga**
Malacca Malaysia *see* **Melaka**
Malacca *state* Malaysia *see* **Melaka**
Malacca, Strait of Indon./Malaysia **58** B1
Malacky Slovakia **37** H4
Malad *r.* U.S.A. **134** D4
Malad City U.S.A. **134** D4
Maladzyechna Belarus **29** C5
Malá Fatra *nat. park* Slovakia **37** I4
Málaga Spain **42** D4
Malaga *NJ* U.S.A. **131** F4
Malaga *NM* U.S.A. **135** F6
Malaga *OH* U.S.A. **130** C4
Malagarasi *r.* Burundi/Tanz. **97** A6
Malagarasi Tanz. **97** A6
Malagón Spain **42** E3
Malagon *r.* Spain **42** C4
Malahar Indon. **108** C2
Malaimbandy Madag. **99** [inset] J4
Malaita *i.* Solomon Is **107** F2
Malaka *mt.* Indon. **59** G5
Malakal Sudan **96** A2
Malakanagiri India **73** D2
Mala Kapela *mts* Croatia **44** E2
Malakheti Nepal **74** D3
Malakula *i.* Vanuatu **107** F3
Malakwal Pak. **81** H3
Malali Guyana **147** G3
Malamala Indon. **57** F6
Malang Indon. **59** F4
Malanga Moz. **97** C8
Malangali Tanz. **97** B7
Malangana Nepal *see* **Malangwa**
Malange Angola *see* **Malanje**
Malangseidet Norway **32** E1
Malangwa Nepal **75** E4
Malanje Angola **95** C7
Malanje *prov.* Angola **95** C7
Malanville Benin **93** F3
Malanzán Arg. **152** D2
Malanzán, Sierra de *mts* Arg. **152** D2
Mälaren *l.* Sweden **33** E4
Malargüe Arg. **152** C3
Malaripo Brazil **147** H4
Malartic Canada **124** E3
Malaspina Arg. **153** D6
Malaspina Glacier U.S.A. **122** A3
Malatya Turkey **79** D3
Malaut India **74** B3
Malavate Fr. Guiana **147** H4
Malāvī Iran **80** A3
Malawali *i.* *Sabah* Malaysia **59** G1
▶**Malawi** *country* Africa **97** B8
africa **86–87, 100**
Malawi, Lake Africa *see* **Nyasa, Lake**
Malawi National Park Zambia *see* **Nyika National Park**
Malawiya Sudan **89** H6
Malax Fin. **32** F3
Malaya *pen.* Malaysia *see* **Peninsular Malaysia**
Malaya Pera Rus. Fed. **28** J2
Malaya Vishera Rus. Fed. **28** E4
Malāyer Iran **80** B3
Malay Reef Australia **111** G3
▶**Malaysia** *country* Asia **59** F2
asia **52–53, 82**
Malbaie *r.* Canada **125** G4
Malbaza Niger **93** G2
Malbon Australia **111** E4
Malbork Poland **37** I1
Malbrán Arg. **152** E2
Malchin Germany **37** F2
Malcolm Australia **109** C7
Malcolm, Point Australia **109** C8
Malcolm Inlet Oman *see* **Ghazira, Ghubbat al**
Maldegem Belgium **36** A3
Malden U.S.A. **133** D4
Malden Island Kiribati **165** H6
▶**Maldives** *country* Indian Ocean **71** D11
asia **52–53, 82**
Maldonado Uruguay **152** G3

▶**Male** Maldives **69** F6
Capital of the Maldives.

Male Myanmar **60** B3
Maléa Guinea **92** C3
Maleas, Akra *pt Lesbos* Greece **47** E5
Maleas, Akra *pt* Greece **47** C6
Male Atoll Maldives **71** D11
Malebogo S. Africa **98** E6
Malegaon *Maharashtra* India **72** B1
Malegaon *Maharashtra* India **72** C2
Malei Moz. **99** H3
Malé Karpaty *hills* Slovakia **37** H4
Malek Sīāh, Kūh-e *mt.* Afgh. **81** E4
Malela Dem. Rep. Congo **95** E6
Malélé Congo **95** B6
Malele Dem. Rep. Congo **95** B6
Malema Moz. **99** H2
Malendo *watercourse* Nigeria **93** G3
Malerås Sweden **33** D4
Maler Kotla India **74** B3
Maleševske Planine *mts* Bulg./Macedonia **46** C4
Malesherbes France **38** E2
Malesina Greece **47** C5
Mālestān Afgh. **81** F3
Malestroit France **38** B3
Malgobek Rus. Fed. **29** H8
Malgomaj *l.* Sweden **32** E2
Malha Sudan **89** E6
Malhada Brazil **150** D5
Malham Saudi Arabia **80** A5
Malhargarh India **74** B4
Malheur *r.* U.S.A. **134** C3
Malheur Lake U.S.A. **134** C4
▶**Mali** *country* Africa **93** E1
africa **86–87, 100**
Mali Dem. Rep. Congo **94** E5
Mali Guinea **92** B2
Malia Greece **47** D7
Maliana East Timor **57** G7
Malibu U.S.A. **136** C4
Mali Hka *r.* Myanmar **60** B2
Malikdin Afgh. **81** G3
Malik Naro *mt.* Pak. **81** E4
Mali Kyun *i.* Myanmar **61** B5
Malili Indon. **57** F6
Mali Lošinj Croatia **44** E2
Malimba, Monts *mts* Dem. Rep. Congo **95** F6
Malin Rep. of Ireland **34** C4
Malin Ukr. *see* **Malyn**
Malindi Kenya **96** D5
Malines Belgium *see* **Mechelen**
Malinga Gabon **94** B5
Malin Head Rep. of Ireland **34** C4
Malinovka *r.* Rus. Fed. **64** C3
Malinyi Tanz. **97** C7
Malipo China **66** C4
Maliq Albania **46** B4
Mali Raginac *mt.* Croatia **44** E2
Mali i Thatë, Qafa e *pass* Albania **46** B3
Maliwun Myanmar **61** B6
Maliya India **74** A5
Malka *r.* Rus. Fed. **29** H8
Malka Mary Kenya **96** D3
Malkapur *Maharashtra* India **72** B2
Malkapur *Maharashtra* India **72** C1
Malkara Turkey **78** A2
Malko Tŭrnovo Bulg. **46** E4
Mallacoota Australia **112** D5
Mallaig U.K. **34** D3
Mallanga *well* Chad **88** D5
Mallawī Egypt **89** F3
Mallee Cliffs National Park Australia **112** B4
Mållejus *hill* Norway **32** F1
Mallery Lake Canada **123** L1
Mallét Brazil **151** B8
Mallia Greece *see* **Malia**
Mallorca *i.* Spain *see* **Majorca**
Mallow Rep. of Ireland **35** B5
Mallowa Well Australia **108** D5
Malm Norway **32** C2
Malmberget Sweden **32** F2
Malmédy Belgium **39** G1
Malmesbury S. Africa **98** C7
Malmesbury U.K. **35** E6
Malmköping Sweden **33** E4
Malmö Sweden **33** D5
Malmö-Sturup *airport* Sweden **33** D5
Malmslätt Sweden **33** D4
Malmyzh Rus. Fed. **28** I4
Maloca *Amazonas* Brazil **147** F5
Maloca *Pará* Brazil **147** H4
Maloca Salamaim Brazil **149** E3
Malo Crniće Yugo. **46** B2
Malombe, Lake Malawi **97** B8
Malone U.S.A. **131** F1
Malong China **66** B3
Małopolska, Wyżyna *hills* Poland **37** J3
Maloshuyka Rus. Fed. **28** F3
Malovan *pass* Bos.-Herz. **44** F3
Malovăț Romania **46** C2
Malowera Moz. **97** A8
Måløy Norway **33** B3
Maloyaroslavets Rus. Fed. **29** F5
Malozemel'skaya Tundra *lowland* Rus. Fed. **28** I2
Malpelo, Isla de *i.* N. Pacific Ocean **165** M5
Malpica Spain **42** B1
Malprabha *r.* India **72** C2
Malpura India **74** B4
Malše *r.* Czech Rep. **37** G4
Malsiras India **72** B2
▶**Malta** *country* Europe **45** E7
europe **24–25, 48**
Malta Latvia **33** G4
Malta *i.* Malta **45** E7
Malta U.S.A. **134** F2
Maltahöhe Namibia **98** C5
Maltam Cameroon **88** B6
Malton U.K. **35** F4
Maluera Moz. *see* **Malowera**
Malukken *is* Indon. *see* **Moluccas**
Maluku *is* Indon. *see* **Moluccas**
Ma'lūlā, Jabal *mts* Syria **77** C3
Malumfashi Nigeria **93** G3
Malundano Zambia **95** E9
Malung Sweden **33** D3
Maluti Mountains Lesotho **99** F6
Malu'u Solomon Is **107** F2
Malvan India **72** B2
Malvasia Greece *see* **Monemvasia**
Malvern *AR* U.S.A. **133** C5
Malvern *OH* U.S.A. **130** C3
Malvérnia Moz. *see* **Chicualacuala**
Malvinas, Islas *terr.* S. Atlantic Ocean *see* **Falkland Islands**
Malwal Sudan **96** A2
Malý Dunaj *r.* Slovakia **37** I5
Malyn Ukr. **29** D6
Malyy Anyuy *r.* Rus. Fed. **27** Q3
Malyy Irgiz *r.* Rus. Fed. **29** I5
Malyy Kavkaz *mts* Asia *see* **Lesser Caucasus**
Malyy Lyakhovskiy, Ostrov *i.* Rus. Fed. **27** O2
Malyy Taymyr, Ostrov *i.* Rus. Fed. **27** K2
Malyy Uzen' *r.* Kazakh./Rus. Fed. **29** I6
Mama *r.* Rus. Fed. **27** O3
Mamadysh Rus. Fed. **28** I5
Mamafubedu S. Africa **99** F5
Mambahenauhan *i.* Phil. **59** G1
Mambai Brazil **150** C5
Mambal Cameroon **93** I4
Mambali Tanz. **97** B6
Mambasa Dem. Rep. Congo **94** F4
Mambéré *r.* Cent. Afr. Rep. **94** C4
Mambéré-Kadéï *pref.* Cent. Afr. Rep. **94** B3
Mambili *r.* Congo **94** C4
Mambolo Sierra Leone **92** B3
Mambrui Kenya **96** D5
Mamelodi S. Africa **99** F5
Mamers France **38** D2
Mamfé Cameroon **93** H4
Mamiá Brazil **147** F6
Mamili National Park Namibia **98** D3
Mamiña Chile **148** C5
Mamison Pass Georgia/Rus. Fed. **79** E2
Mamison Pass Rus. Fed. **29** G8
Mammoth U.S.A. **137** G5
Mammoth Cave National Park U.S.A. **128** B4
Mammoth Lakes U.S.A. **136** C3
Mamonovo Rus. Fed. **37** I1
Mamoré *r.* Bol./Brazil **148** D2
Mamori Brazil **146** E5
Mamoriá Brazil **148** D1
Mamou Guinea **92** B3
Mampikony Madag. **99** [inset] J3
Mampong Ghana **93** E4
Mamry, Jezioro *l.* Poland **37** J1
Mamuju Indon. **59** G3
Mamuno Botswana **98** D4
Mamuras Albania **46** A4
Man Côte d'Ivoire **92** D4
Man *r.* India **72** B2
Man U.S.A. **130** C5

▶**Man, Isle of** *i.* Irish Sea **35** D4
United Kingdom Crown Dependency.
europe **48**

Mana Fr. Guiana **147** H3
Manabí *prov.* Ecuador **146** B5
Manacacias *r.* Col. **146** C3
Manacapuru Brazil **147** F5
Manacor Spain **43** H3
Manado Indon. **57** F5

▶**Managua** Nicaragua **138** G6
Capital of Nicaragua.

Managua, Lago de *l.* Nicaragua **138** G6
Manakara Madag. **99** [inset] J4
Manakau *mt.* N.Z. **113** C3
Manali India **74** C2

▶**Manama** Bahrain **80** B5
Capital of Bahrain.

Manamadurai India **72** C4
Manambaho *r.* Madag. **99** [inset] J3
Manambondro Madag. **99** [inset] J4
Manamelkudi India **72** C4
Manam Island P.N.G. **57** K6
Mananantañana *r.* Madag. **99** [inset] J4
Manankara *r.* Madag. **99** [inset] J4
Mananara, Parc National de *nat. park* Madag. **99** [inset] K3
Mananara Avaratra Madag. **99** [inset] K3
Manangoora Australia **110** D3
Mananjary Madag. **99** [inset] K4
Manankoliva Madag. **99** [inset] J5
Manankoro Mali **92** D3
Manantali, Lac de *l.* Mali **92** C2
Manantavadi India **72** C4
Manantenina Madag. **99** [inset] J5
Mana Pass China/India **74** C3
Mana Pools National Park Zimbabwe **99** F3

▶**Manapouri, Lake** N.Z. **113** A4
Deepest lake in Oceania.

Manapparai India **72** C4
Manarantsandry Madag. **99** [inset] J3
Manas *r.* India **75** F4
Manasa India **74** B4
Manas Hu *l.* China **70** G2

▶**Manaslu** *mt.* Nepal **75** E3
8th highest mountain in the world and in Asia.
asia **50–51**
world **6–7**

Manassas U.S.A. **130** E4
Manastir Macedonia *see* **Bitola**
Manas Wildlife Sanctuary *nature res.* Bhutan **75** F4
Manatang Indon. **108** D2
Manatí Puerto Rico **139** K5
Manatuto East Timor **57** G7
Man-aung Kyun *i.* Myanmar *see* **Cheduba Island**
Manaus Brazil **147** F5
Manavgat Turkey **78** B3
Manawar India **74** B5
Manawashei Sudan **88** E6
Manawatu *r.* N.Z. **113** C3
Manbazar India **75** E5
Manbij Syria **77** C1
Manchar India **72** B2
Manchester U.K. **35** E5
Manchester *CT* U.S.A. **131** G3
Manchester *IA* U.S.A. **132** D3
Manchester *KY* U.S.A. **130** B5
Manchester *MI* U.S.A. **130** A2
Manchester *NH* U.S.A. **131** H2
Manchester *OH* U.S.A. **130** B4
Manchhar Lake Pak. **81** F5
Manciano Italy **44** C3
Mancılık Turkey **78** D3
Mancınık Dağı *mts* Turkey **47** E5
Mancos *r.* U.S.A. **137** H3
Mand Pak. **81** E5
Mand, Rūd-e *r.* Iran **80** B4
Manda Malawi **97** B7
Manda Tanz. **97** B6
Manda, Jebel *mt.* Sudan **94** E2
Manda, Parc National de *nat. park* Chad **94** C2
Mandabe Madag. **99** [inset] J4
Mandai Sing. **58** [inset]
Mandal Afgh. **81** E3
Mandal *Gujarat* India **74** A5
Mandal *Rajasthan* India **74** B4
Mandal Norway **33** B4

▶**Mandala, Puncak** *mt.* Indon. **57** J6
3rd highest mountain in Oceania.
oceania **102–103**

Mandalay Myanmar **60** B3
Mandalay *admin. div.* Myanmar **60** A3
Mandale Myanmar *see* **Mandalay**
Mandale *admin. div.* Myanmar *see* **Mandalay**
Mandalgarh India **74** B4
Mandalgovĭ Mongolia **63** H2
Mandalī Iraq **79** F4
Mandan U.S.A. **134** G3
Mandas *Sardinia* Italy **45** B5
Mandav Hills India **74** A5
Mandé, Mont de *hill* France **39** F3
Mandelieu-la-Napoule France **39** G5
Mandello del Lario Italy **44** B2
Mandera Kenya **96** D4
Manderfield U.S.A. **137** F2
Mandeville Jamaica **139** I5
Mandeville N.Z. **113** B4
Mandha India **74** A4
Mandheera Somalia **96** E2
Mandhoúdhion Greece *see* **Mantoudi**
Mandi India **74** C3
Mandiakui Mali **92** D2
Mandiana Guinea **92** C3
Mandi Burewala Pak. **81** H4
Mandidzuzure Zimbabwe *see* **Chimanimani**
Mandié Moz. **99** G3
Mandimba Moz. **97** B8
Manding, Monts *mts* Mali **92** C2
Mandji Gabon **93** H6
Mandla India **74** D5
Mandor India **74** B4
Mandoro Dem. Rep. Congo **94** F3
Mandoto Madag. **99** [inset] J3
Mandouri Togo **93** F3
Mandra Greece **47** C5
Mandraki Greece **47** E6
Mandrare *r.* Madag. **99** [inset] J5
Mandrenska *r.* Bulg. *see* **Sredetska Reka**
Mandritsara Madag. **99** [inset] K2
Mandsaur India **74** B4
Mandul *i.* Indon. **59** G2
Mandurah Australia **109** A8
Manduria Italy **45** F4
Mandvi *Gujarat* India **74** A5
Mandvi *Gujarat* India **74** B5
Mandya India **72** C3
Manendragarh India **75** D5
Maner India **75** E4
Maner *r.* India **72** C2
Manerbio Italy **44** C2
Maneromango Tanz. **97** C6
Manesht Kūh *mt.* Iran **80** A3
Mănești Romania **46** D2
Manfalūṭ Egypt **89** F3
Manfredonia Italy **44** E4
Manfredonia, Golfo di *g.* Italy **44** F4
Manga Brazil **150** D5
Manga Burkina **93** E3
Mangabeiras, Serra das *hills* Brazil **150** C4
Manga Grande Angola **95** B6
Mangai Dem. Rep. Congo **95** C6
Mangaia *i.* Cook Is **165** H7
Mangakino N.Z. **113** C2
Mangalagiri India **72** D2
Mangaldai India **75** G4
Mangalia Romania **46** F3
Mangalmé Chad **88** C6
Mangalore India **72** B3
Mangalvedha India **72** B2
Mangania Dem. Rep. Congo **94** D4
Mangaon India **72** B2
Mangapet India **72** D2
Mangaung S. Africa **99** E6
Mangawan India **75** D4
Mangaweka N.Z. **113** C2
Mangde Chhu *r.* Bhutan *see* **Trongsa Chhu**
Ma'ngê China *see* **Luqu**
Mangembe Dem. Rep. Congo **95** E6
Manger Norway **33** B3
Manggar Indon. **59** E3
Mangghyshlaq Kazakh. *see* **Mangystau**
Mangghystaū Kazakh. *see* **Mangystau**
Mangghystaū Oblysy *admin. div.* Kazakh. *see* **Mangistauskaya Oblast'**
Mangistau, Gory *hills* Kazakh. **79** G1
Mangistauskaya Oblast' *admin. div.* Kazakh. **79** H2
Manglares, Punta *pt* Col. **146** B4
Mangnai China **70** H4
Mangoaka Madag. **99** [inset] K2
Mangochi Malawi **97** B8
Mangodara Burkina **92** E3
Mangoky *r. Toliara* Madag. **99** [inset] I4
Mangoky *r. Toliara* Madag. **99** [inset] J4
Mangole *i.* Indon. **57** G6
Mangoli India **72** B2
Mangombe Dem. Rep. Congo **94** E5
Mangoro *r.* Madag. **99** [inset] K3
Mangqystaū Shyghanaghy *b.* Kazakh. *see* **Mangyshlakskiy Zaliv**
Mangral India **74** A5
Mangrol India **74** C4
Mangrul India **72** C1
Mangshi China *see* **Luxi**
Mangualde Port. **42** C2
Manguchar Pak. **81** F4
Mangueira, Lago *l.* Brazil **152** G3
Mangueirinha Brazil **151** A8
Manguéni, Plateau du Niger **91** H5
Mangui China **63** K1
Manguinha, Pontal do *pt* Brazil **150** E4
Mangula Zimbabwe *see* **Mhangura**
Mangum U.S.A. **133** B5
Mangunça, Ilha *i.* Brazil **150** C2
Mangyshlak Kazakh. *see* **Mangystau**
Mangyshlak, Poluostrov *pen.* Kazakh. **79** G1
Mangyshlak Oblast *admin. div.* Kazakh. *see* **Mangistauskaya Oblast'**
Mangyshlakskaya Oblast' *admin. div.* Kazakh. *see* **Mangistauskaya Oblast'**
Mangyshlakskiy Zaliv *b.* Kazakh. **29** I7
Mangystau Kazakh. **26** F5
Manhattan U.S.A. **132** B4
Manhuaçu Brazil **151** D7
Mani Chad **88** B6
Mani China **75** E3
Mani Col. **146** C3
Mani Nigeria **93** G2
Mania *r.* Madag. **99** [inset] J3
Maniago Italy **44** D1
Maniari Tank *resr* India **75** D5
Manica Moz. **99** G3
Manica *prov.* Moz. **99** G3
Manicaland *prov.* Zimbabwe **99** G3
Manicoré Brazil **147** F6
Manicoré *r.* Brazil **147** F6
Manicouagan Canada **125** G3
Manicouagan *r.* Canada **125** G3
Manicouagan, Réservoir Canada **125** G3
Manic Trois, Réservoir Canada **125** G3
Maniema *prov.* Dem. Rep. Congo **94** E5
Manīfah Saudi Arabia **80** B5
Maniganggo China **66** A2
Manigotagan Canada **123** L5
Manihari India **75** E4
Manihiki *atoll* Cook Is **165** H6
Maniitsoq Greenland **121** N3
Manija *r.* Pak. **81** F5
Manikchhari Bangl. **75** G5
Manikganj Bangl. **75** F5
Manikpur India **74** D4

▶**Manila** Phil. **57** F3
Capital of the Philippines
world **16–17**

Manila U.S.A. **134** E4
Manilla Australia **112** D3
Maningrida Australia **110** C2
Maninjau, Danau *l.* Indon. **58** C3
Manipur India *see* **Imphal**
Manipur *state* India **75** G4
Manipur *r.* India/Myanmar **75** G5
Manisa Turkey **78** A3
Manisa *prov.* Turkey **47** F5
Manissauá Missu *r.* Brazil **150** A4
Manistee U.S.A. **132** E2
Manistee *r.* U.S.A. **132** E2
Manistique U.S.A. **132** E2
Manitoba *prov.* Canada **123** L4
Manitoba, Lake Canada **123** L5
Manito Lake Canada **123** I4
Manitou Canada **123** L5
Manitou *r.* Canada **125** H3
Manitou Falls Canada **124** A3
Manitou Islands U.S.A. **132** E2
Manitoulin Island Canada **124** D4
Manitouwadge Canada **124** C3
Manitowoc U.S.A. **132** E2
Manizales Col. **146** C3
Manja Madag. **99** [inset] J4
Manjacaze Moz. **99** G5
Manjak Madag. **99** [inset] J3
Manjeri India **72** C4
Manjhand Pak. **81** G5
Man Jiang *r.* China **64** A4
Manjil Iran **80** B2
Manjimup Australia **109** B8
Manjo Cameroon **93** H4
Manjra *r.* India **72** C2
Man Kabat Myanmar **60** B2
Mankachar India **75** F4
Mankanza Dem. Rep. Congo *see* **Makanza**
Mankato *KS* U.S.A. **132** B4
Mankato *MN* U.S.A. **132** C2
Mankono Côte d'Ivoire **92** D3
Mankota Canada **123** J5
Manlleu Spain **43** H2
Manmad India **72** B1
Mann *r.* Australia **110** C2
Mann, Mount Australia **110** B5
Manna Indon. **58** C4
Mannahill Australia **112** A4
Mannar Sri Lanka **72** C4
Mannar, Gulf of India/Sri Lanka **72** C4
Mannargudi India **72** C4
Manneru *r.* India **72** D3
Mannheim Germany **36** D4
Mannicolo Islands Solomon Is *see* **Vanikoro Islands**
Manning Canada **123** G3
Manning U.S.A. **132** A2
Mannington U.S.A. **130** C4
Männlifluh *mt.* Switz. **39** G3
Mann Ranges *mts* Australia **110** E5
Mannsville U.S.A. **131** E2
Mannu *r.* *Sardinia* Italy **45** B4
Mannu *r.* *Sardinia* Italy **45** B5
Mannu *r.* *Sardinia* Italy **45** B5
Mannu, Capo *c.* *Sardinia* Italy **45** B4
Manville Canada **123** I4
Mano *r.* Liberia/Sierra Leone **92** C4
Manoa Bol. **148** D2
Manohar Thana India **74** C4
Manokotak U.S.A. **120** D4
Manokwari Indon. **57** H6
Manombo Atsimo Madag. **99** [inset] I4
Manompana Madag. **99** [inset] K3
Manono Dem. Rep. Congo **95** E6
Manora Head Pak. **81** F5
Mano River Liberia **92** C4
Manos, Cueva de las *tourist site* Arg. **153** C6
Manosque France **39** F5
Manouane, Lac *l.* Canada **125** G3
Man Pan Myanmar **60** B3
Manp'o N. Korea **64** A4
Manpur India **74** B5
Manra *i.* Kiribati **107** H2
Manresa Spain **43** G2
Mansa *Gujarat* India **74** B5
Mansa *Punjab* India **74** B3
Mansa Zambia **95** F7
Mansabá Guinea-Bissau **92** B2
Mansa Konko Gambia **92** B2
Man Sam Myanmar **60** B3
Mansehra Pak. **81** H3
Mansel Island Canada **121** L3
Mansel'kya *ridge* Fin./Rus. Fed. **32** H2
Mansfield Australia **112** C5
Mansfield U.K. **35** F5
Mansfield *AR* U.S.A. **133** C5
Mansfield *LA* U.S.A. **133** C5
Mansfield *OH* U.S.A. **130** B3
Mansfield *PA* U.S.A. **131** E3
Mansi Myanmar **60** A2
Mansidão Brazil **150** D4
Manso *r.* Brazil *see* **Mortes, Rio das**
Manso, Represa do Rio *r.* Brazil **150** A5
Manso-Nkwanta Ghana **93** E4
Mansurlu Turkey **78** C3
Manta Ecuador **146** A5
Mantantale Dem. Rep. Congo **94** D5
Mantaro *r.* Peru **148** B3
Manteca U.S.A. **136** B3
Mantecal Venez. **146** D3
Manteigas Port. **42** C2
Mantena Brazil **151** D6
Manteo U.S.A. **128** E5
Mantes-la-Jolie France **38** D2
Manthani India **72** C2
Mantiqueira, Serra da *mts* Brazil **151** C7
Manton U.S.A. **132** E2
Mantos Blancos Chile **148** C5
Mantoudi Greece **47** C5
Mantova Italy *see* **Mantua**
Mäntsälä Fin. **33** G3
Mänttä Fin. **33** G3
Mantua Italy **44** C2
Mantua U.S.A. **130** C3
Mantuan Downs Australia **111** F5
Manturovo Rus. Fed. **28** H4
Mäntyharju Fin. **33** G3
Mäntyjärvi Fin. **32** G2
Manu *r.* Bol. *see* **Mapiri**
Manú *r.* Peru **148** C3
Manu, Parque Nacional *nat. park* Peru **148** B3
Manuae *atoll* Fr. Polynesia **165** H7
Manua Islands American Samoa **107** I3
Manuel Alves *r.* Brazil **150** B4
Manuel J. Cobo Arg. **152** F3
Manuel Rodriguez, Isla *i.* Chile **153** B8
Manuel Urbano Brazil **148** C2
Manuel Vitorino Brazil **150** D5
Manuelzinho Brazil **150** A3
Manui *i.* Indon. **57** F6
Manūjān Iran **80** D5
Manukau N.Z. **113** C2

Manukau Harbour N.Z. 113 C2
Manupari r. Bol. 148 D2
Manuripi r. Bol. 148 D2
Manus Island P.N.G. 57 K6
Manvi India 72 C3
Manwat India 72 C2
Many U.S.A. 133 C6
Manyame r. Moz./Zimbabwe 99 F2
Manyara, Lake salt l. Tanz. 97 B5
Manyas Turkey 47 E4
Manyas Gölü l. Turkey see Kuş Gölü
Manyberries Canada 123 I5
Manyinga Zambia 95 E8
Many Farms U.S.A. 137 H3
Manyoni Tanz. 97 B6
Manzanal, Puerto del pass Spain 42 C1
Manzanares Spain 42 E3
Manzaneda, Cabeza de mt. Spain 42 C1
Manzanillo Cuba 127 K7
Manzanillo Mex. 126 F8
Manzanza Dem. Rep. Congo 95 F6
Manzariyeh Iran 80 B3
Manzengele Dem. Rep. Congo 95 C6
Manzhouli China 63 J2
Manzini Swaziland 99 F5
Manzovka Rus. Fed. see Sibirtsevo
Mao Chad 88 B6
Maó Spain see Mahón
Mao, Nam r. Myanmar see Shweli
Maocifan China 67 G2
Mao'ergai China 66 B1
Maoke, Pegunungan mts Indon. 57 I6
Maokeng S. Africa 99 F5
Maoming China 67 F4
Ma On Shan hill Hong Kong China 67 [inset]
Maopi Cape Taiwan see Maopi T'ou
Maopi T'ou c. Taiwan 67 C4
Maowen China see Maoxian
Maoxian China 66 B1
Mapai Moz. 99 F2
Mapam Yumco l. China 70 F5
Mapane Indon. 57 F6
Mapanza Zambia 95 E9
Mapastepec Mex. 138 F5
Maphodi S. Africa 98 E6
Mapi r. Indon. 57 I7
Mapiche, Serrania mts Venez. 146 E3
Mapimí Mex. 133 A7
Mapimí, Bolsón de des. Mex. 135 F8
Mapin i. Phil. 59 G5
Mapinhane Moz. 99 G4
Mapire Venez. 147 F3
Mapireme Brazil 147 H4
Mapiri Bol. 148 D2
Mapirpán Col. 146 C4
Maple r. MI U.S.A. 130 A2
Maple r. ND U.S.A. 132 B2
Maple r. ND U.S.A. 132 B2
Maple Creek Canada 134 E2
Mapleton U.S.A. 132 E3
Mapmakers Seamounts sea feature N. Pacific Ocean 164 F4
Mapoon Australia 111 E1
Mapor i. Indon. 58 D2
Maprik P.N.G. 57 J6
Mapuca India 72 B3
Mapuera r. Brazil 147 G5
Mapulanguene Moz. 99 G3
Mapunda Dem. Rep. Congo 95 E7

▶Maputo Moz. 99 G5
Capital of Mozambique.

Maputo prov. Moz. 99 G5
Maputo r. Moz./S. Africa 99 G5
Maputsoe Lesotho 99 E6
Maqanshy Kazakh. see Makanchi
Maqar an Na'am well Iraq 79 E5
Maqat Kazakh. see Makat
Maqên China 66 B1
Maqên Gangri mt. China 70 I5
Maqteïr reg. Mauritania 90 C5
Maqu China 66 B1
Ma Qu r. China see Yellow River
Maquan He r. China 75 E3
Maquela do Zombo Angola 95 B6
Maquinchao Arg. 152 C5
Maquoketa U.S.A. 132 F3
Mar r. Pak. 81 F5
Mar, Serra do mts Rio de Janeiro/São Paulo Brazil 151 C7
Mar, Serra do mts Rio Grande do Sul/Santa Catarina Brazil 151 B9
Mara r. Canada 123 I1
Mara Guyana 147 G3
Mara India 75 D5
Mara admin. reg. Tanz. 96 B5
Maraã Brazil 147 E5
Maraba Brazil 150 B3
Marabahan Indon. 59 F3
Marabatua i. Indon. 59 E4
Maraboon, Lake resr Australia 111 G4
Maracá r. Brazil 150 B2
Maracá, Ilha i. Brazil 147 F4
Maracá, Ilha de i. Brazil 147 I4
Maracaibo Venez. 146 D2
Maracaju Brazil 149 H4
Maracaju, Serra de hills Brazil 149 G5
Maracaná Brazil 150 D2
Maracanaquará, Planalto plat. Brazil 147 H5
Maracanda Uzbek. see Samarkand
Maracás Brazil 150 D5
Maracás, Chapada de hills Brazil 150 D5
Maracay Venez. 147 E2
Marādah Libya 88 C2
Maradi Niger 93 F2
Maradi dept Niger 93 G2
Marāgheh Iran 80 A2
Maragogi Brazil 150 F4
Marah Saudi Arabia 80 A5
Marahuaca, Cerro mt. Venez. 146 E4
Marais des Cygnes r. U.S.A. 132 C4
Marajó, Baía de est. Brazil 150 B2
Marajó, Ilha de i. Brazil 150 B2
Marakkanam India 72 C3
Maralal Kenya 96 C4
Maralbashi China see Bachu
Maralinga Australia 110 B6
Maralwexi China see Bachu
Maramasike i. Solomon Is 107 F2
Maramba Zambia see Livingstone
Marambio research station Antarctica 167 A2
Maran mt. Pak. 81 F4
Marana U.S.A. 137 H5
Marand Iran 80 A2
Marandellas Zimbabwe see Marondera
Maranguape Brazil 150 E2
Maranhão r. Brazil 149 I3
Maranhão state Brazil 150 C3
Maranoa r. Australia 111 D5
Marañón r. Peru 146 C4
Marans France 38 C4
Marão Moz. 99 G5
Marão mt. Port. 42 C2
Marapanim Brazil 150 C2
Marape Brazil 149 F3
Marapi, Gunung vol. Indon. 58 C3

Marari Brazil 146 E6
Mara Rosa Brazil 150 B5
Maraş Cyprus see Varosia
Maraş Turkey see Kahramanmaraş
Marasende i. Indon. 59 G4
Mărăşeşti Romania 46 F2
Mărăşu Romania 46 E2
Maratea Italy 45 E5
Marathon Canada 124 C3
Marathon Greece see Marathonas
Marathon FL U.S.A. 129 C7
Marathon TX U.S.A. 133 A6
Marathonas Greece 47 C5
Marauá Brazil 146 E5
Marauiá r. Brazil 147 E5
Marāwah Libya 88 D1
Marayes Arg. 152 D2
Maray Lake Pak. 81 G4
Marbella Spain 42 D5
Marble Bar Australia 108 B5
Marble Canyon U.S.A. 137 G3
Marble Canyon gorge U.S.A. 137 G3
Marble Hall S. Africa 99 F5
Marble Hill U.S.A. 132 F4
Marble Island Canada 123 N2
Marbul Pass Jammu and Kashmir 74 B2
Marburg S. Africa 99 F6
Marburg Slovenia see Maribor
Marburg an der Lahn Germany 36 D3
Marca, Ponta do pt Angola 95 A9
Marcal r. Hungary 37 H5
Marcapata Peru 148 C3
Marcelino Brazil 146 E3
March r. Austria/Slovakia 37 H4
March U.K. 35 G5
Marche reg. France 38 D3
Marche admin. reg. Italy 44 D3
Marche-en-Famenne Belgium 39 F1
Marchena Spain 42 D5
Mar Chiquita, Lago l. Arg. 152 E2
Marchtrenk Austria 37 G4
Marcona Peru 148 B3
Marcopeet Islands Canada 124 E1
Marcos Juárez Arg. 152 E2
Marcy, Mount U.S.A. 131 G1
Mardan Pak. 81 H3
Mar de Ajó Arg. 152 F4
Mar del Plata Arg. 152 F4
Mardian Afgh. 81 F2
Mardin Turkey 79 E3
Mârdudden Sweden 32 F2
Maré i. New Caledonia 107 F4
Maree, Loch l. U.K. 34 D3
Mareeba Australia 111 F3
Mareh Iran 81 D5
Maréna Mali 92 C3
Marendet Niger 93 G1
Marennes France 38 C4
Marerano Madag. 99 [inset] J4
Mareuil France 38 D4
Mareuil-sur-Lay-Dissais France 38 C3
Marevo Rus. Fed. 29 E1
Marfa U.S.A. 135 F7
Margam r. mts China 75 E2
Märgäng Estonia 33 G4
Marjan Afgh. see Wazi Khwa
Marganets Ukr. see Marhanets'
Margao India see Madgaon
Margaret r. Australia 108 D4
Margaret, Mount Australia 108 B5
Margaret Lake Alta Canada 123 H3
Margaret Lake N.W.T. Canada 123 H1
Margaret River Australia 109 A8
Margaretville U.S.A. 131 F2
Margarita Arg. 152 E2
Margarita, Isla de i. Venez. 147 F2
Margate U.K. 35 G6
Margherita India 75 G4
Margherita, Lake Eth. see Abaya, Lake

▶Margherita Peak Dem. Rep. Congo/Uganda 94 F4
3rd highest mountain in Africa.
africa 84–85

Marghilon Uzbek. see Margilan
Margilan Uzbek. 81 G1
Margo, Dasht-i des. Afgh. 81 E4
Margos Peru 148 A2
Margow, Dasht-e des. Afgh. 81 E4
Marguerite Canada 122 F4
Marguerite, Pic de mt. Dem. Rep. Congo/Uganda see Margherita Peak
Marguerite Bay Antarctica 167 L2
Margyang China 75 F3
Marhaj Khalil Iraq 79 F4
Marhan Dāgh hill Iraq 79 E3
Marhanets' Ukr. 29 E7
Marhoum Alg. 91 E2
Mari P.N.G. 57 J7
Maria r. Brazil 151 A7
Maria atoll Fr. Polynesia 165 H7
María Elena Chile 148 C5
Mariager Denmark 33 C4
Maria Island Australia 110 C2
Maria Island Tas. Australia 112 D6
Marian Australia 111 G4
Marianao Cuba 129 C4

▶Mariana Ridge sea feature N. Pacific Ocean 164 C4

▶Mariana Trench sea feature N. Pacific Ocean 164 C5
Deepest trench in the world.

Mariani India 75 G4
Mariánica, Cordillera mts Spain see Morena, Sierra
Marian Lake Canada 123 G2
Marianna AR U.S.A. 133 D5
Marianna FL U.S.A. 129 B6
Mariannelund Sweden 33 D4
Mariano Loza Arg. 152 F2
Mariano Machado Angola see Ganda
Mariánské Lázně Czech Rep. 37 F4
Mariapiri, Mesa de hills Col. 146 D4
Marias r. U.S.A. 134 E3
Marias, Islas is Mex. 126 E7

▶Mariato, Punta pt Panama 139 H7
Most southerly point of North America.

Maria van Diemen, Cape N.Z. 113 C1
Mariazell Austria 37 G5
Ma'rib Yemen 76 D3
Maribo Denmark 36 E1
Maribor Slovenia 44 F1
Marica r. Bulg. see Maritsa
Maricopa AZ U.S.A. 137 G5
Maricopa CA U.S.A. 136 C4
Maricopa Mountains U.S.A. 137 F5
Maridi Sudan 94 F3
Maridi watercourse Sudan 94 F3
Marié r. Brazil 146 E4
Marie Byrd Land reg. Antarctica 167 J1
Marie-Galante i. Guadeloupe 139 L5
Mariehamn Fin. 33 F3
Mari El aut. rep. Rus. Fed. see Mariy El, Respublika
Mariembero r. Brazil 150 B5
Marienbad Czech Rep. see Mariánské Lázně
Marienburg Poland see Malbork
Mariental Namibia 98 C5

Marienville U.S.A. 130 D3
Marienwerder Poland see Kwidzyn
Mariestad Sweden 33 D4
Marietta GA U.S.A. 129 B5
Marietta OH U.S.A. 130 C4
Marietta OK U.S.A. 133 B5
Mariga r. Nigeria 93 F3
Marignane France 39 F5
Marijampolė Lith. 33 E5
Marikostinovo Bulg. 46 C4
Marília Brazil 149 H5
Marillana Australia 108 B5
Marimba Angola 95 B6
Marín Spain 42 B1
Marina U.S.A. 136 B3
Marina di Gioiosa Ionica Italy 45 F5
Mar"ina Gorka Belarus see Mar"ina Horka
Mar"ina Horka Belarus 29 D5
Marinella, Golfo di b. Sardinia Italy 44 C4
Marinette U.S.A. 132 E2
Maringá Brazil 149 G5
Maringa r. Dem. Rep. Congo 94 C4
Maringue Moz. 99 G3
Marinha Grande Port. 42 B3
Marinjab Iran 80 B3
Mar"insko Rus. Fed. 33 H4
Marion AL U.S.A. 133 B5
Marion AR U.S.A. 133 D5
Marion IL U.S.A. 128 A4
Marion IN U.S.A. 132 E3
Marion KS U.S.A. 132 B4
Marion KY U.S.A. 128 C5
Marion NC U.S.A. 128 C5
Marion OH U.S.A. 130 B3
Marion SC U.S.A. 129 D5
Marion VA U.S.A. 130 C5
Marion, Lake U.S.A. 129 C5
Marion Bay Australia 112 A4
Marion Lake U.S.A. 132 B4
Marion Reef Australia 111 H3
Mariou, Adrar mt. Alg. 91 H5
Maripa Venez. 147 E3
Maripasoula Fr. Guiana 147 H4
Mariposa U.S.A. 136 C3
Mariposa r. U.S.A. 136 B3
Mariquita Col. 146 C3
Mariscal Estigarribia Para. 149 E5
Mărişel Romania 46 C1
Maritime Kray admin. div. Rus. Fed. see Primorskiy Kray
Maritimes, Alpes mts France/Italy see Maritime Alps
Maritsa Bulg. see Simeonovgrad
Maritsa r. Bulg. 46 E4
Maritime, Alpi mts France/Italy see Maritime Alps
Mariupol' Ukr. 29 F7
Mariusa nat. park Venez. 147 F2
Mariusa, Isla i. Venez. 147 F2
Marīvān Iran 80 A3
Mariy El, Respublika aut. rep. Rus. Fed. 28 J4
Märjamaa Estonia 33 G4
Marka Somalia 96 E4
Markala Mali 92 D2
Markam China 66 A2
Markapur India 72 C3
Markaryd Sweden 33 D4
Markazi prov. Iran 80 B3
Markdale Canada 130 C1
Marken S. Africa 99 F4
Markermeer l. Neth. 36 B2
Market Harborough U.K. 35 F5
Market Rasen U.K. 35 F5
Market Weighton U.K. 35 F5
Markha r. Rus. Fed. 27 L3
Markham Canada 130 D2
Markham, Mount Antarctica 167 H1
Markhamet Uzbek. 81 H1
Markitta Sweden 32 F2
Markleeville U.S.A. 136 C2
Markkleeberg Germany 36 F3
Markleysburg U.S.A. 130 D4
Markounda Cent. Afr. Rep. 94 C3
Markovo Rus. Fed. 27 R3
Markoye Burkina 92 E3
Marks Rus. Fed. 29 H6
Marks U.S.A. 133 D5
Marksville U.S.A. 133 C6
Marktheidenfeld Germany 36 D4
Marktoberdorf Germany 36 E5
Marktredwitz Germany 36 F3
Marl Germany 36 C3
Marla Australia 110 C5
Marlborough Australia 111 G4
Marlborough admin. reg. N.Z. 113 G2
Marle France 39 E2
Marlin U.S.A. 133 B6
Marlinton U.S.A. 130 C4
Marlo Australia 112 D5
Marmagao India 72 B3
Marmande France 38 D4
Marmara Turkey 46 E4
Marmara, Sea of g. Turkey 78 B2
Marmara Adası i. Turkey 46 E4
Marmara Denizi g. Turkey see Marmara, Sea of
Marmaraereğlisi Turkey 46 E4
Marmara Gölü l. Turkey 47 F5
Marmaris Turkey 78 B3
Marmaro Greece 47 E5
Marmelos r. Brazil 149 F1
Marmet U.S.A. 130 C4
Marmion, Lake salt l. Australia 109 C7
Marmion Lake Canada 132 D1
Marmolada mt. Italy 44 C1
Marmolejo Spain 42 D3
Marne r. France 38 E2
Marne Germany 36 D2
Marne, Source de la tourist site France 39 F3
Marne-la-Vallée France 39 E2
Marneuli Georgia 79 F2
Maro Chad 94 C2
Maroantsetra Madag. 99 [inset] K2
Marofandilia Madag. 99 [inset] J4
Marol Jammu and Kashmir 74 C2
Marolambo Madag. 99 [inset] K4
Maromokotro mt. Madag. 99 [inset] K2
Marondera Zimbabwe 99 F3
Maroni r. Fr. Guiana 147 H3
Maronne r. France 38 D4
Maroochydore Australia 111 H5
Maroonah Australia 108 A5
Maroon Peak U.S.A. 134 F5
Maros Indon. 57 F4
Maros r. Romania 46 B1
Maroseranana Madag. 99 [inset] K3
Maros-Körös Köze plain Hungary 46 B1
Marosvásárhely Romania see Târgu Mureş
Marotandrano Madag. 99 [inset] K2
Marotolana Madag. 99 [inset] K2
Marovato Madag. 99 [inset] K2
Marovoay Madag. 99 [inset] J3
Marovoay Atsimo Madag. 99 [inset] J3
Marowijne r. Suriname 147 H3
Marqādah Syria 79 E3

Mar Qu r. China 66 B1
Marquesas Islands Fr. Polynesia 165 I6
Marquesas Keys is U.S.A. 129 C7
Marquette France 38 D1
Marquise France 38 D1
Marquises, Îles is Fr. Polynesia see Marquesas Islands
Marra r. Nigeria 93 G3
Marradi Italy 44 D2
Marrakech Morocco see Marrakech
Marrakesh Morocco see Marrakech
Marrakech Morocco 90 D3
Marra Plateau Sudan 88 E6
Marrawah Australia 112 C6
Marree Australia 110 D6
Marromeu Moz. 99 G3
Marrupa Moz. 97 C8
Mars r. France 39 E4
Mars U.S.A. 130 C3
Marsá al 'Alam Egypt 89 G3
Marsabit Kenya 96 C4
Marsabit National Reserve nature res. Kenya 96 C4
Marsa Darur Sudan 89 H5
Marsa Delwein Sudan 89 H5
Marsala Sicily Italy 45 D6
Marsá Matrūh Egypt 89 F2
Mars Bay Bahamas 129 D8
Marsberg Germany 36 D3
Marsciano Italy 44 D3
Marsden Canada 123 I4
Marseille France 39 F5
Marseilles France see Marseille
Marsella Bol. 148 D3
Marsfjället mt. Sweden 32 D2
Marsh watercourse Australia 110 D6
Marshall AR U.S.A. 133 C5
Marshall IL U.S.A. 128 B4
Marshall MI U.S.A. 130 A2
Marshall MN U.S.A. 132 C2
Marshall MO U.S.A. 132 C4
Marshall TX U.S.A. 133 C5
Marshall VA U.S.A. 130 E4

▶Marshall Islands country N. Pacific Ocean 164 E5
oceania 104–105, 114

Marshalltown U.S.A. 132 C3
Marshfield U.S.A. 132 C4
Marsh Harbour Bahamas 129 D7
Mars Hill U.S.A. 128 G2
Marsh Island U.S.A. 127 H6
Marsh Lake Canada 122 C2
Mārsta Sweden 33 E4
Marsyangdi r. Nepal 75 E4
Marta Italy 44 C3
Marta r. Italy 44 C3
Martaban Myanmar 61 B4
Martaban, Gulf of Myanmar 61 B4
Mask, Lough l. Rep. of Ireland 35 C4
Maskanah Syria 77 D1
Maskūtān Iran 81 D5
Maslti Pak. 81 F4
Martapura Sumatera Selatan, Sumatra Indon. 58 D4
Martapura Kalimantan Selatan Indon. 59 F3
Martel France 38 D4
Marten River Canada 124 D3
Marte R. Gómez, Presa resr Mex. 133 B7
Martés, Serra mts Spain 43 F3
Martha's Vineyard i. U.S.A. 131 H3
Martigny Switz. 39 G3
Martigues France 39 F5
Martin Slovakia 37 I4
Martin r. Spain 43 F2
Martin U.S.A. 132 A3
Martin, Lake U.S.A. 129 B5
Martinet Spain 43 G1
Martínez Mex. 126 G7
Martinez GA U.S.A. 129 C5
Martinez CA U.S.A. 136 B2
Martinho Campos Brazil 151 C6

▶Martinique terr. West Indies 139 L6
French Overseas Department.
northamerica 118–119, 140

Martinique Passage Dominica/Martinique 139 L5
Martino Greece 47 C5
Martin Peninsula Antarctica 167 K2
Martinsburg PA U.S.A. 130 D3
Martinsburg WV U.S.A. 130 E4
Martinsville IN U.S.A. 128 B4
Martinsville VA U.S.A. 130 D5

▶Martin Vas, Ilhas is S. Atlantic Ocean 161 M7
Most easterly point of South America.

Martök Kazakh. see Martuk
Marton N.Z. 113 C3
Martorell Spain 43 G2
Martos Spain 42 E4
Martuk Kazakh. 26 F4
Martuni Armenia 79 F2
Maru Nigeria 93 F2
Maruchak Afgh. 81 E3
Marudi Sarawak Malaysia 59 F1
Marudu, Teluk b. Sabah Malaysia 59 G1
Marukhis Ugheltekhili pass Georgia/Rus. Fed. 79 F2
Marum, Mount vol. Vanuatu 107 F3
Mārūn r. Iran 80 B4
Marungu mts Dem. Rep. Congo 95 D9
Maruwa Hills Sudan 96 B3
Marvast Iran 80 C4
Marvejols France 39 E4
Marvine, Mount U.S.A. 137 G2
Marwar Junction India 74 B4
Mary r. N.T. Australia 110 B4
Mary r. Qld Australia 111 H5
Mary r. W.A. Australia 108 D4
Mary Turkm. 81 E2
Mary A.S.S.R. aut. rep. Rus. Fed. see Mariy El, Respublika
Maryborough Qld Australia 111 H5
Maryborough Vic. Australia 112 B5
Marydale S. Africa 98 D6
Mar'yevka Rus. Fed. 29 I5
Maryland state U.S.A. 131 E4
Mary Oblast admin. div. Turkm. see Maryyskaya Oblast'
Mary's Harbour Canada 125 K2
Marystown Canada 125 K4
Marysville CA U.S.A. 136 B2
Marysville KS U.S.A. 132 B4
Marysville MI U.S.A. 130 B2
Marysville OH U.S.A. 130 B3
Marysville WA U.S.A. 134 B2
Maryvale Qld Australia 111 F3
Maryville TN U.S.A. 128 C5
Maryville MO U.S.A. 132 C3
Maryyskaya Oblast' admin. div. Turkm. 81 E2
Marzo, Cabo c. Col. 146 B3
Marzūq Libya 88 B2
Masada tourist site Israel 77 B4
Masai Mara National Reserve nature res. Kenya 96 C4
Masai Steppe plain Tanz. 97 C6
Masaka Uganda 96 B4
Masalanyane Pan salt pan Botswana 99 D4

Masalembu Besar i. Indon. 59 F4
Masalembu Kecil i. Indon. 59 F4
Masallı Azer. 79 G3
Masamba Indon. 57 F6
Masan S. Korea 65 B6
Masasi Tanz. 97 C7
Masbate Phil. 57 F3
Masbate i. Phil. 57 F3
Mascara Alg. 91 F2
Mascarene Basin sea feature Indian Ocean 162 K7
Mascarene Plain sea feature Indian Ocean 162 K7
Mascarene Ridge sea feature Indian Ocean 162 K6
Ma Sekatok b. Indon. 59 G2
Masela i. Indon. 108 E2
Maseno Kenya 96 B4

▶Maseru Lesotho 99 E6
Capital of Lesotho.

Masfjorden Norway 33 B3
Mashaba Zimbabwe see Mashava
Mashai Lesotho 99 F6
Mashala Dem. Rep. Congo 95 D6
Mashan China 66 D4
Mashava Zimbabwe 99 F4
Masherbrum mt. Jammu and Kashmir 74 C2
Mashhad Iran 81 D3
Mashi r. India 74 B3
Mashiko Japan 65 F5
Mashkel r. Pak. 81 E4
Māshkīd r. Iran 81 D5
Mashonaland Central prov. Zimbabwe 99 F3
Mashonaland East prov. Zimbabwe 99 F3
Mashonaland West prov. Zimbabwe 99 F3
Masi-Manimba Dem. Rep. Congo 95 C6
Masindi Uganda 96 A4
Masinyusane S. Africa 98 D6
Masira, Gulf of Oman see Maşīrah, Khalīj
Masīrah, Jazīrat i. Oman 76 F5
Masīrah, Khalīj b. Oman 76 F6
Masira Island Oman see Maşīrah, Jazīrat
Masis Armenia 79 F2
Masisea Peru 148 B2
Masisi Dem. Rep. Congo 95 D6
Masjed Soleymān Iran 80 B4
Massa Italy 44 C2
Massachusetts state U.S.A. 131 G2
Massachusetts Bay U.S.A. 131 H2
Massafra Italy 45 F4
Massaguet Chad 88 B6
Massakory Chad 88 B6
Massalassef Chad 94 C2
Massa Marittima Italy 44 C3
Massangena Moz. 99 G4
Massango Angola 95 A5
Massau Eritrea see Massawa
Massawa Eritrea 89 H6
Massawa Channel Eritrea 89 H5
Massena U.S.A. 128 G2
Massenya Chad 94 C2
Masset Canada 122 C4
Masset Inlet Canada 122 C4
Massiac France 39 E4
Massieville U.S.A. 130 B4
Massif Central mts France 39 E4
Massigui Mali 92 D3
Massillon U.S.A. 130 C3
Massina Mali 92 D2
Massinga Moz. 99 G4
Massingir Moz. 99 G4
Masson Island Antarctica 167 F2
Mastchoh Tajik. 81 G1
Masterton N.Z. 113 C3
Masticho, Akra pt Greece 47 E5
Mastuj Pak. 81 H2
Mastung Pak. 81 F4
Mastūrah Saudi Arabia 89 H4
Masty Belarus 29 C5
Masuda Japan 65 B6
Masuku Gabon see Franceville
Masuku Dem. Rep. Congo 95 D6
Masuleh Iran 80 B2
Masulipatam India see Machilipatnam
Masuna i. American Samoa see Tutuila
Masurai, Bukit mt. Indon. 58 C3
Masvingo Zimbabwe 99 F4
Masvingo prov. Zimbabwe 99 F4
Maswe Tanz. 97 B5
Maşyāf Syria 78 B2
Mat r. Albania 46 A4
Mataba Zambia 95 D8
Matabaan Somalia 96 E3
Matabeleland North prov. Zimbabwe 99 E3
Matabeleland South prov. Zimbabwe 99 F4
Matabhanga India 75 G4
Mata Bia, Gunung mt. East Timor 108 D2
Matadi Dem. Rep. Congo 95 B6
Matador U.S.A. 133 A5
Matagalpa Nicaragua 139 G6
Matagami Canada 124 E3
Matagami, Lac l. Canada 124 E3
Matagorda Island U.S.A. 133 B6
Matak i. Indon. 58 D2
Matak, Jabal hill Saudi Arabia 89 I3
Matam Senegal 92 B2
Matamey Niger 93 H2
Matamoros Coahuila Mex. 133 A7
Matamoros Tamaulipas Mex. 126 G4
Ma'ta Moûlana well Mauritania 92 B1
Matandu r. Tanz. 97 C7
Mata Negra Venez. 147 F2
Matanzas Cuba 127 I4
Matão, Serra do hills Brazil 150 D4
Matapan, Cape pt Greece see Tainaro, Akra
Mata Panew r. Poland 37 I3

Matapédia, Lac l. Canada 125 H3
Mataporquera Spain 42 D1
Maţār well Saudi Arabia 80 A5
Matara Sri Lanka 72 D5
Mataragka Greece 47 B5
Mataram Indon. 59 G5
Mataránga Greece see Mataragka
Mataranka Australia 110 C2
Mataró Spain 43 H2
Matarraña r. Spain 43 G2
Mataruška Banja Yugo. 46 B3
Matasiri i. Indon. 59 F4
Matassi well Sudan 89 F5
Matassi Tanz. 97 C6
Matatiele S. Africa 99 F6
Matatila Dam India 74 C4
Mataura N.Z. 113 B4
Mataura r. N.Z. 113 B4

▶Matā'utu Wallis and Futuna Is 107 H3
Capital of Wallis and Futuna.

Matawai N.Z. 113 C3
Matawin r. Canada 125 F4
Matbakh, Ra's al pt Qatar 80 B5
Matcha Tajik. see Mastchoh
Mategua Bol. 149 E3
Matehuala Mex. 126 F7
Mateke Hills Zimbabwe 99 F4
Matelica Italy 44 D3
Matemanga Tanz. 97 C7
Matende Angola 95 C9
Matera Italy 45 F4
Matese, Monti del mts Italy 44 E4
Matetsi Zimbabwe 99 E3
Mateur Tunisia 45 B6
Matha France 38 C4
Mathews U.S.A. 131 E5
Mathias U.S.A. 130 D4
Mathura India 74 C4
Mati Phil. 57 G4
Matiacoali Burkina 93 F2
Matianxu China 67 G3
Matias Cardoso Brazil 150 D5
Matías Romero Mex. 138 E5
Matibane Moz. 99 I2
Matimekosh Canada 125 H2
Matinicus Island U.S.A. 131 I2
Matla r. India 75 F5
Matli Pak. 81 G5
Matlock U.K. 35 F5
Mato r. Venez. 147 E3
Mato, Cerro mt. Venez. 147 E3
Matobo National Park Zimbabwe 99 E4
Matogrossense, Pantanal marsh Brazil 149 G4
Mato Grosso Brazil 149 F3
Mato Grosso state Brazil 149 G3
Mato Grosso, Planalto do plat. Brazil 150 A3
Mato Grosso do Sul state Brazil 149 G5
Matola Moz. 99 G5
Matondo Moz. 99 G3
Matope Malawi 97 B8
Matos r. Bol. 148 D2
Matosinhos Port. 42 B2
Matou China see Pingguo
Mátra mts Hungary 37 I5
Matrah Oman 76 F5
Matrei in Osttirol Austria 37 F5
Matrosberg mt. S. Africa 98 C7
Maţrūḥ governorate Egypt 78 A5
Matsitama Botswana 99 E5
Matsue Japan 65 C5
Matsumoto Japan 65 D5
Matsusaka Japan 65 D6
Matsu Tao i. Taiwan 67 G3
Matsuyama Japan 65 C6
Mattagami r. Canada 124 D3
Mattamuskeet, Lake U.S.A. 128 D5
Mattawa Canada 124 E3
Mattawa U.S.A. 134 C2
Matterhorn mt. Italy/Switz. 44 A2
Matterhorn mt. U.S.A. 134 D4
Matthews U.S.A. 128 C5
Matthews Ridge Guyana 147 F2
Matthew Town Bahamas 127 L7
Mattituck U.S.A. 131 G3
Mattmar Sweden 32 D3
Mattoon U.S.A. 128 A4
Mättsund Sweden 32 F2
Matturai Sri Lanka see Matara
Matu Sarawak Malaysia 59 E2
Matucana Peru 148 A2
Matugama Sri Lanka 72 D5
Matuku i. Fiji 107 G4
Matumbo Angola 95 B8
Matun Afgh. see Khowst
Maturín Venez. 147 F2
Matusadona National Park Zimbabwe 99 F3
Matveyev, Ostrov i. Rus. Fed. 28 K1
Matveyevka Rus. Fed. 29 J5
Matwabeng S. Africa 99 E5
Matxitxako, Cabo c. Spain 43 E1
Maty Island P.N.G. see Wuvulu Island
Mau Uttar Pradesh India 75 D4
Mau Uttar Pradesh India 75 D4
Ma'ūbas well Mauritania 92 B1
Maubermé, Pic de mt. France/Spain 43 G1
Maubeuge France 39 E1
Maubin Myanmar 60 A4
Ma-ubin Myanmar 60 B2
Maubourguet France 38 D5
Maudaha India 74 D4
Maude Australia 112 C4
Maud Seamount sea feature S. Atlantic Ocean 161 O10
Mau-é-ele Moz. see Marão
Maués Brazil 147 G5
Maués r. Brazil 147 G5
Mauganj India 74 D4
Maug Islands N. Mariana Is 57 K1
Mauguio France 39 F5
Maui i. U.S.A. 135 [inset] Z2
Maukkadaw Myanmar 60 A3
Maule admin. reg. Chile 152 B5
Maule r. Chile 152 B3
Mauléon France 38 C3
Mauléon-Licharre France 38 C5
Maumee U.S.A. 130 B3
Maumee r. U.S.A. 130 B3
Maumee Bay U.S.A. 130 B3
Maumere Indon. 57 F5
Maun Botswana 95 D9
Mauna Kea vol. U.S.A. 135 [inset] Z2
Mauna Loa vol. U.S.A. 135 [inset] Z2
Maungaturoto N.Z. 113 C2
Maungdaw Myanmar 73 G1
Maungmagan Islands Myanmar 61 B5
Maungmagon Myanmar 61 B5
Maupin U.S.A. 134 B3
Mau Rampur India 74 C4
Maurawan India 74 D4
Maurepas, Lake U.S.A. 133 D6
Maures, Massif des hills France 39 F5
Mauriac France 38 E4
Maurice, Lake salt flat Australia 110 B6

▶Mauritania country Africa 90 C5
africa 86–87, 100

▶Mauritius country Indian Ocean 162 K7
africa 86–87, 100

Mauro, Monte mt. Italy 44 E4
Mauron France 38 B2
Mauros mt. Spain 42 C2
Maurs France 38 E4
Mauston U.S.A. 132 D3
Mauvezin France 38 D5
Mauzé-sur-le-Mignon France 38 C3
Mava Dem. Rep. Congo 94 E4
Mavaca r. Venez. 147 E4
Mavago Moz. 97 C8
Mavasjaure l. Sweden 32 E2
Mavengue Angola 95 C9
Mavinga Angola 95 D8
Mavrothalassa Greece 46 C4
Mavrovo nat. park Macedonia 46 B4
Mavume Moz. 99 G4
Mawa, Bukit mt. Indon. 59 F2
Ma Wan i. Hong Kong China 67 [inset]
Mawana India 74 C3
Mawanga Dem. Rep. Congo 95 C6
Mawdaung Pass Myanmar/Thai. 61 B6
Mawei China 67 F3
Māwheranui r. N.Z. see Grey
Mawjib, Wādī al r. Jordan 77 B4
Mawkhi Myanmar 61 B4
Mawkmai Myanmar 60 B3
Mawlaik Myanmar 60 A3
Mawlamyaing Myanmar see Moulmein
Mawlamyine Myanmar see Moulmein
Mawphlang India 75 F4
Mawson research station Antarctica 167 E2
Mawson Coast Antarctica 167 E2
Mawson Escarpment Antarctica 167 E2
Mawson Peninsula Antarctica 167 H2
Maw Taung mt. Myanmar 61 B6
Mawza Yemen 96 D1
Maxaas Somalia 96 E3
Maxán Arg. 152 D2
Maxhamish Lake Canada 122 F3
Maxia, Punta mt. Sardinia Italy 45 B5
Maxixe Moz. 99 G4
Maxwelton Australia 111 E4
Maya Chad 94 C3
Maya i. Indon. 59 E3
Maya r. Rus. Fed. 27 N3
Mayaguana i. Bahamas 127 L7
Mayagüez Puerto Rico 139 K5
Mayak Rus. Fed. 29 J6
Mayakovskogo mt. Tajik. 81 G2
Mayakovskogo, Pik mt. Tajik. see Mayakovskogo
Mayala Dem. Rep. Congo 95 C6
Mayama Congo 95 E5
Mayamba Dem. Rep. Congo 95 C6
Mayamey Iran 80 C2
Maya Mountains Belize/Guat. 138 G5
Mayan China see Mayanhe
Mayang China 67 D3
Mayanhe China 66 C1
Maybeury U.S.A. 130 C5
Maybole U.K. 34 D4
Maych'ew Eth. 96 C1
Maydā Shahr Afgh. 81 G3
Maydh Somalia 96 E2
Maydos Turkey see Eceabat
Mayen Germany 36 C3
Mayenne France 38 C2
Mayenne r. France 38 C3
Mayêr Kangri mt. China 75 E2
Mayerthorpe Canada 123 H4
Mayet France 38 D3
Mayfield N.Z. 113 B3
Mayi r. China 64 B3
Maykhura Tajik. 81 G2
Maykop Rus. Fed. 29 G7
Maymyo Myanmar 60 B3
Mayna Respublika Khakasiya Rus. Fed. 69 H1
Mayna Ul'yanovskaya Oblast' Rus. Fed. 29 H5
Mayna r. Rus. Fed. 62 C1
Mayne watercourse Australia 111 E4
Mayni India 72 B2
Mayo Canada 122 C2
Mayo r. Mex. 135 E8
Mayo r. Peru 146 B6
Mayo Alim Cameroon 93 I3
Mayo-Belwa Nigeria 93 I3
Mayo Darlé Cameroon 93 H4
Mayo-Kébbi pref. Chad 94 B2
Mayoko Congo 94 B5
Mayo Lake Canada 122 C2
Mayo Landing Canada see Mayo
Mayo Lara Cent. Afr. Rep. 94 B3
Mayon vol. Phil. 57 F3
Mayor, Puig mt. Spain see Major, Puig
Mayor Buratovich Arg. 152 E4
Mayor Island N.Z. 113 D2
Mayor Pablo Lagerenza Para. 149 E4
▶Mayotte terr. Africa 97 E8
French Territorial Collectivity.
africa 86–87, 100
Mayraira Point Phil. 67 G5
Maysān governorate Iraq 79 F5
Mayskiy Amurskaya Oblast' Rus. Fed. 64 B1
Mayskiy Kabardino-Balkarskaya Respublika Rus. Fed. 29 H8
Mays Landing U.S.A. 131 F4
Mayson Lake Canada 123 J3
Maysville U.S.A. 130 B4
Mayu r. Myanmar 73 G1
Mayumba Gabon 94 A5
Mayum La pass China 75 D3
Mayuram India 72 C4
Mayville MI U.S.A. 130 B2
Mayville ND U.S.A. 132 B2
Maywood U.S.A. 132 A3
Maya Rus. Fed. 27 N3
Maza Arg. 152 E4
Mazabuka Zambia 95 E8
Mazaca Turkey see Kayseri
Mazagan Morocco see El Jadida
Mazagão Brazil 147 I5
Mazamet France 38 E5
Mazán Peru 146 C5
Māzandarān prov. Iran 80 B2
Mazao Dem. Rep. Congo 95 D7
Mazar China 70 E4
Mazar, Koh-i- mt. Afgh. 81 F3
Mazara, Val di valley Sicily Italy 45 D6
Mazara del Vallo Sicily Italy 45 D6
Mazār-e Sharīf Afgh. 81 F2
Mazarrón Spain 43 F4
Mazaruni r. Guyana 147 G3
Mazatán Mex. 135 E7
Mazatlán Mex. 126 E7
Mazatzal Peak U.S.A. 137 G4
Mazāvī watercourse Iran 80 D5
Mažeikiai Lith. 33 F4
Mazelet well Niger 93 H1
Mazı Turkey 47 E6
Mazie U.S.A. 130 B4
Mazirbe Latvia 33 F4
Mazocahui Mex. 135 E7
Mazomeno Dem. Rep. Congo 95 E6
Mazomora Tanz. 97 C6
Mazowe r. Zimbabwe 99 G3
Mazrub well Sudan 89 F6
Mazsalaca Latvia 33 G4
Māzū Iran 80 B3
Mazunga Zimbabwe 99 F4
Mazyr Belarus 29 D5
Mazzouna Tunisia 91 H2
Mba Cameroon 93 H4
▶Mbabane Swaziland 99 F5
Capital of Swaziland.
Mbacké Senegal 92 B2
Mbaéré r. Cent. Afr. Rep. 94 C4
Mbagne Mauritania 92 B1
Mbahiakro Côte d'Ivoire 92 D4
Mbaïki Cent. Afr. Rep. 94 C4
Mbakaou Cameroon 93 I4
Mbakaou, Lac de l. Cameroon 93 I4
Mbala Zambia 97 A7
Mbalabala Zimbabwe 99 F4
Mbalam Cameroon 93 I5
Mbale Uganda 96 B4
Mbalmayo Cameroon 93 H5
Mbam r. Cameroon 93 H4
Mbamba Bay Tanz. 97 B7
Mbandaka Dem. Rep. Congo 94 C5
Mbandjok Cameroon 93 H4
Mbang Cameroon 93 I5
M'banza Congo Angola 95 B6
Mbanza-Ngungu Dem. Rep. Congo 95 B6
Mbarangandu Tanz. 97 C7
Mbarara Uganda 96 A5
Mbari r. Cent. Afr. Rep. 94 D3
Mbarika Mountains Tanz. 97 C7
Mbata Cent. Afr. Rep. 94 C4
Mbati Zambia 97 A7
Mbé Cameroon 93 I4
Mbé Congo 94 B5
Mbemba Moz. 97 B8
Mbembesi Zimbabwe 99 F3
Mbemkuru r. Tanz. 97 C7
Mbéni Comoros 97 D7
Mbengué Côte d'Ivoire 92 D3
Mberengwa Zimbabwe 99 F4
Mbereshi Zambia 95 F7
Mbeya Tanz. 97 B7
Mbeya admin. reg. Tanz. 97 B7
Mbi r. Cameroon 93 I4
Mbi r. Cent. Afr. Rep. 94 C3
Mbigou Gabon 94 A5
Mbinda Congo 94 B5
Mbinga Tanz. 97 B7
Mbini Equat. Guinea 93 H5
Mbini r. Equat. Guinea 93 H5
Mbizi Zimbabwe 99 F4
Mbizi Mountains Tanz. 97 A7
Mbo Cent. Afr. Rep. 94 C2
Mboki Cent. Afr. Rep. 94 E3
Mbomo Congo 94 B4
Mbomou pref. Cent. Afr. Rep. 94 D3
Mbomou r. Cent. Afr. Rep./Dem. Rep. Congo 94 D3
Mbon Congo 94 B5
Mbour Senegal 92 A2
Mbout Mauritania 92 B1
Mbowela Zambia 95 E8
Mbozi Tanz. 97 B7
Mbrès Cent. Afr. Rep. 94 C3
Mbrostar Albania 46 A4
Mbuji-Mayi Dem. Rep. Congo 95 D6
Mbulu Tanz. 97 B5
Mburucuyá Arg. 152 F2
Mbuyuni Tanz. 97 C6
Mbwewe Tanz. 97 C6
McAdam Canada 125 H4
McAlester U.S.A. 133 C5
McAllen U.S.A. 133 B7
McArthur r. Australia 110 D2
McArthur U.S.A. 130 B4
McBride Canada 122 F4
McCall U.S.A. 134 C3
McCamey U.S.A. 133 A6
McCammon U.S.A. 134 D4
McCarthy U.S.A. 122 A2
McCauley Island Canada 122 D4
McClintock, Mount Antarctica 167 H1
McClintock Channel Canada 121 I2
McClintock Range hills Australia 108 D4
McClure, Lake U.S.A. 136 B3
McClure Strait Canada 121 H2
McClusky U.S.A. 132 A2
McComb U.S.A. 127 H5
McConaughy, Lake U.S.A. 132 A3
McConnellsburg U.S.A. 130 E4
McConnelsville U.S.A. 130 C4
McCook U.S.A. 132 A3
McCormick U.S.A. 129 C5
McCrea r. Canada 123 H2
McCreary Canada 123 L5
McCullum, Mount Canada 122 B1
McDame Canada 122 D3
McDonald Islands Indian Ocean 163 L9
McDonald Peak U.S.A. 134 D3
McDouall Range hills Australia 110 C3
McDowell Peak U.S.A. 137 G5
McFarland U.S.A. 136 C4
McFarlane r. Canada 123 J3
McGill U.S.A. 137 E2
McGivney Canada 125 H4
McGrath AK U.S.A. 120 D3
McGrath MN U.S.A. 132 C2
McGregor r. Canada 122 F4
McGregor, Lake Canada 123 H5
McGregor Range hills Australia 111 E5
McGuire, Mount U.S.A. 134 D3
Mcherrah reg. Alg. 90 D4
Mchinga Tanz. 97 C7
Mchinji Malawi 97 B8
McIlwraith Range hills Australia 111 E2
McInnes Lake Canada 123 M4
McIntosh U.S.A. 132 A2
McKay Range hills Australia 108 C5
McKean i. Kiribati 107 H2
McKee U.S.A. 130 A5
McKeesport U.S.A. 130 D3
McKenney U.S.A. 130 E5
McKenzie U.S.A. 128 A4
McKenzie r. U.S.A. 134 B3
McKinlay Australia 111 E4
McKinlay r. Australia 111 E4
▶McKinley, Mount U.S.A. 120 D3
Highest mountain in North America.
northamerica 116–117
McKinney U.S.A. 133 B5
McKittrick U.S.A. 136 C4
McLennan Canada 123 G4
McLeod r. Canada 123 H4
McLeod Bay Canada 123 I2
McLeod Lake Canada 122 F4
McLeods Island Myanmar 61 B6
McMinnville OR U.S.A. 134 B3
McMinnville TN U.S.A. 128 B5
McMurdo research station Antarctica 167 H1
McMurdo Sound b. Antarctica 167 H1
McNary U.S.A. 137 H4
McNaughton Lake Canada see Kinbasket Lake
McPherson U.S.A. 132 B4
McQuesten r. Canada 122 B2
McRae U.S.A. 129 C5
McTavish Arm b. Canada 123 G1
McVeytown U.S.A. 130 E3
McVicar Arm b. Canada 122 F1
McWhorter U.S.A. 130 C4
Mdantsane S. Africa 99 E7
M'Daourouch Alg. 91 G1
Mead, Lake resr U.S.A. 137 E3
Meade U.S.A. 132 A4
Meade r. U.S.A. 120 D2
Meadow Australia 109 A6
Meadow U.S.A. 137 F2
Meadowbank r. Canada 123 L1
Meadow Bridge U.S.A. 130 C5
Meadow Lake Canada 123 I4
Meadow Valley Wash r. U.S.A. 137 E3
Meadowview U.S.A. 130 C5
Meadville MS U.S.A. 133 D6
Meadville PA U.S.A. 130 C3
Meaford Canada 130 C1
Meaken-dake vol. Japan 64 F4
Mealhada Port. 42 B2
Mealy Mountains Canada 125 J2
Meandarra Australia 111 G5
Meander River Canada 123 G3
Mearim r. Brazil 150 C2
Meaux France 39 E2
Mebridege r. Angola 95 B6
Mebu India 75 G3
Mebulu, Tanjung pt Indon. 59 F5
Mecanhelas Moz. 99 G2
▶Mecca Saudi Arabia 89 H4
asia 52–53
Mecca U.S.A. 135 C6
Mechanicsburg U.S.A. 130 B3
Mechanicsville IA U.S.A. 124 B5
Mechanicsville VA U.S.A. 130 E5
Mechanicville U.S.A. 131 G2
Mechelen Belgium 39 F1
Mecheria Alg. 91 E2
Mechernich Germany 36 C3
Mechimeré Chad 88 B6
Mechka r. Bulg. 46 D3
Meciliye Turkey 46 E4
Mecitözü Turkey 78 C2
Meckenheim Germany 36 C3
Mecklenburger Bucht b. Germany 36 E1
Mecklenburg-Vorpommern land Germany 37 F2
Mecklenburg - West Pomerania land Germany see Mecklenburg-Vorpommern
Mecúburi Moz. 97 C8
Mecúburi r. Moz. 97 D8
Mecúfi Moz. 97 D8
Mecula Moz. 97 C8
Meda r. Australia 108 C4
Meda Port. 42 C2
Meda mt. Spain 42 C1
Medak India 72 C2
Medan Indon. 58 B2
Medang i. Indon. 59 G5
Médanos Buenos Aires Arg. 152 E4
Médanos Entre Ríos Arg. 152 F3
Medanosa, Punta pt Arg. 153 D7
Médanos de Coro, Parque Nacional nat. park Venez. 146 D2
Medchal India 72 C2
Médéa Alg. 91 F1
Medellín Col. 146 C3
Medenine Tunisia 91 H2
Mederdra Mauritania 92 B1
Medford NY U.S.A. 131 G3
Medford OK U.S.A. 133 B4
Medford OR U.S.A. 134 B4
Medford WI U.S.A. 132 D2
Medgidia Romania 46 F2
Mediadilet well Mali 93 E1
Media Luna Arg. 152 D3
Mediaș Romania 46 D1
Medicine Bow r. U.S.A. 134 F4
Medicine Bow Mountains U.S.A. 134 F4
Medicine Bow Peak U.S.A. 134 F4
Medicine Hat Canada 134 E2
Medicine Lodge U.S.A. 132 B4
Medina Brazil 151 D6
Medina Col. 146 C3
Medina Saudi Arabia 89 H3
Medina NY U.S.A. 130 D2
Medina OH U.S.A. 130 C3
Medina r. U.S.A. 133 B6
Medinaceli Spain 43 E2
Medina del Campo Spain 42 D2
Medina de Pomar Spain 42 E1
Medina de Rioseco Spain 42 D2
Médina Gounas Senegal 92 B2
Medina-Sidonia Spain 42 D4
Medinipur India 75 E5
Mediolanum Italy see Milan
Mediterranean Sea 41 I5
Medje Dem. Rep. Congo 94 E4
Mednogorsk Rus. Fed. 68 D1
Mednyy, Ostrov i. Rus. Fed. 164 F2
Médoc reg. France 38 C4
Mêdog China 75 G3
Medora U.S.A. 132 A2
Médouneu Gabon 94 A4
Medstead Canada 123 I4
Medu Kongkar China see Maizhokunggar
Medveda Yugo. 46 B3
Medvedevo Rus. Fed. 28 H4
Medveditsa r. Rus. Fed. 29 G6
Medvednica mts Croatia 44 E2
Medvezh'i, Ostrova is Rus. Fed. 27 Q2
Medvezh'yegorsk Rus. Fed. 28 E3
Medzilaborce Slovakia 37 J4
Meeberrie Australia 109 A6
Meekatharra Australia 109 B6
Meeker U.S.A. 134 F4
Meeladeen Somalia 96 F2
Meelpaeg Reservoir Canada 125 J3
Meerane Germany 37 F3
Meerapalu Estonia 33 G4
Meerut India 74 C3
Mēga Eth. 96 C3
Mega i. Indon. 58 C3
Mega Escarpment Eth./Kenya 96 C3
Megalo Chorio Greece 47 E6
Megalopoli Greece 47 C6
Megalos Anthropofas i. Greece 47 E6
Meganisi i. Greece 47 B5
Mégantic, Lac l. Canada 125 G4
Megara Greece 47 C5
Megezez mt. Eth. 96 C2
▶Meghalaya state India 75 F4
Highest mean annual rainfall in the world.
world 12–13
Meghasani mt. India 75 E5
Meghna r. Bangl. 75 F5
Meghri Armenia 79 F3
Megion Rus. Fed. 26 H3
Megisti i. Greece 78 B3
Megri Armenia see Meghri
Mehadica Romania 46 C2
Mehamn Norway 32 G1
Mehar Pak. 81 F5
Meharry, Mount Australia 108 B5
Mehdia Tunisia see Mahdia
Mehedeby Sweden 33 E3
Mehekar India 72 C1
Meherpur Bangl. 75 F5
Meherrin U.S.A. 130 D5
Meherrin r. U.S.A. 130 E5
Mehidpur India 74 B5
Mehlville U.S.A. 132 D4
Mehmadabad India 74 B5
Mehndawal India 75 D4
Mehrābān Iran 80 A2
Mehrān Iran 80 C5
Mehrān watercourse Iran 80 C5
Mehrān Iraq 79 F4
Mehtar Lām Afgh. 81 G3
Mehun-sur-Yèvre France 38 E3
Meia Ponte r. Brazil 149 H4
Meicheng Anhui China see Qianshan
Meicheng Fujian China see Minqing
Meicheng Zhejiang China see Jiande
Meichengzhen China 67 D2
Meiganga Cameroon 93 I4
Meighen Island Canada 121 J2
Meigu China 66 B2
Meihekou China 64 A4
Meijiang China see Ningdu
Mei Jiang r. China 67 E3
Meikeng China 67 E3
Meiktila Myanmar 60 A3
Meilen Switz. 39 H3
Meilin China see Ganxian
Meilleur r. Canada 122 E2
Meilü China see Wuchuan
Meiningen Germany 36 E3
Meira Spain 42 C1
Meiringen Switz. 39 H3
Meishan Anhui China see Jinzhai
Meishan Sichuan China 66 B2
Meißen Germany 37 F3
Meister r. Canada 122 D2
Meitan China 66 C3
Meitingen Germany 36 E4
Meixi China 64 B3
Meixian Guangdong China see Meizhou
Meixian Shaanxi China 66 C1
Meixing China see Xiaojin
Meizhou China 67 F3
Mej r. India 74 C4
Méjan, Sommet de mt. France 39 F4
Mejaouda well Mauritania 90 D5
Mejez el Bab Tunisia 45 B6
Mejicana mt. Arg. 152 D2
Mejillones Chile 148 C5
Mejillones del Sur, Bahía de b. Chile 148 C5
Mekadio well Sudan 89 G5
Mékambo Gabon 94 B4
Mek'elē Eth. 89 H6
Mékhé Senegal 92 A2
Mekhtar Pak. 81 G4
Mekkaw Nigeria 93 F4
Meknès Morocco 90 D2
Mekong r. Xizang China 70 I6
Mekong r. Xizang/Yunnan China 70 J7
Mekong r. Laos/Thai. 60 D5
also known as Mènam Khong (Laos/Thailand)
Mekong, Mouths of the Vietnam 61 D6
Méla, Mont hill Cent. Afr. Rep. 94 D2
Melaka Malaysia 58 C2
Melaka state Malaysia 58 C2
Melalo, Tanjung pt Indon. 58 D3
Melanesia is Oceania 164 E6
Melanesian Basin sea feature Pacific Ocean 164 E5
Melawi r. Indon. 59 E2
▶Melbourne Australia 112 C5
State capital of Victoria. 2nd most populous city in Oceania.
oceania 104–105
world 16–17
Melbourne U.S.A. 129 C6
Melbu Norway 32 D1
Melchor, Isla i. Chile 153 B6
Meldal Norway 32 C3
Meldorf Germany 36 D1
Meldrum U.S.A. 130 B5
Meldrum Bay Canada 124 D4
Mele, Capo c. Italy 44 B3
Melekess Rus. Fed. see Dimitrovgrad
Melenci Yugo. 46 B2
Melendiz Dağı mt. Turkey 78 C3
Melenki Rus. Fed. 28 G5
Melet Turkey see Mesudiye
Meleuz Rus. Fed. 29 J5
Mélèzes, Rivière aux r. Canada 125 G1
Melfa U.S.A. 131 F5
Mélfi Chad 94 C2
Melfi Italy 44 E4
Melfort Canada 123 J4
Melgaço Brazil 150 B2
Melgar de Fernamental Spain 42 D1
Melhus Norway 32 C3
Meliau, Gunung mt. Sabah Malaysia 59 G1
Melide Spain 42 C1
Meligalas Greece 47 B6
▶Melilla N. Africa 90 E2
Spanish Territory.
africa 100
Melilli Sicily Italy 45 E6
Melimoyu, Monte mt. Chile 153 B6
Melintang, Danau l. Indon. 59 G3
Melipilla Chile 152 C3
Melita Canada 123 K5
Melitene Turkey see Malatya
Melito di Porto Salvo Italy 45 E6
Melitopol' Ukr. 29 E7
Melk Austria 37 G4
Melka Guba Eth. 96 C3
Mellakoski Fin. 32 G2
Mellansjö Sweden 33 D3
Mellanström Sweden 32 E2
Melle Germany 36 D2
Mellègue, Barrage dam Tunisia 45 B6
Mellerud Sweden 33 D4
Mellid Spain see Melide
Mellit Sudan 89 E6
Mellizo Sur, Cerro mt. Chile 153 B7
Mellor Glacier Antarctica 167 E2
Mellrichstadt Germany 36 E3
Melmele watercourse Chad 88 C6
Melmoth S. Africa 99 F6
Mel'nichoye Rus. Fed. 64 C3
Mělník Czech Rep. 37 G3
Mel'nikovo Rus. Fed. 33 H3
Melo Uruguay 152 G3
Melolo Indon. 108 C2
Melozitna r. U.S.A. 120 D3
Melrhir, Chott salt l. Alg. 91 G2
Melrose Australia 109 C6
Melrose U.S.A. 132 C2
Melsetter Zimbabwe see Chimanimani
Melsungen Germany 36 D3
Melta, Mount Sabah Malaysia see Meliau, Gunung
Meltaus Fin. 32 G2
Melton Australia 112 C5
Melton Mowbray U.K. 35 F5
Meluan Sarawak Malaysia 59 E2
Melun France 39 E2
Melur India 72 C4
Melut Sudan 96 B2
Melville Canada 134 G2
Melville, Cape Australia 111 F2
Melville, Lake Canada 125 J2
Melville Bugt b. Greenland see Qimusseriarsuaq
Melville Island Australia 110 B1
Melville Island Canada 121 I2
Melville Peninsula Canada 121 K3
Melvin, Lough l. Rep. of Ireland/U.K. 35 B4
Mélykút Hungary 46 A1
Memaliaj Albania 47 A4
Mêmar Co salt l. China 75 D2
Memba Moz. 97 D8
Memba, Baía de b. Moz. 97 D8
Memberamo r. Indon. 57 I6
Memboro Indon. 57 E7
Memel Lith. see Klaipėda
Memel S. Africa 99 F5
Memmingen Germany 36 E5
Mempakul Sabah Malaysia 59 F1
Mempawah Indon. 55 C6
Memphis tourist site Egypt 89 F2
Memphis MI U.S.A. 130 B2
Memphis TN U.S.A. 127 H4
Memphis TX U.S.A. 133 A5
Mena Eth. 96 C3
Mena Indon. 108 D2
Mena Ukr. 29 E6
Mena U.S.A. 133 C5
Menabe mts Madag. 99 [inset] J4
Ménaka Mali 93 F2
Mènam Khong r. Laos/Thai. 61 D5 see Mekong
Menarandra r. Madag. 99 [inset] J5
Menard U.S.A. 133 B6
Mencal mt. Spain 42 E4
Mencué Arg. 152 C5
Mendanau i. Indon. 59 D3
Mendarda India 74 A5
Mendarik i. Indon. 59 D2
Mendawai Indon. 59 F3
Mendawai r. Indon. 59 F3
Mende France 39 E4
Mendebo Mountains Eth. 96 C3
Mendefera Eritrea 89 H6
Mendeleyev Ridge sea feature Arctic Ocean 166 B1
Mendeleyevsk Rus. Fed. 28 J5
Menden (Sauerland) Germany 36 C3
Mendenhall U.S.A. 133 D6
Mendenhall, Cape U.S.A. 120 C4
Mendenhall Glacier U.S.A. 122 C3
Méndez Mex. 126 G6
Mendī Eth. 68 B6
Mendi P.N.G. 57 J7
Mendip Hills U.K. 35 E6
Mendocino U.S.A. 136 A2
Mendocino, Cape U.S.A. 134 A4
Mendocino, Lake U.S.A. 136 A2
Mendota CA U.S.A. 136 B3
Mendota IL U.S.A. 132 D3
Mendoza Arg. 152 C3
Mendoza prov. Arg. 152 C3
Mene de Mauroa Venez. 146 D2
Menemen Turkey 47 E5
Menez Bré hill France 38 B2
Menfi Sicily Italy 45 D6
Menga, Puerto de pass Spain 42 D2
Mengalum i. Malaysia 59 F1
Mengcheng China 67 F1
Menggala Indon. 58 D4
Menghai China 66 B4
Mengíbar Spain 42 E4
Mengkiang r. Indon. 59 E2
Menglang China see Lancang
Menglie China see Jiangcheng
Mengmeng China see Shuangjiang
Mengong Cameroon 93 H5
Mengshan China 67 D3
Mengxian China see Mengzhou
Mengyang China see Mingshan
Mengzhou China 67 E1
Mengzi China 66 B4
Menihek Canada 125 H2
Menindee Australia 112 B4
Menindee Lake Australia 112 B4
Meningie Australia 112 A4
Menkere Rus. Fed. 27 M3
Mennecy France 39 E2
Menominee r. U.S.A. 132 E2
Menongue Angola 95 C8
Menor, Mar lag. Spain 43 F4
Menorca i. Spain see Minorca
Mensalong Indon. 59 G2
Mentakab Malaysia see Mentekab
Mentarang r. Indon. 59 G2
Mentasta Lake U.S.A. 122 A2
Mentasta Mountains U.S.A. 122 A2
Mentawai, Kepulauan is Indon. 58 B3
Mentawai, Selat sea chan. Indon. 58 C3
Mentaya r. Indon. 59 F3
Mentekab Malaysia 58 C2
Mentiras hill Port. 42 C3
Mentiras mt. Spain 43 E3
Mentok Indon. 58 D3
Menton France 39 G5
Mentone U.S.A. 133 A6
Mentuba r. Indon. 59 F3
Menufia governorate Egypt see Minūfīyah
Menukung Indon. 59 F3
Menyapa, Gunung mt. Indon. 59 G2
Menzel Bourguiba Tunisia 91 H1
Menzelet Barajı resr Turkey 78 D3
Menzelinsk Rus. Fed. 28 J5
Menzel Temime Tunisia 45 C6
Menzies Australia 109 C7
Menzies, Mount Antarctica 167 E2
Meoqui Mex. 135 F7
Mepala Angola 95 B6
Meponda Moz. 97 B8
Meppel Neth. 36 C2
Meppen Germany 36 D5
Meqheleng S. Africa 99 E6
Mequéns r. Brazil 149 E3
Mequinenza, Embalse de resr Spain 43 G2
Mer France 38 D3
Merah Indon. 59 G2
Merak Indon. 58 D4
Meråker Norway 32 C3
Meramec r. U.S.A. 132 D4
Merano Italy 44 C1
Merapi, Gunung vol. Jawa Tengah Indon. 59 E4
Merapi, Gunung vol. Jawa Timur Indon. 59 F5
Merari, Serra mt. Brazil 147 F3
Meratswe r. Botswana 98 E4
Meratus, Pegunungan mts Indon. 59 F3
Merauke Indon. 57 J7
Merawwah i. U.A.E. 80 C5
Merbein Australia 112 B4
Merca Somalia see Marka
Mercadal Spain 43 I3
Mercantour, Parc National du nat. park France 39 G4
Merced U.S.A. 136 B3
Merced r. U.S.A. 136 B3
Mercedario, Cerro mt. Arg. 152 C2
Mercedes Corrientes Arg. 152 F2
Mercedes San Luis Arg. 152 D3
Mercedes Uruguay 152 F3
Mercer ME U.S.A. 131 I1
Mercer OH U.S.A. 130 A3
Mercer PA U.S.A. 130 C3
Mercer WI U.S.A. 132 D2
Mercersburg U.S.A. 130 E4
Mercês Brazil 148 C2
Mercier Bol. 148 C2
Mercury U.S.A. 137 E3
Mercury Islands N.Z. 113 C2
Mercy, Cape Canada 166 K2
Merdenik Turkey see Göle
Meredith U.S.A. 131 H2
Meredith, Cape Falkland Is 153 E8
Meredith, Lake U.S.A. 133 A5
Meredoua Alg. 91 F4
Mereeg Somalia 96 E4
Merefa Ukr. 29 F6
Meremäe Estonia 33 G4
Merga Oasis Sudan 89 E5
Mergui Myanmar 61 B5
Mergui Archipelago is Myanmar 61 B6
Meriç r. Greece/Turkey 46 E4
Meriç r. Greece/Turkey see Evros
Merichas Greece 47 D6
Mérida Mex. 127 I7
Mérida Spain 42 C3
Mérida Venez. 146 D2
Mérida state Venez. 146 D2
Mérida, Cordillera de mts Venez. 146 D3
Meriden U.S.A. 131 G3
Meridian MS U.S.A. 129 A5
Meridian TX U.S.A. 133 B6
Mérignac France 38 C4
Merijärvi Fin. 32 G2
Merikarvia Fin. 33 F3
Merín, Laguna l. Brazil/Uruguay see Mirim, Lagoa
Merinda Australia 111 G4
Meringur Australia 112 B4
Merir i. Palau 57 H5
Merirumã Brazil 147 H4
Merkel U.S.A. 133 A5
Merkinė Lith. 33 G5
Merlimau, Pulau reg. Sing. 58 [inset]
Mermaid Reef Australia 108 B4
Merolia Australia 109 C7
Meron, Har mt. Israel 77 B3
Merošina Yugo. 46 B3
Merowe Sudan 89 F5
Merredin Australia 109 B7
Merrick hill U.K. 34 D4
Merrill MI U.S.A. 130 A2
Merrill WI U.S.A. 132 D2
Merrill, Mount Canada 122 E2
Merriman U.S.A. 132 A3
Merritt Canada 134 B2
Merritt Island U.S.A. 129 C6
Merrygoen Australia 112 D3
Mersa Fatma Eritrea 89 I6
Mersa Gulbub Eritrea 89 H5
Mersa Teklay Eritrea 89 H5
Merse r. Italy 44 C3
Merseburg (Saale) Germany 36 E3
Mersin Turkey see İçel
Mersing Malaysia 58 C2
Mersin Galgalo Eth. 96 E3
Mērsrags Latvia 33 F4
Merta India 74 B4
Merta Road India 74 B4
Merthyr Tydfil U.K. 35 E6
Merti Kenya 96 C4
Merti Plateau Kenya 96 C4
Mértola Port. 42 C4
Mertoutek Alg. 91 G4
Mertz Glacier Antarctica 167 G2
Mertz Glacier Tongue Antarctica 167 G2
Mertzon U.S.A. 133 A6
Méru France 38 E2
Meru Kenya 96 C4
▶Meru vol. Tanz. 96 C5
4th highest mountain in Africa.
africa 84–85
Meru Betiri National Park Indon. 59 F5
Merui Pak. 81 E4
Meru National Park Kenya 96 C4
Merv Turkm. see Mary
Merweville S. Africa 98 D7
Merzifon Turkey 78 C2
Merzig Germany 36 C4
Merz Peninsula Antarctica 167 L2
Mesa r. Spain 43 F2
Mesa U.S.A. 137 G5
Mesabi Range hills U.S.A. 132 C2
Mesagne Italy 45 F4
Mesara, Ormos b. Greece 47 D7
Mesa Verde National Park U.S.A. 135 E5
Meschede Germany 36 D3
Meselefors Sweden 32 E2
Mesfinto Eth. 89 H6
Mesgouez Lake Canada 125 F3
Mesha r. Rus. Fed. 28 I5
Meshed Iran see Mashhad
Meshkān Iran 80 D2
Meshra'er Req Sudan 96 A2
Mesimeri Greece 47 C4
Meslay-du-Maine France 38 C3
Mesola Italy 44 D2
Mesolongi Greece 47 B5
Mesolóngion Greece see Mesolongi
Mesquite U.S.A. 133 B5
Mesquite Lake U.S.A. 137 E4
Messaad Alg. 91 F2
Messak Mellet hills Libya 88 A3
Messalo r. Moz. 97 D7
Messana Sicily Italy see Messina
Messaoud, Oued watercourse Alg. 91 E4
Messier, Canal sea chan. Chile 153 B7
Messina Sicily Italy 45 E5
Messina S. Africa 99 F4
Messina, Strait of Italy 45 E5
Messini Greece 47 C6
Messiniakos Kolpos b. Greece 47 C6
Meßkirch Germany 36 D5
Messlingen Sweden 32 D3
Mesta r. Bulg. 46 D4
Mesta r. Greece see Nestos
Mestghanem Alg. see Mostaganem
Meston, Akra pt Greece 47 D5
Mesudiye Turkey 79 D2
Mesuji r. Indon. 58 D4
Meta dept Col. 146 C4
Meta r. Col./Venez. 146 E3
Métabetchouan Canada 125 G3
Meta Incognita Peninsula Canada 121 M3
Metairie U.S.A. 133 D6
Metaliferi, Munții mts Romania 46 C1
Metallifere, Colline mts Italy 44 C3
Metán Arg. 152 D1
Metanara Eth. 96 C2
Metangula Moz. 97 B8
Metauro r. Italy 44 D3
Metema Eth. 96 C1
Meteora tourist site Greece 47 B5
Meteor Creek r. Australia 111 G5
Methoni Greece 47 B6
Methuen U.S.A. 131 H2
Metionga Lake Canada 124 B3
Metković Croatia 44 F3
Metlakatla U.S.A. 122 D4
Metlaoui Tunisia 91 H2
Metlika Slovenia 44 E2
Metoro Moz. 97 C8
Metro Indon. 58 D4
Metropolis U.S.A. 128 A4
Metsäkylä Fin. 32 H2
Metsovo Greece 47 B5
Metter U.S.A. 129 C5
Mettler U.S.A. 136 C4
Mettuppalaiyam India 72 C4
Mettur India 72 C4
Metu Eth. 96 B2
Metz France 39 G2
Metzingen Germany 36 D4
Meu r. France 38 C2
Meulaboh Indon. 58 B1
Meung-sur-Loire France 38 D3
Meurthe r. France 39 G2
Meuse r. Belgium/France 39 F1
also spelt Maas (Netherlands)
Mēwa China 66 B1
Mexia U.S.A. 133 B6
Mexiana, Ilha i. Brazil 150 B1
Mexicali Mex. 135 D6
Mexican Hat U.S.A. 137 H3
Mexican Water U.S.A. 137 H3

Mexico country Central America **138** D4
2nd most populous and 3rd largest
country in Central and North America.
northamerica 118–119, 140

Mexico MO U.S.A. **132** D4
Mexico NY U.S.A. **131** E2
Mexico, Gulf of Mex./U.S.A. **129** B7

▶**Mexico City** Mex. **138** E5
Capital of Mexico. Most populous city in
North America and 2nd in the world.
world 16–17

Meybod Iran **80** C3
Meyenburg Germany **37** F2
Meyersdale U.S.A. **130** D4
Meymaneh Afgh. **81** F3
Meyme Iran **80** B3
Meynypil'gyno Rus. Fed. **27** R3
Meyo Centre Cameroon **93** H5
Meza Myanmar **60** B2
Mezada tourist site Israel see Masada
Mezas mt. Spain **42** C2
Mezdra Bulg. **46** C3
Mezen' Rus. Fed. **28** H2
Mezen' r. Rus. Fed. **28** G2
Mezenskaya Guba b. Rus. Fed. **28** G2
Mézenc, Mont mt. France **39** F4
Mezenskiy, Ostrov i. Rus. Fed.
26 F2
Mézidon-Canon France **38** C2
Mézin France **38** D4
Mezitli Turkey **77** B1
Mezőberény Hungary **37** J5
Mezőhegyes Hungary **46** B1
Mezőkövácsháza Hungary **46** B1
Mezőkövesd Hungary **37** J5
Mezőtúr Hungary **37** J5
Mezquitic Mex. **138** D4
Mežvidi Latvia **33** O4
Mezzolombardo Italy **44** C1
Mfouati Congo **95** B6
Mfuwe Zambia **97** A8
Mgachi Rus. Fed. **64** E2
Mgbidi Nigeria **93** G4
Mhail, Rubh' a' pt U.K. **34** C4
Mhangura Zimbabwe **99** F2
Mhasvad India **72** B2
Mhow India **74** B5
Mi r. Myanmar **60** A3
Miahuatlán Mex. **138** E5
Miajadas Spain **42** D4
Miaméré Cent. Afr. Rep. **94** C2
Miami AZ U.S.A. **137** G5
Miami FL U.S.A. **129** C7
Miami OK U.S.A. **132** C4
Miami TX U.S.A. **133** A5
Miami Beach U.S.A. **129** C7
Miamitown U.S.A. **130** C4
Miānābād Iran **80** D2
Mianaz Pak. **81** E5
Mianchi China **67** D1
Miāndasht Iran **80** D2
Miandowāb Iran **80** A2
Miandrivazo Madag. **99** [inset] J3
Mianeh Iran **80** A2
Miani Hor b. Pak. **81** F5
Mianmian Shan mts China **66** B3
Mianning China **66** B2
Mianwali Pak. **81** G3
Mianxian China **66** C1
Mianyang Hubei China see Xiantao
Mianyang Sichuan China **66** C2
Mianzhu China **66** C2
Miaogao China see Suichang
Miaoli Taiwan **67** F3
Miarinarivo Antananarivo Madag.
99 [inset] J3
Miarinarivo Toamasina Madag. **99** [inset] J3
Miass Rus. Fed. **26** G4
Miastko Poland **37** H1
Mica, Cerro de mt. Chile **148** C5
Mica Creek Canada **122** G4
Micang Shan mts China **66** C1
Michalovce Slovakia **37** J4
Michel Canada **123** I4
Michelson, Mount U.S.A. **120** E3
Micheng China see Midu
Michigan state U.S.A. **130** A1

▶**Michigan, Lake** U.S.A. **132** E3
3rd largest lake in North America and
5th in the world.
northamerica 116–117
world 6–7

Michigan City U.S.A. **132** E3
Michipicoten Bay Canada **124** C4
Michipicoten Island Canada **124** C4
Michipicoten River Canada **124** C4
Michurin Bulg. see Tsarevo
Michurinsk Rus. Fed. **29** G5
▶**Micronesia** is Pacific Ocean **164** D5
▶**Micronesia, Federated States of**
country N. Pacific Ocean **164** G5
oceania 104–105, 114
Midai i. Indon. **59** D2
Midal well Niger **93** G3
Midale Canada **123** K5
Mid-Atlantic Ridge sea feature
Atlantic Ocean **160** N7
Middelburg Neth. **36** A3
Middelburg E. Cape S. Africa **98** E6
Middelburg Mpumalanga S. Africa **99** D5
Middelfart Denmark **33** C5
Middelharnis Neth. **36** B3
Middelwit S. Africa **99** D4
Middle America Trench sea feature
N. Pacific Ocean **165** L5
Middle Andaman i. India **73** G3
Middle Atlas mts Morocco see
Moyen Atlas
Middle Bay Canada **125** J3
Middleburg PA U.S.A. **131** E3
Middleburg VA U.S.A. **130** D4
Middleburgh U.S.A. **131** F2
Middlebury U.S.A. **131** I1
Middle Concho r. U.S.A. **133** A6
Middle Island U.S.A. **131** G3
Middle Loup r. U.S.A. **132** E3
Middlemarch N.Z. **113** B4
Middlemount Australia **111** G4
Middleport U.S.A. **130** D4
Middle River U.S.A. **131** E4
Middlesboro U.S.A. **130** D5
Middlesbrough U.K. **35** F4
Middlesex U.S.A. **131** I3
Middle Strait India see Andaman Strait
Middleton Australia **111** H5
Middleton Canada **125** H4
Middleton Reef Australia **107** F4
Middletown CA U.S.A. **136** A2
Middletown CT U.S.A. **131** I3
Middletown DE U.S.A. **131** H4
Middletown NY U.S.A. **131** H3
Middletown OH U.S.A. **130** A4
Middletown PA U.S.A. **131** G3
Middletown VA U.S.A. **130** D4
Middleville U.S.A. **131** F2
Midelt Morocco **90** D2
Midhisho well Somalia **96** E2

Midhurst U.K. **35** F6
Midi Yemen **89** I5
Midi, Canal du France **38** E5
Midi de Bigorre, Pic du mt. France **38** D5
Mid-Indian Basin sea feature
Indian Ocean **162** M6
Mid-Indian Ridge sea feature
Indian Ocean **162** L7
Midi-Pyrénées admin. reg. France **38** E4
Midland Canada **130** D1
Midland CA U.S.A. **137** E5
Midland MI U.S.A. **130** A2
Midland TX U.S.A. **133** B6
Midlands prov. Zimbabwe **99** F3
Midleton Rep. of Ireland **35** B6
Midlothian TX U.S.A. **133** B5
Midlothian VA U.S.A. **130** D5
Midnapore India see Medinipur
Midongy Atsimo Madag. **99** [inset] J4
Midou r. France **38** D5
Midouze r. France **38** D5
Mid-Pacific Mountains sea feature
N. Pacific Ocean **164** G4
Midu China **66** B3
Midway Oman see Thamarīt
Midway U.S.A. **130** A4

▶**Midway Islands** N. Pacific Ocean **164** G4
United States Unincorporated Territory.
oceania 114

Midway Well Australia **108** C5
Midwest U.S.A. **134** F4
Midwest City U.S.A. **133** B5
Midyat Turkey **79** E3
Midye Turkey see Kıyıköy
Midzhur mt. Bulg./Yugo. **46** C3
Miechów Poland **37** J3
Miedwie, Jezioro l. Poland **37** G2
Międzychód Poland **37** G2
Międzylesie Poland **37** H3
Międzyrzecz Poland **37** G2
Miekojärvi l. Fin. **28** C2
Mielec Poland **37** J3
Miembwe Tanz. **97** C7
Mień r. Poland **37** J3
Mienga Angola **95** C5
Miengela Angola **95** C5
Miengela Tanz. **97** C7
Mienhua Yü i. Taiwan **67** G3
Mieraslompolo Fin. **32** G1
Mierašluoppal Fin. see Mieraslompolo
Miercurea-Ciuc Romania **46** D1
Mieres Spain **42** D1
Mieres del Camín Spain see Mieres
Mieres del Camino Spain see Mieres
Mierzeja Helska pen. Poland **37** I1
Mierzeja Wiślana spit Poland **37** I1
Miesbach Germany **36** E5
Mi'ēso Eth. **96** D2
Mietoinen Fin. **33** F3
Mifflin U.S.A. **131** E3
Mifflinburg U.S.A. **131** E3
Mifflintown U.S.A. **131** E3
Migennes France **39** E3
Miguasha National Park Canada
125 H3
Miguel Alemán, Presa resr Mex. **138** E5
Migyaunye Myanmar **60** A4
Mihăilești Romania **46** D2
Mihalıçcık Turkey **78** B3
Mihijam India see Chittaranjan
Mihumo Chini Tanz. **97** C7
Mijares r. Spain **43** F3
Mikashevichy Belarus **29** C5
Mikha Tskhakaia Georgia see Senaki
Mikhailov Rus. Fed. **29** F5
Mikhaylovgrad Bulg. see Montana
Mikhaylovka Amurskaya Oblast'
Rus. Fed. **64** B2
Mikhaylovka Primorskiy Kray Rus. Fed.
64 C4
Mikhaylovka Tul'skaya Oblast' Rus. Fed.
see Kimovsk
Mikhaylovka Volgogradskaya Oblast'
Rus. Fed. **29** G6
Mikhaylovskiy Rus. Fed. **26** H1
Mikines tourist site Greece see Mycenae
Mikir Hills India **75** G4
Mikkeli Fin. **33** O3
Mikkwa r. Canada **123** H3
Mikonos i. Greece see Mykonos
Mikoyan Armenia see Yeghegnadzor
Mikulkin, Mys c. Rus. Fed. **28** H2
Mikulov Czech Rep. **37** H4
Mikumi Tanz. **97** C6
Mikumi National Park Tanz. **97** C6
Mikun' Rus. Fed. **28** I3
Mikura-jima i. Japan **65** D6
Mila Alg. **91** G1
Milaca U.S.A. **132** C2
Miladhunmadulu Atoll Maldives **72** B5
Milagres Brazil **150** E3
Milagro Arg. **152** D2
Milagro Ecuador **146** B5
Milan Italy **44** B2
Milan MI U.S.A. **130** B2
Milan MO U.S.A. **132** C3
Milan OH U.S.A. **130** B3
Milando Angola **95** C7
Milange Moz. **99** D3
Milano Italy see Milan
Milano (Malpensa) airport Italy **44** B2
Milas Turkey **78** A3
Milazzo Sicily Italy **45** E5
Milazzo, Capo di c. Sicily Italy **45** E5
Milbank U.S.A. **132** B2
Milde r. Germany **36** E2
Mildura Australia **112** B4
Mile China **66** B3
Mile Eth. **96** D2
Miles Australia **111** G5
Milesburg U.S.A. **130** E3
Miles City U.S.A. **134** F3
Mileura Australia **109** B6
Milevsko Czech Rep. **37** G4
Milford CT U.S.A. **131** I3
Milford DE U.S.A. **131** H4
Milford NE U.S.A. **132** B3
Milford NH U.S.A. **131** H2
Milford PA U.S.A. **131** H3
Milford UT U.S.A. **137** F2
Milford VA U.S.A. **131** G4
Milford Haven U.K. **35** D6
Milford Sound N.Z. **113** A4
Milford Sound inlet N.Z. **113** A4
Milgarra Australia **111** E3
Milgun Australia **109** B6
Milh, Baḩr al l. Iraq see
Razāzah, Buḩayrat ar
Miliana Alg. **43** H6
Milicz Poland **37** H3
Milid Turkey see Malatya
Milikapiti Australia **110** B1
Miling Australia **109** B7
Milingimbi Australia **110** C2
Milip Vanuatu **107** F3
Milk r. U.S.A. **134** F2
Milk, Wadi el watercourse Sudan **89** F5
Mil'kovo Rus. Fed. **27** P4
Milk River Canada **134** D2
Millaa Millaa Australia **111** F3
Millàrs r. Spain see Mijares
Millau France **39** E4
Millboro U.S.A. **130** D5

Mill City U.S.A. **134** B3
Mill Creek r. U.S.A. **136** B1
Milledgeville U.S.A. **129** C5
Mille Lacs lakes U.S.A. **132** C2
Mille Lacs, Lac des l. Canada **124** B3
Millen U.S.A. **129** C5
Millenium Island Kiribati see
Caroline Island
Miller watercourse Australia **110** C6
Miller U.S.A. **132** B2
Miller, Mount U.S.A. **122** A2
Millerovo Rus. Fed. **29** G6
Millersburg U.S.A. **130** C3
Millers Creek Australia **110** D6
Millers Creek U.S.A. **130** B5
Millers Falls U.S.A. **131** G3
Millerton U.S.A. **131** G3
Millerton Lake U.S.A. **136** C3
Mill Hall U.S.A. **130** E3
Millicent Australia **112** B5
Millington MI U.S.A. **130** C2
Millington TN U.S.A. **133** D5
Millinocket U.S.A. **128** F2
Milliri, Cerro mt. Bol. **148** C5
Mill Island Antarctica **163** N10
Millmerran Australia **111** G5
Millom U.K. **35** E4
Millsboro U.S.A. **131** F1
Mills Creek watercourse Australia
111 F4
Mills Lake Canada **123** G2
Millstone U.S.A. **130** C4
Millstream Australia **108** B5
Millstream-Chichester National Park
Australia **108** B5
Millungera Australia **111** E3
Millville U.S.A. **131** H4
Millwood Lake U.S.A. **133** C5
Milly Milly Australia **109** B6
Milne Land i. Greenland see
Ilimananngip Nunaa
Milo r. Guinea **92** C3
Milo U.S.A. **128** F2
Milogradovo Rus. Fed. **64** C4
Milolii U.S.A. **135** [inset] Z2
Milos i. Greece **47** D6
Miloud well Alg. **90** D4
Milparinka Australia **111** E6
Milpitas U.S.A. **136** B3
Milroy U.S.A. **130** E3
Milton Canada **130** D2
Milton DE U.S.A. **131** H4
Milton FL U.S.A. **129** B6
Milton VT U.S.A. **131** G1
Milton WV U.S.A. **130** B4
Milton-Freewater U.S.A. **134** C3
Milton Keynes U.K. **35** F5
Miluo China **67** E2
Milverton Canada **130** C2
Milwaukee U.S.A. **130** B2

▶**Milwaukee Deep** sea feature
Caribbean Sea **160** J4
Deepest point in the Atlantic Ocean
(Puerto Rico Trench).
oceans 156–157, 168

Mimbelly Congo **94** C4
Mimbres watercourse U.S.A. **135** F6
Mimili Australia **110** C5
Mimisal India **72** C4
Mimizan France **38** C4
Mimoň Czech Rep. **37** G3
Mimongo Gabon **94** C4
Mimosa Rocks National Park Australia
112 C4
Mina Mex. **133** A7
Mina U.S.A. **136** C2
Mīnāb Iran **80** D5
Mina Clavero Arg. **152** D2
Minaçu Brazil **150** B5
Minago r. Canada **123** L4
Minahasa, Semenanjung pen. Indon.
57 F5
Minahassa Peninsula Indon. see
Minahasa, Semenanjung
Mina Jebel Ali U.A.E. **80** C5
Minaker Canada see Prophet River
Minaki Canada **123** M5
Minamata Japan **65** B6
Minami Australia **110** C2
Minami Alps National Park Japan **65** D6
Minami-Daitō-jima i. Japan **63** M6
Minami-Iō-jima vol. Japan **57** J1
Min'an China see Longshan
Minas Indon. **58** C2
Minas Uruguay **152** G3
Minas Gerais state Brazil **149** I4
Minā' Sa'ūd Kuwait **79** G5
Minas, Serra do hills Brazil **149** H5
Minatitlán Mex. **138** F5
Minbu Myanmar **60** A3
Minbya Myanmar **60** A3
Minchinabad Pak. **74** B3
Minchinmávida vol. Chile **153** B5
Mincio r. Italy **44** D2
Mincivan Azer. **79** H3
Mindanao i. Phil. **57** G4
Mindat Sakan Myanmar **60** A3
Mindelheim Germany **36** D2
Mindelo Cape Verde **92** [inset]
Minden Germany **36** D2
Minden LA U.S.A. **133** C5
Minden NE U.S.A. **132** B3
Minden NV U.S.A. **136** C2
Minden City U.S.A. **130** B2
Minderoo Australia **108** A5
Mindon Myanmar **60** A4
Mindona Lake imp. l. Australia **112** B4
Mindoro i. Phil. **57** G3
Mindoro Strait Phil. **57** F3
Mindouli Congo **95** B6
Mindszent Hungary **37** J5
Minehead U.K. **35** E6
Mineiros Brazil **149** G2
Mineola U.S.A. **133** C5
Mineral U.S.A. **130** D4
Mirond Lake Canada **123** K4
Mironovka Ukr. see Myronivka
Mineral del Monte Mex. **126** F7
Mineral'nyye Vody Rus. Fed. **29** G7
Mineral Wells U.S.A. **133** B5
Minersville U.S.A. **131** G3
Minervino Murge Italy **44** F4
Minfeng China **70** D4
Minga Dem. Rep. Congo **95** E7
Mingäçevir Azer. **79** H2
Mingäçevir Su Anbarı resr Azer. **79** F2
Mingan Canada **127** N1
Mingechaur Azer. see Mingäçevir
Mingechaurskoye Vodokhranilishche
resr Azer. see Mingäçevir Su Anbarı
Mingela Australia **111** F3
Mingenew Australia **109** A7
Mingfeng China see Yuan'an
Minggang China **67** E1
Mingguang China **67** H1
Mingin Myanmar **60** A2
Minglanilla Spain **43** F3
Mingo Junction U.S.A. **130** D3
Mingora Pak. see Saidu Sharif
Mingoyo Tanz. **97** C7
Mingshan Chongqing China see Fengdu
Mingshan Sichuan China **66** B2
Mingshui China **64** A3

Mingteke China **74** B1
Minguez, Puerto de pass Spain **43** F2
Mingulay i. U.K. **34** C3
Mingxi China **67** F3
Minhe Jiangxi China see Jinxian
Minhe Qinghai China **62** G4
Minhla Myanmar **60** A4
Minho reg. Port. **42** B2
Minhou China **67** F3
Minicoy i. India **72** B4
Minigwal, Lake salt flat Australia **109** C7
Minilya r. Australia **108** A5
Minilya r. Australia **108** A5
Miñiміñe Chile **148** C3
Minion China **66** C1
Mininian Côte d'Ivoire **92** D3
Minipi Lake Canada **125** I2
Ministra, Sierra mts Spain **43** E2
Minitonas Canada **123** K4
Minjian China see Mabian
Min Jiang r. Sichuan China **66** C2
Min Jiang r. China **67** F3
Minjilang Australia **110** C1
Minlaton Australia **112** A4
Minna Nigeria **93** G3
Minna, Jibāl al mts Saudi Arabia **89** I3
Minneapolis KS U.S.A. **132** B4
Minneapolis MN U.S.A. **132** C2
Minnedosa Canada **134** H2
Minnehaha Springs U.S.A. **130** D4
Minnesota r. U.S.A. **132** C2
Minnesota state U.S.A. **132** C2
Minnewaukan U.S.A. **132** B1
Minnitaki Lake Canada **124** B3
Miño r. Port./Spain **42** B2
Minorca i. Spain **43** H2
Minot U.S.A. **134** C2
Minqar, Ghadīr imp. l. Syria **77** C3
Minqin China **67** F3
Minquan China **67** E1
Min Shan mts China **66** B1
Minsin Myanmar **60** A2

▶**Minsk** Belarus **29** C5
Capital of Belarus.

Mińsk Mazowiecki Poland **37** J2
Mintaka Pass China/Jammu and Kashmir
74 B1
Mintlaw U.K. **34** G3
Minto, Lac l. Canada **125** F1
Minto, Mount Antarctica **167** H2
Mintom Cameroon **93** H5
Minton Canada **123** J5
Minturn U.S.A. **134** F5
Minturnae Italy see Minturno
Minturno Italy **44** D4
Minudasht Iran **80** D2
Minūf Egypt **78** B5
Minūfiyah governorate Egypt **78** B5
Minusinsk Rus. Fed. **62** E1
Minutang India **66** A1
Minvoul Gabon **94** C3
Minxian China **66** C1
Minya Konka mt. China see Gongga Shan
Minyar Rus. Fed. **28** K5
Minywa Myanmar **60** A3
Minzong India **60** B2
Mio well Niger **93** H1
Mio U.S.A. **130** A1
Miquelon Canada **124** E3
Miquelon i. St Pierre and Miquelon **125** J4
Mira r. Col. **146** B3
Mira Port. **42** B2
Mira r. Port. **42** B4
Mira, Sierra de mts Spain **43** F3
Miracema do Norte Brazil see
Miracema do Tocantins
Miracema do Tocantins Brazil **150** B4
Mirador, Parque Nacional de nat. park
Brazil **150** C3
Miraflores Col. **146** C3
Mirāh, Wādī al watercourse
Iraq/Saudi Arabia **79** E4
Miraj India **72** B2
Miramar Arg. **152** F4
Miramas France **39** F5
Miramichi Canada **125** H4
Miramichi Bay Canada **125** H4
Miram Shah Pak. **81** G3
Miranda r. Brazil **149** F4
Miranda Moz. see Macaloge
Miranda U.S.A. **136** A1
Miranda state Venez. **146** E1
Miranda de Ebro Spain **42** E1
Miranda do Douro Port. **42** C2
Mirande France **38** D5
Mirandela Port. **42** C2
Mirandola Italy **44** C2
Mirante, Serra do hills Brazil **149** H5
Mirapinima Brazil **147** F5
Miras Albania **46** C4
Mirassol Brazil **149** H5
Mirbāt Oman **76** E6
Mirebeau France **38** D3
Mirecourt France **39** G2
Mirepoix France **38** D5
Mirganj India **75** E4
Miri Sarawak Malaysia **59** F1
Miri mt. Pak. **81** E4
Miria Niger **93** H2
Mirjāveh Iran **81** F4
Mirkovo Bulg. **46** D3
Mirna r. Croatia **44** E2
Miroč hills Yugo. **46** C3
Mirokovy Vale Australia **111** G5
Mirina Greece see Myrina
Mirintu watercourse Australia **111** E6
Mirjan India **72** B3
Mirnyy Rus. Fed. **27** L3
Mironovka Ukr. see Myronivka
Mironovka Ukr. see Myronivka
Mirow Germany **36** F1
Mirpur Pak. **81** H3
Mirpur Batoro Pak. **81** G5
Mirpur Khas Pak. **81** G5
Mirpur Sakro Pak. **81** F5
Mirsale Somalia **96** E3
Mirs Bay Hong Kong China **67** [inset]
Mirtoan Sea Greece see Mirtoö Pelagos
Mirtoö Pelagos sea Greece **47** C6
Miruro Moz. **97** A8
Miryalaguda India see Mirialguda
Miryang S. Korea **65** B6
Mirza Chirla Turkm. see Murzechirla
Mirzachul Uzbek. see Gulistan
Mirzapur India **75** E4
Misau Nigeria **93** H3
Miziziya Bulg. **46** D3
Mizo Hills state India see Mizoram
Mizoram state India **75** G5
Mizque r. Bol. **148** D4
Mizque Bol. **148** D4
Mizusawa Japan **65** F5
Mjelde Norway **32** H2
Mjølfjell Norway **33** B3
Mjölby Sweden **33** D4
Mjøsa l. Norway **33** C3
Mkata Tanz. **97** C6
Mkoani Tanz. **97** C6
Mkokotoni Tanz. **97** C6
Mkujani Tanz. **97** C7
Mkumbura Zimbabwe see Mukumbura
Mkunja Tanz. **97** C7
Mkurusi Tanz. **97** C6
Mkushi Zambia **95** F8

Mingteke China **74** B1
Mi-shima i. Japan **65** B6
Mishmi Hills India **60** A1
Misima Island P.N.G. **111** H1
Misis Dağ hills Turkey **77** B1
Miskah Saudi Arabia **89** I3
Miskitos, Cayos is Nicaragua **139** H6
Miskitos, Costa de coastal area
Nicaragua see Mosquitos, Costa de
Miskolc Hungary **37** J4
Mismā, Jibāl al mts Saudi Arabia **89** I3
Mismā, Tall al hill Jordan **77** C3
Misoöl i. Indon. **57** H6
Misr country Africa see Egypt
Misraç Turkey see Kurtalan
Miṣrātah Libya **88** B1
Missinaibi r. Canada **124** D3
Missinaibi Lake Canada **124** D3
Missinipe Canada **123** J4
Mission U.S.A. **133** B7
Mission Beach Australia **111** F3
Mission Viejo U.S.A. **136** D5
Missisa r. Canada **124** D3
Missisa Lake Canada **124** D3
Missisicabi r. Canada **124** E3
Missisagi r. Canada **124** D3
Mississauga Canada **130** D2
Mississippi r. Canada **128** D2

▶**Mississippi** r. U.S.A. **133** D6
4th longest river in North America. Part
of the longest (Mississippi-Missouri).
northamerica 116–117

Mississippi state U.S.A. **129** A5
Mississippi Delta U.S.A. **129** A6

▶**Mississippi-Missouri** U.S.A. **127** H6
Longest river in North America and
4th in world.
northamerica 116–117
world 6–7

Mississippi Sound sea chan. U.S.A.
129 A6
Missolonghi Greece see Mesolongi
Missoula U.S.A. **134** D3
Missour Morocco **90** E2

▶**Missouri** r. U.S.A. **134** E3
3rd longest river in North America. Part
of the longest (Mississippi-Missouri).
northamerica 116–117

Missouri state U.S.A. **127** H4
Missouri Valley U.S.A. **132** C3
Mistake Creek r. Australia **111** F4
Mistanipisipou r. Canada **125** I3
Mistassibi r. Canada **125** F3
Mistassini Canada **125** F3
Mistassini r. Canada **125** F3
Mistassini, Lac l. Canada **125** F3
Mistastin Lake Canada **125** I2
Mistelbach Austria **37** H4
Misterbianco Sicily Italy **45** E6
Mistissini Canada **125** F3
Mistras tourist site Greece **47** C6
Misty Fiords National Monument
Wilderness nat. park U.S.A. **120** F4
Misurata Libya see Miṣrātah
Misvær Norway **32** D2
Mitande Moz. **97** B8
Mitaraca hill Suriname **147** H4
Mitatib Sudan **89** H6
Mitchell r. Qld Australia **111** E2
Mitchell r. Vic. Australia **112** C5
Mitchell Canada **130** C2
Mitchell OR U.S.A. **134** B3
Mitchell SD U.S.A. **132** B3
Mitchell, Lake Australia **111** F3
Mitchell, Mount U.S.A. **128** C5
Mitchell and Alice Rivers National
Park Australia **111** E2
Mitchell Point Australia **110** B1
Mitchell Range hills Australia **110** C2
Mitchelstown Rep. of Ireland **35** B5
Mithi Pak. **81** G5
Mithimna Greece see Mithymna
Mithrani Can canal Pak. **81** G5
Mithymna Greece **47** E5
Mitilini Greece see Mytilini
Mitkof Island U.S.A. **122** C3
Mito Japan **65** E5
Mitomoni Tanz. **97** B7
Mitre mt. N.Z. **113** B4
Mitre, Península pen. Arg. **153** D8
Mitre Island Solomon Is **107** G3
Mitrofanovka Rus. Fed. **29** F6
Mitrovica Yugo. see Kosovska Mitrovica
Mitsikeli mt. Greece **47** B5
Mits'iwa Eritrea see Massawa
Mittelwald Germany **36** E5
Mittersill Austria **37** F5
Mitterteich Germany **37** F3
Mittimatalik Canada see Pond Inlet
Mitú Col. **146** D4
Mituas Col. **146** D4
Mitumba, Chaîne des mts
Dem. Rep. Congo **95** E7
Mitumba, Monts mts Dem. Rep. Congo
94 F5
Mitwaba Dem. Rep. Congo **95** F7
Mitzic Gabon **94** A4
Miughalaigh i. U.K. see Mingulay
Miura Japan **65** D6
Mixian China see Xinmi
Miyāh, Wādī al watercourse Syria **79** D4
Miyake-jima i. Japan **65** D6
Miyako Japan **65** E5
Miyakonojō Japan **65** B7
Miyako-rettō is Japan **63** K7
Miyaluo China **66** B2
Miyaly Kazakh. **29** J6
Miyang China see Mile
Miyani India **74** A5
Miyazaki Japan **65** B7
Miyi China **66** B3
Miyoshi Japan **65** C6
Mizan Teferi Eth. **96** B3
Mizdah Libya **88** B1
Mizen Head Rep. of Ireland **35** B6
Mizil Romania **46** E2

Mladenovac Yugo. **46** B2
Mlala Hills Tanz. **97** A6
Mlandizi Tanz. **97** C6
Mlava r. Yugo. **46** B2
Mljet i. Croatia **44** F3
Mljet nat. park Croatia **44** F3
Mljetski Kanal sea chan. Croatia **44** F3
Mluńgisi S. Africa **99** E6
Mmabatho S. Africa **98** E5
Mmadinare Botswana **99** E4
Mmashoro Botswana **99** E4
Mmathethe Botswana **98** E5
Mo Norway **33** B3
Moa r. Brazil **148** B1
Moa i. Indon. **108** D2
Moab U.S.A. **137** H2
Moabi Gabon **94** A5
Moaco r. Brazil **148** C1
Moa Island Australia **57** J8
Moala i. Fiji **107** G3
Moamba Moz. **99** G5
Moanda Gabon **94** B4
Moatize Moz. **99** G3
Moba Dem. Rep. Congo **95** F6
Mobārakābād Iran **80** C3
Mobārakeh Iran **80** B3
Mobaye Cent. Afr. Rep. **94** C3
Mobayi-Mbongo Dem. Rep. Congo see
Mobayi-Mbongo
Mobayi-Mbongo Dem. Rep. Congo **94** C3
Mobeka Dem. Rep. Congo **94** C4
Moberly U.S.A. **132** C4
Moberly Lake Canada **122** F4
Mobile AL U.S.A. **129** A6
Mobile AZ U.S.A. **137** F5
Mobile Bay U.S.A. **129** A6
Moble watercourse Australia **111** F5
Mobridge U.S.A. **132** B2
Mobutu, Lake Dem. Rep. Congo/Uganda
see Albert, Lake
Mobutu Sese Seko, Lake
Dem. Rep. Congo/Uganda see
Albert, Lake
Moca Geçidi pass Turkey **77** A1
Mocajuba Brazil **150** B2
Moçambicano, Planalto plat. Moz. **99** H2
Moçambique country Africa see
Mozambique
Moçâmedes Angola see Namibe
Moccasin U.S.A. **134** E3
Moccasin Gap U.S.A. **130** B5
Mộc Châu Vietnam **60** D3
Mocha Yemen **76** C7
Mocha, Isla i. Chile **152** B4
Mochirma, Parque Nacional nat. park
Venez. **147** E2
Mochudi Botswana **99** E5
Mocimboa da Praia Moz. **97** D7
Mociu Romania **46** D1
Möckeln l. Sweden **33** D4
Mocó r. Brazil **146** D4
Mocoa Col. **146** B4
Mococa Brazil **151** C7
Moctezuma Chihuahua Mex. **135** F7
Moctezuma Sonora Mex. **135** E7
Moctezuma Mex. **135** E7
Mocuba Moz. **99** H3
Modasa India **74** B5
Modder r. S. Africa **98** E6
Modena Italy **44** C2
Modena U.S.A. **137** F3
Modesto U.S.A. **136** B3
Modica Sicily Italy **45** E6
Modriča Bos.-Herz. **44** G2
Modugno Italy **44** F4
Moe Australia **112** C5
Moebase Moz. **99** H3
Moel Sych hill U.K. **35** E5
Moelv Norway **33** C3
Moen Norway **32** E1
Moengo Suriname **147** H3
Moenkopi U.S.A. **137** G3
Moeraki Point N.Z. **113** B4
Moero, Lake Dem. Rep. Congo/Zambia
see Mweru, Lake
Moers Germany **36** C3
Moffat U.K. **34** E4
Moga India **74** B3

▶**Mogadishu** Somalia **96** E4
Capital of Somalia.

Mogador Morocco see Essaouira
Mogadouro Port. **42** C2
Mogadouro, Serra de mts Port. **42** C2
Mogalo Dem. Rep. Congo **94** C4
Mogalturra India **72** D2
Mogandjo Dem. Rep. Congo **94** E4
Mogaung Myanmar **60** B2
Mogdy Rus. Fed. **64** C2
Moggar Alg. **91** G2
Moghrar-Foukani Alg. **91** E2
Mogilev Belarus see Mahilyow
Mogilev Podol'skiy Ukr. see Mohyliv
Mohyliv Podil's'kyy
Mogilno Poland **37** H2
Mogocha Rus. Fed. **63** J2
Mogi-Mirim Brazil **151** C7
Mogocha Rus. Fed. **63** J2
Mogod mts Tunisia **91** H1
Mogogh Sudan **96** A2
Mogollon Plateau U.S.A. **137** G4
Mogontiacum Germany see Mainz
Mogor Eth. **96** D2
Mogoro Sardinia Italy **45** B5
Mogroum Chad **93** H2
Moguer Spain **42** C4
Mohács Hungary **46** A2
Mohaka r. N.Z. **113** D2
Mohala India **72** D1
Mohale's Hoek Lesotho **99** E6
Mohall U.S.A. **132** A1
Mohammad Iran **81** F2
Mohammadabad Iran see Darreh Gaz
Mohammadia Alg. **91** F2
Mohammad, India/Nepal **74 D3
Mohana India **74** E5
Mohanganj Bangl. **75** F4
Mohave, Lake U.S.A. **137** E4
Mohawk r. U.S.A. **131** G2
Mohawk Mountains U.S.A. **137** F5
Moheda Sweden **33** D4
Mohéli i. Comoros see Mwali
Mohembo Botswana **98** D3
Mohenjo Daro tourist site Pak. **81** G5
Möhne r. Germany **36** D3
Mohnyin Myanmar **60** B2
Moho Peru **148** D3
Mohol India **72** B2
Mohon Peak U.S.A. **137** F4
Mohoro Tanz. **97** C7
Mohyliv Podil's'kyy Ukr. **29** C6
Moi Norway **33** B4
Moijabana Botswana **99** E4
Moincêr China **74** D3
Moinda China **75** F3
Moineşti Romania **46** E1
Mointy Kazakh. see Moyynty
Moirai Greece see Moires
Mo i Rana Norway **32** D2

Moirang India 75 G4
Moires Greece 47 D7
Mõisaküla Estonia 33 G4
Moisie r. Canada 125 H3
Moissac France 38 D4
Moïssala Chad 94 C2
Moitaco Venez. 147 E3
Mojácar Spain 43 F4
Mojados Spain 42 D2
Mojave U.S.A. 136 C4
Mojave r. U.S.A. 136 D4
Mojave Desert U.S.A. 137 D4
Mojerda r. Tunisia 45 C6
Mojiang China 66 B4
Mojikō Japan 65 B6
Mojkovac Yugo. 46 A3
Mojo Bol. 148 D5
Mojo Eth. 96 C2
Mojones, Cerro mt. Arg. 152 D1
Mojos, Llanos de plain Bol. 148 D3
Mojo Shet' r. Eth. 96 D3
Mojotoro Bol. 148 D4
Moju Brazil 150 B2
Mokama India 75 E4
Mokambo Dem. Rep. Congo 95 F8
Mokaria Dem. Rep. Congo 94 D4
Mokau N.Z. 113 C2
Mokau r. N.Z. 113 C2
Mokèko Congo 94 B4
Mokelumne r. U.S.A. 136 B2
Mokelumne Aqueduct canal U.S.A. 136 B2
Mokhotlong Lesotho 99 F6
Mokhsogollokh Rus. Fed. 27 M3
Mokimbo Dem. Rep. Congo 95 F6
Moknine Tunisia 45 C7
Mokohinau Islands N.Z. 113 C1
Mokokchung India 75 G4
Mokolo Cameroon 93 I3
Mokolo r. S. Africa 99 E4
Mokp'o S. Korea 65 A6
Mokra Gora mts Yugo. 46 B3
Mokrin Yugo. 46 B2
Mokrous Rus. Fed. 29 H6
Moksha r. Rus. Fed. 29 G5
Mokshan Rus. Fed. 29 H5
Mōktama Myanmar see Martaban
Mokundurra India see Mukandwara
Mokwa Nigeria 93 G3
Mola di Bari Italy 44 F4
Molango Mex. 126 G7
Molaoi Greece 47 C6
Molat i. Croatia 44 E2
Molatón mt. Spain 43 F3
Moldavia country Europe see Moldova
Moldavskaya S.S.R. country Europe see Moldova
Molde Norway 32 B3
Moldefjorden inlet Norway 32 B3
Moldjord Norway 32 D2
▶Moldova country Europe 29 D7
europe 24–25, 48
Moldova Nouă Romania 46 B2
Moldoveanu, Vârful mt. Romania 46 D2
Moldovei, Podișul plat. Romania 46 E1
Moldovei Centrale, Podișul plat. Moldova 29 C7
Moldovei de Sud, Cîmpia plain Moldova 46 F1
Molega Lake Canada 125 H4
Molegbe Dem. Rep. Congo 94 D3
Mole National Park Ghana 93 E3
Molepolole Botswana 98 E5
Molėtai Lith. 33 G5
Molfetta Italy 44 F4
Molières France 38 D4
Molina Arg. 152 C3
Molina de Aragón Spain 43 F2
Molina de Segura Spain 43 F3
Moline U.S.A. 132 D3
Molinella Italy 44 C2
Molinos Arg. 152 D1
Moliro Dem. Rep. Congo 97 A7
Molise admin. reg. Italy 44 E4
Molkom Sweden 33 D4
Molledo Spain 42 D1
Mol Len mt. India 75 G4
Mollendo Peru 148 C4
Mollerussa Spain 43 G2
Mölln Germany 36 E2
Mölnlycke Sweden 33 D4
Molochnoye Rus. Fed. 28 F4
Molodechno Belarus see Maladzyechna
Molodezhnaya research station Antarctica 167 D2
Molokai i. U.S.A. 135 [inset] Z1
Moloma r. Rus. Fed. 28 I4
Molong Australia 112 D4
Molopo watercourse Botswana/S. Africa 98 D6
Molos Greece 47 C5
Molotov Rus. Fed. see Perm'
Molotovsk Arkhangel'skaya Oblast' Rus. Fed. see Severodvinsk
Molotovsk Kirovskaya Oblast' Rus. Fed. see Nolinsk
Molotovskaya Oblast' admin. div. Rus. Fed. see Permskaya Oblast'
Moloundou Cameroon 94 B4
Molowaie Dem. Rep. Congo 95 D6
Molsheim France 39 G2
Molson Lake Canada 123 L4
Molu i. Indon. 57 H7
Moluccas is Indon. 57 G6
Molucca Sea Indon. 57 G6
Moluengo mt. Spain 43 F3
Molumbo Moz. 99 H2
Molwe Dem. Rep. Congo 95 E7
Moma Moz. 99 H3
Momba Australia 112 B3
Mombaça Brazil 150 E3
Mombasa Kenya 97 C5
Mombenzélé Dem. Rep. Congo 94 C4
Mombetsu Japan see Monbetsu
Momboyo r. Dem. Rep. Congo 94 C5
Mombuca, Serra da hills Brazil 149 G4
Momchilgrad Bulg. 46 D4
Momeik Myanmar see Mōng Mit
Mompono Dem. Rep. Congo 94 D4
Mompós Col. 146 C2
Momskiy Khrebet mts Rus. Fed. 27 O3
Møn i. Denmark 33 D5
Mon India 75 G4
Mon state Myanmar 61 B4
Mona U.S.A. 137 G2
Monach Islands U.K. 34 C3
▶Monaco country Europe 39 G5
europe 24–25, 48
Monaco Basin sea feature N. Atlantic Ocean 160 M4
Monadhliath Mountains U.K. 34 D3
Monagas state Venez. 147 F2
Monaghan Rep. of Ireland 35 C4
Monahans U.S.A. 133 A6
Mona Passage Dom. Rep./Puerto Rico 139 K5
Monapo Moz. 99 I2
Mona Quimbundo Angola 95 C7
Monar, Loch l. U.K. 34 D3
Monarch Mountain Canada 122 E5
Monarch Pass U.S.A. 135 F5
Monashee Mountains Canada 122 G5
Monasterio del Suso tourist site Spain 43 E1
Monastery of St Catherine tourist site Egypt 77 A5
Monastery of St Anthony tourist site Egypt 77 A5
Monastery of St Paul tourist site Egypt 77 A5
Monastir Macedonia see Bitola
Monastir Tunisia 91 H2
Monastyrishche Ukr. see Monastyryshche
Monastyryshche Ukr. 29 D6
Monbetsu Japan 64 E3
Monboré Cameroon 93 I3
Moncalieri Italy 44 A2
Moncalvo mt. Spain 42 C1
Monchegorsk Rus. Fed. 32 I2
Mönchengladbach Germany 36 C3
Monchique Port. 42 B4
Monchique, Serra de mts Port. 42 B4
Monclova Mex. 126 F6
Moncton Canada 125 H4
Mondai Brazil 151 A8
Mondego r. Port. 42 B2
Mondego, Cabo c. Port. 42 B2
Mondimbi Dem. Rep. Congo 94 D4
Mondim de Basto Port. 42 C2
Mondlo S. Africa 99 F5
Mondo Chad 88 B6
Mondolfo Italy 44 D3
Mondoñedo Spain 42 C1
Mondovì Italy 44 A2
Mondragón Spain see Arrasate
Mondragone Italy 44 D4
Mondsee l. Austria 37 F5
Mondúver hill Spain 43 F3
Monemvasia Greece 47 C6
Moneron, Ostrov i. Rus. Fed. 64 E3
Monessen U.S.A. 130 D3
Moneta U.S.A. 130 D5
Monéteau France 39 E3
Monfalcone Italy 44 D2
Monflanquin France 38 D4
Monfort Col. 146 D4
Monforte Port. 42 C3
Monforte Spain 42 C1
Monfurado hill Port. 42 B3
Monga Katanga Dem. Rep. Congo 95 E7
Monga Orientale Dem. Rep. Congo 94 D3
Mongala r. Dem. Rep. Congo 94 C4
Mongar Bhutan 75 F4
Mongbwalu Dem. Rep. Congo 94 F4
Mông Cai Vietnam 60 D3
Mongemputu Dem. Rep. Congo 95 D5
Mongers Lake salt flat Australia 109 B7
Mong Hang Myanmar 60 B3
Mong Hpayak Myanmar 60 B3
Mong Hsat Myanmar 60 B3
Monghyr India see Munger
Mong Kung Myanmar 60 B3
Mong Kyawt Myanmar 60 B4
Mongla Bangl. 75 F5
Mong La Myanmar 60 C3
Mong Lin Myanmar 60 C3
Mong Loi Myanmar 60 C3
Mōng Mit Myanmar 60 B3
Mong Nai Myanmar 60 B3
Mong Nawng Myanmar 60 B3
Mongo Chad 88 C6
▶Mongolia country Asia 62 F2
asia 52–53, 82
Mongolküre China see Zhaosu
Mongol Uls country Asia see Mongolia
Mongomo Equat. Guinea 93 H5
Mongonu Nigeria 93 I2
Mongora Pak. 81 H3
Mongororo Chad 88 D6
Mongoumba Cent. Afr. Rep. 94 C4
Mong Pan Myanmar 60 B3
Mong Ping Myanmar 60 B3
Mongu Zambia 95 D8
Mongua Angola 95 B9
Mong Yai Myanmar 60 B3
Mong Yang Myanmar 60 B3
Mong Yawng Myanmar 60 C3
Mong Yu Myanmar 60 B3
Monhegan Island U.S.A. 131 I2
Mönh Hayrhan Uul mt. Mongolia 70 H2
Monistrol-sur-Loire France 39 F4
Monitor Mountain U.S.A. 137 D2
Monitor Range mts U.S.A. 137 D2
Moñitos Col. 146 B2
Monkey Bay Malawi 97 B8
Monkey Mia Australia 109 A6
Mońki Poland 37 K2
Monkira Australia 111 E5
Monkoto Dem. Rep. Congo 94 D5
Monmouth U.K. 35 E6
Monmouth U.S.A. 132 D3
Monmouth Mountain Canada 122 F5
Monnett U.S.A. 130 B3
Mono r. Togo 93 F4
Mono, Punta del pt Nicaragua 139 H6
Mono Lake U.S.A. 136 C2
Monolithos Greece 47 E6
Monopoli Italy 44 F4
Monor Hungary 37 I5
Monongahela r. U.S.A. 130 D3
Monou Chad 88 D5
Monóvar Spain 43 F3
Monreal del Campo Spain 43 F2
Monreale Sicily Italy 45 D5
Monroe IA U.S.A. 132 C3
Monroe LA U.S.A. 133 C5
Monroe MI U.S.A. 130 B3
Monroe NC U.S.A. 128 C5
Monroe VA U.S.A. 130 D5
Monroe WA U.S.A. 134 B3
Monroe WI U.S.A. 132 D3
Monroe Center U.S.A. 132 D2
Monroe City U.S.A. 132 D4
Monroe Lake U.S.A. 128 B4
Monroeville U.S.A. 130 A3
▶Monrovia Liberia 92 C4
Capital of Liberia.
Mons Belgium 39 E1
Monselice Italy 44 C2
Møns Klint cliff Denmark 37 F1
Mönsterås Sweden 33 E4
Montabaur Germany 36 C3
Montagu S. Africa 98 D7
Montague Canada 125 I4
Montague U.S.A. 133 B5
Montague Island U.S.A. 120 E3
Montague Range hills Australia 109 B6
Montaigu France 38 C3
Montaigu-de-Quercy France 38 D4
Montalto mt. Italy 45 E5
Montalto di Castro Italy 44 C3
Montalto Uffugo Italy 45 F5
Montalvo Ecuador 146 B5
Montana Bulg. 46 C3
Montana state U.S.A. 134 E3
Montánchez hill Spain 42 C3
Montánchez, Sierra de mts Spain 42 C3
Montargis France 39 E3
Montauban France 38 D4
Montauk U.S.A. 131 H3
Montauk Point U.S.A. 131 H3
Montbard France 39 F3
Montbéliard France 39 G3
Montblanc Spain 43 G2
Montblanch Spain see Montblanc
Montbrison France 39 F4
Montcalm U.S.A. 130 C5
Montceau-les-Mines France 39 F3
Montchanin France 39 F3
Montcuq France 38 D4
Mont-de-Marsan France 38 C5
Montdidier France 39 E2
Monte, Lago del l. Arg. 152 E4
Monteagudo Bol. 149 D4
Monte Alegre Brazil 147 H5
Monte Alegre de Goiás Brazil 150 C5
Montealegre del Castillo Spain 43 F3
Monte Alegre de Minas Brazil 149 H4
Montebello Canada 128 E2
Montebello Islands Australia 108 A5
Montebelluna Italy 44 D2
Monte Buey Arg. 152 E3
Monte-Carlo Monaco 39 G5
Monte Carlo Monaco see Monte-Carlo
Monte Caseros Arg. 152 F2
Montech France 38 D5
Monte Christo S. Africa 99 E4
Monte Cristi Dom. Rep. 127 L8
Montecristi Ecuador 146 A5
Monte Cristo Bol. 149 E3
Montecristo, Isola di i. Italy 44 C3
Monte Dinero Arg. 153 C8
Monte Dourado Brazil 147 H5
Monte Falterona, Campigna e delle Foreste Casentinesi, Parco Nazionale del nat. park Italy 44 C3
Montefiascone Italy 44 D3
Montegiorgio Italy 44 D3
Montego Bay Jamaica 139 I5
Monteiro Brazil 150 E3
Montejinnie Australia 110 B3
Montejunto, Serra de hill Port. 42 B3
Monte León Arg. 153 C7
Monte Líbano Col. 146 C2
Montélimar France 39 F4
Monte Lindo r. Para. 149 F5
Montellano Spain 42 D4
Montemayor, Meseta de plat. Arg. 153 D6
Montemorelos Mex. 126 G6
Montemor-o-Novo Port. 42 B3
Montendre France 38 C4
Montenegro aut. rep. Yugo. see Crna Gora
Monte Patria Chile 152 C2
Montepuez Moz. 97 C8
Montepuez r. Moz. 97 D8
Monte Quemado Arg. 152 E1
Montereau-faut-Yonne France 39 E2
Monterey Mex. see Monterrey
Monterey CA U.S.A. 136 B3
Monterey VA U.S.A. 130 D4
Monterey Bay U.S.A. 136 A3
Montería Col. 146 C2
Montero Bol. 149 E4
Monteros Arg. 152 D1
Monterotondo Italy 44 D3
Monterrey Baja California Mex. 137 E5
Monterrey Nuevo León Mex. 126 F6
Montes Altos Brazil 150 C3
Montesano U.S.A. 134 B3
Montesano sulla Marcellana Italy 45 E4
Monte Sant'Angelo Italy 44 E4
Monte Santo Brazil 150 E4
Monte Santu, Capo di c. Sardinia Italy 45 B4
Montes Claros Brazil 151 D6
Montesilvano Italy 44 E3
▶Montevideo Uruguay 152 F3
Capital of Uruguay.
Montevideo U.S.A. 132 C2
Monte Vista U.S.A. 135 F5
Montezuma U.S.A. 132 C3
Montezuma Creek U.S.A. 137 H3
Montezuma Creek r. U.S.A. 137 H3
Montezuma Peak U.S.A. 136 D3
Montfort-le-Gesnois France 38 D2
Montgomery U.K. 35 E5
▶Montgomery AL U.S.A. 129 B5
State capital of Alabama.
Montgomery PA U.S.A. 131 E3
Montgomery WV U.S.A. 130 C4
Montgomery Islands Australia 108 C3
Monthey Switz. 39 G3
Monti Sardinia Italy 45 B4
Monticello AR U.S.A. 127 H5
Monticello FL U.S.A. 129 C6
Monticello IL U.S.A. 132 D3
Monticello IN U.S.A. 132 E3
Monticello KY U.S.A. 130 A5
Monticello MO U.S.A. 132 D3
Monticello MS U.S.A. 133 D6
Monticello NY U.S.A. 131 F3
Monticello UT U.S.A. 137 H3
Montichiari Italy 44 C2
Montiel, Cuchilla de hills Arg. 152 F2
Montignac France 38 D4
Montijo Spain 42 C3
Montilla Spain 42 D4
Monti Sibillini, Parco Nazionale dei nat. park Italy 44 D3
Mont-Joli Canada 125 G3
Mont-Laurier Canada 124 F4
Mont Louis Canada 125 H3
Montluçon France 39 E3
Montmagny Canada 121 L5
Montmélian France 39 G4
Montmirail France 39 E2
Montmoreau-St-Cybard France 38 D4
Montmorillon France 38 D3
Monto Australia 111 G5
Montoro Spain 42 D3
Montour Falls U.S.A. 131 E2
Montoursville U.S.A. 131 E3
Mont Peko, Parc National du nat. park Côte d'Ivoire 92 D4
Montpelier ID U.S.A. 134 E4
Montpelier OH U.S.A. 130 A3
▶Montpelier VT U.S.A. 131 G1
State capital of Vermont.
Montpellier France 39 E5
Montpon-Ménestérol France 38 D4
▶Montréal Canada 125 F4
northamerica 140
Montreal r. Ont. Canada 124 C4
Montréal-Dorval airport Canada 125 F4
Montreal Lake Canada 123 J4
Montreal Lake l. Canada 123 J4
Montréal-Mirabel airport Canada 125 F4
Montreal River Canada 124 C4
Montreuil France 38 D1
Montreux Switz. 39 G3
Montrose well S. Africa 98 D5
Montrose U.K. 34 E3
Montrose CO U.S.A. 135 F5
Montrose MI U.S.A. 130 B2
Montrose PA U.S.A. 131 F3
Montrose WV U.S.A. 130 D4
Mont-St-Aignan France 38 D2
Mont-St-Michel, Baie du b. France 38 C2
Montsalvy France 39 E4
Mont Sangbé, Parc National du nat. park Côte d'Ivoire 92 D4
▶Montserrat terr. West Indies 139 L5
United Kingdom Overseas Territory.
northamerica 118–119, 140
Mont St Michel tourist site France see Le Mont-St-Michel
Montvale U.S.A. 130 D5
Monument Valley reg. U.S.A. 137 G3
Monveda Dem. Rep. Congo 94 D4
Monywa Myanmar 60 A3
Monza Italy 44 B2
Monze Zambia 95 E9
Monze, Cape pt Pak. see Muari, Ras
Monzhukly Turkm. 80 C2
Monzón Peru 148 A2
Monzón Spain 43 G2
Mookane Botswana 99 E4
Moolawatana Australia 111 D6
Moomba Australia 111 G5
Moonda Lake salt flat Australia 111 E5
Moonie Australia 111 G5
Moonie r. Australia 112 D3
Moonta Australia 112 A4
Moora Australia 109 B7
Mooraberree Australia 111 E5
Moorcroft U.S.A. 134 F3
Moore r. Australia 109 A7
Moore U.S.A. 134 E3
Moore, Lake salt flat Australia 109 B7
Moore Embayment b. Antarctica 167 H1
Moorefield U.S.A. 130 D4
Moore Haven U.S.A. 129 C7
Moore Reef Australia 111 G3
Moore Reservoir U.S.A. 131 H1
Moore River National Park Australia 109 A7
Moorhead U.S.A. 132 B2
Moornanyah Lake imp. l. Australia 112 B4
Mooroopna Australia 112 C5
Moorpark U.S.A. 136 C4
Moorrinya National Park Australia 111 F4
Moose r. Canada 124 D3
Moose Factory Canada 124 D3
Moosehead Lake U.S.A. 128 F2
Moose Jaw Canada 134 F2
Moose Jaw r. Canada 123 J5
Moose Lake U.S.A. 132 C2
Moose Mountain Creek r. Canada 123 K5
Moose River Canada 124 D3
Moosomin Canada 134 G2
Moosonee Canada 124 D3
Mootwingee National Park Australia 112 B3
Mopane S. Africa 99 F4
Mopeia Moz. 99 G3
Mopipi Botswana 98 E4
Mopti Mali 92 D2
Mopti admin. reg. Mali 92 E2
Moquegua Peru 148 C4
Moquegua dept Peru 148 C4
Mór Hungary 37 I5
Mora Cameroon 93 I3
Mora Port. 42 B3
Mora Spain 42 E3
Mora Sweden 33 D3
Mora MN U.S.A. 132 C2
Mora NM U.S.A. 135 F6
Mora r. U.S.A. 135 F6
Morača r. Yugo. 46 A3
Morad r. Pak. 81 F4
Moradabad India 74 C3
Morada Nova Amazonas Brazil 148 C1
Morada Nova Ceará Brazil 150 E3
Morafenobe Madag. 99 [inset] J3
Morąg Poland 37 I2
Moraine Lake Canada 123 J1
Moraleda, Canal sea chan. Chile 153 B6
Moraleja Spain 42 C2
Moram India 72 C2
Moramanga Madag. 99 [inset] K3
Moran U.S.A. 134 E4
Moranbah Australia 111 G4
Morang Nepal see Biratnagar
Moranhat India 75 G4
Morappur India 72 C3
Morar, Loch l. U.K. 34 D3
Moratalla Spain 43 F3
Moratuwa Sri Lanka 72 C5
Morava reg. Czech Rep. see Moravia
Morava r. Europe 37 H4
Moraveh Tappeh Iran 80 C2
Moravia reg. Czech Rep. 37 H4
Moravica r. Yugo. 46 B3
Moravica r. Yugo. 46 B3
Moravice r. Czech Rep. 37 H4
Moravské Budějovice Czech Rep. 37 G4
Moravskoslezské Beskydy mts Czech Rep. 37 I4
Morawa Australia 109 A7
Morawhanna Guyana 147 G2
Moray Firth b. U.K. 34 D3
Moray Range hills Australia 110 B2
Morbach Germany 36 C4
Morbegno Italy 44 B1
Morbi India 74 A5
Morcenx France 38 C4
Mordaga China 63 K1
Mor Dağı mt. Turkey 79 F3
Mordelles France 38 C2
Mordovia aut. rep. Rus. Fed. see Mordoviya, Respublika
Mordoviya, Respublika aut. rep. Rus. Fed. 29 H5
Mordovo Rus. Fed. 29 G5
Mordovskaya A.S.S.R. aut. rep. Rus. Fed. see Mordoviya, Respublika
Mordvinia aut. rep. Rus. Fed. see Mordoviya, Respublika
Mordy Poland 37 K2
Moreau r. U.S.A. 132 A2
Morecambe Bay U.K. 35 E4
Moree Australia 111 G6
Morehead P.N.G. 57 J7
Morehead U.S.A. 130 B4
Moreira Brazil 147 F5
Morel-Iz, Gora hill Rus. Fed. 28 L1
Morel r. India 74 C4
Moreland U.S.A. 130 A5
Morelia Col. 146 C4
Morelia Mex. 126 F8
Morella Australia 111 E4
Morella Spain 43 F2
Morena India 74 C4
Morena, Sierra mts Spain 42 C4
Morenci U.S.A. 137 H5
Moreni Romania 46 D2
Moreno Mex. 135 E7
Moreno Valley U.S.A. 136 D5
Møre og Romsdal county Norway 32 B3
Morerú r. Brazil 149 F2
Mores Sardinia Italy 45 B4
Moresby Island Canada 122 C4
Moreton Bay Australia 111 H5
Moreton Island Australia 111 H5
Moreuil France 39 E2
Moreyu r. Rus. Fed. 28 K1
Morez France 39 G3
Morfou Cyprus 77 A2
Morfou Bay Cyprus 77 A2
Morgam-Viibus hill Fin. 32 G1
Morgan Australia 112 A4
Morgan City U.S.A. 127 H6
Morgan Hill U.S.A. 136 B3
Morganton U.S.A. 128 C5
Morgantown KY U.S.A. 128 B4
Morgantown WV U.S.A. 130 D4
Morgenzon S. Africa 99 F5
Morges Switz. 39 G3
Morgex Italy 44 A2
Morhar r. India 75 E4
Mori China 70 H3
Mori Japan 64 E4
Moriah, Mount U.S.A. 137 E2
Moriarty U.S.A. 135 F6
Moriarty's Range hills Australia 111 F6
Moribaya Guinea 92 C3
Moricetown Canada 122 E4
Morichal Col. 146 D4
Moriki Nigeria 93 G2
Morin Dawa China see Nirji
Morine pass Bos.-Herz. 44 G3
Morioka Japan 65 E5
Moris Moz. 99 G3
Morjärv Sweden 32 F2
Morjen r. Pak. 81 E4
Morki Rus. Fed. 28 I4
Morlaix France 38 B2
Morley Canada 123 H5
Mormant France 39 E2
Mormon Lake U.S.A. 137 G4
Mormugao India see Marmagao
Morne Diablotins vol. Dominica 139 L5
Mornington, Isla i. Chile 153 B7
Mornington Abyssal Plain sea feature S. Atlantic Ocean 161 I9
Mornington Island Australia 110 D3
Mornos r. Greece 47 B5
Moro Pak. 81 F5
Moro U.S.A. 134 B3
Morobe P.N.G. 106 D2
▶Morocco country Africa 90 D3
africa 86–87, 100
Morogoro Tanz. 97 C6
Morogoro admin. reg. Tanz. 97 C7
Moro Gulf Phil. 57 F4
Morokweng S. Africa 98 D5
Morombe Madag. 99 [inset] I4
Moromoro Bol. 149 D4
Moron Arg. 152 E5
Mörön Mongolia 62 G2
Morona Ecuador 146 B5
Morona r. Peru 146 B6
Morona-Santiago prov. Ecuador 146 B5
Morondava Madag. 99 [inset] J4
Morón de la Frontera Spain 42 D4
Morondo Côte d'Ivoire 92 D3
▶Moroni Comoros 97 D7
Capital of the Comoros.
Moroni U.S.A. 137 G2
Moron Us He r. China 75 G2
Moros r. Spain 42 D2
Morotai i. Indon. 57 G5
Moroto Uganda 96 B4
Moroto, Mount Uganda 96 B4
Morozovsk Rus. Fed. 29 G6
Morpara Brazil 150 D4
Morpeth U.K. 34 F4
Morphou Cyprus see Morfou
Morrill U.S.A. 130 A5
Morrilton U.S.A. 133 C5
Morrin Canada 123 H5
Morrinhos Brazil 149 H4
Morris Canada 123 L5
Morris IL U.S.A. 132 D3
Morris MN U.S.A. 132 C2
Morris PA U.S.A. 131 E3
Morrisburg Canada 131 F1
▶Morris Jesup, Kap c. Greenland 121 P1
Most northerly point of North America.
Morristown AZ U.S.A. 137 F5
Morristown NJ U.S.A. 131 F3
Morristown NY U.S.A. 131 F1
Morristown TN U.S.A. 128 C4
Morrisville NY U.S.A. 131 F2
Morrisville VT U.S.A. 131 G1
Morro, Punta pt Chile 152 C1
Morro Bay U.S.A. 136 B4
Morro d'Anta Brazil 151 E6
Morro do Chapéu Brazil 150 D4
Morro do Sinal hills Brazil 149 G2
Morros Brazil 150 C2
Morrosquillo, Golfo de b. Col. 146 C2
Morrumbala Moz. 99 G3
Morrumbene Moz. 99 G4
Mors reg. Denmark 33 C4
Morse Canada 134 F2
Morse, Cape Antarctica 167 G2
Morshanka Rus. Fed. 29 G5
Morshansk Rus. Fed. see Morshanka
Morsi India 74 C5
Morsott Alg. 45 B7
Mørsvikbotn Norway 32 D2
Mort watercourse Australia 111 E4
Mortagne-au-Perche France 38 D2
Mortagne-sur-Sèvre France 38 C3
Mortain France 38 C2
Mortara Italy 44 B2
Morteau France 39 G3
Morteros Arg. 152 E2
Mortes, Rio das r. Brazil 150 B4
Mortimer's Bahamas 129 E8
Mortlach Canada 123 J5
Mortlake Australia 112 B5
Mortlock Islands Micronesia 164 E5
Mortlock Islands P.N.G. see Tauu Islands
Morton IL U.S.A. 132 D3
Morton TX U.S.A. 133 A5
Morton WA U.S.A. 134 B3
Morton National Park Australia 112 D4
Morundah Australia 112 C4
Moruya Australia 112 D4
Morven Australia 111 F5
Morven hill U.K. 34 E2
Morvern reg. U.K. 34 D3
Morvi India see Morbi
Morwell Australia 112 C5
Morzhovets, Ostrov i. Rus. Fed. 28 G2
Mosbach Germany 36 D4
Mosby U.S.A. 134 F3
Moscarter, Punta des pt Spain 43 G3
▶Moscow Rus. Fed. 28 F5
Capital of the Russian Federation and 3rd most populous city in Europe.
world 16–17
Moscow ID U.S.A. 134 C3
Moscow PA U.S.A. 131 F3
Moscow Oblast admin. div. Rus. Fed. see Moskovskaya Oblast'
Moscow University Ice Shelf Antarctica 167 G2
Mosel r. Germany 36 C3
Moselebe watercourse Botswana 98 D5
Moselle r. France 39 G2
Moses, Mount U.S.A. 136 D1
Moses Lake U.S.A. 134 C3
Mosgiel N.Z. 113 B4
Moshannon U.S.A. 130 D3
Moshchnyy, Ostrov i. Rus. Fed. 33 G4
Moshi r. Nigeria 93 G3
Moshi Tanz. 96 C5
Mosina Poland 37 H2
Mosi-oa-Tunya National Park Zimbabwe see Victoria Falls National Park
Mosjøen Norway 32 D2
Moskal'vo Rus. Fed. 27 O4
Moskenesøy i. Norway 32 D2
Moskenestraumen sea chan. Norway 32 D2
Moskkugáisi mt. Norway 32 F1
Moskosel Sweden 32 E2
Moskovskaya Oblast' admin. div. Rus. Fed. 31 N2
Moskva Rus. Fed. see Moscow
Moskva Tajik. 81 G2
Mosonmagyaróvár Hungary 37 H5
Mosor mts Croatia 44 F3
Mosquera Col. 146 B4
Mosquero U.S.A. 135 F6
Mosquito Creek Lake U.S.A. 130 C3
Mosquito Lake Canada 123 K2
Mosquitos, Costa de coastal area Nicaragua 139 H6
Moss Norway 33 C4
Mossaka Congo 94 C5
Mossâmedes Angola see Namibe
Mossburn N.Z. 113 B4
Mosselbaai S. Africa see Mossel Bay
Mossel Bay S. Africa 98 D7
Mossendjo Congo 94 B5
Mossgiel Australia 112 C4
Mossman Australia 111 F3
Mossoró Brazil 150 E3
Moss Vale Australia 112 D4
Mossy r. Canada 123 K4
Most Bulg. 46 D4
Most Czech Rep. 37 F3
Mostaganem Alg. 91 F2
Mostar Bos.-Herz. 44 F3
Mostardas Brazil 152 H2
Mosteni Romania 46 D2
Moștiștea r. Romania 46 E2
Móstoles Spain 42 E2
Mostoos Hills Canada 123 I4
Mostovskoy Rus. Fed. 29 G7
Mosty Belarus see Masty
Mosul Iraq 79 E3
Møsvatnet l. Norway 33 C4
Mot'a Eth. 96 C2
Motaba r. Congo 94 C4
Mota del Cuervo Spain 43 E3
Motala Sweden 33 D4
Mota Lava i. Vanuatu 107 F3
Motaze Moz. 99 G5
Motenge-Boma Dem. Rep. Congo 94 C4
Moth India 74 C4
Motherwell U.K. 34 E4
Motihari India 75 E4
Motilla hill Spain 42 D3
Motilla del Palancar Spain 43 F3
Motiti Island N.Z. 113 D2
Motloutse r. Botswana 99 F4
Motokwe Botswana 98 D5
Motovskiy Zaliv sea chan. Rus. Fed. 32 I1
Motril Spain 42 E4
Motru Romania 46 C2
Motru r. Romania 46 C2
Mott U.S.A. 132 A2
Motul Mex. 127 I7
Mouali Gbangba Congo 94 C4
Mouan, Nam r. Laos 60 D4
Mouaskar Alg. see Mascara
Mouchalagane r. Canada 125 G3
Mouchet, Mont mt. France 39 E4
Moudjéria Mauritania 92 B1
Moudon Switz. 39 G3
Moudros Greece 47 D5
Mouhijärvi Fin. 33 F3
Mouhoun r. Africa 92 E3 see Black Volta
Mouila Gabon 94 B5
Moul well Niger 93 I2
Moulamein Australia 112 C4
Moulamein Creek r. Australia 112 B4
Moulavibazar Bangl. see Moulvibazar
Moulèngui Binza Gabon 94 A5
Moulhoulé Djibouti 96 D1
Moulins France 39 E3
Moulle de Jaut, Pic du mt. France 38 C5
Moulmein Myanmar 61 B4
Moulmeingyun Myanmar 61 A4
Moulouya, Oued r. Morocco 90 E2
Moulton U.S.A. 129 B5
Moultrie U.S.A. 129 C6
Moultrie, Lake U.S.A. 129 D5
Moulvibazar Bangl. 75 F4
Mound City MO U.S.A. 132 C3
Mound City SD U.S.A. 132 A2
Moundou Chad 94 C2
Moundsville U.S.A. 130 C4
Mounta, Akra pt Greece 47 B5
Mount Abu India 74 B4
Mountain City U.S.A. 130 C5
Mountain Grove U.S.A. 132 C4
Mountain Home AR U.S.A. 133 C4
Mountain Home ID U.S.A. 134 D4
Mountain Home UT U.S.A. 137 G1
Mountain Lake Park U.S.A. 130 D4
Mountain Pass U.S.A. 137 E4
Mountain View AR U.S.A. 133 C5
Mountain View HI U.S.A. 135 [inset] Z2
Mount Airy MD U.S.A. 131 E4
Mount Airy NC U.S.A. 130 C5
Mount Aspiring National Park N.Z. 113 B4
Mount Augustus Australia 109 B6
Mount Ayr U.S.A. 132 C3
Mount Barker S.A. Australia 112 A4
Mount Barker W.A. Australia 109 E8
Mount Barnett Australia 108 D4
Mount Bellew Rep. of Ireland 35 B5
Mount Brydges Canada 130 C2
Mount Buffalo National Park Australia 112 C5
Mount Carmel IL U.S.A. 128 B4
Mount Carmel TN U.S.A. 130 B5
Mount Carmel Junction U.S.A. 137 F3
Mount Carroll U.S.A. 132 D3
Mount Clere Australia 109 B6
Mount Cook N.Z. 113 B3
Mount Cook National Park N.Z. 113 B3
Mount Coolon Australia 111 F4
Mount Darwin Zimbabwe 99 F3
Mount Denison Australia 110 C4
Mount Desert Island U.S.A. 128 F2
Mount Eba Australia 110 C6
Mount Eccles National Park Australia 112 B5
Mount Elgon National Park Kenya 96 B4
Mount Field National Park Australia 112 C6
Mount Fletcher S. Africa 99 F6
Mount Forest Canada 130 C2
Mount Frankland National Park Australia 109 B8
Mount Gambier Australia 112 B5
Mount Garnet Australia 111 F3
Mount Hagen P.N.G. 57 J7
Mount Holly U.S.A. 131 F4
Mount Holly Springs U.S.A. 131 E3
Mount Hope N.S.W. Australia 112 C4
Mount Hope S.A. Australia 109 F8
Mount Hope U.S.A. 130 C5
Mount House Australia 108 D4
Mount Ida U.S.A. 133 C5
Mount Isa Australia 111 D4
Mount Jackson U.S.A. 130 D4
Mount Jewett U.S.A. 130 D3
Mount Kaputar National Park Australia 112 D3
Mount Keith Australia 109 C6
Mount Kenya National Park Kenya 96 C5
Mount Lebanon U.S.A. 130 C3
Mount Lofty Range mts Australia 112 A4
Mount Magnet Australia 109 B7
Mount Manara Australia 112 B4
Mount McKinley National Park U.S.A. see Denali National Park and Preserve
Mount Meadows Reservoir U.S.A. 136 B1

Mount Molloy Australia 111 F3
Mount Moresby Canada 122 C4
Mount Morgan Australia 111 G4
Mount Morris U.S.A. 130 E2
Mount Nebo U.S.A. 130 C4
Mount Olivet U.S.A. 130 A4
Mount Orab U.S.A. 130 B4
Mount Pearl Canada 125 K4
Mount Pleasant Canada 125 H4
Mount Pleasant IA U.S.A. 132 D3
Mount Pleasant MI U.S.A. 130 A2
Mount Pleasant PA U.S.A. 130 D3
Mount Pleasant TX U.S.A. 133 C5
Mount Pleasant UT U.S.A. 137 G2
Mount Rainier National Park U.S.A. 134 B3
Mount Remarkable National Park Australia 112 A4
Mount Revelstoke National Park Canada 122 G5
Mount St Helens National Volcanic Monument nat. park U.S.A. 134 B3
Mount Sanford Australia 110 B3
Mount's Bay U.K. 35 D6
Mount Shasta U.S.A. 134 B4
Mount Sterling KY U.S.A. 130 B4
Mount Sterling OH U.S.A. 130 B4
Mount Storm U.S.A. 130 D4
Mount Surprise Australia 111 F3
Mount Vernon Australia 109 B6
Mount Vernon GA U.S.A. 129 C5
Mount Vernon IL U.S.A. 128 A4
Mount Vernon KY U.S.A. 130 A5
Mount Vernon MO U.S.A. 132 C4
Mount Vernon OH U.S.A. 130 B3
Mount Vernon TX U.S.A. 133 C5
Mount Vernon WA U.S.A. 134 B2
Mount Wedge Australia 110 C4
Mount William National Park Australia 112 D6
Mount Willoughby Australia 110 C5
Moura Australia 111 G5
Moura Brazil 147 F5
Moura Port. 42 C3
Mourão Port. 42 C3
Mouraya Chad 94 D2
Mourdi, Dépression du depr. Chad 88 D5
Mourdiah Mali 92 D2
Mourenx France 38 C5
Mourne Mountains hills U.K. 35 C4
Mourre de Chanier mt. France 39 G5
Mouscron Belgium 39 E1
Mousgougou Chad 94 C2
Moussafoyo Chad 94 C2
Moussoro Chad 88 C6
Mouth of Wilson U.S.A. 130 C5
Moûtiers France 39 G4
Moutong Indon. 57 F5
Mouydir, Monts du plat. Alg. 91 F4
Mouyondzi Congo 95 B5
Mouzaki Greece 47 B5
Mouzarak Chad 88 B6
Movila Miresii Romania 46 E2
Movileni Romania 46 D2
Mowbullan, Mount Australia 111 G5
Moxahala U.S.A. 130 B4
Moxey Town Bahamas 129 D7
Moxico prov. Angola 95 C8
Moy r. Rep. of Ireland 35 B4
Moyale Eth. 96 C4
Moyamba Sierra Leone 92 B3
Moyen Atlas mts Morocco 90 D2
Moyen-Chari pref. Chad 94 C2
Moyen Congo country Africa see Congo
Moyeni Lesotho 99 E6
Moyenne-Guinée admin. reg. Guinea 92 B3
Moyen-Ogooué prov. Gabon 94 A5
Moynaq Uzbek. see Muynak
Moyo i. Indon. 59 G5
Moyo Uganda 96 A4
Moyobamba Peru 146 B6
Moyowosi r. Tanz. 97 A6
Møysalen mt. Norway 32 D1
Moyum waterhole Kenya 96 C4
Moyynty Kazakh. 70 D2
▶Mozambique country Africa 99 G4
africa 86–87, 100
Mozambique Channel Africa 99 I4
Mozambique Ridge sea feature Indian Ocean 163 J7
Mozdok Rus. Fed. 29 H8
Mozdūrān Iran 81 E2
Mozelle U.S.A. 130 B5
Mozhga Rus. Fed. 28 J4
Mozhong China 66 A1
Mozo Myanmar 60 A3
Mozyr' Belarus see Mazyr
Mpal Senegal 92 A2
Mpanda Tanz. 97 A6
Mpandamatenga Botswana 98 E3
Mpé Congo 94 B5
Mpessoba Mali 92 D2
Mpigi Uganda 96 B4
Mpika Zambia 97 A7
Mpongwe Zambia 95 F8
Mporokoso Zambia 95 F7
Mpouya Congo 94 C5
Mpui Tanz. 97 A7
Mpulungu Zambia 97 A7
Mpumalanga prov. S. Africa 99 F5
Mpwapwa Tanz. 97 C6
Mqinvartsveri mt. Georgia/Rus. Fed. see Kazbek
Mrągowo Poland 37 J2
Mrewa Zimbabwe see Murehwa
Mrežnica r. Croatia 44 E2
Mrkonjić-Grad Bos.-Herz. 44 F2
Mrocza Poland 37 H2
Mroga r. Poland 37 I2
M'Saken Tunisia 45 C7
Msambweni Kenya 97 C6
Msata Tanz. 97 C6
M'Sila Alg. 91 G2
Msta r. Rus. Fed. 28 D4
Mstislavl' Belarus see Mstsislaw
Mstsislaw Belarus 31 L2
Mszana Dolna Poland 37 J4
Mtama Tanz. 97 C7
Mtelo Kenya 96 B4
Mtera Reservoir Tanz. 97 B6
Mtoko Zimbabwe see Mutoko
Mtorashanga Zimbabwe see Mutorashanga
Mtsensk Rus. Fed. 29 F5
Mts'khet'a Georgia 79 F2
Mtukula Tanz. 97 C7
Mtwara Tanz. 97 D7
Mtwara admin. reg. Tanz. 97 C7
Mu r. Myanmar 60 A3
Mu hill Port. 42 B4
Muaguide Moz. 97 C8
Mualama Moz. 99 H3
Muana Brazil 150 B2
Muanda Dem. Rep. Congo 95 B6
Muang Khammouan Laos 60 D4
Muang Không Laos 61 D5
Muang Khôngxédôn Laos 61 D5
Muang Luang r. Thai. 61 E6
Muang Pakbeng Laos 60 C4
Muang Pakxan Laos 60 C4
Muang Phin Laos 61 D4
Muang Phôn-Hông Laos 60 C4
Muang Sam Sip Thai. 61 D5
Muang Sing Laos 60 C3
Muang Thai country Asia see Thailand
Muang Vangviang Laos 60 C4
Muang Xaignabouri Laos 60 C4
Muanza Moz. 99 G3
Muar Malaysia 58 C2
Muar r. Malaysia 58 C2
Muara Brunei 59 F1
Muaraancalong Indon. 59 G2
Muaraatap Indon. 59 G2
Muarabeliti Indon. 58 C3
Muarabungo Indon. 58 C3
Muaradua Indon. 58 D4
Muaraenim Indon. 58 C3
Muarainu Indon. 59 F3
Muarakaman Indon. 59 G3
Muaralesan Indon. 59 G2
Muararupit Indon. 58 C3
Muarasoma Indon. 58 B2
Muaras Reef Indon. 59 G2
Muaratebo Indon. 58 C3
Muaratembesi Indon. 58 C3
Muarateweh Indon. 59 F3
Muarawahau Indon. 59 G2
Muari, Ras pt Pak. 81 F5
Mubārak, Jabal mt. Jordan/Saudi Arabia 77 B5
Mubarakpur India 75 D4
Mubarek Uzbek. 81 F2
Mubarraz well Saudi Arabia 89 I2
Mubende Uganda 96 A4
Mubi Nigeria 93 I3
Muborak Uzbek. see Mubarek
Mubur i. Indon. 58 D2
Mucaba Angola 95 B6
Mucajá Brazil 147 G5
Mucajaí r. Brazil 147 F4
Mucajaí, Serra do mts Brazil 147 F4
Mučanj mt. Yugo. 46 B3
Muchinga Escarpment Zambia 95 F8
Muchiri Bol. 149 E4
Muchuan China 66 B2
Muck i. U.K. 34 C3
Muco r. Col. 146 D3
Mucojo Moz. 97 D8
Muconda Angola 95 D7
Mucubela Moz. 99 H3
Mucuim r. Brazil 147 E6
Mucumbura Moz. 99 F3
Mucundi Angola 95 C9
Mucunha Angola 95 C8
Mucupia Moz. 99 H3
Mucur Turkey 78 C3
Mucura Brazil 147 F5
Mucuri Brazil 151 E6
Mucuri r. Brazil 151 E6
Mucuripe Brazil 146 D5
Mucussueje Angola 95 D7
Muda r. Malaysia 58 C1
Mudabidri India 72 B3
Mudanjiang China 64 B3
Mudan Jiang r. China 64 B3
Mudan Ling mts China 64 A4
Mudanya Turkey 78 B2
Mudayrah Kuwait 79 F5
Mudaysisāt, Jabal al hill Jordan 77 C4
Muddebihal India 72 C2
Muddus nationalpark nat. park Sweden 32 E2
Muddy r. U.S.A. 137 E3
Muddy Boggy Creek r. U.S.A. 133 C5
Muddy Creek r. U.S.A. 137 G2
Muddy Gap Pass U.S.A. 134 F4
Muddy Peak U.S.A. 137 E3
Mūd-e-Dahanāb Iran 81 D3
Mudgal India 72 C3
Mudgee Australia 112 D4
Mudhol India 72 B2
Mudigere India 72 B3
Mudjatik r. Canada 123 J3
Mudkhed India 72 C2
Mud Lake U.S.A. 136 D3
Mudon Myanmar 61 B4
Mudraya country Africa see Egypt
Mudug admin. reg. Somalia 96 E3
Mudukani Tanz. 97 B5
Mudumu National Park Namibia 98 D3
Mudurnu Turkey 78 B2
Mud'yuga Rus. Fed. 28 F3
Muecate Moz. 99 H2
Mueda Moz. 97 C7
Muela de Arés mt. Spain 43 F2
Mueller Range hills Australia 108 D4
Muende Moz. 97 B8
Muertos Cays is Bahamas 129 C7
Muftah well Sudan 89 G4
Muftyuga Rus. Fed. 28 H2
Mufulira Zambia 95 F8
Mufumbwe Zambia 95 E8
Mufu Shan mts China 67 E2
Muğan Düzü lowland Azer. 79 G3
Muge r. Port. 42 B3
Mugeba Moz. 99 H3
Mughalbhin Pak. see Jati
Mughal Sarai India 75 D4
Mūghār Iran 80 C3
Mughayrā' Saudi Arabia 89 H2
Mugila, Monts mts Dem. Rep. Congo 95 F6
Muğla Turkey 78 B3
Muğla prov. Turkey 47 F6
Mug Qu r. China 62 E5
Mugua Moz. 97 C8
Mugu Karnali r. Nepal 75 D3
Mugxung China 75 G2
Mūḩ, Sabkhat imp. l. Syria 77 D2
Muhagiriya Sudan 94 E2
Muhala China see Yutian
Muhala Dem. Rep. Congo 95 F6
Muḩammad, Ra's pt Egypt 89 G3
Muhammadabad India 75 D4
Muhammad Qol Sudan 89 H4
Muhammarah Iran see Khorramshahr
Muhashsham, Wādī al watercourse Egypt 77 B4
Muḩaysh, Wādī al watercourse Jordan 77 C5
Mühlacker Germany 36 D4
Mühlberg Germany 37 F3
Mühldorf am Inn Germany 37 F4
Mühlhausen (Thüringen) Germany 36 E3
Mühlig-Hofmann Mountains Antarctica 167 C2
Muhos Fin. 32 G2
Muḩradah Syria 77 C2
Muhu i. Estonia 33 F4
Muhula Moz. 97 C8
Muhulu Dem. Rep. Congo 94 E5
Mui Eth. 96 B3
Mui Bai Bung c. Vietnam see Mui Ca Mau
Mui Ca Mau c. Vietnam 61 D6
Mui Dinh hd Vietnam 61 E6
Mui Độc pt Vietnam 60 D4
Muidumbe Moz. 97 C7
Muineachán Rep. of Ireland see Monaghan
Muine Bheag Rep. of Ireland 35 C5
Muirkirk U.K. 34 D4
Mui Ron hd Vietnam 60 D4
Muisne Ecuador 146 B4
Muite Moz. 97 C8
Muju S. Korea 65 A5
Mujuí Joboti Brazil 147 H5
Mukačevo Ukr. see Mukacheve
Mukacheve Ukr. 31 J3
Mukachevo Ukr. see Mukacheve
Mukah Sarawak Malaysia 59 F2
Mukah r. Sarawak Malaysia 59 F2
Mukalla Yemen 76 D7
Mukandwara India 74 C4
Mukanga Dem. Rep. Congo 95 D6
Mukawwar, Gezirat i. Sudan 89 H4
Mukdahan Thai. 61 D4
Mukden China see Shenyang
Mukerian India 74 B3
Mukhen Rus. Fed. 64 D2
Mukhino Rus. Fed. 64 A1
Mukhtuya Rus. Fed. see Lensk
Mukinbudin Australia 109 B7
Mu Ko Chang National Park Thai. 61 C6
Mukomuko Indon. 58 C3
Mukono Uganda 96 B4
Mukoshi Zambia 95 F7
Mukry Turkm. 81 F2
Muktinath Nepal 75 D3
Muktsar India 74 B3
Mukuku Zambia 95 F8
Mukumbura Zimbabwe 99 F3
Mukunsa Zambia 95 F7
Mukur Kazakh. 29 J7
Mukutawa r. Canada 123 L4
Mul India 72 C1
Mula r. India 72 B2
Mula r. Pak. 81 F4
Mula Spain 43 F3
Mulakatholhu Atoll Maldives 71 D11
Mulaku atoll Maldives see Mulakatholhu Atoll
Mulan China 64 B3
Mulapula, Lake salt flat Australia 110 D6
Mula-tupo Panama 146 B2
Mulayh salt pan Saudi Arabia 77 D5
Mulayjah Saudi Arabia 80 B5
Mulayz, Wādī al watercourse Egypt 77 A4
Mulbagal India 72 C3
Mulbekh Jammu and Kashmir 74 C2
Mulchatna r. U.S.A. 120 D3
Mulchén Chile 152 B4
Mulde r. Germany 37 F3
Muleba Tanz. 96 A5
Mule Creek U.S.A. 134 F4
Mulegé Mex. 135 D8
Mulekatembo Zambia 97 B7
Muleshoe U.S.A. 135 G6
Mulevala Moz. 99 H3
Mulgathing Australia 109 F7
Mulhacén mt. Spain 42 E4
Mülhausen France see Mulhouse
Mulhouse France 39 G3
Muli China 66 B3
Muli Rus. Fed. see Vysokogorniy
Mulilansolo Zambia 97 B7
Muling Heilong. China 64 B3
Muling Heilong. China 64 B3
Muling r. China 64 C3
Mull i. U.K. 34 D3
Mulla Ali Iran 80 B2
Mullaaxe Beyle Somalia 96 E2
Mullaittivu Sri Lanka 72 D4
Muller, Pegunungan mts Indon. 59 F2
Mullett Lake U.S.A. 132 E2
Mullewa Australia 109 A7
Müllheim Germany 36 C5
Mullica r. U.S.A. 131 F4
Mulligan watercourse Australia 110 D5
Mullingar Rep. of Ireland 35 C5
Mull of Galloway c. U.K. 35 D4
Mull of Kintyre hd U.K. 34 D4
Mull of Oa hd U.K. 34 C4
Müllrose Germany 37 G2
Mullsjö Sweden 33 D4
Mulobezi Zambia 95 E9
Mulondo Angola 95 B8
Mulonga Plain Zambia 95 D9
Mulongo Dem. Rep. Congo 95 E6
Mulsanne France 38 D3
Mulshi Lake India 72 B2
Multai India 74 C5
Mūltān Iran 81 E5
Multan Pak. 81 G4
Multia Fin. 33 G3
Mulu, Gunung mt. Sarawak Malaysia 59 F1
Mulug India 72 C2
Mulumbe, Monts mts Dem. Rep. Congo 95 E7
Mulurulu Lake Australia 112 B4
Muma Dem. Rep. Congo 94 D4
Mūmān Iran 81 E5

▶Mumbai India 72 B2
2nd most populous city in Asia and 5th in the world.
world 16–17

Mumbeji Zambia 95 D8
Mumbondo Angola 95 B7
Mumbwa Zambia 95 E8
Mumbwi Tanz. 97 C6
Mume Dem. Rep. Congo 95 E7
Muminabad Tajik. see Leningrad
Mu'minobod Tajik. see Leningrad
Mumra Rus. Fed. 29 H7
Mun, Mae Nam r. Thai. 61 D5
Muna i. Indon. 57 F7
Muna Mex. 127 I7
Muna r. Rus. Fed. 27 M3
Munabao Pak. 81 G5
Munaðarnes Iceland 32 [inset]
Munagala India 72 C2
Munayshy Kazakh. 79 H2
Münchberg Germany 36 E3
München Germany see Munich
München-Gladbach Germany see Mönchengladbach
Munchique, Parque Nacional nat. park Col. 146 B4
Muncho Lake Canada 122 E3
Munch'ŏn N. Korea 65 A5
Muncie U.S.A. 132 E3
Muncoonie West, Lake salt flat Australia 110 D5
Muncy U.S.A. 131 E3
Munda Solomon Is 107 E2
Mundel Lake Sri Lanka 72 C5
Mundemba Cameroon 93 H4
Mundiwindi Australia 108 C5
Mundo r. Spain 43 F3
Mundo Novo Brazil 150 D4
Mundra India 74 A5
Mundrabilla Australia 109 D7
Munds Park U.S.A. 137 G4
Mundubbera Australia 111 G5
Mundwa India 74 B4
Muneru r. India 72 D2
Munfordville U.S.A. 128 B4
Mungallala Australia 111 F5
Mungallala Creek r. Australia 111 F6
Mungana Australia 111 F3
Mungaoli India 74 C4
Mungári Moz. 99 G3
Mungbere Dem. Rep. Congo 94 F4
Mungeli India 75 D5
Munger India 75 E4
Munger U.S.A. 130 B2
Mungeranie Australia 110 D6
Mu Nggava i. Solomon Is see Rennell
Mungguresak, Tanjung pt Indon. 59 E2
Mungindi Australia 112 D3
Mungo Angola 95 C7
Mungo National Park Australia 112 B4
Mun'gyŏng S. Korea 65 A5
Munhango Angola 95 C8
Munhino Angola 95 B8
Munich Germany 36 E4
Munising U.S.A. 132 E2
Munkács Ukr. see Mukacheve
Munkedal Sweden 33 C4
Munku-Sardyk, Gora mt. Mongolia/Rus. Fed. 62 G1
Munro, Mount Australia 112 D6
Munshiganj Bangl. 75 F5
Münsingen Switz. 39 G3
Münster Niedersachsen Germany 36 E2
Münster Nordrhein-Westfalen Germany 36 C3
Munster reg. Rep. of Ireland 35 B5
Münster-Osnabrück airport Germany 36 C2
Muntadgin Australia 109 B7
Muntele Mare, Vârful mt. Romania 46 C1
Munteni Romania 46 E2
Mununga Zambia 95 F7
Munyal-Par sea feature India see Bassas de Pedro Padua Bank
Munyati r. Zimbabwe 99 F3
Munzur Vadisi Milli Parkı nat. park Turkey 79 D3
Muodoslompolo Sweden 32 F2
Muojärvi l. Fin. 32 H2
Muonio Fin. 32 F2
Muonioälven r. Fin./Sweden 32 F2
Muonionjoki r. Fin./Sweden see Muonioälven
Mupa Angola 95 B9
Mupa, Parque Nacional da nat. park Angola 95 B8
Mupfure r. Zimbabwe 99 F3
Muqaddam watercourse Sudan 89 F5
Muqdisho Somalia see Mogadishu
Muqshin, Wādī r. Oman 76 E6
Muquem Brazil 150 B5
Muqui Brazil 151 D7
Muqyr Kazakh. see Mukur
Mur r. Austria 37 H5
Muradiye Manisa Turkey 47 E5
Muradiye Turkey 79 E3
Murai, Tanjong pt Sing. 58 [inset]
Murai Reservoir Sing. 58 [inset]
Murakami Japan 65 D5
Murallón, Cerro mt. Chile 153 B7
Muramvya Burundi 94 F5
Muráň r. Slovakia 37 J4
Muranga Kenya 96 C5
Muras Spain 42 C1
Murashi Rus. Fed. 28 I4
Murat France 39 E4
Murat r. Turkey 79 D3
Muratlı Turkey 78 A2
Murayr, Jabal hill Saudi Arabia 89 I3
Muraysah, Ra's al pt Libya 88 E2
Murça Port. 42 C2
Murcheh Khvort Iran 80 B3
Murchison Australia 112 C5
Murchison watercourse Australia 109 A6
Murchison, Mount Antarctica 167 H2
Murchison Falls Uganda 96 A4
Murchison Falls National Park Uganda 96 A4
Murcia Spain 43 F4
Murcia aut. comm. Spain 43 F4
Mûr-de-Bretagne France 38 B2
Murdo U.S.A. 132 A3
Murdochville Canada 125 H3
Mürefte Turkey 46 E4
Muregi Nigeria 93 G3
Murehwa Zimbabwe 99 F3
Mureş r. Romania 46 B1
Muret France 38 D5
Murewa Zimbabwe see Murehwa
Murfjället mt. Norway 32 D2
Murfreesboro NC U.S.A. 131 E5
Murfreesboro TN U.S.A. 128 B5
Murgab Tajik. see Murghob
Murgab r. Tajik. 81 H2
Murgab Turkm. see Murgap
Murgab r. Turkm. see Murgap
Murgap Turkm. 81 E2
Murgap r. Turkm. 81 E2
Murgeni Romania 46 F1
Murge Tarantine hills Italy 45 F4
Murghab r. Afgh. 81 E3
Murgha Kibzai Pak. 81 G4
Murghob Tajik. 81 H2
Murgh Pass Afgh. 81 G3
Murgon Australia 111 G5
Murgoo Australia 109 B6
Muri India 75 E5
Mūrī Iran 80 D2
Muria, Gunung mt. Indon. 59 E4
Muriaé Brazil 151 D7
Muriege Angola 95 D7
Müritz l. Germany 37 F2
Müritz, Nationalpark nat. park Germany 37 F2
Murjek Sweden 32 F2
Murkong Selek India 75 G4
Murmansk Rus. Fed. 32 I1
Murmanskaya Oblast' admin. div. Rus. Fed. 32 I1
Murmanskiy Bereg coastal area Rus. Fed. 28 E1
Murmansk Oblast admin. div. Rus. Fed. see Murmanskaya Oblast'
Murmashi Rus. Fed. 32 I1
Muro, Capo di c. Corsica France 44 B4
Muro Lucano Italy 45 E4
Murom Rus. Fed. 28 G5
Muroran Japan 64 E4
Muros Spain 42 B1
Muroto Japan 65 C6
Muroto-zaki pt Japan 65 C6
Murphy ID U.S.A. 134 C4
Murphy NC U.S.A. 128 C5
Murphys U.S.A. 136 B2
Murrah, Wādī watercourse Egypt 77 B5
Murra Murra Australia 111 F6

▶Murray r. S.A. Australia 112 A4
3rd longest river in Oceania. Part of the longest (Murray-Darling).
oceania 102–103

Murray r. W.A. Australia 109 A8
Murray r. Canada 122 F3
Murray U.S.A. 128 A4
Murray, Lake P.N.G. 57 J7
Murray, Lake U.S.A. 129 C5
Murray, Mount Canada 122 D2
Murray Bridge Australia 112 A4
Murray City U.S.A. 130 B4

▶Murray-Darling Australia 106 B5
Longest river in Oceania.
oceania 102–103

Murray Downs Australia 110 C4
Murray Range hills Australia 109 E6
Murraysburg S. Africa 98 D6
Murray Sunset National Park Australia 112 B4
Murree Pak. 81 H3
Murroa Moz. 99 H3

▶Murrumbidgee r. Australia 112 B4
4th longest river in Oceania.
oceania 102–103

Murrupula Moz. 99 H2
Murshidabad India 75 F4
Murska Sobota Slovenia 44 F1
Murtajapur India 72 C1
Murten Switz. 39 G3
Murter Croatia 44 E3
Murter i. Croatia 44 E3
Murtoa Australia 112 B5
Murtovaara Fin. 32 H2
Muru r. Brazil 148 C2
Murua i. P.N.G. see Woodlark Island
Murud India 72 B2
Murud, Gunung mt. Indon. 59 F2
Murui r. Indon. 59 F3
Murung r. Indon. 59 F3
Murung r. Indon. 59 F3
Murupara N.Z. 113 D2
Mururoa atoll Fr. Polynesia 165 I7
Murviedro Spain see Sagunto
Murwara India 74 D5
Murygino Rus. Fed. 28 I4
Mürz r. Austria 37 G5
Murzechirla Turkm. 81 E2
Murzūq Libya 88 B3
Mürzzuschlag Austria 37 G5
Muş Turkey 79 E3
Musa Dem. Rep. Congo 94 C4
Mūša r. Latvia/Lith. 33 G4
Mūsa r. Latvia/Lith. 33 G4
Mûsa, Gebel mt. Egypt see Sinai, Mount
Mūsá, Jabal mt. Egypt see Sinai, Mount
Mūsā, Khowr-e b. Iran 80 B4
Musa Āli Terara vol. Africa 89 I6
Musabani India 75 E5
Muşabih Saudi Arabia 89 I5
Musa Khel Bazar Pak. 81 G4
Musala mt. Bulg. 46 C3
Musala i. Indon. 58 B2
Musan N. Korea 64 B4
Musandam admin. reg. Oman 80 D5
Musandam Peninsula Oman/U.A.E. 80 D5
Musa Qala, Rūd-i r. Afgh. 81 F3
Musay'īd Qatar see Umm Sa'id
Musbat well Sudan 88 E6

▶Muscat Oman 76 F5
Capital of Oman.

Muscat and Oman country Asia see Oman
Muscatine U.S.A. 132 D3
Muscongus Bay U.S.A. 131 I2
Musgrave Australia 111 E2
Musgrave Harbour Canada 125 K3
Musgrave Ranges mts Australia 110 B5
Mūshakī Afgh. 81 G3
Mushash al Kabid well Jordan 77 C5
Mushash Dabl well Saudi Arabia 77 C5
Mushāsh Muḍayyān well Saudi Arabia 77 D5
Mushayyish, Wādī al watercourse Jordan 77 C4
Mushenge Dem. Rep. Congo 95 D6
Mushie Dem. Rep. Congo 94 C5
Mushin Nigeria 93 F4
Musi r. India 72 C2
Musi r. Indon. 58 D3
Musica mt. Macedonia 46 B4
Music Mountain U.S.A. 137 F4
Musikot Nepal 75 D3
Musinia Peak U.S.A. 137 G2
Muskeg r. Canada 122 F2
Muskeget Channel U.S.A. 131 H3
Muskegon U.S.A. 132 E3
Muskegon r. U.S.A. 132 E3
Muskeg River Canada 122 G4
Muskingum r. U.S.A. 130 C4
Muskogee U.S.A. 133 C5
Muskoka, Lake Canada 124 E4
Muskrat Dam Lake Canada 124 B2
Muskwa r. Canada 122 F3
Muslimbagh Pak. 81 F4
Muslim-Croat Federation aut. div. Bos.-Herz. see Federacija Bosna i Hercegovina
Musoma Tanz. 96 B5
Musombe Tanz. 97 B6
Musquanousse, Lac l. Canada 125 I3
Musquaro Canada 125 I3
Musquaro, Lac l. Canada 125 I3
Mussau Island P.N.G. 106 D2
Musselburgh U.K. 34 E4
Musselshell r. U.S.A. 134 F3
Mussende Angola 95 C8
Musserra Angola 95 B6
Mussidan France 38 D4
Mussolo Angola 95 C7
Mussoorie India 74 C3
Mussuma Angola 95 D8
Mussuma r. Angola 95 D8
Mustafabad India 75 D4
Mustafakemalpaşa Turkey 78 B2
Mustahīl Eth. 96 E3
Mustang Draw watercourse U.S.A. 133 A6
Musters, Lago l. Arg. 153 C6
Mustique i. St Vincent 147 F1
Mustjala Estonia 28 B4
Mustjõgi r. Estonia 33 G4
Mustla Estonia 33 G4
Mustvee Estonia 28 C4
Musu-dan pt N. Korea 65 B4
Muswellbrook Australia 112 D4
Mūţ Egypt 89 F3
Mut Turkey 78 C3
Mutá, Ponta do pt Brazil 150 E5
Mutanda Zambia 95 E8
Mutare Zimbabwe 99 G3
Mutina Italy see Modena
Mutis Col. 146 B3
Mutis, Gunung mt. Indon. 108 D2
Mutnyy Materik Rus. Fed. 28 J2
Mutoko Zimbabwe 99 G3
Mutombo Dem. Rep. Congo 95 D6
Mutooroo Australia 112 B4
Mutorashanga Zimbabwe 99 F3
Mutsamudu Comoros 97 E8
Mutshatsha Dem. Rep. Congo 95 E7
Mutsu Japan 64 E4
Mutsu-wan b. Japan 64 E4
Muttaburra Australia 111 F4
Muttonbird Islands N.Z. 113 A4
Mutuali Moz. 99 H2
Mutum r. Brazil 146 D6
Mutum Biyu Nigeria 93 H3
Mutungu-Tari Dem. Rep. Congo 95 C6
Mutur Sri Lanka 72 D4
Muuga Estonia 33 G4
Muurame Fin. 33 G3
Muurola Fin. 32 G2
Mu Us Shamo des. China 63 H4
Muxaluando Angola 95 B7
Muxi China see Muchuan
Muxima Angola 95 B7
Muyezerskiy Rus. Fed. 28 E3
Muyinga Burundi 96 A5
Muynak Uzbek. 76 F1
Muynoq Uzbek. see Muynak
Muyombe Zambia 97 B7
Muyuka Cameroon 93 H4
Muyumba Dem. Rep. Congo 95 E6
Muyunkum, Peski des. Kazakh. 70 C3
Muyuping China 67 D2
Muzaffarabad Pak. 81 H3
Muzaffargarh Pak. 81 G4
Muzaffarnagar India 74 C3
Muzaffarpur India 75 E4
Muzamane Moz. 99 G4
Muze Moz. 97 A8
Muzillac France 38 B3
Mūzīn Iran 81 E5
Muzon, Cape U.S.A. 122 C4
Múzquiz Mex. 133 A7
Muztag mt. Xinjiang China 70 F4
Muztag mt. Xinjiang China 70 G4
Mvadi Gabon 94 B4
Mvolo Sudan 94 F3
Mvomero Tanz. 97 C6
Mvoung r. Gabon 94 B4
Mvouti Congo 95 B6
Mvuma Zimbabwe 99 F3
Mwali i. Comoros 97 D8
Mwanisenga Tanz. 97 B6
Mwanya Zambia 97 B8
Mwanza Malawi 97 B8
Mwanza Tanz. 96 B5
Mwanza admin. reg. Tanz. 96 B5
Mwape Zambia 97 A8
Mweho Dem. Rep. Congo 95 E6
Mweka Dem. Rep. Congo 95 D6
Mwenda Zambia 95 F7
Mwene-Biji Dem. Rep. Congo 95 D7
Mwene-Ditu Dem. Rep. Congo 95 D6
Mwenezi Zimbabwe 99 F4
Mwenezi r. Zimbabwe 99 F4
Mwenga Dem. Rep. Congo 94 F5
Mwereni Kenya 97 C6
Mweru, Lake Dem. Rep. Congo/Zambia 95 F7
Mweru Plateau Tanz. 97 C7
Mweru Wantipa, Lake Zambia 95 F7
Mweru Wantipa National Park Zambia 95 F7
Mwimba Dem. Rep. Congo 95 D7
Mwingi Kenya 96 C5
Mwinilunga Zambia 95 E7
Mya, Oued watercourse Alg. 91 G3
Myaing Myanmar 60 A3
Myajlar India 74 A4
Myakit Rus. Fed. 27 P3
Myall Lakes National Park Australia 112 E4
Myanaung Myanmar 60 A4
▶Myanmar country Asia 60 A3
asia 52–53, 82
Myaundzha Rus. Fed. 27 O3
Myaungmya Myanmar 61 A4
Mycenae tourist site Greece 47 C6
Myeik Myanmar see Mergui
Myers U.S.A. 130 B4
Myingyan Myanmar 60 A3
Myinmoletkat mt. Myanmar 61 B5
Myinmu Myanmar 60 A3
Myitkyina Myanmar 60 B2
Myitson Myanmar 60 B3
Myitta Myanmar 61 B5
Myittha Myanmar 60 B3
Myittha r. Myanmar 75 G5
Myjava Slovakia 37 H4
Mykines i. Faroe Is 34 [inset]
Mykines tourist site Greece see Mycenae
Mykolayiv Ukr. 29 E7
Mykonos Greece 47 D6
Mykonos i. Greece 47 D6
Myla Rus. Fed. 28 I2
Mylae Sicily Italy see Milazzo
Mylasa Turkey see Milas
Mymensing Bangl. see Mymensingh
Mymensingh Bangl. 75 F4
Mynämäki Fin. 33 F3
Myohaung Myanmar 60 A3
Myŏnggan N. Korea 64 B4
Myory Belarus 28 C5
Myotha Myanmar 60 A3
Mýrdalsjökull ice cap Iceland 32 [inset]
Myre Norway 32 D1
Myrheden Sweden 32 F2
Myrhorod Ukr. 29 E6
Myrina Greece 47 D5
Myrnam Canada 123 I4
Myrnopillya Ukr. 46 F1
Myronivka Ukr. 29 D6
Myrtle Beach U.S.A. 129 D5
Myrtle Creek U.S.A. 134 B4
Myrtleford Australia 112 C5
Myrzakent Kazakh. 81 G1
Mysen Norway 33 C4
Mys Lazareva Rus. Fed. see Lazarev
Myślenice Poland 37 I4
Myślibórz Poland 37 G2
My Son tourist site Vietnam 61 E5
Mysore India 72 C3
Mysore state India see Karnataka
Mysovsk Rus. Fed. see Babushkin
Mys Shmidta Rus. Fed. 27 S3
Myszków Poland 37 I3
Myszyniec Poland 37 J2
Myt Rus. Fed. 28 G4
My Tho Vietnam 61 D6
Mytilene i. Greece see Lesbos
Mytilini Greece 47 E5
Mytilinioi Greece 47 E6
Mytilini Strait Greece/Turkey 47 E5
Mytishchi Rus. Fed. 28 F5
Myton U.S.A. 137 H1
Mývatn l. Iceland 32 [inset]
M'Zab Valley tourist site Alg. 91 F2
Mzamomhle S. Africa 99 E6
Mže r. Czech Rep. 37 F4
Mziha Tanz. 97 C6
Mzingwani r. Zimbabwe 99 F4
Mzuzu Malawi 97 B7

↓ N

Na, Nam r. China/Vietnam 66 B4
Naab r. Germany 36 F4
Naalehu U.S.A. 135 [inset] Z2
Naam Sudan 94 F2
Naama Alg. 91 E2
Naantali Fin. 33 F3
Naas Rep. of Ireland 35 C5
Näätämö Fin. 32 H1
Naba Myanmar 60 B2
Nabadwip India see Navadwip
Nabão r. Port. 42 B3
Nabarangapur India 73 D2
Nabatîyet et Tahta Lebanon 77 B3
Nabberu, Lake salt flat Australia 109 C6
Naberera Tanz. 97 C6
Naberezhnyye Chelny Rus. Fed. 28 J5
Nabesna U.S.A. 122 A2
Nabeul Tunisia 91 H1
Nabha India 74 C3
Nabileque r. Brazil 149 F5
Nabinagar India 75 E4
Nabire Indon. 57 I6
Nabi Younés, Ras en pt Lebanon 77 B3
Nablus West Bank see Nābulus
Nabolo Ghana 93 E3
Naboomspruit S. Africa 99 F5
Nabra r. India 74 C2
Nābulus West Bank 77 B3
Nacala Moz. 99 I2
Nacaome Hond. 138 G6
Nacaroa Moz. 97 C8
Nacebe Bol. 148 D2
Nachingwea Tanz. 97 C7
Nachna India 74 A4
Náchod Czech Rep. 37 H3
Nachuge India 73 G4
Nacimiento Chile 152 B4
Nacimiento Reservoir U.S.A. 136 B4
Nacogdoches U.S.A. 133 C6
Nacozari de García Mex. 135 E7
Nada China see Danzhou

Nadaleen r. Canada 122 C2
Nådendal Fin. see Naantali
Nadi Fiji 107 G3
Nadiad India 74 B5
Nădlac Romania 46 B1
Nador Morocco 90 E2
Nădrag Romania 46 C2
Nadúshan Iran 80 C3
Nadvirna Ukr. 29 C6
Nadvornaya Ukr. see Nadvirna
Nadym Rus. Fed. 26 H3
Naenwa India 74 B4
Næstved Denmark 33 C5
Naf r. Bangl./Myanmar 75 G5
Nafas, Ra's an mt. Egypt 77 B5
Nafḥa, Har hill Israel 77 B4
Nafpaktos Greece 47 B5
Nafplio Greece 47 C6
Naft r. Iran see Âb Naft
Naft-e Safid Iran see Naft Shahr
Naft-e Shāh Iran see Naft Shahr
Naft Shahr Iran 80 A3
Nafūd ad Daḥl des. Saudi Arabia 76 D5
Nafūd al 'Urayq des. Saudi Arabia 89 I3
Nafūd as Surrah des. Saudi Arabia 89 I4
Nafūsah, Jabal hills Libya 88 A2
Nafy Saudi Arabia 89 I3
Nag, Co l. China 75 F2
Naga Phil. 57 F3
Nagagami r. Canada 124 C3
Nagagami Lake Canada 124 C3
Naga Hills India 75 G4
Naga Hills state India see Nagaland
Nagaland state India 75 G4
Nagaoka Japan 65 D5
Nagaon India 75 G4
Nagapatnam India see Nagappattinam
Nagappattinam India 72 C4
Nagar r. Bangl./India 75 F4
Nagar Himachal Pradesh India 74 C2
Nagar Rajasthan India 74 C4
Nagaram India 72 C2
Nagarjuna Sagar Reservoir India 72 C2
Nagarzê China 75 F3
Nagasaki Japan 65 B6
Nagato Japan 65 B6
Nagaur India 74 B4
Nagavali r. India 72 D2
Nagda India 74 B5
Nagercoil India 72 C4
Nagha Kalat Pak. 81 F5
Nagina India 74 C3
Nagineh Iran 80 D3
Nagma Nepal 75 E3
Nagod India 74 D4
Nagold Germany 36 D4
Nagong Chu r. China see Parlung Zangbo
Nagorno-Karabakh aut. reg. Azer. see Dağlıq Qarabağ
Nagornyy Rus. Fed. 27 M4
Nagornyy Karabakh aut. reg. Azer. see Dağlıq Qarabağ
Nagorsk Rus. Fed. 28 I4
Nagoya Japan 65 D5
Nagpur India 74 C5
Nagqu China 75 G3
Nag Qu r. China 75 J3
Nagu Fin. 33 F3
Nagurskoye Rus. Fed. 26 E1
Nagyatád Hungary 44 F1
Nagybecskerek Yugo. see Zrenjanin
Nagyenyed Romania see Aiud
Nagyhalász Hungary 37 J4
Nagykanizsa Hungary 44 F1
Nagykáta Hungary 37 I4
Nagykörös Hungary 37 I5
Nagyvárad Romania see Oradea
Naha Japan 63 L6
Nahan India 74 C3
Nahang r. Iran/Pak. 81 E5
Nahanni Butte Canada 122 F2
Nahanni National Park Canada 122 E2
Nahanni Range mts Canada 122 F2
Nahariyya Israel 77 B3
Nahâvand Iran 80 B3
N'Ahnet, Adrar mts Alg. 91 F4
Nahr Ouassel, Oued watercourse Alg. 43 H5
Nahuel Huapi, Parque Nacional nat. park Arg. 152 C5
Nahuel Mapá Arg. 152 D3
Nahunta U.S.A. 133 D6
Naica Mex. 135 F8
Naidor well Tanz. 97 C6
Naikliu Indon. 108 C2
Nailung China 75 G3
Na'ima Sudan 89 G3
Nain Canada 125 I1
Nā'īn Iran 80 C3
Naina India 75 D4
Naini Tal India 74 C3
Nainpur India 74 D5
Naiopué Moz. 99 H3
Nairn U.K. 34 E3

▶Nairobi Kenya 96 C5
Capital of Kenya.

Naissaar i. Estonia 33 G4
Naissus Yugo. see Niš
Naivasha Kenya 96 C5
Najafābād Iran 80 B3
Najd reg. Saudi Arabia 76 C4
Nájera Spain 43 E1
Najibabad India 74 C3
Najin N. Korea 64 B4
Najmah Saudi Arabia 80 B5
Najrān Saudi Arabia 76 C6
Nakalele Point U.S.A. 135 [inset] Z1
Nakambé watercourse Burkina/Ghana 93 E3 see White Volta
Nakamura Japan 65 C6
Nakano Rus. Fed. 27 K3
Nakano-shima i. Japan 65 B7
Nakapanya Tanz. 97 C7
Nakasongola Uganda 96 B4
Nakatsu Japan 65 C6
Nakatsugawa Japan 65 D6
Nakfa Eritrea 89 H5
Nakhichevan' Azer. see Naxçıvan
Nakhl Egypt 89 G3
Nakhl-e Taqi Iran 80 D5
Nakhodka Rus. Fed. 64 C4
Nakhon India 75 G4
Nakhon Nayok Thai. 61 C5
Nakhon Pathom Thai. 61 C5
Nakhon Phanom Thai. 60 D3
Nakhon Ratchasima Thai. 61 C5
Nakhon Sawan Tha. 61 C4
Nakhon Si Thammarat Thai. 61 B6
Nakhtarana India 74 A5
Nakło nad Notecią Poland 37 H2
Naknek U.S.A. 120 C4
Nakodar India 74 B3
Nakonde Zambia 97 B7
Nakskov Denmark 33 C5
Näkten l. Sweden 32 D3
Nakuru Kenya 96 C5
Nakusp Canada 134 C2
Nalázi Moz. 99 G5
Nalbari India 75 G4
Naldurg India 72 C2

Nałęczów Poland 37 K3
Nalerigu Ghana 93 E3
Nalgonda India 72 C2
Nalhati India 75 E4
Nallamala Hills India 72 C3
Nallıhan Turkey 78 B2
Nalolo Zambia 95 D8
Nalón r. Spain 38 A5
Nālūt Libya 88 A2
Namaacha Moz. 99 G5
Namacunde Angola 95 B9
Namacurra Moz. 99 H3
Namadgi National Park Australia 112 D4
Namahadi S. Africa 99 F5
Namak, Daryácheh-ye salt l. Iran 80 B3
Namak-e Mīqhän, Kavir-e salt flat Iran 80 B3
Nāmaki watercourse Iran 80 C4
Namakkal India 72 C4
Namakzar-e Shadad salt flat Iran 80 D4
Namanga Kenya 96 C5
Namangan Uzbek. 70 D3
Namapa Moz. 97 C8
Namaponda Moz. 99 H2
Namaqua National Park S. Africa 98 C6
Namarrói Moz. 99 H2
Namasale Uganda 96 B4
Namatanai P.N.G. 107 E2
Namba Angola 95 B7
Nambour Australia 111 H5
Nambucca Heads Australia 112 E3
Nambung National Park Australia 109 A7
Năm Căn Vietnam 61 D6
Namcha Barwa mt. China see Namjagbarwa Feng
Namch'ŏn N. Korea 65 A5
Namco China 75 F3
Nam Co salt l. China 70 H5
Namdalen valley Norway 32 D2
Namdalseid Norway 32 C2
Nam Đinh Vietnam 60 D2
Namen Belgium see Namur
Náměstovo Slovakia 37 I4
Nametil Moz. 99 H2
Namew Lake Canada 123 K4
Nam-gang r. N. Korea 65 A5
Namhkam Myanmar 60 B3
Namhsan Myanmar 60 B3
Namialo Moz. 99 H2
Namib Desert Namibia 98 B5
africa 86–87
Namibe Angola 95 B8
Namibe prov. Angola 95 B8
Namibia country Africa 98 B4
africa 86–87, 100
Namib-Naukluft Game Park nature res. Namibia 98 B5
Namichiga Tanz. 97 C7
Namicunde Moz. 97 C7
Namidobe Moz. 99 H3
Namin Iran 80 B2
Namina Moz. 99 H2
Namitete Malawi 97 B8
Namjagbarwa Feng mt. China 62 E4
Namka China see Doilungdêqên
Namlan Myanmar 60 B3
Namlang r. Myanmar 60 B3
Namlea Indon. 57 G6
Namling China 75 F3
Nam Nao National Park Thai. 60 C4
Namoi r. Australia 112 D3
Nampa Canada 123 G3
Nampa mt. Nepal 74 D3
Nampa U.S.A. 134 C4
Nampala Mali 92 D2
Namp'o N. Korea 65 A5
Nampuecha Moz. 97 D8
Nampula Moz. 99 H2
Nampula prov. Moz. 99 H2
Nam Pung Reservoir Thai. 60 C4
Namrup India 75 G4
Namsai Myanmar 60 B3
Namsang Myanmar 60 B3
Namsos Norway 32 C2
Namsskogan Norway 32 D2
Namtari Nigeria 93 I3
Namtok Myanmar 60 B4
Nam Tok Thai. 61 B5
Namtok Chattakan National Park Thai. 60 C4
Namtok Mae Surin National Park Thai. 60 B4
Namton Myanmar 60 B3
Namtsy Rus. Fed. 27 M3
Namtu Myanmar 60 B3
Namu Canada 122 E5
Namuli, Monte mt. Moz. 99 H2
Namuno Moz. 97 C8
Namur Belgium 39 F1
Namutoni Namibia 99 B5
Namwala Zambia 95 D8
Namwera Malawi 97 B8
Namwŏn S. Korea 65 A6
Namya Ra Myanmar 60 B2
Namyit Island S. China Sea 56 D3
Namysłów Poland 37 H3
Nan Thai. 60 C3
Nan, Mae Nam r. Thai. 60 C5
Nana r. Cent. Afr. Rep. 94 B3
Nana Bakassa Cent. Afr. Rep. 94 B3
Nana Barya r. Cent. Afr. Rep./Chad 94 B3
Nana-Grébizi pref. Cent. Afr. Rep. 94 C3
Nanaimo Canada 134 B3
Nana-Mambéré pref. Cent. Afr. Rep. 94 B3
Nan'an China 67 H3
Nanango Australia 111 H5
Nananib Plateau Namibia 98 C5
Nan'ao China see Dayu
Nanao Japan 65 D5
Nanatsu-shima i. Japan 65 D5
Nanay r. Peru 146 C5
Nanbai China see Zunyi
Nanbin China see Shizhu
Nanbu China 66 C2
Nancha China 64 C3
Nanchang Jiangxi China 67 G3
Nanchang Jiangxi China 67 G2
Nancheng China 67 H3
Nanchong China 66 C2
Nanchuan China 66 C2
Nanchuan China see Nanchuan
Nanci China see Nanchang
Nanco India 74 B4
Nanda Devi mt. India 74 D3
Nanda Kot mt. India 74 D3
Nandan China 66 C3
Nander India see Nanded
Nandewar Range mts Australia 112 D3
Nandgaon India 72 B1
Nandikotkur India 72 C3
Nanding He r. China 66 B4
Nandod India 74 B5
Nandu Jiang r. China 67 D4
Nandurbar India 74 B5
Nandyal India 72 C3
Nanfeng Guangdong China 67 D4
Nanfeng Jiangxi China 67 F3

Nang China 75 G3
Nangade Moz. 97 C7
Nanga Eboko Cameroon 93 I4
Nangah Dedai Indon. 59 E3
Nangahembaloh Indon. 59 E2
Nangahpinoh Indon. 59 E3
Nangahkemangai Indon. 59 F3
Nangahtempuai Indon. 59 F2
Nangalala Australia 110 C2
Nanganga Tanz. 97 C7
Nangar Shan mts China 64 B4
▶Nanga Parbat mt. Jammu and Kashmir 74 B2
9th highest mountain in the world and in Asia.
asia 50–51
world 6–7
Nangarhār prov. Afgh. 81 G3
Nangatayap Indon. 59 E3
Nangbéto, Retenue de resr Togo 93 E4
Nangin Myanmar 61 B6
Nangis France 38 E2
Nangqên China 66 A1
Nangulangwa Tanz. 97 C7
Nanguneri India 72 C4
Nanhua China 66 B3
Nanhui China 67 G2
Nani Afgh. 81 G3
Nanisivik Canada 121 K2
Nanjian China 66 B3
Nanjiang China 66 C1
Nanjie China see Guangning
Nanjing China 67 F1
Nanji Shan i. China 67 G3
Nanka Jiang r. China 66 B4
Nankang Jiangxi China 67 E3
Nankang Jiangxi China see Xingzi
Nanking China see Nanjing
Nankoku Japan 65 C6
Nankova Angola 95 C9
Nanlan He r. China 66 A4
Nanling China 67 F2
Nan Ling mts China 67 D3
Nanliu Jiang r. China 67 D4
Nanlong China see Nanbu
Nanmulingzue China see Namling
Nannine Australia 109 B6
Nanning China 67 D4
Nannup Australia 109 A8
Nanortalik Greenland 121 O3
Nanpan Jiang r. China 66 C3
Nanpara India 75 D4
Nanping Fujian China 67 F3
Nanping Sichuan China 66 C1
Nanpu China see Pucheng
Nanpu Xi r. China 67 F3
Nanqiao China see Fengxian
Nanri Dao i. China 67 F3
Nansa r. Spain 42 D1
Nansebo Eth. 96 C3
Nansei-shotō Japan see Ryukyu Islands
Nansen Basin sea feature Arctic Ocean 166 H1
Nansenga Zambia 95 E8
Nansen Land Greenland 121 O1
Nansen Sound sea chan. Canada 121 J1
Nanshan Island S. China Sea 56 E3
Nansha Qundao is S. China Sea see Spratly Islands
Nansio Tanz. 96 B5
Nantais, Lac l. Canada 125 H3
Nantes France 38 D3
Nantes à Brest, Canal de France 38 B3
Nanthi Kadal lag. Sri Lanka 72 C4
Nantiat France 38 D3
Nanticoke Canada 130 C2
Nanticoke MD U.S.A. 131 F4
Nanticoke PA U.S.A. 131 E3
Nanticoke r. U.S.A. 131 F4
Nanton Canada 123 H5
Nantong China 67 H1
Nantou China 67 [inset]
Nant'ou Taiwan 67 G4
Nantucket U.S.A. 131 H3
Nantucket Island U.S.A. 131 I3
Nantucket Sound g. U.S.A. 131 H3
Nantulo Moz. 97 C8
Nanumanga i. Tuvalu see Nanumanga
Nanumanga i. Tuvalu 107 G2
Nanumea i. Tuvalu 107 G2
Nanuque Brazil 151 D6
Nanusa, Kepulauan is Indon. 57 G5
Nanutarra Roadhouse Australia 108 A5
Nanxi China 66 C2
Nanxian China 67 E2
Nanxiong China 67 F3
Nanyang China 67 F1
Nanyang China see Zhao'an
Nanzhang China 67 F1
Nanzhou China see Nanxian
Naogaon Bangl. 75 F4
Naokot Pak. 81 G5
Naoli r. China 64 C3
Naousa Greece 46 C4
Napa U.S.A. 134 A2
Napaktulik Lake Canada 123 H1
Napanee Canada 131 E1
Napasar India 74 B4
Napasoq Greenland 121 N3
Naperville U.S.A. 132 D3
Napier N.Z. 113 F4
Napier Peninsula Australia 110 C2
Napier Range hills Australia 108 D4
Naples Italy 45 E4
Naples FL U.S.A. 129 C7
Naples ME U.S.A. 131 H2
Naples NY U.S.A. 131 E2
Naples UT U.S.A. 137 H1
Napo prov. Ecuador 146 C4
Napo r. Ecuador 146 D4
Napoleon ND U.S.A. 132 B2
Napoleon OH U.S.A. 130 A3
Napoli Italy see Naples
Napoli, Golfo di b. Italy 45 E4
Napoopoo U.S.A. 135 [inset]
Naqb Mälihah mt. Egypt 77 A5
Nara Japan 65 C6
Nara Mali 92 D3
Narach Belarus 33 G5
Narach, Vozyera l. Belarus 33 G5
Naracoorte Australia 112 B5
Naradhan Australia 112 C4
Naraini India 74 B4
Naranjal Ecuador 146 B5
Naranjal Peru 146 C5
Naraq Iran 80 B3
Narasannapeta India 73 E2
Narasapatnam, Point India 73 E2
Narasaraopet India 73 D2
Narathiwat Thai. 61 C7
Narayanganj Bangl. 75 F5
Narayanganj India 74 D5
Narayangaon India 72 B2
Narayanpet India 72 C2
Naray Kelay Afgh. 81 G3

Narbada r. India see Narmada
Narbo France see Narbonne
Narbonne France 39 E5
Narbuvoll Norway 33 A5
Narcea r. Spain 42 C1
Narcondam Island India 73 G3
Nardin Iran 80 C2
Nardò Italy 45 G4
Narechi r. Pak. 81 G4
Narembeen Australia 109 B8
Nares Abyssal Plain sea feature S. Atlantic Ocean 160 J4
Nares Deep sea feature N. Atlantic Ocean 160 J4
Nares Strait Canada/Greenland 121 J2
Naretha Australia 109 D7
Narew r. Poland 37 J2
Nari r. Pak. 81 G4
Narib Bangl. 75 F5
Narib Namibia 98 C5
Narie, Jezioro l. Poland 37 J2
Narin Afgh. 81 G2
Narince Turkey 79 D3
Narin Gol watercourse China 75 G1
Nariño dept Col. 146 B3
Narizon, Punta pt Mex. 135 E8
Narken Sweden 32 F2
Narmada r. India 74 B5
Narnaul India 74 C3
Narni Italy 44 D3
Narnia Italy see Narni
Narodnaya, Gora mt. Rus. Fed. 28 L2
Naro-Fominsk Rus. Fed. 28 F5
Narok Kenya 96 C5
Narona Belarus 33 G5
Narrabri Australia 112 D3
Narragansett Bay U.S.A. 131 H3
Narran r. Australia 112 C3
Narrandera Australia 112 C4
Narrogin Australia 109 B8
Narromine Australia 112 D4
Narrows U.S.A. 130 C5
Narrowsburg U.S.A. 131 F3
Narsalik Greenland 121 O3
Narsaq Greenland 121 O3
Narsarsuaq Greenland 121 O3
Narsimhapur India 74 C5
Narsingdi Bangl. 75 F5
Narsinghgarh India 74 C5
Narsipatnam India 73 D2
Nartê Albania 46 A4
Nartkala Rus. Fed. 79 F2
Narto Japan 65 D5
Narva Estonia 28 D4
Narva r. Estonia/Rus. Fed. 33 H4
Narva Bay Estonia/Rus. Fed. 28 C4
Narva-Jõesuu Estonia 33 H4
Narvik Norway 32 F1
Narvskiy Zaliv b. Estonia/Rus. Fed. see Narva Bay
Narva Reservoir Estonia/Rus. Fed. see Narvskoye Vodokhranilishche
Narvskoye Vodokhranilishche resr Estonia/Rus. Fed. 33 H4
Narwana India 74 C3
Narwar India 74 C4
Nar'yan-Mar Rus. Fed. 28 J2
Naryn Kyrg. 62 E3
Naryn r. Kyrg./Uzbek. 70 D3
Nasby Sweden 32 J3
Naseby N.Z. 113 B7
Nashik India see Nashik
Nashua U.S.A. 131 H2
Nashville AR U.S.A. 133 C5
▶Nashville TN U.S.A. 128 C4
State capital of Tennessee.

Našice Croatia 44 G2
Nasielsk Poland 37 J2
Näsijärvi l. Fin. 33 F3
Nasik India see Nashik
Nasir Sudan 96 B3
Nasirabad Bangl. see Mymensingh
Nasirabad India 74 B4
Nasirabad Pak. 81 G4
Naskaupi r. Canada 125 I2
Nasmganj India 75 E7
Nasondoye Dem. Rep. Congo 95 E7
Nasosnyy Azer. see Hacı Zeynalabdin
Naşr Egypt 78 B5
Naşrābād Eşfahān Iran 80 B3
Naşrābād Khorāsān Iran 80 C3
Naşrānī, Jabal an mts Syria 77 C3
Nasratabad Iran see Zābol
Naşrīan-e-Pā'īn Iran 80 A3
Nass r. Canada 122 D4
Nassarawa Nigeria 93 G3
Nassarawa state Nigeria 93 H3
Nassau i. Australia 111 E2
▶Nassau Bahamas 129 D7
Capital of The Bahamas.

Nassau i. Cook Is 165 G6
Nassau U.S.A. 131 G2
Nassawadox U.S.A. 131 F5
Nasser, Lake resr Egypt 89 G4
Nassian Côte d'Ivoire 92 E3
Nässjö Sweden 33 I4
Nastapoca r. Canada 124 E1
Nastapoka Islands Canada 124 E1
Nasu-dake vol. Japan 65 D5
Nasva Rus. Fed. 28 D4
Nata Botswana 99 E4
Nata watercourse Botswana/Zimbabwe 99 E4
Natal Brazil 150 F3
Natal Indon. 58 B2
Natal prov. S. Africa see Kwazulu-Natal
Natal Basin sea feature Indian Ocean 163 J4
Natal Drakensberg National Park S. Africa 99 F6
Națanz Iran 80 B3
Natashquan Canada 125 I3
Natashquan r. Canada 125 I3
Natchez U.S.A. 127 F6
Natchitoches U.S.A. 133 C6
Nathalia Australia 112 B5
Nathana India 74 C3
Nathdwara India 74 B4
Natingou Benin 93 F3
Natividade Brazil 150 C4
Natla r. Canada 122 F2
Natmauk Myanmar 60 A3
Natogyi Myanmar 60 A3
Nátora Mex. 135 E7
Natore Bangl. 75 F4
Natori Japan 65 E5
Natron, Lake salt l. Tanz. 96 C5
Nattai National Park Australia 112 D4
Nattaung mt. Myanmar 60 B3
Nattavaara Sweden 32 F2
Na'tu Iran 81 E5
Natuna, Kepulauan is Indon. 59 D1
Natuna Besar i. Indon. 59 E1
Natural Bridge U.S.A. 130 D5

Natural Bridges National Monument nat. park U.S.A. 137 G3
Naturaliste, Cape Australia 109 A8
Naturaliste Channel Australia 109 A6
Naturaliste Plateau sea feature Indian Ocean 163 O8
Nau Tajik. see Nov
Naucelle France 38 E4
Nauchas Namibia 98 C2
Nau Co l. China 75 D2
Nauen Germany 37 F2
Naugatuck U.S.A. 131 G3
Nau Hissar Pak. 81 F4
Naujoji Akmenė Lith. 33 F4
Naukh India 74 B4
Naukluft mts Namibia 98 C2
Naumburg (Saale) Germany 36 E3
Naungpale Myanmar 60 B4
Na'ūr Jordan 78 C5
Naurskaya Rus. Fed. 79 F2
▶Nauru country S. Pacific Ocean 107 F2
oceania 104–105, 114
Naushahro Firoz Pak. 81 G5
Naushara India 75 G4
Naustdal Norway 33 B3
Nautaca Uzbek. see Karshi
Nautonwa India 75 D4
Nava r. Dem. Rep. Congo 94 E4
Nava Mex. 133 C7
Navabad Tajik. see Novobod
Navacerrada, Puerto de pass Spain 42 E2
Navachica mt. Spain 42 D4
Navadwip India 75 F5
Navahermosa Spain 42 D3
Navahrudak Belarus 31 L2
Navajo U.S.A. 135 F5
Navajo Mountain U.S.A. 137 G3
Navalmoral de la Mata Spain 42 D3
Navalvillar de Pela Spain 42 D3
Navan Rep. of Ireland 35 C5
Navangar India see Jamnagar
Navapolatsk Belarus 31 L2
Navarin, Mys c. Rus. Fed. 27 R3
Navarino, Isla i. Chile 153 C9
Navarra aut. comm. Spain 43 F1
Navarra, aut. comm. Spain see Navarra
Navarre aut. comm. Spain see Navarra
Navarrenx France 38 C5
Navarro Peru 146 C5
Navarro r. U.S.A. 136 A2
Navashino Rus. Fed. 28 G5
Navasota U.S.A. 133 B6
Navasota r. U.S.A. 133 B6
▶Navassa Island terr. West Indies 139 J5
United States Unincorporated Territory.
northamerica 118–119, 140
Naver r. U.K. 34 E2
Navia Spain 42 C1
Navia r. Spain 42 C1
Navidad Chile 152 C5
Navidad r. U.S.A. 133 B6
Naviraí Brazil 151 A7
Navlakhi India 74 A5
Navlya Rus. Fed. 29 E5
Năvodari Romania 46 N2
Navoi Uzbek. 81 F1
Navoiy Uzbek. see Navoi
Navoy Oblast admin. div. Uzbek. see Navoiyskaya Oblast'
Navojoa Mex. 135 E8
Navoy Oblast admin. div. Uzbek. see Navoiyskaya Oblast'
Navsari India 72 B1
Nawá Syria 78 D4
Nawabganj Bangl. 75 F4
Nawabganj India 75 D4
Nawabshah Pak. 81 G5
Nawada India 75 F4
Nāwah Afgh. 81 F3
Nawakot Nepal 75 E4
Nawalgarh India 74 C4
Nawar, Dasht-i imp. l. Afgh. 81 F3
Nawāşif, Ḥarrat lava field Saudi Arabia 89 I4
Nawnghkio Myanmar 60 B3
Nawngleng Myanmar 60 B3
Nawoiy Uzbek. see Navoi
Nawoiy Wiloyati admin. div. Uzbek. see Navoiyskaya Oblast'
Naxçıvan Azer. 79 G3
Naxi China 66 C2
Naxos Greece 47 D6
Naxos i. Greece 47 D6
Naya Col. 146 B4
Nayagarh India 73 E1
Nayak Afgh. 81 F3
Näy Band, Kūh-e mt. Iran 80 D3
Nayong China 66 C3
Nayoro Japan 64 F3
Nayudupeta India 72 C3
Nayyāl, Wādī watercourse Saudi Arabia 79 D5
Nazaré Brazil 146 C5
Nazaré Brazil 147 H6
Nazareth Israel 77 B3
Nazareth U.S.A. 131 F3
Nazário Brazil 149 H4
Nazas Mex. 126 F6
Nazca Peru 146 C6
Nazca Ridge sea feature S. Pacific Ocean 165 M7
Nāzik Iran 80 A2
Nazilli Turkey 78 B3
Nazimiye Turkey 79 D3
Nazinon r. Burkina/Ghana 93 E3 see Red Volta
Nazira Bangl. 75 F5
Nazir Hat Bangl. 75 F5
Nazko Canada 122 F4
Nazko r. Canada 122 F4
Nazran' Rus. Fed. 29 H8
Nazrēt Eth. 96 C2
Nazwá Oman 76 E6
Nazyvayevsk Rus. Fed. 26 H4
Nbâk Mauritania 92 B3
Ncheu Malawi see Ntcheu
Ncue Equat. Guinea 93 H5
Ndala Tanz. 96 B5

▶Ndjamena Chad 88 B6
Capital of Chad.

Ndji r. Cent. Afr. Rep. 94 C3
Ndjim r. Cameroon 93 H4
Ndjolé Gabon 94 A5
Ndjouna Gabon 94 B5

Ndogo, Lagune lag. Gabon 94 A5
Ndoi i. Fiji see Doi
Ndok Cameroon 94 B3
Ndola Zambia 95 F8
Ndoto mt. Kenya 96 C4
Ndougou Gabon 94 A5
Nduke i. Solomon Is see Kolombangara
Ndumbwe Tanz. 97 C7
Nduye Dem. Rep. Congo 94 D4
Nea Anchialos Greece 47 C5
Nea Apollonia Greece 46 C4
Neagh, Lough l. U.K. 35 C4
Neah Bay U.S.A. 134 A2
Neajlov r. Romania 46 D2
Nea Karvali Greece 46 D4
Neale, Lake salt flat Australia 110 B5
Neales watercourse Australia 110 D5
Nea Liosia Greece 47 C5
Nea Makri Greece 47 D5
Nea Moudania Greece 47 C4
Nea Peramos Greece 46 D4
Neapoli Kriti Greece 47 C7
Neapoli Peloponnisos Greece 47 C6
Neapolis Italy see Naples
Nea Roda Greece 47 C4
Nea Santa Greece 46 C4
Neath U.K. 35 E6
Nea Zichni Greece 46 C4
Nebbi Uganda 96 A4
Nebbou Burkina 93 E3
Nebine Creek r. Australia 111 F6
Nebitdag Turkm. 80 C2
Nebo Australia 111 E4
Nebolchi Rus. Fed. 28 E4
Nebraska state U.S.A. 134 G4
Nebraska City U.S.A. 132 C3
Nebrodi, Monti mts Sicily Italy 45 E6
Neches r. U.S.A. 133 C6
Nechí r. Col. 146 C2
Nechisar National Park Eth. 96 C3
Neckarsulm Germany 36 D4
Necker Island U.S.A. 165 H4
Necochea Arg. 152 F5
Necocli Col. 146 C2
Nedelišće Croatia 44 F1
Nederland country Europe see Netherlands
Nederlandse Antillen terr. West Indies see Netherlands Antilles
Neder Rijn r. Neth. 36 B3
Nedlouc, Lac l. Canada 125 F1
Nedluk Lake Canada see Nedlouc, Lac
Nêdong China 75 G3
Nedre Soppero Sweden 32 F1
Nedstrand Norway 33 B4
Needham U.S.A. 131 H2
Needles U.S.A. 137 E4
Needmore U.S.A. 130 C4
Neemuch India see Nimach
Neepawa Canada 123 L5
Nefta Tunisia 91 G2
Neftçala Azer. 79 G3
Neftechala Azer. see Neftçala
Neftechala Azer. see 26 Baki Komissari
Neftegorsk Rus. Fed. 29 I5
Neftekamsk Rus. Fed. 28 J4
Neftekumsk Rus. Fed. 29 H7
Nefteyugansk Rus. Fed. 26 H3
Neftezavodsk Turkm. see Seydi
Nefza Tunisia 45 B6
Negada Weyn well Eth. 96 E3
Negage Angola 95 B6
Négala Mali 92 C3
Negār Iran 80 D4
Negara Bali Indon. 59 F5
Negara Kalimantan Selatan Indon. 59 F3
Negara r. Indon. 59 F3
Negēlē Oromia Eth. 96 C3
Negēlē Oromia Eth. 96 C3
Negeri Sembilan state Malaysia 58 C2
Negev des. Israel 77 B4
Negomane Moz. 97 C7
Negombo Sri Lanka 72 C5
Negotin Yugo. 46 C2
Negotino Macedonia 46 C4
Negra, Cordillera mts Peru 148 A2
Negra, Lago l. Uruguay 152 G3
Negra, Serranía de mts Bol. 149 E3
Negrais, Cape Myanmar 61 A4
Negratín, Embalse de resr Spain 43 E4
Nègrepelisse France 38 D4
Negri r. Australia 110 B3
Négrine Alg. 91 G2
Negeri Sembilan state Malaysia see Negeri Sembilan
Negritos Peru 146 A6
Negro r. Arg. 152 E5
Negro r. Brazil 149 F6
Negro r. Para. 149 F6
Negro r. S. America 147 G5
Negro r. Uruguay 152 F4
Negro, Cabo c. Morocco 42 D5
Negroponte i. Greece see Evvoia
Negros i. Phil. 57 F4
Negru Vodă Romania 46 E2
Nehalem r. U.S.A. 134 B3
Nehavand Iran 80 B3
Nehbandān Iran 81 E4
Nehe China 63 K2
Nehoiu Romania 46 E2
Nehone Angola 95 C9
Neiafu Tonga 107 H3
Neijiang China 66 C2
Neill Island India 73 G4
Nei Mongol Zizhiqu aut. reg. China 64 A4
Neiße r. Poland/Germany 37 G2
Neiva Col. 146 C4
Neixiang China 67 F1
Nejanilini Lake Canada 123 L3
Nejd reg. Saudi Arabia see Najd
Neka Iran 80 C2
Neka r. Iran 80 C2
Nek'emtē Eth. 96 C2
Nekso Denmark 33 F5
Nela r. Spain 42 E1
Nelamangala India 72 C3
Nelas Port. 42 C2
Nelia Australia 111 E4
Nelidovo Rus. Fed. 28 E4
Nel'kan Khabarovskiy Kray Rus. Fed. 27 M3
Nel'kan Rus. Fec. 27 O3
Nelson r. Canada 123 M3
Nelson N.Z. 113 C3
Nelson AZ U.S.A. 137 F4
Nelson NE U.S.A. 132 B3
Nelson NV U.S.A. 137 E4
Nelson, Cape Australia 112 B5
Nelson Bay Australia 112 E4
Nelson Forks Canada 122 F3
Nelson House Canada 123 L4
Nelson Lakes National Park N.Z. 113 C3
Nelspruit S. Africa 99 F5
Nem r. Rus. Fed. 28 J3
Néma Mauritania 92 D1
Nema Rus. Fed. 28 I4
Neman Rus. Fed. 33 F3
Ne'matābād Iran 81 D4
Nemausus France see Nîmes
Nembe Nigeria 93 G4
Nemda r. Rus. Fed. 28 G4

Nemea Greece 47 C6
Nemed Rus. Fed. 28 J3
Nemenčine Lith. 33 G5
Nemetocenna France see Arras
Nemetskiy, Mys c. Rus. Fed. 32 H1
Nemirov Ukr. see Nemyriv
Némiscau r. Canada 124 E3
Nemor r. China 64 A2
Nemours Alg. see Ghazaouet
Nemours France 39 E2
Nemrut Dağı mt. Turkey 79 E3
Nemta r. Rus. Fed. 64 C2
Nemunas r. Lith. 33 F5
Nemuro Japan 64 F4
Nemyriv Ukr. 29 D6
Nenagh Rep. of Ireland 35 E5
Nenana U.S.A. 120 E3
Nene r. U.K. 35 G5
Nenets Autonomous Okrug admin. div. Rus. Fed. see Nenetskiy Avtonomnyy Okrug
Nenetskiy Avtonomnyy Okrug admin. div. Rus. Fed. 28 J2
Nenjiang China 63 L2
Nen Jiang r. China 64 A3
Neo Karlovasi Greece 47 E6
Neola U.S.A. 137 G1
Neo Monastiri Greece 47 C5
Néon Karlovásion Greece see Neo Karlovasi
Neosho U.S.A. 132 C4
Neosho r. U.S.A. 132 C4
Neos Marmaras Greece 47 C4
▶Nepal country Asia 75 D3
asia 52–53, 82
Nepalganj Nepal 75 D3
Nepanagar India 74 C5
Nepean Canada 124 F4
Nephi U.S.A. 137 G2
Nephin hill Rep. of Ireland 30 B2
Nephin Beg Range hills Rep. of Ireland 35 B4
Nepisiguit r. Canada 121 M5
Neptune U.S.A. 131 F3
Ner r. Poland 37 I2
Nera r. Italy 44 D3
Neral India 72 B2
Nerang Australia 111 H5
Nera Tso l. China 75 G3
Nerchinsk Rus. Fed. 27 L4
Nerekhta Rus. Fed. 28 G4
Nereta Latvia 33 G4
Neretva r. Bos.-Herz./Croatia 44 F3
Neretvanski Kanal sea chan. Croatia 44 F3
Neri India 72 C1
Nêri Pünco l. China 75 F3
Neriquinha Angola 95 D8
Neris r. Lith. 33 F5
Nerl' Rus. Fed. 28 F4
Nerl' r. Rus. Fed. 28 F4
Neroyka, Gora mt. Rus. Fed. 28 K2
Neryungri Rus. Fed. 27 M4
Nes' Rus. Fed. 28 H2
Nesa' Iran 80 B2
Nesbyen Norway 33 C3
Nesebŭr Bulg. 46 E3
Neskaupstaður Iceland 32 [inset]
Nesna Norway 32 D2
Nesque r. France 39 F4
Nesri India 72 B2
Ness, Loch l. U.K. 34 D3
Ness City U.S.A. 132 B4
Nesse r. Germany 36 E3
Nesselrode, Mount Canada/U.S.A. 122 C3
Nesselwang Germany 36 E5
Neste r. France 38 D5
Nesterov Rus. Fed. 37 K1
Nestor Falls Canada 124 A3
Nestos r. Greece 46 D4
Nesvizh Belarus see Nyasvizh
Netanya Israel 77 B3
Netarhat India 75 E5
Netcong U.S.A. 131 F3
▶Netherlands country Europe 36 B2
europe 24–25, 48

▶Netherlands Antilles terr. West Indies 146 D1
Self-governing Netherlands Territory.
northamerica 118–119, 140

Neto r. Italy 45 F5
Netrakona Bangl. 75 F4
Netrang India 74 B5
Nettilling Lake Canada 121 L3
Nettuno Italy 44 D4
Neubari r. Sudan 96 B3
Neubrandenburg Germany 37 F2
Neubukow Germany 36 E1
Neuburg an der Donau Germany 36 E4
Neuchâtel Switz. 39 G3
Neuchâtel, Lac de l. Switz. 39 G3
Neuenhagen Berlin Germany 37 F2
Neuenkirchen-Seelscheid Germany 36 C3
Neufchâteau Belgium 39 F2
Neufchâteau France 39 F2
Neufchâtel-en-Bray France 38 D2
Neuhausen Rus. Fed. see Gur'yevsk
Neuhof Germany 36 D3
Neuillé-Pont-Pierre France 38 D3
Neumarkt in der Oberpfalz Germany 36 E4
Neumayer research station Antarctica 167 B2
Neumünster Germany 36 D1
Neun, Nam r. Laos 60 D4
Neunkirchen Austria 37 H5
Neunkirchen Germany 36 C4
Neuquén Arg. 152 C4
Neuquén prov. Arg. 152 C4
Neuquén r. Arg. 152 D4
Neuruppin Germany 37 F2
Neu Sandez Poland see Nowy Sącz
Neuse r. U.S.A. 128 D5
Neusiedler See l. Austria/Hungary 37 H5
Neusiedler See Seewinkel, Nationalpark nat. park Austria 37 H5
Neuss Germany 36 C3
Neustadt (Wied) Germany 36 C3
Neustadt am Rübenberge Germany 36 D2
Neustadt an der Aisch Germany 36 E4
Neustadt an der Hardt Germany see Neustadt an der Weinstraße
Neustadt an der Weinstraße Germany 36 D4
Neustadt in Holstein Germany 36 E1
Neustift im Stubaital Austria 39 I3
Neustrelitz Germany 37 F2
Neuves-Maisons France 39 G2
Neuville-aux-Bois France 38 E2
Neuville-lès-Dieppe France 38 D2
Neuwerk i. Germany 36 D2
Neuwied Germany 36 C3
Nevada IA U.S.A. 132 C3
Nevada MO U.S.A. 132 C4
Nevada state U.S.A. 136 D2
Nevada, Sierra mt. Arg. 152 C1
Nevada, Sierra mts Spain 42 E4
Nevada, Sierra mts U.S.A. 136 B1
Nevada City U.S.A. 136 B2
Nevado, Cerro mt. Arg. 152 C3
Nevasa India 72 B2
Nevdubstroy Rus. Fed. see Kirovsk
Neve, Serra da mts Angola 95 B8
Nevel' Rus. Fed. 31 L1
Nevel'sk Rus. Fed. 64 E3
Nevers France 39 E3
Nevertire Australia 112 C3
Nevesinje Bos.-Herz. 44 G3
Nevėžis r. Lith. 33 F5
Nevinnomyssk Rus. Fed. 29 G7
Nevşehir Turkey 78 C3
New r. CA U.S.A. 137 E5
New r. WV U.S.A. 130 C5
New Aiyansh Canada 122 D4
Newala Tanz. 97 C7
New Albany IN U.S.A. 128 B4
New Albany MS U.S.A. 129 A5
New Amsterdam Guyana 147 G3
New Angledool Australia 112 C3
Newark DE U.S.A. 131 F4
Newark NJ U.S.A. 131 F3
Newark NY U.S.A. 131 E2
Newark OH U.S.A. 130 B3
Newark airport U.S.A. 131 F3
Newark Lake U.S.A. 137 E2
Newark-on-Trent U.K. 35 F5
Newark Valley U.S.A. 131 E2
New Bedford U.S.A. 131 H3
New Berlin U.S.A. 131 F2
New Bern U.S.A. 128 D5
Newberry MI U.S.A. 132 E2
Newberry SC U.S.A. 129 C5
Newberry National Volcanic Monument nat. park U.S.A. 134 B4
Newberry Springs U.S.A. 137 D4
New Bethlehem U.S.A. 130 D3
New Bight Bahamas 129 E7
New Bloomfield U.S.A. 131 E3
Newboro Canada 124 E4
New Boston OH U.S.A. 130 B4
New Boston TX U.S.A. 133 C5
New Braunfels U.S.A. 133 B6
New Brighton U.S.A. 130 C3
New Britain i. P.N.G. 107 D2
New Britain Trench sea feature S. Pacific Ocean 164 E6
New Brunswick prov. Canada 125 H4
New Brunswick U.S.A. 131 F3
Newburg U.S.A. 130 E3
Newburgh U.S.A. 131 F3
Newbury U.K. 35 F6
Newburyport U.S.A. 131 H2

▶New Caledonia terr. S. Pacific Ocean 107 F4
French Overseas Territory.
oceania 104–105,114

New Caledonia Trough sea feature Tasman Sea 164 E7
New Carlisle Canada 125 H3
Newcastle Australia 112 D4
Newcastle Canada 130 D2
Newcastle U.K. 35 D4
New Castle DE U.S.A. 131 F4
New Castle IN U.S.A. 128 B4
New Castle PA U.S.A. 130 C3
Newcastle UT U.S.A. 137 F3
New Castle VA U.S.A. 130 C5
Newcastle WY U.S.A. 134 F4
Newcastle Creek r. Australia 110 C3
Newcastle Range hills Australia 111 E3
Newcastle-under-Lyme U.K. 35 E5
Newcastle upon Tyne U.K. 34 F4
Newcastle Waters Australia 110 C3
New Church U.S.A. 131 F5
Newchwang China see Yingkou
New City U.S.A. 131 G3
Newcomerstown U.S.A. 130 C3
New Concord U.S.A. 130 C4
Newdegate Australia 109 B8

▶New Delhi India 74 C3
Capital of India.

New Don Pedro Reservoir U.S.A. 136 B3
Newell, Lake salt flat Australia 109 D6
Newell, Lake Canada 123 I5
New England Range mts Australia 112 D3
New England Seamounts sea feature N. Atlantic Ocean 160 K3
Newenham, Cape U.S.A. 120 C4
Newfound Lake U.S.A. 131 H2
Newfoundland i. Canada 125 J3
Newfoundland and Labrador prov. Canada 121 N4
Newfoundland Evaporation Basin salt l. U.S.A. 134 D4
New Galloway U.K. 34 D4
New Georgia i. Solomon Is 107 E2
New Georgia Islands Solomon Is 107 E2
New Georgia Sound sea chan. Solomon Is 107 E2
New Glasgow Canada 125 I4
Newgrange Tomb tourist site Rep. of Ireland 35 C5

▶New Guinea i. Indon./P.N.G. 57 J7
Largest island in Oceania and 2nd in the world.
oceania 102–103
world 6–7

New Hampshire state U.S.A. 131 H1
New Hanover i. P.N.G. 106 E2
New Hartford U.S.A. 131 F2
New Haven CT U.S.A. 131 G3
New Haven MI U.S.A. 130 B2
New Haven WV U.S.A. 130 C4
New Hebrides country S. Pacific Ocean see Vanuatu
New Hebrides Trench sea feature S. Pacific Ocean 164 F7
New Holland country Oceania see Australia
New Holland U.S.A. 131 E3
New Iberia U.S.A. 133 D6
New Ireland i. P.N.G. 107 E2
New Jersey state U.S.A. 131 F4
New Kandla India 74 A5
New Kensington U.S.A. 130 D3
New Kent U.S.A. 131 E5
Newkirk U.S.A. 132 B4
New Lanark tourist site U.K. 34 E4
Newland Range hills Australia 109 C7
New Lexington U.S.A. 130 B4
New Liskeard Canada 124 E4
New London U.S.A. 131 G3
New Madrid U.S.A. 133 D4
Newman Australia 108 B5
Newman U.S.A. 136 B3
Newmarket Canada 130 D1
Newmarket U.K. 35 G5
New Market U.S.A. 130 D4
New Martinsville U.S.A. 130 C4
New Meadows U.S.A. 134 C3
New Mexico state U.S.A. 135 F6
New Miami U.S.A. 130 A4
New Milford CT U.S.A. 131 G3
New Milford PA U.S.A. 131 F3
Newnan U.S.A. 129 B5
New Norcia Australia 109 B7
New Norfolk Australia 112 C6
New Orleans U.S.A. 127 H6
New Paltz U.S.A. 131 F3
New Philadelphia U.S.A. 130 C3
New Plymouth N.Z. 113 C2
Newport Isle of Wight, England U.K. 35 F6
Newport Newport, Wales U.K. 35 E6
Newport AR U.S.A. 127 H4
Newport DE U.S.A. 131 F4
Newport NH U.S.A. 131 G2
Newport OR U.S.A. 134 A3
Newport PA U.S.A. 131 E3
Newport RI U.S.A. 131 H3
Newport TN U.S.A. 128 C5
Newport VT U.S.A. 127 L3
Newport WA U.S.A. 134 C2
Newport Beach U.S.A. 136 D5
Newport News U.S.A. 131 E5
New Providence i. Bahamas 129 D7
Newquay U.K. 35 D6
New Richmond U.S.A. 132 C2
New River U.S.A. 137 F5
New Roads U.S.A. 133 D6
New Rockford U.S.A. 132 B2
New Ross Rep. of Ireland 35 C5
Newry Australia 110 B3
Newry U.K. 35 C4
New Siberia Islands Rus. Fed. 27 O2
New Smyrna Beach U.S.A. 129 C6
New South Wales state Australia 111 F6
New Stanton U.S.A. 130 D3
New Tazewell U.S.A. 130 B5
Newton IA U.S.A. 132 C3
Newton IL U.S.A. 128 A4
Newton KS U.S.A. 132 B4
Newton MA U.S.A. 131 H2
Newton MS U.S.A. 129 A5
Newton NJ U.S.A. 131 F3
Newton TX U.S.A. 133 C6
Newton Abbot U.K. 35 E6
Newton Falls U.S.A. 131 F1
Newton Stewart U.K. 34 D4
Newtontoppen mt. Svalbard 26 B2
Newtown U.K. 35 E5
New Town U.S.A. 132 A1
Newtown U.S.A. 131 F3
Newtownabbey U.K. 35 D4
Newtownards U.K. 35 D4
Newtownbarry Rep. of Ireland see Bunclody
Newtown St Boswells U.K. 34 E4
Newtownstewart U.K. 34 C4
New Ulm U.S.A. 132 C2
New Vienna U.S.A. 130 B4
Newville U.S.A. 130 E3

▶New York U.S.A. 131 G3
2nd most populous city in North America and 4th in the world.
northamerica 118–119
world 14–15, 16–17

New York state U.S.A. 131 F2
New York Mountains U.S.A. 137 E4

▶New Zealand country Oceania 113 B2
3rd largest and 3rd most populous country in Oceania.
oceania 104–105, 114

Neya Rus. Fed. 28 G4
Neya r. Rus. Fed. 28 G4
Ney Bīd Iran 80 D4
Neyestānak Iran 80 C3
Neyrīz Iran 80 C4
Neyshābūr Iran 81 D2
Nezhin Ukr. see Nizhyn
Ngabang Indon. 59 E2
Ngabé Congo 94 C5
Nga Chong, Khao mt. Myanmar/Thai. 61 B5
Ngadda watercourse Nigeria 93 I2
Ngagahtawng Myanmar 60 B2
Ngajira Tanz. 97 B6
Ngala Nigeria 93 I2
Ngalu Indon. 108 C2
Ngam Chad 94 C2
Ngama Chad 94 C2
Ngamaseri watercourse Botswana 98 D3
Ngambé Cameroon 93 H4
Ngamda China 66 A2
Ngamiland admin. dist. Botswana 98 D3
Ngamring China 70 G6
Ngangala Sudan 96 A3
Ngangla Ringco salt l. China 70 F5
Nganglong Kangri mt. China 70 F5
Nganglong Kangri mts China 70 F5
Ngangzê Co salt l. China 70 G5
Ngangzê Shan mts China 75 E3
Ngan Sau, Sông r. Vietnam 66 C5
Ngao Thai. 60 B4
Ngaoundal Cameroon 93 I4
Ngaoundéré Cameroon 93 I4
Ngara Malawi 97 B7
Ngara Tanz. 96 A5
Ngarrab China see Gyaca
Ngaruawahia N.Z. 113 C2
Ngaruroro r. N.Z. 113 D2
Ngathainggyaung Myanmar 60 A4
Ngawa China see Aba
Ngawan Chaung r. Myanmar 61 B5
Ngawi Indon. 59 E4
Ngcheangel atoll Palau see Kayangel Atoll
Ngeaur i. Palau see Angaur
Ngegera Tanz. 97 A6
Ngeruangel i. Palau 57 H4
Ngezi Zimbabwe 99 F4
Nggelelevu i. Fiji see Qelelevu
Nghabe r. Botswana 98 D4
Ngiap r. Laos 60 C4
Ngilmina Indon. 108 D2
Ngiva Angola see Ondjiva
Ngo Congo 94 B5
Ngoc Linh mt. Vietnam 61 D5
Ngoïla Cameroon 93 I5
Ngoin, Co salt l. China 75 F3
Ngoko r. Cameroon/Congo 94 C4
Ngoma Zambia 95 E8
Ngoma Bridge Botswana 98 E3
Ngomba Tanz. 97 B7
Ngom Qu r. China 62 F5
Ngong Cameroon 93 I3
Ngongola Angola 95 C8
Ngoqumaima China 75 E2
Ngoring Hu l. China 66 A1
Ngorongoro Conservation Area nature res. Tanz. 96 B5
Ngorongoro Crater Tanz. 96 B5
Ngoumou Cameroon 93 H5
Ngounié prov. Gabon 94 A5
Ngounié r. Gabon 94 A5
Ngouoni Gabon 94 B5
Ngoura Chad 88 C6
Ngouri Chad 88 B6
Ngourti Niger 93 I2
Ngoutchey well Chad 88 C5
Ngozi Burundi 94 F5
Nguigmi Niger 93 I2
Nguiu Australia 110 B1
Ngukurr Australia 110 C2
Ngulu atoll Micronesia 57 I4
Ngum, Nam r. Laos 60 C4
Ngundu Zimbabwe 99 F4
Ngunza Angola see Sumbe
Ngunza-Kabolu Angola see Sumbe
Nguru Nigeria 93 H2
Nguru Mountains Tanz. 97 C6
Nguyên Binh Vietnam 60 D3
Ngwaketse admin. dist. Botswana 98 E5
Ngwako Pan salt pan Botswana 98 D4
Ngwane country Africa see Swaziland
Ngwezi r. Zambia 95 E9
Nhamatanda Moz. 99 G3
Nhamundá Brazil 147 G5
Nhamundá r. Brazil 147 G5
N'harea Angola 95 C7
Nha Trang Vietnam 61 E5
Nhecolândia Brazil 149 F4
Nhill Australia 112 B5
Nhlangano Swaziland 99 F5
Nhoma Namibia 98 D3
Nho Quan Vietnam 60 D3
Nhulunbuy Australia 110 D2
Nhu Pora Brazil 152 G2
Niabembe Dem. Rep. Congo 94 E5
Niablé Ghana 92 E4
Niacam Canada 123 J4
Niafounké Mali 92 E2
Niagara U.S.A. 132 E2
Niagara Falls Canada 130 D2
Niagara Falls waterfall Canada/U.S.A. 130 D2
Niagara Falls U.S.A. 130 D2
Niagara-on-the-Lake Canada 130 D2
Niagassola Guinea 92 C2
Niagouelé, Mont du hill Guinea 92 C3
Niagzu Aksai Chin 74 C2
Niah Sarawak Malaysia 59 F2
Niak Nepal 75 E3
Niakaramandougou Côte d'Ivoire 92 D3

▶Niamey Niger 93 F2
Capital of Niger.

Niamina Mali 92 D2
Niandan r. Guinea 92 C3
Niandankoro Guinea 92 C3
Niangandu Tanz. 97 C6
Niangara Dem. Rep. Congo 94 E4
Niangay, Lac l. Mali 92 E2
Niangoloko Burkina 92 D3
Niangua r. U.S.A. 132 C4
Nia-Nia Dem. Rep. Congo 94 E4
Niantic U.S.A. 131 G3
Niari admin. reg. Congo 94 B5
Nias i. Indon. 58 B2
Niassa prov. Moz. 97 C8
Niassa, Lago l. Africa see Nyasa, Lake
Niaur i. Palau see Angaur
Nibil Well Australia 108 D5
Nīca Latvia 33 F4

▶Nicaragua country Central America 139 G6
4th largest country in Central and North America.
northamerica 116–117, 140

Nicaragua, Lake Nicaragua 139 G6
Nicastro Italy 45 F5
Nice France 39 G5
Nicephorium Syria see Ar Raqqah
Niceville U.S.A. 129 B6
Nichicun, Lac l. Canada 125 G2
Nichlaul India 75 D4
Nicholas Channel Bahamas/Cuba 129 C8
Nicholasville U.S.A. 130 A5
Nicholl's Town Bahamas 129 D7
Nichols U.S.A. 131 E2
Nicholson Australia 108 E4
Nicholson r. Australia 110 D3
Nicholson U.S.A. 131 F3
Nicholson Lake Canada 123 K2
Nicholson Range hills Australia 109 B6
Nicholville U.S.A. 131 F1
Nicobar Islands India 73 G4
Nicolae Bălcescu Romania 46 F2
Nicolaus U.S.A. 136 B2
Nicomedia Turkey see Kocaeli
Nico Pérez Uruguay 152 G3
Nicopolis Bulg. see Nikopol

▶Nicosia Cyprus 77 A2
Capital of Cyprus.

Nicosia Sicily Italy 45 E6
Nicotera Italy 45 E5
Nicoya, Península de pen. Costa Rica 139 G7
Nicuadala Moz. 99 H3
Nida Lith. 33 F5
Nida r. Poland 37 J3
Nidadavole India 73 D2
Nidagunda India 72 C2
Nidym Rus. Fed. 27 J3
Nidže mt. Greece/Macedonia 46 B4
Nidzica Poland 37 J2
Nidzkie, Jezioro l. Poland 37 J2
Niebüll Germany 36 D1
Nied r. France 39 G2
Niedere Tauern mts Austria 37 F5
Niedersachsen land Germany 36 D2
Niedersächsisches Wattenmeer, Nationalpark nat. park Germany 36 C2
Niefang Equat. Guinea 93 H5
Niellé Côte d'Ivoire 92 D3
Niem Cent. Afr. Rep. 94 B3
Niemba Dem. Rep. Congo 95 F6
Niemegk Germany 37 F2
Niemisel Sweden 32 F2
Niéna Mali 92 D3
Nienburg (Weser) Germany 36 D2
Niéri Ko watercourse Senegal 92 B2
Niers r. Germany 36 B3
Niesky Germany 37 G3
Nieuw Amsterdam Suriname 147 H3
Nieuw Nickerie Suriname 147 G2
Nieuwoudtville S. Africa 98 C6
Nieuwpoort Belgium 36 A3
Nieves Spain see As Neves
Niğde Turkey 78 C3
▶Niger country Africa 93 H1
africa 86–87, 100

▶Niger r. Africa 92 G4
3rd longest river in Africa.
africa 84–85

Niger state Nigeria 93 G3
▶Niger, Mouths of the Nigeria 93 G4
africa 100
Niger, Source of the tourist site Guinea 92 C3
Niger Cone sea feature S. Atlantic Ocean 160 O5

▶Nigeria country Africa 93 G3
Most populous country in Africa and 10th in the world.
africa 86–87, 100
world 16–17

Nighasan India 74 D3
Nighthawk Lake Canada 124 D3
Nigrita Greece 46 C4
Nihing Pak. 81 F4
Nihommatsu Japan see Nihonmatsu
Nihon country Asia see Japan
Nihonmatsu Japan 65 E5
Niigata Japan 65 D5
Niihama Japan 65 C6
Niihau i. U.S.A. 135 [inset] Y1
Nii-jima i. Japan 65 D6
Niimi Japan 65 C6
Niitsu Japan 65 D5
Nijar Spain 43 E4
Nijerāne well Mauritania 92 C1
Nijil, Wādī watercourse Jordan 77 B4
Nijmegen Neth. 36 B3
Nijverdal Neth. 36 C2
Nikaia Greece 47 C5
Nikel' Rus. Fed. 32 H1
Nikiniki Indon. 108 D2
Nikkaluokta Sweden 32 E2
Nikki Benin 93 F3
Nikkō National Park Japan 65 D5
Nikolaevo Bulg. 46 D3
Nikolayev Ukr. see Mykolayiv
Nikolayevka Rus. Fed. 29 H5
Nikolayevsk Rus. Fed. 29 H6
Nikolayevskiy Rus. Fed. see Nikolayevsk
Nikolayevsk-na-Amure Rus. Fed. 27 O4
Nikol'sk Penzenskaya Oblast' Rus. Fed. 29 H5
Nikol'sk Vologod. Obl. Rus. Fed. 28 H4
Nikol'skaya Pestravka Rus. Fed. see Nikol'sk
Nikol'skiy Kazakh. see Satpayev
Nikol'skoye Rus. Fed. 27 Q4
Nikol'skoye Vologod. Obl. Rus. Fed. see Sheksna
Nikopol Bulg. 46 D3
Nikopol' Ukr. 29 E7
Nīk Pey Iran 80 B2
Niksar Turkey 78 D2
Nīkshahr Iran 81 E5
Nikšić Yugo. 46 A3
▶Nikumaroro i. Phoenix Is Kiribati 107 H2
oceania 104–105
Nikunau i. Kiribati 107 G2
Nīl, Bahr el r. Africa see Nile
Nilagiri India 75 E5
Nilakka l. Fin. 32 G3
Nilakkottai India 72 C4
Nilambur India 72 C4
Niland U.S.A. 137 E5
Nilandhoo Atoll Maldives 71 D11
Nilanga India 72 C2
Nilaveli Sri Lanka 72 D4

▶Nile r. Africa 89 F2
Longest river in the world and in Africa.
africa 84–85
world 6–7

Nile state Sudan 89 G5
Niles MI U.S.A. 132 E3
Niles OH U.S.A. 130 C3
Nileswaram India 72 B3
Nilgiri Hills India 72 C4
Nil Pass Afgh. 81 F3
Nilphamari Bangl. 75 F4
Nilsiä Fin. 32 H3
Nilüfer r. Turkey 47 F4
Nimach India 74 B4
Nimaj India 74 B4
Niman r. Rus. Fed. 64 C2
Nimba, Monts mts Africa see Nimba Mountains
Nimbahera India 74 B4
Nimbal India 72 B2
Nimba Mountains Africa 92 C4
Nimberra Well Australia 108 C5
Nimbhera India see Nimbahera
Nimelen r. Rus. Fed. 64 D1
Nîmes France 39 F5
Nimka Thana India 74 B4
Nimmitabel Australia 112 D5
Nimrod Glacier Antarctica 167 H1
Nīmrūz prov. Afgh. 81 E4
Nimu Jammu and Kashmir 74 C2
Nimule Sudan 96 B4
Nimwegen Neth. see Nijmegen
Ninawá governorate Iraq 79 E4
Ninawá tourist site Iraq see Nineveh
Ninda Angola 95 D8
Nindai Tanz. 97 B7
Nindigully Australia 111 G6
Nine Degree Channel India 72 B4
Nine Islands P.N.G. see Kilinailau Islands
Ninepin Group is Hong Kong China 67 [inset]
Ninetyeast Ridge sea feature Indian Ocean 162 M8
Ninety Mile Beach Australia 112 C5
Ninety Mile Beach N.Z. 113 C1
Nineveh tourist site Iraq 79 E3
Ninfas, Punta pt Arg. 153 D5
Ning'an China 64 B3
Ningbo China 67 G2
Ningde China 67 F3
Ningdu China 67 E3
Ning'er China see Pu'er
Ningguo China 67 F2
Ninghai China 67 G2
Ninghsia aut. reg. China see Ningxia Huizu Zizhiqu
Ninghsia Hui Autonomous Region aut. reg. China see Ningxia Huizu Zizhiqu
Ninghua China 67 F3
Ningi Nigeria 93 H3
Ninging India 75 G3
Ningjiang China see Songyuan
Ningjing Shan mts China 66 A2
Ninglang China 66 B3
Ningming China 66 C4
Ningnan China 66 B3
Ningqiang China 66 C1
Ningshan China 66 D1
Ningxia aut. reg. China see Ningxia Huizu Zizhiqu
Ningxia Huizu Zizhiqu aut. reg. China 63 H4
Ningxiang China 67 E2
Ningyuan China 67 D3
Ninh Binh Vietnam 60 D3
Ninh Hoa Vietnam 61 E5
Ninigo Group is P.N.G. 57 J6
Ninnis Glacier Antarctica 167 G2
Ninnis Glacier Tongue Antarctica 167 H2
Ninohe Japan 64 E4
Nioaque Brazil 149 G5
Niobrara r. U.S.A. 134 H4
Nioki Dem. Rep. Congo 94 C5
Niokolo Koba, Parc National du nat. park Senegal 92 B2
Niono Mali 92 D2
Nioro Mali 92 C2
Niort France 38 C3
Nioût well Mauritania 92 D2
Nipani India 72 B2
Nipawin Canada 123 J4
Niphad India 72 B1
Nipigon Canada 124 B3
Nipigon, Lake Canada 124 B3
Nipishish Lake Canada 125 I2
Nipissing, Lake Canada 124 E4
Nippon country Asia see Japan
Nippon Hai sea N. Pacific Ocean see Japan, Sea of
Nippur tourist site Iraq 79 F4
Niquelândia Brazil 150 B5
Nīr Ardabīl Iran 80 A2
Nīr Yazd Iran 80 C4
Nira r. India 72 B2
Nirji China 64 A2
Nirmal India 72 C2
Nirmali India 75 E4
Nirmal Range hills India 72 C2
Niš Yugo. 46 B3
Nişāb Yemen 76 D7
Nisah, Wādī watercourse Saudi Arabia 80 A5
Nišava r. Yugo. 46 B3
Niscemi Sicily Italy 45 E6
Nīshāpūr Iran see Neyshābūr
Nishi-Sonogi-hantō pen. Japan 65 B6
Nisibis Turkey see Nusaybin
Nísiros i. Greece see Nisyros
Niskanselkä l. Fin. 32 G2
Niskibi r. Canada 124 B1
Nisko Poland 37 K3
Nisling r. Canada 122 B2
Nissan r. Sweden 33 D4
Nisser l. Norway 33 C4
Nissum Bredning b. Denmark 33 C4
Nistru r. Moldova 31 L4 see Dniester
Nisutlin r. Canada 122 C2
Nisyros i. Greece 47 E6
Nitchequon Canada 125 G2
Nitendi i. Solomon Is see Ndeni
Niterói Brazil 151 D7
Nith r. U.K. 34 E4
Niti Pass China 74 C3
Nitmiluk National Park Australia 110 C2
Nitra Slovakia 37 I4
Nitra r. Slovakia 37 I5
Nitro U.S.A. 130 C4
Nittedal Norway 33 C3
Niuafo'ou i. Tonga 107 H3
Niuafu i. Tonga see Niuafo'ou
Niuatoputopu i. Tonga 107 H3

▶Niue terr. S. Pacific Ocean 107 I3
Self-governing New Zealand Overseas Territory.
oceania 104–105, 114

Niujing China see Binchuan
Niulakita i. Tuvalu 107 G3
Niulan Jiang r. China 66 B3
Niur, Pulau i. Indon. 58 C3
Niushan China see Donghai
Niutao i. Tuvalu 107 G2
Nivala Fin. 32 G3
Nivastroy Rus. Fed. 32 I2
Nive r. France 38 C5
Nive Downs Australia 111 F5
Nivelles Belgium 39 F1
Niwai India 74 B4
Niwari India 74 C4
Niwas India 74 D5
Nixia China see Sêrxü
Nixon U.S.A. 136 C2
Niya China see Minfeng
Niyut, Gunung mt. Indon. 59 E2
Nizamabad India 72 C2
Nizampatnam India 72 D3
Nizam Sagar l. India 72 C2
Nizhegorodskaya Oblast' admin. div. Rus. Fed. 28 H4
Nizhneangarsk Rus. Fed. 27 K4
Nizhnedevitsk Rus. Fed. 29 F6
Nizhnekamsk Rus. Fed. 28 I5
Nizhnekamskoye Vodokhranilishche resr Rus. Fed. 28 J5
Nizhnekolymsk Rus. Fed. 27 Q3
Nizhneudinsk Rus. Fed. 62 F1
Nizhnevartovsk Rus. Fed. 26 H3
Nizhnevolzhsk Rus. Fed. see Narimanov
Nizhneyansk Rus. Fed. 27 N2
Nizhneye Kuyto, Ozero l. Rus. Fed. 32 H2
Nizhniye Kresty Rus. Fed. see Cherskiy
Nizhniy Lomov Rus. Fed. 29 G5
Nizhniy Novgorod Rus. Fed. 28 G4
Nizhniy Novgorod Oblast admin. div. Rus. Fed. see Nizhegorodskaya Oblast'
Nizhniy Odes Rus. Fed. 28 J3
Nizhniy Pyandzh Tajik. see Panji Poyon
Nizhniy Tagil Rus. Fed. 26 F4
Nizhnyaya Mola Rus. Fed. 28 H2
Nizhnyaya Omra Rus. Fed. 28 J3
Nizhnyaya Pesha Rus. Fed. 28 H2
Nizhnyaya Pirenga, Ozero l. Rus. Fed. 32 I2
Nizhnyaya Poyma Rus. Fed. 27 J4
Nizhnyaya Tunguska r. Rus. Fed. 27 I3
Nizhnyaya Tura Rus. Fed. 26 F4
Nizhyn Ukr. 29 D6
Nizina Mazowiecka reg. Poland 37 J2
Nizip Turkey 79 D3
Nízke Beskydy hills Slovakia 37 J4
Nízke Tatry mts Slovakia 37 I4
Nízke Tatry nat. park Slovakia 37 I4
Nizwā Oman see Nazwá
Nizza France see Nice
Nizza Monferrato Italy 44 B2
Njavve Sweden 32 E2
Njazidja i. Comoros 97 D7
Njegoš mts Yugo. 46 A3
Njinjo Tanz. 97 C7
Njombe Tanz. 97 B7
Njombe r. Tanz. 97 B6
Nkai Zimbabwe see Nkayi
Nkasi Tanz. 97 A6
Nkawkaw Ghana 93 E4
Nkayi Zimbabwe 99 F3
Nkhaïlé well Mauritania 92 D1
Nkhata Bay Malawi 97 B7
Nkhotakota Malawi 97 B8
Nkomfap Nigeria 93 H4
Nkomi, Lagune lag. Gabon 94 A5
Nkondwe Tanz. 97 A6
Nkongsamba Cameroon 93 H4
Nkoteng Cameroon 93 I4
Nkululeko S. Africa 99 E6
Nkundi Tanz. 97 A6
Nkungwi Tanz. 97 A6
Nkurenkuru Namibia 98 C3
Nkwanta Ghana 93 F3
Nkwenkwezi S. Africa 99 E7
Nmai Hka r. Myanmar 60 B2
Noa Dihing r. India 60 B2
Noakhali Bangl. 75 F5
Noamundi India 75 E5
Noatak r. U.S.A. 120 C3
Nobeoka Japan 65 B6
Noboribetsu Japan 64 E4
Noccundra Australia 111 E5
Noce r. Italy 44 C1
Nocera Terinese Italy 45 F5
Noci Italy 45 F4
Nockatunga Australia 111 E5
Nocona U.S.A. 133 B5
Nodeland Norway 33 B4
Noel Kempff Mercado, Parque Nacional nat. park Bol. 149 E3
Nogales Mex. 135 E7
Nogales U.S.A. 135 E7
Nogaro France 38 C5
Nogat r. Poland 37 I1
Nōgata Japan 65 B6
Nogent-le-Rotrou France 38 D2
Nogent-sur-Seine France 39 E2
Noginsk Rus. Fed. 27 J3
Noginsk Moskovskaya Oblast' Rus. Fed. 28 F5
Nogliki Rus. Fed. 64 E2
Nogo r. Australia 111 G5
Nogoa r. Australia 111 G4
Nogoyá Arg. 152 F3
Nohar India 74 B3
Noheji Japan 64 E4
Nohfelden Germany 36 C4
Nohili Point U.S.A. 135 [inset] Y1
Nohur Turkm. see Nokhur
Noia Spain 42 B1
Noire, Montagne mts France 38 E5
Noires, Montagnes hills France 38 B2
Noirmoutier, Île de i. France 38 B3
Noirmoutier-en-l'Île France 38 B3
Nokesville U.S.A. 130 E4
Nokha India 74 B4

Nokhowch, Kūh-e mt. Iran 81 E5
Nokhur Turkm. 80 D2
Nokia Fin. 33 F3
Nōkis Uzbek. see Nukus
Nok Kundi Pak. 81 E4
Nokomis Canada 123 J5
Nokomis Lake Canada 123 K3
Nokou Chad 88 B6
Nokrek Peak India 75 F4
Nola Cent. Afr. Rep. 94 C4
Nolinsk Rus. Fed. 28 I4
Nólsoy i. Faroe Is 34 [inset]
Nome U.S.A. 120 C3
Nomhon China 75 H1
Nomonde S. Africa 99 E6
Nomuka Tonga 107 H4
Nomzha Rus. Fed. 28 G4
Nonacho Lake Canada 123 I2
Nong'an China 64 A3
Nong Hong Thai. 61 C5
Nonghui China see Guang'an
Nong Khai Thai. 60 C4
Nongoma S. Africa 99 F5
Nongstoin India 75 F4
Nonni r. China see Nen Jiang
Nonoava Mex. 135 F8
Nonouti atoll Kiribati 164 F6
Nonsan S. Korea 65 A5
Nonthaburi Thai. 61 C5
Nontron France 38 D4
Nonzwakazi S. Africa 98 E6
Nookawarra Australia 109 B6
Noolyeanna Lake salt flat Australia 110 D5
Noonamah Australia 110 B2
Noondie, Lake salt flat Australia 109 B7
Noonkanbah Australia 108 D4
Noonthorangee Range hills Australia 112 B3
Noorama Creek watercourse Australia 111 F5
Noordbeveland i. Neth. 36 A3
Noordoost Polder Neth. 36 B2
Noormarkku Fin. 33 F3
Nootka Island Canada 122 E5
Nóqui Angola 95 B6
Nora r. Rus. Fed. 64 B2
Norak Tajik. 81 G2
Noranda Canada 124 E3
Nor-Bayazet Armenia see Kamo
Norberg Sweden 33 D3
Nord prov. Cameroon 93 I3
Nord Greenland see Station Nord
Nord, Canal du France 36 A3
Nordaustlandet i. Svalbard 26 C2
Nordbotn Norway 32 F1
Nordegg Canada 123 G4
Norden Germany 36 C2
Nordenshel'da, Arkhipelag is Rus. Fed. 27 J2
Nordenskiold r. Canada 122 B2
Nordenskjold Archipelago is Rus. Fed. see Nordenshel'da, Arkhipelag
Norder Hever sea chan. Germany 36 D1
Norderney Germany 36 C2
Norderstedt Germany 36 E2
Nordfjord Norway 32 H1
Nordfjord inlet Norway 33 B3
Nordfjordeid Norway 33 B3
Nordfold Norway 32 D2
Nordhausen Germany 36 E3
Nordholz Germany 36 D2
Nordhorn Germany 36 C2
Nordishavet sea Norway 32 F1
Nord Kap c. Iceland see Horn
Nordkapp c. Norway see North Cape
Nord-Kivu prov. Dem. Rep. Congo 94 F5
Nord-Kvaløy i. Norway 32 E1
Nordkynhalvøya i. Norway 32 G1
Nordland county Norway 32 D2
Nordli Norway 32 D2
Nördlingen Germany 36 E4
Nord- og Østgrønland, Nationalparken i nat. park Greenland 121 P2

▶Nordostrundingen c. Greenland 166 I1
Most easterly point of North America.

Nord-Ouest prov. Cameroon 93 H4
Nord - Pas-de-Calais admin. reg. France 39 E1
Nordrhein-Westfalen land Germany 36 C3
Nordstrand i. Germany 36 D1
Nord-Trøndelag county Norway 32 D2
Nordvik Rus. Fed. 27 L2
Nordvika Norway 32 C3
Nore r. Rep. of Ireland 35 C5
Nore, Pic de mt. France 38 E5
Noreg country Europe see Norway
Norfolk NE U.S.A. 132 B3
Norfolk NY U.S.A. 131 F1
Norfolk VA U.S.A. 131 E5

▶Norfolk Island terr. S. Pacific Ocean 107 F4
Australian External Territory.
oceania 104–105, 114

Norfolk Island Ridge sea feature Tasman Sea 164 F7
Norfork Lake U.S.A. 133 C4
Norge country Europe see Norway
Noril'sk Rus. Fed. 27 I3
Norkyung China see Bainang
Norland Canada 130 D1
Norlina U.S.A. 130 D5
Norman r. Australia 111 E3
Norman U.S.A. 133 B5
Norman, Lake resr U.S.A. 128 C5
Normanby r. Australia 111 F2
Normanby Island P.N.G. 107 E2
Normanby Range hills Australia 111 G4
Normandes, Îles is English Chan. see Channel Islands
Normandia Brazil 147 G4
Normandie, Collines de hills France 38 C2
Normandy reg. France 38 C2
Normanton Australia 111 E3
Norman Wells Canada 122 E1
Norogachic Mex. 135 F8
Ñorquinco Arg. 153 C5
Norråker Sweden 32 D2
Norra Kvarken strait Fin./Sweden 32 F3
Norrbotten county Sweden 32 E2
Nørre Nebel Denmark 33 C5
Norrent-Fontes France 39 E1
Norrfjärden Sweden 32 F2
Norristown U.S.A. 131 F3
Norrköping Sweden 33 E4
Norrtälje Sweden 33 E4
Norseman Australia 109 C8
Norsk Rus. Fed. 64 B1
Norsup Vanuatu 107 F3
Norte, Punta pt Buenos Aires Arg. 152 F4
Norte, Punta pt Arg. 153 E5
Norte, Serra do hills Brazil 149 F2
Norte de Santander dept Col. 146 C2
Nortelândia Brazil 149 F3
North salt flat Australia see Eyre, Lake
North, Cape Antarctica 167 H2
North, Cape Canada 125 I4
North Adams U.S.A. 131 G2
Northallerton U.K. 35 F4
Northam Australia 109 B7
Northampton Australia 109 A7
Northampton U.K. 35 F5
Northampton MA U.S.A. 131 G2
Northampton PA U.S.A. 131 F3
Northampton Downs Australia 111 F5
North Andaman i. India 73 G3
North Anna r. U.S.A. 130 E5
North Arm b. Canada 123 H2
North Australian Basin sea feature Indian Ocean 162 O6
North Baltimore U.S.A. 130 B3
North Battleford Canada 123 I4
North Bay Canada 124 E4
North Bennington U.S.A. 131 G2
North Berwick U.K. 34 E3
North Berwick U.S.A. 131 H2
North Borneo state Malaysia see Sabah
North Branch U.S.A. 130 B2
North Canadian r. U.S.A. 132 C5
North Cape Canada 125 H4
North Cape Norway 32 G1
North Cape N.Z. 113 C1
North Cape S. Georgia 153 [inset]
North Cape U.S.A. 120 B4
North Caribou Lake Canada 124 B2
North Carolina state U.S.A. 128 D4
North Cascades National Park U.S.A. 134 B2
North Channel lake channel Canada 124 D4
North Channel strait U.K. 34 C4
North Charleston U.S.A. 129 D5
Northcliffe Australia 109 B8
Northcliffe Glacier Antarctica 167 F2
North Collins U.S.A. 130 D2
North Concho r. U.S.A. 133 A6
North Conway U.S.A. 131 H1
North Cowichan Canada 122 F5
North Creek U.S.A. 131 G2
North Dakota state U.S.A. 134 G3
North Downs hills U.K. 35 F6
North East admin. dist. Botswana 99 E4
North East U.S.A. 130 D2
North East Cay reef Australia 111 H4
North-Eastern prov. Kenya 96 D4
North-East Frontier Agency state India see Arunachal Pradesh
Northeast Pacific Basin sea feature N. Pacific Ocean 165 H4
Northeast Providence Channel Bahamas 129 D7
North Edwards U.S.A. 136 D4
Northeim Germany 36 D3
Northern admin. reg. Ghana 93 E3
Northern admin. reg. Malawi 97 B7
Northern prov. Sierra Leone 92 C3
Northern state Sudan 89 F4
Northern prov. Zambia 95 F7
Northern Aegean admin. reg. Greece see Voreio Aigaio
Northern Areas admin. div. Pak. 81 H2
Northern Bahr el Ghazal state Sudan 94 E2
Northern Cape prov. S. Africa 98 C6
Northern Darfur state Sudan 89 E5
Northern Donets r. Rus. Fed./Ukr. see Severskiy Donets
Northern Dvina r. Rus. Fed. see Severnaya Dvina
Northern Indian Lake Canada 123 L3
Northern Ireland prov. U.K. 35 C4
Northern Kordofan state Sudan 89 F6
Northern Lau Group is Fiji 107 H3
Northern Light Lake Canada 124 B3

▶Northern Mariana Islands terr. N. Pacific Ocean 57 J2
United States Commonwealth.
oceania 104–105, 114

Northern Rhodesia country Africa see Zambia
Northern Sporades is Greece see Voreioi Sporades
Northern Territory admin. div. Australia 110 C3
Northern Transvaal prov. S. Africa see Limpopo
North Fabius r. U.S.A. 132 D4
Northfield MA U.S.A. 131 G2
Northfield MN U.S.A. 132 C2
Northfield VT U.S.A. 131 G1
North Foreland c. U.K. 35 G6
North Fork Pass Canada 122 B1
North French r. Canada 124 D3
North Frisian Islands Germany 36 D1
North Geomagnetic Pole (2000) Arctic Ocean 166 K1
North Haven U.S.A. 131 G3
North Head N.Z. 113 C2
North Henik Lake Canada 123 L2
North Highlands U.S.A. 136 B2
North Horr Kenya 96 C4
North Hudson U.S.A. 131 G2
North Island India 72 B4

▶North Island N.Z. 113 C2
3rd largest island in Oceania.
oceania 102–103

North Jadito Canyon gorge U.S.A. 137 G4
North Knife r. Canada 123 M3
North Knife Lake Canada 123 L3
North Koel r. India 75 D4
North Komelik U.S.A. 137 G5
▶North Korea country Asia 65 A4
asia 52–53, 82
North Lakhimpur India 75 G4
North Land is Rus. Fed. see Severnaya Zemlya
North Las Vegas U.S.A. 137 E3
North Little Rock U.S.A. 133 C5
North Loup r. U.S.A. 132 B3
North Luangwa National Park Zambia 97 B7
North Maalhosmadulu Atoll Maldives 72 B5
North Magnetic Pole (2000) Arctic Ocean 166 L1
North Mam Peak U.S.A. 134 F5
North Moose Lake Canada 123 K4
North Muiron Island Australia 108 A5
North Nahanni r. Canada 122 F2
North Ossetia aut. rep. Rus. Fed. see Severnaya Osetiya-Alaniya, Respublika
North Palisade mt. U.S.A. 136 C3
North Platte U.S.A. 132 A3
North Platte r. U.S.A. 134 G4
North Pole Arctic Ocean 166 I1
Northport U.S.A. 129 B5
North Rhine - Westphalia land Germany see Nordrhein-Westfalen
North Rona i. U.K. see Rona
North Ronaldsay i. U.K. 34 E2
North Saskatchewan r. Canada 123 J4
North Schell Peak U.S.A. 137 E2
North Sea Europe 34 G3
North Seal r. Canada 123 L3
North Sentinel Island India 73 G4
North Shoal Lake Canada 123 L5
North Siberian Lowland Rus. Fed. 27 K2
North Simlipal National Park India 75 E5
North Sinai governorate Egypt see Shamāl Sīnā'
North Slope plain U.S.A. 120 E3
North Spirit Lake Canada 123 M4
North Stradbroke Island Australia 111 H5
North Stratford U.S.A. 131 H1
North Taranaki Bight b. N.Z. 113 C2
North Thompson r. Canada 122 F5
North Tonawanda U.S.A. 130 D2
North Trap reef N.Z. 113 A4
North Twin Island Canada 124 E2
North Uist i. U.K. 34 C3
Northumberland National Park U.K. 34 E4
Northumberland Strait Canada 125 H4
North Umpqua r. U.S.A. 134 B4
North Vancouver Canada 122 F5
Northville U.S.A. 131 F2
North Wabasca Lake Canada 123 H3
North Walsham U.K. 35 G5
North Waterford U.S.A. 131 H1
Northway U.S.A. 122 A2
Northway Junction U.S.A. 122 A2
North West prov. S. Africa 98 E5
Northwest Atlantic Mid-Ocean Channel N. Atlantic Ocean 160 K1
North West Cape Australia 108 A5
North-Western prov. Zambia 95 D8
North West Frontier prov. Pak. 81 G3
North West Nelson Forest Park nat. park N.Z. see Kahurangi National Park
Northwest Pacific Basin sea feature N. Pacific Ocean 164 E3
Northwest Providence Channel Bahamas 129 D7
North West River Canada 125 J2
Northwest Territories admin. div. Canada 123 J2
North Windham U.S.A. 131 H2
Northwind Ridge sea feature Arctic Ocean 166 B1
Northwood IA U.S.A. 132 C3
Northwood NH U.S.A. 131 H2
North York Canada 130 D2
North York Moors moorland U.K. 35 F4
North York Moors National Park U.K. 35 F4
Norton U.S.A. 132 B4
Norton de Matos Angola see Balombo
Norton Sound sea chan. U.S.A. 120 C3
Nortorf Germany 36 D1
Nort-sur-Erdre France 38 C3
Norvegia, Cape Antarctica 167 B2
Norwalk U.S.A. 130 B3
▶Norway country Europe 32 C3
europe 24–25, 48
Norway U.S.A. 131 H1
Norway House Canada 123 L4
Norwegian Basin sea feature N. Atlantic Ocean 160 N1
Norwegian Bay Canada 121 J2
Norwegian Sea N. Atlantic Ocean 166 H2
Norwich Canada 130 C2
Norwich U.K. 35 G5
Norwich CT U.S.A. 131 G3
Norwich NY U.S.A. 131 F2
Norwood NY U.S.A. 131 F1
Norwood OH U.S.A. 130 A4
Nose Lake Canada 123 I1
Noshiro Japan 65 E4
Noshul' Rus. Fed. 28 I3
Nosivka Ukr. 29 D6
Nosovaya Rus. Fed. 28 J1
Nosovka Ukr. see Nosivka
Noşratābād Iran 81 D4
Nossa Senhora da Glória Brazil 148 B1
Nossa Senhora do Livramento Brazil 149 F3
Nossob watercourse Africa 98 C5
Nosy Varika Madag. 99 [inset] K4
Nota r. Fin./Rus. Fed. 32 H1
Notch Peak U.S.A. 137 F2
Noteć r. Poland 37 G2
Notikewin r. Canada 122 G3
Notio Aigaio admin. reg. Greece 47 E6
Nótion Aiyaíon admin. reg. Greece see Notio Aigaio
Notios Evvoïkos Kolpos sea chan. Greece 47 C5
Notio Steno Kerkyras sea chan. Greece 47 B5
Noto Sicily Italy 45 E6
Noto, Golfo di g. Sicily Italy 45 E6
Notodden Norway 33 C4
Noto-hantō pen. Japan 65 D5
Notre Dame, Monts mts Canada 125 G4
Notre Dame Bay Canada 125 K3
Notre-Dame-de-Koartac Canada see Quaqtaq
Notsé Togo 93 F4
Nottawasaga Bay Canada 130 C1
Nottaway r. Canada 124 E3
Nottingham U.K. 35 F5
Nottingham Island Canada 121 L3
Nottoway U.S.A. 130 D5
Nottoway r. U.S.A. 130 E5
Nouabalé-Ndoki, Parc National de nat. park Congo 94 C4
Nouâdhibou Mauritania 90 A5
Nouâdhibou, Râs c. Mauritania 90 A5

▶Nouakchott Mauritania 92 B1
Capital of Mauritania.

Noual well Mauritania 92 D1
Nouâmghâr Mauritania 92 A1
Nouei Vietnam 61 D5

▶Nouméa New Caledonia 107 F4
Capital of New Caledonia.

Noun r. Cameroon 93 H4
Nouna Burkina 92 E2
Noupoort S. Africa 98 E6
Nousu Fin. 32 H2
Nouveau-Comptoir Canada see Wemindji
Nouvelle Anvers Dem. Rep. Congo see Makanza
Nouvelle Calédonie i. S. Pacific Ocean 107 F4
Nouvelle Calédonie terr. S. Pacific Ocean see New Caledonia
Nouvelles Hébrides country S. Pacific Ocean see Vanuatu
Nov Tajik. 81 G1
Nõva Estonia 33 F4
Nova América Brazil 149 H3
Novabad Tajik. see Novobod
Novabad Tajik. see Novobod
Nová Baňa Slovakia 37 I4
Nova Chaves Angola see Muconda
Novaci Romania 46 C2
Nova Crnja Yugo. 46 B2
Nova Cruz Brazil 150 F3
Nova Esperança Angola see Buengas
Nova Freixa Moz. see Cuamba
Nova Friburgo Brazil 151 D7
Nova Goa India see Panaji
Nova Gorica Slovenia 44 D2
Nova Gradiška Croatia 44 F2
Nova Iguaçu Brazil 151 D7
Nova Kakhovka Ukr. 29 E7
Nova Lima Brazil 151 D6
Nova Lisboa Angola see Huambo
Nova Londrina Brazil 149 G5
Novalukoml' Belarus 29 D5
Nova Mambone Moz. 99 G4
Nova Nabúri Moz. 99 H3
Nova Odesa Ukr. 29 D7
Nová Paka Czech Rep. 37 G3
Nova Paraiso Brazil 147 F4
Nova Pazova Yugo. 46 B2
Nova Pilão Arcado Brazil 150 D4
Nova Ponte Brazil 149 I4
Novara Italy 44 B2
Nova Remanso Brazil 150 D4
Nova Russas Brazil 150 D3
Nova Scotia prov. Canada 125 H5
Nova Sento Sé Brazil 150 D4
Nova Soure Brazil 150 E4
Novate Mezzola Italy 44 B1
Novato U.S.A. 136 A2
Nova Topola Bos.-Herz. 44 F2
Nova Vandúzi Moz. 99 G3
Nova Varoš Yugo. 46 A3
Nova Venécia Brazil 151 D6
Nova Vida Brazil 146 E5
Nova Xavantino Brazil 149 G3
Novaya Kakhovka Ukr. see Nova Kakhovka
Novaya Kazanka Kazakh. 29 I6
Novaya Odessa Ukr. see Nova Odesa
Novaya Pismyanka Rus. Fed. see Leninogorsk
Novaya Sibir', Ostrov i. Rus. Fed. 27 O2

▶Novaya Zemlya is Rus. Fed. 26 F2
3rd largest island in Europe.
europe 22–23

Nova Zagora Bulg. 46 E3
Novelda Spain 43 F3
Novellara Italy 44 C2
Nové Město nad Metuj Czech Rep. 37 H3
Nové Mlýny, Vodní nádrž resr Czech Rep. 37 H4
Nové Zámky Slovakia 37 I5
Novgorod Rus. Fed. see Velikiy Novgorod
Novgorodka Rus. Fed. 33 H4
Novgorod Oblast admin. div. Rus. Fed. see Novgorodskaya Oblast'
Novgorod-Severskiy Ukr. see Novhorod-Sivers'kyy
Novgorodskaya Oblast' admin. div. Rus. Fed. 28 E4
Novgorod-Volynskiy Ukr. see Novohrad-Volyns'kyy
Novhorod-Sivers'kyy Ukr. 29 E6
Novi Bečej Yugo. 46 B2
Novi Grad Bos.-Herz. see Bosanski Novi
Novi Iskŭr Bulg. 46 C3
Novikovo Rus. Fed. 64 E3
Novi Kritsim Bulg. see Stamboliyski
Novi Ligure Italy 44 B2
Novi Marof Croatia 44 F1
Novi Pazar Bulg. 46 E3
Novi Pazar Yugo. 46 B3
Novi Sad Yugo. 46 A2
Novi Vinodolski Croatia 44 E2
Novo, Lago l. Brazil 147 I4
Novoaleksandrovsk Rus. Fed. 64 E3
Novoaltaysk Rus. Fed. 62 C1
Novoanninskiy Rus. Fed. 29 G6
Novo Aripuanã Brazil 147 F6
Novoazovs'k Ukr. 29 F7
Novo Beograd Yugo. 46 B2
Novobod Tajik. 81 G2
Novobod Tajik. 81 G2
Novobogatinsk Kazakh. see Novobogatinskoye
Novobogatinskoye Kazakh. 29 I7
Novobureyskiy Rus. Fed. 64 B2
Novocheboksarsk Rus. Fed. 28 H4
Novocherkassk Rus. Fed. 29 G7
Novo Cruzeiro Brazil 151 D6
Novodvinsk Rus. Fed. 28 G2
Novogeorgiyevka Rus. Fed. 64 A2
Novo Hamburgo Brazil 151 B9
Novohrad-Volyns'kyy Ukr. 29 C6
Novokazalinsk Kazakh. see Ayteke Bi
Novokhopersk Rus. Fed. 29 G6
Novokiyevskiy Uval Rus. Fed. 64 B2
Novokubansk Rus. Fed. 79 E1
Novokubanskiy Rus. Fed. see Novokubansk
Novokuybyshevsk Rus. Fed. 29 I5
Novokuznetsk Rus. Fed. 62 D1
Novolazarevskaya research station Antarctica 167 C2
Novolukoml' Belarus see Novalukoml'
Novo Marapi Brazil 147 E5
Novo Mesto Slovenia 44 E2
Novomichurinsk Rus. Fed. 29 F5
Novomikhaylovskiy Rus. Fed. 29 F7
Novo Miloševo Yugo. 46 B2
Novomirgorod Ukr. see Novomyrhorod
Novomoskovsk Rus. Fed. 29 F5
Novomoskovs'k Ukr. 29 E6
Novomyrhorod Ukr. 29 D6
Novonazyvayevka Rus. Fed. see Nazyvayevsk
Novonikolayevsk Rus. Fed. see Novosibirsk
Novonikolayevskiy Rus. Fed. 29 G6
Novooleksiyivka Ukr. 29 E7
Novo Olinda do Norte Brazil 147 G5
Novo Oriente Brazil 150 D3
Novo Parnarama Brazil 150 D3
Novopashiyskiy Rus. Fed. see Gornozavodsk
Novopokrovka Rus. Fed. 64 C3
Novopolotsk Belarus see Navapolatsk
Novopskov Ukr. 29 F6
Novo Redondo Angola see Sumbe
Novorossiysk Rus. Fed. 29 F7
Novorybnaya Rus. Fed. 27 K2
Novorzhev Rus. Fed. 28 D4
Novoselskoye Rus. Fed. see Achkhoy-Martan
Novosel'ye Rus. Fed. 28 D4
Novosergiyevka Rus. Fed. 29 J5
Novoshakhtinsk Rus. Fed. 29 F7
Novosheshminsk Rus. Fed. 28 I5
Novosibirsk Rus. Fed. 26 I4
Novosibirskiye Ostrova is Rus. Fed. see New Siberia Islands
Novosokol'niki Rus. Fed. 28 D4
Novospasskoye Rus. Fed. 29 H5
Novotroyits'ke Ukr. 29 E7
Novoukrainka Ukr. see Novoukrayinka
Novoukrayinka Ukr. 29 D6
Novouzensk Rus. Fed. 29 I6
Novovolyns'k Ukr. 29 C6
Novovoronezh Rus. Fed. 29 F6
Novovoronezhskiy Rus. Fed. see Novovoronezh
Novo-Voskresenovka Rus. Fed. 64 A1
Novozhilovskaya Rus. Fed. 28 I2
Novozybkov Rus. Fed. 29 D5
Novska Croatia 44 F2
Nový Bor Czech Rep. 37 G3
Nový Jičín Czech Rep. 37 H4
Novyy Bor Rus. Fed. 28 J2
Novyye Petushki Rus. Fed. see Petushki
Novyy Izborsk Rus. Fed. 33 G4
Novyy Kholmogory Rus. Fed. see Archangel
Novyy Margelan Uzbek. see Fergana
Novyy Nekouz Rus. Fed. 31 N1
Novyy Oskol Rus. Fed. 29 F6
Novyy Port Rus. Fed. 26 H3
Novyy Urengoy Rus. Fed. 26 H3
Novyy Urgal Rus. Fed. 64 C2
Novyy Uzen' Kazakh. see Zhanaozen
Novyy Zay Rus. Fed. 28 J5
Now Iran 80 C4
Nowa Dęba Poland 37 J3
Nowa Ruda Poland 37 H3
Nowa Sól Poland 37 G3
Nowata U.S.A. 133 C4
Now Dezh Iran 80 B3
Nowe Poland 37 I2
Nowe Miasto Lubawskie Poland 37 I2
Now Gombad Iran 80 C3
Nowgong Assam India see Nagaon
Nowgong Madhya Pradesh India 74 C4
Now Kharegan Iran 80 C2
Nowleye Lake Canada 123 K2
Nowogard Poland 37 G2
Nowogród Poland 37 J2
Nowogród Bobrzański Poland 37 G3
Nowood r. U.S.A. 134 F3
Noworadomsk Poland see Radomsko
Nowra Australia 112 D4
Nowshahr Iran 80 B2
Now Shahr Iran 76 E2
Nowshera Pak. 81 H3
Nowsūd Iran 80 A3
Nowy Dwór Gdański Poland 37 I1
Nowy Dwór Mazowiecki Poland 37 J2
Nowy Sącz Poland 37 J4
Nowy Targ Poland 37 J4
Nowy Tomyśl Poland 37 H2
Noxen U.S.A. 131 E3
Noy, Xé r. Laos 60 D4
Noya Spain see Noia
Noyabr'sk Rus. Fed. 26 H3
Noyant France 38 D3
Noyil r. India 72 C4
Noyon France 39 G2
Nozay France 38 C3
Nozhay-Yurt Rus. Fed. 29 H8
Nsalamu Zambia 97 A8
Nsambi Dem. Rep. Congo 94 C5
Nsawam Ghana 93 E4
Nseluka Zambia 97 A7
Nsoc Equat. Guinea 93 H5
Nsombo Zambia 95 F7
Nsukka Nigeria 93 G4
Nsumbu National Park Zambia see Sumbu National Park
Ntalfa well Mauritania 90 B5
Ntambu Zambia 95 E8
Ntandembele Dem. Rep. Congo 94 C5
Ntcheu Malawi 97 B8
Ntchisi Malawi 97 B8
Ntem r. Cameroon 93 H5
Ntha S. Africa 99 E5
Ntiona Chad 88 B6
Ntomba, Lac l. Dem. Rep. Congo 94 C5
Ntoroko Uganda 96 A4
Ntoum Gabon 94 A4
Ntui Cameroon 93 H4
Ntungamo Uganda 96 A5
Ntwetwe Pan salt pan Botswana 98 E4
Nuanetsi r. Zimbabwe see Mwenezi
Nuba, Lake resr Sudan 89 F4
Nuba Mountains Sudan 96 A2
Nubian Desert Sudan 89 G4
Nubivarri hill Norway 32 F1
Nueces r. U.S.A. 133 B7
Nueltin Lake Canada 123 L2
Nueva, Isla i. Chile 153 D8
Nueva Alejandría Peru 146 C6
Nueva Ciudad Guerrero Mex. 133 B7
Nueva Esparta state Venez. 147 E2
Nueva Florida Venez. 146 D2
Nueva Germania Para. 149 F5
Nueva Harberton Arg. 153 D8
Nueva Imperial Chile 152 B4
Nueva Loja Ecuador 146 B4
Nueva Lubecka Arg. 153 C6
Nueva Rosita Mex. 126 F6
Nueva San Salvador El Salvador 138 G6
Nueve de Julio Arg. see 9 de Julio
Nuevitas Cuba 127 K7
Nuevo, Golfo g. Arg. 153 D5
Nuevo Casas Grandes Mex. 135 F7
Nuevo Ideal Mex. 126 E7
Nuevo Laredo Mex. 126 G6
Nuevo León state Mex. 133 B7
Nugaal admin. reg. Somalia 96 F2
Nugaal watercourse Somalia 96 F3
Nugget Point N.Z. 113 B4
Nugu r. India 72 C3
Nuguria Islands P.N.G. 107 E2
Nuh, Ras pt Pak. 81 E5
Nuhaka N.Z. 113 D2
Nui i. Tuvalu 107 G2
Nui Con Voi r. Vietnam see Red River
Nui Ti On mt. Vietnam 61 D5
Nuits-St-Georges France 39 F3
Nu Jiang r. China see Salween
Nukey Bluff hill Australia 109 F8
Nukha Azer. see Şäki

▶Nuku'alofa Tonga 107 H4
Capital of Tonga.

Nukufetau i. Tuvalu 107 G2
Nuku Hiva i. Fr. Polynesia 165 I6
Nukulaelae i. Tuvalu 107 G2
Nukulailai i. Tuvalu see Nukulaelae
Nukumanu Islands P.N.G. 107 E2
Nukunau i. Kiribati see Nikunau
Nukunono atoll Tokelau see Nukunonu
Nukunonu atoll Tokelau 107 H2
Nukus Uzbek. 76 F1
Nulato U.S.A. 120 D3
Nules Spain 43 F3
Nullagine Australia 108 C5
Nullagine r. Australia 108 C5
Nullarbor Australia 109 E7
Nullarbor National Park Australia 109 E7
Nullarbor Plain Australia 109 E7
Nullarbor Regional Reserve park Australia 109 E7
Nuluarniavik, Lac l. Canada 124 E1
Num i. Indon. 57 I6
Num Nepal 75 E4
Numan Nigeria 93 I3
Numata Japan 65 D5
Numazu Japan 65 D6
Numbulwar Australia 110 C2
Numfoor i. Indon. 57 H6
Numin r. China 64 A3
Numkaub Namibia 98 C3
Nummi Fin. 33 F3
Nunap Isua c. Greenland see Farewell, Cape
Nunavik reg. Canada 125 E1
Nunavut admin. div. Canada 123 L2
Nunda U.S.A. 130 E2
Nuneaton U.K. 35 F5
Nungatta National Park Australia 112 D5
Nungesser Lake Canada 123 M5
Nungo Moz. 97 C8
Nunivak Island U.S.A. 120 C4
Nunkapasi India 73 E1
Nunkun mt. Jammu and Kashmir 74 C2
Nunligran Rus. Fed. 27 S3
Nuñomoral Spain 42 C2
Nunukan i. Indon. 59 G2
Nuojiang China see Tongjiang
Nuoro Sardinia Italy 45 B4
Nupani i. Solomon Is 107 F3
Nuqayy, Jabal mts Libya 88 C4
Nuqrah Saudi Arabia 89 I3
Nuqruş, Jabal mt. Egypt 89 G3
Nuquí Col. 146 B3
Nur r. Iran 80 C2
Nūrābād Iran 80 B4
Nurakita i. Tuvalu see Niulakita
Nurata Uzbek. 81 F1
Nuratau, Khrebet mts Uzbek. 81 F1
Nur Dağları mts Turkey 78 C3
Nure r. Italy 44 B2
Nurek Tajik. see Norak
Nuremberg Germany 36 E4
Nūr Gal Afgh. 81 G3
Nuri Mex. 135 E7
Nuri Sudan 89 G5
Nuri, Teluk b. Indon. 59 E3
Nurla Jammu and Kashmir 74 C2
Nurlat Rus. Fed. 29 I5
Nurmes Fin. 32 H3
Nürnberg Germany see Nuremberg
Nurota Uzbek. see Nurata
Nurpur Pak. 81 G4
Nurri, Mount Australia 112 C3
Nurzec r. Poland 37 K2
Nusaybin Turkey 79 E3
Nu Shan mts China 66 A3
Nushki Pak. 81 F4
Nutak Canada 125 I1
Nutarawit Lake Canada 123 L2
Nutrioso U.S.A. 137 H5
Nutwood Downs Australia 110 C2
Nuugaatsiaq Greenland 121 N2

▶Nuuk Greenland 121 N3
Capital of Greenland.

Nuupas Fin. 32 G2
Nuussuaq Greenland 121 N2
Nuussuaq pen. Greenland 121 N2
Nuwakot Nepal 75 D3
Nuwaybi' al Muzayyinah Egypt 89 G2
Nuwerus S. Africa 98 C6
Nuweveldberge mts S. Africa 98 D7
Nuyts, Point Australia 109 B8
Nuyts Archipelago is Australia 109 F8
Nxai Pan National Park Botswana 98 E3
Nxaunxau Botswana 98 D3
Nyabessan Cameroon 93 H5
Nyabing Australia 109 B8
Nyack U.S.A. 131 G3
Nyagan' Rus. Fed. 26 G3
Nyagquka China see Yajiang
Nyagrong China see Xinlong
Nyahua Tanz. 97 B6
Nyahururu Kenya 96 C4
Nyainqêntanglha Feng mt. China 70 H5
Nyainqêntanglha Shan mts China 70 H6
Nyainrong China 75 G2
Nyakahura Kagera Tanz. 96 A5
Nyakahura Kagera Tanz. 96 A5
Nyakaliro Tanz. 96 B5
Nyakanazi Tanz. 96 A5
Nyåker Sweden 32 E3
Nyakh Rus. Fed. see Nyagan'
Nyakrom Ghana 93 E4
Nyala Sudan 88 E6
Nyalam China 70 G6
Nyamandhiovu Zimbabwe 99 F3
Nyamapanda Zimbabwe 99 G3
Nyambiti Tanz. 96 B5
Nyamlell Sudan 94 E2
Nyamtumbo Tanz. 97 C7
Nyande Zimbabwe see Masvingo
Nyandoma Rus. Fed. 28 G3
Nyandomskiy Vozvyshennost' hills Rus. Fed. 28 F3
Nyanga Congo 94 A5
Nyanga Gabon 94 A5
Nyanga prov. Gabon 94 A5
Nyanga Zimbabwe 99 G3
Nyanga National Park Zimbabwe 99 G3
Nyang Qu r. China 75 F3
Nyang Qu r. China 75 G3
Nyankpala Ghana 93 E3
Nyanza prov. Kenya 96 B5
Nyapongeth Sudan 96 B3
Nyar r. India 74 C3
Nyarling r. Canada 123 H2

▶Nyasa, Lake Africa 97 B7
3rd largest lake in Africa and 10th in the world.
africa 84–85
world 6–7

Nyasaland country Africa see Malawi
Nyashabozh Rus. Fed. 28 J2
Nyasvizh Belarus 29 C5
Nyathi Zimbabwe 99 F3
Nyaunglebin Myanmar 60 B4
Nyaungu Myanmar 60 A3
Nyays r. Rus. Fed. 28 L3
Nyazura Zimbabwe 99 G3
Nyborg Denmark 33 C5
Nyborg Norway 32 H1
Nybro Sweden 33 D4
Nyeboe Land reg. Greenland 121 N1
Nyêmo China 75 F3
Nyenchen Tanglha Range mts China see Nyainqêntanglha Shan
Nyeri Kenya 96 C5
Nyhammar Sweden 33 D3
Nyi, Co l. China 75 E2
Nyika National Park Zambia 97 B7
Nyika Plateau Malawi 97 B7
Nyima China 70 G5
Nyimba Zambia 97 A8
Nyingchi China 70 H6
Nyinma China see Maqu
Nyíregyháza Hungary 37 J5
Nyiri Desert Kenya 96 C5
Nyiru, Mount Kenya 96 C4
Nykøbing Denmark 33 C5
Nykøbing Mors Denmark 33 C4
Nykøbing Sjælland Denmark 33 C5
Nyköping Sweden 33 E4
Nykvarn Sweden 33 E4
Nylstroom S. Africa 99 F5
Nymagee Australia 112 C4
Nymboida National Park Australia 112 E3
Nymburk Czech Rep. 37 G3
Nynäshamn Sweden 33 E4
Nyngan Australia 112 C3
Nyogzê China 75 D3
Nyon Switz. 39 G3
Nyong r. Cameroon 93 H5
Nyons France 39 F4
Nýřany Czech Rep. 37 F4
Nyrob Rus. Fed. 28 K3
Nyrud Norway 32 H1
Nysa Poland 37 H3
Nysa Kłodzka r. Poland 37 H3
Nysa Łużycka r. Germany/Poland see Neiße
Nysäter Sweden 33 D4
Nysätern Sweden 33 D3
Nysh Rus. Fed. 64 E2
Nyssa U.S.A. 134 C4
Nystad Fin. see Uusikaupunki
Nyuk, Ozero l. Rus. Fed. 32 H2
Nyuksenitsa Rus. Fed. 28 H3

Nyunzu Dem. Rep. Congo 95 F6
Nyurba Rus. Fed. 27 L3
Nyuvchim Rus. Fed. 28 I3
Nyuya Rus. Fed. 27 L3
Nyuya r. Rus. Fed. 27 L3
Nyyskiy Zaliv lag. Rus. Fed. 64 E1
Nyzhn'ohirs'kyy Ukr. 29 E7
Nzambi Congo 95 A5
Nzara Sudan 94 F3
Nzega Tanz. 97 B6
Nzérékoré Guinea 92 C4
N'zeto Angola 95 B6
Nzi r. Côte d'Ivoire 92 D4
Nzilo, Lac l. Dem. Rep. Congo 95 E7
Nzingu Dem. Rep. Congo 94 E5
Nzo r. Côte d'Ivoire 92 D4
Nzobe Dem. Rep. Congo 95 B6
Nzoia r. Kenya 96 B4
Nzwani i. Comoros 97 E8

O

Oahe, Lake U.S.A. 132 A2
Oahu i. U.S.A. 135 [inset] Y1
Oaitupu i. Tuvalu see Vaitupu
Oakbank Australia 112 B4
Oak City U.S.A. 137 F2
Oakdale CA U.S.A. 136 B3
Oakdale LA U.S.A. 133 C6
Oakes U.S.A. 132 B2
Oakey Australia 111 G5
Oak Grove U.S.A. 133 D5
Oakham U.K. 35 F5
Oak Harbor OH U.S.A. 130 B3
Oak Harbor WA U.S.A. 134 B2
Oak Hill OH U.S.A. 130 B4
Oak Hill WV U.S.A. 130 C5
Oakhurst U.S.A. 136 C3
Oak Lake Canada 132 A1
Oakland CA U.S.A. 136 A3
Oakland MD U.S.A. 130 D4
Oakland ME U.S.A. 131 I1
Oakland NE U.S.A. 132 B3
Oakland airport U.S.A. 136 A3
Oaklands Australia 112 C4
Oak Lawn U.S.A. 132 E3
Oakley KS U.S.A. 132 A4
Oakley MI U.S.A. 130 A2
Oakover r. Australia 108 C5
Oakridge U.S.A. 134 B4
Oak Ridge U.S.A. 128 B4
Oakville Canada 130 D2
Oamaru N.Z. 113 B4
Oaro N.Z. 113 C3
Oasis U.S.A. 136 D3
Oatlands Australia 112 C6
Oaxaca Mex. 138 E5
Ob' r. Rus. Fed. 26 G3
Ob, Gulf of sea chan. Rus. Fed. see Obskaya Guba
Oba Canada 124 C3
Oba i. Vanuatu see Aoba
Obala Cameroon 93 H4
Obama Japan 65 C6
Oban U.K. 34 D3
Obanazawa Japan 65 E5
Obanbori Qayroqqum resr Tajik. 81 G1
Oban Hills mt. Nigeria 93 H4
O Barco Spain 42 C1
Obbia Somalia see Hobyo
Obbola Sweden 32 F3
Obdorsk Rus. Fed. see Salekhard
Óbecse Yugo. see Bečej
Obed Canada 123 G4
Obeliai Lith. 33 G5
Oberau Germany 36 E5
Oberlin KS U.S.A. 132 A4
Oberlin LA U.S.A. 133 C6
Obernai France 39 G2
Oberpfälzer Wald mts Germany 37 F4
Oberpullendorf Austria 37 H5
Oberstdorf Germany 36 E5
Oberwart Austria 37 H5
Obi i. Indon. 57 G6
Óbidos Brazil 147 H5
Obigarm Tajik. 81 G2
Obihiro Japan 64 E4
Obilić Yugo. 46 B3
Obil'noye Rus. Fed. 29 H7
Obion r. U.S.A. 133 D4

▶Ob'-Irtysh Asia 26 G3
2nd longest river in Asia and 5th in the world.
asia 50–51
world 6–7

Obispos Venez. 146 D2
Obluch'ye Rus. Fed. 64 B2
Obninsk Rus. Fed. 29 F5
Obo Cent. Afr. Rep. 94 E3
Obock Djibouti 96 D2
Obokote Dem. Rep. Congo 94 E5
Obolo Nigeria 93 G4
Oborniki Poland 37 H2
Obouya Congo 94 B5
Oboyan' Rus. Fed. 29 F6
Obozerskiy Rus. Fed. 28 G3
Obra India 75 D4
Obra r. Poland 37 G2
Obrage Arg. 152 F2
Obregón, Presa resr Mex. 135 E8
Obrenovac Yugo. 46 B2
O'Brien U.S.A. 134 B4
Obrochishte Bulg. 46 F3
Obruk Turkey 78 C3
Observatory Hill Australia 110 C6
Obshchiy Syrt hills Rus. Fed. 29 I6
Obskaya Guba sea chan. Rus. Fed. 26 H3
Obuasi Ghana 93 E4
Obubra Nigeria 93 H4
Obudu Nigeria 93 H4
Obva r. Rus. Fed. 28 J4
Ob"yachevo Rus. Fed. 28 I3
Ocala U.S.A. 129 C6
Ocampo Mex. 133 A7
Ocaña Col. 146 C2
Ocaña Peru 148 B3
Ocaña Spain 42 E3
Occidental, Cordillera mts Chile 148 C4
Occidental, Cordillera mts Col. 146 B4
Occidental, Cordillera mts Peru 148 C4
Oceana U.S.A. 130 C5
Ocean Beach U.S.A. 131 G3
Ocean Cape U.S.A. 122 B3
Ocean City MD U.S.A. 131 F4
Ocean City NJ U.S.A. 131 F4
Ocean Falls Canada 122 E4
Oceans Cay i. Bahamas 129 D7
Oceanside U.S.A. 136 D5
Ochakiv Ukr. 29 D7
Och'amch'ire Georgia 79 E2
Ocher Rus. Fed. 28 J4
Ochi mt. Greece 47 D5
Ochiishi-misaki pt Japan 64 F4
Ochil Hills U.K. 34 E3
Ochlockonee r. U.S.A. 129 B6
Ochrida, Lake Albania/Macedonia see Ohrid, Lake
Ochthonia, Akra pt Greece 47 D5
Ocilla U.S.A. 129 C6
Ockelbo Sweden 33 E3
Ocmulgee r. U.S.A. 129 C6
Ocna Mureș Romania 46 C1
Ocna Sibiului Romania 46 D2
Ocoña Peru 148 B4
O'Connell Creek r. Australia 111 E4
Oconto U.S.A. 132 E2
O Corgo Spain 42 C1
Ocoruro Peru 148 C3
October Revolution Island Rus. Fed. see Oktyabr'skoy Revolyutsii, Ostrov
Ocurí Bol. 148 D4
Ocussi East Timor see Pantemakassar
Ocussi enclave East Timor 108 D2
Oda Ghana 93 E4
Ōda Japan 65 C6
Oda, Jebel mt. Sudan 89 H4
Odae-san National Park S. Korea 65 B5
Ōdate Japan 65 E4
Odda Norway 33 B3
Odei r. Canada 123 L3
Odem U.S.A. 133 B7
Odemira Port. 42 B4
Ödemiş Turkey 78 A3
Ödenburg Hungary see Sopron
Odense Denmark 33 C5
Oder r. Germany 37 D3
also spelt Odra (Poland)
Oderbucht b. Germany 37 G1
Oderhaff b. Germany 37 G2
Oderzo Italy 44 D2
Odesa Ukr. 29 D7
Ödeshog Sweden 33 D4
Odessa Ukr. see Odesa
Odessa U.S.A. 133 A6
Odessus Bulg. see Varna
Odi watercourse Sudan 89 H5
Odiel r. Spain 42 C4
Odienné Côte d'Ivoire 92 D3
Odintsovo Rus. Fed. 28 F5
Odobeștilor, Măgura hill Romania 46 E2
Odolanów Poland 37 H3
Odorheiu Secuiesc Romania 46 D1
Odra r. Poland 37 I4
also spelt Oder (Germany)
Odra r. Spain 42 D1
Odžaci Yugo. 46 A2
Odzala, Parc National d' nat. park Congo 94 B4
Odzi r. Zimbabwe 99 G3
Oea Libya see Tripoli
Oeiras Brazil 150 D3
Oelde Germany 36 D3
Oelrichs U.S.A. 132 A3
Oelsnitz Germany 36 F3
Oelwein U.S.A. 132 D3
Oenpelli Australia 110 C2
Oesel i. Estonia see Hiiumaa
Oeufs, Lac des l. Canada 125 F2
Oeversee Germany 36 D1
Of Turkey 79 E2
O'Fallon r. U.S.A. 134 F3
Ofanto r. Italy 45 F4
Offa Nigeria 93 G3
Offenbach am Main Germany 36 D3
Offenburg Germany 36 C4
Offerdal Sweden 32 D3
Ofidoussa i. Greece 47 E6
Ofotfjorden sea chan. Norway 32 E1
Ōfunato Japan 65 E5
Oga r. Indon. 59 F2
Oga Japan 65 D5
Ogadēn reg. Eth. 96 E3
Oga-hantō pen. Japan 65 D5
Ōgaki Japan 65 D6
Ogallala U.S.A. 132 A3
Ogan r. Indon. 58 D3
Ogasawara-shotō is Japan see Bonin Islands
Ogbomosho Nigeria see Ogbomoso
Ogbomoso Nigeria 93 G3
Ogden IA U.S.A. 132 C3
Ogden UT U.S.A. 134 E4
Ogden, Mount Canada 122 C3
Ogdensburg U.S.A. 131 F1
Ogeechee r. U.S.A. 129 C6
Ogidaki Canada 124 C4
Ogilvie Mountains Canada 122 A1
'Oglât el Khnâchîch well Mali 90 E5
Oglat Sbot well Alg. 90 D4
Oglio r. Italy 44 C2
Ogmore Australia 111 G4
Ognon r. France 39 F3
Ognut Turkey see Göynük
Ogoja Nigeria 93 H4
Ogoki r. Canada 124 C3
Ogoki Lake Canada 124 C3
Ogoki Reservoir Canada 124 B3
Ogooué r. Gabon 94 A5
Ogooué-Ivindo prov. Gabon 94 B5
Ogooué-Lolo prov. Gabon 94 B5
Ogooué-Maritime prov. Gabon 94 A5
Ogosta r. Bulg. 46 C3
Ogou r. Togo 93 F4
Ogražden mts Bulg./Macedonia 46 C4
Ograzhden mts Bulg./Macedonia see Ogražden
Ogre Latvia 33 G4
Ogre r. Latvia 33 G4
Ogulin Croatia 44 E2
Ogun state Nigeria 93 F4
Ogurchinskiy, Ostrov i. Turkm. 79 H3
Ogurjaly Adasy i. Turkm. see Ogurchinskiy, Ostrov
Oğuz Azer. 29 H8
Ohafia Nigeria 93 G4
Ohai N.Z. 113 A4
Ohakune N.Z. 113 C2
Ohanet Alg. 91 H3
Ohangwena admin. reg. Namibia 98 C3
Ohcejohka Fin. see Utsjoki
O'Higgins Chile 148 C5
O'Higgins admin. reg. Chile 152 C3
O'Higgins, Lago l. Chile 153 B7
Ohio r. U.S.A. 130 C4
Ohio state U.S.A. 130 B3
Ohio Range mts Antarctica 163 X11
Ohm r. Germany 39 H1
'Ohonua Tonga 107 H4
Ohře r. Czech Rep. 37 G3
Ohre r. Germany 36 E2
Ohrid Macedonia 46 B4
Ohrid, Lake Albania/Macedonia 46 B4
Ohridsko Ezero l. Albania/Macedonia see Ohrid, Lake
Ohrigstad S. Africa 99 F5
Ohrit, Liqeni i l. Albania/Macedonia see Ohrid, Lake
Ohura N.Z. 113 C2
Oiapoque Brazil 147 I4
Oiapoque r. Brazil/Fr. Guiana 147 I3
Oiba Col. 146 C3
Oil City U.S.A. 130 D3
Oildale U.S.A. 136 C4
Oi Qu r. China 66 A2
Oise r. France 39 E2
Oiseaux du Djoudj, Parc National des nat. park Senegal 92 A1
Ōita Japan 65 B6
Oiti mt. Greece 47 C5
Oiti nat. park Greece 47 C5
Oituz r. Romania 46 E1
Oiuru well Libya 88 C4
Ojai U.S.A. 136 C4
Ojailén r. Spain 42 E3
Ojalava i. Samoa see Upolu
Ojcowski Park Narodowy nat. park Poland 37 I3
Öje Sweden 33 D3
Ojinaga Mex. 135 F7
Ojiya Japan 65 D5
Ojobo Nigeria 93 G4
Ojo de Laguna Mex. 135 F7

▶Ojos del Salado, Nevado mt. Arg./Chile 152 C1
2nd highest mountain in South America.
southamerica 142–143

Öjung Sweden 33 D3
Oka Nigeria 93 G4
Oka r. Rus. Fed. 29 G4
Okahandja Namibia 98 C4
Okahukura N.Z. 113 C2
Okaka Nigeria 93 F3
Okakarara Namibia 98 C4
Okak Islands Canada 125 I1
Okanagan Lake Canada 134 C2
Okanogan U.S.A. 134 C2
Okanogan r. U.S.A. 134 C2
Okanogan Range mts U.S.A. 134 B2
Okaputa Namibia 98 C4
Okara Pak. 81 H4
Okarem Turkm. 80 C2
Okaukuejo Namibia 98 B3
Okavango r. Botswana/Namibia 98 D3
Okavango admin. reg. Namibia 98 C3

▶Okavango Delta swamp Botswana 98 D3
Largest oasis in the world.
africa 84–85

Okaya Japan 65 D5
Okayama Japan 65 C6
Okazaki Japan 65 D6
Okeechobee U.S.A. 129 C7
Okeechobee, Lake U.S.A. 129 C7
Okefenokee Swamp U.S.A. 129 C6
Okene Nigeria 93 G4
Oker r. Germany 36 E2
Okha India 74 A5
Okha Rus. Fed. 27 O4
Okhadunga Nepal see Okhaldhunga
Okhaldhunga Nepal 75 E4
Okhansk Rus. Fed. 28 J4
Ókhi Óros mt. Greece see Ochi
Okhotka r. Rus. Fed. 27 O4
Okhotsk Rus. Fed. 27 O4
Okhotsk, Sea of Japan/Rus. Fed. 64 F3
Okhotskoye More sea Japan/Rus. Fed. see Okhotsk, Sea of
Okhtyrka Ukr. 29 E6
Okinawa i. Japan 63 L6
Okinawa-guntō is Japan see Okinawa-shotō
Okinawa-shotō is Japan 63 L6
Okino-Daitō-jima i. Japan 63 M7
Okino-Tori-shima i. Japan 57 I1
Oki-shotō is Japan 65 C5
Okitipupa Nigeria 93 G4
Okkan Myanmar 60 A4
Oklahoma state U.S.A. 135 H6

▶Oklahoma City U.S.A. 133 B5
State capital of Oklahoma.

Oklawaha r. U.S.A. 129 C6
Okmulgee U.S.A. 133 B5
Oko, Wadi watercourse Sudan 89 H4
Okola Cameroon 93 H4
Okolona U.S.A. 129 A5
Okondja Gabon 94 B5
Okonek Poland 37 H2
Okor r. Hungary 44 F2
Okotoks Canada 123 H5
Okotusu well Namibia 98 A3
Okovskiy Les for. Rus. Fed. 28 E5
Okoyo Congo 94 B5
Oksbøl Denmark 33 C5
Øksfjord Norway 32 F1
Oksskolten mt. Norway 32 D2
Oksu r. Tajik. 81 H2
Oktemberyan Armenia see Hoktemberyan
Oktumkum, Peski des. Turkm. 80 C1
Oktwin Myanmar 60 B4
Oktyabr' Kazakh. see Kandyagash
Oktyabr'sk Kazakh. see Kandyagash
Oktyabr'sk Rus. Fed. 29 I5
Oktyabr'skiy Belarus see Aktsyabrski
Oktyabr'skiy Amurskaya Oblast' Rus. Fed. 64 B1
Oktyabr'skiy Arkhangel'skaya Oblast' Rus. Fed. 28 G3
Oktyabr'skiy Rus. Fed. 27 P4
Oktyabr'skiy Rus. Fed. 28 J5
Oktyabr'skiy Sverdlovskaya Oblast' Rus. Fed. 28 K4
Oktyabr'skiy Volgogradskaya Oblast' Rus. Fed. 29 G7
Oktyabr'skoye Khanty-Mansiyskiy Avtonomnyy Okrug Rus. Fed. 26 G3
Oktyabr'skoye Orenburgskaya Oblast' Rus. Fed. 29 J5
Oktyabr'skoy Revolyutsii, Ostrov i. Rus. Fed. 27 J2
Okučani Croatia 44 F2
Okulovka Rus. Fed. 28 E4
Okushiri-tō i. Japan 64 D4
Okwa watercourse Botswana 98 E4
Ola Rus. Fed. 27 P4
Ola U.S.A. 133 C5
Ólafsvík Iceland 32 [inset]
Olaine Latvia 33 F4
Olancha Peak U.S.A. 136 C3
Öland i. Sweden 33 E4
Olanga Rus. Fed. 32 H2
Olary Australia 112 B4
Olary watercourse Australia 112 B4
Olathe U.S.A. 132 C4
Olavakod India 72 C4
Olavarría Arg. 152 E4
Oława Poland 37 H3
Olbernhau Germany 37 F3
Olbia Sardinia Italy 44 B4
Olcott U.S.A. 130 D2
Old Bastar India 73 D2
Old Cherrabun Australia 108 D4
Old Cork Australia 111 E4
Old Crow Canada 120 F3
Oldeide Norway 33 B3
Oldenburg Germany 36 D2
Oldenburg in Holstein Germany 36 E1
Oldenzaal Neth. 36 C2
Olderdalen Norway 32 F1
Oldfield r. Australia 109 C8
Old Forge U.S.A. 131 F2
Old Gidgee Australia 109 B6
Oldham U.K. 35 E5
Old Head of Kinsale Rep. of Ireland 35 B6
Oldmeldrum U.K. 34 E3
Old Mkushi Zambia 95 F8
Old Perlican Canada 125 K3
Old River U.S.A. 136 C4
Olds Canada 123 H5
Old Speck Mountain U.S.A. 131 H1
Olduvai Gorge tourist site Tanz. 96 B5
Old Wives Lake Canada 134 F2
Old Woman Mountains U.S.A. 137 E4
Olean U.S.A. 130 D2
Olecko Poland 37 K1
Oleggio Italy 44 B2
Olekma r. Rus. Fed. 27 M3
Olekminsk Rus. Fed. 27 M3
Oleksandriys'k Ukr. see Zaporizhzhya
Oleksandriya Ukr. 29 E6
Ølen Norway 33 B4
Olenegorsk Rus. Fed. 32 I1
Olenek Rus. Fed. 27 L3
Olenek r. Rus. Fed. 27 L2
Olenek Bay Rus. Fed. see Olenekskiy Zaliv
Olenekskiy Zaliv b. Rus. Fed. 27 M2
Olenino Rus. Fed. 28 E4
Olenitsa Rus. Fed. 28 E2
Olenivs'ki Kar"yery Ukr. see Dokuchayevs'k
Oleniy, Ostrov i. Rus. Fed. 26 H2
Olenya Rus. Fed. see Olenegorsk
Oléron, Île d' i. France 38 C4
Oleshky Ukr. see Tsyurupyns'k
Oleśnica Poland 37 H3
Olesno Poland 37 I3
Olet Tongo mt. Indon. 59 G5
Olevs'k Ukr. 29 C6
Ølfjellet mt. Norway 32 D2
Ol'ga Rus. Fed. 64 C4
Olga, Lac l. Canada 124 E3
Olga, Mount Australia 110 B5
Olhão Port. 42 C4
Olhava Fin. 32 G2
Olia Chain mts Australia 110 B5
Oliana Spain 43 G1
Olib i. Croatia 44 E2
Olifants watercourse Namibia 98 C5
Olifants r. W. Cape S. Africa 98 C6
Olifants r. W. Cape S. Africa 98 D7
Olifants r. S. Africa 99 F4
Olifantshoek S. Africa 98 D5
Olimarao atoll Micronesia 57 K4
Olimbos hill Cyprus see Olympos
Olimbos mt. Greece see Olympus, Mount
Olímpia Brazil 149 H5
Olimpos Beydağları Milli Parkı nat. park Turkey 78 B3
Olinda Entrance sea chan. Australia 111 F1
Olinga Moz. 99 H3
Olio Australia 111 E4
Oli Qoltyq Sory dry lake Kazakh. see Sor Mertvyy Kultuk
Olisipo Port. see Lisbon
Olite Spain 43 F1
Oliva Spain 43 F3
Oliva hill Spain 42 C3
Oliva, Cordillera de mts Arg./Chile 152 C2
Oliva de la Frontera Spain 42 C3
Olivares, Cerro de mt. Arg./Chile 152 C2
Olive Hill U.S.A. 130 B4
Olivehurst U.S.A. 136 B2
Oliveira Brazil 151 C7
Oliveira dos Brejinhos Brazil 150 D5
Olivença Moz. see Lupilichi
Olivenza r. Port./Spain 42 C3
Olivenza Spain 42 C3
Oliver Canada 134 C2
Olivet U.S.A. 132 B3
Olivia U.S.A. 132 C2
Oljoro Wells Tanz. 97 C6
Ol'khovatka Rus. Fed. 29 F6
Olkusz Poland 37 I3
Ollagüe Chile 148 C5
Ollioules France 39 F5
Ollita, Cordillera de mts Arg./Chile 152 C2
Ollitas mt. Arg. 152 C2
Öllölä Fin. 32 H3
Ollombo Congo 94 B5
Olmedo Spain 42 D2
Olmeto Corsica France 44 B4
Olmos Peru 146 B6
Olmütz Czech Rep. see Olomouc
Olney IL U.S.A. 128 A4
Olney MD U.S.A. 131 E4
Olney TX U.S.A. 133 B5
Olomane r. Canada 125 I3
Olomouc Czech Rep. 37 H4
Olonets Rus. Fed. 28 E3
Olongapo Phil. 57 F3
Olongliko Indon. 59 F3
Oloron-Ste-Marie France 38 C5
Olosenga i. American Samoa see Swains Island
Olot Spain 43 H1
Olot Uzbek. see Alat
Olovo Bos.-Herz. 44 G2
Olovyannaya Rus. Fed. 27 L4
Oloy, Qatorkŭhi mts Asia see Alai Range
Olpad India 74 B5
Olpe Germany 36 C3
Olše r. Czech Rep. 37 I4
Olsztyn Poland 37 J2
Olsztynek Poland 37 J2
Olt r. Romania 46 D3
Olta Arg. 152 D2
Olte, Sierra de mts Arg. 153 C5
Olten Switz. 39 G3
Oltenița Romania 46 E2
Olteț r. Romania 46 D2
Oltintopkan Tajik. 81 G1
Oltu Turkey 79 E2
Oluan Cape Taiwan see Oluan Pi
Oluan Pi c. Taiwan 67 G4
Ólvega Spain 43 F2
Olvera Spain 42 D4
Ol'viopol' Ukr. see Pervomays'k
Olymbos hill Cyprus see Olympos
Olympia tourist site Greece 47 B6

▶Olympia U.S.A. 134 B3
State capital of Washington.

Olympic National Park U.S.A. 134 B3
Olympos hill Cyprus 77 A2
Olympos mt. Greece see Olympus, Mount
Olympos nat. park Greece 47 C4
Olympus, Mount Greece 47 C4
Olympus, Mount U.S.A. 134 B3
Olyutorskiy Rus. Fed. 27 Q3
Olyutorskiy, Mys c. Rus. Fed. 27 R4
Olyutorskiy Zaliv b. Rus. Fed. 27 Q4
Olzheras Rus. Fed. see Mezhdurechensk
Oma China 75 D2
Ōma Japan 64 E4
Oma r. Rus. Fed. 28 H2
Omagh U.K. 35 C4
Omaguas Peru 146 C6
Omaha U.S.A. 132 C3
Omaheke admin. reg. Namibia 98 C4
Omal'skiy Khrebet mts Rus. Fed. 64 D1
Omalur India 72 C4
▶Oman country Asia 76 E6
asia 52–53, 82
Oman, Gulf of Asia 80 D5
Omangambo Namibia 98 B4
Omarama N.Z. 113 B4
Omarska Bos.-Herz. 44 F2
Omaruru Namibia 98 B4
Omatako watercourse Namibia 98 D3
Omate Peru 148 C4
Omba i. Vanuatu see Aoba
Ombai, Selat sea chan. Indon. 108 D2
Ombalantu Namibia see Uutapi
Ombella-Mpoko pref. Cent. Afr. Rep. 94 C3
Ombika waterhole Namibia 98 B3
Omboué Gabon 94 A5
Ombrone r. Italy 44 C3
Ombu China 75 E3
Omdraaisvlei S. Africa 98 D6
Omdurman Sudan 89 G6
Omegna Italy 44 B2
Omeo Australia 112 C5
Ometepec Mex. 138 E5
Om Hajēr Eritrea 89 H6
Omīdīyeh Iran 80 B4
Omineca Mountains Canada 122 E3
Omiš Croatia 44 F3
Omitara Namibia 98 C4
Ōmiya Japan 65 D6
Ommaney, Cape U.S.A. 122 C3
Ommen Neth. 36 C2
Omodeo, Lago l. Sardinia Italy 45 B4
Omoku Nigeria 93 G4
Omolon Rus. Fed. 27 Q3
Omolon r. Rus. Fed. 27 P3
Omo National Park Eth. 96 B3
Omo Wenz r. Eth. 96 C3
Omsk Rus. Fed. 26 H4
Omsukchan Rus. Fed. 27 P3
Ōmū Japan 64 E3
Omu, Vârful mt. Romania 46 D2
Omu-Aran Nigeria 93 G3
Omulew r. Poland 37 J2
Ōmura Japan 65 B6
Omurtag Bulg. 46 E3
Omusati admin. reg. Namibia 98 B3
Omutninsk Rus. Fed. 28 J4
Onaman Lake Canada 124 C3
Onancock U.S.A. 131 F5
Onang Indon. 59 G3
Onangué, Lac l. Gabon 94 A5
Onavas Mex. 135 E7
Onawa U.S.A. 132 B3
Onbingwin Myanmar 61 B5
Oncativo Arg. 152 E2
Oncócua Angola 95 B9
Onda Spain 43 F3
Ondal India see Andal
Ondangwa Namibia 98 B3
Ondava r. Slovakia 37 J4
Ondjiva Angola 95 B9
Ondo Nigeria 93 G4
Ondo state Nigeria 93 G4
Öndörhaan Mongolia 63 I2
One Botswana 98 D4
One and a Half Degree Channel Maldives 71 D11
One and a Half Mile Opening sea chan. Australia 111 F2
Onega Rus. Fed. 28 F3
Onega r. Rus. Fed. 28 F3
Onega, Lake Rus. Fed. 26 D3

▶Onega, Lake Rus. Fed. 28 E3
3rd largest lake in Europe.
europe 22–23

Onega Bay g. Rus. Fed. see Onezhskaya Guba
One Hundred and Fifty Mile House Canada see 150 Mile House
One Hundred Mile House Canada see 100 Mile House
Oneida NY U.S.A. 131 F2
Oneida TN U.S.A. 130 A5
Oneida Lake U.S.A. 131 F2
O'Neill U.S.A. 132 B3
Onekotan, Ostrov i. Rus. Fed. 54 H2
Oneonta AL U.S.A. 129 B5
Oneonta NY U.S.A. 131 F2
Onești Romania 46 E1
Onezhskaya Guba g. Rus. Fed. 28 E2
Onezhskoye Ozero l. Rus. Fed. see Onega, Lake
Onezhskoye Ozero l. Rus. Fed. see Onega, Lake
Ong r. India 73 D1
Onga Gabon 94 B5
Ongeri Dem. Rep. Congo 95 E6
Ongers watercourse S. Africa 98 D6
Ongiyn Gol r. Mongolia 70 J3
Ongjin N. Korea 65 A5
Ongole India 72 D3
Oni Georgia 79 E2
Onida U.S.A. 132 A2
Onilahy r. Madag. 99 [inset] I4
Onistagane, Lac l. Canada 125 G3
Onitsha Nigeria 93 G4
Onjati Mountain Namibia 98 C4
Onjiva Angola see Ondjiva
Onkamo Fin. 32 H3
Onkivesi l. Fin. 32 G3
Onnes Rus. Fed. 27 N3
Ōno Japan 65 D6
Ono-i-Lau i. Fiji 107 H4
Onomichi Japan 65 C6
Onor, Gora mt. Rus. Fed. 64 E2
Onotoa atoll Kiribati 107 G2
Ons, Illa de i. Spain 42 B1
Onseepkans S. Africa 98 C6
Onslow Australia 108 A5
Onslow Bay U.S.A. 129 D5
Onsŏng N. Korea 64 B4
Ontake-san vol. Japan 65 D6
Ontario prov. Canada 123 N5
Ontario CA U.S.A. 136 D4
Ontario OR U.S.A. 134 C3
Ontario, Lake Canada/U.S.A. 130 E2
Onteniente Spain see Ontinyent
Ontinyent Spain 43 F3
Ontojärvi l. Fin. 32 H2
Ontong Java Atoll Solomon Is 107 E2
Ontur Spain 43 F3
Onutu atoll Kiribati see Onotoa
Onverwacht Suriname 147 H3
Onyx U.S.A. 136 C4
Oodnadatta Australia 110 C5
Oodweyne Somalia 96 E2
Ooldea Range hills Australia 110 B6
Oologah Lake resr U.S.A. 133 C4
Ooratippra r. Australia 110 D4
Oos-Londen S. Africa see East London
Oostanaula r. U.S.A. 129 B5
Oostende Belgium see Ostend
Oosterhout Neth. 36 B3
Oosterschelde est. Neth. 36 A3
Ootacamund India see Udagamandalam
Ootsa Lake Canada 122 E4
Ootsa Lake l. Canada 122 E4
Opari Sudan 96 B4
Oparino Rus. Fed. 28 I4
Opasatika r. Canada 124 D3
Opasatika Lake Canada 124 D3
Opasquia Canada 123 M4
Opataca, Lac l. Canada 125 F3
Opatija Croatia 44 E2
Opatów Poland 37 J3
Opava Czech Rep. 37 H4
Opava r. Czech Rep. 37 I4
Opelika U.S.A. 129 B5
Opelousas U.S.A. 133 C6
Opeongo Lake Canada 124 E4
Opheim U.S.A. 134 F2
Ophir, Gunung vol. Indon. 58 C2
Opihi r. N.Z. 113 B4
Opinaca r. Canada 124 E2
Opinaca, Réservoir Canada 124 E2
Opinnagau r. Canada 124 D2
Opis tourist site Iraq 79 F4
Opiscotéo, Lac l. Canada 125 G2
Opobo Nigeria 93 G4
Opochka Rus. Fed. 28 D4
Opoczno Poland 37 J3
Opodepe Mex. 135 E7
Opole Poland 37 H3
Oporto Port. 42 B2
Opotiki N.Z. 113 D2
Opp U.S.A. 129 B6
Oppdal Norway 32 C3
Oppedal Norway 33 B3
Oppeln Poland see Opole
Oppido Lucano Italy 45 E4
Oppland county Norway 33 C3
Opportunity U.S.A. 134 C3
Oprișor Romania 46 C2
Opunake N.Z. 113 C2
Opuwo Namibia 98 B3
Oqtosh Uzbek. see Aktash
Øra Norway 32 F1
Oradea Romania 31 J4
Orahovac Yugo. 46 B3
Orahovica Croatia 44 F2
Orai India 74 C4
Oraibi U.S.A. 137 G4
Oraibi Wash watercourse U.S.A. 137 G4
Orajärvi Fin. 32 G2
Oral Kazakh. see Ural'sk
Oran Alg. 91 E2
Orán Arg. 149 D5
Oran, Sebkha d' salt pan Alg. 43 F5
Ŏrang N. Korea 64 B4
Orange Australia 112 D4
Orange France 39 F4
Orange r. Namibia/S. Africa 99 C6
Orange CA U.S.A. 136 D5
Orange TX U.S.A. 133 C6
Orange VA U.S.A. 130 D4
Orange, Cabo c. Brazil 147 I3
Orangeburg U.S.A. 129 C5
Orange Cone sea feature S. Atlantic Ocean 161 O8
Orange Cove U.S.A. 136 C3
Orange Free State prov. S. Africa see Free State
Orangerie Bay P.N.G. 111 G1
Orangeville Canada 130 C2
Orange Walk Belize 138 G5
Orani Sardinia Italy 45 B4
Oranienburg Germany 37 F2
Oranje Gebergte hills Suriname 147 H4
Oranjemund Namibia 98 C6

▶Oranjestad Aruba 146 D1
Capital of Aruba.

Orapa Botswana 98 E4
Orašac Bos.-Herz. 44 F2
Orăștie Romania 46 C2
Orașul Stalin Romania see Brașov
Orava r. Slovakia 37 I4
Orava, Vodná nádrž resr Slovakia 37 I4
Oravița Romania 46 B2
Oravská Magura mts Slovakia 37 I4
Orba Co l. China 74 D2
Orbassano Italy 44 A2
Orbec France 38 D2
Orbetello Italy 44 C3
Orbieu r. France 39 E5
Orbisonia U.S.A. 130 E3
Orbost Australia 112 D5
Orcadas research station S. Atlantic Ocean 167 A2
Orcera Spain 43 E3
Orchha India 74 C4
Orchila, Isla i. Venez. 147 E2
Orchomenos Greece 47 C5
Orchy r. U.K. 34 D3
Orcia r. Italy 44 C3
Orco r. Italy 44 A2
Orcutt U.S.A. 136 B4
Ord r. Australia 110 B2
Ord U.S.A. 132 B3
Ord, Mount Australia 110 A3
Orda Rus. Fed. 28 K4
Ördenes Spain see Ordes
Ordes Spain 42 B1
Ordesa - Monte Perdido, Parque Nacional de nat. park Spain 43 G1
Ord River Dam Australia 108 E4
Ordu Hatay Turkey see Yayladağı
Ordu Turkey 79 D2
Ordubad Azer. 79 F3
Ordway U.S.A. 132 A4
Ordzhonikidze Rus. Fed. see Vladikavkaz
Ordzhonikidzeabad Tajik. see Kofarnihon
Ordzhonikidzevskaya Rus. Fed. see Sleptsovskaya
Ore Nigeria 93 G4
Öreälven r. Sweden 32 E3
Oreälven r. Sweden 33 D3
Oreana U.S.A. 136 C1
Örebro Sweden 33 D4
Örebro county Sweden 33 D4
Oregon U.S.A. 130 B3
Oregon state U.S.A. 134 B4
Oregon City U.S.A. 134 B3
Orekhov Ukr. see Orikhiv
Orekhovo-Zuyevo Rus. Fed. 28 F5
Orel Orlovskaya Oblast' Rus. Fed. 29 F5
Orel Permskaya Oblast' Rus. Fed. 28 K4
Orel', Ozero l. Rus. Fed. 27 N4
Orelek mt. Bulg. 46 C4
Orellana Peru 146 C6
Orellana, Embalse de resr Spain 42 D3
Orel Oblast admin. div. Rus. Fed. see Orlovskaya Oblast'
Orem U.S.A. 137 G1
Ore Mountains Czech Rep./Germany see Erzgebirge
Ören Turkey 78 A3
Orenburg Rus. Fed. 29 J6
Orenburg Oblast admin. div. Rus. Fed. see Orenburgskaya Oblast'
Orenburgskaya Oblast' admin. div. Rus. Fed. 29 I6
Orense Arg. 152 F4
Orense Spain see Ourense
Oreón, Dhiavlos sea chan. Greece see Oreon, Diavlos
Oreon, Diavlos sea chan. Greece 47 C5
Oreor Palau see Koror
Orepuki N.Z. 113 A4
Oresh Bulg. 46 D3
Öreskilsälven r. Sweden 33 C4
Orestiada Greece 46 E4
Orestiás Greece see Orestiada
Öresund strait Denmark/Sweden 33 D5
Oretana, Cordillera mts Spain see Toledo, Montes de
Orewa N.Z. 113 C2
Orfane well Niger 93 G1
Orfanou, Kolpos b. Greece 46 C4
Orford Ness hd U.K. 35 G5
Organabo Fr. Guiana 147 H3
Organ Pipe Cactus National Monument nat. park U.S.A. 135 D6
Orgiva Spain 42 E4
Orgūn Afgh. 81 G3
Orhaneli Turkey 47 F5
Orhangazi Turkey 46 F4
Orhon Gol r. Mongolia 70 K1
Orhy, Pic d' mt. France/Spain 43 F1
Oria Spain 43 E4
Oriental, Cordillera mts Bol. 148 D4
Oriental, Cordillera mts Col. 146 C3
Oriental, Cordillera mts Peru 148 C3

Orientale *prov.* Dem. Rep. Congo **94** E4
Oriente Brazil **149** D2
Orihuela Spain **43** F3
Orikhiv Ukr. **29** E7
Orikum Albania **47** A4
Orillia Canada **130** D1
Orimattila Fin. **33** G3
Orin U.S.A. **134** F4
▶Orinoco *r.* Col./Venez. **147** F2
southamerica **154**
Orinoco Delta Venez. **147** F2
Oripää Fin. **33** F3
Oriskany U.S.A. **131** F2
Orissa *state* India **73** E1
Orissaare Estonia **33** J1
Oristano *Sardinia* Italy **45** B5
Oristano, Golfo di *b. Sardinia* Italy **45** B5
Orivesi Fin. **33** G3
Orivesi *l.* Fin. **32** H3
Oriximiná Brazil **147** H5
▶Orizaba, Pico de *vol.* Mex. **126** G5
3rd highest mountain in North America.
northamerica **116–117**

Orjonikdzeobod Tajik. *see* Kofarnihon
Örkelljunga Sweden **33** D4
Orkhomenós Greece *see* Orchomenos
Orkney *is* U.K. **34** F2
Orla *r.* Poland **37** H2
Orla *r.* Poland **37** H3
Orland U.S.A. **136** A2
Orlando U.S.A. **129** C6
Orleaes Brazil **151** B9
Orleans France **38** D3
Orléans U.S.A. **131** I3
Orléans, Île d' *i.* Canada **125** G4
Orléansville Alg. *see* Ech Chélif
Orlické Hory *mts* Czech Rep. **37** H3
Orlik Rus. Fed. **62** F1
Orlík, Vodní nádrž *resr* Czech Rep. **37** G4
Orlov Rus. Fed. **28** I4
Orlov Gay Rus. Fed. **29** I6
Orlovo Rus. Fed. **29** F6
Orlovskaya Oblast' *admin. div.* Rus. Fed. **29** F5
Orlovskiy Rus. Fed. **29** G7
Orly *airport* France **38** E2
Ormara, Ras *hd* Pak. **81** F5
Ormara, Ras *hd* Pak. **81** F5
Ormília Greece *see* Ormylia
Ormoc Phil. **57** F3
Ormond Beach U.S.A. **129** C6
Ormskirk U.K. **35** E5
Ormylia Greece **47** C4
Orne *r.* France **38** C2
Orne *r.* France **38** D2
Orneta Poland **37** J1
Örnö *i.* Sweden **33** E4
Örnsköldsvik Sweden **32** E3
Oro, Lac *l.* Mali **92** E1
Orobayaya Bol. **149** D3
Orobie, Alpi *mts* Italy **44** B1
Orocó Brazil **150** E4
Orocué Col. **146** D3
Orodara Burkina **92** D3
Orofino U.S.A. **134** C3
Oro Grande U.S.A. **136** D4
Orol Dengizi *salt l.* Kazakh./Uzbek. *see* Aral Sea
Oromia *admin. reg.* Eth. **96** C2
Oromocto Canada **125** H4
Oron Israel **77** B4
Oron Nigeria **93** H4
Orona *i.* Kiribati **107** H2
Orono U.S.A. **128** F2
Oronoque Guyana **147** G4
Oronoque *r.* Guyana **147** G4
Orontes *r.* Lebanon/Syria **77** C2
Oroqen Zizhiqi China *see* Alihe
Ororbia Spain **43** F1
Orós Brazil **150** E3
Orós, Açude *resr* Brazil **150** E3
Orosei *Sardinia* Italy **45** B4
Orosei, Golfo di *b. Sardinia* Italy **45** B4
Orosháza Hungary **37** J5
Oroszlány Hungary **37** I5
Oro Valley U.S.A. **137** G5
Oroville *CA* U.S.A. **136** B2
Oroville *WA* U.S.A. **134** C2
Orrkjølen *hill* Norway **33** C3
Orsa Sweden **33** D3
Orsha Belarus **29** C5
Orsjön *l.* Sweden **33** E3
Orsk Rus. Fed. **26** F4
Orșova Romania **46** C2
Ørsta Norway **33** B3
Ortaca Turkey **47** F6
Orta Nova Italy **44** F4
Orta Toroslar *plat.* Turkey **77** A1
Orte Italy **44** E3
Ortegal, Cabo *c.* Spain **42** C1
Orteguaza *r.* Col. **146** C4
Orthez France **38** C5
Ortigueira Spain **42** C1
Ortiz Mex. **135** F7
Ortiz Venez. **146** E2
Ortles *mt.* Italy **44** C1
Ortona Italy **44** E3
Ortonville *MI* U.S.A. **130** D2
Ortonville *MN* U.S.A. **132** B2
Ortospana Afgh. *see* Kābul
Örtülü Turkey *see* Şenkaya
Orulgan, Khrebet *mts* Rus. Fed. **27** M3
Orumbo Boka *hill* Côte d'Ivoire **92** D4
Orūmīyeh Iran *see* Urmia
Orūmīyeh, Daryācheh-ye *salt l.* Iran *see* Urmia, Lake
Oruro Bol. **148** D4
Oruro *dept* Bol. **148** D4
Orūzgān *prov.* Afgh. **81** F3
Orvault France **38** C3
Orvieto Italy **44** D3
Orville Coast Antarctica **167** L1
Orwell *OH* U.S.A. **130** C3
Orwell *VT* U.S.A. **131** I2
Oryol Rus. Fed. *see* Orel
Oryokgok China *see* Gade
Oryu *r.* Poland **37** J2
Oryshkany U.S.A. **131** G2
Orzyc *r.* Poland **37** J2
Orzysz Poland **37** J2
Os Norway **33** C3
Osa *r.* Poland **37** I2
Osa Rus. Fed. **28** R4
Osa, Península de *pen.* Costa Rica **139** H7
Osage U.S.A. **130** C4
Osage *r.* U.S.A. **132** E4
▶Osaka Japan **65** C6
world **16–17**
Osborne U.S.A. **132** B4
Oscar Fr. Guiana **147** H4
Oscar Range *hills* Australia **108** D4
Osceola *AR* U.S.A. **133** D5
Osceola *IA* U.S.A. **132** E3
Osceola *MO* U.S.A. **132** E4
Osceola *NE* U.S.A. **132** B3
Oschersleben (Bode) Germany **36** E2
Oschiri *Sardinia* Italy **45** B4
Osečina Yugo. **46** B2
Osel *i.* Estonia *see* Hiiumaa
Osensjøen *l.* Norway **33** C3
Osetr *r.* Rus. Fed. **29** F5

Osgoode Canada **124** F4
Osgood Mountains U.S.A. **134** C4
Osh Kyrg. **70** D3
Osh *admin. div.* Kyrg. **81** H1
Oshakati Namibia **98** B3
Oshana *admin. reg.* Namibia **98** B3
Oshawa Canada **130** D2
Oshika-hantō *pen.* Japan **65** E5
Oshikango Namibia **98** B3
Oshikoto *admin. reg.* Namibia **98** C3
Oshikuku Namibia **98** B3
Oshin *r.* Nigeria **93** G3
Oshivelo Namibia **98** B3
Oshkosh *NE* U.S.A. **132** A3
Oshkosh *WI* U.S.A. **130** B2
Oshmyany Belarus *see* Ashmyany
Oshnovīyeh Iran **80** B3
Oshobgo Nigeria **93** G4
Oshper Rus. Fed. **28** L2
Oshskaya Oblast' *admin. div.* Kyrg. *see* Osh
Oshtorān Kūh *mt.* Iran **80** B3
Oshun *state* Nigeria **93** G4
Osica de Sus Romania **46** D2
Osijek Croatia **44** F2
Osikovitsa Bulg. **46** D3
Osilinka *r.* Canada **122** E3
Osimo Italy **44** D3
Osipaonica Yugo. **46** B2
Osipenko Ukr. *see* Berdyans'k
Osipovichi Belarus *see* Asipovichy
Osire Namibia **98** C1
Osiyan India **74** B4
Osizweni S. Africa **99** F5
Osječenica *mts* Bos.-Herz. **44** F2
Oskaloosa U.S.A. **132** E3
Oskarshamn Sweden **33** E4
Oskarström Sweden **33** D4
Öskemen Kazakh. *see* Ust'-Kamenogorsk
Oskol *r.* Rus. Fed. **29** F6
Oslava *r.* Czech Rep. **37** H4
▶Oslo Norway **33** C4
Capital of Norway.

Oslo *airport* Norway *see* Gardermoen
Oslofjorden *sea chan.* Norway **33** C4
Osmanabad India **72** C2
Osmancık Turkey **78** D2
Osmaniye Turkey **78** D3
Os'mino Rus. Fed. **28** D4
Osmussaar *i.* Estonia **33** F1
Osnabrück Germany **36** D2
Osno Lubuskie Poland **37** G2
Osogbo Nigeria *see* Oshogbo
Osogovske Planine *mts* Bulg./Macedonia **46** C3
Osor *hill* Croatia **44** E2
Osório Brazil **151** A8
Osorno Chile **152** B5
Osorno Spain **42** D1
Osoyoos Canada **134** C2
Osøyri Norway **30** F1
Osprey Reef Australia **111** F2
Oss Neth. **36** E3
Ossa *hill* Port. **42** C3
Ossa, Mount Australia **112** C6
Osse *r.* Nigeria **93** G4
Ósseo U.S.A. **132** D2
Ossining U.S.A. **131** G3
Ossokmanuan Lake Canada **125** H2
Ossora Rus. Fed. **27** Q4
Ostashkov Rus. Fed. **28** E4
Oste *r.* Germany **36** D1
Ostend Belgium *see* Ostend
Ostende Belgium *see* Ostend
Osterburg (Altmark) Germany **36** E2
Österbybruk Sweden **33** E3
Österbymo Sweden **33** D4
Österdalälven *l.* Sweden **33** D3
Österfärnebo Sweden **33** J3
Östergötland *county* Sweden **33** D4
Osterholz-Scharmbeck Germany **36** D2
Ostermundigen Switz. **39** G3
Österreich *country* Europe *see* Austria
Östersund Sweden **32** D3
Östervåla Sweden **33** J3
Østfold *county* Norway **33** C4
Østhammar Sweden **33** E3
Östra Kvarken *strait* Fin./Sweden **32** F3
Ostrava Czech Rep. **37** I4
Ostróda Poland **37** I2
Ostrogozhsk Rus. Fed. **29** F6
Oštro Koplje *mt.* Yugo. **46** B3
Ostrołęka Poland **37** J2
Ostrov Czech Rep. **37** F3
Ostrov Romania **46** E2
Ostrov Romania **46** E2
Ostrov Rus. Fed. **28** D4
Ostrovets Poland *see* Ostrowiec Świętokrzyski
Ostrovskoye Rus. Fed. **28** I4
Ostrów Poland *see* Ostrów Wielkopolski
Ostrowiec Poland *see* Ostrowiec Świętokrzyski
Ostrowiec Świętokrzyski Poland **37** J3
Ostrów Mazowiecka Poland **37** J2
Ostrowo Poland *see* Ostrów Wielkopolski
Ostrów Wielkopolski Poland **37** H3
Ostrzeszów Poland **37** H3
Ostseebad Binz Germany **37** F1
Ostuni Italy **45** F4
Osum *r.* Albania **47** A4
Osŭm *r.* Bulg. **46** D3
Ōsumi-kaikyō *sea chan.* Japan **65** B7
Ōsumi-shotō *is* Japan **65** B7
Osun *state* Nigeria *see* Oshun
Osuna Spain **42** D4
Oswego *KS* U.S.A. **132** C4
Oswego *NY* U.S.A. **131** E2
Oswestry U.K. **35** E5
Oświęcim Poland **37** I3
Ōta Japan **65** D5
Otago Peninsula N.Z. **113** B4
Otaki N.Z. **113** E4
Otaru Japan **64** E4
Otava Fin. **33** G3
Otavalo Ecuador **146** B4
Otavi Namibia **98** B3
Ōtawara Japan **65** E5
Otdia *atoll* Marshall Is *see* Wotje
Otelnuc, Lac *l.* Canada **125** H2
Oțelu Roșu Romania **46** C2
Otematata N.Z. **113** B4
Otepää Estonia **33** O3
Otepää kõrgustik *hills* Estonia **33** G4
Oteren Norway **32** F1
Oteros *r.* Mex. **135** E8
Othello U.S.A. **134** C3
Othonoi *i.* Greece **47** A5
Oti *r.* Ghana/Togo **93** F4
Otira N.Z. **113** B3
Otis *Monts hills* Canada **125** G3
Otjenene Namibia **98** C3
Otjitambi Namibia **98** B3

Otjiwarongo Namibia **98** C4
Otjivasandu *waterhole* Namibia **98** B3
Otjozondjupa *admin. reg.* Namibia **98** C4
Otočac Croatia **44** E2
Otok Croatia **44** G2
Otoka Bos.-Herz. **44** F2
Otoro, Jebel *mt.* Sudan **96** A2
Otorohanga N.Z. **113** E4
Otpor Rus. Fed. *see* Zabaykal'sk
Otradnoye Rus. Fed. *see* Otradnyy
Otradnyy Rus. Fed. **29** K5
Otranto Italy **45** H4
Otranto, Strait of Albania/Italy **31** I5
Otrogovo Rus. Fed. *see* Stepnoye
Otrokovice Czech Rep. **37** H4
Otrozhnyy Rus. Fed. **27** R3
Otsego Lake U.S.A. **131** F2
Ōtsu Japan **65** C6
Otta Norway **33** C3
Otta *r.* U.K. **35** E4
Otterburn U.K. **34** E4
Otterstad Sweden **33** D4
Ottignies Belgium **36** D4
Ottumwa U.S.A. **132** E3
Otukpa Nigeria **93** G4
Otukpo Nigeria **93** H4
▶Ottawa Canada **124** F4
Capital of Canada.

Ottawa *r.* Canada **124** F4
Ottawa *IL* U.S.A. **132** D3
Ottawa *KS* U.S.A. **132** C4
Ottawa *OH* U.S.A. **130** A3
Ottawa Islands Canada **124** D1
Otter *r.* U.K. **35** E4
Otterøy Norway **32** C2
Otway Australia **130** D2
Otway, Bahía *b.* Chile **152** B8
Otway, Cape Australia **112** B5
Otway, Seno *b.* Chile **152** C8
Otway National Park Australia **112** B5
Otwock Poland **37** J2
Ötztaler Alpen *mts* Austria **36** E5
Ou, Nam *r.* Laos **60** C3
Ouacha Niger **93** H2
Ouachita *r.* U.S.A. **133** D6
Ouachita, Lake U.S.A. **133** C5
Ouachita Mountains *AR/OK* U.S.A. **127** I5
Ouadâne Mauritania **90** C5
Ouadda Cent. Afr. Rep. **94** C3
Ouaddaï *pref.* Chad **88** C6
Ouadjinkarem *well* Niger **91** G5
Ouâd Nâga Mauritania **92** B1
Ouagadougou Burkina **93** E2
Capital of Burkina.

Ouahigouya Burkina **93** E2
Ouahran Alg. *see* Oran
Ouaka *pref.* Cent. Afr. Rep. **94** D3
Ouaka *r.* Cent. Afr. Rep. **94** D3
Ouâlâta Mauritania **92** D1
Oualé *r.* Burkina **93** F3
Oualia Mali **92** C2
Ouallam Niger **93** F2
Ouallene Alg. **91** F4
Ouanary Fr. Guiana **147** I3
Ouanazein *well* Chad **88** C5
Ouanda-Djallé Cent. Afr. Rep. **94** D3
Ouandago Cent. Afr. Rep. **94** C3
Ouandja *r.* Cent. Afr. Rep. **94** D2
Ouandja Vakaga Cent. Afr. Rep. **94** D2
Ouango Cent. Afr. Rep. **94** C4
Ouangolodougou Côte d'Ivoire **92** D3
Ouani Kalaoua *well* Niger **93** G2
Ouanne *r.* France **38** E3
Ouaqui Fr. Guiana **147** H4
Ouara *r.* Cent. Afr. Rep. **94** D3
Ouargaye Burkina **93** F3
Ouargla Alg. **91** G2
Ouarissibiti *well* Mali **93** F1
Ouaritoufoulout *well* Mali **93** F1
Ouarkziz, Jbel *ridge* Alg./Morocco **90** C3
Ouarogou Burkina *see* Ouargaye
Ouatagouna Mali **93** F2
Oubangui *r.* Cent. Afr. Rep./Dem. Rep. Congo *see* Ubangi
Oubergpas *pass* S. Africa **98** E7
Oudenaarde Belgium **39** E1
Oudon *r.* France **38** C3
Oudtshoorn S. Africa **98** D7
Oued Zem Morocco **90** D2
Ouéléssébougou Mali **92** C3
Ouémé *r.* Benin **93** F4
Ouessa Burkina **92** E3
Ouessant, Île d' *i.* France **38** A2
Ouesso Congo **94** C4
Ouest *prov.* Cameroon **93** H4
Ouezzane Morocco **90** D2
Oughterard Rep. of Ireland **35** B5
Ouham *pref.* Cent. Afr. Rep. **94** C3
Ouham *r.* Cent. Afr. Rep./Chad **94** C3
Ouham Pendé *pref.* Cent. Afr. Rep. **94** C3
Ouidah Benin **93** F4
Ouindarene Mali **93** E1
Ouiriego Mex. **135** E8
Ouistreham France **38** D2
Oujaft *well* Mauritania **92** D1
Oujda Morocco **91** F2
Oujeft Mauritania **92** B1
Oulad Teïma Morocco **90** C3
Oulainen Fin. **32** N4
Oulangan kansallispuisto *nat. park* Fin. **32** H2
Ould Yenjé Mauritania **92** C2
Ould Djellal Alg. **91** G2
Ouled Farès Alg. **43** G5
Ouled Naïl, Monts des *mts* Alg. **91** F2
Ouled Saïd *well* Alg. **91** F3
Ouli Cameroon **94** B3
Oullins France **39** F4
Oulu Fin. **32** N4
Oulu *prov.* Fin. **32** O3
Oulujärvi *l.* Fin. **32** O4
Oulujoki *r.* Fin. **32** O4
Oulx Italy **44** A2
Oum-Chalouba Chad **88** D6
Oumé Côte d'Ivoire **92** D4
Oum el Bouaghi Alg. **91** G2
Oumm ed Droûs Guebli, Sebkhet *salt flat* Mauritania **90** C5
Oumm ed Droûs Telli, Sebkha *salt flat* Mauritania **90** C4
Oumm el A'sel *well* Mali **90** D5
Ounara Morocco **90** C3
Oungre Canada **123** I5
Ounianga Kébir Chad **88** D5
Ounianga Sérir Chad **88** D5
Ounissoui *well* Niger **93** I1
Our *r.* Lux. **39** E2
Ourcq *r.* France **39** E2
Ouré Kaba Guinea **92** C3
Ouricuri Brazil **150** H5
Ourinhos Brazil **149** H5
Ourique Port. **42** B4
Ouro Brazil **150** C4

Ouro Preto Brazil **151** D7
Ourthe *r.* Belgium **39** F1
Ouse *r.* France **38** D1
Oust *r.* France **38** B3
Outamba Kilimi National Park Sierra Leone **92** B3
Outaouais, Rivière des *r.* Canada *see* Ottawa
Outardes *r.* Canada **125** G3
Outardes Quatre, Réservoir Canada **125** G3
Outat Oulad el Haj Morocco **90** E2
Outer Hebrides *is* U.K. **34** A3
Outer Mongolia *country* Asia *see* Mongolia
Outer Santa Barbara Channel U.S.A. **136** C5
Outjo Namibia **98** C4
Outlook Canada **123** J5
Outokumpu Fin. **32** P5
Out Skerries *is* U.K. **34** F1
Ouvéa *i.* New Caledonia **107** F4
Ouyanghai Skuiku *resr* China **67** E3
Ouyen Australia **112** B4
Ova *r.* Turkey **46** E4
Ovace, Punta d' *mt. Corsica* France **44** B4
Ovada Italy **44** B2
Ovaeymiri Turkey **47** E6
Ovalle Chile **152** C2
Ovamboland *reg.* Namibia **98** B3
Ovan Gabon **94** B4
Ovar Port. **42** B2
Oveng Cameroon **93** I5
Ovens *r.* Australia **112** C5
Overhalla Norway **32** C2
Överkalix Sweden **32** F2
Overlander Roadhouse Australia **109** A6
Overland Park U.S.A. **132** C4
Övermark Fin. **33** M3
Overton U.S.A. **137** F3
Övertorneå Sweden **32** F2
Överum Sweden **33** E4
Överuman *l.* Sweden **32** D2
Ovid *MI* U.S.A. **130** A2
Ovid *NY* U.S.A. **131** E2
Ovidiu Romania **46** F2
Oviedo Spain **42** D1
Ovišrags *hd* Latvia **32** F3
Øvre Anarjokka Nasjonalpark *nat. park* Norway **32** G1
Øvre Dividal Nasjonalpark *nat. park* Norway **32** E1
Øvre Pasvik Nasjonalpark *nat. park* Norway **32** H1
Övre Soppero Sweden **32** F1
Ovruch Ukr. **29** D6
Owaka N.Z. **113** B4
Owando Congo **94** B5
Owase Japan **65** D6
Owatonna U.S.A. **132** E2
Owbeh Afgh. **81** E3
Owego U.S.A. **131** E2
Owen Falls Dam Uganda **96** B4
Owen Island Myanmar **61** B6
Owen River N.Z. **113** D5
Owens *r.* U.S.A. **136** D3
Owensboro U.S.A. **128** B4
Owens Lake U.S.A. **136** D3
Owen Sound Canada **130** C1
Owen Springs Australia **110** C1
Owen Stanley Range *mts* P.N.G. **106** D2
Owensville U.S.A. **132** D4
Owenton U.S.A. **130** A4
Owerri Nigeria **93** G4
Owikeno Lake Canada **122** E5
Owingsville U.S.A. **130** C4
Owl *r.* Canada **123** M3
Owl Creek *r.* U.S.A. **134** C4
Owo Nigeria **93** G4
Owosso U.S.A. **130** A2
Owyhee *r.* U.S.A. **134** C4
Owyhee Mountains U.S.A. **134** C4
Owyhee North Fork *r.* U.S.A. **134** C4
Owyhee South Fork *r.* U.S.A. **134** C4
Oxapampa Peru **148** C3
Oxbow Canada **123** K5
Ox Creek *r.* U.S.A. **132** C1
Oxelösund Sweden **33** J4
Oxford N.Z. **113** D6
Oxford U.K. **35** F6
Oxford *MA* U.S.A. **131** H2
Oxford *ME* U.S.A. **131** H1
Oxford *MS* U.S.A. **127** I5
Oxford *NC* U.S.A. **128** D4
Oxford *NY* U.S.A. **131** F2
Oxford *OH* U.S.A. **130** A4
Oxford House Canada **123** M4
Oxford Lake Canada **123** M4
Oxley Australia **112** B4
Oxleys Peak Australia **112** D4
Oxley Wild Rivers National Park Australia **112** E3
Ox Mountains *hills* Rep. of Ireland *see* Slieve Gamph
Oxnard U.S.A. **136** C4
Oxus *r.* Asia *see* Amudar'ya
Oxylithos Greece **47** D5
Oya *r.* Sarawak Malaysia **59** E2
Oyabe Japan **65** D5
Ō-yama *vol.* Japan **65** D6
Oyapock *r.* Brazil/Fr. Guiana **147** I3
Oyem Gabon **94** A4
Oyen Canada **123** I5
Øyeren *l.* Norway **33** C4
Oykel *r.* U.K. **34** E3
Oymyakon Rus. Fed. **27** O3
Oyo Congo **94** B5
Oyo Nigeria **93** F4
Oyo *state* Nigeria **93** F3
Oyón Peru **148** C3
Oyonnax France **39** F3
Oy-Tal Kyrg. **81** H1
Oytograk China **75** D1
Oyukludağı *mt.* Turkey **77** A1
Oyyl Kazakh. *see* Uil
Ozalp Turkey **79** F3
Ozamiz Phil. **57** F5
Ozark *AL* U.S.A. **129** B6
Ozark *AR* U.S.A. **133** C5
Ozark *MO* U.S.A. **132** C4
Ozark Plateau U.S.A. **132** C4
Ozarks, Lake of the U.S.A. **132** C4
Ozárow Poland **37** J3
Ozbaşı Turkey **47** E6
Ózd Hungary **37** J4
Özdere Turkey **47** E6
Ozerne Ukr. **46** F1
Ozernovskiy Rus. Fed. **27** P4
Ozernyy Rus. Fed. **31** M2
Ozero *r.* Rus. Fed. **64** B2
Ozery Rus. Fed. **29** F5
Ozhogina *r.* Rus. Fed. **27** O3
Ozieri *Sardinia* Italy **45** B4
Ozimek Rus. Fed. **29** F5
Ozinki Rus. Fed. **29** J6
Ozona U.S.A. **133** A6

Ouro Preto Brazil **151** D7
Ozorków Poland **37** I3
Ozurget'i Georgia **79** E2

Pâ Burkina **92** E3
Paakkola Fin. **32** G2
Pa-an Myanmar **60** B4
Paamiut Greenland **121** O3
Pa-an S. Africa **60** B3
Paarl S. Africa **98** D7
Paatsjoki *r. Europe see* Patsoyoki
P'abal-li N. Korea **65** B4
Pabianice Poland **37** I3
Pabianitz Poland *see* Pabianice
Pabna Bangl. **75** F4
Pabradė Lith. **33** G5
Pab Range *mts* Pak. **81** F5
Pacaás Novos, Parque Nacional *nat. park* Brazil **149** E2
Pacahuaras *r.* Bol. **148** D2
Pacajus Brazil **150** E4
Pacaraimã, Serra *mts* S. America *see* Pakaraima Mountains
Pacaraima Mountains S. America *see* Pakaraima Mountains
Pacarán Peru **148** B3
Pacasmayo Peru **148** A1
Pacatuba Brazil **150** E4
Pacaya Samiria, Reserva Nacional *nature res.* Peru **146** C6
Paceco *Sicily* Italy **45** C6
Pachia *i.* Greece **47** D6
Pachino *Sicily* Italy **45** E6
Pachmarhi India **74** C5
Pachor India **72** B1
Pachora India **72** B1
Pachpadra India **74** B4
Pachuca Mex. **126** G7
Pachthon *mt.* Iran **80** B3
Pacific-Antarctic Ridge *sea feature* S. Pacific Ocean **165** H9
Pacific Grove U.S.A. **136** B3
▶Pacific Ocean **165** J5
Largest ocean in the world.
oceans **156–157,168**

Pacific Rim National Park Canada **122** E5
Pacinan, Tanjung *pt* Indon. **59** F4
Pačir Yugo. **46** A2
Pacitan Indon. **59** E5
Packsattel *pass* Austria **37** G5
Pacov Czech Rep. **37** G4
Pacoval Brazil **147** H5
Padali Rus. Fed. *see* Amursk
Padampur India **74** D5
Padang *Kalimantan Barat* Indon. **59** E3
Padang *Sumatera Barat, Sumatra* Indon. **58** C3
Padang *i.* Indon. **58** C2
Padangpanjang Indon. **58** C3
Padangsidimpuan Indon. **58** B2
Padangtikar Indon. **59** E3
Padangtikar *i.* Indon. **59** E3
Padany Rus. Fed. **28** G3
Padasjoki Fin. **33** G3
Padatha, Kūh-e *mt.* Iran **80** B3
Padauiri *r.* Brazil **146** F4
Padcaya Bol. **148** D5
Paddington Australia **112** C4
Paderborn Germany **36** D3
Padeșu, Vârful *mt.* Romania **46** C2
Padilla Bol. **149** D4
Padina Romania **46** E2
Padina Yugo. **46** B2
Padinska Skela Yugo. **46** B2
Padjelanta nationalpark *nat. park* Sweden **32** E2
Padmanabhapuram India **72** C4
Padmapur India **74** D5
Padova Italy *see* Padua
Padra India **74** B5
Padrão, Ponta do *pt* Angola **95** B4
Padrauna India **75** E4
Padre Caro *hill* Spain **42** C4
Padre Island U.S.A. **133** B7
Padrón Spain **42** B1
Padua Italy **44** D2
Paducah *KY* U.S.A. **128** B4
Paducah *TX* U.S.A. **133** A5
Padum Jammu and Kashmir **74** C2
Pădurea Craiului, Munții *mts* Romania **46** C1
Paekdu-san *mt.* China/N. Korea **64** C4
Paengnyŏng-do *i.* S. Korea **65** A5
Paeroa N.Z. **113** E3
Paestum *tourist site* Italy **45** E4
Pafúri Moz. **99** D3
Pag Croatia **44** E2
Pag *i.* Croatia **44** E2
Paga Conta Brazil **147** H6
Pagadian Phil. **57** G5
Pagai Selatan *i.* Indon. **58** C3
Pagai Utara *i.* Indon. **58** C3
Pagalu *i. Equat. Guinea see* Annobón
Pagan *i.* N. Mariana Is **57** K2
Pagaralam Indon. **58** C3
Pagasitikos Kolpos *b.* Greece **47** C4
Pagatan *Kalimantan Selatan* Indon. **59** F3
Pagatan *Kalimantan Tengah* Indon. **59** F3
Page U.S.A. **137** G3
Pagerdewa Indon. **58** D3
Pagėgiai Lith. **33** G5
Pageland U.S.A. **129** D5
Pagirai Lith. **33** G5
Pago *r.* Croatia *see* Pag
Pagon *i.* N. Mariana Is *see* Pagan
Pagosa Springs U.S.A. **135** F5
Pagouda Togo **93** F3
Pagqên China *see* Gadê
Pagri China **75** G4
Pagwa River Canada **124** D3
Pahala U.S.A. **135** [inset] Z2
Pahang *r.* Malaysia **58** C2
Pahang *state* Malaysia **58** C2
Paharpur Pak. **81** G3
Pahasu India **72** C4
Pahaunan Indon. **59** E2
Pahlavi Dezh Iran *see* Āq Qal'eh
Pahlgam Jammu and Kashmir **74** C2
Pahra Kariz Afgh. **81** E3
Pahranagat Range *mts* U.S.A. **137** F3
Pahrump U.S.A. **137** E3
Pahuj *r.* India **74** C4
Pahute Mesa *plat.* U.S.A. **137** D3
Paiaguás Brazil **149** F4
Paicines U.S.A. **136** B3
Paide Estonia **28** D4
Paignton U.K. **35** D6
Paiján Peru **148** A1
Päijänne *l.* Fin. **33** G3
Paikü Co *l.* China **75** E3
Paila *r.* Bol. **149** D4
Pailing China *see* Chun'an
Pailin Cambodia **61** C4
Pailitas Col. **146** D2
Pailolo Channel U.S.A. **135** [inset] J1
Pailolo Channel U.S.A. **135** [inset]
Paillaco Chile **152** B5

Paimpol France **38** B2
Painan Indon. **58** C3
Paine Chile **152** C3
Paine, Cerro *mt.* Chile **153** B7
Painesville U.S.A. **130** C3
Painted Desert U.S.A. **137** G3
Painted Rock Dam U.S.A. **137** F5
Paint Hills Canada *see* Wemindji
Paint Lake Canada **123** L4
Paint Rock U.S.A. **133** B6
Paintsville U.S.A. **130** B5
Pairi *r.* India **73** D1
Paisley Canada **130** C1
Paisley U.K. **34** E4
Païsu Vasco *aut. comm.* Spain **43** E1
Paita Peru **146** A6
Paitan, Teluk *b. Sabah* Malaysia **59** G1
Paithan India **72** B2
Paitou China **67** G2
Paiva *r.* Port. **42** B2
Paiva Couceiro Angola *see* Quipungo
Paizhou China **67** G2
Pajala Sweden **32** F2
Pajan Ecuador **146** A5
Pajęczno Poland **37** H3
Pakala India **72** C3
Pakanbaru Indon. *see* Pekanbaru
Pakaraima Mountains S. America **147** F3
Pakaur India **75** E4
Pakch'ŏn N. Korea **65** A5
Pakesley Canada **124** D4
Pakhachi Rus. Fed. **27** Q3
Pakhiá *i.* Greece *see* Pachia
Pakhoi China *see* Beihai
▶Pakistan *country* Asia **81** F4
4th most populous country in Asia and 6th in the world.
asia **52–53, 82**
world **16–17**

Pakkat Indon. **58** B2
Paklenica *nat. park* Croatia **44** E2
Paknampho Thai. *see* Nakhon Sawan
Pakokku Myanmar **60** A3
Pakowki Lake *imp. l.* Canada **123** I5
Pakpattan Pak. **81** H4
Pak Phanang Thai. **61** C6
Pak Phayun Thai. **61** C7
Pakrac Croatia **44** F2
Pakruojis Lith. **33** F5
Paks Hungary **37** I5
Pakse Laos **61** D5
Pak Tam Chung *Hong Kong* China **67** [inset]
Pak Thong Chai Thai. **61** C5
Paktiā *prov.* Afgh. **81** G3
Paktīkā *prov.* Afgh. **81** G3
Pakwash Lake Canada **124** D4
Pakxé Laos **61** D5
Pal Senegal *see* Mpal
Pala Chad **94** B3
Pala Myanmar **61** B5
Palabuanbaru Indon. **59** D4
Palabuhanratu, Teluk *b.* Indon. **58** D4
Palacios Bol. **148** D2
Palaestinia *reg.* Asia *see* Palestine
Palafrugell Spain **43** H2
Palagiano Italy **45** F4
Palagruža *i.* Croatia **44** F3
Palaia Fokaia Greece **47** C6
Palaiochora Greece **47** C7
Palaiokastron Greece *see* Palaikastro
Palaikastro Greece **47** E7
Palairos Greece **47** B5
Palakkat India *see* Palghat:
Palamakoloi Botswana **98** D1
Palam Pur India **74** C2
Palana India **74** B4
Palana Rus. Fed. **27** P4
Palancia *r.* Spain **43** F3
Palandur India **72** D1
Palanga Lith. **33** F5
Palangán, Kūh-e *mts* Iran **81** F3
Palangkaraya Indon. **59** F3
Palani India **72** C4
Palanpur India **74** B4
Palantak Pak. **81** F5
Palapye Botswana **99** E4
Palapye Botswana **99** E4
Palasbari India **75** F4
Palas de Rei Spain **42** C1
Palatka Rus. Fed. **27** P3
Palatka U.S.A. **129** C6
Palau *Sardinia* Italy **45** B4
▶Palau *country* N. Pacific Ocean **57** H4
asia **52–53, 82**
Palau Islands Palau **57** H4
Palauk Myanmar **61** B5
Palaw Myanmar **61** B5
Palawan *i.* Phil. **56** F5
Palawan Trough *sea feature* N. Pacific Ocean **164** D5
Palayankottai India **72** C4
Paldiski Estonia **33** N7
Pale Bos.-Herz. **44** G3
Palembang Indon. **58** C3
Palena *Aisén* Chile **153** B6
Palena Los Lagos Chile **153** B5
Palencia Spain **42** D1
Palermo Arg. **149** D6
Palermo *Sicily* Italy **45** D5
Palermo Punta Raisi *airport Sicily* Italy **45** D5
Palestine *reg.* Asia **77** B3
Palestine U.S.A. **133** C6
Paletwa Myanmar **60** A3
Palghar India **72** B2
Palghat India **72** C4
Pali *Madhya Pradesh* India **74** D5
Pali *Maharashtra* India **72** B2
Pali *Rajasthan* India **74** B4
▶Palikir Micronesia **164** E5
Capital of Micronesia.

Palinuro, Capo *c.* Italy **45** E4
Paliouri Greece **47** C5
Paliouri, Akra *pt* Greece **47** C5
Palisade U.S.A. **134** F4
Palitana India **74** A5
Palja *hill* Sweden **32** H2
Paljakka *hill* Fin. **32** O4
Pälkäne Fin. **33** G3
Palk Bay Sri Lanka **72** C4
Palkohda India **75** E5
Palkonda Range *mts* India **72** C3
Palkot India **75** E5
Palk Strait India/Sri Lanka **72** C4
Pallapalle *mt.* India **72** C4
Pallani India **72** D2
Pallas ja Ounastunturin kansallispuisto *nat. park* Fin. **32** F1
Pallasovka Rus. Fed. **29** H6
Palleru *r.* India **72** D2
Pallinup *r.* Australia **109** B8
Pallisa Uganda **96** B3
Palliser, Cape N.Z. **113** E5
Palliser, Îles *is* Fr. Polynesia **165** I7
Palliser Bay N.Z. **113** C3

Pallu India 74 B3
Palma r. Brazil 150 C5
Palma Moz. 97 D7
Palma del Río Spain 42 D4
Palma di Montechiaro Sicily Italy 45 D6
Palmaner India 72 C3
Palmares Acre Brazil 148 D2
Palmares Pernambuco Brazil 150 F4
Palmares do Sul Brazil 151 B9
Palmarito Venez. 146 D2
Palmarola, Isola i. Italy 45 D4
Palmas Paraná Brazil 151 B8
Palmas Tocantins Brazil 150 D4
Palmas, Cape Liberia 92 C4
Palmas, Golfo di b. Sardinia Italy 45 B5
Palm Bay U.S.A. 129 C7
Palmdale U.S.A. 136 C4
Palm Desert U.S.A. 137 D5
Palmeira das Missões Brazil 151 A8
Palmeira dos Índios Brazil 150 E4
Palmeirais Brazil 150 D3
Palmeiras r. Brazil 150 C5
Palmeiras de Goiás Brazil 149 H4
Palmeirinhas, Ponta das pt Angola 95 B7
Palmer research station Antarctica 167 L2
Palmer r. Australia 111 E3
Palmer watercourse Australia 110 C5
Palmer U.S.A. 120 C3
Palmerston N.T. Australia 167 L2
Palmerston N.T. Australia 110 B2
Palmerston N.T. Australia see Darwin
Palmerston Canada 130 C2
Palmerston atoll Cook Is 165 H7
Palmerston, Cape Australia 111 G4
Palmerston North N.Z. 113 B4
Palmerton U.S.A. 131 F3
Palmerville Australia 111 F2
Palmi Italy 45 E5
Palmira Col. 146 B4
Palmnicken Rus. Fed. see Yantarnyy
Palm Springs U.S.A. 137 D5
Palmyra Syria see Tadmur
Palmyra NY U.S.A. 131 E3
Palmyra PA U.S.A. 131 F3
Palmyra VA U.S.A. 130 D5

► Palmyra Atoll N. Pacific Ocean 165 H5
United States Unincorporated Territory.
oceania 104–105, 114

Palmyras Point India 73 E1
Palni Hills India 72 C4
Palo Alto U.S.A. 136 A3
Palo Blanco Arg. 152 D1
Palo Blanco Mex. 133 B7
Palo Chino watercourse Mex. 135 D7
Palo de las Letras Col. 146 B3
Paloh Sarawak Malaysia 59 E2
Paloich Sudan 86 D3
Palojoensuu Fin. 32 F1
Palomani mt. Peru 148 C3
Palomar Mountain U.S.A. 136 D5
Palomera, Sierra mts Spain 43 F2
Palomitas Arg. 148 D6
Paloncha India 72 D2
Palopo Indon. 57 F7
Palos, Cabo de c. Spain 43 F4
Palo Santo Arg. 152 E1
Palouse r. U.S.A. 134 C3
Palovesi l. Fin. 33 F3
Palpa Peru 148 B3
Palsana India 74 B5
Paltamo Fin. 32 G2
Paltaselkä l. Fin. 32 G2
Palu Indon. 57 E6
Palu i. Indon. 108 C2
Palu Turkey 79 D3
Palung Co China 75 D3
Pal'vart Turkm. 81 F2
Palwal India 74 C3
Palwancha India see Paloncha
Palyavaam r. Rus. Fed. 27 R3
Palyeskaya Nizina marsh Belarus/Ukr.
see Pripet Marshes
Pama Burkina 93 F3
Pama r. Cent. Afr. Rep. 94 C3

► Pamana i. Indon. 108 C2
Most southerly point of Asia.

Pamanukan Indon. 59 D4
Pamar Col. 146 D3
Pamban Channel India 72 C4
Pambarra Moz. 99 G4
Pambula Australia 112 D6
Pamekasan Indon. 59 F4
Pameungpeuk Indon. 59 D4
Pamfylla Greece 47 K5
Pamidi India 72 C3
Pamiers France 38 D5
Pamir r. Afgh./Tajik. 81 H2
Pamir mts Asia 70 D4
Pamlico r. U.S.A. 128 E5
Pampa U.S.A. 133 A5
Pampachiri Peru 148 B3
Pampa Grande Arg. 152 D1
Pampas r. Peru 148 B3
Pampeluna Spain see Pamplona
Pamplin U.S.A. 130 D5
Pamplona Col. 146 C3
Pamplona Spain 43 F1
Pamukan, Teluk b. Indon. 59 G3
Pamukçu Turkey 47 L5
Pamukkale Turkey 47 F6
Pamukova Turkey 78 B2
Pamunkey r. U.S.A. 131 E5
Pamzal Jammu and Kashmir 74 C2
Pana Gabon 94 B5
Pana U.S.A. 128 A4
Panaca U.S.A. 137 E3
Panache, Lake Canada 124 D4
Panaeati Island P.N.G. 111 H1
Panagar India 74 D5
Panagia i. Greece 46 D4
Panagi India 72 C3
Panaguyurishte Bulg. 46 D3
Panaitan i. Indon. 58 D4

► Panama country Central America 139 H7
northamerica 118–119, 140

Panamá, Bahía de b. Panama 146 B2
► Panama, Gulf of Panama 146 B3
► Panama Canal Central America 146 B2
northamerica 118–119

► Panama City Panama 146 B2
Capital of Panama.

Panama City U.S.A. 129 E6
Panamint Range mts U.S.A. 136 D3
Panamint Valley U.S.A. 136 D3
Panao Peru 148 A2
Panar r. India 75 F4
Panarea, Isola i. Isole Lipari Italy 45 E5
Panarik Indon. 59 E2
Panaro r. Italy 44 C2
Panatinane Island P.N.G. 111 H1
Panay i. Phil. 57 C4

Panayarvi Natsional'nyy Park nat. park
Rus. Fed. 32 H2
Panayia i. Greece see Panagia
Pancake Range mts U.S.A. 137 E2
Pančevo Yugo. 46 B2
Panchagarh Bangl. 75 F4
Panch'iao Taiwan 67 H3
Pancingapan, Bukit mt. Indon. 59 D4
Panciu Romania 46 F2
Pancsova Yugo. see Pančevo
Panda Moz. 99 G3
Pandan, Selat strait Sing. 58 [inset]
Pandan Reservoir Sing. 58 [inset]
Pandaria India 75 D5
Pandavapura India 72 C3
Pan de Azúcar Chile 152 C1
Pan de Azúcar, Parque Nacional
nat. park Chile 152 C1
Pandhana India 74 C5
Pandharpur India 72 B2
Pandhurna India 74 C5
Pando dept Bol. 148 D2
Pando Uruguay 152 E4
Pandokrátor hill Greece see
Pantokratoras
Pandora Entrance sea chan. Australia
111 F1
Pandrup Denmark 33 C4
Paneas Syria see Bāniyās
Panelas Brazil 149 E2
Panevėžys Lith. 33 G5
Panfilov Kazakh. see Zharkent
Pang r. China 64 A1
Pang, Nam r. Myanmar 60 B3
Panga Dem. Rep. Congo 94 E3
Pangai Tonga 107 H3
Pangal Andhra Pradesh India 72 C2
Pangal Andhra Pradesh India 72 C2
Pangani Tanz. 97 C6
Pangani r. Tanz. 97 C6
Panghsang Myanmar 60 B3
Pangi Dem. Rep. Congo 94 E5
Pangi Range mts Pak. 74 C2
Pangkah, Tanjung pt Indon. 59 F4
Pangkalanbuun Indon. 59 E3
Pangkalanlunang Indon. 58 B2
Pangkalansusu Indon. 58 B1
Pangkalpinang Indon. 58 D3
Pangkalsiang, Tanjung pt Indon. 57 F6
Panglang Myanmar 60 B2
Pangman Canada 123 J5
Pangnirtung Canada 121 M3
Pango Aluquém Angola 95 B7
Pangody Rus. Fed. 26 I3
Pangonda Cent. Afr. Rep. 94 C3
Pangong Tso salt l. China/
Jammu and Kashmir see Bangong Co
Pangrango mt. Indon. 59 D4
Pang Sida National Park Thai. 61 C5
Pang Sua, Sungai r. Sing. 58 [inset]
Pangtara Myanmar 60 B3
Panguipulli Chile 152 B4
Panguitch U.S.A. 137 F3
Panhandle U.S.A. 133 A5
Pania-Mwanga Dem. Rep. Congo 95 F6
Pani Mines India 74 B5
Panipat India 74 C3
Panj r. Afgh./Tajik. see Pyandzh
Panj Tajik. 81 G2
Panjāb Afgh. 81 F3
Panjakent Tajik. 81 F2
Panjang r. Indon. 59 E2
Panjang i. Indon. 58 D3
Panjang, Bukit Sing. 58 [inset]
Panjang, Selat sea chan. Indon. 58 C2
Panjgur Pak. 81 F5
Panjhra r. India 74 B5
Panjim India see Panaji
Panji Poyon Tajik. 81 G2
Panjkora r. Pak. 81 G3
Panjnad r. Pak. 81 G4
Pankakoski Fin. 32 H3
Panlian China see Miyi
Pan Ling mts China 64 B4
Panlong China see Queshan
Panna India 74 D4
Pannawonica Australia 108 B5
Pannonhalma Hungary 37 H5
Pano Aqil Pak. 81 G5
Panopah Indon. 59 E3
Panoplis Egypt see Akhmīm
Panorama Brazil 149 H5
Panormus Sicily Italy see Palermo
Panruti India 72 C4
Panshi China 64 A4
Panshui China see Pu'an
Pantaicermin, Gunung mt. Indon. 58 C3

► Pantanal marsh S. America 149 F4
Largest area of wetlands in the world.

Pantanal de São Lourenço marsh Brazil
149 F4
Pantanal do Taquari marsh Brazil
149 F4
Pantanal Matogrossense, Parque
Nacional do nat. park Brazil 149 F4
Pantar i. Indon. 108 D2
Pantelaria Sicily Italy see Pantelleria
Pantelleria Sicily Italy 45 C7
Pantelleria, Isola di i. Sicily Italy 45 D6
Pantemakassar East Timor 57 F7
Pantha Myanmar 60 A3
Panticapaeum Ukr. see Kerch
Pantokratoras hill Greece 47 A5
Pantoowarinna, Lake salt flat Australia
110 C5
Panu Dem. Rep. Congo 95 C5
Pánuco Mex. 126 G7
Panvel India 72 B2
Panwari India 74 C4
Panxian China 62 G6
Panzhihua China 66 B3
Panzi Dem. Rep. Congo 95 C6
Pao r. Venez. 147 E2
Pão de Açúcar Brazil 150 E4
Paola Italy 45 F5
Paola U.S.A. 132 C4
Paoli U.S.A. 130 B4
Paonia U.S.A. 134 F5
Paoua Cent. Afr. Rep. 94 C3
Paôy Pêt Cambodia 61 C5
Pápa Hungary 37 H5
Papa, Monte del mt. Italy 45 E4
Papagni r. India 72 C3
Papakura N.Z. 113 C3
Papanasam India 72 C4
Paparhahandi India 73 D2
Paparoa National Park N.Z. 113 B5
Papas, Akra pt Greece 47 D6
Papa Stour i. U.K. 34 F1
Pápateszér Hungary 37 H5
Papatoetoe N.Z. 113 C3
Papa Westray i. U.K. 34 G2
Papay i. U.K. see Papa Westray

► Papeete Fr. Polynesia 165 I7
Capital of French Polynesia.

Papenburg Germany 36 H1
Paphos Cyprus 77 A2
Paphus Cyprus see Paphos
Papigochic r. Mex. 135 F7
Papikio mt. Bulg./Greece 46 D4

Papillion U.S.A. 132 B3
Papiya hill Bulg. 46 E3
Paposo Chile 152 C1
Papua, Gulf of P.N.G. 57 J7

► Papua New Guinea country Oceania
106 D2
2nd largest and 2nd most populous
country in Oceania.
oceania 104–105, 114

Papun Myanmar 60 B4
Papunya Australia 110 B4
Pará r. Brazil 151 C6
Pará state Brazil 147 I5
Pará, Rio do r. Brazil 150 B2
Paraburdoo Australia 108 B5
Paracaima, Sierra mts S. America see
Pakaraima Mountains
Paracas Peru 148 A3
Paracas, Península pen. Peru 148 A3
Paracatu Brazil 151 C6
Paracatu r. Brazil 151 C6
Paracel Islands S. China Sea 56 D2
Parachilna Australia 112 A3
Parachinar Pak. 81 G3
Paracín Yugo. 46 C3
Parada, Punta pt Peru 148 B3
Pará de Minas Brazil 151 C6
Paradise r. Canada 125 J2
Paradise Guyana 147 G3
Paradise CA U.S.A. 136 B2
Paradise NV U.S.A. 137 E3
Paradise Gardens Canada 123 H2
Paradise Hill Canada 123 I4
Paradise Peak U.S.A. 136 D2
Paradise River Canada 125 J2
Paradise Valley U.S.A. 137 G5
Paradwip India 73 E1
Paraetonium Egypt see Marsá Maṭrūḥ
Paraf"yanava Belarus 33 G5
Paragominas Brazil 150 C2
Paragould U.S.A. 127 H4
Paragua r. Bol. 149 E3
Paragua i. Phil. see Palawan
Paragua r. Venez. 147 F3
Paraguaçu r. Brazil 150 E4
Paraguaçu Paulista Brazil 151 B7
Paraguaípoa Venez. 146 D2
Paraguari Para. 149 F6
Paraguay r. Arg./Para. 149 F6
► Paraguay country S. America 149 F5
southamerica 142–145, 154
Paraíba r. Brazil 150 F3
Paraíba state Brazil 150 F3
Paraíba do Sul r. Brazil 151 D7
Parainen Fin. see Pargas
Paraíso Brazil 149 G4
Paraíso do Norte Brazil 150 B4
Parakka Sweden 32 F2
Parakou Benin 93 F3
Parakylia Australia 109 G7
Paralakhemundi India 73 E2
Paralia Greece 47 C5
Paramagudi India see Paramakkudi
Paramakkudi India 72 C4
Paramaribo Suriname 147 H3
Capital of Suriname.

Paramillo mt. Col. 146 C3
Paramillo, Parque Nacional nat. park
Col. 146 B3
Paramirim r. Brazil 150 C4
Páramo de Masa, Puerto del pass
Spain 42 E1
Paramonga Peru 148 A2
Paramushir, Ostrov i. Rus. Fed. 27 P4
Paramythia Greece 47 B5
Paran watercourse Israel 77 B4
Paraná Arg. 152 E2
Paraná Brazil 150 C3
Paraná r. Brazil 150 B5
Paraná state Brazil 149 H6
► Paraná r. S. America 152 F3
Part of the Rio de la Plata - Paraná, 2nd
longest river in South America.
southamerica 142–143

Paranaguá Brazil 151 B8
Paranaíba Brazil 149 H4
Paranaíba r. Brazil 151 B7
Paraná Ibicuy r. Brazil 152 F3
Paranaíta r. Brazil 149 F3
Paranaiacaba, Serra mts Brazil
151 B8
Paranari Brazil 147 E5
Paranavaí Brazil 149 G5
Parandak Iran 80 B3
Parang i. Indon. 59 F5
Parangi Aru r. Sri Lanka 72 D4
Parangipettai India 72 C4
Parang Pass India 74 C2
Parângul Mare, Vârful mt. Romania
46 C2
Parantij India 74 B5
Paraopeba r. Brazil 151 C6
Parapanda mt. Spain 42 E4
Paraparaumu N.Z. 113 C3
Parapeti r. Bol. 148 E5
Parapól, Serrania mts Venez. 147 E3
Parapuá Brazil 151 B7
Pararú Iran 80 E5
Paras Mex. 133 A7
Parasnath mt. India 75 E4
Parati Brazil 151 C7
Paratoo Australia 112 A4
Parãú, Kūh-e mt. Iraq 79 F4
Parauapebas r. Brazil 150 B3
Parauaquara, Serra hill Brazil 147 H5
Paraúna Brazil 149 H4
Paray-le-Monial France 39 F3
Parbati r. India 74 C4
Parbatipur Bangl. 75 F4
Parbhani India 72 C2
Parchim Germany 36 E2
Pardina Romania 46 F2
Pardo r. Arg. 152 E5
Pardo r. Bahia Brazil 150 E5
Pardo r. Mato Grosso do Sul Brazil
149 G5
Pardo r. São Paulo Brazil 149 H5
Pardoo Australia 108 B5
Pardubice Czech Rep. 37 G3
Pare Indon. 59 F4
Parecis r. Brazil 149 F3
Parecis, Serra dos hills Brazil 149 E2
Paredes de Nava Spain 42 D2
Paredón Mex. 133 A7
Parent Canada 125 H3
Parentis-en-Born France 38 C4
Pareora N.Z. 113 B4
Parepare Indon. 57 E6
Parga Greece 47 B5
Pargas Fin. 33 F3
Parghelia Italy 45 E5
Pari India 72 C2
Paria r. U.S.A. 137 G3
Paria, Gulf of Trin. and Tob./Venez.
139 L6
Paria, Península de pen. Venez. 147 F2
Pariaman Indon. 58 C3
Paricutín vol. Mex. 133 B7
Parikkala Fin. 33 H3
Parikud Islands India 73 E2

Parima, Serra mts Brazil 147 E4
Parima-Tapirapecó, Parque Nacional
nat. park Venez. 147 E4
Parinari Peru 146 C6
Parintins Brazil 147 G5
Paris Canada 130 C2

► Paris France 38 E2
Capital of France and most populous
city in Europe.
europe 48
world 16–17

Paris IL U.S.A. 128 B4
Paris KY U.S.A. 130 A4
Paris MO U.S.A. 132 C4
Paris TN U.S.A. 128 A4
Paris TX U.S.A. 133 A5
Parish U.S.A. 131 E2
Pârîz Iran 80 D4
Pârk Iran 81 F5
Park r. U.S.A. 132 B1
Parka Dem. Rep. Congo 94 E3
Parkajoki Sweden 32 F2
Parkal India 72 C2
Parkano Fin. 33 F3
Parke Lake Canada 125 J2
Parker U.S.A. 137 E4
Parker Lake Canada 123 M2
Parker Range hills Australia 109 B8
Parkersburg U.S.A. 130 C4
Parkers Lake U.S.A. 130 A5
Parkes Australia 112 D4
Park Falls U.S.A. 132 C2
Parkhar Tajik. see Farkhor
Parkhill Canada 130 C2
Parkman Canada 123 K5
Park Rapids U.S.A. 132 C2
Parksley U.S.A. 131 F5
Parkston U.S.A. 132 B3
Parksville Canada 122 E5
Parla Spain 42 E2
Parlakimedi India see Paralakhemundi
Parla Kimedi India 73 E2
Parli Vaijnath India 72 C2
Parlung Zangbo r. China 66 A2
Parma r. Italy 44 C2
Parma Italy 44 C2
Parma Rus. Fed. 28 K2
Parma ID U.S.A. 134 C4
Parma OH U.S.A. 130 C3
Parmana Venez. 147 E3
Parnaíba Brazil 150 D1
Parnaíba r. Mato Grosso Brazil 150 C4
Parnaíba r. Maranhão Piauí Brazil 150 D2
Parnaíbinha r. Brazil 150 D2
Parnamirim Brazil 150 E3
Parnarama Brazil 150 D3
Parnassós mts Greece 47 C5
Parnassos nat. park Greece 47 C5
Parnassus N.Z. 113 C3
Parnitha mt. Greece 47 C6
Parnon mts Greece 47 C6
Pärnu Estonia 28 C4
Pärnu r. Estonia 28 C4
Pärnu-Jaagupi Estonia 28 C4
Pärnu laht b. Estonia 33 G4
Paro Bhutan 75 F4
Paroo watercourse Australia 111 E6
Paroo Channel watercourse Australia
112 B3
Paropamisus mts Afgh. 81 E3
Paros Greece 47 D6
Paros i. Greece 47 D6
Parowan U.S.A. 137 F3
Parque Nacional Alto Madidi nat. park
Bol. 148 D2
Parque Nacional Constitución de 1857
nat. park U.S.A. 135 D7
Parral Chile 152 C4
Parral r. Mex. 135 F8
Parramatta Australia 112 D4
Parramore Island U.S.A. 131 F5
Parras Mex. 133 A7
Parrsboro Canada 125 H4
Parry, Cape Canada 121 H2
Parry Islands Canada 121 H2
Parry Range hills Australia 108 A5
Parry Sound Canada 124 C4
Pars prov. Iran see Fārs
Parsa prov. Iran see Fārs
Parsęta r. Poland 37 G1
Parsons KS U.S.A. 132 C4
Parsons WV U.S.A. 130 D4
Parsons Range hills Australia 110 C2
Partabpur Chhattisgarh India 72 D2
Partabpur Chhattisgarh India 75 D5
Partakko Fin. 32 G1
Partanna Sicily Italy 45 D6
Pärte mt. Sweden 32 E2
Partenstein Germany 36 E4
Parthenay France 38 D3
Partinico Sicily Italy 45 D5
Partizansk Rus. Fed. 64 C4
Partizansk Sicily Italy see Partinico
Partridge r. Canada 124 D3
Paru r. Brazil 147 H5
Paru de Oeste r. Brazil 147 G5
Parur India 72 C4
Parvân prov. Afgh. 81 G3
Parvatipuram India 73 D2
Parvatsar India 74 B4
Paryang China 75 D3
Parys S. Africa 99 E7
Pas r. Spain 42 E1
Pasa Dağı mt. Turkey 78 C3
Pasadena CA U.S.A. 136 C4
Pasadena TX U.S.A. 133 C6
Pasado, Cabo c. Ecuador 146 A5
Pasaje Ecuador 146 B5
Pa Sak, Mae Nam r. Thai. 61 C5
Pasan India 75 D5
Pasawng Myanmar 60 B4
Pascagoula U.S.A. 129 A6
Pascani Romania 31 K4
Pasco dept Peru 148 A2
Pasco U.S.A. 134 C3
Pascoag U.S.A. 131 H3
Pascoal, Monte hill Brazil 151 E6
Pascua, Isla de i. S. Pacific Ocean see
Easter Island
Pas de Calais strait France/U.K. see
Dover, Strait of
Pasewalk Germany 37 G2
Pasfield Lake Canada 123 J3
Pasha Rus. Fed. 28 E3
Pashaly Rus. Fed. 64 D2
Pashkovo Rus. Fed. 64 D2
Pashtun Zarghun Afgh. 81 E3
Pasighat India 75 H3
Pasinler Turkey 79 E3
Pasir Gudang Malaysia 58 [inset]
Pasirian Indon. 59 F5
Pasir Mas Malaysia 58 C1
Pasirpangarayan Indon. 58 C2
Pasir Panjang hill Sing. 58 [inset]
Pasir Putih Malaysia 58 C1
Pasküh Iran 81 F5
Pasłęk Poland 37 I1
Pasłęka r. Poland 37 I1

Pašman i. Croatia 44 E3
Pasni Pak. 81 E5
Paso de Caballo Venez. 146 E2
Paso de Indios Arg. 152 C5
Paso de los Libres Arg. 152 F2
Paso de los Toros Uruguay 152 E3
Paso del Sapo Arg. 152 C5
Paso de Patria Para. 149 F6
Paso de San Antonio Mex. 133 A6
Paso Río Mayo Arg. 153 C6
Paso Robles U.S.A. 136 B4
Passa Quatro Brazil 151 C7
Passage Franca Brazil 150 D3
Passaic U.S.A. 131 F3
Passau Germany 37 F4
Passo Fundo Brazil 151 A9
Passos Brazil 151 C7
Passo Real, Barragem resr Brazil
151 A9
Pastavy Belarus 28 C5
Pastaza prov. Ecuador 146 B5
Pastaza r. Peru 146 B6
Pasto Col. 146 B4
Pasto Grande Brazil 149 E1
Pastora Peak U.S.A. 137 I3
Pasu Jammu and Kashmir 74 B1
Pasuquín Phil. 67 G5
Pasur Turkey see Kulp
Pasuruan Indon. 59 F4
Pasvalys Lith. 33 G4
Pásztó Hungary 37 I5
Pata Bol. 148 D2
Pata Senegal 92 B2
Patagonia reg. Arg. 153 C7
Pataliputra India see Patna
Patan Gujarat India see Somnath
Patan Gujarat India 74 B5
Patan Madhya Pradesh India 74 C5
Patan Maharashtra India 72 B2
Patan Nepal 75 E4
Patancheru India 72 C2
Patandar, Koh-i- mt. Pak. 81 F5
Patativum Italy see Padua
Patay Arg. 152 D1
Patchewollock Australia 112 A6
Patchogue U.S.A. 131 G3
Patea N.Z. 113 C2
Pate Island Kenya 96 D5
Paternò Sicily Italy 45 E6
Paterson U.S.A. 131 F3
Paterson Range hills Australia 108 C5
Pathalgaon India 75 D5
Pathanamthitta India 72 C4
Pathankot India 74 C2
Pathein Myanmar see Bassein
Pathfinder Reservoir U.S.A. 134 F4
Pathiu Thai. 61 B6
Pathri India 72 C2
Pathum Thani Thai. 61 C5
Pati Indon. 59 E4
Patía r. Col. 146 B3
Patiala India 74 C3
Patitíri Greece 47 C5
Pativilca r. Peru 148 A2
Patkai Bum mts India/Myanmar 75 H3
Patkaklik China 75 F1
Patlangiç Turkey 47 F6
Patmos i. Greece 47 E6
Patna India 75 E4
Patnagarh India 73 D1
Patnos Turkey 79 E3
Pato, Cerro mt. Chile 153 B6
Pato Branco Brazil 151 A8
Patos Albania 46 A4
Patos Brazil 150 E3
Patos, Lagoa dos l. Brazil 151 B9
Patos de Minas Brazil 151 C6
Patquia Arg. 152 D2
Patra Greece 47 C5
Patrae Greece see Patras
Patras Greece 47 C5
Patraïkos Kolpos b. Greece 47 B5
Patreksfjörður Iceland 32 [inset]
Patricio Lynch, Isla i. Chile 153 B7
Patrick Creek watercourse Australia
111 F1
Patrimônio Brazil 149 H4
Patrocínio Brazil 151 C6
Patsoyoki r. Europe 28 D1
Pattadakal tourist site India 72 B2
Pattani Thai. 61 C7
Pattani r. Thai. 61 C7
Pattaya Thai. 61 C5
Patterson CA U.S.A. 136 B3
Patterson LA U.S.A. 133 D6
Patterson r. U.S.A. 130 D4
Patterson, Mount Canada 122 C1
Patti India 74 D4
Patti Indon. 108 D4
Patti Sicily Italy 45 E5
Pättikkä Fin. 32 F1
Pattukkottai India 72 C4
Pattullo, Mount Canada 122 D3
Patu Brazil 150 E3
Patuakhali Bangl. 75 F5
Patuanak Canada 123 J4
Patuca, Punta pt Hond. 139 H5
Patur India 72 C1
Patuxent r. U.S.A. 131 E4
Patuxent Range mts Antarctica 167 L1
Patvinsuon kansallispuisto nat. park
Fin. 32 H3
Pau France 38 D5
Paucartambo r. Peru see Yavero
Pau d'Arco Brazil 150 B3
Pauillac France 38 C4
Pauini Brazil 148 D1
Pauini r. Brazil 147 E5
Pauini r. Brazil 148 D1
Pauk Myanmar 60 A3
Paukkaung Myanmar 60 A4
Paulatuk Canada 120 G3
Paulden U.S.A. 137 F4
Paulis Dem. Rep. Congo see Isiro
Pauliya Romania 46 E1
Paulista Brazil 150 F3
Paulistana Brazil 150 D3
Paulo Afonso Brazil 150 E4
Paulpietersburg S. Africa 99 I6
Pauls Valley U.S.A. 133 B5
Paungbyin Myanmar 60 A3
Paungde Myanmar 60 A4
Pauni India 72 C1
Pauri India 74 C3
Pausa Peru 148 B3
Pavagada India 72 C3
Pavão Brazil 151 D6
Pavarandocito Col. 146 B3
Pāveh Iran 80 A3
Pavia Italy 44 B2
Pavilion U.S.A. 130 D2
Pāvilosta Latvia 33 F4
Pavino Rus. Fed. 28 J4
Paviśtyčio kalnas hill Lith. 37 K1
Pavlikeni Bulg. 46 D3
Pavlodar Kazakh. 26 H4
Pavlof Volcano U.S.A. 120 C4
Pavlograd Ukr. see Pavlohrad
Pavlohrad Ukr. 29 E6

Pavlovka Rus. Fed. 28 K5
Pavlovka Ul'yanovskaya Oblast' Rus. Fed.
29 H5
Pavlovo Rus. Fed. 28 G5
Pavlovsk Rus. Fed. 29 G6
Pavlovskaya Rus. Fed. 29 F7
Pavlovskoye Vodokhranilishche resr
Rus. Fed. 28 K5
Pavullo nel Frignano Italy 44 C2
Pawai India 74 D4
Pawan r. Indon. 59 E3
Pawayan India 74 D3
Pawhuska U.S.A. 133 B4
Pawling U.S.A. 131 G3
Pawn r. Myanmar 60 B4
Pawnee U.S.A. 133 B4
Pawnee r. U.S.A. 132 B4
Paw Paw MI U.S.A. 132 E3
Paw Paw WV U.S.A. 130 D4
Paxaro mt. Spain 42 D1
Paximadia i. Greece 47 D7
Paxoí i. Greece 47 B5
Paxson U.S.A. 120 C3
Paxton U.S.A. 132 D3
Payakumbuh Indon. 58 C3
Paya Lebar Sing. 58 [inset]
Payerne Switz. 39 G3
Payette U.S.A. 134 C3
Payette r. U.S.A. 134 C3
Pay-Khoy, Khrebet hills Rus. Fed. 28 L1
Payne Canada see Kangirsuk
Payne, Lac l. Canada 125 F1
Paynes Creek U.S.A. 136 B1
Payne's Find Australia 109 B7
Paynesville U.S.A. 132 C2
Paysandú Uruguay 152 F3
Pays de la Loire admin. reg. France
38 C3
Payshanba Uzbek. 81 F1
Payson U.S.A. 137 I4
Payún, Cerro vol. Arg. 152 C4
Payyer, Gora mt. Rus. Fed. 26 M2
Paz, Río de r. Brazil 150 B4
Pazar Turkey 79 E2
Pazarcık Turkey 78 D3
Pazardzhik Bulg. 46 D3
Pazarköy Turkey 47 E5
Paz de Río Col. 146 C3
Pazin Croatia 44 D2
Pazña Bol. 148 D4
Pčinja r. Macedonia 46 B4
Pe Myanmar 61 B5
Peabody U.S.A. 132 B4
Peace r. Canada 123 I3
Peace r. U.S.A. 129 C7
Peace Point Canada 123 H3
Peace River Canada 123 G3
Peachland Canada 134 C2
Peach Springs U.S.A. 137 F4
Peaima Falls Guyana 147 F3
Peak Charles National Park Australia
109 C8
Peak District National Park U.K. 35 F5
Peake watercourse Australia 110 D6
Peaked Mountain U.S.A. 136 B5
Peak Hill N.S.W. Australia 112 D4
Peak Hill W.A. Australia 109 B6
Peale, Mount U.S.A. 137 H2
Peanut U.S.A. 136 A1
Pearce Point Australia 110 B3
Pearisburg U.S.A. 130 C5
Pearl r. U.S.A. 127 I5
Pearl River r. China see Zhu Jiang
Pearsall U.S.A. 133 B6
Pearson U.S.A. 129 C6
Peary Channel Canada 121 J2
Peary Land reg. Greenland 121 P1
Pease r. U.S.A. 133 B5
Peawanuck Canada 124 C2
Pebane Moz. 99 H3
Pebas Peru 146 D5
Pebble Island Falkland Is 153 F7
Peć Yugo. 46 B3
Pecan Bayou r. U.S.A. 133 B6
Péces Hungary 37 I5
Pecha r. Rus. Fed. 32 I1
Pechenga r. Rus. Fed. 32 H1
Pechora r. Rus. Fed. 28 K2
Pechora Rus. Fed. 28 L2
Pechora Sea Rus. Fed. see
Pechorskoye More
Pechorskaya Guba b. Rus. Fed. 28 J1
Pechorskoye More sea Rus. Fed. 28 J1
Pechory Rus. Fed. 28 C4
Pecica Romania 46 B1
Peck U.S.A. 130 D2
Pecora, Capo c. Sardinia Italy 45 B5
Pecos U.S.A. 133 G7
Pecos r. U.S.A. 135 G7
Pécs Hungary 44 G1
Pécsvárad Hungary 46 G1
Peddavagu r. India 72 C2
Pedder, Lake Australia 112 C5
Peddie S. Africa 99 E7
Pededze r. Latvia 33 G4
Pedernales Ecuador 146 A4
Pedernales Mex. 135 F7
Pedernales r. U.S.A. 133 B6
Pedernales Venez. 147 F2
Pedersöre Fin. 32 F2
Pediva Angola 95 B9
Pedra Azul Brazil 151 D6
Pedrafita do Cebreiro Spain 42 C1
Pedras Negras Brazil 149 E3
Pedregal Venez. 146 D2
Pedregulho Brazil 149 I5
Pedreiras Brazil 150 D2
Pedro, Point Sri Lanka 72 D4
Pedro Afonso Brazil 150 C3
Pedro Avelino Brazil 150 E3
Pedro Chico Col. 146 D4
Pedro Gomes Brazil 151 A6
Pedro II, Ilha reg. Brazil/Venez. 146 E4
Pedro Juan Caballero Para. 149 G5
Pedro Leopoldo Brazil 151 C6
Pedro Luro Arg. 152 D5
Pedro Osório Brazil 152 G2
Pedroso Port. 42 B2
Peebles U.K. 34 F5
Peebles U.S.A. 130 B4
Pee Dee r. U.S.A. 129 D5
Peekskill U.S.A. 131 G3
Peel r. Canada 122 C1
Peel Isle of Man 35 D4
Peera r. Fin. 32 F1
Peera Peera Poolanna Lake salt flat
Australia 110 C5
Peerless Lake Canada 123 H3
Peers Canada 123 G4
Pegasus Bay N.Z. 113 C3
Pegnitz Germany 36 E4
Pegu Myanmar 60 B4
Pegu admin. div. Myanmar 60 B4
Pegu Yoma mts Myanmar 60 A4
Pehlivanköy Turkey 46 E4
Pehowa India 74 C3
Pehuajó Arg. 152 E3
Peikang Taiwan 67 G4
Peine Chile 148 D4
Peine Germany 36 E2
Peineta, Cerro mt. Arg. 153 C7
Peint India 72 B1
Peipsi järv l. Estonia/Rus. Fed. see
Peipus, Lake

Peipus, Lake Estonia/Rus. Fed. 28 C4
Peiraias Greece see Piraeus
Peitz Germany 37 G3
Peixe Brazil 150 B5
Peixe r. Brazil 149 H3
Peixian Jiangsu China 67 F1
Peixian Jiangsu China see Pizhou
Peixoto de Azevedo Brazil 150 A4
Peixoto de Azevedo r. Brazil 149 G2
Pejantan i. Indon. 59 D2
Peje Yugo. see Peć
Pek r. Yugo. 46 B2
Pekalongan Indon. 59 E4
Pekan Malaysia 58 C2
Pekanbaru Indon. 58 C2
Pékans, Rivière aux r. Canada 125 H2
Peki Ghana 93 F4
Pekin U.S.A. 132 D3
Peking China see Beijing
Pelabuhan Kelang Malaysia 58 C2
Pelabuhan Sandakan inlet Sabah Malaysia 59 G1
Pelada, Pampa hills Arg. 153 C6
Pelado mt. Spain 43 F3
Pelagie, Isole is Sicily Italy 45 D7
Pelagonija plain Macedonia 46 B4
Pelagonisou, Diavlos sea chan. Greece 47 D5
Pelaihari Indon. 59 F3
Pelalawan Indon. 58 C2
Pelapis i. Indon. 59 E3
Pelasgia Greece 47 C5
Pelasyía Greece see Pelasgia
Pelat, Mont mt. France 39 G4
Pelawanbesar Indon. 59 G2
Peleaga, Vârful mt. Romania 46 C2
Pelechuco Bol. 148 C3
Pelee Island Canada 130 B3
Pelee Point Canada 130 B3
Peleliu i. Palau 57 H4
Peleng i. Indon. 57 F6
Peles Rus. Fed. 28 I3
Pelhřimov Czech Rep. 37 G4
Pelican Lake Canada 123 K4
Pelican Narrows Canada 123 K4
Pelister mt. Macedonia 46 B4
Pelister nat. park Macedonia 46 B4
Pelješac pen. Croatia 44 F3
Pelkosenniemi Fin. 32 G2
Pellatt Lake Canada 123 I1
Pellegrue France 38 D4
Pelleluhu Islands P.N.G. 57 J6
Pello Fin. 32 F2
Pellworm i. Germany 36 D1
Pelly r. Canada 122 B2
Pelly Crossing Canada 122 B2
Pelly Lake Canada 123 K1
Pelly Mountains Canada 122 C2
Pelokang is Indon. 59 G4
▶Peloponnese reg. Greece 47 C6
europe 24–25
Peloponnisos admin. reg. Greece 47 C6
Peloritani, Monti mts Sicily Italy 45 E6
Pelotas Brazil 152 G2
Pelotas, Rio das r. Brazil 151 B8
Pelovo Bulg. 46 D3
Pelplin Poland 37 I2
Peltovuoma Fin. 32 G1
Pelusium tourist site Egypt 77 A4
Pelusium, Bay of Egypt see Ţînah, Khalīj aţ
Pelvoux, Massif du mts France 39 G4
Pemalang Indon. 59 E4
Pemangkat Indon. 59 E2
Pemarung, Pulau i. Indon. 59 G3
Pematangsiantar Indon. 58 B2
Pemba Moz. 97 D8
Pemba Zambia 95 E9
Pemba, Baía de b. Moz. 97 D8
Pemba Channel Tanz. 97 C6
Pemba Island Tanz. 97 C6
Pemba North admin. reg. Tanz. 97 C6
Pemba South admin. reg. Tanz. 97 C6
Pemberton Canada 122 F5
Pembina r. Canada 123 H4
Pembina r. U.S.A. 132 B1
Pembroke Canada 124 E4
Pembroke U.K. 35 D6
Pembroke U.S.A. 129 C5
Pembroke, Cape Falkland Is 153 F7
Pembroke Pines U.S.A. 129 C7
Pembrokeshire Coast National Park U.K. 35 D6
Pembuanghulu Indon. 59 F3
Pen India 72 B2
Pen r. Myanmar 60 A3
Pena Barrosa Bol. 148 D5
Peña Cabollera mt. Spain 42 E2
Peña de Francia mt. Spain 42 C2
Peña de Izaga mt. Spain 43 F1
Peña de Oroel mt. Spain 43 F1
Peñafiel Spain 42 D2
Peñagolosa mt. Spain 43 F2
Peñalara mt. Spain 42 E2
Peñalba de Santiago tourist site Spain 42 C1
Peñalsordo Spain 42 D3
Penamacor Port. 42 C2
Penambo Range mts Sarawak Malaysia see Tama Abu, Banjaran
Peña Mira mt. Spain 42 C2
Peña Nevada, Cerro mt. Mex. 126 G7
Penang state Malaysia see Pinang
Peñaranda de Bracamonte Spain 42 D2
Penarie Australia 112 B4
Peñarroya mt. Spain 43 F2
Peñarroya-Pueblonuevo Spain 42 D3
Peñas, Cabo de c. Spain 42 D1
Penas, Golfo de g. Chile 153 B6
Peñasco watercourse U.S.A. 135 F6
Peña Ubiña mt. Spain 42 D1
Peña Utrera hill Spain 42 C3
Pench r. India 74 C5
Pencheng China see Ruichang
Pench National Park India 74 C5
Pendé r. Cent. Afr. Rep. 94 C3
Pendik Turkey 46 F4
Pendleton U.S.A. 134 C3
Pendleton Bay Canada 122 E4
Pendopo Indon. 58 C3
Pend Oreille r. U.S.A. 134 C2
Pend Oreille Lake U.S.A. 134 C2
Pendra India 75 D5
Pendzhikent Tajik. see Panjakent
Penebangan i. Indon. 59 E3
Peneda Gerês, Parque Nacional da nat. park Port. 42 B2
Pene-Mende Dem. Rep. Congo 95 F6
Penetanguishene Canada 130 D1
Penfield U.S.A. 130 D3
Penfro U.K. see Pembroke
Peng'an China 66 C2
Penganga r. India 72 C2
Peng Chau i. Hong Kong China 67 [inset]
P'engchia Yü i. Taiwan 67 G3
Penge Dem. Rep. Congo 95 E6
P'enghu Ch'üntao is Taiwan 67 F4
P'enghu Liehtao is Taiwan see P'enghu Ch'üntao
P'enghu Tao i. Taiwan 67 F4
Pengiki i. Indon. 59 E2
Pengshan China 66 B2
Pengshui China 66 D2
Peng Siang, Sungai r. Sing. 58 [inset]
Pengwa Myanmar 60 A3
Pengxi China 66 C2
Pengze China 67 F2
Penhalonga Zimbabwe 99 G3
Penhook U.S.A. 130 D5
Peniche Port. 42 B3
Penicuik U.K. 34 E4
Penida i. Indon. 59 F5
Peninga Rus. Fed. 28 E3
Peninsular Malaysia Malaysia 58 D1
Penitente, Serra do hills Brazil 150 C4
Pěnjwīn Iraq 79 F4
Penmarch France 38 A3
Penmarch, Pointe de pt France 38 A3
Penn U.S.A. see Penn Hills
Penna, Punta della pt Italy 44 E3
Penne Italy 44 D3
Pennell Coast Antarctica 167 H2
Penner r. India 72 D3
Penneshaw Australia 109 G8
Penn Hills U.S.A. 130 D3
Pennine, Alpi mts Italy/Switz. 44 A2
Pennine Alps mts Italy/Switz. see Pennine, Alpi
Pennines hills U.K. 35 E4
Pennington Gap U.S.A. 130 B5
Pennsboro U.S.A. 130 C4
Pennsville U.S.A. 131 F4
Pennsylvania state U.S.A. 130 D3
Penny Icecap Canada 121 M3
Penny Point Antarctica 167 H1
Penobscot Bay U.S.A. 131 I1
Penola Australia 112 B5
Penong Australia 109 F7
Penonomé Panama 139 H7
Penrhyn atoll Cook Is 165 H6
Penrhyn Basin sea feature S. Pacific Ocean 165 H6
Penrith U.K. 35 E4
Pensacola U.S.A. 129 B6
Pensacola Bay i. U.S.A. 129 B6
Pensacola Mountains Antarctica 167 L1
Pensamiento Bol. 149 E3
Pentadaktylos Range mts Cyprus 77 A2
Pentakota India 73 D2
Pentecost Island Vanuatu 107 F3
Pentecôte r. Canada 125 H3
Pentecôte, Île i. Vanuatu see Pentecost Island
Penteleu, Vârful mt. Romania 46 E2
Penticton Canada 134 C2
Pentland Australia 111 F4
Pentland Firth sea chan. U.K. 34 E2
Penukonda India 72 C3
Penunjok, Tanjong pt Malaysia 58 C1
Penwegon Myanmar 60 B4
Penygadair hill U.K. 35 E5
Penylan Lake Canada 123 J2
Penza Rus. Fed. 29 H5
Penzance U.K. 35 D6
Penza Oblast admin. div. Rus. Fed. see Penzenskaya Oblast'
Penzenskaya Oblast' admin. div. Rus. Fed. 29 H5
Penzhinskaya Guba b. Rus. Fed. 27 Q3
Peoples Creek r. U.S.A. 134 E2
Peoria AZ U.S.A. 137 F5
Peoria IL U.S.A. 132 D3
Pepel Sierra Leone 92 B3
Peper Sudan 96 B3
Pëqin Albania 46 A4
Pequop Mountains U.S.A. 137 E1
Pera Head Australia 111 E2
Peraitepuy Venez. 147 F3
Perak i. Malaysia 58 B1
Perak r. Malaysia 58 C1
Perak state Malaysia 58 C1
Perama Greece 47 D7
Perambalur India 72 C4
Perämeren kansallispuisto nat. park Fin. 32 G2
Perä-Posio Fin. 32 G2
Perche, Collines du hills France 38 D2
Percival Lakes salt flat Australia 108 D5
Percy France 38 C2
Percy Isles Australia 111 G4
Perdida r. Brazil 150 C4
Perdido r. Brazil 149 F5
Perdido, Monte mt. Spain 43 G1
Perdiguère, Pic mt. France/Spain 43 G1
Perdika Greece 47 B5
Perdizes Brazil 149 I4
Perdu, Lac l. Canada 125 G3
Peregrebnoye Rus. Fed. 26 G3
Pereira Col. 146 C3
Pereira Barreto Brazil 149 H5
Pereira de Eça Angola see Ondjiva
Pereiro Brazil 150 E3
Perelyub Rus. Fed. 29 I6
Peremetnoye Kazakh. 29 I6
Peremul Par reef India 72 B4
Peremyshlyany Ukr. 29 C6
Perené r. Peru 148 B2
Perenjori Australia 109 B7
Pereslavl'-Zalesskiy Rus. Fed. 28 F4
Peretu Romania 46 D2
Perevolotskiy Rus. Fed. 29 J6
Pereyaslavka Rus. Fed. 64 C3
Pereyaslav-Khmel'nitskiy Ukr. see Pereyaslav-Khmel'nyts'kyy
Pereyaslav-Khmel'nyts'kyy Ukr. 29 D6
Pérez Chile 152 C1
Perg Austria 37 G4
Pergamino Arg. 152 E3
Pergola Italy 44 D3
Perhentian Besar i. Malaysia 58 C1
Perho Fin. 32 G3
Periam Romania 46 B1
Péribonca r. Canada 125 F3
Pericos Mex. 126 E6
Peridot U.S.A. 137 G5
Périers France 38 C2
Périgueux France 38 D4
Perijá, Parque Nacional nat. park Venez. 146 C2
Perija, Sierra de mts Venez. 146 C2
Peringat Malaysia 58 C1
Periprava Romania 46 F2
Perişoru Romania 46 E2
Peristera i. Greece 47 C5
Peristerio Greece 47 C6
Perito Moreno Arg. 153 C6
Perito Moreno, Parque Nacional nat. park Arg. 153 B6
Perivar r. India 72 C4
Perlas, Punta de pt Nicaragua 139 H6
Perleberg Germany 36 E2
Perlis state Malaysia 58 C1
Perm' Rus. Fed. 28 K4
Permas Rus. Fed. 28 H4
Përmet Albania 47 B4
Perm Oblast admin. div. Rus. Fed. see Permskaya Oblast'
Permskaya Oblast' admin. div. Rus. Fed. 28 K4
Permuda i. Croatia 44 E2
Pernambuco Brazil see Recife
Pernambuco state Brazil 150 E4
Pernambuco Plain sea feature S. Atlantic Ocean 160 M6
Pernatty Lagoon salt flat Australia 112 A3
Pernik Bulg. 46 C3
Perniö Fin. 33 F3
Pernov Estonia see Pärnu
Peron Islands Australia 110 B2
Péronnas France 39 F3
Péronne France 39 E2
Perote Mex. 126 G8
Perpignan France 39 E5
Perrégaux Alg. see Mohammadia
Perris U.S.A. 136 D5
Perros-Guirec France 38 B2
Perry r. Canada 123 K1
Perry FL U.S.A. 129 C6
Perry MI U.S.A. 130 A2
Perry OK U.S.A. 133 B4
Perry Hall U.S.A. 131 E4
Perrysburg U.S.A. 130 B3
Perryton U.S.A. 133 A4
Perryville AR U.S.A. 133 C5
Perryville KY U.S.A. 130 A5
Persepolis tourist site Iran 80 C4
Persia country Asia see Iran
Persian Gulf Asia see The Gulf
Persis prov. Iran see Fārs
Pertek Turkey 79 D3
Perth Tas. Australia 112 C6
▶Perth W.A. Australia 109 A7
State capital of Western Australia. 4th most populous city in Oceania.
Perth Canada 131 E1
Perth U.K. 34 E3
Perth-Andover Canada 125 H4
Perth Basin sea feature Indian Ocean 163 O7
Pertominsk Rus. Fed. 28 F2
Pertuis France 39 F5
Pertuis Breton sea chan. France 38 C3
Pertuis d'Antioche sea chan. France 38 C3
Pertunmaa Fin. 33 G3
Pertusato, Capo c. Corsica France 44 B4
Perú Bol. 148 D3
Peru atoll Kiribati see Beru
▶Peru country S. America 148 B2
3rd largest and 4th most populous country in South America.
southamerica 144–145, 154
Peru U.S.A. 132 E3
Peru-Chile Trench sea feature S. Pacific Ocean 165 M6
Perugia Italy 44 D3
Peruíbe Brazil 149 I6
Perusia Italy see Perugia
Pervomaysk Rus. Fed. 29 G5
Pervomays'k Ukr. 29 D6
Pervomayskiy Arkhangel'skaya Oblast' Rus. Fed. see Novodvinsk
Pervomayskiy Orenburgskaya Oblast' Rus. Fed. 29 J6
Pervomayskiy Tambovskaya Oblast' Rus. Fed. 29 G5
Pervomays'kyy Ukr. 29 F6
Pervorechenskiy Rus. Fed. 27 Q3
Pesaguan r. Indon. 59 E3
Pesaro Italy 44 D3
Pescadores is Taiwan see P'enghu Ch'üntao
Pescadores, Punta pt Peru 148 B4
Pescara Italy 44 E3
Pescara r. Italy 44 E3
Pescari Romania 46 B2
Peschanokopskoye Rus. Fed. 29 G7
Peschanoye Rus. Fed. see Yashkul'
Peschanyy, Mys pt Kazakh. 79 G2
Peschici Italy 44 F4
Pescia Italy 44 C3
Pesha r. Rus. Fed. 28 H2
Peshanjan Afgh. 81 E3
Peshawar Pak. 81 G3
Peshkopi Albania 46 B4
Peshnyye, Ostrova is Kazakh. see Bol'shiye Peshnyye, Ostrova
Peshtera Bulg. 46 D3
Peshtigo r. U.S.A. 128 B2
Peski Turkm. 81 E2
Peski Karakumy des. Turkm. see Karakum Desert
Peskovka Rus. Fed. 28 J4
Pesnica Slovenia 44 E1
Peso da Régua Port. 42 C2
Pesqueira Brazil 150 E4
Pesqueria Mex. 135 F8
Pessac France 38 C4
Pestovo Rus. Fed. 28 E4
Pestravka Rus. Fed. 29 I5
Petah Tiqwa Israel 77 B3
Petäjävesi Fin. 33 G3
Petalidi Greece 47 B6
Petalioi i. Greece 47 D6
Petaluma U.S.A. 136 A2
Pétange Lux. 39 F2
Petangis Indon. 59 F3
Petare Venez. 146 E2
Petas Greece 47 B5
Petatlán Mex. 138 D5
Petauke Zambia 97 A8
Petenwell Lake U.S.A. 132 D2
Peterbell Canada 124 D3
Peterborough Australia 112 A4
Peterborough Canada 130 D1
Peterborough U.K. 35 F5
Peterborough U.S.A. 131 H2
Peterhead U.K. 34 F3
Peter I Island Antarctica 167 K2
Petermann Bjerg nunatak Greenland 121 Q2
Petermann Ranges mts Australia 110 B5
Peter Pond Lake Canada 123 I4
Petersburg AK U.S.A. 122 C3
Petersburg IL U.S.A. 132 D4
Petersburg NY U.S.A. 131 G2
Petersburg OH U.S.A. 130 C3
Petersburg VA U.S.A. 130 E5
Petersburg WV U.S.A. 130 D4
Petershagen Germany 36 D2
Peters Mine Guyana 147 G3
Peterstown U.S.A. 130 C5
Petersville U.S.A. 120 D3
Peter the Great Bay Rus. Fed. see Petra Velikogo, Zaliv
Pétervárad Yugo. see Petrovaradin
Peterwardein Yugo. see Petrovaradin
Peth India 72 B2
Petilia Policastro Italy 45 F5
Petit Atlas mts Morocco see Anti Atlas
Petite Creuse r. France 38 D3
Petitjean Morocco see Sidi Kacem
Petit Lac Manicouagan l. Canada 125 H2
Petit Maine r. France 38 C3
Petit Mécatina r. Nfld. and Lab./Que. Canada see Little Mecatina
Petit Mécatina r. Nfld. and Lab./Que. Canada 125 J3
Petit Mécatina, Île du i. Canada 125 J3
Petit Morin r. France 39 E2
Petitot r. Canada 122 F2
Petit St-Bernard, Col du pass France 39 G4
Petkula Fin. 32 G2
Petlad India 74 B5
Peto Mex. 138 G4
Petoskey U.S.A. 132 E2
Petra tourist site Jordan 78 C5
Petra tou Romiou tourist site Cyprus see Aphrodite's Birthplace
Petra Velikogo, Zaliv b. Rus. Fed. 64 B4
Petre, Point Canada 131 E2
Petrich Bulg. 46 C4
Petrified Forest National Park U.S.A. 137 H4
Petrikau Poland see Piotrków Trybunalski
Petrikov Belarus see Pyetrykaw
Petrinja Croatia 44 F2
Petro, Cerro de mt. Chile 152 C2
Petroaleksandrovsk Uzbek. see Turtkul'
Petrograd Rus. Fed. see St Petersburg
Petrokov Poland see Piotrków Trybunalski
Petrolândia Brazil 150 E4
Petrolia Canada 130 B2
Petrolina Amazonas Brazil 146 E5
Petrolina Pernambuco Brazil 150 D4
Petron, Limni l. Greece 46 B4
Petropavl Kazakh. see Petropavlovsk
Petropavlovsk Kazakh. 26 G4
Petropavlovsk Rus. Fed. see Petropavlovsk-Kamchatskiy
Petropavlovsk-Kamchatskiy Rus. Fed. 27 P4
Petroşani Romania 46 C2
Petrovac Bos.-Herz. see Bosanski Petrovac
Petrovac Yugo. 46 B2
Petrovaradin Yugo. 46 A2
Petrovsk Rus. Fed. 29 H5
Petrovskoye Rus. Fed. see Svetlograd
Petrovsk-Zabaykal'skiy Rus. Fed. 27 K4
Petrov Val Rus. Fed. 29 H6
Petrozavodsk Rus. Fed. 28 E3
Petsamo Rus. Fed. see Pechenga
Pettau Slovenia see Ptuj
Petukhovo Rus. Fed. 26 G4
Petushki Rus. Fed. 28 F5
Peuetsagu, Gunung vol. Indon. 58 B1
Peurasuvanto Fin. 32 G2
Peureula Indon. 58 B1
Pevek Rus. Fed. 27 R3
Pêxung China 75 G2
Peza r. Rus. Fed. 28 H2
Pézenas France 39 E5
Pezinok Slovakia 37 H4
Pfaffenhofen an der Ilm Germany 36 E4
Pfälzer Wald hills Germany 36 C4
Pfarrkirchen Germany 37 F4
Pforzheim Germany 36 D4
Pfullendorf Germany 36 D5
Pfungstadt Germany 36 D4
Phagwara India 74 B3
Phahameng S. Africa 99 E6
Phalaborwa S. Africa 99 F4
Phalia Pak. 81 H3
Phalodi India 74 B4
Phalsbourg France 39 G2
Phalsund India 74 A4
Phaltan India 72 B2
Phalut Peak India/Nepal 75 F4
Phangan, Ko i. Thai. 61 C6
Phangnga Thai. 61 B6
Phan Rang Vietnam 61 E6
Phan Ri Vietnam 61 E6
Phan Thiêt Vietnam 61 E6
Phan Thiêt, Vinh b. Vietnam 61 E6
Phaplu Nepal 75 E4
Phat Diêm Vietnam 60 D3
Phatthalung Thai. 61 C7
Phayao Thai. 60 B4
Phek India 75 G4
Phelp r. Australia 110 C2
Phenix U.S.A. 130 D5
Phenix City U.S.A. 129 B5
Phet Buri Thai. 61 B5
Phetchabun Thai. 61 C4
Phichit Thai. 61 C4
Philadelphia Jordan see 'Ammān
Philadelphia Turkey see Alaşehir
Philadelphia MS U.S.A. 129 A5
Philadelphia NY U.S.A. 131 F1
Philadelphia PA U.S.A. 131 F4
Philae tourist site Egypt 89 G4
Philip U.S.A. 132 A2
Philip Atoll Micronesia see Sorol
Philippeville Alg. see Skikda
Philippeville Belgium 39 F1
Philippi U.S.A. 130 C4
Philippi, Lake salt flat Australia 110 D5
Philippine Basin sea feature N. Pacific Ocean 164 C4
▶Philippines country Asia 57 F3
asia 52–53, 82
Philippine Sea N. Pacific Ocean 164 C4
▶Philippine Trench sea feature N. Pacific Ocean 164 C4
3rd deepest trench in the world.
Philippopolis Bulg. see Plovdiv
Philip Smith Mountains U.S.A. 120 E3
Phillips U.S.A. 132 D2
Phillips Arm Canada 122 E5
Phillipsburg U.S.A. 132 B4
Phillipson, Lake salt flat Australia 110 C6
Phillips Range hills Australia 108 D4
Philomelium Turkey see Akşehir
Philpott Reservoir U.S.A. 130 C5
Phimun Mangsahan Thai. 61 D5
Phiritona S. Africa 99 E5
Phitsanulok Thai. 60 C4
▶Phnom Penh Cambodia 61 D6
Capital of Cambodia.
Pho, Laem pt Thai. 61 C7
▶Phoenix U.S.A. 137 F5
State capital of Arizona.
Phoenix Island Kiribati see Rawaki
Phoenix Islands Kiribati 107 H2
Phoenixville U.S.A. 131 F3
Phon Thai. 61 C5
Phong Nha Vietnam 60 D4
Phôngsali Laos 60 C3
Phong Saly Laos see Phôngsali
Phong Thô Vietnam 60 C3
Phosphate Hill Australia 111 E4
Phrae Thai. 60 C4
Phra Nakhon Si Ayutthaya Thai. see Ayutthaya
Phra Saeng Thai. 61 B6
Phra Thong, Ko i. Thai. 61 B6
Phuchong-Nayoi National Park Thai. 61 D5
Phu Cuong Vietnam see Thu Dâu Môt
Phuduhudu Botswana 98 E4
Phuentsholing Bhutan 75 F4
Phuket Thai. 61 B7
Phuket, Ko i. Thai. 61 B7
Phulabani India 73 E1
Phulpur India 75 D4
Phu Lung Wildlife Reserve Thai. 60 C4
Phu Ly Vietnam 60 D3
Phumĭ Chhuk Cambodia 61 D6
Phumĭ Kâmpóng Trâlach Cambodia 61 D5
Phumĭ Mlu Prey Cambodia 61 D5
Phumĭ Prâmaôy Cambodia 61 C5
Phumĭ Sâmraông Cambodia 61 C5
Phuntsholing Bhutan see Phuentsholing
Phu Phac Mo mt. Vietnam 60 C3
Phu Phan National Park Thai. 60 C4
Phu Quôc, Đao i. Vietnam 61 C6
Phu Tho Vietnam 60 D3
Phu Vinh Vietnam see Tra Vinh
Piabung, Gunung mt. Indon. 59 F2
Piaca Brazil 150 C3
Piacenza Italy 44 B2
Piacouadie, Lac l. Canada 125 G3
Piadena Italy 44 C2
Piagochioui r. Canada 124 E2
Piana di Catania plain Sicily Italy 45 E6
Piangil Australia 112 B4
Pianoro Italy 44 C2
Pianosa, Isola i. Italy 44 C3
Piaseczno Poland 37 J2
Piatã Brazil 150 D5
Piatra Romania 46 D3
Piatra Neamţ Romania 31 K4
Piatra Olt Romania 46 D2
Piauí r. Brazil 150 D3
Piauí state Brazil 150 D3
Piauí, Serra de hills Brazil 150 D4
Piave r. Italy 44 D2
Piazza Armerina Sicily Italy 45 E6
Piazzi, Isla i. Chile 153 B7
Pibor r. Sudan 96 B2
Pibor Post Sudan 96 B3
Pic r. Canada 124 C3
Pica Chile 148 C5
Picacho U.S.A. 137 G5
Picachos, Cerro dos mt. Mex. 135 D7
Picardie admin. reg. France 39 E2
Picardie reg. France 38 D2
Picassent Spain 43 F3
Picayune U.S.A. 127 I5
Pichácnic Mex. 135 F7
Pichanal Arg. 149 D5
Pichilemu Chile 152 B3
Pichilingue Mex. 126 D7
Pichi Mahuida Arg. 152 D4
Pichincha prov. Ecuador 146 B5
Pichor India 74 C4
Pickens U.S.A. 130 C4
Pickering U.K. 35 F4
Pickle Lake Canada 124 B3
Pico da Neblina, Parque Nacional do nat. park Brazil 147 E4
Picos Brazil 150 D3
Picos, Punta dos pt Spain 42 B2
Picota Peru 146 B6
Pico Truncado Arg. 153 D6
Picton Australia 112 D4
Picton Canada 131 E2
Picton N.Z. 113 C3
Picton, Mount Australia 112 C6
Picuí Brazil 150 E3
Picún Leufú Arg. 152 C4
Pidarak Pak. 81 E5
Pidurutalagala mt. Sri Lanka 72 D5
Pie de Palo, Sierra mts Arg. 152 C2
Piedimonte Matese Italy 44 E4
Piedmont admin. reg. Italy see Piemonte
Piedmont MO U.S.A. 132 D4
Piedmont OH U.S.A. 130 C3
Piedra r. Spain 43 F2
Piedrabuena Spain 42 D3
Piedra de Aguila Arg. 152 C5
Piedrafita Spain see Pedrafita do Cebreiro
Piedrahita Spain 42 D2
Piedralaves Spain 42 D2
Piedras, Punta pt Arg. 152 F3
Piedras Blancas Point U.S.A. 136 B4
Piedras Negras Guat. 138 F5
Piedras Negras Mex. 126 F6
Pieksämäki Fin. 33 G3
Pielavesi Fin. 32 G3
Pielavesi l. Fin. 32 G3
Pielinen l. Fin. 32 H3
Pieljekaise nationalpark nat. park Sweden 32 E2
Piemonte admin. reg. Italy 44 A2
Pieniężno Poland 37 J1
Pieniński Park Narodowy nat. park Poland 37 J4
Pieninský nat. park Slovakia 37 J4
Pieńsk Poland 37 G3
Pierce U.S.A. 132 B3
Pierce Lake Canada 123 M4
Pierceland Canada 123 I4
Pieria mts Greece 47 C4
▶Pierre U.S.A. 132 A2
State capital of South Dakota.
Pierre, Bayou r. U.S.A. 133 D6
Pierrelatte France 39 F4
Pieskehaure l. Sweden 32 E2
Piešťany Slovakia 37 H4
Pietermaritzburg S. Africa 99 F6
Pietersaari Fin. see Jakobstad
Pietersburg S. Africa 99 F4
Pietraperzia Sicily Italy 45 E6
Pietrasanta Italy 44 C3
Pietra Spada, Passo di pass Italy 45 F5
Pietrosa mt. Romania 31 K4
Pietrosu, Vârful mt. Romania 29 C7
Pieve di Cadore Italy 44 D1
Pievepelago Italy 44 C2
Pigeon r. Canada/U.S.A. 132 D1
Pigeon Bay Canada 130 B3
Pigeon Lake Canada 123 H4
Pigg r. U.S.A. 130 D5
Piggott U.S.A. 133 D4
Pigg's Peak Swaziland 99 F5
Pigon, Limni l. Greece 47 B5
Pigüé Arg. 152 E4
Pi He r. China 67 F1
Pihkva järv l. Estonia/Rus. Fed. see Pskov, Lake
Pihlajavesi l. Fin. 33 H3
Pihtipudas Fin. 32 G3
Piispajärvi Fin. 32 H2
Piji China see Puge
Pikalevo Rus. Fed. 28 E4
Pikelot i. Micronesia 164 D5
Pikes Peak U.S.A. 134 F5
Piketberg S. Africa 98 C7
Piketon U.S.A. 130 B4
Pikeville U.S.A. 130 B5
Pikounda Congo 94 C4
Pila Arg. 152 F4
Piła Poland 37 H2
Pilanesberg National Park S. Africa 99 E5
Pilani India 74 B3
Pilar Buenos Aires Arg. 152 F3
Pilar Córdoba Arg. 152 E2
Pilar Para. 149 F6
Pilas Spain 42 C4
Pilat, Mont mt. France 39 F4
Pilaya r. Bol. 149 D5
Pilcaniyeu Arg. 152 C5
Pilcomayo r. Bol./Para. 149 F6
Pilenkovo Georgia see Gant'iadi
Piler India 72 C3
Pili Greece see Pyli
Pili, Cerro mt. Chile 148 D5
Pilibhit India 74 C3
Pilica r. Poland 37 J3
Pilipinas country Asia see Philippines
Pillau Rus. Fed. see Baltiysk
Pillcopata Peru 148 C3
Pilliga Australia 112 D3
Pillsbury, Lake U.S.A. 136 A2
Pil'na Rus. Fed. 28 H5
Pil'nya, Ozero l. Rus. Fed. 28 K1
Pilões, Serra dos mts Brazil 151 C6
Pilón r. Mex. 133 B7
Pilos Greece see Pylos
Pilot Peak U.S.A. 136 D2
Pilot Point U.S.A. 120 D4
Pilot Rock U.S.A. 134 C3
Pilot Station U.S.A. 120 C3
Pilsen Czech Rep. see Plzeň
Pilu, Nam r. Myanmar 60 B4
Pima U.S.A. 137 H5
Pimenta Bueno Brazil 149 E2
Pimpalner India 72 B1
Pimpri India 72 B1
Pimu Dem. Rep. Congo 94 D4
Pin r. Myanmar 60 A3
Pinahat India 74 C4
Pinaleno Mountains U.S.A. 137 G5
Pinang Malaysia see George Town
Pinang i. Malaysia 58 C1
Pinang state Malaysia 58 C1
Pinar mt. Spain 42 D4
Pinar, Puerto del pass Spain 43 E3
Pınarbaşı Turkey 78 D3
Pinar del Río Cuba 127 J7
Pinarhisar Turkey 46 E4
Piñas Ecuador 146 B5
Pinatubo, Mt vol. Phil. 57 F2
Pincher Creek Canada 123 H5
Pinconning U.S.A. 130 B2
Pińczów Poland 37 J3
Pindaíba Brazil 149 G3
Pindar Australia 109 A7
Pindar r. India 74 C3
Pindaré r. Brazil 150 C2
Píndhos Óros mts Greece see Pindus Mountains
Pindi Bhattian Pak. 81 H4
Pindi Gheb Pak. 81 H3
Pindobal Brazil 150 B2
Pindos mts Greece see Pindus Mountains
Pindos nat. park Greece 47 B5
Pindus Mountains Greece 47 B5
Pindwara India 74 B4
Pine watercourse Australia 112 B4
Pine r. U.S.A. 130 A2
Pine, Cape Canada 125 K4
Pine Bluff U.S.A. 127 H5
Pine Bluffs U.S.A. 134 F4
Pine City U.S.A. 132 C2
Pine Creek Australia 110 B2
Pine Creek r. U.S.A. 130 E3
Pine Creek watercourse U.S.A. 137 D1
Pinecrest U.S.A. 136 B2
Pinedale U.S.A. 134 E4
Pine Dock Canada 123 L5
Pine Falls Canada 123 L5
Pinega Rus. Fed. 28 G2
Pinega r. Rus. Fed. 28 G2
Pinegrove Australia 109 A6
Pine Hills CA U.S.A. 136 D4
Pine Hills FL U.S.A. 129 C6
Pinehouse Lake Canada 123 J4
Pinehouse Lake l. Canada 123 J4
Pineimuta r. Canada 124 B2
Pineios r. Greece 47 C5
Pineiou, Techniti Limni resr Greece 47 B6
Pine Island Bay Antarctica 163 A10
Pine Island Glacier Antarctica 167 K1
Pine Islands FL U.S.A. 129 C7
Pine Islands FL U.S.A. 129 C7
Pine Knot U.S.A. 130 A5
Pine Peak U.S.A. 137 F4
Pine Point Canada 123 H2
Pineridge U.S.A. 136 C3
Pine Ridge U.S.A. 134 G4
Pinerolo Italy 44 A2
Pines, Isle of i. Cuba see La Juventud, Isla de
Pines, Isle of i. New Caledonia see Pins, Île des
Pineto Italy 44 E3
Pinetop U.S.A. 137 H4
Pine Valley U.S.A. 131 E2
Pineville KY U.S.A. 130 B5
Pineville LA U.S.A. 133 C6
Pineville WV U.S.A. 130 C5
Ping, Mae Nam r. Thai. 61 C5
Pingal Jammu and Kashmir 74 B1
Pingba China 66 C3
Pingbian China 66 B4
Pingchang China 66 C2
Pingdingshan China 67 E1
Pingdong Taiwan see P'ingtung
Pingdu China see Anfu
Pingguo China 66 C4
Pinghai China 67 E4
Pinghe China 67 F3
Pinghu China 67 G2
Pingjiang China 67 E2
Pingle China 67 D3
Pingli China 67 D1
Pingliang China 63 H4
Pinglu China 67 D1
Pingma China see Tiandong
Pingnan China 67 D4
Pingshan Guangdong China see Huidong
Pingshan Sichuan China 66 C2
Pingshan Yunnan China see Luquan
Pingshi China 67 E3
Pingtan China 67 F3
Pingtan Dao i. China see Haitan Dao
P'ingtung Taiwan 67 G4
Pingwu China 66 C1
Pingxi China see Yuping
Pingxiang Guangxi China 66 C4
Pingxiang Jiangxi China 67 E3
Pingyang Heilong. China 64 A2
Pingyang Zhejiang China 67 G3
Pingyu China 67 E1
Pingyuan China 67 E3
Pingyuanjie China 66 B4
Pingzhai China 66 D3
Pinhal Novo Port. 42 B3
Pinheiro Brazil 150 C2
Pinheiro Machado Brazil 152 G2
Pinhel Port. 42 C2
Pini i. Indon. 58 B2
Pinilla r. Spain 43 E3
Piniós r. Greece see Pineios
Pinjarra Australia 109 A8
Pinkafeld Austria 37 H5
Pink Mountain Canada 122 F3
Pinlaung Myanmar 60 B3
Pinlebu Myanmar 60 A2
Pinnacle hill U.S.A. 130 D4
Pinnacles National Monument nat. park U.S.A. 136 B3
Pinnaroo Australia 112 B4
Pinneberg Germany 36 D2
Pinnes, Akra pt Greece 47 D4
Pinofranqueado Spain 42 C2
Pinoh r. Indon. 59 E3
Pinos, Isla de i. Cuba see La Juventud, Isla de
Pinos, Mount U.S.A. 136 C4
Pinoso Spain 43 F3
Pinoso mt. Spain 43 E2
Pinotepa Nacional Mex. 138 E5
Pins, Île des i. New Caledonia 107 F4
Pins, Pointe aux pt Canada 130 C2
Pinsk Belarus 29 C5
Pintados Chile 148 C5
Pintasan Sabah Malaysia 59 G1
Pinto Spain 42 E2
Pintura U.S.A. 137 F3

Pinzolo Italy 44 C1
Pioche U.S.A. 137 E3
Piombino Italy 44 C3
Pioneer U.S.A. 130 A3
Pioneer Mountains U.S.A. 134 D3
Pioner, Ostrov i. Rus. Fed. 27 J2
Pionki Poland 37 J3
Piopio N.Z. 113 C2
Piopiotahi inlet N.Z. see Milford Sound
Piorini r. Brazil 147 F5
Piorini, Lago l. Brazil 147 F5
Piotrków Trybunalski Polanc 37 I3
Piove di Sacco Italy 44 D2
Pip Iran 81 E5
Pipa Dingzi mt. China 64 B4
Pipanaco, Salar de salt flat Arg. 152 D2
Pipar India 74 B4
Pipar Road India 74 B4
Piperi i. Greece 47 D5
Piper Peak U.S.A. 136 D3
Pipestone U.S.A. 123 K5
Pipestone r. U.S.A. 132 E3
Pipiriki N.Z. 113 C2
Pipli India 74 B3
Pipmuacan, Réservoir Canada 125 G3
Pipriac France 38 C3
Piqua U.S.A. 130 B3
Piqueras, Puerto de pass Spain 43 E1
Piquiri r. Brazil 147 A8
Piracicaba r. Brazil 151 D6
Piraçununga Brazil 149 I5
Piracuruca Brazil 150 D2
Piraeus Greece see Peiraeus
Piraí do Sul Brazil 151 B8
Piráievs Greece see Peiraeus
Piraju Brazil 149 H5
Pirajuí Brazil 149 H5
Pirallahı Adası Azer. 79 G2
Pirané Arg. 152 F1
Piranhas Alagoas Brazil 150 E4
Piranhas Amazonas Brazil 147 F6
Piranhas Goiás Brazil 149 H4
Piranhas r. Brazil 150 E3
Pirapemas Brazil 150 D2
Pirapetinga Brazil 149 I4
Pirapora Brazil 151 C6
Pirara Guyana 147 G4
Pirawa India 74 C4
Pire Mahuida, Sierra mts Arg. 153 C5
Pires do Rio Brazil 149 H4
Pirganj Bangl. 75 F4
Pírgos Greece see Pyrgos
Piriápolis Uruguay 152 G3
Pirin mts Bulg. 46 C4
Pirin nat. park Bulg. 46 C4
Pirineos mts Europe see Pyrenees
Piripiri Brazil 150 D3
Piritu Venez. 146 F2
Pirmasens Germany 36 C4
Pirna Germany 37 F3
Pirojpur Bangl. 75 F5
Pirón r. Spain 42 D2
Pirot Yugo. 46 C3
Pirpainti India 75 F4
Pir Panjal Pass Jammu and Kashmir 74 B2
Pir Panjal Range mts India/Pak. 74 B2
Pirsaatçay r. Azer. 79 G2
Piru Indon. 57 G6
Piryatin Ukr. see Pyryatyn
Piryetós Greece see Pyrgetos
Piryíon Greece see Pyrgi
Pirzada Afgh. 81 F4
Pisa Italy 44 C3
Pisa r. Poland 37 J2
Pisae Italy see Pisa
Pisagua Chile 148 B5
Pisaurum Italy see Pesaro
Pisba, Parque Nacional nat. park Col. 146 C3
Pisco Peru 148 A3
Pisco r. Peru 148 A3
Písek Czech Rep. 37 G4
Pisha China see Ningnan
Pishin Iran 81 E5
Pishin Pak. 81 F4
Pishin Lora r. Pak. 81 F4
Pishkan, Ras pt Pak. 81 E5
Pishpek Kyrg. see Bishkek
Pisidia Turkey 78 B3
Piso Firme Bol. 149 E3

▶Pissis, Cerro mt. Arg. 152 C1
4th highest mountain in South America.
southamerica 142–143

Pista r. Rus. Fed. 32 H2
Pisticci Italy 45 F4
Pistoia Italy 44 C3
Pistoriae Italy see Pistoia
Pisuerga r. Spain 42 D2
Pisz Poland 37 J2
Pit r. U.S.A. 134 B4
Pita Guinea 92 B3
Pitaga Canada 125 H2
Pitalito Col. 146 B4
Pitanga Brazil 151 B8
Pitangui Brazil 151 C6
Pitarpunga Lake imp. l. Australia 112 B4
Pitcairn Island Pitcairn Is 165 J7

▶Pitcairn Islands terr. S. Pacific Ocean 165 J7
United Kingdom Overseas Territory.
oceania 104–105, 114

Piteå Sweden 32 F2
Piteälven r. Sweden 32 F2
Pitelino Rus. Fed. 29 G5
Piterka Rus. Fed. 29 H6
Piteşti Romania 46 D2
Pithiviers France 38 E2
Pithoragarh India 74 D3
Pitiquito Mex. 135 D7
Pitkyaranta Rus. Fed. 28 D3
Pitlochry U.K. 34 E4
Pitoa Cameroon 93 I3
Pitomača Croatia 44 F2
Pitrufquén Chile 152 B4
Pitti i. India 72 B4
Pitt Island Canada 122 D4
Pitt Island S. Pacific Ocean 107 H6
Pitt Islands Solomon Is see Vanikoro Islands
Pittsburg KS U.S.A. 132 C4
Pittsburg TX U.S.A. 133 C5
Pittsburgh U.S.A. 130 D3
Pittsfield MA U.S.A. 131 G2
Pittsfield VT U.S.A. 131 G2
Pituri Creek watercourse Australia 110 D4
Pitz Lake Canada 123 L2
Pium Brazil 150 B4
Piura Peru 146 A6
Piura r. dept Peru 146 A6
Piute Mountains U.S.A. 137 E4
Piute Peak U.S.A. 136 C4
Piuthan Nepal 75 E4
Pivabiska r. Canada 124 D3
Pivijay Col. 146 C2
Pivka Yugo. 46 A3
Piwniczna Poland 37 J4
Pixaría mt. Greece see Pyxaria
Pixian China 66 B2

Pixley U.S.A. 136 C4
Pizacoma Peru 148 C4
Pizhi Nigeria 93 G3
Pizhma Rus. Fed. 28 H4
Pizhma r. Rus. Fed. 28 I4
Pizhma r. Rus. Fed. 28 J2
Pizhou China 67 F1
Piz Kesch mt. Switz. 44 B1
Pizol mt. Switz. 39 H3
Piz Pisoc mt. Switz. 39 I3
Piz Platta mt. Switz. 39 H3
Pizzo Italy 45 F5
Pizzo Carbonara mt. Sicily Italy 45 E6
Pizzuto, Monte mt. Italy 44 D3
Placentia Italy see Piacenza
Placentia Bay Canada 125 K4
Placerville U.S.A. 135 E5
Placetas Cuba 127 K7
Plácido de Castro Brazil 148 D2
Plain Dealing U.S.A. 133 C5
Plainfield IN U.S.A. 128 B4
Plainfield NJ U.S.A. 131 F3
Plains U.S.A. 134 D2
Plainview NE U.S.A. 132 B3
Plainview NY U.S.A. 131 G3
Plainview TX U.S.A. 133 A5
Plainville U.S.A. 132 B4
Plaisance France 38 D5
Plaju Indon. 58 D3
Plampang Indon. 59 G5
Planada U.S.A. 136 B3
Planaltina Brazil 149 I3
Plancoët France 38 C2
Plandište Yugo. 46 B2
Planeta r. Germany 37 F2
Plankinton U.S.A. 132 B3
Plano U.S.A. 133 B5
Planura Brazil 149 H5
Plaquemine U.S.A. 133 D6
Plasencia Spain 42 C2
Plaški Croatia 44 E2
Plastun Rus. Fed. 64 D3
Platamonas Greece 47 C5
Platanal Peru 148 C1
Platani r. Sicily Italy 45 D6
Platanos Greece 47 B6

▶Plateau Antarctica
Lowest recorded annual mean temperature in the world.
world 12–13

Plateau state Nigeria 93 G3
Plateaux admin. reg. Congo 94 B5
Platičevo Yugo. 46 A2
Platina U.S.A. 136 A1
Platinum U.S.A. 120 C4
Plato Col. 146 C2
Plato de Sopa Chile 152 C1
Platte r. MO U.S.A. 132 C4
Platte r. NE U.S.A. 132 D3
Platte City U.S.A. 132 C4
Plattenberg hill Germany 37 G4
Plattling Germany 37 F4
Plattsburgh U.S.A. 131 G1
Plattsmouth U.S.A. 132 C3
Platy Greece 46 C4
Plau Germany 37 F2
Plauen Germany 37 F3
Plauer See l. Germany 37 F2
Plav Yugo. 46 A3
Plavinas Latvia 33 G4
Plavsk Rus. Fed. 29 F5
Playa de Castilla coastal area Spain 42 C4
Playas Ecuador 146 A5
Plây Cu Vietnam 61 E4
Playgreen Lake Canada 123 L4
Playones de Santa Ana l. Col. 146 C2
Plaza del Judío mt. Spain 42 D3
Plaza Huincul Arg. 152 C4
Pleasant, Lake U.S.A. 137 F5
Pleasanton U.S.A. 133 B6
Pleasant Point N.Z. 113 B4
Pleasantville U.S.A. 131 F4
Pleaux France 38 E4
Plechý mt. Czech Rep. 37 F4
Plei Doch Vietnam 61 D5
Plenty watercourse Australia 110 D5
Plenty, Bay of g. N.Z. 113 D2
Plentywood U.S.A. 134 F2
Plesetsk Rus. Fed. 28 G3
Pleshchentsy Belarus see Plyeshchanitsy
Pleszew Poland 37 H3
Pleternica Croatia 44 F2
Pletipi, Lac l. Canada 125 G3
Plettenberg Germany 36 C3
Plettenberg Bay S. Africa 98 D7
Pleven Bulg. 46 D3
Plevna Bulg. see Pleven
Pleyben France 38 B2
Plieran r. Sarawak Malaysia 59 F2
Pliszka r. Poland 37 G2
Plješevica mts Croatia 44 E2
Pljevlja Yugo. 46 A3
Ploaghe Sardinia Italy 45 B4
Ploče Croatia 44 F3
Płock Poland 37 I2
Plöckenpass pass Austria/Italy 37 F5
Pločno mt. Bos.-Herz. 44 F3
Plodovoye Rus. Fed. 28 D3
Ploemeur France 38 B3
Ploërmel France 38 B3
Ploeşti Romania see Ploieşti
Ploieşti Romania 46 E2
Plomari Greece 47 E5
Plomb du Cantal mt. France 39 E4
Plombières-les-Bains France 39 H3
Plön Germany 36 E1
Płońsk Poland 37 J2
Ploskoye Rus. Fed. see Stanovoye
Płoty Poland 37 G2
Ploudalmézeau France 38 A2
Ploufragan France 38 B2
Plouguerneau France 38 A2
Plouha France 38 B2
Plouzané France 38 A2
Plovdiv Bulg. 46 D3
Plover Cove Reservoir Hong Kong China 67 [inset]
Płozk Poland see Płock
Pluckemin U.S.A. 131 F3
Plum U.S.A. 130 D3
Plum Coulee Canada 123 L5
Plummer U.S.A. 134 C3
Plumridge Lakes salt flat Australia 109 D7
Plumtree Zimbabwe 99 E4
Plungė Lith. 33 E5
Plutarco Elías Calles, Presa resr Mex. 135 E7
Pluto, Lac l. Canada 125 G2
Plužine Yugo. 46 A3
Plyeshchanitsy Belarus 33 G5
Ply Huey Wati, Khao mt. Myanmar/Thai. 61 B4

▶Plymouth Montserrat 139 L5
Capital of Montserrat, largely abandoned in 1997 owing to volcanic activity.

Plymouth Trin. and Tob. 147 F2
Plymouth U.K. 35 D6
Plymouth CA U.S.A. 136 B2
Plymouth IN U.S.A. 128 B3
Plymouth NC U.S.A. 128 C5
Plymouth NH U.S.A. 131 H2

Plymouth Bay U.S.A. 131 H3
Plynlimon hill U.K. 35 E5
Plyussa Rus. Fed. 31 L5
Plyussa r. Rus. Fed. 33 H4
Plzeň Czech Rep. 37 F4
Pniewy Poland 37 H2
Pô Burkina 93 E3
Po r. Italy 44 B1
Pô, Parc National de nat. park Burkina 93 E3
Po, Tanjong pt Sarawak Malaysia 59 E2
Pobeda, Gora mt. Rus. Fed. 27 O3
Pobeda Peak China/Kyrg. 70 D3
Pobedy, Pik mt. China/Kyrg. see Pobeda Peak
Pobiedziska Poland 37 H2
Poca U.S.A. 130 C4
Pocahontas U.S.A. 132 C3
Pocatalico r. U.S.A. 130 C4
Pocatello U.S.A. 134 D4
Pochala Sudan 96 B3
Poções Brazil 150 D5
Pocheon S. Korea 65 B5
Pochep Rus. Fed. 31 M2
Pochinki Rus. Fed. 29 H5
Pochinok Rus. Fed. 29 E5
Pochutla Mex. 138 E5
Pocklington Reef Australia 109 C8
Pocomoke City U.S.A. 131 F4
Pocomoke Sound b. U.S.A. 131 F5
Pocona Bol. 148 D4
Poconé Brazil 149 F4
Pocono Mountains hills U.S.A. 131 F3
Poco Ranakah vol. Indon. 108 C2
Poços de Caldas Brazil 151 C7
Podberez'ye Rus. Fed. 28 D4
Podbořany Czech Rep. 37 F3
Podcher'ye r. Rus. Fed. 28 K3
Poddor'ye Rus. Fed. 31 L1
Podensac France 38 C4
Podgorac Yugo. 46 B3
Podgorenskiy Rus. Fed. 29 F6
Podgorica Yugo. 46 A3
Podgorie Albania 46 B4
Podgornoye Rus. Fed. 26 I4
Podile India 72 C3
Podişul Transilvaniei plat. Romania see Transylvanian Basin
Podkamennaya Tunguska Rus. Fed. 27 J3
Podkamennaya Tunguska r. Rus. Fed. 27 J3
Podlesnoye Rus. Fed. 29 H6
Podocarpus, Parque Nacional nat. park Ecuador 146 B6
Podol'sk Rus. Fed. 28 F4
Podor Senegal 92 B1
Podporozh'ye Rus. Fed. 28 E3
Podujevo Yugo. 46 B3
Poel i. Germany 36 E1
Poetovio Slovenia see Ptuj
Pofadder S. Africa 98 C6
Pogar Rus. Fed. 29 E5
Poggibonsi Italy 44 C3
Poggio Ballone hill Italy 44 C3
Poggio di Montieri mt. Italy 44 C3
Poggio Rusco Italy 44 C2
Pogled mt. Yugo. 46 B3
Pogradec Albania 46 B4
Pogrebishche Ukr. see Pohrebyshche
Po Hai g. China see Bo Hai
P'ohang S. Korea 65 B5
Pohja Fin. 33 F3
Pohnpei atoll Micronesia 164 E5
Pohrebyshche Ukr. 29 D6
Pohri India 74 C4
Poiana Mare Romania 46 C3
Poiana Ruscă, Munţii mts Romania 46 C2
Poieniţa, Vârful mt. Romania 46 C1
Poindimié New Caledonia 107 F4
Point au Fer Island U.S.A. 133 D6
Pointe a la Hache U.S.A. 133 D6
Pointe-à-Pitre Guadeloupe 139 L5
Pointe-Noire Congo 95 A6
Point Hope U.S.A. 120 C3
Point Kenny Australia 109 F8
Point Lake Canada 123 H1
Point Nepean National Park Australia 112 C5
Point of Rocks MD U.S.A. 130 E4
Point of Rocks WY U.S.A. 134 E4
Point Pelee National Park Canada 130 B3
Point Pleasant U.S.A. 131 F3
Poisevo Rus. Fed. 28 J5
Poitiers France 38 D3
Poitou, Plaines et Seuil du plain France 38 D3
Poitou-Charentes admin. reg. France 38 C3
Poix-de-Picardie France 38 D2
Pojo Bol. 148 D4
Pokaran India 74 A4
Pokataroo Australia 112 D3
Pokcha Rus. Fed. 28 K3
Pokhara Nepal 75 D3
Pokhvistnevo Rus. Fed. 29 J5
Pokigron Suriname 147 H3
Pokka Fin. 32 G1
Pok Liu Chau i. Hong Kong China see Lamma Island
Pokrov Rus. Fed. 28 G4
Pokrovka Orenburgskaya Oblast' Rus. Fed. 29 J5
Pokrovka Yevreyskaya Avtonomnaya Oblast' Rus. Fed. see Priamurskiy
Pokrovsk Rus. Fed. see Engel's
Pokrovskoye Rus. Fed. 29 G7
Pokshen'ga r. Rus. Fed. 28 H3
Pola Croatia see Pula
Polacca Wash watercourse U.S.A. 137 G4
Pola de Allande Spain 42 C1
Pola de Laviana Spain 42 D1
Pola de Lena Spain 42 D1
Pola de Siero Spain 42 D1
Polán Spain 42 D3
Poľana mt. Slovakia 37 I4
Poland country Europe 37 I2
europe 24–25, 48
Polanica Poland 37 J3
Polanów Poland 37 H1
Polar Plateau Antarctica 167 A1
Polatlı Turkey 78 C3
Polatsk Belarus 28 D5
Polavaram India 72 D2
Polazna Rus. Fed. 28 K4
Polcirkeln Sweden 32 F2
Pol-e Fāsā Iran 80 C4
Pol-e Khomrī Afgh. 81 G3
Polessk Rus. Fed. 29 F6
Poles'ye marsh Belarus/Ukr. see Pripet Marshes
Polewali Indon. 56 E6
Poli Cameroon 93 I3
Poli Cyprus see Polis
Poliaigos i. Greece see Polyaigos
Poliçan Albania 46 B4
Policastro, Golfo di b. Italy 45 F5
Police Poland 37 G2
Polichnitos Greece 47 E5

Policoro Italy 45 F4
Polídhrosos Greece see Polydroso
Polignano a Mare Italy 44 F4
Poligny France 39 F3
Políkastron Greece see Polykastro
Polikhnítos Greece see Polichnitos
Polillo Islands Phil. 57 F2
Polis Cyprus 77 A2
Polis'ke Ukr. 29 D6
Polistena Italy 45 F5
Politovo Rus. Fed. 28 I2
Políyiros Greece see Polygyros
Polk U.S.A. 130 D3
Polkowice Poland 37 H3
Polla Italy 45 F4
Pollachi India 72 C4
Pollença Spain 43 H3
Pollensa Spain see Pollença
Pollino, Monte mt. Italy 45 F5
Pollino, Parco Nazionale del nat. park Italy 45 F5
Pollock Pines U.S.A. 136 B2
Pollock Reef Australia 109 C8
Polmak Norway 32 G1
Polnovat Rus. Fed. 26 G3
Pologi Ukr. see Polohy
Polohy Ukr. 29 F7
Polokwane S. Africa see Pietersburg
Polonnaruwa Sri Lanka 72 D5
Polonne Ukr. 29 D6
Polonnoye Ukr. see Polonne
Polotsk Belarus see Polatsk
Polovinka Rus. Fed. see Ugleural'skiy
Polovragi Romania 46 C2
Pöls r. Austria 37 G5
Polska country Europe see Poland
Polski Trümbesh Bulg. 46 D3
Polson U.S.A. 134 D3
Polta r. Rus. Fed. 28 G2
Poltár Slovakia 37 I4
Poltava Ukr. 29 E6
Poltavka Rus. Fed. 64 B3
Poltoratsk Turkm. see Ashgabat
Põltsamaa Estonia 33 G3
Põltsamaa r. Estonia 33 G4
Põlur r. Rus. Fed. 26 I3
Põlva Estonia 28 C4
Polvadera U.S.A. 135 F6
Polvijärvi Fin. 32 H3
Polyaigos i. Greece 47 D6
Polyanovgrad Bulg. see Karnobat
Polyarnoye Rus. Fed. 33 H3
Polyarnyy Murmanskaya Oblast' Rus. Fed. 32 I1
Polyarnyy Ural mts Rus. Fed. 28 L2
Polyarnyye Zori Rus. Fed. 32 I2
Polydroso Greece 47 C5
Polygyros Greece 47 C4
Polykastro Greece 47 C4
Polyiagou-Folegandrou, Steno sea chan. Greece 47 D6
Polynesia is Oceania 165 G6
Pomabamba Peru 148 A2
Pomarance Italy 44 C3
Pomba r. Brazil 151 D7
Pomba r. Brazil 151 D7
Pomene Moz. 99 G4
Pomeroy OH U.S.A. 130 B4
Pomeroy WA U.S.A. 134 C3
Pomezia Italy 44 D4
Pomfret S. Africa 98 D5
Pomio P.N.G. 107 E2
Pomokaira reg. Fin. 32 G2
Pomona Namibia 98 B5
Pomona U.S.A. 136 D4
Pomorie Bulg. 46 E3
Pomorska, Zatoka b. Poland 37 G2
Pomorskie, Pojezierze reg. Poland 37 H2
Pomorskiy Bereg coastal area Rus. Fed. 28 E2
Pomorskiy Proliv sea chan. Rus. Fed. 28 I1
Pomo Tso l. China see Puma Yumco
Pompei Italy 45 E4
Pompeii Italy see Pompei
Pompton Lakes U.S.A. 131 F3
Ponask Lake Canada 123 M4
Ponazyrevo Rus. Fed. 28 H4
Ponca U.S.A. 132 B3
Ponce Puerto Rico 139 K5
Poncha Springs U.S.A. 135 F5
Pondicherry India 72 C4
Pondicherry union terr. India 72 C4
Pondichéry India see Pondicherry
Pond Inlet Canada 121 L2
Ponds Bay Canada see Pond Inlet
Ponente, Riviera di coastal area Italy 44 A3
Ponferrada Spain 42 C1
Pongara, Pointe pt Gabon 94 A4
Pongaroa N.Z. 113 D3
Pongo watercourse Sudan 94 E3
Pongo de Manseriche gorge Peru 146 B6
Poniatowa Poland 37 K3
Ponnaiyar r. India 72 C4
Ponnani India 72 B4
Ponneri India 72 D3
Ponnyadaung Range mts Myanmar 60 A3
Ponoka Canada 134 D1
Ponomarevka Rus. Fed. 29 J5
Ponorogo Indon. 59 E4
Ponoy r. Rus. Fed. 28 G2
Pons r. Canada 125 G2
Pons France 38 C4
Pons Spain see Ponts
Ponsul r. Port. 42 C3
Pontacq France 38 C5

▶Ponta Delgada Azores 160 M3
Capital of the Azores.

Ponta de Pedras Brazil 150 B2
Ponta dos Índios Brazil 147 I3
Ponta do Sol Cape Verde 92 [inset]
Ponta Grossa Brazil 151 B8
Pont-à-Mousson France 39 G2
Pontax r. Canada 124 E3
Pontchartrain, Lake U.S.A. 133 D6
Pont-d'Ain France 39 F3
Pont de Suert Spain 43 G1
Ponte Alta do Norte Brazil 150 C4
Pontebba Italy 44 D1
Ponte de Pedra Brazil 149 F5
Pontedera Italy 44 C3
Ponte de Sor Port. 42 B3
Ponte do Rio Verde Brazil 151 A6
Ponte Nova Brazil 151 D7

Pontes-e-Lacerda Brazil 149 F3
Pontevedra Spain 42 B1
Pontevedra, Ría de est. Spain 42 B1
Ponthierville Dem. Rep. Congo see Ubundu
Pontiac IL U.S.A. 132 D3
Pontiac MI U.S.A. 130 B2
Pontiae is Italy see Ponziane, Isole
Pontianak Indon. 59 E3
Pontine Islands Italy see Ponziane, Isole
Pontivy France 38 B2
Pont-l'Abbé France 38 A3
Pontoetoe Suriname 147 H4
Pontoise France 38 E2
Ponton watercourse Australia 109 C7
Ponton Canada 123 L4
Pontremoli Italy 44 B2
Ponts Spain 43 G2
Pont-St-Esprit France 39 F4
Pont-sur-Yonne France 39 E2
Pontypool Canada 130 D1
Pontypool U.K. 35 E6
Pontypridd U.K. 35 E6
Ponza Italy 45 D4
Ponza, Isola di i. Italy 45 D4
Ponziane, Isole is Italy 45 D4
Poochera Australia 109 F8
Pool admin. reg. Congo 95 B5
Poole U.K. 35 F6
Poona India see Pune
Poopelloe Lake Australia 112 C3
Poopó, Lago de l. Bol. 148 D4
Poor Knights Islands N.Z. 113 C1
Popa Mountain Myanmar 60 B3
Popayán Col. 146 B4
Popes Creek U.S.A. 131 E4
Popigay r. Rus. Fed. 27 K2
Popilta Lake imp. l. Australia 112 B4
Poplar r. Canada 123 L4
Poplar U.S.A. 134 F2
Poplar Bluff U.S.A. 127 H4
Poplar Camp U.S.A. 130 C5
Poplar Plains U.S.A. 130 B4
Poplarville U.S.A. 133 D6

▶Popocatépetl, Volcán vol. Mex. 126 G8
5th highest mountain in North America.
northamerica 116–117

Popokabaka Dem. Rep. Congo 95 C6
Popoli Italy 44 D3
Popondetta P.N.G. 106 E2
Popovichskaya Rus. Fed. see Kalininskaya
Popovo Bulg. 46 E3
Popovo Polje plain Bos.-Herz. 44 F3
Poppberg hill Germany 36 E4
Poppenberg hill Germany 36 E3
Poprad r. Poland 37 J4
Poprad Slovakia 37 J4
Poquoson U.S.A. 131 E5
Porali r. Pak. 81 F5
Porangahau N.Z. 113 D3
Porangatu Brazil 150 B5
Porbandar India 74 A5
Porcher Island Canada 122 D4
Porco Bol. 148 D4
Porcos r. Brazil 151 C6
Porcupine r. Canada/U.S.A. 120 D3
Porcupine, Cape Canada 125 J2
Porcupine Abyssal Plain sea feature N. Atlantic Ocean 160 M2
Porcupine Creek r. U.S.A. 134 F2
Porcupine Gorge National Park Australia 111 C4
Porcupine Hills Canada 123 K4
Porcupine Plain Canada 123 K4
Pordenone Italy 44 D2
Pordim Bulg. 46 D3
Pore Col. 146 C2
Poreč Croatia 44 D2
Porecatu Brazil 149 H5
Poretskoye Rus. Fed. 28 H5
Porga Benin 93 F3
Pori Fin. 33 F3
Porjus Sweden 32 F2
Porkhov Rus. Fed. 28 D4
Porlamar Venez. 147 F2
Porma r. Spain 42 D1
Pornic France 38 B3
Poronaysk Rus. Fed. 27 O5
Porong China see Baingoin
Pörönge, Stœng r. Cambodia 61 D5
Poros Greece 47 C6
Poros r. Greece 47 C6
Porosozero Rus. Fed. 28 E3
Porpoise Bay Antarctica 167 G2
Porquerolles, Île de i. France 39 G5
Porrentruy Switz. 39 H3
Porriño Spain 42 B1
Porsangen sea chan. Norway 32 G1
Porsangerhalvøya pen. Norway 32 G1
Porsgrunn Norway 33 C4
Porsuk r. Turkey 78 B3
Portadown U.K. 35 C4
Portaferry U.K. 35 D4
Portage PA U.S.A. 130 D3
Portage WI U.S.A. 132 D3
Portage Lakes U.S.A. 130 C3
Portage la Prairie Canada 123 L5
Portal U.S.A. 132 A1
Port Alberni Canada 134 A2
Port Albert Australia 112 C5
Portalegre Port. 42 C3
Portalegre admin. dist. Port. 42 C3
Portales U.S.A. 135 G6
Port-Alfred Canada see La Baie
Port Alfred S. Africa 98 E7
Port Alice Canada 122 E5
Port Allegany U.S.A. 130 D3
Port Alma Australia 111 G4
Port Angeles U.S.A. 134 B3
Portarlington Rep. of Ireland 35 C5
Port Arthur Australia 112 C6
Port Arthur U.S.A. 133 C6
Port Askaig U.K. 34 C4
Port Augusta Australia 112 A4
Port-au-Port Bay Canada 125 J3

▶Port-au-Prince Haiti 139 J5
Capital of Haiti.

Port aux Choix Canada 125 J3
Port Beaufort S. Africa 98 D7
Port Blair India 73 G4
Port Bolster Canada 130 D1
Portbou Spain 43 H1
Port Broughton Australia 112 A4
Port Burwell Canada 130 C2
Port Campbell Australia 112 B5
Port Campbell National Park Australia 112 B5
Port Canning India 75 F5
Port-Cartier Canada 125 H3
Port Chalmers N.Z. 113 B4
Port Charlotte U.S.A. 129 C7
Port Clements Canada 122 C4
Port Clinton U.S.A. 130 B3
Port Clyde U.S.A. 131 I2
Port Colborne Canada 130 D2
Port-de-Paix Haiti 127 L8
Port Dickson Malaysia 58 C2
Port Dover Canada 130 C2
Port Edward Canada 122 D4

Port Edward S. Africa 99 F6
Porteira Brazil 147 G4
Porteirinha Brazil 150 D5
Portel Brazil 150 B2
Portel Port. 42 C3
Port Elgin N.B. Canada 125 H4
Port Elgin Ont. Canada 130 C1
Port Elizabeth S. Africa 98 E7
Port Ellen U.K. 34 C4
Port Erin Isle of Man 35 D4
Porter Lake N.W.T. Canada 123 J1
Porter Lake Sask. Canada 123 J3
Porter Landing Canada 122 D3
Porterville U.S.A. 136 C3
Port Étienne Mauritania see Nouâdhibou
Port Everglades U.S.A. see Fort Lauderdale
Port Fairy Australia 112 B5
Port Fitzroy N.Z. 113 C2
Port Francqui Dem. Rep. Congo see Ilebo
Port-Gentil Gabon 94 A5
Port Harcourt Nigeria 93 G4
Port Hardy Canada 122 E5
Port Harrison Canada see Inukjuak
Port Hawkesbury Canada 125 I4
Porthcawl U.K. 35 E6
Port Hedland Australia 108 B5
Port Henry U.S.A. 131 G1
Porthmos Zakynthou sea chan. Greece 47 B6
Port Hope Canada 130 D2
Port Hope U.S.A. 130 B2
Port Hope Simpson Canada 125 K2
Port Hueneme U.S.A. 136 C4
Port Huron U.S.A. 130 C2
Port-Ilīç Azer. see Port-Iliç
Portimão Port. 42 B4
Port Jackson Australia see Sydney
Port Kaituma Guyana 147 G3
Port Keats Australia see Wadeye
Port Kent U.S.A. 131 G1
Port Klang Malaysia see Pelabuhan Kelang
Port Láirge Rep. of Ireland see Waterford
Portland Australia 112 B5
Portland IN U.S.A. 130 B3
Portland ME U.S.A. 131 H2
Portland MI U.S.A. 130 A2
Portland OR U.S.A. 134 B3
Portland Bill hill U.K. see Bill of Portland
Portland Canal inlet Canada 122 D4
Portland Roads Australia 111 E2
Portlaoise Rep. of Ireland 35 C5
Port Lavaca U.S.A. 133 B6
Port Lincoln Australia 109 F8
Port Loko Sierra Leone 92 B4

▶Port Louis Mauritius 162 K7
Capital of Mauritius.

Port-Lyautrey Morocco see Kénitra
Port Macquarie Australia 112 E3
Port Manvers inlet Canada 125 I1
Port McNeill Canada 122 E5
Port-Menier Canada 125 H3
Port Moller b. U.S.A. 120 C4

▶Port Moresby P.N.G. 57 K7
Capital of Papua New Guinea.

Portnahaven U.K. 34 C4
Port Neches U.S.A. 133 C6
Port Neill Australia 109 G8
Portneuf r. Canada 125 G3
Port Nis U.K. 34 C2
Port Nolloth S. Africa 98 C6
Port Norris U.S.A. 131 F4
Port-Nouveau-Québec Canada see Kangiqsualujjuaq
Porto Brazil 150 D2
Porto Port. see Oporto
Porto admin. dist. Port. 42 B2
Porto, Golfe de b. Corsica France 44 B3
Porto Acre Brazil 148 D2
Porto Alegre Mato Grosso do Sul Brazil 151 A7
Porto Alegre Pará Brazil 147 H6
Porto Alegre Rio Grande do Sul Brazil 151 B9
Porto Alexandre Angola see Tombua
Porto Amarante Brazil 149 E3
Porto Amboim Angola 95 B7
Porto Amélia Moz. see Pemba
Porto Artur Brazil 149 E3
Porto Belo, Parque Nacional nat. park Panama 146 C2
Porto Camargo Brazil 151 A7
Porto da Lontra Brazil 147 H6
Porto de Meinacos Brazil 150 A5
Porto de Moz Brazil 147 H5
Porto do Barka Brazil 147 H6
Porto dos Gaúchos Óbidos Brazil 149 F2
Porto do Son Spain 42 B1
Porto Esperança Brazil 149 F4
Porto Esperidão Brazil 149 F3
Porto Estrêla Brazil 149 F3
Portoferraio Italy 44 C3
Porto Franco Brazil 150 C3

▶Port of Spain Trin. and Tob. 147 F2
Capital of Trinidad and Tobago.

Porto Grande Brazil 147 I4
Portogruaro Italy 44 D2
Porto Inglês Cape Verde 92 [inset]
Porto Jofre Brazil 149 F4
Portola U.S.A. 136 B2
Portomaggiore Italy 44 C2
Porto Mauá Brazil 151 A8
Porto Murtinho Brazil 149 F4
Porto Nacional Brazil 150 B4

▶Porto-Novo Benin 93 F4
Capital of Benin.

Porto Novo Cape Verde 92 [inset]
Porto Novo India see Parangipettai
Porto Primavera, Represa resr Brazil 149 G5
Port Orchard U.S.A. 134 B3
Port Orford U.S.A. 134 A4
Porto San Giorgio Italy 44 D3
Porto Santana Brazil 147 I5
Porto Sant'Elpidio Italy 44 D3
Porto Santo, Ilha de i. Madeira 90 A2
Porto Seguro Brazil 151 E6
Porto Tolle Italy 44 D2
Porto Torres Sardinia Italy 45 B4
Porto-Vecchio Corsica France 31 I5
Porto Velho Brazil 149 E2
Portoviejo Ecuador 146 A5
Porto Wälter Brazil 148 D2
Portpatrick U.K. 34 D5
Port Perry Canada 130 D1
Port Phillip Bay Australia 112 C5
Port Pirie Australia 112 A4
Port Radium Canada see Echo Bay
Portree U.K. 34 C3
Port Renfrew Canada 122 E5
Port Rexton Canada 125 K3
Port Rowan Canada 130 C2
Port Royal U.S.A. 131 E4
Port Royal Sound inlet U.S.A. 129 C5
Port Said Egypt 82 B5
Port St Joe U.S.A. 129 B6
Port St Johns S. Africa 99 F6

Port St-Louis Madag. see
  Antsohimbondrona
Port Saint Lucie City U.S.A. **129** C7
Port Salvador Falkland Is **153** F7
Ports de Beseit mts Spain **43** G2
Port Shelter b. Hong Kong China
  67 [inset]
Port Shepstone S. Africa **99** F6
Port Simpson Canada see
  Lax Kw'alaams
Portsmouth NH U.S.A. **131** H2
Portsmouth OH U.S.A. **130** B4
Portsmouth VA U.S.A. **131** E5
Port Stanley Falkland Is see Stanley
Port Stephens Falkland Is **153** E8
Port Sudan Sudan **89** H5
Port Sulphur U.S.A. **133** D6
Port-sur-Saône France **39** G3
Port Swettenham Malaysia see
  Pelabuhan Kelang
Port Talbot U.K. **35** E6
Porttipahdan tekojärvi l. Fin. **32** G1
Port Townsend U.S.A. **134** B2
▶**Portugal** country Europe **42** C3
  europe 24–25, 48
Portugalete Spain **42** E1
Portugália Angola see Chitato
Portuguesa state Venez. **146** D2
Portuguese East Africa country Africa
  see Mozambique
Portuguese Guinea country Africa see
  Guinea-Bissau
Portuguese Timor ccuntry Asia see
  East Timor
Portuguese West Africa country Africa
  see Angola
Portumna Rep. of Ireland **35** B5
Portus Herculis Monoeci country
  Europe see Monaco
Port-Vendres France **39** E5
Port Victoria Australia **112** A4
▶**Port Vila** Vanuatu **107** F3
  Capital of Vanuatu.

Portville U.S.A. **130** D2
Port Vladimir Rus. Fed. **32** I1
Port Wakefield Australia **112** A4
Port Warrender Australia **110** A2
Port Washington U.S.A. **132** E3
Porumamilla India **72** C3
Porvenir Pando Bol. **148** C2
Porvenir Santa Cruz Bol. **149** E3
Porvenir Chile **153** C8
Porvoo Fin. **32** H3
Poryŏng S. Korea **65** A5
Porzuna Spain **42** D3
Posada Sardinia Italy **45** B4
Posada r. Sardinia Italy **45** B4
Posada Spain **42** D1
Posadas Arg. **152** G1
Posadas Spain **42** D4
Poschiavo Switz. **39** I3
Poseidonia Greece **47** D6
Poseidonia tourist site Italy see Paestum
Posen Poland see Poznań
Poshekhon'ye Rus. Fed. **28** F4
Poshekon'ye-Volodarsk Rus. Fed. see
  Poshekhon'ye
Posht watercourse Iran **81** D4
Posht-e Badam Iran **80** D3
Poshteh-ye Chaqvir mt. Iran **81** D4
Posht-e Küh mts Iran **80** A3
Posht Küh hill Iran **80** B2
Posio Fin. **32** H2
Poso Indon. **57** F6
Posof Turkey **77** C3
Posorja Ecuador **146** A5
Posse Brazil **150** C5
Pößneck Germany **36** E3
Post U.S.A. **133** A5
Poşta Câlnău Romania **46** E2
Poşta Câlnău Roman a see Poşta Câlnău
Postavy Belarus see Pastavy
Poste-de-la-Baleine Canada see
  Kuujjuarapik
Postmasburg S. Africa **98** D5
Postojna Slovenia **44** E2
Poston U.S.A. **137** E4
Postville Canada **125** J2
Postville U.S.A. **132** D3
Post Weygand Alg. **91** F4
Postysheve Ukr. see Krasnoarmiys'k
Posušje Bos.-Herz. **44** F3
Pota Indon. **108** C2
Potamia Greece **46** D4
Potamos Greece **47** C6
Potcoava Romania **46** D2
Poté Brazil **151** D6
Poteau U.S.A. **133** C5
Potegaon India **72** C2
Potentia Italy see Potenza
Potenza Italy **44** F4
Potenza r. Italy **44** E3
Potgietersrus S. Africa **99** F5
Poti r. Brazil **150** D3
Pot'i Georgia **79** F2
Potiragua Brazil **150** E5
Potiskum Nigeria **93** H3
Potnarvin Vanuatu **107** F3
Poto Peru **148** C3
Potomac r. U.S.A. **131** E4
Potomac, South Branch r. U.S.A.
  130 D4
Potomana, Gunung mt. Indon. **108** D2
Potoru Sierra Leone **92** C4
Potosí Bol. **148** D4
Potosí dept Bol. **148** D4
Potosi Mountain U.S.A. **137** E4
Potrerillos Chile **152** C1
Potrero del Llano Mex. **135** F7
Potro r. Peru **146** B4
Potsdam Germany **37** F2
Potsdam U.S.A. **131** H1
Pottangi India **73** D2
Potter Valley U.S.A. **136** A2
Potterville U.S.A. **130** C3
Pottsville U.S.A. **131** G3
Pouce Coupe Canada **122** F4
Pouch Cove Canada **125** K4
Poughkeepsie U.S.A. **131** H3
Poultney U.S.A. **131** H2
Pouma Cameroon **93** H5
Pouso Alegre Brazil **151** C7
Poutasi Samoa **107** H3
Poŭthisăt Cambodia **61** C5
Považská Bystrica Slovakia **37** I4
Povenets Rus. Fed. **28** E3
Poverty Bay N.Z. **113** G3
Povlen mt. Yugo. **46** A2
Póvoa de Varzim Port. **42** B2
Povorino Rus. Fed. **29** G6
Povorotnyy, Mys hd Rus. Fed. **64** C4
Powder r. MT U.S.A. **134** F3
Powder r. OR U.S.A. **134** C3
Powder, South Fork r. U.S.A. **134** F4
Powell U.S.A. **134** F3
Powell r. U.S.A. **130** B5
Powell, Lake resr U.S.A. **137** G3
Powell Creek watercourse Australia
  111 E3
Powell River Canada **134** A2
Powhatan U.S.A. **130** E5

Powhatan Point U.S.A. **130** C4
Powidzkie, Jezioro l. Poland **37** H2
Powo China **66** A1
Poxoréu Brazil **150** A5
Poyang China see Boyang
Poyang Hu l. China **67** F2
Poyan Reservoir Sing. **58** [inset]
Poyarkovo Rus. Fed. **64** B2
Poyo, Cerro mt. Spain **43** E4
Poysdorf Austria **37** H4
Pozantı Turkey **78** C3
Požarevac Yugo. **46** B2
Poza Rica Mex. **126** D7
Požega Croatia **44** F2
Požega Yugo. **46** B3
Pozhva Rus. Fed. **28** K4
Poznań Poland **37** H2
Pozo Alcón Spain **42** E4
Pozo Betbeder Arg. **152** D1
Pozoblanco Spain **42** D3
Pozo Colorado Para. **149** F5
Pozo del Tigre Arg. **149** E6
Pozo Hondo Arg. **152** D1
Pozohondo Spain **43** F3
Pozo Nuevo Mex. **135** E7
Pozos, Punta pt Arg. **153** D6
Pozuzo Peru **148** B2
Pozzallo Sicily Italy **45** E6
Pozzuoli Italy **45** E4
Pra r. Ghana **93** E4
Prabumulih Indon. **58** D3
Prabuty Poland **37** I2
Prachatice Czech Rep. **37** G4
Prachi r. India **73** E2
Prachin Buri Thai. **61** C5
Prachuap Khiri Khan Thai. **61** B6
Pradairo mt. Spain **42** C1
Praděd mt. Czech Rep. **37** H3
Prades France **39** E5
Prado Brazil **151** E6

▶**Prague** Czech Rep. **37** G3
  Capital of the Czech Republic.

Praha Czech Rep. see Prague
Prahova r. Romania **46** E2

▶**Praia** Cape Verde **92** [inset]
  Capital of Cape Verde.

Praia do Bilene Moz. **99** G5
Praia Rica Brazil **149** G3
Prainha Amazonas Brazil **149** E1
Prainha Pará Brazil **147** H5
Prairie Australia **111** F4
Prairie City U.S.A. **134** C3
Prairie Dog Town Fork r. U.S.A. **133** A5
Prairie du Chien U.S.A. **132** D3
Prakhon Chai Thai. **61** C5
Pram r. Austria **37** F4
Pramanta Greece **47** B5
Pran r. Thai. **61** C5
Pran Buri Thai. **61** B5
Pranhita r. India **72** C2
Prapat Indon. **58** B2
Prasonísi, Akra pt Greece **47** G7
Praszka Poland **37** I3
Prat i. Chile **153** B7
Prata Brazil **149** H4
Pratapgarh India **74** B4
Pratas Islands China see
  Dongsha Qundao
Prat de Llobregat Spain see
  El Prat de Llobregat
Prathes Thai country Asia see Thailand
Prato Italy **44** C3
Pratt U.S.A. **132** B4
Prattville U.S.A. **129** B5
Pravara r. India **72** B2
Pravdinsk Rus. Fed. **37** J1
Pravia Spain **42** C1
Praya Indon. **59** G5
Preah, Prêk r. Cambodia **61** D5
Preăh Vihéar Cambodia **61** C5
Prechistoye Rus. Fed. **28** G4
Precipice National Park Australia
  111 E5
Predazzo Italy **44** C1
Predeal Romania **46** D2
Preeceville Canada **134** G2
Pré-en-Pail France **38** C2
Preetz Germany **36** E1
Pregolya r. Rus. Fed. **37** J1
Prekornica mts Bos.-Herz. **44** A3
Prémery France **39** E3
Premnitz Germany **37** F2
Prenai mts Bos.-Herz. **44** F3
Prentiss U.S.A. **133** D6
Prenzlau Germany **37** F2
Preobrazheniye Rus. Fed. **64** C4
Preparis Island Cocos Is **61** A5
Preparis North Channel Cocos Is **61** A5
Preparis South Channel Cocos Is **61** A5
Přerov Czech Rep. **37** H4
Presanella, Cima mt. Italy **44** C1
Prescott AR U.S.A. **133** C5
Prescott AZ U.S.A. **137** F4
Prescott Valley U.S.A. **137** F4
Preševo Yugo. **46** B3
Presidencia Roca Arg. **152** F1
Presidencia Roque Sáenz Peña Arg.
  152 E1
Presidente Dutra Brazil **150** D2
Presidente Eduardo Frei
  research station Antarctica **167** A2
Presidente Epitácio Brazil **149** G5
Presidente Hermes Brazil **148** E2
Presidente Juan Perón prov. Arg. see
  Chaco
Presidente Olegário Brazil **151** C5
Presidente Prudente Brazil **149** H5
Presidio U.S.A. **135** F7
Preslav Bulg. see Veliki Preslav
Prešov Slovakia **37** J4
Prespa, Lake Europe **46** B4
Prespansko Ezero l. Europe see
  Prespa, Lake
Prespes nat. park Greece **46** B4
Prespës, Liqeni i. Europe see
  Prespa, Lake
Presque Isle U.S.A. **128** F2
Pressbaum Austria **37** H4
Pressburg Slovakia see Bratislava
Prestea Ghana **93** E4
Presteigne U.K. **35** E5
Preston U.K. **35** E5
Preston ID U.S.A. **134** E4
Preston MD U.S.A. **131** H4
Preston MN U.S.A. **132** C3
Preston, Cape Australia **108** B5
Prestoríbsord U.S.A. **130** D3
Prestwick U.K. **34** D4
Preto r. Bahia Brazil **150** D4
Preto r. Minas Gerais Brazil **151** C6
Preto r. Rondônia Brazil **149** E2

▶**Pretoria** S. Africa **99** F5
  Official capital of South Africa.
  world 8–9

Pretoria-Witwatersrand-Vereeniging
  prov. S. Africa see Gauteng
Preussisch-Eylau Rus. Fed. see
  Bagrationovsk

Preußisch Stargard Poland see
  Starogard Gdański
Preveza Greece **47** B5
Prey Vêng Cambodia **61** D5
Priamurskiy Rus. Fed. **64** C2
Priaral'skiye Karakumy, Peski des.
  Kazakh. **70** B2
Priargunsk Rus. Fed. **63** J1
Pribilof Islands U.S.A. **120** B4
Priboj Yugo. **46** A3
Příbram Czech Rep. **37** G4
Price r. Australia **110** B2
Price Canada **125** G3
Price NC U.S.A. **130** D5
Price UT U.S.A. **137** G2
Price r. U.S.A. **137** G2
Prichard AL U.S.A. **129** A6
Prichard WV U.S.A. **130** B4
Priego de Córdoba Spain **42** D4
Priekule Latvia **33** F4
Priekulė Lith. **33** F5
Prienai Lith. **33** F5
Prieska S. Africa **98** D6
Prieto hill Spain **42** D4
Prievidza Slovakia **37** I4
Prijedor Bos.-Herz. **44** F2
Prijepolje Yugo. **46** A3
Prikaspiyskaya Nizmennost' lowland
  Kazakh./Rus. Fed. see Caspian Lowland
Prilep Macedonia **46** B4
Priluki Ukr. see Pryluky
Primavera Bol. **148** D2
Primavera do Leste Brazil **150** A5
Primeira Cruz Brazil **150** D2
Primorsk Rus. Fed. **28** D3
Primorsk Ukr. see Prymors'k
Primorskiy Kray admin. div. Rus. Fed.
  64 C3
Primorsko-Akhtarsk Rus. Fed. **29** F7
Primrose Lake Canada **123** I4
Prince Albert Canada **123** J4
Prince Albert S. Africa **98** D7
Prince Albert Mountains Antarctica
  167 H1
Prince Albert National Park Canada
  123 J4
Prince Albert Peninsula Canada
  121 H2
Prince Albert Road S. Africa **98** D7
Prince Albert Sound sea chan. Canada
  121 H2
Prince Alfred, Cape Canada **120** G2
Prince Charles Island Canada **121** L3
Prince Charles Mountains Antarctica
  167 E2
Prince Edward Island prov. Canada
  125 I4

▶**Prince Edward Islands** Indian Ocean
  163 J9
  Part of South Africa.

Prince Edward Point Canada **131** E2
Prince Frederick U.S.A. **131** E4
Prince George Canada **122** F4
Prince Harald Coast Antarctica **167** D2
Prince Karl Foreland i. Svalbard see
  Prins Karls Forland
Prince of Wales, Cape U.S.A. **120** C3
Prince of Wales Island Australia
  111 E1
Prince of Wales Island Canada **121** J2
Prince of Wales Island U.S.A. **120** F4
Prince of Wales Strait Canada **121** H2
Prince Patrick Island Canada **121** H2
Prince Regent r. Australia **108** D3
Prince Regent Inlet sea chan. Canada
  121 J2
Prince Rupert Canada **122** D4
Princess Anne U.S.A. **131** H4
Princess Astrid Coast Antarctica
  167 C2
Princess Charlotte Bay Australia
  111 E2
Princess Elizabeth Land reg. Antarctica
  167 E2
Princess Mary Lake Canada **121** L1
Princess May Range hills Australia
  108 D3
Princess Ragnhild Coast Antarctica
  167 C2
Princess Royal Island Canada **122** D4
Princeton Canada **134** B2
Princeton CA U.S.A. **136** B2
Princeton IL U.S.A. **132** D3
Princeton IN U.S.A. **128** B4
Princeton KY U.S.A. **128** B4
Princeton MO U.S.A. **132** C3
Princeton NJ U.S.A. **131** H3
Prince William Sound b. U.S.A. **120** E3
Principe i. São Tomé and Príncipe **93** G5
Prineville U.S.A. **134** B3
Prinos Greece **46** D4
Prins Karls Forland i. Svalbard **26** B2
Prinzapolca Nicaragua **139** H6
Prior, Cabo c. Spain **42** B1
Priozersk Rus. Fed. **28** D3
Priozyorsk Rus. Fed. see Priozersk
Pripet r. Belarus/Ukr. **29** C5
  also spelt Pryp"yat' (Ukraine) or
  Prypyats' (Belarus)
Pripet Marshes Belarus/Ukr. **29** C6
Pripolyarnyy Ural mts Rus. Fed. **28** K2
Pirrechnyy Rus. Fed. **32** I1
Priseka hill Croatia **44** F2
Priština Yugo. **46** B3
Prithvipur India **74** C4
Pritzwalk Germany **37** F2
Privas France **39** F4
Privlaka Croatia **44** F2
Privolzhsk Rus. Fed. **28** G4
Privolzhskaya Vozvyshennost' hills
  Rus. Fed. **29** H6
Privolzhskiy Rus. Fed. **29** H6
Privolzh'ye Rus. Fed. **29** I5
Priyutnoye Rus. Fed. **29** G7
Prizren Yugo. **46** B3
Prizzi Sicily Italy **45** D6
Prnjavor Bos.-Herz. **44** F2
Probištip Macedonia **46** C3
Probolinggo Indon. **59** F4
Prochowice Poland **37** H3
Proctorville U.S.A. **130** B4
Proddatur India **72** C3
Proença-a-Nova Port. **42** C3
Professor van Blommestein Meer resr
  Suriname **147** H3
Progreso Hond. **138** G5
Progreso Coahuila Mex. **133** A7
Progreso Mex. **127** I7
Progress Rus. Fed. **64** B2
Progresso Brazil **148** C2
Prokhladnyy Rus. Fed. **29** H8
Prokletije mts Albania/Yugo. **46** A3
Prokop'yevsk Rus. Fed. **62** D1
Prokuplje Yugo. **46** B3
Proletarsk Rus. Fed. **29** G7
Proletarskaya Rus. Fed. see Proletarsk
Prome Myanmar see Pyè
Promissão Brazil **151** B7
Promontorio del Gargano plat. Italy
  44 F4
Pronino Rus. Fed. **28** G4
Prophet r. Canada **122** F3
Prophet River Canada **122** F3
Propriá Brazil **150** E4
Proserpine Australia **111** B4

Proskurov Ukr. see Khmel'nyts'kyy
Prosna r. Poland **37** H3
Prosotsani Greece **46** C4
Prospect NY U.S.A. **131** H2
Prospect OH U.S.A. **130** B3
Prospect OR U.S.A. **134** B4
Prospect PA U.S.A. **130** C3
Prostějov Czech Rep. **37** H4
Proston Australia **111** E5
Proszowice Poland **37** J3
Proti i. Greece **47** B6
Provadiya Bulg. **46** E3
Prøven Greenland see Kangersuatsiaq
Provence-Alpes-Côte-d'Azur
  admin. reg. France **39** G5
▶**Providence** RI U.S.A. **131** H3
  State capital of Rhode Island.

Providence, Cape N.Z. **113** A4
Providence Atoll i. Seychelles **97** F7
Providence Island i. Seychelles see
  Providence Atoll
Providence Mountains U.S.A. **137** E4
Providencia Rus. Fed. **27** S3
Providencia, Isla de i. Caribbean Sea
  139 H6
Providencia, Serra de hills Brazil
Provideniya Rus. Fed. **27** S3
Providential Channel Australia **111** E2
Provincetown U.S.A. **131** H2
Provincia Col. **146** C3
Provins France **39** E2
Provo U.S.A. **137** G1
Provost Canada **123** I4
Prrenjas Albania **46** B4
Pru r. Ghana **93** E3
Prub r. Rus. Fed. **28** J3
Prudentópolis Brazil **151** B8
Prudhoe Bay U.S.A. **120** E2
Prudhoe Island Australia **111** G4
Prudnik Poland **37** H3
Prüm Germany **36** C3
Prundeni Romania **46** D2
Prundu Romania **46** D2
Pruntytown U.S.A. **130** C4
Prusa Turkey see Bursa
Prushkov Poland see Pruszków
Pruszcz Gdański Poland **37** I1
Pruszków Poland **37** J2
Prut r. Europe **46** F2
Prydz Bay Antarctica **167** E2
Pryelbrussky Natsional'nyy Park
  nat. park Rus. Fed. **79** E2
Pryluky Ukr. **29** E6
Prymors'k Ukr. **29** F7
Prymors'ke Ukr. **46** F1
Pryp"yat' r. see Pripet
Prypyats' r. Belarus **29** C5 see Pripet
Przasnysz Poland **37** J2
Przedbórz Poland **37** I3
Przemyśl Poland **31** J3
Przheval'sk Kyrg. see Karakol
Przysucha Poland **37** J3
Psachna Greece **47** C5
Psakhná Greece see Psachna
Psara i. Greece **47** D5
Psara Greece **47** D5
Psathoura i. Greece **47** D5
Psebay Rus. Fed. **79** E1
Pserimos i. Greece **47** E6
Pskov Rus. Fed. **28** D4
Pskov, Lake Estonia/Rus. Fed. **28** C4
Pskov Oblast admin. div. Rus. Fed. see
  Pskovskaya Oblast'
Pskovskaya Oblast' admin. div.
  Rus. Fed. **28** C4
Pskovskoye Ozero l. Estonia/Rus. Fed.
  see Pskov, Lake
Psunj mts Croatia **44** F2
Ptolemaïda Greece **46** B4
Ptolemais Israel see 'Akko
Ptuj Slovenia **44** E1
Pu r. Indon. **58** C3
Puaka hill Sing. **58** [inset]
Pu'an Guizhou China **66** C3
Pu'an Sichuan China see Jiange
Pucacuro Peru **146** C4
Pucacuro r. Peru **146** C5
Pucalá Peru **148** B6
Pucará Bol. **148** D4
Pucarani Bol. **148** C4
Puca Urco Peru **146** C4
Pucheng Fujian China **67** F3
Pucheng Shaanxi China **67** D1
Puchezh Rus. Fed. **28** G4
Puch'ŏn S. Korea **65** A5
Pucioasa Romania **46** D2
Puck Poland **37** I1
Pucka, Zatoka b. Poland **37** I1
Puçol Spain **43** F3
Pucón Chile **152** B4
Pudai watercourse Afgh. see Dor
Pūdanū Iran **80** D3
Pudasjärvi Fin. **32** G2
Puding China **66** C3
Pudozh Rus. Fed. **28** F3
Puducherry Pondicherry India see
  Pondicherry
Puducherry India see Pondicherry
Pudukkottai India **72** C4
Puebla Mex. **126** G8
Puebla Baja California Mex. **137** E5
Puebla de Don Fadrique Spain **43** E4
Puebla de Obando Spain **42** C3
Puebla de Zaragoza Mex. see Puebla
Pueblo U.S.A. **135** F5
Pueblo Hundido Chile **152** C1
Pueblo Viejo Col. **146** C1
Pueblo Yaqui Mex. **135** D7
Puech de Rouet hill France **38** E4
Puelches Arg. **152** D4
Puelén Arg. **152** D4
Puenteareas Spain see Ponteareas
Puente del Inca Arg. **152** C3
Puente-Genil Spain **42** D4
Puente la Reina Spain **43** F1
Puentes de García Rodríguez Spain
  see Puentes de García Rodríguez
Puente Torres Venez. **146** D2
Puer China see Ning'er
Puerco watercourse AZ U.S.A. **137** G4
Puerco watercourse NM U.S.A. **135** F6
Puerto Aisén Chile **153** B6
Puerto Alegría Col. **146** D5
Puerto Alfonso Col. **146** D5
Puerto Ángel Mex. **138** E5
Puerto America Peru **146** C5
Puerto Armuelles Panama **139** H7
Puerto Asís Col. **146** C4
Puerto Ayacucho Venez. **146** E3
Puerto Bajo Pisagua Chile **153** B6
Puerto Barrios Guat. **138** G5
Puerto Berrío Col. **146** C2
Puerto Boyacá Col. **146** C2
Puerto Cabello Venez. **146** D2
Puerto Cabezas Nicaragua **139** H6
Puerto Carreño Col. **146** E2
Puerto Casado Para. **149** F5
Puerto Cavinas Bol. **148** D3
Puerto Cerpera Peru **148** B6
Puerto Chabuco Chile **153** B6
Puerto Chicama Peru **148** B4
Puerto Cisnes Chile **153** B6
Puerto Coig Arg. **153** C7

Puerto Córdoba Col. **146** D5
Puerto Cortés Costa Rica **139** H7
Puerto Cortés Mex. **126** D7
Puerto Cumarebo Venez. **146** D2
Puerto de Cabras Canary Is see
  Puerto del Rosario
Puerto Definitivo Peru **148** C2
Puerto del Rosario Canary Is **90** B3
Puerto del Son Spain see Porto do Son
Puerto de Nutrias Venez. **146** D2
Puerto de Pollensa Spain see
  Port de Pollença
Puerto Escondido Mex. **138** E5
Puerto Estrella Col. **146** D1
Puerto Flamenco Chile **152** C'**
Puerto Francisco de Orellana Ecuador
  146 B5
Puerto Génova Bol. **148** D3
Puerto Grether Bol. **148** D4
Puerto Guaraní Para. **149** F5
Puerto Harberton Arg. **153** D8
Puerto Heath Bol. **148** D3
Puerto Huitoto Col. **146** C4
Puerto Ingeniero Ibáñez Chile **153** B6
Puerto Inírida Col. **146** E4
Puerto Isabel Bol. **149** F4
Puerto La Paz Arg. **149** E5
Puerto Leguizamo Col. **146** C5
Puerto Lempira Hond. **139** H5
Puerto Libertad Mex. **135** D7
Puerto Lobos Arg. **153** C5
Puerto Lopez Col. **146** D2
Puerto López Col. **146** C2
Puerto López Ecuador **146** A5
Puerto Lumbreras Spain **43** F4
Puerto Madryn Arg. **153** C5
Puerto Maldonado Peru **148** D3
Puerto Mamoré Bol. **148** D4
Puerto Máncora Peru **146** A6
Puerto María Auxiliadora Para. **149** F5
Puerto Marquez Bol. **148** D3
Puerto Melinka Chile **153** B5
Puerto México Mex. see Coatzacoalcos
Puerto Miranda Venez. **146** C3
Puerto Montt Chile **153** B5
Puerto Natales Chile **153** B7
Puerto Nuevo Col. **146** D3
Puerto Ordaz Venez. **147** F2
Puerto Ospina Col. **146** C4
Puerto Páez Venez. **146** E3
Puerto Pando Bol. **148** D3
Puerto Pardo Peru **146** D5
Puerto Peñasco Mex. **135** D7
Puerto Pirámides Arg. **153** D5
Puerto Pirítu Venez. **147** F2
Puerto Pizarro Col. **146** C5
Puerto Plata Dom. Rep. **127** L3
Puerto Portillo Peru **148** C2
Puerto Prado Peru **148** C3
Puerto Presidente Stroessner Para.
  see Ciudad del Este
Puerto Princesa Phil. **56** F5
Puerto Quepos Costa Rica **139** H7
Puerto Real Spain **42** C5
Puerto Rico Arg. **152** G1
Puerto Rico Bol. **148** D3
Puerto Rico Col. **146** C4
▶**Puerto Rico** terr. West Indies **139** K5
  United States Commonwealth.
  northamerica 118–119, 140

▶**Puerto Rico Trench** sea feature
  Caribbean Sea **160** L2
  Deepest trench in the Atlantic Ocean.

Puerto Saavedra Chile **152** B4
Puerto Salgar Col. **146** C3
Puerto San Agustin Peru **146** D5
Puerto San Carlos Bol. **148** D4
Puerto San José Guat. **138** F6
Puerto Sastre Para. **149** F5
Puerto Siles Bol. **148** D3
Puerto Socorro Peru **146** D5
Puerto Suárez Bol. **149** F4
Puerto Tahuantisuyo Peru **148** C3
Puerto Tejado Col. **146** B4
Puerto Tunigrama Peru **146** C5
Puerto Vallarta Mex. **126** D7
Puerto Varas Chile **153** B5
Puerto Victoria Peru **148** C2
Puerto Villamil Arg. **149** E3
Puerto Visser Arg. **153** C6
Puerto Wilches Col. **146** C2
Puerto Yartou Chile **153** C7
Pugachev Rus. Fed. **29** I5
Pugal India **74** B3
Pugwash Canada **125** I4
Pühäl-e Khamir, Küh-e mts Iran **80** D5
Puhja Estonia **33** G4
Pui Romania **46** C2
Puigmal mt. France/Spain **43** H1
Pui O Wan b. Hong Kong China **67** [inset]
Puiseaux France **39** E2
Puits 29 well Chad **88** C6
Puits 30 well Chad **88** C6
Puji China **67** F2
Pujiang China **67** F2
Pujiang Zhejiang China see Pujiang
Pukaki, Lake N.Z. **113** C7
Puk'an-san National Park S. Korea
  65 A5
Pukapuka atoll Cook Is **105** G6
Pukaskwa National Park Canada
  124 C3
Pukatawagan Canada **123** K4
Pukch'ŏng N. Korea **65** B4
Pukë Albania **46** A3
Pukekohe N.Z. **113** C2
Pukeuri Junction N.Z. **113** B4
Puksoozero Rus. Fed. **28** G3
Puksubaek-san mt. N. Korea **65** A4
Pula China see Nyingchi
Pula Sardinia Italy **45** B5
Pula Croatia **44** E2
Pulandian Bol. **148** D5
Pulangpisau Indon. **59** F3
Pular, Cerro mt. Chile **148** C6
Pulaski NY U.S.A. **131** F2
Pulaski TN U.S.A. **128** B5
Pulaski VA U.S.A. **130** C5
Pulau r. Indon. **57** I7
Pulau Pinang state Malaysia see Pinang
Pulheim Germany **36** C3
Pulicat Lake inlet India **72** D3
Pulivendla India **72** C3
Pulkau r. Austria **37** H4
Pulkkila Fin. **32** G2
Pullman U.S.A. **134** D2
Pulo Anna i. Palau **57** H5
Pulog, Mount Phil. **57** F2
Pülümür Turkey **79** D3
Pulu China **74** D1
Pułtusk Poland **37** J2
Puma Yumco l. China **75** F3
Pumiao China see Yongning

Pumpkin Creek r. U.S.A. **134** F3
Puná, Isla i. Ecuador **146** A5
Puna de Atacama plat. Arg. **152** D1
Punakha Bhutan **75** F4
Punata Bol. **148** D4
Punch Pak. **74** B2
Punchaw Canada **122** F4
Punda Maria S. Africa **99** F4
Pundri India **74** C3
Pune India **72** B2
Punganuru India **72** C3
Punggol Sing. **58** [inset]
Punggol, Sungai r. Sing. **58** [inset]
Púnguè r. Moz. **99** G5
Punia Dem. Rep. Congo **94** C5
Puning China **67** F4
Punitaqui Chile **152** B2
Punjab state India **74** B3
Punjab prov. Pak. **81** G4
Punmah Glacier China/Jammu and Kashmir **74** C2
Puno Peru **148** C3
Puno dept Peru **148** C3
Punpun r. India **75** E4
Punta, Cerro de mt. Puerto Rico **139** K5
Punta Alta Arg. **152** E4
Punta Arenas Chile **153** C8
Punta Balestrieri mt. Sardinia Italy **45** B4
Punta de Bombón Peru **148** C4
Punta de Diaz Chile **152** C2
Punta Delgada Arg. **153** D5
Punta de los Llanos Arg. **152** D2
Punta Gorda Belize **138** G5
Punta Negra, Salar salt flat Chile **148** C6
Puntarenas Costa Rica **139** H6
Punto Fijo Venez. **146** C1
Puntón de Guara mt. Spain **43** F1
Punxsutawney U.S.A. **130** D3
Puolanka Fin. **32** G2
Puquio Peru **148** C3
Pur r. Rus. Fed. **26** J3
Puracé, Parque Nacional nat. park Col.
  146 B4
Puranpur India **74** D3
Purari r. P.N.G. **57** J7
Purbalingga Indon. **59** E4
Purcell U.S.A. **133** B5
Purcell Mountains Canada **134** C3
Purcellville U.S.A. **130** E4
Purén Chile **152** B4
Purgatoire r. U.S.A. **132** A4
Puri India **73** E2
Purmerend Neth. **36** B2
Purna r. Maharashtra India **72** C2
Purna r. Maharashtra India **74** C5
Purnabhaba r. India **75** F4
Purnea India see Purnia
Purnia India **75** E4
Purnululu National Park Australia
  108 E4
Puruandiro Chile **152** B5
Purranque Chile **152** B4
Pursat Cambodia see Poŭthisăt
Puruê r. Brazil **146** D5
Purukcahu Indon. **59** F3
Puruliya India **75** E5

Purus r. Peru **147** F5
  3rd longest river in South America
  southamerica 142–143

Puruvesi l. Fin. **33** H3
Pürvomay Bulg. **46** D3
Purwakarta Indon. **59** E4
Purwareja Indon. **59** E4
Purwodadi Indon. **59** E4
Purwokerto Indon. **59** E4
Puryŏng N. Korea **64** B4
Pus r. India **72** C2
Pusa r. Spain **42** D3
Pusad India **72** C2
Pusan S. Korea **65** B6
Pusatdamai Indon. **59** F3
Pushemskiy Rus. Fed. **28** H3
Pushkin Rus. Fed. **28** D4
Pushkino Azer. see Bilāsuvar
Pushkino Rus. Fed. **29** H9
Pushkinskaya, Gora mt. Rus. Fed. **64** C3
Pusht-i Āšmän spring Iran **80** D3
Püspökladány Hungary **37** J5
Pusti Lisac mt. Yugo. **46** A3
Pustoshka Rus. Fed. **31** L1
Pusur r. Bangl. **75** F5
Puszcza Natecka for. Poland **37** G2
Putahow Lake Canada **123** K3
Putao Myanmar **60** B2
Putbus Germany **37** F1
Puteoli Italy see Pozzuoli
Putian China **67** F3
Putignano Italy **45** F4
Putina Peru **148** C3
Puting China see De'an
Puting, Tanjung pt Indon. **59** F3
Putlitz Germany **36** F2
Putna r. Romania **46** E2
Putnam U.S.A. **131** H3
Putney U.S.A. **131** H2
Putoi i. Hong Kong China see Po Toi
Putorana, Gory mts Rus. Fed. **27** J3

▶**Putrajaya** Malaysia **58** C2
  Administrative capital of Malaysia.

Putre Chile **148** C4
Putsonderwater S. Africa **98** D6
Puttalam Sri Lanka **72** C4
Puttalam Lagoon Sri Lanka **72** C4
Puttgarden Germany **36** E1
Puttur India **72** B3
Putumbumba Dem. Rep. Congo **95** C6
Putumayo dept Col. **146** C4
Putumayo r. Col. **146** D4
Putusibau Indon. **59** F2
Puula l. Fin. **33** H3
Puumala Fin. **33** H3
Puuwai U.S.A. **135** [inset] Y1
Puvurnituq Canada **121** L3
Puwakkadu Sri Lanka see Pinang
Puyallup U.S.A. **134** B3
Puyang Henan China **63** J4
Puyang Zhejiang China see Pujiang
Puy de Dôme mt. France **39** E4
Puy de Montoncel mt. France **39** F4
Puy de Sancy mt. France **39** E4
Puyehue, Parque Nacional nat. park
  Chile **152** C5
Puy Gris mt. France **39** G4
Puyo Ecuador **146** B5
Puysegur Point N.Z. **113** A4
Puzol Spain see Puçol
Pwani admin. reg. Tanz. **95** D5
Pweto Dem. Rep. Congo **95** C5
Pwllheli U.K. **35** C5
Pyalitsa Rus. Fed. **28** F2
Pyal'ma Rus. Fed. **28** F3
Pyamalaw r. Myanmar **61** A5
Pyandzh r. Afgh./Tajik. **81** G2
Pyandzh Khatlon Tajik. see Panj
Pyandzh Khatlon Tajik. see Dusti
Pyaozero, Ozero l. Rus. Fed. **32** H2
Pyaozerskiy Rus. Fed. **32** H2
Pyapon Myanmar **61** A4

Pyasina *r.* Rus. Fed. **27** I2
Pyasino, Ozero *l.* Rus. Fed. **27** I3
Pyasinskiy Zaliv *b.* Rus. Fed. **27** I2
Pyatigorsk Rus. Fed. **29** G7
Pyatikhatki Ukr. *see* **P"yatykhatky**
Pyatimar Kazakh. *see* **Pyatimarskoye**
Pyatimarskoye Kazakh. **29** I6
P"yatykhatky Ukr. **29** E6
Pyaunglaung *r.* Myanmar **60** B4
Pyawbwe Myanmar **60** B3
Pyè Myanmar **60** A4
Pye, Mount N.Z. **113** B4
Pyetrykaw Belarus **29** D5
Pygmalion Point India **73** G5
Pyhäjärvi *l.* Fin. **32** G3
Pyhäjärvi *l.* Fin. **32** G3
Pyhäjärvi *l.* Fin. **33** F3
Pyhäjärvi *l.* Fin. **33** H3
Pyhäjoki Fin. **32** G2
Pyhäjoki *r.* Fin. **32** G2
Pyhäntä Fin. **32** G2
Pyhäranta Fin. **33** F3
Pyhäsalmi Fin. **32** G3
Pyhäselkä Fin. **32** H3
Pyhäselkä *l.* Fin. **32** H3
Pyhätunturin kansallispuisto *nat. park* Fin. **32** G2
Pyhtää Fin. **33** G3
Pyin Myanmar *see* **Pyè**
Pyingaing Myanmar **60** A3
Pyinmana Myanmar **60** B4
Pyli Greece **47** E6
Pyl'karamo Rus. Fed. **26** I3
Pylos Greece **47** B6
Pymatuning Reservoir U.S.A. **130** C3
Pyŏksŏng N. Korea **65** A5
Pyŏktong N. Korea **65** A4
P'yŏnggang N. Korea **65** A5
P'yŏngsong N. Korea **65** A5
P'yŏngt'aek S. Korea **65** A5

▶**P'yŏngyang** N. Korea **65** A5
Capital of North Korea.

Pyŏnsan Bando National Park S. Korea **65** A6
Pyramid Lake U.S.A. **136** C1
Pyramid Range *mts* U.S.A. **136** C2
▶**Pyramids of Giza** *tourist site* Egypt **89** F2
africa 86–87
Pyrenees *mts* Europe **43** H1
Pyrénées *mts* Europe *see* **Pyrenees**
Pyrénées Occidentales, Parc National des *nat. park* France/Spain **43** F1
Pyrgetos Greece **47** C5
Pyrgi Greece **47** D5
Pyrgos Greece **47** B6
Pyryatyn Ukr. **29** E6
Pyrzyce Poland **37** G2
Pyshchug Rus. Fed. **28** H4
Pyszna *r.* Poland **37** I3
Pytalovo Rus. Fed. **28** C4
Pyu Myanmar **60** B4
Pyxaria *mt.* Greece **47** C5

↓ Q

Qā', Wādī al *watercourse* Saudi Arabia **89** H3
Qaa Lebanon **77** C2
Qaanaaq Greenland *see* **Thule**
Qābil Oman **76** F5
Qabka China *see* **Xaitongmoin**
Qabnag China **75** G3
Qabqa China *see* **Gonghe**
Qabr Bandar *tourist site* Iraq **79** E5
Qacentina Alg. *see* **Constantine**
Qacha's Nek Lesotho **99** F3
Qadamgāli Iran **81** D2
Qādes Afgh. **81** E3
Qaḑīmah Saudi Arabia **89** H4
Qādir Karam Iraq **79** F4
Qādisīyah, Sadd *dam* Iraq **79** E4
Qadisiyah Dam Iraq *see* **Qādisīyah, Sadd**
Qā'emiyeh Iran **80** B4
Qagan Nur China **63** I3
Qagan Nur *l.* China **64** A3
Qagan Tohoi China **75** G2
Qagan Us China *see* **Dulan**
Qagca China **66** A1
Qagchêng China *see* **Xiangcheng**
Qā' Ḩazawzā' *depr.* Saudi Arabia **89** H2
Qahd, Wādī *watercourse* Saudi Arabia **89** I3
Qahremānshahr Iran *see* **Kermānshāh**
Qaidam He *r.* China **75** G1
Qaidam Pendi *basin* China **70** H4
Qainaqangma China **75** F2
Qaisar Afgh. **81** F3
Qaisar *r.* Afgh. **81** F2
Qaisar, Koh-i- *mt.* Afgh. **81** F3
Qalā Diza Iraq **79** F3
Qala'en Nahl Sudan **89** G6
Qala-i-Fateh Afgh. **81** E4
Qala-i-Kang Afgh. **81** E4
Qal'aikhum Tajik. **81** G2
Qalamat ar Rakabah *oasis* Saudi Arabia **76** E5
Qalamat Fāris *oasis* Saudi Arabia **76** E6
Qalansīyah Yemen **76** E7
Qala Shinia Takht Afgh. **81** F3
Qalāt Afgh. **81** F3
Qal'at al Azlam Saudi Arabia **89** G3
Qal'at al Ḩiṣn *tourist site* Syria **77** C2
Qal'at al Marqab *tourist site* Syria **77** B2
Qal'at al Mu'azzam Saudi Arabia **89** H3
Qal'at Bīshah Saudi Arabia **89** I4
Qal'at Muqaybirah, Jabal *mt.* Syria **77** D2
Qal'at Şāliḩ Iraq **79** F5
Qala Vali Afgh. **81** E3
Qal'eh Iran **80** C2
Qal'eh Dāgh *mt.* Iran **80** A2
Qal 'eh-ye Bost Afgh. **81** F4
Qal 'eh-ye Now Afgh. **81** E3
Qalīb Bāqūr *well* Iraq **79** F5
Qalqīlya West Bank **77** B3
Qalti el Adusa *well* Sudan **89** E5
Qalyūb Egypt **78** B5
Qalyūbīyah *governorate* Egypt **78** B5
Qamalung China **66** A1
Qamanirjuaq Lake Canada **123** M2
Qamanittuaq Canada *see* **Baker Lake**
Qamar, Ghubbat al *b.* Yemen **76** E6
Qamar Bay Yemen *see* **Qamar, Ghubbat al**
Qamashi Uzbek. *see* **Kamashi**
Qamdo China **66** A2
Qam Hadīl Saudi Arabia **89** I5
Qamīnis Libya **88** C2
Qamruddin Karez Pak. **81** G4
Qamşar Iran **80** B3
Qandahar Afgh. *see* **Kandahār**
Qandala Somalia **96** F2
Qandaranbashi *mt.* Iran **80** A2
Qandyaghash Kazakh. *see* **Kandyagash**
Qangzê China **74** C3
Qapshagay Kazakh. *see* **Kapchagay**
Qapshagay Bögeni *resr* Kazakh. *see* **Kapchagayskoye Vodokhranilishche**
Qaqortoq Greenland **121** O3
Qara Āghach *r.* Iran *see* **Mand, Rūd-e**
Qarabutaq Kazakh. *see* **Karabutak**
Qaraçala Azer. **80** B2
Qarachōq, Jabal *mts* Iraq **79** E4
Qara Ertis *r.* China/Kazakh. *see* **Ertix He**
Qaraghandy Kazakh. *see* **Karaganda**
Qaraghayly Kazakh. *see* **Karagayly**
Qārah Egypt **78** A5
Qārah Saudi Arabia **89** I2
Qārah, Jabal al *hill* Saudi Arabia **76** C6
Qarah Bāgh *Ghaznī* Afgh. **81** G3
Qarah Bāgh *Kābul* Afgh. **81** G3
Qaraköl Kazakh. *see* **Karakol'**
Qaranqu *r.* Iran **80** A2
Qaraqum *des.* Kazakh. *see* **Karakum Desert**
Qaraqum *des.* Turkm. *see* **Karakum Desert**
Qara Şū Chāy *r.* Syria/Turkey *see* **Karasu**
Qara Tarai *mt.* Afgh. **81** F3
Qarataū Kazakh. *see* **Karatau**
Qarataū Zhotasy *mts* Kazakh. *see* **Karatau, Khrebet**
Qaratöbe Kazakh. *see* **Karatobe**
Qaraton Kazakh. *see* **Karaton**
Qardho Somalia **96** F2
Qardud Sudan **94** F2
Qareh Chāy *r.* Iran **80** B3
Qareh Dāgh *mts* Iran **80** A2
Qareh Qāch, Kūh-e *mts* Iran **80** C3
Qareh Sū *r.* Iran **80** A2
Qarhan China **75** G1
Qarkilik China *see* **Ruoqiang**
Qarn al Kabsh, Jabal *mt.* Egypt **89** G2
Qarnayṭ, Jabal *hill* Saudi Arabia **89** I4
Qarokŭl *l.* Tajik. **81** H2
Qarqan China *see* **Qiemo**
Qarqan He *r.* China **70** G4
Qarqaraly Kazakh. *see* **Karkaralinsk**
Qarqīn Afgh. **81** F2
Qarrit, Qafa e *pass* Albania **46** B4
Qarshi Uzbek. *see* **Karshi**
Qarshi Chŭli *plain* Uzbek. *see* **Karshinskaya Step'**
Qartaba Lebanon **77** B2
Qārūh, Jazīrat *i.* Kuwait **79** G5
Qārūn, Birkat *l.* Egypt **89** F2
Qaryat al Ulyā Saudi Arabia **80** A5
Qasamī Iran **80** D3
Qasa Murg *mts* Afgh. **81** E3
Qasba India **75** E4
Qāsemābād *Khorāsan* Iran **80** D3
Qāsemābād *Khorāsan* Iran **81** D2
Qashqadaryo *r.* Uzbek. *see* **Kashkadar'ya**
Qashqadaryo Wiloyati *admin. div.* Uzbek. *see* **Kashkadar'inskaya Oblast'**
Qasigiannguit Greenland **121** N3
Qaşr al Azraq Jordan **77** C4
Qaşr al Farāfirah Egypt **89** E3
Qasr al Ḩayr *tourist site* Syria **77** C2
Qasr al Khubbāz Iraq **79** E4
Qaşr 'Amrah *tourist site* Jordan **77** C4
Qaşr aş Şabīyah Kuwait **79** G5
Qaşr Burqu' *tourist site* Jordan **77** C3
Qaşr-e-Qand Iran **81** E5
Qaşr-e Shīrīn Iran **79** F4
Qaşr Larocu Libya **88** B3
Qaşr Shaqrah *tourist site* Iraq **79** F5
Qaṭanā Syria **77** C3
▶**Qatar** *country* Asia **80** B5
asia 52–53, 82
Qatlish Iran **80** D2
Qaṭrānī, Jabal *esc.* Egypt **89** F2
Qaṭrūyeh Iran **80** C4
Qattara Depression Egypt **89** E2
Qaṭṭārah, Munkhafaḑ al Egypt *see* **Qattara Depression**
Qaṭṭārah, Ra's *esc.* Egypt **89** E2
Qaṭṭīnah, Buḩayrat *resr* Syria **77** C2
Qavāmābād Iran **80** D4
Qax Azer. **79** F2
Qāyen Iran **81** D3
Qaynar Kazakh. *see* **Kaynar**
Qayroqqum Tajik. **81** G1
Qaysīyah, Qa' al *imp. l.* Jordan **77** C4
Qayyārah Iraq **79** E4
Qazaq Shyghanaghy *b.* Kazakh. *see* **Kazakhskiy Zaliv**
Qazaqstan *country* Asia *see* **Kazakhstan**
Qazax Azer. **79** F2
Qazımämmäd Azer. **79** G2
Qazvīn Iran **80** B2
Qazvīn *prov.* Iran **80** B2
Qelelevu *i.* Fiji **107** H3
Qena Egypt *see* **Qinā**
Qeqertarsuaq Greenland **121** N3
Qeqertarsuaq *i.* Greenland **121** N3
Qeqertarsuatsiaat Greenland **121** N3
Qeqertarsuup Tunua *b.* Greenland **121** N3
Qeshlāq Iran **80** A3
Qeshm Iran **80** D5
Qeshm *i.* Iran **80** D5
Qeydār Iran **80** B2
Qeys *i.* Iran **80** C5
Qezel Owzan, Rūdkhāneh-ye *r.* Iran **80** B2
Qeẕi'ot Israel **77** B4
Qian *r.* China **66** C1
Qiancheng China **67** D3
Qiang *r.* China **67** F1
Qian Gorlos China *see* **Qianguozhen**
Qianguozhen China **64** A3
Qianjiang *Chongqing* China **67** D2
Qianjiang *Hubei* China **67** E2
Qianjin China **64** C3
Qianning China **66** B2
Qianshan China **67** F2
Qianwei China **66** B2
Qianxi China **66** C3
Qianxian China **66** D1
Qianyang *Hunan* China **67** D3
Qianyang *Shaanxi* China **66** C1
Qianyang *Zhejiang* China **67** F2
Qianyou China *see* **Zhashui**
Qiaojia China **66** B3
Qiaotou China **66** B3
Qiaowa China *see* **Muli**
Qibā' Saudi Arabia **89** J3
Qibing S. Africa **99** E6
Qichun China **67** E2
Qidong *Hunan* China **67** E3
Qidong *Jiangsu* China **67** G2
Qiemo China **70** G4
Qijiang China **66** C2
Qijiaojing China **70** H3
Qikiqtarjuaq Canada **121** M3
Qila Ladgasht Pak. **81** E5
Qila Safed Pak. **81** E4
Qila Saifullah Pak. **81** G4
Qili China *see* **Shitai**
Qilian Shan *mts* China **70** I4
Qillak *i.* Greenland **121** P3
Qimantag *mts* China **75** F1
Qimen China **67** F2
Qimusseriarsuaq *b.* Greenland **121** M2
Qinā Egypt **89** G3
Qinā, Wādī *watercourse* Egypt **89** G3
Qin'an China **66** C1
Qincheng China *see* **Nanfeng**
Qing *r.* China **64** A4
Qing'an China **64** A3
Qingdao China **63** K4
Qinggang China **64** A3
Qingguandu China **67** D2
Qinghai *prov.* China **70** I4
Qinghai Hu *salt l.* China **70** J4
Qinghai Nanshan *mts* China **70** I4
Qingjiang *Jiangsu* China *see* **Huaiyin**
Qingjiang *Jiangxi* China *see* **Zhangshu**
Qing Jiang *r.* China **67** D2
Qingliu China **67** F3
Qingpu China **67** G2
Qingquan China *see* **Xishui**
Qingshan China *see* **Dedu**
Qingshuihe China **66** A1
Qingshuilang Shan *mts* China **66** A3
Qingtian China **67** G2
Qingyang *Anhui* China **67** F2
Qingyang *Jiangsu* China *see* **Sihong**
Qingyuan *Gansu* China *see* **Weiyuan**
Qingyuan *Guangdong* China **67** E4
Qingyuan *Guangxi* China *see* **Yizhou**
Qingyuan *Liaoning* China **64** A4
Qingyuan *Zhejiang* China **67** F3
Qingzang Gaoyuan *plat.* China *see* **Tibet, Plateau of**
Qingzhen China **66** C3
Qingzhou China **67** D2
Qinhuangdao China **63** J4
Qinjiang China *see* **Shicheng**
Qin Ling *mts* China **67** C1
Qinting China *see* **Lianhua**
Qinzhou China **67** D4
Qinzhou Wan *b.* China **67** D4
Qionghai China **67** D5
Qiongjiexue China *see* **Qonggyai**
Qionglai China **66** B2
Qionglai Shan *mts* China **66** B2
Qiongshan China **67** D5
Qiongxi China *see* **Hongyuan**
Qiongzhou Haixia *strait* China *see* **Hainan Strait**
Qiqihar China **63** K2
Qīr Iran **80** C4
Qira China **74** D1
Qiryat Gat Israel **77** B4
Qiryat Shemona Israel **77** B3
Qishan China *see* **Qimen**
Qishn Yemen **76** E6
Qishon *r.* Israel **77** B3
Qishrān Island Saudi Arabia **89** I4
Qitab ash Shāmah *vol. crater* Saudi Arabia **89** H2
Qitaihe China **64** B3
Qiubei China **66** C3
Qiujin China **67** E2
Qixian China **67** E1
Qixing *r.* China **64** C3
Qiyang China **67** D3
Qizhou Liedao *i.* China **67** D5
Qızılağac Körfäzi *b.* Azer. **80** B2
Qizil-Art, Aghbai *pass* Kyrg./Tajik. *see* **Kyzylart Pass**
Qogir Feng *mt.* China/Jammu and Kashmir *see* **K2**
Qojūr Iran **80** A2
Qom Iran **80** B3
Qom *prov.* Iran **80** B3
Qomdo China *see* **Qumdo**
Qomishēh Iran **80** B3
Qomolangma Feng *mt.* China/Nepal *see* **Everest, Mount**
Qonaqkänd Azer. **79** G2
Qonggyai China **75** F3
Qongrat Uzbek. *see* **Kungrad**
Qooriga Neegro *b.* Somalia **96** F3
Qoornoq Greenland **121** N3
Qoqek China *see* **Tacheng**
Qornet es Saouda *mt.* Lebanon **77** C2
Qorowulbozor Uzbek. *see* **Karaulbazar**
Qoroy, Gardaneh-ye *pass* Iran **80** B2
Qorveh Iran **80** A3
Qosh Tepe Iraq **79** E3
Qosshaghyl Kazakh. *see* **Koschagyl**
Qostanay Kazakh. *see* **Kostanay**
Qoṭbābād Iran **80** D5
Qoṭūr Iran **79** F3
Quabbin Reservoir U.S.A. **131** G2
Quadra Island Canada **122** E5
Quadros, Lago dos *l.* Brazil **151** B9
Quail Mountains U.S.A. **137** D4
Quairading Australia **109** B8
Quakenbrück Germany **36** C2
Quamby Australia **111** E4
Quanah U.S.A. **133** B5
Quanbao Shan *mt.* China **67** D1
Quân Đao Cô Tô *is* Vietnam **60** D3
Quan Dao Hoang Sa *is* S. China Sea *see* **Paracel Islands**
Quân Đao Nam Du *i.* Vietnam **61** D6
Quan Dao Truong Sa *is* S. China Sea *see* **Spratly Islands**
Quang Ngai Vietnam **61** E5
Quang Tri Vietnam **60** D4
Quan He *r.* China **67** E1
Quanjiang China *see* **Suichuan**
Quan Long Vietnam *see* **Ca Mau**
Quannan China **67** E3
Quan Phu Quoc *i.* Vietnam *see* **Phu Quôc, Đao**
Quanshang China **67** F3
Quanwan *Hong Kong* China *see* **Tsuen Wan**
Quanzhou *Fujian* China **67** F3
Quanzhou *Guangxi* China **67** D3
Qu'Appelle *r.* Canada **134** G2
Quaqtaq Canada **121** M3
Quaraí Brazil **152** F2
Quarry Bay *Hong Kong* China **67** [inset]
Quarryville U.S.A. **131** E4
Quarteira Port. **42** B4
Quartu Sant'Elena *Sardinia* Italy **45** B5
Quartzite Mountain U.S.A. **137** D3
Quartzsite U.S.A. **137** E5
Quaryat al Faw *tourist site* Saudi Arabia **76** D6
Quba Azer. **79** G2
Quchan Iran **81** D2
Queanbeyan Australia **112** D4

▶**Québec** Canada **125** G4
Provincial capital of Québec.

Québec *prov.* Canada **125** F2
Quedas Moz. **99** G3
Quedlinburg Germany **36** E3
Queen Adelaide Islands Chile *see* **La Reina Adelaida, Archipiélago de**
Queen Alia *airport* Jordan **77** B4
Queen Charlotte Canada **122** C4
Queen Charlotte Bay Falkland Is **153** E7
Queen Charlotte Islands Canada **122** C4
Queen Charlotte Sound *sea chan.* Canada **122** D5
Queen Charlotte Strait Canada **122** E5
Queen Elizabeth Islands Canada **121** I2
Queen Elizabeth National Park Uganda **96** A5
Queen Mary Land *reg.* Antarctica **167** F2
Queen Maud Gulf Canada **121** I3
Queen Maud Land *reg.* Antarctica **167** B2
Queen Maud Land *reg.* Antarctica **167** O10
Queen Maud Mountains Antarctica **167** J1
Queenscliff Australia **112** C5
Queensland *state* Australia **111** F4
Queenstown Australia **112** C6
Queenstown N.Z. **113** B4
Queenstown Rep. of Ireland *see* **Cóbh**
Queenstown S. Africa **99** E6
Queenstown Sing. **58** [inset]
Queenstown U.S.A. **131** E4
Quehua Bol. **148** D4
Queiba *well* Chad **88** D5
Queimada Brazil **149** E2
Queimada, Ilha *i.* Brazil **150** B2
Queimadas Brazil **150** E4
Quela Angola **95** C7
Quelimane Moz. **99** H3
Quellón Chile **153** B5
Quelpart Island S. Korea *see* **Cheju-do**
Quemado U.S.A. **135** E6
Quembo *r.* Angola **95** D8
Quemoy *i.* Taiwan *see* **Chinmen Tao**
Quemú-Quemú Arg. **152** E4
Quepem India **72** B3
Que Que Zimbabwe *see* **Kwekwe**
Querência Brazil **150** A5
Querétaro Mex. **126** F7
Querfurt Germany **36** E3
Querobabi Mex. **135** E7
Querpon Peru **146** B6
Quesada Spain **42** E4
Quesat *watercourse* W. Sahara **90** C4
Queshan China **67** E1
Quesnel Canada **122** F4
Quesnel *r.* Canada **122** F4
Quesnel Lake Canada **122** F4
Quetena de Lipez *r.* Bol. **148** D5
Quetta Pak. **81** F4
Quetzaltenango Guat. **138** F6
Queuco Chile **152** C4
Queulat, Parque Nacional *nat. park* Chile **153** B6
Queupán Arg. **152** D5

▶**Quezon City** Phil. **57** F3
Former capital of the Philippines.

Qugayatang China **75** F3
Quibala Angola **95** B7
Quibaxe Angola **95** B7
Quibdó Col. **146** B3
Quiberon France **38** B3
Quíbor Venez. **146** D2
Quicama, Parque Nacional do *nat. park* Angola **95** B7
Quiet Lake Canada **122** C2
Quilán, Cabo *c.* Chile **153** B5
Quilandi India **72** B4
Quilca Peru **148** B4
Quilenda Angola **95** B7
Quilengues Angola **95** B8
Quillacollo Bol. **148** D4
Quillan France **38** E5
Quill Lakes Canada **134** F2
Quillota Chile **152** C3
Quilmes Arg. **152** F3
Quilon India **72** C4
Quilpie Australia **111** F5
Quilpué Chile **152** C3
Quimbele Angola **95** C6
Quimilí Arg. **152** E1
Quimper France **38** A3
Quimperlé France **38** B3
Quinault *r.* U.S.A. **134** A3
Quince Mil Peru **148** C3
Quincinetto Italy **44** A2
Quincy *CA* U.S.A. **136** B2
Quincy *FL* U.S.A. **129** B6
Quincy *IL* U.S.A. **132** D4
Quincy *MI* U.S.A. **130** A3
Quincy *OH* U.S.A. **130** B3
Quines Arg. **152** D3
Quinga Moz. **99** I2
Quinhagak U.S.A. **120** C4
Quinhámel Guinea-Bissau **92** B3
Qui Nhon Vietnam **61** E5
Quinn *r.* U.S.A. **134** C4
Quinn Canyon Range *mts* U.S.A. **137** E3
Quinnimont U.S.A. **130** C5
Quiñones Bol. **148** D2
Quintanar de la Orden Spain **42** E3
Quintin France **38** B2
Quinto *r.* Arg. **152** D3
Quinto Spain **43** F2
Quinzau Angola **95** B6
Quipapá Brazil **150** F4
Quipungo Angola **95** B8
Quiquive *r.* Bol. **148** D3
Quirihue Chile **152** B4
Quirima Angola **95** C7
Quirindi Australia **112** D3
Quirinópolis Brazil **149** H4
Quiroga Bol. **148** D4
Quiroga Spain **42** C1
Quisiro Venez. **146** D2
Quissac France **39** F5
Quitapa Angola **95** C7
Quiterajo Moz. **97** D7
Quitexe Angola *see* **Dange**
Quitilipi Arg. **152** E1
Quitman *GA* U.S.A. **129** C6
Quitman *MS* U.S.A. **129** A5

▶**Quito** Ecuador **146** B5
Capital of Ecuador.

Quitovac Mex. **135** D7
Quitralco, Parque Nacional *nat. park* Chile **153** B6
Quixadá Brazil **150** E3
Quixeramobim Brazil **150** E3
Qujiang China *see* **Quxian**
Qu Jiang *r.* China **66** C2
Qujing China **66** B3
Qulandy Kazakh. *see* **Kulandy**
Quljuqtow Toghi *hills* Uzbek. *see* **Kul'dzhuktau, Gory**
Qulsary Kazakh. *see* **Kul'sary**
Qumar He *r.* China **70** H5
Qumarheyan China **75** G2
Qumarlêb China **75** G2
Qumdo China **75** G3
Qunayyin, Sabkhat al *salt marsh* Libya **88** D2
Qŭnghirot Uzbek. *see* **Kungrad**
Qu'nyido China **66** A2
Quoich *r.* Canada **123** M1
Quoin Island Australia **110** B2
Quong Muztag *mt.* China **75** D2
Quorn Australia **112** A4
Quoxo *r.* Botswana **98** E4
Quqên China *see* **Jinchuan**
Qŭqon Uzbek. *see* **Kokand**
Qurayyah *tourist site* Saudi Arabia **77** C5
Qurayyah, Wādī *watercourse* Egypt **77** B4
Qurayyat al Milḩ *l.* Jordan **77** C4
Qŭrghonteppa Tajik. **81** G2
Qusar Azer. **79** G2
Qushan China *see* **Beichuan**
Qūshchī Iran **80** A2
Qūsheh Dāgh *mts* Iran **80** A2
Qusmuryn Kazakh. *see* **Kushmurun**
Qusum China **75** G3
Quthing Lesotho *see* **Moyeni**
Quttinirpaaq National Park Canada **121** L1
Qutū' Island Saudi Arabia **89** I5
Quwayq, Nahr *r.* Syria/Turkey **77** C2
Quxar China *see* **Lhazê**
Quxian China **66** C2
Qüxü China **75** F3
Quyang China *see* **Jingzhou**
Qūyūn Eshek *i.* Iran **80** A2
Quzhou China **67** F2
Qvareli Georgia **79** F2
Qypshaq Köli *salt l.* Kazakh. *see* **Kypshak, Ozero**
Qyteti Stalin Albania *see* **Kuçovë**
Qyzan Kazakh. *see* **Kyzan**
Qyzylorda Kazakh. *see* **Kyzylorda**
Qyzyltū Kazakh. *see* **Kishkenekol'**
Qyzylzhar Kazakh. *see* **Kyzylzhar**

↓ R

Raab *r.* Austria **37** H5
Raab Hungary *see* **Győr**
Raahe Fin. **32** G2
Rääkkylä Fin. **32** H3
Raalte Neth. **36** C2
Ra'an, Khashm ar *hill* Saudi Arabia **89** I3
Raanujärvi Fin. **32** G2
Raas *i.* Indon. **59** F4
Raasay *i.* U.K. **34** C3
Rab *i.* Croatia **44** E2
Rába *r.* Hungary **37** H5
Raba Indon. **59** G5
Raba *r.* Poland **37** J3
Rabaale Somalia **96** F2
Rabak Sudan **89** G6
Rabang China **74** D2
Rabat *Gozo* Malta *see* **Victoria**
Rabat Malta **45** E7

▶**Rabat** Morocco **90** D2
Capital of Morocco.

Rabatakbaytal Tajik. *see* **Akbaytal**
Rabāt-e Kamah Iran **81** D3
Rabaul P.N.G. **107** E2
Rabbath Ammon Jordan *see* **'Ammān**
Rabbi *r.* Italy **44** D2
Rabbit *r.* Canada **122** E3
Rabbit Flat Australia **110** B4
Rabbitskin *r.* Canada **122** F2
Rábca *r.* Hungary **37** H5
Rabidine *well* Niger **93** G2
Rābigh Saudi Arabia **89** H4
Rabka Poland **37** I4
Rabkob India *see* **Dharmjaygarh**
Rabnabad Islands Bangl. **75** F5
Râbniţa Moldova *see* **Rîbniţa**
Rābor Iran **80** D4
Rabotoqbaytal Tajik. *see* **Akbaytal**
Rabt Sbayta *des.* W. Sahara **90** B5
Rabyānah *oasis* Libya **88** D3
Racaka China *see* **Riwoqê**
Racalmuto *Sicily* Italy **45** D6
Racconigi Italy **44** A2
Raccoon Creek *r.* U.S.A. **130** B4
Race, Cape Canada **160** K2
Raceland U.S.A. **133** D6
Race Point U.S.A. **131** H2
Rachaïya Lebanon **77** B3
Rachel U.S.A. **137** E3
Rach Gia Vietnam **61** D6
Rach Gia, Vinh *b.* Vietnam **61** D6
Raciąż Poland **37** J2
Racibórz Poland **37** I3
Racine *WI* U.S.A. **132** E3
Racine *WV* U.S.A. **130** C4
Râciu Romania **46** D1
Racoş Romania **46** D1
Radashkovichy Belarus **33** G5
Rădăuţi Romania **31** K4
Radbuza *r.* Czech Rep. **37** F4
Radcliff U.S.A. **128** B4
Radde Rus. Fed. **64** B2
Rade Norway **33** C4
Radebeul Germany **37** F3
Radew *r.* Poland **37** G1
Radford U.S.A. **130** C5
Radhanpur India **74** A5
Radisson *Que.* Canada **124** E2
Radisson *Sask.* Canada **123** J4
Radium Hot Springs Canada **123** G5
Radlinski, Mount Antarctica **167** K1
Radnevo Bulg. **46** D3
Rado de Tumaco *inlet* Col. **146** B4
Radom Poland **37** J3
Radom Sudan **94** E2
Radomir Bulg. **46** C3
Radomir *mt.* Bulg./Greece **46** C4
Radomka *r.* Poland **37** J3
Radom National Park Sudan **94** D2
Radomsko Poland **37** I3
Radoshkovichi Belarus *see* **Radashkovichy**
Radovets Bulg. **46** E4
Radoviš Macedonia **46** C4
Radovljica Slovenia **44** E1
Radstock, Cape Australia **109** F8
Radunia *r.* Poland **37** I1
Radviliškis Lith. **33** F5
Raḑwá, Jabal *mt.* Saudi Arabia **89** H3
Rae Bareli India **74** D4
Raecreek *r.* Canada **122** B1
Rae-Edzo Canada **123** G2
Raeford U.S.A. **128** D5
Rae Lakes Canada **123** G1
Raeside, Lake *salt flat* Australia **109** C7
Raetihi N.Z. **113** C2
Rāf *hill* Saudi Arabia **89** H2
Rafaela Arg. **152** E2
Rafaḩ Gaza *see* **Rafiaḩ**
Rafaï Cent. Afr. Rep. **94** D3
Raffadali *Sicily* Italy **45** D6
Rafḩā' Saudi Arabia **89** I2
Rafiaḩ Gaza **77** B4
Rafina Greece **47** D5
Rafsanjān Iran **80** C4
Raga Sudan **94** E2
Ragag Sudan **94** E2
Ragana Latvia **33** G4
Ragged, Mount Australia **109** C8
Raghogarh India **74** C4
Rago Nasjonalpark *nat. park* Norway **32** E2
Ragueneau Canada **125** G3
Ragusa Croatia *see* **Dubrovnik**
Ragusa *Sicily* Italy **45** E6
Raha India **75** G4
Raha Indon. **57** F6
Rahachow Belarus **29** D5
Rahad *r.* Sudan **89** G6
Rahad Canal Sudan **89** G6
Rahad el Berdi Sudan **94** D2
Rahad Wahal *well* Sudan **88** E6
Rahaeng Thai. *see* **Tak**
Rahaṭ, Ḩarrat *lava field* Saudi Arabia **89** I4
Rahatgaon India **74** C5
Rahimatpur India **72** B2
Rahimyar Khan Pak. **81** G4
Rāhjerd Iran **80** B3
Rahuri India **72** B2
Rahzanak Afgh. **81** E3
Raiatea *i.* Fr. Polynesia **165** H7
Raibu *i.* Indon. *see* **Air**
Raichur India **72** C2
Raiganj India **75** F4
Raigarh *Chhattisgarh* India **75** D5
Raigarh *Orissa* India **73** D2
Raijua *i.* Indon. **108** C2
Railroad Valley U.S.A. **137** E2
Raimangal *r.* Bangl. **75** F5
Raimbault, Lac *l.* Canada **125** G2
Rainbow Lake Canada **122** G3
Raine Island Australia **111** F1
Rainelle U.S.A. **130** C5
Raini *r.* Pak. **81** G4
Rainier, Mount *vol.* U.S.A. **134** B3
Rainy *r.* U.S.A. **132** C1
Rainy Lake Canada **124** A3
Raippaluoto *i.* Fin. **32** F3
Raipur Bangl. **75** F5
Raipur *Chhattisgarh* India **75** D5
Raipur *Rajasthan* India **74** B4
Raipur *W. Bengal* India **75** E5
Rairangpur India **75** E5
Raisen India **74** C5
Raisinghnagar India **74** B3
Raisio Fin. **33** F3
Raistakka Fin. **32** H2
Raitalai India **74** C5
Raivavae *i.* Fr. Polynesia **165** I7
Raiwind Pak. **74** B3
Raja Estonia **33** G4
Raja, Ujung *pt* Indon. **58** B2
Rajabasa, Gunung *vol.* Indon. **58** D4
Rajagangapur India **75** E5
Rajahmundry India **73** D2
Raja-Jooseppi Fin. **32** H1
Rajaldesar India **74** B3
Rajampet India **72** C3
Rajang *r.* *Sarawak* Malaysia **59** E2
Rajanpur Pak. **81** G4
Rajapalaiyam India **72** C4
Rajapur India **72** B2
Rajasthan *state* India **74** B4
Rajasthan Canal India **74** B3
Rajauli India **75** E4
Rajbari Bangl. **75** F5
Rajgarh *Madhya Pradesh* India **74** C4
Rajgarh *Rajasthan* India **74** B3
Rajgarh *Rajasthan* India **74** C4
Rajgród Poland **37** K2
Rájijovsset Fin. *see* **Raja-Jooseppi**
Rajim India **73** D1
Rajkot India **74** A5
Rajmahal Hills India **75** E4
Raj Nandgaon India **74** D5
Rajpipla India **74** B5
Rajpur India **74** B5
Rajpura India **74** C3
Rajputana Agency *state* India *see* **Rajasthan**
Rajsamand India **74** B4
Rajshahi Bangl. **75** F4
Rajshahi *admin. div.* Bangl. **75** F4
Rājū Syria **77** C1
Rajula India **74** A5
Rajur India **72** C1
Rajura India *see* **Ahmadpur**
Raka China **75** E3
Rakai Uganda **96** A5
Rakaia *r.* N.Z. **113** C3
Rakan, Ra's *pt* Qatar **80** B5
Rakaposhi *mt.* Jammu and Kashmir **74** B1
Raka Zangbo *r.* China *see* **Donguxung Zangbo**
Rakhaing *state* Myanmar *see* **Arakan**
Rakhine *state* Myanmar *see* **Arakan**
Rakhiv Ukr. **41** G2
Rakhshan *r.* Pak. **81** E5
Rakiraki Fiji **107** G3
Rakit *i.* Indon. **59** E4
Rakitnitsa *r.* Bulg. **46** D3
Rakitnoye Rus. Fed. **64** C3
Rakiura *i.* N.Z. *see* **Stewart Island**
Rakke Estonia **28** C4
Rakkestad Norway **33** C4
Rakni *r.* Pak. **81** G4
Rakops Botswana **98** E4
Rakovník Czech Rep. **37** F3
Rakovski Bulg. **46** D3
Rakushechnyy, Mys *pt* Kazakh. **79** G2
Rakvere Estonia **28** C4
Raleigh *MS* U.S.A. **133** D5

▶**Raleigh** *NC* U.S.A. **128** D5
State capital of North Carolina.

Ralston Canada **123** I5
Ralston U.S.A. **131** E3
Ram *r.* Canada **122** F2
Ramacca *Sicily* Italy **45** E6
Ramaditas Chile **148** C5
Ramah Canada **125** I1
Ramalho, Serra do *hills* Brazil **150** C5
Ramallah West Bank **77** B4
Ramallo Arg. **152** E3
Ramanagaram India **72** C3
Ramanathapuram India **72** C4
Ramanuj Ganj India **75** D5
Ramas, Cape India **72** B3
Ramatlabama S. Africa **98** E5
Ramayampet India **72** C2
Ramberg Norway **32** D1
Rambervillers France **39** G2
Rambouillet France **38** D2
Ramdurg India **72** B3
Ramechhap Nepal **75** E4
Rame Head U.K. **35** D6
Rameshki Rus. Fed. **31** N1
Rameswaram India **72** C4
Ramezān Kalak Iran **81** E5
Ramgarh Bangl. **75** F5
Ramgarh *Jharkhand* India **75** E5
Ramgarh *Rajasthan* India **74** A4
Rāmhormoz Iran **80** B4
Ramingining Australia **110** C2
Ramit Tajik. *see* **Romit**
Ramla Israel **77** B4
Ramlat al Ghāfah *des.* Saudi Arabia **76** E5
Ramlat Dahm *des.* Saudi Arabia/Yemen **76** D6
Ramlat Rabyānah *des.* Libya *see* **Rebiana Sand Sea**
Ramm, Jabal *mts* Jordan **78** C5
Ramnad India *see* **Ramanathapuram**
Ramnagar *Madhya Pradesh* India **74** D4
Ramnagar *Uttaranchal* India **74** C3
Ramnagar Jammu and Kashmir **74** B2
Ramnäs Sweden **33** E4
Râmnicul Sărat *r.* Romania **46** E2
Râmnicu Sărat Romania **46** E2
Râmnicu Vâlcea Romania **46** D2
Ramokgwebane Botswana **99** E4
Ramona U.S.A. **136** D5
Ramonville-St-Agne France **38** D5
Ramos Arizpe Mex. **133** A7
Ramotswa Botswana **98** E5
Rampart of Genghis Khan *tourist site* Asia **63** I2
Ramparts *r.* Canada **122** D1
Rampur *Uttar Pradesh* India **74** C3
Rampur *Uttar Pradesh* India **74** C3
Rampura India **74** B4
Rampur Boalia Bangl. *see* **Rajshahi**
Rampur Hat India **75** E4
Ramree Myanmar **60** A4
Ramree Island Myanmar **60** A4
Ramsele Sweden **32** E3
Ramsey Isle of Man **35** D4
Ramsey Lake Canada **124** D4
Ramsgate U.K. **35** G6
Ramshai Hat India **75** F4
Rāmshir Iran **80** B4
Ramsing *mt.* India **75** G3
Ramsjö Sweden **33** D3
Ramtek India **74** C5
Ramu Bangl. **75** G5
Ramu *r.* P.N.G. **57** J6
Ramundberget Sweden **32** D3
Ramusio, Lac *l.* Canada **125** I2

Ramvik Sweden **32** E3
Ramygala Lith. **33** G5
Rana, Cerro hill Col. **146** D4
Rañadoiro, Puerto de pass Spain **42** C1
Rañadoiro, Sierra de mts Spain **42** C1
Ranaghat India **75** F5
Ranai i. U.S.A. see Lanai
Rana Pratap Sagar resr India **74** B4
Ranapur India **74** B5
Rånåsfoss Norway **33** C3
Ranau Sabah Malaysia **59** F1
Ranau, Danau l. Indon. **58** C4
Rancagua Chile **152** B5
Rance r. France **38** B2
Rancharia Brazil **149** H5
Rancheria Canada **122** D2
Ranchester U.S.A. **134** F3
Ranchi India **75** E5
Rancho Cordova U.S.A. **136** B2
Rancho de Caçados Tapiúnas Brazil
  149 F2
Ranco, Lago l. Chile **152** B5
Randallstown U.S.A. **131** E4
Randazzo Sicily Italy **45** E6
Randers Denmark **33** C4
Randijaure l. Sweden **32** E2
Randolph MA U.S.A. **131** H2
Randolph NY U.S.A. **130** D2
Randolph UT U.S.A. **134** E4
Randolph VT U.S.A. **131** G2
Randow r. Germany **37** F2
Randsburg U.S.A. **136** D4
Randsfjorden l. Norway **33** C3
Randsjö Sweden **32** E3
Randsverk Norway **33** C3
Rånea Sweden **32** F2
Ranfurly N.Z. **113** B4
Ranga r. India **60** M2
Rangae Thai. **61** C7
Rangamati Bangl. **75** G5
Rangapara North India **75** G4
Rangas, Tanjung pt Indon. **59** G3
Rangasa, Tanjung pt Indon. **59** G3
Rangaunu Bay N.Z. **113** C1
Rangeley U.S.A. **131** H1
Rangely U.S.A. **137** H1
Ranger Lake Canada **124** D4
Rangi India **72** D1
Rangia Patharughat India **75** F4
Rangiauria i. S. Pacific Ocean see
  Pitt Island
Rangiora N.Z. **113** C3
Rangitata r. N.Z. **113** B4
Rangitikei r. N.Z. **113** C3
Rangkasbitung Indon. **58** D4
Rangke China see Zamtang
Rangkül Tajik. **81** H2
Rangôn Myanmar see Rangoon
Rangôn admin. div. Myanmar see Yangôn
►**Rangoon** Myanmar **60** B4
  Capital of Myanmar.

Rangoon admin. div. Myanmar see Yangôn
Rangoon r. Myanmar **61** B4
Rangpur Bangl. **75** F4
Rangsang i. Indon. **58** C2
Rangse Myanmar **60** A2
Rani India **74** B4
Rania India **74** B3
Ranibennur India **72** B3
Raniganj India **75** E5
Ranijula Peak India **75** D5
Ranikhet India **74** C3
Ranipur Pak. **81** G5
Raniwara India **74** B4
Ranken watercourse Australia **110** B3
Rankin U.S.A. **133** A6
Rankin Inlet Canada **123** M2
Rankin Inlet inlet Canada **123** M2
Rankin's Springs Australia **112** C4
Rankovićevo Yugo. see Kraljevo
Rannes Australia **111** E5
Ranneye Rus. Fed. **29** J6
Rannoch, Loch l. U.K. **34** D3
Ranobe r. Madag. **99** [inset] J4
Ranohira Madag. **99** [inset] K3
Ranomafana Madag. **99** [inset] K3
Ranomatana Madag. **99** [inset] J5
Ranong Thai. **61** B6
Ranotsara Avaratra Madag. **99** [inset] J4
Ranpur India **74** A5
Ransiki Indon. **57** H6
Rantasalmi Fin. **33** H3
Rantau Indon. **59** F3
Rantau r. Indon. **58** C2
Rantaukampar Indon. **58** C2
Rantaupanjang Kalimantan Tengah
  Indon. **59** F3
Rantaupanjang Kalimantan Timur Indon.
  59 F2
Rantauprapat Indon. **58** B2
Rantaupulut Indon. **59** F3
Rantoul U.S.A. **132** B3
Rantsila Fin. **32** G2
Ranua Fin. **32** G2
Ranxë Albania **46** A4
Rânya Iraq **79** F3
Ranyah, Wâdî watercourse Saudi Arabia
  89 I4
Rao r. Thai. **61** B7
Raohe China **64** C3
Rapa i. Fr. Polynesia **165** I7
Rapar Gujarat India **74** B5
Rapar Punjab India **74** C3
Rapch watercourse Iran **81** D5
Rapidan r. U.S.A. **130** E4
Rapid Bay Australia **112** A4
Rapid City U.S.A. **134** G3
Räpina Estonia **33** G4
Rapirrän r. Brazil **148** D2
Rapla Estonia **33** G4
Rappahannock r. U.S.A. **131** E5
Rapti r. India **75** D4
Rapulo r. Bol. **148** D3
Rapur Andhra Pradesh India **72** C3
Rapur Gujarat India **74** B5
Raqqa Syria see Ar Raqqah
Raquette r. U.S.A. **131** F1
Raquette Lake U.S.A. **131** F2
Rara National Park Nepal **75** D3
Raritan Bay U.S.A. **131** F3
Raroia atoll Fr. Polynesia **165** I7
Rarotonga i. Cook Is **165** H7
Ras India **74** B4
Raša r. Croatia **44** E2
Rasa, Punta pt Arg. **152** E5
Ra's ad Daqm Oman **76** F6
Ra's al Hikmah Egypt **89** E2
Ra's al Khaimah U.A.E. see
  Ra's al Khaymah
Ra's al Khaymah U.A.E. **80** C5
Ra's al Mish ãb Saudi Arabia **79** G5
Ra's an Naqb Jordan **78** C5
Ra's ash Shaykh Humayd Saudi Arabia
  78 C5
►**Ras Dashen** mt. Eth. **96** C1
  5th highest mountain in Africa.
  africa 84–85

Raseiniai Lith. **33** F5
Ras el Ma Alg. **91** H2
Râs el Mâ Mali **92** D1
Ra's Ghârib Egypt **89** G2

Rashad Sudan **96** A2
Rashîd Egypt **89** F2
Rashid Qala Afgh. **81** F4
Rasht Iran **80** B2
Rasina Estonia **33** G4
Rasina r. Yugo. **46** B3
Rãsjö Sweden **33** D3
Raska r. Yugo. **46** B3
Raška Yugo. **46** B3
Raskam mts China **74** B1
Ras Koh mt. Pak. **81** F4
Raskoh mts Pak. **81** F4
Ras Maskan pt Somalia **96** D2
Râșnov Romania **46** F2
Raso da Catarina hills Brazil **150** E4
Rason Lake salt flat Australia **110** A6
Rasova Romania **46** G2
Rasovo Bulg. **46** C3
Rasra India **75** D4
Rass Jebel Tunisia **45** C6
Rast Romania **46** C3
Ras Tannûrah Saudi Arabia **76** E4
Rastatt Germany **36** D4
Rastede Germany **36** D2
Råstojaure l. Sweden **32** F1
Ratae U.K. see Leicester
Ratai, Gunung mt. Indon. **58** D4
Ratangarh Madhya Pradesh India **74** B4
Ratangarh Rajasthan India **74** B3
Ratanpur Chhattisgarh India **75** D5
Ratanpur Gujarat India **74** B5
Rätansbyn Sweden **33** D3
Rat Buri Thai. **61** B5
Rath India **74** C4
Rathbun Lake U.S.A. **132** C3
Rathedaung Myanmar **73** G1
Rathenow Germany **37** F2
Rathlin Island U.K. **34** C4
Rathluirc Rep. of Ireland **35** B5
Ratibor Poland see Racibórz
Ratisbon Germany see Regensburg
Ratiya India **74** B3
Rat Lake Canada **123** L3
Ratnagiri India **72** B2
Ratnapura Sri Lanka **72** D5
Ratne Ukr. **29** C6
Ratno Ukr. see Ratne
Rato Dero Pak. **81** G5
Raton U.S.A. **135** F4
Rattray Head U.K. **34** F3
Rättvik Sweden **33** D3
Ratz, Mount Canada **122** C3
Ratzeburg Germany **36** E2
Raub Malaysia **58** C2
Rauch Arg. **152** F4
Rauch watercourse Iran **81** D5
Raudanjoki r. Fin. **32** G2
Rău de Mori Romania **46** C2
Raudna r. Estonia **33** G4
Raudhatain Kuwait **79** F5
Raukumara Range mts N.Z. **113** D2
Raul r. India **72** D3
Rauma Fin. **33** F3
Raurkela India see Rourkela
Rauschen Rus. Fed. see Svetlogorsk
Rautalampi Fin. **32** G3
Rautavaara Fin. **32** H3
Rautjärvi Fin. **33** H3
Rauza India see Khuldabad
Rãvansar Iran **80** A3
Rãvar Iran **80** D4
Ravanusa Sicily Italy **45** D6
Ravena U.S.A. **131** G2
Ravenna Italy **44** D2
Ravenna NE U.S.A. **132** B3
Ravenna OH U.S.A. **130** C3
Ravenshoe Australia **111** F3
Ravensthorpe Australia **109** C8
Ravenswood Australia **111** F4
Ravenswood U.S.A. **130** C4
Raver India **74** C5
Ravi r. Pak. **81** F4
Ravna Gora hill Croatia **44** F2
Ravnina Turkm. **81** F3
Rãwah Iraq **79** E4
Rawaki i. Kiribati **107** H2
Rawala Kot Pak. **81** H3
Rawalpindi Pak. **81** H3
Rawalpindi Lake Canada **123** H1
Rawa Mazowiecka Poland **37** J3
Rawãndiz Iraq **79** F3
Rawas r. Indon. **58** C3
Rawatsar India **74** B3
Rawghah watercourse Saudi Arabia
  77 C5
Rawi i. Thai. **61** B7
Rawicz Poland **37** H3
Rawka r. Poland **37** J2
Rawlinna Australia **109** D7
Rawlins U.S.A. **134** F4
Rawlinson, Mount Australia **109** D6
Rawlinson Range hills Australia **109** E6
Rawson Turkm. see Ravnina
Rawson Arg. **153** D5
Rawu China **66** A2
Rawul India **74** C4
Ray, Cape Canada **125** J4
Rayachoti India **72** C3
Rayadurg India **72** C3
Rayagarha India **73** D2
Rayak Lebanon **77** C3
Raychikhinsk Rus. Fed. **64** C2
Rayen Iran **80** D4
Rayes Peak U.S.A. **136** C4
Rayevskiy Rus. Fed. **28** J5
Raymond Canada **123** H5
Raymond U.S.A. **131** H2
Raymondville U.S.A. **133** B7
Raymore Canada **123** J5
Rayna India **75** E5
Rayner Glacier Antarctica **167** C2
Rayones Mex. **133** A7
Rayong Thai. **61** C5
Raystown Lake U.S.A. **130** D3
Rayth al Khayl watercourse
  Saudi Arabia **77** C5
Rayville U.S.A. **133** D5
Raz, Pointe du pt France **38** A2
Razam India **73** D2
Razan Iran **80** B3
Razãzah, Buhayrat ar l. Iraq **79** E4
Razdel'naya Ukr. see Rozdil'na
Razdol'noye Rus. Fed. **64** B4
Razeh Iran **80** B3
Razgrad Bulg. **46** F3
Razhëng Zangbo r. China **75** F3
Razim, Lacul lag. Romania **46** H2
Raz"yezd 3km Rus. Fed. see
  Novyy Urgal
R. D. Bailey Lake U.S.A. **130** C5
Ré, Île de i. France **38** C3
Reading U.K. **35** F6
Reading MI U.S.A. **130** A3
Reading OH U.S.A. **130** A4
Reading PA U.S.A. **131** F3
Reagile S. Africa **99** E5
Real r. Brazil **150** E4

Reales mt. Spain **42** D4
Realicó Arg. **152** D5
Réalmont France **38** E5
Reãng Kesei Cambodia **61** C5
Reata Mex. **133** A7
Reate Italy see Rieti
Rebaa Alg. **91** H3
Rebbenesøy i. Norway **32** E1
Rebecca, Lake salt flat Australia
  109 C7
Rebiana Sand Sea des. Libya **88** D3
Rebollera mt. Spain **42** D3
Reboly Rus. Fed. **32** H3
Rebun-tō i. Japan **64** E3
Recaș Romania **46** B2
Recherche, Archipelago of the is
  Australia **109** C8
Rechitsa Belarus see Rechytsa
Rechna Doab lowland Pak. **81** H4
Rechytsa Belarus **29** D5
Recife Brazil **150** F4
Recife, Cape S. Africa **98** E7
Recinto Chile **152** B5
Recklinghausen Germany **36** C3
Recknitz r. Germany **37** F1
Reconquista Arg. **152** F2
Recreio Brazil **149** F2
Recreo Arg. **152** D3
Rectorville U.S.A. **130** D4
Recz Poland **37** G2
Red r. Australia **111** E3
Red r. Canada **122** C4
Red r. Canada/U.S.A. **123** L5
Red r. U.S.A. **133** D6
Red, North Fork r. U.S.A. **133** B5
Redang i. Malaysia **58** C1
Red Bank U.S.A. **131** F3
Red Basin China see Sichuan Pendi
Red Bay Canada **125** J3
Redberry Lake Canada **123** J4
Red Bluff hill Australia **109** B6
Red Bluff U.S.A. **136** A1
Red Butte mt. U.S.A. **137** F4
Redcar U.K. **35** F4
Redcliff Canada **134** F2
Redcliff Zimbabwe **99** F3
Redcliffe, Mount Australia **109** C7
Red Cliffs Australia **112** B4
Red Cloud U.S.A. **132** B3
Red Deer Canada **123** H4
Red Deer r. Canada **123** I5
Red Deer Lake Canada **123** K4
Redding U.S.A. **136** A1
Redditch U.K. **35** F5
Red Earth Creek Canada **123** H3
Redenção Pará Brazil **150** B3
Redenção Piauí Brazil **150** D4
Redeyef Tunisia **91** H2
Redfield U.S.A. **132** B2
Red Granite Mountain Canada **122** B2
Red Hills U.S.A. **132** B4
Red Hook U.S.A. **131** G3
Red Idol Gorge China **75** F3
Red Indian Lake Canada **125** J3
Redkino Rus. Fed. **28** F4
Redknife r. Canada **122** G2
Red Lake Canada **123** M5
Red Lake U.S.A. **137** E4
Red Lake l. U.S.A. **132** D2
Red Lakes U.S.A. **132** C1
Redlands U.S.A. **136** D4
Red Lion NJ U.S.A. **131** F4
Red Lion PA U.S.A. **131** G4
Red Lodge U.S.A. **134** E3
Redmesa U.S.A. **137** H3
Redmond OR U.S.A. **134** B3
Redmond UT U.S.A. **137** G2
Red Oak U.S.A. **132** C3
Redon France **38** B3
Redondela Spain **42** B1
Redondo Port. **42** C4
Redondo Beach U.S.A. **136** C5
Red Peak U.S.A. **134** D4
Red River r. U.S.A. see Red
Red Rock Canada **124** B3
Red Rock AZ U.S.A. **137** G5
Red Rock PA U.S.A. **131** E3
Red Rock r. U.S.A. **134** D3
Red Sea Africa/Asia **76** A4
Red Sea state Sudan **89** G5
Redstone Canada **122** F4
Red Volta r. Burkina/Ghana **93** E3
  also known as Nazinon (Burkina)
Redwater r. U.S.A. **134** F2
Red Willow Creek r. U.S.A. **132** A3
Red Wing U.S.A. **132** C2
Redwood r. U.S.A. **132** C2
Redwood Falls U.S.A. **132** C2
Redwood National Park U.S.A. **134** A4
Redwood Valley U.S.A. **136** A2
Ree, Lough l. Rep. of Ireland **35** C5
Reed City U.S.A. **132** B2
Reedley U.S.A. **136** C3
Reed Lake Canada **123** K4
Reedsport U.S.A. **134** A4
Reedsville OH U.S.A. **130** C4
Reedsville PA U.S.A. **130** E3
Reedville U.S.A. **131** E5
Reedy Creek watercourse Australia
  111 F4
Reedy Glacier Antarctica **167** J1
Reefton N.Z. **113** B3
Reese r. U.S.A. **136** D2
Reese U.S.A. **130** B2
Refahiye Turkey **79** D3
Reform U.S.A. **129** A5
Refugio U.S.A. **133** B6
Rega r. Poland **37** G1
Regen Germany **37** F4
Regensburg Germany **36** F4
Regentown S. Africa **99** E5
Reggane Alg. **91** F4
Reggio Calabria Italy see
  Reggio di Calabria
Reggio Emilia Italy see
  Reggio nell'Emilia
Reggio di Calabria Italy **45** E5
Reggio Emilia Italy see
  Reggio nell'Emilia
Reggio nell'Emilia Italy **44** C2
Reghin Romania **46** E1
Regi Afgh. **81** F3
►**Regina** Canada **134** F2
  Provincial capital of Saskatchewan.

Régina Fr. Guiana **147** H3
Registro Brazil **149** I6
Regium Lepidum Italy see
  Reggio nell'Emilia
Regozero Rus. Fed. **32** H2
Rehli India **74** C5
Rehoboth Namibia **98** C3
Rehoboth Bay U.S.A. **131** F4
Rehovot Israel **77** B4
Reichenbach Germany **37** F3
Reichshoffen France **39** G2
Reid Australia **109** E7
Reidsville U.S.A. **128** E4
Reiley Peak U.S.A. **137** G5
Reims France **39** F2
Reinach Switz. **39** G3
Reinbek Germany **36** E2
Reindeer r. Canada **123** K4
Reindeer Island Canada **123** L4
Reindeer Lake Canada **123** K3

Reinosa Spain **42** D1
Reinøya Mex. **126** G6
Reyssouze r. France **39** F3
Rejã, Küh-e hill Iran **80** B3
Rezã'iyeh Iran see Urmia
Rezã'iyeh, Daryãcheh-ye salt l. Iran see
  Urmia, Lake
Rezekne Latvia **33** G4
Rezovska Reka r. Bulg./Turkey **46** F4
Rezvãndeh Iran **80** B2
Rezvãnshahr Iran **80** B2
R. F. Magón Mex. **126** D6
  Ricardo Flores Magón
Rgotina Yugo. **46** C2
Rharbi, Oued el watercourse Alg. **91** F3
Rhegium Italy see Reggio di Calabria
Rheims France see Reims
Rhein r. Germany **36** C4 see Rhine
Rheine Germany **36** C2
Rheinland-Pfalz land Germany **36** C4
Rheinsberg Germany **37** F2
Rheinwaldhorn mt. Switz. **39** H3
Rhemilès well Alg. **90** D3
Rhénérif, Oued watercourse Morocco
  90 D3
Rhin r. Germany see Rhine
Rhine r. Europe **36** C4
  also spelt Rhein (Germany) or Rhin (France)
Rhinelander U.S.A. **132** C2
Rhineland-Palatinate land Germany see
  Rheinland-Pfalz
Rhinluch marsh Germany **37** F2
Rhino Camp Uganda **96** A4
Rhinow Germany **37** F2
Rhir, Cap c. Morocco **90** C3
Rho Italy **44** B2
Rhode Island state U.S.A. **131** H3
Rhodes Greece **47** F6
Rhodes i. Greece **47** F6
Rhodesia country Africa see Zimbabwe
Rhodes Inyanga National Park
  Zimbabwe see Nyanga National Park
Rhodes Matopos National Park
  Zimbabwe see Matobo National Park
Rhodope Mountains Bulg./Greece
  46 C4
Rhodus i. Greece see Rhodes
Rhône r. France/Switz. **39** F5
Rhône-Alpes admin. reg. France **39** F4
Rhube, Oasis of Syria see Ruhbah
Rhum i. U.K. see Rum
Rhuthun U.K. see Ruthin
Rhyl U.K. **35** E5
Riachão Brazil **150** C3
Riacho de Santana Brazil **150** D5
Rialma Brazil **149** H3
Rialp, Pantà de resr Spain **43** G2
Rialto U.S.A. **136** D4
Riangnam Sudan **94** F2
Riaño, Embalse de resr Spain **42** D1
Riansáres r. Spain **42** E3
Riasi Jammu and Kashmir **74** B2
Riau prov. Indon. **58** C2
Riau, Kepulauan is Indon. **58** D2
Riaza r. Spain **42** E2
Ribadavia Spain **42** B1
Ribadeo Spain **42** C1
Ribadesella Spain **42** D1
Ribas do Rio Pardo Brazil **151** A7
Ribat Afgh. **81** G2
Ribat-i-Shur waterhole Iran **80** D3
Ribaúè Moz. **99** H2
Ribble r. U.K. **35** E5
Ribe Denmark **33** C5
Ribeirão Preto Brazil **149** I5
Ribera Sicily Italy **45** D6
Ribérac France **38** D4
Riberalta Bol. **148** D2
Ribnica Slovenia **44** E2
Ribnița Moldova **31** L4
Ribnitz-Damgarten Germany **37** F1
Rica Aventura Chile **148** D5
Ricany Czech Rep. **37** G4
Rice CA U.S.A. **137** E4
Rice VA U.S.A. **130** E5
Rice Lake U.S.A. **132** C2
Rice Lake l. Canada **130** D1
Rice Lake U.S.A. **135** E6
Richards Bay S. Africa **99** G6
Richards Inlet Antarctica **167** H1
Richardson r. Canada **123** I3
Richards Island Canada **120** F3
Richardson U.S.A. **133** C5
Richardson Island Canada **123** H1
Richardson Mountains Canada
  120 F3
Richardson Mountains N.Z. **113** B4
Richard Toll Senegal **92** B1
Richelieu r. Canada **124** E4
Richfield U.S.A. **137** G2
Richfield Springs U.S.A. **131** F2
Richford NY U.S.A. **131** E2
Richford VT U.S.A. **128** C2
Richgrove U.S.A. **136** C4
Richibucto Canada **125** H4
Rich Lake Canada **123** I4
Richland U.S.A. **134** C3
Richland Center U.S.A. **132** D3
Richlands U.S.A. **130** C5
Richmond N.S.W. Australia **112** C4
Richmond Qld Australia **111** E4
Richmond Kwazulu-Natal S. Africa **99** F6
Richmond N. Cape S. Africa **98** D6
Richmond Canada **125** G4
Richmond N.Z. **113** C3
Richmond CA U.S.A. **136** A3
Richmond IN U.S.A. **130** A4
Richmond KY U.S.A. **130** A5
Richmond MI U.S.A. **130** B2
►**Richmond** VA U.S.A. **130** E5
  State capital of Virginia.

Richmond Dale U.S.A. **130** B4
Richmond Hill U.S.A. **129** C6
Richmond Range hills Australia **112** F2
Richtersveld National Park S. Africa
  98 C6
Richvale U.S.A. **136** B2
Richwood U.S.A. **130** C4
Rickleån r. Sweden **32** F2
Rickreall U.S.A. **134** B3
Ricobayo, Embalse de resr Spain
  42 D2
Ricomagus France see Riom
Riddell Nunataks nunataks Antarctica
  167 F2
Ridder Kazakh. see Leninogorsk
Riddlesburg U.S.A. **130** D3
Rideau Lakes Canada **131** E1
Ridge r. Canada **124** C3
Ridgecrest U.S.A. **136** D4
Ridgefield U.S.A. **131** G3
Ridgeland MS U.S.A. **133** D5
Ridgeland SC U.S.A. **129** D5
Ridgetown Canada **130** C2
Ridgway U.S.A. **130** D3
Ridgway U.S.A. **130** D3
Riding Mountain National Park Canada
  123 K5
Ridley r. Australia **108** B5
Riecito Venez. **146** D2
Ried im Innkreis Austria **37** F4
Riedlingen Germany **36** D4
Rieppesgai'sa mt. Norway **32** F1
Riesa Germany **37** F3
Riesco, Isla i. Chile **153** B8
Riesi Sicily Italy **45** E6
Riet r. S. Africa **98** D6

Riet watercourse S. Africa **98** D6
Rietavas Lith. **33** F5
Rietfontein S. Africa **98** D5
Rieti Italy **44** D3
Rietschen Germany **37** G3
Rifã'i, Tall mt. Jordan/Syria **77** C3
Rifeng China see Lichuan
Rifle U.S.A. **134** F5
Rift Valley prov. Kenya **96** B4
Rift Valley Lakes National Park Eth.
  see Abijatta-Shalla National Park
Riga Latvia see Rīga
►**Rīga** Latvia **33** G4
  Capital of Latvia.

Riga, Gulf of Estonia/Latvia **33** G4
Rigacikun Nigeria **93** G3
Rigán Iran **81** D4
Rigas jūras līcis b. Estonia/Latvia see
  Riga, Gulf of
Rig-Rig Chad **88** B6
Riguel r. Spain **43** F2
Riia laht b. Estonia/Latvia see
  Riga, Gulf of
Riihimäki Fin. **33** G3
Riiser-Larsen Ice Shelf Antarctica
  167 B2
Riisipere Estonia **33** G4
Riisitunturin kansallispuisto nat. park
  Fin. **32** H2
Riito Mex. **135** D6
Rijau Nigeria **93** G3
Riječki Zaliv b. Croatia **44** E2
Rijeka Croatia **44** E2
Rikuchū-kaigan National Park Japan
  65 E5
Rila mts Bulg. **46** C3
Rila China **75** E3
Riley U.S.A. **134** C4
Rillieux-la-Pape France **39** F4
Rillito U.S.A. **137** G5
Rima watercourse Niger/Nigeria **93** G2
Rimah, Wâdī al watercourse
  Saudi Arabia **89** J4
Rimava r. Slovakia **37** J4
Rimavská Sobota Slovakia **37** J4
Rimbey Canada **123** H4
Rimbo Sweden **33** E4
Rimersburg U.S.A. **130** D3
Rimforsa Sweden **33** D4
Rimini Italy **44** D2
Rîmnicu Sãrat Romania see
  Râmnicu Sãrat
Rîmnicu Vîlcea Romania see
  Râmnicu Vâlcea
Rimouski Canada **125** G3
Rinbung China **75** F3
Rincón, Cerro del mt. Chile **148** D5
Rinconada Arg. **148** D5
Rincón del Bonete, Lago Artificial de
  resr Uruguay **152** F3
Rincón de los Sauces Arg. **152** C5
Rincón de Romos Mex. **126** F7
Rind r. India **74** D4
Rindal Norway **32** C3
Rineia i. Greece **47** E6
Ringas India **74** B4
Ringebu Norway **33** C3
Ringim Nigeria **93** H2
Ringkøbing Denmark **33** C4
Ringkøbing Fjord lag. Denmark **33** C5
Ringsted Denmark **33** C5
Ringvassøy i. Norway **32** E1
Ringwood U.K. **35** F6
Ringwood U.S.A. **131** F3
Rinía i. Greece see Rineia
Rinteln Germany **36** D2
Rinya r. Hungary **44** F2
Rio Alegre Brazil **149** F4
Riobamba Ecuador **146** B5
Rio Blanco U.S.A. **137** H2
Rio Branco Brazil **148** D2
Rio Branco state Brazil see Roraima
Rio Branco, Parque Nacional do
  nat. park Brazil **147** F4
Rio Brilhante Brazil **151** A7
Rio Bueno Chile **152** B5
Rio Caribe Venez. **147** F1
Rio Casca Brazil **151** D7
Rio Chico Arg. **153** C7
Rio Chico Venez. **147** E2
Rio Claro Brazil **149** I5
Rio Claro Trin. and Tob. **147** F2
Rio Colorado Arg. **152** D4
Rio Corrientes Ecuador **146** B5
Rio Cuarto Arg. **152** D3
Rio das Almas r. Brazil **149** H3
►**Rio de Janeiro** Brazil **151** D7
  3rd most populous city in South
  America. Former capital of Brazil.
  southamerica 144–145
  world 16–17

Rio de Janeiro state Brazil **151** D7
►**Río de la Plata-Paraná** S. America
  152 F2
  2nd longest river in South America and
  9th in the world.
  southamerica 142–143
  world 6–7

Rio Dell U.S.A. **134** A4
Rio do Sul Brazil **151** B8
Rio Formoso Brazil **150** F4
Río Gallegos Arg. **153** C8
Rio Grande Arg. **153** D8
Rio Grande Bol. **148** D5
Rio Grande Brazil **152** D3
Rio Grande Mex. **126** F7
Rio Grande r. Mex./U.S.A. **135** H8
Rio Grande City U.S.A. **133** B7
Rio Grande do Norte state Brazil
  150 D3
Rio Grande do Sul state Brazil **151** A9
Rio Grande Rise sea feature
  S. Atlantic Ocean **161** L8
Ríohacha Col. **146** C1
Río Hondo, Embalse resr Arg. **152** D1
Rioja Peru **146** B5
Riom France **39** E4
Rio Maior Port. **42** B3
Riom-ès-Montagnes France **39** E4
Rio Muerto Arg. **152** E1
Rio Mulatos Bol. **148** D4
Rio Muni reg. Equat. Guinea **93** H5
Rio Negro prov. Arg. **152** D5
Rionero in Vulture Italy **44** E4
Rioni r. Georgia **79** E2
Rio Pardo de Minas Brazil **150** D5
Rio Rancho U.S.A. **135** F4
Ríos Spain **42** D2
Riosucio Col. **146** B3
Rio Tercero Arg. **152** D3
Rio Tigre Ecuador **146** B5
Rio Tinto Brazil **150** F3
Riou, Oued watercourse Alg. **43** G5
Riou Lake Canada **123** J3
Rio Verde Brazil **149** H4
Rio Verde Chile **153** C8
Rioverde Ecuador **146** B4

Río Verde Mex. **126** G7
Rio Verde de Mato Grosso Brazil **151** A6
Rio Vista U.S.A. **136** B2
Riozinho Brazil **148** D2
Riozinho r. Brazil **146** E5
Ripanj Yugo. **46** B2
Ripky Ukr. **29** D6
Ripley MS U.S.A. **128** A5
Ripley NY U.S.A. **130** D2
Ripley OH U.S.A. **130** B4
Ripley TN U.S.A. **133** D5
Ripley WV U.S.A. **130** C4
Ripoll Spain **43** H1
Ripon U.K. **35** F4
Ripon U.S.A. **136** B3
Riposto Sicily Italy **45** E6
Risân 'Unayzah hill Egypt **77** A4
Risasi Dem. Rep. Congo **94** E5
Risbäck Sweden **32** D2
Risco Plateado mt Arg. **152** C3
Rishiri-tō i. Japan **64** B3
Rishon Le Ziyyon Israel **77** B4
Rising Sun IN U.S.A. **130** A4
Rising Sun MD U.S.A. **131** E4
Risle r. France **38** D2
Risnjak nat. park Croatia **44** E2
Rîşnov Romania see **Râşnov**
Rison U.S.A. **133** C5
Rissa Norway **32** C3
Ristiina Fin. **33** G3
Ristijärvi Fin. **33** G2
Ristikent Rus. Fed. **32** H1
Risum China **74** C2
Ritan r. Indon. **59** F2
Ritchie U.S.A. **38** E6
Ritchie's Archipelago is India **73** G3
Ritch Island Canada **123** D2
Ritscher Upland mts Antarctica **167** B2
Ritsem Sweden **32** D2
Ritzville U.S.A. **134** C3
Riu, Mount P.N.G. **111** H1
Rivadavia Buenos Aires Arg. **152** E3
Rivadavia Mendoza Arg. **152** C3
Rivadavia Salta Arg. **149** E6
Rivadavia Chile **152** C2
Riva del Garda Italy **44** C2
Riva Palacio Mex. **135** F7
Rivarolo Canavese Italy **44** A2
Rivas Nicaragua **139** G6
Rivash Iran **80** D3
Rive-de-Gier France **39** F4
Rivera Arg. **152** E4
Rivera Uruguay **152** G2
River Cess Liberia **92** C4
Riverhead U.S.A. **131** G3
Riverina Australia **109** C7
Riverina reg. Australia **112** C4
Rivero, Isla i. Chile **153** B6
Rivers state Nigeria **93** G4
Riversdale S. Africa **98** D7
Riverside U.S.A. **136** D5
Riversleigh Australia **110** D3
Riverton N.Z. **113** B4
Riverton UT U.S.A. **137** G1
Riverton WY U.S.A. **134** F3
Riverview Canada **125** H4
River View S. Africa **99** G6
Rives France **39** F4
Rivesaltes France **39** E5
Rivesville U.S.A. **130** C4
Rivière-au-Renard Canada **125** H3
Rivière Bleue Canada **125** G4
Rivière-du-Loup Canada **125** G4
Rivière-Pentecôte Canada **125** H3
Rivière-Pigou Canada **125** H3
Rivne Ukr. **29** C6
Rivoli Italy **44** A2
Riwaka N.Z. **113** C3
Riwoqê China **66** A2

▶Riyadh Saudi Arabia **76** DE
  Capital of Saudi Arabia.

Riza well Iran **80** C3
Rize Turkey **79** E2
Rizhao China **63** J4
Rizokarpaso Cyprus see **Rizokarpason**
Rizokarpason Cyprus **77** B2
Rizū well Iran **80** D3
Rizū'īyeh Iran **80** D4
Rjukan Norway **33** C4
Rkîz, L. Mauritania **92** B1
Roa Norway **33** C3
Roa Spain **42** E2
Roach Lake U.S.A. **137** E4
Roads U.S.A. **130** B4

▶Road Town Virgin Is (U.K.) **139** L5
  Capital of the British Virgin Islands.

Roan Fell hill U.K. **34** E4
Roanne France **39** F3
Roanoke AL U.S.A. **129** B5
Roanoke VA U.S.A. **130** D5
Roanoke r. U.S.A. **130** E5
Roanoke Rapids U.S.A. **130** E5
Roan Plateau U.S.A. **137** H2
Roaringwater Bay Rep. of Ireland **35** B6
Roatán Hond. **138** G5
Robat r. Afgh. **81** E4
Robāt Iran **80** D3
Robāt-e Khān Iran **80** D3
Robāt-e Shahr-e Bābak Iran **80** C4
Robāt-e Torqol Iran **81** D2
Robāt Karim Iran **80** B3
Robāt-Sang Iran **81** E3
Robat Thana Pak. **81** E4
Robb Canada **122** G4
Robbins Island Australia **112** C6
Robe r. Australia **108** A4
Robe, Mount Australia **112** E3
Robel Germany **37** F2
Robert Glacier Antarctica **167** D2
Robert Lee U.S.A. **133** D6
Roberts U.S.A. **134** D4
Roberts, Mount Australia **111** H6
Robertsburg U.S.A. **130** C4
Roberts Butte mt. Antarctica **167** H2
Roberts Creek Mountain U.S.A. **137** D2
Robertsfors Sweden **32** F2
Robertsganj India **75** D4
Robert S. Kerr Reservoir U.S.A. **133** C4
Robertson S. Africa **98** D7
Robertson, Lac l. Canada **125** J3
Robertson Bay Antarctica **167** H2
Robertson Island Antarctica **167** A2
Robertson Range hills Australia **108** C5
Robertsport Liberia **92** C4
Roberval Canada **125** F3
Robert Williams Angola see **Caála**
Robeson Channel Canada/Greenland **121** M1
Robhanais, Rubha a hd U.K. see **Butt of Lewis**
Robinson r. Australia **110** D3
Robinson Canada **122** C2
Robinson U.S.A. **130** A4
Robinson Mountains U.S.A. **122** A2
Robinson Range hills Australia **109** B6
Robinvale Australia **112** B4
Roblin Canada **134** G2
Robore Bol. **149** F4
Robsart Canada **123** I5
Robson, Mount Canada **122** G4

Robstown U.S.A. **133** B7
Roby U.S.A. **133** A5
Roçadas Angola see **Xangongo**
Roca Partida, Isla i. Mex. **126** D8
Rocas, Atol das atoll Brazil **150** F2
Rocca Busambra mt. Sicily Italy **45** D6
Rocca Imperiale Italy **45** F4
Roccastrada Italy **44** D3
Roc de Montalet mt. France **39** E5
Roc d'Enfer mt. France **39** F3
Rocha Uruguay **152** G2
Rochdale U.K. **35** E5
Rochechouart France **38** D4
Roche de Vic hill France **38** D4
Rochedo Brazil **151** A6
Rochefort Belgium **39** F1
Rochefort France **38** D4
Rochefort, Lac l. Canada **125** F1
Rochegda Rus. Fed. **28** G3
Rochelle U.S.A. **132** A3
Rochester IN U.S.A. **132** E3
Rochester MN U.S.A. **132** A2
Rochester NH U.S.A. **131** H2
Rochester NY U.S.A. **131** F2
Roc'h Trévezel hill France **38** B2
Rocina r. Canada **122** E2
Rock r. Canada **122** E2
Rock r. IA U.S.A. **132** B3
Rock r. WI U.S.A. **132** B3
Rockall i. N. Atlantic Ocean **30** A1
Rockall Bank sea feature N. Atlantic Ocean **30** A1
Rock Creek Canada **122** E5
Rock Creek Canada **122** B1
Rock Creek r. U.S.A. **134** D2
Rockdale U.S.A. **133** B6
Rockefeller Plateau Antarctica **167** J1
Rockford AL U.S.A. **129** B5
Rockford IL U.S.A. **132** D3
Rockford OH U.S.A. **130** A3
Rockglen Canada **123** J5
Rock Hall U.S.A. **131** E4
Rockhampton Australia **111** G4
Rockhampton Downs Australia **110** C3
Rock Hill U.S.A. **129** D5
Rockingham Australia **109** A8
Rockingham U.S.A. **128** D5
Rockingham Bay Australia **110** C3
Rockinghorse Lake Canada **123** H1
Rockland Canada **131** I1
Rocklands Reservoir Australia **112** B5
Rocklea Australia **108** B5
Rocknest Lake Canada **123** H1
Rock Point U.S.A. **137** H3
Rock Rapids U.S.A. **132** B3
Rock River U.S.A. **134** F4
Rock Sound Bahamas **129** D7
Rock Springs MT U.S.A. **134** F3
Rocksprings U.S.A. **133** A6
Rock Springs WY U.S.A. **134** F4
Rockstone Guyana **147** G3
Rockville IN U.S.A. **128** B4
Rockville MD U.S.A. **131** E4
Rockwell City U.S.A. **132** C3
Rockwood Canada **130** B2
Rocky Ford U.S.A. **132** A4
Rocky Fork Lake U.S.A. **130** B4
Rocky Harbour Canada **125** J3
Rocky Lane Canada **123** G3
Rocky Mount NC U.S.A. **130** E5
Rocky Mount VA U.S.A. **130** D5
Rocky Mountain House Canada **123** H4
Rocky Mountain National Park U.S.A. **134** F4
Rocroi France **39** F2
Rødberg Norway **33** C3
Rødbyhavn Denmark **33** C5
Roddickton Canada **125** K3
Rödeby Sweden **33** C4
Rodez France **39** E4
Rodholivos Greece see **Rodolivos**
Rodhópolis Greece see **Rodopoli**
Ródhos i. Greece see **Rhodes**
Rodi i. Greece see **Rhodes**
Roding Germany **37** F4
Rødlia Norway **32** D2
Rodnichek Rus. Fed. see **Rodnichok**
Rodnichok Rus. Fed. **74** C1
Rodolfo Sanchez Toboada Mex. **135** D7
Rodolivos Greece **46** C4
Rodonit, Kepi i pt Albania **46** A4
Rodopi Planina mts Bulg./Greece see **Rhodope Mountains**
Rodopoli Greece **46** C4
Rodos Greece see **Rhodes**
Rodos i. Greece see **Rhodes**
Rodosto Turkey see **Tekirdağ**
Rodøya i. Norway **32** D2
Rodrigues Peru **146** C5
Rodrigues Island Mauritius **162** L7
Rødsand Norway **32** H1
Rødsand Norway **32** F1
Roe r. Australia **110** C2
Roper Bar Australia **110** C2
Roebourne Australia **108** B5
Roebuck Bay Australia **108** C4
Roedtan S. Africa **99** F5
Roe Plains Australia **109** D7
Roermond Neth. **36** B3
Roeselare Belgium **39** E1
Roes Welcome Sound sea chan. Canada **123** O1
Rogachev Belarus see **Rahachow**
Rogaguá, Laguna l. Bol. **148** D3
Rogaland county Norway **33** B4
Rogatica Bos.-Herz. **46** A3
Rogers Canada **122** C2
Rogers U.S.A. **133** C4
Rogers City U.S.A. **132** F2
Rogers Lake U.S.A. **136** E4
Roggan, Lac l. Canada **124** E2
Roggeveen Basin sea feature S. Pacific Ocean **165** M8
Roggeveld plat. S. Africa **98** D7
Roggeveldberge esc. S. Africa **98** D7
Rogliano Italy **45** F5
Rognan Norway **32** D2
Rögnitz r. Germany **36** E2
Rogozno Poland **37** P2
Rogue r. U.S.A. **134** A4
Roha India **72** B2
Rohnert Park U.S.A. **136** A2
Rohrbach in Oberösterreich Austria **37** I4
Rohri Pak. **74** A4
Rohtak India **74** C3
Rohuküla Estonia **33** F4
Roi Et Thai. **61** C4
Roi Georges, Îles du is Fr. Polynesia **165** I6
Roine l. Fin. **33** G3
Roja Latvia **33** F4
Rojas Arg. **152** D4
Röjdåfors Sweden **33** D3
Rojhan Pak. **81** G4
Rojo Aguado, Laguna l. Bol. **148** D3
Rokan r. Indon. **58** C2
Rokeby Australia **111** E2
Rokeby National Park Australia **111** E2
Rokiškis Lith. **33** G5
Roknäs Sweden **32** F2
Rokycany Czech Rep. **37** F4
Rokytne Ukr. **29** C6
Rola Kangri mt. China **75** F2
Rolas, Ilha das i. São Tomé and Principe **93** G5
Rolim de Moura Brazil **149** E2
Roll U.S.A. **137** F5

Rolla MO U.S.A. **132** D4
Rolla ND U.S.A. **132** B1
Rollag Norway **33** C3
Rolleston Australia **111** G5
Rolleston N.Z. **113** C3
Rolleville Bahamas **129** E8
Rolling Fork r. U.S.A. **133** D5
Rolvsøya i. Norway **32** G1
Rom mt. Uganda **96** H1
Roma Australia **111** G5
Roma i. Indon. **57** G7
Roma Italy see **Rome**
Romaine r. Canada **125** I3
Roman Romania **31** K4
Romana, Câmpia plain Romania **46** C2
Romanaţilor, Câmpia plain Romania **46** C2
Romanche Gap sea feature S. Atlantic Ocean **160** M6
Roman-Kosh mt. Ukr. **78** C1
▶Romania country Europe **46** D1
  europe 24–25, 48
Roman-Kosh mt. Rus. Fed. **61** H5
Romanovka Moldova see **Basarabeasca**
Romanovka Rus. Fed. **28** H4
Romanzof, Cape U.S.A. **120** C3
Romão Brazil **147** F5
Rombas France **39** G2

▶Rome Italy **44** D4
  Capital of Italy.

Rome GA U.S.A. **129** B5
Rome NY U.S.A. **131** F2
Romeo U.S.A. **130** D2
Romford U.K. **35** G6
Romilly-sur-Seine France **39** E2
Romit Tajik. **81** G2
Romney U.S.A. **130** E4
Romny Ukr. **29** E6
Rømø i. Denmark **33** C5
Romorantin-Lanthenay France **38** D3
Rompin r. Malaysia **58** C2
Romu mt. Indon. **59** G5
Romulus U.S.A. **130** B2
Ron India **72** B3
Rona i. U.K. **34** D7
Ronas Hill U.K. **34** [inset]
Roncador, Serra do hills Brazil **150** A5
Roncador Reef Solomon Is **107** E2
Ronceverte U.S.A. **130** C5
Ronda Spain **42** D4
Ronda, Serranía de mts Spain **42** D4
Ronda das Salinas Brazil **149** E3
Ronde i. Grenada **147** F1
Rondon Brazil **149** G5
Rondón Col. **146** D3
▶Rondônia state Brazil **149** E2
  southamerica 144–145
Rondonópolis Brazil **151** A6
Rong'an China **67** F3
Rongbaca China **66** A2
Rongcheng Anhui China see **Qingyang**
Rongcheng Guangxi China see **Rongxian**
Rongcheng Hubei China see **Jianli**
Rong Chu r. China **75** F3
Rongelap atoll Marshall Is **164** F6
Rongjiang Guizhou China **67** D3
Rongjiang Jiangxi China see **Nankang**
Rong Jiang r. China **67** D4
Rongjiawan China see **Yueyang**
Rongklang Range mts Myanmar **60** A3
Rongmei China see **Hefeng**
Rongxian Guangxi China **67** D4
Rongxian Sichuan China **66** C2
Rongzhag China see **Danba**
Rønne Denmark **33** I5
Ronneby Sweden **33** I5
Ronne Entrance strait Antarctica **167** L2
Ronne Ice Shelf Antarctica **167** L1
Ronnenberg Germany **36** D2
Ronse Belgium **39** E1
Ronuro r. Brazil **150** A5
Rooke Island P.N.G. see **Umboi**
Roorkee India **74** C3
Roosendaal Neth. **36** B3
Roosevelt AZ U.S.A. **137** G5
Roosevelt UT U.S.A. **137** H1
Roosevelt, Mount Canada **134** E3
Roosevelt Island Antarctica **167** I1
Roosna-Alliku Estonia **33** G4
Root r. Canada **122** F2
Root r. U.S.A. **132** B3
Ropa r. Poland **37** J4
Ropczyce Poland **37** J3
Roper r. Australia **110** C2
Roper Bar Australia **110** C2
Ropi mt. Fiji **107** G3
Roquebrune-sur-Argens France **39** G5
Roquefort France **38** D4
Roquetas de Mar Spain **43** E4
Roraima state Brazil **147** F4
Roraima, Mount Guyana **147** F3
Rori India **74** B3
Rorketon Canada **123** K5
Røros Norway **32** C3
Rorschach Switz. **39** H3
Rørvik Norway **32** C2
Rørvik Norway **32** C2
Roś, Jezioro l. Poland **37** J2
Rosal de la Frontera Spain **42** C4
Rosalia U.S.A. **134** C3
Rosamond U.S.A. **136** C4
Rosamond Lake U.S.A. **136** C4
Rosario Jujuy Arg. **148** D5
Rosario Santa Fé Arg. **152** E4
Rosário Brazil **150** C2
Rosario Baja California Mex. **135** D7
Rosario Coahuila Mex. **133** A7
Rosario Mex. **126** E7
Rosario Sonora Mex. **135** E8
Rosario Para. **149** F6
Rosario Venez. **146** D2
Rosario de la Frontera Arg. **152** D1
Rosario de Lerma Arg. **148** D5
Rosário do Sul Brazil **151** A9
Rosário Oeste Brazil **149** F3
Rosarito Baja California Mex. **135** D7
Rosarito Baja California Mex. **136** D5
Rosarno Italy **45** E5
Rosas Spain see **Roses**
Rosas, Golfo de b. Spain see **Roses, Golf de**
Rosa Zárate Ecuador **146** B4
Roscoff France **38** B2
Roscommon Rep. of Ireland **35** B5
Roscommon U.S.A. **130** A1
Roscrea Rep. of Ireland **35** C5
Rose r. Australia **110** C2
Rose, Mount U.S.A. **136** C2

▶Roseau Dominica **139** L5
  Capital of Dominica.

Roseau U.S.A. **132** C1
Roseau r. U.S.A. **132** B1
Roseberth Australia **111** D5
Rosebery Australia **112** C6
Rose Blanche Canada **125** J4
Rosebud r. Canada **123** H5
Rosebud Creek r. U.S.A. **134** F3
Roseburg U.S.A. **134** B4
Rose City U.S.A. **130** A1
Rosedale U.S.A. **133** D5

Rosendal Norway **33** B4
Rosengarten Germany **36** D2
Rosenheim Germany **36** F5
Rose Peak U.S.A. **137** H5
Rose Point Canada **122** D4
Roses Spain **43** H1
Roses, Golf de b. Spain **43** H1
Roseto degli Abruzzi Italy **44** E3
Rosetown Canada **134** F2
Rosetta Egypt see **Rashīd**
Roseville CA U.S.A. **136** B2
Roseville IL U.S.A. **132** B3
Roshchino Rus. Fed. **28** Q4
Roshkhvār Iran **81** D3
Rosh Pinah Namibia **98** C5
Rosignano Marittimo Italy **44** C3
Roşiori de Vede Romania **46** D2
Rositsa r. Bulg. **46** D3
Roslavl' Rus. Fed. **29** E5
Roslyakovo Rus. Fed. **28** H1
Roslyatino Rus. Fed. **28** H4
Rosolina Italy **44** D2
Rosporden France **38** B3
Rossa Romania **46** D2
Ross r. Australia **110** C4
Ross r. Canada **122** C2
Ross N.Z. **113** D3
Ross, Mount N.Z. **113** C3
Rossan Point Rep. of Ireland **34** B4
Ross Barnett Reservoir U.S.A. **133** D5
Ross Bay Junction Canada **125** H3
Ross Dependency Antarctica **167** I2
Rossel P.N.G. **111** H1
Ross Ice Shelf Antarctica **167** I1
Rössing Namibia **98** B4
Ross Island Myanmar see **Daung Kyun**
Ross Island Antarctica **167** H1
Rossiyskaya Sovetskaya Federativnaya Sotsialisticheskaya Respublika country Asia/Europe see **Russian Federation**
Rossland Canada **122** G5
Rosslare Rep. of Ireland **35** C5
Rosslare Harbour Rep. of Ireland **35** C5
Rosso Mauritania **92** B1
Rosson China **67** E3
Ross-on-Wye U.K. **35** E6
Rossoh' Rus. Fed. **29** F6
Ross River Australia **110** C4
Ross River Canada **122** C2
Ross Sea Antarctica **167** H1
Røssvatnet l. Norway **32** C2
Rosswood Canada **122** D4
Røst i. Norway **32** C2
Røst Iraq **79** F3
Rostaq Afgh. **81** H2
Rostaq Fārs Iran **80** C4
Rostaq Hormozgan Iran **80** C5
Rosthern Canada **123** J4
Rostock Germany **36** F1
Rostonsölkä ridge Sweden **32** F1
Rostov Rus. Fed. **28** H4
Rostov Oblast admin. div. Rus. Fed. see **Rostovskaya Oblast'**
Rostov-na-Donu Rus. Fed. **29** F7
Rostov-on-Don Rus. Fed. see **Rostov-na-Donu**
Rostovskaya Oblast' admin. div. Rus. Fed. **29** G7
Rostrenen France **38** B2
Rosvik Norway **32** D2
Roswell U.S.A. **135** F6
Rota i. N. Mariana Is **57** K3
Rotch Island Kiribati see **Tamana**
Rote i. Indon. **108** C2
Rotenburg (Wümme) Germany **36** D2
Rote Wand mt. Austria **36** D5
Roth Germany **36** E4
Rothenburg ob der Tauber Germany **36** E4
Rothera research station Antarctica **167** L2
Rotherham N.Z. **113** C3
Rotherham U.K. **35** F5
Rothesay U.K. **34** D4
Rothschild Germany **36** D3
Roti Indon. **108** C2
Roti i. Indon. see **Rote**
Roto Australia **112** C4
Rotomagus France see **Rouen**
Rotomanu N.Z. **113** B3
Rotorua N.Z. **113** D2
Rotorua, Lake N.Z. **113** D2
Rott r. Germany **37** F4
Rottenmann Austria **37** G5
Rotterdam Neth. **36** B3
Rottnest Island Australia **109** A8
Rottweil Germany **36** D4
Rotuma i. Fiji **107** G3
Rötviken Sweden **32** D3
Rötz Germany **37** F4
Roubaix France **39** E1
Roudnice nad Labem Czech Rep. **37** F3
Rouen France **38** D2
Rouhia Tunisia **45** B7
Roui, Oued el watercourse Niger **88** A4
Roulers Belgium see **Roeselare**
Roumania country Europe see **Romania**
Roundeyed Lake Canada **125** G2
Round Mountain mt. Australia **112** E3
Round Mountain U.S.A. **136** D2
Round Rock AZ U.S.A. **137** H3
Round Rock TX U.S.A. **133** B6
Roundup U.S.A. **134** F3
Roura Fr. Guiana **147** H3
Rousay i. U.K. **34** F1
Roussillon France **39** F4
Rouyn Canada **124** F4
Rovaniemi Fin. **32** G2
Rovato Italy **44** C2
Roven'ki Rus. Fed. **29** F6
Rovereto Italy **44** C2
Roversi Arg. **152** E1
Rovigo Italy **44** C2
Rovinari Romania **46** C2
Rovinj Croatia **44** D2
Rovkul'skoye, Ozero l. Rus. Fed. **32** R5
Rovno Ukr. see **Rivne**
Rovnoye Rus. Fed. **29** H6
Rovuma r. Moz./Tanz. see **Ruvuma**
Rowena Australia **112** D2
Rowlett U.S.A. **133** D5
Rowley Island Canada **121** L3
Rowley Shoals sea feature Australia **108** B4
Rôwne Ukr. see **Rivne**
Rów Polski r. Poland **37** H3
Roxas Mindoro Phil. **57** G4
Roxas Palawan Phil. **56** E3
Roxas Panay Phil. **57** F3
Roxboro U.S.A. **128** D4
Roxborough Downs Australia **110** D4
Roxburgh N.Z. **113** B4
Roxby Downs Australia **109** G7
Roxen l. Sweden **33** G4
Roxo, Barragem do resr Port. **42** B4
Royal Canal Rep. of Ireland **35** C5
Royal Chitwan National Park Nepal **75** E4
Royale, Île i. Canada see **Cape Breton Island**
Royale, Isle i. U.S.A. **132** D1
Royal Oak U.S.A. **130** D2
Royan France **38** C4
Roye France **39** E2

Roy Hill Australia **108** B5
Royston U.K. **35** F5
Röytä Fin. **32** G2
Rozdil'na Ukr. **29** E7
Rožaj Yugo. **46** B3
Rožaňa Poland **37** J2
Rožany Poland **37** J2
Rozdil'na Ukr. **29** E7
Rozhdestvenskoye Rus. Fed. **28** H4
Rozino Bulg. **46** C3
Rozivka Ukr. **29** F7
Rožňava Slovakia **37** J4
Rozveh Iran **80** C3
Rrëshen Albania **46** A4
Rrogozhinë Albania **46** A4
Ruacana Namibia **98** B3
Ruaha National Park Tanz. **97** B6
Ruahine Range mts N.Z. **113** D3
Ruapehu, Mount vol. N.Z. **113** D3
Ruapuke Island N.Z. **113** B4
Ruarwe Malawi **97** B7
Ruatoria N.Z. **113** D2
Rub' al Khālī des. Saudi Arabia **76** D6
  Largest uninterrupted stretch of sand in the world.
Rubaydā' reg. Saudi Arabia **80** B5
Rubeho Mountains Tanz. **97** C6
Rubi r. Dem. Rep. Congo **94** D3
Rubicon r. U.S.A. **136** B2
Rubondo National Park Tanz. **96** A5
Rubtsovsk Rus. Fed. **26** I1
Rubuga Tanz. **97** B6
Rucăr Romania **46** D2
Ruchany Belarus **33** G5
Rucheng Guangdong China see **Ruyuan**
Rucheng Hunan China **67** E3
Ruciane-Nida Poland **37** J2
Ruckersville U.S.A. **130** D4
Rudall River National Park Australia **108** C5
Rudalpur India **75** D4
Rudarpur India **75** D4
Rudbar Afgh. **81** E4
Rūdbār Iran **80** B2
Rüd-e Kor watercourse Iran **80** C4
Rudina pass Yugo. **46** A3
Rüd-i-Shur watercourse Iran **80** D4
Rūdiškes Lith. **33** G5
Rudkøbing Denmark **33** C5
Rudna Glava Yugo. **46** C2
Rudnaya Pristan' Primorskiy Kray Rus. Fed. **64** D3
Rudnaya Pristan' Primorskiy Kray Rus. Fed. **64** C3
Rudnichnyy Rus. Fed. **28** J4
Rudnik Poland **37** K3
Rudnik Ingichka Uzbek. see **Ingichka**
Rudnya Smolenskaya Oblast' Rus. Fed. **29** D5
Rudnya Volgogradskaya Oblast' Rus. Fed. **29** H6
Rudnyy Kazakh. **26** G4
Rudnyy Rus. Fed. **64** C3
Rudolf, Lake salt l. Eth./Kenya see **Turkana, Lake**
Rudolf Island Rus. Fed. see **Rudol'fa, Ostrov**
▶Rudol'fa, Ostrov i. Rus. Fed. **26** F1
  Most northerly point of Europe.
Rudolph Island Rus. Fed. see **Rudol'fa, Ostrov**
Rudolstadt Germany **36** E3
Rudong China **67** G1
Rudozem Bulg. **46** D4
Rüdsar Iran **80** B2
Rue France **38** D1
Ruen mt. Macedonia see **Rujen**
Ruenya r. Zimbabwe **99** G3
Rufa'a Sudan **89** G6
Ruffec France **38** D3
Rufiji r. Tanz. **97** C7
Rufino Arg. **152** E3
Rufisque Senegal **92** A1
Rufunsa Zambia **95** F8
Rugāji Latvia **33** G4
Rugao China **67** G1
Rugby U.K. **35** F5
Rugby U.S.A. **134** G2
Rügen i. Germany **37** F1
Rugged Mountain Canada **122** E5
Rugheiwa wtl Sudan **89** F5
Ruhango Tanz. **97** C7
Ruhnu i. Estonia **33** F4
Ruhr r. Germany **36** C3
Ruhubu r. Tanz. **97** B7
Ruhudji r. Tanz. **97** B7
Ruhuna National Park Sri Lanka **72** D5
Rui'an China **67** G3
Ruichang China **67** E2
Ruidoso U.S.A. **135** F6
Ruijin China **67** E3
Ruiz Mex. **126** E7
Ruiz, Nevado del vol. Col. **146** C3
Rujaylah, Harrat ar lava field Jordan **77** C3
Rujen mt. Macedonia **46** C3
Rūjiena Latvia **33** G4
Ruki r. Dem. Rep. Congo **94** C4
Rukumkot Nepal **75** D3
Rukwa admin. reg. Tanz. **97** A6
Rukwa, Lake Tanz. **97** B7
Rūl Dadnah U.A.E. **80** D5
Ruleville U.S.A. **133** D5
Rulin China see **Chengbu**
Rulong China see **Xinlong**
Rūm Iran **81** D3
Rum r. U.K. **34** C3
Rum r. U.S.A. **132** A2
Rum, Jebel mts Jordan see **Ramm, Jabal**
Ruma Yugo. **46** B2
Rumāh Saudi Arabia **80** A5
Rumania country Europe see **Romania**
Rumbek Sudan **94** F3
Rumblar r. Spain **42** E3
Rumburk Czech Rep. **37** G3
Rum Cay i. Bahamas **129** E8
Rumford U.S.A. **131** J2
Rumia Poland **37** I1
Rumilly France **39** F4
Rummānā hill Syria **77** D3
Rumoi Japan **64** F1
Rumphi Malawi **97** B7
Runan China **67** E1
Runanga N.Z. **113** D3
Runaway, Cape N.Z. **113** D2
Runcorn U.K. **35** E5
Runcu Romania **46** C2
Runde r. Zimbabwe **99** G3
Rundu Namibia **98** C3
Rundvik Sweden **32** E3
Rüng, Kaôh i. Cambodia **61** C6
Rungan r. Indon. **59** F3

Rungu Dem. Rep. Congo **94** E4
Rungwa Rukwa Tanz. **97** A6
Rungwa Singida Tanz. **97** B6
Rungwa r. Tanz. **97** B6
Runing China see **Runan**
Rūniz-e Bālā Iran **80** C4
Runn l. Sweden **33** D3
Running Springs U.S.A. **136** D4
Running Water watercourse U.S.A. **133** A5
Runton Range hills Australia **108** C5
Ruokolahti Fin. **33** H3
Ruoqiang China **70** G4
Ruovesi Fin. **33** G3
Rupa India **75** G4
Rupat i. Indon. **58** C2
Rupea Romania **46** D1
Rupert r. Canada **124** F3
Rupert U.S.A. **130** C5
Rupert Bay Canada **124** F3
Rupert Coast Antarctica **167** J1
Rupert Creek r. Australia **111** E4
Rupshu reg. Jammu and Kashmir **74** C2
Ruqqād, Wādī ar watercourse Israel **77** B3
Rural Retreat U.S.A. **130** C5
Rurrenabaque Bol. **148** D3
Rus r. Canada **124** D1
Ruschuk Bulg. see **Ruse**
Ruse Bulg. **46** D3
Rusenski Lom nat. park Bulg. **46** D3
Rusera India **75** E4
Ruşeţu Romania **46** E2
Rushan China see **Rushon**
Rushanskiy Khrebet mts Tajik. see **Rushon, Qatorkühi**
Rush Creek r. U.S.A. **132** A4
Rushford U.S.A. **132** B3
Rushmere U.S.A. **131** E5
Rushon Tajik. **81** G2
Rushon, Qatorkühi mts Tajik. **81** G2
Rushville IL U.S.A. **132** B3
Rushville IN U.S.A. **128** B4
Rushville OH U.S.A. **130** C4
Rushworth Australia **112** C5
Rusk U.S.A. **133** C5
Ruskin U.S.A. **129** C7
Ruskele Sweden **32** E2
Rusokastro Bulg. **46** E3
Rušona Latvia **33** G4
Russas Brazil **150** D3
Russell N.Z. **113** C1
Russell U.S.A. **132** D4
Russell Bay Antarctica **167** J2
Russell Island Canada **123** K3
Russell Lake Man. Canada **123** K3
Russell Lake N.W.T. Canada **123** H2
Russellville AL U.S.A. **129** B5
Russellville AR U.S.A. **133** C5
Russellville KY U.S.A. **128** B4
Russellville OH U.S.A. **130** B4
Rüsselsheim Germany **36** D3
Russi Italy **44** D2
▶Russia country Asia/Europe see **Russian Federation**
▶Russian Federation country Asia/Europe **27** F3
  Largest country in the world, Europe and Asia. Most populous country in Europe, 5th in Asia and 7th in the world.
  europe 24–25, 48
  asia 52–53, 82
  world 8–9, 16–17
Russian Soviet Federal Socialist Republic country Asia/Europe see **Russian Federation**
Russkiy Kameshkir Rus. Fed. **29** H5
Russkiy Zavorot, Poluostrov pen. Rus. Fed. **28** J1
Russkoye Ust'ye Rus. Fed. **27** O2
Rust'avi Georgia **79** F2
Rustburg U.S.A. **130** D5
Rustenburg S. Africa **99** E5
Ruston U.S.A. **133** C5
Rutana Burundi **95** F5
Rutba Indon. **57** F7
Rutenga Zimbabwe **99** F4
Rutherfordton U.S.A. **128** C5
Ruther Glen U.S.A. **130** E5
Ruthin U.K. **35** E5
Rutland U.S.A. **131** G2
Rutland Island India **73** G4
Rutland Plains Australia **111** E2
Rutledge Lake Canada **123** I2
Rutög China **74** D2
Rutog Xizang China **75** E3
Rutog Xizang China **75** E3
Rutshuru Dem. Rep. Congo **94** E4
Rutul Rus. Fed. **79** G2
Ruukki Fin. **32** G2
Ruvaslahti Fin. **32** H3
Ruvo di Puglia Italy **44** F4
Ruvozero Rus. Fed. **32** H2
Ruvu Tanz. see **Pangani**
Ruvuma r. Moz./Tanz. **97** D7
Ruvuma admin. reg. Tanz. **97** C7
Ruwayshid, Wādī watercourse Jordan **79** D4
Ruwayţah, Wādī watercourse Jordan **77** C5
Ruweijil pt Saudi Arabia **77** B5
Ruweis U.A.E. **80** D5
Ruwenzori mts Dem. Rep. Congo/Uganda **94** E4
Ruwenzori National Park Uganda see **Queen Elizabeth National Park**
Ruya r. Zimbabwe **99** G3
Ruyuan China **67** E3
Ruza Rus. Fed. **28** F5
Ruzayevka Kazakh. **26** G1
Ruzayevka Rus. Fed. **29** H5
Ruzhou China **67** E1
Ruzomberok Slovakia **37** I4
▶Rwanda country Africa **94** F5
  africa 86–87, 100
Ryābād Iran **80** C2
Ryazan' Rus. Fed. **29** F5
Ryazan Oblast admin. div. Rus. Fed. see **Ryazanskaya Oblast'**
Ryazanskaya Oblast' admin. div. Rus. Fed. **29** G5
Ryazhsk Rus. Fed. **29** G5
Rybachiy, Poluostrov pen. Rus. Fed. **32** I1
Rybach'ye Kyrg. see **Balykchy**
Rybinsk Rus. Fed. **28** F4
Rybinskoye Vodokhranilishche resr Rus. Fed. **28** F4
Rybnik Poland **37** I3
Rybnitsa Moldova see **Rîbnița**
Rybreka Rus. Fed. **28** F3
Rychnov nad Kněžnou Czech Rep. **37** H3
Rycroft Canada **122** G4
Ryd Sweden **33** I4
Rydaberg Peninsula Antarctica **167** L2
Ryde U.K. **35** F6
Rye r. U.K. **35** F4
Rye Patch Reservoir U.S.A. **136** C1
Ryki Poland **37** J3
Rykovo Ukr. see **Yenakiyeve**
Ryl'sk Rus. Fed. **29** E6

Rýmařov Czech Rep. **37** H4
Rymättylä Fin. **33** F3
Ryn Poland **37** J2
Ryn-Peski des. Kazakh. **29** I7
Ryōtsu Japan **65** D5
Rypin Poland **37** I2
Rysjedal Norway **33** B3
Rytterknægten hill Denmark **33** D5
Ryukyu Islands Japan **63** K7
Ryūkyū-rettō is Japan see
  Ryukyu Islands
Ryukyu Trench sea feature
  N. Pacific Ocean **154** C4
Rzav r. Bos.-Herz. **46** A3
Rzepin Poland **37** G2
Rzeszów Poland **37** K3
Rzhaksa Rus. Fed. **29** F5
Rzhev Rus. Fed. **28** E4

Sa'ābād Iran **80** D3
Saacow Somalia **96** D4
Sa'ādah al Barṣā' pass Saudi Arabia
  77 C5
Sa'ādatābād Fārs Iran **80** C4
Sa'ādatābād Hormozgan Iran **80** C4
Saalach r. Germany **36** E3
Saale r. Germany **36** E2
Saalfeld Germany **36** E3
Saalfelden am Steinernen Meer
  Austria **37** F3
Saanen Switz. **36** C3
Saanich Canada **122** F5
Saar land Germany see Saarland
Saar r. Germany **36** C4
Saarbrücken Germany **36** C4
Säare Estonia **28** B4
Saaremaa i. Estonia **28** B4
Saarenkylä Fin. **32** G2
Saari Fin. **33** H3
Saarijärvi Fin. **32** G3
Saari-Kämä Fin. **32** G2
Saarikoski Fin. **32** F1
Saariselkä Fin. **32** G1
Saaristomeren Kansallispuisto nat. park
  Fin. see Skärgårdshavets Nationalpark
Saarland land Germany **36** C4
Saarlouis Germany **36** C4
Saatlı Azer. **79** G3
Saatse Estonia **33** G4
Sab' Ābār Syria **79** D4
Šabac Yugo. **46** A2
Sabadell Spain **43** I2
Sabah state Malaysia **59** G1
Sabak Malaysia **58** C2
Sabaki r. Kenya **96** D5
Sabalan, Kūhhā-ye mts Iran **80** A2
Sabalgarh India **74** C4
Sabana, Archipiélago de is Cuba **129** C8
Sabanalarga Col. **146** D1
Sabang Indon. **58** A1
Sabano Col. **146** C5
Šabanözü Turkey **78** C2
Šabará Brazil **151** D6
Sabari r. India **73** D2
Sabarmati r. India **74** B5
Sabaru i. Indon. **59** G4
Sabastiya West Bank **77** B3
Sabaudia Italy **44** E4
Sabaya Bol. **148** C4
Sabhraï India **74** A5
Sabi r. India **74** C3
Sabie r. S. Africa **99** F5
Sabie U.S.A. **130** B4
Sabinal Mex. **135** F7
Sabiñánigo Spain **43** F1
Sabinar, Punta del mt. Spain **43** E4
Sabinas Mex. **126** F6
Sabinas r. Coahuila Mex. **133** A7
Sabinas r. Nuevo León Mex. **133** C7
Sabinas Hidalgo Mex. **126** F6
Sabine r. U.S.A. **133** C6
Sabine Lake U.S.A. **133** C6
Sabinov Slovakia **37** J4
Sabirabad Azer. **79** G2
Sable, Cape Canaca **125** H5
Sable, Cape U.S.A. **129** C7
Sable, Lac du l. Canada **125** H2
Sable Island Canada **125** J5
Sablé-sur-Sarthe France **38** C3
Sabloiro Brazil **150** E3
Sablon, Pointe du pt France **39** F5
Saboeiro Brazil **150** E3
Sabon Kafi Niger **93** H2
Sabou Burkina **93** E2
Sabres France **39** C4
Sabrina Coast Antarctica **167** F2
Sabugal Port. **42** C2
Şabyā Saudi Arabia **89** I5
Sabzawar Afgh. see Shindand
Sabzevār Iran **80** D2
Sabzvārān Iran see Jīroft
Saca, Vârful mt. Romania **46** D1
Sa Cabaneta Spain **43** H3
Sacaca Bol. **148** D4
Sacandaga r. U.S.A. **131** F2
Sacco r. Italy **44** D4
Sacece Romania **46** D2
Săceni Romania **46** D2
Sachanga Angola **95** C8
Sachigo r. Canada **124** B2
Sachigo Lake Canada **123** M4
Sachin India **74** B5
Sach'on S. Korea **65** C6
Sachsen Germany **37** F3
Sachsen-Anhalt land Germany **36** E2
Sachs Harbour Canada **120** F2
Sacirsuyu r. Syria/Turkey see Sājūr, Nahr
Sackpfeife hill Germany **36** D3
Sackville Canada **125** H4
Saco U.S.A. **131** H2
Sacramento Brazil **149** I4

▶Sacramento U.S.A. **136** B2
  State capital of California.

Sacramento r. U.S.A. **136** B2
Sacramento Mountains U.S.A. **135** F6
Sacramento Valley U.S.A. **136** A1
Sacratif, Cabo c. Spain **42** E4
Sádaba Spain **43** F1
Sa'dābād Iran **81** F4
Sá da Bandeira Angola see Lubango
Şadad Syria **78** D4
Şa'dah Yemen **76** C6
Sadani Tanz. **97** C4
Sadao Thai. **61** C7
Sadaseopet India **72** C2
Saddat al Hindīyah Iraq **79** F4
Saddleback Mesa mt. U.S.A. **133** A5
Saddle Hill Australia **111** D4
Saddle Island Vanuatu see Mota Lava
Saddle Peak hill India **73** D5
Sa Đec Vietnam **61** D6
Sadhaura India **74** C3
Sadi Eth. **96** B2

Sadieville U.S.A. **130** A4
Sadij watercourse Iran **81** D5
Sadiqabad Pak. **81** G4
Sadiya India **62** F6
Sa'diya Saudi Arabia **89** H4
Sa'diyah, Hawr as imp. l. Iraq **79** F4
Sa'diyyat i. U.A.E. **80** C5
Sado r. Port. **42** B3
Sado-shima i. Japan **65** D5
Sadon Myanmar **60** B1
Sadri India **74** B4
Sadulshahar India **74** B3
Saegertown U.S.A. **130** C3
Saena Julia Italy see Siena
Safad Israel see Zefat
Safané Burkina **92** E3
Šafárikovo Slovakia see Tornaľa
Safayal Maqūf well Iraq **79** F5
Safed Khirs mts Afgh. **81** G2
Safed Koh mts Afgh. **81** G3
Safed Koh mts Afgh./Pak. **81** G3
Safed Dasht Iran **80** B3
Safid Kūh mts Afgh. see Paropamisus
Şāfītā Syria **77** C2
Safonovo Arkhangel'skaya Oblast'
  Rus. Fed. **28** J2
Safonovo Smolenskaya Oblast' Rus. Fed.
  31 M2
Safotu Samoa **107** H3
Safranbolu Turkey **78** C2
Safwan Iraq **79** F5
Şag Romania **46** B2
Şaga China **70** D5
Saga Japan **65** B6
Sagaing Myanmar **60** A3
Sagaing admin. div. Myanmar **60** A3
Sagala Mali see Séguéla
Sagamihara Japan **65** D6
Sagami-nada g. Japan **65** D6
Saganthit Kyun i. Myanmar **61** B5
Sagar Karnataka India **72** B3
Sagar Karnataka India **72** C2
Sagar Madhya Pradesh India **74** C5
Sagaredzho Georgia see Sagarejo
Sagarejo Georgia **79** F2
Sagar Island India **75** F5
Sagarmatha mt. China/Nepal see
  Everest, Mount
Sagarmatha National Park Nepal **75** E4
Sagastyr Rus. Fed. **27** M2
Sagauli India **75** F4
Sagavanirktok r. U.S.A. **120** D3
Sage Creek r. U.S.A. **134** E2
Saggi, Har mt. Israel **77** B4
Sagleipie Liberia **92** C4
Saglek Bay Canada **125** I1
Saglouc Canada see Salluit
Sagone, Golfe de b. Corsica France
  44 B3
Sagra mt. Spain **43** E4
Sagres Port. **42** B4
Sagres, Ponta de pt Port. **42** B4
Sagu Indon. **108** C2
Sagu Myanmar **60** A3
Saguache U.S.A. **135** F5
Saguache Creek r. U.S.A. **135** F5
Saguaro National Park U.S.A. **137** G5
Saguenay r. Canada **125** G3
Sagunt Spain see Sagunto
Sagunto Spain **43** F3
Saguntum Spain see Sagunto
Sagwara India **74** B5
Sagyz r. Kazakh. **29** J7
Şaḩāb Jordan **77** C4
Sahabab India **74** C3
Sahagún Spain **42** D1
Sahand, Kūh-e mt. Iran **80** A2

▶Sahara des. Africa **91** G6
  Largest desert in the world.
  africa 84–85

Şaḩara el Gharbīya des. Egypt see
  Western Desert
Şaḩara el Sharqīya des. Egypt see
  Eastern desert
Saharan Atlas mts Alg. see
  Atlas Saharien
Saharanpur India **74** C3
Sahara Well Australia **108** C5
Saharsa India **75** F4
Sahaswan India **74** C3
Sahat, Kūh-e hill Iran **80** C3
Sahavato Madag. **99** [inset] K4
Şahbuz Azer. **79** G3
Sahel reg. Africa **94** A1
Sahibganj India **75** F4
Sahiwal Punjab Pak. **81** H4
Sahiwal Punjab Pak. **81** H4
Sahlābād Iran **81** D3
Sahl al Maṭrān Saudi Arabia **89** H3
Sahl Rakbah plain Saudi Arabia **89** I4
Şaḩm Oman **80** E5
Şaḩneh Iran **80** A3
Şaḩrā al Ḩijārah reg. Iraq **79** F5
Sahu China see Zadoi
Sahuaripa Mex. **135** E7
Sahuayo Mex. **126** D4
Sahy Slovakia **37** I4
Sahyadri mts India see Western Ghats
Sahyadriparvat Range hills India **72** B1
Şaḩyūn tourist site Syria **77** C2
Sai r. India **74** E4
Saibai Island Australia **57** J7
Sai Buri Thai. **61** C7
Sai Buri r. Thai. **61** C7
Saïda Alg. **91** F2
Saïda Lebanon see Sidon
Sai Dao Tai, Khao mt. Thai. **61** C5
Saidpur Bangl. **75** F4
Saidpur India **75** D4
Saidu Pak. **81** H3
Saihan Tal China **63** I3
Saigon Vietnam see Ho Chi Minh City
Saiha India **75** H5
Saikai National Park Japan **65** B6
Saikanosy Masoala pen. Madag.
  99 [inset] K2
Saiki Japan **65** B6
Sai Kung Hong Kong China **67** [inset]
Sailana India **74** B5
Saimaa l. Fin. **33** H3
Saimbeyli Turkey **78** D3
Saindak Pak. **81** F4
Sa'indezh Iran **80** A2

Sa'īn Qal'eh Iran see Sa'īndezh
Saïnsoubou Senegal **92** C2
Saint r. U.S.A. **132** D4
St Abb's Head U.K. **34** E4
St-Affrique France **39** E5
St-Aignan France **38** D3
St Alban's Canada **125** K4
St Albans U.K. **35** F6
St Albans WV U.S.A. **130** C4
St Alban's Head U.K. **35** E6
St Albert Canada **123** H4
St Aldhelm's Head U.K. see
  St Alban's Head
St-Amand-les-Eaux France **39** E1
St-Amand-Montrond France **39** E3
St-Amour France **39** F3
St-André, Cap c. Madag. see
  Vilanandro, Tanjona
St-André-de-Cubzac France **38** C4
St Andrews U.K. **34** E3
St Andrew Sound inlet U.S.A. **129** C6
St Ann's Bay Jamaica **139** I5
St Anthony Canada **125** K3
Saint Anthony U.S.A. **134** E4
St Arnaud Australia **112** D6
St Arnaud Range mts N.Z. **113** C3
St-Astier France **38** D4
St Augustin Canada **125** J3
St Augustine U.S.A. **129** C6
St Aulaye France **38** D4
St Austell U.K. **35** C8
St Barbe Canada **125** J3
St-Barthélemi Canada **125** F4
St-Barthélemy i. West Indies **139** L5
St-Barthélemy, Pic de mt. France **38** D5
St Bees U.K. **34** D4
St-Blaise Switz. **39** G3
St-Brice-en-Coglès France **38** C2
St-Bride's Bay U.K. **35** C6
St-Brieuc France **38** B2
St-Brieuc, Baie de b. France **38** B2
St-Calais France **38** D3
St Catharines Canada **130** D2
St Catherine's Canada **125** K4
St-Céré France **38** D4
St-Chamond France **39** F4
St Charles MD U.S.A. **131** E4
Saint Charles U.S.A. **130** A2
St Charles MO U.S.A. **127** H4
St-Chély-d'Apcher France **39** E4
St Christopher and Nevis country
  West Indies see St Kitts and Nevis
St Clair r. Canada/U.S.A. **132** D3
St Clair U.S.A. **130** B2
St Clair, Lake Canada/U.S.A. **130** B2
St Clairsville U.S.A. **130** C3
St-Claude France **39** F3
St Cloud U.S.A. **132** C2
St Croix r. U.S.A. **132** C2
St Croix Falls U.S.A. **132** C2
St Croix Island Virgin Is (U.S.A.) **139** L5
St-Cyr-sur-Loire France **38** D3
St David's U.K. **35** C6
St David's Head U.K. **35** D6
St-Denis France **38** E2

▶St-Denis Réunion **162** K7
  Capital of Réunion.

St-Dié France **39** G2
St-Dizier France **39** F2
St-Domingue country West Indies see Haiti
Sainte Anne Canada **123** L5
Sainte Anne, Lac l. Canada **125** H3
Ste-Anne-de-Portneuf Canada **125** G3
Ste-Anne-des-Monts Canada **125** H3
Ste-Foy-la-Grande France **38** D4
Sainte Genevieve U.S.A. **132** D4
St-Égrève France **39** F4
Ste-Hermine France **38** C3
St Elias, Cape U.S.A. **120** E4

▶St Elias, Mount U.S.A. **122** A2
  4th highest mountain in North America.
  northamerica 116–117

St Elias Mountains Canada **122** A2
St-Élie Fr. Guiana **147** H3
St-Éloy-les-Mines France **39** E3
Sainte Marguerite r. Canada **125** H3
Ste-Marie, Cap c. Madag. see
  Vohimena, Tanjona
St-Maure-de-Touraine France **38** D3
Ste-Maxime France **39** G5
Ste-Rose-du-Dégelé Canada see Dégelis
Sainte Rose du Lac Canada **134** H2
Saintes France **38** D4
St-Étienne France **39** F4
St-Étienne-de-Tinée France **39** H4
St Eustatius i. Neth. Antilles **139** L5
St-Florentin France **39** E2
St-Florent-sur-Cher France **38** E3
St Floris, Parc National nat. park
  Cent. Afr. Rep. **94** D2
St-Flour France **39** E4
St Francesville U.S.A. **133** D6
St Francis r. U.S.A. **133** D5
St Francis, Cape U.S.A. **128** F2
St Francis Isles Australia **109** F8
St Francis r. Canada **125** I5
St-François France **38** D3
St-François, Lac l. Canada **132** G1
St-Gaudens France **38** D5
St-Geniez-d'Olt France **39** E4
St George Australia **111** G6
St George r. U.S.A. **133** A5
St George Canada **125** H4
St George AK U.S.A. **120** C4
St George UT U.S.A. **137** F3
St George, Point U.S.A. **134** A4
St George Head Australia **112** D4
St George Island U.S.A. **120** C4
St George Range hills Australia **108** D4
St-Georges Canada **125** H3
St-Georges Fr. Guiana **147** I4

▶St George's Grenada **139** L6
  Capital of Grenada.

St George's Bay Nfld. and Lab. Canada
  125 J3
St George's Bay N.S. Canada **125** I4
St George's Channel India **73** G5
St George's Channel P.N.G. **107** F7
St George's Channel
  Rep. of Ireland/U.K. **35** C6
St-Germain-du-Puy France **38** E3
St-Germain-les-Belles France **38** D4
St-Gildas, Pointe de pt France **38** B3
St-Gildas-des-Bois France **38** B3
St-Gilles France **39** F5
St-Gilles-Croix-de-Vie France **38** B3
St Helen U.S.A. **130** C1
St Helena i. S. Atlantic Ocean **160** N7
St Helena U.S.A. **136** B2

▶St Helena and Dependencies terr.
  S. Atlantic Ocean **160** N7
  United Kingdom Overseas territory.
  Consists of St Helena, Ascension,
  Tristan da Cunha and Gough Island.
  africa 100

St Helena Bay S. Africa **98** C7

St Helens Australia **112** D6
St Helens U.K. **35** E5
St Helens U.S.A. **134** B3
▶St Helens, Mount vol. U.S.A. **134** B3
  world 10–11
St Helens Point Australia **112** D6

▶St Helier Channel Is **38** B2
  Capital of Jersey.

St-Hilaire-du-Harcouët France **38** C2
St-Hyacinthe Canada **125** F4
St Ignace U.S.A. **132** E2
St Ignace Island Canada **124** C3
St Ives U.K. **35** D6
St-Jacques, Cap Vietnam see Vung Tau
St-Jacques-de-Dupuy Canada **132** G1
St James France **38** C2
St James MN U.S.A. **132** C3
St James MO U.S.A. **132** D4
St James NY U.S.A. **131** G3
St James, Cape Canada **122** D5
St-Jean r. Canada **125** I3
St-Jean, Lac l. Canada **125** F3
St-Jean-d'Acre Israel see 'Akko
St-Jean-de-la-Ruelle France **38** D3
St-Jean-de-Luz France **38** C5
St-Jean-de-Maurienne France **39** H4
St-Jean-de-Monts France **38** B3
St-Jean-de-Port-Joli Canada **125** F3
St-Jérôme Canada **125** F4
St Joe r. U.S.A. **134** C3
Saint John r. Liberia **92** C4
St John U.S.A. **132** D4
St John r. U.S.A. **128** C2
St John Bay Canada **125** J3
St John Island Virgin Is (U.S.A.) **139** L5

▶St John's Antigua and Barbuda **139** L5
  Capital of Antigua and Barbuda.

▶St John's Canada **125** K4
  Provincial capital of Newfoundland.

St Johns AZ U.S.A. **137** H4
St Johns MI U.S.A. **130** C2
St Johns OH U.S.A. **130** A3
St Johns r. U.S.A. **129** C6
St Johnsbury U.S.A. **131** G1
St Johnsville U.S.A. **131** F2
St Joseph r. Canada **125** H4
St Joseph MI U.S.A. **132** C4
St Joseph r. MI U.S.A. **130** A3
St Joseph, Lake Canada **124** B2
St-Joseph-d'Alma Canada see Alma
St Joseph Island U.S.A. **133** B7
São Vicente, Cabo de c. see
  St Vincent, Cape
St-Juéry France **38** E5
St-Julien-en-Genevois France **39** G3
St-Junien France **38** D4
St-Just-en-Chaussée France **38** E3
St-Just-St-Rambert France **39** F4
St Kilda i. U.K. **34** A3

▶St Kitts and Nevis country
  West Indies **139** L5
  northamerica 118–119, 140

St-Laurent, Golfe du g. Canada see
  St Lawrence, Gulf of
St-Laurent-du-Maroni Fr. Guiana
  147 H3
St Lawrence Australia **111** G4
St Lawrence inlet Canada **125** G3
St Lawrence, Gulf of Canada **125** I3
St Lawrence Island U.S.A. **120** C3
St Lawrence Islands National Park
  Canada **131** F1
St Lawrence Seaway sea chan.
  Canada/U.S.A. **131** F1
St-Léonard N.B. Canada **125** H4
St-Léonard Que. Canada **125** H3
St Leonard U.S.A. **131** E4
St-Léonard-de-Noblat France **38** D4
St Lewis r. Canada **125** J2
St-Lô France **38** C2
St-Louis Senegal **92** A1
St Louis MI U.S.A. **130** A2
St Louis MO U.S.A. **127** H4
St Louis r. U.S.A. **132** C2
St-Loup-sur-Semouse France **39** G3
▶St Lucia country West Indies **139** L6
  northamerica 118–119, 140
St Lucia, Lake S. Africa **99** G6
St Lucia Channel Martinique/St Lucia
  139 L6
St Luke's Island Myanmar see
  Zadetkale Kyun
St Magnus Bay U.K. **34** [inset]
St-Maixent-l'École France **38** C3
St-Malo France **38** C2
St-Malo, Golfe de g. France **38** B2
St-Marcellin France **39** F4
St Margaret's Hope U.K. **34** G2
Saint Maries U.S.A. **134** C3

▶St Martin i. West Indies **139** L5
  Dependency of Guadeloupe (France).
  The southern part of the island is the
  Dutch territory of Sint Maarten.

St Martin, Lake Canada **134** H2
St-Martin-de-Crau France **39** F5
St-Martin-de-Ré France **38** C3
St-Martin-d'Hères France **39** F4
St Mary r. Canada **123** H5
St Mary Peak Australia **112** B4
St Marys Australia **112** D6
St Marys Canada **130** D2
St Mary's i. U.K. **35** C7
St Marys OH U.S.A. **130** A3
St Marys PA U.S.A. **130** D3
St Marys WV U.S.A. **130** C4
St Marys r. U.S.A. **130** A3
St Mary's, Cape Canada **125** K4
St Mary's Bay Canada **125** K4
St Marys City U.S.A. **131** E4
St Matthew Island U.S.A. **120** B3
St Matthew's Island Myanmar see
  Zadetkyi Kyun
St Matthias Group is P.N.G. **106** F7
St-Maximin-la-Ste-Baume France
  39 F5
St Michaels U.S.A. **131** E4
St Michael's Bay Canada **125** J3
St Michael's Mount tourist site U.K.
  35 D6
St-Michel-des-Saints Canada **125** F4
St-Mihiel France **39** F2
St-Nazaire France **38** B3
St Nicolas Belgium see Sint-Niklaas
St-Nicolas-de-Port France **39** G2
St-Omer France **38** E1
St Pais U.S.A. **138** B4
St Paris U.S.A. **130** A3
St Paul Canada **123** I4
St Paul r. Canada **125** J3
St Paul r. Liberia **92** C4

▶St Paul MN U.S.A. **132** C2
  State capital of Minnesota.

St Paul NE U.S.A. **132** D3
St Paul VA U.S.A. **130** B5

St Paul, Île i. Indian Ocean **163** M8
St-Paul-de-Fenouillet France **39** E5
St Paul Island U.S.A. **120** B4
St-Paul-lès-Dax France **38** C5

▶St Peter Port Channel Is **38** B2
  Capital of Guernsey.

St Peter's Canada **125** I4
St Peters Canada **125** I4
St Petersburg Rus. Fed. **28** D4
  world 16–17
St Petersburg U.S.A. **129** C7
St Petrus i. Indon. **59** F2
St-Philbert-de-Grand-Lieu France **38** C3
St-Pierre mt. France **39** F5
St Pierre Mauritius **97** [inset]

▶St-Pierre St Pierre and Miquelon **125** K4
  Capital of St Pierre and Miquelon.

St-Pierre, Lac l. Canada **125** F4

▶St Pierre and Miquelon terr.
  N. America **125** J4
  French Territorial Collectivity.
  northamerica 118–119, 140

St-Pierre-des-Corps France **38** D3
St-Pierre-d'Oléron France **38** C4
St-Pierre-le-Moûtier France **39** F3
St-Pol-sur-Ternoise France **38** E1
St-Pons-de-Thomières France **39** E5
St-Pourçain-sur-Sioule France **39** E3
St Quentin Canada **125** H4
St-Quentin France **38** E2
St-Raphaël France **39** H5
St Regis U.S.A. **134** F1
St-Rigaud, Mont mt. France **39** F3
St-Savin France **38** C4
St-Savinien France **38** C4
St-Sébastien-sur-Loire France **38** C3
St Siméon Canada **125** H3
St-Sorlin, Mont de mt. France **39** G3
St-Symphorien France **38** C4
St Terese U.S.A. **122** C4
St Theresa Point Canada **123** M4
St-Tite-des-Caps Canada **125** F3
St-Tropez France **39** H5
St-Tropez, Cap de c. France **39** G5
St-Vallier Bourgogne France **39** F3
St-Vallier Rhône-Alpes France **39** F4
St-Vincent, Cap c. Madag. see
  Ankaboa, Tanjona
St Vincent, Cape Australia **112** C6
St Vincent, Cape Port. see
  São Vicente, Cabo de
St Vincent, Gulf Australia **112** A4
▶St Vincent and the Grenadines
  country West Indies **139** L6
  northamerica 118–119, 140
St-Vincent-de-Tyrosse France **38** C5
St Vincent Passage St Lucia/St Vincent
  139 L6
St-Yrieix-la-Perche France **38** E4
Saipal mt. Nepal **75** D3
Saipan i. N. Mariana Is **57** K2
Saison r. France **38** C5
Saittarana Sweden **32** I1
Saivomuotka Sweden **32** I1
Sai Yok National Park Thai. **61** B5
Sajama, Nevado mt. Bol. **148** C4
Sajó r. Hungary **37** J5
Šájúr, r. Syria/Turkey **77** D1
Sajzi Iran **80** C3
Sak watercourse S. Africa **98** D6
Saka Eth. **96** C2
Sakai Japan **65** D6
Sakaide Japan **65** C6
Sakaiminato Japan **65** C6
Sakākah Saudi Arabia **89** I2
Sakakawea, Lake U.S.A. **134** C3
Sakala i. Indon. **59** G4
Sakalili Tanz. **97** A7
Sakami r. Canada **124** F2
Sakami Lake Canada **124** F2
Sakaraha Madag. **99** [inset] J4
Sakartvelo country Asia see Georgia
Sakarya Turkey **78** C2
Sakarya r. Turkey **78** C2
Sakassou Côte d'Ivoire **92** C4
Sakata Japan **65** D5
Sakchu N. Korea **65** A4
Sa Keo r. Thai. **61** C5
Sakété Benin **93** F4
Sakhalin i. Rus. Fed. **64** F2
Sakhalin Oblast admin. div. Rus. Fed.
  see Sakhalinskaya Oblast'
Sakhalinskaya Oblast' admin. div.
  Rus. Fed. **64** E2
Sakhalinskiy Zaliv b. Rus. Fed. **27** O4
Sakhile S. Africa **99** I5
Sakhra Syria **77** D2
Sakht-Sar Iran **80** B2
Şāki Azer. **79** F2
Saki Nigeria see Shaki
Saki Ukr. see Saky
Šakiai Lith. **33** M3
Sakishima-shotō is Japan **63** K7
Sa-koi Myanmar **60** B4
Sakrand Pak. **81** G5
Sakri India **74** C3
Sakrivier S. Africa **98** D6
Sakshaug Norway **32** G4
Sakti India **75** D5
Saku Estonia **33** N2
Sakura-jima vol. Japan **65** B7
Saky Ukr. **29** E7
Sal i. Cape Verde **92** [inset]
Sal r. Rus. Fed. **29** G7
Šaľa Slovakia **37** H4
Sala Sweden **33** J4
Salaberry-de-Valleyfield Canada
  125 F4
Sala Consilina Italy **45** E4
Salada, Bahía b. Chile **152** C1
Salada, Laguna salt l. Mex. **137** E5
Saladas Arg. **152** F2
Saladillo Arg. **152** E4
Saladillo r. Córdoba Arg. **152** E3
Saladillo r. Santa Fé Arg. **152** E3
  152 E2
Salado Ecuador **146** B5
Salado r. Mex. **126** G6
Salado r. Spain **42** D4
Salado watercourse U.S.A. **135** F6

Saladou Guinea **92** C3
Salaga Ghana **93** E3
Şalāḩ, Tall hill Jordan **77** D3
Şalāḩ ad Dīn governorate Iraq **79** E4
Šalajwe Botswana **98** F2
Salakh, Jabal mt. Oman **76** F5
Salal Chad **88** C6
Sálala Sudan **89** H4
Şalālah Oman **76** E6
Salalé well Niger **93** I2
Salamá Guat. **138** F7
Salamanca Chile **152** C2
Salamanca Mex. **126** F7
Salamanca Spain **42** D2
Salamanca U.S.A. **130** D2
Salamanga Moz. **99** G5
Salamantica Spain see Salamanca
Salamat pref. Chad **94** D2
Salamina Greece **47** C6
Salamina i. Greece **47** C6
Salamina tourist site Cyprus **77** A2
Salamis i. Greece see Salamina
Salamiyah Syria **77** C2
Salandi r. India **73** E1
Salantai Lith. **33** L3
Salar de Pocitos Arg. **148** D6
Salas Spain **42** C1
Salas de los Infantes Spain **42** E1
Salat r. France **38** D5
Salatiga Indon. **59** E4
Salavat Rus. Fed. **29** J5
Salawati i. Indon. **57** H6
Salawin, Mae Nam r. China/Myanmar
  54 B5 see Salween
Salaya India **74** A5
Salayar i. Indon. **57** G8
Sala y Gómez, Isla i. S. Pacific Ocean
  165 K7
Salazar Angola see N'dalatando
Salazar Arg. **152** E4
Salbris France **38** E3
Salccantay, Cerro mt. Peru **148** B3
Saldae Alg. see Bejaïa
Saldana Col. **146** C2
Saldaña Spain **42** D1
Saldanha S. Africa **98** C7
Saldus Latvia **33** L4
Sale Australia **112** C7
Salé Morocco **90** D1
Sale U.K. **35** E5
Salé, Île i. !sole Lipari Italy **45** E5
Säle U.S.A. **138** F5
Salé Italy **45** E5
Salebabu i. Indon. **57** H6
Salem India **72** C4
Salem AR U.S.A. **133** D4
Salem IL U.S.A. **128** A4
Salem MO U.S.A. **132** D4
Salem NJ U.S.A. **131** F4
Salem NY U.S.A. **131** F2

▶Salem OR U.S.A. **134** B3
  State capital of Oregon.

Salem SD U.S.A. **132** B3
Salem VA U.S.A. **130** C5
Salem WV U.S.A. **130** C4
Salemi Sicily Italy **45** D6
Salerno Italy **45** F4
Salerno, Golfo di g. Italy **45** E4
Salernum Italy see Salerno
Salford U.K. **35** E5
Salgada Brazil **147** F5
Salgótarján Hungary **37** I4
Salgueiro Brazil **150** E3
Sali Alg. **91** E4
Salida U.S.A. **135** F5
Salihli Turkey **78** B3
Salihorsk Belarus **29** C5
Saliméni Senegal **92** B2
Salimi Dem. Rep. Congo **95** D7
Salimo Moz. **97** D5
Salina KS U.S.A. **132** B4
Salina UT U.S.A. **137** G2
Salina, Isola i. Isole Lipari Italy **45** E5
Salinas Brazil **151** D6
Salinas Mex. **126** F7
Salinas r. Mex. **133** B7
Salinas U.S.A. **136** B3
Salinas, Cabo de c. Spain see
  Ses Salines, Cap de
Salinas, Ponta das pt Angola **95** B8
Salinas de Garci Mendoza Bol. **148** D4
Salinas Peak U.S.A. **135** F6
Saline r. U.S.A. **130** B2
Saline r. AR U.S.A. **133** D5
Saline r. KS U.S.A. **132** B4
Saline Valley depr. U.S.A. **136** D3
Salineville U.S.A. **130** C3
Salingyi Myanmar **60** A3
Salinópolis Brazil **150** D3
Salinosó Lachay, Punta pt Peru **148** B3
Salisbury U.K. **35** F6
Salisbury MD U.S.A. **131** F4
Salisbury NC U.S.A. **128** C5
Salisbury Zimbabwe see Harare
Salisbury Plain U.K. **35** E6
Sălişte Romania **46** D2
Salitre r. Brazil **150** D4
Salki r. India **73** E1
Salla Fin. **32** H2
Salliquelló Arg. **152** E4
Sallisaw U.S.A. **133** C5
Salluit Canada **121** L3
Sallum, Khalij as Egypt **88** E2
Sallyana Nepal **75** E3
Salmās Iran **80** A2
Salmi Rus. Fed. **28** D3
Salmo Canada **122** G5
Salmon r. U.S.A. **134** D3
Salmon, Middle Fork r. U.S.A. **134** D3
Salmon Arm Canada **134** G3
Salmon Falls Creek r. U.S.A. **134** D4
Salmon Reservoir U.S.A. **131** F2
Salmon River Mountains U.S.A. **134** D3
Sal'niye Tundry, Khrebet mts Rus. Fed.
  32 H1
Salo Cent. Afr. Rep. **94** C4
Salo Fin. **33** F3
Salò Italy **44** D2
Salon-de-Provence France **39** F5
Salonga r. Dem. Rep. Congo **94** D5
Salonica Greece see Thessaloniki
Salonta Romania **46** B1
Salor r. Spain **42** C3
Salou Spain **43** G2
Salou, Cap de c. Spain **43** G2
Saloum watercourse Senegal **92** A2
Salpausselkä reg. Fin. **33** G3
Salsacate Arg. **152** D2
Salsbruket Norway **32** G4
Salses, Étang de l. France see
  Leucate, Étang de
Sal'sk Rus. Fed. **29** G7
Salso r. Sicily Italy **45** D6
Salsomaggiore Terme Italy **44** C2
Salt Jordan see As Salṭ

Salt watercourse S. Africa 98 D7
Salt Spain 43 H2
Salt r. AZ U.S.A. 137 F5
Salt r. MO U.S.A. 132 D4
Salt r. WY U.S.A. 134 E4
Salta Arg. 148 D6
Salta prov. Arg. 152 D1
Saltaire U.K. 35 F5
Saltash U.K. 35 D6
Salt Creek r. U.S.A. 130 B4
Saltee Islands Rep. of Ireland 35 C5
Saltery Bay Canada 134 A2
Saltfjellet Svartisen Nasjonalpark nat. park Norway 32 D2
Salt Fork Arkansas r. U.S.A. 133 B4
Salt Fork Lake U.S.A. 130 C3
Salt Fork Red r. U.S.A. 133 B5
Saltillo Mex. 126 F6
▶Salt Lake City U.S.A. 134 E4
State capital of Utah.
Salt Lick U.S.A. 130 B4
Salto Arg. 152 E3
Salto Brazil 149 I5
Salto r. Italy 44 D3
Salto Uruguay 152 F2
Salto da Divisa Brazil 151 E6
Salto del Guairá Para. 149 G6
Salto Grande, Embalse de resr Uruguay 152 F2
Salton City U.S.A. 137 D5
Salton Sea salt l. U.S.A. 137 E5
Saltpond Ghana 93 E4
Salt River Canada 123 H2
Saltville U.S.A. 130 C5
Saluda SC U.S.A. 129 C5
Saluda VA U.S.A. 131 E5
Saluda r. U.S.A. 129 C5
Salumbar India 74 B4
Saluq, Kūh-e mt. Iran 80 D2
Salur India 73 D2
Saluzzo Italy 44 A2
Salvador Brazil 150 E5
Salvador country Central America see El Salvador
Salvador, Lake U.S.A. 133 D6
Salvador Mazza Arg. 149 E5
Salvaterra Brazil 150 B2
Salviac France 38 D4
Salwah Saudi Arabia 80 B5
Salwah, Dawhat b. Qatar/Saudi Arabia 80 B5
Salween r. China 70 I7
Salween r. China/Myanmar 60 B4
also known as Mae Nam Khong or Thanlwin (Myanmar) or Nu Jiang (China)
Salyan Azer. 79 G3
Sal'yany Azer. see Salyan
Salyersville U.S.A. 130 B5
Salza r. Austria 37 G5
Salzach r. Austria/Germany 37 F4
Salzburg Austria 37 F5
Salzgitter Germany 36 E2
Salzkotten Germany 36 D3
Salzwedel Germany 36 E2
Sam Gabon 94 A4
Sam India 74 A4
Sam, Nam r. Laos/Vietnam 60 D4
Šamac Bos.-Herz. see Bosanski Šamac
Samae San, Laem pt Thai. 61 C5
Samāh well Saudi Arabia 80 A4
Samaida Iran see Someydeh
Samaipata Bol. 149 E4
Samak, Tanjung pt Indon. 58 D3
Samakoulou Mali 92 C2
Samalayuca Mex. 135 F7
Samālūt Egypt 89 F2
Samana India 74 C3
Samana Cay i. Bahamas 129 E8
Samanala mt. Sri Lanka see Adam's Peak
Samandağı Turkey 78 C3
Samangān prov. Afgh. 81 F2
Samangān Iran 81 E3
Samani Japan 64 E4
Samaniego Col. 146 B4
Samanlı Dağları mts Turkey 46 F4
Samannūd Egypt 78 B5
Samar i. Phil. 57 G3
Samara Rus. Fed. 29 I5
Samara r. Rus. Fed. 29 I5
Samarahan Sarawak Malaysia see Sri Aman
Samarai P.N.G. 107 E3
Samara Oblast admin. div. Rus. Fed. see Samarskaya Oblast'
Samarga Rus. Fed. 64 D3
Samaria nat. park Greece 47 C7
Samariapo Venez. 146 E3
Samarinda Indon. 59 G3
Samarka Rus. Fed. 64 C3
Samarkand Uzbek. 81 F2
Samarkand, Pik mt. Tajik. 81 G2
Samarkand Oblast admin. div. Uzbek. see Samarkandskaya Oblast'
Samarkandskaya Oblast' admin. div. Uzbek. 81 F2
Samarobriva France see Amiens
Samarqand Uzbek. see Samarkand
Samarqand, Qullai mt. Tajik. see Samarkand, Pik
Samarqand Wiloyati admin. div. Uzbek. see Samarkandskaya Oblast'
Sāmarrā' Iraq 79 E4
Samarskaya Oblast' admin. div. Rus. Fed. 29 I5
Samasata Pak. 81 G4
Samassi Sardinia Italy 45 B5
Samastipur India 75 E4
Samaúma Brazil 147 F6
Şamaxı Azer. 79 G2
Samba Dem. Rep. Congo 95 E6
Samba r. Indon. 59 F3
Samba Jammu and Kashmir 74 B2
Samba Cajú Angola 95 B7
Sambaliung mts Indon. 59 G2
Sambalpur India 75 D5
Sambar, Tanjung pt Indon. 59 E3
Sambas Indon. 59 E2
Sambat Ukr. see Kiev
Sambava Madag. 99 [inset] K2
Sambhal India 74 C3
Sambhar India 74 B4
Sambhar Lake India 74 B4
Sambir Ukr. 31 J3
Sambo Angola 95 C8
Sambo Indon. 59 G3
Samboja Indon. 59 G3
Sambor Ukr. see Sambir
Sâmbor Dam Cambodia 61 D5
Samborombón, Bahía b. Arg. 152 F3
Samch'ŏnp'o S. Korea see Sach'on
Sameikkon Myanmar 60 A3
Samer France 38 D1
Samet, Ko i. Thai. 61 C5
Samfya Zambia 95 F7
Samhah i. Yemen 76 E7
Sami India 74 A5
Sami Pak. 81 E5
Samiria r. Peru 146 C6
Samirum Iran see Yazd-e Khvāst
Samka Myanmar 60 B3
Şämkir Azer. 79 F2
Sam Neua Laos see Xam Hua
Samnū Libya 88 B3
▶Samoa country S. Pacific Ocean 107 H3
oceania 104–105, 114
Samoa Basin sea feature S. Pacific Ocean 165 G7
Samoa i Sisifo country S. Pacific Ocean see Samoa
Samobor Croatia 44 E2
Samoded Rus. Fed. 28 G3
Samokov Bulg. 46 C3
Šamorín Slovakia 37 H4
Samos Greece 47 E6
Samos i. Greece 47 E6
Samosir i. Indon. 58 B2
Samothrace i. Greece see Samothraki
Samothraki Greece 46 D4
Samothraki i. Greece 47 D4
Samovodene Bulg. 46 D3
Samoylovka Rus. Fed. 29 G6
Sampa Côte d'Ivoire 92 E4
Sampacho Arg. 152 D3
Sampit Indon. 59 F3
Sampit r. Indon. 59 F3
Sampit, Teluk b. Indon. 59 F3
Sampwe Dem. Rep. Congo 95 E7
Sam Rayburn Reservoir U.S.A. 133 C6
Samreboe Ghana 93 E4
Samrong Cambodia see Phumĭ Sâmraông
Samsang China 75 D3
Sam Sao, Phou mts Laos/Vietnam 60 C3
Samsø i. Denmark 33 C5
Samsø Bælt sea chan. Denmark 33 C5
Sâm Son Vietnam 60 D4
Samsun Turkey 78 D2
Samtens Germany 37 F1
Samthar India 74 C4
Samtredia Georgia 79 E2
Samui, Ko i. Thai. 61 C6
Samundri Pak. 81 H4
Samur r. Azer./Rus. Fed. 79 G2
Samut Prakan Thai. 61 C5
Samut Sakhon Thai. 61 C5
Samut Songkhram Thai. 61 C5
San Mali 92 D2
San r. Poland 37 J3
San, Phou mt. Laos 60 C4
San, Tônlé r. Cambodia 61 D5
Sana r. Bos.-Herz. 44 F2
▶Şan'ā' Yemen 76 C6
Capital of Yemen.
Sanaag admin. reg. Somalia 96 E2
San Adrián, Cabo de c. Spain 42 B1
Sanae research station Antarctica 167 B2
Sanaga r. Cameroon 93 H5
San Agostín U.S.A. see St Augustine
San Agustín Col. 146 B4
Sanak Island U.S.A. 120 C4
Sanandaj Iran 80 A3
Sanando Mali 92 D2
San Andreas U.S.A. 136 B2
San Andrés Bol. 149 D3
San Andrés Col. 146 C3
San Andrés, Isla de i. Caribbean Sea 139 H6
San Andrés del Rabanedo Spain 42 D1
San Andres Mountains U.S.A. 135 F6
San Andrés Tuxtla Mex. 138 E5
San Angelo U.S.A. 133 A6
Sanankoroba Mali 92 D2
San Antolín de Ibias Spain 42 C1
San Antonio Chile 152 C1
San Antonio Peru 146 C5
San Antonio NM U.S.A. 135 F6
San Antonio TX U.S.A. 133 B6
San Antonio r. CA U.S.A. 136 B4
San Antonio r. TX U.S.A. 133 B6
San Antonio, Cabo c. Arg. 152 F4
San Antonio, Cabo c. Cuba 127 J7
San Antonio Abad Spain 43 G3
San Antonio de los Cobres Arg. 148 D6
San Antonio de Palé Equat. Guinea 93 G6
San Antonio de Tamanaco Venez. 147 E2
San Antonio Este Arg. 152 D5
San Antonio Oeste Arg. 152 D5
San Antonio Reservoir U.S.A. 136 B4
San Augustín Arg. 152 F4
San Augustín de Valle Fértil Arg. 152 D2
San Augustine U.S.A. 133 C6
Sanawad India 74 C5
San Bartolomeo in Galdo Italy 44 E4
San Benedetto del Tronto Italy 44 D3
San Benedicto, Isla i. Mex. 126 D8
San Benito r. U.S.A. 136 B3
San Benito Mountain U.S.A. 136 B3
San Bernardino U.S.A. 136 D4
San Bernardino, Passo di pass Switz. 39 H3
San Bernardino Mountains U.S.A. 137 D4
San Bernardo Chile 152 C3
San Blas Arg. 152 D2
San Blas, Archipiélago de is Panama 146 B2
San Blas, Cape U.S.A. 129 B6
San Blas, Cordillera de mts Panama 146 B2
San Borja Bol. 148 D3
Sanborn U.S.A. 132 C3
Sanbornville U.S.A. 131 H2
San Buenaventura Mex. 133 A7
Sança Moz. 99 G3
San Candido Italy 44 D1
San Caprasio hill Spain 43 F2
San Carlos Mendoza Arg. 152 C3
San Carlos Salta Arg. 152 D1
San Carlos Chile 152 C4
San Carlos Equat. Guinea see Luba
San Carlos Mex. 133 A6
San Carlos Para. 149 F5
San Carlos Uruguay 152 G3
San Carlos U.S.A. 137 G5
San Carlos Amazonas Venez. 146 E4
San Carlos Apure Venez. 146 E3
San Carlos Cojedes Venez. 146 D2
San Carlos de Bariloche Arg. 152 C5
San Carlos de Bolívar Arg. 152 E4
San Carlos de la Rápita Spain see Sant Carles de la Ràpita
San Carlos del Zulia Venez. 146 D2
San Carlos Lake U.S.A. 137 G5
San Cayetano Arg. 152 F4
San Celoni Spain see Sant Celoni
Sancerre France 39 E3
Sancerrois, Collines du hills France 39 E3
Sancha China 66 C1
Sanchahe China see Fuyu
Sancha He r. China 66 C3
Sanchi India 74 C5
San Chien Pau mt. Laos 60 C3
Sanchor India 74 A4
San Clemente Chile 152 C3
San Clemente U.S.A. 136 D5
San Clemente del Tuyú Arg. 152 F4
San Clemente Island U.S.A. 136 C5
Sancoins France 39 E3
San Cristóbal Arg. 152 E2
San Cristóbal Potosí Bol. 148 D5
San Cristóbal Santa Cruz Bol. 149 E3
San Cristóbal Col. 146 C5
San Cristobal i. Solomon Is 107 F3
San Cristóbal Venez. 146 C3
San Cristóbal de las Casas Mex. 138 F5
San Cristobal Wash watercourse U.S.A. 137 F5
Sancti Spíritus Cuba 127 K7
Sand r. S. Africa 99 F4
Sandakan Sabah Malaysia 59 G1
Sandakphu Peak India 75 F4
Sandanski Bulg. 46 C4
Sandaré Mali 92 C2
Sanday i. U.K. 34 E2
Sandbukt Norway 32 F1
Sand Cay reef India 72 B4
Sande Sogn og Fjordane Norway 33 B3
Sande Vestfold Norway 33 C4
Sandefjord Norway 33 C4
Sandefjord airport Norway 33 C4
Sandercock Nunataks nunataks Antarctica 167 D2
Sanders U.S.A. 137 H4
Sanderson U.S.A. 133 A6
Sandersville U.S.A. 129 C5
Sandfire Roadhouse Australia 108 C4
Sandfloeggi mt. Norway 33 B4
Sand Hill r. U.S.A. 132 B2
Sand Hills U.S.A. 132 A3
Sandhornøy i. Norway 32 D2
Sandi India 74 D4
Sandia Peru 148 C3
San Diego U.S.A. 136 D5
San Diego, Cabo c. Arg. 153 D8
San Diego, Sierra mts Mex. 135 E7
Sandıklı Turkey 78 B3
Sandila India 74 D4
Sanding i. Indon. 58 C3
Sand Lake Canada 123 M5
Sandnes Norway 33 B4
Sandø i. Faroe Is see Sandoy
Sandoa Dem. Rep. Congo 95 D7
Sandomierz Poland 37 J3
Sândominic Romania 46 D1
San Donà di Piave Italy 44 D2
Sandover watercourse Australia 110 D4
Sandovo Rus. Fed. 28 F4
Sandoway Myanmar 60 A4
Sandoy i. Faroe Is 34 [inset]
Sandpoint U.S.A. 134 C2
Sandray i. U.K. 34 C3
Sandringham Australia 110 D5
Sandsele Sweden 32 E2
Sandspit Canada 122 D4
Sand Springs U.S.A. 133 B4
Sand Springs Salt Flat U.S.A. 136 C2
Sandstone Australia 109 B6
Sandstone U.S.A. 132 C2
Sandu Guizhou China 66 C3
Sandu Hunan China 67 E3
Sandur India 72 C3
Sandusky MI U.S.A. 130 B2
Sandusky OH U.S.A. 130 B3
Sandusky Bay U.S.A. 130 B3
Sandveld mts S. Africa 98 C6
Sandvika Akershus Norway 33 C4
Sandvika Nord-Trøndelag Norway 32 D3
Sandviken Sweden 33 E3
Sandwich U.S.A. 131 H3
Sandwich Bay Canada 125 J2
Sandwich Island Vanuatu see Éfaté
Sandwip Bangl. 75 F5
Sandwip Channel Bangl. 75 F5
Sandy U.S.A. 137 G1
Sandy r. U.S.A. 131 I1
Sandy Bay Canada 123 K4
Sandy Cape Qld Australia 111 H5
Sandy Cape Tas. Australia 112 C6
Sandy Creek r. Australia 111 D3
Sandy Island Australia 108 C3
Sandykachi Turkm. 81 E2
Sandykly Gumy des. Turkm. see Sundukli, Peski
Sandy Lake Canada 123 M4
Sandy Lake l. Canada 123 M4
Sandy Springs U.S.A. 129 B5
Sandyville U.S.A. 130 C4
San Estanislao Para. 149 F6
San Fabián de Alico Chile 152 C4
San Felipe Chile 152 C3
San Felipe Baja California Mex. 135 D7
San Felipe Chihuahua Mex. 135 F8
San Felipe Venez. 146 D2
San Feliú de Guíxols Spain see Sant Feliu de Guíxols
San Fernando Arg. 152 F3
San Fernando Chile 152 C3
San Fernando Baja California Mex. 135 D7
San Fernando Tamaulipas Mex. 126 G7
San Fernando Phil. 57 F2
San Fernando Spain 42 C4
San Fernando Trin. and Tob. 147 F2
San Fernando U.S.A. 136 C4
San Fernando de Apure Venez. 146 E3
San Fernando de Atabapo Venez. 146 E3
San Filipe Creek watercourse U.S.A. 137 E5
Sånfjället nationalpark nat. park Sweden 33 D3
Sanford r. Australia 109 A6
Sanford FL U.S.A. 129 C6
Sanford ME U.S.A. 131 H2
Sanford MI U.S.A. 130 A2
Sanford NC U.S.A. 128 D5
San Francisco Arg. 152 E2
San Francisco Mex. 135 D7
▶San Francisco U.S.A. 136 A3
world 16–17
San Francisco r. U.S.A. 135 E6
San Francisco, Paso de pass Arg. 152 C1
San Francisco Bay inlet U.S.A. 136 A3
San Francisco del Oro Mex. 135 F8
San Francisco de Macorís Dom. Rep. 139 J5
San Francisco de Paula, Cabo c. Arg. 153 D7
San Francisco Javier Spain 43 G3
Sanga Dem. Rep. Congo 95 F6
San Gabriel Ecuador 146 B4
San Gabriel, Punta pt Mex. 135 D7
San Gabriel Mountains U.S.A. 136 C4
Sangai, Parque Nacional nat. park Ecuador 146 B5
Sangaigerong Indon. 58 D3
Sa'ngain China 66 A2
Sangam India 72 C3
Sangameshwar India 72 B2
Sangamner India 72 B2
Sangamon r. U.S.A. 132 D3
Sangān Iran 81 D3
Sangan, Koh-i- mt. Afgh. 81 F3
Sangar r. Pak. 81 G4
Sangaréa Guinea 92 B3
Sangareddi India 72 C2
Sangarédi Guinea 92 B3
Sangaria India 74 B3
Sangasanga Indon. 59 G3
Sangasso Mali see Zangasso
Sangaste Estonia 33 G4
San Gavino Monreale Sardinia Italy 45 B5
Sangay, Volcán vol. Ecuador 146 B5
Sang Bast Iran 81 D3
Sangbé Cameroon 93 I4
Sangbur Afgh. 81 E3
Sangeang i. Indon. 108 B2
Sanger U.S.A. 136 C3
Sangerfield U.S.A. 131 F2
Sangerhausen Germany 36 E3
Sanggar, Teluk b. Indon. 59 G5
Sanggarmai China 66 B1
Sanggau Indon. 59 E2
Sangha admin. reg. Congo 94 B4
Sangha r. Congo 94 C5
Sangha-Mbaéré pref. Cent. Afr. Rep. 94 C4
Sanghar Pak. 81 G5
San Gil Col. 146 C3
San Giovanni in Fiore Italy 45 F5
Sangir India 74 B5
Sangir i. Indon. 57 G5
Sangir, Kepulauan is Indon. 57 F5
Sangju S. Korea 65 B5
Sangkapura Indon. 59 F4
Sângke, Stœng r. Cambodia 61 C5
Sangkulirang Indon. 59 G2
Sangkulirang, Teluk b. Indon. 59 G2
Sangla Pak. 81 H4
Sangli India 72 B2
San Glorio, Puerto de pass Spain 42 D1
Sangmélima Cameroon 93 H5
Sango Zimbabwe 99 F4
Sangod India 74 C4
Sangole India 72 B2
Sangpi China see Xiangcheng
Sang Qu r. China 66 A2
Sangre de Cristo Range mts U.S.A. 135 F5
Sangre Grande Trin. and Tob. 147 F2
Sangri China 75 G3
Sangro r. Italy 44 E3
Sangrur India 74 B3
Sangsang China 75 E3
Sangu r. Bangl. 75 F5
Sangue r. Brazil 149 F2
Sangüesa Spain 43 F1
San Guiliano Milanese Italy 44 B2
Sangū'īyeh Iran 80 D4
Sangzhi China 67 D2
Sanhe China see Sandu
San Hipólito, Punta pt Mex. 135 D8
Sanhūr Egypt 89 F2
San Ignacio Beni Bol. 148 D3
San Ignacio Santa Cruz Bol. 149 E4
San Ignacio Santa Cruz Bol. 149 E4
San Ignacio Mex. 135 D8
San Ignacio Para. 149 F6
San Ignacio Peru 146 B6
San Ignacio, Laguna l. Mex. 135 D8
Sanikiluaq Canada 124 E1
Sanin-kaigan National Park Japan 65 C6
Sanitz Germany 37 F1
Sāniyat al Fawākhir well Libya 88 C3
San Jacinto Peak U.S.A. 137 D5
Sanjai r. India 75 E5
San Jaime Arg. 152 F2
San Javier Arg. 152 F2
San Javier Beni Bol. 148 D3
San Javier Santa Cruz Bol. 149 E4
Sanjawi Pak. 81 G4
Sanjbod Iran 80 B2
Sanjiang Guangxi China 67 D3
Sanjiang Guizhou China see Jinping
Sanjō Japan 65 D5
San Joaquín Bol. 148 D3
San Joaquín Para. 149 F6
San Joaquin U.S.A. 136 B3
San Joaquin r. U.S.A. 136 B2
San Joaquin Valley U.S.A. 136 B3
San Jon U.S.A. 135 G6
San Jorge Arg. 152 E2
San Jorge, Golfo de g. Arg. 153 D6
San Jorge, Golfo de g. Spain see Sant Jordi, Golf de
▶San José Costa Rica 139 H7
Capital of Costa Rica.
San Jose Phil. 57 F2
San Jose CA U.S.A. 136 B3
San Jose NM U.S.A. 135 F6
San Jose watercourse U.S.A. 135 F6
San José Venez. 146 E2
San José, Cabo c. Arg. 153 D6
San José, Cuchilla de hills Uruguay 152 F2
San José, Golfo g. Arg. 153 D5
San José, Isla i. Mex. 126 D7
San José, Volcán vol. Chile 152 C3
San José de Amacuro Venez. 147 F2
San Jose de Buenavista Phil. 57 F3
San José de Chiquitos Bol. 149 E4
San José de Comondú Mex. 126 D6
San José de Gracia Mex. 135 E7
San José de Jáchal Arg. 152 C2
San José de la Dormida Arg. 152 E2
San José del Boquerón Arg. 152 E1
San José del Cabo Mex. 126 E7
San José del Guaviare Col. 146 C4
San José de Mayo Uruguay 152 F3
San José de Ocuné Col. 146 D3
San Juan Arg. 152 C2
San Juan prov. Arg. 152 C2
San Juan Bol. 149 E4
San Juan Col. 146 B2
San Juan r. Col. 146 B3
San Juan r. Costa Rica/Nicaragua 139 H6
San Juan Mex. 135 F8
San Juan Peru 148 B3
▶San Juan Puerto Rico 139 K5
Capital of Puerto Rico.
San Juan r. CA U.S.A. 136 B4
San Juan r. UT U.S.A. 137 G3
San Juan Venez. 147 E3
San Juan, Cabo c. Equat. Guinea 93 H5
San Juan Bautista Para. 149 F6
San Juan Bautista Spain 43 G3
San Juan Bautista Tuxtepec Mex. 138 E5
San Juan Capistrano U.S.A. 136 D5
San Juan de César Col. 146 C2
San Juan dela Costa Chile 152 B5
San Juan de la Peña, Sierra de mts Spain 43 F1
San Juan de los Cayos Venez. 146 D2
San Juan de los Morros Venez. 146 E2
San Juan del Río Mex. 126 G7
San Juan de Salvamento Arg. 153 E8
San Juan Islands U.S.A. 134 B2
San Juanito Mex. 135 F8
San Juan Mountains U.S.A. 135 F5
San Julián Arg. 153 D7
San Just mt. Spain 43 F2
San Justo Arg. 152 E2
Sankarani r. Côte d'Ivoire/Guinea 92 C3
Sankarankovil India 72 C4
Sankeshwar India 72 B2
Sankh r. India 75 E5
Sankosh r. Bhutan see Sunkosh
Sankra Chhattisgarh India 73 D1
Sankra Rajasthan India 74 A4
Sankt Andrä Austria 37 G5
Sankt Gallen Switz. 39 H3
Sankt Gotthard Hungary see Szentgotthárd
Sankt Moritz Switz. 39 H3
Sankt-Peterburg Rus. Fed. see St Petersburg
Sankt Peter-Ording Germany 36 D1
Sankt Pölten Austria 37 G4
Sankt Veit an der Glan Austria 37 G5
Sankt Wendel Germany 36 C4
Sankuru r. Dem. Rep. Congo 95 D6
San Leandro U.S.A. 136 A3
San Leonardo in Passiria Italy 44 C1
Şanlıurfa Turkey 79 D3
San Lorenzo Arg. 152 E3
San Lorenzo Beni Bol. 148 D3
San Lorenzo Pando Bol. 148 D2
San Lorenzo Tarija Bol. 148 D5
San Lorenzo Ecuador 146 B4
San Lorenzo Mex. 135 F7
San Lorenzo Peru 148 C2
San Lorenzo mt. Spain 42 E1
San Lorenzo, Cabo c. Ecuador 146 A5
San Lorenzo, Cerro mt. Arg./Chile 153 B6
Sanlúcar de Barrameda Spain 42 C4
San Lucas Bol. 148 D5
San Lucas Baja California Sur Mex. 126 E7
San Lucas Baja California Sur Mex. 135 D8
San Lucas, Serranía de mts Col. 146 C3
San Luis Arg. 152 D3
San Luis prov. Arg. 152 D3
San Luis Peru 146 C5
San Luis AZ U.S.A. 137 E5
San Luis CO U.S.A. 135 F5
San Luis, Sierra de mts Arg. 152 D3
San Luisito Mex. 135 D7
San Luis Obispo U.S.A. 136 B4
San Luis Obispo Bay U.S.A. 136 B4
San Luis Potosí Mex. 126 F7
San Luis Reservoir U.S.A. 136 B3
San Luis Río Colorado Mex. 135 D6
Sanluri Sardinia Italy 45 B5
San Manuel U.S.A. 137 G5
San Marcello Pistoiese Italy 44 C2
San Marcos Col. 146 C2
San Marcos U.S.A. 133 B6
▶San Marino country Europe 44 D3
europe 24–25, 48
▶San Marino San Marino 44 D3
Capital of San Marino.
San Martín research station Antarctica 167 L2
San Martín Catamarca Arg. 152 D2
San Martín Mendoza Arg. 152 C3
San Martín r. Bol. 149 E3
San Martín dept Peru 148 A1
San Martín, Lago l. Arg./Chile 153 B7
San Martín de los Andes Arg. 152 C5
San Martín de Valdeiglesias Spain 42 D2
San-Martino-di-Lota Corsica France 39 H5
San Mateo Peru 146 D5
San Mateo U.S.A. 136 A3
San Mateo Venez. 147 E2
San Matías Bol. 149 F4
San Matías, Golfo g. Arg. 152 D5
San Mauricio Venez. 146 E2
Sanmen China 67 G2
Sanmen Wan b. China 67 G2
Sanmenxia China 67 D1
San Miguel Bol. 149 E4
San Miguel r. Bol. 149 E3
San Miguel r. Col. 146 C4
San Miguel El Salvador 138 G6
San Miguel Panama 146 B2
San Miguel U.S.A. 136 B4
San Miguel de Horcasitas r. Mex. 135 E7
San Miguel de Huachi Bol. 148 D3
San Miguel de Tucumán Arg. 152 D1
San Miguel do Araguaia Brazil 150 B5
San Miguel Island U.S.A. 136 B4
San Miguel Islands Phil. 59 G1
San Miguelito Panama 146 B2
Sanming China 67 F3
San Miniato Italy 44 C3
Sanndatti India 72 B3
Sanndraigh i. U.K. see Sandray
Sannicandro Garganico Italy 44 E4
San Nicolás de los Arroyos Arg. 152 E3
San Nicolas Island U.S.A. 136 C5
Sânnicolau Mare Romania 46 B1
Sanniquellie Liberia 92 C4
Sanok Poland 31 J3
San Onofre Col. 146 C2
San Pablo Arg. 153 D8
San Pablo Bol. 148 D5
San Pablo r. Bol. 149 E3
San Pablo Col. 146 D3
San Pablo Phil. 57 F3
San Pablo de Manta Ecuador see Manta
San Pedro Buenos Aires Arg. 152 F3
San Pedro Catamarca Arg. 152 D1
San Pedro Jujuy Arg. 148 D6
San Pedro Misiones Arg. 152 G1
San Pedro Bol. 149 E4
San-Pédro Côte d'Ivoire 92 D4
San Pedro Mex. 126 F7
San Pedro r. Mex. 135 F7
San Pedro watercourse U.S.A. 137 G5
San Pedro, Sierra de mts Spain 42 C3
San Pedro Channel U.S.A. 136 C5
San Pedro de Atacama Chile 148 C5
San Pedro de las Colonias Mex. 126 F6
San Pedro del Pinatar Spain 43 F4
San Pedro de Macorís Dom. Rep. 139 K5
San Pedro de Ycuamandyyú Para. 149 F6
San Pedro el Saucito Mex. 135 E7
San Pedro Mártir, Parque Nacional nat. park Mex. 135 D7
San Pedro Sula Hond. 138 G5
San Pietro, Isola di i. Sardinia Italy 45 B5
San Pietro in Cariano Italy 44 C2
San Pitch r. U.S.A. 137 G2
Sanquhar U.K. 34 E4
Sanquianga, Parque Nacional nat. park Col. 146 B4
San Quintín, Cabo c. Mex. 135 C7
San Rafael Arg. 152 C3
San Rafael Bol. 149 E4
San Rafael U.S.A. 136 A3
San Rafael r. U.S.A. 137 G2
San Rafael Venez. 146 D2
San Rafael del Moján Venez. see San Rafael
San Rafael Knob mt. U.S.A. 137 G2
San Rafael Mountains U.S.A. 136 B4
San Ramón Beni Bol. 148 D3
San Ramón Santa Cruz Bol. 149 E4
San Remo Italy 44 A3
San Rodrigo watercourse Mex. 133 A6
San Roque Andalucía Spain 42 D4
San Roque Galicia Spain 42 B1
San Roque Galicia Spain 42 B1
San Saba U.S.A. 133 B6
San Saba r. U.S.A. 133 B6
Sansalé Guinea 92 B3
San Salvador Arg. 152 F2
San Salvador i. Bahamas 129 E7
▶San Salvador El Salvador 138 G6
Capital of El Salvador.
San Salvador de Jujuy Arg. 148 D6
San Salvo Italy 44 E3
Sansanné Haoussa Niger 93 F2
Sansanné-Mango Togo 93 F3
San Sebastián Arg. 153 C8
San Sebastián hill Spain 42 B1
San Sebastián, Bahía de b. Arg. 153 C8
San Sebastián de los Reyes Spain 42 E2
Sansepolcro Italy 44 D3
San Severino Marche Italy 44 D3
San Severo Italy 44 E4
San Silvestre Bol. 148 C2
Sanski Most Bos.-Herz. 44 F2
Sansoral Islands Palau see Sonsorol Islands
Sansui China 67 D3
Santa Peru 148 A2
Santa r. Peru 148 A2
Santa Ana Arg. 152 D1
Santa Ana La Paz Bol. 148 D3
Santa Ana Santa Cruz Bol. 149 F4
Santa Ana El Salvador 138 G6
Santa Ana Mex. 135 E7
Santa Ana U.S.A. 136 D5
Santa Ana de Yacuma Bol. 148 D3
Santa Anna U.S.A. 133 B6
Santa Bárbara Brazil 149 F3
Santa Bárbara Mex. 126 E6
Santa Bárbara mt. Spain 43 E4
Santa Barbara U.S.A. 136 C4
Santa Bárbara Venez. 146 D3
Santa Bárbara, Serra de hills Brazil 151 A7
Santa Barbara Channel U.S.A. 136 B4
Santa Bárbara d'Oeste Brazil 149 I5
Santa Barbara do Sul Brazil 151 A9
Santa Barbara Island U.S.A. 136 C5
Santa Catalina Chile 152 C1
Santa Catalina Venez. 147 F2
Santa Catalina, Gulf of U.S.A. 136 D5
Santa Catalina de Armada Spain 42 B1
Santa Catalina Island U.S.A. 136 C5
Santa Catarina state Brazil 151 B8
Santa Catarina Baja California Mex. 135 D7
Santa Catarina Nuevo León Mex. 133 A7
Santa Catarina, Ilha de i. Brazil 151 B8
Santa Clara Cuba 127 K7
Santa Clara r. Mex. 135 F7
Santa Clara r. U.S.A. 136 C4
Santa Clara, Barragem de resr Port. 42 B4
Santa Clarita U.S.A. 136 C4
Santa Clotilde Peru 146 C5
Santa Coloma de Gramanet Spain 43 H2
Santa Comba Angola see Waku-Kungo
Santa Comba Dão Port. 42 B2
Santa Croce Camerina Sicily Italy 45 E6
Santa Cruz prov. Arg. 153 C7
Santa Cruz r. Arg. 153 C7
Santa Cruz Bol. 149 E4
Santa Cruz dept Bol. 149 E4
Santa Cruz Pará Brazil 147 H5
Santa Cruz Pará Brazil 150 B2
Santa Cruz mt. Spain 43 F2
Santa Cruz U.S.A. 136 A3
Santa Cruz watercourse U.S.A. 137 G5
Santa Cruz Cabrália Brazil 151 E6
Santa Cruz de la Palma Canary Is 90 A3
Santa Cruz del Sur Cuba 127 K7
Santa Cruz de Mudela Spain 42 E3
▶Santa Cruz de Tenerife Canary Is 90 A3
Joint capital of the Canary Islands.
Santa Cruz do Sul Brazil 151 A9
Santa Cruz Island U.S.A. 136 C4
Santa Cruz Islands Solomon Is 107 F3
Santa Elena Arg. 152 F2
Santa Elena Bol. 148 D5
Santa Elena Venez. 147 F3
Santa Elena, Cabo c. Costa Rica 138 G6
Santa Elena, Punta pt Ecuador 146 A5
Santa Eufemia, Golfo di g. Italy 45 F5
Santa Eugenia Spain 42 B1
Santa Eulalia del Río Spain 43 G3
Santa Fé Arg. 152 E2
Santa Fé prov. Arg. 152 E2
Santa Fe Spain 42 E4
▶Santa Fe U.S.A. 135 F6
State capital of New Mexico.
Santa Fé de Bogotá Col. see Bogotá
Santafé de Bogotá municipality Col. 146 C4
Santa Fé do Sul Brazil 149 H5
Sant'Agata di Militello Sicily Italy 45 E5
Santa Helena Brazil 150 C2
Santa Helena de Goiás Brazil 149 H4
Santai China 66 C2
Santa Inês Bahia Brazil 150 E5
Santa Inês Maranhão Brazil 150 C2
Santa Inés, Isla i. Chile 153 B8
Santa Isabel Arg. 152 D4
Santa Isabel Brazil 149 E3
Santa Isabel Equat. Guinea see Malabo
Santa Isabel i. Solomon Is 107 E2
Santa Isabel, Ilha Grande de i. Brazil 150 D2
Santa Isabel, Sierra mts Mex. 135 D7
Santa Isabel do Araguaia Brazil 150 B3
Santalpur India 74 A5
Santa Lucia Chile 148 C5
Santa Lucía Ecuador 146 B5
Santa Lucía, Cerro de mt. Spain 42 D4
Santa Lucia Range mts U.S.A. 136 B3
Santa Luzia Maranhão Brazil 150 C3
Santa Luzia Paraíba Brazil 150 E3
Santa Luzia i. Cape Verde 92 [inset]
Santa Magdalena Arg. 152 E3
Santa Margarita Arg. 152 E2
Santa Margarita U.S.A. 136 B4
Santa Margarita, Isla i. Mex. 126 D7
Santa María Arg. 152 D1
Santa Maria Brazil 149 E3
Santa Maria Amazonas Brazil 147 G5
Santa Maria Pará Brazil 147 H5
Santa Maria Rio Grande do Sul Brazil 151 A9
Santa Maria Cape Verde 92 [inset]
Santa María r. Mex. 135 F7
Santa Maria U.S.A. 136 B4
Santa Maria r. U.S.A. 137 F4
Santa María Venez. 146 E3
Santa Maria, Cabo de c. Moz. 99 G5
Santa Maria, Cabo de c. Port. 42 C4
Santa Maria, Chapadão de hills Brazil 150 C5
Santa María, Punta pt Peru 148 B3
Santa Maria, Serra de hills Brazil 150 C5
Santa Maria das Barreiras Brazil 150 B4
Santa Maria da Vitória Brazil 150 C5
Santa María de Ipire Venez. 147 E2
Santa Maria di Leuca, Capo c. Italy 45 G5
Santa Maria do Suaçuí Brazil 151 D6
Santa María Island Vanuatu 107 F3
Santa María Mountains U.S.A. 137 F4
Santa Marina Salina Isole Lipari Italy 45 E5
Santa Marta Col. 146 C2
Santa Maura i. Greece see Lefkada

Santa Monica U.S.A. **136** C4
Santa Monica Bay U.S.A. **136** C5
Santan Indon. **59** G3
Santana Brazil **150** D5
Sântana Romania **46** B1
Santana da Boa Vista Brazil **152** G2
Santana do Acarau Brazil **150** D4
Santana do Araguaia Brazil **150** B4
Santana do Livramento Brazil **152** G2
Santander Col. **146** B4
Santander *dept* Col. **146** C3
Santander Spain **42** E1
Santa Nella U.S.A. **136** B3
Sant'Angelo Lodigiano Italy **44** B2
Santanilla, Islas *is Caribbean Sea see*
Swan Islands
Santan Mountain U.S.A. **137** G4
Sant'Antioco *Sardinia* Italy **45** B5
Sant'Antioco, Isola di *i. Sardinia* Italy
45 B5
Santañy Spain *see* Santanyí
Santanyí Spain **43** H3
Santa Paula U.S.A. **136** C4
Santapilly India **73** D2
Santa Pola Spain **43** F3
Santa Pola, Cabo de *c.* Spain **43** F3
Santaquin U.S.A. **137** G2
Santa Quitéria Brazil **147** H5
Santarém Brazil **147** H5
Santarém Port. **42** B3
Santarém *admin. dist.* Port. **42** B3
Santa Rita *Mato Grosso* Brazil **149** F1
Santa Rita *Paraíba* Brazil **150** F3
Santa Rita Col. **146** C4
Santa Rita Mex. **133** A7
Santa Rita *Guárico* Venez. **146** E2
Santa Rita *Zulia* Venez. **146** D2
Santa Rita do Pardo Brazil **149** G5
Santa Rita do Weil Brazil **146** D5
Santa Rosa *Corrientes* Arg. **152** F2
Santa Rosa *La Pampa* Arg. **152** D4
Santa Rosa *Río Negro* Arg. **152** D4
Santa Rosa *Salta* Arg. **148** D6
Santa Rosa Bol. **148** C2
Santa Rosa *Acre* Brazil **148** C2
Santa Rosa *Rio Grande do Sul* Brazil
151 A8
Santa Rosa Col. **146** D4
Santa Rosa Ecuador **146** B5
Santa Rosa Para. **149** D6
Santa Rosa *Loreto* Peru **146** C5
Santa Rosa *Puno* Peru **148** C3
Santa Rosa *CA* U.S.A. **136** A2
Santa Rosa *NM* U.S.A. **135** F6
Santa Rosa Venez. **146** E4
Santa Rosa and San Jacinto
Mountains National Monument
nat. park U.S.A. **137** D5
Santa Rosa de Copán *Hond.* **138** G6
Santa Rosa de la Roca Bol. **149** E4
Santa Rosa del Conlara Arg. **152** C3
Santa Rosa de Osos Col. **146** C3
Santa Rosa de Vigo Bol. **148** D3
Santa Rosa Island U.S.A. **136** B5
Santa Rosalía Mex. **135** D8
Santa Rosa Mountains U.S.A. **137** C4
Santa Rosa Range *mts* U.S.A. **134** C3
Santa Rosa Wash *watercourse* U.S.A.
137 F5
Santa Sylvina Arg. **152** E1
Santa Teresa Australia **110** C5
Santa Teresa *r.* Brazil **150** B4
Santa Teresa Mex. **133** B7
Santa Teresa, Embalse de *resr* Spain
42 D2
Santa Teresa di Gallura *Sardinia* Italy
44 B4
Santa Terezinha Brazil **150** B4
Santa Vitória Brazil **149** H4
Santa Vitória do Palmar Brazil **152** G3
Santa Vittoria, Monte *mt. Sardinia* Italy
45 B5
Santa Ynez *r.* U.S.A. **136** B4
Santa Ysabel *i.* Solomon Is *see*
Santa Ysabel
Sant Carles de la Ràpita Spain **43** G2
Sant Celoni Spain **43** H2
Santee *r.* U.S.A. **129** D5
Santerno *r.* Italy **44** D2
Sant Feliu de Guíxols Spain **43** H2
Santiago Brazil **151** A9

▶ **Santiago** Chile **152** C3
Capital of Chile.
southamerica 144–145

Santiago *admin. reg.* Chile **152** C3
Santiago *Baja California Sur* Mex. **126** E7
Santiago *Nuevo León* Mex. **133** A7
Santiago Panama **139** H7
Santiago *r.* Peru **146** B6
Santiago, Cabo *c.* Chile **153** B7
Santiago, Sierra de *hills* Bol. **149** F4
Santiago de Cao Peru **146** B6
Santiago de Compostela Spain **42** B1
Santiago de Cuba Cuba **127** K7
Santiago de la Espada Spain **43** E3
Santiago del Estero Arg. **152** D2
Santiago del Estero *prov.* Arg. **152** E1
Santiago de los Caballeros Dom. Rep.
see Santiago
Santiago de Méndez Ecuador **146** B5
Santiago de Pacaguaras Bol. **148** D3
Santiago do Cacém Port. **42** B3
Santiago Vázquez Uruguay **152** F3
San Timoteo Venez. **146** D2
Santipur India *see* Shantipur
Santisteban del Puerto Spain **42** E3
Sant Jordi, Golf de *g.* Spain **43** G2
Santo Amaro Brazil **150** E6
Santo Amaro de Campos Brazil **151** D7
Santo André Brazil **151** C7
Santo Ángelo Brazil **151** F3

▶ **Santo Antão** *i.* Cape Verde **92** [inset]
Most westerly point of Africa.

Santo Antônio *Amazonas* Brazil **147** F5
Santo Antônio *Maranhão* Brazil **150** C3
Santo Antônio *Rio Grande do Norte*
Brazil **150** F3
Santo Antônio *r.* Brazil **151** D6
Santo Antônio São Tomé and Príncipe
93 G5
Santo Antônio de Jesus Brazil **150** E5
Santo Antônio de Leverger Brazil
149 F3
Santo Antônio do Içá Brazil **146** E5
Santo Antônio dos Cavaleiros Port.
42 B3
Santo Antônio do Zaire Angola *see* Soyo
Santo Corazón Bol. **149** F4

▶ **Santo Domingo** Dom. Rep. **139** K5
Capital of the Dominican Republic.

Santo Domingo Mex. **135** D7
Santo Domingo Peru **148** D3
Santo Domingo *country* West Indies *see*
Dominican Republic
Santo Domingo Pueblo U.S.A. **135** F6
Santo Tirso Port. **42** B2
Santoña Spain **42** E1
Santong *r.* China **64** A4
Santorini *i.* Greece *see* Thira

Santos Brazil **151** C7
Santos Mercado Bol. **148** D2
Santos Plateau *sea feature*
S. Atlantic Ocean **161** K7
Santo Stefano di Camastra *Sicily* Italy
45 E5
Santo Tomás *Chihuahua* Mex. **135** F7
Santo Tomás *Sonora* Mex. **135** D7
Santo Tomás Peru **148** B3
Santo Tomé Arg. **152** F2
Santrampur India **74** B5
San Valentín, Cerro *mt.* Chile **153** B6
San Vicente El Salvador **138** G6
San Vicente Mex. **135** C7
San Vicente de Cañete Peru **148** B3
San Vicente del Caguán Col. **146** C4
San Vicente del Raspeig Spain **43** F3
San Vincenzo Italy **44** C3
San Vito, Capo *c. Sicily* Italy **45** D5
San Vito Chietino Italy **44** F3
San Vito dei Normanni Italy **45** F4
Sanwer India **74** B5
Sanya China **67** D5
San Yanaro Col. **146** D4
Sanyuan China **67** F1
Sanyuan *r.* Zimbabwe **99** F3
Sanza Pombo Angola **95** C6
Sao, Phou *mt.* Laos **60** C4
São Benedito Brazil **150** D4
São Bento *Amazonas* Brazil **148** D1
São Bento *Maranhão* Brazil **150** C2
São Bento *Roraima* Brazil **147** F3
São Bento do Norte Brazil **150** F3
São Bernardo Brazil **150** D2
São Bernardo do Campo Brazil **151** C7
São Borja Brazil **152** F2
São Carlos *Rondônia* Brazil **149** D2
São Carlos *Rondônia* Brazil **149** E2
São Carlos *São Paulo* Brazil **149** I5
São Desidério Brazil **150** C5
São Domingos Brazil **150** C5
São Félix *Mato Grosso* Brazil **150** B4
São Félix *Pará* Brazil **147** I6
São Fidélis Brazil **151** C7
São Francisco *Acre* Brazil **148** C2
São Francisco *Amazonas* Brazil **147** F6
São Francisco *Minas Gerais* Brazil
150 C5
São Francisco *r.* Brazil **148** D2

▶ **São Francisco** *r.* Brazil **150** E4
5th longest river in South America.
southamerica 142–143

São Francisco, Ilha de *i.* Brazil **151** B8
São Francisco de Assis Brazil **151** A9
São Francisco do Sul Brazil **151** B3
São Gabriel Brazil **151** A9
São Gonçalo Brazil **151** D7
São João Brazil **146** E5
São João, Ilhas de *is* Brazil **150** C2
São João, Serra de *hills* Brazil **149** D2
São João da Aliança Brazil **150** C5
São João da Barra Brazil **151** D7
São João da Madeira Port. **42** B2
São João del Rei Brazil **151** C7
São João do Araguaia Brazil **150** B3
São João do Cariri Brazil **150** F3
São João do Paraíso Brazil **150** D5
São João do Piauí Brazil **150** D4
São João do Sul Angola **95** B8
São Joaquim *Amazonas* Brazil **146** E4
São Joaquim *Santa Catarina* Brazil
151 B9
São José *Amazonas* Brazil **146** E5
São José *Santa Catarina* Brazil **151** A9
São José do Anauá Brazil **147** F4
São José de Belmonte Brazil **150** E3
São José do Egito Brazil **150** E3
São José do Norte Brazil **152** G3
São José do Peixe Brazil **150** D3
São José dos Campos Brazil **151** C7
São José dos Pinhais Brazil **151** B8
São Lourenço *r.* Brazil **149** H5
São Lourenço do Sul Brazil **152** H2
São Lucas Angola **95** C7
São Luís *Pará* Brazil **150** C2
São Luís *Maranhão* Brazil **147** G6
São Luís de Montes Belos Brazil
149 H4
São Luís do Quitunde Brazil **150** F4
São Luis Gonzaga Brazil **151** A9
São Manuel Brazil **149** H5
São Marceline Brazil **146** E4
São Marcos *r.* Brazil **149** I4
São Marcos, Baía de *b.* Brazil **150** C2
São Martinho Brazil **147** G6
São Mateus Brazil **151** E6
São Mateus do Sul Brazil **151** B8
São Miguel *i.* Azores **160** M3
São Miguel do Tapuio Brazil **150** D3
São Miguel Jesuit Missions *tourist site*
Brazil **151** A9
Saône *r.* France **39** F4
São Nicolau Angola *see* Bentiaba
São Nicolau *i.* Cape Verde **92** [inset]

▶ **São Paulo** Brazil **149** I5
Most populous city in South America
and 3rd in the world.
world 16–17

São Paulo *state* Brazil **149** H5
São Paulo de Olivença Brazil **146** E5
São Pedro *Amazonas* Brazil **147** G6
São Pedro *Rondônia* Brazil **149** E2
São Pedro da Aldeia Brazil **151** D7
São Pedro do Sul Brazil **151** A9
São Pedro do Sul Port. **42** B2
São Pedro e São Paulo *is*
N. Atlantic Ocean **160** M5
São Pires *r.* Brazil *see* Teles Pires
São Raimundo Nonato Brazil **150** D3
São Romão *Amazonas* Brazil **146** E6
São Romão *Minas Gerais* Brazil **151** C6
São Salvador Angola *see*
M'banza Congo
São Salvador do Congo Angola *see*
M'banza Congo
São Sebastião *Amazonas* Brazil **148** C1
São Sebastião *Pará* Brazil **147** H6
São Sebastião *Rondônia* Brazil **149** E2
São Sebastião *São Paulo* Brazil **151** C7
São Sebastião, Ilha do *i.* Brazil **151** C7
São Sebastião da Boa Vista Brazil
150 B2
São Sebastião do Paraíso Brazil
151 C7
São Simão Brazil **149** F5
São Simão, Barragem de *resr* Brazil
149 H4
Sao-Siu Indon. **57** G5
São Tiago *i.* Cape Verde **92** [inset]

▶ **São Tomé** São Tomé and Príncipe **93** G5
Capital of São Tomé and Príncipe.

São Tomé *i.* São Tomé and Príncipe **93** G5
São Tomé, Cabo de *c.* Brazil **151** D7
São Tomé, Pico de *mt.*
São Tomé and Príncipe **93** G5

▶ **São Tomé and Príncipe** *country* Africa
93 G5
africa 86–87, 100

Saoura, Oued *watercourse* Alg. **90** E3
São Vicente Brazil **151** C7
São Vicente *i.* Cape Verde **92** [inset]
São Vicente, Cabo de *c.* Port. **42** B4
Sápai Greece *see* Sapes
Sapallanga Peru **148** B3
Sapanca Turkey **78** B2
Sapapeguá India *see* Ichapur
Sapo National Park Liberia **92** C4
Sapele Nigeria **93** G4
Sapelo Island U.S.A. **129** D6
Sapes Greece **46** B2
Sapienza *i.* Greece **47** B6
Sapo, Serranía del *mts* Panama **146** B3
Sapouy Burkina **93** G3
Sappa Creek *r.* U.S.A. **132** B3
Sapporo Japan **64** F3
Sapucaia Brazil **147** G5
Sapudi *i.* Indon. **59** F4
Sapulpa U.S.A. **133** D4
Sapulut *Sabah* Malaysia **59** G1
Saqi Iran **81** D3
Saqqaq Greenland **121** N2
Sarā Iran **80** A2
Sarāb Iran **80** A2
Sarābil y al Khādim *tourist site* Egypt
77 A5
Sarābiyum Egypt **77** A4
Sara Buri Thai. **61** C5
Saracá, Lago *l.* Brazil **147** G5
Saragossa Spain *see* Zaragoza
Sarai Sidhu Pak. **81** H4
Saraji Iran **80** B3
Saraktash Rus. Fed. **26** C5
Saramati *mt.* India/Myanmar **75** G4
Sarameriza Peru **146** B6
Saran, Gunung *mt.* Indon. **59** E3
Saranac *r.* U.S.A. **131** G1
Saranac Lake U.S.A. **131** F1
Sarandë Albania **47** B5
Sarandi Brazil **151** A8
Sarandi del Yí Uruguay **152** G3
Sarandi Grande Uruguay **152** G3
Sarangani Islands Phil. **57** G4
Sarangarh India **75** D5
Sarangpur India **74** C5
Saransk Rus. Fed. **28** J4
Saraswati *r.* India **74** A5
Sarata Ukr. **46** M2
Sărata *r.* Moldova **46** M1
Sărata *r.* Romania **46** E2
Sarata Ukr. **29** D7
Sarata *r.* Ukr. **46** F2
Saratoga *CA* U.S.A. **136** A3
Saratoga *WY* U.S.A. **134** F4
Saratoga Springs U.S.A. **131** G2
Saratok *Sarawak* Malaysia **59** E2
Saratov Rus. Fed. **29** H6
Saratov Oblast *admin. div.* Rus. Fed.
see Saratovskaya Oblast'
Saratovskaya Oblast' *admin. div.*
Rus. Fed. **29** H5
Saratovskoye Vodokhranilishche *resr*
Rus. Fed. **29** H5
Saravan Iran **81** F5
Saravan Laos **60** D5
Sarawa *r.* Myanmar **61** B5
Sarawak *state* Malaysia **59** F2
Saray Turkey **78** A2
Saraya Guinea **92** C3
Saraya Senegal **92** C3
Saraya, Pulau *i.* Sing. **58** [inset]
Saraykôy Turkey **78** B3
Sarayönü Turkey **78** B3
Sarbaz Iran **81** E5
Sarbaz *r.* Iran **81** F5
Sârbeni Romania **46** D2
Sarbhang Bhutan **75** F4
Sarbisheh Iran **81** D3
Sarbogárd Hungary **44** G1
Sarcham Iran **80** D2
Sarco Chile **152** C2
Sardab Pass Afgh. **81** G2
Sardarpur India **74** B5
Sardarshahr India **74** B3
Sardasht Iran **80** B4
Sardegna *admin. reg.* Italy **45** B4
Sardegna *i.* Italy *see* Sardinia
Sardica Bulg. *see* Sofia
Sardinia *i.* Italy **45** C4
Sardis Lake *resr* U.S.A. **133** D5
Sardoal Port. **42** B3
Sareb, Rás-as- *pt* U.A.E. **80** B5
Sareks nationalpark *nat. park* Sweden
32 J2
Sarektjåkkå *mt.* Sweden **32** J2
Sarempaka, Gunung *mt.* Indon. **59** F3
Sar-e Pol Afgh. **81** F2
Sar-e Pol Afgh. **81** F2
Sar Eskandar Iran *see* Hashtrud
Sare Yazd Iran **80** C4
Sargasso Sea N. Atlantic Ocean **160** I4
Sargentu Loros Peru **146** C5
Sargodha Pak. **81** H3
Sarh Chad **94** C2
Sarhro, Jbel *mt.* Morocco **90** D1
Sārī Iran **80** C2
Saria *i.* Greece **47** L7
Sar-i-Bum Afgh. **81** F3
Sáric Mex. **135** F7
Sarichioi Romania **46** F2
Sarigöl Turkey **47** M5
Sarıkamış Turkey **79** F2
Sarıkaya Turkey **78** D2
Sarikei *Sarawak* Malaysia **59** E2
Sarikemer Turkey *see* Belören
Sarıköl *mts* China/Tajik. *see*
Sarykol Range
Sarikül, Qatorkühi *mts* China/Tajik. *see*
Sarykol Range
Sarina Australia **111** E4
Sariñena Spain **43** F2
Sari-i-Pul Afgh. **81** F3
Sāri Qamish Iran **80** C2
Sariqamish Kuli *salt l.* Turkm./Uzbek.
see Sarykamyshskoye Ozero
Sarir Tibesti *des.* Libya **88** E2
Sarir Water Wells Field Libya **88** D3
Sarishabari Bangl. **75** F4
Sarita U.S.A. **133** D7
Sariveller Turkey **78** C3
Sariwön N. Korea **65** A5
Sariyer Turkey **78** B2
Sarız Turkey **78** D3
Sarkad Hungary **37** J5
Sark *i.* Channel Is **38** B2
Sarkad Hungary **37** J5
Sarkari Tala India **74** A4

Şarkikaraağaç Turkey **78** B3
Şarkışla Turkey **78** D3
Şarköy Turkey **78** A2
Sarlath Range *mts* Afgh./Pak. **81** F4
Sarlat-la-Canéda France **38** D4
Sarmanovo Rus. Fed. **28** J5
Sarmento *r.* Italy **45** F4
Sarmi Indon. **57** I6
Sarmiento Arg. **152** C6
Sarmiento *r.* Italy **45** F4
Särna Sweden **33** D3
Särnate Latvia **33** L4
Sarnen Switz. **39** I3
Sarni India *see* Amla
Sarnia Canada **130** B2
Sarny Ukr. **29** C6
Sarolangun Indon. **58** C3
Saroma-ko *l.* Japan **64** F3
Saronikos Kolpos *g.* Greece **47** C6
Saros Körfezi *b.* Turkey **78** A2
Sarotra India **74** B4
Sarova Rus. Fed. **29** G5
Sarowbi Afgh. **81** H3
Sarpa, Ozero *l.* Rus. Fed. **29** H7
Sarpan *i.* N. Mariana Is *see* Rota
Sarpol-e Zahab Iran **80** B3
Sarpsborg Norway **33** G7
Sarqant Kazakh. *see* Sarkand
Sarre *r.* France **39** G2
Sarrebourg France **39** G2
Sarreguemines France **39** G2
Sarre-Union France **39** G2
Sarria Spain **42** C1
Sarrión Spain **43** F2
Sarro Mali **92** C3
Sars Rus. Fed. **27** Q4
Sartène *Corsica* France **44** B4
Sarthe *r.* France **38** C3
Sarti Greece **47** C4
Sartu China *see* Daqing
Sarud, Rūdkhāneh-ye *r.* Iran **80** B3
Saruhanlı Turkey **78** A3
Sarupsar India **74** B3
Sarur India **74** B3
Saru Tara *tourist site* Afgh. **81** F4
Sarwar India **74** A4
Sarya *r.* India **72** E3
Sarygamysh Köli *salt l.* Turkm./Uzbek.
see Sarykamyshskoye Ozero
Sary-Ishikotrau, Peski *des.* Kazakh. *see*
Saryyesik-Atyrau, Peski
Sarykamys Kazakh. **29** J7
Sarykamyshskoye Ozero *salt l.*
Turkm./Uzbek. **76** I1
Sarykol Range *mts* China/Tajik. **81** H2
Saryozek Kazakh. **70** E3
Saryqamys Kazakh. *see* Sarykamys
Saryshagan Kazakh. **70** D2
Sarysu *watercourse* Kazakh. **70** C2
Sary-Tash Kyrg. **62** A4
Sary Yazikskoye Vodokhranilishche
resr Turkm. **81** E2
Saryyesik-Atyrau, Peski *des.* Kazakh.
70 E2
Sarzana Italy **44** C2
Sasak Indon. **58** B2
Sasar, Tanjung *pt* Indon. **108** B2
Sasaram India **75** E4
Sásd Hungary **44** G1
Sasebo Japan **65** B6
Saskatchewan *prov.* Canada **134** F1
Saskatchewan *r.* Canada **123** K4
Saskatoon Canada **134** F1
Saskylakh Rus. Fed. **27** L2
Saslaya *mt.* Nicaragua **139** H6
Sasolburg S. Africa **99** C5
Sasovo Rus. Fed. **29** G5
Sassandra Côte d'Ivoire **92** D4
Sassandra *r.* Côte d'Ivoire **92** D4
Sassari *Sardinia* Italy **45** B4
Sassnitz Germany **37** F1
Sasso Marconi Italy **44** D2
Sasso *r.* Italy **44** C3
Sass Town Liberia **92** C4
Sassuolo Italy **44** D2
Sastre Arg. **152** E2
Sasvad India **72** B2
Sasykköl *l.* Kazakh. *see* Sasykkol', Ozero
Satadougou Mali **92** C3
Satahual *i.* Micronesia *see* Satawal
Satana India **72** B1
Satara India **72** B2
Satara India **72** B2
Satawal *i.* Micronesia **57** K4
Sätbaev Kazakh. *see* Satpayev
Satchinez Romania **46** B2
Satéma Cent. Afr. Rep. **94** C3
Satengar *i.* Indon. **59** G4
Satevó Mex. **135** F8
Satilla *r.* U.S.A. **129** D6
Satiri Burkina **92** D3
Satırlar Turkey *see* Yeşilova
Satka Rus. Fed. **26** F4
Satkania Bangl. **75** H5
Satkhira Bangl. **75** F5
Satluj *r.* India/Pak. *see* Sutlej
Satmala Range *hills* India **72** C2
Satna India **74** D4
Sátoraljaújhely Hungary **37** J4
Satorina *mt.* Croatia **44** F2
Satpayev Kazakh. **70** C2
Satpura Range *mts* India **74** B5
Satsuma-hantō *pen.* Japan **65** B7
Sattahip Thai. **61** C4
Sattenapalle India **72** D2
Satthwa Myanmar **60** A4
Satti Jammu and Kashmir **74** C2
Satu Mare Romania **31** J4
Satun Thai. **61** C7
Saubi *i.* Indon. **59** F4
Sauce Arg. **152** E2
Sauceda Mountains U.S.A. **137** D5
Saucillo Mex. **135** F7
Sauda Norway **33** E7
Saúda U.S.A. **135** F7
Saudárkrókur Iceland **32** [inset]

▶ **Saudi Arabia** *country* Asia **76** C5
asia 52–53, 82

Sauêruiná *r.* Brazil **149** F3
Saugeen *r.* Canada **130** C1
Saugerties U.S.A. **131** G2
Saugues France **38** F4
Säüjbolägh Iran *see* Mahābād
Saujil Arg. **152** C2
Saujon France **38** D4
Sauk Center U.S.A. **132** C2
Saul Fr. Guiana **147** H4
Sauland Norway **33** F7
Sauldre *r.* France **38** E3
Saulgau Germany **36** D4
Saulieu France **39** F3
Sault Sainte Marie Canada **124** C4
Sault Sainte Marie U.S.A. **132** D2
Saumalköl Kazakh. **26** F3
Saumarez Reef Australia **111** H4

Saumlakki Indon. **57** H7
Saumur France **38** C3
Saunders, Mount Australia **110** B2
Saunders Island Antarctica **167** J1
Saungka Myanmar **60** B2
Saurimo Angola **95** D7
Sausalito U.S.A. **136** A3
Sausar India **74** C5
Sava *r.* Europe **44** F2
Savai'i *i.* Samoa **107** H3
Savala *r.* Rus. Fed. **29** G6
Savalou Benin **93** F4
Savane *r.* Canada **125** G3
Savane Moz. **99** D5
Savanna U.S.A. **132** D3
Savannah *GA* U.S.A. **129** D5
Savannah *TN* U.S.A. **128** C5
Savannah *r.* U.S.A. **129** D5
Savanna-la-Mar Jamaica **139** I5
Savant Lake Canada **123** M4
Savantvadi India *see* Vadi
Savanur India **72** C3
Sävar Sweden **32** K3
Săvârşin Romania **46** C1
Savaştepe Turkey **78** A3
Savè Benin **93** F3
Save *r.* France **39** D5
Save Moz. **99** D6
Save *r.* Moz./Zimbabwe **99** G4
Säveh Iran **80** B3
Savelugu Ghana **93** E3
Savenay France **38** C3
Savernake Guyana **147** G3
Saverne France **39** G2
Savigliano Italy **44** A2
Savinja *r.* Slovenia **44** F1
Savinskiy Rus. Fed. **28** G3
Savio *r.* Italy **44** D2
Savitaipale Fin. **33** G3
Šavnik Yugo. **46** A3
Savona Italy **44** C2
Savonlinna Fin. **33** H3
Savonranta Fin. **32** H3
Savoonga U.S.A. **120** B3
Savoy *reg.* France **39** G4
Savşat Turkey **79** F2
Sävsjö Sweden **33** D4
Savu *i.* Indon. **57** F8
Savudrija, Rt *pt* Croatia **44** D2
Savukoski Fin. **32** H2
Savur Turkey **79** E3
Savute *r.* Botswana **98** E3
Saw Myanmar **60** B3
Sawah-Lunto Indon. **58** C3
Sawai Madhopur India **74** C4
Sawan Indon. **59** F4
Sawankhalok Thai. **60** B4
Sawanur India **72** C3
Sawara Japan **65** D6
Sawatch Range *mts* U.S.A. **134** F5
Sawda', Jabal as *hills* Libya **88** B2
Sawhāj Egypt **89** F3
Sawi, Ao *b.* Thai. **61** B5
Sawla Ghana **93** E3
Sawmills Zimbabwe **99** F3
Sawn China **66** A4
Şawqirah *b.* Oman **76** F6
Şawqirah Bay Oman *see*
Şawqirah, Dawḩat
Sawtell Australia **112** E3
Sawtooth Range *mts ID* U.S.A. **134** D3
Sawtooth Range *mts WA* U.S.A. **134** B2
Sawu *i.* Indon. **57** F8
Sawu *i.* Indon. *see* Savu
Sawu Sea Indon. **57** F7
Saxby *r.* Australia **111** E3
Saxnäs Sweden **32** I2
Saxon Germany *see* Sachsen
Saxony *land* Germany *see* Sachsen
Saxony-Anhalt *land* Germany *see*
Sachsen-Anhalt
Saxton U.S.A. **130** A5
Say Niger **93** F2
Sayabouri Laos *see* Muang Xaignabouri
Sayak Kazakh. **70** E2
Sayalkudi India **72** C4
Sayam *well* Niger **93** I2
Sayán Peru **148** A2
Sayano-Shushenskoye
Vodokhranilishche *resr* Rus. Fed. **62** E1
Sayaq Kazakh. *see* Sayak
Sayat Turkm. **81** F2
Sayda Lebanon *see* Sidon
Sayер, Ozero *l.* Kazakh. **70** F2
Sayghan Afgh. **81** F3
Sayhūt Yemen **76** E6
Sayingpan China **66** B3
Saykhin Kazakh. **29** H6
Saylac Somalia **96** D2
Saylan *country* Asia *see* Sri Lanka
Saynshand Mongolia **63** J3
Sayot Turkm. *see* Sayat
Say-Ötesh Kazakh. *see* Say-Utes
Şayqal, Baḩr *imp. l.* Syria **77** C3
Saýqyn Kazakh. *see* Saykhin
Sayram Hu *salt l.* China **70** F3
Sayre *PA* U.S.A. **131** F3
Sayre *OK* U.S.A. **133** B5
Sayreville U.S.A. **131** F3
Sayula Mex. **135** F7
Say-Utes Kazakh. **79** H1
Sayward Canada **122** E5
Sayyod Turkm. *see* Sayat
Sazan *i.* Albania **47** A4
Sázava *r.* Czech Rep. **37** F3
Sazonovo Rus. Fed. **28** E4
Sbaa Alg. **91** E3
Sbeïtla Tunisia **91** H7
Sbiba Tunisia **45** B7
Scafell Pike *hill* U.K. **35** E4
Scalea Italy **45** E5
Scaletta Zanclea *Sicily* Italy **45** E5
Scalloway U.K. **34** F1
Scandicci Italy **44** C3
Scansano Italy **44** C3
Scânteia Romania **46** E2
Scapa Flow *inlet* U.K. **34** E2
Scarba *i.* U.K. **34** D3
Scarborough Canada **130** D2
Scarborough Trin. and Tob. **147** F6
Scarborough U.K. **35** F4
Scarborough Shoal *sea feature*
S. China Sea **56** E2
Scarinish U.K. **34** C3
Scarp *i.* U.K. **34** C2
Scarpanto *i.* Greece *see* Karpathos
Scèdro *i.* Croatia **44** F3
Schaalsee *l.* Germany **36** E1
Schaffhausen Switz. **39** H3
Schagen Neth. **36** B2
Schakalskuppe Namibia **98** C5
Schao *watercourse* Afgh./Iran **81** E3
Scharbeutz Germany **36** E1
Schärding Austria **37** F4
Scharhörn *sea feature* Germany **36** D1
Scheeßel Germany **36** D2
Schefferville Canada **125** I2
Schell Creek Range *mts* U.S.A. **137** E2
Schellburg U.S.A. **130** D3

Schellville U.S.A. **136** A2
Schenectady U.S.A. **131** G2
Schenefeld Germany **36** D2
Schertz U.S.A. **133** B6
Schesaplana *mt.* Austria/Switz. **39** H3
Schiermonnikoog *i.* Neth. **36** C2
Schiermonnikoog Nationaal Park
nat. park Neth. **36** C2
Schiers Switz. **39** H3
Schignano Italy **44** C2
Schio Italy **44** D2
Schirmeck France **39** G2
Schiza *i.* Greece **47** B6
Schladen Germany **36** E2
Schladming Austria **37** F5
Schlei *r.* Germany **36** E1
Schleswig Germany **36** D1
Schleswig-Holstein *land* Germany **36** D1
Schleswig-Holsteinisches Wattenmeer,
Nationalpark *nat. park* Germany **36** D1
Schlosshof *tourist site* Austria **37** H4
Schloß Wartburg *tourist site* Germany
36 E3
Schluchsee Germany **36** D5
Schlüchtern Germany **36** D3
Schmidt Island U.S.A. **131** E4
Schmidta, Ostrov
Schneidemühl Poland *see* Piła
Schneverdingen Germany **36** D2
Schoharie U.S.A. **131** F2
Schöllkrippen Germany **36** D3
Schönebeck (Elbe) Germany **36** E2
Schönefeld *airport* Germany **37** F2
Schöpfl *hill* Austria **37** G4
Schorfheide *reg.* Germany **37** F2
Schouten Island Australia **112** D6
Schouten Islands P.N.G. **57** K7
Schrems Austria **37** G4
Schrobenhausen Germany **36** E4
Schroon Lake U.S.A. **131** G2
Schröttersburg Poland *see* Płock
Schulenburg U.S.A. **133** E6
Schull Rep. of Ireland **35** B6
Schultz Lake Canada **123** L1
Schuyler U.S.A. **132** D3
Schuyler Lake U.S.A. **131** F2
Schuylerville U.S.A. **131** G2
Schwabach Germany **36** E4
Schwäbische Alb *mts* Germany **36** D5
Schwäbisch Hall Germany **36** D4
Schwabmünchen Germany **36** E4
Schwanden Switz. **39** H3
Schwandorf Germany **36** F4
Schwaner, Pegunungan *mts* Indon.
59 F3
Schwarzenbek Germany **36** E2
Schwarzenberg Germany **37** F3
Schwarzer Mann *hill* Germany **36** C3
Schwarzrand *mts* Namibia **98** C5
Schwarzwald *mts* Germany *see*
Black Forest
Schwaz Austria **36** E5
Schwedeneck Germany **36** E1
Schwedt an der Oder Germany **37** G2
Schweinfurt Germany **36** E3
Schweiz *country* Europe *see* Switzerland
Schwerin Germany **36** E2
Schweriner See *l.* Germany **36** E2
Schwyz Switz. **39** H3
Sciacca *Sicily* Italy **45** D6
Scicli *Sicily* Italy **45** E6
Science Hill U.S.A. **130** A5
Scilly, Isles of U.K. **35** C7
Scio U.S.A. **130** C3
Scioto *r.* U.S.A. **137** F2
Scobey U.S.A. **134** F2
Scodra Albania *see* Shkodër
Scofield Reservoir U.S.A. **137** G2
Scone Australia **112** D4
Scordia *Sicily* Italy **45** E6
Scoresby Land *reg.* Greenland **121** Q2
Scoresbysund Greenland *see*
Ittoqqortoormiit
Scoresby Sund *sea chan.* Greenland *see*
Kangertittivaq
Scorniceşti Romania **46** D2
Scorpion Bight *b.* Australia **109** D6
Scorzè Italy **44** D2
Scotia Ridge *sea feature*
S. Atlantic Ocean **161** K9
Scotia Sea S. Atlantic Ocean **161** L9
Scotland *admin. div.* U.K. **34** E3
Scotstown Canada **131** I1
Scott, Cape Australia **110** B2
Scott, Mount U.S.A. **133** B5
Scott Base *research station* Antarctica
167 I1
Scottburgh S. Africa **99** F6
Scott City U.S.A. **132** A4
Scott Coast Antarctica **167** H1
Scott Glacier Antarctica **167** I1
Scott Island Antarctica **167** H2
Scott Islands Canada **122** D5
Scott Mountains Antarctica **167** D2
Scottsbluff U.S.A. **134** G4
Scottsboro U.S.A. **129** C5
Scottsburg U.S.A. **128** C4
Scottsdale Australia **112** C6
Scottsville *KY* U.S.A. **128** B5
Scottsville *VA* U.S.A. **130** D5
Scottville U.S.A. **132** C2
Scourie U.K. **34** D2
Scranton U.S.A. **131** F3
Scugog, Lake Canada **130** D1
Scunthorpe U.K. **35** F5
Scuol Switz. **39** I3
Scupi Macedonia *see* Skopje
Scutari Albania *see* Shkodër
Scutari, Lake Albania/Yugo. **46** A3
Seaboard U.S.A. **131** F5
Seabrook, Lake *salt flat* Australia **109** B7
Seaca Romania **46** D3
Seaford U.S.A. **131** F4
Seaforth Canada **130** C2
Seal *r.* Canada **123** M3
Seal, Cape S. Africa **98** D7
Sea Lake Australia **112** B4
Seal Cove Canada **125** J3
Sealy U.S.A. **133** B6
Seaman U.S.A. **130** B4
Searcy U.S.A. **127** H4
Searles Lake U.S.A. **136** D4
Searsport U.S.A. **131** I1
Seascale U.K. **35** E4
Seaside *CA* U.S.A. **136** B3
Seaside Park U.S.A. **131** F4
Seattle U.S.A. **134** B3
Seaview Range *mts* Australia **111** F3
Seaville U.S.A. **131** F4
Seba Indon. **108** C2
Sebago Lake U.S.A. **131** H2
Sebangan, Teluk *b.* Indon. **59** F3
Sebangka *i.* Indon. **58** D2
Sebastea Turkey *see* Sivas
Sebastian U.S.A. **129** C7
Sebastián Vizcaíno, Bahía *b.* Mex.
135 D7
Sebastopol Ukr. *see* Sevastopol'
Sebastopol U.S.A. **136** A2
Sebatik *i.* Indon. **59** G1
Sebauh *Sarawak* Malaysia **59** F3
Sebayan, Bukit *mt.* Indon. **59** E3
Sebba Burkina **93** F2
Sebderat Eritrea **89** H6

Sebdou Alg. 91 E2
Sébékoro Mali 92 C2
Sebenico Croatia see Šibenik
Sebennytos Egypt see Samannūd
Sebeş Romania 46 C2
Sebeş r. Romania 46 C1
Sebewaing U.S.A. 130 B2
Sebezh Rus. Fed. 28 D4
Şebinkarahisar Turkey 79 D2
Sebiş Romania 46 C1
Sebisseb, Oued r. Alg. 43 H5
Seblat, Gunung mt. Indon. 58 C3
Sebuku i. Indon. 59 G3
Sebuku r. Indon. 59 G1
Sebuku, Teluk b. Indon. 59 G2
Sečanj Yugo. 46 B2
Secaş r. Romania 46 C1
Secchia r. Italy 44 C2
Seccia Mountains Eth. 96 C3
Sechelt Canada 122 F5
Sechenovo Rus. Fed. 28 H5
Sechura Peru 146 A6
Sechura, Bahía de b. Peru 146 A6
Second Mesa U.S.A. 137 G4
Second Three Mile Opening sea chan. Australia 111 E2
Sečovce Slovakia 37 J4
Secretary Island N.Z. 113 A4
Secunderabad India 72 C2
Seda Latvia 33 G4
Seda Lith. 33 F4
Seda r. Port. 42 B3
Sedalia U.S.A. 132 C4
Sedam India 72 C2
Sedan France 39 F2
Sedan U.S.A. 132 B4
Sedan Dip Australia 111 E3
Seddon N.Z. 113 C3
Seddonville N.Z. 113 B3
Sedeh Fārs Iran 80 C4
Sedeh Khorāsan Iran 81 D3
Sedgewick Canada 134 E1
Sedgwick U.S.A. 131 I1
Sédhiou Senegal 92 B2
Sedico Italy 44 D1
Sedlčany Czech Rep. 37 G4
Sedlets Poland see Siedlce
Sedom Israel 77 B4
Sedona U.S.A. 137 G4
Šeduva Lith. 33 F5
Sędziszów Poland 37 J3
Seebad Heringsdorf Germany 37 G2
Seeberg pass Austria/Slovenia 37 G5
Seehausen (Altmark) Germany 36 E2
Seeheim Namibia 98 C5
Seela Pass Canada 122 B1
Seeley U.S.A. 137 E5
Seelig, Mount Antarctica 167 K1
Seelow Germany 37 G2
Seenu Atoll Maldives see Addu Atoll
Sées France 38 D2
Seesen Germany 36 E3
Seevetal Germany 36 E2
Seferihisar Turkey 47 E5
Sefīd, Kūh-e mt. Iran 80 B3
Sefīd, Kūh-e mts Iran 80 B4
Sefophe Botswana 99 E4
Ségala Mali 92 C2
Segama r. Sabah Malaysia 59 G1
Segamat Malaysia 58 C2
Şegarcea Romania 46 C2
Ségbana Benin 93 F3
Segen Wenz watercourse Eth. 96 C3
Segera Tanz. 97 C6
Segezha Rus. Fed. 28 E3
Seggeur, Oued watercourse Alg. 91 F2
Seghnān Afgh. 81 G2
Segontia U.K. see Caernarfon
Segontium U.K. see Caernarfon
Segonzac France 38 C4
Segorbe Spain 43 F3
Ségou Mali 92 D2
Ségou admin. reg. Mali 92 D2
Segovia Col. 146 C3
Segovia r. Hond./Nicaragua see Coco
Segovia Spain 42 D2
Segozerskoye, Ozero resr Rus. Fed. 28 E3
Segré France 38 C3
Segre r. Spain 43 G2
Seguam Island U.S.A. 120 B4
Séguédine Niger 88 B4
Séguéla Côte d'Ivoire 92 D4
Séguéla Mali 92 D2
Seguin U.S.A. 133 B6
Segura r. Spain 43 F4
Segura, Sierra de mts Spain 43 E4
Sehithwa Botswana 98 D4
Sehore India 74 C5
Sehulea P.N.G. 111 G1
Sehwan Pak. 81 F5
Seiche r. France 38 C3
Seignelay r. Canada 125 G3
Seikpyu Myanmar 60 A3
Seiland i. Norway 32 F1
Seiling U.S.A. 133 B4
Seille r. France 39 G2
Sein, Île de i. France 38 A2
Seinäjoki Fin. 32 F3
Seine r. Canada 124 B3
Seine r. France 39 D2
Seine, Baie de b. France 38 C2
Seine, Sources de la tourist site France 39 F3
Seine, Val de valley France 39 E2
Seipinang Indon. 59 F3
Seitsemisen kansallispuisto nat. park Fin. 33 F3
Sekadau Indon. 59 E2
Sekanak, Teluk b. Indon. 58 D3
Sekatak Bengara Indon. 59 G2
Sekayu Indon. 58 C3
Seke China see Sêrtar
Seke-Banza Dem. Rep. Congo 95 B6
Sekicau, Gunung vol. Indon. 58 D4
Sekoma Botswana 98 D5
Sekondi Ghana 93 E4
Sek'ot'a Eth. 96 C1
Sekūheh Iran 81 E4
Sela Rus. Fed. see Shali
Selagan r. Indon. 58 C3
Selangor state Malaysia 58 C2
Selaru i. Indon. 57 H7
Selatan, Tanjung pt Indon. 59 F4
Selatpanjang Indon. 58 C2
Selawik U.S.A. 120 C3
Selbu Norway 32 C3
Selby U.K. 35 F5
Selby U.S.A. 132 A2
Selbyville U.S.A. 131 F4
Selçuk Turkey 47 E6
Sele r. Italy 45 E4
Selebi-Phikwe Botswana 99 E4
Selebi-Pikwe Botswana see Selebi-Phikwe
Selečka Planina mts Macedonia 46 B4
Selemdzha r. Rus. Fed. 64 B1
Selemdzhinskiy Khrebet mts Rus. Fed. 64 C1
Selendi Turkey 47 F5

▶Selenga r. Rus. Fed. 62 H1
Part of the Yenisey-Angara-Selenga, 3rd longest river in Asia.
asia 50–51

Selenge Dem. Rep. Congo 94 C5
Selenge Mörön r. Mongolia 62 H1
Selenicë Albania 46 A4
Sélestat France 39 G2
Seletar Sing. 58 [inset]
Seletar, Pulau i. Sing. 58 [inset]
Seletar Reservoir Sing. 58 [inset]
Seletyteniz, Ozero salt l. Kazakh. see Siletiteniz, Ozero
Seleucia Turkey see Silifke
Seleucia Pieria Turkey see Samandağı
Seleznevo Rus. Fed. 33 H3
Selfoss Iceland 32 [inset]
Sel'gon Stantsiya Rus. Fed. 64 C2
Selib Rus. Fed. 28 I3
Sélibabi Mauritania 92 B2
Seliger, Ozero l. Rus. Fed. 28 E4
Seligman U.S.A. 137 F4
Selikhino Rus. Fed. 64 D2
Selîma Oasis Sudan 89 F4
Selimiye Turkey 47 E6
Sélingué, Lac de l. Mali 92 C3
Selinnkegni Mali 92 C2
Selinous r. Greece 47 C5
Selinsgrove U.S.A. 131 E3
Selinunte tourist site Sicily Italy 45 D6
Selishchi Rus. Fed. 29 G5
Seliu i. Indon. 59 D3
Selizharovo Rus. Fed. 28 E4
Selje Norway 33 B3
Seljord Norway 33 C4
Selkirk Canada 123 L5
Selkirk U.K. 34 E4
Selkirk Mountains Canada 134 C1
Sellia Marina Italy 45 F5
Sellore Island Myanmar see Saganthit Kyun
Selma AL U.S.A. 129 B5
Selma CA U.S.A. 136 C3
Selmer U.S.A. 128 A5
Selmęt Wielki, Jezioro l. Poland 37 K2
Selong Indon. 59 G5
Selongey France 39 F3
Sélouma Guinea 92 C3
Selous, Mount Canada 122 C2
Selous Game Reserve nature res. Tanz. 97 C7
Selseleh-ye Pīr Shūrān mts Iran 81 E4
Selsey Bill hd U.K. 35 F6
Sel'tso Rus. Fed. 29 E5
Selty Rus. Fed. 28 J4
Selu i. Indon. 108 E1
Seluan i. Indon. 59 D1
Selukwe Zimbabwe see Shurugwi
Selvagens, Ilhas is Madeira 90 B3
Selvānā Iran 80 A2
Selvas reg. Brazil 146 D6
Selway r. U.S.A. 134 D3
Selwyn Lake Canada 123 J2
Selwyn Mountains Canada 122 D1
Selwyn Range hills Australia 111 D4
Seman r. Albania 46 A4
Semangka, Teluk b. Indon. 58 D4
Semarang Indon. 59 E4
Sematan Sarawak Malaysia 59 E2
Semau i. Indon. 108 C2
Semayang, Danau l. Indon. 59 G3
Sembakung r. Indon. 59 G2
Sembawang Sing. 58 [inset]
Sembawang, Sungai r. Sing. 58 [inset]
Sembé Congo 94 B4
Şemdinli Turkey 79 F3
Semenanjung Malaysia pen. Malaysia see Peninsular Malaysia
Semendire Yugo. see Smederevo
Semendua Dem. Rep. Congo 94 C5
Semenic, Vârful mt. Romania 46 C2
Semenivka Ukr. 29 E5
Semenov Rus. Fed. 28 H4
Semenovka Ukr. see Semenivka
Semeru, Gunung vol. Indon. 59 F5
Semey Kazakh. see Semipalatinsk
Semidi Islands U.S.A. 120 D4
Semigorodnyaya Rus. Fed. 28 G4
Semiluki Rus. Fed. 29 F6
Seminoe Reservoir U.S.A. 134 F4
Seminole U.S.A. 133 A5
Seminole, Lake U.S.A. 129 B6
Semipalatinsk Kazakh. 70 F1
Semīrom Iran 80 B4
Semisopochnoi Island U.S.A. 120 A4
Semitau Indon. 59 E2
Sem Kolodezey Ukr. see Lenine
Semnān Iran 80 C3
Semnān prov. Iran 80 B3
Semois r. Belgium 39 F2
Sempach Switz. 39 H3
Semporna Sabah Malaysia 59 G1
Sempu i. Indon. 59 F5
Sem Tripa Brazil 147 H6
Semuliki National Park Uganda 96 A4
Semyonovskoye Arkhangel'skaya Oblast' Rus. Fed. see Bereznik
Semyonovskoye Kostromskaya Oblast' Rus. Fed. see Ostrovskoye
Sên, Stœng r. Cambodia 61 D5
Senador Pompeu Brazil 150 E3
Senaki Georgia 79 E2
Sena Madureira Brazil 148 C2
Senanayake Samudra l. Sri Lanka 72 D5
Senanga Zambia 95 D9
Sénas France 39 F5
Senatobia U.S.A. 133 D5
Sendai Japan 65 B7
Sendai Japan 65 E5
Sendai-wan b. Japan 65 E5
Senden Germany 36 E4
Sêndo China see Chido
Şendreni Romania 46 E2
Sene r. Ghana 93 E4
Seneca KS U.S.A. 132 B4
Seneca OR U.S.A. 134 C3
Seneca Lake U.S.A. 131 E2
Seneca Rocks U.S.A. 130 D4
Senecaville Lake U.S.A. 130 C4
▶Senegal country Africa 92 B2
africa 86–87, 100
Sénégal r. Mauritania/Senegal 92 A1
Senftenberg Germany 37 G3
Senga Malawi 97 B8
Senga Hill Zambia 97 A7
Sengar r. India 74 C4
Sengata Indon. 59 G2
Sengerema Tanz. 96 B5
Sênggê Zangbo r. China see Indus
Sengiley Rus. Fed. 29 I5
Sengirli, Mys pt Kazakh. see Syngyrli, Mys
Sêngli Co l. China 75 E3
Senguerr r. Arg. 153 C6
Sengwa r. Zimbabwe 99 E3
Senhor do Bonfim Brazil 150 D4
Senica Slovakia 37 H4
Senigallia Italy 44 D3
Senj Croatia 44 E2
Senja i. Norway 32 E1
Şenkaya Turkey 79 E2
Senko Guinea 92 C3
Senkobo Zambia 95 E9
Şenköy Turkey 77 C1
Senku Jammu and Kashmir 74 C2
Senlac S. Africa 98 D5
Senlis France 39 E2
Senmonorom Cambodia 61 D5
Sennar Sudan 89 G6
Sennar state Sudan 89 G6
Senneterre Canada 124 E3
Senorbì Sardinia Italy 45 B5
Senqu r. Lesotho 99 E6
Sens France 39 E2
Sensuntepeque El Salvador 138 G6
Senta Yugo. 46 B2
Sentinel Peak Canada 122 F4
Sentinum Italy see Sassoferrato
Sentosa i. Sing. 58 [inset]
Şenyurt Turkey 79 E3
Seo de Urgell Spain see La Seu d'Urgell
Seonath r. India 75 D5
Seondha India 74 C4
Seoni India 74 C5
Seoni Chhapara India 74 C5
Seoni-Malwa India 74 C5

▶Seoul S. Korea 65 A5
Capital of South Korea.
world 16–17

Séoune r. France 38 D4
Sepanjang i. Indon. 59 F4
Separation Well Australia 108 C5
Separ Shāhābād Iran 80 A3
Sepasu Indon. 59 G2
Sepatini r. Brazil 148 D1
Sepik r. P.N.G. 57 J6
Sepinang Indon. 59 G2
Sepino Italy 44 E4
Sep'o N. Korea 65 A5
Sępólno Krajeńskie Poland 37 H2
Seppa India 75 G4
Septèmes-les-Vallons France 39 F5
Sept-Îles Canada 125 H3
Sepupa Botswana 98 D3
Seputih r. Indon. 58 D4
Sequillo r. Spain 42 D2
Sequoia National Park U.S.A. 136 C3
Serafimovich Rus. Fed. 29 G6
Sêraitang China see Baima
Seram i. Indon. 57 G6
Seram Sea Indon. 57 H6
Serang Indon. 58 D4
Serangoon, Pulau i. Sing. 58 [inset]
Serangoon, Sungai r. Sing. 58 [inset]
Serangoon Harbour b. Sing. 58 [inset]
Serapong, Mount Sing. 58 [inset]
Serasan i. Indon. 59 E2
Serasan, Selat sea chan. Indon. 59 E2
Seraya i. Indon. 59 E2
Serbia aut. rep. Yugo. see Srbija
Sêrbug Co l. China 75 F2
Sêrca China 75 G3
Serdica Bulg. see Sofia
Serdo Eth. 96 D2
Serdoba r. Rus. Fed. 29 H5
Serdobsk Rus. Fed. 29 H5
Serebryanka Rus. Fed. 28 J3
Sered' Slovakia 37 H4
Seredka Rus. Fed. 28 D4
Şereflikoçhisar Turkey 78 C3
Serein r. France 39 E3
Seremban Malaysia 58 C2
Serengeti National Park Tanz. 96 B5
Serengeti Plain Tanz. 96 B5
Serenje Zambia 95 F8
Serezha r. Rus. Fed. 28 G5
Sergach Rus. Fed. 28 H5
Sergen Turkey 46 E4
Sergino Rus. Fed. 26 G3
Sergipe state Brazil 150 E4
Sergiyev Posad Rus. Fed. 28 F4
Sergo Ukr. see Stakhanov
Seria Brunei 59 F1
Serian Sarawak Malaysia 59 E2
Seribu, Kepulauan is Indon. 59 D4
Serifos Greece 47 D6
Serifos i. Greece 47 D6
Serifou, Steno sea chan. Greece 47 D6
Sérigny, Lac l. Canada 125 G2
Serik Turkey 78 B3
Seringa, Serra da hills Brazil 147 I6
Seringapatam Reef Australia 108 C3
Serinhisar Turkey 47 F6
Serio r. Italy 44 B2
Sêrkang China see Nyainrong
Sermata, Kepulauan is Indon. 57 G7
Sermersuaq glacier Greenland 121 M2
Sermersuaq glacier Greenland 121 N2
Sernovodsk Rus. Fed. 29 I5
Sernur Rus. Fed. 28 I4
Sernyy Zavod Turkm. see Kukurtli
Serón Spain 43 E4
Seronga Botswana 98 D3
Serouenout well Alg. 91 G4
Serov Rus. Fed. 26 G4
Serowe Botswana 99 E4
Serpa Port. 42 C4
Serpa Pinto Angola see Menongue
Serpent, Vallée du watercourse Mali 92 C2
Serpentine Lakes salt flat Australia 110 B6
Serpent's Mouth sea chan. Trin. and Tob./Venez. 147 F2
Serpis r. Spain 43 F3
Serpneve Ukr. 46 F1
Serpukhov Rus. Fed. 29 F5
Serra Brazil 151 D7
Serra da Bocaina, Parque Nacional da nat. park Brazil 151 C7
Serra da Canastra, Parque Nacional da nat. park Brazil 151 C7
Serra da Capivara, Parque Nacional da nat. park Brazil 150 D4
Serra da Mesa, Represa resr Brazil 150 B5
Serra de Outes Spain 42 B1
Serradilla Spain 42 C3
Serra do Divisor, Parque Nacional da nat. park Brazil 148 B2
Serra do Navio Brazil 147 H4
Sérrai Greece see Serres
Serramanna Sardinia Italy 45 B5
Serranía de la Neblina, Parque Nacional nat. park Venez. 147 E4
Serrano i. Chile 153 B7
Serraria, Ilha i. Brazil see Queimada, Ilha
Serra Talhada Brazil 150 E3
Serre r. France 39 E2
Serres Greece 46 C4
Serrezuela Arg. 152 D2
Serrinha Brazil 150 E4
Sêrro Brazil 151 D6
Serrota mt. Spain 42 D2
Sers Tunisia 45 B6
Sertã Port. 42 B3
Sertânia Brazil 150 E4
Sertanópolis Brazil 149 H5
Sertão de Campuã reg. Brazil 149 G4
Sertãozinho Brazil 149 I5
Sêrtar China 66 B1
Sertolovo Rus. Fed. 28 D3
Serui Indon. 57 I6
Serule Botswana 99 E4
Serutu i. Indon. 59 E3
Seruyan r. Indon. 59 F3
Servia Greece 47 C4
Servol r. Spain 43 G2
Serwaru Indon. 108 D2
Sêrxü China 66 A1
Sesayap Indon. 59 G2
Sesayap r. Indon. 59 G2
Sese Dem. Rep. Congo 94 E4
Sesfontein Namibia 98 B3
Seshachalam Hills India 72 C3
Sesheke Zambia 95 E9
Sesia r. Italy 44 B2
Sesklio i. Greece 47 E6
Sesostris Bank sea feature India 72 A3
S'Espalmador i. Spain 43 G3
Sessa Angola 95 D8
Ses Salines, Cap de c. Spain 43 H3
Sestri Levante Italy 44 B2
Sestu Sardinia Italy 45 B5
Šešupė r. Lith./Rus. Fed. 33 F5
Sesvete Croatia 44 F2
Set r. Spain 43 G2
Set, Phou mt. Laos 61 D5
Sète France 39 E5
Sete Lagoas Brazil 151 C6
Setermoen Norway 32 E1
Setesdal valley Norway 33 B4
Seti r. Nepal 75 D3
Seti r. Nepal 75 E4
Setia Italy see Sezze
Sétif Alg. 91 G1
Setit r. Africa 89 G6
Seto Japan 65 D6
Seto-naikai sea Japan 63 M5
Seto-naikai sea chan. Japan 65 C6
Seto-naikai National Park Japan 65 C6
Settat Morocco 90 D2
Setté Cama Gabon 94 A5
Settepani, Monte mt. Italy 44 B2
Settimo Torinese Italy 44 A2
Settle U.K. 35 E4
Settlement Creek r. Australia 110 D3
Setúbal Port. 42 B3
Setúbal admin. dist. Port. 42 B3
Setúbal, Baía de b. Port. 42 B3
Seugne r. France 38 C4
Seul, Lac l. Canada 124 A3
Seurre France 39 F3
Sevan Armenia 79 F2
Sevan, Lake Armenia 79 F2
Sevan, Ozero l. Armenia see Sevan, Lake
Sevana Lich l. Armenia see Sevan, Lake
Sevaruyo Bol. 148 D4
Sevastopol' Ukr. 78 C1
Seven Islands Canada see Sept-Îles
Sevenoaks U.K. 35 G6
Seventeen Seventy Australia 111 G5
Seventy Mile House Canada see 70 Mile House
Sévérac-le-Château France 39 E4
Severino Ribeiro Brazil 152 G2
Severn r. Canada 124 C2
Severn S. Africa 98 D5
Severn r. U.K. 35 E6
Severn U.S.A. 131 E5
Severnaya Dvina r. Rus. Fed. 28 G2
Severnaya Mylva r. Rus. Fed. 28 K3
Severnaya Osetiya-Alaniya, Respublika aut. rep. Rus. Fed. 29 H8
Severnaya Sos'va r. Rus. Fed. 26 G3
Severnaya Zemlya is Rus. Fed. 27 K1
Severn Lake Canada 124 B2
Severnoye Rus. Fed. 29 J5
Severnyy Nenetskiy Avtonomnyy Okrug Rus. Fed. 28 I1
Severnyy Respublika Komi Rus. Fed. 28 M2
Severnyy Anyuyskiy Khrebet mts Rus. Fed. 27 R3
Severnyy Kommunar Rus. Fed. 28 J4
Severnyy Suchan Rus. Fed. see Uglekamensk
Severnyy Ural mts Rus. Fed. 28 K3
Severobaykal'sk Rus. Fed. 27 K4
Severo-Baykal'skoye Nagor'ye mts Rus. Fed. 27 L4
Severodonetsk Ukr. see Syeverodonets'k
Severodvinsk Rus. Fed. 28 F2
Severomorsk Rus. Fed. 32 I1
Severoonezhsk Rus. Fed. 28 F3
Severo-Osetinskaya A.S.S.R. aut. rep. Rus. Fed. see Severnaya Osetiya-Alaniya, Respublika
Severo-Sibirskaya Nizmennost' lowland Rus. Fed. see North Siberian Lowland
Severoural'sk Rus. Fed. 28 K3
Severo-Yeniseyskiy Rus. Fed. 27 J3
Severskiy Donets r. Rus. Fed./Ukr. 29 G7
Seveso Italy 44 B2
Sevier U.S.A. 137 F2
Sevier r. U.S.A. 137 F2
Sevier Desert U.S.A. 137 F2
Sevier Lake U.S.A. 137 F2
Sevilla Col. 146 C3
Sevilla Spain see Seville
Seville Spain 42 D4
Sevlievo Bulg. 46 D3
Sevnica Slovenia 44 E1
Sèvre Nantaise r. France 38 C3
Sewani India 74 B3
Seward AK U.S.A. 120 E3
Seward NE U.S.A. 132 B3
Seward PA U.S.A. 130 D3
Seward Mountains Antarctica 167 L2
Seward Peninsula U.S.A. 120 C3
Sewell Chile 152 C3
Sexi Spain see Almuñécar
Sexsmith Canada 122 G4
Sextín r. Mex. 126 E6
Seyah Band Koh mts Afgh. 81 E3
Seyakha Rus. Fed. 26 H2
▶Seychelles country Indian Ocean 162 K6
africa 86–87, 100
Seydi Turkm. 81 E2
Seydişehir Turkey 78 B3
Seyðisfjörður Iceland 32 [inset]
Seyfe Gölü salt flat Turkey 78 C3
Seyhan Turkey see Adana
Seyhan r. Turkey 78 C3
Seyitgazi Turkey 78 B3
Seym r. Rus. Fed./Ukr. 29 E6
Seymchan Rus. Fed. 27 P3
Seymour Australia 112 C5
Seymour IN U.S.A. 128 B4
Seymour TX U.S.A. 133 B5
Seymour Inlet Canada 122 E5
Seymour Range mts Australia 110 C5
Seypan i. N. Mariana Is see Saipan
Seytan r. Turkey 46 E4
Seyyedābād Afgh. 81 G3
Sežana Slovenia 44 D2
Sézanne France 39 E2
Sezze Italy 44 D4
Sfakia Greece 47 D7
Sfântu Gheorghe Romania 46 D2
Sfântu Gheorghe Romania 46 F2
Sfântu Gheorghe, Braţul watercourse Romania 46 F2
Sfax Tunisia 91 H2
Sfendami Greece 47 C4
Sfintu Gheorghe Romania see Sfântu Gheorghe
Sgiersch Poland see Zgierz
's-Gravenhage Neth. see The Hague
Sgurr Alasdair hill U.K. 34 C3
Sgurr Mor mt. U.K. 34 D3
Shaanxi prov. China 67 D1
Shaartuz Tajik. see Shahrtuz
Shaba prov. Dem. Rep. Congo see Katanga
Shabani Zimbabwe see Zvishavane
Shabeellaha Dhexe admin. reg. Somalia 96 E4
Shabeellaha Hoose admin. reg. Somalia 96 D4
Shabestar Iran 80 A2
Shabla Bulg. 46 F3
Shabla, Nos pt Bulg. 46 F3
Shabogamo Lake Canada 125 H2
Shabunda Dem. Rep. Congo 94 E5
Shabwah Yemen 76 D6
Shache China 70 E4
Shackleton Coast Antarctica 167 H1
Shackleton Glacier Antarctica 167 I1
Shackleton Ice Shelf Antarctica 167 F2
Shackleton Range mts Antarctica 167 A1
Shadadkot Pak. 81 F5
Shadaogou China 67 D2
Shādegān Iran 80 B4
Shādkām watercourse Iran 80 C4
Shadrinsk Rus. Fed. 26 G4
Shady Spring U.S.A. 130 C5
Shafer Peak Antarctica 167 H2
Shafī'abad Iran 80 D2
Shafter U.S.A. 136 C4
Shaftesbury U.K. 35 E6
Shagamu r. Canada 124 C2
Shagamu Nigeria 93 F4
Shag Rocks is S. Georgia 161 L9
Shahabad Andhra Pradesh India 72 C2
Shahabad Haryana India 74 C3
Shahabad Karnataka India 72 C2
Shahabad Rajasthan India 74 C4
Shahabad Uttar Pradesh India 74 D4
Shāhābād Iran see Eslāmābād-e Gharb
Shahada India 74 B5
Shah Alam Malaysia 58 C2
Shahana Pak. 81 E5
Shahapur India 72 B3
Shahbā' Syria 77 C3
Shahbazpur sea chan. Bangl. 75 F5
Shahdād Iran 80 D4
Shahdadpur Pak. 81 G5
Shahdol India 75 D5
Shahejie China see Jiujiang
Shahezhen China see Jiujiang
Shah Fuladi mt. Afgh. 81 F3
Shahganj India 75 D4
Shahgarh Madhya Pradesh India 74 C4
Shahgarh Rajasthan India 74 A4
Shāhīn Dezh Iran see Sa'īndezh
Shah Ismail Afgh. 81 F4
Shahjahanpur India 74 C4
Shāh Jehān, Kūh-e mts Iran 80 D2
Shāh Jūy Afgh. 81 F3
Shāh Kūh mt. Iran 81 D4
Shahpur Karnataka India 72 C2
Shahpur Madhya Pradesh India 74 C5
Shāhpūr Iran see Salmās
Shahpur Balochistān Pak. 81 G4
Shahpur Punjab Pak. 81 H3
Shahpur Sindh Pak. 81 G5
Shahpura Madhya Pradesh India 74 D5
Shahpura Rajasthan India 74 B4
Shahr oasis Saudi Arabia 76 E6
Shahrak Afgh. 81 F3
Shāhrakht Iran 81 E3
Shahr-e Bābak Iran 80 C4
Shahr-e Kord Iran 80 B3
Shahr-e-Now Iran 81 E3
Shahrezā Iran see Qomishēh
Shahrisabz Uzbek. see Shakhrisabz
Shahriston Tajik. 81 G2
Shahr Rey Iran 80 B3
Shahrtuz Tajik. 81 G2
Shāhrūd Iran see Emāmrūd
Shāhrūd, Rūdkhāneh-ye r. Iran 80 B2
Shāh Savārān, Kūh-e mts Iran 81 D4
Shāh Taqī Iran see Emām Taqī
Sha'ībān el Jiraniyat watercourse Saudi Arabia 77 D4
Shaikh Husain mt. Pak. 81 F4
Shā'īr, Jabal mts Syria 77 C2
Sha'īrah, Jabal mt. Egypt 77 B5
Shaistaganj Bangl. 75 F4
Shaj'ah, Jabal hill Saudi Arabia 80 B5
Shajapur India 74 C5
Shakawe Botswana 98 D3
Shakh Tajik. 81 G2
Shakhbuz Azer. see Şahbuz
Shakhovskaya Rus. Fed. 28 E4
Shakhrisabz Uzbek. 81 F2
Shakhristan Tajik. see Shahriston
Shakhtars'k Ukr. 29 F6
Shakhtersk Ukr. see Shakhtars'k
Shakhty Respublika Buryatiya Rus. Fed. see Gusinoozersk
Shakhty Rostovskaya Oblast' Rus. Fed. 29 G7
Shakhtyorsk Ukr. see Shakhtars'k
Shakhun'ya Rus. Fed. 28 H4
Shaki Nigeria 93 F3
Shakotan-hantō pen. Japan 64 E4
Shakou China 67 E4
Shala Hāyk' l. Eth. 96 C3
Shalakusha Rus. Fed. 28 G3
Shālamzār Iran 80 B3
Shali Rus. Fed. 29 H8
Shalim Oman 76 F6
Shaliuhe China see Gangca
Shalkar Kazakh. 70 A2
Shalkar, Ozero salt l. Kazakh. 29 I6
Shalqar Kazakh. see Shalkar
Shalqar Kōli salt l. Kazakh. see Shalkar, Ozero
Shaluli Shan mts China 66 A2
Shaluni mt. India 66 A2
Shama r. Tanz. 97 B6
Shamāl Sīnā' governorate Egypt 77 A4
Shamalzā'ī Afgh. 81 F4
Shamary Rus. Fed. 28 K4
Shāmat al Akbād des. Saudi Arabia 89 I2
Shamattawa Canada 123 M3
Shamattawa r. Canada 124 C2
Shambār Iran 80 B3
Shambe Sudan 96 A3
Shambu Eth. 96 C2
Shambuanda Dem. Rep. Congo 95 D6
Shamgarh India 74 B4
Shamgong Bhutan see Zhemgang
Shamkhal Rus. Fed. 79 F2
Shamkhor Azer. see Şämkir
Shamrock U.S.A. 133 A5
Shan state Myanmar 60 B3
Shancheng China see Shanxian
Shand Afgh. 81 E4
Shandan China 70 J4
Shandiz Iran 81 D2
Shandong prov. China 63 J4
Shandong Bandao pen. China 63 K4
Shandrūkh Iraq 79 F4
Shandur Pass Pak. 81 H2
Shangani r. Zimbabwe 99 E3
Shangcai China 67 E1
Shangcheng China 67 E2
Shangchuan Dao i. China 67 E4
Shangchuankou China see Minhe
Shanggao China 67 E2

▶Shanghai China 67 G2
4th most populous city in Asia and 8th in the world.
world 16–17

Shanghai municipality China 67 G2
Shanghang China 67 F3
Shanghekou China 65 A4
Shangji China see Xichuan
Shangjie China see Yangbi
Shangnan China 67 D1
Shangombo Zambia 95 D9
Shangpai China see Feixi
Shangpaihe China see Feixi
Shangqiu Henan China 67 E1
Shangqiu Henan China 67 E1
Shangrao China 67 F2
Shangshui China 67 E1
Shangsi China 66 D4
Shangtang China see Yongjia
Shangyou China 67 E3
Shangyou Shuiku salt flat China 70 F3
Shangyu China 67 G2
Shangzhi China 64 A3
Shangzhou China 67 D1
Shanhetun China 64 A3
Shani Nigeria 93 I3
Shannon airport Rep. of Ireland 35 B5
Shannon est. Rep. of Ireland 35 B5
Shannon r. Rep. of Ireland 35 B5
Shannon, Mouth of the Rep. of Ireland 35 B5
Shannon National Park Australia 109 B8
Shannon Ø i. Greenland 121 R2
Shan Plateau Myanmar 60 B3
Shansi prov. China see Shanxi
Shantarskiye Ostrova is Rus. Fed. 27 N4
Shan Teng hill Hong Kong China see Victoria Peak
Shantipur India 75 F5
Shantou China 67 F4
Shantung prov. China see Shandong
Shanwei China 67 E4
Shanxi prov. China 63 I4
Shanxian China 67 F1
Shanyang China 67 D1
Shaodong China 67 D3
Shaoguan China 67 E3
Shaoshan China 67 E3
Shaowu China 67 F3
Shaoxing China 67 G2
Shaoyang China 67 D3
Shapa China 67 D4
Shapembe Dem. Rep. Congo 95 D6
Shaping China see Ebian
Shapinsay i. U.K. 34 E2
Shapkina r. Rus. Fed. 28 J2
Shaqq el Giefer, Wadi watercourse Sudan 89 E6
Shaqq el Khadir Sudan 89 E6
Shaqrā' Saudi Arabia 76 D4
Sharaf well Iraq 79 E5
Sharafa Sudan 89 E6
Sharāh, Jibāl ash mts Jordan 77 B4
Sharan Jogizai Pak. 81 G4
Sharātīb, Ra's pt Egypt 77 A5
Sharawrā, Jabal hills Saudi Arabia 77 C5
Sharbithāt, Ra's c. Oman 76 F6
Shardi Pak. 74 B2
Shargun' Uzbek. 81 F2
Shari r. Cameroon/Chad see Chari
Sharjah U.A.E. 80 C5
Sharka-leb La pass China 75 F3
Sharkawshchyna Belarus 33 G5
Shark Bay Australia 109 A6
Shark Reef Australia 111 F2
Sharlyk Rus. Fed. 29 J5
Sharmah Saudi Arabia 89 G2
Sharm ash Shaykh Egypt 89 G3
Sharon U.S.A. 130 C3
Sharon, Plain of Israel 77 B3
Sharon Springs U.S.A. 132 A4
Sharonville U.S.A. 130 A4
Sharpe Lake Canada 123 M4
Sharp Peak hill Hong Kong China 67 [inset]
Sharpsburg U.S.A. 130 C4
Sharqat Iraq see Ash Sharqāṭ
Sharqīya governorate Egypt see Ash Sharqīyah
Sharqī, Jabal ash mts Lebanon/Syria 77 B3
Sharqpur Pak. 74 B3
Sharur Azer. see Şärur
Shar Us Gol r. Mongolia 70 I2
Shary well Saudi Arabia 89 I3
Shar'ya Rus. Fed. 28 H4
Shashe r. Botswana/Zimbabwe 99 F4
Shashemenē Eth. 96 C3
Shashi China see Jingzhou
Shasta, Mount vol. U.S.A. 134 B4
Shasta Lake U.S.A. 134 B4
Shāṭī', Wādī ash watercourse Libya 88 B3
Shatilki Belarus see Svyetlahorsk
Sha Tin Hong Kong China 67 [inset]
Shatki Rus. Fed. 28 H5
Shatnat as Salmās, Wādī watercourse Syria 77 D2
Shatoy Rus. Fed. 29 H8
Shatsk Rus. Fed. 29 G5
Shaṭṭ, Ra's osh pt Iran 80 B4
Shaṭṭ al 'Arab r. Iran/Iraq 80 B4
Shaṭṭ al Gharrāf r. Iraq 79 F5
Shattuck U.S.A. 133 B4
Shatura Rus. Fed. 28 F5
Shaubak Jordan see Ash Shawbak
Shaunavon Canada 123 I5
Shavers Fork r. U.S.A. 130 D4
Shaw r. Australia 108 B5
Shawangunk Mountains hills U.S.A. 131 F3
Shawano U.S.A. 132 D2
Shawāq well Saudi Arabia 89 H3
Shawnee U.S.A. 133 B5
Shawsville U.S.A. 130 C5
Sha Xi r. China 67 F3
Shaxian China 67 F3
Shayang China 67 E2
Shaybārā i. Saudi Arabia 89 H3
Shayboveyem r. Rus. Fed. 27 Q3
Shay Gap Australia 108 C5
Shaykh, Wādī ash watercourse Egypt 77 A5
Shaykh Jūwī Iraq 79 F4
Shaykh Sa'd Iraq 79 F4
Shāzand Iran 80 B3
Shazud Tajik. 81 H2
Shchekino Rus. Fed. 29 F5
Shchel'yayur Rus. Fed. 28 J2
Shcherbakov Rus. Fed. see Rybinsk
Shchigry Rus. Fed. 29 F6
Shchors Ukr. 29 D6
Shchuchin Belarus see Shchuchyn
Shchuchinsk Kazakh. 26 H4
Shchuchyn Belarus 29 C5
Shchuger r. Rus. Fed. 28 K2
Shea Guyana 147 G4
Shebekino Rus. Fed. 29 F6
Sheberghān Afgh. 81 F2
Sheboygan U.S.A. 132 E3
Shebshi Mountains Nigeria 93 H3
Shebunino Rus. Fed. 64 E3
Shediac Canada 125 H4
Shedin Peak Canada 122 E4
Shedok Rus. Fed. 29 G7
Sheelin, Lough l. Rep. of Ireland 35 C5
Sheep Peak U.S.A. 137 E3
Sheerness U.K. 35 G6
Sheet Harbour Canada 125 I4
Shefar'am Israel 77 B3
Sheffield N.Z. 113 C3
Sheffield U.K. 35 F5
Sheffield PA U.S.A. 130 D3
Sheffield TX U.S.A. 133 A6
Sheffield Lake Canada 125 J3
Shegaon India 72 C1
Shēh Husēn Eth. 96 D3
Shehong China 66 C2

Sheikh, Jebel esh *mt.* Lebanon/Syria see Hermon, Mount
Sheikh Othman Yemen *see* Ash Shaykh 'Uthman
Shekak *r.* Canada 124 C3
Shekhupura Pak. 74 B3
Sheki Azer. *see* Şäki
Shek Kwu Chau *i.* Hong Kong China 67 [inset]
Shekou China 67 [inset]
Sheksna Rus. Fed. 28 F4
Sheksninskoye Vodokhranilishche *resr* Rus. Fed. 28 F4
Shek Uk Shan *mt.* Hong Kong China 67 [inset]
Shela China 75 G3
Shelag *watercourse* Afgh./Iran 81 E4
Shelagskiy, Mys *pt* Fus. Fed. 166 C2
Shelbiana U.S.A. 130 B5
Shelburne *N.S.* Canada 125 H5
Shelburne *Ont.* Canada 130 C1
Shelburne Bay Australia 111 E1
Shelburne Falls U.S.A. 131 G2
Shelby *MS* U.S.A. 133 D5
Shelby *MT* U.S.A. 134 C2
Shelby *NC* U.S.A. 128 C5
Shelby *OH* U.S.A. 130 B3
Shelbyville *IL* U.S.A. 128 B5
Sheldon U.S.A. 132 C3
Sheldrake Canada 125 H3
Shelek Kazakh. *see* Chilik
Shelikhova, Zaliv *g.* Rus. Fed. 27 P3
Shelikof Strait U.S.A. 120 C4
Shellbrook Canada 123 J4
Shell Lake Canada 123 J4
Shell Mountain U.S.A. 136 A1
Shelter Bay Canada *see* Port-Cartier
Shelter Island U.S.A. 131 G3
Shelton U.S.A. 134 B3
Shelton U.S.A. 134 B3
Sheltozero Rus. Fed. 28 E3
Shemakha Azer. *see* Şamaxi
Shemankar *r.* Nigeria 93 H4
Shemonaikha Kazakh. 70 F1
Shemordan Rus. Fed. 28 I4
Shenandoah *IA* U.S.A. 132 C3
Shenandoah *PA* U.S.A. 131 E3
Shenandoah *VA* U.S.A. 130 D4
Shenandoah *r.* U.S.A. 130 E4
Shenandoah Mountains U.S.A. 130 D4
Shenandoah National Park U.S.A. 130 D4
Shendam Nigeria 93 H3
Shendi Sudan 89 G6
Shending Shan *hill* China 64 C3
Shenge Sierra Leone 92 B4
Shengli China 67 G2
Shengli Feng *mt.* China/Kyrg. *see* Pobeda Peak
Shengrenjian China *see* Pinglu
Shengsi China 67 G2
Shengsi Liedao *is* China 67 G2
Shengxian China *see* Shengzhou
Shengzhou China 67 G2
Shenkursk Rus. Fed. 28 G3
Shenqiu China 67 F1
Shenshu China 64 B3
Shensi *prov.* China *see* Shaanxi
Shentala Rus. Fed. 29 I5
Shenton, Mount Australia 109 C7
Shenyang China 63 <3
Shenzhen China 67 [inset]
Shenzhen Wan *b.* Hong Kong China *see* Deep Bay
Sheopai China 74 B4
Sheopur India 74 C4
Shepetivka Ukr. *see* Shepetivka
Shepetovka Ukr. *see* Shepetivka
Shepherd Islands Vanuatu 107 F3
Shepparton Australia 112 C5
Sherabad Uzbek. 74 B2
Sherborne U.K. 35 E6
Sherbro Island Sierra Leone 92 B4
Sherbrooke *N.S.* Canada 125 I4
Sherbrooke *Que.* Canada 125 G4
Sherburne U.S.A. 131 G2
Shercock Rep. of Ireland 35 C5
Sherda *well* Chad 88 B5
Shereiq Sudan 68 B5
Shergarh India 74 B4
Sherghati India 75 E4
Sheridan *AR* U.S.A. 133 C5
Sheridan *WY* U.S.A. 134 F3
Sherman *NY* U.S.A. 130 D2
Sherman *TX* U.S.A. 133 D5
Sherobod Uzbek. *see* Sherabad
Sherpur *Dhaka* Bangl. 75 G5
Sherpur *Rajshahi* Bangl. 75 F4
Sherridon Canada 123 K4
Shertally India 72 C4
's-Hertogenbosch Neth. 36 B3
Sherwood U.S.A. 130 A3
Sheryshevo Rus. Fec. 64 B2
Sheshtamad Iran 80 D2
Sheslay Canada 122 C3
Sheslay *r.* Canada 122 C3
Shethanei Lake Canada 123 L3
Shetland *is* U.K. 34 F1
Shetland *admin. div.* U.K. 34 F1
Shetpe Kazakh. 26 F5
Sheung Shui *Hong Kong* China 67 [inset]
Sheung Sze Mun *sea chan.* Hong Kong China 67 [inset]
Shevaroy Hills India 72 C4
Shevchenko Kazakh. *see* Aktau
Shevgaon India 72 B2
Shevli *r.* Rus. Fed. 64 C1
Shexian China 67 F2
Sheya Rus. Fed. 27 L3
Sheyang China 67 G1
Sheyenne *r.* U.S.A. 132 B2
Sheykh Sho'eyb *i.* Iran 80 C5
Shey Phoksundo National Park Nepal 75 E3
Shiant Islands U.K. 34 C3
Shiashkotan, Ostrov *i.* Rus. Fed. 54 H1
Shibam Yemen 68 C5
Shibar Pass Afgh. 81 G3
Shibata Japan 65 D5
Shibazhan China 64 A1
Shibetsu Japan 64 E3
Shibetsu Japan 64 F4
Shibin al Kawm Egypt 89 E2
Shibing China 66 D3
Shibogama Lake Canada 124 B3
Shibotsu-jima *i.* Rus. Fed. *see* Zelenyy, Ostrov
Shicheng *Fujian* China *see* Zhouning
Shicheng *Jiangxi* China 67 F3
Shickshinny U.S.A. 131 E3
Shidād al Mismā' *hill* Saudi Arabia 77 D4
Shiel, Loch *I.* U.K. 34 C3
Shieli Kazakh. *see* Chiili
Shifa, Jabal ash *mts* Saudi Arabia 89 D4
Shifang China 66 C2
Shigatse China *see* Xigazê
Shihezi China 70 G3
Shihkiachwang China *see* Shijiazhuang
Shihmen China *see* Shijiazhuang
Shijiao China *see* Fogang

Shijiazhuang China 63 I4
Shijiu Hu *l.* China 67 F2
Shijiusuo China *see* Rizhao
Shikag Lake Canada 124 B3
Shikar *r.* Pak. 81 F4
Shikarpur Pak. 81 G5
Shikengkong *mt.* China 67 E3
Shikhany Rus. Fed. 29 H5
Shikohabad India 74 C4
Shikoku *i.* Japan 65 C6
Shikoku-sanchi *mts* Japan 65 C6
Shikotsu-Tōya National Park Japan 64 F4
Shilega Rus. Fed. 28 H2
Shiliguri India 75 F4
Shilipu China 67 E2
Shiliu China *see* Changjiang
Shilla *mt.* Jammu and Kashmir 74 C2
Shillelagh Rep. of Ireland 35 C5
Shillo *r.* Israel 77 B3
Shilovo Rus. Fed. 29 G5
Shimabara Japan 65 B6
Shimada Japan 65 D6
Shimbiris *mt.* Somalia 96 E2
Shimen China 67 D2
Shimian China 66 B2
Shimla India 74 C3
Shimoda Japan 65 D6
Shimokita-hantō *pen.* Japan 64 E4
Shimoni Kenya 97 C6
Shimonoseki Japan 65 B6
Shimsha *r.* India 72 C3
Shimshal Jammu and Kashmir 74 B1
Shimsk Rus. Fed. 28 D4
Shin, Loch *l.* U.K. 34 D2
Shinafiyah Iraq *see* Ash Shanafiyah
Shinan Afgh. 81 F2
Shindand Afgh. 81 F3
Shingbwiyang Myanmar 60 B2
Shinghshai Pass Pak. 74 B1
Shinglehouse U.S.A. 130 D3
Shingletown U.S.A. 136 B1
Shingū Japan 65 D6
Shinjō Japan 65 E5
Shinkai Hills Afgh. 81 G3
Shinkāy Afgh. 81 F4
Shinnston U.S.A. 130 E4
Shinyanga Tanz. 96 B5
Shinyanga *admin. reg.* Tanz. 97 B5
Shiogama Japan 65 E5
Shiono-misaki *c.* Japan 65 C6
Shioya-zaki *pt* Japan 65 E5
Shipai China *see* Huaining
Shipchenski Prokhod *pass* Bulg. 46 D3
Shiping China 66 B4
Shipki Pass China/India 74 C3
Shippegan Canada 125 H4
Shippensburg U.S.A. 131 G3
Shippenville U.S.A. 130 D3
Shiprock U.S.A. 135 F5
Shiprock Peak U.S.A. 137 H3
Shipu China 67 G2
Shiqian China 66 D3
Shiqizhen China *see* Zhongshan
Shiquan China 67 F1
Shiquanhe *Xizang* China *see* Gar
Shiquanhe *Xizang* China *see* Ali
Shirā'awh *i.* Qatar 80 C5
Shīrābād Iran 80 D2
Shirane-san *mt.* Japan 65 D6
Shirane-san *mt.* Japan 65 E5
Shirase Coast Antarctica 167 J1
Shirase Glacier Antarctica 167 D2
Shirati Tanz. 96 B5
Shīrāz Iran 80 C4
Shirbīn Egypt 78 E5
Shire *r.* Malawi 97 B9
Shiretoko National Park Japan 64 F3
Shirinab *r.* Pak. 81 F4
Shīrīn Tagāb Afgh. 81 F2
Shiriya-zaki *pt* Japan 64 E4
Shirkala *reg.* Kazakh. 70 A2
Shirpur India 74 B5
Shiroro Reservoir Nigeria 93 G3
Shirpur India 74 B5
Shirten Holoy Gobi *des.* China 70 I3
Shirvān Iran 80 D2
Shisanzhan China 64 A1
Shishaldin Volcano U.S.A. 120 C4
Shisha Pangma *mt.* China *see* Xixabangma Feng
Shishou China 67 F2
Shitai China 67 F2
Shitang China 67 G2
Shiv India 74 A4
Shivpuri India 74 C4
Shivta *tourist site* Israel 77 B4
Shivwits U.S.A. 137 F3
Shivwits Plateau U.S.A. 137 F3
Shiwan Dashan *mts* China 66 E4
Shiwa Ngandu Zambia 97 A7
Shixing China 67 E3
Shiyan China 67 D1
Shizhu China 66 D2
Shizipu China 67 F2
Shizong China 66 B3
Shizuishan China 63 H4
Shizuoka Japan 65 D6

Shkhara *mt.* Georgia/Rus. Fed. 79 E2
3rd highest mountain in Europe.
europe 22–23
Shklov Belarus *see* Shklow
Shklow Belarus 31 L2
Shkodër Albania 46 A4
Shkodrës, Ligeni I *l.* Albania/Yugo. *see* Scutari, Lake
Shkumbin *r.* Albania 46 A4
Shmidta, Ostrov *i.* Rus. Fed. 27 J1
Shoal Lake *Man.* Canada 123 L5
Shoal Lake *Sask.* Canada 123 K4
Shoalwater Bay Australia 111 G4
Shōbara Japan 65 C6
Shoemakersville U.S.A. 131 F3
Shoh Tajik. *see* Shakh
Shohi Pass Pak. *see* Tal Pass
Sholapur India *see* Solapur
Shona Ridge *sea feature* S. Atlantic Ocean 161 O9
Shongar Bhutan 75 F4
Shoranur India 72 C4
Shorap Pak. 81 F5
Shorapur India 72 C2
Shor Barsa-Kel'mes *salt marsh* Uzbek. 76 F1
Shorghun Uzbek. *see* Shargun'
Shorobe Botswana 98 D3
Shortsville U.S.A. 131 E2
Shoshone *CA* U.S.A. 137 D4
Shoshone *ID* U.S.A. 134 D4
Shoshone *r.* U.S.A. 134 E3
Shoshone Mountains U.S.A. 136 D2
Shoshong Botswana 99 E4
Shoshoni U.S.A. 134 E4
Shostka Ukr. 29 E6
Shouxian China 67 F1
Shouzhou China *see* Shouxian
Show Low U.S.A. 137 G4
Shoyna Rus. Fed. 28 H2
Shpola Ukr. 29 D6

Shqipërisë, Republika e *country* Europe see Albania
Shreve U.S.A. 130 B3
Shreveport U.S.A. 133 C5
Shrewsbury U.K. 35 E5
Shrigonda India 72 B2
Shri Lanka *country* Asia *see* Sri Lanka
Shri Mohangarh India 74 B4
Shrirampur India 75 F5
Shrirangapattana India 72 C3
Shtefan-Vode Moldova *see* Ştefan Vodă
Shtërmen Albania 46 A4
Shu Kazakh. 70 D3
Shu'aiba Iraq 79 B5
Shuajingsi China 66 C1
Shuangbai China 66 B3
Shuangcheng *Fujian* China *see* Zherong
Shuangcheng *Heilong.* China 64 A3
Shuanghe China 67 E2
Shuanghechang China 66 C2
Shuanghedagang China 64 C3
Shuangjiang *Guizhou* China *see* Jiangkou
Shuangjiang *Hunan* China *see* Tongdao
Shuangjiang *Yunnan* China 66 C4
Shuangjiang *Yunnan* China *see* Eshan
Shuangpai China 67 D3
Shuangshipu China *see* Fengxian
Shuangyang China 64 A4
Shuangyashan China 64 C3
Shuangzhong China *see* Hukou
Shubarkuduk Kazakh. 70 A2
Shubrā al Khaymah Egypt 78 E4
Shubrāmiyah *well* Saudi Arabia 89 I4
Shucheng China 67 F2
Shuganu India 75 G4
Shughnon, Qatorkühi *mts* Tajik. 81 G2
Shughnanskiy Khrebet *mts* Tajik. *see* Shughnon, Qatorkühi
Shugozero Rus. Fed. 28 E4
Shuicheng China *see* Lupanshui
Shuidong China *see* Dianbai
Shuihu China *see* Changfeng
Shuiji China 67 F3
Shuijing China 66 C2
Shuikou *Guangdong* China 67 E4
Shuikou *Hunan* China 66 C3
Shuikouguan China 66 C4
Shuikoushan China 67 F3
Shuituo He *r.* China 66 B3
Shuizhai China *see* Wuhua
Shujaabad Pak. 81 H4
Shulan China 64 A4
Shul'mak Tajik. *see* Novobod
Shumagin Islands U.S.A. 120 C4
Shumen Bulg. 46 E3
Shumensko Plato *nat. park* Bulg. 46 E3
Shumerlya Rus. Fed. 28 H5
Shumyachi Rus. Fed. 31 M2
Shūnat Nimrin Jordan 77 B4
Shunde China *see* Wuhua
Shuoxian China *see* Shuozhou
Shuozhou China 63 I4
Shuqrah Yemen 76 D7
Shūr *r.* Iran 80 C4
Shūr *r.* Iran 81 E3
Shūr *r.* Iran 81 E3
Shūr *watercourse* Iran 80 C4
Shūr *watercourse* Iran 80 C5
Shūr *watercourse* Iran 80 C5
Shūr *watercourse* Iran 80 C4
Shūr *watercourse* Iran 80 C4
Shūrāb *Chahār Mahall va Bakhtiāri* Iran 80 B3
Shūr Āb Iran 80 B3
Shūrāb *Khorāsan* Iran 80 D3
Shūrāb *Yazd* Iran 76 F3
Shūr Āb *watercourse* Iran 80 C4
Shurab Tajik. *see* Shürob
Shurchi Uzbek. 81 F2
Shūr Gaz Iran 81 E4
Shūrjestān Iran 80 C4
Shūrob Tajik. 81 G1
Shūrū Iran 81 F4
Shurma Rus. Fed. 28 I4
Shūrāb Tajik. *see* Shürob
Shurugwi Zimbabwe 99 F3
Shuruppak *tourist site* Iraq 79 F5
Shusf Iran 80 D3
Shūsh Iran 80 B3
Shushicë *r.* Albania 47 A4
Shushtar Iran 80 B3
Shutar Khun Pass Afgh. 81 F3
Shuwaysh, Tall ash *hill* Jordan 79 D5
Shuya *Ivanovskaya Oblast'* Rus. Fed. 28 G4
Shuya *Respublika Kareliya* Rus. Fed. 28 G3
Shuyak Island U.S.A. 120 D4
Shuyang China 67 F1
Shuyskoye Rus. Fed. 28 G4
Shwebandaw Myanmar 60 A4
Shwebo Myanmar 60 A3
Shwedaung Myanmar 60 A4
Shwedwin Myanmar 60 A2
Shwegun Myanmar 60 B4
Shwegyin Myanmar 60 B4
Shwelaung *r.* Myanmar 61 A4
Shweli *r.* Myanmar 60 B3
Shwenyaung Myanmar 60 B3
Shweudaung *mt.* Myanmar 60 B3
Shyghanaq Kazakh. *see* Chiganak
Shymkent Kazakh. 70 C3
Shynggyrlaü Kazakh. *see* Chingirlau
Shyok India 74 D1
Shyok *r.* Jammu and Kashmir 74 C2
Shypuvate Ukr. 29 F6
Sia Indon. 57 H7
Siabost U.K. 34 C2
Siachen Glacier Jammu and Kashmir 74 C2

Siahan Range *mts* Pak. 81 E5
Sīah Chashmeh Iran 80 A2
Siahgird Afgh. 81 F2
Siah Koh *mts* Afgh. 81 F3
Sīāh Kūh *mts* Iran 80 C2
Siak *r.* Indon. 58 C2
Siak Sri Inderapura Indon. 58 C2
Sialkot Pak. 81 H3
Siam *country* Asia *see* Thailand
Sian China *see* Xi'an
Sianów Poland 37 H1
Siantan *i.* Indon. 58 C2
Siapa *r.* Venez. 147 E4
Siargao *i.* Phil. 57 H4
Siasi *i.* Phil. 57 G5
Siau *i.* Indon. 57 G6
Siauliai Lith. 33 N5
Siavonga Zambia 95 F9
Siazan' Azer. *see* Siyäzän
Sibay, Lake S. Africa 99 G5
Sibbo Fin. 33 G3
Šibenik Croatia 44 B3
Siberia *reg.* Rus. Fed. 27 J3
Siberut *i.* Indon. 58 B3
Siberut, Selat *sea chan.* Indon. 58 B3
Siberut National Park Indon. 58 B3
Sibi Pak. 81 F4
Sibidiri P.N.G. 57 J7
Sibigo Indon. 58 A2
Sibiloi National Park Kenya 96 D3
Sibir' Rus. Fed. *see* Siberia
Sibiryakova, Ostrov *i.* Rus. Fed. 26 H2
Sibiti Congo 95 B5
Sibiu Romania 46 D2
Sibley U.S.A. 132 C3
Sibolga Indon. 58 B2

Siborongborong Indon. 58 B2
Sibsagar India 75 G4
Sibu *Sarawak* Malaysia 59 E2
Sibut Cent. Afr. Rep. 94 C3
Sibutu *i.* Phil. 56 E5
Sibuyan *i.* Phil. 57 F3
Sibuyan Sea Phil. 57 F3
Sicamous Canada 122 G5
Sicasica Bol. 146 E7
Sicheng China *see* Lingyun
Sichon Thai. 61 B5
Sichuan *prov.* China 66 B2
Sichuan Pendi *basin* China 66 C2
Sicié, Cap *c.* France 39 F5
Sicilia *admin. reg.* Italy *see* Sicily
Sicilian Channel Italy/Tunisia 45 D6
Sicily *i.* Italy 45 D6
Sicuani Peru 148 C3
Šid Yugo. 46 I2
Siddhapur India 74 B5
Siddharthanagar Nepal *see* Bhairawa
Siddipet India 72 C2
Sideby Fin. 33 F3
Sideia Island P.N.G. 111 G1
Sidensjö Sweden 32 J3
Sideros, Akra *pt* Greece 47 E7
Sidesaviwa S. Africa 98 D7
Sidhi India 75 E4
Sidhirókastron Greece *see* Sidirokastro
Sidhpur India *see* Siddhapur
Sidi Aïssa Alg. 43 H5
Sidi Ali Alg. 43 G5
Sidi Barrāni Egypt 89 E2
Sidi Bel Abbès Alg. 91 E2
Sidi Bennour Morocco 90 B4
Sidi Bou Sa'id Tunisia *see* Sidi Bouzid
Sidi Bouzid Tunisia 91 H2
Sidi el Mokhtâr *well* Mali 92 D3
Sidi Ifni Morocco 90 C3
Sidi Kacem Morocco 90 D2
Sidikalang Indon. 58 B2
Sidi Khaled Alg. 91 F1
Sidi Mannsour *well* Tunisia 91 H2
Sidi Mhamed *well* W. Sahara 90 B5
Sidi Okba Alg. 91 G2
Sidirokastro Greece 46 C4
Sidi Saâd, Barrage *dam* Tunisia 45 B7
Sid Lake Canada 123 J2
Sidlaw Hills U.K. 34 F4
Sidley, Mount Antarctica 167 J1
Sidmouth U.K. 35 D6
Sidney *MT* U.S.A. 134 F3
Sidney *NE* U.S.A. 134 G4
Sidney *NY* U.S.A. 131 F2
Sidney *OH* U.S.A. 130 A3
Sido Mali 92 C3
Sidoan Indon. 57 F5
Sidoarjo Indon. 59 E4
Sidoktaya Myanmar 60 A3
Sidon Lebanon 77 B3
Sidorovo Rus. Fed. 28 G4
Sidr, Ra's as *pt* Egypt 77 A5
Sidrī, Wādī *watercourse* Egypt 77 A5
Sidrolândia Brazil 151 A7
Siedlce Poland 37 E1
Sieg *r.* Germany 36 C3
Siegen Germany 36 D3
Siĕmréab Cambodia 61 C5
Siem Reap Cambodia *see* Siĕmréab
Si'en China *see* Huanjiang
Siena Italy 44 D3
Sieppijärvi Fin. 32 F2
Sieradz Poland 37 I3
Sierakowo Poland 37 H2
Sieraków Poland 37 I2
Sierpc Poland 37 I2
Sierpienica *r.* Poland 37 I2
Sierra Blanca U.S.A. 135 F7
Sierra Colorada Arg. 152 D5
Sierra del Gistral *mts* Spain *see* Xistral, Serra do
Sierra Grande Arg. 152 D5
Sierra Leone *country* Africa 92 C3
africa 86–87, 100
Sierra Leone Basin *sea feature* N. Atlantic Ocean 160 M5
Sierra Leone Rise *sea feature* N. Atlantic Ocean 160 M5
Sierra Madre Mountains U.S.A. 136 C4
Sierra Mojada Mex. 131 C7
Sierra Nevada, Parque Nacional *nat. park* Venez. 146 D2
Sierra Nevada de Santa Marta, Parque Nacional *nat. park* Col. 146 C1
Sierra San Francisco Mex. 135 C7
Sierraville U.S.A. 136 C2
Sierra Vista U.S.A. 135 E7
Sierre Switz. 39 G3
Sieve *r.* Italy 44 D3
Sievi Fin. 32 G3
Sifang Ling *mts* China 66 C4
Sifeni Eth. 96 D1
Sifié Côte d'Ivoire 92 C4
Sifnos *i.* Greece 47 D6
Sifnou, Steno *sea chan.* Greece 47 D6
Sigatoka Fiji 107 H3
Sigave Wallis and Futuna Is 107 H3
Sigean France 39 E5
Siggiup Nunaa *pen.* Greenland 121 N2
Sighetu Marmaţiei Romania 31 J4
Sighişoara Romania 46 D1
Sigiriya Sri Lanka 72 D1
Siglap Sing. 58 [inset]
Sigli Indon. 58 A1
Siglufjörður Iceland 32 [inset]
Sigmaringen Germany 36 D4
Signal de Mailhebiau *mt.* France 39 E4
Signal de Randon *mt.* France 39 F4
Signal du Pic *hill* France 38 D4
Signal Peak U.S.A. 137 E5
Signy-l'Abbaye France 39 F2
Signy-l'Abbaye France 39 F2
Sigoisooinan Indon. 58 B3
Sigourney U.S.A. 132 C3
Sigri, Akra *pt* Greece 47 D4
Sigsbee Deep *sea feature* G. of Mexico 160 M4
Siguatepeque Hond. 142 G5
Sigüeiro Spain 42 B1
Sigüenza Spain 42 E2
Siguiri Guinea 92 C3
Sigulda Latvia 33 N4
Sigurd U.S.A. 137 G2
Sihanoukville Cambodia 61 C6
Sihanoukville, Chhâk *b.* Cambodia 61 C6
Sihaung Myauk Myanmar 60 A3
Sihawa India 73 D1
Sihong China 67 F1
Sihora *Madhya Pradesh* India 74 D5
Sihora *Madhya Pradesh* India 74 C5
Sihui China 67 E4
Siikainen Fin. 33 F3
Siikajoki Fin. 32 G2
Siikajoki *r.* Fin. 32 G2
Siilinjärvi Fin. 32 O3
Siippy Fin. *see* Sideby
Siirt Turkey 79 E3
Sijunjung Indon. 58 C3
Sika India 74 A5
Sikakap Indon. 58 B3
Sikandarabad India 74 C3
Sikandra India 74 D4
Sikandra Rao India 74 C4
Sikanni Chief Canada 122 F3
Sikanni Chief *r.* Canada 122 F3
Sikar India 74 C4
Sikaram *mt.* Afgh. 81 G3
Sikasso Mali 92 D3

Sikasso *admin. reg.* Mali 92 D3
Sikaw Myanmar 60 B3
Sikea Greece 47 C4
Sikeston U.S.A. 133 F4
Sīkelī Indon. 57 I4
Sikhote-Alin' *mts* Rus. Fed. 64 C4
Sikinos Greece 47 D6
Sikinos *i.* Greece 47 D6
Sikkim *state* India 75 F4
Sikonge Tanz. 97 B6
Sikongo Zambia 95 D8
Sikta India 75 E4
Sil *r.* Spain 42 C1
Silale Lith. 33 M5
Silandro Italy 44 C1
Silao Mex. 142 D4
Silba *i.* Croatia 44 E2
Silchar India 75 G4
Sildegapet *sea chan.* Norway 32 D5
Silchar India 75 G4
Silda Zambia 95 E9
Silgadi Nepal *see* Silgarhi
Silgarhi Nepal 74 E3
Silghat India 75 G4
Siliana Tunisia 91 H1
Silifke Turkey 78 C3
Siliguri India *see* Shiliguri
Siling Co *salt l.* China 70 G5
Silipur India 74 C4
Silisili, Mount Samoa 107 H3
Silistat Turkey *see* Bozkir
Silistra Bulg. 46 E2
Silistria Bulg. *see* Silistra
Silivri Turkey 78 B3
Siljan *l.* Sweden 33 H3
Silkeborg Denmark 33 G4
Silla Spain 43 F3
Sillamäe Estonia 28 C4
Sillaro *r.* Italy 44 C2
Sillé-le-Guillaume France 38 C2
Silli India 75 F5
Sillod India 72 B1
Sillon de Talbert *pen.* France 38 B2
Siloam Springs U.S.A. 133 C4
Silobela S. Africa 99 F4
Silovayakha *r.* Rus. Fed. 28 L2
Silsbee U.S.A. 133 C6
Silsby Lake Canada 123 M4
Silsden U.K. 34 F5
Siltaharju Fin. 32 O2
Siltou *well* Chad 88 B5
Siluas Indon. 58 D2
Silūp *r.* Iran 81 E5
Silute Lith. 33 L5
Silvan Turkey 79 E3
Silvânia Brazil 149 H4
Silvassa India 72 B1
Silver Bank Passage Turks and Caicos Is 127 L7
Silver Bay U.S.A. 132 D2
Silver City Canada 122 F3
Silver City U.S.A. 135 E6
Silver Creek U.S.A. 130 D2
Silver Lake U.S.A. 137 D4
Silvermine Mountains *hills* Rep. of Ireland 35 C5
Silver Peak Range *mts* U.S.A. 136 D3
Silver Spring U.S.A. 131 E4
Silver Springs U.S.A. 136 C2
Silverthrone Mountain Canada 122 E5
Silvertip Mountain Canada 134 B2
Silverton Canada 122 G5
Silverton U.S.A. 135 F5
Silves Brazil 147 G5
Silves Port. 42 B4
Silvia Col. 146 B4
Silvies *r.* U.S.A. 134 C4
Sim *r.* Rus. Fed. 28 K5
Sima Comoros 97 E8
Simao China 66 B4
Simão Dias Brazil 150 E4
Simara *Jharkhand* India 75 E4
Simaria *Madhya Pradesh* India 74 D4
Simav Turkey 78 B3
Simav Dağları *mts* Turkey 78 B3
Simayr *i.* Saudi Arabia 89 I5
Simba Dem. Rep. Congo 94 D4
Simbirsk Rus. Fed. *see* Ul'yanovsk
Simbruini, Monti *mts* Italy 44 E4
Simcoe Canada 130 D1
Simcoe, Lake Canada 130 D1
Simdega India 75 E5
Simên Mountain National Park Eth. 96 C1
Simên Mountains Eth. 96 C1
Simeonovgrad Bulg. 46 D3
Simeria Romania 46 C2
Simeto *r. Sicily* Italy 45 E6
Simeulue *i.* Indon. 58 A2
Simferopol' Ukr. 29 E7
Simi *i.* Greece *see* Symi
Simikot Nepal 75 E3
Simití Col. 146 C2
Simi Valley U.S.A. 136 D4
Simla India *see* Shimla
Simla U.S.A. 134 G5
Simleu Silvaniei Romania 46 C1
Simmern (Hunsrück) Germany 36 C3
Simmesport U.S.A. 133 D6
Simo Fin. 32 G2
Simojärvi *l.* Fin. 32 O2
Simojovel Mex. 135 F7
Simonette *r.* Canada 122 G4
Simonhouse Canada 123 K4
Šimonka *mt.* Slovakia 37 J4
Simons U.S.A. 130 E3
Simontornya Hungary 37 I5
Simoom Sound Canada 122 E5
Simpang Indon. 58 C3
Simpang Mangayau, Tanjong *pt Sabah* Malaysia 59 G1
Simplicio Mendes Brazil 150 E5
Simplon Pass Switz. 39 H3
Simpson Canada 123 J5
Simpson Desert Australia 110 D5
Simpson Desert National Park Australia 110 D5
Simpson Desert Regional Reserve *nature res.* Australia 110 D5
Simpson Park Mountains U.S.A. 137 D2
Simpson Peninsula Canada 121 K3
Simpsonville U.S.A. 129 C5
Simra Nepal 75 F4
Simrishamn Sweden 33 H5
Simuku *i.* Indon. 58 B3
Simunjan *Sarawak* Malaysia 59 E2
Simushir, Ostrov *i.* Rus. Fed. 54 H2
Sina *r.* India 72 B2
Sinā', Shibh Jazīrat *pen.* Egypt *see* Sinai
Sinabang Indon. 58 A2
Sinabung *vol.* Indon. 58 B2
Sinadhaqa Somalia 96 E3
▶Sinai *pen.* Egypt 89 G2
africa 100
Sinai, Mont *hill* France 39 E4
Sinai, Mount Egypt 77 A5
Sinaia Romania 46 D2

Sinai al Janūbīya *governorate* Egypt *see* Janūb Sīnā'
Sinai ash Shamālīya *governorate* Egypt *see* Shamāl Sīnā'
Si Nakarin Reservoir Thai. 61 B5
Sinamaica Venez. 146 D1
Sinan China 66 D3
Sinancha Rus. Fed. *see* Cheremshany
Sinanju N. Korea 65 A5
Sinarades Greece 47 A5
Sinäwin Libya 88 A2
Sinazongwe Zambia 95 E9
Sinbaungwe Myanmar 60 A4
Sinbo Myanmar 60 B2
Sinbyugyun Myanmar 60 A3
Sincan Turkey 79 D3
Sincé Col. 146 C2
Sincelejo Col. 146 C2
Sinchu Taiwan *see* T'aoyüan
Sinclair U.S.A. 129 C5
Sinclair, Lake U.S.A. 129 C5
Sinclair Mills Canada 122 F4
Sincora, Serra do *hills* Brazil 150 D5
Sind *r.* India 74 C4
Sind Rus. Fed. 64 D2
Sinda Rus. Fed. 64 D2
Sinda Zambia 97 A8
Sindal Denmark 33 G4
Sindangbarang Indon. 59 D4
Sindara Gabon 94 A5
Sindari India 74 A4
Sindelfingen Germany 36 D4
Sindgi India 72 C2
Sindh *prov.* Pak. 81 G5
Sindhnur India 72 C3
Sindhuli Garhi Nepal 75 E4
Sindhulimadi Nepal *see* Sindhuli Garhi
Sindi India 72 C1
Sındırgı Turkey 78 B3
Sindkhed India 72 C2
Sindominic Romania *see* Sândominic
Sindor Rus. Fed. 28 I3
Sindou Burkina 92 D3
Sindphana *r.* India 72 C2
Sindri India 75 E5
Sind Sagar Doab *lowland* Pak. 81 G4
Sinekçi Turkey 47 E4
Sinel'nikovo Ukr. *see* Synel'nykove
Sinendé Benin 93 F3
Sines Port. 42 B4
Sines, Cabo de *c.* Port. 42 B4
Sinettä Fin. 32 G2
Sinfra Côte d'Ivoire 92 D4
Sing Myanmar 60 B3
Singa Sudan 89 G6
Singahi India 74 D3
Singaingmyo Myanmar 60 B3
▶Singapore *country* Asia 58 C2
asia 52–53, 82
Singapore Sing. 58 C2
Capital of Singapore.
Singapore *r.* Sing. 58 [inset]
Singapore, Strait of *Indon./Sing.* 58 C2
Singapura *country* Asia *see* Singapore
Singaraja Indon. 59 F5
Singareni India 72 D2
Singatoka Fiji *see* Sigatoka
Singave Wallis and Futuna Is *see* Sigave
Sing Buri Thai. 61 C5
Singen (Hohentwiel) Germany 36 D5
Singhampton Canada 130 C1
Singida Tanz. 97 B6
Singida *admin. reg.* Tanz. 97 B6
Singidunum Yugo. *see* Belgrade
Singkaling Hkamti Myanmar 60 A2
Singkawang Indon. 59 E2
Singkep *i.* Indon. 58 C3
Singkil Indon. 58 B2
Singleton Australia 112 D4
Singleton, Mount *N.T.* Australia 110 E4
Singleton, Mount *W.A.* Australia 109 B7
Singoli India 74 C4
Singon Myanmar 60 A3
Singora Thai. *see* Songkhla
Sin'gosan N. Korea *see* Kosan
Singra India 75 F4
Singu Myanmar 60 A3
Sin'gye N. Korea 65 A4
Sinhala *country* Asia *see* Sri Lanka
Sinharaja Forest Reserve *nature res.* Sri Lanka 72 D5
Sinhüng N. Korea 65 A4
Sining China *see* Xining
Siniscola *Sardinia* Italy 45 B4
Sini Vrükh *mt.* Bulg. 46 D4
Sinj Croatia 44 A3
Sinjai Indon. 57 F7
Sinjär Iraq 79 E3
Sinjār, Jabal *mt.* Iraq 79 E3
Sinkat Sudan 89 H5
Sinkiang *aut. reg.* China *see* Xinjiang Uygur Zizhiqu
Sinkiang Uighur Autonomous Region *aut. reg.* China *see* Xinjiang Uygur Zizhiqu
Sinmi-do *i.* N. Korea 65 A5
Sinnar India 72 B2
Sinn Bishr, Jabal *hill* Egypt 77 A5
Sinneh Iran *see* Sanandaj
Sinni *r.* Italy 44 F4
Sinnicolau Mare Romania *see* Sânnicolau Mare
Sinoia Zimbabwe *see* Chinhoyi
Sinoie, Lacul *lag.* Romania 46 F2
Sinop Brazil 149 G6
Sinop Turkey 78 C2
Sinope Turkey *see* Sinop
Sinoquipe Mex. 135 E7
Sinp'a N. Korea 64 A4
Sinp'o N. Korea 65 B4
Sinsheim Germany 36 D4
Sintang Indon. 59 E2

▶Sint Maarten *i.* Neth. Antilles 139 L5
Part of the Netherlands Antilles. The northern part of the island is the French territory of St Martin.
Sint-Niklaas Belgium 36 A3
Sinton U.S.A. 133 B6
Sint-Vith Belgium 39 G1
Sinú *r.* Col. 146 C2
Sinúiju N. Korea 65 A4
Sinujiif Somalia 96 E3
Sinyaya *r.* Rus. Fed. 33 H4
Sioma Zambia 95 D8
Sioma Ngwezi National Park Zambia 95 D9
Sion Switz. 39 G3
Sioraipaluk Greenland 121 L2
Sioule *r.* France 39 E3
Sioux Center U.S.A. 132 B3
Sioux City U.S.A. 132 B3
Sioux Falls U.S.A. 132 B3
Sioux Lookout Canada 124 B3
Šipan *i.* Croatia 44 F3
Siping China 64 A4
Sipiwesk Canada 123 L4
Sipiwesk Lake Canada 123 L4
Siple, Mount Antarctica 167 J2
Siple Coast Antarctica 167 I1
Siple Island Antarctica 167 J2
Sipolilo Zimbabwe *see* Guruve
Sipul P.N.G. 57 F2
Sipura *i.* Indon. 58 B3

Sipura, Selat sea chan. Indon. 58 B3
Sīq, Wādī as watercourse Egypt 77 A5
Siquisique Venez. 146 D2
Sir r. Pak. 81 G5
Sira India 72 C3
Sira Norway 33 B4
Şīr Abū Nu'āyr i. U.A.E. 80 C5
Si Racha Thai. 61 C5
Siracusa Sicily Italy see Syracuse
Siraha Nepal see Sirha
Sirajganj Bangl. 75 F4
Sir Alexander, Mount Canada 122 F4
Şiran Turkey 79 D2
Sirathu India 75 D4
Sirba r. Burkina/Niger 93 F2
Sirbāl, Jabal mt. Egypt 77 A5
Şīr Banī Yās i. U.A.E. 80 C5
Sircilla India see Sirsilla
Sirdaryo r. Asia see Syrdar'ya
Sirdaryo Uzbek. see Syrdar'ya
Sirdaryo Wiloyati admin. div. Uzbek. see Syrdar'inskaya Oblast'
Sirdingka China see Lhari
Sire Tanz. 97 A6
Sir Edward Pellew Group is Australia 110 D2
Siret r. Romania 46 F2
Sir Graham Moore Islands Australia 108 D3
Sirha Nepal 75 E4
Sirḩān, Wādī as watercourse Jordan/Saudi Arabia 77 C4
Şiria Romania 46 B1
Sīrīk Iran 80 D5
Sirik, Tanjong pt Sarawak Malaysia 59 E2
Siri Kit Dam Thai. 60 C4
Sirikit Reservoir Thai. 60 C4
Sirina i. Greece see Syrna
Siritoi r. Pak. 81 G4
Sīrjā Iran 81 E5
Sir James MacBrien, Mount Canada 122 E2
Sīrjān Iran 80 C4
Sirjan salt flat Iran 80 C4
Sirkka Fin. 32 G2
Sirmaur India 74 C3
Sirmilik National Park Canada 121 L2
Sirmium Yugo. see Sremska Mitrovica
Sirmour India 75 D4
Sirmour India see Sirmaur
Şırnak Turkey 79 E3
Sirniö Fin. 32 H2
Sirohi India 74 B4
Sironcha India 72 D2
Sironj India 74 C4
Síros i. Greece see Syros
Siroua, Jbel mt. Morocco 90 D3
Sirpur India 72 C2
Sirrei Eth. 96 D3
Sirretta Peak U.S.A. 136 C4
Sīrrī, Jazīreh-ye i. Iran 80 C5
Sirsa India 74 B3
Sir Sandford, Mount Canada 122 G5
Sirsi Karnataka India 72 B3
Sirsi Uttar Pradesh India 74 C3
Sirsilla India 72 C2
Sirte Libya 88 C2
Sirte, Gulf of Libya 88 C2
Sir Thomas, Mount Australia 110 B5
Siruguppa India 72 C3
Sirupa r. Mex. 135 E7
Sirur India 72 B2
Širvintos Lith. 33 G5
Sīrwān r. Iraq 79 F4
Sir Wilfrid Laurier, Mount Canada 122 G4
Sir William Thompson Range hills Australia 111 E2
Sis Turkey see Kozan
Sisak Croatia 44 F2
Sisaket Thai. 61 D5
Sisante Spain 43 E4
Siscia Croatia see Sisak
Sishen S. Africa 98 D5
Sisian Armenia 79 F3
Sisimiut Greenland 121 N3
Sisipuk Lake Canada 123 K4
Sisogúichic Mex. 135 F8
Sisŏphŏn Cambodia 61 C5
Sisquoc r. U.S.A. 136 B4
Sisseton U.S.A. 132 B2
Sissili r. Burkina 93 E3
Sissonville U.S.A. 130 C4
Sīstan, Daryācheh-ye marsh Afgh. 81 E4
Sisteron France 39 F4
Sisters U.S.A. 134 B3
Sistersville U.S.A. 130 C4
Sisto r. Italy 44 D4
Sitalike Tanz. 97 A6
Sitamarhi India 75 E4
Sitamau India 74 B4
Sitampiky Madag. 99 [inset] J3
Sitang China see Sinan
Sitapur India 74 D4
Siteia Greece 47 E7
Siteki Swaziland 99 F5
Sithonia pen. Greece 47 C4
Sitía Greece see Siteia
Sitila Moz. 99 G4
Siting China 66 C3
Sítio da Abadia Brazil 150 C5
Sítio do Mato Brazil 150 D5
Sitka U.S.A. 120 F4
Sitnica r. Yugo. 46 B3
Sitno mt. Slovakia 37 I4
Sitrah oasis Egypt 89 E2
Sittang r. Myanmar 60 B4
Sittard Neth. 36 B3
Sittaung Myanmar 60 A2
Sittaung r. Myanmar see Sittang
Sittoung r. Myanmar see Sittang
Sittwe Myanmar 62 E7
Situbondo Indon. 59 F4
Siumpain, Rubha an t- hd U.K. see Tiumpan Head
Siuri India 75 E5
Sivaganga India 72 C4
Sivakasi India 72 C4
Sivaki Rus. Fed. 64 A1
Sivand Iran 80 C4
Sivas Turkey 78 D3
Sivaslı Turkey 78 B3
Siverek Turkey 79 D3
Siverskiy Rus. Fed. 28 D4
Sivers'kyy Donets' r. Rus. Fed./Ukr. see Severskiy Donets
Sivomaskinskiy Rus. Fed. 28 L2
Sivrice Turkey 79 D3
Sivrihisar Turkey 78 B3
Sīwah Egypt 89 E2
Sīwah, Wāḩāt Egypt 89 E2
Siwalik Range mts India/Nepal 74 C3
Siwan India 75 E4
Siwana India 74 B4
Six Cross Roads Barbados 147 G1
Six-Fours-les-Plages France 39 F5
Sixian China 67 F1
Sixtymile Canada 122 A1
Siyabuswa S. Africa 99 F5
Siyang Guangxi China see Shangsi
Siyang Jiangsu China 67 F1
Siyäzän Azer. 79 G2
Sīyunī Iran 80 C3
Sjenica Yugo. 46 B3
Sjoa Norway 33 C3
Sjöbo Sweden 33 D5
Sjøholt Norway 32 B3
Sjona sea chan. Norway 32 D2
Sjoutnäset Sweden 32 D2
Sjøvegan Norway 32 E1
Skäckerfjällen mts Sweden 32 D3
Skadarsko Jezero nat. park Yugo. 46 A3
Skadovs'k Ukr. 29 E7
Skærbæk Denmark 33 C5
Skaftafell nat. park Iceland 32 [inset] C2
Skagafjörður inlet Iceland 32 [inset]
Skagen Denmark 33 C4
Skagern l. Sweden 33 D4
Skagerrak strait Denmark/Norway 33 C4
Skagit r. U.S.A. 134 B2
Skagway U.S.A. 120 F4
Skaidi Norway 32 G1
Skala Notio Aigaio Greece 47 E6
Skala Peloponnisos Greece 47 C6
Skala Kallonis Greece 47 E5
Skaland Norway 28 A1
Skallelv Norway 32 H1
Skalmodal Sweden 32 D2
Skanderborg Denmark 33 C4
Skåne county Sweden 33 D5
Skaneateles U.S.A. 131 E2
Skaneateles Lake U.S.A. 131 E2
Skånevik Norway 33 B4
Skantzoura i. Greece 47 D5
Skara Sweden 33 D4
Skara Brae tourist site U.K. 34 E2
Skarberget Norway 32 E1
Skardarsko Jezero l. Albania/Yugo. see Scutari, Lake
Skardu Jammu and Kashmir 74 B2
Skare Norway 33 B4
Skärgårdshavets Nationalpark nat. park Fin. 33 F4
Skarnes Norway 33 C3
Skärplinge Sweden 33 E3
Skärsjövålen Sweden 33 D3
Skarszewy Poland 37 I1
Skarvedalseggen mt. Norway 33 C3
Skarvsjöby Sweden 32 E2
Skaryszew Poland 37 J3
Skarżysko-Kamienna Poland 37 J3
Skaudvilė Lith. 33 F5
Skaulo Sweden 32 F2
Skawa r. Poland 37 I3
Skawina Poland 37 I4
Skaymat W. Sahara 90 B4
Skeena r. Canada 122 D4
Skeena Mountains Canada 122 D3
Skegness U.K. 35 G5
Skeiðarársandur sand area Iceland 32 [inset]
Skeleton Coast Game Park nature res. Namibia 98 B3
Skellefteå Sweden 32 F2
Skellefteälven r. Sweden 32 F2
Skeppshamn Sweden 33 E3
Skerries Rep. of Ireland 35 C5
Skhimatárion Greece see Schimatari
Skhira Tunisia 40 E5
Skhiza i. Greece see Schiza
Ski Norway 33 C4
Skiathos Greece 47 C5
Skiathos i. Greece 47 C5
Skibbereen Rep. of Ireland 35 B6
Skibotn Norway 32 F1
Skiddaw hill U.K. 35 E4
Skien Norway 33 C4
Skierniewice Poland 37 J3
Skikda Alg. 91 G1
Skinari, Akra pt Greece 47 B6
Skio Jammu and Kashmir 74 C2
Skipton Australia 112 B5
Skipton U.K. 35 E5
Skiropoúla i. Greece see Skyropoula
Skíros i. Greece see Skyros
Skive Denmark 33 C4
Skjálfandafljót r. Iceland 32 [inset]
Skjerkeknuten hill Norway 33 B4
Skjern Denmark 33 C5
Skjern Norway 32 G2
Skobelev Uzbek. see Fergana
Skobeleva, Pik mt. Kyrg. 81 H2
Skocjanske Jame tourist site Slovenia 44 D2
Škofja Loka Slovenia 44 E1
Skog Sweden 33 E3
Skoganvarre Norway 32 G1
Skogfoss Norway 32 H1
Skoki Poland 37 H2
Sköllersta Sweden 33 D4
Skomvær is Norway 32 C2
Skopelos i. Greece 47 C5
Skopia hill Greece 47 D5
Skopin Rus. Fed. 29 F5

▶Skopje Macedonia 46 B4
Capital of Macedonia.

Skoplje Macedonia see Skopje
Skopunarfjørður sea chan. Faroe Is 34 [inset]
Skórcz Poland 37 I2
Skorodnoye Rus. Fed. 29 F6
Skørping Denmark 33 C4
Skotoussa Greece 46 C4
Skotterud Norway 33 D4
Skoutari Greece 46 C4
Skoutaros Greece 47 E5
Skövde Sweden 33 D4
Skovorodino Rus. Fed. 27 M4
Skowhegan U.S.A. 128 F2
Skrīveri Latvia 33 G4
Skröven Sweden 32 F2
Skrunda Latvia 33 F4
Skrwa r. Poland 37 I2
Skúgvoy i. Faroe Is 34 [inset]
Skukum, Mount Canada 122 C2
Skukuza S. Africa 99 F5
Skuleskogens nationalpark nat. park Sweden 32 E3
Skull Valley U.S.A. 137 F4
Skultuna Sweden 33 E4
Skunk r. U.S.A. 132 D3
Skuodas Lith. 33 F4
Skurup Sweden 33 D5
Skŭt r. Bulg. 46 C3
Skutskär Sweden 33 E3
Skvyra Ukr. 29 D6
Skwierzyna Poland 37 G2
Skye i. U.K. 34 C3
Skykula hill Norway 33 B4
Skyring, Seno b. Chile 153 B8
Skyropoula i. Greece 47 D5
Skyros Greece 47 D5
Skyros i. Greece 47 D5
Skytrain Ice Rise Antarctica 167 L1
Slættaratindur hill Faroe Is 34 [inset]
Slagelse Denmark 33 C5
Slagnäs Sweden 32 E2
Slamet, Gunung vol. Indon. 59 E4
Slana U.S.A. 122 A2
Slaney r. Rep. of Ireland 35 C5
Slănic r. Romania 46 E2
Slănic Moldova Romania 46 E1
Slanské Vrchy mts Slovakia 37 J4
Slantsy Rus. Fed. 28 D4
Slaný Czech Rep. 37 G3
Slapovi Krke nat. park Croatia 44 E3
Slashers Reefs Australia 111 F3
Śląska, Wyżyna hills Poland 37 I3
Slatina Croatia 44 F2
Slatina Romania 46 D2
Slatina-Timiş Romania 46 C2
Slaty Fork U.S.A. 130 C4
Slautnoye Rus. Fed. 27 Q3
Slave r. Canada 123 H2
Slave Coast Africa 93 F4
Slave Lake Canada 123 H4
Slave Point Canada 123 H2
Slavgorod Belarus see Slawharad
Slavgorod Rus. Fed. 62 B1
Slavonska Požega Croatia see Požega
Slavonski Brod Croatia 44 G2
Slavutych Ukr. 29 D6
Slavyanka Kazakh. see Myrzakent
Slavyanka Rus. Fed. 64 B4
Slavyansk Ukr. see Slov"yans'k
Slavyanskaya Rus. Fed. see Slavyansk-na-Kubani
Slavyansk-na-Kubani Rus. Fed. 29 F7
Sława Poland 37 H3
Slawharad Belarus 29 D5
Sławno Poland 37 H1
Slayton U.S.A. 132 C3
Sleaford U.K. 35 F5
Sleat, Sound of sea chan. U.K. 34 D3
Sled Lake Canada 123 J4
Sleeper Islands Canada 124 E1
Sleptsovskaya Rus. Fed. 29 H8
Slessor Glacier Antarctica 167 B1
Ślęża hill Poland 37 H3
Slick Rock U.S.A. 137 H2
Slidell U.S.A. 133 D6
Slide Mountain U.S.A. 131 F3
Slidre Norway 33 C3
Slieve Car hill Rep. of Ireland 35 B4
Slieve Donard hill U.K. 35 D4
Slieve Gamph hills Rep. of Ireland 35 B5
Slieve Mish Mountains hills Rep. of Ireland 35 A5
Sligachan U.K. 34 C3
Sligeach Rep. of Ireland see Sligo
Sligo Rep. of Ireland 35 B4
Sligo U.S.A. 130 D3
Sligo Bay Rep. of Ireland 35 B4
Slippery Rock U.S.A. 130 C3
Sliven Bulg. 46 E3
Slivnitsa Bulg. 46 C3
Slivo Pole Bulg. 46 E3
Sljeme mt. Croatia 44 E2
Sloan r. Canada 123 G1
Sloan U.S.A. 137 E4
Sloat U.S.A. 136 B2
Sloboda Rus. Fed. see Ezhva
Slobodchikovo Rus. Fed. 28 I3
Slobodskoy Rus. Fed. 28 I4
Slobozia Romania 46 E2
Slobozia Bradului Romania 46 E2
Słomniki Poland 37 J3
Slonim Belarus 29 C5
Slough U.K. 35 F6
▶Slovakia country Europe 37 I4
europe 24–25, 48
▶Slovenia country Europe 44 E1
europe 24–25, 48
Slovenija country Europe see Slovenia
Slovenj Gradec Slovenia 44 E1
Slovenska Bistrica Slovenia 44 E1
Slovenske Gorice hills Slovenia 44 E1
Slovenské Rudohorie mts Slovakia 37 I4
Slovensko country Europe see Slovakia
Slovenský kras mts Slovakia 37 J4
Slovenský raj nat. park Slovakia 37 J4
Slov"yans'k Ukr. 29 F6
Słowiński Park Narodowy nat. park Poland 37 H1
Słubice Poland 37 G2
Slunj Croatia 44 E2
Słupca Poland 37 H2
Słupia r. Poland 37 H1
Słupsk Poland 37 H1
Slussfors Sweden 32 E2
Slutsk Belarus 29 C5
Slyne Head Rep. of Ireland 35 A5
Slyudyanka Rus. Fed. 27 K4
Smackover U.S.A. 133 C5
Smålandsstenar Sweden 33 D4
Small Point U.S.A. 131 I2
Smallwood Reservoir Canada 125 H2
Smalyavichy Belarus 29 D5
Smarhon' Belarus 29 C5
Smeaton Canada 123 J4
Smederevo Yugo. 46 B2
Smederevska Palanka Yugo. 46 B2
Smeeni Romania 46 E2
Smela Ukr. see Smila
Smethport U.S.A. 130 D3
Smila Ukr. 29 D6
Smiltene Latvia 33 G4
Smirnykh Rus. Fed. 64 E2
Smith Canada 123 H4
Smith r. MT U.S.A. 134 E3
Smith r. VA U.S.A. 130 D5
Smith Arm b. Canada 122 F1
Smith Center U.S.A. 132 B4
Smithers Canada 122 E4
Smithers Landing Canada 122 E4
Smithfield UT U.S.A. 134 E4
Smithfield VA U.S.A. 131 E5
Smith Glacier Antarctica 167 K1
Smith Island India 73 G3
Smith Island U.S.A. 131 E4
Smith Mountain Lake U.S.A. 130 D5
Smith River Canada 122 E3
Smithsburg U.S.A. 130 E4
Smiths Falls Canada 131 E1
Smithton Australia 112 C6
Smithville TN U.S.A. 128 B5
Smithville WV U.S.A. 130 C4
Smjörfjöll mts Iceland 32 [inset]
Smoke Creek Desert U.S.A. 136 C1
Smoky r. Canada 122 G3
Smoky Bay Australia 109 F8
Smoky Cape Australia 112 E3
Smoky Falls Canada 124 D3
Smoky Hill r. U.S.A. 132 A4
Smoky Hill, North Fork r. U.S.A. 134 G5
Smoky Hills KS U.S.A. 126 G4
Smoky Hills KS U.S.A. 132 B4
Smoky Lake Canada 123 H4
Smoky Mountains U.S.A. 134 D4
Smøla i. Norway 32 B3
Smolensk Rus. Fed. 29 E5
Smolenskaya Oblast' admin. div. Rus. Fed. 29 E5
Smolensk Oblast admin. div. Rus. Fed. see Smolenskaya Oblast'
Smolensko-Moskovskaya Vozvyshennost' hills Rus. Fed. 31 M2
Smolevichi Belarus see Smalyavichy
Smolikas mt. Greece 47 B4
Smolyan Bulg. 46 D4
Smolyoninovo Rus. Fed. 64 C4
Smooth Rock Falls Canada 124 D3
Smoothrock Lake Canada 124 B3
Smoothstone Lake Canada 123 J4
Smørfjord Norway 32 G1
Smorgon' Belarus see Smarhon'
Smyadovo Bulg. 46 E3
Smyley Island Antarctica 167 L2
Smyrna Turkey see İzmir
Smyrna DE U.S.A. 131 F4
Smyrna GA U.S.A. 129 B5
Smyrna TN U.S.A. 128 B5
Snæfell mt. Iceland 32 [inset]
Snaefell hill Isle of Man 35 D4
Snæfellsnes pen. Iceland 32 [inset]
Snake r. Canada 122 C1
Snake r. U.S.A. 134 C3
Snake Range mts U.S.A. 137 E2
Snake River Canada 122 F3
Snake River Plain U.S.A. 134 D4
Snare r. Canada 123 G2
Snare Lake Canada 123 J3
Snare Lakes Canada see Wekweti
Snares Islands N.Z. 107 F6
Snåsa Norway 32 D2
Snåsvatn l. Norway 32 D2
Sneedville U.S.A. 130 B5
Sneek Neth. 36 B2
Sneem Rep. of Ireland 35 B6
Sneeuberge mts S. Africa 98 E6
Snegamook Lake Canada 125 I2
Sněžka mt. Czech Rep. 37 G3
Snežnik mt. Slovenia 44 E2
Śniardwy, Jezioro l. Poland 37 J2
Sniečkus Lith. see Visaginas
Śnieżka mt. Czech Rep. see Sněžka
Śnieżnik mt. Poland 37 H3
Snihurivka Ukr. 29 E7
Snøhetta mt. Norway 33 C3
Snønuten mt. Norway 33 B4
Snovsk Ukr. see Shchors
Snowbird Lake Canada 123 K2
Snowdon mt. U.K. 35 D5
Snowdonia National Park U.K. 35 E5
Snowdrift Canada see Łutselk'e
Snowdrift r. Canada 123 I2
Snowflake U.S.A. 137 G4
Snow Hill MD U.S.A. 131 F4
Snow Hill NC U.S.A. 128 D5
Snow Lake Canada 123 K4
Snowtown Australia 112 A4
Snowy r. Australia 112 D5
Snowy Mountain U.S.A. 131 F2
Snowy Mountains Australia 112 C5
Snug Harbour Canada 125 K2
Snyder OK U.S.A. 133 B5
Snyder TX U.S.A. 133 A5
Soahany Madag. 99 [inset] J3
Soaigh i. U.K. see Soay
Soalala Madag. 99 [inset] J3
Soanierana-Ivongo Madag. 99 [inset] K3
Soan-kundo is S. Korea 65 A6
Soata Col. 146 C3
Soay i. U.K. 34 B3
Sobaek-sanmaek mts S. Korea 65 A6
Sobaek-san National Park S. Korea 65 B5
Sobat r. Sudan 96 A2
Soběslav Czech Rep. 37 G4
Sobger r. Indon. 57 J6
Sobinka Rus. Fed. 28 G5
Sobradinho, Barragem de resr Brazil 150 D4
Sobrado Brazil 150 D4
Sobral Brazil 150 D2
Soča r. Italy see Isonzo
Sochaczew Poland 37 J2
Sochi Rus. Fed. 29 F8
Sochos Greece 46 C4
Society Islands Fr. Polynesia 165 H7
Socol Romania 46 B2
Socompa Chile 148 C6
Socorro Col. 146 C3
Socorro U.S.A. 135 F6
Socorro, Isla i. Mex. 126 D8
Socotra i. Yemen 76 E7
Socovos Spain 43 F4
Soc Trăng Vietnam 61 D6
Socuéllamos Spain 42 E3
Soda Lake CA U.S.A. 136 C4
Soda Lake CA U.S.A. 137 D4
Sodankylä Fin. 32 G2
Soda Plains Aksai Chin 74 C2
Soda Springs U.S.A. 134 E4
Söderhamn Sweden 33 E3
Söderköping Sweden 33 E4
Södermanland county Sweden 33 E4
Södertälje Sweden 33 E4
Sodiri Sudan 89 F6
Sodo Eth. 96 C3
Södra Kvarken strait Fin./Sweden 33 E3
Soë Indon. 57 F7
Soekmekaar S. Africa 99 F4
Soerabaia Indon. see Surabaya
Soest Germany 36 D3
Sofades Greece 47 C5
Sofala Moz. 99 G4
Sofala prov. Moz. 99 G3
Sofala, Baía de b. Moz. 99 G4

▶Sofia Bulg. 46 C3
Capital of Bulgaria.

Sofia r. Madag. 99 [inset] J2
Sofiko Greece 47 C6
Sofiya Bulg. see Sofia
Sofiyevka Ukr. see Vil'nyans'k
Sofiysk Khabarovskiy Kray Rus. Fed. 64 C1
Sofiysk Khabarovskiy Kray Rus. Fed. 64 D2
Sofporog Rus. Fed. 32 H2
Softa Kalesi tourist site Turkey 77 A1
Sōfu-gan i. Japan 65 E7
Sog China 70 H5
Sogamoso Col. 146 C3
Sogda Rus. Fed. 64 C2
Sogma China 74 D2
Søgne Norway 33 B4
Sognefjorden inlet Norway 33 B3
Sogn og Fjordane county Norway 33 B3
Sogo Hills Kenya 96 C4
Sogolle well Chad 88 B6
Sog Qu r. China 75 G2
Söğüt Turkey 78 B2
Söğüt Dağı mts Turkey 78 B3
Sohâg Egypt see Sawhāj
Sohagpur India 74 C5
Sohan r. Pak. 81 G3
Sohano P.N.G. 107 E2
Sohar Oman see Şuḩār
Sohela India 75 D5
Sohna India 74 C3
Sohng Gwe, Khao hill Myanmar/Thai. 61 B5
Soignies Belgium 39 F1
Soila China 66 A2
Soini Fin. 32 G3
Soissons France 39 E2
Sojat India 74 B4
Sojat Road India 74 B4
Sok r. Rus. Fed. 29 I5
Sokch'o S. Korea 65 B5
Söke Turkey 78 A3
Sokele Dem. Rep. Congo 95 E7
Sokhós Greece see Sochos
Sokhumi Georgia 79 E2
Sokiryany Ukr. see Sokyryany
Sokobanja Yugo. 46 B3
Sokodé Togo 93 F3
Soko Islands Hong Kong China 67 [inset]
Sokol Rus. Fed. 28 G4
Sokolac Bos.-Herz. 44 G3
Sokolo Mali 92 D2
Sokolov Czech Rep. 37 F3
Sokołów Podlaski Poland 37 K2
Sokolozero, Ozero l. Rus. Fed. 32 H2
Sokosti hill Fin. 32 H1
Sokoto Nigeria 93 G2
Sokoto r. Nigeria 93 G3
Sokoto state Nigeria 93 G2
Sokourala Guinea 92 C3
Sokyryany Ukr. 29 C6
Soła r. Poland 37 I4
Sola i. Tonga see Ata
Solan India 74 C3
Solander Island N.Z. 113 A4
Solapur India 72 B2
Soldado Bartra Peru 146 C5
Soldotna U.S.A. 120 D3
Solec Kujawski Poland 37 I2
Soledad Arg. 152 E2
Soledad U.S.A. 136 B3
Soledad Venez. 147 F2
Soledade Brazil 146 D6
Sølen mt. Norway 33 C3
Solenzo Burkina 92 D2
Solfjellsjøen Norway 32 D2
Solginskiy Rus. Fed. 28 G3
Solhan Turkey 79 E3
Soligalich Rus. Fed. 28 G4
Soligorsk Belarus see Salihorsk
Solihull U.K. 35 F5
Solikamsk Rus. Fed. 28 K4
Sol'-Iletsk Rus. Fed. 29 J6
Soliman Tunisia 45 C6
Solingen Germany 36 C3
Solita Col. 146 C4
Sol-Karmala Rus. Fed. see Severnoye
Sollefteå Sweden 32 E3
Sollentuna Sweden 33 E4
Sóller Spain 43 H3
Solling hills Germany 36 D3
Solnechnyy Khabarovskiy Kray Rus. Fed. 64 D2
Solnechnyy Khabarovskiy Kray Rus. Fed. see Gornyy
Solo r. Indon. 59 F4
Solofra Italy 45 E4
Solok Indon. 58 C3
Solomon U.S.A. 137 H5
Solomon r. U.S.A. 132 B4
Solomon, North Fork r. U.S.A. 132 B4
Solomon, South Fork r. U.S.A. 132 B4

▶Solomon Islands country S. Pacific Ocean 107 F2
4th largest and 5th most populous country in Oceania.
oceania 104–105, 114

Solomon Sea P.N.G./Solomon Is 107 E2
Solor i. Indon. 108 C2
Solor, Kepulauan is Indon. 57 F7
Solotcha Rus. Fed. 29 F5
Solothurn Switz. 39 G3
Solovetskiye Ostrova is Rus. Fed. 28 E2
Solsona Spain 43 G2
Solt Hungary 37 I5
Šolta i. Croatia 44 F3
Soltānābād Khorāsan Iran 80 D2
Soltānābād Khorāsan Iran 81 D3
Soltānābād Tehrān Iran 80 B3
Soltān-e Bakva Afgh. 81 E3
Soltānī, Khowr-e b. Iran 80 B4
Soltanqolī Iran 80 A3
Soltau Germany 36 D2
Sol'tsy Rus. Fed. 28 D4
Soltvadkert Hungary 37 I5
Solunska Glava mt. Macedonia 46 B4
Solvay U.S.A. 131 E2
Sölvesborg Sweden 33 D4
Solway Firth est. U.K. 34 E4
Solwezi Zambia 95 E8
Sōma Japan 65 E5
Soma Turkey 78 A3
Somabhula Zimbabwe 99 F3
Somabula Zimbabwe see Somabhula
Somali admin. reg. Eth. 96 D3
▶Somalia country Africa 96 E4
africa 86–87, 100
Somali Basin sea feature Indian Ocean 162 K6
Somali Republic country Africa see Somalia
Somanga Tanz. 97 C7
Somanya Ghana 93 E4
Sombo Angola 95 D7
Sombor Yugo. 46 A2
Sombrerete Mex. 126 F7
Sombrero Chile 153 C8
Sombrero Channel India 73 G5
Somdari India 74 B4
Somero Fin. 33 F3
Somerset KY U.S.A. 130 A5
Somerset MI U.S.A. 130 A2
Somerset OH U.S.A. 130 B4
Somerset PA U.S.A. 130 D4
Somerset East S. Africa 98 E7
Somerset Island Canada 121 J2
Somerset West S. Africa 98 C7
Somersworth U.S.A. 131 H2
Somerton U.S.A. 137 E5
Somerville U.S.A. 131 F3
Someşu Cald r. Romania 46 C1
Someydeh Iran 80 A3
Sommarøy Norway 32 E1
Somme r. France 38 D1
Sommen l. Sweden 33 D4
Sömmerda Germany 36 E3
Somnath India 72 A1
Somosomo Fiji 107 H3
Sompolno Poland 37 I2
Somport, Col du pass France/Spain 43 F1
Šomrda hill Yugo. 46 B2
Somuncurá, Mesa Volcánica de plat. Arg. 152 D5
Somvarpet India 72 B3
Son r. India 74 E4
Sonag China see Zêkog
Sonai r. India 75 G4
Sonai r. India 75 G4
Sonakhan India 75 D5
Sonamukhi India 75 E5
Sonapur India 73 D1
Sonari India 75 G4
Sondalo Italy 44 C1
Sønderborg Denmark 33 C5
Sondershausen Germany 36 E3
Sønderup Denmark 33 C4
Søndre Strømfjord Greenland see Kangerlussuaq
Søndre Strømfjord inlet Greenland see Kangerlussuaq
Sondrio Italy 44 B1
Song Nigeria 93 I3
Songad India 74 A5
Songbai China see Shennongjia
Songbu China 67 E2
Sông Cau Vietnam 61 E5
Songcheng China see Xiapu
Sông Đa, Hồ resr Vietnam 60 D3
Songea Tanz. 97 B7
Sŏnggan N. Korea 65 A4
Sông Hông r. Vietnam see Red River
Songhua Hu resr China 64 A4
Songhua Jiang r. China 64 C3
Songjiang Jilin China 64 B4
Songjiang Shanghai China 67 G2
Songjianghe China 64 A4
Sŏngjin N. Korea see Kimch'aek
Songkan China 66 C2
Songkhla Thai. 61 C7
Song Khram, Mae Nam r. Thai. 60 D4
Songmai China see Dêrong
Songming China 66 B3
Sŏngnam S. Korea 65 A5
Songnim N. Korea 65 A5
Songni-san National Park S. Korea 65 A5
Songo Angola 95 B6
Songo Moz. 99 G2
Songololo Bas-Congo Dem. Rep. Congo 95 B6
Songololo Bas-Congo Dem. Rep. Congo see Mbanza-Ngungu
Songpan China 66 B1
Songsak India 75 F4
Sŏngsan S. Korea 65 A6
Songshan China see Ziyun
Song Shan mt. China 67 E1
Songtao China 67 D2
Songxi China 67 F3
Songxian China 67 E1
Songyang China see Songming
Songyuan Fujian China see Songxi
Songyuan Jilin China 64 A3
Songzi China 67 D2
Sonhat India 75 D5
Sonid Youqi China see Saihan Tal
Sonipat India 74 C3
Sonkach India 74 C5
Sonkajärvi Fin. 28 C3
Sonkovo Rus. Fed. 28 F4
Son La Vietnam 60 C3
Sonmiani Bay Pak. 81 F5
Sonneberg Germany 36 E3
Sonnenjoch mt. Austria 36 F5
Sono r. Minas Gerais Brazil 151 C6
Sono r. Tocantins Brazil 150 B4
Sonoita watercourse Mex. 135 D7
Sonoma U.S.A. 136 A2
Sonora r. Mex. 135 E7
Sonora state Mex. 137 E5
Sonora CA U.S.A. 136 B3
Sonora TX U.S.A. 133 A6
Sonoran Desert National Monument nat. park U.S.A. 137 F5
Sonqor Iran 80 A3
Sonseca Spain 42 E3
Son Servera Spain 43 H3
Sonsón Col. 146 C3
Sonsonate El Salvador 138 G6
Sonsorol Islands Palau 57 H4
Son Tây Vietnam 60 D3
Sonthofen Germany 36 E5
Soochow China see Suzhou
Soomaaliya country Africa see Somalia
Sopo watercourse Sudan 94 E2
Sopot Bulg. 46 D3
Sopot Poland 37 I1
Sopron Hungary 37 H5
Sopu-Korgon Kyrg. 81 H1
Sopur Jammu and Kashmir 74 B2
Sôr r. Port. 42 B3
Sor r. Spain 42 C1
Sora Italy 44 D4
Sorab India 72 B3
Soråker Sweden 33 E3
Sŏrak-san mt. S. Korea 65 B5
Sorak-san National Park S. Korea 65 B5
Sorata Bol. 148 C3
Sorbas Spain 43 E4
Sorbe r. Spain 42 E2
Sor Donyztau dry lake Kazakh. 70 A2
Soreq r. Israel 77 B4
Sorgono Sardinia Italy 45 B4
Sorgues France 39 F4
Sorgues r. France 39 E5
Sorgun Turkey 78 C3
Sorgun r. Turkey 77 B1
Soria Spain 43 E2
Sorikmarapi vol. Indon. 58 B2
Sørkappøya i. Svalbard 26 B2
Sor Kaydak dry lake Kazakh. 79 H1
Sorkh, Kūh-e mts Iran 80 C3
Sorkheh Iran 80 C3
Sørland Norway 32 D2
Sørli Norway 32 D2
Sor Mertvyy Kultuk dry lake Kazakh. 29 J7
Sorø Denmark 33 C5
Soro India 75 E5
Soro, Monte mt. Sicily Italy 45 E6
Soroca Moldova 29 D6
Sorocaba Brazil 149 I5
Sorochinsk Rus. Fed. 29 J5
Soroki Moldova see Soroca
Sorol atoll Micronesia 57 J4
Sorong Indon. 57 H6
Sororó r. Brazil 150 B3
Soroti Uganda 96 B4
Sørøya i. Norway 32 F1
Sorp Turkey see Reşadiye
Sorraia r. Port. 42 B3
Sorrento Italy 45 E4
Sorsatunturi hill Fin. 32 H2
Sorsele Sweden 32 E2
Sorso Sardinia Italy 45 B4
Sorsogon Phil. 57 F3
Sortavala Rus. Fed. 28 D3
Sortland Norway 32 D1
Sortot Sudan 89 F5
Sør-Trøndelag county Norway 32 C3
Sørvær Norway 32 F1
Sørvågen Norway 32 D2
Sõrve väin sea chan. Estonia/Latvia see Irbe Strait
Soshanguve S. Africa 99 F5
Sosna r. Rus. Fed. 29 F5
Sosnogorsk Rus. Fed. 28 J3
Sosnovka Arkhangel'skaya Oblast' Rus. Fed. 28 H3
Sosnovka Murmanskaya Oblast' Rus. Fed. 28 G2
Sosnovka Tambovskaya Oblast' Rus. Fed. 29 G5
Sosnovo Rus. Fed. 28 D3
Sosnovo-Ozerskoye Rus. Fed. 63 I1
Sosnovyy Rus. Fed. 32 I2
Sosnovyy Bor Rus. Fed. 28 D4
Sosnowiec Poland 37 I3
Sosnowitz Poland see Sosnowiec
Sosso Cent. Afr. Rep. 94 B4
Sota r. Benin 93 F3
Sotang China 75 G3
Sotério r. Brazil 149 D2
Sotillo r. Spain 42 D3
Sotkamo Fin. 32 H2
Soto Arg. 152 D2
Sotouboua Togo 93 F3
Sotteville-lès-Rouen France 38 D2
Souanké Congo 94 B4
Soubré Côte d'Ivoire 92 D4
Souda Greece 47 D7
Soudan Australia 110 D4
Soúdha Greece see Souda
Soufli Greece 46 E4
Soufrière St Lucia 139 L6
Soufrière vol. St Vincent 139 L6
Sougueta Guinea 92 B3
Souillac France 38 D4
Souk Ahras Alg. 91 G1
Souk el Arbaâ du Rharb Morocco 90 D2
Soukoukoutane Niger 93 F2
Souk Tleta Taghramet Morocco 42 D5
Sŏul S. Korea see Seoul
Soulac-sur-Mer France 38 C4
Sounding Creek r. Canada 123 I4
Sounfat well Mali see Tessoûnfat
Sounio nat. park Greece 47 D6
Soûr Lebanon see Tyre
Soure Brazil 150 B2
Sour el Ghozlane Alg. 43 H4
Souris Man. Canada 134 G2
Souris P.E.I. Canada 125 I4
Souris r. Canada 134 H2

Souriya *country* Asia *see* Syria
Souroumelli *well* Mauritania 92 C1
Sous, Oued *watercourse* Morocco 90 C3
Sousa Brazil 150 E3
Sousa Lara Angola *see* Bocoio
Sousel Port. 42 C3
Sousse Tunisia 91 H2
Soustons France 38 C5
South *salt flat* Australia *see* Eyre (South), Lake
South Africa *country* Africa *see* South Africa, Republic of
▶South Africa, Republic of *country* Africa 98 E6
5th most populous country in Africa.
africa 86–87, 100
South Alligator *r.* Australia 110 C2
Southampton Canada 130 C1
Southampton U.K. 35 F6
Southampton U.S.A. 131 G3
Southampton Island Canada 123 C1
South Andaman *i.* India 73 G4
South Anna *r.* U.S.A. 130 E5
South Atlantic Ocean 161 P8
South Aulatsivik Island Canada 125 I1
South Australia *state* Australia 110 C6
South Australian Basin *sea feature* Indian Ocean 163 O8
Southaven U.S.A. 133 D5
South Baldy *mt.* U.S.A. 135 F6
South Bend *IN* U.S.A. 132 E3
South Bend *WA* U.S.A. 134 B3
South Boston U.S.A. 130 D5
Southbridge U.S.A. 131 G2
South Brook Canada 125 J3
South Burlington U.S.A. 131 G1
South Carolina *state* U.S.A. 129 C5
South Charleston *OH* U.S.A. 130 B4
South Charleston *WV* U.S.A. 130 C4
South China Sea N. Pacific Ocean 56 E3
South Coast Town Australia *see* Gold Coast
South Dakota *state* U.S.A. 134 G3
South Downs *hills* U.K. 35 F6
South East Cape Australia 112 C6
Southeast Indian Ridge *sea feature* Indian Ocean 163 M8
South East Isles Australia 109 C8
Southeast Pacific Basin *sea feature* S. Pacific Ocean 165 K10
Southend Canada 123 K3
Southend-on-Sea U.K. 35 G6
Southern *admin. reg.* Eth. 96 C3
Southern *admin. reg.* Malawi 97 B8
Southern *prov.* Sierra Leone 92 B4
Southern *prov.* Zambia 95 E9
Southern Aegean *admin. reg.* Greece *see* Notio Aigaio
Southern Alps *mts* N.Z. 113 B3
Southern Cross Australia 109 B7
Southern Darfur *state* Sudan 94 E2
Southern Indian Lake Canada 123 L3
Southern Kordofan *state* Sudan 96 A2
Southern Lau Group *is* Fiji 107 H3
Southern National Park Sudan 94 F3
Southern Ocean 165 F10
Southern Rhodesia *country* Africa *see* Zimbabwe
Southern Uplands *hills* U.K. 34 D4
South Esk Tableland *reg.* Australia 108 D4
Southey Canada 123 J5
South Fabius *r.* U.S.A. 132 D4
Southfields U.S.A. 131 F3
South Fiji Basin *sea feature* S. Pacific Ocean 164 F7
South Fork *CA* U.S.A. 136 A1
South Fork *CO* U.S.A. 135 F5
South Fork *PA* U.S.A. 130 D3
Southgate *r.* Canada 134 A2
South Geomagnetic Pole (2000) Antarctica 167 F1
South Georgia *terr.* S. Atlantic Ocean 153 [inset]
▶South Georgia and South Sandwich Islands *terr.* S. Atlantic Ocean 161 L9
United Kingdom Overseas Territory.
southamerica 144–145, 154
South Grand *r.* U.S.A. 132 C4
South Hatia Island Bangl. 75 F5
South Henik Lake Canada 123 L2
South Hill U.S.A. 130 D5
South Honshu Ridge *sea feature* N. Pacific Ocean 164 D3
South Horr Kenya 96 C4
South Indian Lake Canada 123 L3
South Island India 72 B4
▶South Island N.Z. 113 C4
2nd largest island in Oceania.
oceania 102–103
South Junction Canada 123 M5
South Kitui National Reserve *nature res.* Kenya 96 C5
South Koel *r.* India 75 E5
▶South Korea *country* Asia 65 A5
asia 52–53, 82
South Lake Tahoe U.S.A. 136 B2
South Loup *r.* U.S.A. 132 B3
South Luangwa National Park Zambia 97 A8
South Macmillan *r.* Canada 122 C2
South Magnetic Pole (2000) Antarctica 167 G2
South Mills U.S.A. 131 E5
Southminster U.K. 35 G6
South Moose Lake Canada 123 K4
South Mountains *hills* U.S.A. 131 E4
South Muiron Island Australia 108 A5
South Nahanni *r.* Canada 122 D1
South New Berlin U.S.A. 131 F2
South Orkney Islands S. Atlantic Ocean 161 L10
South Paris U.S.A. 131 H1
South Platte *r.* U.S.A. 134 G4
South Point U.S.A. 135 [inset] Z2
South Pole Antarctica 167 L1
Southport Australia 112 C6
Southport U.K. 35 E5
Southport U.S.A. 131 E2
South Portland U.S.A. 131 H2
South Ronaldsay *i.* U.K. 34 E2
South Royalton U.S.A. 131 G2
South Salt Lake U.S.A. 137 G1
South Sandwich Islands S. Atlantic Ocean 167 B3
South Sandwich Trench *sea feature* S. Atlantic Ocean 161 M9
South San Francisco U.S.A. 136 A3
South Saskatchewan *r.* Canada 134 F1
South Seal *r.* Canada 123 L3
South Shetland Islands Antarctica 167 A2
South Shetland Trough *sea feature* S. Atlantic Ocean 161 J10
South Shields U.K. 34 F4
South Sinai *governorate* Egypt *see* Janūb Sīnā'
South Solomon Trench *sea feature* S. Pacific Ocean 164 E6
South Taranaki Bight *b.* N.Z. 113 C2
South Tasman Rise *sea feature* Australia 163 Q9
South Tent *mt.* U.S.A. 137 G2
South Tons *r.* India 75 D4
South Twin Island Canada 124 E2
South Uist *i.* U.K. 34 C3
South Umpqua *r.* U.S.A. 134 B4
South Wellesley Islands Australia 111 D3
South-West Africa *country* Africa *see* Namibia
South West Cape N.Z. 113 A4
South West Cay *reef* Australia 111 H4
South West Entrance *sea chan.* P.N.G. 111 G1
Southwest Indian Ridge *sea feature* Indian Ocean 163 J8
South West National Park Australia 112 C6
Southwest Pacific Basin *sea feature* S. Pacific Ocean 165 H8
Southwest Peru Ridge *sea feature* S. Pacific Ocean *see* Nazca Ridge
South Williamson U.S.A. 130 B5
South Windham U.S.A. 131 H2
Southwold U.K. 35 G5
Southwood National Park Australia 111 G5
Soutpansberg *mts* S. Africa 99 F4
Souttouf, Adrar *mts* W. Sahara 90 B5
Souvigny France 39 E3
Sovata Romania 46 D1
Soveja Romania 46 E1
Soverato Italy 45 F5
Sovetsk *Kaliningradskaya Oblast'* Rus. Fed. 28 B5
Sovetsk *Kirovskaya Oblast'* Rus. Fed. 28 I4
Sovetskaya Gavan' Rus. Fed. 64 E2
Sovetskiy *Khanty-Mansiyskiy Avtonomnyy Okrug* Rus. Fed. 26 G3
Sovetskiy *Leningradskaya Oblast'* Rus. Fed. 28 D3
Sovetskiy *Respublika Mariy El* Rus. Fed. 28 I4
Sovetskoye *Chechenskaya Respublika* Rus. Fed. *see* Shatoy
Sovetskoye *Stavropol'skiy Kray* Rus. Fed. *see* Zelenokumsk
Soviči Bos.-Herz. 44 F3
Sowa Botswana 99 E4
Sowa China 66 A2
Sowa Pan *salt pan* Botswana 99 E4
Soweto S. Africa 99 E5
Sōya-kaikyō *strait* Japan/Rus. Fed. *see* La Pérouse Strait
Sōya-misaki *c.* Japan 64 E3
Soyana *r.* Rus. Fed. 28 G2
Soyang-ho *l.* S. Korea 65 A5
Soyaux France 38 D4
Soylan Armenia *see* Vayk'
Soyma *r.* Rus. Fed. 28 I2
Soyo Angola 95 B6
Sozh *r.* Europe 26 D4
Sozopol Bulg. 46 E3
▶Spain *country* Europe 42 E2
4th largest country in Europe.
europe 24–25,48
Spalato Croatia *see* Split
Spalatum Croatia *see* Split
Spalding U.K. 35 F5
Spanish *r.* Canada 124 D4
Spanish Fork U.S.A. 137 G1
Spanish Guinea *country* Africa *see* Equatorial Guinea
Spanish Netherlands *country* Europe *see* Belgium
Spanish Point Rep. of Ireland 35 B5
Spanish Sahara *terr.* Africa *see* Western Sahara
Spanish Town Jamaica 139 I5
Spanish Wells Bahamas 129 D7
Sparks U.S.A. 136 C2
Sparta Greece *see* Sparti
Sparta *airport* Greece 47 C6
Sparta *GA* U.S.A. 129 C5
Sparta *NC* U.S.A. 130 C5
Sparta *TN* U.S.A. 128 B5
Spartanburg U.S.A. 128 C5
Spartansburg U.S.A. 130 D3
Spartel, Cap *c.* Morocco 42 D5
Sparti Greece 47 C6
Spartivento, Capo *c. Sardinia* Italy 45 B5
Spartivento, Capo *c.* Italy 45 F6
Sparwood Canada 123 H5
Spas-Demensk Rus. Fed. 31 M2
Spas-Klepiki Rus. Fed. 29 G5
Spassk-Dal'niy Rus. Fed. 64 C3
Spatha, Akra *pt* Greece 47 C7
Spean Bridge U.K. 34 D3
Spearfish U.S.A. 134 G3
Spearman U.S.A. 133 A4
Speightstown Barbados 147 G1
Speikkogel *mt.* Austria 37 G5
Speke Gulf Tanz. 96 B5
Spence Bay Canada *see* Taloyoak
Spencer *IA* U.S.A. 132 C3
Spencer *ID* U.S.A. 134 D3
Spencer *IN* U.S.A. 128 B4
Spencer *MA* U.S.A. 131 H2
Spencer *NY* U.S.A. 131 E2
Spencer *VA* U.S.A. 130 C5
Spencer, Cape U.S.A. 122 B3
Spencer Gulf *est.* Australia 112 A4
Spencer Range *hills* Australia 110 B2
Spences Bridge Canada 122 F5
Spercheios *r.* Greece 47 C5
Sperkhiós *r.* Greece *see* Spercheios
Sperrin Mountains *hills* U.K. 34 C4
Sperryville U.S.A. 130 D4
Spétsai *i.* Greece *see* Spetses
Spetses Greece 47 C6
Spetses *i.* Greece 47 C6
Spey *r.* U.K. 34 E3
Speyer Germany 36 D4
Spezand Pak. 81 F4
Spice Islands Indon. *see* Moluccas
Spiez Switz. 39 G3
Spijkenisse Neth. 36 B3
Spil Dağı Milli Parkı *nat. park* Turkey 47 E5
Spilimbergo Italy 44 D1
Spīn Būldak Afgh. 81 F4
Spirit Lake U.S.A. 132 C3
Spiritwood Canada 123 J4
Spišská Nová Ves Slovakia 37 J4
Spitak Armenia 79 F2
Spiti *r.* India 74 C3
▶Spitsbergen *i.* Svalbard 26 B2
5th largest island in Europe.
world 14–15
Spitsyno Rus. Fed. 33 G4
Spittal an der Drau Austria 37 F5
Spitzbergen *i.* Svalbard *see* Spitsbergen
Split Croatia 44 F3
Split Lake Canada 123 L3
Split Lake *l.* Canada 123 L3
Spokane U.S.A. 134 C3
Spokane *r.* U.S.A. 134 C3
Spoon *r.* U.S.A. 132 D3
Spooner U.S.A. 132 D2
Spotsylvania U.S.A. 130 E4
Sprague *r.* U.S.A. 134 B4
Spranger, Mount Canada 122 F4
Spratly Island S. China Sea 56 D4
Spratly Islands S. China Sea 56 D3
Spreča *r.* Bos.-Herz. 44 G2
Spree *r.* Germany 37 F2
Spremberg Germany 37 G3
Springbok S. Africa 98 C6
Springdale Canada 121 N5
Springdale U.S.A. 133 C4
Springe Germany 36 D2
Springer U.S.A. 135 F5
Springerville U.S.A. 135 E6
Springfield *CO* U.S.A. 135 G5
Springfield *GA* U.S.A. 129 C5
▶Springfield *IL* U.S.A. 127 I4
State capital of Illinois.
Springfield *MA* U.S.A. 131 G2
Springfield *MN* U.S.A. 132 C2
Springfield *MO* U.S.A. 132 C4
Springfield *OH* U.S.A. 130 B4
Springfield *OR* U.S.A. 134 B3
Springfield *TN* U.S.A. 128 B4
Springfield *VT* U.S.A. 131 G2
Springfield *WV* U.S.A. 130 D4
Spring Garden Guyana 147 G3
Spring Grove U.S.A. 131 E5
Spring Hill U.S.A. 129 C6
Springhouse Canada 134 B2
Spring Mountains U.S.A. 137 E3
Springs Junction N.Z. 113 C3
Springsure Australia 111 G5
Springview U.S.A. 132 B3
Springville *CA* U.S.A. 136 C3
Springville *NY* U.S.A. 130 D2
Springville *PA* U.S.A. 131 F3
Springville *UT* U.S.A. 137 G1
Springwater U.S.A. 130 E2
Spruce Grove Canada 123 H4
Spruce Knob *mt.* U.S.A. 130 D4
Spruce Mountain U.S.A. 137 E1
Spulico, Capo *c.* Italy 45 F5
Spur, Mount *vol.* U.S.A. 120 D3
Spurn Head U.K. 35 G5
Spuzzum Canada 122 F5
Squamish Canada 134 B2
Squamish *r.* Canada 122 F5
Squam Lake U.S.A. 131 H2
Square Lake U.S.A. 128 F2
Squillace Italy 45 F5
Squillace, Golfo di *g.* Italy 45 F5
Squinzano Italy 45 G4
Squire U.S.A. 130 C5
Squires, Mount Australia 109 D6
Sragen Indon. 59 E4
Srbija *aut. rep.* Yugo. 46 B3
Srbinje Bos.-Herz. *see* Foča
Srbobran Bos.-Herz. *see* Donji Vakuf
Srbobran Yugo. 46 A2
Srebărna *tourist site* Bulg. 46 E2
Srebrenica Bos.-Herz. 46 A2
Sredets Bulg. 46 E3
Sredets Bulg. *see* Sofia
Sredetska Reka *r.* Bulg. 46 E3
Sredinnyy Khrebet *mts* Rus. Fed. 27 P4
Sredishte Bulg. 46 E3
Sredna Gora *mts* Bulg. 46 C3
Srednebelaya Rus. Fed. 64 A2
Srednekolymsk Rus. Fed. 27 P3
Sredne-Russkaya Vozyshennost' *see* Central Russian Upland
Sredne-Sibirskoye Ploskogor'ye *plat.* Rus. Fed. *see* Central Siberian Plateau
Sredneye Kuyto, Ozero *l.* Rus. Fed. 32 H2
Srednogorie Bulg. 46 D3
Srednyaya Akhtuba Rus. Fed. 29 H6
Śrem Poland 37 H2
Sremska Mitrovica Yugo. 46 A2
Srêpok, Tônlé *r.* Cambodia 61 D5
Sretensk Rus. Fed. 63 J1
Sri Aman *Sarawak* Malaysia 59 E2
Sriharikota Island India 72 D3
▶Sri Jayewardenepura Kotte Sri Lanka 72 C5
Capital of Sri Lanka.
Srikakulam India 73 E2
Sri Kalahasti India 72 C3
▶Sri Lanka *country* Asia 72 D5
asia 52–53, 82
Sri Madhopur India 74 B4
Srimangal Bangl. 75 F4
Srinagar India 74 C3
Srinagar Jammu and Kashmir 74 B2
Sringeri India 72 B3
Sri Pada *mt.* Sri Lanka *see* Adam's Peak
Srirangam India 72 C4
Srisailam India 72 C2
Srivaikuntam India 72 C4
Srivardhan India 72 B2
Srivilliputtur India 72 C4
Srnetica *mts* Bos.-Herz. 44 F2
Srnice Bos.-Herz. 44 G2
Środa Wielkopolska Poland 37 H2
Srpska Crnja Yugo. 46 B2
Srpska Kostajnica Bos.-Herz. *see* Bosanska Kostajnica
Srpski Brod Bos.-Herz. *see* Bosanski Brod
Srungavarapukota India 73 D2
Staaten *r.* Australia 111 E3
Staaten River National Park Australia 111 E3
Stabbursdalen Nasjonalpark *nat. park* Norway 32 G1
Staberhuk *c.* Germany 36 E1
Stabroek Guyana *see* Georgetown
Stade Germany 36 D2
Stadskanaal Neth. 36 C2
Stadtallendorf Germany 36 D3
Staffa *i.* U.K. 34 C3
Stafford U.K. 35 E5
Stafford Creek Bahamas 129 D7
Stafford Springs U.S.A. 131 G3
Staicele Latvia 33 G4
Stakhanov Ukr. 29 F6
Stakhanovo Rus. Fed. *see* Zhukovskiy
Stalin Bulg. *see* Varna
Stalinabad Tajik. *see* Dushanbe
Stalingrad Rus. Fed. *see* Volgograd
Stalingradskaya Oblast' *admin. div.* Rus. Fed. *see* Volgogradskaya Oblast'
Staliniri Georgia *see* Ts'khinvali
Stalino Ukr. *see* Donets'k
Stalinogorsk Rus. Fed. *see* Novomoskovsk
Stalinogród Poland *see* Katowice
Stalinsk Rus. Fed. *see* Novokuznetsk
Stalowa Wola Poland 37 K3
Stâlpu Romania 46 E2
Stamboliyski Bulg. 46 D3
Stamford Australia 111 E4
Stamford U.K. 35 F5
Stamford *CT* U.S.A. 131 G3
Stamford *NY* U.S.A. 131 F2
Stamford *TX* U.S.A. 133 B5
Stampalia *i.* Greece *see* Astypalaia
Stampriet Namibia 98 C5
Stanardsville U.S.A. 130 D4
Stancomb-Wills Glacier Antarctica 167 B1
Standish U.S.A. 130 B2
Stanfield U.S.A. 137 G5
Stanford *KY* U.S.A. 130 A5
Stanford *MT* U.S.A. 134 E3
Stangenestind *hill* Norway 32 H1
Stanger S. Africa 99 F6
Stănilești Romania 46 F1
Stanišić Yugo. 46 A2
Stanislav Ukr. *see* Ivano-Frankivs'k
Stanke Dimitrov Bulg. *see* Dupnitsa
Stanley Australia 112 C6
Stanley *Hong Kong* China 67 [inset]
▶Stanley Falkland Is 153 F7
Capital of the Falkland Islands.
Stanley *ID* U.S.A. 134 D3
Stanley *ND* U.S.A. 132 A1
Stanley *VA* U.S.A. 130 D4
Stanley, Chutes *waterfall* Dem. Rep. Congo *see* Boyoma Falls
Stanley, Mount Australia 110 B4
Stanley, Mount Dem. Rep. Congo/Uganda *see* Margherita Peak
Stanley Reservoir India 72 C4
Stanleyville Dem. Rep. Congo *see* Kisangani
Stanmore Zimbabwe 99 F4
Stanos Greece 47 B5
Stanovoye Rus. Fed. 29 F5
Stanovoye Nagor'ye *mts* Rus. Fed. 27 L4
Stanovoy Khrebet *mts* Rus. Fed. 27 M4
Stans Switz. 39 H3
Stansmore Range *hills* Australia 108 E5
Stansted *airport* U.K. 35 G6
Stanthorpe Australia 111 G6
Stanton *KY* U.S.A. 130 B5
Stanton *MI* U.S.A. 132 E3
Stanton *TX* U.S.A. 133 A5
Stantsiya-Yakkabag Uzbek. *see* Yakkabag
Staples U.S.A. 132 C2
Stapleton U.S.A. 132 A3
Starachowice Poland 37 J3
Stará Ľubovňa Slovakia 37 J4
Stara Pazova Yugo. 46 B2
Stara Planina *mts* Bulg./Yugo. *see* Balkan Mountains
Staraya Russa Rus. Fed. 31 L1
Stara Zagora Bulg. 46 D3
Starbuck Island Kiribati 165 H6
Starcke National Park Australia 111 F2
Stargard in Pommern Poland *see* Stargard Szczeciński
Stargard Szczeciński Poland 37 G2
Stari Ras and Sopoćani *tourist site* Yugo. 46 B3
Staritsa Rus. Fed. 28 E4
Starke U.S.A. 129 C6
Starkey U.S.A. 130 D5
Starkville U.S.A. 129 A5
Star Lake U.S.A. 131 F1
Starnberg Germany 36 E5
Starnberger See *l.* Germany 36 E5
Starobel'sk Ukr. *see* Starobil's'k
Starobil's'k Ukr. 29 F6
Starogard Gdański Poland 37 I2
Starokonstantinov Ukr. *see* Starokostyantyniv
Starokostyantyniv Ukr. 29 C6
Starokozache Ukr. 46 F1
Starominskaya Rus. Fed. 29 F7
Staro Oryakhovo Bulg. 46 E3
Staro Selo Bulg. 46 E3
Staroshcherbinovskaya Rus. Fed. 29 F7
Staroyur'yevo Rus. Fed. 29 G5
Star Peak U.S.A. 136 C1
Start Point U.K. 35 E6
Staryya Darohi Belarus 29 D5
Staryye Dorogi Belarus *see* Staryya Darohi
Staryy Kayak Rus. Fed. 27 K2
Staryy Nadym Rus. Fed. 26 H3
Staryy Oskol Rus. Fed. 29 F6
Staßfurt Germany 36 E3
Staszów Poland 37 J3
State College U.S.A. 130 E3
Staten Island Arg. *see* Los Estados, Isla de
Statesboro U.S.A. 129 C5
Statesville U.S.A. 128 C5
Stathelle Norway 33 C4
Station No. 6 Sudan 89 G4
Station No. 10 Sudan 89 G5
Station Nord Greenland 121 R1
Statzberg *hill* Austria 37 G4
Staunton U.S.A. 130 D4
Stavanger Norway 33 B4
Stavertsi Bulg. 46 D3
Stavropol' Rus. Fed. 29 G7
Stavropol Kray *admin. div.* Rus. Fed. *see* Stavropol'skiy Kray
Stavropol'-na-Volge Rus. Fed. *see* Tol'yatti
Stavropol'skaya Vozvyshennost' *hills* Rus. Fed. 29 G7
Stavropol'skiy Kray *admin. div.* Rus. Fed. 29 G7
Stavros Greece 46 C4
Stavros, Akra *pt* Greece 47 D6
Stawell Australia 112 B5
Stawell *r.* Australia 111 E4
Stawiski Poland 37 K2
Stawiszyn Poland 37 I3
Stayner Canada 130 C1
Steamboat U.S.A. 136 C2
Steamboat Springs U.S.A. 134 F4
Stebbins U.S.A. 120 C3
Steel *r.* Canada 124 C3
Steele Island Antarctica 167 L2
Steelton U.S.A. 128 D3
Steelville U.S.A. 132 D4
Steen *r.* Canada 123 G3
Steen River Canada 123 G3
Steens Mountain U.S.A. 134 C4
Steenstrup Gletscher *glacier* Greenland *see* Sermersuaq
Steenvoorde France 39 E1
Steenwijk Neth. 36 C2
Stefanoviki Greece 47 C5
Stefansson Bay Antarctica 163 L10
Stefansson Island Canada 121 I2
Ştefan Vodă Moldova 46 F1
Ştefan Vodă Romania 46 E2
Stege Denmark 33 D5
Stegi Swaziland *see* Siteki
Ştei Romania 46 C1
Steigerwald *mts* Germany 36 E4
Steinar Iceland 32 [inset]
Steinbach Canada 123 L5
Steinfurt Germany 36 C2
Steinhausen Namibia 98 C4
Steinkjer Norway 32 C2
Steinkopf S. Africa 98 C6
Stella Maris Bahamas 129 E8
Stellenbosch S. Africa 98 C7
Steller, Mount U.S.A. 122 A2
Stello, Monte *mt. Corsica* France 39 H5
Stelvio, Parco Nazionale dello *nat. park* Italy 44 C1
Stelvio, Passo dello *pass* Italy 44 C1
Stenay France 39 F2
Stendal Germany 36 E2
Stende Latvia 33 F4
Stenudden Sweden 32 E2
Stenungsund Sweden 33 C4
Steornabhagh U.K. *see* Stornoway
Stepanakert Azer. *see* Xankändi
Stephens *watercourse* Australia 112 B4
Stephens, Cape N.Z. 113 C3
Stephens Lake Canada 123 M3
Stephenville Canada 125 J3
Stephenville U.S.A. 133 B5
Stepnoy Rus. Fed. *see* Elista
Stepnoye Rus. Fed. 29 H6
Stepojevac Yugo. 46 B2
Sterea Ellas *admin. reg.* Greece 47 C5
Sterlibashevo Rus. Fed. 29 J5
Sterling *CO* U.S.A. 134 G4
Sterling *IL* U.S.A. 132 D3
Sterling *UT* U.S.A. 137 G2
Sterling City U.S.A. 133 A6
Sterling Heights U.S.A. 130 E2
Sterlitamak Rus. Fed. 29 J5
Sternberg Germany 36 E2
Stęszew Poland 37 H2
Stettin Poland *see* Szczecin
Stettiner Haff *b.* Germany *see* Oderhaff
Stettler Canada 134 D1
Steubenville *KY* U.S.A. 130 A5
Steubenville *OH* U.S.A. 130 C3
Stevenage U.K. 35 F6
Stevenson U.S.A. 134 B3
Stevenson Lake Canada 123 L4
Stevens Point U.S.A. 132 D2
Stevensville *MD* U.S.A. 131 E4
Stevensville *PA* U.S.A. 131 E3
Stewart Canada 122 D4
Stewart *r.* Canada 122 B2
Stewart, Cape Australia 110 C1
Stewart, Isla *i.* Chile 153 C8
Stewart Crossing Canada 122 B2
Stewart Island N.Z. 113 A4
Stewart Islands Solomon Is 107 F2
Stewarts Point U.S.A. 136 A2
Stewart Valley Canada 123 J5
Stewiacke Canada 125 I4
Steyr Austria 37 G4
Steytlerville S. Africa 98 E7
Stif Alg. *see* Sétif
Stigtomta Sweden 33 E4
Stikine *r.* Canada 122 C3
Stikine Plateau Canada 122 D3
Stilis Greece *see* Stylida
Stillwater U.S.A. 133 B4
Stillwater *r.* U.S.A. 134 E3
Stillwater Range *mts* U.S.A. 136 C2
Stilo Italy 45 F5
Stilo, Punta *pt* Italy 45 F5
Štilt *mt.* Bos.-Herz. 44 F3
Štimlje Yugo. 46 B3
Stinnett U.S.A. 133 A5
Štip Macedonia 46 C4
Stipanov Grič *mt.* Croatia 44 E2
Stirling Australia 110 C4
Stirling Canada 130 E1
Stirling U.K. 34 E3
Stirling Creek *r.* Australia 110 B3
Stirling Range National Park Australia 109 B8
Stjernøya *i.* Norway 32 F1
Stjørdalshalsen Norway 32 C3
Stockach Germany 36 D5
Stockbridge U.S.A. 130 A2
Stockerau Austria 37 H4
▶Stockholm Sweden 33 E4
Capital of Sweden.
Stockholm *county* Sweden 33 E4
Stockinbingal Australia 112 C4
Stockport U.K. 35 E5
Stocks Seamount *sea feature* S. Atlantic Ocean 160 L6
Stockton *CA* U.S.A. 136 B3
Stockton *KS* U.S.A. 132 B4
Stockton *MO* U.S.A. 132 C4
Stockton *UT* U.S.A. 137 F1
Stockton Lake U.S.A. 132 C4
Stockton-on-Tees U.K. 35 F4
Stockton Plateau U.S.A. 133 A6
Stoczek Łukowski Poland 37 J3
Stöde Sweden 33 E3
Stœng Trêng Cambodia 61 D5
Stogovo Planina *mts* Macedonia 46 B4
Stoke-on-Trent U.K. 35 E5
Stokes Point Australia 112 B6
Stokkseyri Iceland 32 [inset]
Stokkvågen Norway 32 D2
Stokmarknes Norway 32 D1
Stol *mt.* Yugo. 46 C2
Stolac Bos.-Herz. 44 F3
Stolberg (Rheinland) Germany 36 C3
Stolbovoy Rus. Fed. 26 F2
Stolbovoy, Ostrov *i.* Rus. Fed. 27 N2
Stolbtsy Belarus *see* Stowbtsy
Stolice *hill* Bos.-Herz. 44 G2
Stolin Belarus 29 C6
Stolp Poland *see* Słupsk
Stolzenau Germany 36 D2
Stone U.K. 35 E5
Stoneboro U.S.A. 130 C3
Stonecliffe Canada 124 E4
Stonecutters' Island *pen. Hong Kong* China 67 [inset]
Stonehaven U.S.A. 134 G4
Stonehaven U.K. 34 E3
Stonehenge Australia 111 E5
Stonehenge *tourist site* U.K. 35 F6
Stoneville U.S.A. 130 D5
Stonewall Canada 123 L5
Stoney Creek Canada 130 D2
Stoney Point Canada 130 B2
Stonington U.S.A. 131 I1
Stony Creek U.S.A. 130 E5
Stony Gorge Reservoir U.S.A. 136 A2
Stony Lake Canada 123 L3
Stony Point U.S.A. 131 E2
Stony Rapids Canada 123 J3
Stooping *r.* Canada 124 D2
Stör *r.* Germany 36 D2
Stora Lulevatten *l.* Sweden 32 E2
Stora Sjöfallets nationalpark *nat. park* Sweden 32 E2
Storavan *l.* Sweden 32 E2
Storbäcken Sweden 33 D3
Storbekkfjellet *mt.* Norway 33 C3
Stord *i.* Norway 33 B4
Store *mt.* Norway 33 C3
Store Bælt *sea chan.* Denmark *see* Great Belt
Store Heddinge Denmark 33 D5
Store Jukleeggi *mt.* Norway 33 C3
Store Koldewey *i.* Greenland 121 R2
Store Moss nationalpark *nat. park* Sweden 33 D4
Støren Norway 32 C3
Store Sotra *i.* Norway 33 B3
Storfjärden *l.* Sweden 33 E3
Storfjorden *sea chan.* Svalbard 26 B2
Storjola Sweden 32 D2
Storjord Norway 32 D2
Storjuktan *l.* Sweden 32 E2
Storkerson Peninsula Canada 121 I2
Storm Bay Australia 112 C6
Storm Lake U.S.A. 132 C3
Stornoway U.K. 34 C2
Storo Italy 44 C2
Storozhevsk Rus. Fed. 28 J3
Storseleby Sweden 32 E2
Storsjøen *l.* Norway 33 C3
Storsjön *l.* Sweden 32 D3
Storsjön *l.* Sweden 33 E3
Storskarhø *mt.* Norway 32 C3
Storskog Sweden 32 D2
Storslett Norway 32 F1
Storuman Sweden 32 E2
Storuman *l.* Sweden 32 E2
Storvigelen *mt.* Norway 33 D3
Storvik Sweden 33 E3
Storvorde Denmark 33 C4
Storvreta Sweden 33 E4
Stoughton Canada 123 K5
Stoŭng, Stœng *r.* Cambodia 61 D5
Stour *r. Dorset, England* U.K. 35 F6
Stour *r. Essex/Suffolk, England* U.K. 35 G6
Stour *r. Kent, England* U.K. 35 G6
Stovall U.S.A. 130 D5
Stowbtsy Belarus 31 K2
Stowmarket U.K. 35 G5
Stoyba Rus. Fed. 64 B1
Strabane U.K. 34 C4
Stradella Italy 44 B2
Strahan Australia 112 C6
Strakonice Czech Rep. 37 F4
Straldzha Bulg. 46 E3
Stralsund Germany 37 F1
Stranda Norway 33 B3
Strangford Lough *inlet* U.K. 35 D4
Strängnäs Sweden 33 E4
Strangways *r.* Australia 110 C2
Stranraer U.K. 34 D4
Strasbourg France 39 G2
Strasburg Germany 37 F2
Strasburg *OH* U.S.A. 130 C3
Strasburg *PA* U.S.A. 131 E4
Strasburg *VA* U.S.A. 130 D4
Strassburg France *see* Strasbourg
Straßwalchen Austria 37 F5
Stratford Canada 130 C2
Stratford N.Z. 113 C2
Stratford *CA* U.S.A. 136 C3
Stratford *TX* U.S.A. 133 A4
Stratford-upon-Avon U.K. 35 F5
Strathalbyn Australia 112 A4
Strathgordon Australia 112 C6
Strathmore Canada 123 H5
Strathmore U.S.A. 136 C3
Strathnaver Canada 122 F4
Strathpeffer U.K. 34 D3
Strathroy Canada 130 C2
Strathspey *valley* U.K. 34 E3
Stratton Mountain U.S.A. 131 G2
Straubing Germany 37 F4
Straume Norway 32 D1
Straumen Norway 32 D2
Straumnes *pt* Iceland 32 [inset]
Strawberry U.S.A. 137 G4
Strawberry Mountain U.S.A. 134 C3
Strawberry Reservoir U.S.A. 137 G1
Straža *mt.* Macedonia 46 C3
Streaky Bay Australia 109 F8
Streaky Bay *b.* Australia 109 F8
Streator U.S.A. 132 D3
Strehaia Romania 46 C2
Strei *r.* Romania 46 C2
Střela *r.* Czech Rep. 37 F4
Strelcha Bulg. 46 D3
Strelka Rus. Fed. 27 P3
Strelley Australia 108 B5
Strel'na *r.* Rus. Fed. 28 F2
Strenči Latvia 33 G4
Streymoy *i.* Faroe Is 34 [inset]
Strezhevoy Rus. Fed. 26 H3
Stříbro Czech Rep. 37 F4
Strickland *r.* P.N.G. 57 J7
Strimonas *r.* Greece 46 C4
Strizivojna Croatia 44 G2
Stroeder Arg. 152 E5
Strofades *i.* Greece 47 B6
Ströhen Germany 36 D2
Stromboli, Isola *i. Isole Lipari* Italy 45 E5
Stromeferry U.K. 34 D3
Stromness S. Georgia 153 [inset]
Stromness U.K. 34 E2
Strömstad Sweden 33 C4
Strömsund Sweden 32 D3
Strongsville U.S.A. 130 C3
Stronsay *i.* U.K. 34 E2
Stropkov Slovakia 37 J4
Stroud U.K. 35 E6
Struer Denmark 33 C4
Struga Macedonia 46 B4
Strugi-Krasnyye Rus. Fed. 28 D4
Struis Bay S. Africa 98 D7
Struma *r.* Bulg. 46 C4
Strumica Macedonia 46 C4
Strumica *r.* Macedonia 46 C4
Struthers U.S.A. 130 C3
Stryama *r.* Bulg. 46 D3
Strydenburg S. Africa 98 D6
Stryn Norway 33 B3
Stryy Ukr. 41 G2
Strzelce Krajeńskie Poland 37 G2
Strzelce Opolskie Poland 37 I3
Strzelecki, Mount Australia 110 C4
Strzelecki Creek *watercourse* Australia 111 D6
Strzelecki Regional Reserve *nature res.* Australia 111 D6
Strzelin Poland 37 H3
Strzelno Poland 37 I2
Strzyżów Poland 37 J4
Stuart *r.* Australia 111 G5
Stuart *FL* U.S.A. 129 C7
Stuart *IA* U.S.A. 132 C3
Stuart *VA* U.S.A. 130 C5
Stuart Lake Canada 122 E4
Stuart Range *hills* Australia 110 C6
Stuarts Draft U.S.A. 130 D4
Stubaier Alpen *mts* Austria 36 E5
Stuchka Latvia *see* Aizkraukle
Stučka Latvia *see* Aizkraukle
Studenica *tourist site* Yugo. 46 B3
Studen Kladenets, Yazovir *resr* Bulg. 46 D4
Studholme Junction N.Z. 113 B4
Stugun Sweden 32 D3
Stung Treng Cambodia *see* Stœng Trêng
Stupart *r.* Canada 123 M4
Stupino Rus. Fed. 29 F5
Stura di Demonte *r.* Italy 44 A2
Sturge Island Antarctica 167 H2
Sturgeon *r. Ont.* Canada 124 E4
Sturgeon *r. Sask.* Canada 123 J4
Sturgeon Bay U.S.A. 132 E2
Sturgeon Lake Canada 130 D1
Sturgis *KY* U.S.A. 128 B4
Sturgis *MI* U.S.A. 132 E3
Sturgis *SD* U.S.A. 132 A2
Šturlić Bos.-Herz. 44 E2
Sturt Creek Australia 108 E4
Sturt Creek *watercourse* Australia 110 A3
Sturt National Park Australia 112 B3
Sturt Stony Desert Australia 111 E6
Stutterheim S. Africa 99 E7
Stuttgart Germany 36 D4
Stuttgart U.S.A. 127 H5
Stykkishólmur Iceland 32 [inset]
Stylida Greece 47 C5
Suaçuí Grande *r.* Brazil 151 D6
Suai East Timor 108 D2
Suaita Col. 146 C3
Suakin Sudan 89 H5
Suakin Archipelago *is* Sudan 89 H5
Suana Dem. Rep. Congo 95 D6
Suao Taiwan 67 G3
Suaqui Grande Mex. 135 E7
Suara, Mount Eritrea 89 H5
Suardi Arg. 152 E2

Suata Venez. **147** E2
Suau P.N.G. **111** G1
Subang Indon. **59** D4
Subansiri *r.* India **60** A2
Subarnarekha *r.* India **75** E5
Sūbāshī Iran **80** B3
Subaşı Turkey **46** F4
Şubayḩah Saudi Arabia **89** H2
Subcetate Romania **46** D1
Subeita *tourist site* Israel *see* **Shivta**
Subiaco Italy **44** D4
Subi Besar *i.* Indon. **59** E2
Subi Kecil *i.* Indon. **59** E2
Sublette U.S.A. **132** A4
Subotica Yugo. **46** A1
Subucle *mt.* Eritrea **89** I6
Success, Lake U.S.A. **136** C3
Suceava Romania **31** K4
Sucha Beskidzka Poland **37** I4
Suchan Rus. Fed. *see* **Partizansk**
Suchan *r.* Rus. Fed. **64** C4
Suchedniów Poland **37** J3
Sucio *r.* Col. **146** B3
Suck *r.* Rep. of Ireland **35** B5

▶**Sucre** Bol. **148** D4
Legislative capital of Bolivia.
world 8–9

Sucre *dept* Col. **146** C2
Sucre *state* Venez. **147** F2
Sucuaro Col. **146** D3
Sucumbíos *prov.* Ecuador **146** B5
Sucunduri *r.* Brazil **147** G6
Sucuriú *r.* Brazil **149** H5
Suczawa Romania *see* **Suceava**
Sud *prov.* Cameroon **93** H5
Suda Rus. Fed. **28** F4
Sudak Ukr. **78** C1

▶**Sudan** *country* Africa **89** F5
Largest country in Africa and 10th largest in the world.
africa 86–87, 100
world 8–9

Suday Rus. Fed. **28** G4
Sudayr, Sha'īb *watercourse* Iraq **79** F5
Sudbury Canada **124** D4
Sudbury U.K. **35** G5
Sudd *swamp* Sudan **96** A3
Sudest Island P.N.G. *see* **Tagula Island**
Sudetenland *mts* Czech Rep./Poland *see* **Sudety**
Sudety *mts* Czech Rep./Poland **37** G3
Sudislavl' Rus. Fed. **28** G4
Sud-Kivu *prov.* Dem. Rep. Congo **94** F5
Sudlersville U.S.A. **131** F4
Sudoeste Alentejano Costa Vicentina, Parque Natural do *nature res.* Port. **42** B4
Sudogda Rus. Fed. **28** G5
Sud-Ouest *prov.* Cameroon **93** H4
Sudr Egypt **89** G2
Suðuroy *i.* Faroe Is **34** [inset]
Suðuroyarfjørður *sea chan.* Faroe Is **34** [inset]
Sue *watercourse* Sudan **94** F3
Sueca Spain **43** F3
Sŭedinenie Bulg. **46** D3
Suez Egypt **89** G2
Suez, Gulf of Egypt **89** G2
Suez Bay Egypt **77** A5
▶**Suez Canal** Egypt **89** G2
africa 86–87
Şufaynah Saudi Arabia **89** I4
Suffolk U.S.A. **131** E5
Sūfīān Iran **80** A2
Sufi-Kurgan Kyrg. *see* **Sopu-Korgon**
Sugarbush Hill U.S.A. **132** D2
Sugarloaf Mountain U.S.A. **128** F2
Sugarloaf Point Australia **112** E4
Sugut *r.* *Sabah* Malaysia **59** G1
Sugut, Tanjong *pt* *Sabah* Malaysia **59** G1
Suhaia Romania **46** D3
Sūhāj Egypt *see* **Sawhāj**
Şuḩār Oman **76** F5
Şuhaymī, Wādī as *watercourse* Egypt **77** A4
Sühbaatar Mongolia **62** H1
Suheli Par *i.* India **72** B4
Suhl Germany **36** E3
Suhopolje Croatia **44** F2
Suhum Ghana **93** E4
Şuhut Turkey **78** B3
Suiá Missur *r.* Brazil **150** A4
Sui'an China *see* **Zhangpu**
Suibin China **64** B3
Suichang China **67** F2
Suicheng *Fujian* China *see* **Jianning**
Suicheng *Guangdong* China *see* **Suixi**
Suichuan China **67** E3
Suid-Afrika *country* Africa *see* **South Africa, Republic of**
Suidzhikurmsy Turkm. *see* **Madau**
Suifen *r.* China **64** B4
Suifenhe China **64** B3
Suigam India **74** A4
Suihua China **64** A3
Suijiang China **66** B2
Suileng China **64** A3
Suining *Hunan* China **67** D3
Suining *Jiangsu* China **67** F1
Suining *Sichuan* China **66** C2
Suiping China **67** E1
Suippes France **39** F2
Suir *r.* Rep. of Ireland **35** C5
Suisse *country* Europe *see* **Switzerland**
Suixi *Anhui* China **67** F1
Suixi *Guangdong* China **67** D4
Suixian *Henan* China **67** E1
Suixian *Hubei* China *see* **Suizhou**
Suiyang China **66** C3
Suizhai China *see* **Xiancheng**
Suizhou China **67** E2
Sujangarh India **74** B4
Sujawal Pak. **81** G5
Sukabumi Indon. **59** D4
Sukadana *Kalimantan Barat* Indon. **59** E3
Sukadana *Lampung, Sumatra* Indon. **58** D4
Sukadana, Teluk *b.* Indon. **59** E3
Sukagawa Japan **65** E5
Sukaramai Indon. **59** E3
Sukarnapura Indon. *see* **Jayapura**
Sukarno, Puntjak *mt.* Indon. *see* **Jaya, Puncak**
Suket India **74** C4
Sukeva Fin. **32** G3
Sukhinichi Rus. Fed. **29** E5
Sukhona *r.* Rus. Fed. **28** H3
Sukhothai Thai. **60** B4
Sukhumi Georgia *see* **Sokhumi**
Sukhum-Kale Georgia *see* **Sokhumi**
Sukkertoppen Greenland *see* **Maniitsoq**
Sukkozero Rus. Fed. **28** E3
Sukkur Pak. **81** G5
Sukkur Barrage Pak. **81** G5
Sukma India **73** D2
Sukpay Rus. Fed. **64** D3
Sukpay *r.* Rus. Fed. **64** D3
Sukri *r.* India **74** B4
Sukses Namibia **98** C4
Suktel *r.* India **73** D1
Sukumo Japan **65** C6
Sukun *i.* Indon. **108** C2
Sula *r.* Rus. Fed. **28** I2
Sula, Kepulauan *is* Indon. **57** G6
Sula, Ozero *l.* Rus. Fed. **32** H3
Sulabesi *i.* Indon. **57** G6
Sulaiman Ranges *mts* Pak. **81** G4
Sulak Rus. Fed. **79** F2
Sulak *r.* Rus. Fed. **79** F2
Sūlār Iran **80** B4
Sula Sgeir *i.* U.K. **34** C2
Sulawesi *i.* Indon. *see* **Celebes**
Sulaymān Beg Iraq **79** F4
Sulci *Sardinia* Italy *see* **Sant'Antioco**
Sulcis *Sardinia* Italy *see* **Sant'Antioco**
Sulechów Poland **37** G2
Suledeh Iran **80** B2
Sulejów Poland **37** I3
Sulejowskie, Jezioro *l.* Poland **37** I3
Sule Skerry *i.* U.K. **34** D2
Sule Stack *i.* U.K. **34** D2
Sulima Sierra Leone **92** C4
Sulina Romania **46** F2
Sulina, Braţul *watercourse* Romania **46** F2
Suliskongen *mt.* Norway **32** E2
Sulitjelma Norway **32** E2
Sulkava Fin. **33** H3
Sullana Peru **146** A6
Sullivan U.S.A. **128** B4
Sullivan Bay Canada **122** E5
Sullivan Island Myanmar *see* **Lanbi Kyun**
Sullivan Lake Canada **123** I5
Sully-sur-Loire France **38** E3
Sulmo Italy *see* **Sulmona**
Sulmona Italy **44** D3
Sülüoğlu Turkey **46** E4
Sulphur *LA* U.S.A. **133** C6
Sulphur *OK* U.S.A. **133** B5
Sulphur *r.* U.S.A. **133** C5
Sulphur Springs U.S.A. **133** C5
Sulphur Springs Draw *watercourse* U.S.A. **133** A5
Sultan Canada **124** D4
Sultan, Koh-i- *mts* Pak. **81** E4
Sultanabad Iran *see* **Arāk**
Sultanbeyli Turkey **46** F4
Sultanhanı Turkey **78** C3
Sultaniça Turkey **46** E4
Sultaniye Turkey *see* **Karapınar**
Sultanpur India **75** D4
Sultansandzharskoye Vodokhranilische *resr* Turkm. **81** E1
Sulu Dem. Rep. Congo **95** E6
Sulu Archipelago *is* Phil. **57** F4
Sulu Basin *sea feature* N. Pacific Ocean **164** C5
Sülüklü Turkey **78** C3
Sülüktü Kyrg. **81** G2
Suluntah Libya **88** D1
Sulūq Libya **88** D2
Suluru India **72** D3
Sulu Sea N. Pacific Ocean **164** B5
Sulyukta Kyrg. *see* **Sülüktü**
Sulzbach-Rosenberg Germany **36** E4
Sulzberger Bay Antarctica **167** I1
Sumampa Arg. **152** E2
Sumapaz, Parque Nacional *nat. park* Col. **146** C4
Sumatera *i.* Indon. *see* **Sumatra**
Sumatera Barat *prov.* Indon. **58** C3
Sumatera Selatan *prov.* Indon. **58** C3
Sumatera Utara *prov.* Indon. **58** B2

▶**Sumatra** *i.* Indon. **58** B2
2nd largest island in Asia and 6th in the world.
asia 50–51
world 6–7

Sumaúma Brazil **149** E1
Šumava *mts* Czech Rep. **37** F4
Šumava *nat. park* Czech Rep. **37** F4
Sumba *i.* Indon. **57** F7
Sumba, Île *i.* Dem. Rep. Congo **94** C4
Sumba, Selat *sea chan.* Indon. **57** E7
Sumbar *r.* Turkm. **80** C2
Sumbawa *i.* Indon. **59** G5
Sumbawabesar Indon. **59** G5
Sumbawanga Tanz. **97** A6
Sumbay Peru **148** C3
Sumbe Angola **95** B7
Sumbing, Gunung *vol.* Indon. **58** C3
Sumbu Zambia **97** A7
Sumbu National Park Zambia **95** F7
Sumburgh U.K. **34** F2
Sumburgh Head U.K. **34** F2
Sumbuya Sierra Leone **92** C4
Sumdo Aksai Chin **74** C2
Sumdo China **66** B2
Sumdum, Mount U.S.A. **122** C3
Sumé Brazil **150** E3
Sumedang Indon. **59** D4
Sume'eh Sarā Iran **80** B2
Sümeg Hungary **37** H5
Sumeih Sudan **94** E2
Sumenep Indon. **59** F4
Sumerpur India **74** B4
Sumgait Azer. *see* **Sumqayıt**
Sumisu-jima *i.* Japan **65** E7
Summēl Iraq **79** E3
Summer Beaver Canada **124** B2
Summerdown Namibia **98** C4
Summerford Canada **125** K3
Summerland Canada **122** G5
Summerside Canada **125** I4
Summersville U.S.A. **130** C4
Summersville Lake U.S.A. **130** C4
Summerville *GA* U.S.A. **129** B5
Summerville *SC* U.S.A. **129** C5
Summit Lake *B.C.* Canada **122** E3
Summit Lake *B.C.* Canada **122** F4
Summit Mountain U.S.A. **137** D2
Summit Peak U.S.A. **135** F5
Sumnal Aksai Chin **74** C2
Sumner N.Z. **113** C3
Sumner U.S.A. **133** D5
Sumner Strait U.S.A. **122** C3
Šumperk Czech Rep. **37** H4
Sumprabum Myanmar **60** B2
Sumpu Japan *see* **Shizuoka**
Sumqayıt Azer. **79** G2
Sumqayıt *r.* Azer. **79** G2
Sumskiy Posad Rus. Fed. **28** E2
Sumter U.S.A. **129** C5
Sumur Jammu and Kashmir **74** C2
Sumy Ukr. **29** E6
Sun *r.* U.S.A. **134** E3
Suna Rus. Fed. **28** I4
Sunam India **74** B3
Sunamganj Bangl. **75** F4
Sunan N. Korea **65** A5
Sunbula Kuh *mts* Iran **80** A3
Sunbury Australia **112** C5
Sunbury *NC* U.S.A. **131** E5
Sunbury *OH* U.S.A. **130** B3
Sunbury *PA* U.S.A. **131** E3
Sunchales Arg. **152** E2
Suncho Corral Arg. **152** E1
Sunch'ŏn N. Korea **65** A5
Sunch'ŏn S. Korea **65** A6
Sun City S. Africa **99** E5
Sun City U.S.A. **137** F5
Suncook U.S.A. **131** H2
Sunda, Selat *strait* Indon. **58** D4
Sunda Kalapa Indon. *see* **Jakarta**
Sundance U.S.A. **134** F3
Sundarbans *reg.* Bangl./India **75** F5
Sundarbans National Park Bangl./India **75** F5
Sundargarh India **75** E5
Sundarnagar India **74** C3
Sunda Shelf *sea feature* Indian Ocean **162** O5
Sunda Strait Indon. *see* **Sunda, Selat**
Sunda Trench *sea feature* Indian Ocean *see* **Java Trench**
Sunday Strait Australia **108** C4
Sunderland U.K. **34** F4
Sündiken Dağları *mts* Turkey **78** B3
Sundre Canada **123** H5
Sundridge Canada **124** E4
Sundsvall Sweden **33** E3
Sundukli, Peski *des.* Turkm. **81** E2
Sunga Tanz. **97** C6
Sungaiapit Indon. **58** C2
Sungaiguntung Indon. **58** C2
Sungailiat Indon. **58** D3
Sungaipenuh Indon. **58** C3
Sungaipinyuh Indon. **59** E2
Sungari *r.* China *see* **Songhua Jiang**
Sungei Petani Malaysia **58** C1
Sungei Seletar Reservoir Sing. **58** [inset]
Sungikai Sudan **89** F6
Sungkiang China *see* **Songjiang**
Sung Kong *i.* *Hong Kong* China **67** [inset]
Sungo Moz. **99** G3
Sungqu China *see* **Songpan**
Sungurlare Bulg. **46** E3
Sungurlu Turkey **78** C2
Sunja Croatia **44** F2
Sunkosh *r.* Bhutan **75** F4
Sun Kosi *r.* Nepal **75** E4
Sunndal Norway **33** B3
Sunndalsøra Norway **32** C3
Sunne Sweden **33** D4
Sunnyside *UT* U.S.A. **137** G2
Sunnyside *WA* U.S.A. **134** C3
Sunnyvale U.S.A. **136** A3
Sunset House Canada **123** G4
Sunset Peak *hill* *Hong Kong* China **67** [inset]
Suntar Rus. Fed. **27** L3
Suntsar Pak. **81** E5
Sunwi-do *i.* N. Korea **65** A5
Sunwu China **64** A2
Sunyani Ghana **93** E4
Suojanperä Fin. **32** H1
Suolahti Fin. **32** G3
Suoločielgi Fin. *see* **Saariselkä**
Suoluvuobmi Norway **32** F1
Suomenniemi Fin. **33** G3
Suomi *country* Europe *see* **Finland**
Suō-nada *b.* Japan **65** B6
Suonenjoki Fin. **32** G3
Suŏng Cambodia **61** D6
Suong *r.* Laos **60** C4
Suontee Fin. **32** G3
Suontienselkä *l.* Fin. **32** G3
Suoyarvi Rus. Fed. **28** E3
Supa India **72** B3
Supai U.S.A. **137** F3
Supaul India **75** E4
Superfosfatnyy Uzbek. **81** F2
Superior *AZ* U.S.A. **137** G5
Superior *MT* U.S.A. **134** D3
Superior *WI* U.S.A. **132** C2

▶**Superior, Lake** Canada/U.S.A. **132** E2
Largest lake in North America and 2nd in the world.
northamerica 116–117
world 6–7

Supetar Croatia **44** F3
Suphan Buri Thai. **61** C5
Süphan Dağı *mt.* Turkey **79** E3
Supiori *i.* Indon. **57** I6
Suponevo Rus. Fed. **29** E5
Support Force Glacier Antarctica **167** A1
Sup'sa *r.* Georgia **79** E2
Supung N. Korea **65** A4
Sūq ar Rubū' Saudi Arabia **89** I4
Sūq ash Shuyūkh Iraq **79** F5
Suqian China **67** F1
Sūq Suwayq Saudi Arabia **89** H3
Suquṭrā *i.* Yemen *see* **Socotra**
Sūr *r.* Ghana **93** E3
Sūr Hungary **37** I5
Şūr Oman **76** F5
Sur, Point U.S.A. **136** B3
Sur, Punta *pt* Arg. **152** F4
Sura *r.* Rus. Fed. **29** H4
Surab Pak. **81** F4
Surabaya Indon. **59** F4
Surajpur India **75** D5
Sūrak Iran **81** D5
Surakarta Indon. **59** E4
Şura Mare Romania **46** D2
Sūran Iran **81** E5
Şūrān Syria **77** C2
Surára Brazil **147** F6
Surat Australia **111** G5
Surat India **74** B5
Suratgarh India **74** B3
Surat Thani Thai. **61** B6
Surazh Rus. Fed. **29** E5
Surbiton Australia **111** F4
Surdāsh Iraq **79** F4
Surdila-Greci Romania **46** E2
Surdulica Yugo. **46** C3
Sûre *r.* Germany/Lux. **39** G2
Surendranagar India **74** A5
Surf U.S.A. **136** B4
Surgères France **38** C3
Surgut Rus. Fed. **26** H3
Suri India *see* **Siuri**
Suriapet India **72** C2
Surigao Phil. **57** G4
Surimena Col. **146** C4
Surin Thai. **61** C5
Surinam *country* S. America *see* **Suriname**
▶**Suriname** *country* S. America **147** G3
southamerica 144–145, 154
Suriname *r.* Suriname **147** H3
Suripá Venez. **146** D3
Suriyān Iran **80** C4
Surkhābād Iran **80** C3
Surkhandar'inskaya Oblast' *admin. div.* Uzbek. **81** F2
Surkhandar'ya *r.* Uzbek. **81** F2
Surkhandarya Oblast *admin. div.* Uzbek. *see* **Surkhandar'inskaya Oblast'**
Surkhet Nepal **75** D3
Surkhob *r.* Tajik. **81** G2
Surkhondaryo *r.* Uzbek. *see* **Surkhandar'ya**
Surkhondaryo Wiloyati *admin. div.* Uzbek. *see* **Surkhandar'inskaya Oblast'**
Surmāq Iran **80** C4
Sürmene Turkey **79** E2
Surnadalsøra Norway **32** C3
Sŭrnevo Bulg. **46** D3
Surovikino Rus. Fed. **29** G6
Surprise Canada **122** C3
Surrey Canada **122** F5
Surskoye Rus. Fed. **29** H5
Surt Libya *see* **Sirte**
Surt, Khalīj *g.* Libya *see* **Sirte, Gulf of**
Surtsey *i.* Iceland **32** [inset]
Sūrū Iran **80** D5
Suru, Vârful *mt.* Romania **46** D2
Surubiú *r.* Brazil **150** B2
Sürüç Turkey **79** D3
Surud, Raas *pt* Somalia **96** E2
Surud Ad *mt.* Somalia *see* **Shimbiris**
Suruga-wan *b.* Japan **65** D6
Surulangun Indon. **58** C3
Surumú *r.* Brazil **147** F4
Suryapet India *see* **Suriapet**
Susa Italy **44** A2
Sušac *i.* Croatia **44** F3
Susah Tunisia *see* **Sousse**
Susaki Japan **65** C6
Susan U.S.A. **131** E5
Süsangerd Iran **80** B4
Susanville U.S.A. **136** B1
Suşehri Turkey **79** D2
Sušice Czech Rep. **37** F4
Susner India **74** C5
Susong China **67** F2
Susquehanna U.S.A. **131** F3
Susquehanna *r.* U.S.A. **131** E4
Susquehanna, West Branch *r.* U.S.A. **130** E3
Susques Arg. **148** D5
Sussex Canada **125** H4
Sussex U.S.A. **131** F3
Susuman Rus. Fed. **27** O3
Susurluk Turkey **78** B3
Suswa, Mount Kenya **96** B5
Susz Poland **37** I2
Sutak Jammu and Kashmir **74** C2
Sutherland Australia **112** D4
Sutherland S. Africa **98** D7
Sutherland *NE* U.S.A. **132** A3
Sutherland *VA* U.S.A. **130** E5
Sutherland Range *hills* Australia **109** D6
Sutjeska *nat. park* Bos.-Herz. **44** G3
Sutlej *r.* India/Pak. **74** A3
Sütlüce Turkey **77** A1
Sutter U.S.A. **136** B2
Sutton *r.* Canada **124** D2
Sutton U.S.A. **130** C4
Sutton Coldfield U.K. **35** F5
Sutton Lake Canada **124** C2
Sutton Lake U.S.A. **130** C4
Suttor *r.* Australia **111** F4
Sutwik Island U.S.A. **120** D4
Sutyr' *r.* Rus. Fed. **64** C2
Suure-Jaani Estonia **33** G4
Suurpea Estonia **33** G4

▶**Suva** Fiji **107** G3
Capital of Fiji.

Suvalki Poland *see* **Suwałki**
Suvorov Rus. Fed. **29** F5
Suvorove Ukr. **46** F2
Suvorovo Moldova *see* **Ştefan Vodă**
Suwakong Indon. **59** F3
Suwałki Poland **37** K1
Suwannaphum Thai. **61** C5
Suwannee *r.* U.S.A. **129** C6
Suwanose-jima *i.* Japan **65** B7
Suwaran, Gunung *mt.* Indon. **59** G2
Suwarrow *atoll* Cook Is **165** H6
Suwaylih Jordan **77** B3
Suwayqīyah, Hawr as *imp. l.* Iraq **79** F4
Suwayr *well* Saudi Arabia **89** I2
Suways, Khalīj as *g.* Egypt *see* **Suez, Gulf of**
Suways, Qanāt as *canal* Egypt *see* **Suez Canal**
Suweilih Jordan *see* **Suwaylih**
Suweis, Khalîg el *g.* Egypt *see* **Suez, Gulf of**
Suweis, Qanâ el *canal* Egypt *see* **Suez Canal**
Suwŏn S. Korea **65** A5
Suz, Mys *pt* Kazakh. **79** H2
Sūzā Iran **80** D5
Suzaka Japan **65** D5
Suzdal' Rus. Fed. **28** G4
Suzhou *Anhui* China **67** F1
Suzhou *Gansu* China *see* **Jiuquan**
Suzhou *Jiangsu* China **67** G2
Suzi *r.* China **64** A4
Suzu Japan **65** D5
Suzuka Japan **65** D6
Suzu-misaki *pt* Japan **65** D5
Suzzara Italy **44** C2
Sværholthalvøya *pen.* Norway **32** G1

▶**Svalbard** *terr.* Arctic Ocean **26** B2
Part of Norway.

Svalenik Bulg. **46** E3
Svanstein Sweden **32** F2
Svappavaara Sweden **32** F2
Svärdsjö Sweden **33** D3
Svartälven *r.* Sweden **33** D4
Svartenhuk Halvø *pen.* Greenland *see* **Sigguup Nunaa**
Svatove Ukr. **29** F6
Svay Riĕng Cambodia **61** D6
Svecha Rus. Fed. **28** H4
Svėdasai Lith. **33** G5
Sveg Sweden **33** D3
Svegsjön *l.* Sweden **33** D3
Sveio Norway **33** B4
Svelgen Norway **33** B3
Svellingen Norway **32** C3
Švenčionėliai Lith. **33** G5
Švenčionys Lith. **33** G5
Svendborg Denmark **33** C5
Svenljunga Sweden **33** D4
Svenstavik Sweden **32** D3
Sverdlovsk Rus. Fed. *see* **Yekaterinburg**
Sverdlovs'k Ukr. **29** F6
Sverdlovsk Uzbek. **81** F2
Sverdlovskaya Oblast' *admin. div.* Rus. Fed. **28** L4
Sverdlovsk Oblast *admin. div.* Rus. Fed. *see* **Sverdlovskaya Oblast'**
Sverdrup Channel Canada **121** J2
Sverdrup Islands Canada **121** J2
Sverige *country* Europe *see* **Sweden**
Sveta Andrija *i.* Croatia **44** E3
Sveti Ivan Zelina Croatia *see* **Zelina**
Sveti Jure *mt.* Croatia **44** F3
Sveti Nikole Macedonia **46** B4
Svetlaya Rus. Fed. **64** D3
Svetlodarskoye Rus. Fed. **64** E2
Svetlogorsk Belarus *see* **Svyetlahorsk**
Svetlogorsk *Kaliningradskaya Oblast'* Rus. Fed. **33** F5
Svetlogorsk *Krasnoyarskiy Kray* Rus. Fed. **27** I3
Svetlograd Rus. Fed. **29** G7
Svetlopolyansk Rus. Fed. **28** J4
Svetlovodsk Ukr. *see* **Svitlovods'k**
Svetlyy Rus. Fed. **37** J1
Svetlyy Yar Rus. Fed. **29** H6
Svetogorsk Rus. Fed. **28** D3
Svetozarevo Yugo. *see* **Jagodina**
Svíahnúkar *vol.* Iceland **32** [inset]
Svidník Slovakia **37** J4
Svilaja *mts* Croatia **44** F3
Svilajnac Yugo. **46** B2
Svilengrad Bulg. **46** E4
Svinecea Mare, Vârful *mt.* Romania **31** J4
Svinø *i.* Faroe Is *see* **Svínoy**
Svínoy *i.* Faroe Is **34** [inset]
Svintsovyy Rudnik Turkm. **81** F2
Svir Belarus **33** G5
Svir' *r.* Rus. Fed. **28** E3
Svishtov Bulg. **46** D3
Svitava *r.* Czech Rep. **37** H4
Svitavy Czech Rep. **37** H4
Svitlovods'k Ukr. **29** E6
Svizzera *country* Europe *see* **Switzerland**
Svoboda Rus. Fed. **37** J1
Svobodnyy Rus. Fed. **64** B2
Svoge Bulg. **46** C3
Svolvær Norway **32** D1
Svrljig Yugo. **46** C3
Svrljiške Planine *mts* Yugo. **46** C3
Svyatoy Nos, Mys *c.* Rus. Fed. **28** I2
Svyetlahorsk Belarus **31** L2
Swabi Pak. **81** H3
Swain Reefs Australia **111** H4
Swainsboro U.S.A. **129** C5
Swains Island American Samoa **107** H3
Swakop *watercourse* Namibia **98** B4
Swakopmund Namibia **98** B4
Swale *r.* U.K. **35** F4
Swallow Islands Solomon Is **107** F3
Swampy *r.* Canada **125** G1
Swan *r.* Australia **109** A7
Swan *r.* *Man./Sask.* Canada **123** K4
Swan *r.* *Ont.* Canada **124** D2
Swanage U.K. **35** F6
Swana-Mume Dem. Rep. Congo **95** E7
Swandale U.S.A. **130** C4
Swan Hill Australia **112** B4
Swan Hills Canada **123** H4
Swan Island Caribbean Sea **139** H5
Swan Lake Canada **123** K4
Swan Lake U.S.A. **132** C2
Swanlinbar Rep. of Ireland **35** C4
Swanquarter U.S.A. **128** D5
Swan River Canada **134** G1
Swansea Australia **112** D6
Swansea U.K. **35** E6
Swansea Bay U.K. **35** E6
Swanton U.S.A. **136** A3
Swart Nossob *watercourse* Namibia *see* **Black Nossob**
Swartruggens S. Africa **99** E5
Swartz Creek U.S.A. **130** B2
Swarzędz Poland **37** H2
Swasey Peak U.S.A. **137** F2
Swat *r.* Pak. **81** G3
Swatow China *see* **Shantou**
▶**Swaziland** *country* Africa **99** F5
africa 86–87, 100

▶**Sweden** *country* Europe **33** D3
5th largest country in Europe.
europe 24–25, 48

Sweet Home U.S.A. **134** B3
Sweet Springs U.S.A. **130** C5
Sweetwater U.S.A. **133** A5
Sweetwater *r.* U.S.A. **134** F4
Swellendam S. Africa **98** D7
Świder *r.* Poland **37** J3
Świdnica Poland **37** H3
Świdwin Poland **37** G2
Świebodzice Poland **37** H3
Świebodzin Poland **37** G2
Świecie Poland **37** I2
Świętokrzyskie, Góry *hills* Poland **37** J3
Świętokrzyski Park Narodowy *nat. park* Poland **37** J3
Swift *r.* U.S.A. **131** H1
Swift Current Canada **134** F2
Swilly, Lough *inlet* Rep. of Ireland **34** C4
Swindon U.K. **35** F6
Świnoujście Poland **37** G2
Swiss Confederation *country* Europe *see* **Switzerland**
Swiss National Park Switz. **39** I3
▶**Switzerland** *country* Europe **39** H3
europe 24–25, 48
Swords Rep. of Ireland **35** C5
Swords Range *hills* Australia **111** E4
Syamozero, Ozero *l.* Rus. Fed. **28** E3
Syamzha Rus. Fed. **28** G3
Syang Nepal **75** D3
Syas'troy Rus. Fed. **28** E3
Sychevka Rus. Fed. **28** E5
Syców Poland **37** H3

▶**Sydney** Australia **112** D4
State capital of New South Wales. Most populous city in Oceania.
oceania 104–105
world 16–17

Sydney Canada **125** I4
Sydney Island Kiribati *see* **Manra**
Sydney Lake Canada **123** M5
Syeverodonets'k Ukr. **29** F6
Sykesville U.S.A. **130** D3
Sykkylven Norway **32** B3
Syktyvkar Rus. Fed. **28** I3
Sylacauga U.S.A. **129** B5
Sylhet Bangl. **75** F4
Sylhet *admin. div.* Bangl. **75** F4
Sylt *i.* Germany **36** D1
Sylva *r.* Rus. Fed. **28** K4
Sylva U.S.A. **128** C5
Sylvania *GA* U.S.A. **129** C5
Sylvania *OH* U.S.A. **130** B3
Sylvan Lake Canada **123** H4
Sylvester, Lake *salt flat* Australia **110** C3
Sylvia, Mount Canada **122** E3
Symi Greece **47** E6
Symi *i.* Greece **47** E6
Synel'nykove Ukr. **29** E6
Syngyrli, Mys *pt* Kazakh. **79** H2
Synnagyn, Khrebet *mts* Rus. Fed. **27** M4
Synnfjell *mt.* Norway **33** C3
Synnott Range *hills* Australia **108** D4
Synya Rus. Fed. **28** K2
Synya *r.* Rus. Fed. **28** M2
Syowa *research station* Antarctica **167** D2
Syracusae *Sicily* Italy *see* **Syracuse**
Syracuse *Sicily* Italy **45** E6
Syracuse *KS* U.S.A. **132** A4
Syracuse *NY* U.S.A. **131** E2
Syrdar'inskaya Oblast' *admin. div.* Uzbek. **81** G1
Syr Darya *r.* Asia *see* **Syrdar'ya**
Syrdar'ya *r.* Asia **70** C3
Syrdar'ya Uzbek. **81** G1
Syrdarya Oblast *admin. div.* Uzbek. *see* **Syrdar'inskaya Oblast'**
Syrdaryinskiy Uzbek. *see* **Syrdar'ya**
▶**Syria** *country* Asia **79** D4
asia 52–53, 82
Syriam Myanmar **60** B4
Syrian Desert Asia **79** D4
Syrna *i.* Greece **47** E6
Syros *i.* Greece **47** D6
Syrskiy Rus. Fed. **29** F5
Sysmä Fin. **33** G3
Sysola *r.* Rus. Fed. **28** I3
Syumsi Rus. Fed. **28** I4
Syun *r.* Rus. Fed. **28** J5
Syurkum Rus. Fed. **64** E2
Syurkum, Mys *pt* Rus. Fed. **64** E2
Syzran' Rus. Fed. **29** I5
Szabadka Yugo. *see* **Subotica**
Szadek Poland **37** I3
Szamocin Poland **37** H2
Szamotuły Poland **37** H2
Szarvas Hungary **37** J5
Százhalombatta Hungary **37** I5
Szczecin Poland **37** G2
Szczecinek Poland **37** H2
Szczekociny Poland **37** I3
Szczucyn Poland **37** K2
Szczytno Poland **37** J2
Szechwan *prov.* China *see* **Sichuan**
Szeged Hungary **46** B1
Szeghalom Hungary **37** J5
Székesfehérvár Hungary **37** I5
Szekszárd Hungary **46** A1
Szentes Hungary **37** J5
Szentgotthárd Hungary **37** H5
Szentlőrinc Hungary **44** F1
Szerencs Hungary **37** J4
Szeska Góra *hill* Poland **37** K1
Szigetszentmiklós Hungary **37** I5
Szigetvár Hungary **44** F1
Szkwa *r.* Poland **37** J2
Szolnok Hungary **37** J5
Szombathely Hungary **37** H5
Szprotawa Poland **37** G3
Sztálinváros Hungary *see* **Dunaújváros**
Sztum Poland **37** I2
Szubin Poland **37** H2
Szydłowiec Poland **37** J3
Szypliszki Poland **33** F5

↓ T

Taabo, Lac de *l.* Côte d'Ivoire **92** D4
Taagga Duudka *reg.* Somalia **96** D2
Tab Hungary **37** I5
Tābah Saudi Arabia **89** I3
Tabajara Brazil **149** E2
Tabakat *well* Mali **91** E5
Tabanan Indon. **59** F5
Tabang Indon. **59** G2
Tabang *r.* Indon. **59** F2
Ţabaqah Syria **77** D2
Tabar Islands P.N.G. **107** E2
Tabarka Tunisia **45** B6
Ţabas Iran **80** D3
Tabāsin Iran **80** D4
Tābask, Kūh-e *mt.* Iran **80** B4
Tabatinga Brazil **146** D6
Tabatinga, Serra da *hills* Brazil **150** C4
Tabédé *well* Chad **88** B6
Tabelbala Alg. **90** E3
Taber Canada **123** H5
Tabernas Spain **43** E4
Tabernes de Valldigna Spain *see* **Tavernes de la Valldigna**
Tabet, Nam *r.* Myanmar **60** B2
Tabia Tsaka *salt l.* China **75** E3
Tabīr *r.* Indon. **58** C3
Tabiteuea *atoll* Kiribati **164** F6
Table Cape N.Z. **113** D2
Table Islands India **61** A5
Table Rock Reservoir U.S.A. **133** C4
Tabligbo Togo **93** F4
Taboca Brazil **147** F5
Tabocal *r.* Brazil **147** F6
Tabong Myanmar **60** B2
Tábor Czech Rep. **37** G4
Tabora Tanz. **97** B6
Tabora *admin. reg.* Tanz. **97** B6
Taboshar Tajik. **81** G1
Tabou Côte d'Ivoire **92** D4
Tabrichat *well* Mali **93** F1
Tabrīz Iran **80** A2
Tabuaeran *i.* Kiribati **165** H5
Tabūk Saudi Arabia **89** H2
Tabūk *prov.* Saudi Arabia **77** B5
Tabulam Australia **112** E3
Tabuyung Indon. **58** B2
Täby Sweden **33** E4
Tacaipu, Serra *hills* Brazil **147** H5
Tachdaït *well* Mali **93** F1
Tacheng China **70** F2
Tachie Canada **122** E4
Táchira *state* Venez. **146** C2
Tachiumet *well* Libya **88** A3
Tachov Czech Rep. **37** F4
Tacina *r.* Italy **45** F5
Taciuã, Lago *l.* Brazil **147** F6
Tacloban Phil. **57** G3
Tacna Col. **146** D5
Tacna Peru **148** C4
Tacna *dept* Peru **148** C4
Tacoma U.S.A. **134** B3
Taco Pozo Arg. **152** E1
Tacuarembó Uruguay **152** G2
Tadélaka *well* Niger **93** G1
Tademaït, Plateau du Alg. **91** F3
Tademaït Plateau Alg. *see* **Tademaït, Plateau du**
Tadine New Caledonia **107** F4
Tadjentourt *hill* Alg. **91** H4
Tadjeraout, Oued *watercourse* Alg. **91** F5
Tadjikistan *country* Asia *see* **Tajikistan**
Tadjoura Djibouti **96** D2
Tadjoura, Golfe de *g.* Djibouti **96** D2
Tadjrouna Alg. **91** F2
Tadmur Syria **79** D4
Tadó Col. **146** B3
Tadohae Haesang National Park S. Korea **65** A6
Tadoule Lake Canada **123** L3
Tadpatri India **72** C3
Tadrart Acacus *tourist site* Libya **88** A3
Tadwale India **72** C2
Tadzhikabad Tajik. *see* **Tojikobod**
Tadzhikskaya S.S.R. *country* Asia *see* **Tajikistan**
T'aean Haean National Park S. Korea **65** A5
T'aebaek-sanmaek *mts* N. Korea/S. Korea **65** A5
Taebla Estonia **33** F4
Taech'ŏn S. Korea *see* **Poryŏng**
Taech'ŏng-do *i.* S. Korea **65** A5
Taedong-man *b.* N. Korea **65** A5
Taegu S. Korea **65** B6
Taehŭksan-kundo *is* S. Korea **65** A6
Taejŏn S. Korea **65** A5
Taejŏng S. Korea **65** A6
T'aepaek S. Korea **65** B5
Ta'erqi China **63** K2
Tafahi *i.* Tonga **107** H3
Tafalla Spain **43** F1
Tafassasset, Oued *watercourse* Alg./Niger **91** H5
Tafelberg *mt.* Suriname **147** G4
Tafila Jordan *see* **Aţ Ţafilah**
Tafiré Côte d'Ivoire **92** D3
Tafi Viejo Arg. **152** D1
Tafjord Norway **33** B3
Tafresh Iran **80** B3
Taft Iran **80** C4
Taft U.S.A. **135** C6
Taftān, Kūh-e *mt.* Iran **81** E4
Taftanāz Syria **77** C2
Tagab Sudan **89** F5
Tagânet Keyna *well* Mali **92** E1
Taganrog Rus. Fed. **29** F7
Taganrog, Gulf of Rus. Fed./Ukr. **29** F7
Taganrogskiy Zaliv *b.* Rus. Fed./Ukr. *see* **Taganrog, Gulf of**
Tagant *admin. reg.* Mauritania **92** C1
Tagarev, Gora *mt.* Iran/Turkm. **80** D2
Tagay Rus. Fed. **29** H5
Tagaza *well* Niger **93** G1
Tagbilaran Phil. **57** F4
Tagchagpu Ri *mt.* China **75** D2
Tagdempt Alg. *see* **Tiaret**
Taghmanant *well* Mali **90** D4
Tagish Canada **122** C2
Tagish Lake Canada **122** C3
Tagliamento *r.* Italy **44** D2
Tagnout Chaggueret *well* Mali **91** E5
Tagourâret *well* Mauritania **92** D1
Tagtabazar Turkm. **81** E3

Taguatinga Brazil **150** C5
Taguenout Hagguereut *well* Mali *see* Tagnout Chaggueret
Tagula P.N.G. **111** H1
Tagula Island P.N.G. **107** E3
Tagus *r.* Port./Spain **42** C3
also known as Tajo (Portugal) or Tejo (Spain)
Tah, Sabkhat *salt pan* Morocco **90** B4
Taha China **64** A3
Tahan, Gunung *mt.* Malaysia **58** C1
Tahanroz'ka Zatoka *b.* Rus. Fed./Ukr. *see* Taganrog, Gulf of
Tahat, Mont Alg. **91** G5
Tahaurawe *i.* U.S.A. *see* Kahoolawe
Tahe China **64** A1
Taheke N.Z. **113** C1
Tahifet Alg. **91** G5
Tahiti *i.* Fr. Polynesia **165** I7
Tahlab, Dasht-i *plain* Pak. **81** E4
Tahlab *r.* Iran/Pak. **81** E4
Tahlequah U.S.A. **133** C5
Tahltan Canada **122** D3
Tahoe, Lake U.S.A. **136** B2
Tahoe City U.S.A. **136** B2
Tahoe Vista U.S.A. **136** B2
Tahoka U.S.A. **131** C5
Tahoua *dept* Niger **93** G2
Tahoua Niger **93** G2
Tahrud Iran **80** D4
Tahrūd *r.* Iran **80** D4
Tahtā Egypt **89** F3
Tahtsa Peak Canada **122** E4
Tahua Bol. **148** D4
Tahuamanú Peru **148** C2
Tahulandang *i.* Indon. **57** G5
Taï Côte d'Ivoire **92** C4
Taï, Parc National de *nat. park* Côte d'Ivoire **92** D4
Tai'an China **66** C1
Taibai China **66** C1
Taibai Shan *mt.* China **66** C1
Taibei Taiwan *see* T'aipei
Taibilla *r.* Spain **43** E3
Taibilla, Sierra de *mts* Spain **43** E3
Taibus Qi China *see* Baochang
T'aichung Taiwan **67** G3
Taidong Taiwan *see* T'aitung
Taieri *r.* N.Z. **113** B4
Taihe Anhui China **67** E1
Taihe *r.* China **67** E3
Taihe *Jiangxi* China **67** E3
Taihe *Sichuan* China *see* Shehong
Taihezhen China *see* Shehong
Tai Ho Wan Hong Kong China **67** [inset]
Taihu China **67** F2
Tai Hu *l.* China **67** G2
Taikang *Heilong.* China **64** A3
Taikang *Henan* China **67** E1
Taikkyi Myanmar **60** A4
Tailako East Timor **108** D3
Tai Lam Chung Reservoir Hong Kong China **67** [inset]
Taileleo Indon. **58** B3
Tailem Bend Australia **112** A4
Tai Long Wan *b.* Hong Kong China **67** [inset]
Tailuge Taiwan *see* T'ailuko
T'ailuko Taiwan **67** G3
Taim Brazil **152** E3
Tai Mo Shan *hill* Hong Kong China **67** [inset]
Tain *r.* Ghana **93** E3
Tain U.K. **34** E2
T'ainan Taiwan **67** G4
Tainaro, Akra *c.* Greece **47** C6
Tai O Hong Kong China **67** [inset]
Taiobeiras Brazil **151** D5
Taipa Fin. **33** H3
Tai Pang Wan *b.* Hong Kong China *see* Mirs Bay

▶ **T'aipei** Taiwan **67** G3
Capital of Taiwan.

Taipei Taiwan *see* T'aipei
Taiping *Guangdong* China *see* Shixing
Taiping Guangxi China **67** E4
Taiping *Guangxi* China *see* Chongzuo
Taiping *Guangxi* China **67** G3
Taiping Malaysia **58** C1
Tai Po Hong Kong China **67** [inset]
Tai Poutini National Park N.Z. *see* Westland National Park
Taipu Brazil **150** F3
Taipudia India **75** G4
Tairbeart U.K. *see* Tarbert
Tai Rom Yen National Park Thai. **61** B4
Tairuq Iran **80** A3
Tais Indon. **58** C4
Taishan China **67** E4
Tai Shek Mo *hill* Hong Kong China *see* Crest Hill
Taishun China **67** F3
Taita Hills Kenya **96** C5
Taitaitanepo *i.* Indon. **58** C3
Taitanu N.Z. **113** C3
Taitao, Península de *pen.* Chile **153** B6
Taitao, Punta *pt* Chile **153** B6
Taiti *mt.* Kenya **96** B4
Tai To Yan *mt.* Hong Kong China **67** [inset]
T'aitung Taiwan **67** G4
Taivalkoski Fin. **32** H2
Taivaskero *hill* Fin. **32** G1
▶ **Taiwan** country Asia **67** G4
asia 52–53, 82
Taiwan Haixia *strait* China/Taiwan *see* Taiwan Strait
Taiwan Shan *mts* Taiwan *see* Chungyang Shanmo
Taiwan Strait China/Taiwan **67** F4
Taixian China *see* Jiangyan
Taixing China **67** I4
Taïyetos Oros *mts* Greece *see* Tavgetos
Taiyuan China **63** I4
Tai Yue Shan *i.* Hong Kong China *see* Lantau Island
Taizhong Taiwan *see* T'aichung
Taizhou *Jiangsu* China **67** F1
Taizhou *Zhejiang* China **67** G2
Taizhou Liedao *i.* China **67** G2
Ta'izz Yemen **76** C7
Tajamulco, Volcán de *vol.* Guat. **138** C3
Tajarhī Libya **88** B3
Tajem, Gunung *hill* Indon. **59** D3
Tāj-e Malekī Iran **80** B3
Tajerouine Tunisia **45** B7
▶ **Tajikistan** *country* Asia **81** G2
asia 52–53, 82
Tajitos Mex. **135** D7
Taj Mahal *tourist site* India **74** C4
Tajo *r.* Spain **42** E2 *see* Tagus
Tajsara, Cordillera de *mts* Bol. **148** D5
Tajuña *r.* Spain **43** E2
Tak Thai. **60** B4
Takāb Iran **80** A2
Takabba Kenya **96** E3
Takada Japan **65** D5
Takahe, Mount Antarctica **162** J1
Takahagi Japan **65** F5
Takalous, Oued *watercourse* Alg. **91** G5
Takama Guyana **147** G3
Takamatsu Japan **65** C6
Takaoka Japan **65** D5
Takapau N.Z. **113** D3
Takapuna N.Z. **113** C2

Takasaki Japan **65** D5
Takatokwane Botswana **98** E5
Takatshwaane Botswana **98** D4
Takatu *r.* Brazil/Guyana **147** G4
Takayama Japan **65** D5
Tak Bai Thai. **61** C7
Takefu Japan **65** D6
Takengon Indon. **58** B1
Takeo Cambodia *see* Takêv
Takeo Japan **65** B6
Take-shima *i.* N. Pacific Ocean *see* Liancourt Rocks
Takestān Iran **80** B2
Taketa Japan **65** B6
Takêv Cambodia **61** D6
Takfon Tajik. **81** G2
Takhādīd *well* Iraq **79** F5
Takhar *prov.* Afgh. **81** G2
Takhatpur India **75** D5
Takhiatash Uzbek. *see* Gulabie
Takhini *r.* Canada **122** C2
Takhini Hotspring Canada **122** C2
Ta Khli Thai. **61** C4
Ta Khmau Cambodia **61** D6
Takhta-Bazar Turkm. *see* Tagtabazar
Takht-i-Sulaiman *mt.* Iran **80** B2
Takht-i-Suleiman *mt.* Pak. **81** G4
Takiéta Niger **93** G3
Takijuq Lake Canada *see* Napaktulik Lake
Takikawa Japan **64** E4
Takisung Indon. **59** F3
Takla Lake Canada **122** E4
Takla Landing Canada **122** E4
Takla Makan *des.* China *see* Taklimakan Desert
▶ **Taklimakan Desert** China **70** F4
asia 50–51
Taklimakan Shamo *des.* China *see* Taklimakan Desert
Takoradi Ghana **93** E4
Takpa Shiri *mt.* China **75** G3
Taku Canada **122** C3
Taku *r.* Canada/U.S.A. **120** F4
Takua Pa Thai. **61** B6
Takum Nigeria **93** H4
Takundi Dem. Rep. Congo **95** C6
Tala Uruguay **152** E4
Talachyn Belarus **29** F5
Talagang Pak. **81** H3
Talaiassa, Sant *hill* Spain **43** G3
Talaja India **74** B5
Talakan *Amurskaya Oblast'* Rus. Fed. **64** B2
Talakan *Khabarovskiy Kray* Rus. Fed. **64** C2
Talala India **72** A1
Talandzha Rus. Fed. **64** B2
Talangbatu Indon. **58** D4
Talara Peru **146** A6
Talar-i-Band *mts* Pak. **81** E5
Talas Kyrg. **70** D3
Talas *r.* Kyrg. **70** D3
Talata-Mafara Nigeria **93** G3
Ţal 'at Mūsá *mt.* Lebanon/Syria **77** C2
Talaud, Kepulauan *is* Indon. **57** G5
Talavera de la Reina Spain **42** D3
Talawanta Australia **111** C3
Talawgyi Myanmar **60** A1
Talaya Rus. Fed. **27** P3
Talayuelo *mt.* Spain **43** E3
Talbehat India **74** C4
Talbotton U.S.A. **129** B5
Talbragar *r.* Australia **112** D4
Talca Chile **152** C3
Talca, Punta *pt* Chile **152** C3
Talcahuano Chile **152** B4
Talcher India **73** E1
Taldan Rus. Fed. **64** A1
Taldom Rus. Fed. **28** F4
Taldyk, Pereval *pass* Kyrg. **81** H2
Taldy-Kurgan Kazakh. *see* Taldykorgan
Taldyqorghan Kazakh. *see* Taldykorgan
Talen Indon. **58** [inset]
Tälesh Iran **80** B2
Talguharai Sudan **86** E6
Ţalḩah Saudi Arabia **89** I5
Taliabu *i.* Indon. **57** F6
Talikota India **72** C2
Talimardzhan Uzbek. **81** F2
Taliouine Morocco **90** D3
Taliparamba India **72** B3
Tali Post Sudan **96** A3
Talisay Phil. **57** F3
Talisayan Indon. **59** F2
Talış Dağları *mts* Azer./Iran **79** G3
Talitsa Rus. Fed. **28** H4
Taliwang Indon. **58** C4
Tallacootra, Lake *salt flat* Australia **109** F7
Talladega U.S.A. **129** B5
▶ **Tallahassee** U.S.A. **129** B6
State capital of Florida.

Tallangatta Australia **112** C5
Tallapoosa *r.* U.S.A. **129** B5
Tall Baydar Syria **79** E3

Tamai, Nam *r.* Myanmar **60** B2
Tamala Australia **109** A6
Tamale Ghana **93** E3
Tamalelt *well* Mali **93** F2
Tamalung Indon. **59** F3
Tamana *i.* Kiribati **107** G2
Tamanar Morocco **90** C3
Tamanco Peru **146** C6
Tamanhint Libya **88** B3
Tamani Mali **92** D2
Tamanrasset Alg. **91** G5
Tamanrasset, Oued *watercourse* Alg. **91** F5
Tamanthi Myanmar **60** A2
Tamaqua U.S.A. **131** F3
Tamar *r.* India **75** E5
Tamar Syria *see* Tadmur
Tamar *r.* U.K. **35** D6
Tamaradit *well* Mali **93** F1
Tamarugal, Pampa de *plain* Chile **148** C4
Tamási Hungary **37** I5
Tamaulipas *state* Mex. **133** B7
Tambach Kenya **96** B4
Tambacounda Senegal **92** B3
Tambangsawah Indon. **58** C3
Tambaoura, Falaise de *esc.* Mali **92** C2
Tambaqui Brazil **147** F6
Tambelan, Kepulauan *is* Indon. **59** D2
Tambelan Besar *i.* Indon. **59** D2
Tambellup Indon. **59** F4
Tambo Australia **111** F5
Tambo *r.* Australia **112** C5
Tambo *r.* Peru **148** C3
Tambobamba Peru **148** B3
Tambo Grande Peru **146** A6
Tambohorano Madag. **99** [inset] I3
Tambopata *r.* Peru **148** C3
Tambor Angola **95** B9
Tambora, Gunung *vol.* Indon. **59** G5
Tamboril Brazil **150** D3
Tamboryacu *r.* Peru **146** C5
Tambouna Cont. Afr. Rep. **94** E3
Tambov Rus. Fed. **29** G5
Tambovka Rus. Fed. **64** B2
Tambov Oblast *admin. div.* Rus. Fed. *see* Tambovskaya Oblast'
Tambovskaya Oblast' *admin. div.* Rus. Fed. **29** G5
Tambre *r.* Spain **42** B1
Tambunan Malaysia **59** G1
Tambunan, Bukit *hill* Sabah Malaysia **59** G1
Tambura Sudan **94** E3
Tâmchekket Mauritania **92** C1
Tame Col. **146** D3
Tâmega *r.* Port. **42** C2
Tamel Aike Arg. **153** C7
Tamelos, Akra *pt* Greece **47** D6
Tamenghest Alg. *see* Tamanrasset
Tamenghest, Oued *watercourse* Alg. **91** G5
Tamesna *reg.* Niger **93** G1
Tamgak, Adrar *mt.* Niger **93** H1
Tamgout de Lalla Khedidja *mt.* Alg. **43** I4
Tamgué, Massif du *mt.* Guinea **92** B2
Tamia India **74** C5
Tamiahua, Laguna de *lag.* Mex. **126** C7
Tamiami Canal U.S.A. **129** C7
Tamiang *r.* Indon. **58** B1
Tamiang, Ujung *pt* Indon. **58** B1
Tamil Nadu *state* India **72** C4
Tamiš *r.* Yugo. **46** B2
Ţāmiyah Egypt **89** F2
Tamiyah, Jabal *hill* Saudi Arabia **89** I3
Tamjit *well* Mali **93** F2
Tamlelt, Plaine de *plain* Morocco **90** D2
Tamluk India **75** F5
Tammar *r.* Italy **44** E4
Tammarvi *r.* Canada **123** K1
Tammela Fin. **32** H2
Tammerfors Fin. *see* Tampere
Tammisaaren Saariston Kansallispuisto *nat. park* Fin. *see* Ekenäs skärgårds Nationalpark
Tammisaari Fin. *see* Ekenäs
Tamnava *r.* Yugo. **46** B2
Tamou Niger **93** F3
Tampa U.S.A. **129** C7
Tampa Bay U.S.A. **129** C7
Tampang Indon. **58** D4
Tampico Mex. **126** D7
Tampines, Sungai *r.* Sing. **58** [inset]
Tampines Sing. **58** [inset]
Tamsagbulag Mongolia **63** J2
Tamshiyacu Peru **146** C6
Tamsweg Austria **37** H5
Tamu Myanmar **60** A2
Tamur *r.* Nepal **75** F4
Tamworth Australia **112** D3
Tamworth U.K. **35** F5
Tana *r.* Fin./Norway *see* Tenojoki
Tana *r.* Kenya **96** D5
Tana Madag. *see* Antananarivo
Tana *i.* U.S.A. **122** A2
Tana *i.* Vanuatu *see* Tanna
Tana, Lake Eth. **96** C2
Tanabe Japan **65** C6
Tana Bru Norway **32** H1
Tanacross U.S.A. **122** A2
Tanaga Island U.S.A. **120** A4
Tanagro *r.* Italy **45** E4
Tanah, Tanjung *pt* Indon. **59** E4
Tanahbala *i.* Indon. **58** B3
Tanahgrogot Indon. **59** G3
Tanahjampea *i.* Indon. **57** F7
Tanahmasa *i.* Indon. **58** B3
Tanahmerah Indon. **58** G3
Tanahputih Indon. **58** C2
Tanakpur India **74** D3
Tanami Australia **110** B3
Tanami Desert Australia **110** B3
Tân An Vietnam **61** D6
Tana River *r.* U.S.A. **122** A2
Tananarive Madag. *see* Antananarivo
Tanāqīb, Ra's *pt* Saudi Arabia **80** B5
Tanaro *r.* Italy **44** D2
Tanbar Australia **111** E5
Tancheng Fujian China *see* Pingtan
Tanch'ŏn N. Korea **65** B4
Tanda Côte d'Ivoire **92** E4
Tanda *Uttar Pradesh* India **74** D4
Tanda *Uttar Pradesh* India **75** D4
Tăndărei Romania **46** E2
Tandaué Angola **95** B9
Tandek *Sabah* Malaysia **59** G1
Tandil Arg. **152** F4
Tandil, Sierra del *hills* Arg. **152** F4
Tandjilé *préf.* Chad **94** C3
Tando Adam *r.* Pak. **81** G5
Tando Allahyar Pak. **81** G5
Tando Bago Pak. **81** G5
Tando Muhammad Khan Pak. **81** G5
Tandou Lake *imp. l.* Australia **112** B4
Tandula *r.* India **74** D5
Tandur *Andhra Pradesh* India **72** C2
Tandur *Andhra Pradesh* India **72** C2
Tane, Serra de *hills* Brazil **147** H5
Tanega-shima *i.* Japan **65** C7
Tanen Taunggyi *mts* Thai. **60** B4
Tanezrouft Rio Grande do Sul Brazil **151** A9
Tapera *Rio Grande do Sul* Brazil **151** A9

Tanezrouft *reg.* Alg./Mali **91** E5
Tanezrouft Tan-Ahenet *reg.* Alg. **91** E5
Ţanf, Jabal aţ *hill* Syria **77** D3
Tanga Tanz. **97** C4
Tanga *admin. reg.* Tanz. **97** C6
Tangaehe N.Z. **113** C2
Tangail Bangl. **75** G4
Tangalla Sri Lanka **72** C5
Tanganyika *country* Africa *see* Tanzania
▶ **Tanganyika, Lake** Africa **95** F6
Deepest and 2nd largest lake in Africa and 7th largest in the world.
africa 84–85
world 6–7

Tangar Iran **80** C2
Tangasseri India **72** C4
Tangdan China **66** B3
Tangeli China **80** C2
Tange Promontory *hd* Antarctica **163** K10
Tanger Morocco *see* Tangier
Tangerang Indon. **59** D4
Tangermünde Germany **36** E2
Tang-e Sarkheh Iran **80** D5
Tanggor China **66** B1
Tanggu China *see* Tuotuoheyan
Tanggulashan China *see* Tuotuoheyan
Tanggula Shan *mt.* China **70** G5
Tanggula Shan *mts* China **70** G5
Tanggula Shankou *pass* China **70** H5
Tangguo China **75** G3
Tanghe China **67** E1
Tang He *r.* China **67** E1
Tangi Pak. **81** G3
Tangier Morocco **90** D2
Tangkittebak, Gunung *mt.* Indon. **58** D4
Tang La *pass* China **75** F4
Tanglin Sing. **58** [inset]
Tangmai China **75** G3
Tangor Indon. **58** C2
Tangra Yumco *salt l.* China **70** G5
Tangse Indon. **58** B1
Tangshan China **63** J4
Tangtou China **67** G3
Tanguma China **75** F4
Tangtse Jammu and Kashmir **74** C2
Tangudi *r.* India *see* Tengri Nur
Tanguieta Benin **93** F3
Tangwang He *r.* China **64** B3
Tangxianzhen China **67** E2
Tang-yan Myanmar **60** B3
Tangyan He *r.* China **67** D2
Tangyuan China **64** B3
Tanhaçu Brazil **150** D5
Tanhua Fin. **32** G2
Taniantaweng Shan *mts* China **66** A1
Tanimbar, Kepulauan *is* Indon. **57** H7
Tanintharyi Myanmar *see* Tenasserim
Tanintharyi Myanmar **60** B4
Tanintharyi *admin. div.* Myanmar *see* Tenasserim
Taninthayi Myanmar *see* Tenasserim
Tanjah Morocco *see* Tangier
Tanjay Phil. **57** F4
Tanjore India *see* Thanjavur
Tanjung *Kalimantan Selatan* Indon. **59** F3
Tanjung *Jambi, Sumatra* Indon. **58** D3
Tanjung *Sumatera Utara, Sumatra* Indon. **58** B2
Tanjungbalai *Sumatera Utara, Sumatra* Indon. **58** B2
Tanjungbatu *Kalimantan Timur* Indon. **59** G2
Tanjungbatu *Riau, Sumatra* Indon. **58** C2
Tanjungbuayabuaya, Pulau *i.* Indon. **59** G2
Tanjungpandan Indon. **58** D3
Tanjungpinang Indon. **58** C2
Tanjungpura Indon. **58** B2
Tanjung Puting National Park Indon. **59** F3
Tanjungredeb Indon. **59** G2
Tanjungsaleh *i.* Indon. **59** E3
Tanjungselor Indon. **59** G2
Tank Pak. **81** G3
Tankara India **74** A5
Tankhala India **74** B5
Tankse Jammu and Kashmir **74** C2
Tankuhi India **75** E4
Tankwa-Karoo National Park S. Africa **98** C7
Tanlwe *r.* Myanmar **60** A4
Tanna *i.* Vanuatu **107** F3
Tännäs Sweden **33** G4
Tanner, Mount Canada **122** G5
Tannila Fin. **32** G2
Tannu-Ola, Khrebet *mts* Rus. Fed. **62** E1
Tannu Tuva *aut. rep.* Rus. Fed. *see* Tyva, Respublika
Tanot India **74** A4
Tanout Niger **93** H2
Tansen Nepal **75** D4
Tanshui Taiwan **67** G3
Tansilla Burkina **92** D3
Ţanţā Egypt **89** F2
Tantabin Myanmar **60** A3
Tantoyuca Mex. **126** D7
Tantpur India **74** C4
Tantura Israel **77** B3
Tanuku India **73** D2
Tanumshede Sweden **33** G4
Tanwakka, Sabkhat *well* W. Sahara **90** B5
▶ **Tanzania** *country* Africa **97** B6
africa 86–87, 100
Tanzilla *r.* Canada **122** D3
Tao, Ko *i.* Thai. **61** B6
Tao'an China *see* Taonan
Taocheng *Fujian* China *see* Yongchun
Taocheng *Guangdong* China *see* Daxin
Taodeni Mali *see* Taoudenni
Tao He *r.* China **66** B1
Taohong China *see* Longhui
Taohuaping China *see* Longhui
Taojiang China **67** E2
Taolanaro Madag. *see* Tôlañaro
Taonan China **63** K2
Taongi *atoll* Marshall Is **164** F5
Taormina *Sicily* Italy **45** F6
Taos U.S.A. **135** F5
Taoudenni *well* Mali **93** F1
Taoudrart *well* Mali **93** E2
Taounate Morocco **90** D2
Taourirt Morocco **90** E2
Taouz Morocco **90** D2
Taoxi China *see* Tangier
Taoyuan *Hunan* China **67** E2
T'aoyüan Taiwan **67** G3
Taozhou China *see* Guangde
Tapa Estonia **28** C4
Tapachula Mex. **138** F6
Tapajós *r.* Brazil **147** G4
Tapaktuan Indon. **58** B2
Tapalqué Arg. **152** E4
Tapan Indon. **58** C3
Tapanui N.Z. **113** B4
Tapara, Serra de *hills* Brazil **147** H5
Tapauá Brazil **147** E6
Tapauá *r.* Brazil **147** E6
Tapera *Rio Grande do Sul* Brazil **151** A9
Taroudannt Morocco **90** C3

Tapera Roraima Brazil **147** F5
Tapera Chile **153** C6
Tapes Brazil **152** H2
Tapeta Liberia **92** C4
Tapi *r.* India **74** B5
Tapia, Sierra de *hills* Bol. **149** F4
Tapiau Rus. Fed. *see* Gvardeysk
Tapiche *r.* Peru **146** C6
Tápió *r.* Hungary **37** I5
Tapiós Hungary **37** I5
Tapiracanga Brazil **150** D3
Tapirapé *r.* Brazil **150** B4
Tapirapuã Brazil **149** G3
Tapis *mt.* Malaysia **58** C1
Taquara Brazil **151** A6
Taquari *r.* Brazil **149** F4
Taquaritinga Brazil **149** H5
Tara Australia **111** E5
Tara *r.* Bos./Yugo./Yugo. **46** A3
Taraba *r.* Nigeria **93** H3
Taraba *state* Nigeria **93** H3
Tarabuco Bol. **148** E4
Ţarābulus Libya *see* Tripoli
Ţarābulus Lebanon *see* Tripoli
Taracua Brazil **146** D4
Taräghin Libya **88** B3
Taraira *r.* Brazil *see* Traíra
Taraju Indon. **59** G2
Tarakan *i.* Indon. **59** G2
Taraklı Turkey **78** B2
Tarakliya Moldova *see* Taraclia
Taran, Mys *pt* Rus. Fed. **31** I2
Tarana India **74** C5
Taranagar India **74** B3
Tarancón Spain **42** E2
Tarangambadi India **72** C4
Tarangara Chad **94** C2
Tarangire National Park Tanz. **97** C6
Taranto Italy **45** H4
Taranto, Golfo di *g.* Italy **45** F4
Tarapacá Col. **146** D5
Tarapacá *admin. reg.* Chile **148** C4
Tarapoto Peru **146** B6
Tarare France **39** F4
Tararua Range *mts* N.Z. **113** C3
Tarascon-sur-Ariège France **38** D5
Tarasovskiy Rus. Fed. **29** G6
Tarat Alg. **91** H4
Tarata Peru **148** C4
Tarauacá Brazil **148** C2
Tarauacá *r.* Brazil **148** C2
Taravo *r.* Corsica France **44** B4
Tarawera N.Z. **113** D2
Tarawera, Mount N.Z. **113** D2
Taraz Kazakh. **70** D3
Tarazona Spain **43** F2
Tarazona de la Mancha Spain **43** F3
Tarbagatay, Khrebet *mts* Kazakh. **70** F2
Tarbat Ness *pt* U.K. **34** E3
Tarbela Dam Pak. **81** G3
Tarbert *Argyll and Bute, Scotland* U.K. **34** D4
Tarbert *Rep. of Ireland* **35** B5
Tarbert *Western Isles, Scotland* U.K. **34** C3
Tarbes France **38** D5
Tarboro U.S.A. **128** D5
Tarcoola Australia **109** F7
Tărculeşti, Munţii *mts* Romania **46** C2
Tardes *r.* France **38** E3
Tardoire *r.* France **38** D4
Tardoki-Yani, Gora *mt.* Rus. Fed. **64** D2
Taree Australia **112** E3
Tareifing Sudan **96** B2
Tärendö Sweden **32** F2
Tareya Rus. Fed. **27** J2
Ţarfā, Ra's aţ *pt* Saudi Arabia **89** I5
Tarfaya Morocco **90** C4
Targa *well* Niger **93** H2
Targhee Pass U.S.A. **134** D3
Târgoviște Romania **46** D2
Târgu Bujor Romania **46** D1
Târgu Jiu Romania **46** C2
Târgu Mureş Romania **46** D1
Târgu Ocna Romania **46** D2
Târgu Secuiesc Romania **46** E1
Targuist Morocco **90** E5
Târgu Jiu Romania **46** C2
Tarhmanant *well* Mali *see* Taghmanant
Tarhūnah Libya **88** B1
Tari P.N.G. **57** J7
Tarif U.A.E. **80** C5
Tarifa Spain **42** D5
Tarifa, Punta de *pt* Spain **42** D5
Tarija Bol. **149** F5
Tarija *dept* Bol. **149** D5
Tarikere India **72** B3
Tariku *r.* Indon. **57** I6
Tarim Yemen **76** D6
Tarim *r.* China **70** G3
Tarim Basin China **70** F4
Tarime Tanz. **96** B5
Tarim He *r.* China **70** G3
Tarim Pendi *basin* China *see* Tarim Basin
Taringuiti Bol. **149** E5
Tarin Kowt Afgh. **81** F3
Taritatu *r.* Indon. **57** I6
Taritipan *Sabah* Malaysia *see* Tandek
Tarka, Vallée de *watercourse* Niger **93** G2
Tarkio U.S.A. **132** C3
Tarko-Sale Rus. Fed. **26** I3
Tarkwa Ghana **93** E4
Tarlac Phil. **57** F2
Tarlo River National Park Australia **112** D4
Tarlton U.S.A. **130** D4
Tarma Peru **148** B2
Tarn *r.* France **39** D4
Tarna *r.* Hungary **37** I5
Tarnak *r.* Afgh. **81** F4
Târnava Mare *r.* Romania **46** C1
Târnava Mică *r.* Romania **46** C1
Târnăveni Romania **46** C1
Tarnobrzeg Poland **37** J3
Tarnogskiy Gorodok Rus. Fed. **28** G3
Tarnopol Ukr. *see* Ternopil'
Tarnów Poland **37** J3
Tarnowitz Poland *see* Tarnowskie Góry
Tarnowskie Góry Poland **37** I3
Taro *r.* Italy **44** D2
Taro Co *salt l.* China **75** D3
Tārom Iran **80** D4
Taroom Australia **111** E5
Taroudannt Morocco **90** C3

Tarpaulin Swamp Australia **110** D3
Tarpon Springs U.S.A. **129** C6
Tarq Iran **80** C3
Tarquinia Italy **44** C3
Tarquinii Italy *see* Tarquinia
Tarracina Italy *see* Terracina
Tarraco Spain *see* Tarragona
Tarragona Spain **43** G2
Tárrajaur Sweden **32** J2
Tarrant Point Australia **111** D3
Tarras N.Z. **113** B4
Tàrrasa Spain *see* Terrassa
Tàrrega Spain **43** G2
Tarrong China *see* Nyêmo
Tarso Ahon *mt.* Chad **88** C4
Tarso Emissi *mt.* Chad **88** C4
Tarso Kobour *mt.* Chad **88** C4
Tarsus Turkey **78** C3
Tarta Turkm. *see* Darta
Tartagal *Salta* Arg. **149** E5
Tartagal *Santa Fé* Arg. **152** F2
Tārtār *r.* Azer. **80** A1
Tartas France **38** D5
Tartu Estonia **28** I2
Ţarţūs Syria **78** B3
Ţarţūs *governorate* Syria **77** C2
Tarumovka Rus. Fed. **79** F1
Tarung Hka *r.* Myanmar **60** B2
Ţārūt Saudi Arabia **80** B5
Tarutina Indon. **58** B2
Tarutyne Ukr. **46** F1
Tarvisio Italy **44** D1
Tarvisium Italy *see* Treviso
Tarvo Bol. **149** E3
Tarz Iran **80** D4
Taseko Mountain Canada **122** F5
Tasendjanet, Oued *watercourse* Alg. **91** F4
Tasgaon India **72** B2
Tashauz Turkm. *see* Dashkhovuz
Tashauzskaya Oblast' *admin. div.* Turkm. *see* Dashkhovuzskaya Oblast'
Tashbunar *r.* Ukr. **46** F2
Tashi Chho Bhutan *see* Thimphu
Tashigang Bhutan *see* Trashigang
Tashino Rus. Fed. *see* Pervomaysk
Tashir Armenia **79** F2
Tashk, Daryācheh-ye *l.* Iran **80** C4
▶ **Tashkent** Uzbek. **70** C3
Capital of Uzbekistan.

Tashkent Oblast *admin. div.* Uzbek. *see* Tashkentskaya Oblast'
Tashkentskaya Oblast' *admin. div.* Uzbek. **81** G2
Tashkepri Turkm. **81** E2
Tash-Kömür Kyrg. **70** D3
Tash-Kumyr Kyrg. *see* Tash-Kömür
Tashla Rus. Fed. **29** J6
Tāshqurghān Afgh. *see* Kholm
Tasialujjuaq, Lac *l.* Canada **125** I1
Tasiat, Lac *l.* Canada **125** F1
Tasiilaq Greenland *see* Ammassalik
Tasikmalaya Indon. **59** D4
Tasiujaq Canada **125** G1
Task *well* Niger **93** I3
Tasker Niger **93** H2
Taskesken Kazakh. **70** F2
Taşköprü Turkey **78** C2
Tasman Abyssal Plain *sea feature* Tasman Sea **163** R8
Tasman Bay *sea feature* Tasman Sea **163** R8
Tasman Bay N.Z. **113** C3
▶ **Tasmania** *state* Australia **106** D6
4th largest island in Oceania.
oceania 102–103, 114

Tasman Mountains N.Z. **113** C3
Tasman Peninsula Australia **112** D6
Tasman Sea S. Pacific Ocean **107** G6
Taşova Turkey **78** C2
Tăssara Niger **93** G2
Tassara Gabon **94** A5
Tassialouc, Lac *l.* Canada **125** F1
Tassili du Hoggar *plat.* Alg. **91** G5
Tassili n'Ajjer *plat.* Alg. **91** G4
Tas-Tumus Rus. Fed. **27** M3
Tasty Kazakh. **70** C3
Tasu Canada **122** D4
Taşucu Turkey **77** A1
Tas-Yuryakh Rus. Fed. **27** L3
Tata Hungary **37** I5
Tataba Indon. **57** F6
Tatabánya Hungary **37** I5
Tatamagouche Canada **125** I4
Tata Mailau, Gunung *mt.* East Timor **57** G7
Tatanagar India **75** E5
Tataouine Tunisia **91** H2
Tatarbunary Ukr. **29** D7
Tatarpur India **74** C4
Tatarsk Rus. Fed. **26** I4
Tatarskaya A.S.S.R. *aut. rep.* Rus. Fed. *see* Tatarstan, Respublika
Tatarskiy Proliv *strait* Rus. Fed. **64** E2
Tatarstan, Respublika *aut. rep.* Rus. Fed. **28** I5
Tatau Sarawak Malaysia **59** F2
Tatavi *r.* Iran **80** A2
Tate *r.* Australia **111** E3
Tateyama Japan **65** D6
Tathlina Lake Canada **123** G2
Tathlith Saudi Arabia **89** I5
Tathlith, Wādī *watercourse* Saudi Arabia **68** C4
Tathra Australia **112** D5
Tatinnai Lake Canada **123** L1
Tatitlek U.S.A. **120** D3
Tatkon Myanmar **60** B3
Tatla Lake Canada **122** F5
Tatlayoko Lake Canada **122** F5
Tatnam, Cape Canada **123** N3
Tatra Mountains Poland/Slovakia **37** I4
Tatranský *nat. park* Slovakia **37** J4
Tatra Poland/Slovakia *see* Tatra Mountains
Tatrzański Park Narodowy *nat. park* Poland **37** I4
Tatshenshini *r.* Canada **122** B3
Tatta Pak. **81** F5
Tatui Brazil **149** I5
Tatuk Mountain Canada **122** E4
Tatum U.S.A. **135** G6
Tatvan Turkey **79** F3
Tau *i.* American Samoa **107** I3
Taua Brazil **150** D3
Tauapeçaçu Brazil **147** F5
Tauariã Brazil **147** F6
Tauató Brazil **151** C7
Taubaté *r.* Germany **36** D4
Tauber *r.* Germany **36** D4
Tauberbischofsheim Germany **36** D4
Tauchik Kazakh. **79** I1
Taufikia Sudan **96** A3
Taufkirchen (Vils) Germany **36** F4
Taumarunui N.Z. **113** C3
Taumaturgo Brazil **148** B2
Taung S. Africa **98** E5

Taungdwingyi Myanmar 60 A3
Taunggyi Myanmar 60 B3
Taunglau Myanmar 60 B3
Taungnyo Range mts Myanmar 61 B4
Taungtha Myanmar 60 A3
Taunqup Myanmar 60 A4
Taunsa Pak. 81 G4
Taunton U.K. 35 E6
Taunton U.S.A. 131 H3
Taunus hills Germany 36 C3
Taupo N.Z. 113 D2
Taupo, Lake N.Z. 113 C2
Tauragė Lith. 33 F5
Tauramena Col. 146 C3
Tauranga N.Z. 113 D2
Taurasia Italy see Turin
Taurianova Italy 45 F5
Taurion r. France 38 D4
Tauroa Point N.Z. 113 C1
Taurus Mountains Turkey 78 C3
Taūshyq Kazakh. see Tauchik
Tauste Spain 43 F2
Tauu Islands P.N.G. 107 E2
Tauz Azer. see Tovuz
Tavagnacco Italy 44 D1
Tavas Turkey 78 B3
Tavastehus Fin. see Hämeenlinna
Tavda Rus. Fed. 26 G4
Tavelsjö Sweden 32 F2
Tavernes de la Valldigna Spain 43 F3
Taveuni i. Fiji 107 H3
Taygetos mts Greece 47 C6
Taviano Italy 45 G5
Tavignano r. Corsica France 44 B3
Tavil'dara Tajik. 81 G2
Tavira Port. 42 C4
Tavistock Canada 130 C2
Tavistock U.K. 35 D6
Tavoy Myanmar 61 B5
Tavoy b. Myanmar 61 B5
Tavoy Island Myanmar see Mali Kyun
Tavoy Point Myanmar 61 B5
Tavşanlı Turkey 78 B3
Taw r. U.K. 35 D6
Tawakoni, Lake U.S.A. 133 C5
Tawallah Range hills Australia 110 C2
Tawang India 75 F4
Tawas Bay U.S.A. 130 B1
Tawas City U.S.A. 130 B1
Tawau Sabah Malaysia 59 G1
Tawau, Telukan b. Sabah Malaysia 59 G1
Tawè Myanmar see Tavoy
Taweisha Sudan 89 E6
Tawi r. India 74 B2
Ṭawī Ḥafīr well U.A.E. 80 C5
Tawila Sudan 88 E6
Ṭawī Murra well U.A.E. 80 C5
Tawitawi i. Phil. 57 F4
Tawmaw Myanmar 60 B2
Tawu Taiwan 67 G4
Taxkorgan China 70 E4
Tay r. Canada 122 C2
Tay r. U.K. 34 E3
Tay, Firth of est. U.K. 34 E3
Tay, Lake salt flat Australia 109 C8
Tay, Loch l. U.K. 34 D3
Tayan Indon. 59 E2
Tayeeglow Somalia 96 E3
Tayga Rus. Fed. 27 I4
Taylor Canada 122 F3
Taylor NE U.S.A. 132 B3
Taylor TX U.S.A. 133 B6
Taylor, Mount U.S.A. 135 F5
Taylorsville U.S.A. 128 B4
Taylorville U.S.A. 128 A4
Taymā' Saudi Arabia 89 H3
Taymura r. Rus. Fed. 27 J3
Taymyr, Ozero l. Rus. Fed. 27 K2
Taymyr, Poluostrov pen. Rus. Fed. see Taymyr Peninsula
Taymyr Peninsula Rus. Fed. 27 I2
Tây Ninh Vietnam 61 D6
Taypak Kazakh. 29 I6
Taypaq Kazakh. see Taypak
Tayshet Rus. Fed. 27 J4
Taysoygan, Peski des. Kazakh. 29 J6
Tayspun tourist site Iraq see Ctesiphon
Taytay Phil. 56 E3
Tayu Indon. 59 E4
Tayuan China 64 A2
Tayyebād Iran 81 E3
Tayynsha Kazakh. 26 G4
Taz r. Rus. Fed. 26 H3
Taza Morocco 90 E2
Tāza Khurmātū Iraq 79 F4
Taze Myanmar 60 A3
Tazeh Kand Azer. 80 A2
Tazenakht Morocco 90 D3
Tazewell TN U.S.A. 130 B5
Tazewell VA U.S.A. 130 C5
Tazin r. Canada 123 I2
Tāzirbū Libya 88 D3
Tazirbu Water Wells Field Libya 88 D3
Tazizilet well Niger 93 H1
Tazlău Romania 46 E1
Tazlău r. Romania 46 E1
Tazmalt Alg. 43 I4
Tazoghrane Tunisia 45 C6
Tazouikert hill Mali 91 E5
Tazovskaya Guba sea chan. Rus. Fed. 26 H3
Tazovskiy Rus. Fed. 26 H3
Tazrouk Alg. 91 G5
Tazzarine Morocco 90 D3
Tazzouguert Morocco 90 E2
Tbessa Alg. see Tébessa
Tbilisi Georgia see T'bilisi

▶T'bilisi Georgia 79 F2
Capital of Georgia.

Tchabal Mbabo mt. Cameroon 93 I4
Tchad country Africa see Chad
Tchamba Togo 93 F3
Tchaourou Benin 93 F3
Tchetti Benin 93 F4
Tchibanga Gabon 94 A5
Tchidoutene watercourse Niger 93 G1
Tchié well Chad 88 C5
Tchigaï, Plateau du Niger 91 I5
Tchin-Tabaradene Niger 93 G2
Tcholliré Cameroon 93 I3
Tczew Poland 37 I1
Te, Prêk r. Cambodia 61 D5
Tea r. Brazil 146 E5
Te Anau N.Z. 113 A4
Te Anau, Lake N.Z. 113 A4
Teano Italy 44 E4
Teanum Sidicinum Italy see Teano
Teapa Mex. 138 F5
Te Araroa N.Z. 113 D2
Te Aroha N.Z. 113 C2
Teate Italy see Chieti
Te Awamutu N.Z. 113 C2
Tébarat Niger 93 G2
Tebedu Sarawak Malaysia 59 E2
Teberda Rus. Fed. 29 G8
Tebesjuak Lake Canada 123 L2
Tébessa Alg. 91 H2
Tébessa, Monts de mts Alg. 91 H2
Tebicuary Para. 149 F6
Tebicuary r. Para. 149 F6
Tebingtinggi Sumatera Utara, Sumatra Indon. 58 B2
Tebingtinggi Sumatera Selatan, Sumatra Indon. 58 C3
Tebo r. Indon. 58 C3
Tébourba Tunisia 45 B6
Téboursouk Tunisia 45 B6
Tebulos Mt'a Georgia/Rus. Fed. 29 H8
Tecate Mex. 137 D5
Tece Turkey 77 B1
Tech r. France 39 E5
Techiman Ghana 93 E4
Tecka Arg. 153 C5
Tecka r. Arg. 153 C5
Tecoripa Mex. 135 E7
Técpan Mex. 138 D5
Tecuci Romania 46 E2
Tecumseh U.S.A. 132 B3
Ted Somalia 96 D3
Tedzhen Turkm. 81 E2
Tedzhen r. Turkm. 81 E2
Tedzhenstroy Turkm. 81 E2
Teec Nos Pos U.S.A. 137 H3
Teeli Rus. Fed. 27 J4
Tees r. U.K. 35 F4
Teeswater Canada 130 C1
Tefé Brazil 147 E5
Tefé r. Brazil 147 E5
Tefé, Lago l. Brazil 147 E5
Tefedest mts Alg. 91 G4
Téfoûlet well Mali 93 F1
Tegal Indon. 59 E4
Tegel airport Germany 37 F2
Tegina Nigeria 93 G3

▶Tegucigalpa Hond. 138 G6
Capital of Honduras.

Teguidda-n-Tessoumt Niger 93 G1
Tehachapi U.S.A. 136 C4
Tehachapi Mountains U.S.A. 136 C4
Tehachapi Pass U.S.A. 136 C4
Tehek Lake Canada 123 M1
Teheran Iran see Tehrān
Tehery Lake Canada 123 M1
Téhini Côte d'Ivoire 92 E3
Tehran Iran see Tehrān

▶Tehrān Iran 80 B3
Capital of Iran.

Tehrān prov. Iran 80 B3
Tehri Madhya Pradesh India see Tikamgarh
Tehri Uttaranchal India 74 C3
Tehuacán Mex. 138 E5
Tehuantepec, Gulf of Mex. 138 F5
Tehuantepec, Istmo de isthmus Mex. 138 F5
Teide, Pico del vol. Canary Is 90 A3
Teifi r. U.K. 35 D5
Teïskot well Mali 93 F1
Teiu Romania 46 D2
Teiuş Romania 46 C1
Teixeira Brazil 150 E3
Teixeira de Sousa Angola see Luau
Tejakula Indon. 108 A2
Tejen Turkm. see Tedzhen
Tejgaon Bangl. 75 F5
Tejira well Niger 93 H2
Tejo r. Port. 42 B2 see Tagus
Tekapo, Lake N.Z. 113 B3
Tekari India 75 E4
Tekezē Wenz r. Eritrea/Eth. 89 H6
Tekiliktag mt. China 74 D1
Tekin Rus. Fed. 64 C2
Tekirdağ Turkey 78 A2
Tekirdağ prov. Turkey 46 E4
Tekkali India 73 E2
Tekman Turkey 79 E3
Teknaf Bangl. 75 G5
Tekong Kechil, Pulau i. Sing. 58 [inset]
Tekouiat, Oued watercourse Alg. 91 F5
Tékro well Chad 88 D5
Te Kuiti N.Z. 113 C2
Tel r. India 73 D1
Tela Dem. Rep. Congo 95 F8
Telanaipura Indon. see Jambi
Télataï Mali 93 F1
T'elavi Georgia 79 F2
Tel Aviv-Yafo Israel 77 B3
Telč Czech Rep. 37 G4
Telchac Puerto Mex. 127 I7
Tele r. Dem. Rep. Congo 94 D4
Télé, Lac l. Mali 92 E1
Teleajen r. Romania 46 D2
Telegapulang Indon. 59 F3
Telegraph Creek Canada 122 D3
Telêmaco Borba Brazil 151 B8
Telemark county Norway 33 C4
Telén Arg. 152 D4
Telen r. Indon. 59 G2
Teleorman r. Romania 46 D3
Telertheba, Djebel mt. Alg. 91 G4
Telescope Peak U.S.A. 136 D3
Teles Pires r. Brazil 149 F1
Telfer Mining Centre Australia 108 C5
Telford U.K. 35 E5
Telfs Austria 36 E5
Telīg well Mali 90 E5
Télimélé Guinea 92 B3
Télissour well Chad 88 D5
Teljo, Jebel mt. Sudan 89 E6
Tell Atlas mts Alg. see Atlas Tellien
Teller U.S.A. 120 C3
Tell es-Sultan West Bank see Jericho
Tellicherry India 72 B4
Telluride U.S.A. 135 F5
Tel Megiddo tourist site Israel 77 B3
Telo Indon. 58 B3
Telo Martius France see Toulon
Tel'pos-Iz, Gora mt. Rus. Fed. 28 K3
Telsen Arg. 153 D5
Telšiai Lith. 33 F5
Teluk Anson Malaysia 58 C1
Telukbajur Indon. see Telukbayur
Telukbatang Indon. 59 E3
Telukbayur Indon. 58 C3
Telukbetung Indon. see Bandar Lampung
Telukdalam Indon. 58 B2
Teluk Intan Malaysia see Teluk Anson
Telukkuantan Indon. 58 C3
Teluknaga Indon. 59 D4
Telukpakedai Indon. 59 E3
Tema Ghana 93 F4
Temagami Lake Canada 124 E4
Temaju i. Indon. 59 E2
Temanggung Indon. 59 E4
Temba S. Africa 99 F5
Tembagapura Indon. 57 I6
Tembenchi r. Rus. Fed. 27 J3
Tembesi r. Indon. 58 C3
Tembilahan Indon. 58 C3
Tembisa S. Africa 99 F5
Tembo Aluma Angola 95 C6
Tembwe Zambia 97 B7
Teme r. U.K. 35 E5
Temecula U.S.A. 136 D5
Temengor, Tasik resr Malaysia 58 C1
Teméra Mali 93 E1
Temerin Yugo. 46 A2
Temerluh Malaysia 58 C2
Teminabuan Indon. 57 H6
Temirtau Kazakh. 70 D1
Témiscamie r. Canada 125 F3
Témiscaming Canada 124 E4
Témiscouata, Lac l. Canada 125 G4
Temiyang i. Indon. 58 D2
Temmes Fin. 32 G2
Temnikov Rus. Fed. 29 G5
Temo r. Sardinia Italy 45 B4
Temora Australia 112 C4
Temósachic Mex. 135 F7
Tempe U.S.A. 137 G5
Tempe Downs Australia 110 C5
Tempelhof airport Germany 37 F2
Tempio Pausania Sardinia Italy 44 B4
Temple U.S.A. 133 B6
Temple Bay Australia 111 E2
Templemore Rep. of Ireland 35 C5
Templeton watercourse Australia 110 D4
Templin Germany 37 F2
Tempué Angola 95 C8
Temryuk Rus. Fed. 29 F7
Temryukskiy Zaliv b. Rus. Fed. 29 F7
Temuco Chile 152 B4
Temuka N.Z. 113 B4
Tena Ecuador 146 B5
Tenabo Mex. 127 H7
Tenabo, Mount U.S.A. 137 D1
Tenali India 72 D2
Tenasserim Myanmar 61 B5
Tenasserim admin. div. Myanmar 61 B5
Tenasserim r. Myanmar 61 B5
Tenby U.K. 35 D6
Tence France 39 F4
Tendaho Eth. 96 D2
Tende France 39 G4
Tende, Col de pass France/Italy 44 A2
Ten Degree Channel India 73 G4
Tendelti Sudan 89 F6
Te-n-Dghâmcha, Sebkhet salt marsh Mauritania 92 B1
Tendō Japan 65 E5
Tendrara Morocco 90 E2
Tendre, Mont mt. Switz. 39 G3
Tendukheda India 74 C5
Téné r. Guinea 92 C3
Tenedos i. Turkey see Bozcaada
Ténenkou Mali 92 D2
Ténéré du Tafassâsset des. Niger 88 A4
Tenerife i. Canary Is 90 A3
Ténès Alg. 91 F1
Ténès, Cap c. Alg. 43 G4
Tenevo Bulg. 46 E3
Teng, Nam r. Myanmar 60 B4
Tengah, Kepulauan is Indon. 59 G4
Tengah, Sungai r. Sing. 58 [inset]
Tengcheng China see Tengxian
Tengchong China 66 A3
Tenge Kazakh. 79 H2
Tengeh Reservoir Sing. 58 [inset]
Tenggarong Indon. 59 G3
Tengger Shamo des. China 62 G4
Tengiz, Ozero salt l. Kazakh. 70 C1
Tengréla Côte d'Ivoire 92 D3
Ten'gushevo Rus. Fed. 29 G5
Tengxian China 67 D4
Teniente Enciso, Parque Nacional nat. park Para. 149 E5
Te-n-Ioubrar, Sebkhet salt marsh Mauritania 92 A1
Tenkasi India 72 C4
Tenke Dem. Rep. Congo 95 E7
Tenkeli Rus. Fed. 27 O2
Tenkodogo Burkina 93 E3
Ten Mile Lake salt flat Australia 109 C6
Tenna r. Italy 44 D3
Tennant Creek Australia 110 C3
Tennessee r. U.S.A. 128 A4
Tennessee state U.S.A. 130 A5
Tennessee Pass U.S.A. 134 F5
Tennholmfjorden sea chan. Norway 32 D2
Tenniöjoki r. Fin./Rus. Fed. 32 H2
Teno Chile 152 C3
Tenojoki r. Fin./Norway 32 H1
Tenom Sabah Malaysia 59 F1
Tenosique Mex. 138 F5
Tenteno Indon. 57 F6
Tenterfield Australia 112 E3
Ten Thousand Islands U.S.A. 129 C7
Tentudia mt. Spain 42 C3
Tenu r. France 38 C3
Teodoro Sampaio Brazil 149 G5
Teófilo Otôni Brazil 151 D6
Teonthar India 75 D4
Teopisca Mex. 138 F5
Tepa Indon. 57 G7
Tepache Mex. 135 E7
Te Paki N.Z. 113 C1
Tepasto Fin. 32 G2
Tepehuanes Mex. 126 E6
Tepeköy Turkey see Karakoçan
Tepelenë Albania 47 B4
Tepelská Vrchovina hills Czech Rep. 37 F4
Tepequem, Serra mts Brazil 147 F4
Tepic Mex. 126 F7
Teplá r. Czech Rep. 37 F3
Teplaya Gora Rus. Fed. 28 K4
Teplice Czech Rep. 37 F3
Teploye Rus. Fed. 29 F5
Tepopa, Punta pt Mex. 135 D7
Tequila Mex. 126 F7
Ter r. Spain 43 H1
Téra Niger 93 F2
Tera r. Port. 42 B3
Tera r. Spain 42 D2
Terakeka Sudan 96 A3
Teram Kangri mt. China/Jammu and Kashmir 74 C2
Teramo Italy 44 D3
Terang Australia 112 B5
Teratani r. Pak. 81 G4
Tercan Turkey 79 E3
Terebovlya Ukr. 29 C6
Teregova Romania 46 C2
Terek Rus. Fed. 79 F2
Terek r. Rus. Fed. 29 H8
Teren'ga Rus. Fed. 29 I5
Terengganu state Malaysia 58 C1
Terenos Brazil 151 A7
Terentang Indon. 59 E3
Terentang, Pulau i. Indon. 59 G3
Tereshka r. Rus. Fed. 29 H6
Teresina Brazil 150 D3
Teresina de Goias Brazil 150 C5
Teresita Col. 146 D4
Teressa Island India 73 G4
Terges r. Port. 42 C4
Tergeste Italy see Trieste
Tergnier France 39 E2
Teriberka r. Rus. Fed. 32 I1
Terka Reba Eth. 96 D3
Terkezi well Chad 88 D5
Terlingua Creek r. U.S.A. 133 A6
Termas de Socos Chile 152 C2
Terme Turkey 78 D2
Termez Uzbek. 81 F2
Termination Island Australia 109 C8
Termini Imerese Sicily Italy 45 D6
Termini Imerese, Golfo di b. Sicily Italy 45 D5
Términos, Laguna de lag. Mex. 138 F5
Termit well Niger 88 A5
Termit, Massif de hill Niger 93 H1
Termit-Kaoboul Niger 93 H2
Termiz Uzbek. see Termez
Termoli Italy 44 E4
Termonde Belgium see Dendermonde
Tern r. U.K. 35 E5
Ternate Indon. 57 G5
Terneuzen Neth. 36 A3
Terney Rus. Fed. 64 D3
Terni Italy 44 D3
Ternitz Austria 37 H5
Ternopil' Ukr. 29 C6
Ternopol' Ukr. see Ternopil'
Terpeniya, Mys c. Rus. Fed. 64 F2
Terpeniya, Zaliv g. Rus. Fed. 64 E2
Terra Alta U.S.A. 130 D4
Terra Bella U.S.A. 136 C4
Terrace Canada 122 D4
Terracina Italy 44 D4
Terralba Sardinia Italy 45 B5
Terra Nova Bay Antarctica 167 H1
Terra Nova National Park Canada 125 K3
Terranuova Bracciolini Italy 44 C3
Terra Preta Brazil 147 G6
Terrasini Sicily Italy 45 D5
Terrassa Spain 43 H2
Terrasson-la-Villedieu France 38 D4
Terrazas Mex. 135 F7
Terrebonne Bay U.S.A. 133 D6
Terre Haute U.S.A. 128 B4
Terrell U.S.A. 133 B5
Terre Plaine plain France 39 F3
Terril mt. Spain 42 D4
Terry U.S.A. 134 F3
Terschelling i. Neth. 36 B2
Terskey Alatau, Khrebet mts Kyrg. see Terskey Ala-Too
Terskey Ala-Too mts Kyrg. 70 E3
Terskiy Bereg coastal area Rus. Fed. 28 F2
Tersko-Kumskiy Kanal canal Rus. Fed. 79 F1
Tertenia Sardinia Italy 45 B5
Teruel Spain 43 F2
Terutao i. Thai. 61 B7
Terutao National Park Thai. 61 B7
Tervel Bulg. 46 E3
Tervola Fin. 32 G2
Tešanj Bos.-Herz. 44 F2
Teseney Eritrea 89 H6
Tesha r. Rus. Fed. 28 G5
Teshekpuk Lake U.S.A. 120 D2
Teshio-dake mt. Japan 64 E4
Teshio-gawa r. Japan 64 E3
Tešica Yugo. 46 B3
Teslin Canada 122 C2
Teslin r. Canada 122 C2
Teslin Lake Canada 122 C2
Teslui r. Romania 46 D2
Teso Santo hill Spain 42 D2
Tesovo-Netyl'skiy Rus. Fed. 28 D4
Tessalit Mali 91 F5
Tessaoua Niger 93 G2
Tesséroukane well Niger 93 G1
Tessolo Moz. 99 G4
Tessoûnfat well Mali 91 F5
Test r. U.K. 35 F6
Testour Tunisia 45 B6
Têt r. France 39 E5
Tete Moz. 99 G3
Tete prov. Moz. 99 G2
Tetehosi Indon. 58 B2
Tête Jaune Cache Canada 122 G4
Te Teko N.Z. 113 D2
Teteriv r. Ukr. 29 D6
Teterow Germany 37 F2
Teteven Bulg. 46 D3
Tetlin U.S.A. 122 A2
Tetlin Junction U.S.A. 122 A2
Tetlin Lake U.S.A. 122 A2
Teton r. U.S.A. 134 E3
Tétouan Morocco 90 D2
Tetovo Macedonia 46 B3
Tetuán Morocco see Tétouan
Tetulia sea chan. Bangl. 75 F5
Tetyukhe Rus. Fed. see Dal'negorsk
Tetyukhe-Pristan' Rus. Fed. see Rudnaya Pristan'
Tetyushi Rus. Fed. 28 I5
Teuchezhsk Rus. Fed. see Adygeysk
Teuco r. Arg. 149 E6
Teulada Sardinia Italy 45 B5
Teulada, Capo c. Sardinia Italy 45 B5
Teunom Indon. 58 A1
Teunom r. Indon. 58 A1
Teutoburger Wald hills Germany 36 D2
Teuva Fin. 33 F3
Tevere r. Italy see Tiber
Teverya Israel see Tiberias
Teviot r. U.K. 34 E4
Teviothead U.K. 34 E4
Te Waewae Bay N.Z. 113 A4
Te Waipounamu i. N.Z. see South Island
Tewane Botswana 99 E4
Tewantin Australia 111 H5
Teweh r. Indon. 59 F3
Te Wharau N.Z. 113 C3
Têwo China 66 B1
Texarkana AR U.S.A. 133 C5
Texarkana TX U.S.A. 133 C5
Texas Australia 111 G6
Texas state U.S.A. 135 H7
Texel i. Neth. 36 B2
Texoma, Lake U.S.A. 133 B5
Teyateyaneng Lesotho 99 E6
Teykovo Rus. Fed. 28 G4
Teyvareh Afgh. 81 F3
Teza r. Rus. Fed. 28 G4
Tezpur India 75 G4
Tezu India 60 B2
Tfaritiy W. Sahara 90 C4
Tha, Nam r. Laos 60 C3
Tha-anne r. Canada 123 M2
Thabana-Ntlenyana mt. Lesotho 99 F6
Thaba Putsoa mt. Lesotho 99 E6
Thaba-Tseka Lesotho 99 F6
Thabazimbi S. Africa 99 E5
Thabeikkyin Myanmar 60 B3
Thab Lan National Park Thai. 61 C5
Tha Bo Laos 60 C4
Thabong S. Africa 99 E5
Thabyedaung Myanmar 60 B3
Thac Ba, Hô l. Vietnam 60 D3
Thade r. Myanmar 60 A4
Thagyettaw Myanmar 61 B5
Tha Hin Thai. see Lop Buri
Thai Binh Vietnam 60 D3
▶Thailand country Asia 61 C4
asia 52–53, 82
Thailand, Gulf of Asia 61 C6
Thai Muang Thai. 61 B6
Thai Nguyên Vietnam 60 D3
Thaj Saudi Arabia 80 B5
Thakurgaon Bangl. 75 F4
Thakurtola India 74 D5
Thal Pak. 81 G3
Thala Tunisia 91 H2
Thalang Thai. 61 B6
Thalassery India see Tellicherry
Thal Desert Pak. 81 G4
Thale (Harz) Germany 36 E3
Thale Luang lag. Thai. 61 C7
Thalgau Austria 37 F5
Tha Li Thai. 60 C4
Thaliparamba India see Taliparamba
Thallon Australia 111 G6
Thamad Bū Hashishah well Libya 88 C3
Thamaga Botswana 98 E5
Thamar, Jabal mt. Yemen 76 D7
Thamarīt Oman 76 E6
Thames r. Canada 130 B2
Thames N.Z. 113 C2
Thames est. U.K. 35 G6
Thames r. U.K. 35 G6
Thamesford Canada 130 C2
Thamesville Canada 130 C2
Thamūd Yemen 76 D6
Thamugadi tourist site Alg. see Timgad
Thana India see Thane
Thana Ghazi India 74 C4
Thanatpin Myanmar 60 B4
Thanbyuzayat Myanmar 61 B5
Thandla India 74 B5
Thandwè Myanmar see Sandoway
Thane India 72 B2
Thangadh India 74 A5
Thangoo Australia 108 C4
Thanh Hoa Vietnam 60 D4
Thanjavur India 72 C4
Than Kyun i. Myanmar 61 B6
Thanlwin r. Myanmar see Salween
Thano Bula Khan Pak. 81 F5
Thaoge r. Botswana 98 D3
Thaolintoa Lake Canada 123 L2
Thap Put Thai. 61 B6
Thap Sakae Thai. 61 B6
Thara India 74 A5
Tharad India 74 A4
Tharaka Kenya 96 C5
Thar Desert India/Pak. 74 A4
Thargomindah Australia 111 E5
Tharrawaddy Myanmar 60 A4
Tharrawaw Myanmar 60 A4
Tharthār, Buḥayrat ath l. Iraq 79 E4
Thasos Greece 46 D4
Thasos i. Greece 46 D4
Thatë, Mali i mt. Albania 46 B4
Thât Khê Vietnam 60 D3
Thaton Myanmar 60 B4
Thau, Bassin de lag. France 39 E5
Thaungdut Myanmar 60 A2
Thaungyin r. Myanmar/Thai. 60 B4
Tha Uthen Thai. 60 D4
Thawr, Jabal mt. Jordan 77 B5
Thayawthadangyi Kyun i. Myanmar 61 B5
Thayetmyo Myanmar 60 A4
Thazi Myanmar 60 B3
The Aldermen Islands N.Z. 113 D2
Theba U.S.A. 137 F5
Thebae tourist site Egypt see Thebes
▶The Bahamas country West Indies 129 E7
northamerica 118–119, 140
Thebes tourist site Egypt 89 G3
Thebes Greece see Thiva
The Broads nat. park U.K. 35 G5
The Brothers is Hong Kong China 67 [inset]
The Brothers is Yemen see Al Ikhwān
The Calvados Chain is P.N.G. 111 H1
The Cheviot hill U.K. 34 E4
The Coorong inlet Australia 112 A4
The Dalles U.S.A. 134 B3
Thedford U.S.A. 132 A3
The English Company's Islands Australia 110 D1
The Entrance Australia 112 D4
The Fens reg. U.K. 35 F5
▶The Gambia country Africa 92 A2
africa 86–87, 100
The Grenadines is St Vincent 147 F1
The Gulf Asia 80 B4

▶The Hague Neth. 36 B2
Seat of government of the Netherlands.
world 8–9

The Hunters Hills N.Z. 113 B4
Theinkun Myanmar 61 B6
Theinzeik Myanmar 60 B4
The Key N.Z. 113 A4
Thekulthili Lake Canada 123 I2
The Lakes National Park Australia 112 C5
Thelon r. Canada 123 L1
The Lynd Junction Australia 111 F3
Themar Germany 36 E3
Thembalihle S. Africa 99 F5
The Minch sea chan. U.K. 34 C2
The Mullet b. Rep. of Ireland 35 A4
Theni India 74 C5
Thenia Alg. 43 H4
Theniet El Had Alg. 43 H5
Thenon France 38 D4
Theodore Australia 111 G5
Theodore Canada 123 K5
Theodore Roosevelt r. Brazil 149 E1
Theodore Roosevelt Lake U.S.A. 137 G5
Theodore Roosevelt National Park U.S.A. 132 A2
Theodosia Ukr. see Feodosiya
The Officer Creek watercourse Australia 110 C5
The Paps hill Rep. of Ireland 35 B5
The Pas Canada 123 K4
Thera i. Greece see Thira
Thérain r. France 38 E2
Theresa U.S.A. 131 F1
Theresa Creek r. Australia 111 G4
Thermaïkos Kolpos g. Greece 47 C4
Thermo Greece 47 B5
Thérmon Greece see Thermo
Thermopolis U.S.A. 134 E4
The Salt Lake salt flat Australia 112 B3

▶The Settlement Christmas I. 164 B6
Capital of Christmas Island.

The Skaw spit Denmark see Grenen
The Slot sea chan. Solomon Is see New Georgia Sound
The Solent strait U.K. 35 F6
Thessalia admin. reg. Greece 47 B5
Thessalon Canada 124 D4
Thessalonica Greece see Thessaloniki
Thessaloniki Greece 46 C4
Thessaly admin. reg. Greece see Thessalia
The Terraces hills Australia 109 C7
Thetford U.K. 35 G5
Thetford Mines Canada 125 G4
Thetkethaung r. Myanmar 61 A5
The Triangle mts Myanmar 60 B2
The Twins Australia 110 C6
Theun r. Laos 60 D4
Theva-i-Ra reef Fiji see Ceva-i-Ra

▶The Valley Anguilla 139 L5
Capital of Anguilla.

Thevenard Island Australia 108 A5
Theveste Alg. see Tébessa
The Wash b. U.K. 35 G5
The Woodlands U.S.A. 133 C6
Thíamis r. Greece see Thyamis
Thibodaux U.S.A. 133 D6
Thief River Falls U.S.A. 132 B1
Thiel Neth. see Tiel
Thiel Mountains Antarctica 167 K1
Thielsen, Mount U.S.A. 134 B4
Thielt Belgium see Tielt
Thiers France 39 E4
Thiès Senegal 92 A2
Thika Kenya 96 C5
Thikombia i. Fiji see Cikobia
Thiladhunmathee Atoll Maldives 72 B5
Thilogne Senegal 92 B2
Thimbu Bhutan see Thimphu

▶Thimphu Bhutan 75 F4
Capital of Bhutan.

Thingvallavatn (Þingvallavatn) l. Iceland 32 [inset]
Thingvellir (Þingvellir) Iceland 32 [inset]
Thionville France 39 G2
Thira Greece 47 D6
Thira i. Greece 47 D6
Thirasia i. Greece 47 D6
Thirsk U.K. 35 F4
Thirty Mile Lake Canada 123 L2
Thiruvananthapuram India see Trivandrum
Thiruvarur India 72 C4
Thiruvattiyur India see Tiruvottiyur
Thissavros, Techniti Limni resr Greece 46 D4
Thisted Denmark 33 C4
Thistilfjörður (Þistilfjörður) b. Iceland 32 [inset]
Thistle Creek Canada 122 B2
Thityabin Myanmar 60 A3
Thiva Greece 47 C5
Thívai Greece see Thiva
Thiviers France 38 D4
Thjórsá (Þjórsá) r. Iceland 32 [inset]
Thlewiaza r. Canada 123 M2
Thoa r. Canada 123 I2
Thô Chu, Đao i. Vietnam 61 C6
Thoen Thai. 60 B4
Thoeng Thai. 60 C4
Thohoyandou S. Africa 99 F4
Tholen i. Neth. 36 B3
Thomas Hubbard, Cape Canada 121 J1
Thomaston CT U.S.A. 131 G3
Thomaston GA U.S.A. 129 B5
Thomaston ME U.S.A. 131 I1
Thomastown Rep. of Ireland 35 C5
Thomasville AL U.S.A. 129 B6
Thomasville GA U.S.A. 129 C6
Thomasville NC U.S.A. 128 C5
Thompson Canada 123 L4
Thompson r. Canada 122 F5
Thompson U.S.A. 137 H2
Thompson r. U.S.A. 132 C4
Thompson Falls U.S.A. 134 D3
Thompson Peak U.S.A. 135 F6
Thompson's Falls Kenya see Nyahururu
Thompson Sound Canada 122 E5
Thomson watercourse Australia 111 E5
Thomson U.S.A. 129 C5
Thon Buri Thai. 61 C5
Thongwa Myanmar 60 B4
Thonon-les-Bains France 39 G3
Thoreau U.S.A. 135 E6
Thorhild Canada 123 H4
Thórisvatn (Þórisvatn) l. Iceland 32 [inset]
Thorn Poland see Toruń
Thorne U.K. 35 F5
Thorne U.S.A. 136 C2
Thornhill U.K. 34 E4
Thornton r. Australia 110 D3
Thorsby Canada 123 H4
Thorshavn Faroe Is see Tórshavn
Thorshavnheiane reg. Antarctica 167 C2
Thórshöfn (Þórshöfn) Iceland 32 [inset]
Thorvaldsfell (Þorvaldsfell) vol. Iceland 32 [inset]
Thouars France 38 C3
Thouet r. France 38 C3
Thourout Belgium see Torhout
Thousand Islands Canada/U.S.A. 131 E1
Thousand Lake Mountain U.S.A. 137 G2
Thousand Oaks U.S.A. 136 C4
Thousandsticks U.S.A. 130 B5
Thrace reg. Turkey 78 A2
Thraki reg. Turkey see Thrace
Thrakiko Pelagos sea Greece 47 D4
Three Forks U.S.A. 134 E3
Three Gorges Project resr China 67 D2
Three Hummock Island Australia 112 C6
Three Kings Islands N.Z. 113 C1
Three Pagodas Pass Myanmar/Thai. 61 B5
Three Points, Cape Ghana 93 E4
Three Rivers CA U.S.A. 136 C3
Three Rivers TX U.S.A. 133 B6
Three Sisters mt. U.S.A. 134 B3
Three Springs Australia 109 A7
Thrissur India see Trichur
Throckmorton U.S.A. 133 B5
Throssell, Lake salt flat Australia 109 D6
Throssel Range hills Australia 108 C5
Thrushton National Park Australia 111 F5
Thubun Lakes Canada 123 I2
Thu Dâu Môt Vietnam 61 D6
Thuin Belgium 39 F1
Thul Sudan 96 B2
Thul watercourse Sudan 96 A2
Thule Greenland 121 M2
Thuli Zimbabwe 99 F4
Thuli r. Zimbabwe 99 F4
Thun Switz. 39 G3
Thunda Australia 111 E5
Thundelarra Australia 109 B7
Thunder Bay Canada 124 B3
Thunder Creek r. Canada 123 J5
Thuner See l. Switz. 39 G3
Thung Salaeng Luang National Park Thai. 60 C4
Thung Song Thai. 61 B6
Thung Wa Thai. 61 B7
Thur r. Switz. 39 H3
Thüringen land Germany 36 E3
Thüringer Becken reg. Germany 36 E3
Thüringer Wald mts Germany 36 E3
Thuringia land Germany see Thüringen
Thuringian Forest mts Germany see Thüringer Wald
Thurles Rep. of Ireland 35 C5
Thursby U.K. 34 E4
Thursday Island Australia 111 E1
Thurso U.K. 34 E2
Thurso r. U.K. 34 E2
Thurston Island Antarctica 167 K2
Thusis Switz. 39 H3
Thwaites Glacier Tongue Antarctica 167 K1
Thyamis r. Greece 47 B5
Thyatira Turkey see Akhisar
Thyborøn Denmark 33 C4
Thylungra Australia 111 E5
Thyolo Malawi 97 B9
Thyou Burkina 93 E3
Thyou Burkina see Tiou
Thysville Dem. Rep. Congo see Mbanza-Ngungu
Tīāb Iran 80 D5
Tiahuanaco Bol. 148 C4
Tiancang China 70 I3
Tianchang China 67 F1
Tiancheng China see Chongyang
Tianchi China see Lezhi
Tiandeng China 66 C4
Tiandiba China see Jinyang
Tiandong China 66 C4
Tian'e China 66 C3
Tianfanjie China 67 F2

Tiângol Lougguéré *watercourse* Senegal **92** B2
Tianguá Brazil **150** D2
Tianjin China **63** J4
Tianjin *municipality* China **63** J4
Tianjun China **70** I4
Tiankoye Senegal **92** B2
Tianlin China **66** C3
Tianmen China **67** E2
Tianmu Shan *mts* China **67** F2
Tianqiaoling China **64** B4
Tianshan China **66** C3
Tian Shan *mts* China/Kyrg. *see* Tien Shan
Tianshifu China **64** A4
Tianshui China **66** C1
Tianshuihai Aksai Chin **74** C2
Tiantai China **67** G2
Tiantang China *see* Yuexi
Tianyang China **66** C4
Tianzhou China *see* Tianyang
Tianzhu China **62** G4
Tiaret Alg. **91** F1
Tiassalé Côte d'Ivoire **92** D4
Tibabar *Sabah* Malaysia *see* Tamburan
Tibagi Brazil **149** H5
Tibagi *r.* Brazil *see* Tibagi
Tibal, Wādī *watercourse* Iraq **79** E4
Tibati Cameroon **93** I4
Tibba Pak. **81** G4
Tibé, Pic de *mt.* Guinea **92** C3
Tiber *r.* Italy **44** D4
Tiberghamine Alg. **91** F3
Tiberias Israel **77** B3
Tiberias, Lake Israel *see* Galilee, Sea of
Tiber Reservoir U.S.A. **134** E2
Tibesti *mts* Chad **88** C2
Tibet *aut. reg.* China *see* Xizang Zizhiqu
Tibet, Plateau of China **70** F5
Tibet Autonomous Region *aut. reg.* China *see* Xizang Zizhiqu
Tibiri Niger **93** G2
Tiboku Falls Guyana **147** G3
Tibooburra Australia **112** B3
Tibrikot Nepal **75** D3
Tibur Italy *see* Tivoli
Tiburón, Isla *i.* Mex. **135** D7
Ticha *r.* Bulg. **46** E3
Tichak *mt.* Bulg. **46** C3
Tichau Poland *see* Tychy
Tichborne Canada **131** E1
Tichégami *r.* Canada **125** F3
Tichet *well* Mali **93** I1
Tichît Mauritania **92** C1
Tichla W. Sahara **90** B5
Ticino *r.* Italy/Switz. **44** B2
Ticinum Italy *see* Pavia
Ticleni Romania **46** C2
Ticonderoga U.S.A. **131** G2
Ticumbia *i.* Fiji *see* Cikobia
Tiddim Myanmar **60** A3
Tideridjaouine, Adrar *mts* Alg. **91** F5
Tidikelt, Plaine du *plain* Alg. **91** F4
Tidioute U.S.A. **130** D3
Tidjerouene *well* Mali **93** F1
Tidjikja Mauritania **92** C1
Tiéboro Chad **88** C1
Tiel Neth. **36** B3
Tiel Senegal **92** B2
Tieli China **64** A3
Tieling China **63** K3
Tielongtan Aksai Chin **74** C2
Tielt Belgium **39** E1
Tiémé Côte d'Ivoire **92** D3
Tiene Liberia **92** C4
Tienen Belgium **39** =1
Tien Shan *mts* China/Kyrg. **70** E3
Tientsin China *see* Tianjin
Tientsin *municipality* China *see* Tianjin
Tiên Yên Vietnam **60** D3
Tierp Sweden **33** F3
Tierra Amarilla U.S.A. **135** F5
Tierra Blanca Mex. **138** E5
Tierra Blanca Peru **146** C6
Tierra Colorada Mex. **138** E5
Tierra del Fuego *prov.* Arg. *see* **153** D8
▶Tierra del Fuego, Isla Grande de *i.* Arg./Chile **153** C8
Largest island in South America.
southamerica 142–143
Tierra del Fuego, Parque Nacional *nat. park* Arg. **153** D8
Tierra Llana de Huelva *plain* Spain **42** C4
Tiétar *r.* Spain **42** D3
Tiétar, Valle de *valley* Spain **42** D2
Tieyon Australia **110** C5
Tiffin U.S.A. **130** D3
Tiflis Georgia *see* T'bilisi
Tifton U.S.A. **129** D6
Tigănești Romania **46** D3
Tigapuluh, Pegunungan *mts* Indon. **58** C3
Tigh Āb Iran **81** E5
Tigheciului, Dealurile *hills* Moldova **46** F2
Tighina Moldova **29** D7
Tigiria India **73** E1
Tignère Cameroon **93** I4
Tignish Canada **125** H4
Tigranocerta Turkey *see* Siirt
Tigre *r.* Ecuador/Peru **146** C6
Tigray *admin. reg.* Eth. **96** C1
Tigre *r.* Ecuador/Peru **146** C6
Tigris *r.* Asia **79** F5
also known as Dicle (Turkey) or Dijlah, Nahr (Iraq/Syria)
Tiguent Mauritania **92** B1
Tiguesmat *hills* Mauritania **90** C4
Tiguidit, Falaise de *esc.* Niger **93** G1
Tiguir *well* Niger **93** H1
Tīh, Jabal at *plat.* Saudi Arabia **89** I5
Tihāmah *reg.* Saudi Arabia **89** I5
Tijamuchí *r.* Bol. **148** D3
Tijara India **74** C4
Tiji Libya **88** A1
Tijuana Mex. **135** C6
Tijucas Brazil **151** B8
Tijucas, Bahía de *b.* Brazil **151** B8
Tikamgarh India **74** C4
Tikherón Greece *see* Tychero
Tikhoretsk Rus. Fed. **29** G7
Tikhvin Rus. Fed. **29** F6
Tikhvinskaya Gryada *ridge* Rus. Fed. **28** E4
Tiki Basin *sea feature* S. Pacific Ocean **165** J7
Tikiktene *well* Niger **93** G1
Tikkakoski Fin. **33** O3
Tikokino N.Z. **113** D2
Tikrit Iraq **79** E4
Tiksheozero, Ozero *l.* Rus. Fed. **32** I3
Tiksi Rus. Fed. **27** M2
Tikumbia *i.* Fiji *see* Cikobia
Tikveš Ezero *l.* Macedonia **46** B4
Tila *r.* Nepal **75** D3
Tilaiya Reservoir India **75** E4
Tilavar Iran **80** C2
Tilbooroo Australia **111** F5
Tilburg Neth. **36** B3
Tilbury Canada **130** B2
Tilbury U.K. **35** G6
Tilcara Arg. **148** C3
Tilemsès Niger **93** G2
Tilemsi, Vallée du *watercourse* Mali **93** F1

Tilghman U.S.A. **131** E4
Tilhar India **74** C4
Tilia, Oued *watercourse* Alg. **91** F4
Tilimsen Alg. *see* Tlemcen
Tilin Myanmar **60** A3
Tillabéri Niger **93** F3
Tillabéri *dept* Niger **93** F2
Tillamook U.S.A. **134** B3
Tillanchong Island India **73** G4
Tille *r.* France **39** F3
Tilley Canada **123** I5
Tillsonburg Canada **130** C2
Tiloa Niger **93** F2
Tilogne Senegal *see* Thilogne
Tilomonte Chile **148** C5
Tilos *i.* Greece **47** E6
Tilton U.S.A. **131** H2
Tim Rus. Fed. **29** F6
Tīmā Egypt **89** B4
Timakara *i.* India **72** B4
Timane *r.* Para. **149** F2
Timanskiy Kryazh *ridge* Rus. Fed. **28** I2
Timar Turkey **79** E3
Timaru N.Z. **113** B4
Timashevsk Rus. Fed. **29** F7
Timashevskaya Rus. Fed. *see* Timashevsk
Timbákion Greece *see* Tympaki
Timbaúba Brazil **150** F3
Timbedgha Mauritania **92** C1
Timber Creek Australia **110** B2
Timber Lake U.S.A. **132** C2
Timber Mountain U.S.A. **135** C5
Timbiquí Col. **146** C3
Timbué, Ponta *pt* Moz. **99** H3
Timbuktu Mali **92** E1
Timbun Mata *i. Sabah* Malaysia **59** G1
Timétrine Mali **93** E1
Timétrine *reg.* Mali **93** E1
Timgad *tourist site* Alg. **91** G2
Timia Niger **93** H1
Timía *r.* Niger **93** H1
Timiaouine Alg. **91** F5
Timimoun Alg. **91** F3
Timirist, Râs *pt* Mauritania **92** A1
Timiş *r.* Romania **46** B2
Timişoara Romania **46** B2
Timişului, Câmpia *plain* Romania **46** B2
Timis Ford Lake U.S.A. **128** B5
Timishr *r.* Rus. Fed. **28** J3
Ti.n, Jabal *hill* Saudi Arabia **89** I3
Timmiarmiut Greenland **121** O3
Tin-Aba *well* Mali **93** G2
Timmins Canada **124** D4
Timms Hill U.S.A. **132** D2
Timok *r.* Yugo. **46** C2
Timokhino Rus. Fed. **28** F4
Timon Brazil **150** D3
Timor *i.* Indon. **57** G7
Timor Sea Australia/Indon. **106** B3
Timor Timur *country* Asia *see* East Timor
Timoudi Alg. **91** E3
Timrå Sweden **33** F3
Timsâh, Buhayrat at *l.* Egypt **77** A4
Tîmush *well* Mali **93** E1
Timzgadiouine, Adrar *mts* Alg. **91** G5
Tinaca Point Phil. **57** H5
Tinaco Venez. **146** E2
Tin Alkoum Libya **88** A3
Tin Amzi, Oued *watercourse* Alg. **91** G5
Tin-n-Azabo *well* Mali **93** E1
Tin-n-Bessaïs *well* Mauritania **90** C5
Tin Can Bay Australia **111** H5
Tinchebray France **38** C2
Tin-n-Didine *well* Mali **91** E5
Tindivanam India **72** C3
Tindouf Alg. **90** C4
Tiné Chad **88** D6
Tin-n-Echeri *well* Mali **93** E1
Tinée *r.* France **39** G5
Tineo Spain **42** C1
Tinerhir Morocco **90** D3
Tin-n-Etissane *well* Mali **93** E1
Tinfouchy Alg. **90** D3
Tinggi *i.* Malaysia **58** D2
Tingi Mountains Sierra Leone **92** C4
Ting Jiang *r.* China **67** F3
Tinglev Denmark **33** C5
Tingo María Peru **148** C2
Tingrela Côte d'Ivoire *see* Tengréla
Tingri China **70** G6
Tingsryd Sweden **33** D4
Tingvoll Norway **32** E3
Tingzhou China *see* Changting
Tinharé, Ilha de *i.* Brazil **150** E5
Tinian *i.* N. Mariana Is **57** K3
Tiniéré *well* Mauritania **92** B1
Tiniguea, Parque Nacional *nat. park* Col. **146** C4
Tini Heke *is* N.Z. *see* Snares Islands
Tinja *r.* Bos.-Herz. **44** G2
Tinjar *r. Sarawak* Malaysia **59** F1
Tinkisso *r.* Guinea **92** C3
Tinn Norway **33** C4
Tinnelvelly India *see* Tirunelveli
Tinnoset Fin. *see* Tirunelveli
Tinnoset Fin. **33** C4
Tinnsjø *l.* Norway **33** C4
Tinogasta Arg. **152** C2
Tinos Greece **47** D6
Tinos *i.* Greece **47** D6
Ti-n-Rerhoh *well* Alg. **91** G5
Tinrhert, Plateau du Alg. **91** G3
Ti-n-Srir *well* Mali **93** F1
Tinsukia India **75** G4
Tîntâne Mauritania **92** C1
Tintina Arg. **152** E1
Tintejert, Adrar *mt.* Alg. **91** F4
Ti-n-Tersi *well* Mali **93** E1
Tintina Arg. **152** E1
Tin Tounnant *well* Mali *see* Taounnant
Ti-n-Zaouâtene Mali **93** F2
Tioga *ND* U.S.A. **132** A1
Tioga *PA* U.S.A. **131** E3
Tioga *r.* U.S.A. **131** G3
Tioman *i.* Malaysia **58** D2
Tioribougou Mali **92** C2
Tiou Burkina **93** E2
Tioughnioga *r.* U.S.A. **131** F2
Tipasa Alg. **91** H1
Tippecanoe *r.* U.S.A. **132** E3
Tiptala Bhanjyang *pass* Nepal **75** E4
Tipton *CA* U.S.A. **136** C3
Tipton *MO* U.S.A. **132** C4
Tiptop U.S.A. **130** C5
Tip Top Hill Canada **124** C3
Tiptur India **72** C3
Tipuani Bol. **148** C3
Tiquié *r.* Brazil **146** D4
Tiquisate Guat. **138** F6
Tirahart, *watercourse* Alg. **91** F4
Tīrān *i.* Saudi Arabia **89** G3
▶Tirana Albania **46** A4
Capital of Albania.
Tiranë Albania *see* Tirana
Tirano Italy **44** D1
Tiraouene *well* Niger **93** G1
Tirap India **60** A2
Tiraraoune *well* Mali **93** E1
Tirari Desert Australia **110** D5
Tirari *r.* Myanmar **61** B4
Tiraspol Moldova **29** D7

Tiraz Mountains Namibia **98** C5
Tire Turkey **47** L5
Tirek *well* Mali **91** F5
Tirest *well* Mali **91** F5
Tîrgovişte Romania *see* Târgovişte
Tirgu Bujor Romania *see* Târgu Bujor
Tîrgu Cărbunești Romania *see* Târgu Cărbunești
Tirgu Jiu Romania *see* Târgu Jiu
Tîrgu Mureş Romania *see* Târgu Mureş
Tirgu Ocna Romania *see* Târgu Ocna
Tirgu Secuiesc Romania *see* Târgu Secuiesc
Tirich Mir *mt.* Pak. **81** G2
Tirîne *r.* India **72** C2
Tîrnăveni Romania *see* Târnăveni
Tírnavos Greece *see* Tyrnavos
Tiro *r.* India **72** C2
Tirodi India **74** C5
Tiros Brazil **151** C6
Tiroungoulou Cent. Afr. Rep. **94** D2
Tirreno, Mare France/Italy *see* Tyrrhenian Sea
Tirso *r.* Sardinia Italy **45** B5
Tirthahalli India **72** B3
Tiruchchendur India **72** C4
Tiruchchirappalli India **72** C4
Tiruchengodu India **72** C4
Tirukkoyilur India **72** C4
Tirumangalam India **72** C4
Tiruntán Peru **148** B1
Tirupati India **72** C3
Tiruppattur *Tamil Nadu* India **72** C3
Tiruppattur *Tamil Nadu* India **72** C4
Tiruppur India **72** C4
Tiruttani India **72** C3
Tiruttanippuram India **72** C4
Tiruvallur India **72** D3
Tiruvannamalai India **72** C3
Tiruvottiyur India **72** D3
Tiru Well Australia **108** D5
Tiryns *tourist site* Greece **47** C6
Tirza *r.* Latvia **33** O4
Tisa *r.* Yugo. **46** B2
Tisa *r.* Yugo. **46** B3
Tisaiyanvilai India **72** C4
Tiska, Mont *mt.* Alg. **91** H5
Tisdale Canada **123** J4
Tissemsilt Alg. **91** F2
Tista *r.* India **75** F4
Tisza *r.* Hungary **37** J5
Tiszaföldvár Hungary **37** J5
Tiszafüred Hungary **37** J5
Tiszakécske Hungary **37** J5
Tiszaújváros Hungary **37** J5
Tiszavasvári Hungary **37** J5
Tit Alg. **91** F4
Tit Alg. **91** G5
Titan Dome *ice feature* Antarctica **167** H1
Titao Burkina **92** E2
Titarisios *r.* Greece **47** C5
Tit-Ary Rus. Fed. **27** M2
Titawin Morocco *see* Tétouan
Titel Yugo. **46** B2
Tithwal Pak. **81** H3
▶Titicaca, Lake Bol./Peru **148** C3
Largest lake in South America.
southamerica 142–143, 154
Tititea *mt.* N.Z. *see* Aspiring, Mount
Titlagarh India **73** D1
Titograd Yugo. *see* Podgorica
Titova Mitrovica Yugo. *see* Kosovska Mitrovica
Titov Drvar Bos.-Herz. **44** F2
Titovka *r.* Rus. Fed. **32** H1
Titovo Užice Yugo. *see* Užice
Titovo Velenje Slovenia *see* Velenje
Titov Veles Macedonia *see* Veles
Titov Vrbas Yugo. *see* Vrbas
Ti Tree Australia **110** C4
Tittabawassee *r.* U.S.A. **130** D2
Titteri *mts* Alg. **43** H4
Titu Romania **46** D2
Titule Dem. Rep. Congo **94** E4
Titusville *FL* U.S.A. **129** C6
Titusville *PA* U.S.A. **130** E3
Tiu Chung Chau *i.* Hong Kong China **67** [inset]
Tiumpan Head U.K. **34** C2
Tiva *watercourse* Kenya **96** C5
Tivari India **74** B4
Tivat Yugo. **46** A3
Tiverton Canada **130** E1
Tiveden nationalpark *nat. park* Sweden **33** D4
Tiverton U.K. **35** E6
Tivoli Italy **44** D4
Tiwal, Wadi *watercourse* Sudan **94** D2
Tiya *tourist site* Eth. **96** C2
Tizi El Arba *hill* Alg. **43** H4
Tizi Mighert *pass* Morocco **90** C3
Tizimín Mex. **127** I7
Tizi-n-Test *pass* Morocco **90** C3
Tizi-n-Tichka *pass* Morocco **90** D3
Tizi Ouzou Alg. **91** G1
Tiznit Morocco **90** C3
Tizoc Mex. **133** A7
Tjaktjajaure *l.* Sweden **32** E2
Tjappsåive Sweden **28** A2
Tjautas Sweden **32** F2
Tjeggelvas *l.* Sweden **32** E2
Tjirebon Indon. *see* Cirebon
Tjirebon Indon. *see* Cirebon
Tjöjo Zimbabwe *see* Tsholotsho
Tjörn *i.* Sweden **33** C4
Tjörnes *pen.* Iceland **32** [inset]
Tjøtta Norway **32** D2
Tkibuli Georgia *see* Tqibuli
Tkvarcheli Georgia *see* Tqvarch'eli
Tlacolula Mex. **138** E5
Tlacotalpán Mex. **126** G8
Tlalnepantla Mex. **126** G8
Tlaxcala Mex. **126** E5
Tlell Canada **122** D4
Tlemcen Alg. **91** E2
Tłuszcz Poland **37** J2
Tlyarata Rus. Fed. **79** F2
Tmaöt, Prêk *r.* Cambodia **61** D6
To *r.* Myanmar **61** B4
Toad *r.* Canada **122** E3
Toad River Canada **122** E3
Toamasina Madag. **99** [inset] K3
Toamasina *prov.* Madag. **99** [inset] K3
Toana *mts* U.S.A. **137** E1
Toano U.S.A. **131** G5
Toa Payoh Sing. **58** [inset]
Toba China **66** B2
Toba, Danau *l.* Indon. **58** B2
Toba, Danau *l.* Indon. *see* Toba, Danau
Toba and Kakar Ranges *mts* Pak. **81** F4
Tobago *i.* Trin. and Tob. **147** F2
Toba Inlet Canada **122** E5
Tobarra Spain **43** F3
Tobas Arg. **152** D3
Toba Tek Singh Pak. **81** H4
Tobelo Indon. **57** G5

Tomamae Japan **64** E3
Tomani *Sabah* Malaysia **59** F1
Tomar Brazil **147** F5
Tomar Port. **42** B3
Tomari Rus. Fed. **64** E3
Tomarza Turkey **78** C3
Tombador, Serra do *hills* Bahia Brazil **150** D4
Tombigbee *r.* U.S.A. **129** B6
Tomboco Angola **95** B6
Tombouctou Mali *see* Timbuktu
Tombouctou *admin. reg.* Mali **92** C2
Tombs of Buganda Kings *tourist site* Uganda **96** A4
Tombstone U.S.A. **135** I7
Tombua Angola **95** A8
Tomé Chile **152** B3
Tome Moz. **99** G4
Tomelilla Sweden **33** D5
Tomelloso Spain **42** E3
Tomenaryk Kazakh. **70** C3
Tomi Romania *see* Constanța
Tominé *r.* Guinea **92** B2
Tomini, Teluk *g.* Indon. **57** F6
Tominian Mali **92** D3
Tomislavgrad Bos.-Herz. **44** F3
Tomkinson Ranges *mts* Australia **110** E5
Tommot Rus. Fed. **27** M4
Tomo Col. **146** E4
Tomo *r.* Col. **146** E3
Tomóchic Mex. **135** F7
Tomorit, Maja e *mt.* Albania **46** B4
Tompo Rus. Fed. **27** N3
Tom Price Australia **108** B5
Tomra China **75** E3
Tomsk Rus. Fed. **27** I4
Toms River U.S.A. **131** F4
Tomtor Rus. Fed. **27** O3
Tomur Feng *mt.* China/Kyrg. *see* Pobeda Peak
Tomuzlovka *r.* Rus. Fed. **29** H7
Tonalá Mex. **138** F5
Tonantins Brazil **146** E5
Tonate Fr. Guiana **147** H3
Tonawanda U.S.A. **130** D2
Tonb-e Bozorg, Jazireh-ye *i.* The Gulf *see* Greater Tunb
Tonb-e Küchek, Jazireh-ye *i.* The Gulf *see* Lesser Tunb
Tonbridge U.K. **35** G6
Tondano Indon. **57** F5
Tondela Port. **42** B3
Tønder Denmark **33** C5
Tondi India **72** C4
Toney Mount Antarctica **167** K1
Tonga Sudan **96** A3
Tongaat S. Africa **99** F6
▶Tonga *country* S. Pacific Ocean **107** H3
oceania 104–105, 114
Tonga Sudan **96** A3
Tong'an China **67** E3
Tonga Plateau Zambia **95** E9
Tongatapu *i.* Tonga **107** H4
▶Tongatapu Group *is* Tonga **107** H4
Tongbai China **67** E1
Tongbai Shan *mts* China **67** E1
Tongcheng *Hubei* China **67** E2
T'ongch'ŏn N. Korea **65** A5
Tongchuan *Shaanxi* China **63** H4
Tongchuan *Sichuan* China *see* Santai
Tongdao China **67** E3
Tongduch'ŏn S. Korea **65** A5
Tongeren Belgium **39** F1
Tonggu Jiao *pt* China **67** [inset]
Tonghae S. Korea **65** B5
Tonghai China **66** B3
Tonghe China **64** C3
Tonghua *Jilin* China **64** A4
Tonghua *Jilin* China **64** A4
Tongi Bangl. *see* Tungi
Tongjiang *Heilong.* China **64** C3
Tongjiang *Sichuan* China **66** C2
Tongken *r.* China **64** B3
Tongking, Gulf of China/Vietnam **66** D2
Tongle China *see* Leye
Tongliao China **63** K3
Tongling *Anhui* China **67** F2
Tongling *Anhui* China **67** F2
Tonglu China **67** F2
Tongo Australia **112** B3
Tongobory Madag. **99** [inset] J4
Tongquan China *see* Malong
Tongren China **67** D3
Tongres Belgium *see* Tongeren
Tongsa Bhutan *see* Trongsa
Tongshan China *see* Xuzhou
Tongshi China **67** D5
Tongtian He *r.* China **70** I5
Tongue U.K. **34** D2
Tongue *r.* U.S.A. **134** F3
Tongue of the Ocean *sea chan.* Bahamas **129** D7
▶T'ongyŏng S. Korea **65** B6
Tongzi China **66** C2
Tonj Sudan **96** F3
Tonj *watercourse* Sudan **94** F3
Tonk India **74** C4
Tonkabon Iran **80** B2
Tonkawa U.S.A. **133** B4
Tonkin *reg.* Vietnam **60** D3
Tônlé Repou *r.* Laos **61** D5
▶Tonle Sap *l.* Cambodia **61** C5
Largest lake in Southeast Asia.
Tonnay-Charente France **38** C4
Tonneins France **38** D4
Tonnerre France **39** E3
Tönning Germany **36** D1
Tono Japan **65** E5
Tonopah *AZ* U.S.A. **137** F5
Tonopah *NV* U.S.A. **136** D2
Tonozang Myanmar **60** A3
Tonstad Norway **33** C4
Tooborac Australia **112** B6
Tooele U.S.A. **137** E1
Tooma *r.* Australia **112** C6
Toompine Australia **111** F5
Toorberg *mt.* S. Africa **98** F7
Toowoomba Australia **111** G5
Tooxin Somalia **96** F2
Top Afgh. **81** G3
▶Topeka U.S.A. **132** C4
State capital of Kansas.

Topia Mex. **138** C3
Topley Canada **122** E4
Toplica *r.* Yugo. **46** B3
Topocalma, Punta *pt* Chile **152** B3
Topock U.S.A. **137** E4
Topol'čany Slovakia **37** I4
Topolampo Mex. **138** C3
Topoli Kazakh. **29** J7
Topolnitsa *r.* Bulg. **46** D3
Topolobampo Mex. **138** C3
Topolog Romania **46** E2
Topolog *r.* Romania **46** D2
Topoloveni Romania **46** D2
Topolovgrad Bulg. **46** E3
Topozero, Ozero *l.* Rus. Fed. **32** I2
Toppenish U.S.A. **134** B3
Topraisar Romania **46** F2
Tor Eth. **96** B3
Tora Dem. Rep. Congo **94** F4
Tor Baldak *mt.* Afgh. **81** F4
Torbalı Turkey **78** A3
Torbat-e Heydarīyeh Iran **81** D3
Torbat-e Jām Iran **81** E3
Torbeyevo Rus. Fed. **29** G5
Torch *r.* Canada **123** K4
Tordesillas Spain **42** D2
Tórdiga, Puerto de *pass* Spain **43** E3
Töre Sweden **32** F2
Töreboda Sweden **33** D4
Torelló Spain **43** H1
Toreno Spain **42** C1
Toretam Kazakh. *see* Baykonur
Torgau Germany **37** F3
Torgelow Germany **37** G2
Torghay Kazakh. *see* Turgay
Torgun *r.* Rus. Fed. **29** H5
Torhamn Sweden **33** D4
Torhout Belgium **39** E1
Tori India **75** E5
Tori *r.* Sudan **96** A3
Torigni-sur-Vire France **38** C2
Torine *pass* Bos.-Herz. **44** E3
Torino Italy *see* Turin
Tori-shima *i.* Japan **65** E7
Torit Sudan **96** B3
Torkaman Iran **80** B2
Torkovichi Rus. Fed. **28** D4
Törmänen Fin. **32** O1
Tormes *r.* Spain **42** C3
Tornado Mountain Canada **123** H5
Tornala Slovakia **37** J4
Tornavacas, Puerto de *pass* Spain **42** D2
Torneå Fin. *see* Tornio
Torneälven *r.* Sweden **32** E2
Torneträsk Sweden **32** E1
Torneträsk *l.* Sweden **32** E1
Torngat, Monts *mts* Canada *see* Torngat Mountains
Torngat Mountains Canada **125** H1
Tornio Fin. **32** G2
Tornquist Arg. **152** E4
Toro Nigeria **93** H3
Toro Spain **42** D2
Toro, Lago del *l.* Chile **153** B7
Torodi Niger **93** F2
Törökszentmiklós Hungary **37** J5
▶Toronto Canada **130** D2
Provincial capital of Ontario and 5th most populous city in North America.
world 16–17
Toronto U.S.A. **130** C3
Toro Peak U.S.A. **137** D5
Toropets Rus. Fed. **28** D4
Tororo Chad **88** C6
Tororo Uganda **96** B4
Toros Dağları *mts* Turkey *see* Taurus Mountains
Toroshino Rus. Fed. **33** O4
Torp *airport* Norway *see* Sandefjord
Torquay U.K. **35** E6
Torrance U.S.A. **136** C5
Torre *mt.* Port. **42** C2
Torreblanca Italy **45** E4
Torreblanca Spain **43** G2
Torre Blanco, Cerro *mt.* Mex. **135** E7
Torrecerredo *mt.* Spain **42** D1
Torrecilla *mt.* Spain **42** D4
Torre del Greco Italy **45** F4
Torre de Moncorvo Port. **40** A3
Torrejón de Ardoz Spain **42** E2
Torrejón-Tajo, Embalse de *resr* Spain **42** D3
Torrelaguna Spain **42** E2
Torrelavega Spain **42** D1
Torremaggiore Italy **44** D4
Torremolinos Spain **42** D4
▶Torrens, Lake *salt flat* Australia **112** A3
2nd largest lake in Oceania.
oceania 102–103
Torrens Creek Australia **111** F4
Torrent Arg. **152** F2
Torrent Spain *see* Torrente
Torrente Spain **43** F3
Torreón Mex. **126** F6
Torre Orsaia Italy **45** F4
Torres Brazil **151** B9
Torres del Paine, Parque Nacional *nat. park* Chile **153** B7
Torres Islands Vanuatu **107** F3
Torres Novas Port. **42** B3
Torres Strait Australia **106** D2
Torres Vedras Port. **42** B3
Torrevieja Spain **43** F4
Torrey U.S.A. **137** G2
Torridge *r.* U.K. **35** D6
Torriglia Italy **44** B2
Torrijos Spain **42** D3
Torrington U.S.A. **134** F4
Torrón *r.* Sweden **32** D3
Torrox Spain **42** E4
Torsa Chhu *r.* Bhutan **75** F4
Torsby Sweden **33** D3

▶Tórshavn Faroe Is **34** [inset]
Capital of the Faroe Islands.

Tortilla Flat U.S.A. **137** G5
Törtköl Uzbek. *see* Turtkul'
Tortoli *Sardinia* Italy **45** B5
Tortona Italy **44** B2
Tortosa Spain **43** G3
Tortum Turkey **79** F2
Torud Iran **80** D3
Torugart, Pereval *pass* China/Kyrg. *see* Turugart Pass
Torul Turkey **79** D2
Toruń Poland **37** I2
Tõrva Estonia **33** G4
Tõrvaoya *mt.* Norway **33** B3
Tory Island Rep. of Ireland **34** E4
Torysa *r.* Slovakia **37** J4
Tory Sound *sea chan.* Rep. of Ireland **34** E4
Torzhok Rus. Fed. **28** E4
Tosashimizu Japan **65** C6
Tosbotn Norway **32** D2
Tosca S. Africa **98** D5
Toscana *admin. reg.* Italy **44** D3
Toscano, Arcipelago *is* Italy **44** D4
Tosenfjorden *inlet* Norway **32** D2
Toshkent Uzbek. *see* Tashkent
Toshkent Wiloyati *admin. div.* Uzbek. *see* Tashkentskaya Oblast'

Tosno Rus. Fed. 28 D4
Tosontsengel Mongolia 70 I2
Tossal de la Baltasana mt. Spain 43 G2
Tossal de l'Orri mt. Spain 43 G1
Tostado Arg. 152 E2
Tõstamaa Estonia 33 F4
Tosu Japan 65 B6
Tosya Turkey 78 C2
Toszek Poland 37 I3
Totana Spain 43 F4
Totapola mt. Sri Lanka 72 D5
Toteng Botswana 98 D4
Tôtes France 38 D2
Tot'ma Rus. Fed. 28 G4
Totness Suriname 147 G3
Totoral Chile 152 C1
Totoralejos Arg. 152 D2
Totoya i. Fiji 107 H3
Tottori Japan 65 C6
Touâret well Niger 93 G1
Touba Côte d'Ivoire 92 D3
Touba Senegal 92 B2
Toubkal, Parc National nat. park Morocco 90 D3
Touboro Cameroon 94 B3
Touchet r. U.S.A. 134 C3
Toucy France 39 E3
Toueïrma well Mauritania 90 B5
Touêrât well Mali 92 E1
Toufourine well Mali 90 D4
Tougan Burkina 92 E2
Touggourt Alg. 91 G2
Tougouri Burkina 93 E2
Touil Mauritania 92 C2
Toukoto Mali 92 C2
Toul France 39 F2
Toulépleu Côte d'Ivoire 92 C4
Touliu Taiwan 67 G4
Toulnustouc r. Canada 125 G3
Toulon France 39 F5
Toulon U.S.A. 132 D3
Toulouk well Niger 93 G1
Toulouse France 38 D5
Toumbélaga well Niger 93 G2
Toummo well Niger 91 I5
Toumodi Côte d'Ivoire 92 D4
Toungo Nigeria 93 I3
Toungoo Myanmar 60 B4
Toupai China 67 D3
Touques r. France 38 D2
Touraine reg. France 38 D3
Tourane Vietnam see Đa Nâng
Tourassine well Mauritania 90 C4
Tourba Chad 88 B6
Tourgis Lake Canada 123 J1
Touriñán, Cabo c. Spain 42 B1
Tourlaville France 38 C2
Tour Matagrin hill France 39 F4
Tournai Belgium 39 E1
Tournavista Peru 148 B2
Tourndo, Oued watercourse Alg./Niger 91 H5
Tournon-sur-Rhône France 39 F4
Tournus France 39 F3
Touros Brazil 150 F3
Touroua Cameroon 93 I3
Tours France 38 D3
Tous, Embalse de resr Spain 43 F3
Toussiana Burkina 92 D3
Tousside, Pic mt. Chad 88 C4
Toussoro, Mont mt. Cent. Afr. Rep. 94 D2
Touwsrivier S. Africa 98 D7
Tovar Venez. 146 D2
Tovarkovo Rus. Fed. 29 E5
Tovarnik Croatia 46 A2
Tovil'-Dora Tajik. see Tavil'dara
Tovu Fiji 107 H3
Tovuz Azer. 79 F2
Towada Japan 64 E4
Towada-Hachimantai National Park Japan 64 E5
Towakaima Guyana 147 G3
Towak Mountain U.S.A. 120 C3
Towanda U.S.A. 131 E3
Tower City U.S.A. 131 E3
Towerhill Creek watercourse Australia 111 F4
Towner U.S.A. 132 A1
Townsend MA U.S.A. 131 H2
Townsend MT U.S.A. 134 E3
Townshend Island Australia 111 G4
Townsville Australia 111 F3
Towori, Teluk b. Indon. 57 F6
Towot Sudan 96 B3
Towr Kham Afgh. 81 G3
Towson U.S.A. 131 E4
Toxkan He r. China 70 F3
Toy U.S.A. 136 C1
Tōya-ko l. Japan 64 E4
Toyama Japan 65 D5
Toyama-wan b. Japan 65 D5
Toyokawa Japan 65 D6
Toyonaka Japan 65 C6
Toyooka Japan 65 C6
Toyota Japan 65 D6
Tozal del Orri mt. Spain see Tossal de l'Orri
Tozê Kangri mt. China 75 D2
Tozeur Tunisia 91 H2
Tqibuli Georgia 79 E2
Tqvarch'eli Georgia 79 E2
Trâblous Lebanon see Tripoli
Trabotivište Macedonia 46 C4
Trabzon Turkey 79 D2
Tracy CA U.S.A. 136 B3
Tracy MN U.S.A. 132 C2
Trading r. Canada 124 B3
Træna i. Norway 32 D2
Trænfjorden sea chan. Norway 32 D2
Trafalgar, Cabo c. Spain 42 C4
Traffic Mountain Canada 122 D2
Traiguén Chile 152 B4
Trail Canada 122 G5
Traill Island Greenland see Traill Ø
Traill Ø i. Greenland 121 Q2
Traipu Brazil 150 E4
Traíra r. Brazil 146 D5
Trairi Brazil 150 E2
Traisen r. Austria 37 G4
Trajectum Neth. see Utrecht
Trakai Lith. 33 G5
Trakai nat. park Lith. 33 G5
Trakiya reg. Turkey see Thrace
Trakt Rus. Fed. 28 I3
Trakya reg. Turkey see Thrace
Tralee Rep. of Ireland 35 B5
Trá Li Rep. of Ireland see Tralee
Trá Mhór Rep. of Ireland see Tramore
Trammel U.S.A. 130 B5
Tramore Rep. of Ireland 35 C5
Tramuntana, Serra de mts Spain 43 H3
Tranås Sweden 33 D4
Trancoso Port. 42 C2
Tranemo Sweden 33 D4
Trang Thai. 61 B7
Trangan i. Indon. 57 H7
Trangie Australia 112 C4
Trani Italy 44 F4
Tranoroa Madag. 99 [inset] J5
Tranqueras Uruguay 152 G2
Transantarctic Mountains Antarctica 167 H2
Trans Canada Highway Canada 123 H5
Transtrand Sweden 33 D3
Transylvanian Alps mts Romania 46 C2
Transylvanian Basin plat. Romania 46 D1
Tra Ôn Vietnam 61 D6
Trapani Sicily Italy 45 D5
Trapezus Turkey see Trabzon
Trapper Peak U.S.A. 134 D3
Trapua r. Brazil 152 G2
Traralgon Australia 112 C5
Trarza admin. reg. Mauritania 92 B1
Trascăului, Munții mts Romania 46 C1
Trashigang Bhutan 75 F4
Trasimeno, Lago l. Italy 44 D3
Trás-os-Montes reg. Port. 42 C2
Trasvase, Canal de Spain 43 E3
Trasvase Tajo-Segura, Canal de Spain 43 E3
Trat Thai. 61 C5
Traun Austria 37 G4
Traun r. Austria 37 G4
Traunreut Germany 37 F5
Traunsee l. Austria 37 F5
Traunstein Germany 37 F5
Trave r. Germany 36 E2
Travellers Lake imp. l. Australia 112 B4
Travers, Mount N.Z. 113 C3
Traverse City U.S.A. 132 E2
Travesía Puntana des. Arg. 152 D3
Travesía Tunuyán des. Arg. 152 D3
Tra Vinh Vietnam 61 D6
Travnik Bos.-Herz. 44 F2
Trbovlje Slovenia 44 E1
Trebebvić nat. park Bos.-Herz. 44 G3
Trebel r. Germany 37 F2
Třebíč Czech Rep. 37 G4
Trebinje Bos.-Herz. 44 G3
Trebisacce Italy 45 F5
Trebišov Slovakia 37 J4
Trebižat r. Bos.-Herz. 44 F3
Trebizond Turkey see Trabzon
Trebnje Slovenia 44 E2
Třeboň Czech Rep. 37 G4
Tree r. Canada 123 I1
Tree Island India 72 B4
Treene r. Germany 36 D1
Trefaldwyn U.K. see Montgomery
Trefynwy U.K. see Monmouth
Tregosse Islets and Reefs Australia 111 G3
Tréguier France 38 C2
Treignac France 38 D4
Treinta y Tres Uruguay 152 G3
Trelew Arg. 153 D5
Trelleborg Sweden 33 D5
Trélon France 36 B3
Trem mt. Yugo. 46 C3
Tremblant, Mont hill Canada 125 F4
Trembleur Lake Canada 122 E4
Tremiti, Isole is Italy 44 E3
Tremont U.S.A. 131 E3
Tremonton U.S.A. 134 D4
Tremp Spain 43 G1
Trenche r. Canada 125 F4
Trenčín Slovakia 37 I4
Trengganu state Malaysia see Terengganu
Trenque Lauquén Arg. 152 E3
Trent Italy see Trento
Trent r. U.K. 35 F5
Trentino - Alto Adige admin. reg. Italy 44 C1
Trento Italy 44 C1
Trenton Canada 130 E1
Trenton FL U.S.A. 129 C6
Trenton GA U.S.A. 128 B5
Trenton MO U.S.A. 132 C3
Trenton NE U.S.A. 132 A3
▶Trenton NJ U.S.A. 131 F3
State capital of New Jersey.
Trepassey Canada 125 K4
Tres Arboles Uruguay 152 F3
Tres Arroyos Arg. 152 E4
Tres Cerros Arg. 153 D7
Três Corações Brazil 151 C7
Tres Cruces Arg. 148 D5
Tres Cruces Chile 152 C2
Tres Esquinas Col. 146 C4
Tres Forcas, Cabo c. Morocco see Trois Fourches, Cap des
Tres Isletas Arg. 152 E1
Treska r. Macedonia 46 B3
Três Lagoas Brazil 149 H5
Tres Lagos Arg. 153 C7
Tres Lomas Arg. 152 E4
Três Marias, Represa resr Brazil 151 C6
Tres Matas Venez. 147 E2
Tres Montes, Península pen. Chile 153 B6
Tres Picachos, Sierra mts Mex. 135 F7
Tres Picos mt. Arg. 153 C5
Tres Picos, Cerro mt. Arg. 152 E4
Tres Piedras U.S.A. 135 F5
Três Pontas Brazil 151 C7
Tres Puntas, Cabo c. Arg. 153 D6
Três Rios Brazil 151 D7
Tretten Norway 33 C3
Treuchtlingen Germany 36 E4
Treuenbrietzen Germany 37 F2
Treungen Norway 33 C4
Trevelín Arg. 153 C5
Treves Germany see Trier
Trevi Italy 44 D3
Treviglio Italy 44 B2
Treviso Italy 44 D2
Trevose Head U.K. 35 D6
Trgovište Yugo. 46 C3
Triabunna Australia 112 C6
Tri An, Hô resr Vietnam 61 D6
Tria Nisia i. Greece 47 E6
Tribal Areas admin. div. Pak. 81 G3
Tribeč mts Slovakia 37 I4
Tribune U.S.A. 132 A4
Tricase Italy 45 G5
Trichinopoly India see Tiruchchirappalli
Trichonida, Limni l. Greece 47 B5
Trichur India 72 C4
Trida Australia 112 C4
Tridentum Italy see Trento
Trier Germany 36 C4
Trieste Italy 44 D2
Trieste, Golfo di g. Europe see Trieste, Gulf of
Trieste, Gulf of Europe 44 D2
Trie-sur-Baïse France 38 D5
Trieux r. France 38 B2
Triggiano Italy 44 F4
Triglavski Narodni Park nat. park Slovenia 44 D1
Trigno r. Italy 44 E3
Trikala Greece 47 B5
Trikkala Greece see Trikala
Trikomo Cyprus see Trikomon
Trikomon Cyprus 77 A2
▶Trikora, Puncak mt. Indon. 57 I6
2nd highest mountain in Oceania.
oceania 102–103
Trikorfa mt. Greece 47 C5
Trilj Croatia 44 F3
Trincheras Mex. 135 E7
Trincomalee Sri Lanka 72 D4
Trindade Brazil 149 H4
Trindade, Ilha da i. S. Atlantic Ocean 161 M7
Tringia mt. Greece 47 B5
Trinidad Bol. 148 D3
Trinidad i. Trin. and Tob. 147 F2
Trinidad Uruguay 152 F3
Trinidad U.S.A. 135 F5
Trinidad, Golfo b. Chile 153 B7
▶Trinidad and Tobago country West Indies 147 F2
northamerica 118–119, 140
Trinitapoli Italy 44 F4
Trinity U.S.A. 133 C6
Trinity r. CA U.S.A. 134 B4
Trinity r. TX U.S.A. 133 C6
Trinity, West Fork r. U.S.A. 133 B5
Trinity Bay Canada 125 K4
Trinity Islands U.S.A. 120 D4
Trinity Range mts U.S.A. 136 C1
Trinkat Island India 73 G4
Trino Italy 44 B2
Trinway U.S.A. 130 B3
Trionto, Capo c. Italy 45 F5
Tripa r. Indon. 58 B2
Tripoli Greece 47 C6
Tripoli Lebanon 77 B2
▶Tripoli Libya 88 B1
Capital of Libya.
Tripolis Greece see Tripoli
Tripolis Lebanon see Tripoli
Tripolitania reg. Libya 88 B2
Tripunittura India 72 C4
Tripura state India 75 F5
Trischen i. Germany 36 D1
▶Tristan da Cunha i. S. Atlantic Ocean 161 N8
Dependency of St Helena.
Tristao, Îles is Guinea 92 B3
Trisul mt. India 74 C3
Triton Canada 125 K3
Triton Island atoll Paracel Is 56 D2
Triunfo Pernambuco Brazil 150 E3
Triunfo Rondônia Brazil 149 D2
Trivandrum India 72 C4
Trivento Italy 44 E4
Trizina Greece 47 C6
Trnava Slovakia 37 H4
Trobriand Islands P.N.G. 107 E2
Trofa Port. 42 B2
Trofaiach Austria 37 G5
Trofors Norway 32 D2
Trogir Croatia 44 F3
Troglav mt. Croatia 44 F3
Troina Sicily Italy 45 E6
Troisdorf Germany 36 C3
Trois Fourches, Cap des c. Morocco 90 E2
Trois-Pistoles Canada 125 G3
Trois-Rivières Canada 125 F4
Troitsa Rus. Fed. 26 G3
Troitsk Rus. Fed. 26 G4
Troitsko-Pechorsk Rus. Fed. 28 K3
Troitskoye Khabarovskiy Kray Rus. Fed. 64 D2
Troitskoye Respublika Kalmykiya - Khalm'g-Tangch Rus. Fed. 29 H7
Trolla well Chad 88 B6
Trollhättan Sweden 33 D4
Trombetas r. Brazil 147 G5
Tromelin, Île i. Indian Ocean 162 K7
Tromelin Island Micronesia see Fais
Tromen, Volcán vol. Arg. 152 C4
Trompsburg S. Africa 98 E6
Troms county Norway 32 E1
Tromsø Norway 32 E1
Trona U.S.A. 136 D4
Tronador, Monte mt. Arg. 152 C5
Tronçais, Forêt de for. France 39 E3
Trondheim Norway 32 C3
Trondheimsfjorden sea chan. Norway 32 C3
Trondheimsleia sea chan. Norway 32 C3
Trongsa Bhutan 75 F4
Trongsa Chhu r. Bhutan 75 F4
Troödos, Mount Cyprus 77 A2
Troödos Mountains Cyprus 77 A2
Tropaia Greece 47 B6
Tropas r. Brazil 147 G6
Tropeiros, Serra dos hills Brazil 150 C5
Trosh Rus. Fed. 28 J2
Trostan hill U.K. 34 C4
Trostberg Germany 37 F4
Trotuș r. Romania 46 E1
Trout r. B.C. Canada 122 E3
Trout r. N.W.T. Canada 122 G2
Trout Dale U.S.A. 130 C5
Trout Lake Alta Canada 123 H3
Trout Lake N.W.T. Canada 122 F2
Trout Lake l. N.W.T. Canada 122 F2
Trout Lake l. Ont. Canada 123 M5
Trout Run U.S.A. 131 E3
Troutville U.S.A. 130 D5
Trowbridge U.K. 35 E6
Trowutta Australia 112 C6
Troy tourist site Turkey 78 A3
Troy AL U.S.A. 129 B6
Troy KS U.S.A. 132 C4
Troy MI U.S.A. 130 B2
Troy MO U.S.A. 132 D4
Troy NC U.S.A. 128 D5
Troy NY U.S.A. 131 G2
Troy OH U.S.A. 130 A3
Troy PA U.S.A. 131 E3
Troyan Bulg. 46 D3
Troyes France 39 F2
Troy Peak U.S.A. 137 E2
Trstenik Yugo. 46 B3
Trubia r. Spain 42 D1
Truc Giang Vietnam see Bên Tre
Trucial Coast country Asia see United Arab Emirates
Trucial States country Asia see United Arab Emirates
Truckee U.S.A. 136 B2
Trudovoy Kazakh. see Kuybyshevskiy
Trufanovo Rus. Fed. 28 H2
Trujillo Hond. 139 G5
Trujillo Peru 148 A2
Trujillo Spain 42 D3
Trujillo Venez. 146 D2
Trujillo state Venez. 146 D2
Trujillo, Monte mt. Dom. Rep. see Duarte, Pico
Trumansburg U.S.A. 131 E2
Trumbull U.S.A. 131 G3
Trumbull, Mount U.S.A. 137 F3
Trumon Indon. 58 B2
Trun France 38 D2
Trŭna mt. Bulg. 46 C3
Trung Khanh Vietnam 60 D3
Truong Sa is S. China Sea see Spratly Islands
Truro Canada 125 I4
Truro U.K. 35 D6
Trusan Sarawak Malaysia 59 F1
Trusan r. Sarawak Malaysia 59 F1
Truskmore hill Rep. of Ireland 35 B4
Trus Madi, Gunung mt. Sabah Malaysia 59 G1
Trutch Canada 122 F3
Trutch Creek r. Canada 122 F3
Truth or Consequences U.S.A. 135 F6
Trutnov Czech Rep. 37 G3
Truva tourist site Turkey see Troy
Truyère r. France 39 E4
Tryavna Bulg. 46 D3
Tryon U.S.A. 132 A3
Trypiti, Akra pt Kriti Greece 47 D7
Trypiti, Akra pt Greece 47 D5
Trysil Norway 33 D3
Trysilfjellet mt. Norway 33 D3
Tržac Bos.-Herz. 44 E2
Trzcianka Poland 37 H2
Trzebiatów Poland 37 G1
Trzebinia Poland 37 I3
Trzebnica Poland 37 H3
Trzemeszno Poland 37 H2
Tržič Slovenia 44 E1
Tsagaannuur Mongolia 62 D2
Tsagan Aman Rus. Fed. 29 H7
Tsagan-Nur Rus. Fed. 29 H7
Tsaidam Basin China see Qaidam Pendi
Tsåktso mt. Sweden 32 F1
Tsama I Congo 94 B5
Tsangatjåkkå mt. Sweden 32 D2
Tsao Botswana 98 D4
Tsaratanana, Massif du mts Madag. 99 [inset] K2
Tsarevo Bulg. 46 E3
Tsaribrod Yugo. see Dimitrovgrad
Tsaritsyn Rus. Fed. see Volgograd
Tsaukaib Namibia 98 B5
Tsavo East National Park Kenya 96 C5
Tsavo West National Park Kenya 97 C5
Tsebanana Botswana 99 E3
Tsefat Israel see Zefat
Tselinograd Kazakh. see Astana
Tsenogora Rus. Fed. 28 H2
Tsentralen Balkan nat. park Bulg. 46 D3
Tsentral'nyy Rus. Fed. 28 I4
Tserovo Bulg. 46 C3
Tsetseng Botswana 98 D4
Tsetserleg Mongolia 62 G2
Tsetserleg Mongolia see Halban
Tsévié Togo 93 F4
Tshabong Botswana 98 D5
Tshad country Africa see Chad
Tshchikskoye Vodokhranilishche resr Rus. Fed. 29 F7
Tshela Dem. Rep. Congo 95 B6
Tshene Dem. Rep. Congo 95 C6
Tshibala Dem. Rep. Congo 95 D6
Tshibuka Dem. Rep. Congo 95 D6
Tshibwika Dem. Rep. Congo 95 D7
Tshikapa Dem. Rep. Congo 95 D6
Tshikapa r. Dem. Rep. Congo 95 D6
Tshimbulu Dem. Rep. Congo 95 D6
Tshipise S. Africa 99 F4
Tshokwane S. Africa 99 F5
Tsholotsho Zimbabwe 99 E3
Tshootsha Botswana 98 D4
Tshuapa r. Dem. Rep. Congo 94 D5
Tshumbiri Dem. Rep. Congo 94 C5
Tsiazonano mt. Madag. 99 [inset] J3
Tsibritsa r. Bulg. 46 C3
Tsiigehtchic Canada 120 F3
Tsil'ma r. Rus. Fed. 28 I2
Tsimlyansk Rus. Fed. 29 G7
Tsimlyanskoye Vodokhranilishche resr Rus. Fed. 29 G7
Tsinan China see Jinan
Tsinghai prov. China see Qinghai
Tsing Shan hill Hong Kong China see Castle Peak
Tsingtao China see Qingdao
Tsing Yi i. Hong Kong China 67 [inset]
Tsining China see Jining
Tsinjomay mt. Madag. 99 [inset] J3
Tsintsabis Namibia 98 C3
Tsiombe Madag. 99 [inset] J5
Tsiroanomandidy Madag. 99 [inset] J3
Tsiteli Tskaro Georgia see Dedop'listsqaro
Tsitondroina Madag. 99 [inset] J4
Tsitsihar China see Qiqihar
Tsitsutl Peak Canada 122 E4
Tsivil'sk Rus. Fed. 28 H5
Tskhakaia Georgia see Senaki
Tskhaltubo Georgia see Tsqaltubo
Ts'khinvali Georgia 79 E2
Tsna r. Rus. Fed. 29 G5
Tsnori Georgia 79 F2
Tsodilo Hills Botswana 98 D3
Tsolo S. Africa 99 F6
Tsomo S. Africa 99 E7
Tso Morari Lake Jammu and Kashmir 74 C2
Tsona China see Cona
Tsopan hill Greece 46 D4
Tsqaltubo Georgia 79 E2
Tsu Japan 65 D6
Tsuchiura Japan 65 E5
Tsuen Wan Hong Kong China 67 [inset]
Tsugarū-kaikyō strait Japan 64 E4
Tsugaru Strait Japan see Tsugarū-kaikyō
Tsumeb Namibia 98 C3
Tsumis Park Namibia 98 C4
Tsumkwe Namibia 98 D3
Tsuruga Japan 65 D6
Tsurugi-san mt. Japan 65 C6
Tsurukhaytuy Rus. Fed. see Priargunsk
Tsuruoka Japan 65 D5
Tsushima is Japan 65 B6
Tsushima-kaikyō strait Japan/S. Korea see Korea Strait
Tsuyama Japan 65 C6
Tswaane Botswana 98 D4
Tswelelang S. Africa 98 E5
Tsyp-Navolok Rus. Fed. 32 I1
Tsyurupyns'k Ukr. 29 E7
Tthenaagoo Canada see Nahanni Butte
Tua r. Port. 42 C2
Tua, Tanjung pt Indon. 58 D4
Tual Indon. 57 H7
Tuam Rep. of Ireland 35 B5
Tuamotu, Archipel des Fr. Polynesia see Tuamotu Islands
Tuamotu Islands Fr. Polynesia 165 I6
Tuân Giao Vietnam 60 C3
Tuangku i. Indon. 58 B2
Tuapse Rus. Fed. 29 F7
Tuaran Sabah Malaysia 59 G1
Tuas Sing. 58 [inset]
Tuatapere N.Z. 113 A4
Tuath, Loch a' b. U.K. see Broad Bay
Tuba City U.S.A. 137 G3
Tuban Indon. 59 F4
Tubarão Brazil 151 B9
Ṭūbās West Bank 77 B3
Tubau Sarawak Malaysia 59 F2
Tubeya Dem. Rep. Congo 95 D6
Tübingen Germany 36 D4
Tubmanburg Liberia 92 C4
Tubo r. Nigeria 93 G3
Tubou Fiji 107 H3
Tubruq Libya 88 D1
Tubu r. Indon. 59 G2
Tubuai i. Fr. Polynesia 165 I7
Tubuai Islands Fr. Polynesia 165 H7
Tubutama Mex. 135 E7
Tucandera Brazil 147 F5
Tucannon r. U.S.A. 134 C3
Tucano Brazil 150 E4
Tucavaca Bol. 149 F4
Tucavaca r. Bol. 149 F4
Tuchitua Canada 122 D2
Tuchodi r. Canada 122 F3
Tuchola Poland 37 H2
Tuchów Poland 37 J4
Tuckanarra Australia 109 B6
Tuckerton U.S.A. 131 F4
Tucson U.S.A. 135 E6
Tucson Mountains U.S.A. 137 G5
Tuctuc r. Canada 125 H1
Tucumán Arg. see San Miguel de Tucumán
Tucumán prov. Arg. 152 D1
Tucumcari U.S.A. 135 G6
Tucunuco Arg. 152 C2
Tucuparé Brazil 147 H6
Tucupita Venez. 147 F2
Tucuracas Col. 146 C2
Tucuruí Brazil 150 B2
Tucuruí, Represa resr Brazil 150 B3
Tuczno Poland 37 H2
Tudela Spain 43 F1
Tudela de Duero Spain 42 D2
Tuder Italy see Todi
Tudu Estonia 33 G4
Tuen Mun Hong Kong China 67 [inset]
Tuensang India 75 G4
Tueré r. Brazil 147 I5
Ṭufayḥ Saudi Arabia 80 B5
Tufi P.N.G. 106 D2
Tufts Abyssal Plain sea feature N. Pacific Ocean 165 I2
Tugela r. S. Africa 99 F6
Tuglung China 75 G3
Tuguancun China 66 B3
Tuguegarao Phil. 57 F2
Tugur Rus. Fed. 27 N4
Tuhemberua Indon. 58 B2
Tui Spain 42 B1
Tuichi r. Bol. 148 D3
Tuilianpui r. Bangl./India 75 G5
Tūja Latvia 33 G4
Tujiabu China see Yongxiu
Tujuh, Kepulauan is Indon. 58 D3
Tukangbesi, Kepulauan is Indon. 57 F7
Tukayel Eth. 96 E2
Tukituki r. N.Z. 113 D2
Tükrah Libya 88 D1
Tuktoyaktuk Canada 120 F3
Tuktut Nogait National Park Canada 120 G3
Tukums Latvia 33 F4
Tukuyu Tanz. 97 B7
Tula Mex. 126 G7
Tula Rus. Fed. 29 F5
Tulach Mhór Rep. of Ireland see Tullamore
Tulagt Ar Gol r. China 75 G1
Tulak Afgh. 81 E3
Tula Mountains Antarctica 167 D2
Tulancingo Mex. 126 G7
Tulangbawang r. Indon. 58 D4
Tula Oblast admin. div. Rus. Fed. see Tul'skaya Oblast'
Tulare U.S.A. 136 C3
Tulare Lake Bed U.S.A. 136 C4
Tularosa U.S.A. 135 F6
Tulasi mt. India 73 D2
Tulcán Ecuador 146 B4
Tulcea Romania 46 F2
Tule r. U.S.A. 136 C3
Tuléar Madag. see Toliara
Tulelake U.S.A. 134 B4
Tulia U.S.A. 133 A5
Tuliszków Poland 37 I2
Tulita Canada 122 E1
Tuljapur India 72 C2
Ṭūlkarm West Bank 77 B3
Tulkarm West Bank see Ṭūlkarm
Tullahoma U.S.A. 128 B5
Tullamore Australia 112 C4
Tullamore Rep. of Ireland 35 C5
Tulle France 38 D4
Tulln Austria 37 H4
Tullow Rep. of Ireland 35 C5
Tully Australia 111 F3
Tully Falls Australia 111 F3
Tulnici Romania 46 E2
Tuloma r. Rus. Fed. 32 I1
Tulos Rus. Fed. 32 H3
Tulppio Fin. 32 H2
Tulsa U.S.A. 133 C4
Tulsequah Canada 122 C3
Tulsipur Nepal 75 D3
Tul'skaya Oblast' admin. div. Rus. Fed. 29 F5
Tuluá Col. 146 B3
Tulucești Romania 46 F2
Tuluksak U.S.A. 120 C3
Tulūl al Ashāqif hills Jordan 77 C3
Tulun Rus. Fed. 62 G1
Tulungagung Indon. 59 E4
Tulu-Tuloi, Serra hills Brazil 147 F4
Tulu Welel mt. Eth. 96 B2
Tulva r. Rus. Fed. 28 J4
Tuma Rus. Fed. 29 G5
Tumaco Col. 146 B4
Tumahole S. Africa 99 E5
Tumain China 75 F2
Tūmān Āqā Iran 81 E3
Tuman-gang r. Asia see Tumen Jiang
Tumannaya r. Asia see Tumen Jiang
Tumannyy Rus. Fed. 28 E1
Tumanskiy Rus. Fed. 27 R3
Tumatumari Guyana 147 G3
Tumba Sweden 33 E4
Tumba, Lac l. Dem. Rep. Congo see Ntomba, Lac
Tumbangmiri Indon. 59 F3
Tumbangsamba Indon. 59 F3
Tumbangtiti Indon. 59 E3
Tumbarumba Australia 112 D4
Tumbes Peru 146 A5
Tumbes dept Peru 146 A5
Tumbler Ridge Canada 122 F4
Tumbou Fiji see Tubou
Tumbur Indon. 108 E1
Tumby Bay Australia 109 G8
Tumcha r. Fin./Rus. Fed. 32 H2
Tumen China 64 B4
Tumen Jiang r. Asia 64 B4
Tumeremo Venez. 147 F3
Tumereng Guyana 147 F3
Tumkur India 72 C3
Tumlingtar Nepal 75 E4
Tummo, Mountains of Libya/Niger 88 B4
Tumnin r. Rus. Fed. 64 E2
Tump Pak. 81 E5
Tumpah Indon. 59 F3
Tumpôr, Phnum mt. Cambodia 61 C5
Tumsar India 74 C5
Tumu Ghana 93 E3
Tumucumaque, Serra hills Brazil 147 G4
Tumudibandh India 73 D2
Tumupasa Bol. 148 D3
Tumusla Bol. 148 D5
Tumut Australia 112 D4
Tuna Ghana 93 E3
Tunapuna Trin. and Tob. 147 F2
Ṭunb al Kubrá i. The Gulf see Greater Tunb
Ṭunb aş Şughrá i. The Gulf see Lesser Tunb
Tunbridge Wells, Royal U.K. 35 G6
Tunçbilek Turkey 47 F5
Tunceli Turkey 79 D3
Tuncurry Australia 112 E4
Tundubai well Sudan 89 F5
Tunduma Tanz. 97 B7
Tundun-Wada Nigeria 93 H3
Tunduru Tanz. 97 C7
Tundzha r. Bulg. 46 E4
Tunes Tunisia see Tunis
Tunga Nigeria 93 H3
Tungabhadra r. India 72 C3
Tungabhadra Reservoir India 72 C3
Tungdor China see Mainling
Tungi Bangl. 75 F5
Tungku Sabah Malaysia 59 G1
Tung Lung Chau i. Hong Kong China see Tung Lung Island
Tung Lung Island Hong Kong China 67 [inset]
Tungozero Rus. Fed. 32 H2
Tungsten Canada 122 D2
Tungun, Bukit mt. Indon. 59 F2
Tungurahua prov. Ecuador 146 B5
Tung Wan b. Hong Kong China 67 [inset]
Tuni India 73 D2
▶Tunis Tunisia 91 H1
Capital of Tunisia.
Tunis, Golfe de g. Tunisia 91 H1
▶Tunisia country Africa 91 H2
africa 86–87, 100
Tunja Col. 146 C3
Tunkhannock U.S.A. 131 F3
Tunnsjøen l. Norway 32 D2
Tuntsa Fin. 32 H2
Tununak U.S.A. 120 C3
Tunungayualok Island Canada 125 I1
Tunuyán Arg. 152 C3
Tunuyán r. Arg. 152 D3
Tunxi China see Huangshan
Tuodian China see Shuangbai
Tuo He r. China 67 F1
Tuojiang Hunan China see Fenghuang
Tuojiang Hunan China see Shuikou
Tuo Jiang r. China 66 C2
Tuolumne U.S.A. 136 B3
Tuolumne r. U.S.A. 136 B3
Tuolumne Meadows U.S.A. 136 C3
Tuoniang Jiang r. China 66 C3
Tuotuo He r. China 75 G2
Tuotuoheyan China 75 G2
Tupã Brazil 149 H5
Tupanaóca Brazil 147 F5
Tupanciretã Brazil 151 A9
Tupelo U.S.A. 133 D5
Tupinambarama, Ilha i. Brazil 147 G5
Tupiza Bol. 148 D5
Tupper Canada 122 F4
Tupper Lake U.S.A. 131 F1
Tüpqaraghan Tübegi pen. Kazakh. see Mangyshlak, Poluostrov
▶Tupungato, Cerro mt. Arg./Chile 152 C3
5th highest mountain in South America.
southamerica 142–143
Tuqayyid well Iraq 80 A4
Túquerres Col. 146 B4
Tuqu Wan b. China 67 D5
Tura India 75 F4
Tura Rus. Fed. 27 K3
Turabah Saudi Arabia 89 I2
Turabah Saudi Arabia 89 I4
Turabah, Wādī watercourse Saudi Arabia 89 I4
Turagua, Serranía mt. Venez. 147 E3
Turakina N.Z. 113 C3
Turana, Khrebet mts Rus. Fed. 64 B2
Turangi N.Z. 113 C2
Turan Lowland Asia 81 D1
Turanskaya Nizmennost' lowland Asia see Turan Lowland
Ţuraq al 'Ilab hills Syria 77 D3
Tura-Ryskulova Kazakh. 70 D3
Turayf Saudi Arabia 89 H2
Turayf well Saudi Arabia 80 B5
Turba Estonia 31 K1
Turbacz mt. Poland 37 J4
Turbat Pak. 81 E5
Turbo Col. 146 B2
Turčianske Teplice Slovakia 37 I4
Turco Bol. 148 C4
Turda Romania 46 C1
Tūreh Iran 80 B3
Turek Poland 37 I2
Turfan China see Turpan
Turfan Depression China see Turpan Pendi
Turgay Kazakh. 70 B2
Turgayskaya Dolina valley Kazakh. 70 B2
Turgayskaya Stolovaya Strana reg. Kazakh. 26 G4
Turgeon r. Canada 124 E3
Tŭrgovishte Bulg. 46 E3
Turgut Turkey 78 B3
Turgut Muğla Turkey 47 F6
Turgutalp Turkey 47 E5
Turgutlu Turkey 78 A3
Turgutreis Turkey 47 E6
Turhal Turkey 78 D2
Türi Estonia 28 C4
Turi Italy 44 F4
Turia r. Spain 43 F3
Turiaçu Brazil 150 C2
Turiaçu r. Brazil 150 C2
Turiamo Venez. 146 E2
Turiec r. Slovakia 37 I4
Turin Canada 134 D2
Turin Italy 44 A2
Turinsk Rus. Fed. 26 G4
Turiy Rog Rus. Fed. 64 B3
Turkana, Lake salt l. Eth./Kenya 96 B4
Türkeli Turkey 46 E4
Türkeli Adası i. Turkey 46 E4
Turkestan Kazakh. 70 C3
Turkestan Range mts Asia 81 F2
Túrkeve Hungary 37 J5
▶Turkey country Asia 78 C3
asia 52–53, 82
Turkey r. U.S.A. 132 D3
Turki Rus. Fed. 29 G6
Türkistan Kazakh. see Turkestan
Türkmenabat Turkm. see Chardzhev
Türkmen Aylagy b. Turkm. see Turkmenskiy Zaliv
Türkmenbashi Turkm. 80 C1
Türkmen Dağı mt. Turkey 78 B3
▶Turkmenistan country Asia 81 D1
asia 52–53, 82
Turkmeniya country Asia see Turkmenistan
Turkmenkarakul' Turkm. 81 E3
Turkmenostan country Asia see Turkmenistan
Turkmenskaya S.S.R. country Asia see Turkmenistan
Turkmenskiy Zaliv b. Turkm. 80 C2
Türkoğlu Turkey 78 D3
▶Turks and Caicos Islands terr. West Indies 127 L7
United Kingdom Overseas Territory.
northamerica 118–119, 140
Turks Islands Turks and Caicos Is 127 L7
Turku Fin. 33 F3
Turkwel watercourse Kenya 96 C4
Turlock U.S.A. 136 B3
Turlock Lake U.S.A. 136 B3
Turmalina Brazil 151 D6
Turnagain r. Canada 122 E3

Turnagain, Cape N.Z. **113** D3
Turnbull, Mount U.S.A. **137** G5
Turneffe Islands Belize **138** G5
Turner *r.* Australia **108** B5
Turner U.S.A. **130** B
Turner River Australia **108** E4
Turner's Peninsula Sierra Leone **92** B4
Turnhout Belgium **36** B3
Turnor Lake Canada **123** I3
Turnor Lake *l.* Canada **123** I3
Turnov Czech Rep. **37** G3
Tŭrnovo Bulg. *see* **Veliko Tŭrnovo**
Turnu Măgurele Romania **46** D3
Turnu Severin Romania *see* **Drobeta - Turnu Severin**
Turon *r.* Australia **112** D4
Turones France *see* **Tours**
Turopolje *plain* Croatia **44** E2
Turpan China **70** G3

▶**Turpan Pendi** *depr.* China **70** G3
Lowest point in northern Asia.

Turriff U.K. **34** E3
Turris Libisonis *Sardinia* Italy *see* **Porto Torres**
Tursāq Iraq **79** F4
Turtkul' Uzbek. **70** B3
Turtleford Canada **123** I4
Turtle Island Fiji *see* **Vatoa**
Turtle Islands Phil. **59** G1
Turtle Lake Canada **123** I4
Turugart Pass China/Kyrg. **70** E3
Turugart Shankou *pass* China/Kyrg. *see* **Turugart Pass**
Turukhansk Rus. Fed. **27** I3
Turvo Brazil **151** B9
Tusayan U.S.A. **137** F4
Tuscaloosa U.S.A. **129** B5
Tuscany *admin. reg.* Italy *see* **Toscana**
Tuscany *reg.* Italy **44** C3
Tuscarawas *r.* U.S.A. **130** C3
Tuscarora Mountains *hills* U.S.A. **130** C3
Tuscola U.S.A. **128** A4
Tuskegee U.S.A. **129** B5
Tussey Mountains *hills* U.S.A. **130** D3
Tuszyn Poland **37** I3
Tutak Turkey **79** E3
Tutayev Rus. Fed. **28** F4
Tutera Spain *see* **Tudela**
Tuticorin India **72** C4
Tutoh *r. Sarawak* Malaysia **59** F2
Tutong Brunei **59** F1
Tutova *r.* Romania **46** E1
Tutrakan Bulg. **46** E2
Tuttle Creek Reservoir U.S.A. **132** B4
Tuttlingen Germany **36** D5
Tutuala East Timor **108** D2
Tutubu P.N.G. **111** G1
Tutubu Tanz. **97** B6
Tutuila *i.* American Samoa **107** H3
Tutume Botswana **99** E4
Tutunendo Col. **146** B3
Tutupaca, Volcán *vol.* Peru **148** C4
Tuun-bong *mt.* N. Korea **64** A4
Tuusniemi Fin. **32** H3
Tuusula Fin. **33** G3
Tuva *aut. rep.* Rus. Fed. *see* **Tyva, Respublika**
▶**Tuvalu** *country* S. Pacific Ocean **107** G2
oceania 104–105, 114
Tuvana-i-Colo *i.* Fiji **107** H4
Tuvana-i-Tholo *i.* Fiji *see* **Tuvana-i-Colo**
Tuve Sweden **33** C4
Tuvinskaya A.S.S.R. *aut. rep.* Rus. Fed. *see* **Tyva, Respublika**
Tuwau *r.* Indon. **59** G2
Tuwayq, Jabal *hills* Saudi Arabia **76** D4
Tuwayq, Jabal *mts* Saudi Arabia **76** D5
Ţuwayyil ash Shihāq *mt.* Jordan **77** C4
Tuwwal Saudi Arabia **89** H4
Tuxer Gebirge *mts* Austria **36** E5
Tuxpan Mex. **126** F8
Tuxpan Mex. **126** G7
Tuxtla Gutiérrez Mex. **138** F5
Túy Spain *see* **Tui**
Tuya Lake Canada **122** D3
Tuy Duc Vietnam **61** D5
Tuyên Quang Vietnam **60** D3
Tuy Hoa Vietnam **61** E5
Tuymazy Rus. Fed. **28** J5
Tuz, Lake *salt l.* Turkey **78** C3
Tuz Gölü *salt l.* Turkey *see* **Tuz, Lake**
Tŭzha Bulg. **46** D3
Tuzha Rus. Fed. **28** H4
Tuz Khurmātū Iraq **79** F4
Tuzla Bos.-Herz. **44** G2
Tuzla Romania **46** F2
Tuzla Turkey **78** C3
Tuzla *r.* Turkey **79** E3
Tuzlov *r.* Rus. Fed. **29** G7
Tuzu *r.* Myanmar **60** A2
Tuzugu *well* Libya **88** C4
Tvärålund Sweden **32** E2
Tvedestrand Norway **33** C4
Tver' Rus. Fed. **28** E4
Tver Oblast *admin. div.* Rus. Fed. *see* **Tverskaya Oblast'**
Tverskaya Oblast' *admin. div.* Rus. Fed. **31** M1
Tvøroyri Faroe Is **34** [inset]
Tvŭrditsa Bulg. **46** D3
Twardogóra Poland **37** H3
Tweed Canada **131** E1
Tweed *r.* U.K. **34** E4
Tweed Heads Australia **112** E3
Tweedie Canada **123** I4
Twee Rivier Namibia **98** C5
Twentynine Palms U.S.A. **137** D4
Twillingate Canada **125** K3
Twin Bridges U.S.A. **136** B2
Twin Buttes Reservoir U.S.A. **133** A6
Twin Falls Canada **125** H2
Twin Falls U.S.A. **134** D4
Twingi Zambia **95** F7
Twin Heads *hill* Australia **108** D5
Twin Mountain U.S.A. **131** H1
Twin Peak U.S.A. **136** B2
Twisp U.S.A. **134** B2
Twitya *r.* Canada **122** D1
Two Butte Creek *r.* U.S.A. **132** A4
Two Harbors U.S.A. **132** D2
Two Hills Canada **123** I4
Two Rivers U.S.A. **132** E2
Tyan' Shan' *mts* China/Kyrg. *see* **Tien Shan**
Tyao *r.* India/Myanmar **75** G5
Tyatya, Vulkan *vol.* Rus. Fed. **64** F3
Tychy Poland **37** I3
Tyczyn Poland **37** K4
Tydal Norway **32** C3
Tyddewi U.K. *see* **St David's**
Tygart Valley U.S.A. **130** D4
Tygda Rus. Fed. **64** A1
Tygda *r.* Rus. Fed. **64** A1
Tyinkrysset Norway **33** C3
Tykhero Greece **46** E4
Tykocin Poland **37** K2
Tyler U.S.A. **133** C5
Tylertown U.S.A. **133** D6
Tym' *r.* Rus. Fed. **64** E2
Tymovskoye Rus. Fed. **64** E2
Tympaki Greece **47** D7
Tynda Rus. Fed. **27** M4
Tyndall U.S.A. **132** B3
Tyndinskiy Rus. Fed. *see* **Tynda**
Tyndrum U.K. **34** D3
Tyne *r.* U.K. **34** E3
Tyngsjö Sweden **33** D3
Týn nad Vltavou Czech Rep. **37** G4
Tynset Norway **33** C3
Tyr Lebanon *see* **Tyre**
Tyras Ukr. *see* **Bilhorod-Dnistrovs'kyy**
Tyre Lebanon **77** B3
Tyree, Mount Antarctica **167** L1
Tyrifjorden *l.* Norway **33** C3
Tyrma Rus. Fed. **64** C2
Tyrma *r.* Rus. Fed. **64** B2
Tyrnavos Greece **47** C5
Tyrnyauz Rus. Fed. **79** E2
Tyrone U.S.A. **130** D3
Tyrrell, Lake *dry lake* Australia **112** B4
Tyrrell Lake Canada **123** J2
Tyrrhenian Sea France/Italy **45** C4
Tyrus Lebanon *see* **Tyre**
Tysnesøy *i.* Norway **33** B4
Tyson Wash *watercourse* U.S.A. **137** E5
Tysse Norway **33** B3
Tytuvėnai Lith. **33** F5
Tyubelyakh Rus. Fed. **27** O3
Tyub-Karagan, Mys *pt* Kazakh. **79** G1
Tyukalinsk Rus. Fed. **26** H4
Tyulen'i, Ostrova *is* Kazakh. **29** I7
Tyul'gan Rus. Fed. **29** K5
Tyul'kino Rus. Fed. **28** K4
Tyumen' Rus. Fed. **26** G4
Tyumen'-Aryk Kazakh. *see* **Tomenaryk**
Tyung *r.* Rus. Fed. **27** M3
Tyuratam Kazakh. *see* **Baykonur**
Tyva, Respublika *aut. rep.* Rus. Fed. **62** F1
Tywi *r.* U.K. **35** D6
Tzaneen S. Africa **99** F4

↓ U

Uacauyén Venez. **147** F3
Uaco Congo Angola *see* **Waku-Kungo**
Uainambi Brazil **146** D4
Uamanda Angola **95** D9
Uape Moz. **99** H3
Uara Brazil **147** E5
Uarc, Ras *c.* Morocco *see* **Trois Fourches, Cap des**
Uari Brazil **147** G6
Uarini Brazil **147** E5
Uaroo Australia **108** A5
Uaruma Brazil **146** D4
Uasadi-jidi, Sierra *mts* Venez. **147** E3
Uatumã *r.* Brazil **147** G5
Uauá Brazil **150** E4
Uaupés Brazil **146** E5
Uaupés *r.* Brazil **146** E4
U'aywij *well* Saudi Arabia **89** J2
U'aywij, Wādī al *watercourse* Saudi Arabia **79** E5
Ub Yugo. **46** B2
Ubá Brazil **151** D7
Ubaid *well* Sudan **89** E6
Ubaitaba Brazil **150** E5
Ubal Karabaur *hills* Uzbek. **76** F1
Ubangi *r.* Cent. Afr. Rep./Dem. Rep. Congo **94** C5
Ubangi-Shari *country* Africa *see* **Central African Republic**
Ubauro Pak. **81** G4
Ubayyiḍ, Wādī al *watercourse* Iraq/Saudi Arabia **79** E4
Ube Japan **65** B6
Úbeda Spain **42** E3
Ubenazomozi Tanz. **97** C6
Uberaba Brazil **149** I4
Uberlândia Brazil **149** H4
Überlingen Germany **36** D5
Ubin, Pulau *i.* Sing. **58** [inset]
Ubinskoye, Ozero *l.* Rus. Fed. **26** I4
Ubly U.S.A. **130** B2
Ubolratna Reservoir Thai. **60** C4
Ubombo S. Africa **99** G5
Ubon Ratchathani Thai. **61** D5
Ubori Sudan **94** F3
Ubrique Spain **42** D4
Ubundu Dem. Rep. Congo **94** E5
Ucar Azer. **79** F2
Ucayali *dept* Peru **148** B2
Ucayali *r.* Peru **146** C6
Ucero *r.* Spain **42** E2
Uch Pak. **81** G4
Uch-Adzhi Turkm. **81** E2
Üchajy Turkm. *see* **Uch-Adzhi**
Üchān Iran **80** B2
Ucharal Kazakh. **70** F2
Uchiura-wan *b.* Japan **64** E4
Uchiza Peru **148** A2
Uchkuduk Uzbek. **70** B3
Uchkyay Uzbek. **81** F2
Uchquduq Uzbek. *see* **Uchkuduk**
Uchte *r.* Germany **36** E2
Uchto *r.* Pak. **81** F5
Uchur *r.* Rus. Fed. **27** N4
Uckfield U.K. **35** G6
Ucluelet Canada **122** E5
Uda *r.* Rus. Fed. **27** N4
Udachnoye Rus. Fed. **29** H7
Udachnyy Rus. Fed. **27** L3
Udagamandalam India **72** C4
Udaipur *Rajasthan* India **74** B4
Udaipur *Tripura* India **75** F5
Udaipura India **74** C5
Udaipur Garhi Nepal **75** E4
Udalguri India **75** G4
Udanti *r.* India/Myanmar **73** D1
Uda Walawe Reservoir Sri Lanka **72** D5
Udayagiri India **72** C3
Uddeholm Sweden **33** D3
Uddevalla Sweden **33** C4
Uddjaure *l.* Sweden **32** E2
Uden Neth. **36** B3
Udgir India **72** C2
Udhagamandalam India *see* **Udagamandalam**
Udhampur Jammu and Kashmir **74** B2
Udimskiy Rus. Fed. **28** H3
Udine Italy **44** D1
Udmalaippettai India *see* **Udumalaippettai**
Udmurtia *aut. rep.* Rus. Fed. *see* **Udmurtskaya Respublika**
Udmurtskaya A.S.S.R. *aut. rep.* Rus. Fed. *see* **Udmurtskaya Respublika**
Udmurtskaya Respublika *aut. rep.* Rus. Fed. **28** J4
Udomlya Rus. Fed. **28** E4
Udon Thani Thai. **60** C4
Udskaya Guba *b.* Rus. Fed. **54** F1
Udumalaippettai India **72** C4
Udupi India **72** B3
Udyl', Ozero *l.* Rus. Fed. **64** D1
Udzhary Azer. *see* **Ucar**
Uéa *i.* New Caledonia *see* **Ouvéa**
Uecker *r.* Germany **37** G2
Ueckermünde Germany **37** G2
Ueda Japan **65** D5
Uekuli Indon. **57** F6
Uele *r.* Dem. Rep. Congo **94** D3
Uelen Rus. Fed. **27** S3
Uel'kal' Rus. Fed. **27** S3
Uelzen Germany **36** E2
Uere *r.* Dem. Rep. Congo **94** E4
Ufa Rus. Fed. **28** J5
Uftyuga *r.* Rus. Fed. **28** H3
Ugab *watercourse* Namibia **98** B4
Ugāle Latvia **33** F4
Ugalla *r.* Tanz. **97** A6
▶**Uganda** *country* Africa **96** B4
africa 86–87, 100
Ugar *r.* Bos.-Herz. **44** F2
Uggdal Norway **33** B3
Ughelli Nigeria **93** G4
Ugine France **39** G4
Uglegorsk Rus. Fed. **64** E2
Uglekamensk Rus. Fed. **64** C4
Ugleural'skiy Rus. Fed. **28** K4
Uglich Rus. Fed. **28** F4
Ugljan *i.* Croatia **44** E2
Uglovoye *Amurskaya Oblast'* Rus. Fed. **64** B2
Uglovoye *Primorskiy Kray* Rus. Fed. **64** C4
Ugol'noye Rus. Fed. **27** O3
Ugolnyy Rus. Fed. *see* **Beringovskiy**
Ugol'nyye Kopi Rus. Fed. **27** R3
Ugra Rus. Fed. **29** E5
Ugut Rus. Fed. **26** H3
Uherské Hradiště Czech Rep. **37** H4
Uhlava *r.* Czech Rep. **37** F4
Uibhist a' Deas *i.* U.K. *see* **South Uist**
Uibhist a' Tuath *i.* U.K. *see* **North Uist**
Uig U.K. **34** C3
Uige Angola **95** B6
Uige *prov.* Angola **95** B6
Uijŏngbu S. Korea **65** A5
Uiju N. Korea **65** A4
Uil Kazakh. **29** J6
Uil *r.* Kazakh. **29** J6
Uimaharju Fin. **32** H3
Uinkaret Plateau U.S.A. **137** F3
Uinskoye Rus. Fed. **28** K4
Uinta *r.* U.S.A. **137** H1
Uinta Mountains U.S.A. **137** G1
Uis Mine Namibia **98** B4
Uitenhage S. Africa **98** E7
Uithuizen Neth. **36** C2
Ujhani India **74** C4
Uji Japan **65** C6
Uji-guntō *is* Japan **65** B7
Ujiyamada Japan *see* **Ise**
Ujjain India **74** B5
Ujohbilang Indon. **59** F2
Ujście Poland **37** H2
Ujung Kulon National Park Indon. **58** D4
Ujung Pandang Indon. *see* **Makassar**
Ujvidék Yugo. *see* **Novi Sad**
Ukal Sagar *l.* India **74** B5
Ukata Nigeria **93** G3
Ukerewe Island Tanz. **96** B5
Ukhaydir *tourist site* Iraq **79** E4
Ukhdūd *tourist site* Saudi Arabia **76** C6
Ukholovo Rus. Fed. **29** G5
Ukhrul India **75** G4
Ukhta *Respublika Kareliya* Rus. Fed. *see* **Kalevala**
Ukhta *Respublika Komi* Rus. Fed. **28** J3
Ukiah U.S.A. **136** A2
Ukimbo Tanz. **97** B6
Ukkusissat Greenland **121** N2
Ukmergė Lith. **33** G5

▶**Ukraine** *country* Europe **29** D6
2nd largest country in Europe.
europe 24–25, 48

Ukrainskaya S.S.R. *country* Europe *see* **Ukraine**
Ukrayina *country* Europe *see* **Ukraine**
Ukrina *r.* Bos.-Herz. **44** F2
Uku Angola **95** B7
Uku-jima *i.* Japan **65** B6
Ukuma Angola **95** B8
Ukwi Botswana **98** D4
Ula Turkey **47** F6
Ulaanbaatar Mongolia *see* **Ulan Bator**
Ulaangom Mongolia **62** E2
Ulan China **70** I4

▶**Ulan Bator** Mongolia **63** H2
Capital of Mongolia.

Ulan Erge Rus. Fed. **29** H7
Ulanhad China *see* **Chifeng**
Ulanhot China **63** K2
Ulan-Khol Rus. Fed. **29** H7
Ulan-Ude Rus. Fed. **27** K4
Ulan Ul Hu *l.* China **70** H5
Ulaş Turkey **78** D3
Ulaş *Tekirdağ* Turkey **46** E4
Ulaya Tanz. **97** C6
Ulbroka Latvia **33** G4
Ulchin S. Korea **65** B5
Ulcinj Yugo. **46** A4
Uleåborg Fin. *see* **Oulu**
Ulefoss Norway **33** C4
Ulfborg Denmark **33** C4
Ulhasnagar India **72** B2
Uliastai China **63** J2
Uliastay Mongolia **62** F2
Ulie *atoll* Micronesia *see* **Woleai**
Ulindi *r.* Dem. Rep. Congo **94** E5
Ulithi *atoll* Micronesia **57** I3
Ülkenözen *r.* Kazakh./Rus. Fed. *see* **Bol'shoy Uzen'**
Ulla *r.* Spain **42** B1
Ulladulla Australia **112** D4
Ullapool U.K. **34** D3
Ullatti Sweden **32** F2
Ulldecona Spain **43** G2
Ulloma Bol. **148** C4
Ullŭng-do *i.* S. Korea **65** B5
Ulm Germany **36** D4
Ul'ma *r.* Rus. Fed. **64** B2
Ulongue Moz. **97** B8
Ulooloo Australia; **Uloowaranie, Lake** *salt flat* Australia **111** D5
Ulricehamn Sweden **33** D4
Ulsan S. Korea **65** B6
Ulsberg Norway **32** C3
Ulsta U.K. **34** F1
Ulsteinvik Norway **32** B3
Ulster *reg.* Rep. of Ireland/U.K. **34** C4
Ulster U.S.A. **131** E3
Ultima Australia **112** B4
Ultraoriental, Cordillera *mts* Peru **148** B2
Ulu Sudan **96** B2
Ulúa *r.* Hond. **138** G5
Ulubat Gölü *l.* Turkey **78** B2
Ulubey Turkey **78** B3
Uluborlu Turkey **78** B3
Uluçay *r.* Turkey **79** E3
Uludağ *mt.* Turkey **78** B2
Uludağ Milli Parkı *nat. park* Turkey **47** F4
Ulugqat China *see* **Wuqia**
Ulu Kali, Gunung *mt.* Malaysia **58** C2
Ulukışla Turkey **78** C3
Ulundi S. Africa **99** G5
Ulungur Hu *l.* China **70** G2
Uluqsaqtuuq Canada *see* **Holman**
▶**Uluru** *hill* Australia **110** B5
oceania 114
Uluru-Kata Tjuta National Park Australia **110** B5
Ulus Dağı *mt.* Turkey **47** F5
Ulutau, Gory *mts* Kazakh. **70** C2
Ulverston U.K. **35** E4
Ulvsjön Sweden **33** E3
Ul'yanovo Uzbek. **81** G1
Ul'yanovsk Rus. Fed. **29** I5
Ul'yanovskaya Oblast' *admin. div.* Rus. Fed. **29** H5
Ulyanovsk Oblast *admin. div.* Rus. Fed. *see* **Ul'yanovskaya Oblast'**
Ulysses *KS* U.S.A. **132** A4
Ulysses *KY* U.S.A. **130** B5
Umag Croatia **44** D2
Umala Bol. **148** D4
'Umān *country* Asia *see* **Oman**
Uman' Ukr. **29** D6
Umango, Cerro *mt.* Arg. **152** C2
'Umarī, Qa' al *salt pan* Jordan **77** C4
Umaria India **74** D5
Umarkhed India **72** C2
Umarkot India **73** D2
Umarkot Pak. **81** G5
Umaroona, Lake *salt flat* Australia **110** D5
Umarpada India **74** B5
Umatilla U.S.A. **134** C3
Umba Rus. Fed. **28** E2
Umbagog Lake U.S.A. **131** H1
Umbakumba Australia **110** D2
Umbeara Australia **110** C5
Umbelasha *watercourse* Sudan **94** E2
Umbertide Italy **44** D3
Umboi *i.* P.N.G. **106** D2
Umbria *admin. reg.* Italy **44** D3
Umeå Sweden **32** F3
Umeälven *r.* Sweden **32** F3
Umet Rus. Fed. **29** G5
Umfreville Lake Canada **123** M5
Umfuli *r.* Zimbabwe *see* **Mupfure**
Umiiviip Kangertiva *inlet* Greenland **121** O3
Umingmaktok Canada **121** I3
Umiujaq Canada **124** E1
Umlazi S. Africa **99** F6
Umma *tourist site* Iraq **79** F5
Umm ad Daraj, Jabal *mt.* Jordan **77** B3
Umm al Birak Saudi Arabia **89** H4
Umm al Qaiwain U.A.E. *see* **Umm al Qaywayn**
Umm al Qaywayn U.A.E. **80** C5
Umm ar Raqabah, Khabrat *imp. l.* Saudi Arabia **77** C5
Umm as Samīm *salt flat* Oman **76** F5
Umm at Qalbān Saudi Arabia **89** I3
Umm Badr Sudan **89** E6
Umm Dam Sudan **89** F6
Umm Keddada Sudan **89** E6
Umm Lajj Saudi Arabia **89** H3
Umm Mafrūḍ, Jabal *mt.* Egypt **77** B5
Umm Mukhbār, Jabal *hill* Saudi Arabia **89** H4
Umm Nukhaylah *hill* Saudi Arabia **77** D5
Umm Nukhaylah *well* Saudi Arabia **77** B5
Umm Qaşr Iraq **79** F5
Umm Qurein *well* Sudan **89** F5
Umm Rumeila *well* Sudan **89** F6
Umm Ruwaba Sudan **89** F6
Umm Sa'ad Libya **88** E2
Umm Sa'īd Qatar **80** B5
Umm Saiyala Sudan **89** F6
Umm Şalāl 'Alī Qatar **80** B5
Umm Shaitiya *well* Jordan **77** C5
Umm Shugeira Sudan **89** F6
Umm Tināşşib, Jabal *mt.* Egypt **77** A5
Umnak Island U.S.A. **120** C4
Umpilua Moz. **97** C8
Umpqua *r.* U.S.A. **134** A4
Umred India **72** C1
Umtali Zimbabwe *see* **Mutare**
Umtata S. Africa **99** F6
Umuahia Nigeria **93** G4
Umuarama Brazil **151** A7
Umurbey Turkey **47** E4
Umvuma Zimbabwe *see* **Mvuma**
Umzingwani *r.* Zimbabwe *see* **Mzingwani**
Una *r.* Bos.-Herz./Croatia **44** F2
Una Brazil **150** E5
Una *r.* Brazil **150** F4
Una India **74** C3
'Unāb, Jabal al *hill* Jordan **77** C5
'Unāb, Wādī al *watercourse* Jordan **77** C4
Unac *r.* Bos.-Herz. **44** F2
Unadilla U.S.A. **131** F2
Unadilla *r.* U.S.A. **131** F2
Unaí Brazil **151** C6
Unai Pass Afgh. **81** G3
Unalaska U.S.A. **120** C4
Unalaska Island U.S.A. **120** C4
Unari Fin. **32** G2
'Unayzah Saudi Arabia **89** I3
'Unayzah, Jabal *hill* Iraq **79** D4
Unchahra India **74** D4
Uncompahgre Plateau U.S.A. **137** H2
Undara National Park Australia **111** F3
Unden *l.* Sweden **33** D4
Underberg S. Africa **99** F6
Underbool Australia **112** B4
Undva Estonia **33** F4
Unecha Rus. Fed. **31** M2
Uneiuxi *r.* Brazil **147** E5
Unga Island U.S.A. **120** C4
Ungarie Australia **112** C4
Ungava, Baie d' *b.* Canada *see* **Ungava Bay**
Ungava, Péninsule d' *pen.* Canada **121** L3
Ungava Bay Canada **125** H1
Ungava Peninsula Canada *see* **Ungava, Péninsule d'**
Ungeny Moldova *see* **Ungheni**
Unggi N. Korea **63** M3
Ungheni Moldova **29** C7
Unguana Moz. **99** G4
Unguja North *admin. reg.* Tanz. *see* **Zanzibar North**
Unguja South *admin. reg.* Tanz. *see* **Zanzibar South**
Unguja West *admin. reg.* Tanz. *see* **Zanzibar West**
Unguz, Solonchakovyye Vpadiny *salt flat* Turkm. **81** D2
Üngüz Angyrsyndaky Garagum *des.* Turkm. *see* **Zaunguzskiye Karakumy**
Ungvár Ukr. *see* **Uzhhorod**
Ungwana Bay Kenya **96** D5
Uni Rus. Fed. **28** I4
União da Vitória Brazil **151** B8
União do Marará Brazil **147** F5
União dos Palmares Brazil **150** F4
Uniara India **74** C4
Uniejów Poland **37** I3
Unije *i.* Croatia **44** E2
Unimak Island U.S.A. **120** C4
Unini *r.* Brazil **147** F5
Unión Arg. **152** D3
Union *MO* U.S.A. **127** H4
Union *OR* U.S.A. **134** C3
Union *WV* U.S.A. **130** C5
Unión, Bahía *b.* Arg. **152** E4
Union, Mount U.S.A. **137** F4
Union City *OH* U.S.A. **130** A3
Union City *PA* U.S.A. **130** D3
Union City *TN* U.S.A. **128** A4

▶**Union of Soviet Socialist Republics**
Divided in 1991 into 15 independent nations: Armenia, Azerbaijan, Belarus, Estonia, Georgia, Kazakhstan, Kyrgyzstan, Latvia, Lithuania, Moldova, the Russian Federation, Tajikistan, Turkmenistan, Ukraine and Uzbekistan.

Union Springs *AL* U.S.A. **129** B5
Union Springs *NY* U.S.A. **131** E2
Uniontown U.S.A. **130** D4
Unionville *MI* U.S.A. **130** B2
Unionville *MO* U.S.A. **132** C3
Unionville *VA* U.S.A. **130** E4
▶**United Arab Emirates** *country* Asia **76** E5
asia 52–53, 82
United Arab Republic *country* Africa *see* **Egypt**

▶**United Kingdom** *country* Europe **34** F4
3rd most populous country in Europe.
europe 24–25, 48

United Provinces *state* India *see* **Uttar Pradesh**

▶**United States of America** *country* N. America **126** E3
Most populous country in North America and 3rd in the world. 3rd largest country in the world and 2nd in North America.
northamerica 118–119, 140
world 8–9, 16–17

United States Range *mts* Canada **121** M1
Unity Canada **123** I4
Unjab *watercourse* Namibia **98** B4
Unjha India **74** B5
Unnao India **74** D4
Ŭnsan N. Korea **65** A5
Unst *i.* U.K. **34** F1
Unstrut *r.* Germany **36** E3
Untari India **75** D4
Unteres Odertal *nat. park* Germany **37** G2
Unturán, Sierra de *mts* Venez. **147** E4
Unuk *r.* Canada/U.S.A. **122** D3
Unuli Horog China **75** F2
Un'ya *r.* Rus. Fed. **28** K3
Unzen-dake *vol.* Japan **65** B6
Unzha Rus. Fed. **28** H4
Úpa *r.* Czech Rep. **37** G3
Upar Ghat *reg.* India **75** E5
Upata Venez. **147** F2
Upemba, Lac *l.* Dem. Rep. Congo **95** E7
Upernavik Greenland **121** N2
Upía *r.* Col. **146** C3
Upington S. Africa **98** D6
Upinniemi Fin. **33** G3
Upland U.S.A. **136** D4
Upleta India **74** A5
Upoloksha Rus. Fed. **32** H2
Upolu *i.* Samoa **107** H3
Upolu Point U.S.A. **135** [inset] Z1
Upper Alkali Lake U.S.A. **134** B4
Upper Arlington U.S.A. **130** B3
Upper Arrow Lake Canada **122** G5
Upper Chindwin Myanmar *see* **Mawlaik**
Upper East *admin. reg.* Ghana **93** E3
Upper Fraser Canada **122** F4
Upper Garry Lake Canada **123** K1
Upper Hutt N.Z. **113** C3
Upper Klamath Lake U.S.A. **134** B4
Upper Liard Canada **122** D2
Upper Lough Erne *l.* U.K. **35** C4
Upper Marlboro U.S.A. **131** E4
Upper Missouri Breaks National Monument *nat. park* U.S.A. **134** E3
Upper Nile *state* Sudan **96** B2
Upper Peirce Reservoir Sing. **58** [inset]
Upper Red Lake U.S.A. **132** C1
Upper Sandusky U.S.A. **130** B3
Upper Saranac Lake U.S.A. **131** F1
Upper Seal Lake Canada *see* **Iberville, Lac d'**
Upper Tunguska *r.* Rus. Fed. *see* **Angara**
Upper Volta *country* Africa *see* **Burkina**
Upper West *admin. reg.* Ghana **93** E3
Uppinangadi India **72** B3
Upplands-Väsby Sweden **33** E4
Uppsala Sweden **33** E4
Uppsala *county* Sweden **33** E3
Upsala Canada **124** B3
Upshi Jammu and Kashmir **74** C2
Upstart, Cape Australia **111** F3
'Uqayqah, Wādī *watercourse* Jordan **77** B4
'Uqayribāt Syria **77** C2
Uqlat al 'Udhaybah *well* Iraq **79** F5
'Uqlat aş Şuqūr Saudi Arabia **89** I3
Urabá, Golfo de *b.* Col. **146** B2
Urad Qianqi China *see* **Xishanzui**
Ūrāf Iran **80** D4
Ura-Guba Rus. Fed. **32** I1
Urakam India **72** C4
Ural *hill* Australia **112** C4
Ural *r.* Kazakh./Rus. Fed. **29** I7
Uralla Australia **112** D3
Ural Mountains Rus. Fed. **28** K2
Uralovka Rus. Fed. **64** B1
Ural'sk Kazakh. **26** F4
Ural'skaya Oblast' *admin. div.* Kazakh. *see* **Zapadnyy Kazakhstan**
Ural'skiye Gory *mts* Rus. Fed. *see* **Ural Mountains**
Ural'skiy Khrebet *mts* Rus. Fed. *see* **Ural Mountains**
Urambo Tanz. **97** B6
Uran India **72** B2
Urana Australia **112** C4
Urandangi Australia **110** D4
Urandi Brazil **150** D5
Uranium City Canada **123** I3
Urapunga Australia **110** C2
Urapuntja Australia **110** C4
Uraricoera Brazil **147** F4
Uraricoera *r.* Brazil **147** F4
Urartu *country* Asia *see* **Armenia**
Uras *Sardinia* Italy **45** B5
Ura-Tyube Tajik. *see* **Üroteppa**
Uravakonda India **72** C3
Uravan U.S.A. **137** H2
Uray Rus. Fed. **26** G3
Uray'irah Saudi Arabia **80** B5
'Urayq Sāqān *des.* Saudi Arabia **80** A5
Urbana *IL* U.S.A. **132** D3
Urbana *OH* U.S.A. **130** B3
Urbania Italy **44** D3
Urbel *r.* Spain **42** E1
Urbino Italy **44** D3
Urbinum Italy *see* **Urbino**
Urbión *mt.* Spain **37** I3
Urbs Vetus Italy *see* **Orvieto**
Urcos Peru **148** C3
Urda Spain **42** E3
Ur'devarri *hill* Fin./Norway *see* **Urtivaara**
Urdoma Rus. Fed. **28** I3
Urdyuzhskoye, Ozero *l.* Rus. Fed. **28** I2
Ure *r.* U.K. **35** F4
Urecheşti Romania **46** E1
Uren' Rus. Fed. **28** H4
Urengoy Rus. Fed. **26** H3
Urenosi *mt.* Norway **33** B4
Uréparapara *i.* Vanuatu **107** F3
Urewera National Park N.Z. **113** D2
Urfa Turkey *see* **Şanlıurfa**
Urga Mongolia *see* **Ulan Bator**
Urgal *r.* Rus. Fed. **64** C2
Urganch Uzbek. *see* **Urgench**
Urgench Uzbek. **76** G1
Ürgüp Turkey **78** C3
Urgut Uzbek. **81** F2
Urho Kekkosen kansallispuisto *nat. park* Fin. **32** G1
Uri Jammu and Kashmir **74** B2
Uribia Col. **146** C2
Urique *r.* Mex. **135** F8
Urisino Australia **112** B3
Urjala Fin. **33** F3
Urk Neth. **36** B2
Urkut Somalia **96** D4
Urla Turkey **78** A3
Urlaţi Romania **46** E2
Urluì *r.* Romania **46** D3
Urmai China **75** E3
Urmetan Tajik. **81** G2
Urmi *r.* Rus. Fed. **64** C2
Urmia Iran **80** A2
Urmia, Lake *salt l.* Iran **80** A2
Urmston Road *sea chan.* Hong Kong China **67** [inset]
Uromi Nigeria **93** G4
Uroševac Yugo. **46** B3
Urosozero Rus. Fed. **28** E3
Üroteppa Tajik. **81** G2
Urru Co *salt l.* China **75** E3
Ursat'yevskaya Uzbek. *see* **Khavast**
Urtivaara *hill* Fin./Norway **32** F1
Urt Moron China **75** G1
Uruáchic Mex. **135** E8
Uruaçu Brazil **150** B5
Uruana Brazil **149** H3
Uruapan *Baja California* Mex. **135** C7
Uruapan Mex. **126** F8
Urubaxi *r.* Brazil **147** E5
Urubu *r.* Brazil **147** G5
Urucara Brazil **147** G5
Urucu *r.* Brazil **147** F6
Uruçuí Brazil **150** C3
Uruçuí, Serra do *hills* Brazil **150** C4
Urucuia Brazil **150** C6
Urucuia *r.* Brazil **150** C6
Uruçuí Preto *r.* Brazil **150** C3
Urucum Brazil **149** F4
Urucurituba Brazil **147** G5
Uruguai *r.* Brazil **151** A8
Uruguaiana Brazil **152** F2
Uruguay *r.* Arg./Uruguay **152** F3
▶**Uruguay** *country* S. America **152** G3
southamerica 144–145, 154
Uruk *tourist site* Iraq *see* **Erech**
Urumchi China *see* **Ürümqi**
Ürümqi China **70** G3
Urundi *country* Africa *see* **Burundi**
Urup *r.* Rus. Fed. **29** G7
Urup, Ostrov *i.* Rus. Fed. **54** H2
Urupá *r.* Brazil **149** E2
Urussu Rus. Fed. **28** J5
Uruwira Tanz. **97** A6
Uryupinsk Rus. Fed. **29** G6
Urzhum Rus. Fed. **28** I4
Urziceni Romania **46** E2
Usa Japan **65** B6
Usa *r.* Rus. Fed. **28** K2
Uşak Turkey **78** B3
Uşak *prov.* Turkey **47** F5
Usakos Namibia **98** B4
Usambara Mountains Tanz. **97** C6
Usangu Flats *plain* Tanz. **97** B7
Usarp Mountains Antarctica **167** H2
Usborne, Mount Falkland Is **153** F7
Usedom Germany **37** F2
Usedom *i.* Germany **37** G2
Useless Loop Australia **109** A6
Usengi Kenya **96** B5
Usfān Saudi Arabia **89** H4
Ushakova, Ostrov *i.* Rus. Fed. **27** H1
Ushant *i.* France *see* **Ouessant, Île d'**
Usharal Kazakh. *see* **Ucharal**
Ushibuka Japan **65** B6
Ushirombo Tanz. **96** A5
Ushtobe Kazakh. **70** E2
Ush-Tyube Kazakh. *see* **Ushtobe**
Ushuaia Arg. **153** C8
Usina Brazil **150** A3
Usinsk Rus. Fed. **28** K2
Usk *r.* U.K. **35** E6
Uska India **75** D4
Uskoplje Bos.-Herz. *see* **Gornji Vakuf**
Üsküdar Turkey **78** B2
Usman' Rus. Fed. **29** F5
Usmas ezers *l.* Latvia **33** F4
Uso *r.* Spain **42** D3
Usogorsk Rus. Fed. **28** I3
Usol'ye-Sibirskoye Rus. Fed. **62** G1
Uspallata Arg. **152** C3
Uspen'ye Rus. Fed. **28** G4
Ussel France **38** E4
Ussuri *r.* Rus. Fed. **64** C2
Ussuriysk Rus. Fed. **64** B4
Ust'-Abakanskoye Rus. Fed. *see* **Abakan**
Ust'-Alekseyevo Rus. Fed. **28** H3
Usta Muhammad Pak. **74** A3
Ust'-Balyk Rus. Fed. *see* **Nefteyugansk**
Ust'-Barguzin Rus. Fed. **63** H1
Ust'-Donetskiy Rus. Fed. **29** G7
Ust'-Dzhegata Rus. Fed. **79** E1
Ust'-Dzhegutinskaya Rus. Fed. *see* **Ust'-Dzheguta**
Ustica, Isola di *i. Sicily* Italy **45** D5
Ust'-Ilimsk Rus. Fed. **27** K4
Ust'-Ilych Rus. Fed. **28** K3
Ústí nad Labem Czech Rep. **37** G3
Ústí nad Orlicí Czech Rep. **37** H4
Ustinov Rus. Fed. *see* **Izhevsk**
Ustirt *plat.* Kazakh./Uzbek. *see* **Ustyurt Plateau**
Ustka Poland **37** H1
Ust'-Kamchatsk Rus. Fed. **27** Q4
Ust'-Kamenogorsk Kazakh. **70** F2
Ust'-Kara Rus. Fed. **28** M1
Ust'-Kulom Rus. Fed. **28** J3
Ust'-Kut Rus. Fed. **27** K4
Ust'-Kuyga Rus. Fed. **27** N2
Ust'-Labinsk Rus. Fed. **29** F7
Ust'-Labinskaya Rus. Fed. *see* **Ust'-Labinsk**
Ust'-Luga Rus. Fed. **33** H4
Ust'-Lyzha Rus. Fed. **28** K2
Ust'-Maya Rus. Fed. **27** N3
Ust'-Nem Rus. Fed. **28** J3
Ust'-Nera Rus. Fed. **27** O3
Ust'-Olenek Rus. Fed. **27** L2
Ust'-Omchug Rus. Fed. **27** O3
Ust-Orda Buryat Autonomous Okrug *admin. div.* Rus. Fed. *see* **Ust'-Ordynskiy Buryatskiy Avtonomnyy Okrug**
Ust'-Ordynskiy Rus. Fed. **62** G1
Ust'-Ordynskiy Buryatskiy Avtonomnyy Okrug *admin. div.* Rus. Fed. **62** G1
Ust'-Port Rus. Fed. **27** I3
Ustrem Bulg. **46** E3
Ust'-Tsil'ma Rus. Fed. **28** J2
Ust'-Umalta Rus. Fed. **64** C2
Ust'-Ura Rus. Fed. **28** H3
Ust'-Usa Rus. Fed. **28** K2
Ust'-Vayen'ga Rus. Fed. **28** G3
Ust'-Voya Rus. Fed. **28** K2
Ust'ya *r.* Rus. Fed. **28** G3
Ust'ye Rus. Fed. **28** F4
Ustyurt, Plato *plat.* Kazakh./Uzbek. *see* **Ustyurt Plateau**
Ustyurt Plateau Kazakh./Uzbek. **70** A3
Ustyurt Platosi *plat.* Kazakh./Uzbek. *see* **Ustyurt Plateau**
Ustyuzhna Rus. Fed. **28** F4
Usulután El Salvador **138** G6
Usumbura Burundi *see* **Bujumbura**
Usun Apau, Dataran Tinggi *plat. Sarawak* Malaysia **59** F2
Uta Indon. **57** I6

Utah state U.S.A. 137 G2
Utah Lake U.S.A. 137 G1
Utajärvi Fin. 32 G2
Utashinai Rus. Fed. see Yuzhno-Kuril'sk
'Utaybah, Buḩayrat al imp. l. Syria 77 C3
Utayyiq Saudi Arabia 80 B5
Utebo Spain 43 F2
Utembo r. Angola 95 D9
Utena Lith. 33 G5
Utete Tanz. 97 C7
Uthai Thani Thai. 61 C5
Uthal Pak. 81 F5
Utiariti Brazil 149 F3
Utica NY U.S.A. 131 F2
Utica OH U.S.A. 130 B3
Utiel Spain 43 F3
Utikuma Lake Canada 123 H4
Utinga r. Brazil 150 D5
Utrata r. Poland 37 J2
Utraula India 75 D4
Utrecht Neth. 36 B2
Utrera Spain 42 D4
Utsjoki Fin. 32 G1
Utsunomiya Japan 65 D5
Utta Rus. Fed. 29 H7
Uttaradit Thai. 60 C4
Uttaranchal state India 74 C3
Uttarkashi India 74 C3
Uttar Pradesh state India 74 C4
Utupua i. Solomon Is 107 F3
Utva r. Kazakh. 29 J6
Uulu Estonia 33 G4
Uummannaq Greenland see Dundas
Uummannaq Greenland 121 N2
Uummannaq Fjord inlet Greenland 121 N2
Uummannarsuaq c. Greenland see Farewell, Cape
Urainen Fin. 32 G3
Uusikaupunki Fin. 33 F3
Uutapi Namibia 98 B3
Uva r. Col. 146 D4
Uva Rus. Fed. 28 J4
Uvac r. Bos.-Herz./Yugo. 46 A3
Uvalde U.S.A. 133 B6
Uvarovo Rus. Fed. 29 G6
Uvéa i. New Caledonia see Ouvéa
Uvinza Tanz. 97 A6
Uvira Dem. Rep. Congo 94 F5
Uvs Nuur salt l. Mongolia 62 E1
Uwajima Japan 65 C6
'Uwaynāt Wannīn Libya 88 B2
'Uwayriḑ, Ḩarrat al lava field Saudi Arabia 89 H3
Uwaysiț well Saudi Arabia 77 D4
Uweinat, Jebel mt. Sudan 88 E4
Uwi i. Indon. 59 D2
Uyar Rus. Fed. 27 J4
Uyo Nigeria 93 G4
Uyu Chaung r. Myanmar 60 A2
Uyun Saudi Arabia 80 B5
Uyuni Bol. 148 D5
Uyuni, Salar de salt flat Bol. 148 D5
Uza r. Rus. Fed. 29 H5
'Uzaym, Nahr al r. Iraq 79 F4
▶Uzbekistan country Asia 70 B3
asia 52–53, 82
Ŭzbekiston country Asia see Uzbekistan
Uzbekskaya S.S.R. country Asia see Uzbekistan
Uzbek S.S.R. country Asia see Uzbekistan
Uzerche France 38 D4
Uzès France 39 F4
Uzhgorod Ukr. see Uzhhorod
Uzhhorod Ukr. 31 J3
Užhorod Ukr. see Uzhhorod
Užice Yugo. 46 A3
Uzlovaya Rus. Fed. 29 F5
Uzola r. Rus. Fed. 28 G4
Uzun Uzbek. 81 G2
Uzun Ada i. Turkey 47 E5
Uzuncaburç Turkey 77 A1
Uzunköprü Turkey 78 A2

↓ V

Vaal r. S. Africa 99 D6
Vaala Fin. 32 G2
Vaalbos National Park S. Africa 98 E6
Vaal Dam S. Africa 99 F5
Vaalwater S. Africa 99 F5
Vaasa Fin. 32 F3
Vabkent Uzbek. 81 F1
Vác Hungary 37 I5
Vacaria Brazil 151 B9
Vacaria r. Mato Grosso do Sul Brazil 151 A7
Vacaria r. Minas Gerais Brazil 151 D6
Vacaville U.S.A. 136 B2
Väckelsång Sweden 33 D4
Vad Rus. Fed. 28 H5
Vad r. Rus. Fed. 29 G5
Vada India 72 B2
Vadakste r. Latvia/Lith. 33 F4
Vădeni Romania 46 E2
Vadi India 72 B3
Vadodara India 74 B5
Vadsø Norway 32 H1
▶Vaduz Liechtenstein 36 D5
Capital of Liechtenstein.
Værøy i. Norway 32 D2
Vaga r. Rus. Fed. 28 G3
Vågåmo Norway 33 C3
Vaganski Vrh mt. Croatia 44 E2
Vágar i. Faroe Is 34 [inset]
Vagnhärad Sweden 33 E4
Vägsele Sweden 32 E2
Vågsfjorden sea chan. Norway 32 E1
Váh r. Slovakia 37 I5
Vahhābī Iran 80 D4
Vahsel, Cape S. Georgia 153 [inset]
Vahto Fin. 33 F3
▶Vaiaku Tuvalu 107 G2
Capital of Tuvalu, on Funafuti atoll.
Vaida Estonia 28 C4
Vaiden U.S.A. 133 D5
Vaigai r. India 72 C4
Vaijapur India 72 B2
Väike-Maarja Estonia 33 G4
Vaikijaur Sweden 32 E2
Vaippar r. India 72 C4
Vair r. France 39 F2
Vairowal India 74 B3
Vaison-la-Romaine France 39 F4
Vaitupu i. Tuvalu 107 G2
Vajrakarur India see Kanur
Vajszló Hungary 44 F2
Vakaga pref. Cent. Afr. Rep. 94 D2
Vakaga r. Cent. Afr. Rep. 94 D2
Vakhsh Tajik. 81 G2
Vakhsh r. Tajik. 81 G2
Vakhstroy Tajik. see Vakhsh
Vakīlābād Iran 80 D4
Vaksdal Norway 33 B3
Valandovo Macedonia 46 C4
Valašské Meziříčí Czech Rep. 37 H4
Valaxa i. Greece 47 D5
Valbo Sweden 31 I1
Vâlcanului, Munţii mts Romania 46 C2
Valcheta Arg. 152 D5
Valdai Hills Rus. Fed. see Valdayskaya Vozvyshennost'
Valday Rus. Fed. 28 E4
Valdayskaya Vozvyshennost' hills Rus. Fed. 28 E4
Valdecañas, Embalse de resr Spain 42 D3
Valdemārpils Latvia 33 F4
Valdemarsvik Sweden 33 E4
Val-de-Meuse France 39 F2
Valdepeñas Spain 42 E3
Valderaduey r. Spain 42 D2
Valderas Spain 42 D1
Val-de-Reuil France 38 D2
▶Valdés, Península pen. Arg. 153 E5
Lowest point in South America.
southamerica 142–143
Valdez U.S.A. 120 E3
Valdivia Chile 152 B4
Valdivia Col. 146 C3
Val-d'Or Canada 124 E3
Valdosa mt. Spain 42 E1
Valdosta U.S.A. 129 C6
Valdres valley Norway 33 C3
Vale Georgia 79 E2
Vale U.S.A. 134 C3
Valemount Canada 122 G4
Valença Brazil 150 E5
Valença do Piauí Brazil 150 D3
Valençay France 38 D3
Valence Midi-Pyrénées France 38 D4
Valence Rhône-Alpes France 39 F4
Valencia Spain 43 F3
Valencia aut. comm. Spain 43 F3
Valencia Venez. 146 E2
Valencia, Golfo de g. Spain 43 G3
Valencia de Alcántara Spain 42 C3
Valencia de Don Juan Spain 42 D1
Valencia Island Rep. of Ireland 35 A6
Valenciana, Comunidad aut. comm. Spain see Valencia
Valenciennes France 39 E1
Vălenii de Munte Romania 46 E2
Valensole, Plateau de France 39 G5
Valentia Spain see Valencia
Valentine U.S.A. 132 A3
Valenza Italy 44 B2
Våler Norway 33 C3
Valera Venez. 146 D2
Valga Estonia 33 G4
Valinco, Golfe de b. Corsica France 44 B4
Valjevo Yugo. 46 A2
Valka Latvia 33 G4
Valkeakoski Fin. 33 G3
Valkyrie Dome ice feature Antarctica 167 D1
Vallabhipur India 74 A5
Valladolid Mex. 127 I7
Valladolid Spain 42 D2
Vallard, Lac l. Canada 125 G2
Valldal Norway 33 B3
Valle dept Col. 146 B4
Valle Norway 33 B4
Vallecito Arg. 152 D2
Valle d'Aosta admin. reg. Italy 44 A2
Valle de la Pascua Venez. 147 E2
Valle de Zaragoza Mex. 135 F8
Valledupar Col. 146 C2
Vallée-Jonction Canada 125 G4
Valle Fértil, Sierra de mts Arg. 152 C2
Valle Hermoso Mex. 133 B7
Vallejo U.S.A. 136 A2
Vallelunga Pratameno Sicily Italy 45 D6
Vallenar Chile 152 C2
▶Valletta Malta 45 E7
Capital of Malta.
Valley City U.S.A. 132 B2
Valley Falls U.S.A. 134 B4
Valley Head U.S.A. 130 C4
Valley of the Kings tourist site Egypt 89 G3
Valley Springs U.S.A. 136 B2
Valley Station U.S.A. 128 B4
Valley Stream U.S.A. 131 G3
Valleyview Canada 123 G4
Valley View U.S.A. 130 A5
Vallo della Lucania Italy 45 E4
Valls Spain 43 G2
Vallsta Sweden 33 E3
Val Marie Canada 134 F2
Valmaseda Spain see Balmaseda
Valmiera Latvia 33 G4
Valnera mt. Spain 42 E1
Valognes France 38 C2
Valona Albania see Vlorë
Valozhyn Belarus 29 C5
Valpaçοs Port. 42 C2
Val-Paradis Canada 124 E3
Valparai India 72 C4
Valparaíso Brazil 149 H5
Valparaíso Chile 152 C3
Valparaíso admin. reg. Chile 152 C3
Valparaiso U.S.A. 132 E3
Valpelline valley Italy 44 A2
Valpoi India 72 B3
Valpovo Croatia 44 G2
Valronquillo hill Spain 42 D3
Vals, Tanjung c. Indon. 57 I7
Valsad India 72 B1
Valshui Wash watercourse U.S.A. 135 D7
Valspan S. Africa 98 E5
Valtimo Fin. 32 H3
Valtou mts Greece 47 B5
Valua i. Vanuatu see Mota Lava
Valuyevka Rus. Fed. 29 G7
Valuyki Rus. Fed. 29 F6
Valverde del Camino Spain 42 C4
Vam Co Đông r. Vietnam 61 D6
Vam Co Tay r. Vietnam 61 D6
Vammala Fin. 33 F3
Vampula Fin. 33 F3
Vamsadhara r. India 73 E2
Vamvakas, Akra pt Greece 47 E5
Van Turkey 79 E3
Van, Lake salt l. Turkey 79 E3
Vanadzor Armenia 79 F2
Vanajavesi l. Fin. 33 G3
Vanån r. Sweden 33 D3
Vânători Romania 46 D1
Vanavara Rus. Fed. 27 K3
Van Buren AR U.S.A. 133 C5
Van Buren MO U.S.A. 132 D4
Van Buren OH U.S.A. see Kettering
Vanceburg U.S.A. 130 B4
Vanch Tajik. see Vanj
Vanchskiy Khrebet mts Tajik. see Vanj, Qatorkŭhi
Vancleve U.S.A. 130 B5
Vancouver Canada 134 B2
Vancouver U.S.A. 134 B3
Vancouver Island Canada 134 A2
Vanda Fin. see Vantaa
Vandalia IL U.S.A. 128 A4
Vandalia OH U.S.A. 130 A4
Vandavasi India 72 C3
Vandekerckhove Lake Canada 123 K3
Vanderhoof Canada 122 E4
Vanderkloof Dam resr S. Africa 98 E6
Vanderlin Island Australia 110 D2
Van Diemen, Cape N.T. Australia 110 B1
Van Diemen, Cape Qld Australia 111 D3
Van Diemen Gulf Australia 110 C1
Van Diemen's Land state Australia see Tasmania
Vändra Estonia 33 G4
Väne Latvia 33 F4
Väner, Lake Sweden see Vänern
▶Vänern l. Sweden 33 D4
4th largest lake in Europe.
europe 22–23
Vänersborg Sweden 33 D4
Vanga Kenya 97 C6
Vangaindrano Madag. 99 [inset] J4
Van Gölü salt l. Turkey see Van, Lake
Vangsvik Norway 32 E1
Vanguard Canada 123 J5
Van Horn U.S.A. 135 F7
Vanikoro Islands Solomon Is 107 F3
Vanil Noir mt. Switz. 39 G3
Vanimo P.N.G. 57 J6
Vanino Rus. Fed. 64 E2
Vanivilasa Sagara resr India 72 C3
Vaniyambadi India 72 C3
Vanj Tajik. 81 G2
Vanj, Qatorkŭhi mts Tajik. 81 G2
Vänjaurträsk Sweden 32 E2
Vânju Mare Romania 46 C2
Vankarem Rus. Fed. 27 S3
Vankavesi l. Fin. 33 F3
Vanna i. Norway 32 E1
Vännäs Sweden 32 E3
Vanne r. France 39 E2
Vannes France 38 B3
Vannes, Lac l. Canada 125 H2
Vannovka Kazakh. see Tura-Ryskulova
Van Rees, Pegunungan mts Indon. 57 I6
Vanrhynsdorp S. Africa 98 C6
Vanrook Australia 111 E3
Vansada India 72 B1
Vansant U.S.A. 130 B5
Vansbro Sweden 33 D3
Vanse Norway 33 B4
Vansittart Island Canada 121 K3
Vantaa Fin. 33 G3
Van Truer Tableland reg. Australia 109 C6
Vanua Balavu i. Fiji 107 H3
Vanua Lava i. Vanuatu 107 F3
Vanua Levu i. Fiji 107 G3
Vanua Mbalavu i. Fiji see Vanua Balavu
▶Vanuatu country S. Pacific Ocean 107 F3
oceania 104–105, 114
Vanua Valavo i. Fiji see Vanua Balavu
Van Wert U.S.A. 130 A3
Vanwyksvlei S. Africa 98 D6
Van Zylsrus S. Africa 98 D5
Vao, Embalse de resr Spain 42 C1
Var r. France 39 G5
Vara Estonia 33 G4
Varada r. India 72 C3
Varadero Cuba 129 C8
Varahi India 74 A5
Varaita r. Italy 44 A2
Varakļāni Latvia 33 G4
Varalé Côte d'Ivoire 92 E3
Varallo Italy 44 B2
Varāmīn Iran 80 B3
Varanasi India 75 D4
Varandey Rus. Fed. 28 K1
Varangerfjorden sea chan. Norway 32 H1
Varangerhalvøya pen. Norway 32 H1
Varanger-halvøya pen. Norway 32 H1
Varano, Lago di lag. Italy 44 E4
Varapayeva Belarus 33 G5
Varaždin Croatia 44 F1
Varazze Italy 44 B2
Varberg Sweden 33 D4
Varbla Estonia 33 F4
Varda Greece 47 B5
Vardak prov. Afgh. 81 G3
Vardannapet India 72 C2
Vardar r. Macedonia 46 C4
Varde Denmark 33 C5
Vardenis Armenia 79 F2
Vardø Norway 32 H1
Varel Germany 36 D2
Varela Arg. 152 D3
Varėna Lith. 33 G5
Vareš Bos.-Herz. 44 G2
Varese Italy 44 B2
Varfolomeyevka Rus. Fed. 64 C3
Vårgårda Sweden 33 D4
Vargem r. Brazil 150 E4
Vargem Grande Brazil 150 D2
Varginha Brazil 151 C7
Varkana Iran see Gorgān
Varkaus Fin. 32 G3
Varmahlíð Iceland 32 [inset]
Varmeln l. Sweden 33 D4
Värmland county Sweden 33 D4
Värmlandsnäs i. Sweden 33 D4
Varna Bulg. 46 E3
Varna r. India 72 B2
Värnamo Sweden 33 D4
Värnäs Sweden 33 D3
Varnavino Rus. Fed. 28 H4
Varnek Rus. Fed. 28 L1
Varniai Lith. 33 F5
Varnja Estonia 33 G4
Várnjárg pen. Norway see Varangerhalvøya
Varnyany Belarus 33 G5
Varosha Cyprus see Varosia
Varosia Cyprus 77 A2
Varpaisjärvi Fin. 32 G3
Várpalota Hungary 37 I5
Varsaj Afgh. 81 G2
Vârşand Romania 46 B1
Varsh, Ozero l. Rus. Fed. 28 H2
Vartashen Azer. see Oğuz
Vartdalsfjorden inlet Norway 32 B3
Vartholomio Greece 47 B6
Varto Turkey 79 E3
Vârtop, Pasul pass Romania 46 C1
Värtsilä Fin. 32 H3
Varzaneh Iran 80 C3
Várzea Alegre Brazil 150 E3
Várzea da Palma Brazil 151 C6
Várzea Grande Brazil 150 D3
Varzo Italy 44 B1
Varzob Tajik. 81 G2
Vasa Fin. see Vaasa
Vasa Barris r. Brazil 150 E4
Vasai India 72 B2
Vasalemma Estonia 33 G4
Vascão r. Port. 42 C4
Vashka r. Rus. Fed. 28 H2
Vasht Iran see Khāsh
Vasilika Greece 47 C4
Vasilkov Ukr. see Vasyl'kiv
Vaskivesi Fin. 33 F3
Vaslui Romania 46 E1
Vassar U.S.A. 130 B2
Vas-Soproni-síkság hills Hungary 37 H5
Vastan Turkey see Gevaş
Västana Sweden 32 E3
Västansjö Sweden 32 E2
Vastenjaure l. Sweden 32 E2
Västerås Sweden 33 E4
Västerbotten county Sweden 32 D2
Västerdalälven r. Sweden 33 D3
Västerhaninge Sweden 33 E4
Västernorrland county Sweden 32 E3
Västervik Sweden 33 E4
Västmanland county Sweden 33 D4
Vasto Italy 44 E3
Västra Götaland county Sweden 33 D4
Vasvár Hungary 37 H5
Vasyl'kiv Ukr. 29 D6
Vatan France 38 D3
Väte Sweden 33 E4
Vaté i. Vanuatu see Éfaté
Vatersay i. U.K. 34 C3
Vathi Greece see Ithaki
Vathia Greece 47 C6
Vathy Greece 47 E6
▶Vatican City Europe 44 D4
Independent papal state, the smallest country in the world.
europe 24–25, 48
world 8–9
Vaticano, Capo c. Italy 45 E5
Vaticano, Città del Europe see Vatican City
Vatio Greece 47 E6
Vatnajökull ice cap Iceland 32 [inset]
Vatne Norway 32 B3
Vatoa i. Fiji 107 H3
Vatomandry Madag. 99 [inset] K3
Vatoussa Greece 47 E5
Vat Phou tourist site Laos 61 D5
Vatra Dornei Romania 31 K4
Vätter, Lake Sweden see Vättern
Vättern l. Sweden 33 D4
Vatulele i. Fiji 107 G3
Vaucluse, Monts de mts France 39 F5
Vaucouleurs France 39 F2
Vaughan Springs Australia 110 B4
Vaughn U.S.A. 135 F6
Vaupés dept Col. 146 D4
Vaupés r. Col. 146 D4
Vauquelin r. Canada 124 E2
Vauvert France 39 F5
Vauxhall Canada 123 H5
Vav India 74 A4
Vavatenina Madag. 99 [inset] K3
Vava'u i. Tonga 107 H3
Vava'u Group is Tonga 107 H3
Vavoua Côte d'Ivoire 92 D4
Vavozh Rus. Fed. 28 I4
Vavuniya Sri Lanka 72 D4
Vawkavysk Belarus 29 C5
Växjö Sweden 33 D4
Vây, Đao i. Vietnam 61 C6
Vayenga Rus. Fed. see Severomorsk
Vaygach, Ostrov i. Rus. Fed. 28 K1
Vayk' Armenia 79 F3
Vazante Brazil 151 C6
Vazáš Sweden see Vittangi
Vazobe mt. Madag. 99 [inset] J3
Veaikevárri Sweden see Svappavaara
Vecht r. Neth. 36 C2
Vechta Germany 36 D2
Vechte r. Germany 36 C2
Vecumnieki Latvia 33 G4
Vedana Rus. Fed. see Vedeno
Vedaranniyam India 72 C4
Vedasandur India 72 C4
Vedea Romania 46 D2
Vedea Romania 46 D3
Vedea r. Romania 46 D3
Vedeno Rus. Fed. 79 F2
Vedia Arg. 152 E3
Vedlozero Rus. Fed. 28 E3
Veendam Neth. 36 C2
Veenendaal Neth. 36 B2
Vega i. Norway 32 C2
Vega U.S.A. 133 A5
Vegadeo Spain 42 C1
Vegarshei Norway 33 C4
Vegoritis, Limni l. Greece 46 B4
Vehmaa Fin. 33 F3
Vehoa r. Pak. 81 G4
Veidnes Norway 32 G1
Veinticinco de Mayo Buenos Aires Arg. see 25 de Mayo
Veinticinco de Mayo La Pampa Arg. see 25 de Mayo
Veinticinco de Mayo Mendoza Arg. see 25 de Mayo
Vejer de la Frontera Spain 42 D4
Vejle Denmark 33 C5
Vela Luka Croatia 44 F3
Velardena Mex. 133 A7
Velasco, Sierra de mts Arg. 152 D2
Velázquez Uruguay 152 G3
Velbŭzhdki Prokhod pass Macedonia 46 C3
Velddrif S. Africa 98 C7
Veldhoven Neth. 36 B3
Velduri India 72 C3
Velebit mts Croatia 44 E2
Veleka r. Bulg. 46 E3
Velenje Slovenia 44 E1
Veles Macedonia 46 B4
Velës, Mali i mt. Albania 46 A4
Velež mts Bos.-Herz. 44 F3
Vélez Col. 146 C3
Vélez-Málaga Spain 42 D4
Vélez-Rubio Spain 43 E4
Velhas r. Brazil 151 C6
Velia tourist site Italy 45 E4
Velibaba Turkey see Aras
Velichayevskoye Rus. Fed. 29 H7
Velika Drenova Yugo. 46 B3
Velika Gorica Croatia 44 F2
Velika Kapela mts Croatia 44 E2
Velika Kladuša Bos.-Herz. 44 E2
Velika Morava canal Yugo. 46 B2
Velika Plana Yugo. 46 B2
Velikaya Rus. Fed. 28 I4
Velikaya r. Rus. Fed. 27 R3
Velikaya r. Rus. Fed. 31 L1
Velikaya Guba Rus. Fed. 28 E3
Velikaya Kema Rus. Fed. 64 D3
Veliki Drvenik i. Croatia 44 F3
Veliki Jastrebac mts Yugo. 46 B3
Veliki Preslav Bulg. 46 E3
Veliki Šturac mt. Yugo. 46 B2
Velikiye Luki Rus. Fed. 28 D4
Velikiy Novgorod Rus. Fed. 28 D4
Velikiy Ustyug Rus. Fed. 28 H3
Velikonda Range hills India 72 C3
Veliko Tŭrnovo Bulg. 46 D3
Velikoye Rus. Fed. 28 F4
Velikoye, Ozero l. Rus. Fed. 31 N1
Vélingara Senegal 92 B2
Vélingara Senegal 92 B2
Velingrad Bulg. 46 D3
Velino r. Italy 44 D3
Velino, Monte mt. Italy 44 D3
Velizh Rus. Fed. 28 D5
Veľká Domaša, Vodná nádrž resr Slovakia 37 J4
Veľká Fatra mts Slovakia 37 I4
Veľká Javorina hill Czech Rep./Slovakia 37 H4
Velké Meziříčí Czech Rep. 37 H4
Veľký Krtíš Slovakia 37 I4
Veľký Meder Slovakia 37 H5
Vella Lavella i. Solomon Is 107 E2
Vellar r. India 72 C4
Vellore India 72 C3
Vel'mo r. Rus. Fed. 27 J3
Velopoula i. Greece 47 C6
Vel'sk Rus. Fed. 28 G3
Velsuna Italy see Orvieto
Vel't Rus. Fed. 28 I1
Velten Germany 31 H2
Veluwezoom, Nationaal Park nat. park Neth. 36 B2
Velykyy Tokmak Ukr. see Tokmak
Vel'yu r. Rus. Fed. 28 J3
Vema Seamount sea feature S. Atlantic Ocean 161 O8
Vema Trench sea feature Indian Ocean 162 L6
Vembanad Lake India 72 C4
Vemor'ye Rus. Fed. 64 E3
Vempalle India 72 C3
Venado Tuerto Arg. 152 E3
Venafro Italy 44 E4
Venamo r. Guyana/Venez. 147 F3
Venamo, Cerro mt. Venez. 147 F3
Venarey-les-Laumes France 39 F3
Venaria Italy 44 A2
Vencedor Brazil 147 F6
Venceslau Bráz Brazil 149 H5
Vendeuvre-sur-Barse France 39 F2
Vendinga Rus. Fed. 28 H3
Vendôme France 38 D3
Vendrell Spain see El Vendrell
Veneta, Laguna lag. Italy 44 D2
Venetia Italy see Venice
Veneto admin. reg. Italy 44 C2
Venev Rus. Fed. 29 F5
Venezia Italy see Venice
Venezia, Golfo di g. Europe see Venice, Gulf of
▶Venezuela country S. America 147 E3
5th most populous country in South America.
southamerica 144–145, 154
Venezuela, Golfo de g. Venez. 146 D2
Venezuelan Basin sea feature S. Atlantic Ocean 160 J4
Vengurla India 72 B3
Veniaminof Volcano U.S.A. 120 D4
▶Venice Italy 44 D2
europe 24–25
Venice FL U.S.A. 129 C7
Venice LA U.S.A. 133 D6
Venice, Gulf of Europe 44 D2
Vénissieux France 39 F4
Venjan Sweden 33 D3
Venkatagiri India 72 C3
Venkatapuram India 72 D2
Venlo Neth. 36 C3
Vennesla Norway 33 B4
Venosa Italy 44 E4
Venosta, Val valley Italy 44 C1
Venray Neth. 36 B3
Venta r. Latvia/Lith. 33 F4
Venta Lith. 33 F4
Venta de Baños Spain 42 D2
Ventimiglia Italy 44 A3
Ventisquero mt. Arg. 153 C5
Ventotene, Isola i. Italy 45 D4
Ventoux, Mont mt. France 39 F4
Ventspils Latvia 33 F4
Ventuari r. Venez. 147 E3
Ventura U.S.A. 136 C4
Venusia Italy see Venosa
Venustiano Carranza, Presa resr Mex. 133 A7
Vera Arg. 152 E2
Verá, Lago l. Para. 149 F6
Vera Cruz Brazil 148 D2
Veracruz Mex. 126 G8
Vera Cruz Mex. see Veracruz
Veraval India 72 A1
Verbania Italy 44 B2
Vercelli Italy 44 B2
Vercors reg. France 39 F4
Vercovicium tourist site U.K. see Housesteads
Verdalsøra Norway 32 C3
Verde r. Arg. 153 D5
Verde r. Bahia Brazil 150 D4
Verde r. Goiás Brazil 149 H4
Verde r. Mato Grosso Brazil 149 G2
Verde r. Mato Grosso do Sul Brazil 149 H5
Verde r. Mex. 126 E6
Verde r. Para. 149 F5
Verde r. U.S.A. 137 G5
Verde, Cabo c. Senegal see Vert, Cap
Verde, Península pen. Arg. 152 E4
Verde Grande r. Brazil 150 D5
Verden (Aller) Germany 36 D2
Verde Pequeno r. Brazil 150 D5
Verdi U.S.A. 136 C2
Verdigris r. U.S.A. 132 C5
Verdinho, Serra do mts Brazil 149 H4
Verdon r. France 39 F5
Verdun France 39 F2
Vereeniging S. Africa 99 E5
Vereshchagino Rus. Fed. 28 J4
Verga, Cap c. Guinea 92 B3
Vergara Uruguay 152 G3
Vergennes U.S.A. 131 G1
Véria Greece see Veroia
Verín Spain 42 C2
Veriora Estonia 33 G4
Veríssimo Sarmento Angola see Camissombo
Verkhneimbatsk Rus. Fed. 27 I3
Verkhnekolvinsk Rus. Fed. 28 K2
Verkhnespasskoye Rus. Fed. 28 H4
Verkhnetulomskoye Vodokhranilishche resr Rus. Fed. 32 H1
Verkhnevilyuysk Rus. Fed. 27 M3
Verkhneye Kuyto, Ozero l. Rus. Fed. 32 H2
Verkhniy Baskunchak Rus. Fed. 29 H6
Verkhniy Vyalozerskiy Rus. Fed. 28 E2
Verkhnyaya Inta Rus. Fed. 28 L2
Verkhnyaya Pakhachi Rus. Fed. 27 Q3
Verkhnyaya Tunguska r. Rus. Fed. see Angara
Verkhoshizhem'ye Rus. Fed. 28 I4
Verkhovazh'ye Rus. Fed. 28 G3
Verkhoyanskiy Khrebet mts Rus. Fed. 27 M2
Verkola Rus. Fed. 28 H3
Verma Norway 33 C3
Vermelho r. Brazil 150 B3
Vermenton France 39 E3
Vermilion Canada 123 I4
Vermilion r. U.S.A. 128 A3
Vermilion Bay U.S.A. 133 D6
Vermilion Cliffs esc. AZ U.S.A. 137 F3
Vermilion Cliffs esc. UT U.S.A. 137 F3
Vermilion Cliffs National Monument nat. park U.S.A. 137 G3
Vermilion Lake U.S.A. 132 C2
Vermillion U.S.A. 132 B3
Vermillion r. U.S.A. 132 B3
Vermillion Bay Canada 124 A3
Vermont state U.S.A. 131 G1
Vernadsky research station Antarctica 167 L2
Vernal U.S.A. 137 H1
Verner Canada 124 D4
Verneuil-sur-Avre France 38 D2
Verneuk Pan salt pan S. Africa 98 D6
Vernier Switz. 39 G3
Vernio Italy 44 C2
Vernon Canada 122 G5
Vernon France 38 D2
Vernon AL U.S.A. 129 A5
Vernon TX U.S.A. 133 B5
Vernon Islands Australia 110 B2
Vernyy Kazakh. see Almaty
Vero Beach U.S.A. 129 C7
Veroia Greece 46 C4
Verona Italy 44 C2
Verona U.S.A. 130 D4
Verres Italy 44 A2
Versailles France 38 E2
Versailles IN U.S.A. 128 B4
Versailles KY U.S.A. 130 A4
Versailles MO U.S.A. 132 C4
Versailles OH U.S.A. 130 A3
Versalles Bol. 149 E3
Versec Yugo. see Vršac
Vert, Cap c. Senegal 92 A2
Vertentes r. Brazil 150 B4
Vertou France 38 C3
Vertus France 39 F2
Verulamium U.K. see St Albans
Verviers Belgium 39 F1
Vervins France 39 E2
Verwood Canada 123 J5
Vesanto Fin. 32 G3
Vescovato Corsica France 40 D3
Vesele Ukr. 29 E7
Veselina r. Bulg. 46 D3
Veselí nad Lužnicí Czech Rep. 37 G4
Veselí nad Moravou Czech Rep. 37 H4
Veselovskoye Vodokhranilishche resr Rus. Fed. 29 G7
Veselyy Rus. Fed. 29 G7
Veshenskaya Rus. Fed. 29 G6
Vesijärvi l. Fin. 33 G3
Vesle r. France 39 E2
Veslyana r. Rus. Fed. 28 J3
Vesontio France see Besançon
Vesoul France 39 G3
Vest-Agder county Norway 33 B4
Vesterålen is Norway 32 D1
Vestfjorddalen valley Norway 33 C4
Vestfjorden sea chan. Norway 32 D2
Vestfold county Norway 33 C4
Vestmanna Faroe Is 34 [inset]
Vestmannaeyjar is Iceland 32 [inset]
Vestnes Norway 32 B3
Vestvågøy i. Norway 32 D1
Vesuvio, Parco Nazionale del nat. park Italy 45 E4
Vesuvius vol. Italy 45 E4
Ves'yegonsk Rus. Fed. 28 F4
Veszprém Hungary 37 H5
Veteran Canada 123 I4
Veternik Yugo. 46 A2
Vetlanda Sweden 33 D4
Vetluga Rus. Fed. 28 H4
Vetluga r. Rus. Fed. 28 H4
Vetovo Bulg. 46 E3
Vetralla Italy 44 D3
Vetren Bulg. 46 E3
Vetrişoaia Romania 46 F1
Vettasjärvi Sweden 32 F2
Vettore, Monte mt. Italy 44 D3
Veurne Belgium 39 E1
Veveno r. Sudan 96 B3
Vevey Switz. 39 G3
Veyle r. France 39 F3
Veynes France 39 F4
Veyo U.S.A. 137 F3
Vézère r. France 38 D4
Vezhen mt. Bulg. 46 D3
Vezirköprü Turkey 78 C2
Viacha Bol. 148 C4
Vialar Alg. see Tissemsilt
Viamao Brazil 151 B9
Viana Angola 95 B7
Viana Brazil 150 C2
Viana del Bollo Spain see Viana do Bolo
Viana do Bolo Spain 42 C1
Viana do Castelo Port. 42 B2
Viana do Castelo admin. dist. Port. 42 B2
Viangchan Laos see Vientiane
Viangphoukha Laos 60 C3
Viar r. Spain 42 D4
Viareggio Italy 44 C3
Viaur r. France 39 D4
Viborg Denmark 33 C4
Viborg Rus. Fed. see Vyborg
Vibo Valentia Italy 45 F5
Vic Spain 43 H2
Vicam Mex. 135 E8
Vicdessos r. France 38 D5
Vic-en-Bigorre France 38 D5
Vicente, Point U.S.A. 136 C5
Vicente Guerrero Mex. 135 C7
Vicenza Italy 44 C2
Vic-Fezensac France 38 D5
Vich Spain see Vic
Vichada dept Col. 146 D3
Vichada r. Col. 146 E3
Vichadero Uruguay 152 G2
Vichuga Rus. Fed. 28 G4
Vichy France 39 E3
Vicksburg AZ U.S.A. 137 F5
Vicksburg MS U.S.A. 127 H5
Vico, Lago di l. Italy 44 D3
Viçosa Brazil 151 D7
Vic-sur-Cère France 39 E4
Victor, Mount Antarctica 167 D2
Victor Harbor Australia 112 A4
Victoria Arg. 152 E3
Victoria r. Australia 110 B2
Victoria state Australia 106 D5
Victoria Cameroon see Limbe
▶Victoria Canada 134 B2
Provincial capital of British Columbia.
Victoria La Araucanía Chile 152 B4
Victoria Magallanes Chile 153 C8
Victoria Malaysia see Labuan
Victoria Malta 45 E6
Victoria Romania 46 D2
▶Victoria Seychelles 162 K6
Capital of the Seychelles.
Victoria TX U.S.A. 133 B6
Victoria VA U.S.A. 130 D5
▶Victoria, Lake Africa 96 B5
Largest lake in Africa and 3rd in the world.
africa 84–85
world 6–7
Victoria, Lake Australia 112 B4
Victoria, Mount Myanmar 60 A3
Victoria, Mount P.N.G. 106 D2
Victoria and Albert Mountains Canada 121 L2
▶Victoria Falls waterfall Zambia/Zimbabwe 95 E9
africa 100
Victoria Falls Zimbabwe 98 E3
Victoria Falls National Park Zimbabwe 99 E3
Victoria Harbour sea chan. Hong Kong China see Hong Kong Harbour
▶Victoria Island Canada 121 I2
3rd largest island in North America and 9th in the world.
northamerica 116–117
world 6–7
Victoria Lake Canada 125 J3

Victoria Land coastal area Antarctica 167 H2
Victoria Peak hill Hong Kong China 67 [inset]
Victoria Range mts N.Z. 113 C3
Victoria River Downs Australia 110 B3
Victoriaville Canada 125 G4
Victoria West S. Africa 98 D6
Victorica Arg. 152 D4
Victorino Venez. 146 E4
Victorville U.S.A. 136 D4
Victory U.S.A. 131 E2
Victory Downs Australia 110 C5
Vicuña Chile 152 C2
Vicuña Mackenna Arg. 152 D3
Vidalia U.S.A. 133 D5
Vidal Junction U.S.A. 137 E4
Videle Romania 46 D2
Vidigueira Port. 42 C3
Vidima r. Bulg. 46 D3
Vidin Bulg. 46 C3
Vidisha India 74 C5
Vidlitsa Rus. Fed. 28 E3
Vidourle r. France 39 F5
Viduša mts Bos.-Herz. 44 G3
Vidzemes Centrālā Augstiene hills Latvia 33 G4
Viechtach Germany 37 F4
Viedma Arg. 152 E5
▶Viedma, Lago l. Arg. 153 B7
southamerica 142–143
Viehberg mt. Austria 37 G4
Viejo, Cerro mt. Mex. 135 D7
Vielha Spain 43 G1
Viella Spain see Vielha
Vielsalm Belgium 39 F1
Vienenburg Germany 36 E3

▶Vienna Austria 37 H4
Capital of Austria.

Vienna GA U.S.A. 129 C5
Vienna IL U.S.A. 128 A4
Vienna MD U.S.A. 131 F4
Vienna MO U.S.A. 132 D4
Vienna WV U.S.A. 130 C4
Vienne France 39 F4
Vienne r. France 38 D3

▶Vientiane Laos 60 C4
Capital of Laos.

Viersen Germany 36 C3
Vierwaldstätter See l. Switz. 39 H3
Vierzon France 38 E3
Viesca Mex. 133 A7
Vieste Italy 44 F4
Vietas Sweden 32 E2
▶Vietnam country Asia 60 D4
asia 52–53, 82
Viet Nam country Asia see Vietnam
Việt Tri Vietnam 60 D3
Vieux Comptoir, Lac du l. Canada 124 E2
Vieux-Fort Canada 125 J3
Vieux Poste, Pointe du pt Canada 125 I3
Vigan Phil. 57 F2
Vigeois France 38 D4
Vigevano Italy 44 B2
Vigia Brazil 150 B2
Vigia hill Port. 42 B4
Viglio, Monte mt. Italy 44 D4
Vignola Italy 44 C2
Vigny France 38 D2
Vigo Spain 42 B1
Vihanti Fin. 32 G2
Vihari Pak. 81 H4
Vihiers France 38 C3
Viiala Fin. 33 F3
Viipuri Rus. Fed. see Vyborg
Viirinkylä Fin. 32 G2
Viitasaari Fin. 32 G3
Vijainagar India 74 B3
Vijapur India 74 B5
Vijayadurg India 72 B2
Vijayapati India 72 C4
Vijayawada India 72 D2
Vik Iceland 32 [inset]
Vikajärvi Fin. 32 G2
Vikarabad India 72 C2
Vikedal Norway 33 B4
Vikeke East Timor see Viqueque
Vikersund Norway 33 C4
Vikhren mt. Bulg. 46 C4
Viking Canada 123 I4
Vikna i. Norway 32 C2
Vikos-Aoos nat. park Greece 47 B5
Vikøyri Norway 33 B3
Vikran Norway 32 E1
Vila Spain 42 B2
Vila Vanuatu see Port Vila
Vila Arriaga Angola see Bibala
Vila Bittencourt Brazil 146 D5
Vila Braga Brazil 147 G6
Vila Bugaço Angola see Camanongue
Vila Cabral Moz. see Lichinga
Vila Caldas Xavier Moz. see Muende
Vilacaya Bol. 148 D4
Vila Coutinho Moz. see Ulongue
Vila da Ponte Angola see Kuvango
Vila da Ribeira Brava Cape Verde 92 [inset]
Vila de Aljustrel Angola see Cangamba
Vila de Almoster Angola see Chiange
Vila de João Belo Moz. see Xai-Xai
Vila de Junqueiro Moz. see Gurué
Vila de Sal Rei Cape Verde 92 [inset]
Vila de Sena Moz. 99 G3
Vila de Trego Morais Moz. see Chókwé
Vila do Tarrafal Cape Verde 92 [inset]
Vila Flor Port. 42 C2
Vila Fontes Moz. see Caia
Vilafranca del Penedès Spain 43 G2
Vila Franca de Xira Port. 42 B3
Vilagarcía de Arousa Spain 42 B1
Vila Gomes da Costa Moz. 99 G5
Vila Gouveia Moz. see Catandica
Vilaine r. France 38 B3
Viļaka Latvia 33 G4
Vilalba Spain 42 C1
Vila Marechal Carmona Angola see Uíge
Vila Miranda Moz. see Macaloge
Vilanandro, Tanjona pt Madag. 99 [inset] J3
Vilanculos Moz. 99 G4
Viļāni Latvia 33 G4
Vila Nova da Fronteira Moz. 99 G3
Vila Nova de Foz Coa Port. 42 C2
Vila Nova de Gaia Port. 42 B2
Vila Nova de Ourém Port. 42 B3
Vila Nova de Paiva Port. 42 C2
Vila Nova do Seles Angola see Uku
Vilanova i la Geltrú Spain 43 G2
Vila Nova Sintra Cape Verde 92 [inset]
Vila Paiva de Andrada Moz. see Gorongosa
Vila Pery Moz. see Chimoio
Vila Real Port. 42 C2
Vila Real admin. dist. Port. 42 C2
Vila-real de los Infantes Spain 43 F3
Vilar Formoso Port. 42 C2
Vila Salazar Angola see N'dalatando
Vila Salazar Zimbabwe see Sango
Vila Teixeira de Sousa Angola see Luau
Vilavankod India 72 C4
Vila Velha Amapá Brazil 147 I4
Vila Velha Espírito Santo Brazil 151 D7
Vila Velha de Ródão Port. 42 C3
Vila Verde Port. 42 B2
Vilcabamba, Cordillera mts Peru 148 B3
Vilcanota, Cordillera de mts Peru 148 C3
Vil'cheka, Zemlya i. Rus. Fed. 26 G1
Viled' r. Rus. Fed. 28 H3
Vileyka Belarus see Vilyeyka
Vil'gort Rus. Fed. 28 K3
Vilhelmina Sweden 32 E2
Vilhena Brazil 149 E3
Viliya r. Belarus/Lith. 33 G5
Viljandi Estonia 28 C4
Viljoenskroon S. Africa 99 E5
Vilkaviškis Lith. 33 F5
Vilkija Lith. 33 F5
Vil'kitskogo, Proliv strait Rus. Fed. 27 J2
Villa Abecia Bol. 148 D5
Villa Adriana tourist site Italy 44 D4
Villa Ahumada Mex. 135 F7
Villa Alba Arg. 152 E4
Villa Angela Arg. 152 E1
Villa Bella Bol. 148 D2
Villa Bens Morocco see Tarfaya
Villablino Spain 42 C1
Villacañas Spain 42 E3
Villacarrillo Spain 42 E3
Villach Austria 37 F5
Villacidro Sardinia Italy 45 B5
Villa Cisneros W. Sahara see Ad Dakhla
Villa Constitución Arg. 152 E3
Villa Constitución Mex. see Ciudad Constitución
Villa del Rosario Arg. 152 E2
Villa del Totoral Arg. 152 D2
Villadiego Spain 42 D1
Villa Dolores Arg. 152 D2
Villadossola Italy 44 B1
Villa Flores Mex. 138 F5
Villafranca Spain 43 F1
Villafranca del Bierzo Spain 42 C1
Villafranca del Cid Spain 43 F2
Villafranca de los Barros Spain 42 C3
Villafranca del Penedès Spain see Vilafranca del Penedès
Villafranca di Verona Italy 44 C2
Villagarcía de Arosa Spain see Vilagarcía de Arousa
Villa Gesell Arg. 152 F4
Villaguay Arg. 152 F2
Villa Guillermina Arg. 152 F2
Villa Hayes Para. 149 F6
Villahermosa Mex. 138 F5
Villaines-la-Juhel France 38 C2
Villa Insurgentes Mex. 138 B3
Villa Iris Arg. 152 E4
Villajoyosa-La Vila Joíosa Spain 43 F3
Villa Juárez Mex. 135 E8
Villaldama Mex. 133 A7
Villalonga Arg. 152 E4
Villa María Arg. 152 E3
Villa María Grande Arg. 152 F2
Villa Martín Bol. 148 D5
Villamartin Spain 42 D4
Villa Matoque Arg. 152 E1
Villa Montes Bol. 149 E5
Villanova Monteleone Sardinia Italy 45 B4
Villanueva Col. 146 C2
Villanueva de Córdoba Spain 42 D3
Villanueva de la Serena Spain 42 D3
Villanueva de los Castillejos Spain 42 C4
Villanueva de los Infantes Spain 42 E3
Villanueva-y-Geltrú Spain see Vilanova i la Geltrú
Villa Ocampo Arg. 152 F2
Villa O'Higgins Chile 153 B7
Villa Ojo de Agua Arg. 152 E2
Villa Oropeza Bol. 148 D4
Villa Pesqueira Mex. 135 E7
Villaputzu Sardinia Italy 45 B5
Villar del Rey Spain 42 C3
Villareal Spain see Vila-real de los Infantes
Villareal de los Infantes Spain see Vila-real de los Infantes
Villa Regina Arg. 152 D4
Villarrica Chile 152 B4
Villarrica Para. 149 F6
Villarrica, Lago l. Chile 152 B4
Villarrica, Parque Nacional nat. park Chile 152 C4
Villarrobledo Spain 43 E3
Villarrubia de los Ojos Spain 42 E3
Villasalazar Zimbabwe see Sango
Villasana de Mena Spain 42 E1
Villa San Giovanni Italy 45 E5
Villa Sanjurjo Morocco see Al Hoceima
Villa San Martín Arg. 152 D2
Villasboas Uruguay 152 F3
Villa Serrano Bol. 149 D4
Villasimius Sardinia Italy 45 B5
Villa Unión Arg. 152 C2
Villa Unión Coahuila Mex. 133 A6
Villa Unión Mex. 126 E7
Villa Valeria Arg. 152 D3
Villavicencio Col. 146 C3
Villaviciosa Spain 42 D1
Villaviciosa de Córdoba Spain 42 D3
Villa Viscarra Bol. 148 D4
Villazon Bol. 148 D5
Villedieu-les-Poêles France 38 C2
Villefranche-de-Lauragais France 38 D5
Villefranche-de-Rouergue France 38 E4
Villefranche-sur-Saône France 39 F4
Ville-Marie Canada see Montréal
Villemur-sur-Tarn France 38 D5
Villena Spain 43 F3
Villenauxe-la-Grande France 39 E2
Villeneuve-de-Marsan France 38 C5
Villeneuve-sur-Lot France 38 D4
Villers-Bocage France 38 C2
Villers-Cotterêts France 39 E2
Villeurbanne France 39 F4
Villicun, Sierra mts Arg. 152 C2
Villingen Germany 36 D4
Villupuram India see Viluppuram
Vilna Canada 123 I4
Vilna Lith. see Vilnius

▶Vilnius Lith. 33 G5
Capital of Lithuania.

Vil'nyans'k Ukr. 29 E7
Vilppula Fin. 33 G3
Vils r. Germany 36 E4
Vils r. Germany 37 F4
Vilsbiburg Germany 37 F4
Vilshofen Germany 37 F4
Viluppuram India 72 C4
Vilvoorde Belgium 39 F1
Vilyeyka Belarus 29 C5
Vilyeyskaye, Vozyera l. Belarus 33 G5
Vilyuy r. Rus. Fed. 27 M3
Vilyuyskoye Vodokhranilishche resr Rus. Fed. 27 L3
Vimbe mt. Zambia 97 A8
Vimercate Italy 44 B2
Vimianzo Spain 42 B1
Vimioso Port. 42 C2
Vimmerby Sweden 33 D4
Vimoutiers France 38 D2
Vimperk Czech Rep. 37 F4
Vina r. Cameroon 93 I4
Vina U.S.A. 136 A2
Viña del Mar Chile 152 C3
Vinalopó r. Spain 43 F3
Vinanivao Madag. 99 [inset] K2
Vinaròs Spain 43 G2
Vinaroz Spain see Vinaròs
Vincelotte, Lac l. Canada 125 F2
Vincennes U.S.A. 128 B4
Vincennes Bay Antarctica 167 F2
Vinchina Arg. 152 C2
Vinchos Peru 148 B3
Vindelälven r. Sweden 32 E3
Vindeln Sweden 32 E2
Vindhya Range hills India 74 B5
Vindobona Austria see Vienna
Vineland U.S.A. 131 F4
Vinga Romania 46 B1
Vingăi, Câmpia plain Romania 46 B1
Vingåker Sweden 33 D4
Vinh Vietnam 60 D4
Vinhais Port. 42 C2
Vinh Long Vietnam 61 D6
Vinh Thuc, Đao i. Vietnam 60 D3
Vinh Yên Vietnam 60 D3
Vinica Macedonia 46 C4
Vinita U.S.A. 133 C4
Vinjhan India 74 A5
Vînju Mare Romania see Vânju Mare
Vinkovci Croatia 44 G2
Vinland i. Canada see Newfoundland
Vinnitsa Ukr. see Vinnytsya
Vinnytsya Ukr. 29 D6

▶Vinson Massif mt. Antarctica 167 L1
Highest mountain in Antarctica.
oceans and poles 168

Vinton U.S.A. 132 C3
Vinukonda India 72 C2
Vinza Congo 94 B5
Viphya Mountains Malawi 97 B8
Vipiteno Italy 44 C1
Viqueque East Timor 108 D2
Vir i. Croatia 44 E2
Viramgam India 74 B5
Virançehir Turkey 79 D3
Virarajendrapet India 72 B3
Virawah Pak. 81 G5
Virchow, Mount Australia 108 B5
Virdáánjarga Fin. see Virtaniemi
Virden Canada 134 G2
Vire France 38 C2
Virei Angola 95 B8
Virful Highiş hill Romania 46 B1
Vírgenes, Cabo c. Arg. 153 C8
Virgilina U.S.A. 130 D5
Virgin r. U.S.A. 137 E3
Virginia S. Africa 99 E6
Virginia U.S.A. 132 C2
Virginia state U.S.A. 130 D5
Virginia Beach U.S.A. 131 F5
Virginia City MT U.S.A. 134 E3
Virginia City NV U.S.A. 136 C2
Virginia Falls Canada 122 E2

▶Virgin Islands (U.K.) terr. West Indies 139 L5
United Kingdom Overseas Territory.
northamerica 118–119, 140

▶Virgin Islands (U.S.A.) terr. West Indies 139 L5
United States Unincorporated Territory.
northamerica 118–119, 140

Virgin Mountains U.S.A. 137 E3
Virginópolis Brazil 151 D6
Virkkala Fin. 33 G3
Virmasvesi l. Fin. 32 G3
Virôchey Cambodia 61 D5
Virolahti Fin. 33 G3
Virovitica Croatia 44 F2
Virrat Fin. 33 F3
Virserum Sweden 33 D4
Virtaniemi Fin. 32 H1
Virton Belgium 39 F2
Virtsu Estonia 33 F4
Virú Peru 148 A2
Virudunagar India 72 C4
Virunga, Parc National des nat. park Dem. Rep. Congo 94 F5
Vis Croatia 44 F3
Vis i. Croatia 44 F3
Visaginas Lith. 33 G5
Visakhapatnam India see Vishakhapatnam
Visalia U.S.A. 136 C3
Visapur India 72 B2
Visavadar India 74 A5
Visayan Sea Phil. 57 F3
Visby Sweden 33 E4
Viscount Melville Sound sea chan. Canada 121 H2
Vise, Ostrov i. Rus. Fed. 26 H2
Višegrad Bos.-Herz. 46 A3
Viseu Brazil 150 C2
Viseu Port. 42 C2
Viseu admin. dist. Port. 42 C2
Vishakhapatnam India 73 D2
Vishegrad hill Bulg. 46 E4
Vishera r. Rus. Fed. 28 J3
Vishera r. Rus. Fed. 28 K4
Vishnyeva Belarus 33 G5
Vișina Romania 46 D2
Viški Kanal sea chan. Croatia 44 F3
Visnagar India 74 B5
Viso, Monte mt. Italy 44 A2
Visoko Bos.-Herz. 44 G3
Visp Switz. 39 G3
Vissannapeta India 72 D2
Vista U.S.A. 136 D5
Vista Alegre Amazonas Brazil 146 D4
Vista Alegre Amazonas Brazil 146 D6
Vista Alegre Amazonas Brazil 147 F6
Vista Alegre Mato Grosso do Sul Brazil 149 F4
Vista Alegre Roraima Brazil 147 F4
Vista Lake U.S.A. 136 C4
Vistonida, Limni lag. Greece 46 D4
Vistula r. Poland 37 I1
Vištytis Lith. 37 K1
Vit r. Bulg. 46 D3
Vita r. Col. 146 E3
Vitao mt. Yugo. 46 A3
Vitebsk Belarus see Vitsyebsk
Viterbo Italy 44 D3
Vitez Bos.-Herz. 44 F2
Vitez pass Bos.-Herz. 44 G3
Vitigudino Spain 42 C2
Viti Levu i. Fiji 107 G3
Vitim r. Rus. Fed. 63 J1
Vitimskoye Ploskogor'ye plat. Rus. Fed. 63 I1
Vitomirica Yugo. 46 B3
Vitor r. Peru 148 B4
Vitória Espírito Santo Brazil 151 D7
Vitória Pará Brazil 147 H5
Vitoria Spain see Vitoria-Gasteiz
Vitória da Conquista Brazil 150 D5
Vitoria-Gasteiz Spain 43 E1
Vitória Seamount sea feature S. Atlantic Ocean 161 L7
Vitosha nat. park Bulg. 46 C3
Vitré France 38 C2
Vitrolles France 39 F5
Vitry-le-François France 39 F2
Vitsyebsk Belarus 28 D5
Vittangi Sweden 32 F2
Vitteaux France 39 F3
Vittel France 39 F2
Vittoria Sicily Italy 45 E6
Vittorio Veneto Italy 44 D2
Vityaz Depth sea feature N. Pacific Ocean 162 R3
Vivarais, Monts du mts France 39 F4
Viveiro Spain 42 C1
Vivero Spain see Viveiro
Vivian U.S.A. 133 C5
Vivo S. Africa 99 F4
Vivonne France 38 D3
Vivoratá Arg. 152 F4
Vizagapatam India see Vishakhapatnam
Vizcaíno Mex. 135 D8
Vizcaíno, Desierto de des. Mex. 135 D8
Vizcaíno, Sierra mts Mex. 135 D8
Vize Turkey 78 A2
Vizhas r. Rus. Fed. 28 H2
Vizianagaram India 73 D2
Vizinga Rus. Fed. 28 I3
Viziru Romania 46 E2
Vizzini Sicily Italy 45 E6
V. J. José Perez Bol. 148 C3
Vjosë r. Albania 47 A4
Vlaardingen Neth. 36 B3
Vlădeasa, Vârful mt. Romania 46 C1
Vladičin Han Yugo. 46 C3
Vladikavkaz Rus. Fed. 29 H8
Vladimir Rus. Fed. 28 G4
Vladimir Oblast admin. div. Rus. Fed. see Vladimirskaya Oblast'
Vladimirskaya Oblast' admin. div. Rus. Fed. 28 G5
Vladimir-Volynskiy Ukr. see Volodymyr-Volyns'kyy
Vladivostok Rus. Fed. 64 B4
Vlăhița Romania 46 D1
Vlajna mt. Yugo. 46 B3
Vlasenica Bos.-Herz. 46 A2
Vlašić Planina mts Yugo. 46 A2
Vlašim Czech Rep. 37 G4
Vlasotince Yugo. 46 C3
Vlieland i. Neth. 36 B2
Vlissingen Neth. 36 A3
Vlorë Albania 46 A4
Vlorës, Gjiri i b. Albania 47 A4
Vlotslavsk Poland see Włocławek
Vltava r. Czech Rep. 37 G3
Vöcklabruck Austria 37 F4
Vodice Croatia 44 E3
Vodlozero, Ozero l. Rus. Fed. 28 F3
Vodňany Czech Rep. 37 G4
Vodnjan Croatia 44 D2
Vogan Togo 93 F4
Vogelkop Peninsula Indon. see Doberai, Jazirah
Vogelsberg hills Germany 36 D3
Voghera Italy 44 B2
Vognill Norway 32 C3
Vogošća Bos.-Herz. 44 G3
Vohémar Madag. see Iharaña
Vohibinany Madag. see Ampasimanolotra
Vohilava Fianarantsoa Madag. 99 [inset] J4
Vohilava Fianarantsoa Madag. 99 [inset] K4
Vohimarina Madag. see Iharaña
Vohimena, Tanjona c. Madag. 99 [inset] J5
Vohipeno Madag. 99 [inset] J4
Võhma Estonia 31 K1
Voi Kenya 96 C5
Voikoski Fin. 33 G3
Voineasa Romania 46 C2
Voinjama Liberia 92 C3
Voiron France 39 F4
Voitsberg Austria 37 G5
Vojvodina prov. Yugo. 46 A2
Vokhma Rus. Fed. 28 H4
Voknavolok Rus. Fed. 32 H2
Voko Cameroon 93 I3
Volaterrae Italy see Volterra
Volcán Arg. 148 D5
Volcán, Cerro vol. Bol. 148 D5
Volcano Bay Japan see Uchiura-wan

▶Volcano Islands N. Pacific Ocean 164 D4
Part of Japan.

Volda Norway 33 B3
Vol'dino Rus. Fed. 28 J3
Volens U.S.A. 130 D5

▶Volga r. Rus. Fed. 29 H7
Longest river in Europe.
europe 22–23

Volga Upland hills Rus. Fed. see Privolzhskaya Vozvyshennost'
Volgodonsk Rus. Fed. 29 G7
Volgograd Rus. Fed. 29 H6
Volgograd Oblast admin. div. Rus. Fed. see Volgogradskaya Oblast'
Volgogradskaya Oblast' admin. div. Rus. Fed. 29 H6
Volgogradskoye Vodokhranilishche resr Rus. Fed. 29 H6
Volissos Greece 47 D5
Völkermarkt Austria 37 G5
Volkhov Rus. Fed. 28 E4
Volkhov r. Rus. Fed. 28 E3
Völklingen Germany 36 C4
Volkovysk Belarus see Vawkavysk
Vol'no-Nadezhdinskoye Rus. Fed. 64 B4
Volnovakha Ukr. 29 F7
Vol'nyansk Ukr. see Vil'nyans'k
Volochanka Rus. Fed. 27 J2
Volochayevka-Vtoraya Rus. Fed. 64 C2
Volochisk Ukr. see Volochys'k
Volochys'k Ukr. 29 C6
Volodars'ke Ukr. 29 F7
Volodarskoye Kazakh. see Saumalkol'
Volodymyr-Volyns'kyy Ukr. 29 C6
Vologda Rus. Fed. 28 F4
Vologda Oblast admin. div. Rus. Fed. see Vologodskaya Oblast'
Vologodskaya Oblast' admin. div. Rus. Fed. 28 G4
Volokonovka Rus. Fed. 29 F6
Volos Greece 47 C5
Volosovo Rus. Fed. 28 D4
Volot Rus. Fed. 28 D4
Volovo Rus. Fed. 29 F5
Volozhin Belarus see Valozhyn
Volsinii, Monti mts Italy 44 C3
Volsinii Italy see Orvieto
Vol'sk Rus. Fed. 29 H5
Volta admin. reg. Ghana 93 F4
Volta r. Ghana 93 F4

▶Volta, Lake resr Ghana 93 F4
5th largest lake in Africa.
africa 84–85

Voltaire, Cape Australia 108 D3
Volta Redonda Brazil 151 C7
Volterra Italy 44 C3
Voltoya r. Spain 42 D2
Volturino, Monte mt. Italy 45 E4
Volturno r. Italy 44 D4
Volubilis tourist site Morocco 90 D2
Voluntari Romania 46 E2
Volunteer Point Falkland Is 153 F7
Volvi, Limni l. Greece 46 C4
Volzhsk Rus. Fed. 28 I5
Volzhskiy Rus. Fed. 29 H6
Vomano r. Italy 44 E3
Vondanka Rus. Fed. 28 H4
Vondrozo Madag. 99 [inset] J4
Vonga Rus. Fed. 28 G2
Vonitsa Greece 47 B5
Võnnu Estonia 33 G4
Vontimitta India 72 C3
Voorheesville U.S.A. 131 G2
Vopnafjörður Iceland 32 [inset]
Vörå Fin. 32 F3
Voranava Belarus 33 G5
Vordingborg Denmark 33 C5
Vordorf Germany 36 E2
Vorë Albania 46 A4
Voreio Aigaio admin. reg. Greece 47 D5
Voreioi Sporades is Greece 47 C5
Voreios Evvoïkos Kolpos sea chan. Greece 47 C5
Vorgashor Rus. Fed. 28 L2
Voriai Sporades is Greece see Voreioi Sporades
Voring Plateau sea feature N. Atlantic Ocean 160 O1
Vorjing mt. India 75 G3
Vorkuta Rus. Fed. 28 M2
Vormsi i. Estonia 33 F4
Vorogovo Rus. Fed. 27 I3
Vorona r. Rus. Fed. 29 G6
Voronezh Rus. Fed. 29 F6
Voronezh r. Rus. Fed. 29 F6
Voronezh Oblast admin. div. Rus. Fed. see Voronezhskaya Oblast'
Voronezhskaya Oblast' admin. div. Rus. Fed. 29 G6
Voronov, Mys pt Rus. Fed. 28 G2
Vorontsovo Rus. Fed. 33 H4
Vorontsovo-Aleksandrovskoye Rus. Fed. see Zelenokumsk
Voroshilov Rus. Fed. see Ussuriysk
Voroshilovgrad Ukr. see Luhans'k
Voroshilovsk Rus. Fed. see Stavropol'
Voroshilovsk Ukr. see Alchevs'k
Vorotynets Rus. Fed. 28 H4
Vorozhba Ukr. 29 E6
Vorpommersche Boddenlandschaft, Nationalpark nat. park Germany 37 F1
Vorskla r. Rus. Fed. 29 E6
Võrtsjärv l. Estonia 28 C4
Võru Estonia 28 C4
Vorukh Tajik. 81 G2
Vosburg S. Africa 98 D6
Vose Tajik. 81 G2
Vosges mts France 39 G3
Voskresensk Rus. Fed. 29 F5
Voskresenskoye Rus. Fed. 29 K5
Voss Norway 33 B3
Vostochnaya Litsa Rus. Fed. 28 F1
Vostochno-Sakhalinskiy Gory mts Rus. Fed. 64 E2
Vostochno-Sibirskoye More sea Rus. Fed. see East Siberian Sea
Vostochnyy Rus. Fed. 28 J4
Vostochnyy Sayan mts Rus. Fed. 62 E1

▶Vostok research station Antarctica 167 F1
Lowest recorded screen temperature in the world.
world 12–13

Vostok Rus. Fed. 64 C3
Vostok Island Kiribati 165 H6
Vostretsovo Rus. Fed. 64 C3
Vostroye Rus. Fed. 28 H3
Võsu Estonia 33 G4
Votkinsk Rus. Fed. 28 J4
Votkinskoye Vodokhranilishche resr Rus. Fed. 28 J4
Votuporanga Brazil 149 H5
Vouga Angola see Cunhinga
Vouga r. Port. 42 B2
Vouillé France 38 D3
Voula Greece 47 C6
Vourinos mt. Greece 47 B4
Vouziers France 39 F2
Voves France 38 D2
Vovodo r. Cent. Afr. Rep. 94 E3
Voxna Sweden 33 D3
Voyageurs National Park U.S.A. 132 C1
Voykar r. Rus. Fed. 28 M2
Voynitsa Rus. Fed. 32 H2
Vöyri Fin. see Vörå
Voyvozh Respublika Komi Rus. Fed. 26 F3
Voyvozh Respublika Komi Rus. Fed. 28 J3
Vozhayel' Rus. Fed. 28 I3
Vozhe, Ozero l. Rus. Fed. 28 F3
Vozhega Rus. Fed. 28 G3
Vozhgora Rus. Fed. 28 I2
Voznesens'k Ukr. 29 D7
Voznesen'ye Rus. Fed. 28 E3
Vozonin Trough sea feature Arctic Ocean 166 F1
Vozrozhdeniya, Ostrov i. Uzbek. 70 A3
Vozzhayevka Rus. Fed. 64 B2
Vrachionas hill Greece 47 B6
Vrachnaika Greece 47 B5
Vrådal Norway 33 C4
Vrakhiónas Óros hill Greece see Vrachionas
Vrakhnaíka Greece see Vrachnaika
Vran mt. Bos.-Herz. 44 F3
Vrana r. Bulg. 46 E3
Vrangel' Rus. Fed. 64 C4
Vrangelya, Mys pt Rus. Fed. 27 N4
Vrangelya, Ostrov i. Rus. Fed. see Wrangel Island
Vranjak Bos.-Herz. 44 G2
Vranje Yugo. 46 B3
Vranov, Vodní nádrž resr Czech Rep. 37 G4
Vranov nad Topľou Slovakia 37 J4
Vrapčište Macedonia 46 B4
Vrasidas, Akra pt Greece 46 D4
Vratnik pass Bulg. 46 E3
Vratsa Bulg. 46 C3
Vrbanja r. Bos.-Herz. 44 F2
Vrbas r. Bos.-Herz. 44 F2
Vrbas Yugo. 46 A2
Vrbovsko Croatia 44 E2
Vrchlabí Czech Rep. 37 G3
Vredenburg S. Africa 98 C7
Vredendal S. Africa 98 C6
Vreed-en-Hoop Guyana 147 G3
Vrhnika Slovenia 44 E2
Vriddhachalam India 72 C4
Vrigstad Sweden 33 D4
Vrnjačka Banja Yugo. 46 B3
Vrrin Albania 46 A4
Vršac Yugo. 46 B2
Vryburg S. Africa 98 E5
Vryheid S. Africa 99 F5
Vsetín Czech Rep. 37 H4
Vsevolozhsk Rus. Fed. 28 D3
Vtáčnik mt. Slovakia 37 I4
Vtáčnik mts Slovakia 37 I4
Vučitrn Yugo. 46 B3
Vučica r. Croatia 44 G2
Vučitrn Yugo. 46 B3
Vučje Yugo. 46 B3
Vuka r. Croatia 44 G2
Vukovar Croatia 44 G2
Vuktyl' Rus. Fed. 28 K3
Vukuzakhe S. Africa 99 F5
Vulcan Canada 123 H5
Vulcănești Moldova 46 F2
Vulcan Island P.N.G. see Manam Island
Vulcano, Isola i. Isole Lipari Italy 45 E5
Vŭlchidol Bulg. 46 E3
Vulkaneshty Moldova see Vulcănești
Vulture Mountains U.S.A. 137 F5
Vung Tau Vietnam 61 D6
Vuohijärvi l. Fin. 33 G3
Vuokatti Fin. 32 H2
Vuoksa r. Rus. Fed. 33 H3
Vuolijoki Fin. 32 G2
Vuollerim Sweden 32 F2
Vuolvojaure l. Sweden 32 E2
Vuostimo Fin. 32 G2
Vuotso Fin. 32 G1
Vŭrbitsa Bulg. 46 E3
Vustsye Belarus 33 G5
Vuyyuru India 72 D2
Vyara India 74 B5
Vyatka Rus. Fed. see Kirov
Vyatka r. Rus. Fed. 28 I5
Vyatskiye Polyany Rus. Fed. 28 I4
Vyazemskiy Rus. Fed. 64 C3
Vyaz'ma Rus. Fed. 29 E5
Vyazniki Rus. Fed. 28 G4
Vyazovka Rus. Fed. 29 H5
Vyborg Rus. Fed. 28 D3
Vyborgskiy Zaliv b. Rus. Fed. 33 H3
Vychegda r. Rus. Fed. 28 H3
Vychegodskiy Rus. Fed. 28 H3
Vyerkhnyadzvinsk Belarus 31 K2
Vyetryna Belarus 28 D5
Vygozero, Ozero l. Rus. Fed. 28 E3
Vyksa Rus. Fed. 28 G5
Vylkove Ukr. 29 D7
Vym' r. Rus. Fed. 28 I3
Vypolzovo Rus. Fed. 28 E4
Vyselki Rus. Fed. 29 F7
Vyshnevolotskaya Gryada ridge Rus. Fed. 28 E4
Vyshniy-Volochek Rus. Fed. 28 E4
Vyškov Czech Rep. 37 H4
Vysoká hill Slovakia 37 I4
Vysoké Mýto Czech Rep. 37 H4
Vysokogorniy Rus. Fed. 64 D2
Vystupovychi Ukr. 29 D6
Vytegra Rus. Fed. 28 F3
Vyya r. Rus. Fed. 28 H3

↓ W

Wa Ghana 93 E3
Waajid Somalia 96 D4
Waal r. Neth. 36 B3
Waalwijk Neth. 36 B3
Waat Sudan 96 B2
Wabag P.N.G. 57 J7
Wabakimi Lake Canada 124 B3
Wabasca r. Canada 123 H3
Wabasca-Desmarais Canada 123 H4
Wabash U.S.A. 132 E3
Wabash r. U.S.A. 132 D4
Wabasha U.S.A. 132 C2
Wabassi r. Canada 124 C3
Wabē Gestro r. Eth. 96 D3
Wabē Mena r. Eth. 96 D3
Wabē Shebelē Wenz r. Eth. 96 E3
Wabigoon Lake Canada 124 A3
Wabowden Canada 123 L4
Wabrah well Saudi Arabia 80 A5
Wąbrzeźno Poland 37 I2
Wabu China 67 F1
Wabuk Point Canada 124 C2
Wabush Canada 125 H2
Waccamaw, Lake U.S.A. 129 D5
Waccasassa Bay U.S.A. 129 C6
Wächtersbach Germany 36 D3
Waco Canada 125 H3
Waco U.S.A. 133 B6
Waconda Lake U.S.A. 132 B4
Wad Pak. 81 F5
Wada'a Sudan 89 E6
Wad Banda Sudan 89 E6
Wadbilliga National Park Australia 112 D5
Waddān Libya 88 C2
Waddān, Jabal hills Libya 88 B2
Waddell Dam U.S.A. 137 F5
Waddeneilanden Neth. see West Frisian Islands
Wadden Islands Neth. see West Frisian Islands
Waddenzee sea chan. Neth. 36 B2
Waddikee Australia 109 G8
Waddington, Mount Canada 122 E5
Wadena Canada 123 K5
Wadena U.S.A. 132 C2
Wad en Nail Sudan 89 G6
Wadeye Australia 110 B2
Wadgaon India 72 B2
Wad Hamid Sudan 89 G5
Wadhwan India see Surendranagar
Wadi India 72 C2
Wadian China 67 E1
Wādī as Sīr Jordan 77 B4
Wadi Halfa Sudan 89 F4
Wādī Mūsā Jordan 77 B4
Wad Medani Sudan 89 G6
Wadsworth NV U.S.A. 136 C2
Wadsworth OH U.S.A. 130 C3
Waenhuiskrans S. Africa 98 D7
Wafangdian China 63 K4
Wafra Kuwait see Al Wafrah
Wagah India 74 B3
Wageningen Neth. 36 B3
Wageningen Suriname 147 G3
Wager Bay Canada 123 N1
Wagga Wagga Australia 112 C4
Wagin Australia 109 B8
Wagner U.S.A. 132 B3
Wagoner U.S.A. 133 C4
Wagon Mound U.S.A. 135 F5
Wągrowiec Poland 37 H2
Wah Pak. 81 H3
Wahai Indon. 57 G6
Wahda state Sudan 94 F2
Wahemen, Lac l. Canada 125 G2
Wahiawa U.S.A. 135 [inset] Y1
Wahpeton U.S.A. 132 B2
Wahran Alg. see Oran
Wah Wah Mountains U.S.A. 137 F2
Wai India 72 B2
Waiau r. N.Z. 113 C3
Waidhofen an der Thaya Austria 37 G4
Waidhofen an der Ybbs Austria 37 G5
Waigeo i. Indon. 57 H6
Waiharoa N.Z. 113 C2
Waiheke Island N.Z. 113 C2
Waihi N.Z. 113 C2
Waikabubak Indon. 56 E7
Waikaia r. N.Z. 113 B4
Waikato r. N.Z. 113 C2
Waikerie Australia 112 A4
Waiklibang Indon. 108 C2

Wailuku U.S.A. 135 [inset] Z1
Waimangaroa N.Z. 113 B3
Waimarama N.Z. 113 D2
Waimea U.S.A. 135 [inset] Z1
Wainganga r. India 72 C2
Waingapu Indon. 57 F7
Waini Point Guyana 147 G2
Wainwright Canada 123 I4
Wainwright U.S.A. 120 D2
Waiouru N.Z. 113 C2
Waipahi N.Z. 113 B4
Waipahu U.S.A. 135 [inset] Y1
Waipaoa r. N.Z. 113 D2
Waipara N.Z. 113 C3
Waipawa N.Z. 113 D2
Waipukurau N.Z. 113 D2
Wairarapa, Lake N.Z. 113 C3
Wairau r. N.Z. 113 C3
Wairoa N.Z. 113 D2
Wairoa r. N.Z. 113 D2
Waitahanui N.Z. 113 D2
Waitahuna N.Z. 113 B4
Waitaki r. N.Z. 113 B4
Waitangi S. Pacific Ocean 107 H6
Waitara N.Z. 113 C2
Waite River Australia 110 C4
Waitoa N.Z. 113 C2
Waiuku N.Z. 113 C2
Waiwera South N.Z. 113 B4
Waiyang China 67 F3
Waiyevu Fiji 107 H3
Wajima Japan 65 D5
Wajir Kenya 96 D4
Waka Dem. Rep. Congo 94 D5
Wakasa-wan b. Japan 65 C6
Wakatipu, Lake N.Z. 113 B4
Wakaw Canada 123 J4
Wakayama Japan 65 C6
WaKeeney U.S.A. 132 B4
Wakefield N.Z. 113 C3
Wakefield U.K. 35 F5
Wakefield MI U.S.A. 132 D2
Wakefield RI U.S.A. 131 H3
Wakefield VA U.S.A. 131 E5
Wakeham Canada see Kangiqsujuaq

Wake Island terr. N. Pacific Ocean 164 F4
United States Unincorporated Territory.
oceania 104–105, 114

Wakema Myanmar 61 A4
Wakkanai Japan 64 E3
Wakool Australia 112 C4
Wakool r. Australia 112 B4
Wakuach, Lac l. Canada 125 H2
Waku-Kungo Angola 95 B7
Walajapet India 72 C3
Wałbrzych Poland 37 H3
Walcha Australia 112 D3
Walcott U.S.A. 134 F4
Wałcz Poland 37 H2
Waldaist r. Austria 37 G4
Waldburg Range mts Australia 109 B6
Walden U.S.A. 131 F3
Waldenburg Poland see Wałbrzych
Waldorf U.S.A. 131 E4
Waldport U.S.A. 134 A3
Waldron U.S.A. 133 C5
Waldron, Cape Antarctica 167 F2
Waldshut Germany 36 D5
Walêg China 66 B2
Wales admin. div. U.K. 35 E5
Walewale Ghana 93 E3
Walgett Australia 111 G6
Walgreen Coast Antarctica 167 K1
Walhalla U.S.A. 132 B1
Walikale Dem. Rep. Congo 94 F5
Walker r. Australia 110 C2
Walker watercourse Australia 110 C5
Walker U.S.A. 132 C2
Walker r. U.S.A. 136 C2
Walker Creek r. Australia 111 E3
Walker Lake l. Canada 123 L4
Walker Lake U.S.A. 136 C2
Walker Lake l. U.S.A. 136 C2
Walkersville MD U.S.A. 131 E4
Walkersville WV U.S.A. 130 C4
Wall, Mount Australia 108 E5
Wallaby Island Australia 111 E2
Wallace U.S.A. 134 C3
Wallaceburg Canada 130 B2
Wallal Downs Australia 108 C4
Wallangarra Australia 112 E3
Wallaroo Australia 109 G8
Walla Walla U.S.A. 134 C3
Walldürn Germany 36 D4
Wallenpaupack, Lake U.S.A. 131 F3
Wallis, Îles Wallis and Futuna Is 107 H3

Wallis and Futuna Islands terr. S. Pacific Ocean 107 H3
French Overseas Territory.
oceania 104–105, 114

Wallis et Futuna, Îles terr. S. Pacific Ocean see Wallis and Futuna Islands
Wallis Lake inlet Australia 112 E4
Wallowa Mountains U.S.A. 134 C3
Walls U.K. 34 F1
Walls of Jerusalem National Park Australia 112 C6
Walmsley Lake Canada 123 I2
Walney, Isle of i. U.K. 35 E4
Walnut Creek U.S.A. 136 A3
Walnut Creek r. U.S.A. 132 B4
Walnut Ridge U.S.A. 133 D4
Walong India 60 B1
Walpole, Île i. New Caledonia 107 F4
Walsall U.K. 35 F5
Walsenburg U.S.A. 135 F5
Walsrode Germany 36 D2
Waltair India 73 D2
Walterboro U.S.A. 129 C5
Walter F. George Reservoir U.S.A. 129 B6
Walter's Range hills Australia 111 F6
Waltham U.S.A. 131 H2
Walton KY U.S.A. 130 A4
Walton NY U.S.A. 131 F2
Walton WV U.S.A. 130 C4
Walton-on-the-Naze U.K. 35 G6
Walvisbaai Namibia see Walvis Bay
Walvis Bay Namibia 98 B4
Walvis Bay b. Namibia 98 B4
Walvis Ridge sea feature S. Atlantic Ocean 161 N8
Wamala, Lake Uganda 96 A4
Wamba Dem. Rep. Congo 94 E4
Wamba r. Dem. Rep. Congo 95 C5
Wamba Nigeria 93 H3
Wami r. Tanz. 97 C6
Wampusirpi Hond. 139 H5
Wanaaring Australia 112 C3
Wanaka N.Z. 113 B4
Wanaka, Lake N.Z. 113 B4
Wanaque Reservoir U.S.A. 131 F3
Wanbi Australia 112 B4
Wanbi China 66 B3
Wanbrow, Cape N.Z. 113 B4
Wanda Arg. 152 G1
Wanda Shan mts China 64 C3
Wandering River Canada 123 H4
Wanding China 66 A3
Wandingzhen China see Wanding
Wandiwash India see Vandavasi
Wandlitz Germany 37 F2
Wandoan Australia 111 G5
Wang, Mae Nam r. Thai. 60 B4
Wanganui N.Z. 113 C2
Wanganui r. N.Z. 113 C2
Wangaratta Australia 112 C5
Wangcang China 66 C1
Wangcheng China 67 E2
Wangda China see Zogang
Wangdue Phodrang Bhutan 75 F4
Wanggamet, Gunung mt. Indon. 108 C2
Wangkui China 64 A3
Wang Mai Khon Thai. see Sawankhalok
Wangmo China 66 C3
Wangolodougou Côte d'Ivoire see Ouangolodougou
Wangqing China 64 B4
Wangying China see Huaiyin
Wangziguan China 66 C1
Wanham Canada 122 G4
Wanhatti Suriname 147 H3
Wan Hsa-la Myanmar 60 B3
Wanie-Rukula Dem. Rep. Congo 94 E4
Wankaner India 74 A5
Wankie Zimbabwe see Hwange
Wanlaweyn Somalia 96 E4
Wanna Lakes salt flat Australia 109 E7
Wannian China 67 F2
Wanning China 67 D5
Wanshan Qundao is China 67 E4
Wantage U.K. 35 F6
Wanxian China 67 D2
Wanyuan China 66 D1
Wanzai China 67 E2
Wanzhi China see Wuhu
Wapakoneta U.S.A. 130 A3
Wapawekka Lake Canada 123 J4
Wapikopa Lake Canada 124 B2
Wapiti r. Canada 122 G4
Wappingers Falls U.S.A. 131 G3
Wapsipinicon r. U.S.A. 132 D3
Wapusk National Park Canada 124 A1
Waqên China 66 B1
Waqf aş Şawwān, Jibāl hills Jordan 77 C4
Wāqişah well Iraq 79 E5
War U.S.A. 130 C5
Warab Sudan 94 F2
Warab state Sudan 94 F2
Waradi waterhole Kenya 96 D4
Warah Pak. 81 F5
Warandab Eth. 96 E3
Warangal India 72 C2
Waraseoni India 74 D5
Warbreccan Australia 111 E5
Warburg Germany 36 D3
Warburton Vic. Australia 112 C5
Warburton W.A. Australia 110 A5
Warburton watercourse Australia 110 D5
Warburton Bay Canada 123 I2
Warche r. Belgium 39 F1
Ward watercourse Australia 111 F5
Ward, Mount N.Z. 113 B3
Wardeglo waterhole Kenya 96 D4
Wardha India 72 C1
Wardha r. India 72 C2
Ward Hill U.K. 34 E2
Ware Canada 122 E3
Ware U.S.A. 131 G2
Wareham U.K. 35 E6
Waremme Belgium 36 B3
Waren Germany 37 F2
Warendorf Germany 36 C3
Warginburra Peninsula Australia 111 G4
Wargla Alg. see Ouargla
War Gunbi waterhole Somalia 96 E2
Warialda Australia 111 G6
Warin Chamrap Thai. 61 D5
Warka Poland 37 J3
Warkworth N.Z. 113 C2
War Idaad Somalia 96 E2
Warli China see Walêg
Warman Canada 123 J4
Warmbad Namibia 98 C6
Warmia reg. Poland 37 J1
Warm Springs NV U.S.A. 135 C5
Warm Springs VA U.S.A. 130 D4
Warner Canada 123 H5
Warner Lakes U.S.A. 134 C4
Warner Mountains U.S.A. 134 B4
Warner Robins U.S.A. 129 C5
Warner Springs U.S.A. 137 D5
Warnes Bol. 149 E4
Waroona Australia 109 A8
Warora India 72 C1
Warra Australia 111 G5
Warracknabeal Australia 112 B5
Warragul Australia 112 C5
Warrambool r. Australia 112 C3
Warrandirinna, Lake salt flat Australia 110 D5
Warrawagine Australia 108 C5
Warrego r. Australia 111 F6
Warrego Range hills Australia 111 F5
Warren Australia 112 C3
Warren r. Australia 109 A8
Warren AR U.S.A. 133 C5
Warren MI U.S.A. 130 B2
Warren MN U.S.A. 132 B1
Warren OH U.S.A. 130 C3
Warren PA U.S.A. 130 D3
Warren Hastings Island Palau see Merir
Warren Island U.S.A. 122 C4
Warrenpoint U.K. 35 C4
Warrensburg MO U.S.A. 132 C4
Warrensburg NY U.S.A. 131 G2
Warrenton MO U.S.A. 132 D4
Warrenton VA U.S.A. 130 E4
Warri Nigeria 93 G4
Warriners Creek watercourse Australia 110 D6
Warrington N.Z. 113 B4
Warrington U.K. 35 E5
Warrington U.S.A. 129 B6
Warrnambool Australia 112 B5
Warroad U.S.A. 132 C1
Warrumbungle National Park Australia 112 D3
Warry Warry watercourse Australia 111 E6

Warsaw Poland 37 J2
Capital of Poland.

Warsaw IN U.S.A. 132 E3
Warsaw KY U.S.A. 130 A4
Warsaw MO U.S.A. 132 C4
Warsaw NY U.S.A. 130 D2
Warsaw VA U.S.A. 131 E5
Warsingsfehn Germany 36 C2
Warszawa Poland see Warsaw
Warta Poland 37 I3
Warta r. Poland 37 G2
Wartburg U.S.A. 128 B4
Waru Indon. 59 G3
Warud India 74 C5
Warwick Australia 111 H6
Warwick NY U.S.A. 131 F3
Warwick RI U.S.A. 131 H3
Warzhong China 66 B2
Wasa Canada 123 H5
Wasagu Nigeria 93 G3
Wasaga Beach Canada 130 C1
Wasatch Range mts U.S.A. 137 G2
Wascana Creek r. Canada 123 J5
Wasco U.S.A. 136 C4
Waseca U.S.A. 132 C2
Washado Suriname 147 G3
Washap Pak. 81 E5
Washburn ND U.S.A. 132 A2
Washburn WI U.S.A. 132 D2
Washim India 72 C1
Washimeska r. Canada 125 F3

Washington DC U.S.A. 131 E4
Capital of the United States of America.
world 8–9

Washington GA U.S.A. 129 C5
Washington IN U.S.A. 128 B4
Washington KS U.S.A. 132 B4
Washington KY U.S.A. 130 B4
Washington NC U.S.A. 128 D5
Washington NJ U.S.A. 131 F3
Washington PA U.S.A. 130 C3
Washington state U.S.A. 134 B3
Washington, Cape Antarctica 167 H2
Washington, Mount U.S.A. 131 H1
Washington Court House U.S.A. 130 B4
Washington Island U.S.A. 128 B2
Washington Land reg. Greenland 121 M2
Washir Afgh. 81 E3
Washita r. U.S.A. 133 B5
Washpool National Park Australia 112 E3
Washtucna U.S.A. 134 C3
Wasi' Saudi Arabia 80 A5
Wasilla U.S.A. 120 E3
Wāsiţ governorate Iraq 79 F4
Wasit tourist site Iraq 79 F4
Waskaganish Canada 124 E3
Waskaiowaka Lake Canada 123 L3
Wasletan Indon. 108 E1
Waspán Nicaragua 139 H6
Wassadou Senegal 92 B2
Wassenaar Neth. 36 B2
Wasser Namibia 98 C5
Wasserkuppe hill Germany 36 D3
Wassou Guinea 92 B3
Wassuk Range mts U.S.A. 136 C2
Wassy France 39 F2
Watampone Indon. 57 F6
Watapi Lake Canada 123 I4
Watarrka National Park Australia 110 B5
Watenstadt-Salzgitter Germany see Salzgitter
Waterberg Plateau Game Park nature res. Namibia 98 C4
Waterbury CT U.S.A. 131 G3
Waterbury VT U.S.A. 131 G1
Water Cays i. Bahamas 129 D8
Wateree r. U.S.A. 129 C5
Waterford Rep. of Ireland 35 C5
Waterford U.S.A. 130 D3
Waterhen r. Canada 123 J4
Waterhen Lake Canada 123 L4
Waterloo Canada 130 C2
Waterloo IA U.S.A. 132 C3
Waterloo IL U.S.A. 132 D4
Waterloo NY U.S.A. 131 E2
Waterpoort S. Africa 99 F4
Waterton Lakes National Park Canada 123 H5
Watertown NY U.S.A. 131 F2
Watertown SD U.S.A. 132 B2
Watertown WI U.S.A. 132 D3
Waterval-Boven S. Africa 99 F5
Water Valley U.S.A. 133 D5
Waterville Rep. of Ireland 35 A6
Waterville ME U.S.A. 131 I1
Waterville WA U.S.A. 134 B3
Watford Canada 130 C2
Watford U.K. 35 F6
Watford City U.S.A. 132 A2
Wathaman r. Canada 123 K3
Wathaman Lake Canada 123 K3
Watheroo Australia 109 B7
Watheroo National Park Australia 109 A7
Watīr, Wādī watercourse Egypt 77 B5
Watkins Glen U.S.A. 131 E2
Watkinsville U.S.A. 129 C5
Watling Island Bahamas see San Salvador
Watonga U.S.A. 133 B5
Watrous Canada 134 F2
Watrous U.S.A. 135 F6
Watsa Dem. Rep. Congo 94 F4
Watseka U.S.A. 132 E3
Watson r. Australia 111 E2
Watson Canada 123 J4
Watson Lake Canada 122 D2
Watsonville U.S.A. 136 B3
Watterson Lake Canada 123 L2
Watts Bar Lake resr U.S.A. 128 B5
Wattsburg U.S.A. 130 D2
Watubela, Kepulauan is Indon. 57 H6
Wau P.N.G. 57 K7
Wau Sudan 94 E3
Wau watercourse Sudan 94 E3
Wauchope N.S.W. Australia 112 E3
Wauchope N.T. Australia 110 C4
Wauchula U.S.A. 129 C7
Waukarlycarly, Lake salt flat Australia 108 C5
Waukegan U.S.A. 132 E3
Waukesha U.S.A. 132 D3
Waupaca U.S.A. 132 D2
Waurika U.S.A. 133 B5
Wausau U.S.A. 132 D2
Wauseon U.S.A. 130 A3
Wautoma U.S.A. 128 A2
Waverly IA U.S.A. 132 C3
Waverly NY U.S.A. 131 E2
Waverly OH U.S.A. 130 B4
Waverly TN U.S.A. 128 B4
Waverly VA U.S.A. 131 E5
Wavre Belgium 39 F1
Waw Myanmar 60 B4
Wawa Nigeria 93 G3
Wawagosic r. Canada 124 E3
Wāw al Kabīr Libya 88 C3
Wāw an Nāmūs waterhole Libya 88 C3
Wawoi r. P.N.G. 57 J7
Waxahachie U.S.A. 133 B5
Waxü China 66 B1
Way, Lake salt flat Australia 109 C6
Waycross U.S.A. 129 C6
Way Kambas National Park Indon. 58 D4
Wayland KY U.S.A. 130 B5
Wayland NY U.S.A. 130 E2
Wayne NE U.S.A. 132 B3
Wayne WV U.S.A. 130 B4
Waynesboro GA U.S.A. 129 C5
Waynesboro MS U.S.A. 129 A6
Waynesboro PA U.S.A. 130 E4
Waynesboro TN U.S.A. 128 B5
Waynesboro VA U.S.A. 130 D4
Waynesburg U.S.A. 130 C4
Waynesville MO U.S.A. 132 C4
Waynesville NC U.S.A. 128 C5
Waza Myanmar 60 B2
Waza, Parc National de nat. park Cameroon 93 I3
Wazi Khwa Afgh. 81 G3
Wazirabad Pak. 74 B2
Wda r. Poland 37 I2
W du Niger, Parcs Nationaux du nat. park Niger 93 F3
We New Caledonia 107 F4
We, Pulau i. Indon. 58 A1
Weagamow Lake Canada 124 B2
Wear r. U.K. 35 F4
Weatherford OK U.S.A. 133 B5
Weatherford TX U.S.A. 133 B5
Weatherly U.S.A. 131 F3
Weaverville U.S.A. 134 B4
Webequie Canada 124 C2
Weber r. U.S.A. 134 D4
Weber, Mount Canada 122 D4
Weber Basin sea feature Indon. 164 C6

Webi Shabeelle r. Somalia 96 D4
5th longest river in Africa.
africa 84–85

Webster MA U.S.A. 131 H2
Webster SD U.S.A. 132 B2
Webster City U.S.A. 132 C3
Webster Springs U.S.A. 130 C4
Webuye Kenya 96 B4
Wecho r. Canada 123 H2
Wecho Lake Canada 123 H2
Wedau P.N.G. 111 G1
Weddell Abyssal Plain sea feature Southern Ocean 163 E10
Weddell Island Falkland Is 153 E7
Weddell Sea Antarctica 167 A2
Wedge Mountain Canada 122 F5
Weed U.S.A. 134 B4
Weedville U.S.A. 130 D3
Weener Germany 36 C2
Weert Neth. 36 B3
Wee Waa Australia 112 D3
Wegberg Germany 36 C3
Węgliniec Poland 37 G3
Węgorzewo Poland 37 J1
Węgorzyno Poland 37 G2
Węgrów Poland 37 K2
Wei r. China 67 D1
Weiden in der Oberpfalz Germany 36 F4
Weidongmen China see Qianjin
Weifang China 63 J4
Weihai China 63 K4
Weihu Ling mts China 64 A4
Weilburg Germany 39 H1
Weilheim in Oberbayern Germany 36 E5
Weimar Germany 36 E3
Weinan China 67 D1
Weingarten Germany 36 D5
Weinheim Germany 36 D4
Weining China 66 C3
Weipa Australia 111 E2
Weir r. Australia 111 G6
Weir River Canada 123 M3
Weiser U.S.A. 134 C3
Weiser r. U.S.A. 134 C3
Weishan China 66 B3
Weishan Hu l. China 67 F1
Weishi China 67 E1
Weißenburg in Bayern Germany 36 E4
Weißenfels Germany 36 E3
Weisshorn mt. Switz. 39 G3
Weiss Lake U.S.A. 133 E5
Weissmies mt. Switz. 39 H3
Weissrand Mountains Namibia 98 C5
Weißwasser Germany 37 G3
Weixin China 66 C3
Weiyuan Gansu China 66 C1
Weiyuan Yunnan China see Jinggu
Weiyuan Jiang r. China 66 B4
Weiz Austria 37 G5
Weizhou China see Wenchuan
Weizhou Dao i. China 67 D4
Wejherowo Poland 37 I1
Wekusko Canada 123 L4
Wekusko Lake Canada 123 L4
Wekweti Canada 123 H1
Wel r. Poland 37 I2
Welatam Myanmar 60 B2
Welbourn Hill Australia 110 C5
Welch U.S.A. 130 C5
Weldiya Eth. 96 C2
Weld Range hills Australia 109 B6
Welford National Park Australia 111 E5
Welk'īt'ē Eth. 96 C2
Welkom S. Africa 99 E5
Welland Canada 130 D2
Welland r. U.K. 35 F5
Welland Canal Canada 130 D2
Wellesley Canada 130 C2
Wellesley Islands Australia 111 D3
Wellesley Lake Canada 122 B2
Wellfleet U.S.A. 131 H3
Wellingborough U.K. 35 F5
Wellington Australia 112 D4
Wellington Canada 131 E2

Wellington N.Z. 113 C3
Capital of New Zealand.
oceania 114

Wellington CO U.S.A. 134 F4
Wellington KS U.S.A. 132 B4
Wellington NV U.S.A. 136 C2
Wellington OH U.S.A. 130 B3
Wellington TX U.S.A. 133 A5
Wellington UT U.S.A. 137 G2
Wellington, Isla i. Chile 153 B7
Wellington Range hills N.T. Australia 108 F3
Wellington Range hills W.A. Australia 109 C6
Wells U.S.A. 134 D4
Wells, Lake salt flat Australia 109 C6
Wellsboro U.S.A. 131 E3
Wellsford N.Z. 113 C2
Wells-next-the-Sea U.K. 35 G5
Wellsville U.S.A. 130 E2
Wellton U.S.A. 137 E5
Wełna r. Poland 37 H2
Weloka U.S.A. 135 [inset] Z2
Wels Austria 37 G4
Welshpool U.K. 35 E5
Welwitschia Namibia see Khorixas
Wema Dem. Rep. Congo 94 D5
Wembere r. Tanz. 97 B6
Wembesi S. Africa 99 F6
Wembley Canada 122 G4
Wemindji Canada 124 E2
Wemyss Bight Bahamas 129 D7
Wenamu r. Guyana/Venez. 147 F3
Wenatchee U.S.A. 134 B3
Wenatchee Mountains U.S.A. 134 B3
Wenchang Hainan China 67 D5
Wenchang Sichuan China see Zitong
Wencheng China 67 G3
Wenchi Ghana 93 E4
Wench'it Shet' r. Eth. 96 C2
Wenchow China see Wenzhou
Wenchuan China 66 B2
Wendelstein mt. Germany 36 F5
Wenden Latvia see Cēsis
Wenden U.S.A. 137 F5
Wendo Eth. 96 C3
Wendover U.S.A. 137 E1
Wenfeng China see Yongfeng
Wengshui China 66 A2
Wengyuan China 67 E3
Wenhua China see Weishan
Wenjiashi China 67 E3
Wenlan China see Mengzi
Wenlin China see Renshou
Wenling China 67 G2
Wenlock r. Australia 111 E2
Wenona U.S.A. 131 F4
Wenping China see Ludian
Wenquan Guizhou China 66 C2
Wenquan Hubei China see Yingshan

Wenquan Qinghai China 75 F2
Highest settlement in the world.

Wenquanzhen China 67 E2
Wenshan China 66 C4
Wensum r. U.K. 35 G5
Wentworth Australia 112 B4
Wentworth U.S.A. 131 H2
Wenxian China 66 C1
Wenzhou China 67 G3
Wer India 74 C4
Werda Botswana 98 D5
Werdau Germany 37 F3
Werder Eth. 96 E3
Werder Germany 37 F2
Werl Germany 36 C3
Wernecke Mountains Canada 122 B1
Werota Eth. 96 C2
Werra r. Germany 36 D3
Werris Creek Australia 112 D3
Werwaru Indon. 108 E2
Wesel Germany 36 C3
Weser r. Germany 36 D2
Weser sea chan. Germany 36 D2
Wesergebirge hills Germany 36 D2
Wesleyville Canada 125 K3
Wessel, Cape Australia 110 D1
Wessel Islands Australia 110 D1
Wessington Springs U.S.A. 132 B2
Westall, Point Australia 109 F8
West Alligator r. Australia 110 C2
West Allis U.S.A. 132 D3
West Antarctica reg. Antarctica 167 J1
West Australian Basin sea feature Indian Ocean 162 N7
West Baines r. Australia 110 B2
West Banas r. India 74 A5

West Bank terr. Asia 77 B4
Territory occupied by Israel.
asia 82

West Bay Canada 125 J2
West Bend U.S.A. 132 D3
West Bengal state India 75 E5
West Branch U.S.A. 130 A1
Westbrook U.S.A. 131 H2
Westby U.S.A. 132 D3
West Cape Howe Australia 109 B8
West Caroline Basin sea feature N. Pacific Ocean 164 D5
West Chester U.S.A. 131 F4
Westcliffe U.S.A. 135 F5
West End Bahamas 129 D7
West End U.S.A. 131 F2
Westerland Germany 33 C5
Western watercourse Australia 111 E4
Western r. Canada 123 J1
Western admin. reg. Ghana 93 E4
Western prov. Kenya 96 B4
Western prov. Zambia 95 D8
Western Area admin. div. Sierra Leone 92 B3
Western Australia state Australia 110 A4
Western Bahr el Ghazal state Sudan 94 E3
Western Cape prov. S. Africa 98 D7
Western Darfur state Sudan 88 D6
Western Desert Egypt 89 F3
Western Dvina r. Europe see Zapadnaya Dvina
Western Equatoria state Sudan 94 F3
Western Ghats mts India 72 B3
Western Kordofan state Sudan 94 F2
Western Province prov. Zambia see Copperbelt

Western Sahara terr. Africa 90 B4
Disputed territory (Morocco).
africa 86–87, 100

Western Samoa country S. Pacific Ocean see Samoa
Western Sayan Mountains reg. Rus. Fed. see Zapadnyy Sayan
Westerschelde est. Neth. 36 A3
Westerstede Germany 36 C2
Westerville U.S.A. 130 B3
Westerwald hills Germany 36 C3
West Falkland i. Falkland Is 153 E7
West Fargo U.S.A. 132 B2
West Fayu atoll Micronesia 57 K4
Westfield MA U.S.A. 131 G2
Westfield NY U.S.A. 130 D2
Westfield PA U.S.A. 130 E3
West Frisian Islands Neth. 36 B2
Westgate Australia 111 F5
West Grand Lake U.S.A. 128 G2
West Hamlin U.S.A. 130 B4
West Hartford U.S.A. 131 G3
West Haven U.S.A. 131 G3
West Ice Shelf Antarctica 167 E2
West Indies N. America 127 L7
West Island India 73 G3
West Jordan U.S.A. 137 G1
West Kazakhstan Oblast admin. div. Kazakh. see Zapadnyy Kazakhstan
West Lafayette U.S.A. 132 E3
West Lamma Channel Hong Kong China 67 [inset]
Westland Australia 111 E4
Westland National Park N.Z. 113 B3
West Liberty KY U.S.A. 130 B5
West Liberty OH U.S.A. 130 B3
Westlock Canada 123 H4
West Lorne Canada 130 C2
West Lunga r. Zambia 95 E8
West Lunga National Park Zambia 95 E8
West MacDonnell National Park Australia 110 C4
West Malaysia pen. Malaysia see Peninsular Malaysia
Westmalle Belgium 36 B3
Westman Islands Iceland see Vestmannaeyjar
Westmar Australia 111 G5
West Mariana Basin sea feature N. Pacific Ocean 164 D4
West Memphis U.S.A. 133 D5
Westminster U.S.A. 131 E4
West Monroe U.S.A. 133 C5
Westmoreland Australia 110 D3
West Nicholson Zimbabwe 99 F4
West Nueces r. U.S.A. 133 B6
Weston OH U.S.A. 130 B3
Weston WV U.S.A. 130 C4
Weston-super-Mare U.K. 35 E6
Westover U.S.A. 131 F4
West Palm Beach U.S.A. 129 C7
West Plains U.S.A. 133 D4
West Point pt Australia 112 C6
West Point CA U.S.A. 136 B2
West Point MS U.S.A. 129 A5
West Point NY U.S.A. 131 G3
West Point VA U.S.A. 131 E5
West Point Lake resr U.S.A. 129 B5
Westport Canada 131 E1
Westport N.Z. 113 B3
Westport Rep. of Ireland 35 B5
Westport CA U.S.A. 136 A2
Westport NY U.S.A. 131 G1
Westray Canada 123 K4
Westray i. U.K. 34 E2
Westray Firth sea chan. U.K. 34 E2
Westree Canada 124 D4
West Road r. Canada 122 F4
West Sacramento U.S.A. 136 B2
West Salem U.S.A. 130 B3
West Siberian Plain Rus. Fed. 26 I3
West Union IA U.S.A. 132 D3
West Union OH U.S.A. 130 B4
West Union WV U.S.A. 130 C4
West Valley City U.S.A. 137 G1
Westville U.S.A. 133 C5
West Virginia state U.S.A. 130 C4
West Walker r. U.S.A. 136 C2
Westwood U.S.A. 136 B1
West Wyalong Australia 112 C4
West York U.S.A. 131 E4
Wetan i. Indon. 108 E1
Wetar i. Indon. 57 G7
Wetar, Selat sea chan. Indon. 108 D2
Wetaskiwin Canada 123 H4
Wete Dem. Rep. Congo 95 E6
Wete Tanz. 97 C6
Wetumpka U.S.A. 129 B5
Wetzlar Germany 36 D3
Wewahitchka U.S.A. 129 B6
Wewak P.N.G. 57 J6
Wexford Rep. of Ireland 35 C5
Wexford Harbour b. Rep. of Ireland 35 C5
Weyakwin Canada 123 J4
Weyburn Canada 134 G2
Weyer Markt Austria 37 G5
Weyhe Germany 36 D2
Weymouth Canada 125 H4
Weymouth U.K. 35 E6
Weymouth U.S.A. 131 H2
Whakaari i. N.Z. 113 D2
Whakatane N.Z. 113 D2
Whakatane r. N.Z. 113 D2
Whale r. Canada see La Baleine, Rivière à
Whale Cove Canada 123 M2
Whaleyville U.S.A. 131 E5
Whalsay i. U.K. 34 F1
Whampoa, Sungai r. Sing. 58 [inset]
Whangamata N.Z. 113 C2
Whangamomona N.Z. 113 C2
Whanganui National Park N.Z. 113 C2
Whangarei N.Z. 113 C1
Whapmagoostui Canada 124 E2
Wharfe r. U.K. 35 F5
Wharncliffe U.S.A. 130 C5
Wharton U.S.A. 133 B6
Wharton Lake Canada 123 L1
Wha Ti Canada 123 G2
Wheatland CA U.S.A. 136 B2
Wheatland WY U.S.A. 134 F4
Wheatley Canada 130 B2
Wheatley U.S.A. 130 A4
Wheaton IL U.S.A. 132 D3
Wheaton MN U.S.A. 132 B2
Wheaton-Glenmont U.S.A. 131 E4
Wheeler U.S.A. 133 A5
Wheeler Lake Canada 123 H2
Wheeler Lake resr U.S.A. 129 B5
Wheeler Peak NM U.S.A. 135 F5
Wheeler Peak NV U.S.A. 137 E2
Wheelersburg U.S.A. 130 B4
Wheeler Springs U.S.A. 136 C4
Wheeling U.S.A. 130 C3
Whim Creek Australia 108 B5
Whinham, Mount Australia 110 B5
Whiskey Jack Lake Canada 123 K3
Whispering Pines U.S.A. 136 A2
Whistler Canada 134 B2
Whitbourne Canada 125 K4
Whitby Canada 130 D2
Whitby U.K. 35 F4
Whitchurch U.K. 35 E5
Whitchurch-Stouffville Canada 130 D2
White r. Canada 124 C3
White r. Canada/U.S.A. 122 B2
White r. AR U.S.A. 133 D5
White r. CO U.S.A. 137 H1
White r. IN U.S.A. 128 B4
White r. NV U.S.A. 137 E3
White r. SD U.S.A. 132 B3
White r. VT U.S.A. 131 G2
White watercourse AZ U.S.A. 137 G5
White watercourse TX U.S.A. 133 A5
White, East Fork r. U.S.A. 128 B4
White, Lake salt flat Australia 110 B4
White, North Fork r. U.S.A. 132 C4
White Bay Canada 125 J3
White Butte mt. U.S.A. 134 G3
White Canyon U.S.A. 137 G3
White Cliffs Australia 112 B3
White Cloud U.S.A. 132 E3
Whitecourt Canada 123 H4
Whiteface Mountain U.S.A. 131 G1
Whitefield U.S.A. 131 H1
Whitefish r. Canada 122 E1
Whitefish U.S.A. 134 D2
Whitefish Bay U.S.A. 132 E2
Whitefish Lake Canada 123 J2
Whitefish Point U.S.A. 132 E2
White Hall U.S.A. 132 D4
Whitehall MT U.S.A. 134 D3
Whitehall NY U.S.A. 131 G2
Whitehall OH U.S.A. 130 B4
Whitehaven U.K. 35 E4
White Haven U.S.A. 131 F3
White Hill Canada 125 I4

Whitehorse Canada 122 C2
Territorial capital of Yukon.

White Horse, Vale of valley U.K. 35 F6
White Island Antarctica 167 D2
White Island N.Z. see Whakaari
White Lake salt flat Australia 109 C6
White Lake U.S.A. 133 C6
Whitemark Australia 112 D6
White Mountain Peak U.S.A. 136 C3
White Mountains U.S.A. 131 H1
White Mountains National Park Australia 111 F4
Whitemouth Lake Canada 132 C1
White Nile state Sudan 96 B1
White Nile r. Sudan/Uganda 96 B2
also known as Abiad, Bahr el or Jebel, Bahr el
White Nile Dam Sudan 89 G6
White Nossob watercourse Namibia 98 C4
White Oak U.S.A. 130 B5
White Otter Lake Canada 124 B3
White Pass Canada/U.S.A. 122 C3
White Pine Range mts U.S.A. 137 E2
White River Canada 124 C3
Whiteriver U.S.A. 137 H5
White River U.S.A. 132 A3
White River Junction U.S.A. 131 G2
White River Valley U.S.A. 137 E2
White Russia country Europe see Belarus
Whitesail Lake Canada 122 E4
Whitesand r. Alta/N.W.T. Canada 123 H2
Whitesand r. Sask. Canada 134 G2

White Sands National Monument nat. park U.S.A. 135 F6
Whitesburg U.S.A. 130 B5
White Sea Rus. Fed. 28 F2
White Stone U.S.A. 131 E5
White Sulphur Springs MT U.S.A. 134 E3
White Sulphur Springs WV U.S.A. 130 C5
Whitesville U.S.A. 130 C5
Whiteville U.S.A. 129 D5
White Volta r. Burkina/Ghana 93 E3
White Volta watercourse Burkina/Ghana 93 E3
White Water U.S.A. 137 D5
Whitewater CO U.S.A. 134 E5
Whitewater WI U.S.A. 132 D3
Whitewater Baldy mt. U.S.A. 135 E6
White Well Australia 109 E7
White Woman Creek r. U.S.A. 132 A4
Whitewood Australia 111 E4
Whitewood Canada 123 K5
Whithorn U.K. 35 D4
Whitianga N.Z. 113 C2
Whitley City U.S.A. 130 A5
Whitmire U.S.A. 129 C5
Whitmore Mountains Antarctica 167 K1
Whitney, Lake U.S.A. 133 B6
Whitney, Mount U.S.A. 136 C3
Whitstable U.K. 35 G6
Whitsunday Group is Australia 111 G4
Whitsunday Island National Park Australia 111 G4
Whitsun Island Vanuatu see Pentecost Island
Whittemore U.S.A. 130 B1
Whittier U.S.A. 136 C5
Whittlesey U.K. 35 F5
Whitton Australia 112 C4
Whitula watercourse Australia 111 E5
Wholdaia Lake Canada 123 J2
Whyalla Australia 112 A4
Whydah Benin see Ouidah
Wiang Kosai National Park Thai. 60 B4
Wiang Pa Pao Thai. 60 B4
Wiang Phran Thai. 60 B4
Wiang Sa Thai. 60 C4
Wiarton Canada 130 C1
Wibaux U.S.A. 134 F3
Wichelen Belgium 36 A3
Wichita U.S.A. 132 B4
Wichita r. U.S.A. 133 B5
Wichita Falls U.S.A. 133 B5
Wichita Mountains U.S.A. 133 B5
Wick U.K. 34 E2
Wickenburg U.S.A. 135 D6
Wickepin Australia 109 B8
Wickham r. Australia 110 B3
Wickham, Cape Australia 112 B5
Wicklow Rep. of Ireland 35 C5
Wicklow Head Rep. of Ireland 35 D5
Wicklow Mountains Rep. of Ireland 35 C5
Wicklow Mountains National Park Rep. of Ireland 35 C5
Widawa r. Poland 37 H3
Widawka r. Poland 37 I3
Wideroe, Mount Antarctica 167 C2
Widgiemooltha Australia 109 C7
Wi-do i. S. Korea 65 A6
Wied r. Germany 36 C3
Wiehengebirge hills Germany 36 D2
Wieleń Poland 37 H2
Wielka Sowa mt. Poland 37 H3
Wielkopolskie, Pojezierze reg. Poland 37 H2
Wielkopolski Park Narodowy nat. park Poland 37 H2
Wieluń Poland 37 I3
Wien Austria see Vienna
Wiener Neustadt Austria 37 H5
Wiensberg mt. Austria 37 G4
Wieprz r. Poland 37 J3
Wieprza r. Poland 37 H1
Wieringerwerf Neth. 36 B2
Wieruszów Poland 37 I3
Wierzyca r. Poland 37 I2
Wiesbaden Germany 36 D3
Wiesloch Germany 36 D4
Wiesmoor Germany 36 C2
Wieżyca hill Poland 37 I1
Wigan U.K. 35 E5
Wiggins U.S.A. 129 A6
Wight, Isle of i. U.K. 35 F6
Wigierski Park Narodowy nat. park Poland 37 K1
Wignes Lake Canada 123 J2
Wigtown U.K. 34 D4
Wigtown Bay U.K. 35 D4
Wikieup U.S.A. 137 F4
Wil Switz. 39 H3
Wilberforce, Cape Australia 110 D1
Wilbur U.S.A. 134 C3
Wilburton U.S.A. 133 C5
Wilcannia Australia 112 B3
Wilcox U.S.A. 130 D3
Wilczek Land i. Rus. Fed. see Vil'cheka, Zemlya
Wildcat Peak U.S.A. 137 D2
Wild Coast S. Africa 99 F6
Wilderness U.S.A. 130 E4
Wildeshausen Germany 36 D2
Wildhay r. Canada 122 G4
Wildhorn mt. Switz. 39 G3
Wild Horse Draw r. U.S.A. 135 F7
Wild Horse Hill mt. U.S.A. 132 A3
Wildon Austria 37 G5
Wild Rice r. MN U.S.A. 132 B2
Wild Rice r. ND U.S.A. 132 B2
Wildwood FL U.S.A. 129 C6
Wildwood NJ U.S.A. 131 F4
Wiley Ford U.S.A. 130 D4
Wilga r. Poland 37 J3
Wilge r. S. Africa 99 F5
Wilgena Australia 109 F7
▶Wilhelm, Mount P.N.G. 57 J7
5th highest mountain in Oceania.
oceania 102–103
Wilhelmina Gebergte mts Suriname 147 G4
Wilhelm-Pieck-Stadt Germany see Guben
Wilhelmsburg Austria 37 G4
Wilhelmshaven Germany 36 D2
Wilhelmstal Namibia 98 C4
Wilkes-Barre U.S.A. 131 F3
Wilkesboro U.S.A. 128 C4
Wilkes Coast Antarctica 167 G2
Wilkes Land reg. Antarctica 167 G2
Wilkie Canada 134 E1
Wilkins Coast Antarctica 167 L2
Wilkins Ice Shelf Antarctica 167 L2
Wilkinson Lakes salt flat Australia 110 C6
Will, Mount Canada 122 D3
Willamette r. U.S.A. 134 B3
Willandra Billabong watercourse Australia 112 C4
Willandra National Park Australia 112 C4
Willapa Bay U.S.A. 134 A3
Willard Mex. 135 E7
Willard NM U.S.A. 135 F6
Willard OH U.S.A. 130 B3
Willards U.S.A. 131 F4
Willcox U.S.A. 135 E6
▶Willemstad Neth. Antilles 146 D1
Capital of the Netherlands Antilles.
Willeroo Australia 110 B2
William r. Canada 123 I3
William, Mount Australia 112 B5
William Creek Australia 110 D6
William Lake Canada 123 L4
Williams Australia 109 B8
Williams r. Australia 111 E4
Williams AZ U.S.A. 137 F4
Williams CA U.S.A. 136 A2
Williamsburg IA U.S.A. 132 C3
Williamsburg KY U.S.A. 130 A5
Williamsburg OH U.S.A. 130 A4
Williamsburg VA U.S.A. 131 E5
Williams Lake Canada 122 F4
Williamson NY U.S.A. 131 E2
Williamson WV U.S.A. 130 B5
Williamsport IN U.S.A. 128 B3
Williamsport OH U.S.A. 130 B4
Williamsport PA U.S.A. 131 E3
Williamston U.S.A. 128 D5
Williamstown KY U.S.A. 130 A4
Williamstown MA U.S.A. 131 G2
Williamstown NY U.S.A. 131 F2
Willimantic U.S.A. 131 G3
Willis Group atolls Australia 111 G3
Willis Islands S. Georgia 153 [inset]
Williston S. Africa 98 D6
Williston FL U.S.A. 129 C6
Williston ND U.S.A. 134 G2
Williston SC U.S.A. 129 C5
Williston Lake Canada 122 F4
Willits U.S.A. 136 A2
Willmar U.S.A. 132 C2
Willoughby U.S.A. 130 C3
Willow r. Canada 122 F4
Willow Bunch Canada 134 F2
Willow Creek r. Canada 123 H5
Willow Creek U.S.A. 134 B4
Willow Hill U.S.A. 130 E3
Willow Lake Canada 122 G2
Willowlake r. Canada 122 F2
Willowmore S. Africa 98 D7
Willows U.S.A. 136 A2
Willow Springs U.S.A. 132 D4
Willowvale S. Africa 99 F7
Wills, Lake salt flat Australia 110 B4
Wills Creek watercourse Australia 111 E4
Wilmington Australia 112 A4
Wilmington DE U.S.A. 131 F4
Wilmington NC U.S.A. 129 D5
Wilmington OH U.S.A. 130 B4
Wilmington VT U.S.A. 131 G2
Wilmington Island U.S.A. 129 C5
Wilmore U.S.A. 130 A5
Wilno Lith. see Vilnius
Wilpattu National Park Sri Lanka 72 D4
Wilpena watercourse Australia 112 A3
Wilson watercourse Australia 111 E5
Wilson atoll Micronesia see Ifalik
Wilson NC U.S.A. 128 D5
Wilson NY U.S.A. 130 D2
Wilson, Mount CO U.S.A. 135 F5
Wilson, Mount NV U.S.A. 137 E2
Wilsonia U.S.A. 136 C3
Wilson Lake resr U.S.A. 128 B5
Wilsons U.S.A. 130 E5
Wilson's Promontory pen. Australia 112 C5
Wilson's Promontory National Park Australia 112 C5
Wilton r. Australia 110 C2
Wilton ME U.S.A. 131 H1
Wilton NH U.S.A. 131 H2
Wiltz Lux. 39 F2
Wiluna Australia 109 C6
Wimmera r. Australia 112 B5
Wina r. Cameroon see Vina
Winamac U.S.A. 132 E3
Winam Gulf Kenya 96 B5
Winbin watercourse Australia 111 F5
Winburg S. Africa 99 E6
Wincanton U.K. 35 E6
Winchester U.K. 35 F6
Winchester IN U.S.A. 130 A3
Winchester KY U.S.A. 130 A5
Winchester NH U.S.A. 131 G2
Winchester TN U.S.A. 128 B5
Winchester VA U.S.A. 130 D4
Wind r. Canada 122 C1
Wind r. U.S.A. 134 E4
Windau Latvia see Ventspils
Windber U.S.A. 130 D3
Wind Cave National Park U.S.A. 132 A3
Windermere U.K. 35 E4
Windham U.S.A. 130 C3
▶Windhoek Namibia 98 C4
Capital of Namibia.
Windigo r. Canada 121 J4
Windigo Lake Canada 124 B2
Windischgarsten Austria 37 G5
Wind Mountain U.S.A. 135 F6
Windom U.S.A. 132 C3
Windorah Australia 111 E5
Window Rock U.S.A. 137 H4
Wind Ridge U.S.A. 130 C4
Wind River Range mts U.S.A. 134 E4
Winds, Bay of Antarctica 167 F2
Windsor Nfld. and Lab. Canada 125 K3
Windsor N.S. Canada 125 H4
Windsor Ont. Canada 130 B2
Windsor U.K. 35 F6
Windsor NC U.S.A. 128 D4
Windsor NY U.S.A. 131 F2
Windsor VA U.S.A. 131 E5
Windsor VT U.S.A. 131 G2
Windsor Locks U.S.A. 131 G3
Windward Islands Caribbean Sea 139 L5
Windward Passage Cuba/Haiti 127 L8
Winefred Lake Canada 123 I4
Winfield AL U.S.A. 129 B5
Winfield KS U.S.A. 132 B4
Winfield WV U.S.A. 130 C4
Wingate Mountains hills Australia 110 B2
Wingham Canada 130 C2
Winifreda Arg. 152 D4
Winisk Canada 124 D3
Winisk r. Canada 124 C2
Winisk Lake Canada 124 C2
Winkana Myanmar 61 B5
Winkelman U.S.A. 137 G5
Winkler Canada 123 L5
Winlock U.S.A. 134 B3
Winneba Ghana 93 E4
Winnebago U.S.A. 132 C3
Winnebago, Lake U.S.A. 132 D2
Winnecke Creek watercourse Australia 110 B3
Winnemucca U.S.A. 134 C4
Winnemucca Lake U.S.A. 136 C1
Winner U.S.A. 132 A3
Winnett U.S.A. 134 E3
Winnfield U.S.A. 133 C6
Winnibigoshish, Lake U.S.A. 132 C2
Winning Australia 108 A5
▶Winnipeg Canada 123 L5
Provincial capital of Manitoba.
Winnipeg r. Canada 123 L5
Winnipeg, Lake Canada 123 L5
Winnipegosis Canada 123 L5
Winnipegosis, Lake Canada 134 G1
Winnipesaukee, Lake U.S.A. 131 H2
Winnsboro U.S.A. 129 C5
Winona AZ U.S.A. 137 G4
Winona MN U.S.A. 132 D2
Winona MO U.S.A. 132 D4
Winona MS U.S.A. 127 I5
Winooski r. U.S.A. 131 G1
Winschoten Neth. 36 C2
Winsen (Aller) Germany 36 D2
Winsen (Luhe) Germany 36 E2
Winslow U.S.A. 137 G4
Winsted U.S.A. 131 G3
Winston-Salem U.S.A. 128 C4
Winterberg Germany 36 D3
Winter Haven U.S.A. 129 C6
Winterport U.S.A. 131 I1
Winters CA U.S.A. 136 B2
Winters TX U.S.A. 133 B6
Winterset U.S.A. 132 C3
Winterswijk Neth. 36 C3
Winterthur Switz. 39 H3
Winthrop U.S.A. 131 I1
Winton Australia 111 E4
Winton N.Z. 113 B4
Winton U.S.A. 128 D4
Wirrabara Australia 112 A4
Wirraminna Australia 109 G7
Wirrulla Australia 109 F8
Wisbech U.K. 35 G5
Wiscasset U.S.A. 131 I1
Wisconsin r. U.S.A. 132 D3
Wisconsin state U.S.A. 132 D2
Wisconsin Rapids U.S.A. 132 D2
Wise U.S.A. 130 B5
Wisil Dabarow Somalia 96 F3
Wisła r. Poland see Vistula
Wisłok r. Poland 37 K3
Wisłoka r. Poland 37 J3
Wismar Germany 36 E2
Wisner U.S.A. 133 D6
Wistaria Canada 122 E4
Witbooisvlei Namibia 98 C5
Witham r. U.K. 35 G5
Withernsea U.K. 35 G5
Withlacoochee r. FL U.S.A. 129 C6
Withlacoochee r. FL U.S.A. 129 C6
Witjira National Park Australia 110 C5
Witkowo Poland 37 H2
Witney U.K. 35 F6
Witnica Poland 37 G2
Wittenberg Germany see Lutherstadt Wittenberg
Wittenberg U.S.A. 128 A2
Wittenberge Germany 36 E2
Wittenburg Germany 36 E2
Wittenheim France 39 G3
Wittenoom Australia 108 B5
Wittenoom Gorge Australia see Wittenoom
Witti, Banjaran mts Sabah Malaysia 59 G1
Wittingen Germany 36 E2
Wittlich Germany 36 C4
Wittmund Germany 36 C2
Wittow pen. Germany 37 F1
Wittstock Germany 37 F2
Witu Kenya 96 D5
Witu Islands P.N.G. 106 D2
Witvlei Namibia 98 C4
Witzenhausen Germany 36 D3
Wivenhoe, Lake Australia 111 H5
Wkra r. Poland 37 J2
Władysławowo Poland 37 I1
Włocławek Poland 37 I2
Włoszczowa Poland 37 I3
Wobkent Uzbek. see Vabkent
Wodonga Australia 112 C5
Wodzisław Śląski Poland 37 I3
Wohko watercourse Sudan 94 F3
Wohlthat Mountains Antarctica 167 C2
Wokam i. Indon. 57 H7
Woken r. China 64 B3
Wokha India 75 G4
Woking U.K. 35 F6
Wokingham watercourse Australia 111 E4
Woko National Park Australia 112 D3
Wolcott U.S.A. 131 E2
Wołczyn Poland 37 I3
Woldegk Germany 37 F2
Wolea atoll Micronesia see Woleai
Woleai atoll Micronesia 57 J4
Woleu-Ntem prov. Gabon 94 A4
Wolf r. Canada 122 C2
Wolf r. U.S.A. 132 D2
Wolf Creek MT U.S.A. 134 D3
Wolf Creek OR U.S.A. 134 B4
Wolf Creek r. U.S.A. 133 B4
Wolf Creek Pass U.S.A. 135 F5
Wolfeboro U.S.A. 131 H2
Wolfen Germany 37 F3
Wolfenbüttel Germany 36 E2
Wolfhagen Germany 36 D3
Wolf Lake Canada 122 D2
Wolf Point U.S.A. 134 F2
Wolfsberg Austria 37 G5
Wolfsburg Germany 36 E2
Wolfville Canada 125 H4
Wolgast Germany 37 F1
Wolin Poland 37 G2
Wolin i. Poland 37 G2
Woliński Park Narodowy nat. park Poland 37 G2
Wolkersdorf Austria 37 H4
Wollaston, Islas is Chile 153 D8
Wollaston Lake Canada 123 K3
Wollaston Lake l. Canada 123 K3
Wollaston Peninsula Canada 121 H3
Wollemi National Park Australia 112 D4
Wollerau Switz. 39 H3
Wollongong Australia 112 D4
Wolmirstedt Germany 36 E2
Wołomin Poland 37 J2
Wołów Poland 37 H3
Wolowaru Indon. 108 C2
Wolseley Australia 112 B5
Wolsztyn Poland 37 H2
Wolvega Neth. 36 C2
Wolverhampton U.K. 35 E5
Wolya r. Indon. 58 B2
Wonarah Australia 110 D3
Wondai Australia 111 G5
Wong Chhu r. Bhutan 75 F4
Wong Chuk Hang Hong Kong China 67 [inset]
Wong Leng hill Hong Kong China 67 [inset]
Wŏnju S. Korea 65 A5
Wonogiri Indon. 59 E4
Wonowon Canada 122 F3
Wonreli Indon. 108 D2
Wŏnsan N. Korea 65 A5
Wonthaggi Australia 112 C5
Woocalla Australia 112 A3
Wood, Mount Canada 122 A2
Woodbourne U.S.A. 131 F3
Woodbridge NJ U.S.A. 131 F3
Woodbridge VA U.S.A. 131 E4
Wood Buffalo National Park Canada 123 H3
Woodburn IN U.S.A. 130 A3
Woodburn OR U.S.A. 134 B3
Woodbury U.S.A. 131 F4
Woodend Australia 112 C5
Woodfords U.S.A. 136 C2
Woodhall Spa U.K. 35 F5
Wood Lake Canada 123 K4
Woodlake U.S.A. 136 C3
Woodland CA U.S.A. 136 B2
Woodland WA U.S.A. 134 B3
Woodlands Sing. 58 [inset]
Woodlark Island P.N.G. 107 E2
Woodridge Canada 123 L5
Woodroffe watercourse Australia 110 D4
Woodroffe, Mount Australia 110 B5
Woods, Lake salt flat Australia 110 C3
Woods, Lake of the Canada/U.S.A. 121 J5
Woodsfield U.S.A. 130 C4
Woods Hole U.S.A. 131 H3
Woodstock Australia 111 F3
Woodstock N.B. Canada 125 H4
Woodstock Ont. Canada 130 C2
Woodstock IL U.S.A. 132 D3
Woodstock VA U.S.A. 130 D4
Woodstock VT U.S.A. 131 G2
Woodstown U.S.A. 131 F4
Woodsville U.S.A. 131 G1
Woodville N.Z. 113 C3
Woodville MS U.S.A. 133 D6
Woodville OH U.S.A. 130 B3
Woodville TX U.S.A. 133 C6
Woodward U.S.A. 133 B4
Woody U.S.A. 136 C4
Woōi Indon. 57 I6
Wooler U.K. 34 E4
Woolgoolga Australia 112 E3
Woolla Downs Australia 110 C4
Woollard, Mount Antarctica 167 K1
Woolwine U.S.A. 130 C5
Woomera Australia 109 G7
Woomera Prohibited Area Australia 110 C6
Woonsocket U.S.A. 132 B2
Wooramel r. Australia 109 A6
Wooster U.S.A. 130 C3
Woqooyi Galbeed admin. reg. Somalia 96 D2
Worak-san National Park S. Korea 65 B5
Worbody Point Australia 111 E2
Worcester S. Africa 98 C7
Worcester U.K. 35 E5
Worcester MA U.S.A. 131 H2
Worcester NY U.S.A. 131 F2
Wörgl Austria 36 F5
Workai i. Indon. 57 H7
Workington U.K. 35 E4
Worland U.S.A. 134 F3
Worms Germany 36 D4
Worofla Côte d'Ivoire 92 D3
Wörth am Rhein Germany 36 D4
Worthing U.K. 35 F6
Worthington MN U.S.A. 132 C3
Worthington OH U.S.A. 130 B3
Wotje atoll Marshall Is 164 F6
Wotu Indon. 57 F6
Wour Chad 88 B4
Wouri r. Cameroon 93 H4
Wowoni i. Indon. 57 F6
Wozrojdeniye Oroli i. Uzbek. see Vozrozhdeniya, Ostrov
Wrangel Island Rus. Fed. 27 S2
Wrangell U.S.A. 122 C3
Wrangell Island U.S.A. 122 C3
Wrangell Mountains U.S.A. 122 A2
Wrangell-St Elias National Park and Preserve AK U.S.A. 122 A2
Wrath, Cape U.K. 34 D2
Wray U.S.A. 134 G4
Wreck Reef Australia 111 H4
Wrecsam U.K. see Wrexham
Wrens U.S.A. 129 C5
Wrexham U.K. 35 E5
Wriezen Germany 37 G2
Wrightmyo India 73 G4
Wright Patman Lake U.S.A. 133 C5
Wrightson, Mount U.S.A. 135 E7
Wrightsville U.S.A. 129 C5
Wrightwood U.S.A. 136 D4
Wrigley Canada 122 F2
Wrigley U.S.A. 130 B4
Wrigley Gulf Antarctica 167 J2
Wrocław Poland 37 H3
Wronki Poland 37 H2
Września Poland 37 H2
Wschowa Poland 37 H3
Wu'an China see Changtai
Wubin Australia 106 A5
Wuchang Heilong. China 64 A3
Wuchang Hubei China 67 E2
Wuchow China see Wuzhou
Wuchuan China 67 D4
Wudang Shan mts China 67 D1
Wuday'ah well Saudi Arabia 76 D6
Wudil Nigeria 93 H3
Wudinna Australia 109 F8
Wudu China 66 C1
Wufeng Hubei China 67 D2
Wufeng Yunnan China see Zhenxiong
Wugang China 67 D3
Wugong China 66 D1
Wuhai China 63 H4
Wuhan China 67 E2
Wuhe China 67 F1
Wuhu Anhui China 67 F2
Wuhu Anhui China 67 F2
Wuhua China 67 E4
Wujang China 74 C2
Wujiang China 67 G2
Wu Jiang r. China 66 C2
Wujin Jiangsu China see Changzhou
Wujin Sichuan China see Xinjin
Wukang China see Deqing
Wukari Nigeria 93 H4
Wulian Feng mts China 66 B2
Wuliang Shan mts China 66 B3
Wuliaru i. Indon. 57 H7
Wuling Shan mts China 67 D2
Wulong China 66 C2
Wulongji China see Huaibin
Wum Cameroon 93 H4
Wumeng Shan mts China 66 B3
Wuming China 67 D4
Wümme r. Germany 36 D2
Wungda China 66 B2
Wuning China 67 E2
Wunnummin Lake Canada 124 B2
Wun Rog Sudan 94 F2
Wun Shwai Sudan 94 F2
Wunstorf Germany 36 D2
Wuntho Myanmar 60 A3
Wupatki National Monument nat. park U.S.A. 137 G4
Wuping China 67 F3
Wuppertal Germany 36 C3
Wuppertal S. Africa 98 C7
Wuqia China 81 H2
Wuquan China see Wuyang
Wuranga Australia 109 B7
Würm r. Germany 36 E4
Wurno Nigeria 93 G2
Wurzbach Germany 36 E3
Würzburg Germany 36 D4
Wurzen Germany 37 F3
Wushan Chongqing China 67 D2
Wushan Gansu China 66 C1
Wu Shan mts China 67 D2
Wusheng China 66 C2
Wüstegarten hill Germany 36 D3
Wusuli Jiang r. Rus. Fed. see Ussuri
Wutong r. China 64 B3
Wuvulu Island P.N.G. 57 J6
Wuwei Anhui China 67 F2
Wuwei Gansu China 62 G4
Wuxi Chongqing China 67 D2
Wuxi Hunan China see Luxi
Wuxi Jiangsu China 67 G2
Wuxia China see Wushan
Wuxing China see Huzhou
Wuxu China 67 D4
Wuxuan China 67 D4
Wuxue China 67 E2
Wuyang Guizhou China see Zhenyuan
Wuyang Henan China 67 E1
Wuyi China 67 F2
Wuyiling China 64 B2
Wuyishan China 67 F3
Wuyi Shan mts China 67 F3
Wuyi Shan tourist site China 67 F3
Wuyuan Jiangxi China 67 F2
Wuyuan Nei Mongol China 63 H3
Wuyuan Zhejiang China see Haiyan
Wuyun China see Jinyun
Wuzhen China 67 D2
Wuzhi Shan mts China 67 D5
Wuzhong China 63 H4
Wuzhou China 67 D4
Wyalkatchem Australia 109 B7
Wyalusing U.S.A. 131 E3
Wyandra Australia 111 F5
Wye r. U.K. 35 E6
Wye Mills U.S.A. 131 E4
Wylliesburg U.S.A. 130 D5
Wyloo Australia 108 B5
Wymondham U.K. 35 G5
Wynbring Australia 109 F7
Wyndham Australia 110 B2
Wyndham-Werribee Australia 112 C5
Wynne U.S.A. 133 D5
Wynyard Canada 134 F2
Wyola Lake salt flat Australia 110 B6
Wyoming DE U.S.A. 131 F4
Wyoming MI U.S.A. 132 E3
Wyoming state U.S.A. 134 F4
Wyoming Range mts U.S.A. 134 E4
Wyong Australia 112 D4
Wyperfeld National Park Australia 112 B4
Wysoka Poland 37 H2
Wyszków Poland 37 J2
Wytheville U.S.A. 130 C5
Wyżnica r. Poland 37 J3

↓ X

Xaafuun Somalia 96 F2
▶Xaafuun, Raas pt Somalia 96 F2
Most easterly point of Africa.
Xaçmaz Azer. 79 G2
Xade Botswana 98 D4
Xagnay China 75 E3
Xago China 75 F3
Xagquka China 75 G3
Xaidulla China 74 C1
Xainza China 75 F3
Xaitongmoin China 75 F3
Xai-Xai Moz. 99 G5
Xalin Somalia 96 F2
Xamba China 63 H3
Xambioá Brazil 150 B3
Xam Hua Laos 60 D3
Xá-Muteba Angola 95 C7
Xan r. Laos 60 C4
Xan, Xé r. Vietnam 61 D5
Xangda China see Nangqên
Xangdoring China see Xungba
Xangongo Angola 95 B9
Xankändi Azer. 79 F3
Xanlar Azer. 79 F2
Xanthi Greece 46 D4
Xanxerê Brazil 151 A8
Xapuri Brazil 148 C2
Xarardheere Somalia 96 E3
Xarba La pass China 75 E3
Xarrama r. Port. 42 B3
Xarrë Albania 47 B5
Xarsingma China see Yadong
Xassengue Angola 95 C7
Xátiva Spain 43 F3
Xau, Lake Botswana 98 E4
Xaudum watercourse Botswana/Namibia 98 D3
Xavantes, Serra dos hills Brazil 150 E5
Xa Vo Đat Vietnam 61 D6
Xenia U.S.A. 130 B4
Xeriuini r. Brazil 147 F5
Xero Potamos r. Cyprus see Xeros
Xeros r. Cyprus 77 A2
Xiabole Shan mt. China 64 A2
Xiachengzi China 64 B3
Xiachuan Dao i. China 67 E4
Xiaguan China see Dali
Xiajiang Jiangxi China 67 E3
Xiajiang Xizang China see Qusum
Xiamen China 67 F3
Xi'an China 67 D1
Xiancheng China 67 E1
Xianfeng China 67 D2
Xiangcheng Henan China 67 E1
Xiangcheng Sichuan China 66 A2
Xiangcheng Yunnan China see Xiangyun
Xiangfan China 67 E1
Xiangfeng China see Laifeng
Xianggang Hong Kong China see Hong Kong
Xianggang Tebie Xingzhengqu special admin. reg. China see Hong Kong
Xianghuang Qi China see Xin Bulag
Xiangjiang China see Huichang
Xiang Jiang r. China 67 E2
Xiangkhoang Laos 60 C4
Xiangkhoang Plateau Laos 60 C4
Xiangkou China see Wulong
Xiangquan He r. China 74 C3
Xiangshan Yunnan China see Menghai
Xiangshan Zhejiang China 67 G2
Xiangshan Gang b. China 67 G2
Xiangshui China 67 F1
Xiangshuiba China 67 D3
Xiangtan China 67 E3
Xiangxiang China 67 E3
Xiangyang China see Xiangfan
Xiangyang Hu l. China 75 F2
Xiangyin China 67 E2
Xiangyun China 66 B3
Xianju China 67 G2
Xianning China 67 E2
Xiannümiao China see Jiangdu
Xianshui China see Dawu
Xianshui He r. China 66 B2
Xiantao China 67 E2
Xianxia Ling mts China 67 F3
Xianyang China 67 D1
Xianyou China 67 F3
Xiaochang China 67 E2
Xiaodong China 67 D4
Xiaogan China 67 E2
Xiao Hinggan Ling mts China 64 A2
Xiaojin China 66 B2
Xiaomei China 67 F3
Xiaonanchuan China 75 G2
Xiaosanjiang China 67 E3
Xiaoshan China 67 G2
Xiao Surmang China 66 A1
Xiaotao China 67 F3
Xiaoxi China see Pinghe
Xiaoxian China 67 F1
Xiaoxiang Ling mts China 66 B2
Xiaoyi China see Gongyi
Xiapu China 67 G3
Xiaqiong China see Batang
Xiayanjing China see Yanjing
Xiayingpan Guizhou China see Lupanshui
Xiayingpan Guizhou China see Luzhi
Xibdê China 66 A2
Xibing China 67 F3
Xibu China see Dongshan
Xichang China 66 B3
Xichou China 66 C4
Xichuan China 67 D1
Xide China 66 B2
Xidu China see Hengyang
Xié r. Brazil 146 E4
Xiemahe' China 67 D2
Xieng Khouang Laos see Xiangkhoang
Xieyang Dao i. China 67 D4
Xifei He r. China 67 F1
Xifeng Guizhou China 66 C3
Xifeng Liaoning China 64 A4
Xigazê China 70 G6
Xihan Shui r. China 66 C1
Xihe China 66 C1
Xi He r. China 66 C2
Xi Jiang r. China 67 E4
Xijir Ulan Hu salt l. China 75 F2
Xilagani Greece see Xylagani
Xiligou China see Ulan
Xilin China 66 C3
Xilinhot China 63 J3
Xilókastron Greece see Xylokastro
Xilópolis Greece see Xylopoli
Ximiao China 70 J3
Xin'an Anhui China see Lai'an
Xin'an Henan China 67 E1
Xin'anjiang Shuiku resr China 67 F2
Xin Bulag China 27 L5
Xincai China 67 E1
Xinchang China see Yifeng
Xincheng Fujian China see Gutian
Xincheng Guangdong China see Xinxing
Xincheng Guangxi China 67 D3
Xincheng Sichuan China see Zhaojue
Xincun China see Dongchuan
Xindi Guangxi China 67 D4
Xindi Hubei China see Honghu
Xindu Guangxi China 67 D4
Xindu Sichuan China see Luhuo
Xindu Sichuan China 66 C2
Xinduqiao China 66 B2
Xinfeng Guangdong China 67 E3
Xinfeng Jiangxi China 67 E3
Xinfengjiang Shuiku resr China 67 E4
Xing'an China 67 D3
Xingan China 67 E3
Xingba China see Lhünzê
Xinge Angola 95 C7
Xingguo Gansu China see Qin'an
Xingguo Jiangxi China 67 E3
Xinghai China 70 I4
Xinghua China 67 F1
Xinghua Wan b. China 67 F3
Xingkai China 64 C3
Xingkai Hu l. China/Rus. Fed. see Khanka, Lake
Xinglong China 64 A2
Xinglongzhen China 64 A3
Xingning China 67 E3
Xingou China 67 E2
Xingping China 67 D1
Xingren China 66 C3
Xingsagoinba China 66 B1
Xingshan Guizhou China see Majiang
Xingshan Hubei China 67 D2
Xingtai China 63 I4
Xingu r. Brazil 147 H5
Xinguara Brazil 150 B3
Xingyang China 67 E1
Xingyi China 66 C3
Xingzi China 67 F2
Xinhua Guangdong China see Huadu
Xinhua Hunan China 67 D3
Xinhua Yunnan China see Qiaojia
Xinhua Yunnan China see Funing
Xinhuang China 67 D3
Xining China 70 J4
Xinji China see Xinxian
Xinjian China 67 E2
Xinjiang aut. reg. China see Xinjiang Uygur Zizhiqu
Xin Jiang r. China 67 F2
Xinjiangkou China see Songzi
Xinjiang Uygur Autonomous Region aut. reg. China see Xinjiang Uygur Zizhiqu
Xinjiang Uygur Zizhiqu aut. reg. China 70 E3
Xinjie China see Yuanyang
Xinjin China 66 B2
Xinjing China see Jingxi
Xinling China see Badong
Xinlong China 66 B2
Xinmi China 67 E1
Xinmian China see Shimian
Xinning Guangxi China see Fusui
Xinning Hunan China 67 D3
Xinning Jiangxi China see Wuning
Xinning Sichuan China see Kaijiang
Xinqing China 64 B2
Xinquan China 67 F3
Xinshi China see Jingshan
Xinshiba China see Ganluo
Xintai China 63 J4
Xintian China 67 E3
Xinxian China 67 E2
Xinxiang China 63 I4
Xinxing China 67 E4
Xinyang China 67 E1
Xinyang Gang r. China 67 G1
Xinye r. China 67 F1
Xinyi Guangdong China 67 D4
Xinyi Jiangsu China 67 F1
Xinying China 67 D5
Xinying Taiwan see Hsinying
Xinyu China 67 E3
Xinyuan Qinghai China see Tianjun
Xinyuan Xinjiang China 70 F3
Xinzheng China 67 E1
Xinzhou Guangxi China see Longlin
Xinzhou Guizhou China see Huangping
Xinzhou Hubei China 67 E2
Xinzhou Shanxi China 63 I4
Xinzhu Taiwan see Hsinchu
Xinzo de Limia Spain 42 C1
Xiongshan China see Zhenghe
Xiongzhou China see Nanxiong
Xipamanu r. Bol./Brazil 148 D2
Xiping Henan China 67 D1
Xiping Henan China 67 E1
Xiqing Shan mts China 66 B1
Xique Xique Brazil 150 D4

Xiro hill Greece 47 C5
Xirokampo Greece 47 E6
Xiruá r. Brazil 146 E6
Xisa China see Xichou
Xishanzui China 63 H3
Xisha China see Xichou
Xishui Guizhou China 66 C2
Xishui Hubei China 67 E2
Xistral, Serra do mts Spain 42 C1
Xitole Guinea-Bissau 92 B3
Xiucaiwan China see Fengdu
Xiugu China see Jinxi
Xi Ujimqin Qi China see Bayan Ul
Xiuning China 67 F2
Xiushan Chongqing China 67 D2
Xiushan Yunnan China see Tonghai
Xiushui China 67 E2
Xiu Shui r. China 67 E2
Xiuying China 67 D4
Xiwu China 66 A1
Xixabangma Feng mt. China 70 G6
Xixia China 67 D1
Xixian China 67 E1
Xixiang China 66 C1
Xixón Spain see Gijón-Xixón
Xiyang Dao i. China 67 F3
Xiyang Jiang r. China 66 C3
Xizang aut. reg. China see
  Xizang Zizhiqu
Xizang Gaoyuan plat. China see
  Tibet, Plateau of
Xizang Zizhiqu aut. reg. China 66 A2
Xocavänd Azer. 79 F3
Xoi China see Qüxü
Xom An Lôc Vietnam 61 D6
Xom Duc Hanh Vietnam 61 D6
Xuancheng China see Xuanzhou
Xuan'en China 67 D2
Xuanhan China 66 C2
Xuanzhou China 67 F2
Xuchang China 67 E1
Xucheng China see Xuwen
Xudat Azer. 79 G2
Xuddur Somalia 96 D3
Xudun Somalia 96 E2
Xueba China see Sangri
Xuefeng China see Mingxi
Xuefeng Shan mts China 67 D3
Xuehua Shan hill China 67 D1
Xue Shan mts China 66 A3
Xugui China 75 G2
Xujiang China see Guangchang
Xümatang China 66 A1
Xun r. China 64 B2
Xundian China 66 B3
Xungba China 75 E2
Xungmai China 75 F3
Xung Qu r. China 75 F3
Xungru China 75 E3
Xunhe China 64 A2
Xun He r. China 67 D1
Xunjiang China see Xunwu
Xunke China 64 B2
Xunwu China 67 E3
Xunyang China 67 D1
Xupu China 67 D3
Xuru Co salt l. China 75 E3
Xuwen China 67 D4
Xuyang China see Rongxian
Xuyi China 67 F1
Xuyong China 66 C2
Xuzhou China 67 F1
Xylagani Greece 46 D4
Xylokastro Greece 47 C5
Xylopoli Greece 46 C4

Ya'an China 66 B2
Yaapeet Australia 112 B4
Yabanabat Turkey see Kızılcahamam
Yabassi Cameroon 93 H4
Yabêlo Eth. 96 C3
Yablanitsa Bulg. 46 D3
Yablonovyy Khrebet mts Rus. Fed.
  27 K4
Yabo Nigeria 93 G2
Yabrūd Syria 78 D4
Yabuli China 64 B3
Yabuyanos Peru 146 C5
Yacha China see Baisha
Yacheng China 67 D5
Yachi He r. China 66 C3
Yacireta, Isla i. Para. 152 F1
Yacireta Apipé, Embalse resr Para.
  152 F1
Yacuiba Bol. 149 E5
Yacurai Venez. 146 C4
Yadé, Massif du mts Cent. Afr. Rep.
  94 B3
Yadgir India 72 C2
Yadiki India 72 C3
Yadkin r. U.S.A. 128 C5
Yadong China 70 G6
Yadrin Rus. Fed. 28 H5
Yaeyama-rettō is Japan 63 C7
Yafa Israel see Tel Aviv-Yafo
Yafran Libya 88 D1
Yagaba Ghana 93 E3
Yagaing state Myanmar see Arakan
Yağcılı Turkey 47 E5
Yağda Turkey see Erdemli
Yaghan Basin sea feature
  S. Atlantic Ocean 161 J9
Yagman Turkm. 80 C2
Yagmo China 75 E3
Yagoda Bulg. 46 D3
Yagodnoye Rus. Fed. 27 O3
Yagodnyy Rus. Fed. 64 D2
Yagoua Cameroon 94 B2
Yagra China 75 D3
Yaguarón r. Brazil/Uruguay see Jaguarão
Yaguas r. Peru 146 D5
Yaha Thai. 61 C7
Yahk Canada 134 C2
Yahya Wana Afgh. 74 A3
Yai, Khao hill Thai. 61 B5
Yaizu Japan 65 D6
Yajiang China 66 A1
Yakacık Turkey 77 C1
Yakhab waterhole Iran 80 D3
Yakhehal Afgh. 81 F4
Yakima U.S.A. 134 B3
Yakima r. U.S.A. 134 C3
Yakinish Iran 80 C3
Yakkabag Uzbek. 81 F2
Yakmach Pak. 81 E4
Yako Burkina 93 E3
Yakobi Island U.S.A. 122 B3
Yakoma Dem. Rep. Congo 94 D3
Yakoruda Bulg. 46 C3
Yakumo Japan 64 F4
Yaku-shima i. Japan 65 B7
Yakutat U.S.A. 122 B3
Yakutat Bay U.S.A. 120 E4
Yakutsk Rus. Fed. 27 M3
Yakymivka Ukr. 29 E7
Yala China 66 C1
Yala Thai. 61 C7

Yalai China 75 E3
Yala National Park Sri Lanka see
  Ruhuna National Park
Yalan Dünya Mağarası tourist site
  Turkey 77 A1
Yale Canada 134 B2
Yale U.S.A. 130 D2
Yalgoo Australia 109 B7
Yalıkavak Turkey 47 E6
Yalikorf Cent. Afr. Rep. 94 D3
Yalıköy Turkey 46 F4
Yalinga Cent. Afr. Rep. 94 C3
Yallahs Burkina 92 E2
Yalleroi Australia 111 F5
Yallo Burkina 92 E2
Yaloké Cent. Afr. Rep. 94 C3
Yalong Jiang r. China 66 B3
Yalova Turkey 78 B2
Yalova prov. Turkey 78 B2
Yalpuh, Ozero l. Ukr. 46 F2
Yalpukh r. Moldova see Yalpuh
Yalta Ukr. 78 C1
Yalu Jiang r. China/N. Korea 65 A4
Yalutorovsk Rus. Fed. 26 G4
Yalvaç Turkey 78 B3
Yamagata Japan 65 F5
Yamaguchi Japan 65 B6
Yamal, Poluostrov pen. Rus. Fed. see
  Yamal Peninsula
Yam Alin', Khrebet mts Rus. Fed.
  64 C1
Yamalo-Nenetskiy Avtonomnyy Okrug
  admin. div. Rus. Fed. 28 M2
Yamal Peninsula Rus. Fed. 26 G2
Yamanie Falls National Park Australia
  111 F3
Yamankhalinka Kazakh. see Makhambet
Yamba Australia 112 E3
Yambacoona Australia 112 B5
Yambarran Range hills Australia 110 B2
Yambéring Guinea 92 B3
Yambi, Mesa de hills Col. 146 D4
Yambio Sudan 94 F3
Yambol Bulg. 46 E3
Yambrasbamba Peru 146 B6
Yamdena i. Indon. 57 H7
Yamethin Myanmar 60 B3

Yamin, Puncak mt. Indon. 57 I6
  4th highest mountain in Oceania.
  oceania 102–103

Yamkanmandi India 72 B2
Yamkhad Syria see Aleppo
Yamm Rus. Fed. 28 D4
Yamma Yamma, Lake salt flat Australia
  111 E5
Yamoussoukro Côte d'Ivoire 92 D4
  Capital of Côte d'Ivoire.

Yampil' Ukr. 29 D7
Yampil' Ukr. see Yampil'
Yamuna r. India 74 D4
Yamzho Yumco l. China 70 H6
Yana r. Rus. Fed. 27 N2
Yanachaga-Chemillen, Parque
  Nacional nat. park Peru 148 C3
Yanam India 73 D2
Yan'an China 63 H4
Yanaon India see Yanam
Yanaul Rus. Fed. 28 J4
Yanayacu Peru 146 C5
Yanbian China 66 B3
Yanbu' al Baḥr Saudi Arabia 89 H3
Yancheng Jiangsu China 67 G1
Yancheng Sichuan China see Jingyan
Yanchep Australia 109 A7
Yanco Creek r. Australia 112 C4
Yanco Glen Australia 112 B3
Yanda watercourse Australia 112 C3
Yandama Creek watercourse Australia
  111 E6
Yandang Shan mts China 67 G3
Yandao China see Yingjing
Yandill Australia 109 B6
Yandina Solomon Is 107 E2
Yandja Dem. Rep. Congo 94 C3
Yanfolila Mali 92 C3
Yangalia Cent. Afr. Rep. 94 C3
Yangambi Dem. Rep. Congo 94 E4
Ya'ngamdo China 75 F3
Yangbi China 66 A3
Yangcheng China see Yangshan
Yangchuan China see Suiyang
Yangchun China 67 D4
Yangdok N. Korea 65 A5
Yang Hu l. China 75 E2
Yangi Davan pass Aksai Chin/China
  74 C2
Yangi-Nishan Uzbek. 81 F2
Yangi Qal'eh Afgh. 81 G2
Yangirabad Uzbek. 81 F1
Yangiyul' Uzbek. 70 C3
Yangjiang China 67 D4
Yangôn Myanmar see Rangoon
Yangôn admin. div. Myanmar 60 B4
Yangping China 67 D2
Yangquan China 63 I4
Yangshan China 67 E3
Yangshuo China 67 E3
Yang Talat Thai. 61 C4
Yangtouyan China 66 B3

Yangtze r. China 67 C2
  Longest river in Asia and 3rd in the world.
  Also known as Chang Jiang or Jinsha
  Jiang or Tongtian He or Zhi Qu.
  asia 50–51
  world 6–7

Yangtze, Mouth of the China 67 G2
Yangudi Rassa National Park Eth.
  96 D2
Yangweigang China 67 F1
Yangxian China 66 C1
Yangzhou China see Hanjiang
Yanhe China 67 D2
Yanji China 64 B4
Yanjin China 66 C2
Yanjing Sichuan China see Yanyuan
Yanjing Xizang China 66 A2
Yanjing China see Yanjin
Yankara National Park Nigeria 93 H3
Yankou China see Wusheng
Yankton U.S.A. 132 D3
Yanling China 67 E3
Yannina Greece see Ioannina
Yano-Indigirskaya Nizmennost' lowland
  Rus. Fed. 27 O2
Yanov-Stan Rus. Fed. 27 I3
Yan Oya r. Sri Lanka 72 D4
Yanqi China 70 G3
Yanrey r. Australia 108 A5
Yanshan Jiangxi China 67 F2
Yanshan Yunnan China 66 C4
Yanshiping China 75 G3
Yanshou China 64 B3
Yanskiy Zaliv b. Rus. Fed. 27 N2
Yantabulla Australia 112 C2
Yantai China 63 K4
Yantarnyy Rus. Fed. 33 E5
Yantongshan China 64 A4
Yantra r. Bulg. 46 D3
Yanûfî, Jabal al hill Saudi Arabia 89 I4

Yanyuan China 66 B3
Yao'an China 66 B3
Yaodu China see Dongzhi

Yaoundé Cameroon 93 H5
  Capital of Cameroon.

Yaoxian China 67 D1
Yao Yai, Ko i. Thai. 61 B6
Yap i. Micronesia 57 I4
Yapacana, Parque Nacional nat. park
  Venez. 146 E3
Yapacani r. Bol. 149 E4
Yapen i. Indon. 57 I6
Yapen, Selat sea chan. Indon. 57 I6
Yap Trench sea feature N. Pacific Ocean
  164 D5
Yapukarri Guyana 147 G4
Yaqui r. Mex. 135 E8
Yar Rus. Fed. 28 J4
Yaracal Venez. 146 D2
Yaracuy state Venez. 146 D2
Yaradzha Turkm. see Yaradzhi
Yaradzhi Turkm. 80 C2
Yaraka Australia 111 F5
Yarangüme Turkey see Tavas
Yaransk Rus. Fed. 28 H4
Yardea Australia 109 F8
Yardımcı Burnu pt Turkey 78 B3
Yardımli Azer. 79 G3
Yardoi China 75 F3
Yardymly Azer. see Yardımli
Yare r. U.K. 35 G5
Yarega Rus. Fed. 28 J3

Yaren Nauru 107 F2
  Capital of Nauru.

Yarensk Rus. Fed. 28 I3
Yargara Moldova see Iargara
Yari r. Col. 146 C5
Yariga-take mt. Japan 65 D5
Yarimca Turkey see Körfez
Yaripo Brazil 147 H4
Yaris well Niger 93 G2
Yarkand China see Shache
Yarkant China see Shache
Yarkant He r. China 70 E4
Yarker Canada 131 F1
Yarkhun r. Pak. 81 H2
Yarlung Zangbo r. China 75 G3 see
  Brahmaputra
Yarmouth Canada 125 H5
Yarmouth U.K. see Great Yarmouth
Yarmouth U.S.A. 131 H2
Yarmūk r. Asia 77 B3
Yarnell U.S.A. 137 F4
Yaroslavl' Rus. Fed. 28 F4
Yaroslavl Oblast admin. div. Rus. Fed.
  see Yaroslavskaya Oblast'
Yaroslavskaya Oblast' admin. div.
  Rus. Fed. 28 F4
Yarra r. Australia 112 C5
Yarrawonga Australia 112 C5
Yarra Yarra Lakes salt flat Australia
  109 A7
Yarrie Australia 108 C5
Yarronvale Australia 111 F5
Yarrowmere Australia 111 F4
Yartsevo Krasnoyarskiy Kray Rus. Fed.
  27 I3
Yartsevo Smolenskaya Oblast' Rus. Fed.
  29 F5
Yaru r. China 75 E3
Yarwa China 66 A2
Yary Rus. Fed. 28 M1
Yarzhong China 66 A2
Yaş Romania see Iaşi
Yasa Dem. Rep. Congo 95 D5
Yasawa Group is Fiji 107 G3
Yasel'da r. Belarus 29 E5
Yashi Nigeria 93 F3
Yashikera Nigeria 93 F3
Yashilkül l. Tajik. 81 H2
Yashkul' Rus. Fed. 29 H7
Yasin Jammu and Kashmir 74 B1
Yasna Polyana Bulg. 46 E3
Yasnogorsk Rus. Fed. 29 F5
Yasnyy Rus. Fed. 64 B1
Yasothon Thai. 61 D5
Yass Australia 112 D4
Yass r. Australia 112 D4
Yäsûj Iran 80 B4
Yasuni nat. park Ecuador 146 C5
Yasur vol. Vanuatu 107 F3
Yat well Niger 88 B4
Yata r. Bol. 148 D2
Yata Cent. Afr. Rep. 94 D2
Yatağan Turkey 78 B3
Yatakala Niger 93 F3
Yata Plateau Kenya 96 C5
Yaté New Caledonia 107 F4
Yates r. Canada 123 H2
Yates Center U.S.A. 132 C4
Yathkyed Lake Canada 123 L2
Yatolema Dem. Rep. Congo 94 E4
Yatsushiro Japan 65 B6
Yatta West Bank 77 B4
Yauca Peru 148 C4
Yauca r. Peru 148 C4
Yauli Peru 148 A2
Yauna Maloca Col. 146 D5
Yauri Peru 148 C3
Yauyos Peru 148 A2
Yavari r. Brazil/Peru 148 A2
Yavarí r. Peru 146 D6
Yavatmal India 72 C1
Yavero r. Peru 148 A3
Yaví, Cerro mt. Venez. 147 E3
Yavne Israel 77 B4
Yavoriv Ukr. 29 D6
Yaw r. Myanmar 60 A2
Yawatahama Japan 65 C6
Yawatongguz He r. China 75 D1
Yaw Chaung r. Myanmar 60 A2
Yawng-hwe Myanmar 60 B3
Yaxian China see Sanya
Yayladağı Turkey 77 C2
Yazagyo Myanmar 60 A2
Yazd Iran 80 D4
Yazd prov. Iran 80 D4
Yazdān Iran 81 F3
Yazd-e Khvāst Iran 80 C4
Yazgulem, Qatorkŭhi mts Tajik. see
  Yazgulom, Qatorkŭhi
Yazgulom, Qatorkŭhi mts Tajik. 81 H2
Yazıhan Turkey 78 D3
Yazoo r. U.S.A. 133 D5
Yazoo City U.S.A. 127 H5
Yaz'va r. Rus. Fed. 27 K3
Ybakoura well Chad 88 B4
Y Bala U.K. see Bala
Ybbs r. Austria 37 G4
Ybycuí Para. 149 F6
Yding Skovhøj hill Denmark 33 C5
Ydra i. Greece 47 C6
Ydras, Kolpos sea chan. Greece 47 C6
Y Drenewydd U.K. see Newtown
Ye Myanmar 61 B5
Ye r. Myanmar 61 B5
Yebawmi Myanmar 60 A2
Yebbi-Bou Chad 88 D2
Yecheng China 70 E4
Yecla Spain 43 F3
Yécora Mex. 135 E7
Yedashe Myanmar 60 B3
Yedatore India 72 C3
Yedi Burun Başı pt Turkey 47 F6
Yedri well Chad 88 D2

Yeed Eth. 96 D3
Yeeda River Australia 108 C4
Yefimovskiy Rus. Fed. 28 E4
Yefremov Rus. Fed. 29 F5
Yêgainnyin China see Henan
Yeggueba well Niger 93 H2
Yeghegnadzor Armenia 79 F3
Yegorlyk r. Rus. Fed. 29 G7
Yegorlykskaya Rus. Fed. 29 G7
Yegorova, Mys pt Rus. Fed. 64 D3
Yegor'yevsk Rus. Fed. 28 F5
Yégué Togo 93 F3
Yei r. Sudan 96 A3
Yeji China 67 E1
Yeji Ghana 93 E3
Yejiaji China see Yeji
Yekaterinburg Rus. Fed. 26 G4
Yekaterinoslav Ukr. see Dnipropetrovs'k
Yekaterinoslavka Rus. Fed. 64 B2
Yekhegnadzor Armenia see
  Yeghegnadzor
Yekokora r. Dem. Rep. Congo 94 D4
Yelabuga Khabarovskiy Kray Rus. Fed.
  64 D2
Yelabuga Respublika Tatarstan Rus. Fed.
  28 I5
Yelan' Rus. Fed. 29 G6
Yelarbon Australia 111 G6
Yelbarsli Turkm. 81 F2
Yelenovka Kar'yery Ukr. see
  Dokuchayevs'k
Yelets Rus. Fed. 29 F5
Yeletskiy Rus. Fed. 28 M2
Yélima well Mali 92 D2
Yelizavetgrad Ukr. see Kirovohrad
Yelizovo Rus. Fed. 27 P4
Yelkhovka Rus. Fed. 29 I5
Yell i. U.K. 34 [inset]
Yellabina Regional Reserve nature res.
  Australia 109 F7
Yellandu India 72 D2
Yellapur India 72 B3
Yellareddi India 72 C2
Yellowdine Australia 109 B7
Yellowhead Pass Canada 122 G4

Yellowknife Canada 123 H2
  Capital of Northwest Territories.

Yellowknife r. Canada 123 H2
Yellow Mountain Australia 112 C4

Yellow River r. China 70 I5
  4th longest river in Asia and 7th in the
  world.
  asia 50–51
  world 6–7

Yellow Sea N. Pacific Ocean 65 A6
Yellow Springs U.S.A. 130 B4
Yellowstone r. U.S.A. 134 G3
Yellowstone Lake U.S.A. 134 E3
Yellowstone National Park U.S.A.
  134 E3
Yelm U.S.A. 134 B3
Yeloten Turkm. 81 E2
Yelovo Rus. Fed. 28 J4
Yel'sk Belarus 29 D6
Yelva r. Rus. Fed. 28 I3
Yelwa Nigeria 93 H3

Yemen country Asia 76 D7
  asia 52–53, 82

Yemetsk Rus. Fed. 28 G3
Yemişenbükü Turkey see Taşova
Yemmiganur India see Emmiganuru
Yemtsa Rus. Fed. 28 G3
Yena Rus. Fed. 32 H3
Yenagoa Nigeria 93 G4
Yenakiyeve Ukr. 29 F6
Yenakiyevo Ukr. see Yenakiyeve
Yenangyat Myanmar 60 A3
Yenangyaung Myanmar 60 A3
Yenanma Myanmar 60 A4
Yên Bai Vietnam 60 D2
Yendi Ghana 93 E3
Yénéganou Congo 95 B5
Yenge r. Dem. Rep. Congo 94 D5
Yengema Sierra Leone 92 C3
Yengo Congo 94 C3
Yengo National Park Australia 112 D4
Yeniceoba Turkey 78 C3
Yeniçiftlik Turkey 46 E4
Yenidere r. Turkey 47 F5
Yenihan Turkey see Yıldızeli
Yenihisar Turkey 47 E6
Yenije-i-Vardar Greece see Giannitsa
Yeniköy Kütahya Turkey 47 F5
Yeniköy Kütahya Turkey 47 F5
Yenipazar Turkey 47 E5
Yenişakran Turkey 47 E5
Yenişehir Greece see Larisa
Yenişehir Turkey 78 B2
Yenisey r. Rus. Fed. 27 I2

Yenisey-Angara-Selenga r. Rus. Fed.
  27 I2
  3rd longest river in Asia and 6th in the
  world.
  asia 50–51
  world 6–7

Yeniseysk Rus. Fed. 27 J4
Yeniseyskiy Kryazh ridge Rus. Fed.
  27 J4
Yeniseyskiy Zaliv inlet Rus. Fed. 166 F2
Yeniugou China 66 A1
Yeniyol Turkey see Borçka
Yenotayevka Rus. Fed. 29 H7
Yeola India 72 B1
Yeo Lake salt flat Australia 110 A5
Yeotmal India see Yavatmal
Yeovil U.K. 35 E6
Yeo Yeo r. Australia see Bland
Yepachi Mex. 135 E7
Yeppoon Australia 111 G4
Yerakarou Greece see Gerakarou
Yerakhtur Rus. Fed. 29 G5
Yéraki, Ákra pt Greece see Geraki, Akra
Yérakion Greece see Geraki
Yeralievo Kazakh. see Kuryk
Yerbent Turkm. 81 E2
Yerbogachen Rus. Fed. 27 K3
Yerevan Armenia 79 F2
  Capital of Armenia.

Yereymentau Kazakh. 62 A1
Yergeni hills Rus. Fed. 29 H7
Yergogu Romania see Giurgiu
Yeriho West Bank see Jericho
Yerilla Australia 109 C7
Yerington U.S.A. 136 C2
Yerköy Turkey 78 C3
Yerla r. India 72 B2
Yermak Kazakh. see Aksu
Yermak Plateau sea feature
  Arctic Ocean 166 H1
Yermentau Kazakh. see Yereymentau
Yermo U.S.A. 136 D4
Yerofey Pavlovich Rus. Fed. 63 K1
Yeroham Israel 77 B4
Yërsa r. Rus. Fed. 28 J2
Yershov Rus. Fed. 29 I6

Yertsevo Rus. Fed. 28 G3
Yerupaja mt. Peru 148 A2
Yerushalayim Israel/West Bank see
  Jerusalem
Yerzhar Uzbek. see Gagarin
Yesil' Kazakh. 26 G4
Yeşilhisar Turkey 78 D3
Yeşilırmak r. Turkey 78 D2
Yeşilova Turkey 78 B3
Yeşilova Turkey see Sorgun
Yessentuki Rus. Fed. 29 G7
Yessey Rus. Fed. 27 K3
Yeste Spain 43 E3
Yes Tor hill U.K. 35 D6
Yeu Myanmar 60 A2
Yeu, Île d' i. France 38 B3
Yevdokimovskoye Rus. Fed. see
  Krasnogvardeyskoye
Yevlakh Azer. see Yevlax
Yevlax Azer. 79 F2
Yevpatoriya Ukr. 29 E7
Yevreyskaya Avtonomnaya Oblast'
  admin. div. Rus. Fed. 64 C2
Yexian China 67 E1
Yeyik China 75 F2
Yezhou China see Jianshi
Yezhuga r. Rus. Fed. 28 H2
Yezo i. Japan see Hokkaidō
Yezyaryshcha Belarus 31 L2
Y Fenni U.K. see Abergavenny
Y Fflint U.K. see Flint
Yi r. Henan China 67 E1
Yi r. Shandong China 67 F1
Yi r. Uruguay 152 F3
Yiali i. Greece see Gyali
Yialousa Cyprus see Aigialousa
Yi'an China 64 A3
Yianisádha i. Greece see Gianysada
Yibin Sichuan China 66 C2
Yibin Sichuan China 66 C2
Yibug Caka salt l. China 75 E2
Yicheng China 67 F2
Yichuan China 67 E1
Yichun Heilong. China 64 B3
Yichun Jiangxi China 67 E3
Yidun China 66 A2
Yifeng China 67 E2
Yiggêtang China see Qumarlêb
Yihuang China 67 F3
Yijiang China see Yiyang
Yilaha China 64 A2
Yilan China 64 B3
Yilan Taiwan see Ilan
Yıldız Dağları mts Turkey 78 A2
Yıldızeli Turkey 78 D3
Yilehuli Shan mts China 64 A2
Yiliang Yunnan China 66 B3
Yiliang Yunnan China 66 C3
Yilliminning Australia 109 B8
Yilong Sichuan China 66 C2
Yilong Yunnan China see Shiping
Yilong Hu l. China 66 B4
Yincheng China see Dexing
Yinchuan China 63 H4
Yindarlgooda, Lake salt flat Australia
  109 C7
Yingcheng China 67 E2
Yingde China 67 E3
Ying He r. China 67 F1
Yingjing China 66 B2
Yingkou China 63 K3
Yingshan Hubei China 67 E2
Yingshan Sichuan China 66 C2
Yingtan China 67 F2
Yining Xinjiang China see Xiushui
Yining Xinjiang China 70 F3
Yinjiang China 67 D3
Yinmabin Myanmar 60 A2
Yinnyein Myanmar 60 B4
Yinxian China see Ningbo
Yi'ong Zangbo r. China 75 G3
Yioúra i. Greece see Gioura
Yipinglang China 66 B3
Yiquan China see Meitan
Yirga Alem Eth. 96 C3
Yirol Sudan 96 A3
Yirrkala Australia 110 D2
Yirshi China 64 B1
Yirxie China 63 J2
Yisa China see Honghe
Yishan Guangxi China see Yizhou
Yishun Sing. 58 [inset]
Yithion Greece see Gytheio
Yitiaoshan China see Jingtai
Yitong China 64 A4
Yitong r. China 64 A3
Yi Tu, Nam r. Myanmar 60 D3
Yiwu China 70 H3
Yixing China 67 F2
Yiyang Hunan China 67 E2
Yiyang Jiangxi China 67 F2
Yizhang China 67 E3
Yizhou China 67 D3
Yizra'el country Asia see Israel
Ylämaa Fin. 33 F3
Yläne Fin. 33 F3
Ylihärmä Fin. 32 F3
Yli-li Fin. 32 G2
Yli-Kärppä Fin. 32 G2
Ylikiiminki Fin. 32 G2
Yli-Kitka l. Fin. 32 H2
Ylistaro Fin. 32 F3
Ylitornio Fin. 32 G2
Ylivieska Fin. 32 G2
Ylläs hill Fin. 32 G2
Ylöjärvi Fin. 32 F3
Ymer Ø i. Greenland 121 Q2
Ymonda China see Yanmou
Ynys Môn i. U.K. see Anglesey
Yoakum U.S.A. 133 B6
Yobe state Nigeria 93 H3
Yoboki Djibouti 96 D2
Yogan, Cerro mt. Chile 153 C8
Yogoum well Chad 88 C3
Yogyakarta Indon. 59 I7
Yogyakarta admin. dist. Indon. 59 I5
Yoho National Park Canada 123 G5
Yokadouma Cameroon 94 B4
Yokkaichi Japan 65 E6
Yoko Cameroon 93 I4
Yokohama Japan 65 D6
Yokosuka Japan 65 E6
Yokote Japan 65 E5
Yola Nigeria 93 I3
Yolo U.S.A. 136 B2
Yolombo Dem. Rep. Congo 94 D4
Yom, Mae Nam r. Thai. 60 C3
Yonan N. Korea 65 A5
Yonezawa Japan 65 E5
Yông-am S. Korea 65 A6
Yong'an Chongqing China see Fengjie
Yong'an Fujian China 67 F3
Yongbei China see Yongsheng
Yǒngch'ŏn S. Korea 65 B6
Yongchun China 67 F3
Yongde China 66 C2
Yongding Fujian China 67 F3

Yongding Yunnan China see Yongren
Yongding Yunnan China see Fumin
Yongfeng Jiangxi China 67 E3
Yongfeng Jiangxi China see Guangfeng
Yongfu China 67 D3
Yonggwang S. Korea 65 A6
Yŏnghŭng N. Korea 65 A5
Yŏnghŭng-man b. N. Korea 65 A5
Yongji China 64 A4
Yongjing Guizhou China see Xifeng
Yongjing Liaoning China see Xifeng
Yŏngju S. Korea 65 B5
Yongju China 67 C5
Yongkang China see Nayong
Yongle Shaanxi China see Zhen'an
Yongle Sichuan China see Nanping
Yongling China 64 A4
Yongning Guangxi China see Xuyong
Yongren China 66 B3
Yongshan China 66 C2
Yongsheng China 66 B3
Yongtai China 67 F3
Yongwol S. Korea 65 B5
Yongxi China see Nayong
Yongxing Hunan China 67 E3
Yongxing Jiangxi China 67 E3
Yongxiu China 67 E2
Yongzhou China 67 E3
Yonkers U.S.A. 131 G3
Yonne r. France 39 E2
Yoo Baba well Niger 93 I1
Yopal Col. 146 C2
Yordu Jammu and Kashmir 74 B2
York Australia 109 B7
York Canada 130 D2
York r. Canada 123 M4
York U.K. 35 F5
York AL U.S.A. 129 A5
York NE U.S.A. 132 B3
York PA U.S.A. 131 E4
York, Cape Australia 111 E1
York Downs Australia 111 E2
Yorke Peninsula Australia 112 A4
Yorkshire Dales National Park U.K.
  35 E4
Yorkshire Wolds hills U.K. 35 F5
York Springs U.S.A. 131 G3
Yorkton Canada 134 G2
Yorktown U.S.A. 131 E5
Yosemite National Park U.S.A. 136 C3
Yosemite Village U.S.A. 136 C3
Yoshino-Kumano National Park Japan
  65 D6
Yoshkar-Ola Rus. Fed. 28 H4
Yos Sudarso i. Indon. see Dolak, Pulau
Yōsu S. Korea 65 A6
Yotau Bol. 149 E4
Yotvata Israel 77 B5
Youbou Canada 134 A2
Youghal Rep. of Ireland 35 C6
You Jiang r. China 66 D1
Young Australia 112 D4
Young Uruguay 152 F3
Younghusband, Lake salt flat Australia
  109 G7
Younghusband Peninsula Australia
  112 A4
Young Island Antarctica 167 H2
Youngstown Canada 123 I5
Youngstown U.S.A. 130 E3
Youngsville U.S.A. 130 D3
You Shui r. China 67 D3
Youssoufia Morocco 90 C2
Youvarou Mali 92 D2
Youxi China 67 F3
Youxian China 67 E3
Youyang China 67 D2
Youyi Feng mt. China/Rus. Fed. 70 G2
Yovon Tajik. 81 G2
Yozgat Turkey 78 C3
Ypé-Jhú Para. 149 G5
Yppäri Fin. 32 G2
Ypres Belgium see Ieper
Ypsilanti U.S.A. 130 D2
Yreka U.S.A. 134 B4
Yrghyz Kazakh. see Irgiz
Yr Wyddfa mt. U.K. see Snowdon
Yser r. France 39 F4
Yssingeaux France 39 F4
Ystad Sweden 33 D5
Ysyk-Köl Kyrg. see Balykchy

Ysyk-Köl salt l. Kyrg. 62 B3
  5th largest lake in Asia.
  asia 50–51

Y Trallwng U.K. see Welshpool
Ytre Vinje Norway see Åmot
Ytyk-Kuyel' Rus. Fed. 27 N3
Yu'alliq, Jabal mt. Egypt 77 A4
Yuan'an China 67 D2
Yuanbao Shan mt. China 67 D3
Yuanjiang Hunan China 67 E2
Yuanjiang Yunnan China 66 B4
Yuan Jiang r. Yunnan China 66 B4
Yuanjiazhuang China see Foping
Yuanling China 67 E2
Yuanma China see Yuanmou
Yuanmou China 66 B3
Yuanquan China see Anxi
Yuanshan China see Lianping
Yuanyang China 66 B4
Yuba City U.S.A. 136 B2
Yūbari Japan 64 F4
Yubei China 66 C2
Yubi, Cap c. Morocco see Juby, Cap
Yucatán pen. Mex. 127 H8
Yucatan Channel Cuba/Mex. 127 I7
Yucca U.S.A. 137 E4
Yucca Lake U.S.A. 137 D3
Yucca Valley U.S.A. 137 D4
Yucheng Guangdong China see Yunan
Yucheng Henan China see Yudu
Yudoma r. Rus. Fed. 27 N4
Yudu China 67 E3
Yuecheng China see Yuexi
Yuelai China see Huachuan
Yuendumu Australia 110 B4
Yuen Long Hong Kong China 67 [inset]
Yueqing China 67 G3
Yuexi Anhui China 67 F2
Yueyang Hunan China 67 E2
Yueyang Hunan China 67 E2
Yueyang Sichuan China see Anyue
Yug r. Rus. Fed. 28 I3
Yugan China 67 F2
Yugo-Kamskiy Rus. Fed. 28 J4
Yugorsk Rus. Fed. 26 H3
Yugorskiy Poluostrov pen. Rus. Fed.
  28 L1

Yugoslavia country Europe 46 B3
  europe 24–25, 48

Yugoslavia
  Up to 1993 included Bosnia-Herzegovina,
  Croatia, Macedonia and Slovenia.

Yuhang China 67 G2
Yuhu China see Eryuan
Yuhuan China 67 G3
Yuin Australia 109 B6
Yujiang China 67 F2